Lecture Notes in Computer Science 1170

Edited by G. Goos, J. Hartmanis and J. van Leeuwen

Advisory Board: W. Brauer   D. Gries   J. Stoer

T0180863

Springer
Berlin
Heidelberg
New York
Barcelona
Budapest
Hong Kong
London
Milan
Paris
Santa Clara
Singapore
Tokyo

Manfred Nagl   (Ed.)

Building Tightly Integrated Software Development Environments: The IPSEN Approach

 Springer

Series Editors

Gerhard Goos, Karlsruhe University, Germany

Juris Hartmanis, Cornell University, NY, USA

Jan van Leeuwen, Utrecht University, The Netherlands

Volume Editor

Manfred Nagl
RWTH Aachen, Lehrstuhl für Informatik III
D-52056 Aachen, Germany
E-mail: nagl@i3.informatik.rwth-aachen.de

Cataloging-in-Publication data applied for

Die Deutsche Bibliothek - CIP-Einheitsaufnahme

Building tightly integrated software development environments:
the IPSEN approach / Manfred Nagl (ed.). - Berlin ;
Heidelberg ; New York ; Barcelona ; Budapest ; Hong Kong ;
London ; Milan ; Paris ; Santa Clara ; Singapore ; Tokyo :
Springer, 1996
  (Lecture notes in computer science ; Vol. 1170)
  ISBN 3-540-61985-2
NE: Nagl, Manfred [Hrsg.]; GT

CR Subject Classification (1991): D.2, G.2.2, D.3.1, K.6.3,F.4.2

ISSN 0302-9743
ISBN 3-540-61985-2 Springer-Verlag Berlin Heidelberg New York

© Springer-Verlag Berlin Heidelberg 1996
Printed in Germany

Typesetting: Camera-ready by author
SPIN 10549145   06/3142 – 5 4 3 2 1 0   Printed on acid-free paper

Preface

This book is a state-of-the-art *report* on the *IPSEN project* which aims to introduce a new quality in integration between tools devoted to the development and maintenance of large software systems. Although there are different subprojects for software development environments and also for environments outside the software context investigated in the group, and different grants have supported our work, we inaccurately speak about *the* IPSEN project in the following book. Indeed, it is more a group of related projects which produced a series of prototypes than one single environment demonstrating all we have achieved. IPSEN is an acronym for *I*ntegrated Software *P*roject *S*upport *En*vironment. The project is long lasting and has required considerable human effort. The results produced in this project are collected in this book.

We shall learn later in this book that integration has different facets which we shall carefully explain in chapters 1–4. To give an impression at the very beginning: By integration we mean *tight integration* on and of software documents which is achieved by specific tools. Integration is not only on coarse-grained document level but also on the level of syntactical and semantical units within these documents. Therefore, integration especially means *fine-grained* integration for different tools on one document and, even more important, between different documents by integration tools. We shall carefully argue in chapter 1 that it is especially this kind of integration which is needed for maintenance and other key activities of software engineering. In chapter 2 we demonstrate how this kind of integration appears from the user's perspective.

The specification of what is going on inside the IPSEN software development environment(s) is done by viewing any document/configuration the user is dealing with internally as a graph belonging to a graph class or a complex of graphs. The tool activities are mapped onto activities of graph processors. A formal specification is given by graph rewriting systems, in short graph grammars. A language for expressing such specifications and an environment for handling them, called PROGRES, has been developed, and a lot of methodology knowledge of how to write down specifications has been found. From a specification the realization of tools is mechanically derived. This overall approach was called *graph technology* and is the most *specific aspect* of IPSEN. It is this graph technology which distinguishes this project from most other software development environment projects (see chapter 3).

Another highlight of IPSEN is the results on *software engineering* level, discussed in detail in chapter 4, based on the IPSEN software architecture. The understanding of the term "architecture" is different from that of other authors: An architecture is not a rough draft but an exact plan across all different logical layers of the software system. For the IPSEN system we present its framework architecture, discuss its standard components, and describe a machinery for deriving its specific components. Furthermore, tools to support this machinery are also discussed. The software engineering results are given in chapter 4.

The main concern of this book is to show *uniformity* throughout different logical levels. These levels are language definition, behavior of tools, internal graph grammar modeling, architectural design, and implementation. The uniformity investigation and the traceability it implies through all these levels may be the key result of the IPSEN approach.

The book and its results are (hopefully) *interesting* to the software development environment community mainly for the following reasons: (a) The project has produced a lot of *practical results* in the form of available prototypes showing this new kind of integration, internal modeling, and tool production. These prototypes have demonstrated that it is worthwhile and possible to transfer the underlying ideas to industrial practice. The project also has (b) a *theoretical side* which demonstrates that theory is necessary for good practice, in this case the practice of tool building. This has two reasons: There is no way to get reliable complex tools without specifying formally the internal behavior of a software development environment. Furthermore, the process of developing software tools and environments can only be made more efficient if handcoding is replaced by more intelligent production mechanisms. This, however, is not possible without a theoretical background and basis of corresponding specifications.

The IPSEN project is a university or *research project*. Therefore, the aim was not to produce industrial tools, although prototypes are efficient and stable. The aim, furthermore, was not to gain completeness, i.e. to support all activities of development and maintenance of software, although a remarkable set of tools has been realized. Being researchers, our interest centered more on learning about how new tools have to behave, to be modeled internally, to be realized, and how realization effort can be reduced, than implementing one tool after the other. Therefore, a new tool was only built if we expected to get new insight in one or more of the above questions. This, however, does not mean that the tools we have built are only valuable for research. In the numerous demonstrations we have given, application programmers were especially enthusiastic in their responses, telling us that they would like to have IPSEN-like tools for their practical work. Nevertheless, the process of transforming results to industrial practice is still in its infancy. However, it has started.

Although the IPSEN project mainly deals with software development environments, the *approach* taken can also be *applied* to any *interactive system* on *complex*, structured, and tightly *connected objects* developed in a group, as is the case with software documents and software projects. We have some results proving this claim.

The IPSEN *approach* or project has *different facets* which are shown in the respective chapters of this book. We summarize them in order so as to clarify the range of discussion. IPSEN is:

(a) a certain idea of how tools of an integrated (software) development environment should behave,

(b) an approach using one key idea, namely that of complex interrelated objects (graphs) at all levels of (software) development environments: language definition, tool behavior, conceptual internal modeling, and realization,

(c) the key modeling idea of separation (separate structures) and integration (fine-grained links between structures) being applicable to different technical grains as documents, subconfigurations, configurations, but also for management information and the interrelation of technical and management information,

(d) a uniform conceptual modeling approach, which makes the internal specification clearer, easier to build up, and maintain and which is the prerequisite for any "intelligence" in the tool production process,

(e) a specification language for the internal specification of tools together with corresponding tools (PROGRES and its environment),

(f) a set of environments built according to these ideas which have been demonstrated at many sites,

(g) an approach to configure integrated environments which all share the same architectural framework and corresponding basic blocks,

(h) an approach to generate specific components within this framework and to realize the corresponding generator tools, i.e. IPSEN is a meta-SDE environment,

(i) an endeavor to build a universal administration component which can be taken to cover the coordination aspects of any (software) project,

(j) a platform project for integrated and distributed environments for data, control, and representation integration, especially an underlying object storage,

(k) an approach which can be transferred to other disciplines outside the software development environment world (e.g. CIM, classification and retrieval systems, intelligent text systems, etc.),

(l) an effort to make languages or methods used in software engineering clear and precise, to learn how to use them, and to build tools for them.

The detailed description of these facets (besides the language and method work) for the scientific world and, especially, for the software development environments community is the main goal of this book.

This book is an effort for the scientific community. It presents material in order to *learn,* to a certain extent, *about software development environments* in general *and IPSEN* in particular. This book should help to spread the essential ideas of IPSEN within the (software) development environments community but also in areas outside of environments.

Besides these outside goals the book also has some *internal goals* for the IPSEN group itself. Up to now we have had no compendium for new group members at the Ph.D. candidate or Master's level to enable them to familiarize themselves with the established results. Furthermore, it was discovered that the preparation of this book, with the knowledge gained during that process, was very stimulating.

After having introduced the aims of this book let me list a number of items the *book* does *not handle*:

(1) It is *not* a textbook on software development environments *in general*. It is a monograph devoted to the IPSEN approach and it discusses (some of the numerous) other approaches only to the extent necessary for characterizing IPSEN. There are also monographs on special topics of the project (/8. Na 79, 4. Schä 86, 5. Eng 86, 4. Lew 88c, 2. ES 89, 5. Schü 91a, 4. Wes 91a, 7. Jan 92, 7. Bör 94, 4. Lef 95, 7. Bee 95, 5. Zün 96, 4. Koh 96/).

(2) This is *not a method book*. Some of the existing methods (better termed notations) for the different working areas are introduced because they are the basis for tools. However, they are only introduced by examples and not given formally, and only to the extent needed for the corresponding tool discussions.

All *persons* on the list on the next page have *contributed* considerably to the success of the IPSEN project. They have contributed by finished or ongoing Ph.D. thesis work, by Master's theses, and as programmers. The *commitment* of all these members as developers of ideas, concepts, languages, mechanisms, components, and prototypes is gratefully *acknowledged*. Especially, the contributions of P. Klein, Dr. A. Schürr, and Dr. B. Westfechtel made it possible to edit this book. Furthermore, the careful text preparation work done by A. Fleck, M. Schürr, and R.P. Rössel is responsible for the layout of this volume. Finally, A. Johnston was responsible for improving our English.

The following *grants* given by national and international research organizations have directly or indirectly given considerable support to the IPSEN project and, therefore, have layed the financial basis for the results of this book:

- German Research Council (DFG): project 'Software Workbench'; project 'Graph Grammar Specifications'; project 'Software Architectures for Interactive Systems'; project 'SU-KITS', subproject 'CIM Manager'; project 'Graduate College Computer Science and Engineering', subproject 'Administration of Development',

- European Community: ESPRIT-project 'COMPLEMENT', subproject 'Requirements Engineering and Programming in the Large', together with CAP debis Aachen,

- German Ministry for Research and Technology: project 'European Software Factory', subproject 'Requirements Engineering Tools', together with CAP debis Aachen; project 'Reengineering of Client/Server Applications', together with AMI and GEZ,

- Stiftung Volkswagenwerk: project 'Intelligent Editors for Technical Documentation',

- Ministry for Science and Research of North-Rhine Westphalia: project 'Tool Generators'; participation in 'Client/Server Applications'; project 'Software Reuse'.

Finally, the basic support given by the state of Lower Saxony, when the group was at the University of Osnabrück, and by the state of North-Rhine Westphalia, the group since 1986 being located at Aachen University of Technology, is gratefully acknowledged.

Aachen, September 1996   *Manfred Nagl*

Persons Engaged in the IPSEN Project

D. Adamcyk	St. Hardt	W. Pickartz
G. v.Amerongen	D. Haßl	A. Poensgen
Dr. V. Bacvanski	H. Hassoun	B. Pohlmann
R. Baumann	H. Heil	M. Rademacher
J. Bausch	P. Heimann	A. Radermacher
J. Beckers	R. Herbrecht	C. Rövenich
Dr. M. von der Beek	M. Heyde	M. Rövenich
C. Beer	F. Höfer	A. Rossow
N. Beermann	F. Høgberg	A. Sandbrink
A. Behle	C. Horbach	Prof. W. Schäfer
U. Belten	P. Hormanns	H. Scharrel
E. Berens	Dr. Th. Janning	U. Schleef
R. Biermanns	A. Joereßen	H. Schlüper
Dr. J. Börstler	G. Joeris	V. Schmidt
Dr. Th. Brandes	N. Kiesel	J. Schmitz–Lenders
H. Brandt	P. Klein	O. Scholz
M. Breuer	J. Kloth	Dr. A. Schürr
R. Breuer	R. Koether	J. Schwartz
M. Broekmans	Dr. Ch. Kohring	A. Speulmanns
T. Bruckhaus	P. Kossing	R. Spielmann
B. Bücken	W. Kothes	T. Spellerberg
St. Coors	C.–A. Krapp	G. Sobbe
K. Cremer	H. Kreten	G. Starke
D. Däberitz	S. Krüppel	O. Steffens
A. Deparade	J. Lacour	J. Theis
J. Derissen	Dr. M. Lefering	M. Thiele
O. Dickoph	Prof. C. Lewerentz	P. Tillmann
H. Docquier	T. Liese	B. Tophoven
R. Dömges	B. Lücken	J. Turek
H.J. Dorka	S. Mau	S. Vaillant
M. Eichstädt	R. Melchiesedech	A. Welbers
U. Eisenmenger	G. Metzen	A. Winter
Prof. G. Engels	M. Meuser	Dr. B. Westfechtel
F. Erdtmann	P. Möckel	A. Winter
A. Feye	E. Nadarzinski	St. Witt
R. Gombert	Prof. M. Nagl	H. Zinnen
Th. Gröger	E. Nourbakhsh	S. Zohren
M. Guhl	M. Pandey	Dr. A. Zündorf
H. Haverkamp	F. Phillip	

Adresses of Contributors

Dipl.-Inform. R. Bauman, Lehrstuhl für Informatik III,
E-Mail: roland@i3.informatik.rwth–aachen.de

Dipl.-Inform. A. Behle, Lehrstuhl für Informatik III,
E-Mail: behle@i3.informatik.rwth–aachen.de

Dipl.-Inform. K. Cremer, Lehrstuhl für Informatik III,
E-Mail: katja@i3.informatik.rwth–aachen.de

Dipl.-Inform. A. Deparade, Lehrstuhl für Informatik III,
E-Mail: deparade@i3.informatik.rwth–aachen.de

Prof. Dr. G. Engels, Dept. of Computer Science, Leiden University, P.O.Box 9512,
NL–2300 RA Leiden, Netherlands, E-Mail: engels@wi.leidenuniv.nl

Dipl.-Inform. P. Heimann, Lehrstuhl für Informatik III,
E-Mail: peter@i3.informatik.rwth–aachen.de

Dr. Th. Janning, Deutsche Krankenversicherung DKV, Aachener Str. 300, D–50933 Köln

Dipl.-Inform. N. Kiesel, Software–Ley GmbH, Venloer Str. 83–85, D–50259 Pulheim,
E-Mail: nk@col.sw–ley.de

Dipl.-Inform. P. Klein, Lehrstuhl für Informatik III,
E-Mail: pk@i3.informatik.rwth–aachen.de

Dr. Ch. Kohring, Burgstr. 13, D–38272 Burgdorf

Dipl.-Inform. C.A. Krapp, Lehrstuhl für Informatik III,
E-Mail: krapp@i3.informatik.rwth–aachen.de

Dr. M. Lefering, Frankenberger Str. 25, D–52066 Aachen,
E-Mail: lef@gs–ac.aachen.cap–debis.de

Prof. Dr. M. Nagl, Lehrstuhl für Informatik III, Aachen University of Technology,
Ahornstr. 55, D–52074 Aachen, Germany, E-Mail: nagl@i3.informatik.rwth–aachen.de

Dipl.-Inform. A. Radermacher, Lehrstuhl für Informatik III,
E-Mail: ansgar@i3.informatik.rwth–aachen.de

Dipl.-Math. R.P. Rössel, Sudetenstr. 27, D–52477 Alsdorf,
E-Mail: Rudolf.Roessel@aachen.netsurf.de

Dipl.-Inform. C. Rövenich, Aachener+Münchener Versicherung AG,
Aureliusstr. 2, D–52064 Aachen

Prof. Dr. W. Schäfer, Universität–GH Paderborn, FB 17, Warburger Str. 100,
D–33098 Paderborn, E-Mail: wilhelm@uni–paderborn.de

Dr. A. Schürr, Lehrstuhl für Informatik III,
E-Mail: andy@i3.informatik.rwth–aachen.de

Dr. B. Westfechtel, Lehrstuhl für Informatik III,
E-Mail: bernhard@i3.informatik.rwth–aachen.de

Dipl.-Inform. A. Winter, Lehrstuhl für Informatik III,
E-Mail: winter@i3.informatik.rwth–aachen.de

Dr. A. Zündorf, Universität–GH Paderborn, FB 17, Warburger Str. 100,
D–33098 Paderborn, E-Mail: zuendorf@uni–paderborn.de

Contents

1 Overview:
Introduction, Classification,
and Global Approach

M. Nagl

The *aim* of this *chapter* is to introduce basic notions of software engineering, to stress the importance of software engineering in general and of software development environments in particular, to introduce the problem areas a developer is facing when trying to build a new software development environment, to give an overview of the IPSEN project, to discuss the highlights of the project, to relate IPSEN to other software development environment projects, and to introduce the structure of this book.

The *general part* of this chapter consists of the introduction of basic notions, the discussion of the importance and important topics of software engineering or software development environments (abbr. SDEs in the following) in section 1.1 or 1.2. Furthermore, an introduction to problem areas in software development environments research and realization is given in section 1.3 and a classification of SDEs in section 1.2 but especially in section 1.7. All these topics are IPSEN independent and, therefore, a discussion about software engineering and software development environments in general. However, as there is no common terminology available in software engineering, some of the notions (working area, extended technical configuration, administration configuration, and overall configuration model) have been developed in the context of the IPSEN project. Therefore, these notions express a very personal view on software engineering.

The *IPSEN overview* and *highlighting* is done by different sections: In 1.4 we sketch that the integration problem is a key problem of software development environments which remains unsolved today. Therefore, environments nowadays lack user acceptance. One of the main motivations of the IPSEN research project is to give solutions to this problem. Section 1.5 gives a sketch of the uniform approach we have taken in IPSEN, called graph technology: Modelling documents as graphs, tools as graph processors, and giving a formal specification for both. The software engineering results of the IPSEN SDE are described in terms of a framework architecture containing standard components and derived specific components. Furthermore, a generator tool machinery in section 1.6. So, the highlights of IPSEN are results due to integration, graph technology, and architecture investigations of SDEs.

The third part of this chapter consists of statements *positioning IPSEN* in the SDE world and relating it to other SDE approaches. This is done by describing the variety of SDEs in section 1.2, by explaining the results of IPSEN due to the SDE problem area grouping of section 1.3, by classifying IPSEN according to a scheme for arbitrary SDEs in section 1.7, and by sketching the history, the current state, and the future work in section 1.8.

At the end of the chapter we summarize and give an *overview* of the *chapter* and the *structure* of this *book*. For the latter, we describe the structure of the main chapters and their relationships by a structure and dependency graph.

1.1 Software Engineering:
Definitions, Problem Fields, and Specialization

The *aim* of this *section* is to introduce some basic terms of software engineering, to argue that different working areas of software engineering are more decisive than others in determining the success of a software project, and to introduce some problem fields in software engineering which are the keys for producing good solutions of software systems. Furthermore, we explain in abstract terms that software engineering, in the same way as any other engineering discipline, implies handling complex overall configurations. Finally, we make clear that specialization is needed in order to get deeper insight into the products and processes of software engineering.

1.1.1 History, Claims, and First Definitions

The term *software engineering* was coined in 1968 /9. BR 69, 9. NR 68/ when the software world felt to be in a crisis. There were no means available to manage the complexity of large software systems and of the process of their development and maintenance. The problem, especially, was that the only formal description of a software system at that time was the program code of a system. This code is too large to be understood, available too late, and contains a huge amount of interdependencies related to the structure of the software system and the structure of the process used to produce it. None of these issues are made explicit. The term software engineering expressed the claim to apply principles, techniques, and procedures similar to that of other engineering disciplines to partition the problem, in order to cope with its complexity.

Since that time, we have learned about the *structure* of *software systems* and the *processes* to produce them. More specifically, we have learned to support the process and to express its results. We have assigned an explicit structure to the process of developing and maintaining software systems, which, on a very coarse level, we call lifecycle models (e.g. /7. Agr 86, 7. Boe 82/). We have learned to refine the structure of the development/maintenance process, to describe and to use it for the coordination of labour within a team thereby managing the structure of a complex system consisting of documents in different states with interrelations, called configuration management (e.g. /3. Bab 86, 3. BHS 80, 3. Con 86, 3. Fei 91, 3. Win 88, 3. WT 89/). We have developed languages and methods for describing results of subactivities occurring in the process (see section 7 of the bibliography), and we have developed tools for supporting these subactivities and their combination in order to end up with a final consistent system (see nearly the whole bibliography, but especially section 4). There are a lot of more or less good books on software engineering on the market reflecting the state of the art, but also documenting that we are far away from having reached the goal of behaving like other classical engineering disciplines. Furthermore, there are still many different personal opinions about the question of what software engineering is, or what it should be.

In software development and maintenance more or less formal descriptions on different logical levels for a software system or its process are built up and modified. These levels correspond to areas of activities in the development and maintenance process. We call these areas in this book *working areas* (cf. fig. 1.1, the relations between working areas being discussed later). Different working areas belong to different perspectives on a software system. We will show in section 1.4 that working areas and their dependencies can be used for defining different lifecycle models. The reader should note that in the working area model there is no distinction between a built and a modify activity and, especially, that there is no distinction when these steps occur, either in development or maintenance. Therefore, working areas do not express any time dependent relations between activities. However, they express that activities are logically grouped corresponding to the level/kind of description. We are now going to define the working areas of fig. 1.1.

The first working area is the construction/modification of the requirements for a software system. The working area is called *requirements engineering* (e.g. /3. AM 81, 3. Ohn 87, 3. RO 85, 3. Rom 85, 3. TD 90/) or requirements modelling, the resulting description the requirements specification. Even on this level rather complex situations have to be modelled. The part of the requirements specification which can be formally described is often called the functional part of the requirements specification. It describes the functions of the system and the relations between these functions, the data of the application area they depend on, and sometimes also the coordination and control of functions. The other parts like efficiency parameters, security determinations, user interface details (/3. Pfa 83, 3. Shn 86/) are mostly called the nonfunctional part. Therefore, requirements engineering delivers a precise and partially formal description of the outside perspective on a system to be developed or modified.

In the next logical working area viewed from outside we find software architecture or design modelling, in the following called *programming in the large* (/7. Boo 90, 7. GG 89, 7. Hoo 89, 7. Mey 88a, 7. Nag 90, 7. PCW 85, 7. PN 86, 3. Pot 89, 7. PS 75/). There we are modelling an inside perspective of the software system on a level where we disregard the internals of components, named modules. Therefore, the aim of this working area to give a static description of the software system consisting of finding all modules and subsystems, giving their detailed behavioral description, and specifying the relations between them. So, programming in the large provides a complete, precise, and static description of a software system in the sense of a blue print. This description goes through all logical levels of a system (from user interface to the underlying basic machine) but ignores the details of module internals.

Abbreviations:
RE Requirements Eng.
PiL Progr. in the Large
PO Project Organization

Explanation:

Thickness of arrow gives approximately the fraction of labour in B determined by A activities and decisions

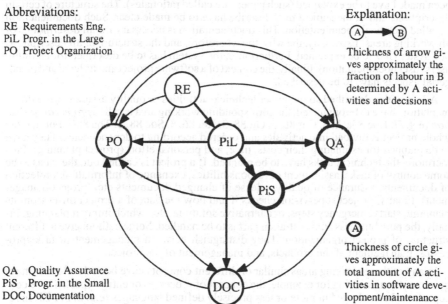

QA Quality Assurance
PiS Progr. in the Small
DOC Documentation

Thickness of circle gives approximately the total amount of A activities in software development/maintenance

Fig. 1.1. Working areas of software engineering, their dependencies, and the special role of architecture modelling

In the working area *programming in the small* we implement the bodies of the modules identified in the architecture using the usual constructs for execution control and data types of programming languages. Although the distinction and chronological separation between programming in the large and programming in the small is an idealization, it is unavoidable from the project organization point of view /7. Nag 90/.

These three working areas are responsible for the *technical side* of a software project. The requirements specification is describing the outside behavior without internals of the system, the architecture the essential structure of the software system, i.e. an inside perspective without implementation details. The architecture information is also contained in the module and subsystem descriptions (export interfaces, import interfaces etc.) which, therefore, after implementation, build up the code for the complete system. Besides these areas there are three *other working areas*, the activities of which *accompany* the work in the technical areas.

The first of these areas to be explained is *quality assurance* (e.g. /3. Cho 85, 3. EM 87/). Quality assurance can be done in different ways. It can be done formally and statically, which is called formal verification (e.g. /7. FBB 82, 9. LS 84/). It can be done experimentally, dynamically, and more or less computer supported, called test (e.g. /3. Bei 84, 3. How 87, 3. Kem 89, 3. MH 81/), which nevertheless has to be carried out systematically and carefully. Tests consist of test planning, test data development, test management and test supervision on module level (module test) and subsystem and system integration level (integration test). Furthermore, human validation in the form of review, inspections, walkthroughs, or ratings are of great importance. Finally, quality assurance can be constructive as guaranteed by tools, procedures etc. which is the topic of this book, or analytical, i.e. checked a posteriori.

Another working area is *documentation* (e.g. /3. BW 82/). The decisions which have been made have to be explained (such papers are called rationales). The structure of certain descriptions and of the subject they describe have to be made clear. Such documentation is called technical documentation. This documentation is necessary for all descriptions of all working areas. Especially, the why, the wherefore, and the structure of all descriptions of a system has to be explained. Furthermore, the system has to be described for its future users (user documentation). Finally, the context of a software project and its legal and managerial aspects have to be described.

All activities described so far, either technical activities or quality assurance and documentation, have to be organized; the corresponding working area is called *project organization* (e.g. /7. Boe 89a, b, 3. Cur 86, 3. Gil 88, 3. Rei 86, 3. Suc 88, 3. Tha 88/). For that the whole project is divided into activities and ordered according to dependencies. They have to be planned for estimating their costs, time, and personal effort (project planning). Furthermore, the technical tasks have to be planned. If a project is carried out, there has to be some control of tasks, assignment of responsibilities, exchange of information, protection of documents, assurance of quality, release of changed documents etc. (project management). Finally, project supervision checks if and how the data of a project differ from its planning, starts emergency steps, or alternative solutions etc., which imply replanning. Finally, the pure business administration part is to be handled. Some authors give a different structure of project organization: They distinguish between management of tasks/processes, management of the products, and management of the project.

In any of these working areas similar or different concepts have been developed (in requirements engineering for example, the concept of processes or entity types). These concepts have been clothed in more or less precisely defined languages (e.g. SA or ER in requirements engineering). There are methods consisting of rules and hints (more or less precisely fixed) on how to apply those languages, and there are tools to handle descriptions in those languages, eventually supporting the methods. Furthermore, there may be successful technical or management procedures to be applied, utilities to be used , components to be taken, experience to be applied, standards to be postulated and later applied etc., when carrying out a software project. We call the sum of all these concepts, ..., standards available within a project, the *technology*, which enables a software system to be realized in a software project. We may regard the restriction of technology to a certain working area (requirements engineering or technology, design technology etc.) or to the development of a portion of the system (e.g. platform subsystem), eventually developed in a different context (e.g. subproject).

Certain *roles* exist for each or any of the working areas mentioned above (requirements engineering, designer, programmer, quality engineer, documentator, project organizer). A certain role is connected with capabilities, education, experience, and expertise expected for a person acting in that role at a certain time. A *person* involved in the development/maintenance process for a software system can have different roles (e.g. designing a subsystem but also implementing the key modules) at the same time or one after the other. Especially, the activities of quality assurance and documentation can be carried out by developers themselves and/or different persons. There are different models to be found in literature detailing how a group of software engineers, i.e. the development *team* of a project, is organized (e.g. hierarchical models, chief programmer team etc.) and how these team or group models are mapped on a company organization, available persons etc.

We call any of the descriptions or meaningful and logically separated portions of descriptions which are developed/maintained in one of the above working areas a *software document*. In particular, a documentation is also treated as a document. A software document may only be a portion of the results of a working area (a subsystem design document which is a part of the complete software architecture). This is due to the fact that the results of a working area reflect different and complementary perspectives, logical hierarchies, different degrees of detail etc. A software document is the portion of a total system or of its descriptions one person is working on interactively for a certain time to give it a certain degree of maturity (rough sketch to be reviewed, elaborated in detail to be quality stamped). This person has a certain role and uses available technology. A software document has a more or less precise structure coming from the language in which it is denoted, the methods to be applied thereby etc. So, a software document belongs to a class of software documents (e.g. a design document). Software documents of one or more working areas contribute to a more complex and comprehensive whole as to be explained soon.

In any of the above working areas there are activities belonging to *analysis* steps (e.g. in architecture modelling the analysis of the corresponding portion of the requirements specification, or analysis whether the architecture which has already been built up is internally consistent, or analysis to check whether an introduced module can later on be implemented efficiently). Furthermore, there are *construction* or *modification* steps (e.g. introducing a new module into the architecture, or making a collection of already existing modules to a new subsystem) which may have preceding planing steps. Furthermore, a software document may be executable (as a module after implementation). Then it can also be instrumented, *executed*, and monitored. These steps may give rise again to analysis and modifications. We call these activities to plan, analyze, build up, modify, instrument, or execute etc. a document of a document class the *modelling* of this document. The modelling of a document is usually restricted by certain assumptions of other already existing documents, of internal quality measures of documents, or of thinking about future documents which are to be derived. Modelling is supported if there are suitable languages, methods, and tools, i.e. if there is technology available. Working areas have been introduced above to collect modelling steps belonging to a certain logical view on the system (RE, PiL, PiS of fig. 1.1) or to a certain group of accompanying activities (QA, DOC, PO).

Software documents of different *working areas* are highly *interrelated* (cf. fig. 1.1 again). All documents besides the requirements specification have to follow the decisions made in the requirements specification, directly or indirectly: The architecture has to be consistent with the requirements, the modules with the architecture, the user documentation with the requirements, the technical documentation with the requirements, the architecture, and the modules, project organization documents are dependent on all three technical working areas etc. These dependencies are shown in the dependency graph of fig. 1.1 and are discussed in more detail in subsection 1.1.3. To give one example already here: If a system is extended in maintenance, we have to change the requirements specification, which induces a change in the architecture and the corresponding modules etc. Validation is necessary for the changed parts and their interplay with the unchanged parts etc. These changes have to be planned, managed, and supervised.

As pointed out, a software system consists of many documents being in different consistency relations with each other (requirements specification, architecture, modules, etc.). Any working area also consists of different documents being consistent with each other (the overall architecture contains subsystems, subsystem contains subsystems and modules etc.). Consistency relations can be bidirectional (different parts of a requirements specification have mutual dependence on each other) or unidirectional (from architecture to modules as the outside description of modules is already contained in the architecture if no architectural changes are allowed in programming). We call such a consistent set of documents for a software system the *configuration* of the software system. The situation is even more complicated: In the development, but especially in the maintenance process, documents live over some time. Not only one state of the document is preserved but a set of states (revisions), revisions being connected by a is–successor–of relation. Therefore, a configuration is a consistent set of revisions of documents /4. Wes 91a/ describing (a part of) the system in a certain state of development or maintenance or to describe alternative states (variants). We come back to configurations in subsection 1.1.4.

A configuration may contain several *subconfigurations*. These may belong to a cutout of the total configuration corresponding to a certain complete perspective (e.g. external behavior of the system for the customer delivered by the requirements specification, user manual, and project handbook), to a certain working area (e.g. the complete architecture of a system consisting of many subsystems and modules), to a certain hierarchy or degree of detail level (e.g. or module/subsystem descriptions according to a certain layer of abstraction within the architecture) or to a certain task of the overall task to be developed independently (i.e. a subsystem being part of the total system consisting of an architecture document, the corresponding modules, documentation etc.). So, a subconfiguration is any group of documents together with their mutual relations which builds up a meaningful portion of the description of the total system to be developed or maintained. A subconfiguration is always embedded in another configuration if it is not developed in an independent project (e.g. for a standard component being used in more than one project).

Comparing the state of software development at the time of the beginning of software engineering and today, the situation is as follows: One amorphous description of a software system (its code) is now divided into different descriptions belonging to different perspectives of the system (outside description, essential structure, management structures etc.). This makes it possible to handle parts of its total complexity, as the documents/subconfigurations have lower complexity than the whole software system description, because they are related to a certain perspective of the system or its development. This makes it also possible to validate documents, before they are usually needed for the preparation of others. The problems of software engineering, however, are not solved but only reduced: Firstly, modelling of software documents is still a very complex task. There are more or less precise languages and more or less suitable tools available on the market to support modelling of certain documents. What is not available in existing tools are appropriate means for building up and maintaining complete configurations. The underlying *integration problem* of documents and their consistency is *not* sufficiently *solved,* or in most cases even unsolved. We come back to this problem in subsections 1.1.3 and 1.1.4 and to the question which integration should be offered by tools in subsection 1.2.4 and section 1.4.

We call a technical solution consisting of hardware and software for a certain problem an *application system.* This solution is the result of a difficult technical process, as sketched above. The application system is embedded into an *organizational system* (company, department of a company etc.) which is running and processing the application system. Furthermore, the organizational system contributes to the development of the application system by helping to specify the requirements, by managing the reorganization induced by the (new) application system etc. This remark makes clear that software engineering is to be seen together with organizational systems. Even more complicated is the situation if a software system which is only a part of a software/hardware system (e.g. real–time system) which, as above, is embedded into an even bigger system (e.g. fabrication control system) being embedded into an organizational system.

1.1.2 Topics of Special Importance

In this subsection we sketch the *topics* of software engineering which are most *problematic* but also *promising* in the sense of achieving good solutions for software systems. We are using the following list of problem fields for two reasons in the following text: Firstly, we measure the usefulness of tools throughout this book by referring to this list. Secondly, we are using the problem fields as parameters for the classification of tools and environments in the next section and in section 1.7.

Each of the working areas of the last subsection is important in the sense that a software project can fail in the short or long run if the area is not executed at all, or not with the necessary effort, competence, and accuracy. However, in *some* of the above *working areas* important decisions have to be made: In project planning the estimation of software system costs, in management the selection of the right people is highly *risky*. In the technical working areas the determination of the outside behavior (requirements specification) and of the essential structure of a software system (the architecture) have a *high impact* on the whole process of development and maintenance.

We know from /7. Zel 79/ that only 11 % of the total activities in a software project are spent for requirements engineering and programming in the large. This is very little and explains the high percentage of maintenance effort of about 60 % /7. Boe 76/. The reference /7. Ram 84/ gives a certification showing that most of the errors are made in requirements engineering and programming in the large. We furthermore know from /7. Ram 84/ that errors detected late, e.g. in maintenance, are 100 to 200 times more expensive than early detected errors. That means that the frequent errors of requirements engineering and programming in the large are the most expensive ones. We conclude that *requirements engineering* and *programming in the large* have to be carried out with much *more competence, effort,* and *support* than done today.

In fig. 1.1 the thickness of arrows reflects the degree of dependency of a document or of documents of a working area from its mastering document or documents. The thickness of circles gives approximately the total amount of work related to a working area. From this figure we see that programming in the large is the most important of the technical working areas. The reason is that the *architecture* is the *essential structure* of the software system which influences most of the structure of all other documents. This essential structure is also the structure on/into which quality properties of a software system (e.g. maintainability) can be measured and built in, and on which decisions of changes in maintenance and essential reuse decisions can be made.

We have argued that those working areas of software engineering where the main decisions are made are risky. On the technical level this is the case in requirements engineering and programming in the large. The reason is that decisions are responsible for later dependencies (the architecture is a plan for a solution according to the requirements specification, the components have to follow their specification given in the architecture, etc.). Looking at fig. 1.1 again, we can conclude that most of the software documents are directly or indirectly, more or less strictly dependent on the architecture of a software system. Therefore, we can argue that the architecture is a rough image of the complete configuration for a software system. So, building up a configuration, modifying a configuration, or administrating alternative configurations is closely connected to architecture modelling, i.e. quality of handling complex *configurations* is *related to* the quality of *architecture modelling*.

As already indicated, one key problem of software engineering is *maintenance* (/3. CSM 89, 3. MM 83, 3. PZ 83/). The main topics of maintenance are distinguished into extension/

change of a software system, porting onto a new hardware/software platform, and correction/perfection of a software system. As argued above this means configuration changes and, especially, architectural changes. Therefore, the problem has very much to do with the question whether the architecture is precisely stated and modelled with state–of–the–art competence. Maintenance entails overall configuration changes and, therefore, is not a working area in our base model of fig. 1.1.

Another big problem field and outstanding current research area is *reusability* (/3. BP 89, 3. Fre 87, 3. Tra 86/). Reuse can take place on model, product, or process level. In any of these topics knowledge, experiences, standards, suitable languages, methods, documents, components, and products can be reused. The current discussion is often narrowed too much on certain parts of documents, collections of documents, and too often on program code level (modules, subsystems, etc.). Here again we can argue from the view point that an architecture is the essential structure. Therefore, this working area either on product or process level is a promising candidate for substantial reuse results.

A big problem of *software engineering* today is its *broad pretension*, it is expected or claims to be able to give solutions for any software system. This is comparable to an Institute of Technology offering an education in general engineering and not in mechanical engineering, electrical engineering etc. which, usually, again are divided into diverse branches of specialization. In our opinion the *nonavailability* of *specialization* in software engineering is to a great part responsible for the rather superficial state of the art. As this is a big problem we come back to it in a dedicated subsection (1.1.5). As can be seen from this book, the IPSEN project attempts to develop and contribute to technology for a specialized domain of software engineering, namely SDEs or, more general, integrated environments.

In the rest of this subsection we are going to discuss novel approaches within software engineering which are problem fields of our list, because the state of the art is not satisfactory. As they are important, they are topics of current research. The first one which is to be discussed is *software metrics* (/3. CDS 86, 3. GC 87, 3. PSS 81/). This involves a process where we quantitatively specify the structure or quality of software documents, configurations of system revisions, and their corresponding processes. There is no metrics approach available today to handle the complex configurations of software systems. Therefore, the ambitious goal of defining practical software metrics again must fail if we do not know more about specific software systems. As above, in our opinion, the most important level for software metrics is the architecture level.

Another problem field of software engineering is the management of the complexity of project organization, especially of project management (coordinating all activities for the working areas of fig. 1.1), but also connections to project planning and supervision. As already mentioned and to be worked out in detail in subsection 1.1.4, software systems during development and maintenance are configurations consisting of lots of complex documents with lots of mutual relations. Furthermore, there are different alternatives of configurations belonging to system variants. Approaches which explicitly describe the corresponding tasks and their dependencies together with their processes and resources, which relate them to (corresponding parts of) a configuration, or to changes of configuration states during development or maintenance, we call *process modelling* (e.g. /3. Dow 86, 3. Tul 89, 3. WD 85/). Process modelling is not a description of a configuration and its internal structure but of the corresponding processes. We come back to this question by describing the problem in more detail.

A further field of problems and interest is *rapid prototyping* (/3. BKM 84/). In the basic model we have introduced so far the first running system is available when all implemented modules have been integrated. If the customer does not like the system, i.e. because of a different understanding of the requirements specification, then there is a problem. Therefore, after having finished the requirements specification, often a rapidly developed prototype is built. Rapid prototyping can be done by (a) directly executing a requirements specification, if the description is executable and the corresponding tools are at hand. This we discuss in chapter 2 of this book. It can, furthermore, be (b) a quick and dirty implementation of the key functions of the system directly in a programming language which is a suitable for this purpose. Finally, it can be (c) a quick implementation of some components of the system, if there is a given architectural framework. The latter is only possible if there is some specialized technology available. The more knowledge in a domain we have, the easier a rapid prototype can be built. We address this problem for software development environments in chapters 3 and 4 of this book.

Let us *summarize:* To get a deep insight into the structure of software systems, configurations, and their development/maintenance process, to be able to apply reusability, to evaluate by metrics, and to build rapid prototypes we have to study the right level, especially the architecture level. We have to develop technologies for specialized fields of software engineering to get more than superficial results. Software engineering as it is understood nowadays claims to be a general engineering or problem solving discipline.

1.1.3 Dependencies between Working Areas and Documents

The *aim* of this *subsection* is to clear up the dependencies between working areas which have appeared in fig. 1.1. This discussion is necessary for the next subsection and for section 1.3, in which we discuss how the scenario of IPSEN looks, e.g. which documents occur, which tools exist, and which integration mechanisms and tools have been developed. Furthermore, this and the next subsection will make clear what we understand by an overall configuration for a software system, which is a key for reading this book.

To one *working area* there may correspond one document, there may correspond a rather independent set of documents, or a complex of interrelated documents. For small projects, there may be one single architecture document. Documentation consists of rather independent documents (technical documentation, user handbook, project handbook). Requirements engineering contains the functional and the nonfunctional system requirements specification, the first being composed of the functional, the information, and the control model each of which is hierarchically decomposed with many mutual relations between these models. So, the standard case, especially for large projects, is that for any working area there is more than one document in existence, i.e. a *subconfiguration*, the documents have *complex* internal *structures* and rather *complex relations* to each other.

We are now going to discuss the arrows of the working area dependency graph of fig. 1.1 in more detail (cf. fig. 1.2 and tables 1.3 and 1.4). If a *binary relation* exists between two *working areas*, A and B, this relation may correspond to different documents of A and B, respectively. Thus regarding the *corresponding documents* the binary relation between working areas is in general a *n:m–relation* between corresponding documents. Regarding, for example, the dependency between requirements engineering and documentation we see that the functional part (being composed internally) and the nonfunctional part of the requirements specification have influence over both the technical and the user documentation (again both being structured internally).

The next question we pose is what the *semantics* of the *binary relation* between working areas (and their corresponding n:m–relations on documents) is. We give an abstract answer to this question, the corresponding concrete dependencies are being discussed later. The semantics are explained by giving all the uses of such binary relations between document(s) of different working areas which have to be consistent. The most important use is that we take the binary relation A–>B for a *construction* or modification step in B, either in development or maintenance: We can (a) use it to produce some portion of a document of B to start with (e.g. module frames for implementation of modules) or (b) to (re)make a document of B consistent with a document of A after this has been changed. We also use the relation in the reverse direction (c) to *analyze* a document of B whether it is consistent with a document of A. This includes the case that the document of B is still empty because we first have to analyze and learn about the structure of the document of A to be transformed. The binary relation is also used (d) for *prognosis* (e.g. to estimate whether a certain change on require-

12

ments engineering level can correspondingly be carried out on architecture and implementation level). So, analysis can go back and forth. Finally, a binary relation is also used for project *organization* issues, e.g. for giving messages again back and forth: Before a change is carried out, the news about the change (e) has to be communicated, such that the developer of the dependent document is prepared for doing this. On the other hand, errors of working area A not detected in this working area but later in B (a module cannot be implemented with the decisions made about it in architecture) yield (f) a message to the person responsible for the document of A. Finally, we see that (g) the results of a technical development step gives rise to management steps in the sense that certain work packages to be fulfilled are identified, e.g. that the design of a subsystem has to be managed and the results of a design may give rise to another management step, as a new subsystem is identified.

Examples (a)–(d) from above use working area *dependency* relations on the *level* of technical developers, (e), (f) to coordinate the collaboration of technical developers, (g) to manage work of developers or identify portions of work to be fulfilled by developers. We will discuss these different cases (a)–(f) in more detail throughout this book after we have made clear how the underlying overall configuration for a software system looks like and after we have explained the functionality of different technical or management tools. We shall see that these different examples are handled on different levels of a complex configuration (see chapter 5). Now we can see another reason for introducing the working area model: Introducing and discussing clean dependency relations is only possible if the source and the target of such a relation have a logical meaning.

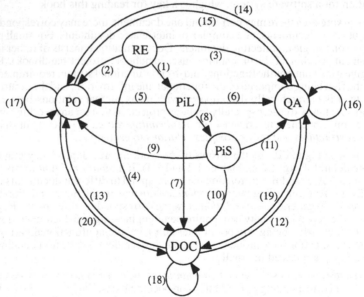

Fig. 1.2. Enumerating the dependency relations between working areas

We summarize that working areas with their dependencies are a very *coarse* view on a complex configuration as working areas are internally structured by subconfigurations and the relations are refined to document dependencies (see below). Being such a very coarse–grained view the working area dependency graph is not dependent on the specific complex configuration of a certain software project and, therefore, is also *invariant* for a whole software project. As structural properties of the graph of fig. 1.2 we see: Technical working areas (RE, PiL, PiS) are mostly sources of binary working area dependency relations, the working areas accompanying the technical working areas (QA, DOC) and the nontechnical working area PO are mostly targets. Furthermore, we see from the dependency graph of fig. 1.2 that PO, QA, and DOC behave symmetrically.

Table 1.3 gives *examples* for most of the *relations between documents* belonging to the working areas and dependency relations of fig. 1.2. All these relations are important and have to be watched carefully during development and maintenance.

(1) Architecture document(s) have to be consistent with the requirements specification documents, e.g. with the functional and nonfunctional description of the system.

(2) Document(s) for project planning (black box estimation) depend on the requirements specification; the activities of requirements engineering are identified as activities to be planned, managed, supervised, and replanned on PO level.

(3) The requirements specification has to be reviewed, or checked/executed by tools (if the description is executable).

(4) The functional and nonfunctional part of the requirements specification has to be documented in the technical documentation and both influence the user documentation.

(5) Project organization documents for cost planning (white box estimation) but especially for management and supervision are highly dependent on the architecture. In the architecture, nearly all work packages of the project can be identified for project organization. Furthermore, architecture modelling itself has to be organized.

(6) The architecture is reviewed or checked giving rise to dependency relations between architecture documents and review protocols, check lists etc. Furthermore, the structure of module and integration test documents (test data collection, test drivers/stubs, test order determination plan etc.) is determined from the architecture especially when black–box test is used.

(7) The architecture determines most of the technical documentation not only from its structure but also from its contents.

(8) The modules to be implemented are determined by the decisions made during architecture modelling. Only the implementation is to be worked out. The resources used for a module body are even fixed in the architecture.

(9) The process of implementing the modules has nearly no influence on the structure of PO documents but on its values (time needed, persons assigned etc.), as the corresponding units are already identified on architecture level.

(10) The implementation ideas are described in the technical documentation.

(11) The modules are tested according to available test methods and tools. In the case of black box tests the structure of module bodies has rather little influence on quality assurance documents. In the case of white box tests we have a strong correspondence between the structure of module bodies and module test documents.

(12) The documentation (user documentation, technical documentation, project handbook) has to be reviewed carefully.

(13) Documentation as an activity has to be organized. The corresponding management documents have a low dependency on the documentation structure.

(14) Quality assurance has to be managed.

(15) All documents of project planning, project management, and project supervision have to be reviewed and/or checked.

(16) Quality assurance, procedures, and strategies to be applied in a project have to be reviewed and evaluated. Furthermore, concrete quality assurance documents (e.g. a module test) may be evaluated by a different quality assurance engineer.

(17) Project organization itself has to be organized (planned, managed, supervised).

(18) The structure of documentation has to be documented.

(19) Quality assurance activities have to be documented.

(20) Project organization activities have to be documented.

Table 1.3. Explanations of major dependency relations by giving examples

We see from this discussion that the edges of fig. 1.2 express dependencies between different working areas and, therefore, dependencies between the documents of different working areas. A dependency A –> B between working areas expresses that the B document is to a smaller or bigger extent *determined* by the results contained in the A document such that either developing the B document or changing the B document one has to obey the pre-determination of, or changes within A. This can be used to support the B developer by appropriate technical tools. These dependencies can also be used to *control* a project w.r.t. installing a suitable working context for a developer or controlling development of back-tracking steps, to control the distribution of problem reports or news about documents, or to build up communication lines between developers etc. All these aspects will be named project administration later in the book. So, it is important to keep in mind that the working area model of fig. 1.2 is not *a* lifecycle model or a project organization model as it contains no time dependencies, milestones etc. and, especially, no information how project organization results are used to control a project. We shall later see that it is a basic model on which different lifecycle models can be mapped.

1.1.4 Software Engineering and Complex Configurations

Software development, maintenance, and reuse of nontrivial software systems deal with *complex overall configurations* (cf. fig. 1.4). Such a configuration mostly contains product information (e.g. of the software system), but also process control information (of the process the result of which is the software system), and further administration information (how to organize the project under the given conditions). Thereby, we have a broad understanding of 'overall configuration', as we define the term such that all perspectives are included. This shall all be explained in this and the next section which are both quite comprehensive as they give a quite specific and personal view on software engineering.

An overall configuration does not only contain the source and/or the object code of the system to be delivered and the dependencies between these parts (*final product configuration*) but also the requirements, the design, the modules, and their mutual dependencies. Let us call all this information the technical information of a configuration as it is written down for software engineers or, in short, the *technical configuration*. So, a technical configuration contains the final product information, but also all information necessary to understand the (development of the) final product. Furthermore, technical activities and their results are accompanied by further activities and results to assure quality (not shown in fig. 1.4), or to guarantee specific documentation etc. We call this next step of comprehensiveness the *extended technical configuration* of a system. Moreover, such a configuration also contains administration information for all of the above aspects, namely to control products, processes, resources etc. developed, carried out, and used by developers, which together we refer to as *administration configuration* (explained in more detail in 1.1.5). Summing up, an overall configuration consists of the extended technical configuration (containing the technical configuration which in turn contains the final product configuration) and the administration configuration with relations between both parts. In chapter 5 we shall see that the situation is even more complex.

We intend to discuss this complete collection of information, together with a bunch of relations between them or between parts of them below, building up the overall configuration of a system in a certain state. It is a good starting point for *further development* of the system, for the *maintenance* of the system, or for the *reuse* of (parts of) the system, or the knowledge of how we got the system. In all three cases we need the information/a part of the information contained in the overall configuration. Such an overall configuration is a complex multi-graph structure. However, this structure only describes the given complexity of a system and its development. Fig. 1.4 gives only a rough picture of the overall complexity, which in a practical case is much more complex. Fig. 1.4 is a conceptual picture and not a user interface description of existing tools.

Fig. 1.4 shows a simple *example software configuration*. The functional requirements specification contains three documents belonging to three perspectives (functional model in SA, data model in EER, control model) in graphical representation for a survey and, furthermore, detailed descriptions (minispecs of data flow processes, control specs, attribute

15

definitions etc.) in textual form in a requirements dictionary. The architecture consists of graphical architecture diagram documents and detailed textual descriptions of components, where any software subsystem has its own representation (as diagram and text, not shown in fig. 1.4). All implementations of modules are given in textual representation (e.g. in Modula-2). Furthermore, there is a textual representation for the technical documentation. Quality assurance documents are not included in the scenario. All of the above representations belong to the extended technical configuration. In addition, there are graphical/textual representations of administration items like configuration control, revision control, process control, and resources control. Therefore, a configuration contains technical information of the product, understanding the term product in a wide sense, and administration information belonging to the product, process, and further aspects.

Such a complex overall configuration consists of a lot of *subconfigurations* (as an architecture of a subsystem together with modules and technical documentation in the technical part, or the configuration description together with its processes in the administration part) which consist of *documents* (the architecture diagram of a subsystem, or the technical documentation of a subsystem). Documents again internally consist of *increments* (a procedure in the export interface of a module, a paragraph of the technical documentation etc.), where increments are derived from the syntax of the underlying language in which the document is written.

Within an overall *configuration* in the above sense, there are a lot of *fine-grained relations* and, therefore, also within (sub)configurations: Within a document there are fine-grained-relations between the increments of the document (intradocument increment–to–increment relations), which are not shown in fig. 1.4. Furthermore, there are a lot of fine-grained relations between increments of different documents which we call interdocument increment–to–increment relations: Objects of entity type E_1 of the data model are stored in the data store S_1 of the function model, the module M_2 of the architecture belongs to data processes P_1, P_2, P_3 of the RE function model, a chapter of the technical documentation is dealing with the design decisions of module M_4, and alike. Such fine-grained relations also exist on the administration configuration side (a revision is contained in a configuration description, a development process control description belongs to a subconfiguration description, a process is carried out by person A, whereby he is using the ABC tool etc.). Relations between the administration configuration and the extended technical configuration are fine-grained (at the administration side, the node is an increment) and *coarse-grained* (at the technical side, the node is a document). The reason is that the administration side only defines which documents, processes etc. occur, but not how they look (see 1.1.5).

An analogous situation we find in *Computer Integrated Manufacturing*. Of course, the technical side of configurations is structured differently (see fig. 1.5 for an example). But again, we have an *overall configuration* consisting of subconfigurations down to increments, fine-grained and one–sided coarse-grained relations. This overall configuration of product development contains again a final product configuration (e.g. the final drawings and NC programs), a technical product configuration (in addition the corresponding documents for analysis, design etc.) and an extended product configuration (furthermore quality assurance and documentation documents). We also have an administration configuration containing the information we need to plan, control, and supervise the development of a product in a CIM-project.

The *technical part* of an overall configuration is *different* in both examples, as it is dependent on the application domain, on procedures/restrictions of a company carrying out a project, on the specific application project etc. The *administration part* is very *similar* as the information is used to plan, control, and supervise a project without going into technical details. Here, the same problems occur independently of the application domain, the specific project, and the division/company carrying out the project.

Why did we introduce a CIM configuration in this introductory chapter of a book on software development environments? The reason is that (a) extended technical configurations,

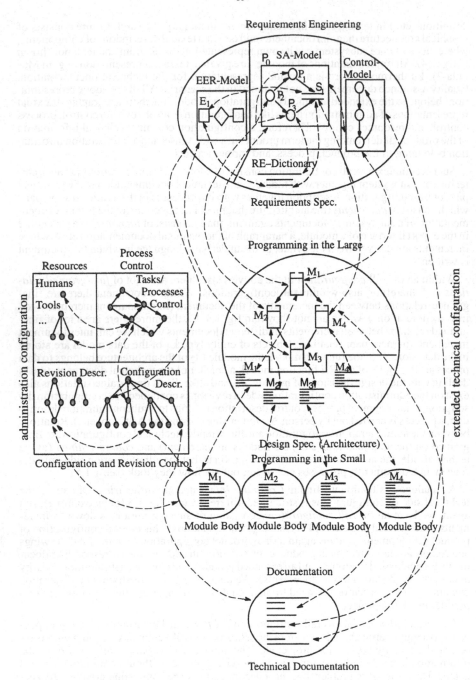

Fig. 1.4. An example of an overall configuration for a software system: technical product information, administration information etc. has to be handled

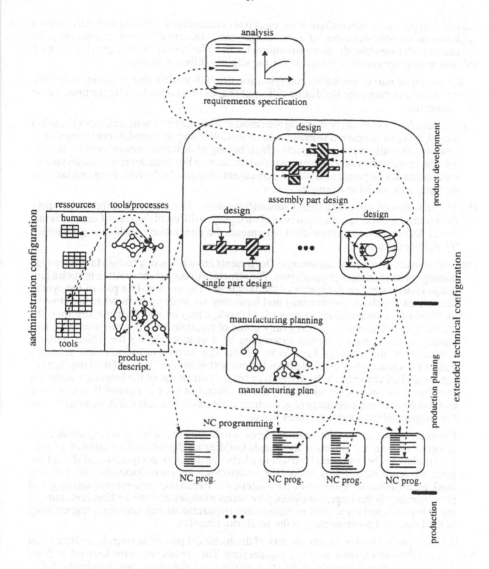

Fig. 1.5. A simple example for an overall configuration in CIM

irrespective of their differences in details, share the *same conceptual structure* (configurations, subconfigurations, documents, increments, together with a lot of fine–grained relations). On this level of abstraction (a1) developing an integrated software or CIM system, or (a2) building an integrated software development environment or integrated support system for developing products in CIM applications is the same problem. Furthermore, (a3) using an integrated software development environment or an integrated CIM development system to build up overall configurations is also the same problem. (b) The administration configuration, to an even larger extent, is not only similar on this level of investigation (again configurations, subconfigurations etc.) it is even *similar* in *structural details*: In both applications we need the same information (process, configuration descriptions etc.). So we can in both cases take the same structures for the administration configuration if, by a suitable parameterization, we provide for the slightly different details.

The *technical part* of a complex configuration depends on different *parameters*, which, each fixed in a certain way, yield quite different shapes of technical configurations. These parameters are:

(a) A coarse *lifecycle model* or working area model: This may be a waterfall model, a spiral model, or, as in our case, a working area model. Working area models center on a division into logically separated aspects which belong to different perspectives of the system/the control of its development, with no distinction between development and maintenance, as development also means permanent changes. In the following, we take the working area model as example.

(b) The *structure* of a *working area's subconfiguration:* There may be different perspectives within a working area, documents belonging to different degrees of detail, hierarchical decomposition, independent documents the integration of which is guaranteed by another document.

(c) The *internal structure* of *documents:* Documents are written in a certain language supporting certain concepts or paradigms. The structure of documents written in such a language is dependent on the syntax of the language. The context-free part of the syntax determines which increments exist and how they are built up from other increments. Furthermore, a methodology to use such a language may impose further restrictions for building up documents (e.g. using only gotos of a certain kind in a programming language), or may impose certain extensions of a syntax (saying for which purpose constructs of the language have to be used). The increment-to-increment relations within a document may originate from the context-sensitive syntax of the language (as e.g. an applied object has to be defined) or from a correct use of the language (anything used has to be set before), or from dynamic semantics (as e.g. control flow), or from methodology to use a language (e.g. a return-code has to be analyzed at the place where the corresponding operation comes back).

(d) *Consistency* and *integration relations* between documents of one working area/of different working areas: Different documents building up the subconfiguration of a working area have to be consistent (consistency between different perspectives, different degrees of detail etc.). Furthermore, the consistency between documents of different working areas has to be observed (consistency between requirements engineering and programming in the large, consistency between modules and the architecture, consistency between technical documentation and requirements engineering, programming in the large, and programming in the small documents).

The example values for the *parameters* of the technical part of an overall configuration have been taken above from software engineering. They could also have been taken from CIM. The parameters (life cycle model etc.) are the *same*, the *values* are completely *different*. Furthermore, in addition to the parameters of the technical part of the configuration we have to regard parameters of the quality assurance part (i.e. structuring quality assurance working area subconfiguration as review for analysis and architecture document, test documents for modules etc.), the internal structure of the corresponding documents, the consistency and integration relations within this subconfiguration and to other parts of the technical configuration. Analogously, documentation parameters have to be determined. So, the parameters we have taken in the above examples for a technical configuration can also be taken for the more comprehensive *extended technical configuration*.

In any application domain where complicated *overall configurations* occur, as in software engineering, CIM etc., development means *building up* a consistent overall configuration by an overall process which contains technical subprocesses resulting in the final product, or subprocesses on documents/subconfigurations to define this product or its built plan, to assure the quality, or to explain and document the products or the processes to get these products. *Maintenance* means to *change* an overall configuration such that starting from a consistent state another consistent state is reached. Reuse (knowledge, components, processes) means to take parts of an overall configuration and to *use* them in another overall configuration.

As we have seen, the technical part of a configuration can have a totally different shape according to the application domain regarded (software development, CIM development) and to the parameters fixed for structuring a certain application development. How can we get rid of this variety in order to build up an administration configuration model which is mostly independent of these details? The key to the solution of this problem is to *separate technical from administration* (organization, management, control, supervision etc.) *information*. This is done by regarding coarse-grained information on administration level and fine-grained information on technical level. In terms of figs. 1.4 and 1.5, we make a vertical cut with models, languages etc. for administration (on the left side) and models, languages etc. for the technical side (at the right side).

In order to factor out technical details on the administration side, we have to regard the suitable level of granularity. This is what we call *coarse-grained* in this section in relation to fine-grained on technical level:

(a) *Internals* of *documents* are not represented on administration level. For documents, we only have information that certain documents exist, but not how they are structured internally (of which increments, which relations between increments etc. they consist of).

(b) *Documents' dependencies* on the administration side only say that documents are dependent, they may have information saying when this dependency is used in order to make documents consistent again, if changes have occurred. However, they contain no information on how the procedure of making inconsistent documents consistent again is to be handled.

(c) *Configuration information* on administration level, therefore, expresses only of which documents and subconfigurations a configuration consists and which dependency relations between these parts exist.

(d) *Revision histories* for documents or configurations on administration level is only expressed by an unsemantical 'is successor of'-relation. This information does not say what has happened if we have derived a new revision of a document, subconfiguration, or configuration from another one.

(e) *Tasks/processes* on administration level only say that tasks/processes exist and, if they are structured internally and if this structure is interesting for administration, of which subtasks/subprocesses they consist. They do not say what these tasks have to do technically, or how processes are carried out in detail on technical level.

(f) This argumentation could be continued for all the *other aspects* of an integrated administration model we shall discuss below. To take only one further example: For a tool on the administration side, it is only registered that it exists, and its characteristics are stored. It is, however, not described how this tool acts on internal structures within or between documents.

Therefore, we have a clear cut between the administration and technical side, with coarse-grained or placeholder information on the administration side (a revision of a document exists, it is empty, in elaboration, inconsistent, consistent with a revision of a master document, is contained in a configuration, the process of development for this revision is in execution, or alike) saying *what* is existing, to be done etc. Technical information saying, *how* something is structured internally, how the process on the technical side is looking like, is not regarded. Therefore, and in order to avoid misunderstandings, we speak in the following paper of *configuration, revision, task* or *process administration* (control, management) etc., if we mean the restriction of the corresponding problem domain to the control part of collaborative development.

As we have seen, overall configurations are very different depending on the application domain and its parameters. Differences are mostly on technical parts. The *administration part* of overall configurations is *similar*. This similarity is quite evident as bookkeeping information of the kind we have in the administration part is necessary in any complex project. However, the administration information is *not the same* if we change the application domain. For example, tasks correspond to the application area, i.e. a software design task in software engineering, a NC-programming task in CIM. These differences can be expressed by a suitable *parameterization* step as is seen later in this book.

This view of separating technical from administration items is in contrast to many articles in software engineering where terms are defined unspecifically. There, *configuration control* (or management) is sometimes not restricted to the administration part but includes technical activities of change and consistency control, configurability control etc. The same situation can be found in process modelling or *process control*, where some authors include all the technical activities involved in developing or maintaining a complete overall configuration, even having the vision such that such an overall process can be fixed by a program /4. Ost 87/. Having in configuration control such a broad view and having also the corresponding activities in mind or, vice versa, regarding all processes in process control on corresponding configurations, means nothing else than replacing the term software engineering or CIM by synonyms, namely e.g. software configuration or CIM process control. This is not useful and results in unprecise terms.

If we look at figs. 1.4 and 1.5, which contain simple overall scenario configurations, we see that on the administration side we find product, process, tool and further information. However, this is product information produced by the manager of a software project. In the same way, on technical side we only have extended technical product information. This is the case in most development environments today. Why do we *not* find *process information* on the both *sides*? The reason is that we do not exactly know today how technical processes (a good design) but also managerial processes (how to manipulate a process net in case of backtracking) are carried out. They are full of creative steps, full of trial and error and, therefore, very hard to formalize. We are not in a position to say what a good process for a certain task is and how it could be denoted. We are at most able to propose some methodological rules on how a product of such a process looks like and how the underlying language should be used to write down intermediate or final results.

On the other hand, if a *subprocess* is *formalizable*, programmable, and automatically executable (e.g. generating a module frame in a certain programming language for the module of an architecture), then in most cases *tools* exist which can perform these subprocesses automatically. How they do this process is then no longer interesting, as it is encoded in the tool. They appear, therefore, on the administration side only with information indicating that the tool exists, which properties it has, whether the corresponding program is available etc. Furthermore, in cases where application technology and structure technology is at hand, it is possible that technical processes and also their control can totally or partially be described (see subsection 1.1.6). In such cases creative, trial and error process steps have been eliminated on the way to inventing the technology. The rest can be mechanized.

Another reason not to regard processes explicitly is the enormous resulting amount of information. We take a subprocess in order to make our point: A complete software design consists of producing a coarse architecture of subsystems and modules, subsystems have to be structured internally by other subsystems and modules, modules contain export and import interfaces which have to be worked out in detail etc. The technical design process description has to define how these details are elaborated, maintained, or reused. Carrying out such a *process* means using small steps *carried* out by tools (from a structure-oriented editor down to a text system), embedded in steps carried *out* by *humans*. So, it is not only the variety of forms, the unpredictability and vagueness of processes, but also the huge amount of process information which would have to be handled in an integrated and distributed environment, which motivates us to concentrate on the product part in this book. Furthermore, process and product descriptions are dual aspects, which are highly interrelated, though not clearly studied yet.

From the arguments of above we see that the IPSEN project does not directly focus on processes. However, the product support on increment, document, intradocument, and interdocument fine–grained level together with its awareness of the administration configuration and its dependencies with the extended technical configuration is also an *indirect* form of *process support*. It facilitates and accelerates processes, guarantees quality of the outcome of subprocesses and of the overall process. The support is mostly on the language level of the underlying languages (requirements specification language, architecture language etc.) and the interrelation of these languages and, at the moment, in some cases also on method level using these languages. If we had adopted the unprecise notion of processes from above, we also could have named IPSEN a process–supporting environment.

In an overall configuration, we have technical product information and also process, product, project etc. control information from an administrative point of view. So, an overall configuration contains information for all these topics. Therefore, we need a *superterm* by which we can refer to all the information corresponding to all above aspects occurring in an overall configuration or process. For that we take the term *project*. So, when a project is running, an overall configuration is built up which contains (indirect) process, product, but also project information, the latter now being restricted in IPSEN to administration aspects like group model, roles, team structure etc. So, 'project' is used in a wide sense throughout the rest of this book and in a narrow sense to regard special aspects of administration.

1.1.5 Management of Complex Configurations and Processes

We have argued that administration (organization, management, control) information has to be kept separate from technical information for certain reasons. Furthermore, all aspects of administration have to be regarded in the administration configuration. Now we shall discuss *separation* and *integration* for the information of an administration configuration in more detail. Especially, we are discussing which aspects of administration have to be regarded, how these aspects are integrated, and how they can be classified. Thereby, we restrict ourselves to the administration of technical tasks, processes, configurations etc. We shall learn later in this book that management has to regard further aspects as well (see chapter 5).

A first problem before we get into details is what we understand under the term *"software project"*, where the term project is used in the wide understanding introduced above. A project can be defined as a *short–term*, limited project, as e.g. the development of a prototype system, or the development of revision 1 of a production system, elimination of errors and weaknesses of the system to get revision 2, porting a system to another hardware or software platform etc. All the different revisions of a system in this sense form a system family, a project is restricted to one member of this family. Another view is that we regard all the revisions of a system family to be developed in one project. This project then is *long–term*, system family-oriented, and consists of a number of short–term projects to be carried out sequentially or in parallel. Therefore, we distinguish between system family and long–term projects and their short–term projects which are logically and closely related. Furthermore, we will later divide projects into *subprojects* corresponding to logical portions of a technical configuration, the development/maintenance of inner subsystems, basic component, high-level tools, or alike. In the following discussion of this subsection we restrict ourselves to subprojects or to short–term projects not cut down to subprojects.

A second item we have to make clear is which *kind of information* we regard on administration level. One view one can find in literature is to regard type information only /6. HW 91/. In this case, only schema information is administrated, as usually done in database systems. This is not sufficient, as administration in our view means keeping track of all information about certain objects of administration, namely of certain configurations, revisions, tasks, processes etc. This is necessary, because one essential point of administration is to be able to make statements about the state of development of all existing objects and their consistency, and not only to know that objects of a certain type may/must exist, must not exist, or may be connected by certain relations of certain types.

The following discussion of this section is devoted to *structure* the working area *project administration* (called project management, organization, or control in software engineering literature) or, consequently, an administration subconfiguration. The aim is to show how this working area can be divided into subareas and how these subareas are intertwined. In the terminology introduced above we restrict ourselves to the administration part of an overall configuration and, even more, to the administration of technical tasks, processes, configurations etc. Therefore, we describe which information is necessary to administrate the work of technical developers. As discussed in the last subsection, it is out of scope to describe the processes which have the administration information explained below as their results. The model for structuring the administration of technical information which we suggest is only one model in a range of possible models. In the form presented in this subsection, it is not application domain specific, as it is not detailed enough to regard the slight differences coming from the application domain.

We find *four subareas* (cf. fig. 1.6). Let us first discuss the project specific subareas at the right side of the vertical dashed line. They deal with the administration aspects of process, product, and abstract resource management/control of a development project. Left of the dashed line we find a subarea which is not specific to one project, but which deals with administration aspects necessary to handle different projects which are carried out 'in parallel' in a certain context. The examples which we use in the explanation are from software engineering.

In *task/process administration* (1), we keep track of all technical tasks to be fulfilled, we assign processes which provide for the solution of these tasks, we denote if tasks are ordered by a 'the result of a task is necessary as the input of another one'-relation. Thereby, we see that task/process nets are built up and modified. For the resulting technical processes there may be more or less precise plans or checklists which have to be followed. These 'plans' may be available or may result from a process to another task. Processes have actors, which at a certain time perform the task. Processes to tasks have attributes for money or duration restrictions, for the absolute start or end time etc. Furthermore, the process to a task is in a certain state (ready, active, suspended, finished, etc.). Such nets can be analyzed (critical paths, flow analysis, etc.). They are stepwise executed if a process is finished therefore making it possible that a process to a dependent task may start. Finally, such nets can be monitored to see whether there is a danger that they run out of time or money restrictions. We shall later discuss that such nets usually cannot be built before project runtime and that they change during project runtime.

Task/process administration is in tight *integration* with *product administration* (2), as any task has an input (revision of a document, subconfiguration, configuration) and has to produce an output of the same kind. To see the integration in the reverse direction, for any component being a part of a configuration which has to be developed, or maintained, or any consistency relation which has to be watched, there must be a corresponding task and, consequently, a corresponding process.

In *product administration* (3) we deal with (sub)configuration and revision administration for (a family of) software (sub)system(s) produced in a project on coarse-grained level. Any (sub)system is represented by a configuration. A configuration contains the information of which parts (revisions of subconfigurations down to documents) it consists. Furthermore, relations (as 'is dependent of', 'is consistent with', etc.) give information about how these parts are related to each other, and in which state the total configuration is. So, a configuration on administration level keeps track of all information of the technical product in the wide understanding of above (extended technical configuration). A system (family) contains lots of 'components' (documents, subconfigurations, configurations) for which different revisions (versions) exist. These revisions are ordered in a 'successor of'-relation. The structure built up by this 'successor of'-relation describes the development history of a 'component'. Thus, such a structure does not describe a specific component contained in a specific configuration but the 'similarities' of specific components which share the same history. However, 'similarities' are not explicit as we have no technology information at hand on administration level and, therefore, do not know about the semantics embedded in 'successor of'-relations. On administration configurations, analyses (e.g. for consistency) can take place at any time of the project. On revision administration level, navigations can take place, especially if revisions and relations have annotations characterizing components or relations (e.g. for what has the revision been introduced, what has happened in a development history by going from one revision to another one).

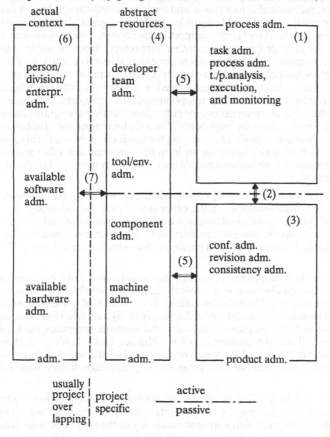

Fig. 1.6. A simple model for administrating the technical configuration of a development project (a simplification, see chapter 5)

Process administration corresponds to the active side, product administration to the passive side of administration. In the same way we distinguish in *abstract resources administration* (4) between active resources (developers, tools) and passive resources (as components used, but not derived in a (sub)project or resources needed to support or to build up active resources). Abstract resources are roles (as a software architect), teams of roles (according to a certain team model), high-level tools (as a transformation tool generating the initial architecture of a software system from a requirements specification) able to perform a process automatically or substantially supporting a manual process for that task, lower-level tools (as a syntax-directed editor) only supporting trivial technical process steps, abstract environments describing collections of more or less integrated tools supporting a process, abstract components describing the properties needed in order to use this component as a given part of a configuration etc. So, the term abstract is used in this paragraph to express that we need resources with certain properties and capabilities and that we do, in the first step, not care about which person, tool, or component is doing the job at project runtime. Of course, the actual developer, tool, component etc. must have the capabilities and properties fixed on abstract level.

Developers, groups, tools, environments play the role of *actors* (machines, processors) for processes or to support processes. Whereas in the case of human actors (roles and teams) we usually have no program for the process fulfilling a task, or we only have a vague and incomplete program, mechanical actors (tools and environments) have to have a detailed and precise program and they must be able to understand the program. High-level tools can replace human actors, low-level tools only support human actors. *Components* may be internal ones (within the same project but in another subproject), from the same company (available in the lab, company, from other projects), or external (from the market). The identification of the right abstract component may be supported by a reuse environment /7.Bör 94/. Finally, other resources have to be administrated, too. They are software or hardware machines, but they can be any facilities like telephones, desks, rooms etc. (not regarded in the following). Machine resources are necessary either for executing a program component being developed, or for executing the program(s) for a tool/environment. Tools/environments have to have a machine capable of executing the program of the tool. This machine may be a software machine which has to be built up by a program and other software or hardware machines together with further components, altogether being part of the abstract resources administration.

The *integration* relations between *task/process* administration and *product administration* on one side and *abstract resources* on the other side (5) are the following: Actors of the task/process model are assigned to roles/teams or high-level tools, low-level tools/environments are assigned to support processes performed by human actors. Components taken from outside are assigned to those parts of a configuration which are not developed/maintained in the project.

The last subarea (6) to be explained describes the *actual context* in a company or lab which has to deliver the actual resources at project runtime. On one hand we have studied this subarea quite superficially. On the other hand it is the border of our model where we can decide to model more or less the real world. Let us give only a sketch: Here, we describe the enterprise, its divisions, the employees, the available software programs, the hardware machines, and alike. All actual resources also have characteristics (abilities and restrictions) describing what we can do with the actual resource and what restrictions to obey (version number, number of software licenses, programming language dialect, hardware restrictions etc.).

Software resources can play different roles when regarding the *connection* to *abstract resources* (7). Software resources may be components of a system which are not developed in the project but taken as they are. Software resources may be the programs of tools or may be the programs of software machines, or components for such a machine necessary to execute the program for a tool. Hardware resources are assigned to the machines of abstract tools supporting a process performed by a human, or to an automatic process determined by a program, which is either given (high-level tool) or developed in the project (a test program run). The employees are assigned to roles.

The dashed line between abstract resources (4) and actual resources (6) corresponds to a *mapping* of abstract resources to actual resources. Thereby, the corresponding abilities and properties have to be delivered by actual resources. Actual resources may have further capabilities not used in a certain mapping. This mapping also has to do with balancing and *scheduling* capacities: Usually, actual resources are shared between different (sub)projects, as the overall resources for a (sub)project change dramatically over the time and resource sharing between different (sub)projects smoothens this time dependency. Only in rare cases, a (sub)project has actual resources which are statically assigned at project start time. In this case, the mapping and scheduling is not performed dynamically during project runtime, but before new projects start.

The *distinction* between *abstract resources* administration on one side and *process* or *product administration* on the other side is sometimes not easy to make. Let us give some examples.

In CIM, there may be a mechanical tool which is developed in the same project in which it is used later on. In most cases, the tool is developed in a separate subproject. In this subproject the tool is on the products' side, in the project where it is used it is on the tools' side. In some cases the development of the tool is intertwined with the development of a product where the tool is used. For example, there are situations in CIM where the development of a production tool cannot be separated from the development of the product in the production of which the tool is used. Other examples come from bootstrapping techniques in compiler construction for extending a language, porting a compiler, or improving a compiler. In these cases, different steps are needed where compilers are developed or modified as products which in the next step are used as high-level tools, or for which, with the help of other tools, new tools are produced /9. Wir 86, 7. Nag 90/. So, usually a tool is taken from outside (developed in another subproject, taken from another project or from the market), but it is sometimes necessary to develop it in the same (sub)project. The model must be able to handle both situations.

In the same way as exists between resources and processes, we can have problems in separation between resources and products. A general component may be developed in a project where it is used although its development should be in a separate (sub)project as it may also be used in other projects. In both cases, development within the same project or in a different project, we have a change of the role of software from product to component, respectively.

On the *abstract resources side* some *difficulties* and *misunderstandings* may also occur. For example, the distinction between developer and tool may change over time: When a tool has a breakdown, a developer may play the role of a tool, when a new tool arrives, a process to a developer's task may from then on be carried out automatically by the tool. Finally, the use of a tool means having the program of the tool, the underlying machine and, furthermore, some components available (e.g. an underlying object storage) which are not necessarily a part of the tool, but a prerequisite. So, a suitable tool may be a combination of abstract software and hardware resources, the components of which are under control of abstract resource administration and have to be combined, sometimes even at process runtime.

Looking at our model for administration of technical information at this point, we see that all aspects and subaspects of administration are regarded as being *tightly integrated*. This integration is broken into increments together with their relations, i.e. to the *fine-grained information* necessary and useful on the administration side. To take only one example: A certain task T may exist, the input and output being each a revision A^i, B^j of two documents. These revisions are contained in a configuration C^m. Each revision is embedded in corresponding revision histories of A, B, and C respectively. The task T has a process P, a role R is responsible for P and is supported by a tool T^k, the role is taken by a person Pe^l. On the other side, as discussed in the last subsection, if we regard the corresponding documents/configurations etc. of the technical configuration, this information is coarse-grained as technical details are disregarded. Documents/configurations on the administration side are only names or references for documents on the technical side.

Up to now we have discussed the administration of technical information at project runtime for which we need nets, configurations, revision histories etc. We have only pointed out that this administration information is necessary at runtime in order to organize or control the technical development. So, we discussed administration information *results*. We did *not* speak about *tasks* or processes etc. responsible for building up or changing this administration information. The tasks or processes on the administration information we mentioned in this section work on subareas (1), (3), (4), (6) of fig. 1.6 (e.g. modifying a task/process net), but also on the integration (2), (5), (7) items. Furthermore, we can build up integrated administration tasks/processes concerned with modifications of all subareas and their integration information. An example was given in the last paragraph. Finally, we did not speak about how the administration subconfiguration discussed here is used to *control* the work of different developers. This is done in chapters 2 and 5 of this book

We get even more complicated examples for integrated administration tasks if we regard *release, quality assurance, access*, or *documentation control*. Quality assurance control, for example, means that on administration level we take care of quality insofar as any development task/process is followed by tasks/processes responsible for quality (review, test, inspection, verification, validation etc.). In the model examined by this subsection this implies that corresponding tasks/processes are inserted into the task/process net, that the corresponding quality assurance documents/subconfigurations are part of the administration configuration, that quality assurance roles and tools are defined and mapped on available persons and tools. The arguments are similar for the areas release, access, or documentation control. So, on administration level, for example, we cannot assure quality as quality is to be found on technical or extended technical configurations, but we take care that the corresponding tasks/processes etc. are regarded at project runtime which, hopefully, assure this quality.

The administration aspects regarded in this section are called *formal* or engineering-like *administration*. They allow the administration of a formal *collaboration* between different members of the project in order to organize a project in which different processes work together to produce a consistent overall configuration. The administration modifications we have offered are suitable to denote the *results* of creative decisions or to denote the implications of problems as tasks or configuration components. However, a creative decision has to be made by a human or a group of humans. For that decision finding, the discussions about different solutions, sketches of vague ideas, or evaluations of different strategies have to be regarded. The same is true for deciding how to react in the event of an unexpected problem. All this is a part of process description, denoting how the technical or management processes of one person or a group of persons are carried out. This kind of human interaction, decision finding, evaluation of alternatives, or problem solution we call *informal* collaboration. For these activities support by tools is also possible /2. MBJ 90, 4. RJG 91/. This, however, is out of the scope of this book. Furthermore, in the SUKITS project multimedia tools are realized to allow different developers discuss the contents of documents by using selection devices, E–Mail, making annotations to documents, and the like. We call such tools, being useful for product–centered environments as described in this book as well as for process–centered environments excluded here, *informal communication* tools.

What we have discussed up to now is horizontal integration, i.e. building up an integrated administration model for technical information by putting certain submodels and integration models into the framework of fig. 1.6. (We shall learn later in this book that we have only discussed one layer of a more complicated situation, see chapter 5.) Another topic is *subproject integration control*. A big project is divided into subprojects which are separate (in the same 'context' as the overall project, in another part of the same lab/company, carried out by an external group) but which on the other side have to be integrated. This means that the 'same' information has to be available for all subprojects, irrespective of where they are carried out. This implies that the model of fig. 1.6 has to be available for any subproject. On the other side such a subproject is embedded in one or more (sub)projects where its results are needed. So, what we need is a model for a hierarchy of subprojects where, on each level of the hierarchy, the overall configuration information for the subproject is available and, on the other side, integration is also guaranteed across the levels of the hierarchy (see also chapter 5 for first ideas).

The *model* for an administration configuration in this subsection has *not* been *fully realized* by us at this point in time. We did not regard all aspects (e.g. context control) and granularity of information (e.g. the software and hardware resources needed to use a tool). We concentrate on its process, product, and on some topics of its resources part in the following.

At the end of this section, let us try to *relate* the notions of this subsection to *notions of software engineering* literature. Project organization (management, control etc.) in literature is understood to contain information belonging to any organizational aspect (product, process, project in the narrow sense etc.) occurring in a software project. Usually, technical aspects are not clearly separated from administration aspects as was seen from the discussion of the term configuration management or process modelling of above. For project organization a lot of different definitions exist. Let us take two widely used ones.

The first divides project organization into project planning, project management (sometimes miscalled programming in the many), and project supervision. Thereby, planning is a quite unprecise term. It can mean (1) estimation of costs, personnel power, or distribution of costs/personnel over the lifetime of a project. Estimation of any kind is not regarded in this book although it can be done using the information of an administration configuration. (Here, we see all tasks/processes, all components of this system in a form suitable for calculations: We can use this information for white–box or for black–box cost estimation as similarity estimation or attribute estimation (e.g. COCOMO /7.Boe 89b/). In the latter case, we would have to extend our administration model by further information for characterizing projects.) On the other side project planning (2) can mean, in a more restricted sense, to plan which technical products, processes are to be developed or are needed. The latter are tasks of what we have called process administration above. Project management in our model is (a) abstract resource administration (roles, groups, tools, environments), integration of abstract and actual resources, and their relation to process administration. It, furthermore, (b) regards other aspects if we assure quality or documentation on organization level (see above). Project supervision (3) is essentially product/process analysis and monitoring.

Closer to our notion is the second definition of project organization distinguishing between management of the processes, the products, and the project, respectively. Not only that we (1) give a more precise definition (by factoring out technical details and concentrating on administration aspects), we also (2) introduce subaspects of this categorization (as quality assurance administration), and we also discuss (3) integration aspects between all these subaspects. We add (4) two further subareas which are also important for project organization, namely abstract resources' administration and administration of the actual resources including, therefore, the context in which a project is carried out.

1.1.6 The Importance of Application and Structure Technology

This section gives again a quite personal view on software engineering. It points out that *specialization* is *needed* in *software engineering* to improve its state of maturity and to get the same level as in other engineering disciplines. We see specialization in three directions as to be pointed out below. Especially, we argue that the right level of details and abstraction is needed to get the desired results. There are examples of software systems where we have deep knowledge.

One specialization yields an improvement of maturity for a certain application area of software engineering. There are different application areas like business applications (booking systems for travel agencies, payroll accounting systems), mathematical/scientific applications (experiment evaluation systems, stability computing systems), process engineering applications (robotic systems, control systems for technical processes, computer–aided manufacturing), communication applications (telephone network software systems, document exchange systems), system software applications (compilers, data base systems, software development environments) etc. We call the products of the above application areas *application* system *'classes'*.

For any of these application classes or special applications concepts, languages, methods, tools, utilities, components etc. can be investigated and developed, and experiences, procedures, techniques etc. can be collected. We have called this variety of knowledge a technology above. So, what we need is *application technology* for different application areas or, according to the statement at the beginning of this subsection, we need a specialization in direction of developing different application technologies. Today the term software engineering stands more or less for all common techniques which are independent from application classes, and not for a collection of specific technologies regarding different applications. The latter, however, is the prerequisite for 'deep' knowledge in software engineering in the sense of seeing differences but also generalizations within an application area. Nowadays, software engineering is a collection of 'methods', i.e. unprecisely defined concepts and languages (w.r.t. syntax, semantics, pragmatics) the application of which is unclear (there are no rules saying what a good specification is, or how to get it). Furthermore, these languages or methods and, consequently, the tools supporting them are not application specific.

Application technology can be local (within a lab, a company, only technical internal reports available) or global (being taught in schools on the basis of good books). There are mainly two *reasons* that *application technology* is *not available* or seen today: (1) Firstly, the awareness for developing such application technology is not to be seen. Developing such a technology means to think in medium or long–term perspectives. Only when concentrating on an application area for a long time can the technology develop and there is a pay–off for the corresponding investment. (2) In some contexts such technology is locally available which, however, is mostly hidden from the competitors. Technology is often implicit and there would be an even greater profit for the company (but also for other companies working in the same field) if developing such technologies were an official business goal.

A second branch of specialization is to regard whether we can find structural patterns in software systems. These structural similarities may also occur in software systems belonging to different application classes. Therefore, we divide different software systems into system *structure 'classes'*. There are transformation systems, interactive systems, reactive systems. Another dimension is to regard sequential systems, concurrent systems, or parallel systems. A further aspect is whether a system is linked, dynamically loadable, or distributed or whether a software system or main component of it is hardwired, generated, or rule–based etc.

Again we call any knowledge from concepts to components together with any knowledge from experience to techniques which is directed towards a structure class a *structure technology*. So, as argued above we have to specialize into different structure technologies and we have to make every effort to distribute structure technologies. The arguments for the nonavailability of structure technology are the same as for the nonavailability of application technology above.

A third branch of specialization is to regard the *project type* for a software system or the character of its output. It may be a new development, the extension/modification of an existing system, a reengineering project, or even a reverse engineering project. It may be oriented to produce just one system or to a machinery to get a member of a family of systems with minor effort. It may yield one complete system, a framework for a family of systems, a platform, or a reusable large component for many systems. As above, we call 'deep' knowledge about different project types *project technology*.

Introducing the term application, structure, and project technology is only a rather trivial attempt to *classify software systems* or their projects. At the moment, no general and reasonable classification system for software systems is known by the author. So, the software engineering community, either researchers or real engineers, act in a field about which they only have a vague understanding either w.r.t. its borders, or what is found inside, or what varieties or similarities can be detected there. There are only global 'missionary' messages from time to time as structured methods, OO methods, or alike. They are attempts to view the problem only in a narrow way. On the other hand, if there were a clear and comprehensive classification system and the technologies according to its dimensions were available, then building a new system would mean starting with a rich set of deep knowledge, suitable reuse units, and suitable application and structure class specific tools.

How do we go about producing the required technologies we miss today? The first question is, on which logical level do we think about software systems. Trivially, it cannot be the requirements specification which gives no results on how a system is built up and, on the other hand, it cannot be the code of the system which contains too much details. The *architecture* of a system is at the ideal level as it is the essential structure which contains all important realization decisions. Therefore, it is both detailed enough and abstract enough to reveal construction patterns, differences, and similarities. Summing up, it is a *specialization* of *design technologies* for different application, structure, or project classes what we need in the future.

There are *fields* of software construction where we have a lot of *deep knowledge*. Let us take the example *compiler construction* (/9. ASU 86, 9. GW 85, 9. Wir 86/) belonging to the application class systems software and to the structure class sequential transformation systems. There is a lot of reuse knowledge available either on the model, product, or process side. The reason is that a remarkable number of researchers have worked for a long time in this field and that many results have been published. By the way, this is also a good example in Computer Science of a symbiosis of theory and practice.

In compiler construction, as in other areas, *reuse* is firstly on the *model* side (formalisms for scanning, parsing, context sensitive analysis, code generation). Furthermore, there is product and process reuse. We have reuse on the *product* and *process* side mainly in multi–phase compilers and process reuse in one–phase compilers.

In the first case (/9. ASU 86, 9. GW 85/), we can extract reusable data structures as standard components for input, output, and intermediate data structures (character stream, list of machine instructions, but also token list, derivation tree, intermediate code etc.). Furthermore, we have a generally applicable pattern between the functional phases, their control, and the underlying data structures. Phases again have basic components as drivers for lexical analysis, or for parsing for a certain class of regular or context–free grammars, but also for the translation stack, the error handling etc. Specifics are put into data structures rather than hardwiring them in program parts. These data structures are often generated by generator systems (scanner, parser, or code generator generator etc.) the results of which are parts of the final product.

In one–phase compilers (/9. Wir 86/) reuse is mostly on the process level, i.e. we automate the production of writing a compiler and do not try to reuse certain components in different compilers. There, the architecture can be derived automatically from the context–free grammar, even the bodies of the modules can be written nearly automatically.

Let us give an *example* of *process reuse*, again from compiler construction, by regarding *bootstrapping* (/9. Wir 86/). Bootstrapping can be used for extending a compiler, for porting a compiler onto another platform, or for improving a compiler. We take *porting* the *compiler* as the example to be discussed. We start with an S_SM compiler and an S_MM compiler as in all bootstrapping tasks (A_BC means that we have a compiler written in B which translates A source code into C target code). The aim is to port the S compiler generating M code and implemented as M code program to another machine M'. This task is fulfilled in three steps (cf. fig. 1.7): In a first step T_1 we manually change the S_SM compiler to produce M' code. Then, this S_SM' compiler is, in a second step T_2, automatically translated by the S_MM compiler running on an M machine. This results in an S_MM' compiler. The result of the first step T_1, namely the S_SM' compiler, is now automatically translated in a third step T_3 using the S_MM' compiler of T_2 which is also running on an M machine. The result is the desired compiler for S running on an M' machine and producing M' code.

We have learned from the examples above on product and process reuse in compiler construction that there can be deep technology in a field of system construction/maintenance such that the corresponding *process* is not vague, unprecise, unforeseeable, and unpredictable but it is *clear*, can be exactly *planned*, either on technical or administration level. Especially, we have seen from the bootstrapping example that the whole process can be *statically determined* (more particularly, it can be taken as a known pattern) before the project starts. Such clearness is a result of specialization. We could also have taken the example of multi–phase compilers showing product reuse, namely that we have a fixed system pattern with reusable components which can be taken, only some components are to be realized and, even more, some are generated such that the whole development process is a precise 'maintenance' process on a given overall configuration.

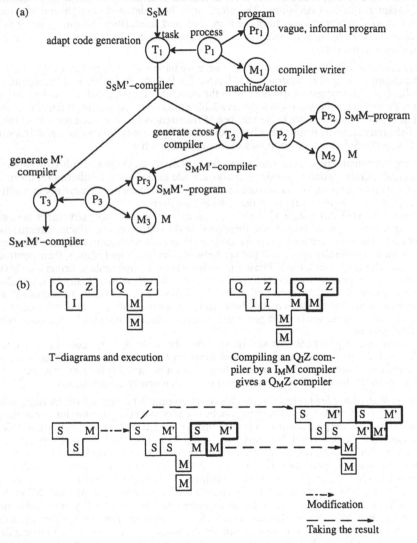

Fig. 1.7. A task/process net for the task of porting a compiler using bootstrapping: (a) task/process net, (b) explanation by T–diagrams /9. Wir 86/

The situation in general software development is far away from this level of maturity. It is also far away from classical engineering disciplines. However, the situation is worse in software engineering: A software engineer changes between different application areas (at one stage, contributing to a business application system, a short time later to a system for process control etc.) and technology is not explicitly available in many fields of software construction. Therefore, the wheel is constantly reinvented all over the world and the processes are vague and unpredictable. What we have in software engineering today is to *claim* that we were able to *educate* the type of a *'general engineer'* being able to build everything what can be realized by software. Although software as an immaterial product in comparison to material products in other engineering disciplines causes some specific problems (cf. /7. Nag 90/) we believe that this unsatisfactory state can only be changed by specialization. This book aims at contributing to a technology for (software) development environments (application class 'system software', structure class 'interactive, integrated, and distributed systems', project type 'new systems with reuse'). Thereby, we shall see that we can learn a lot from compiler construction.

1.2 Software Development Environments: Basic Terms, Goals, Importance, and Variety

The *aim* of this *section* is to introduce the understanding of software development environments we use throughout this book, to explain the importance of software development environments, to discuss the variety of SDEs, and to argue that any approach for software development environments is derived from a certain perception or paradigm.

1.2.1 SDE Definition, Importance, and Goals

Since about 1980 the support of the development and maintenance of software systems by fully or partially automated, more or less integrated tools has received great attention. In the following we call such a tool collection a *software development environment* (abbr. SDE). SDEs have been and are one of the main topics of software engineering research and development. There are a lot of different names for SDEs (fig. 1.8 giving an EBNF generating most of them). Section 1 of the bibliography contains a remarkable set of conference proceedings, monographs, and overview articles giving a survey on the activities in this R&D area. Section 2 of the bibliography gives an overview of the key projects, however, more from an academic point of view. In addition, there are a big number of tools on the industrial market. There is no room in this book to discuss or even enumerate all these different and mostly interesting tools or SDEs (see section 4 of the bibliography).

```
SDE_denotations ::=
             [ attributes ]
             ( Programming | Programmer's | Software ) [ Project | Product | Process | Configuration ]
             ( Development | Production | Support | Engineering )
             ( Tools | Toolbox | Workbench | Environment | Assistant | Apprentice | Factory )
attributes ::=
             ( computer−aided || structure−oriented || integrated || intelligent || incremental ||
             object−oriented || knowledge−based || multi−paradigm || open || distributed || ... )

[ ] option, ( ... | ... | ... ) 1 of n alternative, ( ... || ... || ... ) m of n alternative, terminals
```

Fig. 1.8. An EBNF generating most of the different names for an SDE

The different names derived from fig. 1.8 to a certain extent reflect the range or quality of support and/or the *different approaches* taken. For example, the name Programmer's Workbench is a toolbox approach for an SDE collecting rather conventional tools for programming, the name Software Production Factory expresses the idea of a comprehensive SDE which can be configured according to the actual context. The terms Software Development Environments or Computer–Aided Software Engineering are often associated with a phase or working area oriented and engineering–like approach of software development and maintenance. The Programmer's Assistant or Apprentice gives the imagination of a tool with AI behavior.

Before we continue let us exclude what we do *not understand* under the *term SDE*. The implementation of a certain programming language (editor, compiler, linker, loader, runtime package) or a programming system (a language implementation for a family of languages (usually sharing some intermediate code, possibly extended by a trace, dump etc.)), or a collection of different variants of a compiler (students' compiler, optimizing compiler, incremental compiler) are not regarded to be an SDE. These all are rather conventional tools which have been available before 1980. Furthermore, an SDE should not only support programming, i.e. to build up final product configurations in the definition of the last section. On the other hand, we do not understand the name software development environments in such a wide meaning to include the organization in which a software system is developed, or the persons which are developing, maintaining, or running it, as it was done in the

STARS–Project /2. ST 83/. However, we do demand that the administration of those items is an integrated part of SDEs. The first is a *too narrow* the second *too wide* a definition. Therefore, the name SDE is associated with tools not with human beings. It can include 'intelligent' tools for technical processes as well as for the organization of human labour.

The *overall goal* of *SDEs* is to *improve* the *productivity* of software engineers by automation which reduces the costs in the development and maintenance of software systems. In detail, this is achieved by (1a) *avoiding* unnecessary *clerical* or bookkeeping work, thus allowing the software engineer to concentrate on creative tasks, and (1b) by avoiding *errors* in error–prone activities where it is hard for a human being not to get lost, as e.g. keeping different related software documents consistent. Furthermore, the goal is achieved by (2) giving tools for *improving* the *structure* and *quality* of software documents by offering syntactical and/or semantical operations supporting languages, methods, and paradigms to develop these documents, assuring quality or certain rules for preparation, which altogether are related to certain constraints of one or more classes of software documents. Tools can support and facilitate the work of single software engineers as well as the cooperation of different members in one group or of different groups of a more or less big team of software engineers involved in a project.

The arguments given above have *special instantiations* in some areas, as (a) SDEs facilitate the preparation of documents such that they can better serve as a basis for communication, (b) tools can improve the acceptance of produced software by e.g. offering support for rapid prototyping, (c) tools can improve the commercial success of a software project by e.g. offering support for project planning, project management, and project supervision, (d) tools can facilitate industrial development of software by giving special help for software maintenance, software reuse, and software validation. Any of these instantiations has to do with productivity and quality improvement.

1.2.2 A First Classification of Tools and Environments

In the following subsections we give a short *overview* on *tools* and *environments* to prepare the reader for the realm of possible viewpoints and solutions. A careful classification of SDEs is given in section 1.7. So, this and the next subsection aims only at giving an overview. Thereby, we sketch the variety of tool forms in this subsection, and the influence of underlying perceptions, approaches, and paradigms in the next.

A simple classification of tools and environments is whether they have a *practical relevance* or not. For that we can go through the list of problem topics of the last section and ask whether a given SDE gives substantial support to overcome these problems or not. This practical relevance also has to do with the quality of support (coverage, depth, integration, formalization, granularity; all aspects to be explained later in section 1.7). Therefore, we can conclude that one essential is that an SDE must give at least substantial support for requirements engineering and programming in the large, as both are the most risky technical working areas. Continuing this argument there also should be substantial support for project organization, especially for the planning activities. The latter is rather hard as in this case, if we include estimation of costs, personnel etc., experience knowledge from different projects and intuition have to be used and the question is how to get it, to compare, and evaluate it. Finally, support of maintenance is essential. This, however, has to do with tool integration and is explained in section 1.4 of this book.

For one *working area with a fixed language* there can exist *different tools*. There can exist editor tools to build up or to maintain a document of the corresponding document class. There can exist analyzer tools to check whether a certain constraint of the document class holds true or not. Analysis can be integrated with editing: In this case analysis is implicitly invoked by the editor tool, e.g. to check whether the context sensitive syntax of the document class language is followed or not. We shall see later that many IPSEN–editors have this property. On the other hand, analysis can be explicitly invoked by the user, i.e. in the case of a completeness check. In this case it is not useful to activate this check when a change has been made, because it is only interesting at a certain time. Furthermore, there can be tools for structural changes, e.g. for optimizing transformations in the area programming in the small. There can also exist tools for some kind of monitoring, e.g. for insertion consumption counters and breakpoints to monitor the execution in programming or to observe the number of structural changes in an arbitrary document. There may exist execution tools in the case that a document is executable. An example for this is an interpreter, possibly connected with an incremental compiler, for programming in the small. Finally, there may be a browser by which one can browse through a document. These different tools may exist for all documents of a class of documents or for different document classes. Therefore, this tool classification is *working area*, *language*, and *method* independent.

Usually, a document class is related to one working area and different working areas have different document classes. However, there may be languages which have been defined to fit for different working areas. They are sometimes called *broadband languages*. They have been introduced in so–called transformation approaches (e.g. /2. Bau 85, 87/), where the distinction into different working areas is felt not to be necessary. Another possibility is that a language combines constructs needed and used in different working areas. There may be different opinions about the usability of a language for more than one working area: Some people argue that requirements specification languages like SA or SADT can be used for architecture modelling or, vice versa, an OO architecture modelling language can also be used for requirements engineering. Another example is that modern programming languages, like Ada, are sometimes also used as 'specification languages'. In any of these cases, broadband languages or languages to be used for different working areas, the *tools* listed in the last paragraph are used for *different working areas*.

Accepting that different working areas need different languages in order to express different concepts to be used or that there are different documents in one working area there must be *tools* for *integration* between documents. These tools can be analyzers checking for interdocument consistency (e.g. between requirements specification and architecture), there can be initial transformation tools generating a portion of another document (e.g. module frames from the architecture) to start with, or transformation tools transforming changes of a master document into a dependent document, or a group of dependent documents. There may be browsers going through different documents belonging to different working areas. Integration tools may, furthermore, be devoted to technical or to administration activities. The different forms of integration tools are introduced and classified in subsection 1.6.4.

Having distinguished between different working areas and corresponding languages, methods, and tools, as well as strategies and tools for integration we can find two further aspects of supporting 'quality' in the sense of the first subsection 1.2.1. One is the *degree* of *coverage* and the other the degree of *integration*. The first means for what working areas useful tools exist at all, the second which integration tools exist within and between these working areas and what quality of integration they offer.

The reader should note that coverage and integration or, more generally, any property of an SDE is always to be seen in *correspondence* to underlying *concepts*, *languages*, or *methodologies* determining the use of a language. Therefore, there may be a tool for a working area, supporting the language but not a certain methodology. So, we have coverage corresponding to the language but not w.r.t. the methodology. In the same way, we may have support of certain concepts in the form of representations (e.g. bubbles for processes) but not a specific language explicitly incorporating these concepts (e.g. a clear understanding of processes and their interaction). The same arguments, of course, hold true for integration.

Furthermore, we may distinguish whether certain *tools* have a property, or the *SDE* as a whole, as tools may exist in an SDE having properties which the other tools do not have. Finally, another question is whether a certain *property* is to be seen and can be used at the *user interface* level of a tool/an SDE, or whether it is only, fully or partially, built in.

The arguments of productivity improvement of the last subsection assume that the software engineer is the creative partner in software development and maintenance, the SDE being passive in the sense that it gives only substantial mechanical *support*. Substantial is meant in the *sense* of facilitation and *intelligence*. There are different opinions on what intelligence means and how far it can go. One is that the tools do the clerical work (bookkeeping, support for writing down something, support for remembering something) and check work (being informed if some language or method constraints are violated) on document, collections of documents, process, and combination of processes level. Quite another understanding of intelligence can be found in approaches which come from AI. There the SDE has some role of creativity in the sense that it has deep knowledge about documents and processes and, therefore, does things which otherwise are done by human beings. So, intelligence is a range from stupid mechanical, but useful, to knowledgeable and 'creative'.

Another quite different distinction between *tools* or SDEs is in which form documents are represented to the user of the SDE. They may be represented in *textual* form (e.g. for a programming language editor) or in *graphical* form (e.g. for an architecture editor). In the latter case there is usually an additional textual representation which is used for fixing the details of components. We call different representations of the same internal 'logical' document the different representations (or different views) of this document. Therefore, an SDE can support *multiple* views or *single views* of different forms.

Another possibility for characterizing *tools* is to regard the *level* of concepts, languages, methods, or constraints they are based on. This language may be related to a working area and may incorporate corresponding concepts or not. Therefore, a tool may be *language–independent* (as e.g. a text editor). It may know more or less about a clearly defined language (context free syntax, context free plus context sensitive syntax). In the latter case we speak of *syntax–oriented* editing or structure–oriented editing. (The term language–independent of above is not precise, tools are always language–dependent, but the 'language' may be very low level, as text). On this level the tool may know a method how to use the language. In this case we speak of *method–oriented* tools. Even more, support can mean that knowledge or experience is used, i.e. how to do well or how to apply clear patterns. Only in this case would we call them *knowledge–oriented*.

There is another classification of tools/SDEs which is independent of the language level or the degree of integration which tools support. Tools can be *strict according to* the language/method such that documents they prepare always fulfill the language/method *rules*. On the other side tools may *allow violation* of these restrictions for a certain time within development or maintenance. The most useful tools are those combining both properties: They are watching the restrictions, they allow violations, but they give a complete answer about all violations and their mutual relations.

A further distinction of tools/SDEs comes from the fact whether the *tools* can handle only documents in a certain state and their relation to each other (a certain configuration) or whether they know about different states of documents (revisions, versions) and of different configurations which can be built from them, i.e. they allow control of different revisions of an overall configuration (*system version* or *family*–oriented SDEs). Furthermore, the question is whether the tools only know that documents or configurations are ordered in a time–dependent successor relation or whether the tools know what has happened with a document/ a configuration from one revision to the next and can *exploit* the *structure* and *knowledge* in order to built up/ modify configurations.

Furthermore, tools may be *restricted* to *one* software *(sub)project* or they may keep knowledge and experience of several (sub)projects in order to be used in another project. The latter is the case for tools estimating project costs which are using *experience* of *different (sub)projects* in the form of relevant attributes (black box estimation methods).

Last but not least *tools* may only be devoted to the *standard activities* of software development (for the working areas of fig. 1.2) with corresponding languages and methods or they may, additionally, support *activities* to *overcome* working area independent or working area integrating *specific software problems* such as reuse, process modelling, software metrics. Reuse, for example, can be supported by 'intelligent' browsing, or archiving and retrieval systems on fractions of documents, documents, collections of documents, and configurations level. In any case giving substantial support here means that activities on different document classes and activities of their combination have to be supported.

In the last section we have stated that application, structure, and project technology are key topics required in order to get 'deep' knowledge in software engineering. Therefore, *SDEs* may be built which are devoted to a special *application area* and/or *structure class*. For the first, there may be special application–dependent languages and methods supported by tools. For the second, there may be substantial tool support for standards, architectural frameworks, basic components, generators etc. Tools of both kinds, of course, are project overlapping tools.

Finally, in order to end up with our first characterization scheme, we can ask whether an *SDE* is *configurable* according to the needs of a certain context (working areas, corresponding suitable languages or methods selected etc.) or whether it is *hardwired* for this context. It is clear, that configurability demands for flexibility in the realization of an SDE (exchanging languages, methods, integration mechanisms etc.) but also for portability of the solution, allowing it to be transported to a new hardware or software platform. Another characterization is whether an SDE is *open* to extension by new tools or whether it is *closed*. Openness does not necessarily mean that an SDE is configurable in the above sense. However, at least the interfaces for new tools have to be defined and made public. A last dimension for realization is whether an SDE follows the *bottom–up* or a posteriori approach, as most of the industrial SDEs which try to build integration platforms such that working area tools or integration tools can be taken from the market. Another approach is the *top–down* or a priori one, where new tools (and in some cases also a machinery for building tools) are built for offering new properties, in our case integratedness. We come back to all these properties later in this book.

1.2.3 SDEs and Underlying Models or Paradigms

The *aim* of this *subsection* is to sketch the variety of approaches for SDEs found in literature, especially the difference between academic and industrial approaches. This sketch continues the categorization of SDEs, which we have discussed in the last subsection. However, it gives principle remarks which come from different underlying models and paradigms.

Most of the *SDE approaches* are bound to a certain lifecycle model in the sense that this model is 'hardwired' within the environment. There are quite different models (ranging from waterfall model /7. Boe 82/ to models which are influenced by artificial intelligence /2. RW 90/). Therefore, such SDEs are *dependent* on a certain *lifecycle model*. In the last years in the context of process modelling the question came up of having lifecycle *independent* SDEs in the sense that the corresponding SDE can easily be configured for a certain lifecycle model but, even more, for a more detailed understandings of processes. We discuss this question in chapters 5 and 6.

In some of the approaches, especially from academia, there is one *key concept* for the development of *software* or structuring software and, therefore, determining the whole environment. Examples are object–orientation, functional composition, process–orientation, regarding applications to be rule–based, being specifiable by algebraic specifications, or regarding every activity of software development being a well–defined transformation step. In those approaches the concept is the only one felt to be needed and, therefore, being supported. We call those approaches *mono–paradigm environments*. The other case is that different concepts are regarded to be necessary and, therefore, are supported by tools. In this case the environment is called a *multi–paradigm* environment. Most of the industrial approaches are multi–paradigm environments supporting different concepts, such as e.g. the concept of processes and entity types in requirements engineering, the concepts of modules in programming in the large etc.

Another categorization, which is different from that of the last paragraph, comes from the used language or languages. There can be one language having one key concept (then the environment is usually a mono–paradigm SDE) or different concepts (especially in broadband languages which have been designed for different working areas). We call these approaches *mono–language SDEs*. Correspondingly, we call an SDE *multi–language* SDE if it supports different languages (and then, usually, different paradigms). A standard case of multi–language SDEs is that different concepts useful for a working area are clothed into a language for this area, and different languages for working areas are available. Mono–language SDEs usually lack coverage. This is the case for example for most Smalltalk or Ada environments, which have no expressiveness for requirements engineering and only restricted expressiveness for programming in the large.

The underlying *programming language* in which the final code of systems to be developed/maintained is written often determines the character of the corresponding *SDE*. This is because of two different reasons: (a) The language is *restricted* to a certain *application* area or problem field. For example, most AI languages, like Prolog, are mainly used for prototypes being developed and used in labs. Therefore, requirements engineering or architecture modelling are felt not to be important. As a consequence, these environments have no tools for these working areas. (b) The language *lacks* certain *concepts* and, therefore, is not used if such concepts are needed in applications. To take an example: Nobody would develop a real–time or an operating system in Cobol. Therefore, the concept of a process and synchronization of processes can hardly be found in architecture tools embedded in an SDE based on Cobol.

Another influence from the underlying *programming language* comes from the characteristics of this language: Language design can happen in an interval from emphasizing structural expressiveness, security, and efficiency on one side and flexibility, simplicity, and uniformity on the other. Examples for the two extremes are Ada /7. DoD 83, 7. Nag 92/, or Smalltalk /7. Gr 83/, respectively. Languages of the first category usually have a rich built–in context sensitive syntax, languages of the second miss such rules. In the first category, therefore, we find *compiler–oriented*, in the second *interpreter–oriented* environment. The kind of development mostly corresponds to the category of the environment. Compiler–oriented environments are better for secure software which runs in the field, interpreter–oriented serve for greater flexibility of the development process and, therefore, are mainly used in the lab context. In both environments the drawbacks can be diminished by tools: Tools can serve for flexibility in the first case (most of the IPSEN tools can be subsumed under this goal as we already start with clearly defined languages with a rich underlying syntax) or they can serve for security in the second (e.g. by offering certain checks, how the underlying and flexible language should be used in order to get at least a certain degree of security).

A further classification of environments comes from the way in which the global structure of the software process to be supported is seen. One extreme example is the waterfall model /7. Boe 82/, where in a number of activity blocks with different abstractions corresponding to different views of the system (requirements specification, architectural specification, tested modules, integrated system) are worked out one after the other. Because of this discrete structure of the lifecycle but also of the difference of underlying languages and the fact that a document of an activity block has to be finished before the next starts we call this model *discrete*. An example of the other extreme is the programmer's apprentice /2. RW 90/ where in a long transaction of tiny steps (automatically, or by manual transformations which are later automated) from a 'requirements specification' an efficient program is derived. We call such a model *continuous* because there are no activity blocks and a broadband language must be used. Correspondingly, the *environment* can be classified as discrete, if it supports activities on different levels with corresponding languages and integration between them, or as continuous if it regards the process in the above continuous sense and offers corresponding tools (e.g. language environment for a broadband language /2. Bau 85, 87/). As a clear definition of continuous and discrete and a clear distinction between both approaches is rather important for the following text we summarize the main characteristics of both approaches in the following table 1.9. This table shows that continuous or discrete is rather a combination of different characterization attributes than an atomic attribute. (This characterization might be felt to be unfair as continuous approaches are novel approaches and, therefore, have not been applied to huge practical system.) Roughly speaking, the IPSEN approach is a discrete approach w.r.t. the model side but offering the advantages of the continuous approach by the behavior of its tools.

discrete approaches (engineering–like approaches)	continuous approaches (AI–like or semantical approaches)
• different phases or working areas expressing different separate perspectives of a system (requirements specification, architecture etc.)	• one broad 'working area', no different perspectives are felt to be necessary
• different languages for different document classes usually each incorporating different paradigms (multi–paradigm, multi–language SDEs)	• a broadband language is able to 'handle' all perspectives with one or more paradigms (mono–language, mutli/mono–paradigm SDE), some working areas are ignored
• overall configurations are structured by dependency relations, overall processes contain different technical subprocesses	• there is one big 'program' and a continuous process to build or change it (a system is a moving target /1. GR 83/)
• any document has to be elaborated to a certain state (not necessarily complete as in the waterfall model) and should be quality assured before the work on a dependent document can start, transitions between documents being handled by developers and/or tools	• no restriction about how the portions of the big system are elaborated, process steps are delivered by developers or by tools
• a team of different people, having different roles, is developing a system usually in different subprojects	• no restriction of developer freedom
• the software system to be developed is used in the field, i.e. by many people far away of the development context	• developers are modifiers and users, systems are prototypes or systems usually only used in the same or another lab

Table 1.9. Differences between discrete and continuous approaches

1.2.4 Integrated Environments

This *subsection* tries to *relate* the notions which we have introduced in subsection 1.1.4 on overall *configurations* (containing extended technical configurations and administration configurations) to the basic terms we have learned about *SDEs* in this section. Especially, we make clear in a first step what the *integration* means when we build integrated SDEs. Again, this subsection is a rather personal view w.r.t. some topics, here on integrated environments.

We have learned that in a *working area* a collection of documents is built up reflecting different views (as the function and data view in RE), different degrees of detail (overview graphical and detailed textual views, as in RE and PiL), hierarchical structures (as the decomposition of a subsystem into further ones in PiL). So, in any working area a meaningful *subconfiguration* of the overall configuration is built up/modified which gives a certain (partial) perspective of the overall system. A *subprocess* of the overall process is related to this subconfiguration and handled by *(a) specific person(s)* of the team having the corresponding capabilities and experience. For these subconfigurations/subprocesses *specific environments* have to be offered. Any person working at a certain time on such a subconfiguration should have access to a corresponding specific environment.

We call most of these specific environments *technical environments*, as technical activities are the most probable ones to occur in the overall process. We have a requirements engineering environment, an architectural design environment, and a programming environment. As technical activities are accompanied by further activities we also have further environments for *documentation* and *quality assurance*. Finally, we have seen there has to be an *administration* environment for coordinating the overall process in a project on management level.

We may have a *specialization of* these *environments*. For example, a quality assurance environment may be specialized into a test environment or an environment supporting reviews, a documentation environment into a user documentation environment, or a technical documentation environment. A design environment may be specialized to handle certain perspectives, degree of detail, hierarchical levels in order to support certain subprocesses (as a graphical coarse design environment for the chief designer), or because only a part of the functionality is needed (e.g. an SA/ER environment for requirements specification of business applications where no control model is used), or because persons of a certain role only get access to a restricted functionality (e.g. administration 'environment' for the technical developers which only can use the administration functions which are delegated to them in comparison to the administration environment for the project manager which offers the full functionality).

All these full or specialized environments are *logically centralized instances* which have all aspects of a subconfiguration (in the case of specialized environments it may only be a subset of aspects, the others are not relevant or not allowed) under their control. The reader should note that this is an idealization w.r.t. existing environments as we assume (specialized) environments to offer an integrated set of tools for (a subconfiguration corresponding to) a working area's subconfiguration. Especially, we do assume that logically centralized means that certain aspects are not split over different separate tools or environments such that the fine–grained consistency relations within this subconfiguration are not controlled.

Logical centralization has *nothing to do* with *physical centralization* or placement within a (distributed) platform being the basis of an overall environment. Logical centralization also does not restrain that a certain *number* of *specific* environment *instances* are available for different active persons having the same role at a certain time of the project. So, there may be different programming environment instances available in the main 'phase' of coding a system.

Each of these environment instances can internally handle those parts of the overall configuration its user is responsible for (e.g. a certain subsystem with its internal design structure consisting of modules and subsystems). Furthermore, cooperation of *different people* working on a *working areas subconfiguration* means that different environment instances have to 'work' together (e.g. different design environments). The *control* should be *the same* as if one person had elaborated the complex subconfiguration of the working area (the complete architecture). So, we have the same argumentation as between separate compilation vs. monolithic compilation. Control between different specific environments working on parts of a subconfiguration to a working area means that (a) any environment 'possesses' a portion of this subconfiguration for a certain time (b) gives substantial support for the subprocesses on that part and (c) the change implication on other parts of the subconfiguration are controlled and supported. Within a subconfiguration all fine–grained, increment–to–increment relations have to be observed (see subsection 1.1.4 and section 1.4).

So, *between* different *specific environments* for a *working area* we have a situation as outlined in fig. 1.10.a for the example of different PiL environments. The PiL environment

Env_1 may have been used for a coarse system design D_1, the environment Env_2 for the design of a subsystem which has been defined in D_1, or in Env_1 we have made a graphical design and in Env_2 a detailed design of contained modules. The connection between both is established by an integration tool which is regarded as an integral part of Env_2 and which is needed for consistency control on fine–grained technical level. This integration tool consists of a transformation tool, in the first case of above generating the pre–given interface (of export/import) of the subsystem to be designed. This transformation tool should be incremental such that it can also be taken for the case that the subsystem has (only partially) been defined in D_1 and/or the interface for this subsystem in D_1 is changing. Finally, also changes in Env_2 violating the determinations pre–given from the work on D_1 should be shown, either by not allowing manipulations on the pre–given determinations or by giving corresponding warnings. Interconnection as discussed in this paragraph supports combination of technical processes to bigger technical processes related to one working area.

We have a quite similar situation if we regard the *interconnection* of different subconfigurations for *different working areas* (cf. fig. 1.10.b, where an integration tool is shown for consistency handling between an RE subconfiguration and a PiL subconfiguration). The different forms this integration tool can take are the same as above. The integration tool again is a part of the target environment. Here, we can combine technical and fine–grained processes corresponding to different working areas. Even more complicated is the situation shown in fig. 1.10.c where a PiL environment Env_1, by which the interface of a subsystem is defined, is connected to a *combined* subsystem *development environment* Env_2 which internally is a combination of PiL, PiS, and further environments. The integration tool I_1 has the same functionality as above. In this case, the integration tool supports the composition of processes for subsystem definition and subsystem realization.

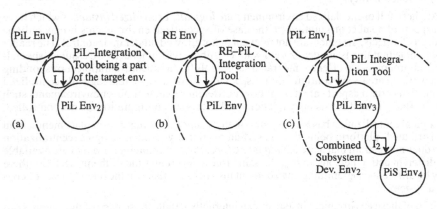

Fig. 1.10. Interconnection of Different Environments (a) between different environments of one working area, (b) between environments of different working areas (both (a) and (b) in one subproject), (c) between different subprojects, (a)–(c) being example situations

So, integration of *technical environments* supports the combination of technical processes or of combined technical processes into bigger ones. These processes are working on subconfigurations of the extended technical configuration which, by these combined subprocesses, are consistently developed or made consistent again. The number of instances of technical environments or integrated technical environments needed at a certain point of the project *reflect* the *state* of the *project*: At the beginning we start with one RE environment, later requiring an integrated RE environment consisting of different RE environments if the requirements specification is worked out by different analysts. Then, we need a growing number of design environments, the number of RE environments is shrinking as they are necessary only for handling requirements errors detected later etc.

The cases regarded in fig. 1.10 are examples for *directed dependencies* between master document(s) and dependent document(s). In such a case the integration tool is usually a part of the target environment, in reverse engineering it is the other way round. For handling *'parallel'* views or dependencies, e.g. in RE where different perspectives are regarded, we need in general an integration tool at both sides of specialized perspective environments, if not an unnatural direction is imposed on all symmetric relations. In both cases, handling directed or undirected dependencies, there has to be some coordination to control the collaboration of technical developers.

So, in addition to integration of technical environments or environments for documentation and quality assurance, altogether on the fine–grained level of extended configurations, we need an administration environment (in more detail different environments) for managing an integrated project. This administration environment and its underlying administration configuration is a central part of an integrated overall environment. This *administration component* can be used in various integrated development environments as a *universal* component. This is true, provided (1) these administration tools cover all aspects and integrate these different aspects on coarse-grained level, (2) such an administration component is configurable according to the administration models needed within a certain context (application domain, special system to be developed, company restrictions etc.), and (3) such an administration component can be integrated with technical environments to form an integrated overall environment, covering and integrating technical and administration aspects as well.

Such an administration component is again a *logically centralized component* where all administration aspects are handled. Logically centralized means, as above, that (a) the administration component is not distributed in total or in parts over the different technical environments, but is a component in its own right, and (b) all aspects of administration are covered. It means furthermore, that (c) integration with the technical environments is obeyed. Again, if we speak of centralized we mean, by no means, physical centralization. It also does not necessarily mean centralization on the outside level inasmuch as only a specialized workstation with a corresponding user interface has to be available for this aspect, or that only special personnel within a group are allowed to work with this administration component. The integration between technical environments and the administration component is handled differently from that of technical environments outlined in fig. 1.10 (see chapter 2, 3, 4).

To support building up or changing overall configurations *integrated environments* have been suggested and built. As in any project where a group of persons has to carry out the overall process for development, maintenance, or reuse, the supporting environments have to be *distributed*. There are quite different types of environments available for an application domain (for software development environments the range of possibilities is described in section 1.7). At the moment, no integrated environment is available, neither as industrial product nor as research prototype, which exploits all the possibilities to support development, maintenance, or reuse processes on overall configurations.

From an abstract view, an *integrated overall environment* is an collection of technical environments and administration environments. Technical environments may have been integrated by the use of integration tools as seen above. There is a *static view* on integrated overall environments showing that technical environments may be connected to other technical environments of the same type (as shown in fig. 1.10.a for PiL). This is the case, whenever in a working area's subconfiguration we have hierarchies such that a subconfiguration can be defined for the elaboration of which we need the same type of environment. It is also the case if different types of environment are connected by a suitable integration tool. Finally, this also holds true for combined development environments (e.g. for a subsystem development containing a PiL and PiS environment). There is also a *dynamic view* on integrated overall environments saying that the number of instances of technical environments, integrated environments of a certain type, and their integration tools at the border of such environments is changing over the time of a project and reflects where current work is done in the overall configuration (see chapter 6).

Regarded from this abstract view the problem of building *integrated overall environments* is *similar* in software engineering, CIM, or *any* other *application area* where we have overall configurations as shown in figures 1.4 and 1.5. There are technical environments to be connected to bigger integrated environments which can look quite different. However, they have common properties. Also, the integration tools have common properties. There is an administration component which is nearly the same, as on coarse–grained level the differences are of minor quality and, therefore, can be handled by a suitable parameterization process.

The state of the art in integrated environments is far away from this view. We restrict ourselves here to list the *deficits* of *existing integrated environments:* (1) They are *incomplete* w.r.t. their coverage of all parts of an overall configuration, therefore leaving many subprocesses without substantial support. (2) Support in many cases is only on *representation level* and not on the level of semantics (a drawing tool which does not know the semantics of representation increments). (3) Environments do not give support or full support w.r.t. establishing/watching/reestablishing consistency relations within a document, or between documents/subconfigurations. (4) Reestablishing consistency after changes and, therefore, also the corresponding processes have to be incremental, i.e. only changes have to be propagated within, or between documents, or into documents. (5) Tools have to support the dynamic behaviour of process and configuration evolution (which is discussed in detail later in this book). We also have deficits on the organization side of a project what we called administration: (6) At the moment integrated development environments often concentrate on the technical part of an overall configuration and have no administration tools at all, (7) only certain aspects of administration are regarded (e.g. process modelling), others are not included, thereby giving up to support other aspects of similar importance. Finally, (8) administration functions (e.g. for versioning) are integrated into certain technical environments, as e.g. into CAD systems, thereby giving up the chance to support all administration aspects and their integration with technical aspects.

Let us conclude this section by giving some *remarks* dedicated to clarifying our position. The first is devoted to *integration*. In literature one distinguishes between (1) *data* integration (how do internal data of environments fit together w.r.t. the way they are modelled, how they can be related to each other, whether they are accessible, wether they are stored in one or different repositories), (2) *granularity* of integration (coarse–grained, document–to–document dependencies, or fine–grained, increment–to–increment dependencies between documents), (3) *process* or *control* integration (how can different tools communicate with each other, which mechanisms are available to connect tools), (4) *representation/UI* integration (do representations of document look similar, do they use common presentation/UI, do they use a common window system), (5) *platform, framework,* or *component* integration (whether a platform, framework, or reusable components are used). This is only to give a first understanding of integration, further aspects of integration are discussed later.

The next remark corresponds to *a priori* versus *a posteriori integration*, a terminology already introduced in subsection 1.2.2 (see also table 1.11). In both cases we need an administration component. (In our case it has been developed in the context of a posteriori CIM integration /6. EMN 92, 6. KSW 92, 6. SW 93/.) At the moment neither a priori– nor a posteriori–environments provide for the integration of a complete administration component (we give our intermediate results on that in chapters 2 and 5). The technical environments themselves look quite different in both cases: In the a priori case they are built for integration. This can end up with tight integration as it is the case in IPSEN. The disadvantage is that we cannot take existing technical environments or tools from the market. The effect of this disadvantage is diminished through the availability of a machinery to easily 'produce' technical environments (as in IPSEN). Using the a posteriori–approach integration of technical environments usually does not go very far as the environments have not been built for integration and their modification and tight coupling would be too cumbersome.

The advantage is, however, that we can take tools from the market. There are two interesting questions in this context: (1) How is the a priori–approach to be combined with configurability, openness, and evolving standards? (2) How far can integration in a posteriori–approaches go in the future and, especially, what requirements can we set for tool or environment builders so that their tools can easily be integrated if, of course, some framework and corresponding interfaces for environments have been defined?

a posteriori	a priori
mostly industrial approaches	mostly academic approaches
technical environments given	technical environments to be developed
different internal structures of environments	environments developed according to a common architecture
different internal data models, in the best case one data base modelling approach (e.g. relational), often specific data structures on top of file system(s)	one data model eventually one meta model or methodology of data modelling
Integration approaches: transmission of data structures via a neutral format, building wrappers for environments delivering some kind of 'semantics' of underlying data or only a 'standarized' interface, building hardwired batch integration tools if internal data structures are open, presenting documents of other environments via a neutral presentation format, administration aspects being distributed (e.g. version control) and, therefore, rather useless	Integration approaches: consistency in the global data space or fine–grained relations of different documents, incremental updating possible using one general mechanism (e.g. method passing), management component possibly included, specific and detailed integration mechanisms
Future directions: porting on a new platform, integration into coarse–grained frameworks, building reusable components for these integration steps, integration of a 'workflow' component	Future directions: detailed platform development, generation machinery for specific environments
Advantages/disadvantages: integration of arbitrary tools possible, but difficult, open only in a poor sense	Advantages/disadvantages: structural support over configurations, difficult to integrate existing tools

Table 1.11. A posteriori vs. a priori integrated environments

The last remark deals with the term *incrementality* which plays a big role in this book. This is not to introduce how this term is used within IPSEN but to make clear that different facets are subsumed under this term and different meanings of incrementality, therefore, can be found. A *rough definition* is that 'The effort for updates/analyses is in the same order of magnitude of changes'. We know this term from incremental compilers where it is used for quite different things (separate compilation on one side, or a mixture between interpreters and compilers to get the flexibility of an interpreter without having the same inefficiency), incremental updates of databases (where only the accessed portion of the database is reorganized according to a change, the rest is left as it is), incremental attribute evaluation, and others. In any case, it means 'not everything is done new, but only for a portion'. As we shall argue later, interactivity and immediateness are to be separated from incrementality (see the separate compiler example of above), they are characteristics for their own but often intermixed with incrementality in the above sense.

We restrict out *explanation* to the *simplest case*: We regard one 'incremental' change and its corresponding 'incremental' update more carefully. This case includes incremental analysis as a part which, therefore, is not separately explained. There are usually more than one change which are to be incrementally handled, we take only one for this discussion. Finally, incrementality can (a) mean to regard more than one document and (b) different incremental updates can be combined. Both are explained later (see section 1.4).

An *incremental* change and its corresponding update are handled by the following *steps* (see fig. 1.12): (1) A certain region around the changed location is regarded, which has to do with the underlying structure, i.e. in our terminology it is an increment. (2) An analysis takes place to find that region, again one or more increments, if any, which are or may be influenced by this changed increment. (3) A change process has to take place in order to inspect and eventually to change these influenced increments. (4) This may give rise to another cycle consisting of (1)–(3), and so on.

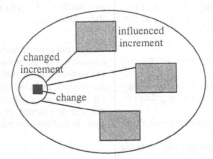

Fig. 1.12. Explanation of incrementality

In step (2), *different mechanisms* may be used (examples below): In general, (a) the influenced increments are computed at increment update time. The latter, of course and to be explained in this book, needs some underlying data structures and/or algorithms to keep track about the detailed structural information. In the case where data structures are used, they have to be updated as well. Often simple computations are used: (a1) take always one and the same specific enclosing increment, or (a2) take one specific increment dependent on the type of the specific changed increment. Furthermore, in step (3) the update is done more or less *mechanically*. It can be done (a) automatically or (b) automatically using some user interaction, or (c) completely manually by the designer. In principle, any of the steps (1)–(3) can be carried out using one of the alternatives (a)–(c). So, the reader should note that the scheme of fig. 1.12 is also applicable if an incremental update is completely carried out by a human, as no tool is available. Finally, also step (1) can use the three different mechanisms (a), (a1), and (a2) described above.

Let us give some explanations for handling steps (1)–(3) from the incrementality examples of above: (1) Separate compilation compiler: In case of changes within a module body as changed increment and influenced increment the body itself is taken. It is (automatically) compiled and is then either O.K. or gives rise by compiler messages to further changes in the body. By changes within the interface of a module, as change increment the complete module interface is taken. As influenced increments we take all modules importing that module which are then (automatically) recompiled. Then the cycle starts again for the body of some modules. In incremental attribute evaluation, some part of an attribute may have changed. As changed increment we take the attribute, then determine all attribute evaluation functions using that increment as influenced increments, automatically evaluate them and, for the changed ones, start the cycle again, taking the changed function values as changes.

1.3 Problem Areas of an SDE Realization

The aim of this *section* is to *introduce* the *problem areas an SDE researcher* and *developer* is *facing*. These problem areas are not to be intermixed with working areas or problem topics of software engineering of section 1.1 nor with classification items of SDEs in section 1.2. The SDE problem areas introduced here build up work packages into which the development process of an SDE realization is divided (SDE lifecycle). This is the IPSEN–*independent* part of this section as these problem areas occur in any SDE project. However, we take IPSEN as the running example of this section. Therefore, this section also introduces the specific work we have done in IPSEN according to the scenario to be discussed below. This is the IPSEN–*specific* part of this section.

Furthermore, we shall use the SDE problem area list of this section later in this book for classifying IPSEN within the SDE world, and for comparing it with other selected approaches in section 1.7. Some of the following subsections are quite short as the corresponding topics are taken up again in the following three sections on IPSEN highlights and, even more, as main chapters of this book.

1.3.1 The Scenario Regarded in this Book

Having introduced the working areas and their mutual dependencies in fig. 1.2 and the structure of overall configurations in fig. 1.4 we *describe* in this subsection the *scenario of IPSEN*. This means that we discuss the portion of the overall scenario given in section 1.1 which is covered by IPSEN, i.e. by the current prototype(s). In detail, we determine the languages for working areas, their interrelations, the documents regarded within working areas, the tools of these working areas, and the integration tools of IPSEN. Furthermore, we give a *rationale* for the chosen scenario. Selecting the scenario is the first work package if an SDE for a certain context is to be realized.

Fig. 1.13 gives the IPSEN scenario at the time of this book's preparation as a cutout of the overall scenario of fig. 1.2. We see that one working area, namely *quality assurance*, is not directly supported. However, it is *indirectly supported* because the mastering documents of RE, PiL, PiS, DOC, and PO are all produced with tools ensuring quality w.r.t. languages and methods defined for these working areas, what we termed *constructive* quality assurance. Consequently, dependencies in direction to QA are not supported by tools. This is not as terrible as it may seem, as quality assurance consists of human reviews and inspections to a great measure which are tremendously facilitated if the documents to be inspected a priori fulfill certain quality measures. The reader should remember the special importance of RE and PiL documents for the success of a software project.

Direct support in IPSEN is given in the following *working areas* (cf. fig. 1.13, integration tools are explained later): Requirements engineering only regards the so–called 'functional' part of the requirements namely the definition of the functionality of the system to be developed, the underlying data structures, and the coordination of processes by a control model (function, data, and control model). So, the 'functional' part of a requirements specification is fully covered, the nonfunctional part is not supported. Documentation only covers the technical documentation. However, the tool developed can also be used to write user and other documentation. For project organization, we have in section 1.1 distinguished between management of the project, its processes, and its products. If we restrict ourselves to the coarse–grained level coordinating work of developers, which was called project administration in section 1.1, then all these aspects are fully covered by the chosen IPSEN scenario (namely process, configuration, revision, and resources control). Planning activities in the sense of estimation are not covered, control activities on technical levels are supported by the corresponding technical tools.

One clarifying remark should be made corresponding to the *term* 'covered' which we have used above in order to sketch what the chosen scenario contains or does not contain.

Covered means that we have developed suitable tools which are necessary and which give substantial support. Covered, however, does not mean that the set of these tools is complete w.r.t. desired functionality. Especially, in offering tools for certain languages or methods we have restricted ourselves to a subset of these languages or methods as our aim is to build prototypes and not industrial tools. In some cases this subset is rather small (as for PiS), in other cases it is rather complex (as in PiL). The criterion for us to select a smaller or bigger subset was how interesting the language was from the scientific point of view (see next subsection) and/or whether we could learn something about SDEs by extending the subset. For example, in the area PiS, neither from the language side nor from the tool building side, did we expect to get results by making the prototypes more practical in the sense of supporting the full language.

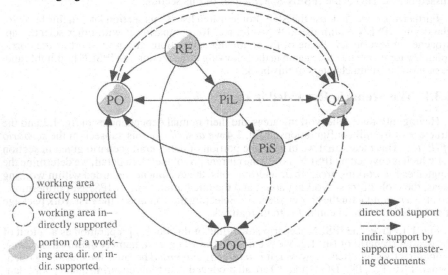

Fig. 1.13. The IPSEN scenario and support of the software developer

The *languages* used in these *working areas* have already been described by introducing the term overall configuration in subsection 1.1.4. There, we gave an example for such an overall configuration which exactly corresponds to our IPSEN scenario. More details are given in the next subsection.

The *tools used* for the above *languages* in certain working areas are the following (a detailed list of the tools of the current prototypes is provided by section 1.8 and a description of the outside behavior in chapter 2): There is a syntax–oriented editor for requirements specifications regarding SA, EER and the control model language. Here, the usual analysis checks corresponding to the combined SA/EER/control model language are intertwined with the editor. Further analyzers can be used on demand for completeness checks. Tools for directly executing a requirements specification have been realized. For architecture modelling, a structure–oriented editor/analyzer as well as demand analyzers are available. For programming in the small there is again an integrated editor/analyzer and a demand analyzer. Furthermore, there is an instrumentation tool and an execution tool. Finally, for documentation there is a structure–oriented editor. For project organization there are tools for revision and configuration control, intermediate steps for process control and resource control have been realized (see chapter 2, 3, 4, our current work is described in chapter 5).

These *tools* for certain *working areas* are *tightly integrated* (for details see again 1.8 and 2). To start with tools for one working area: For example, in programming in the small, editing, analyzing, instrumenting, and executing modules can be performed with arbitrary interleave. Furthermore, even more important, there is a tight integration between tools working on different perspectives or different hierarchical levels of one working area and seeing the integration to others (e.g. between functional, information, and control model in RE, or internal subsystem design and its connection to the document where the subsystem was introduced). Finally, administration tools also work on different perspectives of an integrated whole: product (version, configuration), process, and resources control are mutually interrelated.

The *tools* for *integration* between different working areas are the *following*: Between requirements engineering and programming in the large there is an interactive transformation tool (/7. Jan 92, 4. Lef 95/) which, used by the designer, generates a part of the architecture from the requirements specification, or gives an incremental transformation into an existing architecture, if the requirements specification has changed. Conversely, there is an analyzer finding out if and where the requirements specification is touched if a change takes place on architecture level. From programming in the large to programming in the small there is an automatic transformation generating module frames for Modula–2 (and C). Again, this tool also incrementally transforms changes on architecture level into the corresponding module frames such that, as a consequence, the corresponding changes on module implementation level can be carried out by the programming in the small tools. However, no tight integration tool PiL→PiS to support module maintenance is available (it internally works as other tight integration tools do, the subset of PiS is too small to make it more than a demonstrator). Furthermore, the requirements engineering editor and the architecture editor is integrated with the documentation editor in the sense that the changes on requirements and on architecture level induce changes of the technical documentation. Finally, project organization tools are integrated with all technical environments in a sense which will be explained later.

Now the question arises why we chose just the working areas and integration tools listed above. The answer is a *rationale* for the chosen scenario. Let us split this rationale into two parts and first give an answer corresponding to the *applicability point of view*. The chosen working area and integration tools emphasize the central role of architecture modelling in software development and maintenance (see fig. 1.13). Therefore, the integration tools being connected with programming in the large have been investigated and implemented. Furthermore, the chosen tools also support the development of documents related to the main perspectives of a software system (outside description, essential inside structure, detailed inside description, and organization aspects of the project). As the most interesting working areas and dependencies are covered by tools it is possible to build up a prototype and demonstrate its value to practitioners.

The second thread of arguments is a *rationale* from the *research project point of view*. We shall learn later in this book that the scenario is also chosen to cover different types of document classes and different types of integration tools by taking relevant representatives. As the variety of working area tools and the arguments why the selected tools cover this variety appear later in this book, we restrict ourselves here to arguments corresponding to the classification of integration tools. The integration mechanisms chosen build up a classification of integration tools: The first from requirements engineering to programming in the large is an interactive and, therefore, semiautomatic tool. The designer inputs design decisions, the transformation tool produces a portion of the architecture. The integration tool between programming in the large and programming in the small is an automatic one as the description of modules (export, import etc.) is completely elaborated on architecture level and cannot be changed on programming in the small level. The integration tool from programming in the large and requirements engineering to documentation follows a hypertext approach. The connections between these documents are completely specified by the user (this integration tool can also work differently in an automatic fashion where the structure of the technical documentation is fixed) as the documentator links the portions $S_1, ..., S_n$ of an architecture or requirements specification as mastering documents to a certain portion of the documentation D_m which describe $S_1, ..., S_n$. So, we see that integration tools have quite different characteristics and structure. Finally, the integration between the coarse–grained level of administration configurations and tools on extended technical configuration level are only used to control consistency of products and projects on organization level and to administrate the necessary and available resources. So, we have concentrated on certain investigations from the researcher's point of view.

Another simplification of the real world situation we have made in the current IPSEN prototype is that we regard the *documents* of *one working area* in some cases as being *one internal document* (data base). This restriction is assumed e.g. for project administration, but e.g. not for programming in the small where all the modules are different documents. The assumption is only reasonable for small software projects. In large software projects there has to be again a division of labour in a working area (e.g. for architecture modelling that after having introduced the overall architecture consisting of modules and subsystems, different subsystems are designed independently). Therefore, the restriction has been given up for the different perspectives in RE, their integration, and for PiL. However, for execution of RE specs and for the RE–PiL transformation we need the collection of different documents in one document. This is less a conceptual but only a realization problem.

1.3.2 Concepts, Languages, and Methods

This problem area deals with *developing suitable concepts*, putting them into suitable corresponding *languages,* and developing *methods* or methodologies for applying the languages to certain working areas of software engineering. The same is true for integration where language constructs on both sides of integration have to be conceptually, syntactically, and methodologically related to each other. In the following section and later in this book we briefly speak of 'method' work as abbreviation for work on these topics. This problem area does not deal with tools, it is also important if one works with 'methods' in a paper and pencil mode. However, it is a prerequisite for tools that the underlying languages/relations are precisely defined, based on clear, applicable, and suitable concepts, and that methodological background exists on how to apply them.

As this *book deals with tools* this *method work* is not explicitly and widely discussed in it. There are two arguments for only sketching methods: (1) There is not room enough to incorporate our method work, and (2) if we did, the character of the book would be bipolar. There are readers only interested in methods and others only interested in tools for given methods. So, our method work is only sketched in the form of an *overview* in *this subsection*.

'Method work' consumed a *lot of effort* of the IPSEN–Project. We have spent approximately $1/3$ of the total IPSEN effort for this problem area. The reason is that (except for a single exception) no clear and precise concepts, languages, or methods were available which we could take as the basis of tool development. This is true because of two reasons: In some areas (1) no languages exist in the sense that these languages are widely used or accepted as standards. In other working areas (2) there exist widely used languages which are either not expressive enough to make ideas explicit, or not clearly defined (even the underlying concepts are not clear), or for which only very poor method knowledge is available on how to use them, or which only cover some aspects of one working area and, therefore, have to be extended. The same holds true for integration of these languages. We are discussing these deficits and our work to overcome them in the following paragraphs.

In *requirements engineering,* in order to describe the 'functional' requirements specification, different sublanguages are widely used. In order to describe the functionality *(functional model)* of the system Structured Analysis (e.g. /7. DeM 78/) is a wide–spread standard. SA uses processes, data flows, data stores, and at the upmost level also terminators to build up so–called data flow diagrams. Processes are refined to data flow diagrams down to a level where no further refinement is regarded to be necessary (atomic processes). The internal behavior of atomic processes is described by minispecs usually in an imperative pseudo–language. Refinement is restricted by balancing rules. Only very restricted expressiveness for describing data is available in the so–called data dictionary.

Therefore, in applications handling complex data, especially in information systems, the wish came up to have more explicit facilities for describing the underlying data which may be rather complex corresponding to hierarchical structure, determination of similarities, and mutual relations *(information model)*. Again, in this area a standard called the Entity Relationship Approach exists (e.g. /7. You 89/). In order to improve expressiveness, dialects of the ER–language have been proposed. They can directly express (a restrictive kind of) inheritance or aggregation (e.g. /7. BB 84, 7. SSW 80/). They are called *Extended ER* languages, in short EER.

Finally, especially in real time applications, it is necessary to define events, time constraints, explicit handling of activation/deactivation and synchronization of concurrent processes in order to define cooperation and competition of processes. We call this part of the functional requirements specification the *control model*. Here, a lot of proposals exist (e.g. /7.Har 87, 7.Har 90, 7. HP 87, 7. WM 85/) which are rather different.

In any of these three subareas of requirements engineering (definition of the functional, information, and control model), graphical and textual languages are used. In SA, for example, process decomposition is denoted graphically, the detailed descriptions of data flows, data stores and minispecs are each given textually. Now, when describing an *extended requirements definition language* in order to build tools for it the following *problems* occur:

(1) The sublanguages cited above have severe *deficits* with respect to their *expressiveness*. For example, neither the interface of a process can be precisely defined in SA nor the interface of an entity type in EER (/7. Jan 92/), no object information is available in EER, no type information for processes in SA. Even a greater lack of expressiveness can be found in the sublanguages for the control model (/7. Bee 95/).

(2) The languages are *not precisely defined* according to their syntax and semantics. For example, the decomposition relation can express rather different concepts in both languages SA and EER which no reader can detect when reading corresponding introductions. Even more, severe semantical problems can be found in control model proposals.

(3) The *integration* between these different languages is *not clear*. For example, how should the more explicit data description of a information model interact with the functional model of SA (e.g. /7. You 89/), or how should the control model interact with the functional and information model?

To overcome these problems we took the *following approach* (/7. Jan 92, 7. Bee 95, 4. Koh 96/):

(a) We left the *sublanguages* which are widely used (EER and SA) *mostly unchanged*, although we were aware of the deficits corresponding to expressiveness. However, the control model language was newly defined /7. Bee 95, 4. Koh 96/.

(b) We tried to overcome the deficits in preciseness by *defining* the syntax and the semantics of the corresponding sublanguages *a posteriori*.

(c) We had to define precisely the interrelation of the three sublanguages by defining syntactical and semantical *relations* between these sublanguages.

(d) We tried to develop a *method* on how to use the *sublanguages* and how to use the *integrated* RE language.

Up to now we have a precisely defined, integrated SA/EER/CRT model language, and rules how to use this languages have been elaborated (see references given above). All this RE method work was done in the context of the ESF and COMPLEMENT projects mentioned in the preface and in connection with the industrial partner Cap debis SSP (formally GEI Aachen).

A different situation is found in the working area *architecture modelling*. *No* international *standard* exists which defines the concepts an architecture language should have. There are three worlds which are usually clearly divided (see section 7 of bibliography): firstly, classical ideas of modularization/data abstraction, secondly object–oriented modelling, and thirdly the idea of functional decomposition which comes from early structured techniques and which is still part of practice. The latter, however, if used without data abstraction, is not a reasonable approach from the software engineering point of view.

Starting some time ago on the ground of ideas of tree–like decomposition and data abstraction /7. Alt 79, 7. Gal 82/ we have been working for some time now on concepts, languages, and methods for architecture modelling /7. Nag 82, 7. LN 85, 7. Nag 90, 7. Bör 94/. The *conceptual universe* is the following: There are modules for functional and for data abstraction. On either side there are modules for objects and types (although function type modules are only necessary in some real time applications). Modules can be grouped to subsystems. Modules/subsystems are connected by relations, determined at architecture specification time in order to build up architectures. There are two structural relations between modules, namely locality and inheritance (the latter only being defined between classes). Within locality structures and inheritance structures usability has to be explicitly defined. Furthermore, there is a general usability relation between modules and subsystems. Genericity is defined for modules and subsystems. A lot of consistency conditions can be defined on language or method level.

The architecture *language approach* is an *integrated* one (only some arguments given): (1) Architectures can be built up using concepts of quite different programming languages (locality, realization layers, object–orientation) the architecture language, however, being programming language independent. (2) On module level we can express type as well as object information, the transition between both being important for designing software/ hardware systems or hardware systems alone. (3) Different grains of concern can be expressed, namely modules, subsystems, subarchitectures, and the total system with its connection to the context. (4) Similarities can be expressed (by object–orientation and genericity), and reuse is supported (on architectural pattern as well as on component level; or on process component level when e.g. designing a generator). (5) There is no fixed method. However, a lot of syntactical/methodological rules are given and many example situations have been studied. We believe that all these different concepts have their value and are necessary for different applications.

The concepts mentioned above are embedded into *two languages:* A graphical language for building up architecture diagrams for overviews and a textual description for the details of components. This textual description describes the export interface of a component, structural relations, and imports. An architectural description has to contain all layers of a system, all connections between components, the components in detail, but no details about module bodies.

Another rather big piece of work was on the level of *integrating* the *concepts* and *languages* of *requirements engineering* and *architecture modelling* /7. Jan 92, 4. Lef 93a, b, 4. Lef 95/. Here we think that no fully automatic transformation should take place as architecture modelling is a working area of its own (outside behavior vs. abstract realization view). So, the transformation should be made by the designer and the designer should have the possibility to interact in the sense that he puts in design decisions which drive the translation process. Here, the weaknesses of requirements engineering languages introduced above imply some additional complications: As the expressiveness of these languages is not rich enough (see above), the designer is now entering design decisions which the requirements engineer was not able to state. Furthermore, the insufficient preciseness of the requirements engineering language (see above) also caused some problems. The translation concepts, i.e. the determination which constructs of the requirements engineering language can correspond to which constructs of the architecture language have been directly incorporated into the translator tool. This tool also includes methodological rules w.r.t. the application of correspondences of both languages. So, on the conceptual *integra-*

tion level corresponding *relations* between *increments* of both languages had to be established.

Furthermore, *conceptual work* of minor effort was performed for two *other integration tools,* namely for the translation for programming in the large to programming in the small and from requirements engineering, programming in the large, to technical documentation in the working area documentation. Here, the conceptual work is again which increments of a document from the source language(s) are bound to which increments in a document of the target language in order to realize incremental tool behavior in the same way as for the RE–PiL–integration tool. The integration tools behave differently as sketched above. Here again, there are no languages for the user in order to define the increment relations because they are directly realized within the tool.

No method work was done in the area *programming in the small* where we adopted Modula–2, Eiffel, and C++, as languages to be supported. As stated above, the working area *quality assurance* is supported by IPSEN only in the sense that constructive quality assurance is offered by the RE–, PiL–, PiS–, and DOC–tools. For the working area *documentation* for building up and maintaining the technical documentation the usual structure of textual documents consisting of chapters, subchapters, titles, paragraphs, and subparagraphs was adopted.

In recent time a big bunch of conceptual problems have been addressed for *project organization* (see subsections 1.1.4 and 1.1.5). As a lot of work still has to be done in the future we only give a brief sketch here and postpone a more detailed description to the main chapters and, especially, to chapter 5 of this book. In addition to the coarse structure of an administration configuration outlined in 1.1.5 we gave a formal description of its structure and of its mutual internal relations. Furthermore, we discussed the dynamic situations of software development and maintenance /6. NW 94, 6. Wes 95a, b/. This project organization work includes the results of *version* and *configuration* control which was investigated for some time in the group /4. Wes 89, 4. Wes 91a, b, 5. Wes 95a/.

After having sketched our effort in 'method work' we would like to make some global remarks about modelling in software engineering in general and in the area software development environments in particular, namely on which levels it occurs and how far the support can go. Let us first *recall* that developing/maintaining a software system means that the *developer models* or *specifies* on *different levels*: The outside behavior on RE level, the essential but realization structure on PiL–level, the detailed algorithmic structure on PiS–level. Furthermore, all organizational aspects of the project (i.e. of its processes, products, and the necessary resources) have to be modeled by a *manager.*

Modelling on all these levels by application developers/managers is not only dependent on which concepts, languages, and methods are available. It is also dependent on the habit of thought, used standards and procedures and, especially, on the intellectual power of software engineers to handle abstractions. In any case, even if suitable concepts, languages, and methods are at hand, *modelling* is a *difficult task,* as there is a lot of freedom to do it. The processes are creative and unknown (cf. subsection 1.1.5). Modelling is hard to evaluate, i.e. whether a document has the right or wrong form. *No serious metrics* are available for documents and configurations which give a detailed or specific answer and evaluation.

In the IPSEN project the situation is even more complicated as modelling is not only applying given concepts, languages, and methods in application system development. As pointed out in this subsection, in most cases these concepts, languages, and methods had to be invented before building tools. Therefore, modelling appeared on the level of defining suitable concepts, languages, and methods for certain working areas/perspectives of a system but also for their integration, and the development process. We are going now to describe how this *modelling* on *language/method definition level* is achieved.

For a certain level of abstraction (outside behavior, architecture of a system etc.) the corresponding suitable *concepts* have to be defined or taken. In requirements engineering, for example, for the function model processes, data flows, data stores, and terminators have been taken. Then, it has to be made precise how these constructs can be *combined* as data flow diagrams, and how refinement of processes by data flow diagrams is defined. Then, a lot of *consistency constraints* can be found which have to hold true. All of this falls under the category language definition. Furthermore, a lot a *methodological hints* can be detected, e.g. saying that a certain combination of constructs (fulfilling the consistency constraints) is describing a situation clearly and evidently, or not. Finally, the language, consistency constraints, and hints have to be seen *together* with those of another *level* of *abstraction* (e.g. architecture modelling) in order to see which concepts fit together, to define combined consistency constraints, or combined methodological hints how and when a certain situation on one modelling level induces a certain situation on the other level, or vice versa.

For modelling in a working area (including nontechnical working areas as project organization or technical documentation) we offer one or more corresponding document classes. Defining the language for a document class means fixing the appearance of constructs, their combination, consistency constraints, and also of methodological hints in terms of language constructs. Therefore, constructs, combinations, and consistencies have to be put into a language, and methodology now consists of using certain language patterns and avoiding others. Usually, *conceptual investigations* for languages (concepts, consistencies, method rules) *cannot* clearly *be separated* from *language definition* as we always fix concepts by a certain representation (a language in a broad sense of understanding).

Language definition consists of different steps, also usually intertwined /9. Schn 81/: The context free *syntax* of the language defines the appearance of constructs and, usually, also their local combination. The context sensitive syntax defines static consistency constraints. In executable languages the dynamic *semantics* also have to be defined. For any language the *pragmatics* have to be determined. In the case where methodological hints are precise and two–valued (good situation, bad situation) this *methodology* may be regarded as an 'extension' and 'restriction' of the syntax of the underlying language. It can be regarded as another level of context–free and context–sensitive syntax on top of the language syntax in distinguishing situations as good or bad which on the pure language level are generally permitted.

Whereas for the *working areas* we offer *languages* incorporating concepts allowing a software engineer to write documents in the languages according to a certain methodology, this is *not* so in the *case* of *integration* subjects. In these latter cases we put concepts, consistency constraints, and methodology of the conceptual integration situation directly into the *behavior* of corresponding *tools* acting for integration: The user does not see a document for integration with a specified syntax which can be manipulated by corresponding tools. Instead, he sees the corresponding documents to be integrated together with a certain representation saying which increments of one document are related to which increments of another document and, possibly, why they are related to each other. In some cases the integration or correspondence representation is explicit (the engineer is 'seeing' links), in other cases the links are not seen but rather their consequences in the related document according to these links.

1.3.3 New Tools for Working Areas or Integration

This next problem area deals with the *investigation* of *which tools* are to be realized. This investigation has different facets. These are (1) the question which tools are selected for realization from the rich set of possible tools, (2) which functionality these tools have, (3) which characterizations these tools fulfill, and (4) how the user interface of these tools should appear. This discussion will be very short because a detailed one follows later. So, we do not describe the various tools but only give short answers to the above questions or references to other parts of this book.

The first question *which tools* have been *selected* to be realized in IPSEN was answered above in subsection 1.3.1 where we gave a rationale for the IPSEN scenario of fig. 1.12. It was characterized such that tools give substantial support on one side but, on the other side, the IPSEN environment is limited enough to be realized in a research–oriented context. A complete list of available tools is given in section 1.8.

The *functionality* of *tools* is roughly given by the fact to which of the classes of tools on one document class (editors, analyzers, instrumentation tools, execution tools, browsers), and to which classes of integration tools (transformation tools, consistency checkers, browsers) the available tools belong to. In chapter 2 we extensively discuss the available tools thereby demonstrating their detailed functionality.

A discussion on the *characteristics* of IPSEN *tools* appears in the next section. There, we shall have a special section devoted to explaining the IPSEN understanding of integration and giving reasons why this understanding is necessary for development, maintenance, and reuse. Secondly, we shall discuss the other external characteristics of IPSEN tools, namely interactive and immediate, intelligent, structure–oriented, command–driven, incremental, uniform, and project organization–oriented with respect to their value to the IPSEN user.

Finally, the *user interface* behavior of IPSEN tools will also be postponed to chapter 2 of this book. There, we provide a lot of screen dumps in order to show the user interface style on one side, and the uniformity of style across different tools on the other.

1.3.4 Internal Conceptual Modelling

This subsection will again be rather short. It is aimed only at *introducing* the problem area of *internal conceptual modelling* but not explaining how we handle it. The reason is that the special approach we took for conceptual modelling, namely by graph grammars, is one of the key aspects of the IPSEN project. It is presented in its own section (cf. 1.5) in the introduction and, furthermore, is discussed in detail in chapter 3 in the main part of this book.

Building complex tools which are, furthermore, integrated can hardly be done by directly writing down their code. Instead, one has to think carefully about the *internal structures* on which tools operate and about the *operations* induced by tool activations on these structures. Both are *very complex*. In order to handle this complexity, we have to specify the tools in terms of internal documents and their behavior before encoding these tools in programs. We call modelling on this specification level conceptual (internal) modelling.

The second reason for careful internal conceptual modelling is that it detects many *similarities* between different *internal documents*. The detection and specification of these similarities is a prerequisite and basis for any approach to *reduce* the *effort* of *tool realization* in the sense of building basic blocks for implementation, or building generator tools.

The internal structures serve different *purposes* (more details in section 1.5): We have to handle logical items for what the user is doing in a part of the overall process (e.g. for storing the structure of a subsystem's architecture and to give support for suitable modifications), what we term an *internal logical document*. For this, different representations (external views) may exist, graphical or textual. These again are represented by internal documents, named *representation* documents. Furthermore, integration between different logical documents is stored in an internal document, called the *integration* document. Coordination of technical developers is also handled internally by a corresponding structure (*administration* configuration *document*, with corresponding representations). Internal modelling not only consists of how to structure these internal documents and to support corresponding operations on internal documents but also to determine the various *interrelations* between internal documents. So, what we have called an overall configuration above has an internal pendant, which we call *internal overall configuration* (see subsection 1.4.1).

The *term conceptual modelling* comes from trying to find common concepts, constructs, and methodologies in different areas such as data bases, artificial intelligence, software engineering, and programming languages (/5. BMS 84, 5. SMS 84/). Indeed, we shall see that aspects of all these areas play a role in our internal conceptual modelling approach. What makes conceptual modelling *interesting* but also *difficult* in the IPSEN project is that we are building integrated tools with an understanding of integration as tight integration on one side (with respect to support) but loose integration on the other (with respect to freedom of the technical developers or their coordination).

Let us try to point out why we *need* this *conceptual modelling* for *specifying SDE tools* and their behavior. In many simple dialogue systems, especially in the business application area, we can specify those systems using the wide–spread RE–languages SA (describing the commands and their decomposition), EER (describing underlying data), possibly together with finite automata for describing the micro dialogues corresponding to masks, and a user interface description language for describing how the masks/menus are built up. These dialogs are then combined to bigger automata or nets to define application systems. Different application systems in one company are integrated by using an underlying data base system. This kind of modelling is not appropriate for IPSEN–like integrated SDEs. The reason is that tool specifications for SDEs must be aware of the complex structure of internal documents (the behavior of an inner increment within a block might be different from that of an outer increment), the behavior of tools is dependent on context information (whether an increment is bound to another increment or not), or may be determined by whether a document exists or not (transformation tools must regard existing target documents, or generate new ones). Thus, the specification must be aware of the state representing the knowledge of the complete dialogue of one user (stored in one logical document) or of different users (on an internal overall configuration). Therefore, finite automata approaches on global data fail in this subclass of intelligent dialogue systems. To summarize: In this specification application area of SDEs *common specification techniques* for structuring data base applications are *not sufficient*.

1.3.5 Software Engineering Investigations

This subsection introduces the problem area *architecture modelling* within an SDE realization. Basically, it introduces what we have brought in from software engineering for the overall task of SDE research and realization and what we have learned for software engineering by studying in detail this special application, namely SDEs, for a long time. Again, this subsection is short because there is both an own section on the main ideas of the IPSEN architecture in this introduction (section 1.6) and there is a chapter (4) in the main part of this book.

The reader might assume from the described scenario and from our ambitious understanding of integration that the IPSEN prototype is quite a *big software system* which is rather *complicated* with respect to its internal structure. Therefore, it was especially important to clearly develop and describe its essential structure, i.e. its software *architecture,* in order to be able to realize this complicated system.

The software *architecture* is the *basis* of all structural investigations in direction of reducing the effort of realization for an SDE with a given description of its behavior. This is realized by *reuse*, especially on architecture level. On the *knowledge* side (besides internal modelling which was separately described) we find architectural pattern reuse or human mechanical derivation of code from internal specifications. On the *product* side basic block reuse, platform reuse, and framework reuse is applied. On the *process* side we can find generation of code by generator tools

Thus, the extensive investigation of IPSEN on architecture level contributed to *application* technology, *structure* technology, and to *project* technology in the sense of subsection 1.1.6 (see also chapter 6). If a new environment to be developed is IPSEN–like, then for some tools of the SDE we have a situation of development as for the production of quality compilers: Development is more reuse and maintenance in a predetermined process than a dynamic and unforeseeable process (see next section and chapter 5). Furthermore, the knowledge of IPSEN can be reused and applied to *other applications* within or outside of SDEs.

1.3.6 Implementation

This subsection is again very short. Its aim is to make clear that a considerable portion of the *effort* of a practical SDE research project goes *into implementation activities*, although coding is not the main goal for a research project. However, an efficient and stable prototype able to show new tools, new tool behavior, or new strategies to develop tools means plain realization work.

We had to *implement all components* of the architecture framework, its basic blocks, and the platform. Also the core components, especially for the internal *data structures* and their coupling had to be implemented if not generated. Finally, the generators yielding the specific components had to be developed.

The available *tools* which have been *implemented* will be listed in section 1.8. They belong to all working areas of the scenario of fig. 1.12 together with the corresponding integration and administration tools.

The *code produced* belonging to the IPSEN project is comparable to a medium–size project in a software house. The corresponding figures in terms of LOCs and person years are given later in section 1.8. Furthermore, the PROGRES project, directly devoted to support the internal conceptual work mentioned above, and our contributions to the SUKITS project also took remarkable effort. All environments, fortunately, share a lot of code, namely the framework architecture and its basic components, and they are partially derived by the same generator tools.

1.3.7 Demonstration and Distribution

Demonstration and *distribution efforts* seem to be a rather trivial problem. Nevertheless, the effort spent on activities in this area is remarkable.

IPSEN or, more precisely, its different versions have been *demonstrated* at *many external sites* and, also, locally at Aachen. The most important of them are listed in table 1.14. Furthermore, IPSEN was demonstrated in lectures and project meetings. Finally, a lot of researchers have been visiting our group. Most of them have been interested in getting a demo.

The aim of giving *demos* is not only to demonstrate scientific activities and, therefore, to advertise our efforts in the insider community. In addition to this goal we receive constructive input from people (e.g. from application programmers) when we demonstrate a prototype. These *responses* have improved our system or improved our way of explaining the system.

The overall *effort* required in preparing a *demo*, for showing it, for discussions, or maintaining contact to interested people etc. is rather big. For example, the Hannover Fair 1988 alone cost something like two person months of effort, excluded the time required for preparing the demo, which was often shown later on.

The *prototype* has been *distributed* to other research organizations and to some companies on a non–profit base. Furthermore, the basic component object storage has been sent out to about 20 organizations for use in prototype systems.

location	year	event	prototype
Palo Alto (USA)	1986	2nd ACM Software Eng. Symp. on Pract. SDEs	IPSEN
Kaiserslautern (D)	1986	Softw. Architectures and Modular Programming Workshop	IPSEN
Strasbourg (F)	1987	1st European Conf. on Software Engineering	IPSEN
Dortmund (D)	1987	Workshop on Data Base Systems for Software Eng.	IPSEN
Schloß Banz (D)	1987	13th Int. Workshop on Graphtheoretic Concepts in Computer Science	IPSEN
Hannover (D)	1988	CeBit Hannover Fair	IPSEN
Darmstadt (D)	1988	Workshop on Language–Oriented Programming Env.	IPSEN
Singapore	1988	IEEE Int. Conf. on Software Eng., Tools Fair	IPSEN
Cannes (F)	1988	ACM SIGSMALL Conference	IPSEN
Paris (F)	1988	4eme Exposition Génie Logiciel	IPSEN
Boston (USA)	1988	3rd ACM Softw. Eng. Symp. on Pract. SDEs	IPSEN
Germany and USA	1988	further demos at universities/companies at Nürnberg, München, Oldenburg, Bremen, Providence, Mountain View, Stanford	IPSEN
Berlin (D)	1989	Int. Conf. on Syst. Development Environments & Factories	IPSEN
Rolduc (NL)	1989	15th Int. Workshop on Graphtheoretic Concepts in Computer Science	IPSEN
Marburg (D)	1989	1st German SE Conference	IPSEN
Coventry (GB)	1989	2nd European Conf. on Software Engineering	IPSEN
Bremen (D)	1990	4th Int. Workshop on Graph Grammars and their Appl. to Computer Science	IPSEN and PROGRES
Toulouse (F)	1990	3rd Int. Workshop on Software Eng. and its Appl.	IPSEN
Dortmund (D)	1990	ESF project meeting	IPSEN
further demos	1991	demos in lectures and internal demos at Aachen	IPSEN
nearby		Computer Science Day RWTH Aachen	IPSEN
Berlin (D)	1991	PROGRES Introduction Talk	PROGRES
Aachen (D)	1992	Regina Exhibition	IPSEN
Aachen (D)	1992	Softtec NRW: CASE Workshop State of the Art of Industrial Systems	IPSEN and PROGRES
Aachen (D)	1992	Computer Science day RWTH Aachen	PROGRES
Karlsruhe (D)	1992	Presentations at FZI and GMD	PROGRES
Aachen (D)	1993	Complement Meeting	IPSEN
Aachen (D)	1993	internal demos in lectures and for visitors	IPSEN, IPSEN–RE
Singapore	1993	CASE '93	PROGRES, GRAS
Aachen (D)	1993	SUKITS presentation and evaluation	SUKITS Adm. Comp.
Leiden (NL)	1994	Talk on PROGRES prototype	PROGRES
Amsterdam (NL)	1994	PROGRES presentation	PROGRES
Delft (NL)	1994	PROGRES presentation	PROGRES
Aachen (D)	1994	Technology Center Aachen 'Future from Aachen'	SUKITS, PROGRES, IPSEN–RE
Aachen (D)	1994	Computer Science Day	SUKITS, PROGRES
Umea (S)	1995	Talk on PROGRES	PROGRES
Darmstadt (D)	1995	IEEE Conference VL '95 on Visual Languages	PROGRES
Aachen (D)	1995	WG '95 21st Workshop on Graphtheoretic Concepts in Computer Science	PROGRES, SUKITS
Madrid (E)	1995	ESEC '95 European Conference on Software Engineering	PROGRES
Aachen (D)	1995	Computer Science Day	PROGRES

Table 1.14. IPSEN, PROGRES, SUKITS, GRAS: prototype demos

1.4 Tightly Integrated Tools Are Needed for Software Development Processes

The aim of this section is to motivate the external behavior of IPSEN tools presented to the user (see chapter 2). Thereby, we mainly concentrate on the integration aspect as one of the *highlights* of IPSEN. We introduce a certain kind of integration which we call *tight integration*. Integration has different facets, three of which are explained in this section. These are (1) tight integration on extended technical, fine–grained configurations. Here, we mainly discuss tight integration between different documents /4. Lew 88c, 7. Jan 92, 4. Lef 95/. Furthermore, there is (2) integration between the administration configuration (for the management of a software project) and the extended technical configuration, and (3) within the administration configuration itself /6. NW 94/. The discussion will, furthermore, also show that overall configurations evolve at project runtime.

In addition, we discuss the fact that different lifecycle models can be mapped on the working area model and a corresponding integrated SDE, and we give some remarks that application and structure technologies have impact on the structure of overall configurations. Although, integration is only one of the external characteristics – albeit the most important one – we end this section by discussing all external characteristics of IPSEN.

1.4.1 Tight Integration on Extended Technical Configurations for Development, Maintenance, and Reuse

The *aim* of this *subsection* is to *motivate* and to *introduce* the *understanding of fine–grained integration* on extended technical configurations and the *corresponding support* by *environments* according to the terminology of sections 1.1 and 1.2. In order to show this we regard typical situations occurring in the development or maintenance of software systems, or of reuse within software systems. We discuss tools rather independent of their detailed behavior and user interface. These details of tools are given in the next chapter.

Before we go into details of fine–grained integration let us recall what an overall configuration for a *software system according* to the restricted *scenario* for the users of IPSEN consists of (cf. fig. 1.13 and fig. 1.15). We have the functional requirements specification described in SA, EER, and a control model, all of them with a graphical view for diagrams and a textual view for details. The architecture is represented by diagrams giving an overview device and detailed textual descriptions for corresponding components. For any of the modules contained in the architecture there is a text view containing the implementation (body) of the module. For the working area documentation there are textual views for writing the technical documentation or a part of it, as e.g. the design rationale. Finally, for project organization there are graphical or textual views for configuration, process, and resources control.

As already stated in 1.1, there are many consistencies within and between the documents of a certain working area and between documents of different working areas. The message of this subsection is *not that* these consistencies must be handled. Interesting is the *way* in which these *consistencies* are *handled* by the IPSEN tools, i.e. how fine–grained integration within but, especially, between documents and the corresponding processes on and between these documents is achieved. Fig. 1.15 does not show what our tools present to the software engineer. Instead, only that portion of the information is presented to the user which is important and usable for a certain task. Arguing that this picture is too complex means neglecting reality: At the moment and without integrated SDEs the situation is handled only in the heads of software engineers by discipline, or trial and error.

Before we start with our discussion we have to recall and to heighten the notion of an *increment*. An increment is a portion of a software document which is related to the underlying language, more precisely, to the syntax of this language. To be more general we can dis-

58

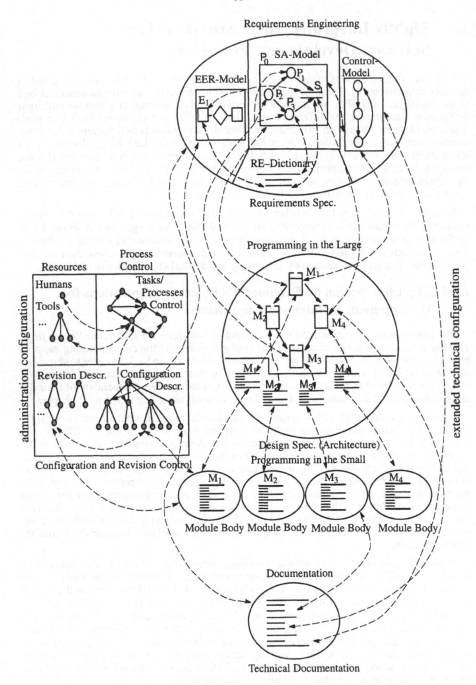

Fig. 1.15. An overall configuration for a software system according to the IPSEN scenario of
fig. 1.13 (fig. 1.4 revisited by which the notion of an overall configuration was introduced)

tinguish increments on different levels: Besides *language* increments (e.g. an assignment statement built up from lexical units and other nonterminals of the programming language) we can define the portions of a document a certain tool is operating on as *user* increments (e.g. only the whole assignment statement is selectable and changeable, modifications within the assignment being done only in a textual mode) and, furthermore, *internal* increments in the internal data base (e.g. a node with two successors for the left and right hand side of the assignment, both with suitable trees). Increments of a more general kind not determined by the context–free syntax of the language may be found on user or *method* level (a declaration of a variable together with its applications; a sequence of statements being a refinement). In the examples of this book user increments, language increments, and internal increments are mostly related 1:1 to each other, and we only regard increments of the context free syntax of the underlying language.

We are now starting to discuss development and maintenance of configurations for software systems as well as reuse within software development or maintenance. We start with *maintenance*. From literature we roughly know (e.g. /7. Ram 84/) that 42% of maintenance effort is applied to extensions or perfections of a software system, 25% into porting and another 20% into corrections. The rest is of minor importance. In any of these cases we have changes on the extended technical configuration of a software system. We are going to discuss these cases in increasing order of severity.

In maintenance due to *correction* (besides the rather seldom case that an error is found and corrected within the body of one module and has no impact outside the body) we have a rather slight *change* of a *technical configuration*: The requirements specification is unchanged, the architecture slightly changed, e.g. by changing the export interface of a module and, correspondingly, some imports, the corresponding bodies of changed modules of the architecture are changed, the technical documentation is also slightly changed (as well as quality assurance documents). The situation is a little bit more complicated when a software *system* is *ported* from one platform to another one. We assume that the architecture has been carefully developed. Besides the fact that the architecture is heavily changed, e.g. by replacing a subsystem the internals of which reflect a certain feature of the basic machine, which induces corresponding changes in dependent documents, the situation is nearly the same as above. A bigger modification of the configuration of a software system appears if this *system* is *extended*, as the requirements definition has to be modified and the architecture plus its dependent documents run through bigger steps of modification.

In any of these cases a rather small number of the total number of documents is changed and, within these changed documents, only a small number of increments. Developers want to be free w.r.t. the *order* of changes. In one document one can either firstly carry out all changes one after the other and then delete the appearing inconsistencies en bloc (batch mode), or make the *modification/inconsistency repair* one after the other (trace mode). A bigger number of modifications might be carried out in the first mode, a small number in the second mode. Analogously, the task of modifying a subconfiguration of documents to make it consistent again can be carried out in different ways. One way is to correct the first document completely and then regard all the 'derived' modifications on a dependent document one after the other and so forth (batch mode). Another way is to trace a change through all documents and then go to the next (trace mode). The developer(s) should be free to choose any of these modes, or a mixture of them.

Another case separately from carrying out modifications involves *estimating* the *consequences of a* (set of) *change(s)* for a configuration. Rather often the situation occurs where a change would not have been made if all the consequences of this change had been clear at the beginning of the change. Estimation can be done only by browsing and inspecting within and between different documents or by changing a new revision of the configuration to see what is happening. Again, browsing as well as changing can be carried out in different modes. It is more probable that it is done in the trace mode, i.e. investigating the implications of a change in one document but also in other documents and so forth before going on to estimate the consequences of the next change.

A rather similar situation as in maintenance is found in the *development* of *software*. Development is not a batch process. Developing one software document means analyzing the (or a portion of the) master document, carrying out a loop of piecewise construction, internal analysis, comparison with the master document, thinking forward about dependent documents etc. So, we have again construction, modification, analysis, and prognosis actions, which can occur in any order. Furthermore, in the same way or even more than in maintenance, backtracking steps take place, i.e. a mastering document has to be changed (e.g. after recognizing that one module cannot be implemented, the architecture has to be changed, see below) which again has consequences for other documents which already exist, either in parts or completely. So, development is often more maintenance like than straightforward construction.

In some cases (it should be nearly always) configurations are not built up from scratch but by using already existing results. This *reuse* can mean that already existing complete documents (code of a module or a subsystem), or parts of documents (the architectural description of a module or of a subsystem within an architecture of another system), related (fractions of) documents or a subconfiguration (architecture description, implementation, and technical documentation of a subsystem), subconfigurations reflecting experience or some standard knowledge (the architecture framework for a system and a corresponding subconfiguration of detailed design and module documents) are taken. We have again less (including a subsystem to be reused by a system) or more (modifying a reused component or modifying the context of a reused component within a subconfiguration) modifications of increments/documents/configurations. So, modifications take place on the level of overall configurations down to the fine–grained increment level, and they take place on the subconfiguration to be reused and the (sub)configuration where the subconfiguration is used.

So, in any of the above situations within *maintenance, development*, and *reuse*, we have a loop of change process steps which consists of construction, modification, analysis, and others within one document, across different documents, and on the extended technical configuration level in order to make or keep documents internally consistent (intradocument consistency) and externally consistent (interdocument consistency) thereby making the overall configuration consistent (configuration consistency). So, the overall *situation is* rather *similar* in all three cases: It may be different corresponding to the severity of changes or the amount of work but it is equal w.r.t. the abstract situation describing what can happen. In any situation, we do not want to be restricted in how we achieve development, maintenance, and reuse processes. This means that the order of subprocesses which determine how to construct, change, or reuse increments, documents, subconfigurations, or configurations should be free to the developer or the team, as a reasonable order cannot be fixed a priori for any situation. (The difficulty in clearly distinguishing between development, maintenance, and reuse was one reason to introduce the working area model of fig. 1.2 which only contains a logical grouping of activities but no time dependency of corresponding technical process steps or processes.)

In development, maintenance, and reuse *processes* are *sequential, overlapped* or *parallel*. Firstly, for example, after the architecture is finished, the modules can be implemented in parallel and independent from the architecture if there is no backtracking step changing the architecture and, thereby, the specifications of the corresponding modules. Secondly, activities can be performed overlapped. For example, the technical documentation is immediately written or updated if corresponding decisions have been fixed in requirements engineering, architecture modelling, or implementation, which are described and substantiated in the technical documentation. Another example is that if the upper layers of an architecture are fixed then, of course, the implementation of some modules identified in the architecture can start, although the architecture is not completed. In both cases, processes of different working areas are carried out in an overlapped manner although these working areas have a directed dependency relation. Thirdly and trivially, there are also sequential orders of activities. In order to handle development, maintenance, and reuse there should be freedom in which order activities in different working areas are carried out. However, management experience recommends some discipline and coordination. Therefore, by ordering complex construction/modification/analysis etc. steps within processes the corresponding developer(s) should be free as long as underlying dependencies between increments/documents/configurations as well as management practices are observed.

To discuss the *needed behavior of tools* let us first discuss the properties of tools on one working area document A, then the properties of integration tools between two documents A and B. Finally, we discuss how the results of the integration tool A → B should be handled by tools on B. Applying this two–document modification scheme iteratively, a change of a complete configuration in the given scenario of fig. 1.15 can be handled (cf. fig. 1.16).

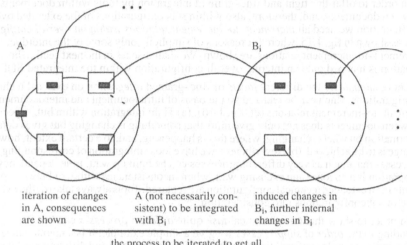

iteration of changes in A, consequences are shown	A (not necessarily consistent) to be integrated with B_i	induced changes in B_i, further internal changes in B_i

the process to be iterated to get all
changes within a (sub)configuration

Fig. 1.16. Needed behavior of document and integration tools

If we firstly discuss the *behavior of tools* on *one document* we see that in order to be free to arrange construction, modification, analysis, and other steps we must have tools (1) showing the consequences of a construction or modification step as precisely as possible. Therefore, no meaningless errors or hints (warning that something has to be completed, which is already known by the developer) and no unspecific errors or hints (an indication that there are some errors in the document) should be given. Instead, the developer is interested in exactly where and which kind of error is occurring, or where a hint is to be applied and how. Furthermore, (2) tools have to handle inconsistent documents: In order to guarantee the above freedom, tools have to tolerate inconsistent documents and should not force the user to delete an inconsistency just after it has occurred. Nevertheless, the tools have to keep track of all inconsistencies and their mutual dependencies. In order to guarantee behavior (1) and (2), tools have to be aware of the full knowledge incorporated in a document belonging to a particular document class.

If a document A is changed and its internal inconsistencies are fully or partially deleted, then the dependent documents $B_1,..., B_m$ usually become inconsistent. To determine these inconsistencies one or more integration tools are invoked. The *behavior* of such an *integration tool* T: A → B_i should be as that of document tools on single documents: (1) The consequences of changes within A have to be made precise corresponding to locality and type in B_i. Furthermore, (2) as inconsistencies of A imply inconsistencies within B_i, the integration tool should not enforce that inconsistencies between both documents A and B_i are repaired immediately or in total. Trivially, the integration tool (3) has to take care of the existing state of the target document B_i. Therefore, it should not produce a new (portion of a) document B'$_i$ of B$_i$ leaving it for the developer to match B$_i$ and B'$_i$ as most integration tools do today.

When the inconsistencies of B$_i$ are determined according to a change of A then the *tools* of the *target document* B$_i$ should help to *keep track* of the *induced modifications* within B$_i$. They should behave again as above: (1) The consequences of the changes within B$_i$ induced by changes of A should be precisely stated corresponding to locality and type, and (2) inconsistencies should be allowed. Altogether, by coupling tools of A, the integration tool, and tools of B$_i$ we get a smooth transition from changes in A to changes within B$_i$, if all tools and their combination have the above characteristics.

In order to offer this tight and fine–grained integration by tools within documents and between documents, and, therefore, also within subconfigurations of the extended overall configuration we need all *increment–to–increment relations within an overall configuration* as shown in fig. 1.15, where for reasons of simplicity only some of the interdocument increment–to–increment relations are shown. We shall discuss in the next section how this situation is mapped onto an internal overall configuration within the integrated SDE.

Let us *summarize* the different *facets* of fine–grained *integration* on external technical configurations which can be realized on the basis of intradocument and interdocument increment–to–increment relations (cf. fig. 1.16): (a) Tight integration within but, especially, between documents does not only give hints that something is changing but gives detailed information on what is changing, where this is happening, and, to a certain extent, how this change is to be achieved. (b) Nevertheless, we have loose integration of corresponding subprocesses inasmuch as very different processes can be built up w.r.t. time dependency. (c) Integration is also loose and excusing w.r.t. when inconsistencies within or between documents in an extended technical configuration are repaired. Tools always take (d) the existing state of subconfigurations into consideration.

In order to show that for a technical *task* quite *different processes* can be taken corresponding to the *order* of *subprocesses* we give a simple example. It is a maintenance task on a simple example configuration consisting of an architecture and different modules (cf. fig. 1.17). The range is from batch–oriented to trace–oriented processes. Fig. 1.17 contains one example for both cases. In the first case, grouping is done according to documents, in the second case grouping is done according to dependencies. The two processes are built up by modifications with tools on one document and integration tools with the above characteristics. A lot of further processes are possible. The example could also have been taken to describe a development or a reuse task.

In the rest of this subsection we discuss the *dynamic situations*, i.e. situations which cannot be predicted before project runtime, on an overall configuration for a software project. Thereby, we restrict ourselves to the dynamic situations on the *extended technical configuration*. Some dynamic situations on the administration configuration are induced by changes on the extended technical configuration. We discuss them later. Dynamics are due to evolution, backtracking, and other reasons at project runtime. We shall see that the integration characteristics of tools, as described above, are necessary to handle these situations.

Let us first start with the *evolution dynamics*. When developing a new system, we do *not know* at the beginning *how* the *extended technical configuration* will *develop* and, therefore, which technical processes are needed. For example, only after having developed the architecture of a system do we know how many modules occur in the system and, therefore, how many module implementation documents but also test data, driver, stub documents, or how many paragraphs in the technical documentation about these documents shall occur. So, we do not know the number of implementation, test, or documentation processes or subprocesses. This situation can elegantly be handled by the integration tools described above as we can start the integration tool between PiL and PiS for generating the corresponding number of module frames the bodies of which are to be implemented, and we can activate the RE, PiL, PiS → DOC integration tool for updating the technical documentation at any time (test is not included in our scenario).

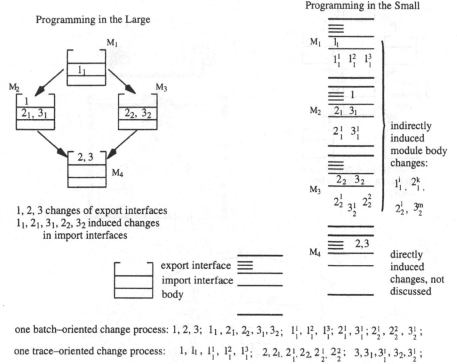

Programming in the Large

Programming in the Small

1, 2, 3 changes of export interfaces
$1_1, 2_1, 3_1, 2_2, 3_2$ induced changes
in import interfaces

export interface
import interface
body

indirectly induced module body changes:
$1_1^i, 2_1^k,$
$2_2^l, 3_2^m$

directly induced changes, not discussed

one batch–oriented change process: $1, 2, 3; \ 1_1, 2_1, 2_2, 3_1, 3_2; \ 1_1^1, 1_1^2, 1_1^3; 2_1^1, 3_1^1; 2_2^1, 2_2^2, 3_2^1;$

one trace–oriented change process: $\quad 1, 1_1, 1_1^1, 1_1^2, 1_1^3; \ 2, 2_1, 2_1^1, 2_2, 2_2^1, 2_2^2; \ 3, 3_1, 3_1^1, 3_2, 3_2^1;$

Fig. 1.17. Tight integration and different change processes shown for one simple maintenance example

To give a simple example for the *backtracking* case of *dynamics* we regard fig. 1.18 which, again, contains a very simple example: In a design document for a subsystem S we have taken a wrong design decision such that the portability of that subsystem is not regarded (cf. fig. 1.18.a). This error was detected much later. A module with a new interface M_n has to be introduced, the architecture below that module is now made to a new subsystem S_1 (cf. fig. 1.18.b). Within the new subsystem S_1, the new interface has to be mapped onto the interfaces of existing modules (here M_4). Above the subsystem, the modules (import interfaces and their bodies; here of M_2, M_3) have to be changed as they now refer to the new subsystem interface. When the error is detected, module M_1 is already in test, M_2, M_3, and M_4 are in implementation (the implementor of M_2 has produced the problem report which, after a problem session, induced the backtracking step), M_5 and M_6 are in detailed design (i.e. writing the export and import interfaces in detail). This example shall later be used to describe dynamic situations on the administration configuration as well.

What has to be done on *technical configuration* level to accomodate this *backtracking step* in development? Firstly, the architecture document is modified to contain the module M_n and its export interface, to correct the imports for M_2 and M_3, and to make M_n together with the modules below of it to a subsystem. This is possible with the PiL editor. As backtracking occurs within development we could work on the same revision of the architecture document to do these modifications. Being cautious, we take a new revision of the architecture document before. After that, we split the architecture document into two documents, one for each subsystem. Splitting as well as making a new revision must preserve the intra-document fine–grained relations but, especially, the interdocument, fine–grained relations,

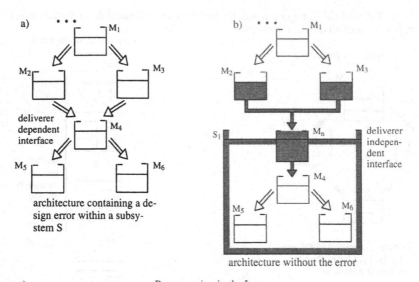

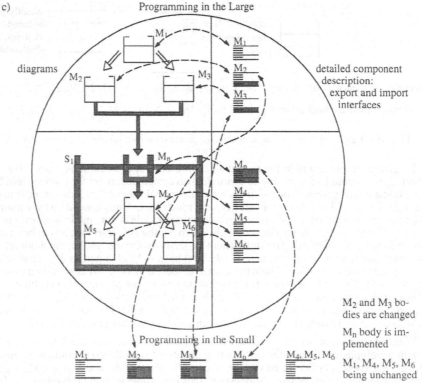

Fig. 1.18. A simple backtracking situation on a technical configuration: a), b) architecture situations before and after error repair, c) changes on technical configuration induced by backtracking

here to the corresponding module bodies. After that, the architecture document for subsystem S_1 can internally be corrected using the PiL editor (introducing the import to M_4). As module bodies of M_1, M_4, M_5, and M_6 remain unchanged the technical configuration is correct w.r.t. the relations between the architecture documents for S or S_1 and these module implementation documents. Then, in any order, the PiL–PiS integration tool for correcting the relations between S_1 and M_2, M_3 or for generating a module frame for M_n can be invoked. As we are cautious, we make a new revision of M_2 and M_3 implementation documents before changing them. After inconsistency repair in the body of M_2 and M_3 and after having implemented M_n the backtracking process is finished.

So, we see that in addition to editors which serve for consistency analysis and repair within a document and, in addition to integration tools working as outlined above, establishing/reestablishing fine–grained increment–to–increment consistency between documents further tool functionality is required: When *splitting* a document (as above for making a subarchitecture to a subsystem), the *fine–grained relations* to other documents have to be *preserved* and the intradocument relations have to be converted into interdocument relations. Analogously, when *taking* a *new revision* for a document before it is changed (either because the old one is still needed for further use, or because we are cautious) the fine–grained relations to dependent document revisions have to be preserved. Conversely, when melting a complete document into another one (e.g. a subsystem is deleted, its internals are put into another architecture document) or when two different revisions are melted we need the functionality that relations to dependent documents are melted and interdocument relations are made to intradocument relations. For introducing a revision the corresponding tool functionality is available, in the other case it still has to be implemented.

IPSEN is a set of *coherent tools* to make and keep documents of different working areas consistent. More particularly, the tools are built for integration in the sense of giving support to end up with a *consistent configuration* whenever an essential *change* has been made either in development, maintenance, or reuse. Tools behave in a fine–grained integration mode. This facilitates any kind of development/maintenance/reuse processes inasmuch as mutual dependencies are explicitly controlled by tools and are not only handled by bookkeeping in mind or by discipline. Secondly, tools are loosely coupled in the sense that they allow very different processes w. r. t. orders of actions. This loose coupling is the prerequisite of distributing labour to different people. So, the tools are well–suited from their character for tight integration within a group of software engineers without restricting the needed freedom of the process in which different people are involved.

1.4.2 Integration of Software Development within a Group

In this subsection we shall discuss *integration* aspects resulting from management of configurations and their processes. This situation has two facets: The first is that we have *all administration* information available, called administration configurations in subsection 1.1.5. Here, the appropriate tool functionality has to be offered. The second topic is how we *integrate* an *administration configuration* with an *extended technical configuration* or, in the terminology of 1.2.4, how to integrate technical environments with the administration component. Especially, the question has to be answered who (the administrator or technical developers) is allowed to use which administration functions.

For the first topic of integration, namely to have an *integrated view* on *all administration information*, we have distinguished between product administration, process administration, and resource administration (cf. subsection 1.1.4 and fig. 1.6). The reader should remember that the administration configuration is coarse–grained information on technical information of a fine–grained nature. On *coarse–grained* administration configurations we only have information of the kind 'that and what' but no information 'how' anything is structured in detail or to be carried out. So, in this subsection we discuss mostly issues on the coarse–grained side in contrast to the last subsection.

Task/process information and *configuration/revision* information are *dual aspects* which describe the two sides of the same coin. If using one aspect the other one has to be built up consistently and the consistency relations between both have to be inserted. Thereby, depending on the situation we may prefer the one or the other to be regarded first. In new system development a manager may take an activity oriented view by creating the corresponding tasks/process descriptions, leaving it for the administration component to insert the corresponding configuration descriptions. On the other hand, in maintenance, we may take the coarse–grained product information to derive the corresponding task and process descriptions.

In the last subsection we have sketched *dynamic situations* on the technical fine–grained level due to evolution and backtracking. These situations are mapped on the coarse–grained *administration configuration*: So, only at project runtime we e.g. know which and how many tasks/processes of a certain kind have to be inserted in the process administration part or, in the backtracking case, which part of the net has to be changed and retraced. Thereby, quite complicated situations arise. We postpone this discussion to later chapters. Furthermore, also on administration level, evolution and problems can give rise to manipulations of the administration configuration at project runtime: For example, a new tool arrives replacing a developer, financial considerations enforce a simpler solution etc.

The rest of this subsection we make some *simplifications* of the more *general situation* described in chapter 5: (1) Parameterization/adaptation of the administration component to a certain scenario takes place before project runtime. (2) We do not explicitly administrate the processes responsible for parameterization or adaptation, nor for the manipulation of the administration information. (3) In the case that there are schemata for how administration information is built up (a design task must be followed by an implementation task; an implementation task follows a certain pattern of coding, test, or documentation tasks), these schemata are also fixed before project runtime. (4) In dynamic situations due to evolution or backtracking etc. it is up to the administrator to interpret the technical or administration information to make the right modifications on administration configurations. (5) We restrict our consideration to one subproject. (6) In the case of backtracking a new net is built up. It is up to the administrator to see the consistency between the original net and the new one being necessary for the time of handling the backtracking step.

We are now discussing which *integrated manipulations* on administration configurations are necessary to keep an administration configuration consistent with the progress or with the problems of a project. Thereby, we do not discuss in the first step who is making the change (administrator, technical developers, tool on extended technical, fine–grained level and/or administration level) and from which environment (administration environment, administration interfaces at the technical environments, or automatically by the tool(s)) the change is made. These aspects are discussed later. We restrict ourselves to sketching some of the possible operations and postpone details to the main chapters of the book. These integrated administration configuration manipulations provide for a controlled distribution of labour within a team. It is clear what each individual of the group has to do and, furthermore, how the activities and results are combined into a team activity or result.

Although the *administration configuration* is coarse–grained w.r.t. the information of an extended technical configuration, it is *internally fine–grained* and has many increment–to–increment links between information belonging to the above administration configuration submodels. We repeat one example of 1.1.5: A certain task T may exist, the input and output being each a revision A^i, B^j of two documents. These revisions are contained in a configuration C^m. Each revision is embedded in corresponding revision histories of A, B, and C respectively. The task T has a process P, which a role R is responsible for, and is supported by a tool T^k, the role is taken by a person Pe^l.

We will now present some *examples* for *administration configuration operations*. They all are taken from system development (not from maintenance, or reuse). Furthermore, they all start from the process model view. We give atomic operations and complex *operations*. Complex operations are either independent of the scenario taken, or scenario–specific.

(1) *Atomic* operations: Insert a new task with two inputs and one output, assign a process to a certain task, or a machine to this process, assign the output to a node of the corresponding product configuration.

(2) *Scenario–independent complex* operations: For a new component of the system to be developed where we have no idea how to do, use documents A, B as input for the corresponding task. This internally is traced back using atomic operations as: Assign a new task with the two inputs and one empty output, insert a node in the product configuration, assign a person as the machine to the process which has no program, relate inputs and outputs of the task to nodes of the product part.

(3) *Scenario–dependent complex* operations: develop a module with a pattern for module implementation on how to proceed. In this case we create a new coding, test data development, test driver/stub development, test execution, and test documentation task together with corresponding processes, create the corresponding nodes on the product side, relate task/inputs/outputs to corresponding product nodes, assign corresponding persons with certain roles as machines etc.

We are now going to discuss the second topic of this subsection, namely integrating the administration configuration with the extended technical configuration. In terms of subsection 1.2.4 this means *integrating technical environments* with the *administration component*. This administration component consists of the administration environment, the functionality of which has been described above, but also of extensions of technical environments for communication with the administration data base containing the administration configuration, and further components (for parameterization and adaptation etc.) to be explained in chapter 5. Clearly, all the integrated administration configuration manipulations can be done by the administrator(s) at the administration environment(s). We are now going to discuss that technical developers also need access to the administration component.

Technical environments have to communicate with the administration data base of the administration component. We are now trying to make clear for *what purpose* such a *communication* is *necessary* by giving some examples:

(1) A certain developer logging into a workstation on which a technical environment or an integrated set of technical environments is installed can get information about the *tasks* he is expected to *fulfill*. This information can be enriched by information which of these tasks are time critical, e.g. by giving tasks in an order of urgency.

(2) Alternatively, with regard to the dual *product* side, he can see which documents/subconfigurations he is expected to build up or to modify, which inconsistent relations between documents/subconfigurations he is expected to repair.

(3) From the administration component, he might also get information on which high-level or low-level tools/environments are supporting the process to the selected task, and at which workstations he may start the process (as the machine must be able to 'understand' the given subconfiguration, the corresponding actual *resources* have to be available). It is also possible that he gets information about alternative resources he can use.

(4) All the examples (1) - (3) only read information from the administration configuration. By starting a task, or by suspending a task for a certain purpose (short break, does not proceed further, is not useful to proceed further), by finishing a task, etc., the developer is also changing administration information. He is changing state attributes, and he is implicitly changing time or money consumption counters, etc.

(5) He is also implicitly changing the product side as, if the task is finished, product attributes (is elaborated, is consistent with etc.) are set. He is also changing resources information implicitly, as e.g. if he takes up a task using a tool then this tool (and possibly

other resources necessary for this tool) is busy now and cannot be used for other tasks. On the other side, if he finishes a task he frees actual resources.

(6) There may be also be rather complex manipulations induced by finishing a task. Let us regard an example: A designer is responsible for a subsystem design, the administration was such that the design result has been reviewed by another person, the documentation process is also finished etc., i.e. all possible precautions have been taken on administration level. Let us, furthermore, assume that there is a tool to find out the number of sub-systems or modules having been defined in the design process, and let us assume that a schema exists on type level saying what to do on administration level with these sub-systems or modules. Then, a quite complex manipulation of the administration information (inserting the corresponding task/process pattern, inserting new and empty documents/subconfigurations, assigning roles etc.) may be induced, provided that such an administration data manipulation is realized at the interface of the administration component.

All the above examples (1) to (6) are nothing else than *delegation* of certain more or less complex *administration tasks* and processes *to developers* or the *administration data base* and allowing activation of corresponding manipulation features from technical environments. In the cases (1) to (3), the administrator could also have distributed a paper list on demand. Instead, he gives the permission to the developers to read the administration information directly. In cases (4) and (5), the events of starting a task, finishing a task etc. could also have been mailed to the administrator who then manipulates the administration data base by himself. In the case (6), a rather complex operation invocation is delegated to the developer which usually is carried out by the administrator. Prerequisites are that such complex operations are realized within the administration component, that this complex operation regards certain restrictions built in, and that such an operation gets suitable information from an analysis tool on technical level.

In order to be able to delegate more or less complex administration tasks, the technical environments have to be extended. In any technical environment a more or less primitive and restricted form of an administration environment is necessary. This *primitive administration environment* (usually only a part of the functionality, usually restricted to that part of the administration information interesting for a certain developer, less demand for representation of the administration information, e.g. tabular instead of graphical form etc.) is part of the *extension* we had to build *for* given *technical environments* in the a-posteriori project SUKITS.

Now a principal problem arises in distributed and integrated projects where administration functions are delegated to technical developers. We have to find a suitable *cooperation model*, especially we have to clear up the interconnections between activities on administration and on technical level. One extreme cooperation model is the *centralized* model where only the administrator of a subproject is able to use administrator functions. For example, any of the above manipulations of the administration data base is done by the administrator, he only gets messages of any form. This is evidently not a good-solution, as changing all status attributes on tasks, processes, products is rather tedious. Another extreme is the fully *decentralized* model where all administration functionality is delegated to technical developers, i.e. any developer automatically has the role of an administrator. This will definitely end up in chaotic situations as a technical developer may not be aware of global implications of a modification. Certainly, *practical models* are *in between* both extremes. So, one has to delegate administrator functionality, but also to be very careful with global implications.

As we have seen from the above discussion, rather *complex* administration *operations* can be offered, provided that *administration knowledge* is available (given object patterns, type patterns, automatic tools deciding which pattern to use/insert, or delivering the right input for administration modifications). Furthermore, delegation can also be made to high-level or complex *administration tools* able to fulfill tasks which, in the case of nonavailabil-

69

ity of such tools, have to be fulfilled by humans. Moreover, an administration *cooperation model* has also to do with group models for technical activities.

Information of the *administration configuration* is responsible for controlling and supervising technical products and their processes. This administration information can also be used to *support* the *technical tasks* on *organization* level. For example, the configuration description information is used to deliver the corresponding fine–grained technical input and output configuration to a developer working on a certain task on a certain workstation, or to ensure the corresponding access rights and access paths. If the process to the task is started, the administration information can be used to provide for the corresponding tools (if dynamic loading of tools is possible, otherwise a suitable workstation has to be chosen according to administration information), or for the availability of 'programs' (as e.g. a checklist) of the process, or for access to used components. Other resources like 'informal communication' channels for direct interaction (e.g. the administration information is used to get out who has delivered an input document, where he is sitting, if he is not available, who can also give answers) can also be offered. So, the administration information can be used to control that the corresponding *technical working context* to a task is built up, where a working context does not only contain access to necessary documents and tools but also communication lines to other members of the group.

Now, the term *administration component* can be made more *precise*: It consists of an administration data base containing the administration configuration. This administration data base can either be manipulated by the administrator (manager) by the use of the administration environment (full functionality). It can also be manipulated by developers. For that, technical environments have an extension, i.e. a poor–mans version of an administration environment. Finally, there may be tools on the fine–grained level to deliver the input for complex administration functions, either invoked manually by the administrator or by an administration tool supporting the administrator. The situation is even more complex as to be outlined in chapter 5: On one side the administration component contains even more parts. On the other side this administration component is only one component of an infrastructure framework for a posteriori– or a priori–integration.

1.4.3 IPSEN and Different Lifecycle Models

The *aim* of this *subsection* is to show that the working area model of fig. 1.2 and the behavior of IPSEN tools as described in subsections 1.4.1 and 1.4.2 can be used as a basis for implementing different lifecycle models. The proof of this claim is on the level that 'in principle it works'. It can be demonstrated for the restricted scenario of fig. 1.15 and the available IPSEN tools of the current prototype.

Let us start with the *implementation* discussion of lifecycle models on top of the basic working area model. We first regard the classical *waterfall model* /7. Boe 82/ of fig. 1.19.a, incorporating a phase–oriented, engineering–like progression. It is a discrete model in the sense of the characterization of subsection 1.2.3. The total development process is cut into portions, namely to develop the requirements specification, the architecture, the implementations, and the integration of the total system. Subprocesses only work on one document/subconfiguration until it is 'completed'. Then, a transformation starts to the next document/subconfiguration. So, the overall process is batch–oriented and sequential. Documentation, quality assurance, and project organization are carried out accompanying the above subprocesses. However, nothing is mentioned about them in the waterfall model. Besides module test and integration test all activities of the above processes are supported by IPSEN tools. To follow the waterfall model the above documents are produced in a top–down manner. Integration tools from RE to PiL and PiL to PiS are used in a batch–like mode producing parts of the next level to initiate the next subprocesses. These transformation tools are only used if and when the preceding document is 'complete' and 'correct'. We see that by using IPSEN tools in a certain restricted manner (thereby using only a part of their ability, intelligence, and flexibility), we can easily simulate the waterfall model. Besides the support by tools on the level of fine–grained, technical configurations we can also give administration support. In this simple case all tasks/processes are fixed, only the number of processes is open and evolves at project runtime. In this simple and idealized case the number of subsequent subprocesses can be determined after a document is completed and put in by the administrator. Test processes can automatically start when coding processes are finished.

The waterfall model reflects the ideal case. In practice many *backtracking steps* occur. We are going to discuss one of these cases (for an example on technical configurations see subsection 1.4.1) and take the management side into consideration: Let us assume that by implementing one module one detects that this is not possible without changing the architecture. Then, in a first step, the architecture has to be inspected to find out the 'region' which will be affected by this change. The corresponding module implementators have to be informed, such that they possibly stop their implementation work which, otherwise, might be senseless as it is overridden by the architecture change, or the implementation processes are suspended. The other implementators may proceed. Then the architecture is changed and the changes are propagated into the corresponding modules by using the integration tool. By using the programming tools (not available) those changes yield corresponding module body changes. We see from this example that the IPSEN tools are well–suited to support the underlying technical work (in our example on architecture and implementation level but also between both) and administration work. At the moment in the case of a 'heavy' backtracking step where new modules are defined and old ones are overridden the administrator has to build up an administration configuration for the backtracking step. He has to take account of consistency between the original development process and the backtracking process.

The next example we take is a modification of the waterfall model including *rapid prototyping*. This can be done in IPSEN in two ways: Using the developed requirements engineering tools, the requirements engineer is able to execute a requirements specification. Therefore, the requirements specification is a rapid prototype (see chapter 2). The other possibility is to derive an architecture by the RE –> PiL transformation tool and to quickly hack the corresponding modules. After the prototype is completed, the RE –> PiL transformation tool is started again, the architecture is developed carefully, the modules are coded etc. So again, we have the corresponding support on fine–grained technical level as well as on administration level (coarse–grained).

To take just one more lifecycle model we regard *continuous development*. To simplify our discussion we take only an easy example (cf. fig. 1.19.b), namely implementing layers of abstract machines, starting directly on architecture level. We regard a continuous design/implementation/test process. In our example we have three layers of abstract machines. In the first step the export interface of module M_1 is determined. When implementing M_1 one detects that two other modules M_2, M_3 are needed, the export interfaces of which and the imports at M_1 are specified. Then implementation/test of M_1 takes place. After that, we proceed with the next layer's implementation thereby detecting and specifying the third layer and its connections to the second. Then, a test of the first two layers can take place. We proceed in the same way throughout all layers. We see that realizing a layer consists of the specification of the next layer down, the implementation using this next layer and an integration test with all upper layers. So again, we see that the necessary basic operations (besides test) are provided by the IPSEN tools on fine–grained technical as well as on administration level (not outlined). This is due to the fact that the tools on extended technical configurations can be used for interleaved processes (here design, programming, and test processes) and the administration tools can be used to define any kind of process model.

These few examples may suffice to prove the statement that *IPSEN tools* may be taken as *basis* for very *different lifecycle models*. The above examples range from discrete, engineering–like to continuous, evolutionary ones. There are many different forms of lifecycle models discussed in literature (spiral model, programmer's apprentice, transformational approach to name a few; for a survey see i.e. /7. Agr 86/). The above discussions have also shown that in any case we need managerial rules and procedures to end up with a certain consistent technical configuration. Process description modelling on management level has to offer means to clearly define these rules and procedures. Furthermore, process description modelling tools have to offer means to easily describe these different models and to execute them.

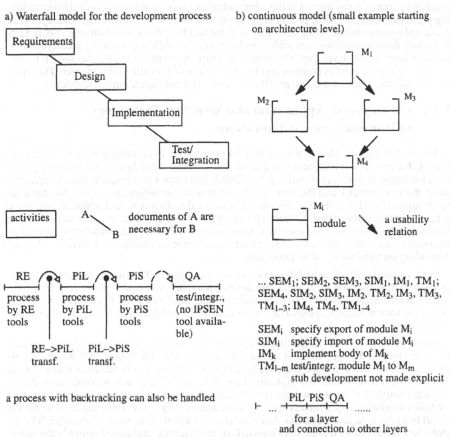

a) Waterfall model for the development process

b) continuous model (small example starting on architecture level)

... SEM_1; SEM_2, SEM_3, SIM_1, IM_1, TM_1; SEM_4, SIM_2, SIM_3, IM_2, TM_2, IM_3, TM_3, TM_{1-3}; IM_4, TM_4, TM_{1-4}

SEM_i specify export of module M_i
SIM_i specify import of module M_i
IM_k implement body of M_k
TM_{l-m} test/integr. module M_l to M_m
stub development not made explicit

a process with backtracking can also be handled

⊢ ... ─┼──┼──┼─ ......
   PiL PiS QA
for a layer
and connection to other layers

Fig. 1.19. Waterfall model and continuous software system development can be simulated by the working area model and the corresponding tools

In section 1.2.3 we have subsumed most IPSEN *tools* (1) as serving for *flexibility* and underlying language/relations between languages support serving for *security*. This is true for all tools working on certain document classes and for integration tools. However, (2) also the structure of a document or the relations between documents can be rather detailed and fixed (PiL document, PiL → PiS integration tool), or only loose and poor (DOC document, RE/PiL/PiS → DOC integration tool). So, there is more or less determination on fine-grained technical configurations for which, in the latter case, there can be only little support by tools. In any case, either due to the flexibility of tools or due to their restricted possible support we need administration tools in order to get more security for processes.

In section 1.2.3 we also have classified environments as *discrete* or *continuous*. We are now going to discuss how this distinction can be applied to *IPSEN*. IPSEN is discrete in the sense that it contains different tools for different perspectives (RE, PiL, PiS etc.) which have underlying tailored languages and corresponding tools. On the other side within these working areas we are rather free as regards how to build up subprocesses (e.g. the programming environment of IPSEN allows editing, analysis, instrumentation, and execution in nearly any order). So we can also classify IPSEN working area tools as being continuous. Integration tools from A to B in the same way are discrete (different languages for documents A, B to be integrated) and continuous (integration for any tiny change of A possible, tool can be started at any time). On the administration level we serve for control by introducing processes, corresponding products, roles etc. So, there is an engineering–like approach of control again combined with flexibility (e.g. for handling dynamic situations). So, IPSEN is discrete from its working area, different languages for different working areas, different tools, different roles, developer/administrator distinction aspect. On the other side, it is continuous (or can be used as continuous) from the view of how the tools interact. This freedom, however, is not paid by insecurity of the overall configuration's consistency.

1.4.4 The Impact of Application and Structure Technology on Processes and Configurations

We are now making clear that *knowledge* and *precision* to organize a reasonable overall *process* for software development, maintenance, and reuse heavily *depends* on the *application*, *structure*, and *project technologies* at hand. The more knowledge in technologies we have, the more precise and the more static the processes/configurations are. We have already argued (see 1.4.1) that the discussion between development, maintenance, and reuse is hard to make if we regard the corresponding processes and their process steps from an abstract perspective. Now, we give two examples where development is more maintenance than new construction. However, this 'maintenance' process is either controlled or chaotic, depending on availability of technologies.

We try to make this clear by taking *two extreme examples:* The first is, taking up the discussion from subsection 1.1.6 again, the development of a new multi–pass compiler front–end in an advanced software house specialized on compiler construction. The other is that another software house develops a new system in an area where it has no experience (which occurs rather often).

In the first *example* of the quality compiler *deep knowledge corresponding* to application, structure, and project *technologies* exists (e.g. /9. ASU 86, 9. GW 85/). More specifically, we know very much about the architecture of such compilers, we even know how to generate them from formal descriptions. Therefore, building up a new compiler in such a software house (e.g. for a new language sharing the same intermediate code) means that we take an existing requirements specification and modify it in certain places. The first is to put in a new lexical and context–free syntax description of the source language. The architecture is not changed at all, only internals of modules are exchanged (namely the corresponding tables of the scanner and parser) which, furthermore, are generated. Analogously, the context–sensitive rules are exchanged in the requirements. The corresponding analysis may also be generated from a formal description by attribute grammars. The same is true for dynamic semantics if, again, a specification and generator machinery is available. So, not only the architectural pattern is reused, but also nearly all of the corresponding modules (basic layer for data structures, drivers for scanning, parsing etc.). The technical documentation is nearly unchanged. Project organization is rather simple as the whole process of development can be exactly planned in advance inasmuch as a static task/process net can be built up before the project starts. Even more, as this net is always the same for compiler development, the net can be taken as it is. Project management and supervision mainly involves decorating this net and executing it. Quality assurance is rather simple, being restricted to the elaboration of formal descriptions, provided the generators are correct. So, most of the overall configuration can be reused on the fine–grained technical level. The changes in the configuration are generated rather than done by hand. Therefore, *software development* in this example *is reusing* a *standard overall configuration* (the requirements specification, the architecture, the reusable modules, the documentation) which has been built according to application and structure class experience and *maintaining* it (by putting in generated tables). The complete configuration is unchanged on the coarse–grained administration level. The whole process of development is not only static and precise, it is nearly mechanical.

The other *example* is a completely new system in a company where *no experience* about the *problem domain* exists. Therefore, the structure of the corresponding software documents as well as the structure of the overall configuration is unclear at the beginning. The *process* of development is highly *dynamic* in the sense that the structure of any of the documents, the overall configuration, and the corresponding processes are evolving at project runtime. Even the knowledge about which documents will exist is evolving. The overall process is full of evolution and backtracking steps: Development is a process with more correction than construction steps as many mistakes are made, have to be corrected, and imply further corrections and backtracking processes. This is also true for the complete configuration. So, there are a lot of modification steps, especially those going through the whole overall configuration to make it consistent again.

What do we learn from this discussion about maintenance, development, and reuse in subsection 1.4.1 and about the impact of technologies of this section? We have already learned that on an abstract level the operations from which *processes* are built up are *similar* in *maintenance* and *development*, either *with* or *without reuse*. So, the question whether we have application, structure, and project technologies is not changing the situation in principal. However, it is changing the situation quantitatively and this change is dramatic. Development/maintenance/reuse processes can be more precise when having these technologies than in those cases where these technologies are not available. This is the statement on knowledge. What we, furthermore, need is tool behavior which is suitable for all these cases on technical as well as on an administration level. What we also see from this discussion is that there is some need for defining processes in general, but especially in those cases where we know exactly how to describe and handle them (see chapters 5 and 6).

1.4.5 Summary of External Characteristics of IPSEN Tools

The following *subsection summarizes* the *characteristics* of IPSEN *tools* as they are presented to the IPSEN–SDE *user*. (At this moment characteristics are more requirements for these tools as the tools have not been introduced yet, see chapter 2.) The most specific of these characteristics, namely integration, has been discussed extensively in the last subsections. We shall see later on that the characterization given here can also be used to characterize IPSEN from its internal mechanisms (next section and chapter 3). Even more, the external characteristics demand corresponding internal mechanisms and, vice versa, the chosen internal mechanisms are responsible for the external behavior described here.

Tightly integrated: As we have seen, all tools for one working area as well as tools on different working areas (integration tools) work tightly integrated. This integration is achieved by fine–grained, increment–to–increment relations controlled by all tools between increments of one document but also between the increments of different documents of an overall configuration belonging to one or to different working areas. Tight integration is provided for the tools on extended technical level as well as for tools on administration level and the interaction of both. This integration allows for arbitrary combination of development, change, analysis, and estimation steps for getting corresponding processes (flexibility). Tight integration is also the basis for establishing/reestablishing consistency within an overall configuration (security).

Interactive and immediate: Immediate response to operations for construction, modification, and analysis (for executable documents also monitoring and execution) is given in the form of acknowledgements, warnings, or error messages after an operation has been carried out. This is also true if a document or a subconfiguration is not complete. For example, analysis (and monitoring/execution) is also possible for incomplete documents (trivially also for construction/modification operations). Furthermore, this is not only the case for operations on one document but also for operations related to different documents. This immediate reaction also applies to project organization operations (e.g. if a process to a development task is suspended, the developer is immediately informed). It has been argued often in literature that immediateness reduces costs, as costs are more expensive if detected late.

Intelligent: Tools on one document but also the integration tools use the full knowledge contained in the document or in (a part of) the overall configuration. This knowledge does not only come from the context free structure of a document but also from its context sensitive structure or from methodological knowledge on how to build up or modify documents. Knowledge of integration tools may come from the correspondences of the languages of related documents (automatic transformation tool), from user selections of alternatives of correspondences (decisions by user), or from the user directly establishing relations (hypertext transformation tool). So, knowledge of an overall configuration comes from languages of documents and their relation but also from how the dialog(s) of user(s) has/have been developing. The tools give more intelligent support for configuration modification than other approaches.

Structure–oriented: All tools operate on 'semantic' increments and not on arbitrary pieces of a document or of different documents. The 'semantical' portions of a document correspond to the context–free syntax of the underlying language, or methodological use of this language. 'Semantical' relations between these increments come from context–sensitive relations within a language, or relations between languages, methods of using these languages/relations, and dialog knowledge. So, structure–oriented involves using the knowledge described in the last paragraph in a 'semantical' way to establish consistency, or to reestablish consistency in an overall configuration. This is true for fine–grained extended technical configurations but also for the administration configuration. In the latter case 'semantic' increments and relations are also used to keep the administration configuration consistent. Moreover, this administration configuration is used to control the extended technical configuration and the corresponding overall process in a 'semantical' way.

Command–driven: Most tools are command–driven, the user does not directly change one view of a document (changing texts, directly changing diagrams). Instead, he invokes a command for doing that on an increment or different increments. Command–driven tools give support in construction or modification steps inasmuch as they generate templates the user has to fill out. Thereby, concrete syntax symbols (delimiters, word symbols, and placeholders) are generated in a correct order by the tool. Therefore, the user cannot make mistakes corresponding to the context free syntax. There has been a big debate in literature between command–driven, syntax–directed, and free input mode. Command–driven mode has advantages in those cases where a lot of concrete syntax has to be input and/or the user is not very familiar with the underlying language. Therefore, IPSEN textual tools can be used in a command–driven as well as in a free input mode (hybrid editing tools).

Incremental: Incrementality (see discussion in 1.2.4) corresponds to the minimization of the effort in defining the consequences of a change (construction, modification, instrumentation operations) or restricting the range of analysis, or the range of preparing/updating internal representations (e.g. code) for execution or for external representations (of all views open for a document). Therefore, incrementality is an internal aspect of an SDE. The user can see only that the above mentioned tight integration, immediateness, intelligence, and structure–orientedness is supported as even complex operations are carried out rather quickly. However, it can hardly be imagined that the above characteristics hold true without tools being incremental.

Uniform: For any working area there is a formally defined document class, a role, and there are corresponding tools (editor, analyzer, browser, instrumentation, and execution tool, the latter two only for executable documents). Furthermore, integration tools are available (transformation tool, consistency checker, browser) whenever different documents of one or of more working areas of the scenario given by figs. 1.13 and 1.15 are regarded. All these tools share the above characteristics. Furthermore, the user interface of all tools on one document is styled uniformly, in the same way for all integration tools. Finally, on the administration level for any technical subconfiguration we have the same information.

Project organization–oriented: The administration component which is integrated with technical environments serves the purpose of configuration/revision control, for task/process control, for team structure and tool/environment control and for mapping these resources on actual ones. The dynamics problems, namely evolution and backtracking, are handled (other kinds of dynamics being realized in the future). Project administration also provides for access, responsibility, quality, or documentation control on the administration level. Furthermore, administration information can be used to establish working contexts. The administration tools in the same way as technical tools are flexible enough to be used to define different processes, different team models, and alike. On the other side by providing administration tools, we provide for security on organization level, i.e. we control and restrict the flexibility offered by technical tools.

At the end of this subsection we relate external characteristics to other topics we have introduced in preceding sections: In section 1.3 we have introduced the *problem areas* when carrying out an SDE research project namely scenario definition, method work, determination of tools and their functionality, conceptual modelling, architecture modelling, and two further ones. These problem areas, in the same way as working areas for software engineering, are not investigated sequentially. Instead, there are *mutually related* to each other. After introducing the external characterization of IPSEN tools, being a subaspect of the tools and their functionality, we regard some of these mutual relations, namely how *external characteristics* influence *method* work, *conceptual* modelling, and *architecture* modelling, respectively.

So, let us start with the relation between external *characteristics* of IPSEN *tools* and ask which *connections* there are to the problem area of *concepts, languages, and methods* modelling we have discussed in 1.3. It is clear, that integration is only possible if the languages defined for document classes incorporate this integration, and if languages for different document classes of one or of different working areas are suitable for integration and the correspondences between different languages have been precisely defined. Interactivity and immediateness is not a question of concepts, languages, or methods modelling but of the corresponding tools. However, especially the concepts and the methods for integration are a prerequisite for an immediate behavior of tools in the sense of making consequences within and across documents clear as outlined in this section. The characteristics intelligence and structure–orientedness also demand for a suitable modelling on the underlying concept/language/methodology level. Command–driven is a pure tool property. The same is true for incrementality. Here, corresponding internal behavior of tools has to be modelled as to be seen in the next section. In order to do this, the underlying concepts/languages/ methodologies have to express which portions (increments) in one document or in different documents can and should be related to each other. The characteristic uniformity also belongs to the concepts/languages/methods modelling level in the sense that if modelling, not on the UI style level but on the semantical level, is done uniformly for different working areas and integration problems then the corresponding tools can behave uniformly. The characteristic project organization–orientation on concepts/languages/methods level means on one side that the administration configuration subconfiguration has to be clearly defined and on the other side that this has to be made precise how administration configurations interfere with extended technical configurations.

The next topic is the relation between *external characteristics* and internal *conceptual modelling* or, vice versa, that the structure of internal overall configurations has to be such that these external characteristics are possible (see also next section). The level of integration within one working area (internal logical document), or of different representations of one working area (logical document and different representation documents), or between different documents (internal integration document and corresponding logical documents) demand for a fine–grained internal modelling on an internal increment–to–increment basis.

The same holds true for internal administration configurations where we again have fine–grained dependencies within the corresponding internal documents. This modelling is also the basis for interactivity and immediateness. Intelligence of the tools means that the whole knowledge is represented in the internal overall configuration and that it is used by the tools. Structure–orientedness means that internal conceptual modelling has to handle the semantic portions a user is thinking of. Command–driven and incremental are user behavior or internal implementation aspects of tools, respectively. However, conceptual modelling has to be such that both are easily possible. Uniformity on conceptual level essentially means that we detect similarity of the static structure and of operations within different logical, or within different representation, or within different integration documents and their coupling. Finally, project organization–orientation implies that the internal administration configuration reflects clear organizational abstractions which are or which contain the suitable portions for product, process, or resources control.

The last topic is the *relation* between *external characteristics* and the *architecture modelling* problem area of SDEs (see also section 1.6). Integration on one document class is mapped on internals of data type subsystems within the architecture. Internal integration between different representations of one document class (logical documents and representation documents) as well as integration between different documents belonging to different document classes is mapped on components for coupling within the architecture. Integration on coarse–grained administration level is handled analogously. Furthermore, integration is achieved by using the same data repository (object storage for all internal documents). The arguments for immediateness, intelligence, and structure–orientedness on document and configuration level are the same as for integration. The property command–driven is a consequence of how the dialogs are styled and, therefore, a local architecture property. Incrementality is a consequence of how integration is handled internally on architecture and implementation level. Uniformity means that subarchitectures for working on certain document classes are similar, and that the same implementation of I/O handling is used throughout the system. The arguments for project organization–orientedness are as above.

1.5   The Realization Approach: Graph Technology

The *aim* of this *section* is to describe the second highlight of the IPSEN project, namely the approach and the procedure we have taken for internal conceptual modelling (cf. subsection 1.1.3), which was named *graph technology*. This name was taken because (1) all internal documents on any level are handled as graphs, (2) construction, modification, analysis, or any other operations the user is applying are internally mapped on operations of graph processors, which are formally specified, (3) the realization of the IPSEN environment can be derived from this specification. We are going to make these points clear in the following subsections.

The question of how the components of the architecture corresponding to the specifications look like and how they are placed within the overall architecture is discussed in the next section. In this section we restrict ourselves to showing the *motivation* for using the graph technology approach and introducing the main ideas. Extensions of these ideas, further interesting concepts, and details are postponed to chapter 3. One special goal of this section is to introduce the notion of *internal overall configurations*, i.e. the form overall configurations of subsection 1.3.4 are handled within an integrated SDE.

1.5.1   Graphs and Their Role within Internal Overall Configurations

In order to understand the approach let us regard the situation of *integrated tools* for *one working area* and on one document which we have called a single environment or technical environment in section 1.2. The situation is simplified, as in one working area (as RE, PiL) there may be a subconfiguration and not only a single document and, furthermore, integration between different working areas has to be regarded. Furthermore, integration between logical document(s), representation document(s), and integration document(s) has to be achieved. We come back to this more complex situation very soon. We know from subsection 1.2.2 that the tools on one document class are editor, analyzer, browser, instrumentation, execution, or monitoring tools, the latter three only appearing if the document is executable.

For any document the user is dealing with an internal persistent data structure exists which above was called *internal logical document*. It contains all structural information of the corresponding document, a user is handling. Fig. 1.20 shows the logical document for one module (body), i.e. for a document belonging to the working area programming in the small. This data structure is changed when a syntax–oriented *editing* or *instrumentation* step by a corresponding tool is activated. This data structure is analyzed when an *analysis* tool command is carried out, traversed when a browser or cursor movement takes place, and it is *executed* and *monitored* if an execution takes place which, furthermore, actualizes consumption data. Therefore, a logical document contains the complete knowledge of the structure of the document and of the state of a dialogue of a user working on a document and, eventually, its execution state.

In addition to these internal operations on one logical document by a transformation step a representation in textual, tabular, or diagram form on the screen is generated. We call this transformation *unparsing*. Conversely, in the context of textual input or in the context of batch input of externally stored textual documents one needs the other transformation building up the logical document from a given representation, which is called *parsing*.

The situation is more complicated, as we already know from above: For any view there exists another internal data structure which we call internal *representation document*. We also know that for a logical document there may be different views (e.g. textual or graphical (Nassi–Shneiderman or flow diagram) form, see fig. 1.20) and, therefore, representation data structures. These representation documents are handled in the same way (structure, dialog knowledge, persistency) as logical documents: They have to be structured as a representation can also be very complex. They contain dialogue information as the user might change the layout of views. He then expects that these layout improvements are stored and not destroyed when an updating step on the logical document takes place. Finally, they are persistent as a user dialogue might be interrupted and continued at any time.

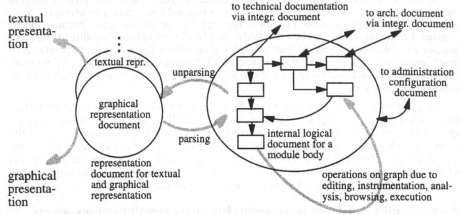

Fig. 1.20. Complex logical documents and example transformation scheme
(example module body, simplified version)

Furthermore, in those cases where for integration between different documents (of one or different working areas) information of an integration tool has to be stored and updated a data–structure on fine–grained internal level connecting two logical documents or sub-configurations is maintained. We call such data structures related to integration tools inter-nal *integration documents*. Integration documents in some cases are only collections of links between two or more logical documents, in other cases they store decisions, depen-dencies of links etc.

So, an extended technical configuration is internally mapped on a collection of logical documents, representation documents, and integration documents, what is called *internal extended technical configuration*. Finally, the administration configuration which contains the information of an extended technical configuration together with tasks/processes and their resources on a coarse–grained level (placeholder information) is also mapped on inter-nal documents, integration documents, and representation documents. We call the internal pendant of an administration configuration the *internal administration configuration*. Cor-respondingly, we call the collection of all internal documents (together with their internal intradocument and interdocument links, see below) the *internal overall configuration*.

Storing different information in different internal documents is done in order to *separate information* belonging to different abstractions: The information contained in logical docu-ments has to be kept separate from representation documents as there may be different rep-resentations for the same logical document (or documents). A new representation with a new unparser/parser pair 'should not touch' the way the modeling of an internal document is done. Separation of integration documents from logical documents is useful because there may be different integration data depending on which kind of integration tool is to be realized between two different logical documents. The integration data may change whereas the logical documents remain the same. Separating administration documents from logical documents is done because administration aspects are rather independent of how an extended technical configuration is internally structured (see subsection 1.1.5). For internal administration configurations the same arguments of separating logical, represen-tation, and integration information can be applied. So, separation is basically done because of abstraction and adaptability reasons. Furthermore, separation cuts the very complex in-ternal overall situation down into pieces which can easier be handled.

Nevertheless, these *different internal data structures* have to be seen together and have to be *integrated* (more details below). This integration has to be done on a fine–grained, internal, increment–to–increment level as shown in figs. 1.20 and 1.21. For any internal logical increment the corresponding representation increments have to be related to and vice versa. Between two internal logical documents corresponding internal increments are related to each other indirectly via an integration document. Finally, from the coarse–grained level of administration documents we have internal relations between their increments representing complex documents and the corresponding technical documents themselves.

Therefore, an 'external document' a developer is working on is internally mapped on a logical document which has connections to one or different representation documents, to other logical documents via integration documents, and to the internal administration configuration (cf. fig. 1.21). (The situation is even more complex as the internal pendant of an external document may be composed, see chapter 5.) An internal logical document may have different views (textual, graphical) which are presentations of corresponding representation documents. So, an *external document* is a composition of different open views the user is working with which belong together. This is *internally realized* in a way that the corresponding representations are all updated whenever the developer is changing the logical document via one view.

Incremental mechanisms with a sophisticated understanding of incrementality (compare subsection 1.2.4) play a big role in IPSEN: If a logical document is changed (by a syntax–directed editing step, for example) then only the corresponding part of the logical document is determined and changed. If this change has an effect on other parts of this logical document, then only these parts are changed. If this change has an impact on other logical documents (via an integration document), then only the corresponding parts of those documents are determined and changed. In a representation document only those parts are changed which correspond to the changes of a logical document. Conversely, in free input mode on a view only that part of a logical document is changed which corresponds to the changed portion of the representation document. The same argument holds also true for the other internal operations on a document (analysis, instrumentation etc.).

In order to determine which parts of a logical document are to be changed, or affected by a change, or on which other logical documents and where in these documents this change has some effect, or which parts of a representation document or integration document have to be modified, we have to *control* all fine–grained internal *dependencies* within and between all these different internal documents. In very much the same way as we have argued for the aspect of incrementality in the last paragraph we could have taken the other external characteristics of IPSEN listed in subsection 1.4.5 to argue that we internally need *linked complexes* of internal documents to guarantee that tools behave according to these external characteristics. Fig. 1.21 is a rather simplified and abstract picture related to the configuration of fig. 1.15.

In order to model these different and various internal documents we take *graphs* as *underlying data model*. We call the internal logical document for a module a module graph, that for a software architecture an architecture graph, that for a technical documentation a documentation graph, and so on. As mentioned above these graphs are the centers of all activities of corresponding tools: Editors, instrumentors, transformation tools internally yield graph changing steps, analyzers yield graph analysis steps, browsers and cursor movement yield graph traversals, executors yield graph execution steps. *Graph processing* on internal documents induces graph processing on other internal documents, namely on logical documents, administration documents, integration documents, and on representation documents, making use of the various links within and between graphs.

The graphs for a document class have specific properties. Therefore, to any external document class there exists, internally, a corresponding *graph class*, the *structure* and the *operations* of which are chosen in order to support the corresponding tool. For example, the graph class belonging to software architecture graphs has operations like 'insert a procedure

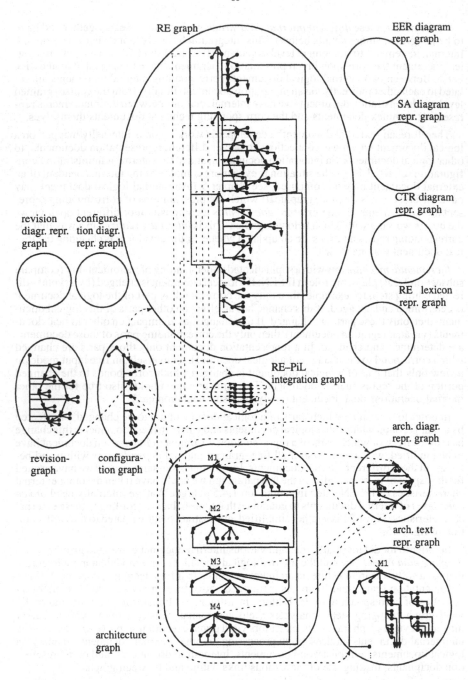

Fig. 1.21. Linked internal graphs on logical, integration, administration, and representation level build up an internal overall configuration as pendant of the external overall configuration (very much simplified)

at the export interface' of a component or 'check whether a certain import is consistent with the corresponding export'. Operations modify a consistent graph with respect to context free or context sensitive syntax (or dynamic semantics in case of executable documents) and, usually, yield another consistent graph. The same is true for representation graphs, integration graphs, and administration graphs. For the representation of architectures, for example, there is internally a diagram representation and a text representation given by specific graph classes offering suitable operations. The integration graph, corresponding e.g. to the RE→PiL integration tool, belongs to the integration graph class.

Of course, these diverse graph classes and their operations are different as they belong to different document classes, tools, and representations. However, we shall learn later in this section and especially in chapter 3 that these different graph classes have structures and operations in common which result in some kind of *uniform modelling* of the *structure* and the *operations* of *different graph classes*. This is true for logical, representation, integration, and administration graphs. This uniform modelling is applied to graph classes and, therefore, automatically applies to a graph of a certain class. This uniform modelling approach is one of the highlights of chapter 3.

To be more *specific* about *diversification* and *similarity*: (1) Internal logical graph classes are each different but have common properties. So, similarity here means that they can be composed by using common structures. (2) Representation document graph classes are the same for all textual representations, all graphical representations, and all mixtures of both. So, for the kinds of representations necessary for software engineering applications we have suitable representation graph classes at hand. (3) In the same way, there is one integration document graph class to be used for any internal integration purpose.

However, even if logical, representation, or integration graph classes are the same, *graphs* of those graph classes look *different* (a specific architecture graph, an architecture diagram representation graph, an RE→PiL integration graph etc.). In the same way, although internal *increment–to–increment dependencies* between nodes of different graphs are the same from a conceptual point of view, we shall later see in this book that dependencies between logical graphs and representation graphs, between logical graphs and integration graphs, and within logical graphs are each *realized differently*.

As logical internal graph classes are different and have to be built up for any new SDE, whereas representation and integration graph classes are chosen from given ones or are the same, we *concentrate* in this book on *internal logical graph classes*. They are the heart of integrated SDEs. Specifying their structure and behavior, their relation to other logical graph classes, and deriving architectural components with corresponding behavior will be the main tasks of chapter 3 and 4.

Internal overall configurations (cf. fig. 1.21) are structured *differently* compared to *external overall configurations* (cf. fig. 1.15) which are seen by users: (1) Internal increments can be finer than external increments, e.g. the external increment 'expression' of an external PiS document appears internally as a subgraph. Correspondingly, logical graphs are richer in structure than external documents. (2) Logically related external presentations (e.g. an architecture diagram and the corresponding architecture text descriptions) are internally mapped on a subconfiguration of logical graphs together with corresponding representation graphs. (3) Fine–grained correspondences of two different external documents are internally represented as logical correspondences of two internal graphs via an integration graph, together with the corresponding representation graphs and fine–grained dependencies between logical graphs and representation graphs.

Fig. 1.21 is a *simplification* of the *structure* of the *internal overall configuration* corresponding to the external overall configuration of fig. 1.15: (1) No intradocument fine–grained links are shown. (2) Only a small portion of logical graphs corresponding to fig. 1.15 is given. (3) The logical RE graph and the architecture graph would have to be split into different logical graphs and integration graphs. (4) Only two representation graphs are explicitly shown. (5) Only very few interdocument, fine–grained dependencies are given.

Although being only a simplification of what has to be handled internally it *looks tremendously complicated*.

The structure of internal overall configurations is on one side determined by the above separation and adaptability considerations and on the other side by the desired behavior of tools. The internal overall configuration forms a *knowledge base* which is used by all tools of an integrated SDE, each tool using a well–defined portion of it. From an abstract perspective we see that the external overall configuration as well as the internal overall configuration are *complex* and *linked multi–graph structures*. The internal overall configuration is richer in structure and structured differently in order to provide the integrated SDE with the functionality to support the user working with portions of the corresponding external overall configuration.

For all the different internal data structures of an internal configuration on logical, integration, representation, and administration level we used attributed *graphs* and *not attributed trees* (/5. RTD 83, 5. KLM 83, 5. Kas 80/) from the very beginning of the project. Graphs as underlying data models have got a lot of attention in recent time (to be seen from actual conference proceedings like /1. Hen 87, 1. Hen 88, 1. Tay 90, 1. Web 92 /). Using graphs is one of the key characteristics of the IPSEN approach in comparison to other SDE approaches.

The *reasons* for *using graphs* and not trees are the following: (1) Graphs are a uniform and powerful description model for expressing any kind of structure. Therefore, there is (1a) not a part of this syntactical structural information namely the context sensitive or non–tree part which has to be expressed outside the regarded data model (tree model) by another kind of formalism (namely attribute evaluation) which is the case with attributed trees. Furthermore, (1b) any kind of structural information which is not necessarily syntactical information (as control flow, data flow, methodological constraints etc.) can be added to these graphs without leaving the data model.

To use graphs is not an argument to *avoid trees*. Usually, an important part of the structure of a graph are tree structures. However, it differs from graph class to graph class whether there is one dominant tree structure and how much of the total structure is already covered by this tree structure. In module graphs abstract syntax trees, for example, are a spanning structure containing a big part of the structural information. In a configuration graph, for example, trees only reflect the is–part–of relation which corresponds poorly to structure.

Furthermore, we do *not avoid attributes*. Attributes are important to store value information (the data when a module was created e.g. is not a structural information). We, therefore, argue to separate structural from nonstructural information (graph vs. value information) and to put only structural information into the graph model. In the attribute tree model, a part of the structural information is put into the attributes.

The internal data model we are using is that of *directed, attributed, node–* and *edge–labelled graphs* (in short danel–graphs). The encoding of structure is usually as follows: elementary objects are nodes, the label (type) of which expresses the kind of objects. Directed edges express directed relations which also are distinguished by their label (type). The universe of node and edge labels for a graph class is finite and determined at graph specification time. Attributes are determined not for objects but for object types. Therefore, all objects of a type share the same attributes, which can be structured internally.

The question where *structural decomposition* internally *ends* and *value information begins* is, apart from conceptual modelling considerations, also determined by which tools we plan to realize. In the technical documentation environment, paragraphs or subparagraphs are internally only nodes, the text of a paragraph/subparagraph being an attribute. This is because the tool does not offer structural operations on syllables, words, or sentences. Analogously, in all our tools the identifiers are attributes as we usually do not offer operations on composition of letters. If, in all these cases, we offered these operations then we would have to decide to realize them on attributes (by runtime computation) or on structure (to keep structural information which, therefore, supports evaluation at runtime).

Using graphs as an internal data model means having a *broad understanding* of structure, i.e. of *syntax* of a *graph class*. In most cases only the context free part of syntax is called syntax, the context sensitive is called static semantics. In the graph model the complete syntax information but also other information (control flow, data flow, method knowledge, and tool information) is handled uniformly as graph syntax. This has consequences not only for the internal modelling but also for realization. Both, modelling and realization are more uniform, we shall see this below and in other sections in this book.

Looking at fig. 1.21 we see again that specifying the structure and the operations of graph classes belonging to a working area is only a portion of specifying the overall internal configuration. Furthermore, the integration graphs (e.g. RE→PiL–integration graph) have to be specified. Even more, the connections between these graphs have to be specified which are used by technical integration tools (the RE→PiL integration tool needs a requirements graph, an RE–PiL integration graph, and an architecture graph; therefore, the concerted action of these graphs has to be specified). In the same way, the integration between the administration graph and the internal pendant of the extended technical configuration has to be specified. We *restrict* ourselves in this section *to single graph classes* and discuss the architecture graph class as a running example. Administration graphs, integration graphs, and representation graphs can be handled analogously. The integration of graphs in the above sense is not discussed because it is too complex for the first example. So, what we describe here about specifications is only one part of the problem.

Fig. 1.22 shows a small cutout of an architecture graph. Furthermore, some of the external relations to other logical documents are sketched (but not regarded in the following). This is only a tiny part of the overall situation of fig. 1.21, namely the internal structure of the architecture graph and, thereby, only the description of two modules. Even this cutout belonging to two modules is not complete. The reader need not understand the picture in detail. Here, we only want to give an impression: *Graphs* for internal modelling used for practical problems become very *big and complex*. The user of an SDE does not see these graphs but the developer of an SDE has to *manage* this complexity. The question is *how* the developer is doing that.

Looking at fig. 1.22 more carefully, we see that the *graph contains* a *tree* which expresses on the topmost level which modules occur in the architecture (is–part–of relation) expressed by ToLElem–edges. On the next level down the tree structure describes from which parts a module specification is built up (consists–of relation) expressed by ToId–, ToBasedOn– etc. edges. On this level we find the resources a module offers and the resources of other modules it depends on. A description of the underlying description language for architecture is given in /4. Lew 88c, 7. Nag 90/. What we can see at one glance is that *tree increments* are divided into certain sorts (elementary increments represented by one node; complex increments, i.e. a node with certain children; list increments, i.e. a node with an arbitrary number of children of the same type) to be explained later.

In addition to this tree part there exist a lot of further edges only some of which can be found in fig. 1.22. Examples are that in the interface of a module for all resources the types of formal parameters are either defined or imported (from BasedOn–part to another module via an ApplToDecl–edge). In our example language, all relations corresponding to the structure of the architecture (different structural relations between different architectural components as locality and inheritance), different import relations (as local import, general import, inheritance import) are mapped onto the non–tree part of the underlying architecture graph syntax. So, *most of* the *structural information* of the architecture language we find in the *context sensitive part* of the graph syntax. The reason is that there are different structural relations within an architecture document which cannot be expressed by one underlying tree skeleton structure. Therefore, we took the consists–of– and is–part–of–relation as spanning tree relation.

Summarizing the last two paragraphs we see that *modelling graphs* starts with *statically composing* them from different structures expressing different parts of the knowledge

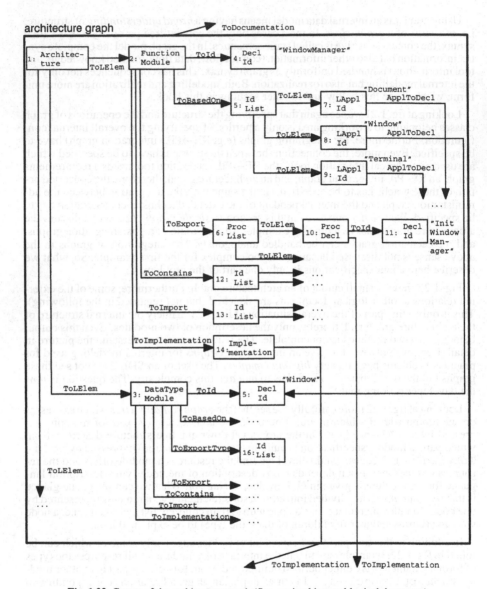

Fig. 1.22. Cutout of the architecture graph (fine–grained internal logical document)

within the underlying document. In our case this means that we start with a rather unsemantical is–part–of relation (the topmost list expressing which components appear in the architecture document) and adjunct different structure relations into the context free (consists–of
relations describing the structure of a component) and context–sensitive graph syntax
(locality, inheritance, different import relations; only one to be seen in fig. 1.22). This way
of structuring graphs can be applied to different applications, i.e. it is a *uniform static* graph
modelling procedure. Other uniform procedures are explained later.

For a certain graph class – in our case the architecture graphs – the types of nodes and
the types of edges which are to occur can be determined before saying anything about opera-

tions. For this determination, similarities between graph node type structures are expressed in an inheritance hierarchy. This static part of a graph class description together with other determinations is called the *schema part* of the *graph class* /5. Schü 91a/. The way a schema is built up is explained in chapter 3. In particular, it is explained there how the schema for our example graph class, namely architecture graphs, has to look like. The schema contains most of the declarative information of a graph class.

At the end of this subsection let us give some remarks on why we need multi–graph structures as internal overall configurations for supporting environments in engineering disciplines, like software engineering or CIM. We discuss this by making clear what differences exist between conventional business administration applications and engineering applications. We do this by firstly characterizing engineering applications and afterwards giving characteristics of business applications. This continues a discussion we have already begun in subsection 1.3.4.

In *engineering applications* (like software engineering) and, therefore, also in their supporting environments (here SDEs) we have the following *characteristics*:

(1) We have web structures of nested data which we have characterized in subsection 1.1.4 and called extended overall configurations: They consist of subconfigurations and documents which, internally, are graph–like structures and which have many intradocument and interdocument relations.

(2) Complex processes on technical overall configurations (e.g. a maintenance process), therefore, are composed of subconfiguration processes which, in turn, are composed of intradocument and interdocument process steps.

(3) Usually, documents or subconfigurations are 'possessed' by technical environments (a programming environment) or combined technical environments (a subsystem realization environment). In a–priori–environments, as IPSEN, these technical environments have the same data model such that integrated processes on fine–grained level in which different technical environments are involved can be supported. In a–posteriori–environments, which are the standard case for industrial tools, such integration is hard to realize as technical environments have different internal models which are not clearly described and which are not open to tool builders outside the offering company.

(4) On coarse–grained level administration integration is necessary, as in complex projects many developers, their activities, and their results have to be controlled. For this, we introduced the administration component which can be parameterized to a certain context.

(5) Dynamics is a standard problem in development, maintenance, and reuse. This is especially true if a project develops a new product and if no deep technologies are at hand.

(6) Process steps on documents cannot be described by a finite automaton model, as nesting and mutual relations are necessary.

If we regard usual business applications then we see some major differences. Some of these differences are due to the current state of the art and not to the fact that a proceeding more or less similar to engineering applications could not be taken. *Business applications* share the following *characteristics*:

(1) The complexity of data is less due to the complexity of structure than to the amount of data: Schemata are usually much simpler but there can be a huge amount of similar data sharing a schema. Usually, there is one global data space which is presented to different applications as 'external' views.

(2) Correspondingly, operations and processes are much simpler. As the data base is not broken down into sub data bases (as subconfigurations or documents in engineering applications) we only have a 'global' view of processes.

(3) In contrast to integrated engineering environments which grew bigger from single different technical environments (with different data models) to more or less integrated

technical overall environments in business applications we usually have a global and homogeneous scheme where certain applications only see a cutout (view) of the total problem. So, business applications are homogeneous (often all data in one server, sharing the same schema) in contrast to integrated technical environments which are heterogeneous.

(4) Integrating the work of different persons is also necessary in business applications in the future. At the moment, integration is seldomly done explicitly. Instead, it is often done implicitly in the form of hardwired programs, or with regard to intermediate states in the data base etc.

(5) Dynamics problems occur rarely in business applications or they have not been studied yet. Processes are often static, i.e. they can be defined a priori. It would be a big progress in comparison to the current situation if the corresponding nets of subprocesses would be clearly defined reflecting the order of process steps or subprocesses.

(6) Process steps are often on the complexity level of a finite automaton (e.g. filling a mask) which then can be combined to process nets.

1.5.2 Operational Specification of Tools

From the task of specifying the changes within the internal overall configuration we restrict ourselves to the subtask of specifying the diverse logical graph classes which occur as parts of the internal overall configuration. So, integration between different logical graphs is not handled within this first course (see chapter 3). We show how the specification of one logical graph class looks, by taking *architecture graphs* as the *example* to be explained. In subsection 1.5.1 we have only discussed the static structure of this graph class, i.e. which description elements are allowed to occur, and which internal structure they have.

Even more important is to *specify* which *operations* on *graphs* of a *graph class* we allow in order to make precise what is happening if internal documents are modified, analyzed, executed, or browsed as implications of tool activations. We concentrate here on the specification of internal changes induced by operations of the editor tool. Other operations can be specified analogously. As already stated, the connection to one or more representation documents and the unparser/parser problem is also not regarded.

For this specification we use formal concepts which have been developed in the context of *graph grammars* (/5. CER 79, 5. EKR 91, 5. ENR 83, 5. ENR 87, 5. Nag 79, 5. Schü 91a/), namely graph rewriting rules and graph tests which we call elementary transactions and from which we build up complex transactions using control structures. This is not the section to discuss details, formalisms, languages, and methods for graph grammars. For this, the reader is referred to the literature cited above and, especially, to chapter 3, where we introduce a formally defined language for graph grammar specifications and give examples of its methodological use in the sense of uniform modelling.

To be more precise we use *sequential, programmed graph rewriting systems* on graphs, to be used in this subsection for the specification of editor operations. Thereby, sequential means that one rewriting step is applied after the other (for other applications outside software development environments, parallel or mixed graph rewriting can be used /5. Nag 79/). Programmed rewriting means that certain control structures control the order in which transactions have to be applied. In the context of software development environments there is always a specific location where rules are applied corresponding to a cursor position on the screen or to an internal position due to the state of a graph processor. Also, control structures behave in most cases *deterministically*. In other specification applications undeterminism is used on replacement and on control level (see chapter 3).

In some cases the external syntax of a *document class* was *given*, as e.g. in programming in the small, where we took Modula-2 /7. Wir 88/ as *language* to be supported by IPSEN. In those cases we built the internal graph syntax such that all syntax information of Modula-2 modules is contained in module graphs. In other cases (e.g. in programming in the large) the languages have been designed *on our own*. In these cases we can define a document class by ourselves by defining the external syntax as usually and then apply the transformation to the internal graph syntax (done with the architecture example), or by defining an internal graph class /5. LN 84/ and then define the external syntax of textual and graphical representations by defining suitable unparsing schemes for corresponding representation graph classes.

By graph rewriting systems we operationally specify the behavior of internal graph processors. That means that we *program* on graphs. However, we do this in a rather *abstract manner*. This is because (1) we regard graphs and not specific data structures to realize graphs, (2) we have rather abstract elementary operations at hand, namely application of graph tests and graph rules, (3) we can control application of these operations in order to build up complex transactions.

Elementary transactions which change a graph, namely the *graph rules*, contain a left hand side (the graph to be replaced) and a right hand side (the graph to be inserted), application conditions (which control whether the application of a graph rule is possible), and an embedding transformation (telling how to embed the right hand side into the host graph depending on how the embedding of the left hand side looked like).

Thereby, a graph grammar specification is a *rule–based specification*. We replace complex graph patterns by other complex graph patterns, test for the occurrence of certain patterns, and we have the possibility to built up even more complex pattern replacements by constructing complex transactions from elementary and other complex transactions. Therefore, although being operational, graph grammar specifications are a rather declarative or rule–based way of specification. We shall learn further constructs for the declarative style of specification in chapter 3.

So, rule–based specifications are built for internal graph classes of all levels (of logical, representation, integration, administration documents). Any such specification has an interface. This interface is built up by some of the interfaces of the transactions the graph class contains. (Other transactions may be designed for internal purposes within the graph class). These transactions (for architecture graph class transactions like 'insert a procedure in the interface of a module') are graph class dependent and designed to offer the appropriate services for tools. To speak in other terms, a graph class specification is the *specification of an abstract data type*. Rule–based programming is inside the abstract data type, i.e. in its body. Therefore, from outside the way a graph grammar specification appears should not be seen. It should not even be seen that we use a graph grammar specification for 'implementing' the body of an abstract data type. So, again, we have encapsulation which serves for adaptability.

In the rest of this section we try to give an *idea how* a *graph grammar specification* for a certain operation of the abstract data type architecture documents can *look like*. We do it in a very sketchy manner here, as graph grammar specifications are explained in detail in chapter 3. There, more advanced specification techniques are presented. We explain this specification only to that extent that the following remarks about structuring a specification in the next subsection are understandable. The example we regard is the transaction to insert a new identifier in the based–on list (list of imported modules necessary to define the interface) of a module (see node 8 in fig. 1.22) and try to bind it within the architecture if there is a module with the corresponding name available (to a DeclId node of another module by an ApplToDecl relation, see again fig. 1.22). Otherwise it is marked as erroneous. So, the operation is a *combined editor/analyzer operation*.

This transaction is built up from a *context free part*, namely to insert a new node with the name of the corresponding module into the corresponding based–on clause. This is a simple tree replacement which is given in fig. 1.23.a). The current node where the replacement is to take place is marked. The mark in the architecture graph corresponds to the cursor placement of the view the user is working in. The rule has an identical embedding for node 1, i.e. all edges ending in or leaving node 1 of the left hand side are replaced identically. This is expressed by having the same node denotation ' 1 on the left and 1 ' on the right hand side of the rule. The rule also sets the value of the Name attribute of node 2 to the name the user is entering.

The marked node characterizes the position in the graph 'around' which the replacement takes place. In order to *fix* this *position*, *different mechanisms* of the specification language PROGRES can be *used* (for details see section 3.1): (1) Within the graph there is a unique location characterized by graph structure information where the rule is to be applied. This can be a unique node label, or a cursor node together with a certain edge pointing to that location. In this case, the marking of fig. 1.23 is refined by structural graph information. (2) The position is determined by a node denotation. In this case, the production of fig. 1.23.a has to be extended by formal parameters such that the location of the left hand side can be specified by an actual parameter and the location of the new current position can be delivered by an output parameter. (3) Finally, the unique position may be delivered by a unique attribute value current which exists at only one node in the graph and which is demanded within the production thereby fixing the place where the production is to be applied. Trivially, this attribute value has to be set to shift the current position.

The *context sensitive part* of the transaction is given in fig. 1.23.b. Here, again, nodes are replaced identically together with their bordering edges. The rule inserts a binding between the node of the based–on clause and the corresponding name node of another module (see fig. 1.22 and 1.23.b). The left hand side contains an application condition which is the description of a path saying how these nodes are connected. If the two nodes of the left hand side are connected according to this path then the right hand side inserts an appropriate relation between these two nodes. The application condition, i.e. the path definition of the context sensitive rule is also given in fig. 1.23.b. It is a declarative description of a way Search-chId through the graph which, for the rule BindToModuleId, is the prerequisite for a binding. The description is easy to read: By ToHeadOfList&<-ToBasedOn-&To-HeadOfList we come to the root node of the architecture graph of fig. 1.22. ToHea-dOfList means in our case only traversing one edge ToLElem from target to source (the trivial path specification is not shown). Then the path ToCorrDefId finds out the identifier node of the appropriate module. As we shall see in chapter 3 the path evaluation uses backtracking: ToCorrDefId is trying one subpath after the other. If it finds a suitable node the subpath is successfully finished, otherwise it fails. Correspondingly, the enclosing path SearchId succeeds or fails.

The *complete transaction* is given in fig. 1.23.c. After inserting the node the binding is tried. If the binding is not possible then a trivial rule (not given here) is applied setting a certain attribute to a failure value. This transaction corresponds to the corresponding editor/ analyzer operation of the architecture editor tool and describes the corresponding graph processing operation on the architecture graph class.

The *rules* in this specification example but also in the whole architecture graph class are very *simple*. Context free replacement is done by rules with a one–node left hand side (which in graph grammar literature sometimes are called context free rules). The right hand side inserts a new node, or a certain number of new nodes into the tree skeleton of the graph. Embedding transformations are trivial. Also, context sensitive rules are simple. They consist of two nodes in left and right hand sides which are not changed. Between those nodes a binary relation is inserted if a certain graph connection structure is available, which can be expressed by a path expression.

Combinations of transactions reflect the static decomposition of the graph class (cf. figs. 1.22 and 1.23). As the *static structure* consists of a tree part and non–tree parts, nearly all *transactions* are built up by a context free part (tree part) and context sensitive parts (for the non–tree parts) of the underlying graph class. Combination is done by control structures, i.e. at transaction execution time.

All *details* are given *chapter 3*. More particularly, the explanation of the underlying specification language PROGRES and the detailed discussion of specification examples is

a) <u>production</u> InsertLApplId (ModuleId : <u>string</u>) =

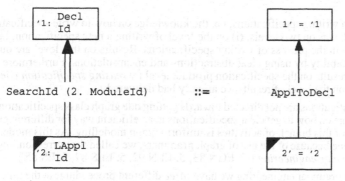

```
'1: IdList  ::=   1' = '1  --ToLElem-->  '2: LAppl
                                              Id
```

    <u>transfer</u> 2.Name := ModuleId =
    <u>end;</u>

b) <u>production</u> BindToModuleId =

```
'1: Decl                         1' = '1
    Id

SearchId (2. ModuleId)  ::=   ApplToDecl

'2: LAppl                        2' = '2
    Id
```

    <u>end;</u>

    <u>path</u> SearchId (Id : <u>string</u>) : LApplId -> DeclId =
        ToHeadOfList   (* & expresses concatenation of paths. *)
        <-ToBasedOn-   (* If the evaluation of a subpath fails,*)
        ToHeadOfList   (* it is reset. A path results in a set *)
        ToCorrDefId (Id)   (* of nodes, or it fails.   *)
    <u>end;</u>
    <u>path</u> ToCorrDefId (Id : STRING) : Architecture -> DeclId =
        ToLElem & ToId.Name
        <u>valid</u> <u>self</u>.Name = Id
    <u>end;</u>

c) <u>transaction</u> CreateAndBindIdInBasedOnPart (ModuleId : STRING) =
    InsertLApplId (ModuleId) &
    <u>choose</u> BindToModuleId
    <u>else</u> (* in case of nonapplicability of BindToModuleId *)
        MarkAsErroneous
    <u>end</u>
    <u>end;</u>

Fig. 1.23. Structuring a complex graph transaction: a) a context–free rule for inserting a node, b) a context–sensitive rule inserting a binding, c) a transaction for the architecture graph class

given later. Furthermore, a rationale for the why the specification language PROGRES contains which constructs and the wherefore of these constructs and their use is presented. Especially, a discussion is given about which different specification paradigms are combined in this language.

1.5.3 Structuring a Graph Grammar Specification

As mentioned above, writing a specification for a graph class means programming an abstract data type on an abstract level. As we have built lots of tools, lots of specifications have also been written. The question whether we can learn from writing a specification in order to produce a better result for the next arose very early. Another question was, how we can reduce the effort of writing specifications. This subsection deals with these questions, namely which *software engineering results* we could find on graph grammar *specification level*.

Learning from writing specifications, i.e. the knowledge on how to write specifications as just discussed, was on two levels: (i) on the level of writing a new specification, i.e. to *reuse knowledge* in the process of writing specifications. Results on this level are due to clarity and adaptability by using clear abstractions and encapsulations. Furthermore, (ii) there were also results on the specification product level by *reusing specification components*, i.e. reuse on the level of results we already had delivered.

As these investigations are not directed towards getting one graph class specification but getting knowledge on how to get clear specifications in an efficient way for different graph classes, the aim of this branch of activities is uniform graph modelling. As this modelling is a rule–based one because of the use of graph grammars, we called the corresponding results *graph grammar engineering* (/5. EGN 83, 5. ELN 92, 5. ELS 87, 5. ES 85/).

For this graph grammar engineering we have *three* different proceedings at the time this book is being written /5. Nag 94/. These different *graph grammar engineering approaches* are sketched now. Each of them has been applied to specify different graph classes in order to show its character of uniformity and its broad applicability. Again, we only provide a sketch of these approaches here, as they are described in chapter 3.

The first approach was already sketched above. Its basic idea is to compose graph syntax from tree syntax (context free syntax) and non–tree syntax (context sensitive syntax, and others). It was called *abstract syntax graph* approach /5 Schü 91a/. Composition can be done statically by melting rules /5. LN 84/ or dynamically by composing rules via control structures as it was done above (upper box in fig. 1.24.a). The next idea not shown above was to factorize out reusable specification portions for tree handling and for context sensitive handling and to make composition rely on those specification portions (again fig. 1.24.a). The result is that the actual tree and non–tree portion for a specific graph class now become much smaller as they use the general and reusable specification portions /5. Zün 96a/. This serves for both aims mentioned above, namely quality improvement for a certain specification and reducing the effort of writing this specification. This approach was found to be especially valuable for tools with textual representations. It is described in detail in section 3.3.

The second approach had its origin in overcoming three problems. Firstly, it is not easy to model a logical document which has both a graphical and a textual representation, i.e. two representation graphs which serve for quite different purposes. The logical document in this case has to be modelled so that both unparsers can be realized easily and efficiently. The second problem was that modelling two different logical documents, namely the requirements and the architecture graph class in order to realize the requirements engineering – programming in the large integration tool, we detected similarities between both external languages and, therefore, also between their corresponding graph classes. The third problem was that in some applications there is no underlying and dominant tree structure available (especially in administration graphs). The approach to overcome this problems was named *metamodelling* /7. Jan 92/. The *essential ideas* are the following: There are logical entities occurring in any situation to be modelled as objects, links, either atomic or complex. Furthermore, there are entities having properties of two of the above entities, e.g. complex objects or links. Proceeding this way we found a general modelling framework which can be used for modelling different graph classes. This general framework can be enriched by specific modelling concepts for a certain graph class. Here, again, the next idea was to factorize out this general metamodelling knowledge into a reusable specification portion (fig. 1.24.b) in order to structure a specification and to reduce the specification effort. This idea is again described in more detail in section 3.3.

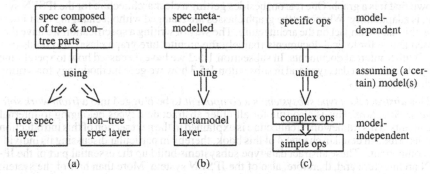

Fig. 1.24. Uniform modelling approaches on specification level

The third idea was developed in the context of project administration (which contains configuration, revision, task/process parts etc., see subsection 1.1.5). All these components have the property that there is no dominant underlying tree skeleton in common. Therefore, a different approach was applied the idea of which is essentially the following (cf. fig. 1.24.c, we discuss it by taking the configuration or revision part of an administration configuration): A revision graph depends on an underlying model for revisions (sequential, tree, DAG model). In the same way a configuration graph depends on the model for configurations and revisions (which dependency relations we have between revisions of components in a configuration and between different configuration revisions, which model we have for handling dependencies etc.). So, the graph classes rely on these special models. In order to be able to exchange these models there is a certain layer where the specific models are introduced. Below this level we have model–independent graphs and operations. Above, we have model–dependent operations. Furthermore, the lower layer, i.e. the model–independent part, is divided into a basic sublayer of reusable primitive operations on which another sublayer of complex operations is defined. This approach was called *layer* and *parameterization* approach /4. Wes 91a/. It is especially useful for specifying administration configurations internally (at the moment in one graph class, namely administration graphs, in the future the different parts are separated graph classes which have to be integrated). The motivation for adopting this proceeding is that an administration configuration is similar for software engineering or CIM (see discussion in section 1.1) but in a parameterization and adaptation process the administration component has to be made suitable for a certain context. However, it should be possible that different models for the parts of an administration configuration (as configuration, revision, task/process, or resources control as well as for their integration) are introduced. This approach is described in detail in section 3.5.

In chapter 5 we shall sketch how these *different ideas* of *uniform modelling* introduced above can be put in a more general framework of introducing spec modules for spec portions and relating these spec modules in order to get an architecture for complex specifications. In chapter 3 we also discuss how integration between different internal documents in order to manage fine–grained, increment–to–increment dependencies is carried out.

1.5.4 Realizing a Specification

A certain internal *document* (logical document, representation document, administration document, integration document, their integration items not being discussed in this introductory section) belongs to a graph class which is realized as an *abstract data type* subsystem within the architecture of the IPSEN system. That means that the interface is designed in order to serve the corresponding tool operations. This has the consequence that within the architecture of the IPSEN system and above these abstract data types it is unknown how the graph class looks internally like. As sketched above, it should even be unknown that it is a graph. One reason, besides getting a clear architecture for the IPSEN system, is adaptability: Whenever the graph classes are changed without changing their interface, this has no impact on the architecture. The way of writing a specification we have discussed above for logical documents (namely the architecture graph class) also holds true for all other internal documents: In subsection 1.5.2 we have discussed how to specify the body of an abstract data type and in subsection 1.5.3 how we get a methodology for writing such specifications.

This *abstract data type subsystem* is a *component* to be plugged into a *framework software architecture*. This is also true for all other abstract data types belonging to internal documents. This framework architecture is explained in the next section of this introduction and described in detail in chapter 4 of this book, thereby in particular discussing its individual components. These abstract data type subsystems build up the essential part of the IPSEN architecture and, therefore, also of the IPSEN system. More than half of the system deals with these internal documents.

Assuming that a framework architecture has been provided, this subsection concentrates on the question of which *different proceedings* exist for *realizing* an abstract data type which has been specified by a graph grammar specification. Essentially, there are four different ways (cf. fig. 1.25), which we are discussing now.

The first possibility consists of *directly executing* a *graph grammar specification* (cf. fig. 1.25.a). The specification consists of executable elements, namely control procedures, graph tests, graph rule applications, and attribute evaluations. For that, a graph grammar specification interpreter has to offer the services to execute these elements in any given syntactically correct order. The graph grammar interpreter is part of the PROGRES environment to be discussed in chapter 3 of this book. In this case the realization of the specification only consists of starting the interpreter on a given specification.

Interpretative execution of a specification is time–consuming which is, however, tolerable: The reader should note that a specification for the changes on an internal document is essentially a deterministic specification. There is mostly one position in the internal document a tool is working at. The positions of other related increments within the same document or in depending documents are found by relations. Therefore, transactions are in most cases built up deterministically. So, there are no global searches for where to apply a change or to find depending increments, and there is rather little backtracking in order to carry out an internal transaction. Nevertheless, this form of realization is only useful for *rapid prototyping*. The prototype consists of the specification together with the graph grammar interpreter being part of a framework architecture.

In order to get an efficient realization, direct interpretation of a specification has to be avoided. This is done by giving a *semantically equivalent* and *efficient implementation*. There are different possibilities for doing that which will be explained now.

The first is to *translate* a graph grammar *specification manually* into an equivalent program component on top of general graph operations (cf. fig. 1.25.c). This was done in the IPSEN 2.0 prototype /4. Lew 88c/. The translation was rather straightforward. Therefore, it was done by a programmer of the group who was familiar with reading and understanding graph grammar specifications. The specification was written by another person.

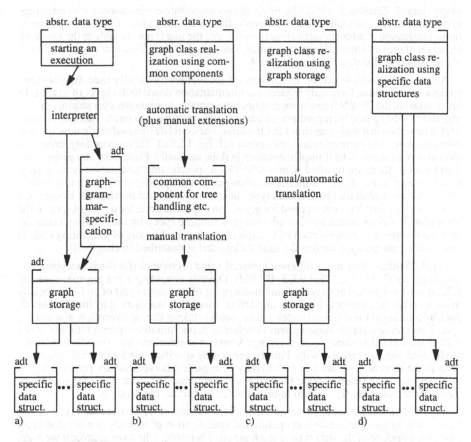

Fig. 1.25. Different proceedings of realizing the operational specification of an abstract data type for an internal document

As this *translation* was rather mechanical, some years ago we started to *automate* it. The chosen approach for the IPSEN system is not a pure compiler–compiler approach (cf. fig. 1.25.b): Basic components in an efficient and handcoded form were built into the system which offer the services for tree handling, for handling context sensitive situations etc. They correspond to the specification components of fig. 1.24.a. Therefore, only for the specification using these basic specification components (see again fig. 1.24.a) equivalent code had to be delivered. Most of this task is done by a generator. However, some portions are still handcoded up to now. So, our generation *approach* for the IPSEN prototype is rather an *engineering–like* one consisting of basic, handcoded components, generated components, and additional portions, all being placed within the IPSEN architecture. This approach (described above for a single internal document class) is the only one which is applicable today for the general complex situation of tight integration discussed in subsection 1.4.1 at least as long as we are not able to handle all integration situations formally and automatically. This is described in detail in chapter 4 of this book.

For prototyping purposes we investigated further possibilities. The first is to *completely generate* a *prototype* from a complete gra gra spec by using a stand–alone architecture framework. The generated code is again using the *graph operations* (see again fig. 1.25.c, now the derivation of code being done automatically). This works for specifications on one graph class /5. Zün 96a, 5. SWZ 95a, b/ yielding a modelling environment for a certain application area. So, integration tools between different working areas, different representations, integration of administration functionality and the like is not possible at the moment. However, there is no manual implementation step to be fulfilled. This way of getting an implementation is also described in chapter 4.

All proceedings (a)–(c) of fig. 1.25, regarded above, namely directly executing or translating a specification, have only regarded implementation down to the level of graphs. In order to do so, the IPSEN framework architecture contains a component for storing, updating, and retrieving graphs, regardless which size and structure they have. This key component is described in detail in section 4.2. Of course, one could *design and implement specific data structures* and corresponding *operations* (cf. fig. 1.25.d). This proceeding, however, has two severe drawbacks if implementation is done manually. Firstly, for any graph class – and a lot of them are handled within IPSEN – a specific implementation is necessary, which causes some effort. Furthermore, changes of the specific data structures induce heavy changes within the abstract data type subsystem for logical documents. However, a new generation line has been opened for *generating* specific code for a gra gra spec in the form of a C++ class hierarchy. The advantage is runtime speed by introducing a specific and *main memory implementation* of a graph class. Again, this way of generating code is restricted to gra gra spec for one document class and is described in chapter 4.

Fig. 1.25 offers ways to get *different forms* of *rapid prototypes* (for the prototyping terminology see /7. Flo 84, 1. SN 90, 3. BP 92/). Directly executing a gra gra spec (see fig. 1.25.a) can be regarded as *experimental* prototyping of the central part of an SDE, namely to see whether the internal behavior of an SDE is 'correct'. It is approved by the SDE developer by looking at the different states a host graph is taking during execution of a gra gra spec. Generating a stand–alone system together with one suitable representation (see fig. 1.25.c) is a form of *explorative* prototyping. A system is generated for a specific modelling application, the user can play with. Finally, generating specific code for internal data structures in the form of C++ (see fig. 1.25.d) may be regarded as *evolutionary* prototyping, as this code may be the starting point for further development. The same is true for generating a part of the code (see fig. 1.25.b) to be extended by further handcoding.

Regarding the different approaches for implementation of an abstract data type of fig. 1.25, given by its interface and an operational specification of its body, we see that in all cases the *interface* of the data type is *unchanged*. Therefore, whatever approach we take, this is not to be seen in the architecture of a system outside the abstract data type subsystem. The *implementation effort* is *growing* from left to right indicated by growing height of the abstract data type's body. The reason is that the layer the implementation is using is of a *decreasing abstraction*.

1.5.5 Graph Technology Summary and Comparison to Data Modelling

In subsection 1.5.1 we have discussed the *differences* between integrated *environments* in *engineering* disciplines (SDEs, CIM etc.) on one hand and *interactive business application systems* on the other by pointing out that the underlying overall configurations look different. Because of the differences between these application classes but also because of the state of the art in information systems (however, new approaches in the data base field go into a similar direction as graph technology) there are differences in realizing both application classes.

We *summarize* now which *differences* we see between graph technology, the approach we have taken in the IPSEN project, and the usual approach taken to implement interactive information systems:
(1) Modelling of internal data structures (internal documents) is hidden in the architecture of IPSEN as implementation details of abstract data types. The kind of data modelling (graph grammar engineering) is not to be seen. In standard data base applications, the schema, or a view as a part of it, is regarded to be global within the system.

(2) We specify internal documents in a data model which is object–oriented corresponding to node types and in a language which is strongly typed (which is to be seen in chapter 3). Moreover, the specification includes the specification of all problem–oriented transactions. This specification uses powerful mechanisms such as rules, tests, and other transactions. In usual database applications only primitive operations are available which are directly used in the application program. Therefore, the complex operations are only implicitly available and they are separated from the underlying data.

(3) Translating a specification into an implementation is done in different forms (rapid prototype, efficient form). In the latter case we transform a specification into an equivalent program which fulfills the static part (schema) and the dynamic part (transactions) of a specification. Therefore, only few checks are necessary at runtime. Consistency is guaranteed by the translation process. In the usual database world, the consistency of operations with the schema is checked at runtime.

(4) Implementation is done using a powerful component for graph implementation (the nonstandard database system GRAS, to be explained in detail). Usual database applications use standard database systems which, for certain reasons, are not suitable for engineering applications.

Let us give a short summary of graph technology now by making clear *on which different logical levels graphs occur* and how they are handled: (1) All internal documents on logical, representation, integration, or administration level are regarded to be graphs. (2) For these graphs schemata are defined (see chapter 3). (3) On dynamic specification level graphs also occur as tests (to see whether a certain pattern holds true) or as operations (as transactions are described by graph rules; the left and right hand side of which are graphs). (4) On implementation level graphs occur (4.a) in the sense of an equivalent program to the specification which is graph–based and (4.b) in the sense that graph implementation is based on a universal graph storage. (5) Graphs, furthermore, also play a big role in the problem area of further development/improvement of languages and methods for software engineering (see subsection 1.3.2). They are based on a certain imagination of an extended overall configuration, or a part of it, which (6) has to be mapped on an internal graph–like configuration.

A second perspective of graph technology is to regard the proceeding taken: Internal documents are *carefully built* up corresponding to their static structure. Operations are formally specified. The *translation* of this specification into code is mechanized. There is a number of differences in the proceeding compared to conventional database applications. The methodology (graph technology) is rather *independent* from the *application* at hand which will be shown later. The aim of the methodology is essentially to get intelligent tools with a reasonable effort.

At the end of this section, after having made clear what we understand by a *specification* of tool behavior by *graph grammars* determining graph processors, we *relate* this understanding of a specification to *other specifications* in *software engineering*:

(a) A specification in the sense of this section is *not* a *requirements specification*. It is not complete corresponding to the requirements as it contains no user interface details nor nonfunctional requirements. On the other hand, it is much more detailed than a usual requirements specification only listing available commands and structuring the underlying data as it makes clear which graph processor steps are connected to tool activations and how these graph transactions look like.

(b) A graph grammar specification is *not* an architectural or *design specification*. This is clear because a design specification is a static view of the system in the sense of a blueprint, and a graph grammar specification is operational. Furthermore, a graph grammar specification is much more detailed as we regard internals of abstract data types even if they are on module body level which is not done in architecture modelling. On the other hand, if a graph grammar specification is clearly structured into components (specification in the large, see chapter 5) then the architectural design of a main part of an SDE, namely the internal data structures, can be derived from such a graph grammar specification.

(c) A graph grammar specification is *not* an *algorithmic specification* in the sense of an abstract or pseudocode implementation. A graph grammar specification is more abstract, and it is mostly declarative in style.

(d) A graph grammar specification is *not* a specification of the *process* of how to get an integrated SDE (either manually or by a generator). On the other hand, the process can be derived from a specification. Even more, it can be automated for arbitrary specifications by building generation tools.

1.6 The Architecture and Reuse: Framework, Standard Components, and Generators

The aim of this section is to sketch the *software engineering results* of the IPSEN project. It is again a sketch as there is a main chapter of this book (chapter 4) which is solely devoted to this aspect. This chapter also shows what we have learned by taking the IPSEN prototype as an important representative of a certain application class (system software) and structure class (integrated dialog systems), i.e. what we have contributed to application and structure technology by this project. As this is a sketch we concentrate on figuring out only the ideas but not the details validating these ideas.

The *contents* of this *section* are as follows: We firstly make clear what we understand by a software architecture. Then, we explain the IPSEN architecture for a technical environment on a coarse level which makes the essential design ideas clear. Thereby, we summarize how the external characteristics of section 1.4, especially the property of integratedness, are mapped on the IPSEN architecture for a technical environment. The next section is devoted to sketching the integration problem between technical environments in order to support fine–grained, increment–to–increment dependencies and the corresponding processes as outlined in subsection 1.4.1. Then, we give some remarks how integration on administration level (project organization level) is achieved by the administration component corresponding to the ideas sketched in subsection 1.4.2.

So, this section is devoted to handling *integration* and *reuse* on *architecture* level for single (technical) environments, integration tools, and the administration component. This is internally mapped on integration of architectural components of logical documents and their representation documents, on integration of the administration configuration with corresponding technical environments, and on reuse of patterns/components to achieve this. Integration and reuse is discussed in the concluding paragraphs of each subsection and in the summary.

1.6.1 Defining the Term Architecture

We firstly make clear that the *term architecture* is mostly *misused* in literature and, therefore, also in connection with investigations of SDEs. To demonstrate this, we take two examples (/4. Som 88, 2. FO 90/, cf. fig. 1.26) from literature. This is not to expose the authors of those articles publicly, as in most articles, wheter in academia or industry, the term software architecture is misused as well (e.g. /6. DEC 91, 6. IBM 89, 6. HP 89/).

We try to explain the misuse by taking the *blueprints* of a *house* as the natural *candidate* for *determining* the *characteristics* a *software architecture description* should have. Such a blueprint contains a static description of the house, its components, and their relation rather than a dynamic description of the later use of the house. Of course, the static description lays ground for a corresponding dynamic use. So, an architecture, although being a statical description and only a blueprint, makes determinations for a dynamic behavior of the complete system. The architecture also contains a description of various abstraction layers: A floor being a part of the topmost abstraction is built from walls forming rooms, walls contain windows and doors etc. It also contains a description of electricity, water, gas etc. infrastructure. It does not contain details as e.g. how many bricks are needed for a wall, how these are composed, how a brick wall has to be plastered, how windows are built. This is left out as being irrelevant on this level and clear for other people to implement those parts. The description contained in an architecture is (mostly) clear to any architect of the world, i.e. he knows syntax, semantics, and pragmatics of such a blueprint. Of course, such a blueprint also describes one (type of a) house and not houses in general. The architecture of a one–family house looks different from that of an apartment house and there are many different architectures for different occurrences of each of them.

We take the *same view for software architecture modelling*: A software architecture forms a static description, namely of components (subsystems, modules) and their relations. The software architecture also has to reflect different layers of abstraction. It has to define all necessary abstraction layers and it has to go down to a granularity where all relevant modules are to be found (that does not mean that we have to design top–down, nor does it mean that there cannot be a hierarchical architecture description with a survey architecture identifying subsystems and more detailed subsystem descriptions). It also leaves details out postponing it to implementation (namely the bodies of modules), thus making a clear distinction between programming in the large (architecture modelling) versus programming in the small (implementation of bodies/coding). So, as in architectures for houses, a software architecture is the essential structure of a system to be developed or maintained which describes the software system from an abstract and statical view. A software architecture has to be denoted in a language which is clearly defined w.r.t. syntax, semantics, and pragmatics. So, again as above, developers which have experience with an architecture description language should be able to understand, to evaluate, and to implement a software system according to this software system blueprint.

We are now going to discuss that both *"architectures"* of fig. 1.26 *do not fulfil* these *characteristics*. Both pictures are much too coarse for being an architecture. Fig. 1.26.a is on the granularity level of describing a house being composed of roof, different floors, and a basement. This is true for all one–family houses and may even be true for skyscrapers. Components are not distinguished by their type. The same holds true for connections. So, they use an unspecified semantics of a component as well as of a connection relation. Therefore, the question is what a component or a connection between components means in detail. Abstraction layers (top = upmost level, down = basic program machine) are not to be found: The user interface is by no means the topmost abstraction. In fig. 1.26.b again components are too coarse–grained, their placement has nothing to do with abstractions, and components and connections are again not clear from their type and semantics. Especially, connections are not clear: Connections may reflect data transmission, or control of mutual activation, or user interaction. Components among others are behavioral objects and they should be behavioral descriptions: An object of the knowledge base is not a part of the architecture, but the component able to organize (to create, to delete, and to give access to) those components at system's runtime is definitely one. Also, the user should not be a part of the architecture, but a component able to react on user interactions should be a part. So, drawings like those of fig. 1.26 are schematic or conceptual pictures and may have some value but they are not architecture descriptions. They lack preciseness in syntax, semantics, and pragmatics. They contain elements which should not be contained in an architecture and they lack the existence of other parts which should. Finally, and this is the most critical point, they lack the necessary detail which should be contained in an architecture.

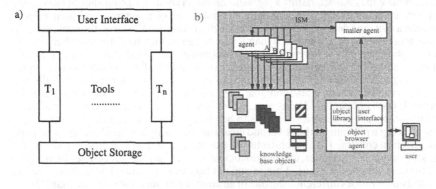

Fig. 1.26. Different examples of so–called architectures

A *software architecture*, therefore, is a special kind of *abstraction* (cf. fig. 1.27): It does not hide abstraction layers (but of course it may make use of the information hiding principle in various ways). Instead, it makes such abstraction layers explicit. It does contain all relevant components on whatever layer and in which other complex component they are found. It does not hide the specifics of a certain system (whether it is small, what characteristics it has, how it is built). Therefore, we may be able to see common parts of different architectures so that we can express the similarities of a class of systems by a framework rather than realizing one single system after the other. In any case, an architecture hides implementation details, namely the bodies of the modules contained in the architecture (coding level). Furthermore, an overview architecture may be only refined down to a certain level of granularity where components are subsystems rather than modules (house survey plan). But then, in the corresponding subarchitecture, we have to deliver more details (exact floor or room plan). In the same way, architectural decomposition may only go down to an abstraction layer of platform components which are available and, therefore, are not part of the system to be designed as they are taken.

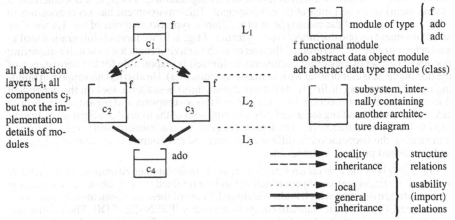

In addition to graphical diagrams for overviews there are detailed descriptions of components and their relations. Within architectures, layers of components as well as encapsulation of subarchitectures (by subsystems) can be expressed.

Fig. 1.27. Abstraction within an architecture: All components and their relation should be given but not their implementation details

Architectures in our sense are *descriptions* in a *well–defined language* (/7. Nag 90, 7. Bör 94/) the concepts of which have been mentioned in subsection 1.3.2 and which is not explicitly introduced here as it is part of our method work and this is a book on tools. However, from studying the IPSEN architecture in various stages of abstraction (in this section for an overview, in chapter 4 for details) the reader will be able to learn the underlying languages at least to the necessary degree for reading this book. Architecture diagrams are used for showing survey pictures of an architecture or of subsystems. Furthermore, there are detailed textual descriptions for the components (export interfaces, structural relations to other components, different import interfaces belonging to different usability relations). This textual language is not shown in this book as textual descriptions would need too much space. Nevertheless, the reader will see that an architecture here is of another quality of precision.

1.6.2 Framework Architecture, Standard or Specific Components, and Generation of Single Environments

In this subsection we explain the IPSEN *architecture* of *one single environment* down to a level of a few components (rather big subsystems of the total system than modules). This is not to be understood as escaping from the problems of architectural description mentioned in the last subsection as the internals of (most of) those subsystems are given later in chapter 4. Although being on a coarse level the reader will recognize that this overall architecture is precise and contains the topmost design decisions. This subsection introduces the overall architecture of such an environment of IPSEN, explains its most important basic reusable components, and some of its specific components. So, it is detailed enough for the explanation given here which discusses the approach used to derive components rather than describing the details of the components.

In this subsection we *assume* the *simplification* that we are regarding a single or isolated environment, i.e. a technical environment (as a programming, a design, a documentation environment) or an administration environment. This environment has no connection to other environments of the same type or of a different type. So, in terms of fig. 1.4 we have an environment on one document type, in terms of fig. 1.10 we have no integration tool to another environment. Therefore, if the user of such an environment has to watch a mastering document or a set of mastering documents he himself is responsible for the consistency of the document he is elaborating with its master document(s). He also has no support in building up a document according to its master document(s) besides the tool on the dependent document itself. In subsection 1.6.3 we give up this assumption and regard integration of environments for handling technical subconfigurations of the overall configuration. In subsection 1.6.4 we, furthermore, sketch how integration on administration level, i.e. for administrating the cooperation of different persons and environments to support integrated and distributed projects, is achieved.

Fig. 1.28 gives the *overall architecture* of such an isolated environment of the IPSEN system. It distinguishes six layers which are to be explained now. Each of its components carries a design decision which is also discussed. Some of these components are basic components and, therefore, are standard components of any IPSEN–like SDE. Their collection forms a framework architecture. Other components are specific and have to be replaced for any occurrence of an IPSEN–like SDE. So, the overall architecture is the combination of the framework together with specific and application–dependent components. There exist different mechanisms to reduce the effort of producing such specific components to be sketched below. It is also discussed how the overall architecture, its components, and the derivation machinery serves for adaptability and extensibility of an IPSEN system.

Fig. 1.28 is the architecture of a PiL environment. This can, however, only be seen from regarding the specific components (e.g. ArchitectureGraph). The *structure* is the *same* for other *isolated environments*. The subsystem components of the architecture are structured internally which is explained in chapter 4, especially for the logical internal graph subsystem (here ArchitectureGraph). There, we also make clear how the subsystems of fig. 1.28 cooperate at runtime. The architecture of fig. 1.28 does not contain a tool for layout improvement to be used by the developer (see again chapter 4). The assumptions are that we have one logical document which may have different views (representation documents) and cutouts of a view are to be shown on the screen (a presentation). Different tools (editor, analyzer etc.) for PiL are working on one logical document. In its control part the architecture is more general than needed for isolated environments to cover the case of integrated environments to be explained in the next subsection.

The following *terminology* and *restrictions* are used for isolated environments: The data type XGraph, here ArchitectureGraph, is used for the logical internal data structure, a representation (being also a graph) contains the representation information of a view, i.e. its geometrical information. Both are persistent. From this geometric representation a certain cutout is shown on the screen, if the view is open, by using presentation elements suitable for this representation. For the presentation on the screen no data structure is built up, the presentation is always build up at runtime when shown. Finally, we are only discussing how elementary commands (e.g. an editor command possibly with analysis) are handled but not combined commands, as putting in all inner details of an increment (so–called implicit command activation), or combined commands (e.g. changing all applied occurrences to a declaring occurrence).

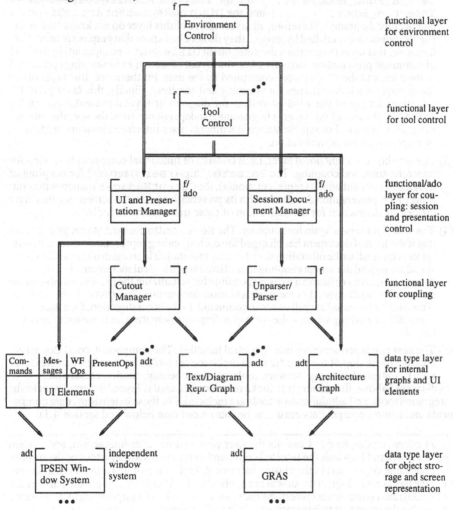

Fig. 1.28. IPSEN overview architecture of an isolated environment (without layout dialog)

Each of the six *layers serves* for a *specific abstraction purpose*. We are explaining them and their components from bottom to top (for design decisions see table 1.29):

(1) The bottom layer serves for (a) persistent storage, modification, and retrieval of graph data structures by the abstract data type subsytem GRAS. The interface of this subsystem does not give any details of how the internals of the subsystem realization looks like. It guarantees the integrity of graph structures on a primitive level (e.g. no edge without

bordering nodes). Furthermore, the adt subsystem (b) `IPSENWindowSystem` offers an independent window system (which can be implemented using standard window systems). Thus, the aim of this layer is essentially to guarantee realization independence (object storage realization, window system realization).

(2) The next layer is again a data abstraction layer serving (a) problem–oriented graph classes. The interface of each adt subsystem is problem–dependent (e.g. `Insert_a_Func_Module` (`...`) for the subsystem `ArchitectureGraph` or `Insert_a_Box` (`...`, `...`) into the `DiagramRepresentationGraph` for architecture diagrams). Therefore, all layers above of this layer do not know how internal documents are modelled by graphs, they do not even know that graphs are used. Furthermore, this layer (b) contains the component `UIElements` encapsulating the kind of command presentation and activation, the layout of messages or warnings presented to the user, and the way they are confirmed by the user. Furthermore, this layer offers commands on window frames for zooming and scrolling. Finally, this layer gives (c) primitives on top of the window system for diagram or textual presentations on the screen. So, the aim of this layer is to guarantee independence from the specific internal modelling of logical or representation documents, user interface elements modelling, or graphic primitives' realization.

(3) The next layer is a functional layer, i.e. it consists of functional components serving for transformation and coupling. The `Parser(s)/Unparser(s)` serve(s) for coupling of a logical document with its representation(s), the `CutoutManager` manages the coupling of a representation document with its presentation(s) on the screen. So, this layer creates an abstraction for the realization of these transformation tools.

(4) The next layer serves again for coupling. The `SessionDocumentManager` ensures that if the logical document has changed the corresponding representation document(s) is (are) changed. In the other direction, for a representation increment it knows the corresponding logical document enabling identification of a logical increment. The `UIandRepresentationManager` is responsible for actualizing the presentation(s) on the screen after (a) change(s) in the representation document(s) has (have) been made, or if the user has selected a scroll or zoom command. In the other direction, for a user selection within a working window the corresponding representation increment can be determined.

(5) The next two layers serve for dialog control handling. The component `ToolControl` controls the dialog of the specific (here architecture) tools, the `EnvironmentControl` controls the change between tools, session opening, session closure etc.

As discussed above, the architecture looks more complicated if layout improvement tools, integration tools, and administration tools are included. For these extensions, data components and control components must also be introduced (see below and section 4.1).

`EnvironmentControl`: Controls the user presentation, user interaction, and system reaction loop and forwards the selected command to the corresponding tool or determines the applicable commands to the chosen increment. In the case of an isolated environment only the tools on one logical document are applicable. (This is more complicated in the case of an integrated environment where the user can switch to layout improvement, to working on another document, or to integration tools etc.) Furthermore, this component is responsible for the dialog at session start and session closure.

`ToolControl`: Controls the actions followed by a tool activation. In the case of an elementary command this is quite simple. In case of a complex command the subdialog of the tool with the user is controlled here.

`UIandPresentationManager`: Handles 'local' commands (e.g. scrolling or zooming); transfers the user action (chosen command, selected representation increment); serves for actualization of window contents on the screen; places subwindows for messages, input or menus relative to the actual window; knows which windows are on the screen; encapsulates the style of user interface (where an input or warning window or a menu is placed, or which command input mode is possible (selection within a menu or short form by keys) etc.).

`SessionDocumentManager`: Keeps track of the logical documents (in the case of an isolated environment this is only one) and the corresponding active representation documents. So, the aim of this subsystem is to coordinate logical documents and their representations (functional part). Furthermore, this subsystem contains all session dependent knowledge (ado part) which, of course, is more interesting if the user is working with different logical documents, their integration, and different representations. This knowledge is not specific to a tool.

`CutoutManager`: Builds up a presentation within a working window on the screen for a certain cutout of the representation. As a representation document contains the complete representation of a logical document the cutout manager is also invoked if the user has selected a scroll or zoom command. In the other direction, the cutout manager replaces a representation structure with a textual representation increment if free text input has taken place. How both transformations work is not to be seen above this coupling component.

`Parser/Unparser`: The unparser realizes an actualization of a representation if a change in the logical graph has taken place. It works incrementally. The parser on the other side determines a logical increment to a representation increment. Furthermore, it actualizes the logical graph if free input on an increment has taken place. The parser also works incrementally. How transformations work is not to be seen above these components. The actualization of the one or the other document is invoked where it has to be clear which logical or representation increment has changed.

`UIElements`: Offers functionality for menu, message, warning etc. windows, text input windows, functionality of window frames for scrolling or zooming. Furthermore, suitable presentation elements are offered for the needed presentation (in textual or graphical form). So, this component encapsulates the style of UI elements (how a menu, message, warning is presented etc.) and offers suitable presentation elements for presenting the representation within a window.

`Text/DiagramRepresentationGraph`: Offers the service for a text or a diagram representation or for a mixed text and diagram representation for a logical document. For a logical document there may be more than one representation. Tools for layout improvement work on representations (which is not shown in fig. 1.28). Representation documents contain the knowledge for the representation of a logical document. This is geometrical information which is free as possible from concrete presentation elements (it contains which box or which connection forms are chosen, where they are placed, but not how a box or a connection looks like). On representation documents automatic layout placement algorithms can take place (not described in this section). The way these representation documents are internally modelled is not to be seen in the architecture.

`ArchitectureGraph (LogicalDocument)`: Is the logical or semantical data base for an isolated environment as described in this section. The way this logical document is modelled is not to be seen above this adt subsystem in the architecture. This document also offers all services for all tools on this document (editor, analyzer, navigator, browser, instrumentation, execution, and monitoring tools, the latter three only in the case of executable documents, the architecture not being an executable document). The internals of this adt subsystem are described in chapter 4.

`IPSENWindowSystem`: Offers standard functionality of a window system thus making the rest of the architecture independent from a chosen window system, which has specific resources and a specific realization.

`GRAS`: Object storage for arbitrary graphs irrespective of their size and structure. The interface offers manipulations of a set of graphs. Within graphs operations like insert/delete nodes/edges, traversing an edge etc. are offered. This graph storage is implemented using advanced techniques (see 4.2). Furthermore, mechanisms like transaction handling, undo/redo, event handling etc. are available.

Table 1.29. Design Decisions and Rationale of Architectural Components

Looking at fig. 1.28 the reader recognizes that the *architecture diagram* is *not symmetric*. This is due to the fact that (1.a) the architecture up to now does not contain tools for layout improvement (middle branch is missing, namely layout tools and their access to representation documents). Furthermore, at the moment (1.b) we have nearly no tools for changing a presentation besides a text editor which is used to change the presentation of a textual increment of arbitrary size. So, the left branch is missing. Our philosophy up to now was mainly to realize structure–oriented and command–driven tools. According to this philosophy (2) the control is usually from right to left: After a change of the logical document the representation(s) is (are) changed by the unparser(s) and the cutout manager corrects the presentation(s). In the future we also plan to realize free mode input tools for graphics (from given presentation elements a drawing is built up, the representation of which is determined and then parsed to correct the logical document. This proceeding is already implemented in the case of textual tools for free input mode. There, the control flow is from left to right. So, future plans for graphical input and layout improvement to be described later make fig. 1.28 fully symmetric.

A second remark corresponds to the dots appearing in fig. 1.28 which stand for *multiple occurrence* of *components*. For one logical document there may be several tools. Furthermore, to a logical document there may exist different representations as outlined above (one or more textual or graphical representations). Analogously, different presentations are possible for a representation.

The rest of this subsection *summarizes reuse* and *integration* aspects for the restricted architecture of an internally integrated single environment we have developed so far. How we get more comprehensive environments by further integration steps is described in subsections 1.6.3 and 1.6.4.

Let us start with the reuse aspect in our explanation. Fig. 1.30.a contains the overall architecture and outlines the components which are reusable. They are *basic* or *standard components* of an *IPSEN–like integrated environment* (up to now an isolated environment, i.e. only tools on one document are integrated) and they build up the framework architecture. We see at one glance that the majority of components are of this kind. The main component GRAS is described in the next paragraph. So, let us concentrate here on the other components. UIElements is reusable if the style of UIElements is accepted: Menus, messages/warnings, window frame operations are presented in a specific style. So, either the style is accepted and then the component can be taken as it is or another style is preferred, then the body of the component has to be changed. In any way, the interface of the component remains unchanged. Furthermore, if other presentation elements are needed (the current presentation elements are suitable for text and diagram presentations in software engineering) then the corresponding elements have to be offered at the interface and they have to be implemented. IPSENWindowSystem only offers a virtual window system which, internally, is mapped on an existing window system. Text/DiagramRepresentationGraph is reusable for usual text representations occurring in the software engineering context and also for diagram representations or mixed diagram/text representations we have studied so far. The CutoutManager does not know specifics of representations or presentations and, therefore, is reusable. The same is true for the UIandPresentationManager. In the same way, the SessionDocumentManager is reusable as it only knows the dependencies between logical and representation documents. The tools of ToolControl are mostly application specific. However, ToolControl also contains reusable portions as e.g. undo/redo control or merging of two documents in order to get a merged form (the latter tool assumes an AST graph form of internal modelling of documents which, therefore, can only be reused in environments following the IPSEN internal AST modelling approach). Finally, EnvironmentControl is mostly reusable as the fact which tools exist determines only a small part of its code.

The *most important basic component* is the object storage GRAS. It is known for some time that standard data base systems are not suitable for engineering applications with highly nested and integrated documents, i.e. internal configurations in the sense of section

1.5 (see also discussions in subsections 1.3.4, 1.5.1, and 1.5.5). The GRAS system offers highly efficient updating and query mechanisms operations on primitive graph level, as e.g. insert a node, delete an edge etc. On top of that, GRAS offers change control (undo/redo, transactions), event handling, and distribution/integration facilities. These internal layers of GRAS are not shown in the simplified architecture. The GRAS system is realized by using rather sophisticated implementation techniques as dynamic hashing, internal semantic paging etc. (/6. Bra 84, 6 BL 85, 6. LS 87, 6. LS 88, 6. Wes 89, 92, 6. KSW 93/). This non-standard data base system shall be explained in detail in section 4.2 as it is one of the key components of the system without which efficient prototypes could have hardly been built. The system can also be used outside the domain SDEs, if graphs are used in an application system and the effort of implementing a suitable component is to be saved.

Fig. 1.30.b shows the *specific components* of the overall architecture which have to be developed for a certain SDE. If realized, they can be hooked into the framework architecture. The specific components to be included into the framework follow a building block approach: They are added in a group (logical document, unparser(s)/parser(s), specific tools, corresponding presentation elements) thereby completing the overall architecture. Certain tools can be deleted if a smaller and tailored system is desired.

These specific components need not be developed from scratch as will be outlined in chapter 4: Logical documents, again, have *internally reusable parts* which need not be redeveloped. Only the rest has to be realized. Unspecific tools (for undo/redo, merging) can be taken as they are. Furthermore, for the remaining specific parts there are *generators* which generate most of this specific code automatically. Therefore, the generator machinery is also reused. This is the case for the specific part of logical documents and for the unparser(s)/parser(s). This is all discussed in detail in chapter 4 of this book.

Let us now *summarize* which *strategies* for *adaptability* and *reuse* we have taken on architecture level by developing the IPSEN prototypes:

(a) The overall architecture consists of a framework architecture, which can be reused for any IPSEN–like SDE, or even for environments in other application areas. Therefore, the overall architecture not only serves one problem, namely building the IPSEN prototype, but is a reusable pattern for IPSEN–like environments also outside the context of SDEs.

(b) The standard components are reusable within an IPSEN–like system or, as GRAS, even in any application system using graphs.

(c) Specific components are grouped. These groups act as building blocks which can be added to an environment or deleted from an environment.

(d) Specific components again contain reusable subcomponents. The remaining rest is, to a big part, automatically generated by generator tools. Hence, the generator is reused.

(e) Parts which are very likely to change have not been put into hardwired code but into data structures which appear as data object modules. They are not to be seen on the coarse level of the overall architecture. Examples are tables for errors, warnings, messages, applicable commands to an increment etc. Also, parsers and unparsers work in a table–driven nature.

(f) Bootstrapping techniques have been used which on the technical and detailed level are described in chapters 3 and 4. On a global level they are (a) the architecture language to be supported by tools (PiL environment) is used to describe the architecture of IPSEN itself. (b) Internal documents are specified by graph grammars. For this specification the PROGRES environment has been built sharing the same architecture as IPSEN. In addition, which is not an architectural aspect, (c) the internal graphs of the graph grammar environment have also been specified by graph grammars and can be prototyped using the PROGRES environment. Efficient code for the PROGRES environment is (d) generated using generator tools, which share similarities with the generator tools used for IPSEN.

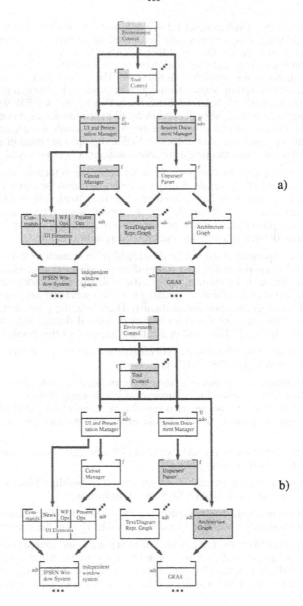

Fig. 1.30. Overall Architecture: a) Framework architecture containing basic components, b) specific components (which again contain reusable parts, see chapter 4)

Now we change to the *second aspect* of the discussion, namely *integration*. We explain this here only for isolated environments. Integration aspects of integrated technical environments, or integrated overall environments are explained in the following two subsections. Even in the restricted systems of isolated environments we have studied up to now we find a bunch of integration aspects.

Different facets of *integration* are found on *different levels*: Integration can be (a) on the user level thereby supporting the developers of a large software system w.r.t. quality and productivity in their business to build up, maintain, and reuse configurations. The discussion of this integration aspect for IPSEN users was already given in section 1.4. It can partially be applied for isolated environments: Tools on documents should be tightly integrated but allow different processes. (Thereby, integration support for users is on a high niveau, namely context–free as well as context–sensitive language level.) The second level of integration is (b) on the SDE product level where we lay the basis for integration w.r.t. user support. The third level of integration is (c) the process which yields an SDE. As already mentioned, the graph grammar engineering approach of IPSEN is also a part of this process level. As it is not directly on architecture level, it is not repeated here. Although it is difficult to distinguish precisely between (b) and (c), we shall discuss the different aspects of integration according to this distinction.

Integration on *SDE product* side can be grouped into framework integration, data integration, control integration, and presentation integration /4. BM 92, 4. MS 92, 4. SN 92/. The following four paragraphs discuss these integration aspects on product level.

Framework integration of IPSEN is due to the aspects that (a) the architectural pattern can be reused, (b) a big part of the components (their description and realization) can be taken as they are (a standard component), and (c) the specific components can be hooked into the frameworking architecture serving for exchangeability.

For *data integration* we have again different aspects to be explained, done in a bottom–up manner: (a) All internal documents are stored in the same underlying object storage. (b) On the top level of that object storage general mechanisms for change control and event handling are placed (not shown in the above figures) which support data integration. (c) Internal documents, either on logical or representation level, are modelled uniformly and, therefore, can share common subcomponents (not shown above). (d) The operations of different tools on one internal logical or representation document are specified and according access operations of the corresponding abstract data type subsystem are offered. (e) Fine–grained relations between increments (here of one graph) are mapped onto the mechanisms of GRAS or on top of GRAS.

Control integration is, correspondingly, to be found on different levels: (a) For all tools on a logical document the functional component EnvironmentControl serves for integration (sometimes called process integration). (b) In the case of complex tools, integration of their elementary steps is realized by the tool itself. (c) Integration between a logical document and its representation(s) is achieved by the corresponding Parser/Unparser component(s) and between a representation and its presentation(s) by the CutoutManager component. (d) Any tool offers the same functionality (sometimes called interface integration).

Presentation integration, on one hand, means uniform user interface modelling, which also reduces the implementation effort for the user interface part of the IPSEN system. On the other hand it is related to the above mentioned tight integration between logical and representation documents and their presentations. Here, we mention (a) the IPSENWindowSystem serving for portability, (b) the component UIElements encapsulating the user interface style of commands, messages/warnings etc., and (c) the UIandRepresentationManager encapsulating global user interface determinations. Finally, as PresentationOps within UIElements have been developed for all environments, it is rather likely that common presentation elements, here for software engineering, have been realized and can be used for all user interfaces.

Let us now discuss the *integration aspects* on process level, i.e. for *producing IPSEN– like* SDEs. The discussion is short as we have no details at hand (see later chapters). Of course (a) the framework architecture, (b) the standard components, and (c) the building block mechanism of above is also a big support on process level. Furthermore, (d) using the reusable subcomponents within specific components and (e) the generator tools for most of the remainder reduce tremendously the effort of producing an SDE. So, the portion of handwritten code to be produced in the process is rather small.

1.6.3 Integration between Different Technical Environments

In this subsection we discuss the architecture of fine–grained integration tools, which establish increment–to–increment links between different external documents. Especially, we explain how this is mapped on internal document integration and which architectural components are achieving this. Thereby, we also find out that integration tools can have different forms to be realized by the same architectural pattern.

The reader should notice that a *single environment* as described so far can *handle* arbitrary *subconfigurations* of one working area (for design, requirements etc.) developed by different software engineers. However, it does this with one internal logical graph in the terminology of the last section. So, this environment can either be used by one developer (e.g. one designer) at a certain time or it can be used by different developers (designers) if they agree on who is working on which portion of the subconfiguration (coarse architecture, different subsystems). This is how technical IPSEN environments (for RE, PiL etc.) were in the past. This agreement by arrangement is supported by version tools (they act on different versions of the big internal graph which are melted later). This view that different developers work on *one graph* can, as the extreme case, even be adopted for the *whole technical configuration*.

This *state* is *unsatisfactory* for the subconfiguration to one working area but, even more, for subconfigurations belonging to different working areas: (1) Different developers work on different parts of the subconfiguration which should be logical units for labour, access, and locking. (2) A melting tool in the above sense can only determine inconsistencies which have to be repaired manually.

In the past we had *technical environments* working on the subconfiguration of one working area where, however, the subconfiguration for this working area was internally represented by one logical graph. *Integration tools* served to couple these technical environments belonging to *different working areas*. This was given up to avoid the disadvantages listed above for cooperative labour of different developers in one working area.

So, the current state of the RE environment /4. Lef 95/ as well as of the design environment /7. Bör 94/ allows that different requirements engineers or designers are each using an RE or a PiL environment. Any developer is working out a part (an external document in the terminology used in this book, internally being represented by one logical document) of the working area's subconfiguration which is the unit for labour, access, and locking. *Integration tools* in the same way as for documents between different working areas help to *overcome consistency problems within* the *subconfiguration to one working area* (e.g. different perspectives of RE, changes within an overview architecture which have implications on subsystems defined there and developed independently). The only exception is PiS, as integration of different modules is done by the corresponding architecture. Version tools, nevertheless, are necessary (for different versions of documents and, even more, for different versions of subconfigurations).

So, the *situation* for working out a subconfiguration for one working area by different developers using technical environments and integration tools is very much *the same* as the next step that technical subconfigurations to be integrated by integration tools belong to different working areas (as RE–PiL integration, see fig. 1.10). The case of handling integrated technical environments (e.g. both a design and a programming environment for developers having both roles, see again fig. 1.10) is also only an *increase* of *quantity* but not of quality. Integration tools in all these three cases have the same shape. The difference is only where they are placed.

So, the discussion of this subsection is how *integration tools* have to be *placed within* the *architecture* of an SDE, *yielding* an *extension* of the results we had in subsection 1.6.2.

This extension then can be applied to cover all three cases of above, e.g. a PiL environment with a PiL integration tool, a PiL environment with an RE→PiL integration tool, or an RE/RE→PiL integration/PiL environment.

Before we go into details we try to *classify* which different *forms* of *integration tools* exist between documents of one or of different working areas. We can detect the following dimensions:

(a) Coupling by an integration tool can be in different *modes*: (a1) automatic (e.g. PiL–PiS transformation), (a2) partially automatic (RE–PiL transformation where a designer selects a transformation rule), or (a3) manual (one form of integration we had between RE, PiL, and DOC).

(b) An integration tool can be different w.r.t. the *size* of the portion to be integrated. So, we can distinguish between (b1) batch integration tools on one side and (b2) piecewise or incremental integration tools on the other.

(c) A further dimension is the *direction*, i.e. whether we regard (c1) unidirectional or (c2) bidirectional dependency relations to be supported by integration tools. According to fig. 1.1 the case of bidirectional relations can only appear if we have different documents within one working area. Dependency relations correspond to logical situations: They are unidirectional, if a mastering document fixes predeterminations to be obeyed (e.g. PiL→PiS), and bidirectional in the case that independent perspectives influence each other (e.g. the function and information model in RE). For explanation see fig. 1.31.

(d) Another topic is in which *direction* a directed or undirected dependency relation is *used*. In the directed case an integration tool can work (d1) in the direction of the directed relation (e.g. a forward engineering transformation tool) or (d2) in the opposite direction (a reverse engineering tool). Analogously, in the undirected case the tool can work in the one or the other direction. For examples see fig. 1.31.

(e) Another classification point is the *time delay* corresponding to integration. Integration can be (e1) immediate (e.g. any change is immediately propagated to dependent documents as suggested in /4. Bar 92, 4. BKH 92/, which is only possible in such cases where the transformation is automatic). In this case, the integration tool can be invoked after a change in the source document, or it can even work (e2) in parallel to the source document tool. The standard case is (e3) that an integration tool works with a delay: If the person working on the target document is able and willing he reacts on changes of the master document which has reached a certain quality to be stated by the developer of the master document (preliminary or final release).

(f) We can classify integration tools whether the *cardinality* of *source* and *target documents* is (f1) 1:1, or (f2) 1:n, (f3) n:1, or (f4) n:m.

(g) Another point comes up if we regard the internals of documents to be integrated. Here, we can distinguish (g1) the *increment* coupling *cardinality* which can be 1:1, 1:n', n':1, or n':m', or (g2) the *strength* of coupling to be either fixed (e.g. determined by the type of bordering increments) or liberal. Any determination corresponding to the number of increments to be coupled or to the strength depends on precise relations between the languages, the documents of which have to be integrated.

(h) A further topic is how integration *information* and how information of the bordering documents is *handled* by the *integration tool*: (h1) Integration information can be inserted/deleted, checked, or used. Analogously, information of bordering documents can be (h2) changed, analyzed, or used. We shall see later, that this point alone gives rise to different typical forms of integration tools.

(i) Yet another dimension, which is less related to the coupling situation or the external behavior of an integration *tool* but has more to do with its *realization* structure is whether the integration tool is (i1) hardwired, (i2) rule–based (where rules are interpreted), or (i3) generated according to a coupling specification.

In *any* of these *cases* (a)–(i) we would like to have one architectural pattern such that the *architecture* is the *same*. Differences come only up if we regard integration tools in more detail which is not done in this section (see chapter 4). In the following, we discuss the architecture of an integration tool between two documents (source and target document) and the unidirectional case. The case that we have more than one source or target document and the bidirectional situation is handled quite similarly. So, e.g., integration of two or more perspectives presented by documents of one working area are mapped onto the same architectural schema.

Whatever integration situation described by the above dimensions we are realizing, one fact holds true in any case: Any integration tool in IPSEN works on another document which we called *integration document*. This integration document is introduced for the following *reasons*: (a) Adaptability: An integration tool may be available or may be not. So, the tools on source and target documents and the corresponding document types should not be changed. (b) Symmetry: An integration situation is not to be added either to the source or to the target document, it is an entity of its own. Furthermore, in the future we may regard integration of integration situations. (c) Decoupling: Independent work on source or target document(s) must be possible. So, the integration tool is only activated at certain points of the time scale, namely when changes on source and target documents have a certain degree of 'maturity'. (d) Behavioral independence: Changes of the behavior of the integration tool (see some of the above dimensions) should be possible with the same integration document by only changing the realization of the integration tool working with this document. (e) Realization independence, e.g. changing a hard–wired to a rule–based realization: The arguments are the same but for other dimensions of above.

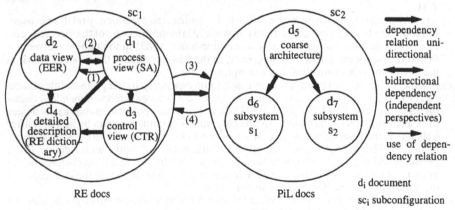

examples of use:
(1) a tool for updating the information model after changes in the functional model (one use of bidirectional dependency), (2) the other direction of use
(3) determining/updating the architecture from a requirements specification or an update of it (transformation tool)
(4) a reverse engineering tool determining the requirements from an architecture (more likely from code). The use is opposite to the logical dependency relation. This situation can be interpreted as working out a requirements specification and directly binding architectural constructs to introduced RE constructs (so, direction as (3) with manual and immediate binding)

Fig. 1.31. Direction and use of dependency relations

Furthermore, changes in integration direction should be possible without changing the integration tool architecture in principle. Such changes may occur (a) in cases where a dependency was first regarded to be unidirectional and later on detected to be symmetrical, i.e. that changes in both directions have to be regarded. (b) Even in the case of a directed relation, an integration tool is useful which goes in the reverse direction of a directed link: It can show the parts of a target document having no connecting links with the master document (backward investigation). Another example is the reverse engineering tool already mentioned above (see fig. 1.31). So, the *integration document internally* should be built up *symmetrically* to cover different integration possibilities even if only one direction is needed.

The integration document is a collection of integration items (logical internal increments). The *integration increment* has links to the source and target document(s). As further information between integration increments has to be introduced (dependency relation between integration increments, a rule selected to describe a certain transformation step etc., see /4. Lef. 95/), an integration document is again a *graph structure*. Because of the symmetrical representation of an integration increment such an increment can express any 'local' integration situation between one or more source or target increments of one or more source and target document(s).

The *integration document* is handled by the integration tool as any other logical internal document inside a technical environment: It is edited, if links between increments are inserted or deleted, it is analyzed, if we try to find out which increments of source or target documents are related to each other or not, it is browsed, if dependency between different relations is regarded. As an integration document is not executable, other operations like instrumentation, execution, or monitoring do not apply.

On the other side *integration documents* are *handled differently inside* the architecture of an IPSEN SDE. This is because: (a) The user is not working on external integration documents (integration specification or integration 'program') which, therefore, are not represented directly, as in /4. BJ 91/. He only sees source and target document(s), links between both are indirectly represented by highlighting the increments corresponding to a relation. So, for an integration document there is no representation document. (b) As there is no direct graphical or textual description of an integration situation, integration items are not described and the description being manipulated by the user, they are only handled by the tool activated by a user. (Of course, one could change the situation such that the user interactively manipulates a description of integration which then is taken for integration handling, see below.) (c) Changes of the integration document can be directly due to an user decision (manual transformation), indirectly due to an user decision (e.g. selection of a transformation rule to be applied), or completely due to a tool (in the case of an automatic translation). In any case, different from those tools operating on logical documents, the user has no idea about the structure inserted for a relation.

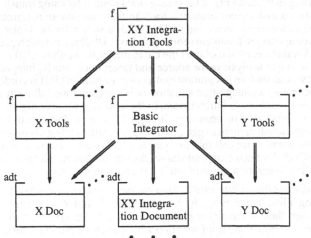

Fig. 1.32. Coarse architecture of integration tools allowing different forms. In any case a basic integrator is involved

Although it has only little influence on the further explanation we now introduce a more *precise notion* for *integration tools* as done above (see figs. 1.32 and 1.33). If the increments in source and target document(s) to be integrated are already given then we call the corresponding coupling tool a *basic integrator*. So, a basic integrator only inserts or deletes links between given increments of the source and target document(s). It is an editing tool on the adt XYIntegrationDocument.

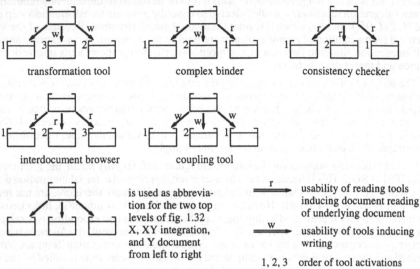

Fig. 1.33. Different forms of integration tools only demand different usability of tools on the second level for reading or writing the underlying documents and different orders of tool activations

Now, according to the possibilities of how integration information is used (see classification of above) and what to be done within the bordering documents we can distinguish *integration tools* into different *forms*: (1) If integration means that we build up (a) target document(s) according to the contents of (a) source document(s) by using transformation rules then we call such a tool a *transformation tool*. In this case, the transformation tool also builds up/changes the target document(s). This holds also true for the bidirectional case if we define source and target documents corresponding to the fact on which place the change is made first. A transformation tool uses the basic integrator of above. (2) In the case, that after some browsing or analysis in the source and target document(s) integration information is inserted we call such an integration tool a *complex binder*. (3) If according to analysis in all three documents an integration situation is investigated we call such an integration tool a *consistency checker*. (4) Furthermore, in the case that we investigate an integration situation by first analyzing or browsing through (a) source document(s) then analyze/browse the integration document to get, possibly again after analysis/browsing, a situation in the target document(s) we call this form an *interdocument browser*. (5) Finally, an integration tool which develops source and target document(s) in parallel thereby introducing the corresponding integration information is called a *coupling tool*.

Let us now *discuss* the *architecture* of *integration tools* on a coarse level (see fig. 1.32). For establishing a link between two increments of the X and Y document, which are selected by the user, there is the above mentioned BasicIntegrator tool. It is a functional subsystem because there is information which has to be put in by the user describing the link (for what, relation to other links etc.) which can be attached to the integration increment in form of structural information to be inserted into the XYIntegrationDocument. The functional subsystem controls the user dialog. Furthermore, the basic integrator can check whether a link is established between two increments of X and Y, it offers navigation operations, e.g. to get the annotation information of a link, or to traverse a link in order to get the target increment in Y to a source increment in X, or vice versa. The basic integrator is nothing else than an editor, analyzer, navigation, and browsing tool on the integration document. So, a basic integrator offers basic functionality for integration needed for all forms of integration tools. A basic integrator does not use the tools of the X or Y environment but only the increment selection facility of their I/O part. On top of the basic integrator we find integration tools using the tools of the X and Y environment to build up different forms of integration tools.

So, an *integration tool* can have different appearances according to the above different forms (cf. figs. 1.32 and 1.33). A transformation tool is building up a structure in Y according to some determined structure in X. Thereby, it changes the underlying integration document by making use of the functionality of the basic integrator. The determination of the structure in the X document is offered by the corresponding tools of the X environment. A complex binder establishes connections between increments of the X and Y document which have been found by analysis, navigation, or browsing tool activations on X or Y documents. A consistency checker finds out whether a group of X increments is bound to a group of Y increments and, if this is the case, gives the corresponding link information. Another form is the interdocument browser which is traversing from a situation in X, which has been found by X operations, via analysis, navigation, or browsing operations in the integration document to a situation in Y, which, again, can be postprocessed by analysis, navigation, or browsing Y operations. Finally, an integration tool can be a coupling tool such that patterns in X and Y are built up in parallel and thereby establishing the links in the integration document at the same time.

These various *forms* of *integration tools cannot be seen* from the architecture diagram of fig. 1.32 as they only can be distinguished by either regarding the usability relations between the topmost subsystem and the subsystems of the next layer in more detail (e.g. by regarding the detailed textual descriptions of the components, or by making annotations as in fig. 1.33), or by regarding the internal structure of the integration tool (see chapter 4). In the case of a consistency checker, for example, usability of tools giving reading access to the underlying documents is necessary. In the case of a coupling tool writing access on all three documents is needed. Furthermore, the direction of links, or the way a directed link is used (forward or backward) cannot be seen from the architecture. Moreover, the architecture only shows the situation modulo multiplicity of involved documents and tools (see dots of fig. 1.32). So, modulo this multiplicity, the situation is the same whether we regard integration of two documents or an arbitrary number of source and target documents. We, therefore, see that the pattern of fig. 1.32 holds true for a big variety of integration tools. The above forms of integration tools and the various appearances of these forms (see above classification) can only be determined by looking at more details.

The *integration tool forms* of above are *not orthogonal*. For example, the functionality of a transformation tool can be simulated by a sequence of Y tool activations and a corresponding sequence of basic integrator activations. To take another example, the above mentioned coupling tool can be simulated by the user if he makes the corresponding modifications of the X and Y document by the X or Y environment tools, and then the corresponding binding by using the basic integrator. Alternatively, he can use the transformation tool after having made the X modifications. So, the functionality of any of the above integration tool forms can be manually simulated by the user, using X tools, Y tools and the functionality of the basic integrator, or by making use of other forms of integration tools.

The *integration tools* we have *realized* in the IPSEN project are *combinations* of occurrences of the above forms: In the case of the RE, PiL→DOC integration tool in the variant in which the user is manually developing the documentation and inserting corresponding links we only have the basic integrator functionality. In the other variant where the structure of the technical documentation is derived we have a transformation tool. In the case of the integration tools integrating different perspectives of requirements engineering we have a complex binder. Furthermore, in the PiL→PiS integration tool we have again a transformer.

Finally, the RE→PiL integration tool includes again a transformer. In any of the above cases, tools internally check if there is already a link and only do link insertion if the check is negative. So, in any of these tools a consistency checker or basic integrator checking is included. Furthermore, in most cases a forward and backward browser is included.

We return to the above topic that a user of our integration tools does not write an integration specification or integration 'program' which is an external representation of the integration document. This case can easily be mapped on the architectural situation of this subsection: If the user describes an integration specification instead of interactively putting it in directly or determining it via tools, then the integration document and the middle column of fig. 1.32 has to be an environment in the sense of fig. 1.28. Then, he can interactively work on this representation (and logical document) and we have more freedom to show the integration situation on the screen.

Let us go back to the discussion of section 1.6.2 on reuse which can be extended now after we have studied integration tools in this subsection. If we combine the architecture of fig. 1.28 of internally integrated but isolated environments with the architecture of fig. 1.32 of integration tools then we end up with the architectural framework of an integrated technical environment not only offering fine–grained integration within documents but also between documents of one or of different working areas. We see that the integration tool architecture again shares basic components as the underlying graph storage, I/O handling (which is necessary despite the fact that the integration document has no own representation and presentation), session document manager, environment control or alike Those components, therefore, have not been drawn in the architecture diagram of fig. 1.32. Thus, no extension of basic components is necessary on this level. Even in the specific components, as e.g. XYIntegrationDocument or XYIntegrationTools, there are a lot of reusable components which cannot be shown on the level of detail of our discussion. The reuse summary of 1.6.2 can exactly be repeated here. There is, however, one difference: Whereas for technical environments we are able to generate most of the remaining specific code this is not done for integration tools yet. They are manually programmed at the moment but derived from an integration specification (for details see chapters 3 and 4).

In subsection 1.6.2 we have classified *integration* into user integration, SDE product integration, and SDE process integration (the process in which an SDE is developed). Product integration was broken down into framework, data, control, and presentation integration. All what we have stated there for single but internally integrated technical environments can be applied as well to integration tools or to integrated technical environments build up by technical environments and integration tools. The explanation of data integration is to be extended now (see corresponding paragraph in subsection 1.6.2): There are also inter-graph edges, event handling, and change control which can be used for different graphs, uniform modelling now also applies to integration graphs, and operations of integration tools are handled according to those of logical or representation graphs. Furthermore, product integration is to be extended by a further dimension, namely *team* integration. Fine–grained integration tools serve for team integration in the way that complex processes involving different technical developers are enormously facilitated: Developers of dependent or parallel documents do not have to make updates by looking at mastering document/other parallel perspectives, interpreting the changes, and making corresponding updates manually. Instead, these subprocesses are directly supported by integration tools.

1.6.4 Integration on Administration and Overall Level

We address now the last integration aspect of integrated environments which gives *support* for the distributed and *cooperative* labour of different persons of a group working on a complex technical configuration. This aspect was studied in the SUKITS project in the application area CIM. Indeed, the aspect and the support we have built up to now are application independent and, therefore, can also be used for SDEs. We give only a sketch here, for details see section 2.5, 3.5, and 4.7, for our ongoing work see 5.1.

We have already discussed in subsection 1.1.5 that we need information of different kind to manage integration on an administration level. We called the subconfiguration of the overall configuration devoted to this aspect the *administration configuration*. The administration configuration contains various coarse–grained information of the technical configuration, e.g. the corresponding processes and products of the technical configuration, but also organizational information which has no pendant on technical level as it is of sheer management interest. We have grouped this information in fig. 1.6 into four subareas namely product, process, abstract resources, and actual context information. We have, furthermore, sketched that we need complex information structures to handle these topics. Finally, we have also pointed out that the information of the four subareas is highly interrelated.

So, according to the IPSEN philosophy, it is not surprising that we *regard* this *administration configuration* internally to be either *one* big *graph* (this is the view on the matter we have realized) or a *complex* of *various graphs* (the view we have for the future) as, again as above, we would like to allow different persons to work on logical portions of the administration configuration. Although, this internal administration configuration only describes course–grained information (e.g. there is a dedicated task for something but no information how the task is solved, see discussion in 1.1.5) it is again an internal configuration which has complex graph structures, complex operations, and where we have many intradocument and interdocument links. Thus, the situation is exactly the same as we had for technical configurations and their internal mapping.

Hence, we can build up an *integrated administration environment* as a universal component to be used in different domains, if it can suitably be parameterized. It has the same internal structure as an integrated technical environment as described in the last two subsections. The way we handled the problem up to now was to realize an administration environment internally working on one big administration graph. Therefore, the administration environment is exactly described by the architectural pattern of an internally integrated but externally isolated technical environment of fig. 1.28. In the future, we plan to have different administration environments to be coupled by integration tools such that different managers can consistently build up the administration configuration. This is the situation we have described for technical configurations in the last section. So, there is nothing to describe, from the architectural point of view, about such an environment which we have called administration environment or project manager workbench. A project manager or different project managers using this environment is/are responsible for handling all management aspects of an integrated project.

There are, however, some problems for an *administration environment*, two of which have already been mentioned in subsection 1.1.5, namely *dynamics* due to evolution and due to backtracking. Both can be handled today. There are some problems due to other forms of dynamics which imply that schema and other form of structural information (which we call schematic information) which determines the structure of the administration configuration is changing not only from project to project but also during a project. Our ideas how to solve this problem and others are reported in section 5.1.

The administration environment described so far, however, is not a practical solution for a project, as it would be internally integrated but externally *isolated*. A *lot* of *human interaction* would be necessary: A developer would have to ask personally, by phone, or by mail etc. what to do next. Conversely, if he has finished a task, the project manager would have to do the corresponding administration change of e.g. setting a token forward in a task/process net after having been informed in one of the above ways. Hence, as a first aspect of administration within an integrated overall environment there has to be a delegation of simple management tasks to developers. This means that any *technical environment* has to have a *simple form* of *an administration environment* (simple operations, simple presentation, simple realization) to be integrated into the technical environment. So, the technical environments have to be *extended* by an administration 'environment' but also by other components for other purposes.

This simplified administration environment by which technical environments are extended besides giving access to the administration configuration via simplified operations has another purpose: In section 1.6.2 we explained the component `SessionDocument-Manager`, which must have administration knowledge about all documents and their dependency relations being 'local' in the technical environment for being read or changed. This knowledge is delivered to the technical environment whenever a new task is started (a working context is installed then) or written back at the end of a task. Furthermore, as the working context can change during a task (if the corresponding management functionality is delegated for taking up another task or extending a task) the local part as well as the global administration configuration has to be changed. So, there has to be an *exchange* of administration *information* between the *administration data base* and the corresponding *cutouts* in the extended technical environments.

Up to now, we have discussed the connection between extended technical environments and the administration data base in order to facilitate management by delegation or to organize work on a portion of the technical configuration. In both cases, coarse–grained administration information is exchanged between the extended technical environments and the administration data base. There is, however, another *integration aspect*, namely between the *administration configuration* and the *fine–grained technical configuration*. The first use of this connection is that a *working context* is installed for a certain task at a technical environment. This working context (besides other topics) means that a certain cutout of the technical fine–grained configuration is available for or at the technical environment. In a priori SDEs which share the same data model and (eventually distributed) data storage this means that the technical environment now has access to this part of the technical configuration. This access is driven by information of the administration configuration. In IPSEN, access means that a technical environment either has remote access to a GRAS object storage at another server, or that a local GRAS object storage is available and the cutout of the technical configuration according to the working context is transported to the local object storage. According to the current state of IPSEN, we assume in the following that the different technical environments or integrated technical environments are bound sequential systems (see however section 5.3). Furthermore, for reasons of simplicity we make in this subsection the assumption that an environment has a local copy of the object storage.

There is a further connection from administration configuration to fine–grained technical configuration besides installing the working context. This topic has to do with facilitating management and delegation of management functionality of above. If a document is completed and, as on the management level all precautions have been taken such that e.g. it is reviewed, then a number of new tasks to be fulfilled may be determined. This is, for example, the case if a subsystem is designed and the number of implementation tasks is now clear. Then, the project manager could extract this management information out of the design document and manipulate the administration configuration by himself using the administration environment. Extracting management information can be done also by the developer himself or by using a tool. The invocation of this tool may be delegated to the technical developer, e.g. the designer. Such tools, if they are connected to the administration configuration (e.g. finishing the design task and correspondingly manipulating the administration configuration), are examples of *connection* between the *two levels* in the *direction* from *technical to administration information*. There is further interplay between the two levels to be sketched in chapter 5.

The *summary* of the *architectural investigations* of this section is given in fig. 1.34. We have different technical environments, which are connected via an administration configuration (all technical environments have an administration extension for this purpose). Furthermore, there is one administration environment (or there are different administration environments) for the project manager(s). In any case, the layer for the administration configuration, therefore, has to offer mutual access. A further integration, which is not only responsible for the integration of technical environments to the administration configuration but also for the integration of the technical environments themselves is given by the object storage. Either all systems use a distributed object storage, or have local object stores (assumed above) such that they are connected on the level of a file system, or there is a mixture of these two cases (see 4.1, 4.2, and 5.3). The second case is shown in fig. 1.34.

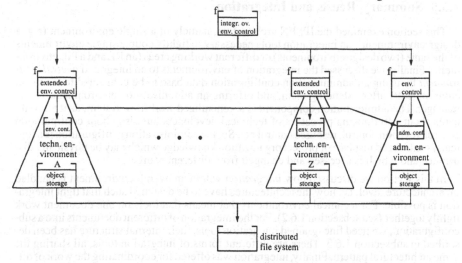

Fig. 1.34. An integrated overall environment: sketch of integrating various technical environments to administration services assuming a basic layer for integration. Internals of technical environments or the administration environment are not shown (see preceding subsections).

Connection here is on the level of *usability* between different technical environments, the layer for the administration configuration, and the object storage (or file system). This connection has to be mapped on basic mechanisms for communication and synchronization (e.g. for rpc implementation, file transfer etc.) which is not shown in fig. 1.34. This figure shows what we have called a *virtual architecture* with replication. How a virtual architecture can be transformed via a sequence of architectural transformations to a distributed architecture running on a real net is presented in /6. KKN 94, 6. LKN 95/ and section 5.3.

We conclude this summary by extending our remarks on *integration* and *reuse*, now corresponding to the administration environment, the extensions of technical environments, and their mutual coupling. There are only a few remarks to be added: All what has been said above on data integration also applies for the administration configuration. *Management integration* is achieved by (a) that all necessary management information is contained in the administration configuration, (b) by coupling of extended technical technical environments with the administration configuration for delegation and working context installation purposes, and (c) by directly manipulating an administration configuration by an administration environment.

Summing up, this subsection dealt with integrating technical environments. These environments are either working on one document (subsection 1.6.2) or on a technical subconfiguration (subsection 1.6.3). Integrating different technical environments, either isolated or integrated, on one side needs an administration infrastructure as the administration environment, access to the administration configuration, the extensions of the technical environments etc. It also needs a basic layer infrastructure (for data storage and retrieval, communication and synchronization of computer processes, but also for the communication and coordination of human developers). This *parameterizable infrastructure* on both levels in the context of a posteriori integration is the topic of the SUKITS project. Therefore, this subsection was on the level of integrating diverse technical environments on one side and integrating technical environments with the administration data base on the other side to end up with an *integrated* (a priori) *overall environment* for handling distributed and coordinated software projects.

1.6.5 Summary, Reuse, and Integration

This section examined the IPSEN architecture, namely of a single environment (e.g. a design environment), on integration tools necessary to tightly couple single environments of the same (two design environments) or different working areas (an RE and a PiL environment). Finally, we discussed the integration of environments to an integrated *overall environment* by using an administration configuration data base to be connected to technical environments, after extending them, and offering an administration environment for the manager. The administration component is a generalized workflow system, as it not only cares about coordinating processes of technical developers but also about configuration control, revision control, resource control etc. So, the administration configuration is a logically centralized instance of project organization knowledge which may be physically distributed and which is accessed and changed from different sources.

In this section we discussed how *integration* within an overall environment is handled on architecture level, i.e. how the architectures have to be designed such that tight integration is possible. For technical environments that means that tools on one document work tightly together (see subsection 1.6.2). For the integration of different documents into a sub-configuration, we need fine–grained integration tools, their internal structure has been described in subsection 1.6.3. There are different forms of integration tools, all sharing the same architectural pattern. Finally, integration was offered for coordinating the work of different developers using different environments, by actions of a manager, delegating management functions, and offering a working context for a technical task. The different *dimensions* of integration were discussed in the corresponding subsections. So, this section sketched our solutions to achieve integration on an external overall configuration (see fig. 1.15) by giving the design patterns for the corresponding tools.

Finally, this section was on *reuse*. Reuse is pattern reuse, if someone wants to adopt the architectural patterns. It is framework reuse, if someone develops an IPSEN–like single environment, integrated environment, or overall environment. In addition, process reuse is utilized in order to get the remaining specific components hooked into the framework, or even for generating a portion of them. Process reuse is described in chapters 3, 4, and 5.

1.7 Classifying SDEs, IPSEN, and Relating It to Other SDE Projects

The *aim* of this *section* is to introduce a classification scheme for SDE projects and SDEs. This scheme is then applied to the IPSEN project. It is also applied to other typical representatives of SDEs. Both are performed for the following reasons: (1) to sketch the realm of different SDE approaches and systems, (2) to clarify the place of IPSEN in the SDE world, and (3) to explain the different dimensions by which SDEs can be characterized. Finally, from the scheme we are able to determine (4) weaknesses of existing SDEs, open problems of today, and research directions of future SDEs.

1.7.1 A Classification Scheme for Software Development Environment Projects

In this subsection we *introduce* and explain a *classification scheme* for SDE projects (see also /1. Nag 93/ for a shorter version). This scheme is the result of a discussion which started some time ago. There are other papers on SDE classifications (e.g. /1. DEF 87, 5. GM 87, 1. HN 87a/) which also try to introduce some order in the SDE terminology. We introduce the scheme in this subsection and give some remarks by which concepts the scheme is built up in the next subsection.

We have already given a *characterization* of SDEs in subsection 1.2.2 and 1.2.3, which the reader should recall as it plays a role in this section. The reason is that all the aspects of these subsections have to fit into the classification scheme introduced here in the sense that the scheme has to offer means to express the characterizations of above.

Without going into details of the classification scheme construction mechanisms (see next subsection) let us make the following remark at the very beginning: A *classification scheme* is a *complex structure* introducing some order in a certain universe, in our case for SDE projects. For this complex structure we can again apply what we have already learned about complex structures as internal documents of an SDE: We shall see that the structure we are building up for an SDE classification shares a lot of similarities with internal documents. It is a graph built up from tree parts together with context sensitive edges. This is a clear evidence that the concepts we are developing in this book are not only applicable for SDEs but are suitable also for other modelling tasks. We shall have further examples for this "universality" in chapters 3, 5, and 6.

We immediately recall that there are five different SDE project types to which the scheme can be applied: An *SDE project* may either introduce (1) a certain and *specific* SDE which is later on used by programmers of an application domain. We shall see that for such specific SDEs quite different instances are possible. On the other hand many SDE projects do not develop one SDE but an environment for developing SDEs, i.e. they are (2) *meta–SDE projects*. In this case, specific SDEs are usually produced only to show that the meta environment approach works well. In this latter case, a more or less complete specification of the SDE to be produced has to be supplied. In order to develop and maintain such a specification a (3) *specification environment* can be built. We mention specification environments separately, although they are usually used in and combined with meta–SDEs, because the specification environment may also be applied in other contexts. The classification scheme can be applied to these three cases. For the reader of this book the first case applies to a certain IPSEN prototype project, the second to the derivation machinery of IPSEN, and the third to the PROGRES environment. Finally, the following classification scheme can also be applied to projects not building SDEs but (4) basic components or *platforms* on top of which an SDE or an arbitrary distributed system or environment can be built, as PCTE /6. BMT 88, 6. GMT 87, 6. ECM 90/, CAIS /6. DoD 88, 6. MOP 88/, ESF Basic Features /6. ESF 90, 6. GKK 87, 6. Ver 91a, b/, Softbench /6. HP 89/, Cohesion /6. Wel 91/, AD/Cycle /6. IBM 89/ etc. An environment of another shape is the (5) administration environment which we discussed at the end of the last section. This environment, together with the extensions of technical environments and the interaction with technical environments serves for the management aspect of a (software) project. So, one has to decide for which of the five different types of projects one wants to apply the scheme to be explained in the following. In addition to the previously mentioned different instances of specific SDEs there are further types to be discussed later.

The classification *scheme* of this subsection is devoted to *SDE projects*. However, it is also applicable to *SDEs* which are the final *products* of SDE projects, or to the *processes* yielding SDEs. This is because the overall project classification has dimensions for all these aspects and, therefore, can be restricted to these aspects. All these aspects are necessary for a complete classification: For example, there may be different processes to get a similar or equal SDE as result, or there may be different projects resulting in the "same" product following the same or a different process.

The following classification scheme cannot only be applied to quite different types of SDE projects, it can also be *read* by quite *different people*. It (1) can be read by people engaged in *application programming* using an SDE. This can either be a manager, or a developer, or anybody else (quality assurance engineering, technical writer etc.). Those people are mainly interested in the outside functionality of an SDE, resulting from an SDE project. SDEs in the form of meta–SDEs, or specification environments are not interesting, platforms may be interesting. The next group of types of people interested in such a scheme are (2) engaged in the *development* or maintenance of SDEs, again ranging from managers, developers, to technical writers. In this case, all types of SDE projects, including meta–SDEs and specification environments are interesting, and all facets of an SDE project including the process facet. The aim here is to see the full variety of existing SDEs, to compare the own SDE project with others, to see what is useful to buy from others etc. Finally, the scheme is (3) also interesting for people only trying to *get* a *survey* of this special field of software engineering.

Nodes of the following scheme are facets (aspects, perspectives). Any node should be prefixed by 'characterization of'. *Edges* from a father to a son node express that the son node is one facet of more facets to determine the father facet. The explanation of the scheme is levelwise from top to bottom and at any level from left to right. For atomic level nodes, we give example *attributes* in order to make the scheme understandable. Classified items, here SDE projects, are attribute value combinations according to the scheme. Further constructs to build up a scheme are given below.

The first level of our overall SDE project classification is given in fig. 1.35. This level distinguishes three nodes below the root node corresponding to different aspects (facets) of an SDE project. The leftmost of these nodes corresponds to fixing the *context* in which the SDE is to be applied, e.g. the different concepts, models, languages, methods etc. which are to be supported by the resulting SDE. Thus, this node characterizes the 'wherefore' of the project's product. The next node corresponds to the characterization of the SDE itself, i.e. the *product* of the project. This characterization will later be split into an external ('how/ what is the outside support') and internal ('how is this realized') characterization. On this level we could also have a characterization of the technical process of investigating/developing an SDE. However, we know very little about these processes from literature. Therefore, and also because the technical process and the resulting product are usually intertwined, we have given the little we know about development processes in the product characterization. We also do not know very much about the organization of an SDE project (configurations, versions, administration processes, resources necessary etc.). The little we know is put into the last facet. This last facet of fig. 1.35 gives a characterization of the *project* by giving some parameters. This facet is rather vague and the scheme below it is not very deep. Summing up, we shall see that the characterization of node 1.1 but, especially, of node 1.2 are the main topics of our classification scheme.

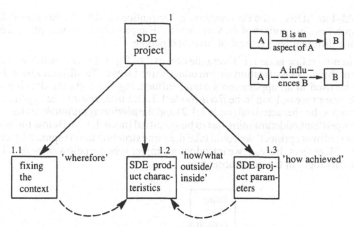

Fig. 1.35. Top–level aspects of an SDE project classification

Considering the top level of our scheme in fig. 1.35 the reader immediately recognizes a strong *correspondence* to our *SDE problem area classification* of section 1.3. The node 1.1 representing the aspect fixing the context directly corresponds to the concepts, languages, methods problem area described in subsection 1.3.2. The next aspect 1.2 which we shall split into external aspects and internal aspects corresponds to the problem areas new tools for working areas or integration of 1.3.3, to conceptual modelling of subsection 1.3.4, and to the problem area software engineering investigations and implementation of 1.3.5 and 1.3.6, respectively. Finally, the aspect project parameters is loosely related to 1.3.7, demonstration and distribution.

All nodes of the second level (and further levels), especially the first node fixing the context, are *important* for the product aspect, even in the case that no *SDE* is to be *built* or *adapted*, as an SDE is *bought*. Even in this case, one has to clarify the development context to see into which context the SDE has to fit, as this is usually the basis of evaluating different SDEs. In this case it may happen that only some aspects are covered by an SDE, others are not, and have to be enforced by discipline and organizational rules. On the other side, this node and its subaspects clearly are of big importance if a project is planning to develop a new SDE, or to extend an existing SDE.

The *aspects* of fig. 1.35 are *mutually dependent*. We give only some of these relations which are given by dashed arrows in fig. 1.35: The aspect fixing the context (which lifecycle model, which languages, which hardware etc.) determines more or less the outside behavior (which tools, which user interface, quality of support etc.) but also the inside 'behavior' (internal mechanisms, architecture), both characterized by node 1.2. Furthermore, the project parameters (one aspect is the background of developers) influences the product characterization, namely the outside as well as the inside behavior. These dashed edges are directed, e.g. it is the context which determines how the SDE should be.

It might be useful to give a remark, explaining in more detail that the *character* of a whole project (product, process) is often *determined* by the *background of developers,* one aspect of node 1.3: Big international projects such as Arcadia /2. TSY 88/, ESF /2. FO 90/ are driven by software engineering people, either from universities or companies. The same is true for CASE /2. Hru 91/ or for platform projects. Language–oriented environments, as e.g. Lisp /2. TM 84/ or Smalltalk /2. Gol 84/ mostly come from programming language people. Most generator projects (as e.g. /2. TR 81, 2. BS 86/) or projects where an SDE is centered around an intermediate code come from compiler writing people. Database modelling tools /3. Jar 94/ are mostly invented by database people. Specification/transformation environments as Larch /7. GG 89, 7. GHM 90/, Prospectra /2. DKP 89/, CiP /2. Bau 85, 87/ come from people involved in the corresponding specification/transformation approaches. Finally, AI–like SDEs as the Programmer's Apprentice /2. RW 90/ have been developed by AI people. So, a big portion of the variety of SDE approaches can be explained by only looking at the different background of involved people.

Let us now refine node 1.1 'fixing the context' of fig. 1.35. The next level is given in fig. 1.36. For this subclassification we introduce three facets: The different *models* to be found and to be used in an application system, influencing the software development/maintenance/reuse process, have to be *fixed* (node 1.1.1). Furthermore, the *application software project* has to be characterized (node 1.1.2) and the *platforms* on/into/on which the software is developed/embedded/running has to be specified (node 1.1.3). Below the node 1.1.2 'application software project' we could take the same structure as on topmost level characterizing the SDE project. Instead, we introduce a simpler scheme below of node 1.1.2. We come back to this topic in the next subsection.

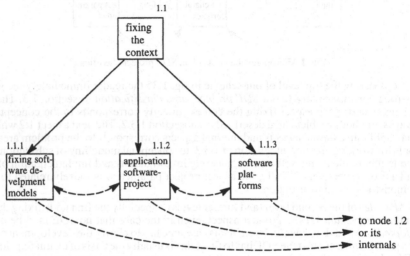

Fig. 1.36. Aspects of the application development context for which an SDE is to be built/bought/selected

Before we continue our schema explanation let us discuss the mutual relations corresponding to the nodes of fig. 1.36. The first kind of those edges results from the refinement of nodes of fig. 1.35. For example, the edge going from node 1.1 to node 1.2 can now be made more precise as the source node of this edge now has an internal structure. These *"refined" edges* are given in fig. 1.36 at its bottom. The refinement is rather trivial in this case: One can easily see that outgoing edges from node 1.1 of fig. 1.35 have to go out from all nodes refining node 1.1 in fig. 1.36. To give an example: Fixing the models for software development environments (which working areas, dependencies, etc.) has influence on node 1.2 and its internals. Therefore, we see that any refinement step elaborating a classification scheme node can result in refined edges according to some balancing rules. Inside of fig. 1.36 we have further relations within this *"local" classification context*. It is easy to see that 'fixing all models' influences 'application software project', and vice versa. In the same way, 'SW platforms' (e.g. target platform) and 'application software project' are in a loose and mutual relation. In the following, for reasons of simplicity, we omit the *discussion* of refining *relations* and defining local relations. So, the following explanation is only dealing with the tree part of the schema.

Let us continue in our breadth–first refinement discussion of the classification schema by refining the node 1.2 'SDE product characteristics'. This node is split into four subaspects as shown in fig. 1.37. Firstly, a classification of the *support* we expect by the SDE, and secondly, a characterization of its *user interface*. These two nodes belong to the outside characterization of the SDE. The next two nodes correspond to the inside characterization of the SDE as the product of the SDE project. There, we have the facets *internal models/ mechanisms* used to develop SDEs, and the software *architecture* of the SDE.

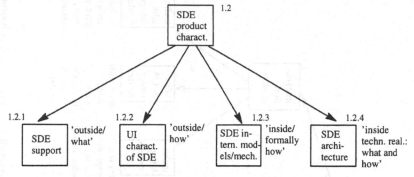

Fig. 1.37. Subaspects of an SDE as the product of an SDE project

The refinement of the last of the bottom nodes of fig. 1.35, namely of node 'SDE project parameters', is given in fig. 1.38. This subscheme is characterizing the SDE from parameters like *project size* (of group), *structure*, *character*, *size* (of product)/*effort* (of process), and from the *background* of its *developers*.

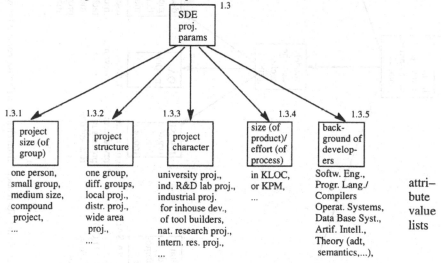

Fig. 1.38. Project parameters of SDE projects extended by possible attribute value lists

As the leaf nodes of figure 1.38 are not refined further – they are called *atomic* – we find *attribute value lists* on these nodes which are possible assignments (one or more attributes per leaf node) for characterizing a special SDE project. This will be done in all cases, where no further refinement is possible or done. The fact that the facets of SDE project parameters are atomic, whereas all other nodes on level 3 are refined further, shows that detailed knowledge about how the projects have been carried out is not available.

We continue the schema discussion by refining the node 1.1.1 fixing the models for development, maintenance, or reuse (cf. fig. 1.39). By model we mean here any paradigms,

124

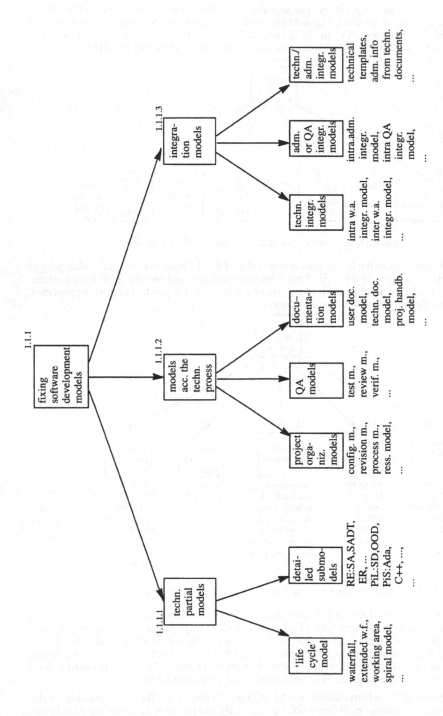

Fig. 1.39. The aspect 'fixing SD models' from characterizing the context for which an SDE is developed, extended, modified, or bought

concepts, languages, methods, procedures which influence the structure of the application system, the corresponding development process, or the project. On the next level we distinguish between the *models* for the *technical part* of software development on the left, the models for all activities *accompanying* the technical *process* in the middle, and *integration* models on the right.

The technical part model node (see again fig. 1.39) is divided into two further facets, namely the *lifecycle* model (waterfall model, spiral model, working area model etc.). For the following explanation we mostly refer to the working area model introduced in section 1.1. For any of these working areas (and correspondingly for phases, or any 'unit' of the lifecycle model) we introduce the corresponding *detailed submodels*, as e.g. SA, ER for requirements engineering, OOD for design, Ada for programming in the small, or alike. For these languages certain methods, rules, or procedures on how to use them may exist. Please note that the models introduced here might cover certain perspectives (as SA or ER), certain degrees of detail (as a data flow diagram in SA and a corresponding minispec), separation aspects (as subsystem of the architecture might be designed and programmed independently after its interface is specified). These submodels may be incomplete (e.g. the perspective of UI–definition is missing in RE). The integration of these submodels has to be defined (see below).

The reader should note that the above introduction of separate working areas or subareas and the usage of different languages/methods for different documents for working areas (as RE) has been called *discrete paradigm* above. Furthermore, the reader might remember that *continuous* paradigms exist (see discussion in subsection 1.2.3). In this case, where the whole development process is acting within one paradigm, one language, and corresponding methodology the characterization of node 1.1.1 becomes trivial. In these continuous approaches the other submodels of fig. 1.39 to be discussed also become obsolete, as continuous approaches have never been applied to big projects.

Technical activities are accompanied by activities on organization/*administration, quality assurance*, and *documentation* level. For these activities corresponding models have to be fixed. For project administration we may have models for the product, process, resources, and actual context description as already discussed. For QA there may be test models (top down incremental integration, white box module test etc.), or review/inspection models (review for the requirements specification, design rationale, and architecture, code–inspection for module bodies). For documentation we have to determine which documentations we are going to have (user documentation, technical documentation, project handbook etc.), and how each of them has to be structured internally. In contrast to the structure below node 1.1.1.1 where we allow different structures (one node determining it on coarse level and the other giving the corresponding details), we have introduced a fixed structure below of node 1.1.1.2. The reason is that whenever a technical development task is regarded the facets project administration, quality assurance, and documentation are needed, the internals of these nodes being selected appropriately. Whereas QA models and DOC models collect models for different tasks which are related to the structure of the technical process (node 1.1.1.1) seen under a superior item, in the case of project administration model we have a characterization which is rather invariant of the technical models (see subsection 1.1.5).

Finally, the integration models have to be determined related to the various models chosen for development, tasks accompanying the development process, or administration (see fig. 1.39). The first part are *technical integration* models. If, for example, different sublanguages are introduced (and not one broadband language is defined), then the consistency relations between these different languages have to be fixed. Examples are consistencies between different perspectives of one working area (functional, data, control model in RE), overview and detailed models (RE diagrams and attribute definitions in RE dictionary), separate definition and use (subsystem defined and developed and its use). All these examples are integration models for subareas within one working area, i.e. intra working area integration models. The next step is to define integration models for different working areas (e.g. the transformation between RE and PiL). We call them inter working area integration models. Furthermore, integration models also have to be defined for the models for tasks accompanying the development process. For example, the *integration* model for *administration* has to be determined (how product, process, resources etc. models play together). Finally, the *integration* between *integrated development* models, *integrated models* for *accompanying* tasks and *integrated administration* models have to be fixed. An example is how an administration configuration can be used to introduce a technical working context or, vice versa, how technical results influence administration procedures. Another is, how QA procedures are guaranteed on organization level or, vice versa, that project organization "enforces" QA.

The part of the schema discussed so far has nothing to do with SDEs, it determines the *context* for an *application project* for which SDE support is wanted. Furthermore, if we look at the 'model' subscheme of fig. 1.39 we see that technical models are only on the product side, i.e. making clear how complex and fine–grained configurations are built up. For these configurations we know very little how the technical *processes* are carried out or how the *project* is carried out in detail on technical level. Therefore, these aspects do *not appear* in our subscheme. On administration level these topics are introduced, but nevertheless, even on this coarse level only little knowledge is available.

The next subscheme to be discussed is the characterization of the application software project which is to be supported by the SDE to be developed, extended, or bought (cf. fig. 1.40). On the level below node 1.1.2 we distinguish three facets, namely a characterization of the *software* to be *developed,* of the *context software* which is available and can be used, and the *software* which is available *for* the development/maintenance *process* of the application system.

'Software to be developed' (node 1.1.2.1) is split into different characterizations which mostly regard the software as a black box. We distinguish between the *application area class* (e.g. mathematical software, process control software etc.), the *structure* class (sequential, concurrent etc. systems; batch, dialog, reactive systems etc.), the *level* class (complete system, component of another software/hardware system, basic layer for certain software systems etc.), the *used* class (in lab, in–house, in field etc.), and the *build* class (new development, change of existing development, etc.).

'Context software' (node 1.1.2.2), i.e. the software to be used within the application system, is characterized by regarding four facets. By application specific *building blocks* we characterize if and how parts of the system can be configured by existing components. In the ideal case, system development is only a configuration process of existing building blocks by tools to be discussed in the next paragraph, i.e. the software to be really developed (node 1.1.2.1) becomes empty. For software systems which are well–studied and standardized, a *framework system* exist into which specific components to be developed have to be hung. Frameworks usually include a *basic layer* of standard components. Conversely, there may be a basic layer for an application but no framework, or the basic layer can be used by different frameworks for different applications. Basic layer components are quite different (DBS/special object storage, window system/UIM system etc.). The last facet to be regarded is *mechanism* software. Such software (for data communication, coordination of processes etc.) is usually used by frameworks and basic layers but it can also be used if frameworks and basic layers are not available.

The last facet to be regarded is software support for the application specific development process. Here, we introduce three facets. *Reuse tools* (classification tools, recherche tools) help to structure a universe of components, to prepare a component for being found later, to find a suitable component etc. *Configuration* tools help to configure a system from available components (automatic, interactive etc.). Finally, *generation* tools try to fully or partially automate the process for that part of the application system which still has to be developed (macro expanders, generic instantiation tools, generators etc.).

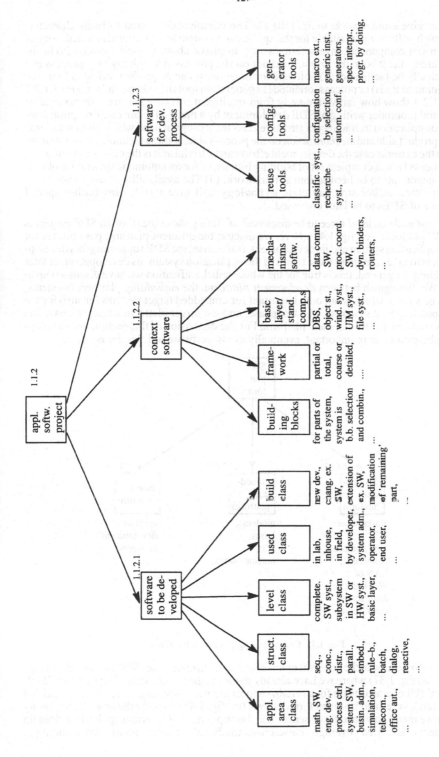

Fig. 1.40. Characterization of the application software project for which an SDE has to give support

Let us give some *remarks* to fig. 1.40: (1) The middle node context software characterizes which software is available for the application system to be built/maintained. Any of the forms of components, layers, frameworks discussed above is itself software (to be directly used), i.e. it is on the *product* and not on the process side although the process can dramatically be facilitated. (2) Software for the *process* can be product–oriented (reuse or configuration tools) or process–oriented (as generation tools). (3) Especially, nodes 1.1.2.2 and 1.1.2.3 show how far we are away from intelligent software construction nowadays: In general (compiler writing or SDE development by a meta–SDE are rare exceptions) we have no application technology or structure class technology at hand which gives *standards* on the product side and *mechanization* on the process side. If these technologies are at hand then in the extreme case the development effort can be trivial as it is the case for a configuration process from a complete set of building blocks, or for an automatic generation of specific components to be hooked into a framework. (4) The availability of *deep knowledge* in application and/or structure class technology will give rise to two further special instances of SDEs to be later discussed.

The last node on level three to be discussed of 'fixing the context' of an SDE project is the 'SW platform' (cf. fig. 1.41). Here, we discuss the different platform possibilities for an an application system and its development. (Of course, the SDE supporting this development, has to take care about these topics of the application system, its development, or later embedding. In general, this is true for the whole subclassification we have discussed up to now.) We distinguish between *development platform*, the *embedding* platform (modems, buses, nets etc.), which is not only important for embedded target systems but also for the corresponding host systems in the test phase, and the *target* platform which can have the same variety as the development platform. For the discussion of this section, the development platform is more important, eventually cross–software utilities are necessary.

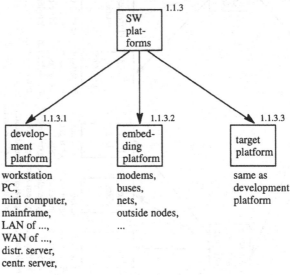

Fig. 1.41. Characterizing platforms for SDEs

Let us come now to the core part of our scheme determining the 'SDE product characteristics' (cf. fig. 1.37) where we have already distinguished four facets. The first of it 'SDE support' (UI characteristics for a certain support are not interesting here, they are regarded separately), is refined by seven further facets (cf. fig. 1.42), namely the *level* of support by which we mean how specific or semantical the support is for a certain application domain or system class. *Area coverage* characterizes the breath of tool support corresponding to

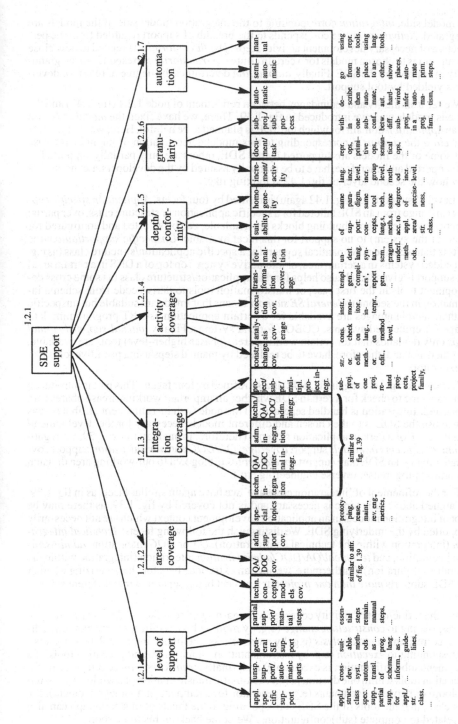

Fig. 1.42. Characterization of the quality of SDE support

the model side, *integration* corresponding to the integration model side, if the models are integrated. *Activity* coverage corresponds to the breadth of support regarded from the perspective of necessary development activity steps. *Depth/conformity* is related to how close the support is to chosen models for a certain context. *Granularity* corresponds to the granularity of support by the SDE. Finally, *automation* determines the degree of relief for developers yielded by tool support.

We see a similarity and redundancy between refinement of node 1.2.1 (fig. 1.42) and the various models we have introduced in fig. 1.39. There, we have fixed the *models* relevant for an *application* domain for which the SDE is planned to be helpful. Here, we characterize *how close* the *support* is corresponding to this model determination. It might be the case that some of the models are supported by the SDE, others are only partially supported or not supported and, therefore, have to be manually assured by the developers. Let us discuss now how the second layer of fig. 1.42 is looking like.

'Level of support' (cf. fig. 1.42 again) is refined by four facets. *Application specific support* can range from an SDE tailored for a specific application or structure class, over partial support given (e.g. some building blocks are available, can be selected and configured for a part of the system) to no support for this facet available. *Unspecific support/automatic parts* is that we have no semantical support for a specific application/structure class (as e.g. embedded systems in a certain area, or interactive systems on top of a DBS in a certain area) but support is given which also helps for this application/structure class (as some cross development tools in the first case, or transformation tools to derive code from schema information in the second). *General SE support* means that important suitable but unspecific methods and languages are available for a certain application as a RT programming language for embedded systems, COBOL for BA systems. Finally, *partial support/manual steps* only demands that for certain working areas/phases higher–level tools are available, for others not and, therefore, have to be replaced by manual steps using primitive tools like a text editor.

'Area coverage' (see again fig. 1.42) is also refined by four facets. This part is introduced in our scheme to check for a certain SDE whether all important working areas/subareas are supported. Integration is handled separately. This node with its refinement attributes says how close the SDE is to the chosen and different models necessary for the development/ maintenance of a certain application system. Therefore, in analogy to fig. 1.39, we regard *technical concepts or models* support *coverage, QA/DOC* and *administration* support coverage. Finally, an SDE may support *special topics* orthogonal to our working area division (as prototyping, reuse, reverse engineering etc.).

For the refinement of 'integration coverage' we have again similar facets as in fig. 1.39. As argued above, this topic is necessary and is not covered by fig. 1.39, as there may be a lot of integration models in an application development context which are not necessarily supported by the underlying SDE. We distinguish the following facets: *Technical integration* (integration within the technical configuration), *QA* or *DOC* integration, *administration* integration, and *technical/QA/DOC/administration* integration (integration within the overall configuration). Furthermore, we have an extra node here for characterizing whether the SDE supports *more than one project* or a project being separated into different subprojects.

For the refinement of activity coverage we regard again four facets. We regard coverage corresponding to *construction/change* (e.g. by more or less intelligent corresponding editors), corresponding to *analysis* (e.g. by more or less intelligent and complete analyzers), corresponding to *execution* (e.g. by instrumentation, monitoring, and execution tools, if a document/subconfiguration is executable) and, finally, *transformation* coverage by transformation tools within one document (e.g. automatic transformation of a while– into an until–loop) or between documents (e.g. a generator for a template of another document). So, it is clear, that the tools of the SDE corresponding to the facets of this paragraph can also be related to complete (sub)configurations. We come back to this topic soon.

'Depth/conformity' is characterized by three facets. *Formalization* says how close the tool support of the SDE is to the underlying chosen formalisms. These may be syntactical or semantical determinations of the underlying languages, formalized methods, but also formalizations of an application/structure class. Furthermore, *suitability* determines whether the support of given tools is suitable for the application development, i.e. the corresponding application/structure class, the chosen models etc., i.e. it measures the distance between the model side and the SDE support side. Finally, if different tools in an SDE exist, the node *homogeneity* characterizes if these tools have the same form of support (paradigm, tool behavior, preciseness etc.).

For the node 1.2.1.6 'granularity' we define three facets which characterize the size of the portions handled by the user using a certain SDE. The granularity may be on *increment/ single activity* level, on *document/*technical *process* level, or on *subconfiguration/configuration* or *integrated process* level. Of course, fine–grained support, i.e. support on increment level is better than coarse–grained support. The best is that within documents or, even more, within complete subconfigurations/configurations we have fine–grained support such that all syntactical, semantical etc. rules in a complete configuration are obeyed.

The last aspect 'automation' of fig. 1.43 is also characterized by three facets. This support is very seldom *automatic* (e.g. described by the user then automatically done by tools, automatism hardwired etc.). In many cases it is *semiautomatic*, i.e. the user is supported by automatic steps (e.g. all localities to be changed are shown, the user makes the modification). The most probable situation nowadays is that steps are carried out *manually* (by using tool support on a more or less suitable level).

Some remarks have to be made regarding nodes on the second level of fig. 1.42: The *support* characterized by the refinement of these nodes can be understood in a more *narrow* or more *wide sense* ranging from documents to complete configurations or from deep support to trivial support. For example, we may have an application/structure class specific environment, where all the single process steps on documents are supported appropriately but no support is given on the more global integration level. Analogously, there may be an integrated editor/analyzer semantically supporting a modification in one document but no integrated set of editor/analyzer/transformation tools supporting the maintenance task across a complete configuration. So, in characterizing a certain SDE, a certain working area may be covered but not all necessary activities, some of the activities are supported by intelligent, some by primitive tools, in some parts the environment is integrated, in others developers have to do this integration by hand. So, the attribute values corresponding to a certain SDE have to make the corresponding determinations for all the models of an SDE and have to give attributes for all single or integrated tools.

The next node on level 2 of SDE as product (cf. fig. 1.37) to be refined is 'UI characteristics of an SDE'. Here, we introduce nine facets (cf. fig. 1.43). *Unit handling* describes on which level units of subdocuments, ..., configurations can be handled by the user. *Granularity* determines the size of these units. *Strictness corresponding* to *errors* is related to how users are bound in handling errors they have made. *Reaction on tool activations* describes how and when the SDE is reacting on a tool activation. Handling *tool integration* describes how tool integration is looking on the UI side. Both nodes, *Views* and *representation/layout*, determine which views are available for tools, and how the layout of single views or of view groups is represented to the user. *User knowledge* characterizes if and how the SDE can interact with users of different degree of expertise. Finally, *user cooperation* characterizes the SDE support for different users cooperating in order to solve a complex task. What we have said in the last paragraph, namely that classification is to be given for any tool (if all tools do not behave homogeneously), can be repeated for the subclassification of node 1.2.2. We discuss and refine this node in the following paragraphs down to the atomic level.

By refining the first facet 'unit handling' we introduce two facets (cf. fig. 1.43 again). *Level* of *structure support* describes how at UI level the underlying structure is directly, indirectly, or not supported (structure–oriented tools corresponding to syntax, semantics,

132

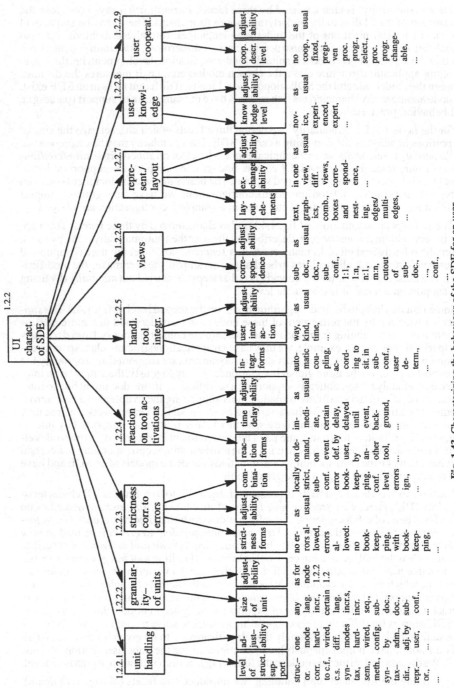

Fig. 1.43. Characterizing the behaviour of the SDE for an user

methodology; presentation–oriented tools on text or graphics possibly with later analyses). The second facet *adjustability* occurs several times in the subclassification of fig. 1.43. It describes if different forms of a UI property, here 'level of structure support', can be chosen or adjusted appropriately (in all tools there may be one or more of the above modes hard-wired, or different modes are hardwired and can be selected; this selection can be made at configuration time by an SDE administrator, or it may be adjusted appropriately by the SDE user at runtime).

Before continuing our discussion a short remark may be useful: The facets introduced below node 1.2.2 look similar to those below of node 1.2.1 (cf. fig. 1.42). There, we handled which *support* is given *in principal*, here we discuss how the support is presented *at the user interface side*, if available. To take one example: There may be support on language syntax level which, at the user interface can be represented in structure–oriented, syntax–directed, or representation–oriented (with batch analysis after a change) form, respectively. These different forms may even be adjustable prior to or during the development process.

The second facet 'granularity of units' describes the size of units to be handled (built up/ changed, analyzed, transformed, executed as step etc.). *Size* of *unit* may be an increment more or less big (any increment of the language from small to big, only large increments the inner increments of which are not separately selectable), a sequence of increments (e.g. the declaration part of a module), a subdocument (e.g. a data flow diagram in a DFD refine-ment structure), a document (e.g. a complete module description), a subconfiguration (e.g. all modules possibly involved in a usual separate compilation), or a complex configuration (e.g. for an analysis tool making a completeness check). The second facet of node 1.2.2.2 *adjustability* of grain size can have the same attribute values as in the last paragraph al-though it now corresponds to another UI property, namely granularity.

'Strictness corresponding to errors' has three facets (cf. fig. 1.43). *Strictness forms* de-scribes how the SDE deals with errors made by the user (no errors allowed, the user has to correct immediately, errors allowed but ignored, errors allowed but a complete bookkeep-ing of errors and their consequences is made). The facet *adjustability* according to strictness forms is as usual. The last facet *combination* corresponds to the fact that strictness forms can be chosen differently on different grains of a complete configuration (e.g. locally strict, on subconfiguration level error bookkeeping, on configuration level errors ignored or, con-versely, strict on global and excusable on local level).

'Reaction on tool activations' is again refined by three facets. *Reaction forms* describes when a tool is activated (on demand by the user, by an event defined by the user, determined by another tool etc.). The facet *time delay* determines when the corresponding tool is acti-vated (immediate, delayed for a certain time, delayed until an event happens, executed in background when appropriate). Finally, the facet *adjustability* is as usual.

Regarding the facet 'handling tool integration' we again refine into three facets. The first facet *integration forms* describes how integration can be determined (automatic coupling, as e.g. an analyzer always being combined with an editor, coupling according to a certain situation in a subconfiguration, as an editor being (re)activated if, after an analysis, some errors have been detected, user predetermined etc.). *User interaction* determines whether the user can interact in fixing the way, kind, and time of coupling. The last facet *adjustability* is as above. The reader should note that we do not describe integration tools here but integra-tion of arbitrary tools. The scheme of fig. 1.43 can be applied to tools of a technical environ-ment, to integration tools, and to administration tools or their coupling as well.

The facet 'views' is refined by two further facets. *Correspondence* characterizes how representation is related to a logical situation contained in one (sub)document, ..., configu-ration (one view, n views, m logical situations related to one view, n:m correspondence). *Adjustability* is as usual.

'Representation/layout' has three facet children. Representation or *layout elements* char-acterizes which elements are available (text elements, graphic elements, text in graphic, ar-bitrary combination in nesting of text/graphic; boxes and nesting; node representation and edge– or multi–edge representation elements etc.). *Exchangeability* determines whether representation elements are exchangeable and determine the range of exchange (exchanged within one separate view, in different views, correspondence of exchange in different views, exchange in separate views determines the exchange in a combined view etc.). Finally, *adjustability* can have values as in all other cases.

The facet 'user knowledge' handling is refined by two nodes. *Knowledge level* describes which degrees of expertise are supported (novice, experienced, expert etc.) and how this is achieved. *Adjustability* describes which ways are available to adjust a given SDE to different knowledge levels, if the SDE is adjustable with respect to this feature.

The last facet 'user cooperation' is also refined by two facets. *Cooperation description level* says if cooperation between different users is supported and if, how it is described (no cooperation supported, fixed models of cooperation, process programs are pre–supplied, possibly selectable, process programs are changeable by the user etc.). *Adjustability* describes if and how an SDE can be adjusted to different cooperation forms if the SDE supports cooperation.

The next node of fig. 1.37 to be refined is 'SDE internal models/mechanisms' (cf fig. 1.44). On the next level down we distinguish four facets. *Internal conceptual data models* characterizes which models we use internally and which properties they have. *Integration models* does the same for integrated tools/environments working on documents/subconfigurations/configurations. *Representation* structures determine formalisms introduced in the environment building process for describing representations and how they are related to logical documents,..., configurations, they represent. Finally, *UI models* characterize models on user interface and interaction level.

The node 'internal conceptual data models' has three facets (cf. fig. 1.44 again). *Model level* characterizes the level of the underlying formalism for modelling (strings, trees, attributed trees, attributed graphs, hypergraphs etc.). *Operation/structure description* determines how the structure and the operations are described using the underlying formalism (schema information extracted, transactions described by complex operations versus primitive ops of the DML, declarative description by derived attributes/relations etc.). The last facet *model variety* says if one model or different models are used and if, if there is a manual or automatic translation between different models.

'Integration models' is refined by two facets. *Integration data models* determines which models exits for grouping/relating different submodels (groups of documents, hierarchical documents, increment–to–increment links, integration documents, administration documents or configurations). *Coupling models* characterizes which models have been introduced to combine operations on different documents (functional coupling by a transformation tool, message passing between 'active' documents, rule–based or event rule coupling, pair model approaches etc.).

'Representation structures' has also two atomic nodes. The first facet, internal *representation data* models, describes where and how representation information is specified (logical documents or separate; representation information is session dependent or persistent; information is on graphics/text level or on conceptual level etc.). The second facet, *logical/representation coupling*, can have the same values as the node coupling models discussed in the last paragraph.

Finally, the facet 'UI models' is refined by three further facets. *Command models* says how commands are prepared for selection by regarding the objects the tool is working on (unspecific commands as 'extend', specific commands for a document as 'append–if' in the case of a module body, specific commands according to the location the user is working at, as e.g. 'insert–type–decl' only if the user is in the type declaration part of a module body). *I/O data representation models* describes how and where the data corresponding to a command are put in (a mask corresponding to a command, in place in the documents etc.). Finally, *selection models* describes selection of objects or of commands corresponding to an object (an object has always to be selected explicitly by the user by movement or selection,

135

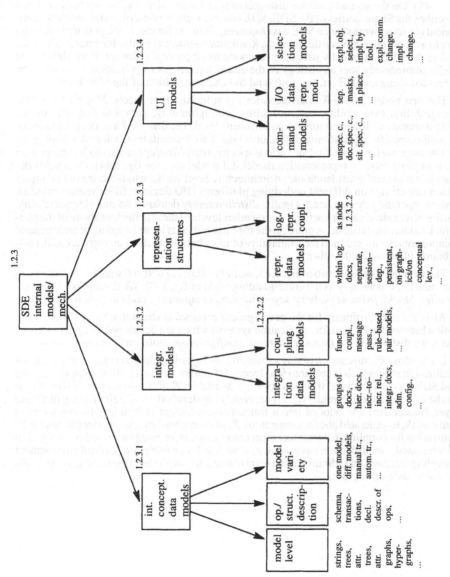

Fig. 1.44. Characterizing the internal mechanisms by which an SDE is built

implicit selection in a complex command; explicit change of a command or command group by the user, implicit change in combined commands etc.), and changes allowed between corresponding modes.

The last node of fig. 1.37 we are regarding in this subsection is 'SDE architecture' (cf. fig. 1.45). On the second level we distinguish four facets. *SDEs software characteristics* describes the SE properties of the SDE. *SDE context software* describes the available components or frameworks for an SDE development, *software* for the *development process* the means available to automate this process. *Realization strategy* finally characterizes how we realize the SDE, eventually using the components or process software, if available. The reader immediately sees an analogy in the characterization of application software to be supported using an SDE (cf. fig. 1.40) and the characterization of the SDE itself.

The first node, 'SDE SW characteristics', is split into three facets: *Modifyability* (exchangeability, extensibility, customizability, configurability, parameterizability) of the SDE demands a clear structure on architecture level, i.e. that we have deep knowledge about this specific application and structure class. This demands that, before developing the architecture, we have specified the various specific parts (data/operation model, integration data/coupling models, representation model, UI model etc., see fig. 1.44). *Portability* demands less general considerations: on architecture level we have to factorize out all topics which can change on different underlying platforms (I/O devices, files systems, window system, operating system, etc.). Finally, *distributability* demands on one side portability. On the other side, clear abstractions also on other levels of the architecture above of the platform level have to be made. A prerequisite for distribution is loose coupling of architectural components on one side and the availability of distribution mechanism software and a distribution platform on the other.

The next node on level two of fig. 1.45, namely 'SDE context software', is structured in very much the same way as the corresponding node of fig. 1.40. We distinguish the facets *building blocks, framework, basic layer/standard components,* and *mechanisms software.*

Also, the node 'software for the development process' is structured similarly as in fig. 1.40 where we have classified application systems which are developed using an SDE. As there, we distinguish the facets *reuse tools, configuration tools,* and *generator tools.*

Let us close the discussion of this subsection by regarding the structure of the last node 'realization strategy'. It is split into four facets. Of course, we do use SDE context software and SDE process software, if such software is available. *Tools* for *subareas/working areas* can be realized quite differently (from completely handcrafted, handcrafted on top of a basic layer, handcrafted and hooked into a framework, selection of building blocks within a framework, to generated and then hung into). *Representation realization, integration tools'* realization for coupling different technical environments, or *integration* realization within an integrated *administration* environment, as well as for an *integrated overall* environment (coupling technical and administration level) can each be realized in the same ways as 'tools for subareas/working areas'.

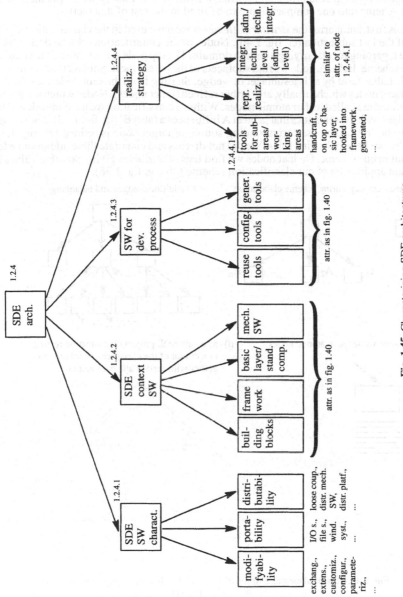

Fig. 1.45. Characterizing SDE architectures

1.7.2 Classification Scheme Structure Summary

In this *subsection* (1) we summarize the classification structure we have used for building up the classification scheme in the last subsection. Furthermore, we (2) make some remarks corresponding to the results of this classification discussion. Finally, we (3) put the classification scheme into one compact figure to be used in the rest of this section.

Let us first summarize the *structural elements* we have used in the classification discussion of the last subsection (cf. fig. 1.46). Nodes of the classification scheme define facets we are regarding for classifying a certain domain. The top node is the representative for the whole scheme. Below a node we find subfacets of the parent facet. Subfacets are connected to their father facet by a 'is a subfacet of'–edge. Starting from the root node we introduce child facet nodes which, usually, are further refined (inner nodes). Nodes which are not further refined are called leaf or atomic nodes. Within a classification we have introduced further edges with the semantics that 'a facet A influences a facet B' (cf. fig. 1.35). Those edges have to be 'refined' if the corresponding source or target node is refined (cf. fig. 1.36). Thereby, we have balancing rules. We did not discuss and elaborate these additional edges in detail in our scheme. On leaf nodes we find lists of attributes giving possible values for a certain application of our classification scheme (cf. e.g. fig. 1.38).

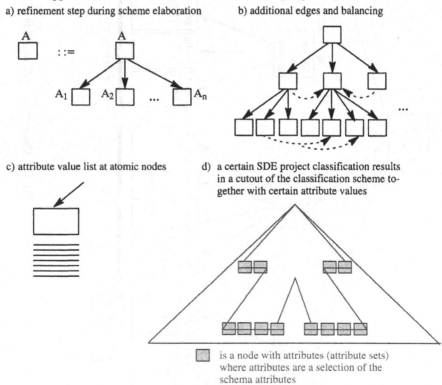

a) refinement step during scheme elaboration
b) additional edges and balancing
c) attribute value list at atomic nodes
d) a certain SDE project classification results in a cutout of the classification scheme together with certain attribute values

is a node with attributes (attribute sets) where attributes are a selection of the schema attributes

Fig. 1.46. Structural elements of the classification scheme and applying the scheme to a certain project

One can use *further elements* for structuring classification schemes: Possibilities are to use common subschemes, to make use of the specialization relation, or some ordering relations on one level of a refinement in addition to the 'is subfacet of'–relation or the local 'influences'–relation we have discussed (cf. /4. Bör 94/).

Any *SDE project* can be *classified* according to this scheme (cf. fig. 1.46.d). In this case we regard the complete classification structure and select suitable attribute values or value lists at the leaf nodes. In a certain SDE project a subtree of the classification scheme may have no values. This may be the case if the SDE project did not regard the facets of this subtree, or no values are known from literature about a specific SDE project. In this case we may regard the overall scheme having only relevant values in certain parts and a certain attribute "not known" on other nodes. Alternatively, we may cut out those parts of the classification scheme having no meaningful values. In both cases we end up with a graph structure being the complete scheme or a simplified version of the scheme having concrete attributes at leaf nodes selected from the attribute lists of the schema leaf nodes. Typical SDE projects (as e.g. language–centered SDE projects) lead to typical classification patterns as we shall see below.

Furthermore, we shall see that the *classification scheme* is *interpreted differently* for the different classes of SDE projects we found at the beginning of the last subsection. Thus, we do not need different classification schemes, we only need a careful use of one globally valid scheme.

Looking at our classification *scheme* of the last subsection (see also fig. 1.48) we see that it is rather *unbalanced*. Whereas the facet 'SDE product characteristics' has been refined three levels down, the facet 'SDE project parameters' has only one further level. The reason is that we do not know very much about how an SDE project should be carried out or has been carried out, neither from experience nor from literature. So, the imbalance of a scheme corresponds to the state of the art of how SDE projects have been carried out and to which results they have delivered. In the future, such parts of the scheme may be more elaborate and, therefore, be richer in structure.

We have refined our classification scheme to the level where specifics of *different* SDE *projects* are expressed by *different attribute values*. This means that the classification scheme need not be changed or repaired if is to be applied to a specific kind of SDE project or product. We have standard or widely used discrete life cycle models today as RE, design, implementation etc. If such a fixed model would have been introduced in our scheme (RE, design and the corresponding transitions being subfacets of the facet life cycle model) then the scheme would have to be changed if, for example, a continuous approach is to be classified. Thus, we did not introduce specific inner nodes thereby getting the differences only at leaf nodes.

Looking at the instrumentarium of structural elements we have *used* for classification and the application domain, SDE projects, we see that classification means building up a complex (classification scheme) structure. For this modelling task we have used an approach which is quite similar to the *AST graph approach* sketched in section 1.5. We use trees for expressing structure with additional edges for dependency relations (the latter not elaborated in detail here). This shows that ideas, concepts, rules, procedures for modelling in one area can be applied to other areas. This is a further confirmation of the term '*universal*' we have used for our internal modelling approach.

Looking at figs. 1.35 and 1.40 (upper part) we detect some similarities. In fig. 1.35 the SDE project is characterized, in fig. 1.40 the SW project for which the SDE is to be used. Unifying and extending these figures, we could roughly characterize any software project as to be seen from fig. 1.47, distinguishing the facets 'context', 'product', 'process', and 'project'. Only the 'context' node is refined, the other nodes could have been refined as well. *Applying this* unified *scheme* to *SDE projects*, for the 'context' we introduce the software development models to be used in the application project. The 'for what' is here the application project(s) in which the SDE is to be applied, 'what available' corresponds to the tools, basic or standard components, framework etc. which are given for the SW project, and 'platform' means the hardware platform. For characterizing the 'product', 'process', and 'project' we have to regard the SDE software parts not given and to be developed, the corresponding 'process', and 'project'. As the 'for what' node of fig. 1.47 is again a software project, the scheme of fig. 1.47 could be applied again for this inner node (to a certain degree this was done in our discussion).

The situation is even more complex for a *meta–SDE* as the 'for what' is then an SDE which, in turn, is to be applied for a certain application system. So, the scheme of fig. 1.47 would have to be applied three times in a nested way. The scheme of fig. 1.47 could also be applied to a usual *application system project*. Then, the 'for what'–node corresponds to a characterization of the places (locations, organizations, software etc.) where this application system is used. 'What available' then corresponds to the context software of the application system, and so on. So, the scheme of fig. 1.47 can be applied in different ways. However, one has to be careful how to apply it (meta–SDEs, SDEs, application systems).

Instead of using the unified scheme of fig. 1.47 in detail and at different locations in our overall classification scheme we have *some deviations* and *simplifications*: (1) On the top level we have only a poor structure for SDE project characterization. (2) Process characterization appears within the facet 'SDE architecture' of the 'SDE product' characterization. The reason is that in most cases no process characterization is available. If it is available then only on the level of products supporting the process (i.e. developing an SDE by using generator tools or a meta–SDE). This intertwining with the product side of the SDEs lead us to discuss process characterization within the SDE product characterization. (3) A similar argument holds true for the available software which in the SDE classification of this section is found within the product characterization. (4) Conversely, in the application software project characterization of fig. 1.40 we miss the project characterization. The reason is that no SDE today gives substantial support for different project forms.

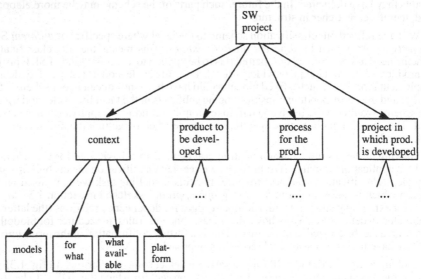

Fig. 1.47. A rough uniform classification for SW projects to be applied for SDEs, meta–SDEs, application software etc.

In order to facilitate the further discussion of classifying typical SDE projects and relating IPSEN to the classification scheme we give an *inline–version* of all figs. 1.35 to 1.45 in fig. 1.48. This summary is drawn slightly differently. Stepping down is now represented as going to the right, going from left to right in figs. 1.35 to 1.45 is now represented by going from top to bottom. Furthermore, without any semantics but only enforced by layout, the leaf nodes are drawn on two "layout levels" in order to get the figure on two pages.

1.7.3 Variety of SDEs and Typical SDE Approaches

In this *subsection* we (1) take up the first SDE classification of section 1.2 and discuss it in terms of the classification scheme of this section. Then, we give (2) a list of typical classes of SDE projects and characterize these classes in the realm of our classification scheme. Thereby, we (3) refer to well–known SDE projects from literature as representatives of these classes.

Let us now discuss how the results of the first classification of SDEs, introduced in subsections 1.2.2 and 1.2.3, are expressed in terms of the classification scheme of fig. 1.48. We go through the characterizations introduced there and give the corresponding attribute combinations according to our scheme. The discussion is on an informal level, i.e. we rather make remarks than giving attribute value assignments for the leaf nodes of (a corresponding cutout of) fig. 1.48.

(a) *discrete/continuous* SDEs: (1) Node 'fixing SD models' and corresponding subtree: In the discrete case we have different working areas and, usually, different languages (multilingual SDEs). Furthermore, we have corresponding integration models. In the continuous case there is only one submodel, the corresponding language being a broadband language. (2) Node 'SDE product characteristics' and subtree: Correspondingly, on the 'SDE support', on the 'UI character of SDE', and on the 'SDE internal models/mechanisms' side in the case of discrete SDEs we have to support different working areas, integration of them by corresponding tools, and we have to regard suitable models/mechanisms etc.

(b) *monoparadigmatic/multiparadigmatic* SDEs: The paradigm(s) the SDE is supporting do(es) not explicitly appear in our scheme. In principal, a monoparadigmatic SDE can be discrete (different working areas, different languages following the same paradigm) or continuous. In the same way, a multiparadigmatic SDE can be discrete or continuous (one broadband language incorporating different paradigms). In practice, monoparadigmatic SDEs are usually continuous and multiparadigmatic SDEs are usually discrete. Thus, we can take the discussion of (a).

(c) *mono view/multiple view* SDEs or *mono representation/multiple representation* SDEs: mono view/multiple view SDEs mostly correspond to the node 'UI characterization of SDEs'. In principal, we can have the mono or multiple view property for any kind of SDE. In practice, we find multiple view SDEs if different languages for one working area appear (graphic view for overviews, text view for details), or in discrete SDEs if documents of different working areas are viewed simultaneously. The same arguments hold true for mono representation (text) or multiple representation SDEs (text, tabular, graphical representation). So, the discussion is again as above.

(d) *complete/partial information* SDEs: In complete information SDEs all information of an application software project is stored in the supporting SDE. Strictly speaking, no existing SDE has this property. In partial information SDE, a certain portion of the information is either not stored at all and has to be handled manually by developers, or it is stored and used by certain tools but not available for further tools (e.g. in a–posteriori environments). Both aspects correspond to the facet 'SDE support' and, especially, to 'area coverage', 'integration', and 'granularity'.

(e) *short term/long term project* SDEs: In long term projects, different states of the development (revisions) of documents/subconfigurations/configurations have to be handled. Therefore, long term projects are directed towards system families rather than certain systems. Therefore, the distinction between short or long term SDEs is wether the SDE supports appropriate version and configuration handling concepts. This is a question of the corresponding models for project organization on coarse and consistency handling on fine–grained level expressed by 'fixing SDE models', of the corresponding tools and UI support on the 'SDE support' side, of the corresponding models/mechanisms on the 'SDE internal models/mechanisms' side, as well as of basic mechanisms for supporting

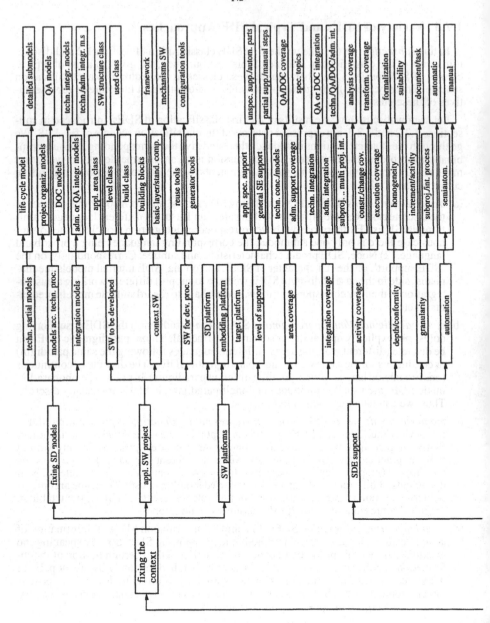

Fig. 1.48. Summary of SDE project classification scheme

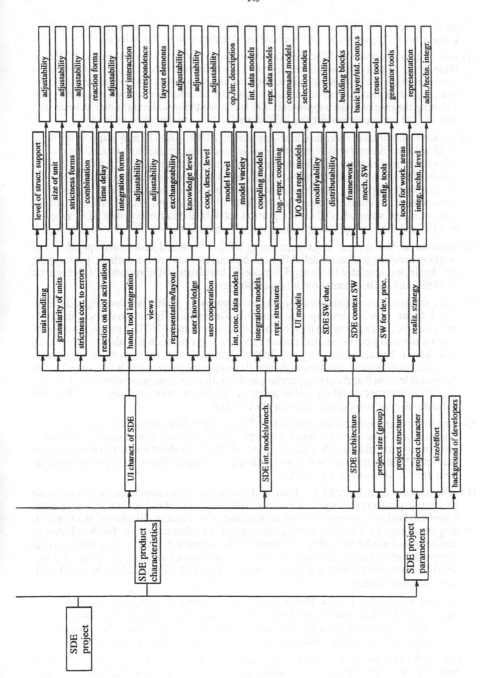

such concepts. No SDE at the moment exploits the possibilities for project families, namely reuse, organization and application domain specific knowledge.

(f) *mono-* or *multi-project* SDEs: If different projects are carried out within one SDE then there is only a quantitative difference to (e). If the different projects have something in common, these common subprojects, their results, and their project organization have to be separated. On the other hand, the results of these subprojects play a role in the project using the results of the subprojects, i.e. subproject/project integration has to be supported. The consequences for the SDE classification are the same as in (e).

(g) *technical* and/or *administration task*–supporting SDEs: An SDE may support the technical tasks in a narrow sense (requirements engineering, architecture modelling etc.) or in a wide sense (together with documentation, quality assurance etc.), or it may, in addition or alone, support administration tasks as product, process administration etc. An environment supporting administration aspects alone will rather be called a "software management environment" than an SDE. This all is a question of the availability of the corresponding submodels, their integration models, the corresponding SDE support, and UI, and the corresponding realization within an SDE (see also discussion of (d)).

(h) *standard* and/or *special tasks*–supporting SDEs: Standard tasks correspond to our working area/integration model of fig. 1.2. Special tasks are reuse, metrics, prototyping etc. Again, this is related to 'fixing SD models', but also to 'SDE support', 'UI character of SDE', and 'SDE internal models/mechanisms'.

(i) *static* or *dynamic configurations/processes–supporting* SDEs: We have argued in section 1.4 that software development demands dynamic configurations/processes (only two examples were discussed there). So, in the case of "static" SDEs, the necessary support on the technical or administration side is not given, such that the corresponding tasks have to be carried out manually. In the "dynamic" case, the corresponding models for configuration/process changes during development process execution time have to be available as well as the corresponding tools. At the moment, no available SDE is "dynamic" with respect to all aspects of software development (see section 5.1). The same subtrees of our classification scheme are touched.

(j) *compiler*– or *interpreter–oriented* SDEs: This is dependent on the languages to be supported. Some languages demand for interpretation, possibly after a small compilation step. In any case, this is only a minor aspect of SDEs. Aside of the fact that interpreters can better be integrated with other tools this aspect is a question of 'SDE product characterization', namely of its realization.

(k) *centralized* or *distributed* SDEs: If we understand centralized/decentralized w.r.t. to the realization platform this aspect is directly reflected by our classification scheme ('basic layer/standard components'). If we understand centralized or distributed w.r.t. who is responsible for the administration (a manager as centralized model or the developers as decentralized model) then this is a question of an administration environment and the integration of technical environments (see (g)), and the availability of a parameterization of the administration component within the overall SDE (model, support, UI character, internal models).

(l) *a priori* or *a posteriori* SDEs: This is mainly a realization ('SDE internal models/mechanisms', 'SDE architecture') aspect. However, the fact that in a posteriori SDEs existing tools are to be integrated has on one side some impact on the facet 'SDE support', and 'UI character' (especially uniformity of the UI can hardly be guaranteed).

In the following we go through *typical projects* of SDEs in literature (our own work is referenced in the next subsection). We shall see that the corresponding SDEs are *representatives* of *classes* of *SDE projects*. The SDEs as well as the corresponding classes are represented by typical scheme/attribute patterns in the sense of fig. 1.47. We distinguish between eight classes of SDEs which are sketched now. Of course, we also find SDEs in literature which belong to more than one class. The discussion again is on an informal level following the same scheme which is made explicit in the first example.

(a) *platform approaches*: Examples are PCTE /6. BMT 88, 6. ECM 90/, CAIS /6. DoD 88/, or the Software Bus /6. ESF 90/. They offer services for structuring persistent data, for defining process interaction, possibly also services for user interface definition. Facet 'SDE project params': They are developed by people in research and development labs of industry with software engineering background, in medium–size projects, and mostly at one place. Facet 'fixing the context': The application domain is systems software, as platforms are basic layers of SDEs or, more general, interactive and distributed software systems. The layer on top of which platforms are built are operating systems, file systems etc. The models are internal models, e.g. of software development environments, which have to be mapped onto the platform resources. The hardware platform is a heterogeneous net, the specifics of which are hidden by the platform. Facet 'SDE product characteristics': The facets 'SDE support' or 'UI characteristics' are interesting only inasmuch as the platform has to be the appropriate base on top of which software systems with suitable properties can be realized. 'Internal models/mechanisms' are that of database systems and operating systems. From the architecture side especially portability is interesting. These systems are usually built manually.

(b) *administration approaches*: These systems again have been developed by developers with software engineering background in industrial or university labs. They support up to now only certain organizational aspects on administration and technical level, as configuration or revision control /4. LC 84, 4. Tic 82, 85/, or process control /6. KO 92/, today with built–in and fixed models. The type of software for which they are used has no importance. As only a tiny portion of the software engineering problems is involved (cf. fig. 1.2), the support and the UI characteristics are restricted to these subareas. The level of support is not very elaborated, as e.g. in configuration/revision control, these systems do not know what languages have been used, what type of software is developed, what specific properties regarded configurations have. Also, these systems are not integrated, they are either useful for configuration/revision or for process control. UI was not a topic regarded too much. The internal models are such that revision, configuration etc. models can be mapped onto. From the architecture side very little can be reported as integrated SDEs were not the focus of development.

(c) *workbench approaches:* The best known representative is Unix PWB /4. DHM 78, 2. KR 84/. It contains different services and, therefore, can hardly be characterized (platform services (see (a)), administration services (see (b)), application specific services as scanner or parser generators, and a programming environment for C). The aim is simple combinability, usability of tools for arbitrary applications, and availability on various platforms. The facets 'fixing the context', 'SDE support', and 'UI character' give few characterizations as the world of ideas is that of plain C programming, files for storage, pipes for coupling, and files/pipes for integration and coupling. Extensions go in direction of more general platform, administration, or UI services.

(d) *language–specific approaches*: They have been developed in industrial R & D or in university labs. Typical representatives are the Interlisp and Smalltalk environment /2. TM 84, 2. Gol 84/ as interpreter–oriented environments, or Ada environments as compiler–oriented environments /4. AD 86/. They are monolingual environments. The SD models are only that of the underlying programming language, the platform is in the case of Smalltalk/Interlisp a single workstation, or in the case of Ada a general purpose machine (from PC to mainframe). 'SDE support' and 'UI characteristics' are also that of programming mostly with one textual view. Remarkable is the tight integration of tools especially in the interpreter–oriented environments. The internal mechanisms/models are sometimes that of the language to be supported. Architectures are seldom made explicit. The Smalltalk realization is impressive inasmuch as it is very extensively using the concepts of the language to be supported.

(e) *method–oriented approaches:* In this class we find most of the SDEs on the market and in daily practical use. They are mainly used for business applications, but also for real-time applications. Representatives are Excelerator, ProMod, Teamwork (in /1. Bal 85, 1. Sch 89/) to name only three of the huge amount of available systems. They usually offer support for requirements engineering (as SA/ER, SADT), architectural design (SD, OOD), as well as tools for generating program templates for one or more programming languages. They are today available on LANs as hardware platforms. The support and UI features are restricted to the supported working areas and to the corresponding transitions between these working areas. Tools are editor, analyzer, execution, and transformation tools. The environments are partially structure–oriented (see (f)) with more than one view in requirements engineering and design. The trend is in direction of taking a general platform (see (a)). Realizations are portable and have been elaborated manually.

(f) *structure–oriented approaches:* This class of SDEs mainly comes from universities. Typical representatives are Gandalf /2. NES 85/, Mentor /2. DHK 84/, and many others. These SDEs are mostly monolingual, some are multilingual. Structure–oriented means that the SDE knows the structure of documents/of underlying languages and uses the inside knowledge (context free and/or context sensitive syntax, dynamic semantics). In the case of multilingual approaches, the fine–grained relations between documents in different languages have to be managed, too. These SDEs are not application specific, the hardware platform is a single workstation, now being extended to an LAN of workstations. For a certain working area we find editor, analyzer, transformer, and executor tools which are closely coupled. Grains are increments of arbitrary size of the underlying language(s), i.e. they are fine–grained approaches. They are mostly command–driven SDEs and tools give an immediate reaction. Internal models are attributed trees or attributed graphs. They usually are based on a self–developed platform and follow the a priori approach. In many of these projects, earlier or later, the steps to mechanize SDE development by a meta–SDE was made (see (h)), such that SDE and meta–SDE can hardly be separated. (We come back to this point in the next subsection, where we have to distinguish between the IPSEN SDE having been realized by using the IPSEN meta–SDE and the IPSEN meta–SDE which could be used also for various other SDEs.)

(g) *theory–based approaches:* Representatives of this class exclusively come from academia or from research labs in industry. They are dominated by one central idea of a software development paradigm (e.g. transformation approach /2. Bau 85, 87/, knowledge–based programming /2. RW 90/, algebraic specification /2. DKP 89/, operational specification /7. Bjo 87/. The character of the SDEs is determined by the background of the developer(s), e.g. formal denotational/axiomatic semantics, abstract data types, specification languages etc. Therefore, the facet 'fixing SD models' is determined by this dominating underlying paradigm. Applications of the resulting SDE are on one side more theoretical, or they are focussed (as specification of ... in the context ...). The facet 'SDE support' is concentrating on this one paradigm/the language incorporating this paradigm. Corresponding to the facet 'UI character of SDE' the representatives of this class are very different as some of them have been developed far away from a software engineering context such that quality of UI support was not in the focus of investigation. In some of these representatives the internal models/mechanisms are that of the supported language. Architecture considerations were in many cases out of the scope of developers.

(h) *meta–SDE approaches:* These approaches completely come from academia. Typical representatives are CPS /2. TR 81/, PSG /2. BS 86/, and Mentor /2. DHK 84/. As mentioned above, we clearly have to separate the case of building an SDE with the help of a meta–SDE, which is not discussed in this paragraph, from the case of developing a meta–SDE. Correspondingly, we have to interpret the scheme of fig. 1.48. If, for example, we regard the facet 'fixing SD models', this facet has one single focus: Not models for general software development are of interest here but only suitable models for developing SDEs, e.g. models for a specialized application domain (systems software) and structure class (intelligent dialog systems on highly complex topics). Technical models are usually restricted up to now to describe internal effects of tool activations on internal data structures of the SDE, structuring these complex data structures, and their mutual relations by a suitable language. The aim of a meta–SDE is to be used to develop and generate various SDEs. Therefore, the models must be complex and broad enough. 'Context software' is the underlying platform. The development of software which supports the development of SDEs (a specification environment, generators) is part of the meta–SDE and, therefore, not context software. The same is true for generally usable components for uniformly structuring internal documents, document–to–document relations, transformation tools etc. Furthermore, for the remaining specific parts mechanization tools (in the best case automatic generators) have to be offered. Meta–SDE projects were never only meta–SDE projects but also projects for getting specific SDEs. The internal models/mechanisms, e.g. architecture models, are usually identical for the meta–SDE and for the SDE mechanically generated with the help of a meta–SDE. Therefore, they usually use the same architecture framework, and within this architecture framework, the same platform.

1.7.4 Classifying IPSEN According to the Scheme

In this *subsection* we shall discuss (1) the different facets of the IPSEN project. In the foreword of this volume we already mentioned that *IPSEN* is not one project but a *bunch* of *projects*. Now, we can make the point and (2) distinguish the various subprojects of the IPSEN endeavor which, however, were not clearly separated but built up as an integrated whole. We shall detect six types of SDE projects within IPSEN. The following explanation (3) goes through the classification scheme of fig. 1.48 and assigns values for any of these six subprojects.

When *applying* the classification *scheme* to the different SDE project types (SDE, meta–SDE, specification environment for a meta–SDE, see below) one has to be very *careful*, as the scheme applies differently. For example, the 'application SW project' of fig. 1.48 in these three cases is of a quite different kind (developing a SW system using an SDE, developing an SDE using a meta–SDE, building a meta–SDE where the specification is to be used as input).

If we speak of *prototypes* in the following explanation, we do not mean rapid prototyping for SDEs. Prototypes are large and rather stable systems (see next section) which have remarkably short reaction times. They are called prototypes to distinguish them from industrial product SDEs, and/or from SDEs which can be applied for large application system development. Our aim was not to get systems for industrial use but demonstrating new behavior, or functionality on one side, and showing that the new realization approach can be applied to get practical systems on the other.

(a) *IPSEN '85, '86, and '88 prototypes* (manually developed integrated SDEs /5. Eng 86, 4. Schä 86, 2. ES 89, 4. Lew 88c/):

These prototypes are integrated SDEs supporting the working areas programming in the large, programming in the small, documentation and access and responsibility control of project organization. The PiL language is self–developed /7. LN 85, 4. Lew 88c/, the PiS language is Modula–2, the documentation "language" consists of the usual structural elements for books (chapter, subchapter, ..., subparagraphs), access and responsibility control are expressed by two tables. Integration is one increment to one increment and automatic between architecture components and module bodies, m:n between architecture and documentation, and there is a role–oriented m:n access model (however, only one person can develop a document at a certain time) between the responsibility/access document and the corresponding technical documents. The facet 'fixing SD models' is described by the above remarks. No assumptions were made about the 'application SW project' or its 'SW platform'. The 'SDE support' was that of general software engineering where only half of the software engineering working areas (see fig. 1.2) was covered. Nevertheless, IPSEN '86/'88 was a multilingual SDE, giving all tools for the scenario chosen, including all integration aspects, and giving homogeneous, semiautomatic support fully harmonized with the chosen languages.

Corresponding to 'UI characterization' all properties are built–in and, therefore, not adjustable. We find structural support for context–free and context–sensitive syntax and dynamic semantics, the latter only for the PiS environment. The size of units can be arbitrarily chosen by the user from given increments of the underlying language. The prototype is strict corresponding to errors. Tool activations can only be started by the user and give immediate reaction. Integration form is batch–oriented between PiL and PiS environment (the reader may remember that the PiS environment was not really integrated but more a stand–alone prototype within the IPSEN '86 or '88 prototype), and alternatively automatic or user–defined (in both cases incremental) between PiL and DOC. It is also incremental between the rudimentary PO tools and the rest of the environment. Views are 1:1 for the DOC environment, 3:1 for the PiL environment, and 2:1 for the PiS environment. For integration tools, views of the source and target document are shown. Representation elements are graphical and textual. No exchangeability is possible other than by reimplementation. Knowledge levels of users are regarded only inasmuch as commands can be put in in menu selection (for novice) and textual form (for experienced users). Cooperation between different users is only coordinated via access to documents.

Corresponding to 'SDE internal models/mechanisms', attributed graphs are used, the operations are described by graph rewriting rules and transactions in a paper and pencil mode by the developers. Integration models in the '86 and '88 prototype are only increment–to–increment links, where links are denoted as attribute values on source and on target side. No coupling of operations on different documents is available on model level, this coupling is hardwired in programs. Internally, logical documents are separated from representation. Representation data structures are not persistent and always built up by an unparser, the coupling again is hardwired. Commands are always specific according to the object type and the location of the object, I/O data representation is always within a text window on top of the representation document, selection models are possible for all modes of subsection 1.7.1 (explicit selection of a new object, implicit change in complex commands, explicit and implicit change of commands).

Corresponding to the classification facet 'SDE architecture', modifiability was regarded on the conceptual architecture level of the SDE but not supported by any tool. Portability was strictly obeyed. As the prototypes are on single machines, nothing can be claimed on distributability. The platform was not available when implementing the above prototypes, they have been developed during prototype development. As we have an own platform paragraph, we shift the explanation to this paragraph (see (c)). Prototypes were built manually and from scratch (specification was only on the level of careful studies beforehand, only experience of IPSEN '86 was used for IPSEN '88). Therefore, nothing can be reported on software for the development process, or tools for building tools for working areas, representation, or integration.

Corresponding to 'SDE project params' the figures are as follows: It was a 10 person group including students which developed the prototypes at one place in a university context. The implementation effort is given in the next section. The background of the group is SE, programming languages, compilers, and graph grammars.

(b) *IPSEN '90 to '95* (developing integrated SDEs by using a meta–SDE): We can proceed faster in our explanation as between the '8X and '9X prototypes there exist some similarities.

As already discussed in subsection 1.3.1, the scenario of the above prototype mostly concentrates on RE and PiL both with submodels (in RE for different perspectives, in PiL for hierarchy to express the development of separate subsystems), and documentation. PiS is again a separate environment. Project organization models are revision and

configuration control and, again, responsibility and access control. As project organization is a topic of its own, we refer for IPSEN '95 to (f). Integration models have explicitly
been regarded for technical submodels (within RE; between RE–PiL; RE/PiL–DOC;
PiL–PiS). As above, the prototypes give general software engineering support. Thus,
we can neither characterize the application software project nor its platform. No support
is given for development if the application software runs on another target platform.

Regarding 'SDE support', the level is general software engineering support but for
nearly all working areas and their integration. Within the regarded scenario the prototype is rather complete w.r.t. activities supported by tools. Integration mainly concentrates on fine–grained integration between technical documents, documentation documents, and administration documents. Subprojects or multiple projects are not supported at the moment. Depth/conformity is as above. Granularity is again fine–grained
in complete technical configurations (according to the scenario). The support is again
mostly semiautomatic.

'UI characterization' is rather similar as above. Strictness with respect to errors is no
longer enforced. Instead, all errors and their consequences are administrated in the SDE.
Again, multiple views for documents and for integration are offered. Representation
documents can be arbitrary nestings of text and graphics. The rest is as above.

Corresponding to 'SDE internal models/mechanisms', for operations or structure description we have learned to declaratively describe big parts of this description. For integration models, integration documents containing increment–to–increment links
have been regarded. Coupling of operations is still on the level of hardwired programs.
However, we have begun to specify integration tools. Representation documents are
now persistent and modelled in the same way as logical documents, unparsers now are
incremental. The rest is as above.

The attributes of 'SDE architecture' have also changed. Modifiability is now, in addition to architecture considerations (product reuse), supported by the generator machinery (process reuse). Portability is as above, distributability is supported inasmuch as the
'94 prototype is based on a distributed platform and cooperation mechanisms software
is available. Context software is the extended framework, the extended platform, and
some mechanisms software. Furthermore, the administration software which was developed in the SUKITS project can also be regarded to be context software (see (f)). Further building blocks are basic components for internal documents, for integration tools
etc. Development process software are generator tools. The realization strategy, as already discussed, is using basic components, frameworks, and a platform, generating the
specific software, and developing the rest manually. The machinery is well–developed
for logical internal documents and representation documents. Corresponding to integration for technical environments we are on the level of having basic components available, generators for integration tools are in development. In the case of the integration
of administration and technical working areas, where we also only have hardwired solutions.

'SDE project params' are the same as with the IPSEN '86 and '88 prototype. Clearly,
the implementation effort was bigger (for figures see next section).

(c) *Platform project(s):* Starting with the first prototype development, the platform proj-
ect(s) was/were carried out in parallel. The platform was improved over the time. We
only describe its latest form. The platform consists of a nonstandard database system
GRAS together with extensions, the biggest component (cf. section 4.2), but furthermore of UI handling components, and in more recent times of components in order to
distribute the internal data over a net of clients and server(s) together with mechanisms
software for cooperation. This platform can also be used in other projects. So, it is not
necessarily restricted to applications within SDEs.

Regarding our classification scheme of fig. 1.48 we have to interpret it appropriately.
'SD models' are now models of the environment in which platforms are used. So, models are internal ones used in systems programming such as, in our case, data structuring
models for internal documents for working areas, or integration between working areas.

The application software is any software project built on top of the platform. So we cannot say very much besides that such systems are distributed systems which have complex internal data structures and which are implemented on top of a platform for a net of workstations.

Even less can be reported on 'SDE support' or 'UI characterization'. All the facets given there apply to SDEs and their behavior to a user. The platform has to offer only corresponding services such that an SDE behavior, e.g. fine granularity, can be appropriately realized using the services of the platform.

Corresponding to 'SDE internal models/mechanisms' the platform offers services for structuring internal logical, representation, administration, and integration documents in the form of attributed graphs. Diverse mechanisms of the upper layers of GRAS (event, schema, change, and distribution management, see section 4.2) serve for handling the internal overall configuration. UI models specific to IPSEN prototypes are not made explicit but offered by an encapsulated I/O system (see fig. 1.28). So, whenever changing the UI model, the handcrafted realization of this component has to be exchanged.

For the facet 'SDE architecture' also only some of the facets are interesting. Portability and distributability are mostly guaranteed by the platform realization, modifiability is not in the center of concern as on one hand the whole platform is reused which, of course, should be extensible for further services. 'Context software' besides primitive operating/file/window systems services have not been available at the beginning of the platform project(s). In the same way 'process software' was not available such that platform(s) had to be realized manually.

(d) *Meta–SDE project* and *framework project:* A framework, usually on top of the platform, is a project on its own, as a framework consisting of all reusable components for an SDE of a certain style can also be used if no generators are available. In many cases, and also in our case, some of the framework components are only understandable as invariant components of the mechanization machinery. This is why we have put both projects into one portion of this subsection.

Again, as in the last paragraph, if we regard the facet 'fixing SD models', we have to especially regard those models by which we can specify how the resulting SDE is to behave. So, again, we have the system developer level (external and internal overall configurations and the corresponding mapping) which we regard for the model facet. Of course, this level has to be suitable on one side to specify the behavior of a variety of SDEs, and on the other side to map the specification onto the services of an underlying platform. Corresponding to this topic, the model of attributed graphs which we use in the meta–SDE is general enough and can easily be mapped, as the platform services are adjusted to that model. At the time being, the models are only on the data side for document types, however including the operations. Specification on technical configuration level for integration tools has started (so, we do not regard the items to be integrated to belong to one big graph). Also, layout or UI behavior specification is not available it is encoded in the corresponding framework components. The next facet, 'application software project', is now the application of the resulting meta–SDE for getting a certain SDE. The 'software to be developed' is only the rest we cannot generate, the context software for the special SDE is, as in other meta–SDE projects, the product part of the meta–SDE itself (framework, basic layer, basic components for logical documents etc.). The software for the development process are the generator tools of the meta–SDE.

The 'SDE support' facet now describes the meta–SDE functionality. It is an application specific support which is not complete w.r.t. coverage (see above). Quality assurance is only involved inasmuch as the specification of a certain SDE is checked at specification time and can be interpreted (see (e)), DOC and administration support are not given (neither for the meta–SDE (described here), nor for the SDE project (see (a), (b)) but for an application project using an IPSEN SDE instance; of course, the DOC and PO environment could be used here if they were not prototypes but industrial systems).

The interpretative execution together with a framework is a rapid prototype. So, prototyping is supported. Tool activities are nearly complete w.r.t. building single technical environments. 'Transformation' is transformation into efficient code by generator tools. Integration aspects are – besides the trivial possibility to regard integration within one big graph – is only partially supported at the moment. Depth/conformity and the corresponding subfacets are strongly supported, if we restrict our evaluation to those parts which are supported by the meta–SDE now. The same holds true for granularity. Automation support is semi–automatic: The specification of an SDE behavior has to be built up manually by support of the PROGRES environment (see (e)), the transformation into efficient code is not complete as certain parts of the resulting SDE have to be programmed manually.

The 'UI character' of the meta–SDE is mainly that of the specification environment, which shall be discussed separately (see (e)) or that of a conventional programming environment for those parts which remain for handcrafting. The 'SDE internal models/ mechanisms' are the same as that for the IPSEN prototype which was realized mechanically using the meta–SDE. The same holds true for the 'SDE architecture' facet. Partially, mechanization of realization is also applied for implementing the meta–SDEs (for details see chapter 3 and 4).

Summing up, the meta–SDE consists of a specification environment and transformation tools for getting efficient code. The meta–SDE is bilingual, PROGRES as specification language and Modula–2 as implementation language for a resulting SDE. There are many similarities between the realization of the meta–SDE and an SDE resulting from a spec by the transformation tools of the meta–SDE.

(e) *Specific SDEs:* As the example to be discussed we take the PROGRES environment which is of value also outside of the meta–SDE context, i.e. as a modelling environment for any kind of complex items which can be suitably modelled by attributed graphs. The environment is a language–centered one for a language which is theoretical on a solid base (/5. Schü 91a/ and section 3.2). We shall sketch further specific environments in chapter 5 and 6, also being built or having been built "along the ideas" of IPSEN.

The model of the PROGRES environment is the world of attributed graphs with description of their structure and changes, whereby as much as possible is described declaratively. As stated above, at the moment models for separation and integration are under investigation. 'Application software' of PROGRES is modelling, e.g. within the meta–SDE to describe the behavior of internal data structures. 'Context software' are pregiven specification sections. 'Software for the development process' is not available, specs have to be built up/maintained manually. (However, some PROGRES spec portions are generated from syntax description of the language to be supported. Furthermore, the reader should note that code generation from PROGRES specs is regarded in the meta–SDE project, see (d).) The platform is described in (c), the framework in (d), as the PROGRES environment shares both with other IPSEN SDE project types. No support is given at the moment to built up complete specs by groups rather than single persons.

'SDE support', 'UI character of SDE' is excellent, provided one accepts the limitation to the language given up to now. DOC or PO support is not necessary, it would be if PROGRES were used for big group efforts. The corresponding attributes are analogous to the IPSEN characterization, as UI handling is the same for the IPSEN '94 and the PROGRES environment.

'SDE internal models/mechanisms' are the same as supported by the PROGRES environment, besides of integration models which are internally hardwired (e.g. between logical and representation structures). UI models are again hardwired within a reusable component which encapsulates the special style of UI interaction.

'SDE architecture' characteristics is the same as for IPSEN generated by meta–SDE as the PROGRES environment underwent the same way of mechanized production. 'SDE project params' are also the same as for the IPSEN '95 prototype. Even the realization effort is comparable.

(f) *Integrated administration component:* This is a project still in development. Most parts of this integrated administration environment have been implemented by now. Details, therefore, shall be given in chapters 3 and 5. All above SDE projects are a priori SDE projects. The same holds true for the integrated administration SDE project. The results of this project, namely the administration component, can, however, also be used for a posteriori integration (see below).

In the case of this administration SDE, we restrict ourselves to administration models (product model, process model, resources model, actual context model etc.) as only this part of the overall problem space is of interest here. Constructive quality assurance is built–in (e.g. analyses, for proving if certain administration conditions hold true, guaranteed by the tools), precautions for quality assurance on technical level (reviews, tests) can be made by the manager using administration tools. Quality assurance on administration level (by reviewing the actions of a manager) or documentation of project organization (e.g. documenting management decisions) could be provided which, however, was not done. Integration models are that of delegating management functionality, extracting management data from technical data, or installing a working context for a developer (see subsection 1.6.4). 'Application SW project' is arbitrary cooperative development, it is to be applied, if we regard software development and not arbitrary development.

'SDE support' is as above, if we take into consideration that only a narrow spectrum of the overall scenario is regarded. Also, 'UI characterization', is as above as the integrated administration environment is built with the same UI ideas. The same is true for 'SDE internal models/mechanisms' and 'SDE architecture'. Also, 'SDE project params' is analogous, the effort is in the order of the above projects for a first version.

An integrated administration environment can be applied to an arbitrary (software) development project, thereby being an isolated environment to support project organization. The more likely case is that it is to be a component of an integrated overall environment integrating different technical environments. In the latter case, the technical environments are either available (a posteriori approach) or have to be developed (a priori approach). For the integration of the administration component to technical environments some provisions have been made which, however, belong to platform of framework projects. The administration component has to be hooked into the overall environment framework (see subsection 1.6.4 and section 4.7) by interfacing extended technical environments with the administration configuration.

The *prototype developments* of the past were not specific SDE projects belonging to one of the six classes explained above. Instead they were a *mixture* of such *projects*. IPSEN '85 and '86 projects were SDE projects for building an integrated SDE manually. In parallel, a first platform was developed. IPSEN '90 to '95 was not only an integrated SDE project realized by making use of a meta–SDE. Again, the platform was improved at the same time. In the same way, the meta–SDE was developed in parallel. Furthermore, the first components of an integrated administration environment have been developed. Finally, not within this project but in parallel, the PROGRES environment took shape (more details in the next section). So, in contrast to the above description, the different kinds of SDE projects within IPSEN were not clearly separated. Instead, we have not even been aware which projects of the above different types we performed in parallel.

All IPSEN–subprojects belong to the category of *a priori SDEs*, as all of the above projects have been developed mainly from the scratch using, of course, existing software when available. In top–down approaches we gain *tight integration,* as a newly developed tool/environment/integrated environment can be built such that tight integration is possible. This tight integration is a "trademark" of IPSEN, as outlined in section 1.4 of this chapter.

The results of some of the above projects, namely parts of the platform or the complete integrated administration environment, can also be used for bottom–up integration of existing technical environments. This administration environment was investigated and developed in the context of building up a heterogeneous integration framework for a posteriori integration in computer–integrated manufacturing (CIM). It can, of course, also be used in the context of integrated SDEs (see chapters 2–5). It should be stated again that in *a posteriori* approaches tight *integration* between existing environments is only *possible* to a *certain degree*, as the corresponding fine–grained data are owned by the technical environments to be integrated and are usually not accessible from outside.

Here, we could continue discussing open problems and *future research* direction which, at least partially, can be *derived from* the classification *scheme* of this section /1. Nag 93/. As these further directions are also further directions for the IPSEN–project, we postpone it to the next section and to chapters 5 and 6.

1.8 History, State, and Future Work

The *aim* of this *section* is (1) to sketch how the IPSEN–project evolved corresponding to the three key topics, namely tight integration, graph technology, and architectural investigations. Furthermore, we (2) discuss which prototypes have been built over the time. For that, we give a detailed list of available tools, size and effort parameters, and we explain how these prototypes are related to each other. Finally, we (3) indicate which main topics of future investigation we see arising from the classification scheme of subsection 1.7. This discussion is not restricted to IPSEN but holds true for SDEs in general. Our ongoing work and future plans for IPSEN are described in chapters 5 and 6.

1.8.1 History of the IPSEN Project

The *origin* of the project is *graph grammar* theory, a discipline which started at the end of the sixties /8. PR 69, 8. Schn 70/ the aim of which was to generalize string grammars for more complex than one–dimensional structures (array grammars, picture description structures, map grammars, tree grammars etc.; for an extended bibliography see /5. Nag 79, 5. ENR 83/). Since then, a lot of results on graph grammars were found. The international workshops on graph grammars give a good survey how this discipline evolved over the time (/5. CER 79, 5. EER 96, 5. EKR 91, 5. ENR 83, 5. ENR 87, 5. SE 94/). There are different branches of graph grammars depending on the underlying formalism as the set theoretic, the algebraic, or the logic approach, which altogether are represented in the Workshop proceedings, cited above.

Graph grammar theory originated from *applications* as grammatical picture analysis, picture description, programming tools etc. and theory conversely was applied to different new application areas (see again the above cited proceedings). In the Erlangen group, different variants of graph grammars and different applications have been studied, namely programming tools /8. Schn 75, 8. BBN 77, 8. Bre 77/, database applications /8. Web 78/, definition of programming languages /8. Göt 77/. The corresponding graph grammar theory of the editor and the above applications of the Erlangen group up to '78 are collected in /5. Nag 79/. Later on, applications in compiler optimization, automatic parallelization /8. Nag 81b/, modularization of program systems /8. Gal 83/, and growth description of plants /8. Nag 76/ were added.

In the mid of the 70ies, the *first experiences* in direction of *implementation* of *graph grammars* were also made. The implementation was in the sense of trying to execute graph grammar examples and not in the more ambitious direction of using graph grammar specification and implementation for implementing integrated tools, which is the topic of this book. Some simple sequential and parallel graph grammars have been implemented /8. Bre 76, 8. BNW 78, 8. Nag 76/. At 1977/'78 also the very first experiences with the graph storage /6. GN 81/ yielding three different implementation variants, namely B–trees /8. Wei 80/, hashing /8. Gal 78/, and associative access by microprogramming /8. Kar 80/ were made. They were derived from a data storage for CAD /8. EW 74/. Furthermore, also the very first investigations on graph layout /8. NZ 79/ took place. Finally, a first proposal of a programming language incorporating graph rewriting was given /8. Nag 80b/.

The next step was to use graph grammars for a bigger example. The application which was selected to be studied in detail was a collection of tools for programming in the small (editor, incremental compiler /8. Bre 77/, and executor). These tools should be tightly integrated, working on one logical document. An integrated programming in the small *environment* was *proposed* /8. Nag 80a/. There were a lot of ideas of combining the compiler and interpreter world around at that time /8. AHK 79, 8. BG 73, 8. EC 72, 8. Kah 79, 8. Kat 69, 8. Ris 70, 8. Schm 72/. Very much later we learned about the Smalltalk projects /2. Gol 84, 2. GR 83/ the aim of which also was to build an integrated programming environment. The proposal in /8. Nag 80a/ was new w.r.t. the idea that these tools should be *based* on *graphs* and be formally specified by graph grammars.

155

Practical work in direction of a programming environment /4. Nag 85a/ really started 1982 at Osnabrück university. There, detailed graph grammar specification investigations for the programming in the small environment were carried out /5. EGN 83, 5. ELS 87, 5. ES 85b, 5. NEG 83/. The architecture of the environment was designed /4. ES 85b/, as well as its input/output and user interface component /6. Schä 85/. At this time the graph storage was rebuilt using dynamic hashing as implementation technique /6. Bra 84, 6. BL 85/. Implementation of tools was mechanically but manually derived from specifications.

The result was a tightly integrated *programming in the small* environment ('84, '85), consisting of a syntax–directed Modula–2 editor, some analysis tools, some instrumentation tools, and an execution tool using incremental compilation /4. ES 87/. The resulting prototype, we call it *IPSEN 1.0,* was finished at about 1984, ran on an IBM AT, and showed tight integration /4. EJS 88/ of all these tools on one logical internal document, namely the module graph. The functionality is described in section 2.1. The prototype was the practical result of two dissertations /5. Eng 86, 4. Schä 86, 2. ES 89/.

The next step was directed to demonstrate tight *integration* for *different working areas*, i.e. different internal logical documents. The working areas to be integrated were programming in the large /5. LN 84, 4. LN 85/, programming in the small, technical documentation, and some aspects of project management, namely responsibility and access control /4. JL 88/. Integration tool functionality was hardwired. The result was another prototype, called *IPSEN 2.0* ('86), showing these features and running again on an IBM AT. It was the practical outcome of a dissertation /4. Lew 88a–c/. At this time we also collected the first results comparing different realizations, namely for the overall architecture /4. ELN 86/, for the structure of different structure–oriented editors /4. ENS 86/, and on different integration mechanisms we had used so far /4. LNW 88/.

In the meantime the group 1986 moved to Aachen. There, more appropriate hardware was at hand. A net of SUN workstations was further on used as underlying development basis. For that new platform, the IPSEN 2.0 prototype had to be ported. Doing so, a lot of restructuring on architecture and implementation level was made. Especially, the graph storage was made more efficient and more stable /6. LS 87, 6. LS 88/. The self–made window system was replaced by X Windows. The whole group was engaged in this endeavor. Basically, the ported prototype *united* the *functionalities* of IPSEN 1.0 and 2.0, i.e. it was an integrated programming in the large, programming in the small, technical documentation, and responsibility/access control environment (integration between PiL and PiS was to be in one program, not in the sense of tight coupling). We call this prototype which was available in spring '88 *IPSEN 2.5* as it contained no new features on tool level.

At about the same time the meta–SDE/IPSEN single environment framework project started. Its first version, related to a textual interface of IPSEN instances, was finished about '90–'91, which we call *Meta–SDE 1.0*. Also, the the first steps were made in order to replace handcoding of logical documents by generation, resulting in an editor generator. The underlying graph storage was extended to incorporate basic features /6. Wes 89, 92/ for integration between different working areas (intergraph edges), for change control (undo, redo, delta mechanisms for revision control), and for event handling (triggers). This meta–SDE was extended over the time by many reusable components. Especially, in 1993 the meta–SDE was extended to produce graphical IPSEN instances. Finally, reusable components for building integration tools were added. The meta–SDE/framework in its current form is called IPSEN *Meta–SDE 2.0*. Its functionality is summarized in the next subsection and described in detail in chapters 3 and 4. The underlying GRAS storage was again a topic of special interest /6. KSW 92, 93, 95a, b/.

In parallel with meta–SDE construction on the tool side new activities started. A first RE prototype /7. DHB 89/ and the RE–PiL integration tool /7. JL 90, 4. BJ 92, 7. BJ 91/ was built /7. Jan 92/. Also, around '91, a new IPSEN prototype integrating PiL, PiS, DOC plus tools for revision control and consistency control (problem–oriented merging of contents of revisions) was implemented /4. Wes 89, 91a, b, 92/. Both prototypes we call *IPSEN 3.0*.

They have been built using the meta–SDE 1.0 thereby generating their editor parts. Only a few parts of IPSEN 3.0 are described in this book.

Using the meta–SDE 2.0, new or improved tool functionality was realized. The RE environment for building up, maintaining, and evaluating a requirements specification consisting of different view and corresponding integration tools was realized, incorporating graphical and textual views /4. Lef 93a, b/. In the same way, executing an RE spec for simulation and rapid prototyping purposes was realized /4. Koh 93a, b, 96/, especially regarding exchangeability of languages, methods, and simulation strategies. The semantics of hierarchical control models was put on a formal basis /7. Bee 93a–c, 94a, b, 95/. The RE–PiL integration tools were newly developed /4. Lef 95/. Integration tools realization started in direction of specification /5. Lef 94, 5. NS 96, 5. Schü 94d/ for later generation. Furthermore, the PiL environment, now incorporating new concepts as genericity, subsystems, object–orientation, and allowing for separate development of designers, was also rebuilt on the 2.0 platform /4. Bör 91, 7. Bör 94/. It incorporates a reuse environment for storing and retrieving components /4. Bör 93, 94, 95/. This functionality, together with a DOC environment, corresponding integration tools for RE, RE–PiL, and RE, PiL, DOC integration together with the administration system to be described separately, was called *IPSEN 4.0*.

Starting from quite another problem domain, namely a posteriori integration of existing CIM components, the SUKITS project /6. EMN 92/ started. Our contribution was the development of an administration system /6. KSW 92/ to integrate CIM–components on management level by realizing the *administration component* and extensions of existing environments to connect both. Thereby, we detected some interesting problem of dynamics /6. NW 94/ some of which have been solved /6. Wes 95a, b, 6. JHK 96/. This approach is also applicable to SDEs thereby yielding integrated and distributed *overall environments*. A first version of this administration component was finished in '93, a second in '96.

Starting with the development of IPSEN 2.5, an environment for building, maintaining, executing, and evaluating *gra gra specs* has been developed, named *PROGRES–environment* /4. NS 91, 5. Schü 91e/. Special effort was put in the development and improvement of the language PROGRES /5. Schü 88, 89, 91b/ and its formal foundation /5. Schü 91a, 94a, b, 5. ZS 92/. Textual editor/analysis tools were finished in '90, graphical tools in '93, execution of gra gra specs in '94 /5. Zün 96a/. The system /5. Schü 94e, 5. SWZ 95c/ and its use for rapid prototyping /5. Schü 94c, 5. SWZ 95a/ are described in this book. For prototyping or for getting efficient environment versions to be put into the IPSEN framework, code generators for Modula–2 and C do exist, which are described in section 4.4.

This *book describes* the outside functionality of most of IPSEN 4.0 tools including the administration environment and some tools of the IPSEN version 2.5 in chapter 2. Furthermore, the outside functionality of the PROGRES environment is described in chapter 3. The available 2.0 meta–SDE is discussed in chapter 4.

The different *relations* between IPSEN *prototypes*, we have introduced so far, are given in fig. 1.49. Neither all versions are given there nor the corresponding relations. The figure nicely shows that IPSEN is not one project and prototype but a complex of projects/prototypes.

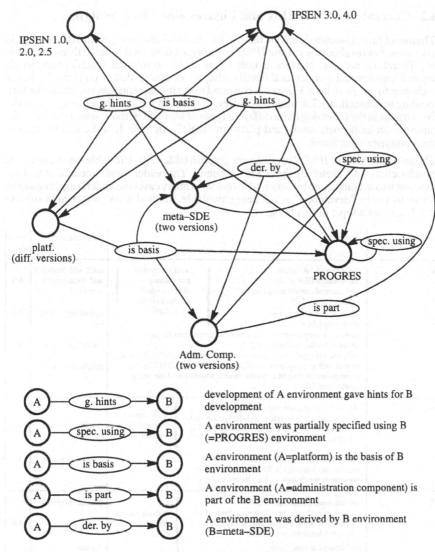

Fig. 1.49. Dependency relations between different IPSEN prototypes and projects

158

1.8.2 Current State of IPSEN and Figures about its Prototypes

The *aim* of this subsection is on one hand to list the *available tools*, and on the other hand to give some *figures* about the current *IPSEN* prototypes described in detail throughout this book. Therefore, no user interface details (chapter 2), no internal specification details (chapter 3), no internal architectural details (chapter 4), and no details on related projects (see chapter 6) are given here. Figures correspond to the implementation volume and effort. According to subsection 1.7.4 where the different facets of the IPSEN project(s) were described we list in the following quite different types of tools (SDE tools, specification tools, administration tools, meta–tools, and platform "tools"). In table 1.14 the main demos of these prototypes were listed.

The *available tools* of *IPSEN* versions are given in table 1.50. This table is to be matched with subsection 1.3.1 sketching the IPSEN scenario. The reader should recall that tool development was accompanied by "method" work as in many cases the underlying languages/methods had to be "developed" as not being available. Method work, sketched in subsection 1.3.2, is not a topic of this book.

Purpose	Tool		Representation	Vers. No.
RE	str.–oriented SA–editor str.–oriented EER–editor str.–oriented control model editor (altogether see 2.2)	with interactive consistency checker which can be switched on and off	each with graphical and textual representation	4.0
	str.–oriented requirements dictionary editor		textual representation	4.0
	horizontal integration tool for different perspectives (consistency checker, binder, browser, see 2.2)		textual/graphical	4.0
	executor for requirement specs for initial (without CSPECs) execution as well as complete execution (with PSPECs, CSPECs), estimation/monitoring of a system model, simulation of the target system (see 2.2)		graphical/textual	4.0
RE ↔ PiL	RE → PiL (transformator, binder, browser): incremental and interactive transformation tool regarding consistency between already existing requirements and design specifications (see 2.3)	with interactive consistency checker	graphical/textual	4.0
	PiL → RE (consistency checker, browser): incremental warnings in RE–documents, if PiL documents are changed which have bindings		graphical/textual	4.0
PiL	str.–oriented architecture editor: for graphical overview diagrams, for textual detailed component (module, subsystem or system) descriptions (see 2.3)	with interactive consistency checker	graphical/textual	4.0
	on–demand analysis tools		textual	
PiL → PiS	incremental and automatic transformation tool generating module frames watching consistency between already existing design specs and module frames written in C++ or Eiffel. Module frames are fixed in PiS, but can be changed in PiL.		textual	4.0
	Furthermore incremental and automatic transformation tool for module text frames in Modula–2.		textual	3.0

PiS	str.–oriented editor for Eiffel and C++ with interactive context–sensitive syntax checker	textual	4.0
	on–demand analysis tools	textual	
	furthermore (see 2.1):		
	str.–oriented editor for a subset of Modula–2 with interactive context–sensitive syntax checker	textual	1.0, 2.5
	on–demand analysis for data and control flow	textual	1.0, 2.5
	tool for inserting conditional and unconditional breakpoints		
	execution tool (incremental compiler) with stepwise or continuous execution showing or hiding the runtime stack	textual	1.0, 2.5
DOC	str.–oriented for writing documentations with or without paraphrasing (see 2.3)	textual	4.0
RE, PiL, PiS → DOC	incremental integration tool either working with an automatic transformation generating a documentation frame, or freely building up documentation. In the first case the links to portions of RE, PiL, PiS documents are generated by the transformation tool, in the second case they are put in by the documentator in a hypertext–like mode (see 2.3)	textual	4.0 (also 2.5 for PiL, PiS, DOC)
general tools and tools for consistency control (for PO tools see table 1.53)	general syntax–oriented editor commands	textual/graphical	
	editor for free input	textual	
	cut, copy, paste	textual	
	file I/O	textual	3.0, 4.0
	layout tools	textual/graphical	
	general undo/redo		
	drawing a revision/melting revisions	textual	
	help and user interface parameterization		

(middle column brace: see 2.4)

Table 1.50. Available SD tools in the IPSEN prototype 4.0 (and earlier prototypes)

Besides these tools for software engineering (IPSEN instances) the *PROGRES* prototype offers *tools* to facilitate handling of graph grammar specs written in the language PROGRES. They are summarized in the upper part of table 1.51. Furthermore, some internal tools for the developer of an IPSEN–like SDE, to support the efficient realization of tools starting with a PROGRES spec are given. These *code generators* are listed in the lower part of table 1.51.

Purpose	Tool	Representation
building, maintaining, and evaluating a Gra Gra Spec (see 3.6)	structure–oriented editor	mixed graphical/textual
	text editor plus parser	textual
	graph schema editor	graphical
	incremental type checker (checks scheme consistency plus rewrite rule schema consistencies)	textual
	PROGRES → Framemaker (textprocessing system) translator generating document interchange format (mif)	textual/graphical
	interpreter/debugger for executing specs	mixed textual/graphical
	host graph viewer with selectable views	graphical
Code generators (see 3.6, 4.4)	PROGRES → Modula–2 code generator for generating specific parts for logical documents of IPSEN tools	
	PROGRES → C + tk/tcl generator for stand–alone prototypes including graphical user interfaces	
	PROGRES → C++ class libraries for implementing abstract data types (under development)	

Table 1.51. PROGRES tools and tools for translating PROGRES specs

Finally, there are a lot of internal tools and components which play a role either as components being a part of any IPSEN–like SDE instance, offering necessary mechanisms, or offering means to get necessary components. These *meta–SDE tools* and *components* are summarized in table 1.52. They consist of platform components and meta–tools. As the derivation machinery includes the support of a gra gra specifier and also of code generation from gra gras all tools of table 1.51 could also be regarded as meta–SDE tools.

Purpose	Tool	Representation

meta–SDE tools	EBNF editor with layout annotations for textual/graphical representations
	generator with annotated EBNF input for generating
	   structure–oriented editors
	   lex/yacc–based parsers } see 4.4
	   incremental unparsers
	EBNF → PROGRES transformation tool (see 4.4)
	PROGRES environment (see table 1.51)
	PROGRES → Modula–2/C generators (see table 1.51)
		textual

framework and its components	generic IPSEN/SDE framework containing
	   tool and user interface coupling
	   generic textual/graphical layout tools
	   document session manager
	   Interviews–based user interface manager
	   GRAS (graph–oriented data base system)
	generic component library for a single environment } see chapter 4
	   persistent representation documents
	   persistent logical documents (AST etc.)
	   incremental type checking tools
	   execution tool framework
	   persistent integration documents
	   integration tool framework	

Table 1.52. Meta–SDE tools used within or components to get an IPSEN–like instance

Finally, the *administration* (project organization) tools are given in table 1.53. There, also the tools for parameterizing an administration configuration (schema definition) are listed. Finally, the extensions (tools, components) for technical environments are listed such that administration functionality is available at technical environments and, conversely, data relevant for administration are delivered back.

Purpose	Component/Code	Representation

project organization	structured–oriented management tools (see 2.5):
	– products (revisions and configurations)
	   editor with incremental, context–sensitive analysis (not
	   tolerating inconsistencies) and many complex commands,
	   e.g. for a complete configuration based on schema information
	   static analysis tool for analyzing the status of configurations,
	   e.g. completeness with respect to the schema
	– processes (process nets)
	   product–centered process management tools (configurations
	   are simultaneously used as process nets) for executing process
	   nets, supporting intertwining of editing and execution, as well as
	   concurrent engineering
	– resources (project team)
	   editor for inserting team members and defining their roles
	– assignment tools
	   assignment of team members to processes, association between
	   processes and input/output documents etc.
		textual/graphical

structuring an administration configuration	schema editor for adapting generic management tools to a chosen scenario by defining document types, configuration types etc., support of consistency–preserving schema modifications	textual/graphical

extending technical environments	– extension for connecting technical environments to the administration configuration: display of agendas and work contexts for processes assigned to developers, commands for starting, suspending, resuming, and terminating development processes, commands for activating technical environments, internal (RPC–based) components for integration between extensions (front ends) and administration configuration	window–based

Table. 1.53. Administration tools and tools/components to get an integrated overall environment

Some *figures* about *realization* by end of '95 give an impression about the complexity of IPSEN products: The total IPSEN framework consists of 245 KLOC usable source code, where 125 KLOC are spent for the underlying distributed nonstandard database system GRAS, 75 KLOC for other components (as UI handling, interface to the windows system, graphical objects, I/O of graphs etc.), 25 KLOC for common tool functionality of editors, integrators etc., and 20 KLOC for general, reusable components internally handling documents. Additionally, there are 275 KLOC specific code for the SDE IPSEN instance from which 105 KLOC are handwritten and 170 KLOC are generated. So, for the IPSEN instance, we have 520 KLOC source code only 105 KLOC of which (20%) are specifically handcoded, assumed that the IPSEN–framework is taken. The PROGRES system also contains the above framework, therefore being another IPSEN–like environment instance with additional 245 KLOC specific source code, namely 215 KLOC for the spec environment and 30 KLOC for the generator. So, both systems are rather big for a university group. Our goal was not sheer code production but a machinery for realizing environments with minimum effort.

The *programming languages* used for *realization* are the following: Most of the code is written/generated in Modula–2. Some parts are written in C, C++, and Modula–3. In future, Modula–3 is used as implementation language. GRAS has been ported to Modula–3. Other parts will follow.

The effort in terms of *person years* is *hard* to *specify* because of the following reasons: The biggest contribution thereof (1) came from students elaborating their Master's Theses. They had to learn about SE in general and SDEs, in particular. But also the other members of the group including the editor learned about SDEs and, as far as they are members of the group now, they are still learning. Corresponding to section 1.3 we had to cover all problem areas for an SDE (methods, tool behavior etc.). So, the learning part should be subtracted but cannot. Method work (2) is not SDEs, but a prerequisite. All members (3) had further duties. So, they could only be part–time SDE developers. The effort figures can (4) only be determined a posteriori. Furthermore, (5) not all work was done in the mainstream but also at its borders, following alternative ideas, which have later been overridden, or applying the concepts outside SDEs. Thus, the figures can hardly be compared to those from industry. In order to correct the numbers we calculated conservatively that about half of the time of the members was spent for SDE research and prototype development.

Going through the different *prototypes* the estimated and already *corrected effort numbers* are as follows: The IPSEN 1.0 prototype needed about 10 person years. About 8 person years were spent for the IPSEN 2.0 prototype. About an effort of 6 p. y. we took for the 2.5 prototype, about 14 for the IPSEN 3.0 prototype, and 18 for the IPSEN 4.0 prototype. For the first and the second version of the meta–SDE the effort was approximately 12 p. y. The numbers for the platform (mostly GRAS) over the whole project time is 16 p. y. The PROGRES prototypes including the code generators also needed 16 p. y. Finally, the administration component (the effort of our group only) is something like 10 p. y. So, the overall effort of the IPSEN project(s) sums up to be approximately 110 person years.

1.8.3 Future Directions of IPSEN and SDEs in General

Again, this subsection is short as we have main chapters (5 and 6) devoted to this aspect. However, we *sketch* the *future plans* here for *two reasons*: (1) A survey, and this introductory chapter is a survey, would not be complete without indicating what is still to be done, or will be done next. (2) From the classification schema of 1.7.1 and from the different project types we have introduced in 1.7.3 we can derive what is still missing and what has to be done. This is not only true for IPSEN–like SDEs but for SDEs in general.

Some of the following remarks are directly related to the introduction of *typical representatives* of SDEs sketched in subsection 1.7.3 and suggest further extensions of such SDE types. Others *combine* and *integrate* different types of SDEs given there. It should be stated that the following discussion mirrors the *personal opinion* of the editor of this book.

(1) *future platform approaches*: The aim of the next generation of platforms for SDEs or, more generally, for integrated, distributed, and interactive applications is to offer a net–wide "operating system" layer of general services. Services are needed for data integration, i.e. for the management of complex overall configurations by a distributed object storage which hides all details of a realization (transparency w.r.t. locality, access, distribution, replication etc.). Services are needed for building up a coarse–grained configuration (named administration configuration above) as well as for fine–grained technical configurations and for the relations between both. So, in our terminology arbitrary internal configurations of graph–like documents, fine–grained links between documents, clustering, nesting, and linking of subconfigurations should be possible. Moreover, data exchange services are needed for heterogeneous environments in the a posteriori context. Furthermore, services are necessary for control integration, remote execution, representation and UI integration, for direct communication of human developers (multi–media services), for archiving nonelectronic and electronic documents, net–wide naming conventions (authentication, authorization, auditing) etc. All technical and administration data models, all tool interactions, UI/layout etc. have to be mapped onto these platform services. The internal heterogeneity of the underlying hardware and software has to be hidden as e.g. different computer internal representations, formats of self–defined data types, communication lines and protocols, low–level control mechanisms etc.

(2) *integrated administration* or project management *services*: As already mentioned, the administration models for software products, processes, and projects are mainly independent from software (product, process, resources, actual context model, cf. subsection 1.1.5). They can be offered for arbitrary integrated and distributed projects on complex technical matters and they are added as a major component to an SDE when building a distributed overall environment. A prerequisite for that is the exchangeability of underlying models (e.g. for revisions, configurations) and the configureability of a suitable administration component w.r.t. chosen models. Thereby, integration has to be obeyed in two respects: On one side administration models and tools have to be integrated to one administration model and environment, respectively. Thereby, as to be seen in section 5.1, the structural knowledge how an administration configuration "looks like" must be changeable during a project. On the other side, a more intelligent integration between the administration and the technical level has to be achieved (e.g. the successful review of a subsystem's architecture can yield the determination of tasks/processes for design or implementation, if the corresponding components are identified in the subsystem's design document). We come back to this question in section 5.1, too.

(3) *Completeness*, *Combination*, and *Configureability*: Even if an SDE can be based on a general platform according to (1) and even if we need not care about administration services according to (2) as both are offered by a corresponding general purpose layer or component, we still have a lot of different models for development, maintenance, and reuse (see node 'fixing the context' in fig. 1.48) which can be supported by an SDE (node 'SDE support') with a variety of outside behaviors of the SDE (node 'UI character

of SDE'). All existing SDEs only cover a small part of the possible support. A useful combination which includes support of consistency across different models means integration (see (4)). Configureability in a posteriori approaches requires that the chosen parts fit together. In a posteriori approaches they are made to fit together. In the case of a priori environments the effort to produce a suitable SDE that can smoothly be integrated with others, has to be of a reasonable order of magnitude (see (5)). In a posteriori environments the effort for integration should be small and the resulting level of integration should be high. The aim of future SDEs must be to support all kinds of tasks/processes of users by tools which, at the moment, are carried out by manual consistency procedures as conventions, rules, discipline etc. As already argued in this chapter, only some of these tasks can be automated and, therefore, taken over by a tool.

(4) *Intelligence, Integration, Flexibility*: Existing SDEs are not very enhanced w.r.t. "intelligence". Intelligence means that the collaborative and distributed elaboration or maintenance of complex overall configurations having a complicated internal structure (cf. fig. 1.15) is essentially supported. For that intelligence SDEs have to "know" what the users are doing. Doing so, integrated SDEs have to offer structure–oriented tools which are not devoted to one document but help to manage the huge amount of structure–to–structure relations in an overall configuration stemming from language, method, convention, or organizational determinations. In the future the borders of integration even have to be extended (organization of projects with different subprojects not necessarily following the same models, organization of related projects of system families, development across companies etc.). This should be possible for arbitrary integrated SDEs configured according to (3). The elaboration of this extended kind of overall configurations must be combined with a corresponding flexibility of integrated processes (according to section 1.4) and has to be obey the topic that evolution and backtracking are everyday problems in technical projects, especially if they face a new task.

(5) *Structuring, Mechanization*: The problem fields (3) and (4) can, because of the great variety of models, selection of models, interrelation of models, configuration of corresponding integrated SDEs, different understanding of intelligence, integration, and flexibility, only be solved if we have a more elaborated model of the internal structure of an SDE or, more generally, an integrated and distributed, interactive system. Suggestions like /6. ECM 90, 6. FO 90/ are too coarse–grained and superficial. These internal structure models have to cover standard solutions for fine–grained integration between different documents, for integration of logical documents and subconfigurations with their representations, lines of distribution for an integrated SDE on a homogeneous or heterogeneous platform, and data, control, representation etc. integration within the SDE and their mapping onto the underlying platform services of (1) etc. Thereby, we can find standard solutions and components of another dimension than sketched in (1) and (2) of above. After such an improved understanding of standard solutions, an extended framework, and a corresponding big number of standard and specific components and their place within the framework can be better identified. These specific components, being dependent on the selected models and their relations, have to be mechanically produced by generators after they have formally be defined. Results on existing meta–SDEs for parts of the total problem are impressive and there is no reason to assume that these results cannot be extended and improved.

(6) *Specific Environments*: A new R&D area is to build new specific or specialized SDEs. Surprisingly, there is nearly no literature about this topic. By those environments we do not understand the selection of corresponding models for a certain application domain and the configuration or generation of a corresponding integrated SDE which gives general support for this application domain (see (3), (4), (5) of above). When developing software, as argued in subsection 1.1.6, we may have deep knowledge about applications, structure classes, and project types. For that we can build specialized and specific SDEs, i.e. an environment which is tailored to an application–dependent and specific platform, an architectural framework, generators, and suitable tools for developing the

remainder of software. A meta–SDE as sketched in (5) is such a specialized and specific SDE, namely for building SDEs. Another example is a compiler–compiler environment. There are many possibilities for such SDEs which are of a great value if a company is working for a long time in the same application domain (application class) and building similar software systems (software structure class).

We find a quite different possibility for a specialized and specific SDE if we look outside of software development. It is related to certain specific application languages and methods of an application area. In this case, the result is not an SDE but a *modelling* or *application environment* for a certain application domain (VLSI, a specialized topic in CIM such as gear construction, a house–building environment). Such an environment has nearly the same internal structure as an SDE and there are the same problems occurring during its realization. SDE builders should look into those fields for applying their ideas and for learning the corresponding application problems and solutions, thereby extending their view of an intelligent, interactive system.

1.9 Summary of the Chapter
and Survey of the Book's Structure

The *aim* of this *section* is (1) to summarize the introduction by pointing out the essential ideas, and (2) to discuss the structure of this book. The latter is done by giving a dependency graph containing chapters and sections as nodes and their dependencies as edges.

1.9.1 Summary of Introductory Chapter

This *subsection* does not repeat the contents of chapter 1 and is not a replication of the corresponding introductions. Instead, it summarizes the main ideas and messages. Furthermore, specific terms/notions are summarized which are important for understanding this book.

In section 1 we presented our view on *software engineering*. A working area model was introduced and its internal relations were discussed. A working area contains the subprocesses which are carried out by persons having a specific role. Modelling in a working area or across different working areas is more change than straightforward construction, either in development, maintenance, or reuse processes. Taking the different documents into account, each usually elaborated/changed by one person, the internal structures of documents, and the many fine–grained relations we end up with a complex structure we called an overall configuration. Thereby, we have a very sharp understanding of the "product" of a development process. Whereas the structure of the extended technical configurations varies from application to application (within or outside SE, even for different applications in SE) the structure of the administration configuration is nearly invariant. The information of the administration configuration is used to manage collaborative processes. Processes and their subprocesses (either on technical or on management level) are often vague, creative, evolve within the project, and are not understood. IPSEN concentrates on the process steps which, according to the structure of the underlying "product", can essentially be supported.

The aim of *SDEs* is to reduce costs of processes and to improve the quality of their results (section 1.2). This section was to give a glimpse on the variety of SDEs, depending on paradigms, languages, and approaches and, furthermore, to introduce the problem of integration for SDEs.

Section 1.3 introduced the *problem fields* when *developing* an *SDE*. They are the work packages of a coarse process model for SDEs. These problem fields (method work, tool behavior determination, internal modelling, realization, marketing (in our case only demonstration)), determines the structure of the introduction and the main part of this book.

The highlights of the IPSEN endeavor were sketched in the three main sections of this introductory chapter. It is the *tight integration* (section 1.4) of tools on one document and between different documents by integration tools, which is our view for future software development and maintenance support. This tight integration on the other hand is loose in the sense that different people can work independently on different documents or integration problems building up quite different forms of overall processes. However, this integrated and distributed labour of different people has to be supported by administration tools in order to organize a complex development or maintenance project. How precise and static, or nondetermined and dynamic this overall process is, depends on the available technology.

The second highlight is the specific proceeding we undertook in realizing such SDEs (section 1.5), called *graph technology* above. The internal overall configuration is the inside pendant to an external overall configuration, i.e. the inside data world on top of which tools are built. This internal configuration is a nested complex of internally structured graphs, with many intra and intergraph relations. For a formal specification of the internals of an SDEs, a uniform data model (danel–graphs) for one internal document was assumed and a calculus to define complex operations specifying internal behavior of tools (graph grammars) was defined. Specification is restricted to one logical document in this chapter. This calculus was enclothed in a specification language (PROGRES) which is supported by a coherent set of tools (PROGRES environment). A uniform modelling approach was given in order to write clear specifications for IPSEN–like tools which is using reusable specification portions.

Another main contribution is to clearly handle the *architecture* (section 1.6) of SDEs and their integration. Architectural considerations are handled on single environments (different tools internally working on one logical document), integration tools supporting fine–grained technical processes on the border of different documents and, finally, on the level of coordinating the work of different developers by the so–called administration component. Single environments are integrated to integrated environments, including integration tools and other environments (mono– or multi–role environments), and are extended (primitive administration functionality) to be integrated into an overall environment. The main message of this section is to use frameworks containing all application–unspecific and, therefore, invariant parts of an SDE (product reuse). Specific components are derived from PROGRES specifications, either automatically, or mechanically and manually (process reuse). The state of automation of this process is different for different parts of IPSEN instances. In any case, it is possible and necessary to add handcoded portions.

Section 1.7 introduced a detailed *classification scheme* for *SDEs*, and SDE projects (cf. fig. 1.48). We have used this scheme on one side to get an overview of the different views on and approaches for SDEs. Furthermore, we have applied this scheme to classify typical SDE approaches known from literature. Moreover, we have applied the scheme to IPSEN itself which results in a clear statement of six SDE projects (subsection 1.7.4) and their mutual relations (fig. 1.49 of 1.8.1). Finally, the scheme was used to derive future trends of SDEs in subsection 1.8.3.

The rest of section 1.8 describes how IPSEN *evolved* over the last 15 years, gives a list of available *tools*/components of its different prototypes, and gives some figures about the *size* of the project or its results.

1.9.2 Structure of the Book

The last subsection is devoted to explain the *structure* of this *book*. How else could it be in our approach than to regard this structure as a *graph* (cf. fig. 1.54). The nodes are the chapters and the sections, the relations are dependencies expressing that a chapter/section is needed in order to understand the chapter/section where this edge ends.

For reasons of *readability*, some *simplifications* are made in fig. 1.54: The whole book and its chapters are given (1) as sequences and not as bunches as it should be. Subsections (2) are not given to keep the number of nodes limited. Summary nodes of chapters and corresponding edges are (3) omitted as, introducing them, implies edges usually go to all other sections of a chapter. The bibliography chapter and its sections are also (4) omitted as we would have dependencies from its nodes to all nodes. For the same reason, the conclusion chapter is omitted. Basic universal dependencies are (5) erased, as e.g. from all nodes to node 1.1 or 1.2, being introductions to SE and SDEs, respectively. Only within chapter 1 these relations are given. Transitive closure edges are (6) omitted: If i node depends on k node and that on j node then, evidently, understanding of i node also depends on j node. Furthermore, if a section depends on a preceding chapter, then it also depends on all sections of this chapter. Finally, (7) lots of relations of minor quality are omitted to keep the figure comprehensible.

167

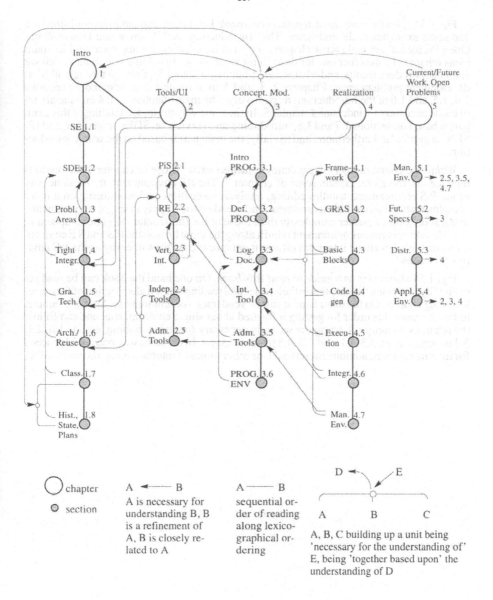

Fig. 1.54. Dependency Graph of this Book (only the most important dependency relations are shown)

Fig. 1.54 gives this *simplified dependency graph*. Let us now explain its overall structure and some examples of dependencies. The 'Introduction' and 'Current and Future Work, Open Problems' are embracing chapters, one for introducing the approach and its main ideas (chapter 1), the other one for describing what we are just doing but about which we cannot report deep results, and what we are planning (chapter 5). Both go through all SDE development problem areas. Chapters 2, 3, and 4 are refining the corresponding sections 1.4, 1.5, and 1.6 of the introduction, respectively. The main chapters 2, 3, 4 en bloc are on one side necessary to understand chapter 5. In the same way the understanding of this main part is based on sections 1.7 and 1.8, introducing an overview on SDEs, in general, and IP-SEN, in particular. Furthermore, and trivially, the main part is based on the whole introduction.

Within the *chapters* many dependency *relations* exist. Those of chapter 1 are obvious now. Let us, therefore, explain some of chapter 2. The RE environment, in the same way as the PiS environment, handles editing, analysis, execution, and monitoring on a more complex matter than the PiS environment. Independent tools apply to single environments. Integration tools of greater complexity than those of RE (horizontal integrators) appear in 2.3. The administration environment is built along the same lines as the PiS and RE environment, on the other side it integrates different perspectives in the same way as the RE environment does.

Fig. 1.54 also serves as a *guide* to *read* this *book*. On one hand the book can be read sequentially following the chapters in their order and reading section after section of the corresponding chapter. On the other hand it can be read trace– or relationwise. So, for example, to find a reasonable order for getting informed about single environments one can follow the relations, thereby collecting the sections necessary for understanding, as 1.1–1.6, 2.1, 3.1 to some extent, 3.3, 4.1, and 4.2–4.5 to some extent. In the same way one could proceed for integration tools, administration tools, or other topics of interest, as e.g. the meta–SDE.

2 The Outside Perspective: Tools, Environments, Their Integration, and User Interface

In *chapter 1* we have introduced which IPSEN *tools* exist, which working areas they belong to, which working areas they integrate, and how administration is done on configuration management and process management level. We have, furthermore, discussed which *external characteristics* the tools share. More particularly, we have made clear what the term 'integrated' in the title of the book means and which facets integration possesses.

The aim of *this chapter* is to *carefully* introduce these *tools in detail*: Which functionality they offer, how they behave in relation to the user, how the user interface is styled, and what characteristics they show. In this explanation we follow an *inductive scheme* by showing tools in an increasing order of complexity. This inductive scheme ranges from tools on one document to tools on different documents and, finally, to tools on administration level. This inductive scheme also roughly reflects the different states and versions in which IPSEN has evolved. The tools discussed here belong to different versions of the IPSEN prototype, most of them to version 4.0. However, only a part of the 4.0 functionality is demonstrated (cf. table 1.50).

In detail, the contents of this chapter are the following: We start in section 2.1 by showing single–user *tools* for one working area, namely Programming in the Small, and their *tight integration*. The next step of section 2.2 is to show how tools integrate different perspectives of one working area expressed by different *languages*. The example is Requirements Engineering where for the functional, information, and for the control model different languages are used. Furthermore, prototyping and simulation are covered by the RE environment. In a further step we show in section 2.3 integration of *different working areas* by taking different examples: We show integration between Requirements Engineering and Programming in the Large, integration between Programming in the Large and Programming in the Small, and integration between Requirements Engineering/architecture modelling/ Programming in the Small, and technical documentation. These three examples will show quite different integrator characteristics in the sense of the integrator classification of chapter 1.

In the above mentioned sections we discuss working area specific tools, and tools for integration of these working areas. In section 2.4 we explain *working area independent* tools of a single environment available on each document and, therefore, being independent of a specific document type. The working area independent functionality of integrator tools is offered by the basic components of the integrator building machinery, discussed in chapter 4.

Up to now we neglected the problem that usually different persons are involved in building up/maintaining a subconfiguration and that for a subconfiguration different versions exist. Therefore, the next section 2.5 is devoted to introduce integration on *project administration* rather than on the level of technical documents or integration between documents. The administration tools work on a *coarse–grained* level keeping track of which revisions and configurations exist and, in the latter case, from which revisions they are built up. Correspondingly, administration also manages which tasks exist, and from which other tasks they are built up. However, there is a *smooth transition* to the tools on fine–grained level as, for example, a revision within a configuration can be handled with the corresponding and specific document class tools.

2.1 Tight Integration on One Document: The Programming Environment

G. Engels, M. Nagl, W. Schäfer, B. Westfechtel

We describe in this chapter the outside functionality and user interface of IPSEN tools, putting a strong emphasis on various aspects of integration. As *starting point*, we have selected the *PiS environment*, to be explained in this section as (1) the language supported by the environment needs no explanation, (2) the functionality is easy to understand, and (3) it nicely shows the IPSEN philosophy of high–level and immediate support of technical work (here programing) without restricting the corresponding process. The PiS environment was already implemented in 1985 as the first prototype within the IPSEN project – IPSEN 1.0 – and was reimplemented in IPSEN 2.5.

2.1.1 Introduction

The PiS environment demonstrates *integration* of different *tools* operating *on* the *same logical document*. Each such document corresponds to a body of a module whose interface is specified in a software architecture. Specification of module interfaces belongs to PiL and is therefore not discussed in this section.

The PiS environment supports *Modula–2* as implementation language. We have to stress that it is an incomplete prototype rather than a full–fledged environment of practical use. Only a subset of Modula–2 is supported which covers most control structures, but is rather limited with respect to data structures. To implement a complete prototype, we would have to apply well–known techniques of compiler construction for all language constructs which was not regarded to be of great scientific value. Rather, we focused on a subset of these constructs to demonstrate the feasibility and main characteristics of our incremental approach to tight tool integration.

In the following, we present a short tour through the PiS environment by showing and explaining snapshots from a *demo session*. The demo illustrates incremental integration of editing, analysis, instrumentation, and execution. A lot of lessons have been learned from IPSEN 2.5. The study of this prototype provides the reader with valuable insights into functionality and user interface of IPSEN environments. All remaining sections of this chapter refer to more recent prototypes, namely IPSEN 3.0 and IPSEN 4.0. Many features of IPSEN 2.5 still apply to them, others have been subject to further improvement. We have refrained from reimplementing the PiS environment once again since this would not have provided us with any new insights.

2.1.2 User Interface, Editing, and Instrumentation

The following sample session illustrates functionality and user interface of the PiS part of IPSEN 2.5 /4. EJS 88, 4. Lew 88b/, a reimplementation of IPSEN 1.0 /4. ES 85b, 4. ES 87, 4. ELN 86, 4. Schä 86, 5. Eng 86/ and IPSEN 2.0. IPSEN 2.5–PiS demonstrates *tight* and *seamless integration* of *different tools* operating on one document. Editing, analysis, instrumentation, and execution commands may be interleaved arbitrarily. The user is not forced through lengthy edit–compile–debug cycles as in compiler–oriented programming systems. Tools provide for immediate response on syntactical and semantical level in order to inform the user about impacts of modifications as soon as possible. Efficient operation is achieved through incremental realization (e.g. only the affected portion of a module is analyzed after an edit command).

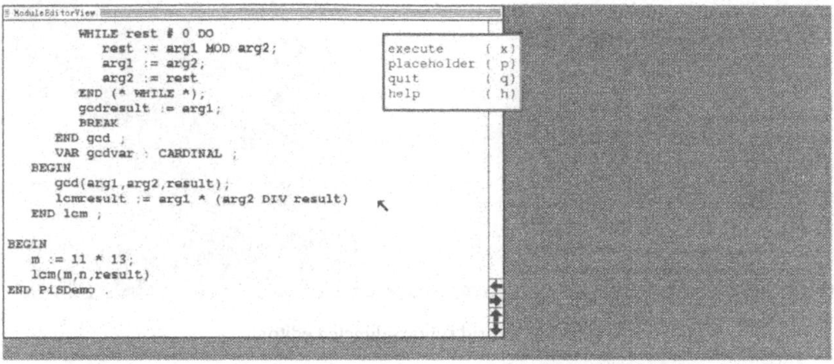

Fig. 2.1. User interface of IPSEN 2.5

The screen dump of fig. 2.1 illustrates the *user interface* of IPSEN 2.5. When this prototype was implemented or reimplemented in 1985/87, no user interface tool kit was available which satisfied our requirements. Therefore, we developed a suitable window system on our own. Of course, the situation is completely different today. Therefore, all prototypes described in the remainder of this chapter provide for an OSF/MOTIF–like user interface whose implementation is based on X Windows. However, many characteristics of IPSEN 2.5 apply to more recent prototypes, as well.

Fig. 2.1 shows different kinds of *windows*. The text window shows a cutout of a small Modula–2 program which will be used throughout the sample session. The program calculates the least common multiple (lcm) of two positive numbers with the help of their greatest common divisor (gcd). The procedure gcd is an inner procedure of the procedure lcm. Only a part of both is displayed in fig. 2.1. The text window is decorated with a title (top bar) and icons for scrolling the text to the left/right/top/bottom (side bar). The small window above the text window contains a menu of commands. Each command refers to the current increment selected in the text window. The current increment is emphasized in bold face (the whole program in fig. 2.1), and it is selected by a mouse click. The contents of the menu window depends on the current increment, i.e. after each selection the set of legal commands is calculated according to the type of the current increment. A command may be activated either by mouse click in the menu window, or by typing in a shortcut which is enclosed in parentheses behind the command name (e.g. x for execute).

Our sample session firstly demonstrates the *editor* which supports both syntax–directed editing and free text input. The advantage of such a *hybrid* approach consists in its flexibility: Syntax–directed editing may be applied by novel users who are not familiar with the underlying language, or it may be used to save typing in case of a verbose concrete syntax. On the other hand, free text input may be preferred by experienced users, or for performing bigger structural changes for which there are no syntax–directed commands.

Our first program modification consists of creating an assignment statement by *syntax–directed editing* (fig. 2.2). We select the assignment m:=11*13, which is the first statement of the main program, as current increment and invoke the command extendassign. Note that the syntax–directed editor only offers commands which do not violate the context–free syntax; e.g. it would not offer a command to create a variable declaration at this point of the program. In response to the command activation, placeholders for the left–hand and right–hand side as well as concrete syntax symbols (:= and ;) are generated, respectively.

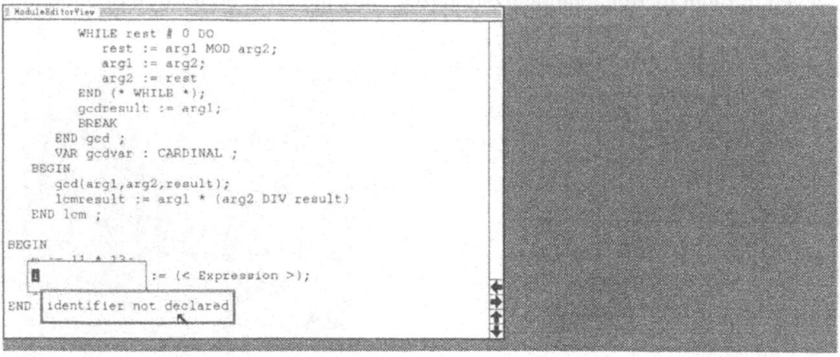

Fig. 2.2. Hybrid syntax–directed editor

Left–hand and right–hand side are treated as *atomic increments* with respect to syntax–directed editing. This means that they are manipulated by free text input in order to avoid syntax–directed editing of variables and expressions. Note, that in IPSEN 2.5 syntax–directed editing ends at this level. In more recent prototypes, any portion of the concrete syntax may be edited either in syntax–directed or in free input mode, i.e. syntax–directed editing ends at the level of lexical units of the underlying language. To use free input on the level of expressions is, however, more friendly to users.

In fig. 2.2, the user has just issued the `extendassign` command and is now editing the left–hand side in *free input mode*. Free input is performed in an input window which initially contains ASCII text of the current increment. During free input, no checks are made with respect to context–free or context–sensitive syntax. The user terminates free input by hitting a function key. Subsequently, context–free and context–sensitive analyses take place. In our example, the user has typed an identifier i which has not been declared before. The user is informed immediately about this error, and free input mode is entered once again. In IPSEN 2.5, free input is accepted only when no context–free or context–sensitive errors are detected; otherwise, all modifications are discarded. In more recent prototypes, we have removed the second restriction, i.e. context–sensitive errors are tolerated temporarily and may be removed later on. Our experience with IPSEN 2.5 has given evidence that exclusion of context–sensitive errors severely restricts the user in his natural way of program construction.

Fig. 2.3 illustrates free input on a complex increment, namely the statement list of the procedure `lcm`. To speed up computation of `lcm`, the original statement list is embedded into an if–statement whose then–part delivers the result in the special case `arg1=1`. In principle, such a *program transformation* could be supported directly by a syntax–directed command (embed current statement list into the else–part of an if–statement). However, this approach would result in a large number of special–purpose commands. The effort of implementing these commands does not seem to be justified as their effects can be achieved conveniently by means of free input and immediate syntax analysis. Note, that the user does not need to care about layout issues during free input. An indented layout is generated by an unparser which transforms the internal document representation into a human–readable text representation (fig. 2.4). In IPSEN 2.5, the user cannot modify the layout of this text representation; more recent prototypes include a layout editor for polishing the output produced by the unparser.

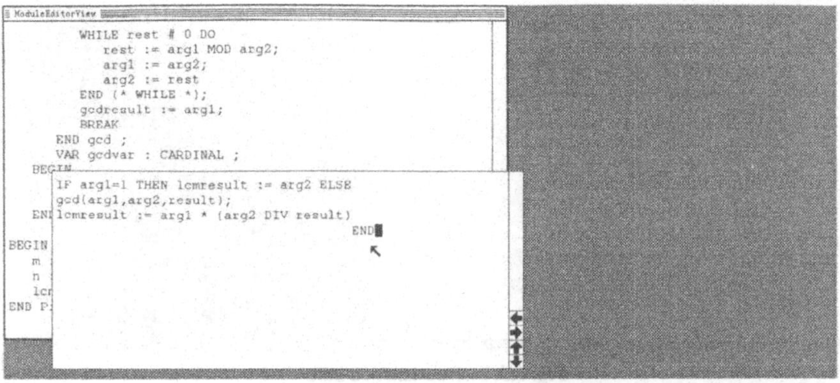

```
ModuleEditorView
          WHILE rest # 0 DO
              rest := arg1 MOD arg2;
              arg1 := arg2;
              arg2 := rest
          END (* WHILE *);
          gcdresult := arg1;
          BREAK
      END gcd ;
      VAR gcdvar : CARDINAL ;
  BEGIN
      IF arg1=1 THEN lcmresult := arg2 ELSE
      gcd(arg1,arg2,result);
  END lcmresult := arg1 * (arg2 DIV result)
                                      END
  BEGIN
      m
      n
      lcm
  END P:
```

Fig. 2.3. Free input mode in editing

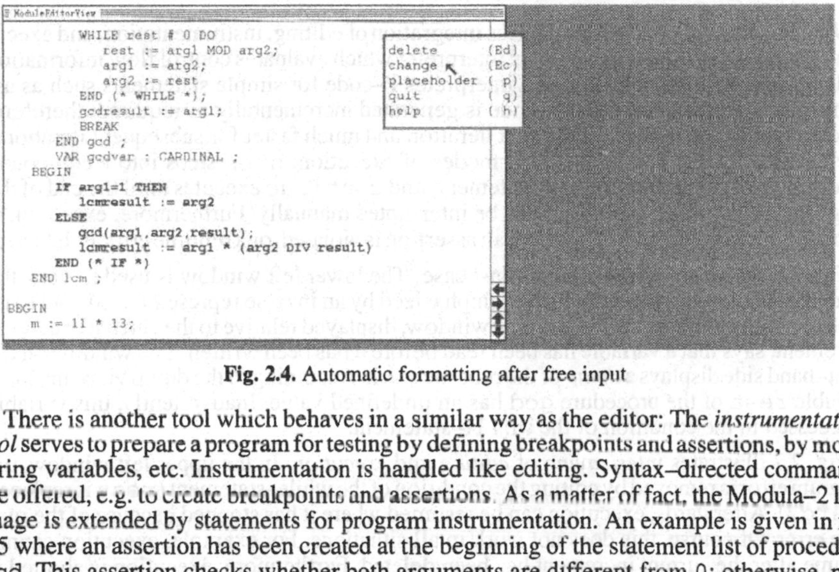

```
ModuleEditorView
          WHILE rest # 0 DO
              rest := arg1 MOD arg2;
              arg1 := arg2;            delete      (Ed)
              arg2 := rest             change      (Ec)
          END (* WHILE *);             placeholder ( p)
          gcdresult := arg1;           quit        ( q)
          BREAK                        help        ( h)
      END gcd ;
      VAR gcdvar : CARDINAL ;
  BEGIN
      IF arg1=1 THEN
          lcmresult := arg2
      ELSE
          gcd(arg1,arg2,result);
          lcmresult := arg1 * (arg2 DIV result)
      END (* IF *)
  END lcm ;

  BEGIN
      m := 11 * 13;
```

Fig. 2.4. Automatic formatting after free input

There is another tool which behaves in a similar way as the editor: The *instrumentation tool* serves to prepare a program for testing by defining breakpoints and assertions, by monitoring variables, etc. Instrumentation is handled like editing. Syntax–directed commands are offered, e.g. to create breakpoints and assertions. As a matter of fact, the Modula–2 language is extended by statements for program instrumentation. An example is given in fig. 2.5 where an assertion has been created at the beginning of the statement list of procedure gcd. This assertion checks whether both arguments are different from 0; otherwise, program execution will stop. The second instrumentation statement BREAK at the end of the statement list denotes an unconditional breakpoint. All instrumentation statements are persistent, i.e. they do not get lost at the end of a session as it is the case with many commercial debugging tools.

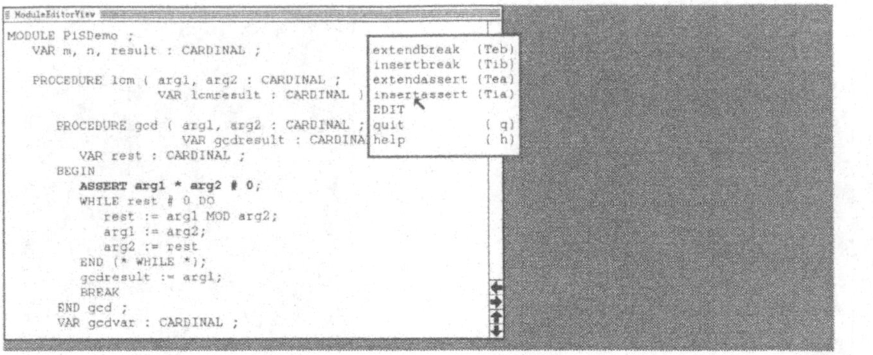

```
 ModuleEditorView
MODULE PiSDemo ;
    VAR m, n, result : CARDINAL ;
                                            extendbreak    (Teb)
                                            insertbreak    (Tib)
    PROCEDURE lcm ( arg1, arg2 : CARDINAL ;  extendassert   (Tea)
                    VAR lcmresult : CARDINAL )  insertassert   (Tia)
                                            EDIT
        PROCEDURE gcd ( arg1, arg2 : CARDINAL ;  quit          ( q)
                        VAR gcdresult : CARDINA  help          ( h)
            VAR rest : CARDINAL ;
        BEGIN
            ASSERT arg1 * arg2 # 0;
            WHILE rest # 0 DO
                rest := arg1 MOD arg2;
                arg1 := arg2;
                arg2 := rest
            END (* WHILE *);
            gcdresult := arg1;
            BREAK
        END gcd ;
        VAR gcdvar : CARDINAL ;
```

Fig. 2.5. Instrumentation input

2.1.3 Execution and Analysis Integrated with Editing

IPSEN 2.5 provides also for seamless integration of editing, instrumentation, and execution. The *execution tool* is a two–level interpreter which evaluates control flow information to determine the next statement and interpretes P–code for simple statements such as assignments and procedure calls. P–code is generated incrementally as required; therefore, execution of a loop is slow for the first iteration and much faster for subsequent iterations. The user may select among different modes of execution: step steps into a compound statement, next executes the next statement, and continue executes until the end of the program. At any time, execution may be interrupted manually. Furthermore, execution is stopped when a breakpoint is reached, an assertion is violated, or a runtime error is detected.

Fig. 2.6 shows an example for the last case. The lower left window is used to view the current *execution increment* (which is emphasized by an inverse representation), and to issue execution commands. The *message* window, displayed relative to the current execution increment, says that a variable has been read before it has been written. The window on the right–hand side displays a *dump* of the runtime stack. According to the dump view, the local variable rest of the procedure gcd has an undefined value. Inadvertently, this variable is accessed in the condition of the while statement.

Fig. 2.7 illustrates *interleaving* of *editing* and *execution*. In the upper left window, the program error is removed by editing the condition of the while–statement (rest is replaced by arg2). Afterwards, execution can be resumed where it has stopped because of the runtime error. Of course, this does not work in all situations. For example, execution cannot resume after the current increment has been deleted. Furthermore, execution is aborted if the formal parameters of a currently executed procedure are modified. On the other hand, interleaving of execution and editing goes far beyond the functionality of conventional edit–compile–debug tools.

To conclude this subsection, let us demonstrate the functionality of the *static analyses tool*. This tool handles the analysis of the context–sensitive syntax. For example, it may be used to determine all *global variables* which are used in a certain procedure. In fig. 2.8, this analysis has been performed for the procedure lcm (current increment in the upper left window). The outcome is displayed in the lower right window. result is a global variable used in procedure lcm.

In fig. 2.9, another analysis has been applied to the same variable result of the whole program (see fig. 2.8), which delivers all *applied occurrences*. Some of them are contained in the procedure lcm. The programmer has used result inadvertently in lcm, where he should have used the local variable gcdvar. Therefore, all occurrences of result in lcm have to be replaced by occurrences of that local variable gcdvar. For that, editing and

ModuleEditorView

```
MODULE PiSDemo ;
  VAR m, n, result : CARDINAL ;

  PROCEDURE lcm ( arg1, arg2 : CARDINAL ;
                  VAR lcmresult : CARDINAL ) ;

    PROCEDURE gcd ( arg1, arg2 : CARDINAL ;
                    VAR gcdresult : CARDINAL ) ;
      VAR rest : CARDINAL ;
    BEGIN
      ASSERT arg1 * arg2 # 0;
      WHILE rest # 0 DO
        rest := arg1 MOD arg2;
        arg1 := arg2;
        arg2 := rest
      END (* WHILE *);
      gcdresult := arg1;
```

DumpView

```
gcd             : < PROCEDURE >

arg1            :   143
arg2            :   221
gcdresult       : < UNDEFINED >
rest            : < UNDEFINED >

lcm             : < PROCEDURE >

arg1            :   143
arg2            :   221
lcmresult       : < UNDEFINED >
gcdvar          : < UNDEFINED >

PiSDemo         : < MODULE >

m               :   143
n               :   221
result          : < UNDEFINED >
```

MInfoView

```
                  VAR lcmresult : CARDINAL ) ;

    PROCEDURE gcd ( arg1, arg2 : CARDINAL ;
                    VAR gcdresult : CARDINAL ) ;
      VAR rest : CARDINAL ;
    BEGIN
      ASSERT arg1 * arg2 # 0;
      WHILE rest # 0 DO
        rest := arg1 MOD arg2;
        arg1 := arg2;
        arg2 := rest
      END (* WHILE *);
      gcdresult := arg1;
      BREAK
    END gcd ;
    VAR gcdvar : CARDINAL ;
  BEGIN
    IF arg1=1 THEN
      lcmresult := arg2
    ELSE
```

ERROR: An applied occurrence of an undefined variable indicates bad programming style.

Fig. 2.6. Execution and analysis

Fig. 2.7. Interleaving editing and execution

analysis are interleaved. Fig. 2.9 shows the situation after the first occurrence of `result` has been replaced. After editing, the analysis does not have to be restarted from scratch; rather, it is resumed seamlessly. Note, that applied occurrences may be retrieved efficiently because the editor, which checks for the context–sensitive correctness, has to establish bindings between declaration and applied occurrences of identifiers anyway.

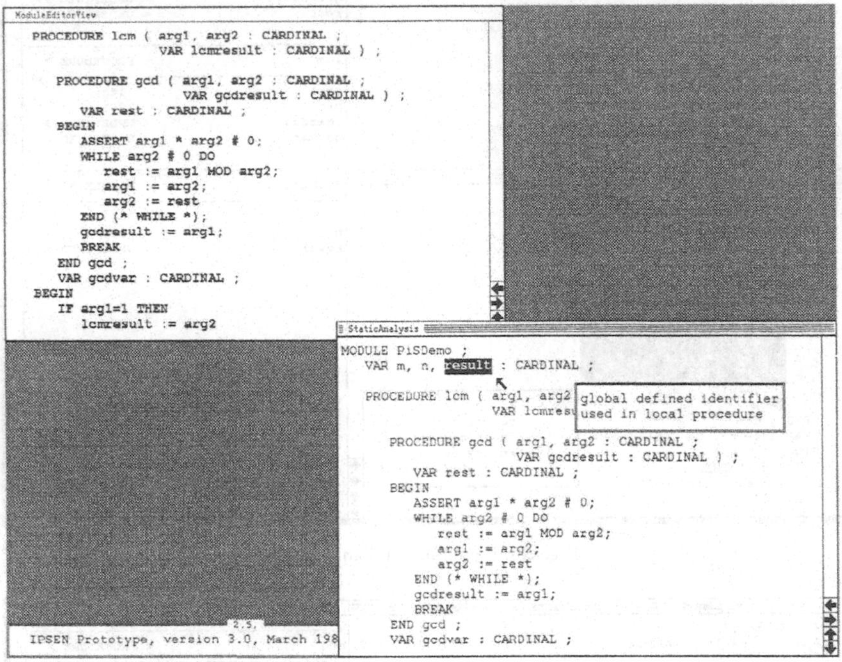

Fig. 2.8. Static analyses: global variables

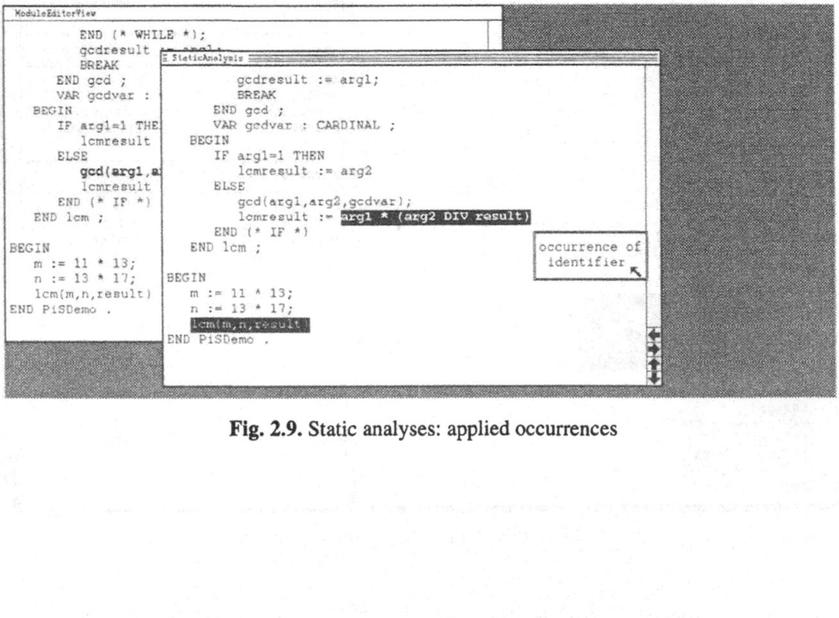

Fig. 2.9. Static analyses: applied occurrences

2.1.4 Summary and Comparison

IPSEN 2.5 offers a *window–based user interface* which distinguishes between windows of different types for editing/instrumentation, analysis, and execution, in the latter case with an additional window to display the run–time stack. Documents in PiS are represented in text windows. Since the layout is generated by an unparser, the user is relieved from formatting. Each command issued by the user refers to the current increment which is selected by mouse click. Commands are displayed in a menu window where they may be selected by mouse click; alternatively, the user may type in a shortcut. The contents of the menu depends o the type of current increment. Messages – e.g. error messages – are displayed in message windows. Finally, input windows are used for free text input.

The PiS part of IPSEN 2.5 offers *tightly integrated tools* which cooperate on one document. IPSEN 2.5 supports programming in Modula–2. Tools are seamlessly integrated, i.e. commands invoking different tools may be interleaved freely. All tools operate on a shared internal representation which represents context–free syntax, context–sensitive syntax, and dynamic semantics. The editor supports syntax–directed program construction as well as free text input. It checks and enforces both context–free and context–sensitive correctness. Programs may be prepared for execution by an instrumentation tool which operates in a similar way to the editor. Program execution is supported by an interpreter which provides for different modes of execution (step, next, continue). Finally, a static analysis tool determines, e.g. global variables used in a certain procedure or all applied occurrences of a certain variable.

The IPSEN programming environment may be compared to other *structure–oriented environments* which were developed in the 80's. Gandalf /2. HN 86/, Mentor /2. DHK 84/, PSG /2. BS 86/, and the Cornell Program Synthesizer /4. RT 84/ are well–known examples of such environments.

A *syntax–aided editor* plays a central role in a structure–oriented programming environment. The spectrum ranges from a purely syntax–directed editors (e.g. Gandalf), which enforce syntax–directed editing down to the level of lexical units, to text editors which are integrated with an incremental parser running in the background (e.g. Magpie /4. DMS 84/). IPSEN provides a hybrid editor which combines syntax–directed editing and free input. In this way, both novel and experienced users are adequately supported. Furthermore, the IPSEN editor performs incremental context–sensitive analysis, which is also done e.g. in PSG, the Cornell Program Synthesizer, and the Pan system /4. BGV 90/.

In addition, IPSEN supports *static analysis*, *instrumentation*, and *execution* in a seamlessly integrated way. Not all structure–oriented environments cover these additional areas. For example, Pan and the Cornell Program Synthesizer are restricted to syntax–aided editing. Those environments which do provide support for the tasks mentioned above achieve seamless integration only rarely. For example, PSG allows for execution of incomplete programs. However, only program extensions (expansions of placeholders) are allowed during program execution. In contrast, IPSEN also allows program modifications at any time as long as they do not cause inconsistencies with respect to execution.

2.2 Integration of Different Perspectives: The Requirements Engineering Environment

M. Lefering, Ch. Kohring, Th. Janning

This section deals with the *tools* that were developed to *support Requirements Engineering*. After a brief introduction of the languages used to describe different perspectives of RE and the motivation supporting their integration, we shortly describe the RE editors and analyzer tools to create/maintain submodels due to these perspectives in the next subsection. The following subsection discusses the interrelationships between the different languages in RE and introduces a consistency checking and binding tool that maintains the consistency between models formulated in these languages. Finally, a prototype of an interpreter for executing a requirements specification is described in the next subsection. In the summary subsection we repeat the main ideas of this section, give a comparison to other literature and, especially, outline a process for getting a validated requirements specification.

So, this section describes again an *integrated environment*, here *for RE*, which, however, is *different* from the PiS environment of section 2.1 in four respects: (1) RE modelling means modelling different perspectives, for which specific tools are available. These different perspectives contain different aspects of information which, however, are related to each other. (2) Tools have a graphical representation for overviews and a textual one for details. In some cases the textual information is given to refine overview information, in other cases to complement a graphical representation of one or more perspectives. (3) This environment allows different developers to work independently. (4) In the terminology introduced in chapter 1, the RE environment works on different logical documents, building up the RE subconfiguration. Nevertheless, integration is as tight as if all tools were working on one document.

An intertwined *process* as in section 2.1 is assumed for building up a complex requirements specification: Different persons work out the different perspectives of a requirements specification. Thereby, the corresponding editor/analyzer checks for intra–document inconsistencies which, therefore, are corrected after a while. After that the different parts are integrated. This, very probably, will show up errors in the corresponding documents, which in turn have to be corrected, which enforces another integration step, and so forth. If the requirements specification is globally and statically consistent, then its initial execution as well as target system simulation will again give rise to diverse changes. This complex process makes clear that besides tools for working out different documents, integrating them to get a consistent subconfiguration, and executing the subconfiguration, there have to be management tools for collaborative work (cf. section 2.5).

The work described here is part of the outcome of our contribution to the ESF and COMPLEMENT project. It reflects the results of a cooperation between CAP debis SSP Aachen and our group for a couple of years. This and the next section describe our efforts on *integration* of documents by intelligent tools, each document containing different logical portions of information. Whereas section 2.1 is restricted to *one working area*, taking RE as example, section 2.2 discusses integration between different working areas.

2.2.1 Supported Languages and the Integrated RE Environment

The RE environment is devoted to support the so–called *functional requirements specification*. The non–functional part (as efficiency parameters, hardware restrictions, and alike) as well as social/behavioral aspects of a group producing a requirements specification, as agreement, decision explanation etc. are not supported (as e.g. in /4. Poh 95/). Again, we give high–level support without restricting the underlying processes which produce a requirements specification. Especially, means for getting a new requirements specification consistent, or making it consistent again after modifications are proposed. All tools work in an incremental way and give support as early as possible. However, we assume some management for the group collaboratively working out a requirements specification (not described in this but in section 2.5): Integration tools for checking and inserting the bindings within a requirements subconfiguration are only invoked by requirements engineers if the corresponding documents for the different perspectives have reached a certain degree of maturity. So, we do not assume that one member of the group is directly changing the other one's documents (as e.g. assumed in some CSCW or groupware approaches).

As already stated in subsection 1.3.2, the emphasis of this book is on tool development and not on method work. Therefore, we *describe* the *languages* used for RE very *briefly* here. (For a more detailed introduction and a comparison with existing literature see /7. Jan 92, 7. Bee 95, 4. Koh 96/.) However, a brief discussion is necessary to understand the behavior of the following RE tools.

In IPSEN, a (functional) *requirements specification* consists of five parts, which are each formulated in a different language. These five parts can be seen as different *perspectives* on the RE subconfiguration:

(a) A *functional model*, formulated in SA, describes the system to be developed as a collection of application processes, which exchange data using data flows and data stores. Data processes transform input data into output data. The synchronization of data processes is described by control processes (see (d)). The complete functional model consists of a hierarchy of data processes, where each dataflow diagram (DFD) describes the internal structure of a data process, and of the declarations of atomic (i.e. not further refined) processes with their interfaces.

(b) An *information model* defines the data types used in the system. It consists of a hierarchy of extended entity relationship diagrams (so–called EER diagrams). As an extension to the regular ER–language, the refinement of entity and relationship types by ER–diagrams is allowed. Furthermore, inheritance can be defined between entity types.

(c) *Process specifications* (PSPECs) describe the internal behavior of atomic data processes, i.e. processes that are not further refined by data flow diagrams. Here, a small pseudo programming language is used in IPSEN.

(d) The behavior of control processes is described by *control specifications* (CSPECs). Control processes exchange information by control flows. For describing the internal behavior of control processes, our prototype uses state transition diagrams (cf. /7. HP 87, 7. WM 85/). Their exchange by timed statecharts has been studied (cf. /7. Bee 95/).

(e) Basic data types used as attributes of entity and relationship types or to define variables in PSPECs are declared in the *requirements dictionary* (RD). Additionally, the RD contains the declaration of control flows and signals used in DFDs and CSPECs. This, again, is a textual model which describes the structure of the data types by EBNF–like rules.

The *integrated environment* for *RE* described in this section, therefore, consists of syntax–directed environments for the above perspective languages, the language–sensitive integration tool, and the execution tool. The requirements engineers are provided with an environment for the full RE functionality. It is up to the requirements engineers and the management to regulate the cooperation.

2.2.2 Different Environments for the Five Perspectives

For these five languages, we have built *syntax–directed editors* and analysis tools: There is a graphical SA editor for drawing DFDs, a graphical editor for drawing EER–diagrams, and a graphical editor for state transition diagrams for CSPECs. PSPECs and the requirements dictionary are built up and modified using textual, syntax–directed editors.

Similar to the Modula–2 Editor described in section 2.1, all these editors include immediate and incremental *analysis tools* to check the context–sensitive syntax of the corresponding language. These include identifier binding as well as further context–sensitive conditions like balancing rules for data flow diagrams in SA.

As the different environments only differ in the representation of the above languages and, especially, whether they are graphical or textual editors, we restrict ourselves to showing the interactions with one of these environments. This is done because (1) other environments appear later, when discussing integration tools and (2) the behavior of these five environments is quite similar (if the reader abstracts from the underlying different concepts and their representation). As an *example* in this subsection we take the *SA environment*.

The *user interface* of this environment (and of the further environments explained in this chapter) is different from the one discussed in section 2.1. The window system is now based on the X11 Window System and was developed using the InterViews toolkit. But the look and feel is still similar: One window is the current window and a menu is displayed at the right side of that window. All the tools offer their commands through this menu. Commands are gathered in so–called command groups (capital letters), which are displayed at the top of the menu. The commands of the currently selected command group (bold font) are listed below of the command groups. All the editor windows contain at the left border several icons and a scrollbar to zoom and scroll the contents of the window (cf. fig. 2.10).

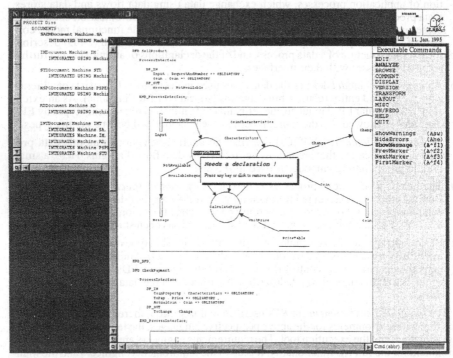

Fig. 2.10. Applied occurrence of a ProcessId without declaration

If the editors work in a syntax–directed and *command–driven* way, errors in the context–free syntax cannot appear. But it is possible to use a *free–insertion* mode that calls a text editor on an arbitrary increment. After finishing editing, an incremental parser is invoked that inserts the corresponding increments into the abstract syntax graph. This mode is sometimes used in textual editors, but usually not in graphical ones.

How the SA environment (other environments operate similarly) deals with context–sensitive errors is explained next. As already mentioned in 2.1, context–sensitive errors are allowed by the editors, if desired by the requirements engineer, to give flexibility during editing. Instead of abandoning context–sensitive errors, inconsistencies are marked by the editor and a message is shown, if wanted. The balancing rules for data flow diagrams are modelled, together with consistency relations between declared and applied occurrences, as *context–sensitive rules* in our SA language. Every process has a unique declaration that consists of the identifier and the process interface which declares incoming and outgoing dataflows (called inlets and outlets, see text preceding the DFD in fig. 2.10). The process declaration also contains the process implementation, which is a data flow diagram, if the process is further refined, and a PSPEC document, if it is an atomic process.

Figs. 2.10 and 2.11 show an *example* of *handling context–sensitive errors* from editing data flow diagrams. The RE engineer has inserted a new process into the DFD SellProduct, which has no process declaration yet. Therefore, the corresponding identifier AcceptChoice is marked and a message that the declaration is missing is shown, as the user has clicked on that increment. After a corresponding process declaration has been inserted (in this case another DFD shown in the lower part of the main window of fig. 2.11), the error disappears as the situation is now consistent again (cf. again fig. 2.11).

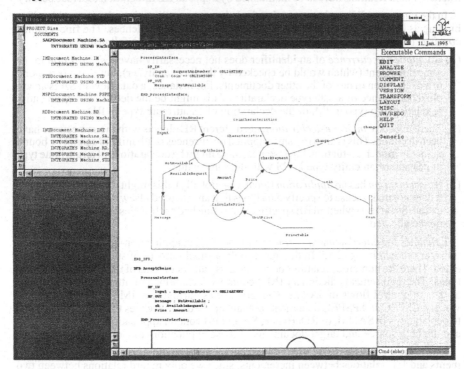

Fig. 2.11. Consistent state after inserting the declaration

2.2.3 Integration of Languages and Tools

Each of the submodels of the requirements specification is stored in an own document. Hence, we have *five* different *documents* and, correspondingly, *document types* in RE: for SA, IM, PSPEC, CSPEC, and RD. In a previous prototype, all these submodels were stored in one single common RE document the type being a composition of the above types. We changed the document realization to multiple documents containing logically separated parts mainly due to the following:

(a) The complete specification consists of models in five different languages each describing a certain aspect/perspective of the requirements. Separation facilitates the *exchangeability* of such languages within RE. For instance, a real programming language could be used instead of our PSPEC language, or StateCharts could be used instead of state transition diagrams. Similarly, the SA or EER language could be changed e.g. to another dialect.

(b) As mentioned above, not a single analyst but a team is working out the requirements. Since documents are the locking units in IPSEN, *concurrent work* on a single document is difficult, because of several technical and management reasons. When using different documents, different analysts can work on separate perspectives of the requirements specification rather independently.

When dividing the requirements specification into several documents, multiple fine–grained *interdocument relations* arise. While the document–local consistency relations are checked by the analyzers within the editors (e. g. document–local identifier binding), these interdocument relations have to be maintained by a special RE integration tool (see below).

In the integrated RE environment sketched above, we realized interdocument identifier binding as language and, correspondingly, document correspondences. The fine–grained *consistency relations* discussed in this section are restricted to the *following cases*:

(1) An *applied occurrence* of an identifier does not necessarily have a *declaration* in the same document (which would be checked by the local analyzer), but may correspond to a declaration in one of the other documents. For instance, a data flow in SA is an applied occurrence of a data type declaration. This might be the declaration of an entity or relationship type in IM, or the declaration of an attribute type in RD.

(2) There may be a *multiple declaration*, i.e. different RE objects with the same name have been declared. This is an error, since applied occurrences of identifiers cannot be bound uniquely in such a situation. For instance, there might be declarations of an attribute type in RD and of an entity type in IM with the same name.

(3) If a *declaration* has no *application* (locally or globally), this might also be an error. E.g., it does not make sense to specify data types that are not used elsewhere within a specification. So, at least when an RE specification is finished such useless declarations should not be allowed.

Examples for *interdocument relations* of type (1), i.e. application–to–declaration–relations, are shown in fig. 2.12. In the figure, only a small number of such relations is presented. There are numerous relations between nearly all documents of the above–mentioned types: The requirements dictionary (RD) contains declarations of attributes that are used as data or control flows in SA (e.g. Cancel) or as attributes in IM (e.g. Value). Conversely, CSPEC and PSPEC documents contain applied occurrences that have to be bound to declarations in SA, IM, or RD. Hence, SA and IM contain applications and declarations and are both source and target documents of these application–to–declaration–relations.

Due to these *consistency relations* within RE, we only have 1:1–relations between documents and 1:1–relations between increments, since we only regard relations between two single (applied and declared, or declared and declared) occurrences of identifiers. On language level, there are 1:n–relations, since e.g. a dataflow identifier can be bound to an entity or relationship type as well as to an attribute type. Of course, more complex fine–grained relations between the RE documents can be found, but are currently not realized by the tool (see below), which maintains the consistency of different documents belonging to different perspectives.

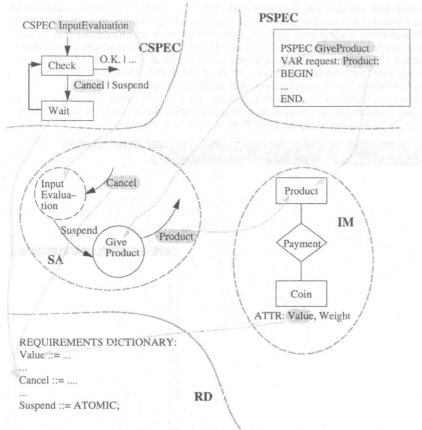

Fig. 2.12. Fine–grained relationships between RE perspectives

2.2.4 A Consistency Checking and Binding Tool for RE–Integration

The consistency relations between different RE documents discussed above are maintained by a so–called *integration tool* for *RE* (cf. subsection 1.6.4). This tool is built as an instance of a framework for building integration tools by reusing most of the framework components and inserting new application–dependent ones (cf. /4. Lef 95/ and chapter 4). The application–dependent components can be derived from a formal specification (cf. chapter 3).

The tool does not change the documents that have to be integrated. It just looks for identifiers that take part in global (i.e. interdocument) consistency relations. If correspondences are found (e.g. an applied identifier and its unique corresponding declaration, or a declaration and a conflicting one in another document) they are stored. This is done by creating a link in a so–called integration document, which is the internal memory of the integration tool (i.e. it is not directly manipulated by the user). These links are used to check the consistency of integrated documents further on. Additionally, they can be used for browsing, e.g.

the tool delivers the according declaration to a currently selected applied occurrence, and vice versa. Hence, according to the classification of integration tools given in subsection 1.6.4, this integrator is a *consistency checker, complex binder,* and *browser.*

All integrators realized with the framework mentioned above (and therefore also the RE integrator) can be driven in two modes: an automatic and a manual mode. In the RE integration, the *automatic mode* is used. Tools that use manual mode are introduced in section 2.3. During an integration process the tool looks for (1) all applied identifiers that need a global declaration, (2) declarations that have a conflicting declaration in another document, and (3) declarations that have no application, but need one. If consistent correspondences can be found (relations between applications and declarations) they are connected by links. If no such correspondences or conflicting correspondences (i.e. multiple declarations) are found, these increments are marked as erroneous within the related documents. This is shown to the user by inverting the identifiers in the editor windows.

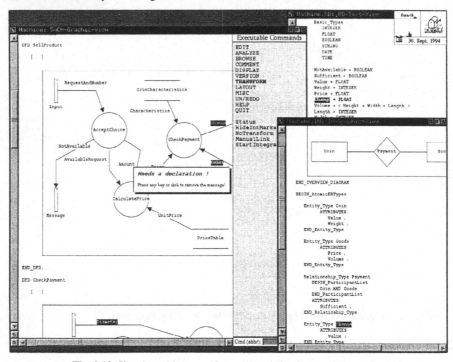

Fig. 2.13. Situation with errors of type (1) and (2) after consistency check

After an integration process has succeeded, i.e. the documents are in a consistent state, *inconsistencies* can occur, when the related *documents* are *modified.* These inconsistencies arise due to the following user actions:

(a) A user has inserted an applied occurrence of an identifier that has to be bound globally, i.e. bound to a declaration in another RE document.

(b) A user has inserted a declaration that needs a global application.

(c) A user has deleted a declaration that was connected to an application by an interdocument link.

(d) A user has deleted an application that was connected with a declaration by an interdocument link.

(e) A user has deleted an interdocument link explicitly, i. e. he has removed an integration relation.

If inconsistencies have occurred and the corresponding documents have been changed, the *documents* have to be *re–integrated*. This is done by starting the integration tool again. Hence, the tool is not running continuously in the background, but has to be started explicitly. The integration is an asynchronous process and the tool integrates with delay (i.e. the tool is of type (e3) according to the classification in subsection 1.6.4).

Fig. 2.13 shows a small part of the *specification* of a vending machine. A view on the SA, IM and RD document can be seen. The integration tool has detected the following *errors*: Firstly, the data type Change is declared twice, namely as entity type in IM and as attribute type in RD (see the two windows on the right side of the screen). Since no unique declaration exists, the dataflow Change (an applied occurrence) cannot be bound and is marked as well. Secondly, the data flow Coins has no declaration at all, since the declaration that was meant is named Coin. The error message corresponding to this error is displayed in the screendump. Finally, the dataflow Diameter is also an application without declaration. Hence, errors of type (1) and (2), according to subsection 2.2.3, occur in the situation presented in the screendump.

As a *reaction* to these errors, the *user* might now rename the data flow Coins as Coin, delete the attribute declaration Change, insert an attribute declaration Diameter (but misprints it as Daimeter) and start the integration tool again.

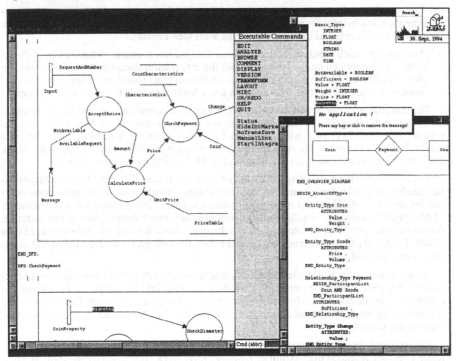

Fig. 2.14. Situation with errors of type (1) and (3) after a further consistency check

The *situation after* the integration tool's run is displayed in fig. 2.14. The data flows Change and Coin have been bound and are consistent now. Since the declaration of the dataflow Diameter was misspelled, it still cannot be bound and remains erroneous. On the other hand, the misspelled declaration Daimeter is erroneous, since it has no application. This is an error of type (3) according to subsection 2.2.3. If the user now changes the declaration `Daimeter` to `Diameter`, restarts the integrator (not shown), and all marks will disappear.

As mentioned above, all links are stored in an integration document. In this situation, several cases – from one integration document for all documents to one integration document for each pair of documents to be integrated – are possible. For our RE integration tool, we use *one integration document* for integrating all five related RE documents. This realization has certain *disadvantages* concerning concurrent work of several analysts within one specification (which was one of the main reasons for using more than one document for a requirements specification). If there is only one integration document, the relations of all related documents are checked during one integration run. That means that all interdocument relations are checked and changed, even if the user only wants to analyze two of the documents, while another analyst is working on different parts of the requirements specification and might not be ready for a consistency check.

Nevertheless, we took this *approach for* the following *reasons* (and realized a way to circumvent the above–mentioned disadvantages, see below):

(a) An integration of several documents is useful only in sensible situations, where the documents to be integrated are in a locally consistent state. Hence, the users of these documents have to agree to be ready for integration and have to prepare their documents for integration before.

(b) The state "partially consistent" which would occur when using multiple integration documents is not helpful for a revision of a requirements specification. As an intermediate state it can be realized in our approach as well (see below).

(c) Another approach would need a two–level integration scenario, where pairs of documents are integrated on the first level and the integration documents are integrated on the second level. This scenario is not realizable with tools based on the integrator framework so far (cf. subsection 4.6) and it is too complicated for the case regarded here.

The integration of documents is realized by using *transformation rules* within an integrator based on the framework. This scheme holds true for all integrators. Hence, the integrators are rule–based systems, where the transformation rules are hard–wired into the code (cf. /4. Lef 93/). However, the rules are specified using a graph grammar approach and the code can be derived from this specification (cf. /4. Lef 95/ and section 3.4).

To give the user the possibility to influence the integration of different documents, *priorities* can be assigned to transformation rules and (more important for integration tools) *rules* can be *switched off*. Hence, it is possible to realize partial integrations even independent of document borders by switching off the inopportune integration relations. For instance, the user could switch off all integrations but those to check the correct declarations of data flows. Then, only the consistency between the data flow diagrams and the IM or RD documents are checked.

Hence, this approach of modelling a complete requirements specification in *several documents* that each embody a perspective written in a different language, and *checking* the consistency of the documents in *certain* discrete *situations* is a safe, highly flexible scenario for specifying requirements in a consistent way, and allows for a suitable management of integration processes.

Future work on the RE integrator will be to extend the available consistency checks. More complex relations than identifier bindings have to be controlled by the tool, like balancing rules if groups of DFDs are to be separated, structural comparisons between merging or splitting dataflows and their type definitions, consistency between data processes and their PSPECs, or between control processes and their CSPECs, respectively.

2.2.5 Prototyping and Simulation by Executing an RE Spec

On one hand this subsection describes the *execution component* of the integrated RE environment. On the other side this component, and necessary preparations in the corresponding requirements definition models, allow not only the specification of *systems* with functional behavior (SA model), possibly connected to complex, structured internal data (EER or RD model) as described above, but also *control behavior* of systems. Therefore, specific aspects of execution have to be regarded.

Compared to the development of standard applications, the development of *embedded systems* requires the consideration of some more specific objectives. We characterize embedded systems as systems with many external events on which such systems have to react. Moreover, the reaction to an external or internal event must take place within some strictly defined time interval, i. e. the correctness of real–time systems crucially relies on the fulfillment of the timing constraints. Hence, requirements have to consider dynamic system behavior and the requirements spec has to declare which timing constraints are critical.

The main topic of this subsection is the *execution* of *requirements specs*. By interpreting requirements specs it is possible to present a rapid *prototype* of the system under consideration. So, the advantage is the *early validation* of the requirements, if possible, together with the customer. The dialogue with the customer is facilitated by the presentation of an animated model.

The idea of executing system specifications for validating and demonstrating system behavior is not new. But there are some obvious *drawbacks* in *existing* methods /7. Har 90, 7. HP 87, 7. BJK 88, 7. WM 85/ and *tools* /4. Ath 89, 4. BH 88, 4. CSE 90, 4. Rze 92/. First of all, the system specifier is fixed to use exactly one method which, in most cases, lacks precise semantics. Secondly, most of the well–known tools support only the execution of a pre–compiled model. This means that no interactive changes of the model are allowed. Thirdly, the relation between the hardware and the software model are not or only roughly considered. Because of these drawbacks we improved the corresponding well–known methods and their tool support.

Besides the syntax–oriented RE–editors used to construct/maintain a requirements spec and explained in 2.2.2, there is a *simulation tool* for the interactive execution (interpretation) of an RE spec. The editor, analysis, and interpreter tools described in this section, form an integrated tool set for **Requirements Engineering and simulation, called RESI** (cf. /4. Koh 93a, b, 4. Koh 96/). The most important goal of the simulation is the early validation of requirements, especially the dynamic system behavior and the timing constraints. As this task cannot be done by reviewing a requirements spec we propose the interpretative execution of the SA/CM/EER model.

By interpreting the requirements spec it is possible to study the internal behavior of the system model. Thereby *validation* delivers quite *different results* and, therefore, gives rise to different improvements corresponding to detected drawbacks, errors, and problems. Detection can (1) correspond to modelling within the different perspectives of a requirements spec and their mutual consistency, to knowledge described elsewhere, or existing in the heads of involved people. One may (2) detect that a concurrent system reaches a deadlock situation. Another interesting question (3) concerns the correctness of the exception handlers. Furthermore, one may (4) check if all timing constraints are fulfilled. Moreover, it is our intention (5) to get data for improvement of the specification, e.g. necessary changes to the global net flow behavior, because one of the processes takes too long and causes delays of others. Finally, during model execution one (6) may get some hints on how to implement the final software, e.g. that some of the software modules should be implemented very efficiently.

The RE–simulation tool is conceived to be *flexible* and *adaptable* in *different ways*. The specified model (1) should be changeable during the simulation. This is realized by an intertwined editing, consistency checking, and execution process. Furthermore (2), the simulation tool should be flexible enough to influence and measure various simulation runs. Finally, the underlying methods (3) should be exchangeable (e.g. the programming language to describe the process specifications in SA).

In regarding the runtime behavior of a specified application system only the *functional* (SA), PSPEC, and *control* part (CSPEC) of a requirements specification are *taken*. These three parts build up the executable model: The SA part described the normal and global interactions of application processes together with implicit synchronization, the PSPEC part the internals of atomic application processes and their runtime behavior, and the control part reacts on events, timing, and activation/suspension of application processes. The EER and the RD part define corresponding data types needed at specification time to build up a consistent overall system model. The objects corresponding to these data types are contained in the SA model. They are inputs and outputs of data processes and/or they are stored, changed, or retrieved from data stores. As PSPECs are part of the SA model we speak in the following of SA/CM execution.

One really important problem for the interpretation of SA/CM is the definition of *precise semantics* corresponding to the dynamic behavior of requirements specs. Our intention was to develop a flexible mechanism which allows the definition of different execution semantics. Above all, we distinguish three process types in the SA/CM methodology: abstract or atomic data processes and control processes. Then, it is possible to define the execution semantics of SA/CM–models through a set of possible internal states for these different process types. As result, we propose the application of a finite state automaton which defines all possible states of processes and describes the allowed transitions between them.

In executing a system model we provide *deadlines* or *priorities* to control the execution times of the processes. This is in order to describe the required system properties. On the other hand, the tool has to simulate the "real" execution times. This will be done by making use of user–defined *execution times* within the PSPEC definitions of the atomic process specification. The simulated values are based on the summations of the execution times of all PSPEC–statements. So, the tool has to check whether the simulated process execution times fulfil the required deadlines/execution times specified in the requirements model.

The requirements model has to be implemented later in the software lifecycle on a concrete hardware configuration. To make the simulation of reactive systems with timing constraints more realistic, in that the implementation on a *target* hardware is able to execute system properly or, vice versa and in order to get hints for the following implementation process, we developed a flexible model for hardware *simulation*. This model comprises virtual processors with different performance rates, different scheduling algorithms for each processor, and the possibility to vary the simulated execution time for each programming language construct.

In order to facilitate the behavior of a system implementation's run on a target hardware, a major goal of our work is the *integration* of the *hardware* model and the *software model*. First of all, the user may define several environment parameters to simulate an adequate hardware environment. Therefore, we developed another syntax–based editor to describe the hardware environment used during the simulation of a requirements spec. The EnvP-editor (EnvP stands for *Env*ironment *P*arameters) enables the definition of several virtual processors with different performance rates and different scheduling algorithms. To simplify the use of the simulation tool all those parameters are filled with default values which are taken if nothing else is specified.

Fig. 2.15 presents a screendump corresponding to a certain *situation* of the *interpreter* tool. The specified example is an access control system that supervises the entrances to critical areas of a factory. The presented situation resembles the process step initial execution of an RE model. At this moment, model execution is started for the first time. Also, the control behaviour is not yet explicitly specified. However, it is possible to interpret the model with real dataflow values and to monitor actual system states. The screendump comprises a window which shows a typical dataflow diagram. The data process Check_Access highlighted in gray is the process currently active in the DFD. The right window of fig. 2.15 is an information window on a (previously selected) data process (here also Check_Access). It, in particular, shows the *state* the process *is in*. In the example, Check_Access is active, which means the process is ready, has got all needed incoming dataflow values, and has been selected from all executable processes. The window on top shows the state of a selected input data flow (here: Entr_Request) of the parent process Checksystem (the process containing Check_Access as applied occurrence). It does not merely show the data currently passed by that data flow (in the example Entr_Request is a record with the three components CardNr, Password, and ReaderNr), but also allows modification of the data at runtime by the user. Hence, it is not only a message window but an input window, too.

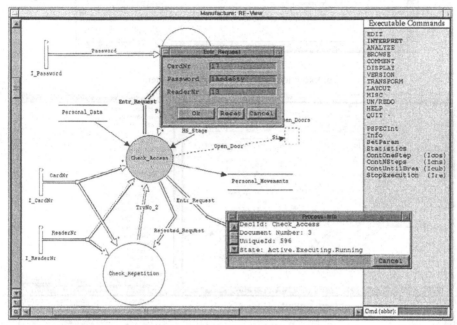

Fig. 2.15. Initial execution by the RE interpreter

Fig. 2.16.a and .b present screendumps corresponding to a subsequent situation during model evaluation. Fig. 2.16.a shows the specification of the target hardware. The virtual hardware model comprises two processors with different performance rates and different scheduling algorithms. Fig. 2.16.b presents the distributed execution of two processes (here: Check_Access and Check_Repetition). Moreover, the DFD is extended by a control process Access_Control (all the processes to be seen in the upper left window). The corresponding CSPEC is shown at the bottom of the screendump. The state Normal_Workstate highlighted in the state transition diagram marks the currently active state of the CSPEC. The upper right window of fig. 2.16.b presents once more a process information window. Here, it can be seen that the process Check_Access is queued. This is because Check_Repetition is to be executed on the same processor and is in state running, which delays the execution of Check_Access. As the strategy chosen is Round Robin and the time slice is 1 Msec, both processes are executed interleaved "in parallel". To improve time behaviour the specifier could assign different processors to both processes.

The interpreter tool offers input and output *windows* for the interactive definition and change of various *model* and *simulation parameters*. For each data process it is possible to assign it to one of the simulated target hardware processors and to define a priority which influences the sequence of process execution. In addition, the specifier has to determine some input values that are attached to the incoming data flows. During the interpretation, all values attached to data or control flows may be changed interactively.

a) Specification of the target system

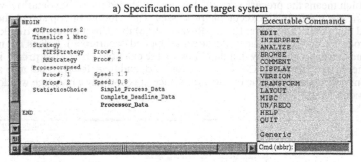

b) Execution on a virtual distributed system

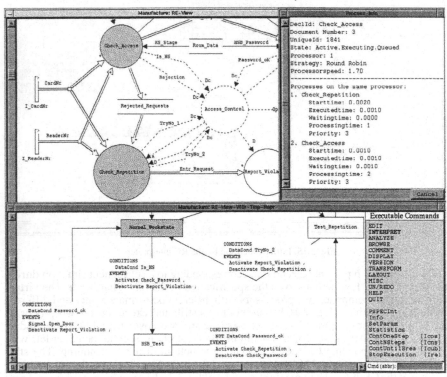

Fig. 2.16. Simulation and monitoring of an RE spec

The proper *interpretation* comprises *four* alternating *phases*: global netflow analysis, CSPEC interpretation, scheduling activities and PSPEC (data process specification) interpretation. Within the netflow analysis the tool determines the current states (e.g. active, inactive, interrupted) of all processes. The interpretation of all CSPECs will be done during one cycle of the global netflow interpreter because the results of the CSPEC interpretation influence the netflow analysis, and vice versa. Thereafter, the scheduler assigns the processes to the virtual processors and determines the order of execution according to the various scheduling algorithms. Finally, the process specifications (PSPECs) are interpreted.

During the interpretation the tool *highlights* all *processes* in state 'active' and in state 'interrupted' to demonstrate the currently interpreted processes. The current state of each CSPEC will be highlighted, too. On the other hand, the tool *presents runtime information* on demand, e.g. current states of processes or waiting queues at each processor.

Finally, we offer some *parameters* to *control* the *simulator* itself. For that purpose, the user is allowed to alter the basic interpretation cycle. This time interval defines the duration between two analysis steps of the simulation tool. Within one cycle, the state of all flows and processes in the SA/CM–model has to be determined. Thus, the user may control the logical accuracy of simulation runs.

In addition, we provide some *statistics* features which allow or facilitate the subsequent *evaluation* of *simulation runs*. Some examples of these statistics are the number of activations of a process, duration of process execution, or information about deadline violations. For these tasks we built instrumentation and monitoring tools which are flexible and easily adaptable to new user demands. The instrumentation tool allows queries on various runtime data, e.g. deadline data, processor data, simple and advanced process data, and time sequences of control flows. The monitoring tool offers many statistics which are based on these information. So, the specifier may analyze and compare different interpretations of the same model at the end of a session.

2.2.6 Summary and Comparison

In this *subsection* we (1) give a summary of the section, we (2) compare our approach to others of literature, and we (3) briefly discuss how an RE process looks, which errors are made, and when they are usually detected.

In this section we introduced an *integrated RE environment* consisting of different editors/analyzer environments for defining/changing the different perspectives of a functional requirements specification (SA, EER, PSPEC, CSPEC, RD). These different perspectives can be worked out in parallel or in any order. An integration tool serves for global consistency (here restricted to declaration and application) within a complete requirements spec. By an execution tool the behavior of the system can be simulated, thereby getting a rapid prototype for a system before its implementation.

The *SA–*, *EER–*, and *CSPEC* environments are graphical, the *PSPEC* and *RD environments* are textual. As there is much similarity between such environments in IPSEN we gave only a brief description, taking the graphical SA environment as example.

The *integration tool* serves for consistency between the different perspectives, i.e. different documents according to the terminology used here. It is a consistency checking, binding, and browsing tool. It is an automatic mode integrator. Other integrators will be presented in the next section. Using priorities and switching off integration rules it can also be used to serve for consistency within a part of the RE subconfiguration.

Execution of requirements specifications especially due to the SA/CM part and to the various simulation influence and control "buttons" of the *RESI tool* delivers *validation* of the system's behavior even in the case of reactive systems. Priorities and deadlines can be assigned to data processes, execution times to PSPEC statements. The interpreter checks/guarantees the corresponding behavior. Even the execution on a target hardware can be simulated and figures for the evaluation of simulation runs are provided.

Hence, the environment provides for *handling* the various *changes* of a *system's specification* due to local and global consistency, or runtime behavior. The corresponding means for supporting the process of working out (editing, changing, analyzing, executing, monitoring, evaluating w.r.t. dynamic behavior or to a later execution on a target hardware) a requirements spec for a system are offered or, as the RE environment is a prototype, it is shown how they should be.

There is a vast amount of *literature*, only some of which can be *sketched* here by enumerating some approaches, systems, and branches of research. *Requirements engineering* deals with the problems of requirements elicitation, capture, validation, and verification /3. Boe 84, 7. RP 92/. There are (1) many papers and systems from the industrial or method–oriented context for building up a requirements spec or executing it which, however, give only weak support for the various perspectives, activities, and roles involved in requirements engineering (see papers cited above). Consequently there are "methods" for supporting requirements engineering that are based on (usually unprecise) representation notations, but these do not give comprehensive support for the system specifier. Another main stream is (2) to stress the human dimension of requirements engineering by costumer–driven or participatory approaches /7. HB 95, 7. Flo 92/, cognitive /7. GC 91, 7. Som 93/, or group interaction approaches /7. Sca 84/. Furthermore, there are (3) formal approaches to requirements engineering by either regarding use of formal requirements spec languages /7. BJ 88, 7. Hoa 90, 7. Spi 90, 7. Zav 82/ or introducing knowledge representation formalisms /7. LC 88/. They offer the advantage of automatic reasoning. Applying them to requirements engineering is by no means straightforward. Moreover, they must be derived from, and integrated with the results of informal requirements engineering /7. GS 90, 7. Joh 88/. Another branch (4) is to focus on the process /7. CKO 88, 92/ of elaborating a requirements spec by giving direct process support /7. PDJ 94, 4. Poh 95/. The requirements process must be traceable and understandable /7. GF 94, 7. RE 93/. The formulation of process steps (how to ...) and their interrelation is the matter of interest. Finally, there are (5) AI approaches either supporting the requirements engineering process by using AI techniques /7. LC 88/ or even by viewing the whole software development process as an automatic and rule–driven activity /3. RW 86/.

Let us compare the RE environment presented here with two *industrial systems*. *STATEMATE* /7. Har 90/ is a comprehensive working environment for the specification and validation of requirements specs. The supported modelling language consist of three different parts (functional, behavioural, and structural view). As model execution is only based on the behavioural view (statecharts), specification is often restricted to this view. Also, the timing behaviour will not be simulated by the STATEMATE environment but can only be measured during the execution of a pre–compiled prototype. Another industrial execution tool is *ShortCut* /4. CSE 90/ which is based on the SA/RT method /7. HP 87/. Although the interpretation and animation facilities are able to demonstrate system behaviour, there are some obvious drawbacks. On one hand, model interpretation is only allowed if the specification is complete and faultless. On the other hand, run–time information is not stored for subsequent evaluation.

Several approaches of *fine–grained integration* support can be found in literature, but most of them are restricted to the method level. The integration of methods within RE is well–studied: The important approaches according to the integration of SA with a real–time–model are introduced by Ward/Mellor /7. WM 85/ and Hatley/Pirbhai /7. HP 87/, respectively. The additional integration of an information model is described in /7. Jan 92/ and /7. Edw 93/. The integration of object–oriented methods in requirements analysis is described in /7. RBP 91/ and /7. Boo 94/.

As already argued, no document or (sub)configuration of a software system is produced in a straightforward manner. Instead, there are usually more modification than construction steps. This is also true for RE. Fig. 2.17.a shows a possible *RE process* and the corresponding backtracking steps which have to be carried out if one or more errors are detected.

193

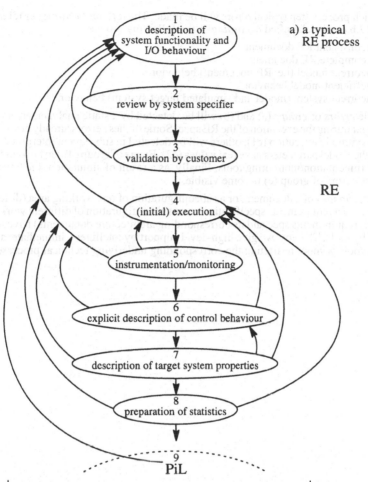

a) a typical
RE process

RE

PiL

process step	type or example of error	error classification
2	– process not declared – violation of balancing rules (data flow or signal in DFD does not match with declaration in process interface)	(b), (a) (a)
3	– semantically incomplete context diagram or DFD (missing terminator/input data flow)	(b)
4/5	– deadlock – delay in process execution because of missing input data – incorrect dynamic process behavior (e.g. error during repeated process execution)	(c1) (d) (c2)
6	– incorrect coordination between DFD and CSPEC (e.g. bad timing of process activation)	(c2)
7	– adverse distribution of processes to virtual processors (delay in process execution because of missing parallelization)	(e), (d)
8	– deadline violation	(c2), (d)
9	– a missing or ambiguous requirement detected in design (PiL)	(a), (b)

Fig. 2.17. A possible process for RE and typical errors detected

In each process step typical errors will be made. The different *error types* referenced in fig. 2.17.b can be classified *according* to the following groups:

(a)   inconsistent RE document
(b)   incomplete RE document
(c)   incorrect model (i.e. RE document) behavior
(d)   inefficient model behavior
(e)   incorrect system (model and simulated target system) behavior.

While *errors* of *groups* (a) and (b) will be detected by a static analyzer, errors of group (c) appear during the execution of the RE spec. Some of these errors already become visible during symbolic execution (c1), others will be detected in subsequent interpretation steps, where the model parameters have real values (c2). Errors of group (d) can be found by using the instrumentation/monitoring tools. Finally, as a result of simulation, the target system property errors of group (e) become visible.

Thus, *changes* of a document, or a subconfiguration of one working area (different perspectives of a requirements specification), or a subconfiguration of different working areas (like the requirements spec and its corresponding architecture documents) have to be *supported* by tools. Thereby, we give high–level support by intelligent, immediate, and incremental tools without restricting the corresponding underlying technical processes.

2.3 Transition Between Different Working Areas: Vertical Integration Tools

M. Lefering, Th. Janning

After having discussed integration of documents within one working area (sometimes called horizontal integration), we now discuss several scenarios to integrate documents of different working areas, which is called *vertical integration*.

Subsection 2.3.1 introduces an integration tool between RE and PiL. This is the most complex of our integration tools. Subsection 2.3.2 describes an integrator between PiL and PiS and, finally, subsection 2.3.3 deals with an integrator to keep the documentation consistent with RE, PiL, and PiS. The two latter integrators are introduced rather coarsely as we concentrate mainly on the differences to the RE–PiL–integrator. According to subsection 1.6.4, this section describes three *different* types of *integration tools*: A semiautomatic transformation tool in subsection 2.3.1, an automatic transformation tool in 2.3.2, and a manual binder and consistency checking tool in subsection 2.3.3.

As in 2.2, this section again describes some results (RE–PiL integration) which have been elaborated in the ESF and COMPLEMENT project in the framework of a cooperation with CAP debis SSP.

2.3.1 Relating RE to PiL: Concepts and Integrator Characteristics

The tool to integrate a requirements spec document of RE and an architecture document of PiL has to fulfil a much more complex task than the RE integrator of subsection 2.2.3. Therefore, we first describe the *background* for this *integration* in this subsection, before being able to introduce the user interface and the behavior of the tool in the next.

According to the classification in subsection 1.6.4, this integrator does not only perform *consistency checking* and *binding*, but also a *transformation* from RE to PiL. Furthermore, it works as a *browser*, since it also allows browsing between related documents, i.e. shows the architecture increments related to requirements increments and vice versa (cf. /4. Lef 93b/, /4. Lef 95/).

In detail the RE–PiL *integration* tool mainly has to solve the following *subtasks* (all steps being carried out incrementally):

(a) it reads a requirements specification worked out with tools of 2.2,

(b) it generates an initial architecture that corresponds to the requirements,

(c) it connects increments that are related to each other by interdocument links, which are stored in an integration document,

(d) and it checks the consistency of hence integrated documents by using the links of the integration document. Inconsistencies are repaired incrementally.

This tool again is *based* on the *integrator framework* which shall be introduced in chapter 4: (1) The application–independent components are reused, (2) the application–dependent parts – i.e. the transformation algorithm – are modelled as a set of transformation rules which are specified. (3) The code for the rules can be derived mechanically from this specification. This is done manually up to now, but can be automated. The derived code is inserted into the code of the framework.

Although the rules were newly specified and coded, the main idea of the rule set was taken over from /7. Jan 92/. Minor modifications are due to new versions of RE and PiL languages, cf. /4. Koh 94, 7. Bör 94/. For explaining the rules we take the SA part of RE and a subpart of the PiL language as examples. The main *characteristics* of the *transformation rules* are the following:

(1) The rules search for or insert *complex patterns* in/into the related documents. Hence, m:n–increment transformations are supported instead of only 1:1–relations of section 2.2.

(2) The rules can be divided into those that (a) transform *declarations* of RE objects (e.g. processes, data stores, entity types, etc.) and those that (b) transform according *applications* of these objects (e.g. process or data store applications, data flows etc. in DFDs).

(3) The languages in RE and PiL support different concepts (e.g. a DFD describes the implementation of a process without defining its interface, while PiL distinguishes interfaces and implementations of modules, cf. /7. Jan 92/). So, the transformation *cannot* be *unambiguous*.

(4) Therefore, the integrator supports three *alternatives* to transform each *declaration* of RE (the user must decide, which alternative is appropriate in a certain situation):
(a) the declaration is transformed into a module of appropriate type (e.g. a process declaration becomes a function module).
(b) the declaration is transformed into an exported resource of an already existing module (e.g. a process declaration becomes an exported procedure of a function module that was, for instance, transformed using the parent–DFD).
(c) the declaration is transformed into a local resource of an already existing module (e.g. a process declaration becomes a local procedure of a function module that was, for instance, transformed taking the parent–DFD).

(5) Each *application* is transformed *depending* on the preceding transformation of related *declarations* (e.g. the transformation of a process application depends on the transformations of the surrounding DFD, i.e. the parent–DFD), and on the transformation of its own declaration (i.e. the DFD). Applications determine relations between related declarations (e.g. process applications determine the refinement relation between DFDs). Hence, they are transformed into relations in PiL (e.g. process applications can become import relations between function modules).

An *example* is given in fig. 2.18. The transformation of process application B depends on the transformation of DFD A (surrounding DFD, parent–DFD) and its own declaration, DFD B. If both declarations became function modules (as shown in fig. 2.18.a) or export procedures in different modules, then process application B becomes an import clause. If the DFDs A and B became procedures in the same function module (as in fig. 2.18.b), then the process application has no correspondence in PiL, i.e. it is not transformed.

Since decisions have to be made by the designer during the transformation process, this integration tool has to be a *semi–automatic tool* (in contrast to the tool described in subsection 2.2.3). RE–PiL transition is a highly creative subprocess, which the designer has to control by suitable decisions The knowledge that has to be added is design knowledge. Therefore, the tool belongs to an integrated PiL environment, as already explained in subsection 1.2.4. However, this integrator massively supports this subprocess by offering transformation rules which only have to be selected, but also allows for quite different transformation solutions.

A second new feature of this integrator is that single *transformations* are *not independent* of each other, because the transformation of applications depends on the transformation of declarations. Transformations are modelled as a set of transformation rules. Therefore, dependencies between transformations means dependencies between rule applications. To guarantee only sensible orders of rule applications, the tool determines in each step which rules can be applied independently of other transformations. The according increments that can be transformed independently of others not yet transformed ones are called *safe transformable* increments. The set of safe transformable increments consists of increments the transformation of which is independent of other transformations or which have been transformed already. Only safe transformable increments are candidates for the next integration step. For our example, this means that process declarations have to be transformed before the integrator allows the transformation of process applications (cf. /4. Lef 93a/).

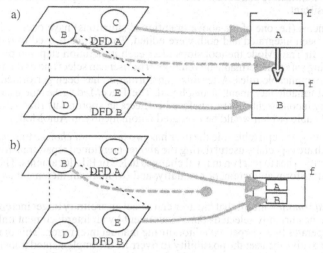

Fig. 2.18. Possible transformation of process applications

The integrator can be driven in two modes: a semi–automatic mode (AutoMode) and a (guided) manual mode (TraceMode). In *AutoMode* the tool applies rules for safe transformable increments automatically, as long as only one rule is applicable for an increment, i.e. as long as the transformation is unambiguous. If conflicts occur, i.e. if more than one rule is applicable (like the transformation of process declarations in the above–mentioned example) the user is asked to select one of these possibilities. Then the tool continues automatically, until the next conflict occurs. The AutoMode is used mainly in *initial transformations*, i.e. when a requirements specification is transformed for the first time and a new initial architecture is generated.

After documents have been integrated initially, they are usually changed later. Hence, after a certain time the documents are inconsistent. *Inconsistencies* occur in the following *situations*:

- Target increments of an integration have been deleted and the corresponding interdocument link is incomplete.

- The applied rule is no longer applicable, e.g. because some change in the context of the source increments, checked by the rule, has been changed.

- An integration (i.e. a link) has been removed by the user explicitly and thus a source increment has no correspondence.

- A new source increment has been added and has to be transformed.

No inconsistencies or only those that are *repaired automatically* by the tool occur in the following *situations*:

- The source increments of an integration has been deleted. In this case the tool deletes the corresponding interdocument link as well. This scenario is sensible, because the semantics of integration is "there is an element in the source document that should have a correspondence in the target document". If a source no longer exists, the integration link is useless as well.

- New target increments were added. This is no inconsistency, but the usual situation, because only parts of the system are modelled in the requirements and can be transformed into parts of the architecture. The rest has to be modelled manually in PiL. Hence, increments of the architecture that have no correspondence in the requirements are not necessarily inconsistent.

If inconsistencies (i.e. one of the above–mentioned situations) have occurred after the documents had been integrated and both were edited, *TraceMode* is used to *repair* these *inconsistencies*. In TraceMode the tool stops after each integration step and presents the user the remaining safe transformable increments. The user can select one of them and then select one of the applicable rules. After this transformation has been performed, the new set of safe transformable increments is displayed. The TraceMode gives the user a chance to examine every inconsistent situation before he selects an appropriate rule – even if only one rule is applicable (which would be executed automatically in AutoMode).

Besides selecting an applicable rule the user has two *additional choices* to *repair inconsistencies*, which are especially useful during the above–mentioned repair transformations, where the integration has to react on manual changes in RE or PiL documents. These possibilities are (a) transform an increment manually, and (b) mark an increment as not to be transformed.

Manual transformation means that the user can select an arbitrary target increment to be connected with the currently selected source increment by an interdocument link. Hence, the integrator operates like a hypertext editor during manual integration. This option is especially helpful to give the user the possibility to overrule the implemented transformation rule set in certain situations: The tool should help the designer to keep his architecture consistent with the requirements, it should not restrict his work.

Additionally, the user can mark an *increment* as *not to be transformed*. In this situation the integration is consistent, although the marked increment has no correspondence in the target document and applicable rules exist. This option gives the user the possibility to realize partial integrations, i.e. to escape from transformation rules for certain increments.

2.3.2 A Transformation Example Session for RE–PiL Integration

The following *example* illustrates the *process* of *incrementally updating* the *consistency* between RE and PiL documents. The requirements of a vending machine were modelled and transformed into an initial architecture (probably in semi–automatic mode). After the integration was finished, the analyst inserted a new process declaration (DFD CheckPayment) and an application (a process application CheckPayment in the DFD SellProduct, see fig. 2.19). Hence, the documents are inconsistent and an incremental repair-transformation has to be started, which just corrects the inconsistent parts of the documents. This means that the new inserted increments have to be transformed.

As mentioned above, the transformation of applications depends on the transformation of the according declarations. Therefore, only the *process declaration* can be transformed (is safe transformable) in the first step and is marked black in the SA model in fig. 2.19. *Three* transformation *rules* are applicable for this declaration and are presented as selectable commands in the menu: A rule to transform the DFD into a functional module (command PDToFM), a rule to transform it into an exported procedure of an existing module (command PDToExpResource), and – since there is only one application of the process declaration – a rule to transform it into a local procedure of the parent module (command PDToLocalResource). Furthermore, the two *standard options* are presented: The increment can be transformed manually by drawing a link to an arbitrary PiL increment to circumvent the transformation rules, or it can be marked as not to be transformed. (The remaining options in the menu are for switching off the markers in the documents and to quit the integration process.)

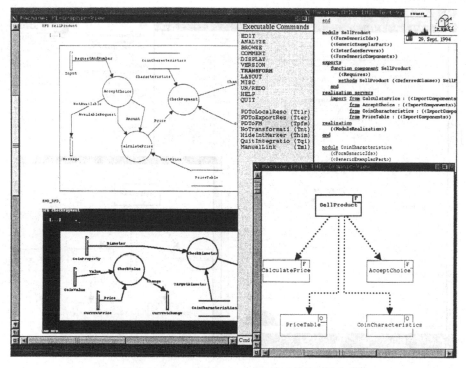

Fig. 2.19. RE–PiL transformation after insertion of a new process

We can see from fig. 2.20, that the rule transforming the process declaration into a module was selected. The module has been inserted by the integrator. Now, the process application of `CheckPayment` is transformable (see fig. 2.20). Furthermore, the process applications within the DFD `CheckPayment` are transformable as well, as we assume that their declarations have been transformed in the meantime. Transformable increments are marked black. We choose to transform the process application `CheckPayment` first. Only one rule is applicable, namely to transform this process application into an import (of module `CheckPayment` for module `SellProduct`), presented as command PAToRealImport in the menu. Again, the standard options are selectable as well. If the rule is selected, an import relation between `SellProduct` and `CheckPayment` will be inserted by the integration tool. If semi–automatic mode were selected, this rule would be applied automatically, since it is the only applicable rule.

Similar to the horizontal integration described in section 2.2, the user can *influence* the *transformation by* assigning *priorities* to rules. In this interactive integration scenario, the rules can be used to decrease the number of necessary user interactions. If several rules are applicable for a transformation (as during the transformation of process declarations described above) the user can assign different priorities to the rules for a specific increment type when transforming a specific RE specification. If he regards a certain alternative to be more appropriate for the transformation of all increments of a type, he assigns a higher priority. The integrator will regard only the rules with the highest priorities. Only, if no rule with this priority is applicable (e.g. because none of its patterns can be matched), it regards the rules with the second highest priorities, and so on. Hence, by assigning different priorities to all the rules for a certain increment type the user can change the semi–automatic transformation to a more or less automatic one.

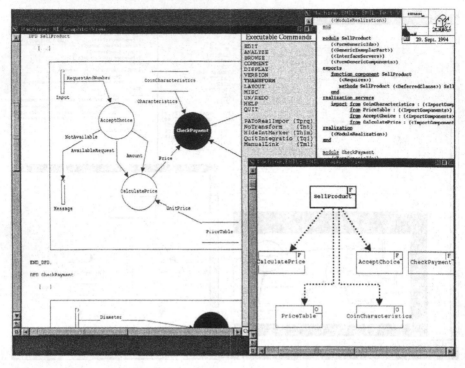

Fig. 2.20. RE–PiL transformation of a process application

Besides assigning priorities to rules the user can again *switch off* single transformation *rules* explicitly. By doing so, the according alternatives for the transformation of a certain increment type will not be applied during a transformation, even if all alternatives with a higher priority might not be applicable. Thus, there is a difference between assigning a low priority to a rule or switching it off.

In fig. 2.21 an example of a *rule set* having priorities and switched off rules is presented. Priority assignment and activation/deactivation of rules can be done by using a textual *syntax–directed editor*. In the example, the effect of the presented priority set is that only the graphical elements of requirements specification are transformed while the transformations for fine–grained textual elements, like parameters or attributes, are switched off. The standard priority used in the example is 5. Most rules get this priority. In the transformation of process, data store, entity, or relationship declarations the first alternative (transforming the declaration into an according module) is preferred and gets the higher priority 10. Hence, during an initial transformation in semi–automatic mode the integrator will apply these rules automatically.

Summarizing, the *user* has several possibilities to *influence* a *transformation*:

(1) He can leave the rule set unchanged, select one of the presented rules in any conflict and thus perform the transformation step.

(2) He can assign priorities to rules to prefer certain alternatives in situations, where several rules are applicable according to the transformation rule set. These priorities are valid for all occurrences of the according increment types.

(3) He can even override the transformation rules for a single instance of an increment type by using the manual transformation facility instead of applying a transformation rule.

(4) He can switch off transformation rules and thereby remove them from the transformation rule set. This rule is then switched off for all occurrences of the according increment type. If all rules for a certain increment type are deactivated, this increment type cannot be transformed at all. Thereby, he can realize partial transformations according to specific increment types.

(5) To realize a partial transformation on instance level, i.e. prevent a single object of an increment type from being transformed, the user can select the NoTransform alternative for this increment during the transformation.

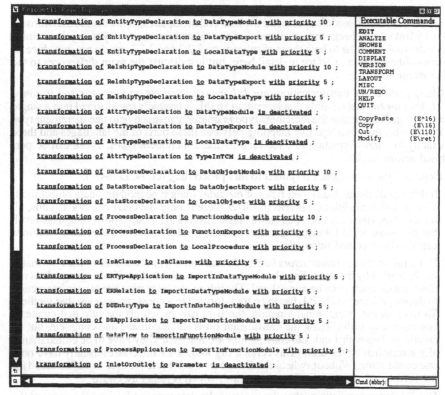

Fig. 2.21. Assigning priorities to RE–PiL transformation rules

Hence, the user is able to realize *various integration scenarios* within the scope given by the implemented transformation rule set. The only action that is not possible is to extend the set of transformation rules by adding new rules during runtime of the integrator. Therefore, the developer of a new integration tool should include the largest possible set of rules. It can be sized down later and customized by the user (mentioned above).

2.3.3 Automatic PiL–PiS Transformation

In /4. Lew 88b,c, 4. Wes 91a/ different versions of a transformation tool transforming module specifications into Modula–2 or C code templates are described. We *redeveloped* that *integrator* between *PiL* and *PiS* within the above integrator framework for the following *reasons*:

- The version of the PiL language used in former integrators has been revised, the integrator should support the new version /7. Nag 90, 7. Bör 94/.

- The new PiL language incorporates new design concepts like genericity or object–orientation. Since these concepts are neither supported in Modula–2 nor C, a new PiS language was selected. We chose Eiffel (cf. /7. Mey 88a, 7. Mey 88b/), because it directly supports these concepts and has a well–defined context–free syntax.

- Since module specifications in the old PiL language were nearly identical to the according parts of Modula–2, a context–free 1:1–transformer, as described in /4. Wes 91a/, was sufficient. The new PiL language is more general and, therefore, sometimes complex m:n–transformations are required.

The new PiL–PiS–integrator has a *similar functionality* to the other ones described above: It transforms module specifications into code templates, connects the transformed parts by links, and checks the consistency of the related documents by using these links. Since the tool is similar to both those of subsection 2.2.3 and 2.3.1, we do not introduce its functionality and user interface in detail here, but just discuss the main *differences* to the other integrators.

Many parts of the transformations are *1:1 transformations* on *language* and *instance level*. That means that not only one increment in PiL is uniquely transformed into a single increment in PiS, but also the increment type is uniquely mapped onto one increment type in PiS. Hence, there is a bijective mapping between these parts of the languages and there is exactly one transformation rule for each of these increment types. These can be performed automatically.

However, there are some *exceptions* to this proceeding (cf. /4. Lef94b/):

- In PiL we distinguish different *types* of *modules* (data type modules, data object modules, function modules), whereas in Eiffel there is only the *class construct*. Thus, all module types have to be mapped onto a class. This is a 3:1 relation on the language level, but, of course, still a 1:1 mapping on the instance level. Therefore, these transformations can also be executed automatically.

- Eiffel distinguishes *constructors* (methods that create a new instance of the type that is implemented by the according class) from *other methods*. Our PiL language does not have this distinction on language level. Therefore, the integrator needs user interaction to decide, if a method in PiL has to be transformed to a constructor or another method. To have an automatic transformation, the user can switch off the rule that creates a constructor in Eiffel. Then, the transformation is still automatic and complete, but no creation–clauses that indicate constructors are inserted. They have to be edited manually afterwards by the user. (This is not a big loss, since the classes usually have only one constructor.) Without switching off the constructor rule the user would be asked for the correct transformation of every method, which is rather awkward.

- Our PiL language distinguishes the name of the data type *module* and the name of the encapsulates *data type*. In Eiffel, as in most OO languages, both are the same. Therefore, an Eiffel class that is transformed from a data type module does not get the name of the module, but that of the datatype.

- In abstract data types every procedure/method needs a *parameter* that indicates the *instance* of that type which is manipulated by this method (cf. /7. Na 90/). In Eiffel, as in most object–oriented languages, this parameter is not explicitly given. Method calls are denoted differently (i.e. x.a() in Eiffel instead of a(x) e.g. in Ada for a call of method a with the actual parameter x). For the transformation this means that all procedures in data type modules in PiL have one parameter more than the corresponding methods in Eiffel (cf. fig. 2.22), while the parameter profile of methods of data object and function modules are not changed during a transformation. This transformation is a 2:1 or 1:1 transformation on instance level, but still can be executed automatically.

203

- Similar to the transformation of modules is the transformation of parameters. Here again our PiL language distinguishes three *modes* of parameters (in, out and inout parameters), while in Eiffel there is only one kind. Therefore, all the three parameter types are transformed to the same parameter type in Eiffel automatically.

So, the complete PiL–PiS–*transformation* can be *performed automatically.* This is due to the fact that, although there are other than 1:1 relations, no 1:n relations occur on language correspondence level, i.e. no PiL increment type that can optionally be transformed into different PiS increment types. Such 1:n relations imply corresponding user interactions.

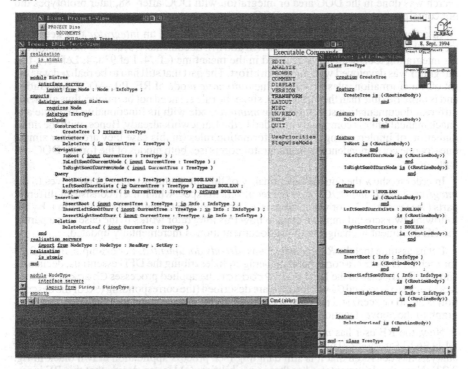

Fig. 2.22. Screendump after a successful PiL–PiS–transformation

Fig. 2.22 shows an *example*, where the PiL specification of an abstract data type Bin-Tree that encapsulates a binary tree is transformed into a class TreeType. The node types are imported from a module Node. In the automatic PiL–PiS–transformation the Eiffel class declaration in the right window is generated from the PiL specification in the left window. As the integrator is again a part of the target working area environment (here: PiS) no command to start a transformation is presented in the PiL menu, but only commands to switch to manual or stepwise mode (which is seldomly used in this scenario) or to switch usage of priorities on and off.

2.3.4 Consistency Checking and Linking between RE, PiL, and Documentation: Manual and Automatic Integration

As already mentioned in subsections 1.7.4 and 1.8.1, the IPSEN–prototypes '86 and '88 contained an *integrator* to *keep* the technical *documentation consistent* with PiS ('86) or PiL and PiS ('88), respectively (cf. /4. Lew 88c/). That integrator could be driven in *two modes*: The first mode was an automatic mode that generated the chapter/section/paragraph structure of a documentation from the architecture and checked the consistency between these documents (i.e. for each module and procedure in the architecture a section or subsection in the documentation was generated). The generated documentation structure was completely fixed, links between PiL and DOC were automatically inserted, no additional references in the documentation and corresponding links to other PiL increments could be inserted. Therefore, a second manual mode was realized, where arbitrary links could be drawn between a freely composed documentation and PiL or PiS documents by the user himself (hypertext mode integrator). The consistency of these links was checked as well, e.g. the user was notified, if a referenced increment was deleted or changed. Since no research was done in the DOC area or integration with DOC after '88, later prototypes did not contain a new integrator for the DOC environment.

To complete the current prototype, we have redeveloped an *integrator* that keeps the technical *documentation* consistent with *RE* and *PiL* documents. Because of the framework for integration tools which was realized in the meantime (cf. /4. Lef 93a, 4. Lef 95/), this integrator was developed with minimum effort. The part that still had to be realized was the set of transformation rules. It realizes the *automatic* mode of RE, PiL→DOC integration and is more flexible than the former one, since the rule set need not be unique, thus allowing different documentation structures. The *manual* mode with its functionality to create and check manual links is completely included in the framework already. Hence, with the minimal effort of implementing some transformation rules (in this case they are rather simple one–to–one correspondences) the integrator comprises both modes of the former DOC–integrator.

In order to show the outside functionality of this integrator, we *restrict* ourselves to the *integration* of *RE* and *DOC*, i.e. to the requirements spec, which itself consists of different parts (see section 2.2), for which there is a corresponding technical documentation. By the following two screendumps we explain how this integrator works in the case that a part of the RE document is changed and the documentation is incrementally updated.

Let us assume that the *RE document* was *already documented*. For example, in fig. 2.23 for each DFD there is a corresponding paragraph describing the DFD essentials, decisions, and the like. In case of the DFD SellProduct the applied processes CheckPayment, AcceptChoice, and GiveChange are described (the corresponding text of the description is not to be seen) and the corresponding references have been inserted from this paragraph to the above–mentioned RE increments, either automatically or manually.

Now, the RE user has *inserted* a *new* applied *occurrence* CalculatePrice in the DFD SellProduct. This increment is not bound to a DOC increment yet. An integrator analysis has delivered that it is still dangling (see process application drawn black in fig. 2.23). Now, the documentator has three possibilities: (a) He can decide that this RE increment is *not* to be documented at all (alternative NoTransformation in the menu). If it is to be documented the documentator can (b) either use the command ProcToDOCU *automatically* generating a documentation reference increment and a corresponding link to that reference increment connected to the text paragraph already existing for the DFD. Alternatively, he can use (c) the documentation editor, insert a reference increment in the documentation document, and then bind this increment to the new process application *manually* by using the ManualLink command. This documentation reference increment can be inserted at any documentation increment (paragraph, section etc.) thereby allowing to structure the documentation freely.

The *situation after applying* alternative (b) or (c) (in the latter case the reference increment having been inserted at Paragraph_1) is shown in fig. 2.24 in the upper right corner. The screendump shows by grey increments that the DFD SellProduct and Paragraph_1 together with the list of references are bound to each other. (The inverted reference and the error message correspond to the next step to be explained.) In the last two cases (b) and (c) the text of the documentation has to be modified appropriately.

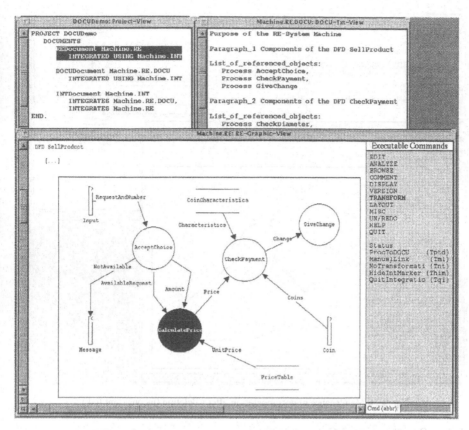

Fig. 2.23. A new increment to be documented (no corresponding link existing)

As the next step, the RE user rearranges the DFD SellProduct by *deleting* the applied process *application* GiveChange. After that change the transformer to DOC is started again. In this situation it does not detect an RE increment not bound by a missing link as above, but a link which is inconsistent as the source increment of that link is missing. It is shown in fig. 2.24 that the reference to object GiveChange is inconsistent showing the corresponding line in inverted mode. As the user has clicked the corresponding Analyze command, an error message is shown in the corresponding window. After modifying the text of the corresponding paragraph to DFD SellProduct the documentator can either remove the link by using the ManualLink command. Alternatively, he could have used the incremental transformer in a mode where all target increments and links according to erased source increments are deleted and, therefore, also for the GiveChange increment.

We have seen that this RE, PiL–DOC integrator (we have only shown the RE–DOC part of it) for a part of RE can work in automatic mode. Then, for any type of increment specified in the transformation rules a corresponding documentation increment is generated by using a corresponding command (as ProcToDOCU of above), and the *link is inserted*. Alternatively, the integration tool can be used in manual mode, where the documentator is completely free how to structure the documentation. In this case, he can add lists of references to any text documentation portion (paragraph, section etc.) and *control links by himself*.

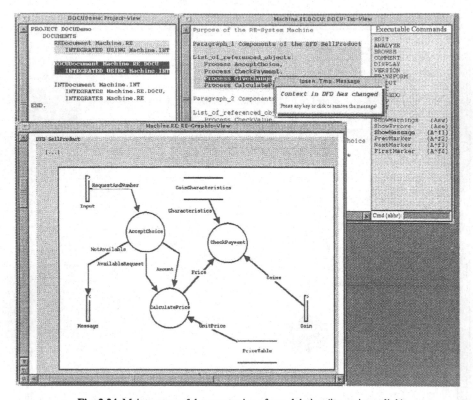

Fig. 2.24. Maintenance of documentation after a deletion (inconsistent link)

2.3.5 Summary and Comparison

This subsection introduced some integrators which we have built for making a subconfiguration consistent or reestablishing consistency after a change. The documents to be integrated stem from different working areas: *vertical integration*. As explained in chapter 1 any integrator is an add–on to the corresponding target environment in the unidirectional case (the RE–PiL transformer to the PiL environment). The bidirectional case handling different perspectives appears in the IPSEN scenario only as horizontal integration within RE (see 2.2).

The tools introduced in this section have *multiple functionality* according to the classification of chapter 1: They are transformers, consistency checkers, binding tools, and browsers.

They represent quite different *modes* of *integration*: The Pil–PiS integrator of 2.3.3 is working automatically. That this due to the fact that relations between a PiL and a PiS document can be derived from the corresponding languages to be integrated. The RE–PiL integrator of 2.3.1, or 2 is semiautomatic as for any increment of RE there are different alternatives in PiL which can be taken. So, the user has to decide which one to choose. However, we have seen that by assigning priorities and switching off rules the integrator can be modified to behave more or less automatically. The DOC integrator of 2.3.4, in the form explained here, may be used to work completely manually. The user has to decide which increments of different documents are related to DOC increments. For pragmatical reasons such a feature was also added to the RE–PiL integrator. Finally, in the case of nonautomatic integrators the completeness of the transformation can be controlled by the user.

Motivation for IPSEN integrators was given in chapter 1 and the usefulness was explained there. This is not to be repeated here. We have seen that for any integrator the *same basic functionality* is used: Generating target increments, checking increments on both sides of the relation, binding increments by links, or traversing links. Whatever type of integrator we introduced, there was one characteristic to be fulfilled by all of them: incrementality. This all is the basis for a general integrator building machinery we have developed and which is to be explained in the next chapters.

Studies of *method integration* between working areas can be divided in *literature* into those supporting structured methods (SA/SD) like /7. BST 92/ and /4. TR 88/, those transforming structured analysis into an object–oriented design (e.g. /7. War 89, 7. SI 90, 7. LH 89, 7. Shu 91/), and those supporting object–oriented analysis and design methods as /7. Boo 94/ and /7. RBP 91/. The integration of the integrated IPSEN RE method and the IPSEN PiL method was firstly introduced in /7. Jan 92/.

Tool support for fine–grained integration is also presented by some of the above–mentioned approaches (e.g. /7. SI 90, 7. LH 89/), but the emphasis is on the method level. A tool to control consistency between different parts of a requirements spec, called requirements assistant, is introduced by Shekaran and Tremlett /7. ST 92/. An example of an integration tool between different working areas in the development of information systems is the integration tool IRIS, developed within the DAIDA project (cf. /7. VMK 90, 7. CKM 93/). IRIS supports the integration of a requirements spec with a design model. Like our RE–PiL–integrator it is a semi–automatic tool, where transformation rules can be derived from defined dependencies between requirements and design objects. A mapping tool between design and the implementation called DBPL–MAP was also developed within DAIDA /7. BMM 89/. Furthermore, it should be mentioned that most of the CASE frameworks on the market (like ProMod, Teamwork, or Software through Pictures) include transformation tools, but these are often batch–like, automatically working tools and, therefore, restricted in their integration support.

2.4 Document Type Independent Tools: Common Services for Manipulation, Layout, and User Support

B. Westfechtel

While the preceding sections of this chapter have focused on various aspects of tool *integration*, the current section represents general *support tools* which are independent of a certain document type. We describe the functionality and user interface of IPSEN tools as they are provided by *IPSEN 3.0* and later prototypes. Thereby, we focus on tools which operate on the contents of documents such as requirements definitions, software architectures, or module implementations. Tools for managing these documents on a coarse–grained level are described in the next section.

2.4.1 General User Interface Characteristics

By and large, *IPSEN 3.0* and its successors have a *similar user interface* as *IPSEN 2.5*, which was described in section 2.1. Documents are displayed in windows which are decorated with vertical and horizontal scrollbars on the left–hand side and at the bottom, respectively. The window title is shown on the top. On the right–hand side, a menu bar displays the commands which are offered on the currently selected increment. Entries in uppercase letters denote command groups. The commands belonging to the currently selected command group appear at the bottom of the menu bar. The long name of a command is constructed in a Modula–2–like fashion with upper case letters denoting the beginning of a subword. The short name is enclosed in parentheses following the long name. Short names either refer to function keys or lower case letters. By typing in a short name, an experienced user avoids selecting a command from the menu by mouse click. Note that the line at the bottom of the menu bar is used for editing short names.

However, there are also some important *differences* compared to IPSEN 2.5. In addition to *textual representations*, current IPSEN prototypes also support *graphical representations* of documents. Furthermore, both types of representations may even be mixed (*hybrid representations*). In general, a representation consists of a tree of subrepresentations each of which is either textual or graphical. An example from requirements engineering was given in fig. 2.10 (section 2.2), which shows the interface of a complex process in a textual notation and the refining data flow diagram in a graphical notation, respectively.

In contrast to IPSEN 2.5, current IPSEN prototypes rely on the *X11 window system* which offers many advantages compared to the IPSEN–specific window system of IPSEN 2.5. IPSEN prototypes may now co–exist with other applications running under X. Furthermore, windows are now provided with some standard facilities which were not supported by IPSEN 2.5: Windows may be iconized, the window contents may be displayed in varying sizes, and the window size may also be manipulated by the user. Finally, a window may be moved by dragging the window to the desired position.

2.4.2 Logical Editors

For each document type, a *syntax–aided editor* is provided which offers commands for manipulating the logical structure of documents. Edit *commands* change the underlying abstract syntax graphs and are *classified* as follows:

(a) *Syntax–directed commands* are used to construct the abstract syntax graph by expanding placeholders, inserting list elements, extending identifiers, or deleting arbitrary increments.

(b) *Free input* is offered to escape from syntax–directed editing. It is useful in many situations (experienced users, input of arithmetic expressions, etc.). Arbitrary increments may be modified in free input mode. To this end, we have integrated a text editor which offers a subset of the commands provided by the well–known Emacs editor.

(c) *Cut* deletes an arbitrary increment and loads its text into a buffer. Similarly, *Copy* loads the buffer without modifying the underlying abstract syntax graph. *Paste* may be viewed as a shortcut for free text input. The parser is supplied with the buffer and the current increment and then proceeds as if the user had directly typed in the buffer contents.

(d) *File I/O* provides for reading/writing arbitrary increments from/to a text file. This facility is useful e.g. when documents are archived in a space–efficient form (an abstract syntax graph needs about 20 times more space than the corresponding text file).

(e) *Comments* may be attached to arbitrary increments. For editing comments, the same editor is used as for free input. Of course, comments may be edited together with free input of increments, as well.

While IPSEN 2.5 enforced free input of procedure calls and expressions, the user of current IPSEN prototypes may choose between syntax–directed editing and free input on any level of the abstract syntax. This *hybrid approach* is very flexible. Syntax–directed editing is preferred by users who are not familiar with the underlying language. Furthermore, it saves typing in case of a rich concrete syntax with many and/or long keywords. Free input is typically employed by experienced users who know the underlying language very well. Moreover, some changes are performed more easily in free input. For example, a while-statement may be converted into a repeat–statement in a convenient way by using the text editor. To achieve the same ease of use in case of syntax–directed editing, a lot of special-purpose commands for transforming language constructs would have to be implemented.

As we have already mentioned in section 2.1, editing is tightly integrated with *context–sensitive analysis*. Unlike IPSEN 2.5, all of its successors tolerate errors with respect to the context–sensitive syntax. The user is informed about errors and warnings by means of markers (inverted display). For each marked increment, the user may have a message displayed which explains the corresponding error or warning. Analysis may be switched on and off as desired. When analysis is switched on, the user is provided with immediate response about errors and warnings after each edit step. When analysis is switched off, all markers disappear. Furthermore, increments are only marked for analysis, but no analysis is performed internally. When the user switches analysis on again, all marked increments are analyzed, and errors and warnings are reported to the user as described above.

Finally, the current IPSEN machinery supports *graphical editing* which had not been provided by IPSEN 2.5. As has been demonstrated in sections 2.2 and 2.3, a document may now have a hybrid representation consisting of textual and graphical increments. Graphically represented increments are edited in a syntax–directed way. Although they are part of the underlying abstract syntax graph, the internal realization is hidden at the user interface. This means that the user is provided with commands for creating/deleting objects and links rather than with low–level syntax–directed commands (e.g. insert a list element). Referential integrity is guaranteed, i.e. when an object is deleted, all adjacent links are deleted, as well.

From the categories listed above, only *syntax–directed commands* are available for *graphical editing*. Of course, all categories may be applied to textual increments nested into a graphically represented increment. Furthermore, for each graphical subrepresentation the IPSEN environment also maintains an equivalent textual subrepresentation which can be edited by the user on demand. Again, all command categories may be applied there, including free input, cut & paste, and editing of comments. After editing the textual representation, the environment constructs an equivalent graphical representation. Inconsistent parts (e.g. pending links) are ignored until the inconsistencies are resolved (e.g. by editing the text representation again). Finally, file I/O is extended to graphical subrepresentations by using the equivalent text representation when generating an output file. The text representation is annotated with pseudo comments indicating the layout of graphically represented increments. In this way, the layout is reconstructed correctly when an output file is parsed in again.

2.4.3 Showing and Changing Representations

As mentioned in chapter 1, we distinguish between the logical structure of a document and its external representation. The former is called *logical document*, the latter *representation document*. In general, one logical document may have multiple representations. For example, in PiL both a textual and a graphical representation of a software architecture are provided.

The *logical editor* described in the last subsection manipulates a logical document and triggers corresponding updates of all representation documents. After execution of an edit command, all representation documents are modified incrementally by means of unparsers which generate the representations according to a table containing formatting information. The *representation editor* may then be employed to adapt representations according to the user's needs. The representation editor changes a representation document without affecting the underlying logical document. The commands offered by the representation editor are subdivided into two groups.

The first group controls the *visibility* of increments. The following *commands* are provided:

(a) *Placeholders* for *optional increments* may be *hidden* (e.g. return type of a procedure). Such placeholders may disturb the representation of a document. Of course, hidden placeholders may be made *visible* again when they are going to be filled in by the user. Note that `HidePlaceholders` only refers to placeholders for optional increments because placeholders for mandatory increments have to be filled in anyway.

(b) Furthermore, *arbitrary increments* may be *holophrased*, as well. In particular, this is useful in large documents in order to get a quick and rough overview (e.g. holophrasing of procedure bodies in a module implementation in order to display the whole module body on one screen). When an expanded increment is holophrased, its representation is replaced with [. . .] to remind the user of a holophrased part of the document (in contrast to this, optional placeholders vanish completely). An example is given in fig. 2.25.

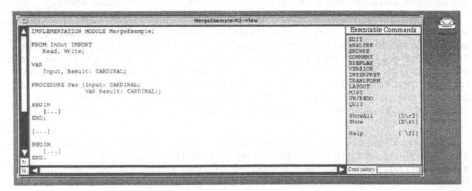

Fig. 2.25. Hiding of increments

The second group is concerned with the *layout* of displayed increments. Layout *commands* directly refer to representation increments and not to logical increments. Normally, the user selects a representation increment which is then mapped onto a logical increment for which commands are offered in the menu. Therefore, a layout *mode* is provided in order to restrict commands to the representation of increments. To make the user aware that he is operating in layout mode, the current increment is differently visualized (i.e. it is enclosed in a rectangle rather than printed in bold face). This is demonstrated in fig. 2.25.

According to the types of subrepresentations, the layout editor is further subdivided into two components the first of which is responsible for *textual layout*. The unparser automatically generates a default layout which can then be improved by means of the layout editor. When a document is edited in syntax–directed mode, its layout has to be generated, anyway. Since free input is realized by internally applying syntax–directed commands after parsing, the layout of the text which has been typed in by the user gets lost, as well.

Although the layout produced by the unparser is satisfactory in most cases, it is still necessary to support manual layout modifications. To this end, various *layout commands* are provided in order to control line breaks and indentations. By means of these commands, the user may manipulate the *layout* of *individual increments*. For example, in fig. 2.26 the user has selected the second parameter of the procedure Fac. Furthermore, he has already started command selection by choosing the command prefix Vertical from the menu. Now, all commands are displayed in the menu which place the current increment below its predecessor:

(a) NoSpace places the current increment in the next line at the same level of indentation as its predecessor (the result of applying this command is shown in fig. 2.25).

(b) Space inserts a blank line and then proceeds in the same way as NoSpace.

(c) Indent places the current increment in the next line at the next level of indentation.

(d) SpaceIndent combines Space and Indent.

(e) Finally, Conditional performs a line break only in case of overflow.

Fig. 2.26. Layout mode

The *layout* for *increment types* is determined by the developer of a syntax–oriented editor. For each increment type, a formatting rule is inserted into an unparser table which directs a generic incremental unparser. In order to provide the developer with more flexibility, the unparser table is not realized as program code but as a text file which can be manipulated by the end user. The formatting rules in the unparser table are defined in an elegant way: They are generated from the layout of EBNF–like rules which define the concrete syntax and the indentation rules of the language to be supported. The layout of these rules is manipulated by the same layout commands which have been explained above. In this way, the context–free part of a syntax–directed editor, parser, and unparser are generated from a single description. Note that the generated program code for formatting rules can still be manipulated by the developer whenever the generated code proves unsatisfactory.

While textual layout commands are used to improve an automatically generated layout, *graphical layout* is mostly *determined* by the *user* when editing the logical document. For example, when creating a logical increment, the position of the corresponding representation increment is fixed by a mouse click. However, the layout has to be generated in some situations, e.g. when the user edits a textual representation of a software architecture and whishes to have the corresponding diagram updated. Furthermore, an automatic layout algorithm can also be used to beautify a quick and dirty manual layout. Therefore, IPSEN provides a collection of *layout algorithms*. The user may experiment with these algorithms in order to find the most suitable layout of a certain diagram.

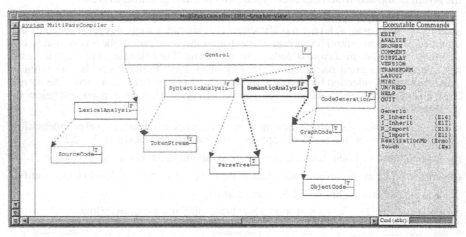

a) manual layout

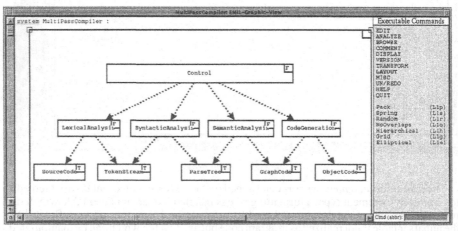

b) automatic layout

Fig. 2.27. Applying layout algorithms

An example is given in fig. 2.27 which is taken from the current PiL editor. In part 2.27.a, the user has quickly edited a diagram which shows the (simplified) architecture of a multi–pass compiler. Rather than spending much time in improving the layout manually, he has invoked a layout algorithm which is particularly suitable for hierarchical graphs (no cycles). The result is shown in fig. 2.27.b.

Furthermore, *commands* are offered for *improving* the *graphical layout manually*. Objects may be moved together with their links, boxes for objects may be resized according to their label size, labels of links may be moved, link attachments to objects may be moved, etc.

2.4.4 Moving Around

In this subsection, we briefly describe some tools which do not perform any changes on documents, but support the user in working with the IPSEN environment. The first of these tools is the *browser* which offers commands for *manipulating* the *current increment* position. These commands are classified as follows:

(a) The current increment may be changed by *cursor keys* which may be used both for textual and graphical representations. In edit and layout mode, cursor keys apply to logical and representation increments, respectively. In both cases, there is a spanning tree in terms of which the effects of cursor keys have to be defined. However, a straightforward definition results in strange effects at the user interface because internal and external moves do not coincide. For example, if –> were used to step to the next list element, the user would have to employ this key to step vertically (and not horizontally) through a list of declarations. Therefore, we have developed more intuitive definitions of cursor keys. For example, –> moves to the next leaf of the tree with respect to depth–first traversal. When applied to the variable declaration in fig. 2.28, the cursor is moved to the name of the procedure below the variable declaration. Cursor commands can be invoked both via selection from the menu and via cursor keys.

(b) Cursor keys refer to context–free relations between increments. They are complemented by browser commands which access *context–sensitive information*. These commands are used to move from an applied occurrence of an identifier to its declaration and vice versa from a declaration to all applied occurrences (which are delivered step by step via FirstAppl and NextAppl).

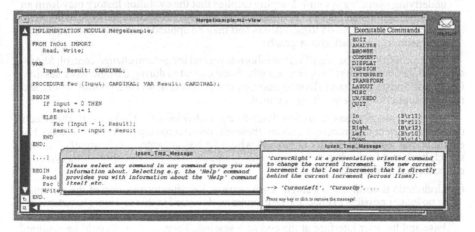

Fig. 2.28. Cursor keys

(c) Furthermore, the user may browse through all *errors* and *warnings* by applying `FirstMarker` and `NextMarker`, which automatically invoke the `ShowMessage` command to describe the type of error or warning.

(d) Finally, *text–based searches* are supported which may be applied both in edit and layout mode. Instances of a pattern may be searched either in forward or backward direction; case sensitivity (distinction between upper case and lower case letters) may be switched on and off as desired. The search returns the smallest enclosing increment of a pattern match.

2.4.5 Undo/Redo

In the current and the next subsection, two tools are presented which support *change control*. In general, change control subsumes tools and services which refer to sequences of change operations. More specifically, the following tools and services belong to this category:

(a) *Undo/redo*, which are described in the current subsection, are meta commands which revert/restore the effect of other commands issued during a work session.

(b) Similarly, *database transactions* are used by tools of the IPSEN environment to implement consistency–preserving sequences of operations. Transactions will be discussed in chapter 4.

(c) *Revision control* is used to manage the evolution histories of software documents. Each revision corresponds to a snapshot of a document which captures a certain state in its evolution history. Revision control on the coarse–grained level, where each revision is considered an atomic unit, will be covered in section 2.5.

(d) A *delta* is a difference between two revisions of the same document. The difference is defined in terms of a sequence of operations which transform one revision into the other. A *logical delta* describes the differences from the user's point of view. Logical deltas will be described in the next subsection. A *physical delta* is used by the underlying database system to store revisions in a space–efficient form. Physical deltas will be discussed in chapter 4.

(e) Finally, *merging* is used to combine changes performed on different branches of the evolution history (e.g. combination of a bug fix and adaptation to a new revision of the underlying operating system). Merging implies that the evolution history may form an acyclic graph (rather than a tree) in general. In the next subsection, a merge tool will be presented which relies on logical deltas and may be applied to all software documents represented as abstract syntax graphs.

Change control may be classified into short–term and long–term change control. *Short–term* change control refers to operations which are executed during a single work session. Undo/redo and transactions belong to this category. In contrast, revision control, deltas, and merging support *long–term* change control.

After these preparations, let us now describe the *undo/redo tool*. Undo reverts the effects of a sequence of commands; redo restores these effects after having performed an undo. For example, the user may undo a command which he has activated inadvertently, he may switch back and forth when debugging a program, etc. The functionality of undo/redo is characterized as follows:

(a) Undo/redo is confined to a *single work session*, i.e. after termination of the session it is no longer possible to undo and redo commands issued in this session. (In order to remove this restriction, IPSEN would have to snapshot the complete state of both the database and the user interface at the end of a session. Then, a session could be resumed seamlessly.)

(b) Within a session, undo/redo refers to an *unbounded command sequence*. There is no limit to the number of commands which may be undone or redone.

(c) All commands issued during a session are arranged in a *single sequence*. This means that each command is viewed as performing a global state change. This approach guarantees that integration commands, which affect multiple documents, are handled correctly. Attaching a separate sequence to each open document would result in severe consistency problems in case of partial undo/redo of the effects of an integration command.

(d) Undo/redo refers to *arbitrary commands*, including editing, analysing, layout modification, increment selection, cursor movements, etc. However, undo/redo is confined to those commands which manipulate the contents of documents. Administrative commands such as creation, deletion, opening, and closing of documents cannot be undone for similar reasons as those mentioned under (a).

(e) Undo and redo are *meta commands*, i.e. they cannot be applied to themselves. Undo and redo do not appear in the command sequence for the work session. This solution has been selected in order to avoid potentially confusing effects of self–referential commands.

(f) Undo and redo are *state–constrained*. Undo of a sequence s of commands may be invoked only in the state which has been produced by the original execution of s. This ensures that undo produces a consistent state, but it excludes selective undo (i.e. undo of some sequence s which is followed by a non–empty sequence s'). Similarly, redo may be applied only after a corresponding undo, and it may not be used to repeat the same action several times. Thus, undo and redo are constrained to step back and forth in the command sequence.

The *user interface* of the undo/redo tool is shown in fig. 2.29. The command sequence is displayed in a window, where each command is represented by a human readable text string and states before and after command execution are indicated by dashed lines. The current state is marked by an inverted representation (state 18). In order to undo a command sequence, the user selects the state he wants to have established and then activates the Undo command. In the same way, a Redo command is invoked.

Fig. 2.29. Undo/redo tool

Undo/redo are supported in a *wide range* of *interactive systems* in different ways. Mostly, undo and redo are confined to a single work session (a). In some systems (e.g. some commercial text processing systems), there is an upper bound to the number of undoable commands (b). Multi–threaded undo – separately for each document – is supported e.g. in the

Intermedia hypertext system /6. YHM 88/, but leads to consistency problems in an integrated environment (c). Usually, the scope of undo/redo is more or less restricted, since some commands (e.g. with side effects) cannot be undone (d). In Interlisp /2. TM 84/, undo commands can be undone (i.e. they are no meta commands as e.g. in /4. ACS 84/), leading to potentially confusing effects (e). Finally, in Interlisp any command can be undone in any state without ensuring consistency (f).

2.4.6 Deltas and Merging

Undo/redo is closely related to *revision control*. While undo/redo is concerned with short–term change control, revision control addresses long–term change control. In order to support the maintenance of long–lived software systems, it is essential to record snapshots of documents which reflect their evolution histories. These snapshots are called *revisions*.

Revision control may be performed for the following reasons:

(a) *Maintenance* of software systems. In order to maintain a software system over a long period, revisions must be kept to make certain states in the evolution history reproducible (e.g. for bug fixes).

(b) *Backup*. In order to recover from erroneous modifications, revisions are used to provide for a backup facility.

(c) *Coordination*. If only one revision is maintained for each document, each user is immediately affected by changes performed by other users. Revision control allows for establishing stable workspaces. Each user can rely on frozen, old revisions of other documents until he explicitly decides to incorporate a new revision into his workspace.

A *delta* is a sequence of commands which describes the differences between two revisions of a certain software document. IPSEN provides a general Diff tool which may be applied to arbitrary software documents represented as abstract syntax graphs. An example is shown in fig. 2.30 where two revisions of a simple module body (written in Modula–2) are compared. Increments occurring in only one revision are marked in grey (e.g. ELSIF part in the left revision shown on the left). Increments which occur differently in both revisions (e.g. different identifiers of the procedure Fact and Factorial, respectively) are marked in black.

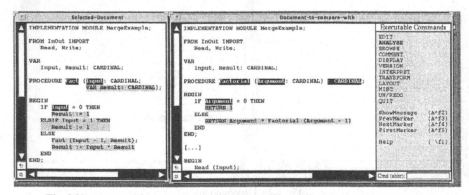

Fig. 2.30. Diff tool for comparing software documents realized as abstract syntax graphs

The Merge tool is closely related to the Diff tool. In the simplest case, the revisions of a document are *ordered linearly* along the time axis. However, the evolution history may also *branch*, e.g. when bugs in an old revision have to be fixed while simultaneously a new revision is being developed. Later on, it may be desirable to *merge* the changes performed on different branches, i.e. to produce a common successor that incorporates all of these changes.

Fig. 2.31 states the merge *problem* in *two* different *ways*:

(a) *Merging of branches*. Starting from a *base revision* b, two *alternative revisions* a_1 and a_2 were developed. Now, a *merge revision* m is to be constructed which combines a_1 and a_2 with respect to b.

(b) *Merging of deltas*. The merge algorithm is supplied with two *deltas* (sequences of change operations) $d_i=\text{delta}(b,a_i)$, from which a single *merge delta* $d=\text{delta}(b,m)$ is to be constructed.

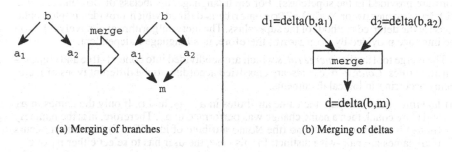

| (a) Merging of branches | (b) Merging of deltas |

Fig. 2.31. The merge problem

Merging revisions manually is both time–consuming and error–prone. Thus, a *tool* is needed which *automates* the process of *merging* as far as possible. Since the changes performed on different branches may interfere, merging cannot be automated completely. Rather, the merge tool should combine non–interfering changes automatically and consult the user when interference is detected.

The designer of a merge tool has to balance the following *contradictory requirements*:

(a) On the one hand, the merge tool should be *general*, i.e. it should be applicable to arbitrary software documents. To this end, the tool has to abstract from the languages in which the documents are written.

(b) On the other hand, the merge tool should be *intelligent*, i.e. it should be based on a high–level concept of change in order to produce a result which makes sense. To this end, the tool has to incorporate language–specific knowledge.

Our merge tool /4. Wes 91b/ *balances* these *requirements* in the following way:

(a) It is applicable to documents written in *arbitrary languages*.

(b) It preserves the *context–free correctness*: Starting from context–free correct revisions, the merge tool produces a result which is also correct with respect to the context–free syntax of the underlying language.

(c) It detects *context–free conflicts*, i.e. interfering changes to the context–free structure.

(d) It detects and partially removes certain *context–sensitive conflicts*. However, it does not preserve context–sensitive correctness because this cannot be achieved through a general tool for arbitrary languages.

The merge tool presented above balances generality with intelligence. Therefore, it *differs* from other *merge tools* which may be classified as follows:

(a) On the one hand, there are merge tools based on *text files* /4. AGM 86, 4. LCS 88, 4. Tic 85/. These tools do a good job in tool–kit environments, but they are not suited for a structure–oriented environment because they do not take the underlying syntactic and semantic structures into account. In particular, they are not able to detect syntactical or semantical conflicts.

(b) On the other hand, there are approaches tailored to a *specific language* /4. HPR 89, 4. YHR 90, 4. Ber 86/. These approaches allow more intelligent merge decisions to be made (they even consider semantics of programs), but they are highly specialized. Furthermore, practical tools relying on such approaches are not yet available.

The merge tool operates on *logical documents*. Its language independence is accomplished by means of an object–oriented design: The class Document is an abstract superclass (i.e. a class which has no instance) which provides a uniform interface to documents written in arbitrary languages. These operations are deferred methods (i.e. no implementations are provided in the superclass). For each language, a subclass of Document (e.g. EiffelDocument or Modula2Document) is defined which provides implementations for the deferred methods of the superclass. The merge algorithm exclusively relies on the interface provided by Document; therefore, it is language independent.

The merge tool applies *merge rules* which are subdivided into context–free and context–sensitive rules. *Context–free rules* are classified according to the different types of increments occurring in logical documents:

(a) *Identifier rules* compare the name attributes in a_1, a_2, and b. If only the names in a_1 and b are equal, then a name change was performed in a_2. Therefore, in m the name n_2 (in a_2) is assigned to i.Name (the Name attribute of identifier i). A conflict occurs if all names are pair–wise distinct. In this case, the user has to select either n_1 or n_2.

(b) *Structure rules* compare corresponding components (the first child, the second child etc.) of record–like structures. If a component was replaced on exactly one branch, it is automatically copied into m. A conflict occurs if the same component was replaced on both branches. In this case, the user has to determine which component is copied into m.

(c) *List rules* handle changes to list structures. If a list element i_1 is both in a_1 and b, but not in a_2, it was deleted from a_2 and therefore is excluded from m. If i_1 is not in the base, it was inserted into a_1. In this case, it is inserted into m. A conflict occurs if two elements were inserted at the same position. Then the user has to determine the order in which the elements appear in m.

Fig. 2.32 shows an *example* of applying the merge tool. The top window displays the base revision, the alternatives to be merged are presented in the windows at the bottom. The example refers to the evolution of a simple Modula–2 program for calculating the factorial of a non–negative integer. By means of an identifier rule, a context–free conflict is detected between changes to the names of the procedure. The conflict is emphasized by marking the names, and the user may then choose between the left and the right alternative.

In addition to the modification of the procedure name, the following changes have been applied to the base revision:

(a) b -> a_1 : In the body of the procedure Fac, an extra case was added (ELSIF) to avoid one recursive call.

(b) b -> a_2 : The procedure was turned into a function. Furthermore, the name of the input parameter was replaced with Argument.

With respect to the context–free structures, these changes do not interfere. Thus, context–free merging proceeds without user interactions. However, the result is not what we desire: The merge algorithm fails to apply the changes of the procedure heading to the extension of the IF statement in its body. Furthermore, the situation is extremely bad because the merge result does not contain context–sensitive errors: The applied occurrences of Input and Result are bound to the declarations in the enclosing block. Thus, the inadequacy of the merge result might turn out only at run–time. Note that the program crashes only

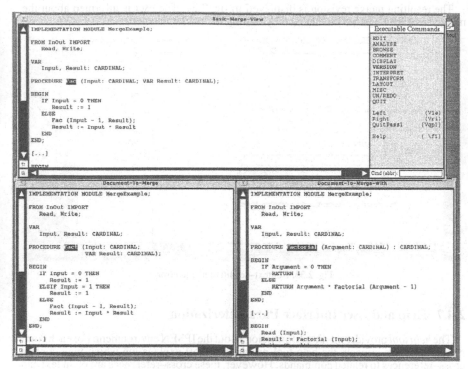

Fig. 2.32. Context–free merge conflict

when the user inputs the value 1. In general, such a rarely occurring error might cause considerable trouble when it creeps into a large and complex software system.

In addition to context–free rules, the merge tool applies *context–sensitive rules* which refer to bindings of applied occurrences to their declarations. Context–free rules are restricted such that identifier rules apply to declarations only. Context–sensitive rules are applied after context–free merging has been completed. For applied occurrences, bindings to declarations are analysed rather than names (i.e. strings). An expected binding in m is inferred from the bindings in b, a1, and a2. If the expected binding is unique and differs from the actual binding, the merge tool tries to remove the difference by replacing the name. If this attempt fails, an error is recorded in the merge revision which has to be handled by the user later on. For further details concerning context–sensitive merge rules, the reader is referred to /4. Wes 91b/.

In our example, context–sensitive rules are applied as follows:

(a) The applied occurrence of `Input` (see condition of `ELSIF` part) is a new one which comes from a₁. In a₁, it was bound to the declaration of the value parameter. From these facts, the algorithm infers that the applied occurrence should be bound to the same declaration in m. To achieve this goal, it automatically changes the applied occurrence from `Input` to `Argument`.

(b) Similarly, the algorithm detects that the applied occurrence of `Result` (see condition of `ELSIF` part) is bound to different declarations in a₁ and m. In this case, it is not possible to make the applied occurrence refer to the original declaration. Therefore, the algorithm produces a warning which indicates a potential problem to the user. Note that error correction would require language specific knowledge (the assignment has to be turned into a `RETURN` statement).

The resulting merge revision is displayed in fig. 2.33. The user is informed about the merge error which has to be removed by editing the merge revision.

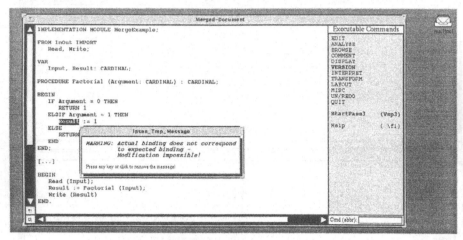

Fig. 2.33. Context–sensitive merge error

2.4.7 Help and User Interface Parameterization

The *help tool* provides on–line information about the IPSEN environment. For each command offered in a menu, the help tool provides a short explanation which may contain cross–references to related commands. However, these cross–references are plain text and are not interpreted by the help system. In order to make the user familiar with the help tool, the command `SelectMeFirst` provides on–line information about the help tool itself. To obtain a description of a certain command, the user activates the `Help` command and then selects the interesting command from the menu. The help tool retrieves its description and displays it in a message window (see fig. 2.28 which shows information about `CursorRight`).

Finally, IPSEN provides some limited facilities for *user interface parameterization*:

(a) *Window parameters* such as default position, size, and font size may be adapted by the `StoreWinParam` command which stores the actual parameter values of the current window as defaults. These defaults are used for initialization when the next window of the same type is opened.

(b) The *command table* may be edited in order to change various command properties. These include the long name appearing in the menu, the short name used for activation through the keyboard, command priority, and implicit activation. A command to be invoked implicitly is activated automatically when an increment is selected. In this way, the user is relieved from explicit command selection. A useful application of implicit activation refers to editing of expressions: many users prefer free input of expressions and therefore switch on the implicit activation flag of the change command. Command priorities are used to guide the selection among multiple commands which can be activated implicitly.

All parameterization facilities mentioned above can be employed by the user of an IPSEN environment during a session (*on–line parameterization*). Since user interface parameters are stored in text files, *off–line parameterization* is also supported by editing these text files before running a session. IPSEN developers supply reasonable default parameterizations which can be tailored by end users to their individual needs.

2.4.8 Summary

This section explained quite *different functionalities* available on an IPSEN environment: Context–free textual and graphical editing, showing and changing representations, moving around by direct selection, navigation and browsing, undo/redo, deltas and merging, getting help or changing the user interface of a corresponding environment.

This section showed generally available functions which *support* the work of single *members* of a group of developers. So, we introduced services in this section existing on the same level as those of preceding sections of this chapter. They have been summarized in an own section because they are available for any document of the working areas PiS, RE, PiL, or whatsoever. Aspects supporting the collaboration of different members of a group are presented in the next section.

When we speak of document type independent tools, this document type independence has *different semantics*: (1) The service of the tool is directly available as part of any environment. This is the case e.g. for undo/redo. (2) A service which has to be implemented but is implemented in the same way for all IPSEN environments. This, for example, is true for syntax–directed editing commands. (3) A general service is available which requires certain assumptions made by IPSEN. An example for this is the merging tool which assumes AST modelled internal documents.

Parameterization is also done on different levels. One branch is that the SDE developer can parameterize a certain environment, e.g. the layout for the type of increments. Another level is parameterization of the development before usage. Neither were presented here. In this section we have only discussed parameterization features which can be changed at SDE runtime.

There are *further general services* on a document which, however, are used by the developer of a new tool, like transaction management, which are explained in chapter 4. Transaction management is also a topic of change control as undo/redo or merging which were explained here. Furthermore, there are services for users or basic mechanisms for tool developers not restricted to one document but available for different documents. They are both encoded in basic components of the IPSEN framework. Some of them will be explained in chapter 4.

2.5 Integration on Coarse–Grained Level: Tools for Managing Products, Processes, and Resources

B. Westfechtel

All preceding sections described tools operating on the *fine–grained level*. This means that these tools operate on the contents of software documents such as requirements definitions, software architectures, and module implementations. Sections 2.1 and 2.4 focused on tools operating on single documents, while sections 2.2 and 2.3 were devoted to integration between multiple software documents. In order to apply these tools, an organizational framework is needed which determines the structure of a software system, the processes to be carried out, and the resources which are required to this end. This organizational framework operates on the *coarse–grained level*.

Using the terminology introduced in chapter 1, the tools presented below operate on *administrative configurations*. So, if we consider documents, subconfigurations, or complete configurations on technical level, software documents are regarded as atomic units, i.e. we are not interested in their internal structure and the detailed technical processes for editing, analyzing, or executing these documents. Analogously, subconfigurations on administrative level only give information about the documents they consist of, and the relations between these documents. Processes for making technical subconfigurations consistent or reestablishing consistency again after a change, regarding the internals of documents and fine–grained dependencies between documents, are not considered. Again, only coarsegrained information between documents (a document depends on another document) is interesting. As we are only interested in coarse–grained information in this section, we speak of configuration and consistency *control* and the term configuration is restricted to coarsegrained or administrative configurations throughout this section.

The tools presented in this section constitute a *management environment* which integrates management of products, processes, and resources on the coarse–grained level and provides hooks for integrating tools operating on the fine–grained level. As outlined in chapter 1, restriction to the coarse–grained level implies that the underlying concepts are very general. Therefore, they may be applied not only to software engineering, but also to related engineering disciplines (e.g. mechanical or electrical engineering). Actually, the tools presented below have been applied in a joint project with mechanical engineers (the SUKITS project, /6. EMN 92/). Here, however, we shall focus on software engineering applications.

The *development* of the management environment follows the *same line* of *ideas* as for other environments introduced in this chapter: We have internal subdocuments for products, processes, and resources, and we maintain fine–grained increment–to–increment relations within and between these subdocuments. So, from the tool builder's point of view the problems are very similar to those of building an RE environment and integration tools between different views. Therefore, it is not surprising that we *apply* the *IPSEN machinery* to build the management environment.

2.5.1 Product Management

In the current subsection, we provide a survey of tools for *product management*. These tools aid in maintaining versions and configurations of software systems, where documents appear at the leaves of composition hierarchies. Thus, the tools described below belong to the software configuration management domain /3. Win88/.

Goals and Principles

In the following, we will introduce the basic *notions* and *principles* underlying *product management*. The reader will notice that the terminology slightly differs from and extends the terminology used in chapter 1. It is, therefore, defined and related to the notions used above.

Early efforts in the field of *software configuration management* succeeded in providing isolated tools for solving specific problems. Make /4. Fel 79/, which supports consistent production of derived objects, and SCCS /4. Roc 75/ or RCS /4. Tic 85/, which both efficiently store revisions of text files, may be quoted as classical examples. Subsequently, tool–kit environments such as DSEE /4. LCS 88, 4. CL 84/ and Shape /4. ML 88, 4. ML 90/ were built which integrate and extend the functionality of first–generation tools. All tools and environments mentioned above were built on top of file–based operating systems and focused on programming–related issues. In contrast, our product management system relies on graphs and covers the whole software life cycle. Version, configuration, and consistency control are supported in an integrated way. Furthermore, the product management system aids in managing system families existing in many variants.

Product management is concerned with the following *tasks*:

(a) *Version control.* During their lifetimes, both software systems and their components evolve into multiple versions. A version is a snapshot of an object which is used to record a certain state of its evolution. Versions are recorded for various purposes: maintenance of old versions of software systems delivered to customers, backup to previous versions after erroneous modifications have been performed, team coordination by providing stable and reliable workspaces consisting of released versions, etc. Version control is used to manage the evolution history of arbitrary objects (systems, subsystems, documents).

(b) *Configuration control.* In general, non–trivial software systems consist of many components which are organized into a composition hierarchy and are connected by manifold dependencies. Configuration control is concerned with recording and manipulating the structure of complex objects such as systems and subsystems. Configuration control has to be integrated with version control; in particular, it must accurately record which component versions make up a certain configuration of a system or subsystem.

(c) *Consistency control.* Consistency control is concerned with analyzing and establishing the correctness of configurations. In particular, the following aspects of consistency need to be considered: structural consistency (does a configuration consist of correctly typed components and dependencies, are any mandatory elements missing?), internal consistency (are the contents of components consistent?), and external consistency (is a dependent component, e.g. a software architecture, consistent with its master, e.g. a requirements definition?).

Let us now introduce some basic notions for product management: A technical document is a logical unit of reasonable size which is typically manipulated by a single software engineer (see chapter 1). Any artifact produced in the software life cycle may be recorded in a document (e.g. a module implementation). The product management system does not rely on any assumptions regarding the internal structure of documents (coarse–grained approach). So, a *product management document* (in this section only called *document*) contains that information necessary to control the different states of a technical document can have.

Logically related technical documents are collected in technical configurations (see chapter 1). For example, a technical subconfiguration may comprise all documents describing a certain software system or some subsystem thereof. In general, technical subconfigurations may be nested so that they form a composition hierarchy of arbitrary depth. Documents, in the sense of this section, act as leaves of the composition hierarchy and correspond e.g. to modules of a program. For controlling the different states of a software system on coarse–grained level, the term *product management document group* is introduced (called *document group* in short). (We shall see that a document group in fact controls the states of a family of software systems.)

Components of a document group are related by various kinds of *dependencies*. Such dependencies may either connect components belonging to the same working area (e.g. dependencies between modules of a program), or they may cross working area boundaries (e.g. dependencies between software architectures and requirements definitions). Accurate management of dependencies is an essential prerequisite for consistency control, i.e. for keeping interdependent components consistent with each other. The semantics of dependencies are *application–dependent*. For example, if A depends on B, then A might import from B, A might inherit from B, A might realize a specification given in B, or A might reference increments in B, etc.

Product management supports uniform version control for both documents and document groups. Therefore, we subsume both notions under the term *object*. Each object has an evolution history represented by a graph of versions interconnected by *history relations*. Versions of documents and document groups are denoted as *revisions* and *configurations*, respectively. Due to uniform versioning, all benefits gained from version control (e.g. reuse, change management) may be exploited on arbitrary levels of the composition hierarchy.

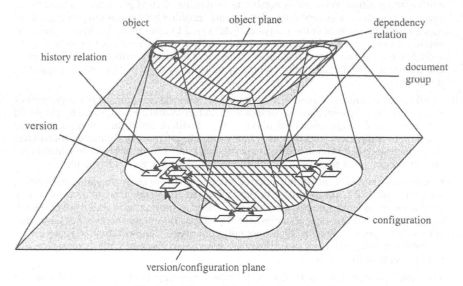

Fig. 2.34. Object and version/configuration plane

According to the distinction between objects and their versions, the product management model distinguishes between an *object plane* and a *version/configuration plane* (fig. 2.34). An object represents a set of versions. The version/configuration plane refines the object plane: each object is refined into its versions, and each relation between two objects is refined into relations between corresponding versions. Furthermore, history relations between versions of one object represent its evolution. While the object plane provides an overview by abstracting version–independent structural information, the version/configuration plane accurately represents actual versions (revisions and configurations, respectively) as well as their mutual relations.

A *(product management) database* comprises all objects, versions, and relations for a certain software system or subsystem. In order to structure the information contained in such a database, the product management system provides different kinds of views each of which corresponds to a certain subgraph of the database:

(a) The evolution history of an object is represented by a *version graph* whose nodes and edges correspond to versions and history relations, respectively. In fig. 2.34, version graphs are shown within large ellipses in the version/configuration plane. Furthermore, objects are represented by small ellipses in the object plane.

(b) A configuration is described by a *configuration graph* which is composed of version components and dependencies. In fig. 2.34, a configuration graph is represented as a hatched region in the version/configuration plane.

(c) Analogously, a *document group graph* consists of object components and dependencies. In fig. 2.34, a document group graph is represented as a hatched region in the object plane. A document group graph for a particular object is composed of all components and dependencies which occur in a configuration graph for some particular version of this object.

The main advantage of the object–version–plane model consists in its support for *system families*. A document group graph represents a family of related configurations. The members of a family may exist in many variants. For example, a multi–pass compiler might vary with respect to the following attributes: target machine, host machine, algorithms for lexical, syntactic, or semantic analysis, presence/absence of an optimization pass, etc. In the simplest case, all configurations, i.e. all family members are structured identically. Then, the document group graph represents the structure of each configuration, abstracting from the version numbers of components.

However, in more complicated cases, *structural variation* does occur. Then, the document group graph is divided into a common part, which is shared by all members of the family, and a varying part, whose elements occur in a proper subset of the family members. Since structural variation does occur in practice, product management has to support this. It is up to the user to break up a document group (i.e. divide and distribute the family) into different document groups if structural variations become too large.

Note that all information described above refers to the coarse–grained level, i.e. revisions of documents are considered atomic units. On the coarse–grained level, the product management model supports *two* different *kinds* of *refinement* or *decomposition* (cf. fig. 2.34):

(a) The version/configuration plane *refines* the object plane. This refinement has *OR*–semantics. Versions are alternative instances of some object. Consequently, in order to construct a configuration from a document group, one alternative version has to be selected for each component (provided that it belongs to that configuration, see remark on structural variation above).

(b) Within the version/configuration plane, each configuration is *decomposed* into its components and their interdependencies. This decomposition has *AND*–semantics. The configuration actually consists of all components and dependencies. Decomposition stops at the level of document revisions.

Fig. 2.35 shows the *relation* between *administrative* and *technical configurations*. Each document revision contained in an administrative configuration is composed of a set of interrelated increments, and each dependency consists of a set of links between increments which belong to different document revisions. Note that inter–document links are stored in separate data structures (integration documents, see sections 2.2 and 2.3).

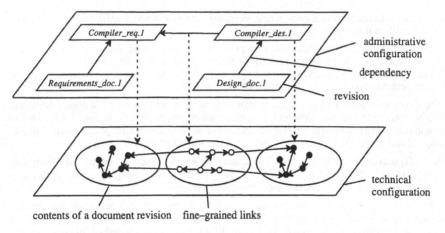

contents of a document revision   fine–grained links

Fig. 2.35. Relation between administrative and technical configurations

Functionality and User Interface

After having discussed goals and principles of product management, we take a closer look at the product management system by presenting a small *sample session*. The example refers to the maintenance of a multi–pass compiler. We consider two changes of the compiler, namely a bug fix and an extension, namely the addition of an optimization phase. To keep the example simple, we assume that both requirements definition and software architecture are contained in one document, respectively. In practice, these objects are too large to be represented in a single document. Therefore, they would be represented by subconfigurations on technical level and document groups on administration level, respectively.

Fig. 2.36 shows the *document group graph* of the multi–pass compiler. The document group graph contains a requirements definition and a software architecture which are related by a dependency. The passes of the compiler are fixed in the software architecture document. For each module specification in the software architecture, a corresponding module implementation is contained in the document group. One module is introduced for each pass of the compiler (lexical analysis, syntactic analysis, semantic analysis, and code generation), and a control module is required for calling these passes in turn. Finally, the document group contains three documentations each of which corresponds to one working area of the software life cycle (suffix _doc).

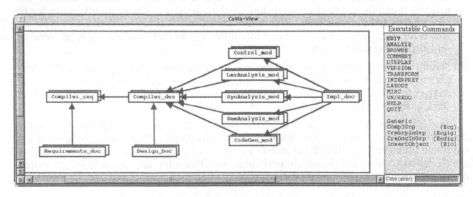

Fig. 2.36. Document group graph of the multi–pass compiler

We assume that two configurations of the compiler (versions 1 and 2 of fig. 2.37) have already been developed sequentially which share the structure given in fig. 2.36. Now, let us consider a typical situation in *software maintenance*. The following changes are performed concurrently, both starting from the second configuration:

(a) A bug fix is removed in the code generation pass (version 3).

(b) The compiler is enhanced by adding an optimization pass (version 4).

Concurrent changes typically need to be performed when bug fixes have to be applied to an old version delivered to a customer, while enhancements are already under way which are to be incorporated into a new version. In this way, *branches* are introduced into the version graph (fig. 2.37). In order to *merge* the changes, a common successor (version 5) is eventually created which contains both the bug fix and the optimization pass. In general, the version graph must not contain cycles, but branches and merges are allowed.

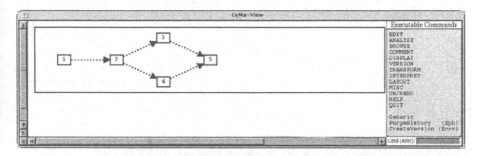

Fig. 2.37. Version graph of the multi–pass compiler

The first change is simple: In order to perform the *bug fix*, a successor of configuration 2 is created by means of the `DeriveVersion` command. `DeriveVersion` creates a shallow copy of the configuration, i.e. references to component versions are copied, but new versions of these components are created on demand only. In order to fix the bug, the code generation module is replaced with a new revision. We assume that no other changes are required (in particular, both the module interface and the documentation remain unaffected).

To manipulate a configuration, a graphical editor is provided which is constructed such that *no view switches* have to be performed. Configuration graphs play a central role in executing development and maintenance processes. Most activities are carried out in the work context of some configuration. In particular, new versions of components may be created via the configuration graph editor rather than by operating on the version graphs directly (see below). Furthermore, the configuration graph editor offers commands for maintaining consistency of a configuration graph with the corresponding document group graph (to be explained later on).

In order to make creation of component versions more convenient, the *configuration graph editor* offers a command `DeriveVersionInConfiguration` which calls `DeriveVersion` and inserts the new version into the configuration. To carry out the bug fix, this command is used to replace the code generation module with a new revision. The configuration graph editor is illustrated in fig. 2.38, where the user has invoked the `Help` command which displays on–line information about a selected command. Note that components of configurations are drawn as single–framed boxes (representing single versions, see fig. 2.38) while components of document groups are drawn as double–framed boxes (representing sets of versions, see fig. 2.36).

So far, all configurations of the multi–pass compiler are structured identically. Each configuration is specific with respect to the versions of its constituting components. For exam-

228

ple, configuration 3 contains another version of the code generation module than configuration 2. By abstracting from the version numbers of components, we obtain the corresponding document group graph (see fig. 2.36). As long as all configurations are structured identically, the document group graph represents the unique structure of the multi–pass compiler. In case of structural variants, the situation gets more complicated. Then, we have to distinguish between common parts and varying parts (see below).

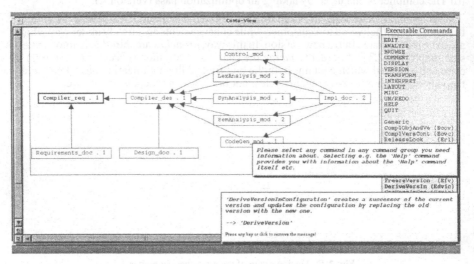

Fig. 2.38. Configuration graph for version 3 of the multi–pass compiler (before bug fix)

The second change, which is performed in parallel to the first, consists of the addition of an *optimization pass* which operates on the intermediate code (i.e. optimization is performed between semantic analysis and machine code generation). Again, a successor of configuration 2 is created by applying CreateVersion (we assume that bug fix and optimization cannot be handled sequentially, which is a realistic scenario in software maintenance). In order to add the optimization pass, most components of the current configuration have to be modified (requirements definition, software architecture, some modules of the implementation, and all documentations). To this end, new component versions are derived, edited, and frozen.

Note that new *component versions* are created *on demand* only. A deep copy of the configuration, which creates new versions of all components, does not allow for sharing of components and results in a huge amount of new versions which partially do not differ from their predecessors. This approach does not allow for reuse of versions among multiple configurations, and it also makes it difficult to figure out actual differences between configurations.

In contrast to the bug fix, addition of an optimization pass requires a *structural change* to the current configuration: a new module Optimize_mod has to be created and connected to the software architecture and the implementation documentation by means of dependencies. Up to now, all configuration graphs have been structured identically, i.e. abstraction from version numbers results in identical graphs. This is no longer the case. The product management system allows for structural variations among the configurations of a document group. This allows for managing families of related configurations which, however, need not be structured identically. The following consistency constraint must hold between a document group graph and its configuration graphs: For each version component/ dependency in some configuration graph, the document group graph must contain the corresponding object component/dependency. Loosely speaking, the document group graph is a union of all configuration graphs.

The product management system provides two ways to perform a structural change:

(a) *Top down*: First, the document group is modified. Second, these modifications are propagated to the current configuration. The second step is supported by a complex editor command named CompleteConfiguration which inserts all components and dependencies occurring in the document group, but not yet in the current configuration.

(b) *Bottom up*: The current configuration is modified by complex commands which maintain the relations between object and version/configuration plane. Whenever a component or dependency is inserted into a configuration, the corresponding modification is applied to the document group, if necessary.

The bottom view of fig. 2.39 shows the final configuration including the optimization pass. An analysis has been invoked to detect the *differences* between this configuration and its predecessor. Components which occur in identical versions in both configurations are shown as white boxes. Dark grey boxes denote components which occur in different versions in both configurations (e.g. Compiler_req). Light grey boxes represent components which belong to only one configuration (Optimize_mod). Note that the Diff command also detects differing dependencies, but they are marked only if their ends belong to both configurations (not demonstrated by the example).

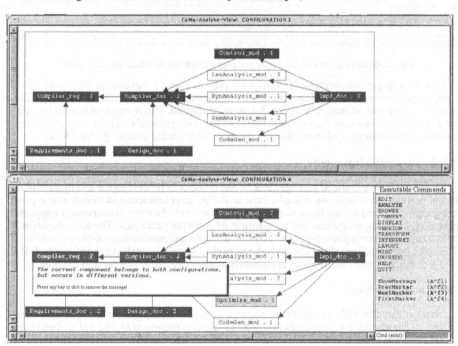

Fig. 2.39. Differences between configuration graphs of the multi-pass compiler

Fig. 2.40 displays the updated document group graph. An analysis has been invoked to detect the *varying parts* of the document group, i.e. components and dependencies which are not shared by all configurations. Varying components are represented by black boxes, while shared components are shown as white boxes.

After having completed both the addition of the optimization pass and the bug fix, these modifications are *merged*. Merging may be performed e.g. in the following way: First, a successor of the configuration including the optimization pass is created. Since we intend to merge the bug fix into the new configuration, another history relation is added which connects the bug fix configuration and the new configuration. Second, a complex command is applied which is called UpdateConfiguration and replaces all components which are not up–to–date with most recent versions. In our example, the binding of component CodeGen_mod is updated because a revision has been derived from the one which has been used so far. The resulting version graph was already shown in fig. 2.37.

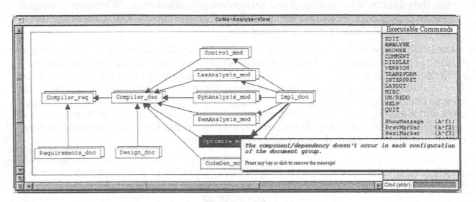

Fig. 2.40. Varying parts of the document group graph for the multi–pass compiler

Note that in general merging of configurations may *imply merging* of the contents of component versions (when a component was modified on both branches). In such a situation, the merge tool presented in section 2.4. may be applied. This merge tool is used to combine revisions of documents, i.e. it operates on the *fine–grained level*. In contrast, in the context of the current section we discuss merging only on the coarse–grained level.

2.5.2 Process Management

So far, we have discussed management of the product to be developed and maintained. In the current subsection, we describe how software development and maintenance processes are managed on the basis of product management. *Process management* supports planning, analysis, execution, and monitoring of software processes. The tools described below support process planning and execution; analysis and monitoring are not covered yet. The work presented here should be considered preliminary inasmuch as the design of a full–fledged management environment is currently under way (/6. NW 94a/ and chapter 5).

Goals and Principles

Many different models for process management have been designed which rely on a wide variety of paradigms, e.g. rule bases /4. KF 87a/, process programs /4. Ost 87/, or Petri nets /4. DG 90/. We believe that *net–based approaches* are particularly well suited for process management. A net represents the structure of a complex process in a graphical and natural way. It shows the steps to be carried out and their interrelations. A process net is a valuable aid for a project manager who wants to plan a complex process and monitor its execution. However, many conventional approaches assume a static process net. In practice, nets have to be modified at runtime. First, the product structure is frequently not known a priori. Since the steps to be carried out depend on the product to be developed, the process net has to be extended dynamically. Second, feedbacks during process execution cannot be predicted statically and cause dynamic net modifications, as well.

There are two *alternatives* w.r.t. the *modeling* of software processes:

(a) *Separation of product and process management.* In this case, products and processes are covered by separate structures. These structures are mutually dependent: Process execution drives product development and maintenance. Conversely, the results of technical processes (e.g. design of an architecture) influence the structure of process nets.

(b) *Product–centered process management.* This is the approach realized in the current prototype. A configuration is interpreted as a process net: Each component of a configuration corresponds to a process which has to produce this component (i.e. a component process). Analogously, dependencies between components correspond to data flows between component processes.

Clearly, the *explicit solution* (a) is *more general* and powerful than the *implicit* solution (b). In general, many different processes may eventually result in the same product. On the (coarse) level of life cycle models, a certain product may be created e.g. according to a waterfall, prototyping, or continuous model (see also subsection 1.4.3). Furthermore, forward and reverse engineering approaches may be distinguished. When inspecting a given product, it is usually impossible to derive from its statical description the process by which it was created. Product–centered process management has a severe drawback: Since there is no separation between products and processes, it is not possible to select among different processes to create some target product.

In spite of this limitation, we have selected the product–centered approach for an initial implementation of process management. Its advantage lies in its *simplicity*: By interpreting a configuration of interdependent components as a process net, we avoid the conceptual overhead which is implied by separating product and process structure and keeping both consistent with each other. Furthermore, we shall demonstrate below that many interesting aspects of process management – in particular some problems of *dynamics* – can *already* be *studied* in this restricted framework.

Process management must cope with *dynamic evolution* of *process nets*. Only rarely may a process net be built up completely before execution is started. In many cases, decisions are made during execution which determine how to proceed. Either these decisions cannot be anticipated in their totality, or taking all possible execution paths into account yields a huge and complex process net which is hard to understand and to follow. Therefore, it is essential to support modifications of process nets during execution.

The following *types* of *process evolution* are supported:

(a) *Incremental net extensions.* A process net is extended incrementally as execution proceeds. For example, processes for module implementations are inserted only after the corresponding modules have been introduced in the software architecture document.

(b) *Simultaneous engineering.* In order to shorten development or maintenance cycles significantly, interdependent processes which are executed with delay in waterfall–like approaches may start as soon as possible, be carried out concurrently or overlapping.

(c) *Iterations.* Processes may be restarted after termination either because their inputs have changed later on, or because feedbacks from dependent processes have to be taken into account.

Process management is *formalized* by attaching *state transition diagrams* to component processes (fig. 2.41). The state of a process determines the operations which may be applied to it. Both edit operations, which change the structure of the net, and execution operations, which are concerned with the 'token flow', are taken into account. State transitions either refer to operations applied to the current process (e.g. Start), or to operations which have a side–effect on it (events, e.g. Enable). The state transitions are arranged in three columns:

(a) The middle column represents a straight–line life cycle from process creation to successful process termination. Created serves as initial state where the process is defined. Outgoing dependencies are created in order to define its inputs. The process has a single output, namely some version of the object to which the component refers. If no version number is specified, the output is created from scratch (development process). Otherwise, the specified version serves as starting point for the output to be created (maintenance process). In the state Waiting, the process waits for its input data. As soon as they are available, the process is moved into the state Ready. Starting promotes the process to the state Active, whose duration depends on the complexity of the task to be solved. In particular, multiple tool activations (e.g. multiple edit sessions) may be performed while a process is active. Finally, the process terminates and proceeds to the state Done.

(b) The left column deals with interruption and failure. Process execution may be interrupted either because of an external event (e.g. pre–releases of inputs have been revoked, see below) or because of an internal event (e.g. execution is suspended by the actor, i.e. the engineer who is responsible for process execution). Blocked and Suspended handle the former and the latter case, respectively. Furthermore, the state Failed indicates that the process could not be executed successfully.

(c) The right column deals with iterations. The state Undecided is an intermediate state where a decision about process iteration needs to be performed. In this way, processes may be marked which are potentially affected by an iteration (impact analysis). Later on (when enough information is available), a process is either moved back into the state Done or into the state Created.

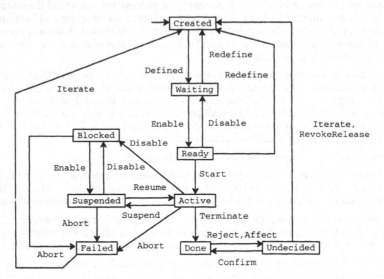

Fig. 2.41. State diagram for component processes

Simultaneous engineering is supported in several ways:

(a) *Decomposition.* Simultaneous engineering allows for overlapping execution of processes belonging to different 'phases' of the software life cycle. This can be achieved by decomposing a phase into multiple processes and specifying the data flows not on the level of phases, but on the control level of cooperative processes. Since e.g. the design of a subsystem s depends only on those requirements which are relevant for s, subsystem design need not be delayed until requirements for all subsystems have been completed.

(b) *Delayed consumption*. When a process needs multiple inputs, it is sometimes possible to start its execution before all inputs are available. For example, a subsystem design may start even when not all interfaces of imported subsystems have already been specified. However, termination of process execution requires that all inputs have eventually been consumed.

(c) *Pre–releases*. In order to accelerate overall process execution, pre–releases of intermediate results may be delivered to dependent processes. There are various motivations of pre–releases, including parallelization of processes on the critical path, early quality assurance, or timely feedback from processes belonging to later 'phases' of the software life cycle.

Delayed consumption is supported by qualifying inputs with *activation attributes* (not further discussed here). Depending on the value of the activation attribute, the input must be available in order to start the process, or it may be supplied later on.

To support pre–releases, each process maintains a *release set* indicating which dependent processes may access the result produced so far. An 'all or nothing' approach to releasing results is too coarse because it depends on the nature of a dependent process when data should be propagated from a master to a dependent process. Therefore, the release set contains the working areas to which the result of the corresponding process has been (pre–) released. For example, consider creation of a requirements definition. In order to enable concurrent documentation of the requirements definition, the requirements definition is released early for documentation. On the other hand, the requirements definition has to reach a certain level of maturity and stability in order to start designing the software architecture. Therefore, the requirements definition is released for design later on.

Pre–releases may even be controlled in a more fine–grained way by boolean *propagation attributes* which are attached to data flows. A dependent process may access data produced by a master process only if its component type is included in the master's release set and propagation is enabled along the flow. For example, design may pre–release its result for implementation of module A. On the other hand, the interface of B may still be under work so that propagation of the software architecture to the implementation process for B is disabled.

As a consequence of simultaneous engineering, each component process operates in a *constantly changing context*. Thus, inputs are consumed and outputs are produced during process execution. A conservative definition of the execution semantics would couple consumption of inputs with process start and production of outputs with process termination, respectively. However, we consider such an approach to be too restrictive. In particular, it does not take the long duration of software processes into account.

In order to control potential chaos, the actor responsible for some process may *control consumption* of inputs and *production* of outputs. In particular, when a new input version arrives, it does not replace a previously consumed old version automatically. Rather, the actor may decide when it is appropriate to update his work context. Symmetrically, (s)he also controls production of outputs by explicit release operations.

Functionality and User Interface

After having described process management in general terms, we give an *example* of both a development and a maintenance *process*. To this end, we pick up the example used in subsection 2.5.1, i.e. the multi–pass compiler.

Let us start our short tour with *initial development* of the multi–pass compiler. Fig. 2.42 shows snapshots of three early development states. Rounded boxes display attributes attached to components. In all snapshots, the configuration developed so far merely consists

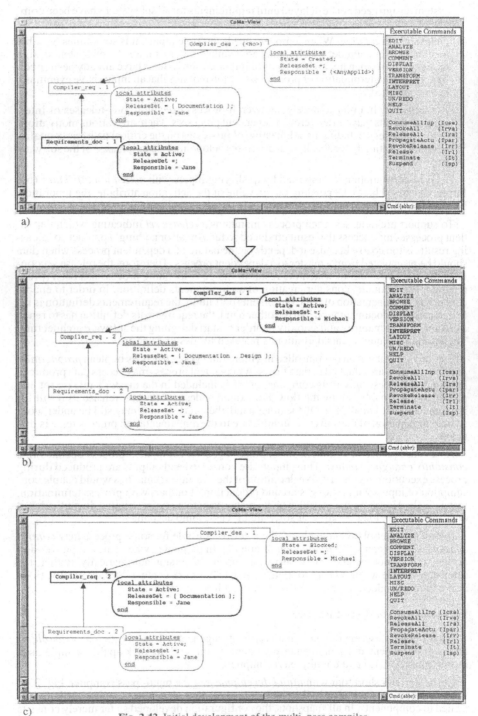

Fig. 2.42. Initial development of the multi–pass compiler

235

of three components for requirements, documentation of requirements, and software architecture, respectively. As development proceeds, the configuration is extended incrementally.

Let us now explain the three snapshots (fig. 2.42.a–c):

(a) Jane has been assigned to both requirements definition and documentation (attribute `Responsible`). Initial revisions of both documents are under development. The corresponding component processes are concurrently active. To exclude uncontrolled activation, the requirements definition process must have pre–released its result to the dependent component process. Thus, the `ReleaseSet` attribute of the former must contain the component type (`Documentation`) of the latter. Finally, the design component `Compiler_des` has already been inserted into the configuration, but no work assignment has been performed so far. Therefore, the component is still unbound, i.e. the version number is still unexpanded.

(b) Jane has continued her work and has decided to keep intermediate revisions of requirements definition and documentation for backup purposes. Thus, she is currently working on the second revisions of these documents. Furthermore, Michael has been assigned to design the compiler. He has already started working because Jane has extended the release set of the requirements definition.

(c) Jane has contacted the customer who has performed some significant changes to the requirements. Therefore, the requirements definition has to be updated, as well. Since these changes are expected to affect the software architecture considerably, Jane revokes the pre–release of the requirements definition for design. As a consequence, the design process is forced into state `Blocked`, and Michael has to wait until the requirements definition is pre–released again.

Fig. 2.43 shows another snapshot which demonstrates *individual releases*. Meanwhile, Michael has produced a draft design which separates the compiler into multiple passes which are called by a control module. Michael has pre–released the design for documentation and implementation purposes. However, the pre–release for implementation is filtered so that some modules may already be implemented, while others still have to wait for a sufficiently precise and stable specification. For example, John is already implementing the control module, while code generation will be implemented later on. Individual pre–releases are controlled by means of the boolean `Propagate` attribute attached to dependencies. In case of the control module, propagation is switched on; in case of the code generation module, it is switched off.

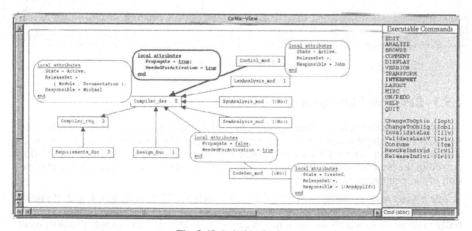

Fig. 2.43. Individual releases

Development is finished when the configuration is complete and all component processes have arrived in state Done. *Maintenance processes* are then handled as follows: First, a new version of the configuration is created. Since the contents of the new version initially equals the contents of its predecessor, all component processes are initially in state Done. When some component process is reactivated, changes are propagated to dependent processes incrementally. This means that only those processes are reactivated which may actually be affected by a change.

As a simple example, consider again the *bug fix* in the code generation module. This is a small, local change which only affects this module and potentially its documentation. After having carried out the corresponding processes, all component processes are again in state Done so that the new configuration may be frozen.

A more comprehensive change is illustrated in fig. 2.44. Since the code produced by the compiler has proved to be too inefficient, an optimization pass has to be added (see last subsection, the example now being regarded from the process view). To this end, Michael is *revising* the *software architecture*. As a consequence, all implementation processes are forced into state Undecided. Furthermore, a new implementation process is created for implementing the optimization pass. The resulting situation is shown in fig. 2.44. Later on, processes in state Undecided will either return to state Done immediately because they are not affected by the change (state transition Confirm), or they will iterate once more through the process transition diagram (state transition Iterate or RevokeRelease of fig. 2.41). In our simple example, we assume that only the control module is affected because it has to call the optimization pass. All other modules remain unaffected and can be reused without revising them.

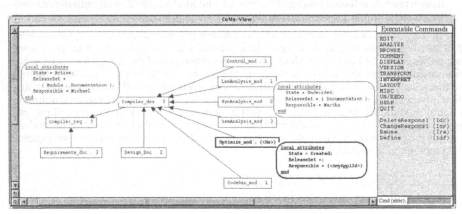

Fig. 2.44. Maintenance process

2.5.3 Resource Management

Resource management has already been covered partially in the last subsection. In order to execute a development process, both human and technical resources have to be allocated. In this subsection, we only deal with *human resources*. Technical resources will be discussed in the next subsection because they are considered primarily during parameterization of the management environment.

The *project team* is managed in a similar way as in IPSEN 2.5 /4. JL 88/. Fig. 2.45 shows a sample team for the scenario of the previous subsection. Each team member plays potentially multiple *roles* which are contained in a role set. Each role corresponds to a document type. By assigning a role T to a team member, the team member may be assigned to processes which produce documents of type T. For example, the role set of Michael contains Design and Documentation. Therefore, Michael may be assigned to design and documentation processes. The role concept is very flexible and allows for customizing a team according to the needs of a certain project and the capabilities of the team members.

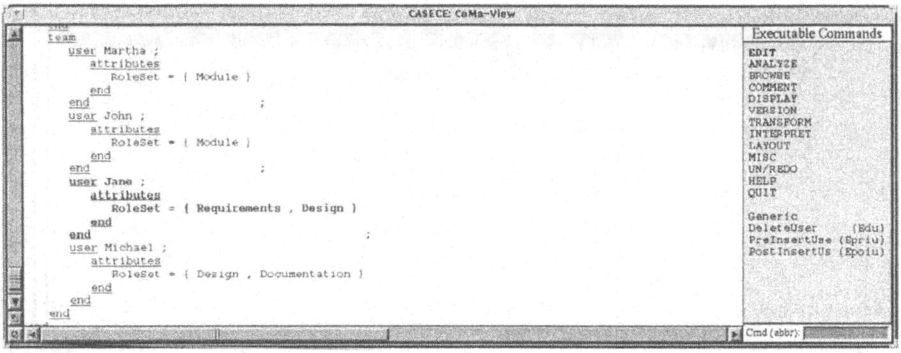

Fig. 2.45. Project team

However, there is an important difference between IPSEN 2.5 and the prototype described in this section. In IPSEN 2.5, team members are made responsible for certain documents without controlling or supporting the development process in any way. For example, software architectures, documentations, and module implementations can be developed in any order in IPSEN 2.5. In contrast, the prototype described here *assigns* team *members to* development *processes* and *controls* the order of their execution. Processes which are ready to execute appear in the agenda of the responsible software developers. Only such processes may be executed, and the access rights for versions of inputs and outputs are granted automatically.

A typical *agenda* is displayed in the top window of fig. 2.46.a. The agenda lists all tasks which have been assigned to Michael in the project MultiPassCompiler. The tasks are sorted by deadline in ascending order. No filter has been applied in this example. In general, it is possible to filter according to task states or cut–off dates for deadlines (e.g. show only tasks in state Ready to execute whose deadlines fall into the current week). The task list shows for each task the following entries: task name, expected duration, deadline, employee, and annotations. Although the employee column is redundant in this example, it is needed in other situations. For example, activation of the PREDECESSOR button results in a list of predecessors to a certain task in the task list. In the predecessor list, the employee column is then needed to identify the responsible employees. Finally, annotations are messages referring to tasks (for example, a project manager could send a message when a deadline has been missed). The annotation column shows the numbers of total and read messages (e.g. 2 / 1 means that one of two messages was read).

By clicking the SHOWTASK button, a detailed *task description* is displayed (fig. 2.46.b). The buttons below the task name are used to show/manipulate task attributes, to send or read annotations, or to perform state transitions (e.g. start execution). In the region below these buttons, four scroll lists are displayed which contain input, output, auxiliary, and guideline documents, respectively. Auxiliary documents are only valid during task execution and can be used e.g. to maintain private notes about issues still to be considered. Guidelines may describe e.g. style guides or other general information to support adequate task execution. Each element of a scroll list consists of the document name, an abbreviation indicating its type (e.g. MOD), and an annotation entry. Annotations may be attached not only to tasks, but also to documents. The sender of a document or an annotation need not specify the receiver, distribution is performed automatically (e.g. attaching an annotation to an input doc-

238

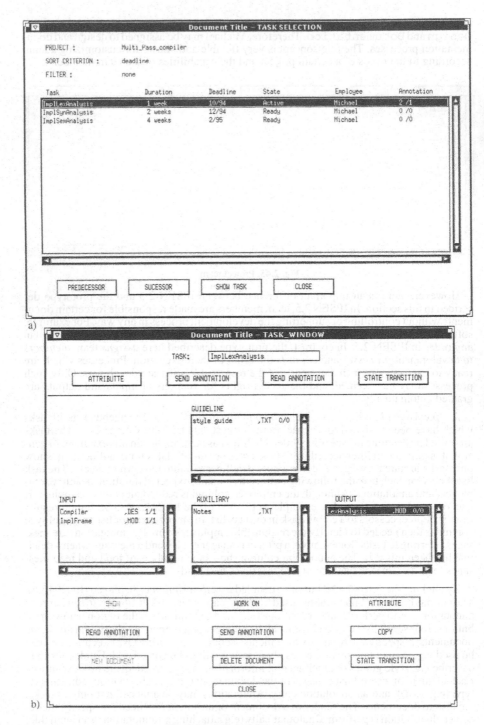

Fig. 2.46. Agenda and task description

ument results in delivering a message to the creator of this document). Finally, the buttons at the bottom are used to activate commands on the currently selected document (LexAnalysis). For example, WORK_ON is used for tool activation.

2.5.4 Parameterization

In order to reuse the management environment in *different application domains*, it does not embody any domain–specific assumptions with respect to types of products, processes, and resources. In particular, this *generic* environment is not aware of the document types used in the examples of the previous subsections. In order to obtain a *specific* environment for a certain application domain, the generic environment must therefore be parameterized by supplying an application–specific schema. In this way, application–specific consistency constraints may be checked and enforced, and application–specific support (e.g. tool invocation) may be provided.

So far, *parameterization* has been realized for product management only. Process types are defined implicitly through the product management schema. Similarly, role types follow from the object types defined in the product management schema. To the date of writing, management of technical resources has only been addressed in an ad hoc manner and will therefore be skipped here (see also comments at the end of this subsection).

The product management system is adapted to a specific application domain by means of an ER–like *schema* defining types of entities, relationships, and attributes. A schema for our sample session is displayed in fig. 2.47. Boxes and arrows correspond to component and dependency types, respectively. Boxes are labeled by names of component types. Dependency types need not be named as long as there is at most one dependency type for some pair of component types. In general, attributes may be attached to entity and relationship types, but this is not shown in the screen dump.

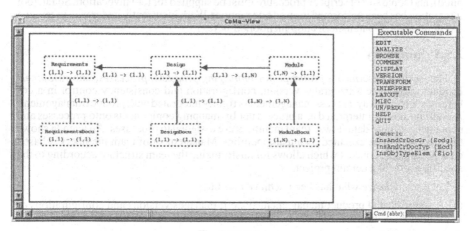

Fig. 2.47. Schema

Cardinalities constrain both component and dependency types. A cardinality is written as $(l_1, u_1) \rightarrow (l_2, u_2)$, where l and u represent lower and upper bounds, respectively. The first and the second pair constrain the numbers of outgoing and incoming relations, respectively. Cardinalities attached to component types refer to composition relations from document groups to components. So, they also refer to a relation which, however is not represented explicitly by arrows in the graphical notation.

Please note that the interpretation of cardinalities does not depend on the graphical layout. For example, consider the cardinality of dependency type Design<-Module (dependency of a module implementation on the design). Since the first pair – i.e. (1,1) – always refers to the source of the dependency type – i.e. Module –, it is associated to the right end rather than to the left end of the arrow.

The sample schema reads as follows: A software system consists of a requirements definition, a design, and multiple modules. These documents are described in corresponding documentations. The first pairs of cardinalities attached to component types (shown inside the dashed boxes) ensure that there is exactly one component of type Requirements, RequirementsDocu, Design, and DesignDocu, respectively. Furthermore, a software system may contain multiple components of type Module and ModuleDocu, respectively. The second pairs of these cardinalities are always (1,1), meaning that each component is contained in exactly one software system. The (1,1)->(1,1) cardinalities attached to the dependency types in the left half of the diagram imply that the single–instance, mandatory components are connected by single–instance, mandatory dependencies. Furthermore, the (1,1)->(1,N) cardinality for dependencies between modules and design ensures that each module has a single, mandatory outgoing dependency to the design and that the design has multiple (at least one) incoming dependencies emanating from modules. Finally, many–to–many relations are allowed between modules and their corresponding documentations (cardinality (1,N)->(1,N) attached to the dependency type).

As mentioned above, *process* and *resource management* are *parameterized implicitly* through the product management schema. This approach is simple, but not very powerful. Additional facilities are needed for parameterizing process and resource management (e.g. specification of conditions for state transitions or definition of project types which constrain the assignment of roles to team members). Finally, parameterization must also cover tool integration (management of technical resources). To this end, the functionality of a tool must be specified (in terms of inputs and outputs, as well as further parameters to be supplied), and some sort of script or procedure must be supplied for tool invocation. So far, tool integration has been performed in an ad hoc manner. Work is currently under way to remove the limitations of parameterization mentioned here.

2.5.5 Summary

This section described a *prototype* for *managing products*, *processes*, and *resources*. Product management integrates version, configuration and consistency control in a coherent, adaptable way. Process management is tightly integrated with product management. A configuration is interpreted as a process net by mapping components onto processes and dependencies onto data flows. Team members are assigned to processes. An agenda shows the processes to be executed by a team member. Management of team members is based on a flexible role concept which allows for customizing the team structure according to the specific needs of a certain project.

Let us *summarize* what has been *achieved* so far:

(a) A sophisticated product management system manages versions and configurations of software documents.

(b) The process management system supports integration of editing, analysis, and execution of process nets. In particular, it takes incremental extensions, feedbacks, and concurrent engineering into account.

(c) The resource management system allows for flexible team definitions and checks work assignments for compatibility with roles played in a project.

The management environment described above serves as a starting point for a *future* powerful and comprehensive *environment* along the lines of /6. NW 94a/. This environment will realize the following improvements compared to the current prototype:

(a) Products will be separated from processes, resulting in additional flexibility of the process management system (e.g. different life cycle models, forward and reverse engineering may be applied to the same product).

(b) So far, the processes for building the process net, for supervising process execution, etc. have not been represented explicitly. Above the technical processes (for creating/modifying requirements, software architectures, module implementations), a layer of management processes will be introduced which controls technical processes (i.e. management tasks such as planning, execution, and supervision of technical processes will be represented by process nets, as well).

(c) Resource management will be extended significantly in order to represent realistic organizational structures (e.g. staff and line organization, or n–dimensional organization which includes matrix organization as a special case).

(d) Parameterization will be extended such that it provides complete coverage of products, processes, and resources. Furthermore, parameterization activities will be modeled as processes, as well. In particular, this allows for modeling schema evolution explicitly.

2.6 Summary of Tools:
Variety, UI Characteristics, and Flexibility

M. Nagl

In this short section we summarize chapter 2 under *three perspectives*. We first discuss the variety of available tools we have introduced in this chapter. Furthermore, we explain the common user interface characteristics, all IPSEN tools share. Finally, we take up our discussion of chapter 1 on flexible processes and incrementality.

2.6.1 Tool Functionality and Variety

This chapter is *not* intended as a *user handbook* for IPSEN. Its aim is to give an impression about the set of available tools in order to explain their behavior, namely integratedness, immediateness, and incrementality, as outlined in chapter 1. This should give a good motivation for the tool builder's aspects presented in the next two chapters. As already mentioned this chapter was also *not* a *method* chapter for the languages or methods underlying their use. Both were only explained to the extent that tool behavior became clear.

Only a *part* of the *functionality of tools* (see tables 1.50 and 1.53) was discussed in this chapter even for those which were introduced. For example, only the SA environment for supporting RE was sketched, the PiS support for EIFFEL and C++ was not discussed. Further tools, of e.g. the architecture modelling environment, or the documentation environment were only touched upon when corresponding integrator tools were discussed. The available facilities for reuse /4. Bör 94/ were not discussed at all. Although IPSEN covers a remarkable part of the needed software engineering support there are further tools which could be built according to the philosophy of this book, as explained in the next two main chapters. This is especially true for quality assurance (e.g. test), where we restricted ourselves to constructive quality assurance guaranteed by tools for the other working areas which assure syntactical or semantical properties as built–in features. Finally, support given for all tools presented here was on language level. In the PiL environment /4. Bör 94/ we also gave some support on the method level how to use a certain language, here the architecture description language. This, again, was not discussed.

This chapter essentially described the *functionality* of *IPSEN prototype 4.0* and, thereby, also the functionality which was taken over from earlier prototypes. However, some tools available in earlier prototypes have not been reimplemented. This is, for example, true for PiS (see 2.1). The new prototype only contains editor/analyzer tools for EIFFEL and C++ which were not discussed here.

The following table summarizes the *tools* we have discussed by giving a *categorization* thereby enumerating the sections in which we can find corresponding occurrences and their explanation. For a detailed list of all available tools and a detailed characterization we refer back to sections 1.8 and 1.7, respectively. Categorization is due to the part of an overall configuration which is supported (from documents to subconfigurations), due to the kind of tool (from editing to monitoring and statistics), which type of working area (technical versus management), which kind of model (static, dynamic, target system) is supported, whether we describe behavior of tool instances or how to parameterize instances, whether tools are document type specific or document type independent, which kind of documents/versions tools work on, how errors are handled, and which input behavior tools possess.

documents/configurations and integration
    one document and intradocument integration: 2.1, 2.2, 2.4, 2.5
    integration tools: horizontal: 2.2, vertical: 2.3
tool kind
    editor: 2.1–2.5
    analyzer: 2.1, 2.2, 2.4, 2.5
    instrumentation: 2.1, 2.2
    executor: 2.1, 2.2, 2.5
    monitoring and statistics: 2.2
    transformer, consistency checker, binder, browser: 2.2, 2.3
working area and level
    technical and fine–grained: 2.1–2.3, part of 2.4
    administration and coarse–grained: 2.5
support of models for documents, subconfigurations, configurations
    building up and maintaining static models: 2.1–2.3, 2.5
    model execution: 2.1, 2.2, 2.5
    simulation of target system: 2.2
instance and parameterization
    behavior of instance environments: 2.1–2.5
    parameterization of instances: 2.4, 2.5
document type
    type specific tools: 2.1–2.3, 2.5
    independent tools: 2.4
working on
    logical documents: 2.1, 2.2, 2.4, 2.5
    representation documents: 2.4
    one version: 2.1–2.3, 2.5
    different versions: 2.4, 2.5
handling errors
    strict: 2.1
    permitting errors: 2.2–2.5
tool behavior
    syntax–directed 2.1–2.5
    free input 2.1, 2.4
    textual representation 2.1–2.5
    graphical representation 2.2–2.5

Table 2.48. Types and variety of tools introduced in chapter 2

2.6.2 UI Features

Let us first summarize the *UI features* of *specific environments* (PiS, ..., administration environment). For any document there may exist different representations presented in windows corresponding to different views (RE, see 2.2), different forms of representation (graphical for overview, textual for details, again 2.2), or different tools (editor, analyzer etc., see 2.1) representing static/structure information or execution information (2.1, 2.2, 2.5). The user is working in one window, the current window, the others being updated if changes occur. Windows have scrolling and zooming facilities. The current increment is shown in bold being selected by mouse click, cursor movement, or being set by the tool (e.g. executor). Commands are sensitive w.r.t. the current increment and are selected via menu selection, function key, or keyboard input, respectively. On text windows structure–oriented and free input mode is possible for simple or complex increments. The latter avoids transformation commands which are better handled by cut, paste, copy, editing, and syntax–analysis. Commands are collected to command groups, only the commands of the current group are shown explicitly. Different types of tools (of editor, analyzer, instrumentation, execution) have been demonstrated for different environments (PiS, RE, PiL, DOC, and PO). Tools are on language level giving support for syntactical or semantical properties of documents in a language.

Integration tools serve for horizontal or vertical integration of documents belonging to one or different working areas. They have the following *behavior*: Integration is on fine–grained, increment–to–increment basis between documents shown here for three occurrences of integrators. Integrators work with at least one window of the corresponding documents where related or inconsistent increments are shown in inverted mode. Integrators again are of different types (transformers, analyzers, binders, browsers), the integrator examples presented here being a mixture of these types for reasons of flexibility for a certain integration task. For example, the RE–PiL integrator needs all those features for a certain RE–PiL integration task. Integrators work automatically (in case of rules for declaring and applied occurrences in RE), semiautomatic to allow a user decision (RE–PiL), or manually (in case of the RE, PiL, PiS–DOC integrator) with hypertext features. The behavior of transformers is internally (by the tool builder) expressed by transformation rules. These rules can get priorities and can be switched on and off (by the tool administrator or by the user) in order to customize the tool.

Working area independent tools within specific environments are of different forms (see 2.4). There are features implemented for all specific environments, as editor behavior, or navigation, see first paragraph. Other general features are available for any IPSEN environment, being a part of the basic layer any environment is based on. This is the case, for example, for undo/redo. Further ones are based on the assumption that internal logical documents are modelled in the same way. This is true for the merging tool. Finally, parameterization tools can be used during tool building, configuration, and even at tool runtime.

So, IPSEN gives *support* for *different roles* of the member of a team. Specific tools give support for the technical developers (the RE environment for Requirements Engineering, the documentation environment for documentation, see 2.1–2.4). Furthermore, the management of a software project is supported by administration tools (e.g. configuration or version control, see 2.5). Moreover, users can parameterize environments at runtime. Further parameterization before tool use is possible but was not presented here. Both are for the tool builder or for an environment system's administrator. Further support, by components/generators, so not for end users but for tool builders – is possible which will be discussed in the next two chapters.

2.6.3 Processes and Incrementality

Processes due to technical or management activities can hardly be predicted or determined. This is why we *support* these processes by *intelligent tools* but we do *not* fix and *restrict* the corresponding processes carried out by human actors. This allows a variety of possible subprocesses and quite different forms of global processes to develop/maintain a software system (see subsections 1.4.1–1.4.3). Support is given by tightly integrated, inter-active/immediate, structure–oriented etc. (see subsection 1.4.5) tools and their property of incrementality guaranteed by their realization.

We come back to the claim given in section 1.4 that quite different processes are possible and such processes, occurring in practice, are substantialy supported by IPSEN tools. To demonstrate this, we summarize the use of IPSEN tools for a *process* which is as *fast* and *open* as possible but which is *managed* in order to avoid chaotic project situations. So, the scenario is between classical and too narrow process models (as waterfall model) which do not work as they cannot handle situations of practice on one side, and continuous process models suggested in literature which cannot be controlled in practice.

The *example overall process* is the following: Different team members are working out the different perspectives of a requirements specification. These actors can perform any kind of processes. Integration of perspectives for finding global inconsistencies within the requirements spec can be started at any time, even when the perspective models are not complete. They will find errors in submodels to be corrected. Even when executing a requirements specification and simulating the later system the requirements specification need not be complete. However, a certain degree of completeness (e.g. information, function, and control model refinement to a certain level is elaborated) is recommended. Transformation to architecture can be started and module specification and then even implementation can be done for "stable" components. Technical documentation can be worked out early. Changes of the requirements can be propagated to an existing architecture, corresponding module implementations, and their documentation. So, development and maintenance happens at the same time, as argued in 1.4. This is possible only by the incrementality of environments and integrator tools. The process of collaboration can be managed on a coarse–grained level such that the project manager is able to control the activities of different group members for quality, responsibility, efficiency etc. purposes and to see whether the project is on schedule and within budget.

So, the process is fast inasmuch as an activity can be begun even before all corresponding working area activities are complete (a module implementation can start although the design is still in process). Furthermore, incomplete documents/subconfigurations can be propagated to actors which have to start with them later or to quality assurance engineers to get hints for errors or necessary modifications before they are released. Both is often subsumed under the term *simultaneous engineering*. Furthermore, as in Requirements Engineering for the different perspectives to be worked out, activities are carried out concurrently. This can happen with mutual dependencies as in RE or with dependencies to a mastering document, as e.g. simultaneous design of two subsystems, the interfaces of which are fixed in a mastering coarse architecture. So, IPSEN gives support by only using the dependency between documents/subconfigurations as partial order therefore allowing the start of dependent tasks to be started as early as possible and even accelerating a process by the exchange of prereleases.

3 Internal Conceptual Modeling: Graph Grammar Specifications

This *chapter* follows the *same train* of *thought* as the last chapter on tool functionality. However, it describes the tools not from their external behavior, but rather from the modelling of their internal documents, or coupling of documents. Thus, we are now switching from the user's to the tool builder's or, more precisely, to the specifier's point of view. This modelling follows the increasing complexity and growing generality of the last chapter, ranging from tools on one internal document, over integration tools for different documents, to tools on administration level.

The chapter's main part about document modelling is *embraced* by *two further parts*. At the beginning, we introduce the specification language PROGRES and at the end the environment which was built for constructing, maintaining, evaluating, and prototyping such specifications.

The *introduction* of the graph grammar specification language *PROGRES* is given by two sections: In section 3.1 the language is informally introduced by an example showing the diverse constructs the language contains for internal modelling, i.e. specification of a graph class. In section 3.2, the formal definition of the language is discussed in an exemplary manner by tracing the language semantics definition back to a graph grammar calculus based on predicate logic.

The kernel part of this chapter (sections 3.3–3.5) shows our *experience* in *internal* conceptual *modelling* using the PROGRES language. This is shown by different specification examples. In section 3.3 we show how to model a logical document such that it is both suitable for textual as well as diagrammatic representation. Furthermore, besides editor operation specification also analysis and execution occur. Section 3.4 describes integrator tool specification by so–called correspondences. The notation used there is an extension of PROGRES. Finally, in section 3.5 we give specification examples corresponding to administration tools. In all cases different specification techniques are used for good reasons.

The final section of this chapter describes the means which were developed for editing, analyzing, and executing graph grammar specifications, i.e. the *PROGRES environment*. Its tools allow, similar to the tools described in chapter 2, quite different interrelated specification processes. As the internal structure of the PROGRES environment is the same as that of the IPSEN environment, all internals about framework architecture, basic components, generators etc. are postponed to chapter 4. So, section 3.6 concentrates on showing the use of the PROGRES environment for a specifier.

One *example*, namely that of a simplified module interconnection language is used as extensively as possible *throughout* this *chapter*, continuing the discussion of section 1.5. It is used for the informal definition of the language in 3.1, for its formal foundation in 3.2, for the specification of an editor and analysis tool in 3.3, and for showing the functionality of the PROGRES environment in 3.6. The remaining sections, namely 3.4 on integration tools and 3.5 on administration tools have and need to use other examples of graph grammar specifications. Trivially, all the examples presented in this chapter are simplifications of practical ones in order to cope with the limited space available and not to bore the reader.

In the last section 3.7 a *summary* of the chapter is given. Furthermore, corresponding to graph grammar engineering, it is outlined how specifications have changed over the years in order to make them as general and declarative as possible.

3.1 Introduction to the Specification Language PROGRES

A. Schürr

This section is an *informal introduction to PROGRES*, the specification language of the IPSEN project, which supports PROgramming with Graph REwriting Systems and which has already been used in chapter 2. We will use a single running example, the specification of a small software design and configuration tool, to present its most important constructs and properties. Although being a kind of "toy" example compared with real software engineering tools, it is complex enough to discuss all important language features. A complete description of PROGRES is outside the scope of this book (see /5. Schü 91a/).

The *section* is *organized* as follows: subsection 3.1.1 gives a short overview of other tool specification languages, discusses their deficiencies and thereby motivates why it was necessary to develop a specification language like PROGRES. Subsection 3.1.2 explains our running example, which will be used throughout this section and reused later on in sections 3.2 through 3.6. Subsection 3.1.3 shows how software engineering documents are internally represented by attributed graphs and, especially, how graph schema definitions may be used to characterize the static properties of a class of internal documents. Subsections 3.1.4 and 3.1.5 deal with the definition of rather complex document querying and manipulating activities as subgraph searching and rewriting programs, whereas subsection 3.1.6 discusses advanced features for improving the runtime behavior of specifications and for writing highly reusable specifications. Finally, subsection 3.1.7 summarizes the main characteristics of our specification language and the basic ideas of its accompanying *graph grammar engineering* approach.

3.1.1 Other Tool Specification Languages

The specification language PROGRES is a strongly and even almost statically typed language that is based on the concept of *programmed graph rewriting systems*. Considering its expressiveness and its derivation history, the underlying formalism belongs to the so-called *set-theoretic branch* of the *algorithmic graph grammar approach* /5. Nag 79, 5. Nag 87/ (cf. section 3.2). To our knowledge, it is the first language approach to evolve the theoretically well-founded calculus of programmed graph rewriting systems into a technique that is applicable to the specification of rather complex software engineering tools.

Other *graph grammar based specification languages* proposed by Göttler /5. Göt 88, 5. GGN 90/, Kaplan and Goering /5. KGL 91/ or Schütte /5. Schü 87/ are more limited in their expressiveness and do not possess any kind of typing concept. Furthermore, they do not support the definition of derived relationships and have no or much more primitive control structures. Finally, all of them attach the definition of derived attributes to graph rewrite rules instead of keeping them separate as PROGRES does, i.e. they relate attribute derivations to the derivation of parse trees. They are therefore more suited for syntax analysis of graph classes than for specifying complex document manipulating software engineering tools (graph rewriting processes).

Comparing our approach with the rather popular formalism of *attribute tree grammars* used in other software engineering environment projects (e.g. in the Cornell Synthesizer Generator /4. RT 88a/ and in PSG /4. SB 90/) or in compiler generator projects (e.g. in OPTRAN /5. LMW 89/), we identify at least three principal differences:
   (a)   Over here, *directed attribute equations* are used to describe attribute dependencies between adjacent graph nodes. They do not describe attribute flows along the edges

of a parse tree, as is customary in attribute tree grammars /5. Kas 80, 4. RT 88a/.
Productions for generating parse trees only are not sufficient for specifying tool
operations which manipulate or analyze already existing software document parts.
We, therefore, believe that the specification of graph schemata and *attribute dependencies* and that of *graph rewriting rules* should be *kept separate* from each other.
(b) Of course, in an attributed graph it is impossible to identify directions like "up" and
"down". Consequently, our derived attributes are *not classified into inherited and
synthesized attributes* as they are in attribute tree grammar projects /4. RT 88a, 4.
SB 90/. Thus the development of nonnaive (incremental) *attribute evaluation algorithms* is much more difficult than in the case of attribute tree grammars.
(c) Our *graph model*, which is *more general* than attributed trees, frees the specifier
from the somewhat artificially different treatment of relationships representing either
context-free or context-sensitive syntax, the latter one also called static semantics.
Using (derived) labeled directed edges in particular does not enforce putting context-
sensitive information into very complex structured attributes, which is a severe hand-
icap for any incremental attribute evaluation algorithm /5. DRT 81, 5. Rep 84/.

Some research has been undertaken to *overcome the disadvantages* and principal restrictions of the "classical" *attribute tree grammar formalism* in modelling context-sensitive relations /5. DRZ 85, 4. Hor 85/. This research still adheres to the data model of an
attributed tree, proposes the introduction of remote references (relations) and/or tree-val-
ued attributes, and still suffers from the above-mentioned problems, when inherently
graph-like structures and operations have to be specified (cf. example of subsection 3.1.2).

Comparing the approach presented here to the research on *conceptual modelling in the
database area*, PROGRES specifications can be viewed as conceptual database specifications, which determine the static structure as well as the allowed dynamic behavior of a
database. Our underlying data model has a lot of similarities to so-called semantic data
models /5. HK 87/, and especially to the binary relationship model /5. EW 83/. However,
while in the database area, the specification is usually restricted to modelling the static
structure of a database or to define queries for an already existing database /5. ACS 90, 5.
AE 94/, our specification language also offers sophisticated features for specifying the
allowed *dynamic behavior of a database* in a rule-oriented graphical style. In this sense,
PROGRES may be considered a visual database programming language, which is similar
to the graph grammar based database manipulation language GOOD /6. GPT 93/. It offers
additional means for defining derived data and for nondeterministic programming.

Taking into account that PROGRES is a graphical and executable specification language, it might be useful to have a final look onto *visual rule-oriented languages* like
BITPICT /5. Fur 91/ and ChemTrains /5. BL 93/. Their deficiencies come from the following sources: They have their main focus on *manipulation of data structures*. Even a
language like VAMPIRE with its class hierarchies and icon rewriting rules /5. MG 92/
comes without a rigid type concept and *without any type checking tools*. Therefore, all
these languages postpone recognition of programming errors to runtime and suffer from
the same disadvantages as any untyped or weakly typed programming language.

To summarize, the overall argument for using programmed graph rewriting systems in
IPSEN-like projects is that *graph structures appear frequently* within SDEs. These graph
structures require a suitable specification mechanism covering *static as well as dynamic
aspects of complex data structures to the same extent*. The specifier should not be forced
to mentally transform a real-world graph-like model into a tree-like one. Furthermore, he
should not be forced to write "code" which checks and preserves static properties of these
data structures instead of specifying them in a completely declarative manner. But the main
argument for a graph rewriting based language is, in fact, its *generality*. It can be applied
in any situation where complex graph-like structures have to be modeled, and queries as
well as update operations on these structures have to be specified.

3.1.2 The Running Example

As an example for motivating and explaining our graph technology approach, we assume the development of a particular software engineering tool. It is a syntax-directed *software design editor* with included configuration management functionality (cf. /4. Lew 88/). In order to keep the resulting specification as simple as possible, its supported *module interconnection (MIL) language* is a subset of the language which is used within the IPSEN project. It offers three types of modules, namely data type modules, data object modules, and function modules, and distinguishes between interface imports and realization (body) imports. It has no support for building subsystems or for using concepts like inheritance or genericity which are a strict necessity in practice (cf. /7. Bör 94, 7. Nag 90/ for further details).

Fig. 3.1 displays a *simple software architecture* which contains examples for all above-mentioned concepts. A functional Main module has one realization variant V1 which needs an abstract data object module UserInterface and an abstract data type module Files. The implementation of the module Files is independent from any available window system platform. It has one variant V1 for UNIX like operating systems and one variant V2 for MSDOS systems. The other module UserInterface imports the module Files in its interface (its interface operations have parameters of type File). Its only available implementation variant V1 uses a UNIX implementation of the window system X. As a consequence, only one consistent configuration of the whole system exists. It consists of variant V1of Main (which has no restrictions concerning an underlying operating system or window system), the variant V1 of the module UserInterface, and the variant V1 of the module Files.

The extension of the chosen module interconnection language for *variants of module realizations* with different body imports and properties is *motivated* as follows: In general, the configuration of a consistent system implementation with a required set of properties is a rather difficult task (cf. section 2.4 and 2.5). It shows very well that graph rewrite rules with complex application conditions and control structures with backtracking are rather useful for specifying software development tasks. It has the consequence that the software design document Example of fig. 3.1 models a *family of system designs* instead of representing a single design decision, where all possibly existing module variants share their implementation imports.

Finally, please note that our design editor maintains information about "sizes" of modules, variants, systems, etc. These *sizes are derived data* which will be computed from text (file) lengths of module interface descriptions as well as implementation variants. They are a good example for explaining the PROGRES language's support for derived attributes.

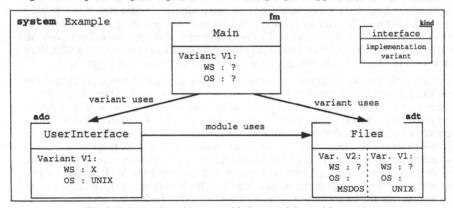

Fig. 3.1. A sample architecture with three modules and four variants

The following basic text sizes are assumed in the sequel (in lines of code):

Module interface text file size		Variant implementation text file size			
`Main:`	100	variant `V1:` 2000			
`UserInterface:`	1000	variant `V1:` 5000			
`Files:`	500	variant `V1:` 3000	variant `V2:`	2000

3.1.3 Definition of Graph Schemata

Generally speaking, the internal representation of all software documents is a *directed attributed graph*. Such a graph consists of labeled nodes and directed labeled edges, where attributes may be attached to nodes only. Node and edge labels distinguish different types of objects and relationships between objects, respectively. They are called *node types and edge types*. *Attributes* are needed to store additional information that is not necessarily to be represented in the graph structure as, for example, the detailed structure of module names. In other words, attributes represent the information that is local to a particular node and which has an unimportant structure from the current point of view. In our simple running example even all properties of a module variant or a system configuration are stored in a single set-valued attribute.

Fig. 3.2 shows the *internal graph representation* of the software system of fig. 3.1, from now on called MIL graph. Any module and any module variant is modeled as an own node; `has`-edges connect module nodes to their implementation variants. The whole software system is represented by a single node of type `System` with `contains` edges to all existing module nodes. An additional `Config` node stores all available information about the only currently existing system configuration. It has the Name `"C"`, needs a `UNIX` implementation of the window system `X`, and has a `Size` of 10000 lines of code. It `contains` one variant of each module.

The language features provided to define static properties of MIL graphs in the form of a graph schema will now be explained in detail. Note that we use the term *graph schema* in the same sense as the term database schema is used in database design.

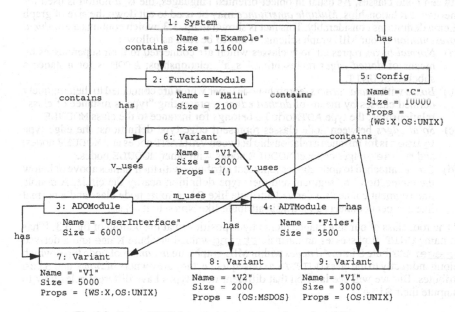

Fig. 3.2. Internal "MIL" graph representation of sample architecture

PROGRES offers the following syntactic constructs for defining the components of a particular class of graphs and their legal combinations. These are

(a) *node types* like System or FunctionModule, which determine the static properties of their nodes instances,

(b) *intrinsic relationships*, henceforth called *edge types* like v(ariant body)_uses or m(odule interface)_uses, which are explicitly manipulated and possess restrictions concerning the types of their sources and targets,

(c) *derived relationships*, which model often needed paths of a given graph, as for instance the path from a particular module to all directly or indirectly needed other module implementations, and which are defined by means of *path expressions*,

(d) *intrinsic attributes* like the Name of a system component, which are defined for a particular set of node types and which are explicitly manipulated, too,

(e) and finally *derived attributes* like the Size of a system component, which are defined by means of directed equations and which may have different definitions for different node types.

A situation that occurs very frequently when defining graph schemata in general is that many *node types* and corresponding *edge type definitions* become very *similar*. As an example, consider node types FunctionModule, ADTModule, and ADOModule. Nodes of all these types are legal sources of has and m_uses edges, legal targets of contains, m_uses, and v_uses edges, and they possess Name and Size attributes. As we will see later on, even the definition of the Size attribute is the same for all three types of nodes. Therefore, it was natural to introduce an additional concept into PROGRES, which allows us to define common node type properties once and for all and to inherit them to node types as needed. These are so-called *node classes*, which are from a theoretical point of view types of node types. Compared with abstract syntax definition notations, node classes play about the same role as phyla or nonterminal classes, whereas node types are the counterparts to operators or terminal classes (cf. /4. RT 88a/ and section 3.3).

Rather than just introducing node classes as second-order types, PROGRES enables us to build *hierarchies of node classes* by exploiting *multiple inheritance* as the relation between node classes. As usual in object-oriented languages, the *is_a* notion is used for inheritance relationships. *Multiple inheritance* may be used to cut down the size of graph schema definitions considerably. This fact is shown in fig. 3.3, which contains a *graphical representation* of our MIL graph schema. It has to be read as follows:

(a) *Normal boxes* represent node classes which are connected to their superclasses by means of *dotted edges* representing "is_a" relationships; ATOM is for instance a subclass of UNIT.

(b) *Boxes* with *round corners* represent node types which are connected to their uniquely defined classes by means of *dashed edges* representing "type is instance of class" relationships; the type ADTModule belongs for instance to the class MODULE.

(c) *Solid edges* between node classes represent edge type definitions; the edge type v_uses is for instance a relationship between VARIANT nodes and MODULE nodes, and m_uses edges connect MODULE nodes with other MODULE nodes.

(d) *Circles* attached to node classes represent attributes with their names above or below the connection line segment and their type definition nearby the circle. A double line segment connects a derived attribute like Size to its node class and a normal line segment connects an intrinsic attribute like Name to its class.

The root class of our inheritance hierarchy is positioned at the bottom of fig. 3.3. It has the name UNIT. It possesses an intrinsic string-valued attribute Name and a derived integer-attribute Size. *All nodes* within MIL graphs are *instances* of node types which belong indirectly to the class UNIT. As a consequence, they are owners of Name and Size attributes. But we will see later on that different node types have different rules how to compute their Size.

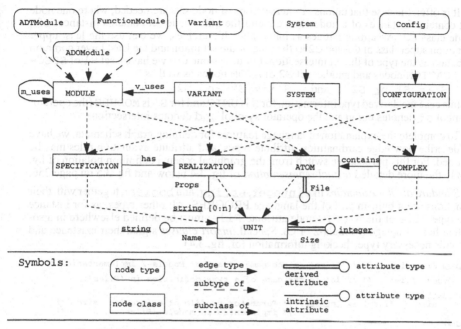

Fig. 3.3. The graph schema of MIL graphs (without derived relationships)

The rest of the graph schema is based on the *distinction between* SPECIFICATION and REALIZATION *nodes* as well as on the distinction between COMPLEX and AT-OM(ic) nodes. Any SPECIFICATION has an arbitrary number of REALIZATION nodes. REALIZATION nodes, on the other hand, are characterized by certain implementation properties, which are stored as a set of strings in the attribute Props. Any COMPLEX node contains a set of ATOM nodes which have in turn a File attribute to refer to their contents. It is worth-while to notice that has edges and contains edges form flat hierarchies which share their leaf nodes. Therefore, it would be rather difficult to model such a software design document as an attributed tree, even if import/export relationships are disregarded (see below).

All remaining node *classes* are then just *combinations* of these four classes and inherit their properties. A SYSTEM is a complex specification of a software system architecture. A CONFIGURATION is a realization of a complex software system with certain properties. A MODULE is an atomic specification of a system component and a VARIANT is an atomic module realization with certain properties. MODULE and VARIANT nodes have additional m_uses and v_uses edge type definitions. This expresses the fact that a module (interface) specification may import types from an arbitrary number of different modules and that realization variants may import additionally needed resources from other modules.

The top layer of fig. 3.3 introduces finally all *needed node types*. MODULE is the only node class with more than one node type, since we did not distinguish variants of different module types and since there is only one type of system or configuration, respectively.

Any two classes of a constructed class hierarchy have to possess at most one least upper common superclass and at most one least lower common subclass. This requirement, that class hierarchies have to be lattices, guarantees that common properties of classes are always represented within a common superclass. This facilitates the detection of misuses of the multiple inheritance concept and simplifies the task of type checking specifications considerably.

It is often the case that unions or intersections of node sets are needed, where one node set contains instances of a node class C1 and the other node set contains instances of a node class C2. Assuming lattices as inheritance hierarchies, we can use the least upper common superclass of C1 and C2 as the type of the set union and the least lower common subclass as the type of the set intersection. Let us assume that we have a set S1 of SPEC-IFICATION nodes and another set S2 of ATOM nodes as well as

  S := S1 or S2   and   S' := S2 and S2.

In this case the derived type information for S is UNIT and for S' is MODULE (the operator symbol or denotes union and the operator symbol and denotes intersection).

To complete the explanation of language features for defining graph schemata, we have to describe how edge cardinalities, attribute types, and attribute evaluation rules may be defined. For this purpose we switch from the graphical schema definition notation of fig. 3.3 to the more detailed *textual representation* of fig. 3.4 below and fig. 3.5 on page 256.

Standard attribute domains like integer, string, and boolean together with their functions are a built-in part of the language PROGRES. All other types, as for instance the type file of the ATOMIC node attribute File, must be defined elsewhere in a so-called host language (Modula-2 or C). Special *import clauses* signal their existence and provide necessary type checking information (cf. fig. 3.4).

```
from Files import  (* 'Files' is the name of a C or Modula-2 implementation *)

types  file;  (* 'file' is the name of a type definition in 'Files'.  *)

functions
    size: ( file ) -> integer; (* Parameter profile of a function 'size' *)
                               (* implemented in module 'Files'.         *)
end;

function select: ( PName:string ; (* 'PName'default cardinality :'[1:1]'. *)
                   PSet: string [0:n] ) -> string [0:n] =
   use P: string := elem( PSet ) ::
      [ propName( P ) = PName :: P | nil ]
   end
end;  (* Returns all ('PName', ?) pairs in a given property set *)
      (* 'PSet' which have 'PName' as their first component.    *)

function merge: ( PSet1, PSet2 : string [0:n] ) -> string [0:n] =
   use NSet1: string [0:n] := propName( PSet1 ) but not propName( PSet2 );
       NSet2: string [0:n] := propName( PSet2 ) but not propName( PSet1 ) ::
          select( NSet1, PSet1 )
          (* Return all (n,v) in PSet1 such that not exist (n:v') in PSet2. *)
       or select( NSet2, PSet2 )
          (* Return all (n,v) in PSet2 such that not exist (n:v') in PSet1. *)
       or ( PSet1 and PSet2 )
          (* Return all (n,v) in PSet1 and PSet2. *)
   end
end;

function addSize: ( Val : integer ; Atom : ATOM ) -> integer =
   Val + Atom.Size
end;
```

Fig. 3.4. Import clauses of external types and functions as well as definition of local functions

Additional *functions* for imported or built-in types may be defined in an *application-oriented style* of programming. Fig. 3.4 contains the definition of three functions (select, merge, and addSize). The first two functions select and merge deal with configuration or module variant properties, which are represented as (sets of) strings of the form "name:value", in short called property pairs. These functions use another function propName, which is defined elsewhere and selects the substring of its argument preceding ":". The function select gets a particular property name of type string and a set of property pairs as input and returns all those pairs which have the given name as first component. The *cardinality clause* [0:n] within the declaration of PSet is a hint for the type checker that its actual value may be an arbitrary set of strings, including the case of an empty set. A nonempty set of strings would have the type definition string [1:n], and an either undefined or uniquely defined string parameter the type definition <u>string</u> [0:1]. Remains the case [1:1], the default, for an always defined and single valued parameter (or local variable). In a similar way, -> <u>string</u> [0:n] indicates that our function returns a possibly empty set of values and not just a single <u>string</u> value.

The definition of the function select uses a *local variable* P, which gets any possible element of PSet as its value. Its declaration has the form

use P: <type> := <values for P> :: <body over P> <u>end</u>.

It evaluates its body for each value in PSet bound to P and returns the union of the resulting values. The evaluated body is a conditional expression with a Boolean condition between [and : :, the true branch between : : and |, and the false branch between | and].

[propName(P) = PName :: P | <u>nil</u>]

has to be read as "include P into the result set if its name component is equal to PName, otherwise include nothing into the result set".

Please note that it is not required, or better even not possible, to program an explicit loop over the elements in PSet within functions. It is an inherent property of the language PROGRES that it deals properly with any kind of *nondeterminism*, in this case with the nondeterministic selection of a set element and its assignment to the single value containing variable P. From a specifier's point of view it makes no difference whether a call to function select computes the return values for all possible assignments to the variable P immediately (the calling function selects then needed elements from the result set) or whether it returns first an arbitrarily chosen value and computes additionally needed values later on (if the calling function needs all possible result values). Any call to function select with a set of property names as its first actual parameter is,therefore, *implicitly expanded to the union* of all possible function calls with different set elements as a first parameter (its first formal parameter is not declared as a set). A call of the form

select({"WS", "OS"}, PSet)

is for instance equivalent to

select("WS", PSet) <u>or</u> select("OS", PSet).

The following function merge makes extensive use of the *set operators* <u>and</u> (intersection), <u>or</u> (union), and <u>but not</u> (difference). Its first line

NSet_1 := propName(PSet_1) <u>but not</u> propName(PSet_2)

computes the set of all property names used in PSet_1, but not used in PSet_2, and assigns it to the variable NSet_1. The next line does the same with exchanged indices 1 and 2. Afterwards, the union of property pair sets is built which are either exclusively defined in the first set or the second set or which have consistent definitions in both sets.

The function merge will be used later on to combine a required set of properties of a partially constructed system configuration with the requirements of a still needed module variant. Let us assume that we start with the requirement of the window system "X" and select a module variant which makes no assumptions about an underlying window system, but requires either a "UNIX" or "MSDOS" operating system. This leads to the call of

merge({"WS:X"}, {"OS:UNIX", "OS:MSDOS"})

with the result (cf. case 1 and case 2 of merge comments in fig. 3.4)

{"WS:X", "OS:UNIX", "OS:MSDOS"}.

Let us assume furthermore that the next selected module variant requires the operating system "UNIX". This leads to the call of

merge({"WS:X", "OS:UNIX", "OS:MSDOS"}, {"OS:UNIX"})

which returns the result (cf. case 1 and 3 of merge comments in fig. 3.4)

{"WS:X", "OS:UNIX"}.

The last declaration of fig. 3.4 defines an auxiliary function addSize, which takes a node of class ATOM as input and adds its Size attribute value to another given <u>integer</u> value. It is used in fig. 3.5 to compute derived Size attributes of COMPLEX nodes.

```
node class UNIT
   derived
      Size : integer = 0;
   intrinsic
      Name : string := "";
end;      (* Root of class hierarchy. *)

node class SPECIFICATION is a UNIT
   redef derived
      Size = max( 0, all self.-has->.Size );
           (* The 'Size' of a specification is the maximum of   *)
           (* the size of all its realizations, instead of      *)
           (* being the sum (which would reasonable, too).       *)
end;       (* A 'SPECIFICATION' is either the complete design of *)
           (* a software system or a design of one its parts.   *)

node class REALIZATION is a UNIT
   intrinsic
      Props : string [0:n];   (* Set of guaranteed properties *)
end;       (* A 'REALIZATION' is an implementation of a 'SPEC.' *)
           (* which fulfills a given set of properties like      *)
           (* needed hardware platforms, operating system, ...  *)

edge type has : SPECIFICATION [1:1] -> REALIZATION [0:n];
           (* A 'SPECIFICATION' 'has' an arbitrary number of   *)
           (* 'REALIZATIONS', but a 'REALIZATION' belongs to a  *)
           (* uniquely defined 'SPECIFICATION'.                 *)

node class COMPLEX is a UNIT
   redef derived
      Size = addSize( 0, all self.-contains-> );
           (* The 'Size' of a complex unit is the sum of *)
           (* the 'Size' of all its children.           *)
end;

node class ATOM is a UNIT
   intrinsic
      File : file;    (* Pointer to externally stored file. *)
   redef derived
      Size = size( self.File );
                (* 'Size' is the length of the attached File. *)
end;

edge type contains : COMPLEX [1:1] -> ATOM [0:n];

node class SYSTEM is a SPECIFICATION, COMPLEX
   redef derived
      Size = addSize( 0, all self.-contains-> );
           (* Resolves inheritance conflict of attribute   *)
           (* definitions in 'SPECIFICATION' and 'COMPLEX' *)
           (* by prefering definition in 'SPECIFICATION'.  *)
end;

node class CONFIGURATION is a REALIZATION, COMPLEX end;
     (* A 'CONFIGURATION' is a set of variants of module    *)
     (* realizations which fulfill all required properties. *)

node class MODULE is a SPECIFICATION, ATOM
   redef derived
      Size = size( self.File ) + max( 0, all self.-has->.Size );
           (* Resolves inheritance conflict of attribute     *)
           (* definitions in 'SPECIFICATION' and 'COMPLEX'   *)
           (* by building the sum of both definitions which  *)
           (* are in conflict to each other.                 *)
end;       (* A 'SYSTEM' contains a set of 'MODULES' which    *)
           (* have 'VARIANTS' as their realizations.         *)

node class VARIANT is a REALIZATION, ATOM end;
```

Fig. 3.5. Defining derived node attributes

Fig. 3.5 contains a cutout of the *textual graph schema representation* which contains more information than the graphical schema declaration of fig. 3.3. It reveals additional cardinality constraints for edges like "any SPECIFICATION has an arbitrary number of REALIZATION nodes, but a REALIZATION belongs always to a single SPECIFI-CATION". More precisely, the same four *cardinality constraints* are available for the definition of edge types as presented above for the definition of formal function parameters. A cardinality constraint of the form [min:max] behind the target class within an edge type declaration defines lower and upper boundaries for the bundle of outgoing edges at a single source node. Such a constraint behind the source class defines lower and upper boundaries for the bundle of incoming edges at a single target node.

The most important part of fig. 3.5 are its derived *attribute evaluation rules*. The default rule within the declaration of the Size attribute requires that "pure" UNIT nodes have no size at all. It is only a part of the specification for completeness reasons and could be omitted. All node types of our example, which have the Size attribute, inherit a *redefined* evaluation rule. For demonstration purposes, we assume that SPECIFICATION nodes have a size which is the maximum of the sizes of their realizations. Furthermore, COMPLEX nodes have a size which is the sum of all their component sizes, and ATOMIC nodes compute their size from the contents of their File attribute.

As a consequence, SYSTEM nodes as well as MODULE nodes inherit two different evaluation rules from their superclasses (see also fig. 3.6). This constitutes a so-called *inheritance conflict* which has to be resolved manually. In the case of the class SYSTEM it seems to be logical to use the same evaluation function as in the class COMPLEX, i.e. one of the inherited evaluation rules *overwrites* the other one. In the case of the class MODULE the new rule has to be a *combination* of the rules which constitute the inheritance conflict. It computes just the sum of the two inherited evaluation rules.

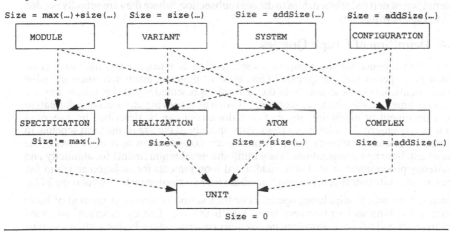

Size = explicitly defined evaluation rule   Size = inherited evaluation rule

Fig. 3.6. Various forms of inheritance conflicts and conflict resolution strategies

The two remaining classes VARIANT and CONFIGURATION exemplify a slightly different situation. They inherit one evaluation rule from the class UNIT directly and another rule from a subclass of UNIT (VARIANT inherits a redefinition from ATOM and CON-FIGURATION a redefinition from COMPLEX). In this case, PROGRES and many object-oriented programming languages *resolve the conflict automatically* in favor of the more specific rule (method).

The values of derived attributes are automatically kept in a consistent state. For this purpose an *incrementally working lazy attribute evaluation mechanism* is used. It is a variant of the well-known two-phase attribute evaluation algorithm in /5. Hud 87/, which is an integral part of our graph-oriented database system GRAS /6. KSW 95/. It works as follows applied to the sample graph of fig. 3.2. At the beginning all derived attributes have uncomputed values. A read access to the `Size` attribute of the `System` node triggers then the evaluation of all derived attributes, which are needed for the computation of the directly needed attribute. In our case, all `Size` attributes (except the attribute of the `Config` node 5) are needed and evaluated in the correct order of their dependencies. `Variant` nodes 6 through 9 compute the sizes of their files. Afterwards, `Module` nodes 2, 3, and 4 compute the sum of their own file size and the maximum of the sizes of their variants. The `System` node itself computes finally the sum of the sizes of all its modules.

Afterwards, any *modification* of the given MIL graph *invalidates* all those computed *attributes* whose values *maybe affected* by the changes. Adding for instance a new variant to the module `Main` would affect the attribute values of the module `Main` itself and the `System` node. For further information concerning the evaluation of derived attributes see section 4.2 about the underlying database system GRAS.

In summary, so far we have explained all language features for the definition of graph schemata with node types, edge types, and attributes as basic components and with node classes as a means for grouping node types with common properties. We shall see within the next section how graph schema definitions may be checked against graph rewrite rules, thereby guaranteeing that any attempt to construct a *schema inconsistent graph* is detected at *compile time* (cf. section 3.6 about tools). Furthermore, we shall see how node classes are used to define *generic graph rewrite rules* that have actual node type parameters and formal node class parameter types. Finally, we should mention that we have postponed the definition of derived relationships to the next subsection, where they are actually needed within graph rewrite rules.

3.1.4 Definition of Graph Queries

The graph schema definition part of a specification as introduced in the last section enables us to specify static properties of any class of directed, attributed, node and edge labeled graphs. Using these graphs as the internal representations of documents implies that all document manipulating tool operations such as retrieving any kind of information from a document or modifying any part of a document can be described by *subgraph selection and subgraph replacement steps*. Analogously to the use of the term schema, in the sense of a database schema, these operations are considered to be *transactions* in the sense of database update operations. They fulfill the usual requirements for atomicity and consistency preservation as well as the additional requirements for isolation and duration in the case of multi-user access to a graph database (see discussion on bottom of page 271).

Such a document manipulating operation or transaction is usually composed of basic subgraph matching and replacement steps, which are specified by means of so-called subgraph *tests* and subgraph rewriting *productions* (rewrite rules). In this section, we start with the explanation of how tests and productions are specified and introduce then further concepts to compose these basic operations to more complex graph queries or graph modifying transactions later on.

Fig. 3.7 contains representative examples for those language constructs which may be used to formulate *complex queries*. The most important components are *subgraph tests*, which search for the existence or nonexistence of a certain subgraph pattern in a host graph. Please note that a selected subgraph in the host graph contains a corresponding node and edge for any (positive) node and edge of the regarded pattern. It may contain *additional edges* between selected nodes in the host graph. All subgraph tests use so-called *restrictions* (double arrows pointing to a node) and *paths* (double arrows between two nodes) as complex application conditions. They are defined later on in fig. 3.9.

```
query ConsistentConfiguration( out CName : string ) =
    (* A configuration is consistent if:
    (* 1) it contains a variant of the system's main module, *)
    (* 2) it contains a variant for any module which is      *)
    (*     needed by another included variant, and           *)
    (* 3) it does not contain variants which are not needed  *)
    (*     by needed variants.                               *)
    use LocalName: string do
        ConfigurationWithMain( out LocalName )
      & not UnresolvedImportExists( LocalName )
      & not ConfigurationWithUselessVariant( LocalName )
      & CName := LocalName
    end
end;

test ConfigurationWithMain( out CName : string ) =
```

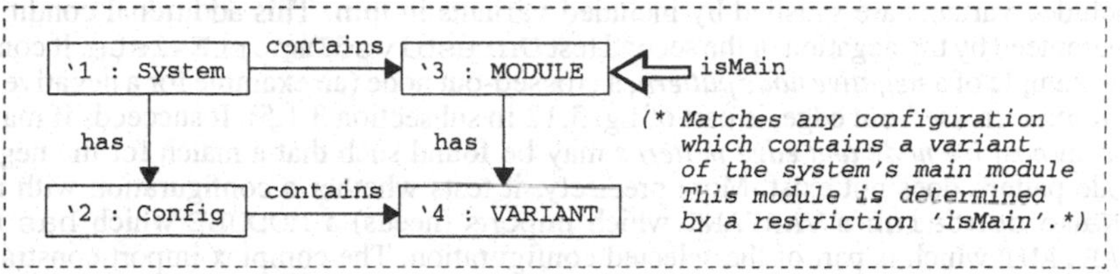

```
                    contains
   ┌───────────┐ ──────────── ┌──────────────┐
   │ '1 : System│             │ '3 : MODULE  │ ⇐ isMain
   └───────────┘              └──────────────┘
                                                (* Matches any configuration
      has              has                         which contains a variant
                                                    of the system's main module
   ┌───────────┐  contains  ┌──────────────┐       This module is determined
   │ '2 : Config│ ───────── │ '4 : VARIANT │       by a restriction 'isMain'.*)
   └───────────┘            └──────────────┘
```

```
    return CName := '2.Name;
end;

test UnresolvedImportExists( CName : string ) =
```

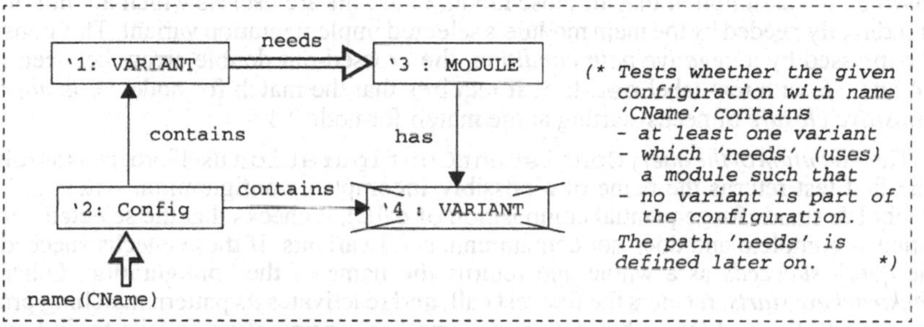

```
                      needs
   ┌─────────────┐ ─────────→ ┌──────────────┐
   │ '1: VARIANT │            │ '3 : MODULE  │      (* Tests whether the given
   └─────────────┘            └──────────────┘         configuration with name
         ↑                                             'CName' contains
      contains                  has                    - at least one variant
                                                        - which 'needs' (uses)
   ┌─────────────┐  contains  ┌──────────────┐           a module such that
   │ '2: Config  │ ─────────→ │ '4 : VARIANT │         - no variant is part of
   └─────────────┘            └──────────────┘           the configuration.
         ⇧                                            The path 'needs' is
    name(CName)                                       defined later on.     *)
```

```
end;

test ConfigurationWithUselessVariant( CName : string ) =
```

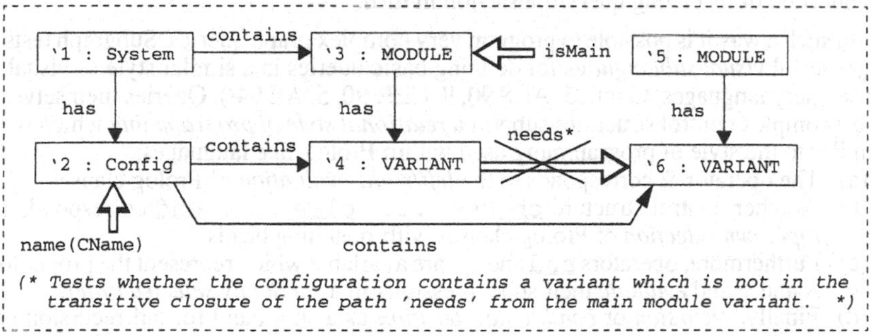

```
                     contains
   ┌───────────┐ ──────────── ┌──────────────┐          ┌──────────────┐
   │ '1 : System│             │ '3 : MODULE  │ ⇐ isMain │ '5 : MODULE  │
   └───────────┘              └──────────────┘          └──────────────┘
      has              has                                   has
                                            needs*
   ┌───────────┐ contains ┌──────────────┐ ═══╳══→ ┌──────────────┐
   │ '2 : Config│ ──────── │ '4 : VARIANT │         │ '6 : VARIANT │
   └───────────┘           └──────────────┘         └──────────────┘
      ⇧                                              ↑
  name(CName)                 contains
```

```
    (* Tests whether the configuration contains a variant which is not in the
       transitive closure of the path 'needs' from the main module variant.  *)
end;
```

Fig. 3.7. Specification of atomic subgraph tests and complex graph queries

The test `ConfigurationWithMain` matches any subgraph consisting of the following nodes and edges, by binding its identifiers `'1`, `'2`, etc. to nodes of the host graph:

  (a) the identifier `'1` is bound to a node of the type `System`,
  (b) the identifier `'2` is bound to a node of type `Config` which is the target of a has-edge from the `System` node,
  (c) the identifier `'3` is bound to a node of (a type belonging to) class `MODULE`, which is part of the selected `System` and fulfills the additional *restriction* `isMain` (expressed by the double arrow pointing to node `'3`; cf. fig. 3.9),
  (d) and the identifier `'4` to a node of (a type of) the class `VARIANT`, which is part of the selected configuration and a realization variant of the selected main module.

The test returns either the `Name` of such a configuration, an *arbitrarily* selected one if several configurations do exist in parallel, or *fails*. It is used within `ConsistentConfiguration` for retrieving any minimal but complete configuration, where imports of included variants are satisfied by included variants in turn. This additional condition is guaranteed by the negation of the second test `UnresolvedImportExists`. It contains an example of a *negative node pattern*, a crossed-out node (an example for a negative edge pattern, a crossed-out edge, is part of fig. 3.12 in subsection 3.1.5). It succeeds if matches for all *positive node and edge patterns* may be found such that a match for the negative node pattern does not exist. More precisely, it tests whether a configuration with name `CName` contains a `VARIANT` which imports (needs) a `MODULE` which has *not* a `VARIANT` which is part of the selected configuration. The complex import constraint is modeled as a *positive path condition*, the double arrow between nodes `'1` and `'3` with text label `needs` (cf. fig. 3.9 for the definition of `needs`).

The last test of fig. 3.7 checks whether a given configuration contains useless variants based on the assumption that all those module variants are useless which are not directly or indirectly needed by the main module's selected implementation variant. This constraint is expressed by a *negative path condition*, the crossed-out double arrow between nodes `'4` and `'6` with text label `needs*`. It requires that the match for node `'6` is *not in the transitive closure* of needs starting at the match for node `'4`.

The *execution of the query* `ConsistentConfiguration` itself proceeds as follows: The first test returns the name of a possibly incomplete configuration. Afterwards (the symbol & stands for sequential composition of calls), it checks that the selected configuration is complete and does not contain unneeded variants. If these checks succeed then the query *succeeds* as a whole and returns the name of the configuration. Otherwise, *backtracking starts*, reenters the first test call, and reactivates its pattern matching process. As a result, the first test either determines another configuration or fails to find another match. In the first case, the execution of the query is continued with checking consistency of the new configuration; in the second case, the whole query fails and triggers backtracking or abortion of its calling query/transaction in turn.

In such a way it is possible to program very complex graph queries. Subgraph tests offer a powerful *visual sublanguage* for defining basic queries in a similar style as visual database query languages do (cf. /5. ACS 90, 9. CER 90, 5. AE 94/). Queries themselves with their complex control structures support a *relational style of programming* which is rather similar to the style of programming used within Prolog-like languages:

  (a) The operator & corresponds to the *left/right-evaluation* of Prolog clauses.
  (b) Another control structure <u>choose</u> ... <u>else</u> ... <u>end</u> corresponds to the *top/down selection* of Prolog clauses with matching heads.
  (c) Furthermore, operators <u>and</u> and <u>or</u> are available which represent the proper logical ∧ and ∨ and *evaluate* their subexpressions in a *randomly selected order*.
  (d) Finally, *recursion* or *conditional iteration* as a shorthand for tail recursion can be used to specify even more complex graph queries with the usual risk of nonterminating evaluation processes.

```
query AllConsistentConfigurations( out CNameSet : string [0:n] ) =
    use LocalNameSet, ResultNameSet : string [0:n] do
        ResultNameSet := nil              (* Start with the empty result set. *)
        & GetAllConfigurations( out LocalNameSet ) (* Get all 'Config' nodes. *)
        & for all LocalCName := elem( LocalNameSet ) do
                        (* Loop through all configurations and check the same   *)
                        (* consistency conditions as in ConsistentConfiguration. *)
            choose
                when ConfigurationWithMain( LocalCName )
                and not ConfigurationWithUselessVariant( LocalCName )
                and for all LocalMName := elem( LocalCName.-has->.=needs=> ) do
                        (* Tests for all 'Variants' which are the targets  *)
                        (* of 'has' edges of a selected configuration:     *)
                        (*    do all needed modules have variants which are *)
                        (*    also part of the selected configuration?      *)
                        ModuleInConfiguration( LocalCName, LocalMName )
                    end
                then ResultNameSet := (ResultNameSet or LocalCName)
                        (* Includes new configuration name into result. *)
                else
                    skip          (* Else branch does nothing and may be omitted. *)
                end
        end
        & CNameSet := ResultNameSet        (* Returns all correct configurations *)
    end
end;

test GetAllConfigurations( out CName : string [0:n] ) =
```

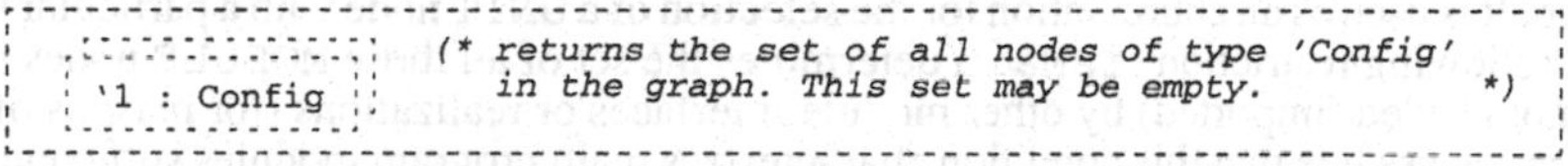

```
    return CName := `1.Name;
end;

test ConfigurationWithMain( CName : string ) =
```

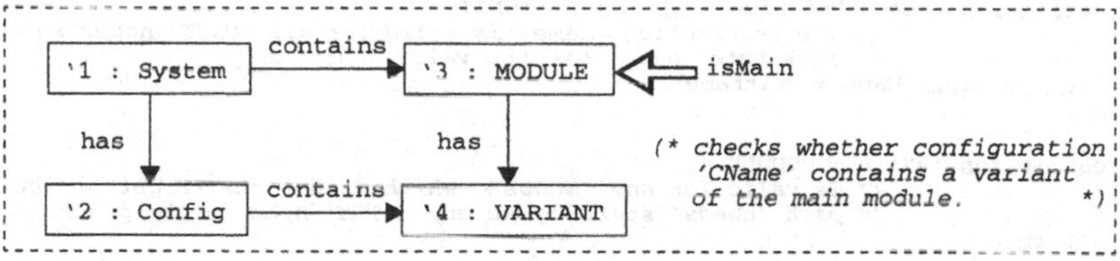

```
    condition CName = `2.Name;
end;

test ModuleInConfiguration( CName : string ; MName : string ) =
```

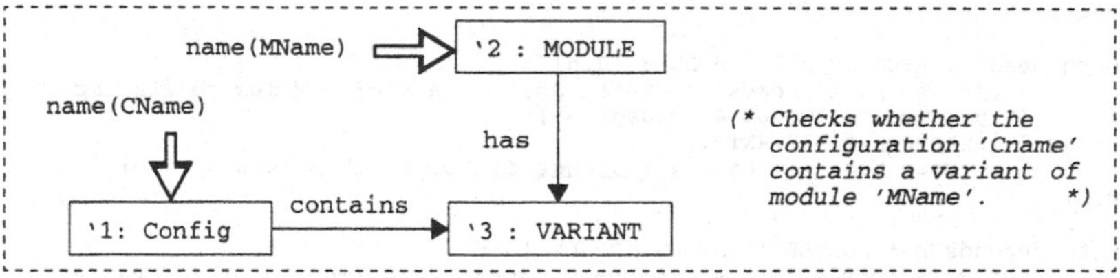

```
end;
```

Fig. 3.8. Replacing implicit backtracking in query implementation by explicit control structures

Beside the relational style of programming, a completely *imperative style of programming* is supported. Fig. 3.8 contains for instance a deterministic reformulation of the query from fig. 3.7, which makes in addition less usage of double negations and implicit existential quantification. The previously used subquery

<u>not</u> UnresolvedImportExists(LocalName)

is replaced by an inner <u>for all</u> loop (explicit quantification), which tests whether all imports of all variants in a configuration also have variants in the configuration. Furthermore, nondeterministic assignments to the LocalName variable in fig. 3.7 together with backtracking is replaced by an outer <u>for all</u> loop, which determines first all existing configurations and selects then the subset of consistent configurations.

It is often a matter of taste (and experience) whether a nondeterministically working query (transaction) or a deterministically working one is more readable. In general, people familiar with the relational style of programming will and should make *extensive usage* of *nondeterminism* and backtracking, since resulting specifications are more compact and are more in the *flavor of rule-oriented visual programming*. People influenced by programming languages like C or Pascal tend to produce and prefer specifications with very primitive subgraph tests and productions, where almost all complex computation steps are performed within queries and transactions in an imperative style of programming.

Until now, we did not explain the purpose of so-called *restrictions* and *path declarations* which were used in fig. 3.7, but which are declared in fig. 3.9. They are the means for defining derived sets of nodes with certain properties and derived binary relationships. Both restrictions and path expressions are used within attribute evaluation rules to *determine context nodes* with needed attribute values and within subgraph tests and productions as *application conditions*. The restriction name selects a subset of all UNIT nodes in a graph. It is used as an abbreviation for the selection of a UNIT node with a particular name. The following restriction isMain determines the set of all those MODULE nodes which are not needed (imported) by other module interfaces or realizations (for reasons of simplicity we assume that this condition characterizes main program modules sufficiently). It is true for all those MODULE nodes which are not reachable from another ATOM node via a separately defined path needs (expressed by the double arrow with label needs).

```
restriction name ( UnitName : string ) : UNIT =
                  (* The restriction 'name' is valid for all 'UNIT' nodes whose *)
                  (* attribute 'Name' has the value 'UnitName'.                 *)
     valid (self.Name = UnitName)
end;

restriction isMain : MODULE =
                  (* Is valid for any 'MODULE' which is not the target of the  *)
                  (* path 'needs' starting at any 'ATOM' node in the graph.     *)
     `1 in
```

```
end;

path needs : ATOM [0:n] -> MODULE [0:n] =
          (* The path 'needs' connects any variant or modules to its imports. *)
     ( instance of MODULE & -m_uses-> )
     or ( instance of VARIANT &
     ( -v_uses-> or ( <-has- & instance of MODULE & -m_uses-> ) ) )
end;

path dependsOn : MODULE [0:n] -> MODULE [0:n] =
     (* connects module to its interface imports and imports of its variants. *)
     ( self or -has-> ) & =needs=>⁺
end;
```

Fig. 3.9. Specification of derived node sets (restrictions) and binary relationships (paths)

The last two declarations of fig. 3.9 define derived binary relations in the form of complex *path expressions*. Path expressions are primarily relational definitions of derived relationships. Nevertheless, they may also be understood as functions, which navigate from a given set of source nodes along certain edges in a host graph and return their target nodes. The notion of a *path expression* within the area of graph grammars was originally introduced to determine and manipulate the embedding of matched subgraphs in their host graph (cf. following subsection 3.1.5 and /5. Nag 79/). They are nowadays more important for defining complex application conditions of subgraph tests and graph rewrite rules. Therefore, our notion of path expressions is almost equivalent to the notion of path expressions as it is used within the database community together with object-oriented or ER-like data models (e.g. in /5. EW 83/).

Basic path expressions were already used for the definition of attribute evaluation rules. They belong to one of the following categories:
(a) *edge operators* of the form -e-> and <-e- allow the traversal of e-labeled edges from source to sink or vice versa,
(b) *attribute conditions* of the form valid expr, as used within the restriction name, require that a given node on a path has certain attribute values,
(c) *context restrictions* of the form with path require that a given node n is related via a path expression path to at least one node m,
(d) and *node type restrictions* of the form instance of type_set require that the type of a node is an element of the given type set.

Many *path operators* are available for composing more complex expressions from basic ones. Often used operators are the *concatenation* p1 & p2 for evaluate first p1 and apply then p2 to the result of p1, p1 or p2 for evaluate both p1 and p2 and construct the *union* of their results, and finally p+ (or p*) for computing the transitive (and reflexive) *closure* of a given path expression p. These constructs are presented within fig. 3.9. The path needs, for instance, relates ATOM nodes to MODULE nodes as follows:
(a) Its first subexpression relates any ATOM node n, which belongs to class MODULE, to a node m, if n is the source and m is the target of an m_uses-edge.
(b) The second subexpression relates an ATOM node n of class VARIANT to another node m, if either (1) n is the source and m is the target of a v_uses-edge or (2) there exists a MODULE node x(n) such that n is the target and x(n) is the source of a has-edge and x(n) is the source and m is the target of an m_uses-edge.
As a result, the relationship $\{(3, 4)\} \cup (\{(6, 3),(6, 4)\} \cup \{(7, 4)\})$ with x(7) = 3 is the semantics of the path declaration needs for the graph of fig. 3.2. Interpreting needs not as a binary relationship between nodes, but as a function which returns for a given node n a set of nodes, we have e.g.: needs(6) := {3,4}. The semantics of the following path declaration dependsOn, the *transitive closure* of needs restricted to MODULE nodes, is then the relationship $\{(2,3),(2,4),(3,4\}$.

Please note that the presented examples do not make usage of all existing path operators. Additionally available operators are offered for computing *intersections* (p1 and p2) or *differences* (p1 but not p2) of intermediate result sets as well as for conditional branching and iteration:

    [not with -m_uses-> :: -has-> & -v_uses-> | -m_uses->]

is a more or less meaningless example for *conditional branching*. It returns for a given node n the result of -has-> & -v_uses-> if n is not the source of an m_uses-edge, it returns the result of -m_uses-> otherwise. An equivalent shorthand without an explicitly mentioned condition (before : :) is

    [-m_uses-> | -has-> & -v_uses->].

Replacing the square brackets [and] of any conditional path expression by curly braces { and } we get an example for *conditional iteration* of path expressions:

    { -m_uses-> | -has-> & -v_uses-> }

iterates as long as one of its two branches returns a nonempty result with a preference for results of the first branch. Its application to the node 2 of fig. 3.2 is computed as follows:

(a) The evaluation of the first branch fails, but the evaluation of the second branch returns the intermediate result {3,4}.

(b) The final result is now the union of the application of the iteration construct to any node of the previously computed intermediate result.

(c) The evaluation with 4 as input fails for both branches and returns, therefore, the node 4 itself.

(d) The evaluation with 3 as input results in another intermediate result set {4} which is already an element of a maintained set of already visited nodes and, therefore, no longer of any importance for the final result set.

(e) The final result of the evaluation process is then the result of step (c), the set {4}.

Please note that *conditional iteration* has a rather different behavior than transitive closure; it returns not the set of all visited nodes, but only those nodes which are end points of the iteration process. Its *termination in the presence of cycles* is guaranteed by maintaining an internal set of already visited nodes. This has the consequence that conditional iteration never returns its input nodes, except the case where the first iteration step fails. Let us assume for instance that the graph of fig. 3.2 contains an additional m_uses-edge from 3 to 2. In this case, the evaluation of our conditional path expression returns the same result as before, the set {4}.

To summarize, all *visual constructs* available for the definition of subgraph tests and many *textual control structures* (similar to those used for the definition of complex queries or attribute expressions) can be used for the declaration of paths and restrictions. The textual style of programming should only be preferred when transitive closures are needed or when alternatives must be considered. Finally, we have to mention that it is a matter of additional pragmas whether a restriction or a path is recomputed every time when it is needed or whether its results are *materialized* once and *incrementally maintained* in a consistent state using an extension of the afore-mentioned attribute evaluation mechanism (cf. subsection 3.1.6).

3.1.5 Definition of Graph Transformations

Subgraph tests and queries together with path declarations and restrictions were the main constructs for inspecting already existing graphs, whereas productions and transactions are their counterparts for creating and modifying schema consistent graphs. *Productions* have a *left-* and a *right-hand side graph pattern* as their main components, where left-hand side patterns are the same as already presented subgraph patterns of tests. *Transactions* use control structures to construct complex graph transformations from basic production applications in the same way as queries use them to combine basic subgraph tests.

The first production of fig. 3.10 selects the System node and verifies that a module with the name MName is not already part of our software design. In that case, the match of its left-hand side is *replaced* by an image of its right-hand side in the following manner (note that we will use the words "node/edge" not only in their usual sense but also as an abbreviation for "image or match of node/edge pattern in host graph" in the sequel):

(a) All nodes in the right-hand side which are bound to nodes of the left-hand side are *preserved* without performing any not explicitly required intrinsic attribute value or edge context modifications. This means in our case that the matched System node '1 is preserved.

(b) All positive nodes and edges of the left-hand side which have no counterparts in the right-hand side have to be *deleted*, including all incident edges of deleted nodes. The left-hand side of our example contains only an identically replaced node '1, a negative node '2 (which must not exist), and an implicitly negative edge from the positive node '1 to the negative node '2. Therefore, nothing is deleted at all.

(c) All nodes and edges of the right-hand side with no counterparts in the left-hand side are *added* to the host graph, i.e. a new node of type MType is created which is connected to the already existing System node via a new contains-edge.

(d) Finally, *new attribute values* are computed by evaluating expressions which may reference input parameters as well as old attribute values (these expressions are computed before any modification of the host graph is performed).

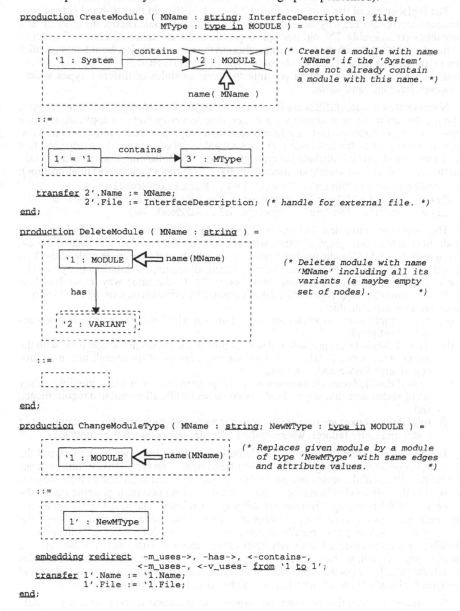

```
production CreateModule ( MName : string; InterfaceDescription : file;
                          MType : type in MODULE ) =

                      contains                          (* Creates a module with name
   '1 : System   --------------->   '2 : MODULE           'MName' if the 'System'
                                                          does not already contain
                                                          a module with this name. *)
                              name( MName )

   ::=

                      contains
   1' = '1       --------------->   3'  : MType

   transfer 2'.Name := MName;
            2'.File := InterfaceDescription; (* handle for external file. *)
end;

production DeleteModule ( MName : string ) =

   '1 : MODULE   <---  name(MName)             (* Deletes module with name
                                                  'MName' including all its
       has                                       variants (a maybe empty
        |                                        set of nodes).          *)
        v
   '2 : VARIANT

   ::=


end;

production ChangeModuleType ( MName : string; NewMType : type in MODULE ) =

   '1 : MODULE   <---  name(MName)             (* Replaces given module by a module
                                                  of type 'NewMType' with same edges
                                                  and attribute values.          *)

   ::=

   1'  : NewMType

   embedding redirect  -m_uses->, -has->, <-contains-,
                       <-m_uses-, <-v_uses- from '1 to 1';
   transfer   1'.Name := '1.Name;
              1'.File := '1.File;
end;
```

Fig. 3.10. Specification of basic graph transformations

This example illustrates the possibility to define *parametrized productions* which must be instantiated (in the sense of a procedure call) with actual attribute values and node types. In this way, a single production may abstract from a set of productions which differ only with respect to used attribute values and types of matched or created nodes. In almost all cases, node type parameters are not used for matching purposes, but provide concrete types for new nodes of the right-hand side.

The replacement of the node inscription ` 2   :   MODULE` in the left-hand side of production `CreateModule` by the inscription ` 2   :   MType` would change the production's semantics considerably. The old inscription prohibits the existence of a node of *any type* of the class `MODULE` with the same name, whereas the new inscription would only prohibit the existence of a node of *exactly the same type* of the class `MODULE` as the node we are going to create. It would then be possible to create modules of different types which, however, have the same name.

Note that the class `MODULE` is used to denote a *type for the node type parameter* `MType`. Having this information available we are then able to verify that any application of the production `CreateModule` to a *schema consistent graph* produces another schema consistent graph, i.e. that the new node is always a legal target of a `contains`-edge and that it carries indeed a `Name` attribute (of type <u>`string`</u>). The following lines would produce all three modules of our sample architecture in fig. 3.1 (without their import relationships):

```
CreateModule("Main", TextFile1, FunctionModule) &
CreateModule("UserInterface", TextFile2, ADOModule) &
CreateModule("Files", TextFile3, ADTModule)
```

The following production `DeleteModule` of fig. 3.10 removes a specified `Module` node from a MIL host graph together with all its `VARIANT` nodes. The dashed double borders of the node ` 2` indicate that it may not only be bound to a single node in the host graph, but to the *maximum set of all nodes* fulfilling all required constraints (they must be the targets of `has`-edges emanating from node ` 1`). In the same way as we had four different options for edge type and variable/parameter cardinalities, *four different kinds of node patterns* are available:

(a) Solid simple boxes are *mandatory node patterns* which match single node instances in the host graph,

(b) dashed simple boxes are *optional node patterns* which match a single node with the required properties if existent, but do not cause failure of the overall matching process if such a node does not exist,

(c) dashed double boxes are *optional node set patterns* which match a possibly empty set of nodes such that any node of the given set fulfills all mentioned requirements, and

(d) solid double boxes are *mandatory node set patterns* which match a nonempty set of nodes and cause failures, where dashed (double) boxes match the empty set.

Taking all these additional kinds of node patterns into account, we have to extend the overall *proceeding for finding matches* of left-hand sides. The first step is to find matches for all dashed or solid *simple node patterns and edge patterns* such that all positive constraints in the left-hand side are taken into account and no two node patterns match the same node in the host graph (isomorphic subgraph matching). The next step then is to find maximal matches for all *node set patterns* such that no two node (set) patterns match the same node in the host graph. Finally, one *negative node or edge pattern* after the other is handled by trying to extend the already determined subgraph with a match of the negative node or edge. Again, we have to ensure that (negative) node patterns do not match nodes which are already part of the selected subgraph. Any existing extension causes failure and initiates backtracking, which tries to find another match within the host graph.

Sometimes it is useful to override the above-mentioned restriction to *isomorphic subgraph matching*. If two node (set) patterns with identifiers ` x` and ` y` may (but need not) share their matches then an explicit *folding clause* of the form <u>`fold`</u> ` x,  ` y` has to be added to a production. For further details concerning (nonisomorphic) pattern matching and the treatment of positive as well as negative application conditions the reader is referred to /5. Zün 96a/. For further details concerning the problem of *finding matches efficiently*, the reader is referred to /5. Zün 96b/ or section 3.6 about PROGRES tools. There, we shall discuss the implementation of pattern matching briefly.

Using identical replacement of nodes or node sets together with the options to allow nonisomorphic matches and to connect nodes in the left-hand side via arbitrarily complex path expressions, offers a language user powerful means to construct and to modify so-called *embeddings*. The general problem, postponed until now, is that we have to create or modify connections between the unmodified rest of the host graph and the new nodes or the identically replaced nodes. There exist *two strategies* for solving this problem in graph grammar literature (cf. section 3.2). The first one is based on *identical replacement* of nodes and was used in the first two productions of fig. 3.10. Its "traditional" form became popular with the so-called algebraic graph grammar approach, where it is restricted to identical replacement of single nodes (cf. /5. Ehr 79/). PROGRES, on the contrary, allows for the identical replacement of arbitrarily large sets of nodes.

Using the identical replacement strategy, when many different types of edges have to be redirected, results in unreadable large left- and right-hand sides with many set node patterns and folding clauses (folding clauses are necessary when two embedding edges may have the same context node). Therefore, PROGRES offers also the second embedding strategy based on *additional embedding clauses* and path expressions, which became popular with the algorithmic (set-theoretic) branch of graph grammars (cf. /5. Nag 79/).

The production `ChangeModuleType` of fig. 3.10 contains an example of an embedding clause. The notation
```
redirect e1, e2,... from 'n to m';
```
is a shorthand for
```
redirect e1 from 'n to m'; redirect e2 from 'n to m'; ...
```
and
```
redirect -x-> from 'n to m';
```
is in turn a shorthand for
```
remove -x-> from 'n; (* not necessary for deleted 'n *)
copy -x-> as -x-> from 'n to m';
```
It affects any x-edge which connects before the rewriting step the match of 'n to another (not matched) context node v. It replaces it by another x-edge which connects the match of the (new) node m' to the context node v after the rewrite step. Using <-y- instead of -x-> at certain places within the lines above, it is also possible to change the type or direction of a whole bundle of edges, which leave the match of the left-hand side or enter it, by a single embedding rule.

Both embedding strategies have their specific (dis-)advantages. The first one, based on identical replacement and node set patterns, has a *graphical notation* and is more readable if edges of a single type have to be redirected and if additional conditions about context node types etc. have to be considered. The second one, based on embedding clauses and path expressions, has a very compact *textual notation*; it is preferable if edges of many different types may or may not exist, which simply have to be redirected.

Returning from these general remarks about the embedding problem, we apply the following sequence of productions
```
DeleteModule("Files") &
CreateModule("FileSystem", TextFile, ADOModule) &
ChangeModuleType("UserInterface", FunctionModule)
```
to the graph of fig. 3.2. This results in another MIL graph which is displayed in fig. 3.11 and computed as follows:

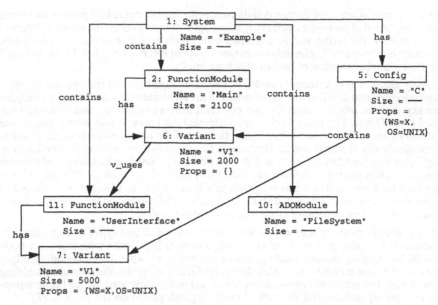

Fig. 3.11. A modified "MIL" graph derived from the previously presented MIL graph

(a) The first production call deletes the node 4 including its `Variant` nodes 8 and 9 as well as all incident edges of these three nodes.

(b) The next production call creates a new node `10` which is connected via a `contains`-edge to the old `System` node `1`.

(c) The last call deletes the `ADOModule` 3 with all its incident edges, creates a new `FunctionModule` node `11`, and redirects all previously existing connections of the deleted node to the new node.

Note that the figure does not display any `File` attributes and uses "—" to mark all possibly affected values of derived `Size` attributes, which must be recomputed when needed.

Until now, we did not use any *complex application conditions* within productions in the form of path expressions or attribute expressions (but we know them from the definition of subgraph tests). The following fig. 3.12 contains examples for these features of the language PROGRES. The first production `CreateMUse` creates a single edge of type `m_uses` and deletes nothing at all. This edge represents an import from a client module `ClientMName` to a server module `ServerMName`. The crossed out double arrow (negative path expression) with label `dependsOn` (cf. fig. 3.9) prohibits the application of the production, if the server module already depends, directly or indirectly, on the client module. In this case, the creation of cyclic (interface) import chains is prohibited.

The following production `InitConfig` implements the first step of the configuration of a system variant, which fulfills the given set of requirements `ReqProps`. It requires that a software system has a uniquely determined main module, which has in turn at least one variant fulfilling the initial set of requirements. The *complex attribute condition* is expressed using the function `'are_in'` (any binary/unary function with a name of the form `'...'` or a name which consists of special symbols like `!@#$$%^&*+-=<>?/` may only be called using infix/prefix notation). It tests whether all required properties in `ReqProps` are covered by the set of guaranteed properties `'4.Props` of the regarded module variant. Its specification is rather similar to the specification of the function `merge` of fig. 3.4 and, therefore, omitted over here.

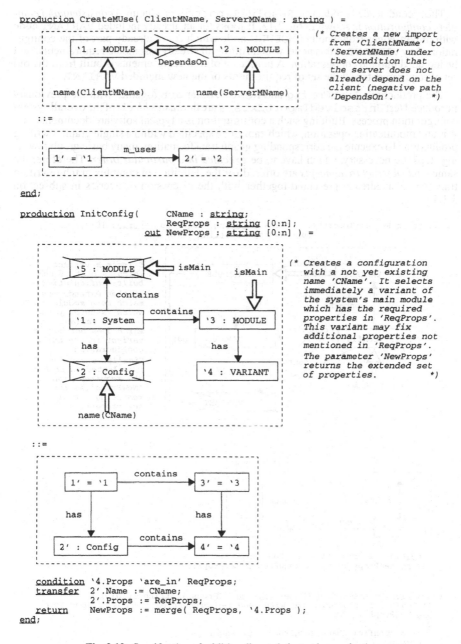

```
production CreateMUse( ClientMName, ServerMName : string ) =
```

(* Creates a new import
from 'ClientMName' to
'ServerMName' under
the condition that
the server does not
already depend on the
client (negative path
'DependsOn'.   *)

```
::=
```

```
end;
```

```
production InitConfig(        CName : string;
                              ReqProps : string [0:n];
                          out NewProps : string [0:n] ) =
```

(* Creates a configuration
with a not yet existing
name 'CName'. It selects
immediately a variant of
the system's main module
which has the required
properties in 'ReqProps'.
This variant may fix
additional properties not
mentioned in 'ReqProps'.

The parameter 'NewProps'
returns the extended set
of properties.   *)

```
::=
```

```
condition  '4.Props 'are_in' ReqProps;
transfer   2'.Name := CName;
           2'.Props := ReqProps;
return     NewProps := merge( ReqProps, '4.Props );
end;
```

Fig. 3.12. Specification of additionally needed complex productions

A selected variant may have additional requirements concerning its runtime platform. These additional requirements are merged with the original set of requirements and returned as an *out parameter* to a calling transaction. In such a way it is possible to take additional restrictions for the rest of the configuration process into account.

270

The second needed production `ResolveImport` for producing a *consistent and complete configuration* is shown in fig. 3.13. It looks for an already included `VARIANT` node with import-edges from another `MODULE` node which is not already part of the configuration. Any `VARIANT` of this node, which fulfills all already assembled requirements, will be included into the configuration. Again, a set of new requirements is built from the old set of requirements and the set of requirements of the new included `VARIANT`.

The productions `InitConfig` and `ResolveImport` together with the previously introduced test `UnresolvedImportExists` are the *basics blocks* of the overall system configuration process. Building such a configuration is a typical software document analysis and modification operation, which cannot be specified within a single graph rewriting production. To execute the corresponding graph transformation, many basic graph rewriting steps are necessary, which have to be *executed in a particular order*. Therefore, the same *control structure concepts* are offered for the definition of complex graph rewriting transactions as already presented together with the discussion of queries in subsection 3.1.4.

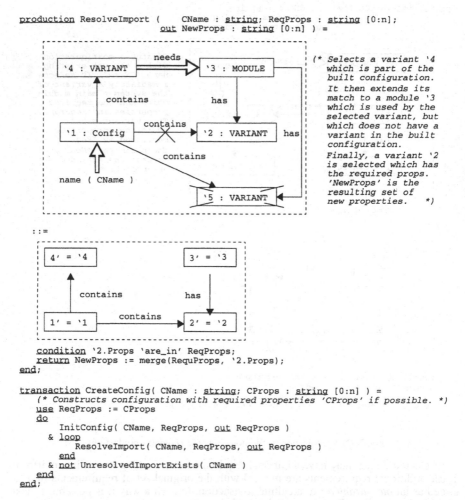

Fig. 3.13. The main transaction for producing a configuration and one of its needed productions

The transaction `CreateConfig` (cf. fig. 3.13) needs the *sequential composition operator* &, the *negation* <u>not</u> of a test, and the *conditional iteration* <u>loop</u> ... <u>end</u>. The hidden termination condition of this loop is that its body is no longer executable. It could be written down explicitly as follows:

```
loop when def( ResolveImport( ... ) then
    ResolveImport( ... )
end
```

The used <u>def</u> operator has about the same semantics as the <u>with</u> operator in path expressions. It tests whether the execution of its argument would be successful or not without modifying the host graph (all temporary modifications during the execution of its argument are cancelled afterwards using backtracking). It is a general rule that the conditions of branching or iterating control structures, also called *guards*, *may not have any side effects*. This is guaranteed by the PROGRES language's static semantics rules.

Other control structures support conditional deterministic branching (see below), *nondeterministic branching* (t <u>or</u> t' applies either t or t' to a graph), and *nondeterministic sequential composition* (t <u>and</u> t' is equivalent to (t & t') or (t' & t), i.e. executes both t and t' in an arbitrarily selected order). It would, for instance, be possible to replace the above explained conditional iteration by a call to the *recursively defined transaction*

```
transaction Iter( ... ) =
    choose
        ResolveImport( ... ) & Iter
    else
        skip
    end
end;
```

which shows an example for *conditional deterministic branching*. The condition of the choose statement's branches are again hidden and could be added as follows:

```
transaction Iter( ... ) =
    choose
        when def( ResolveImport( ... ) & Iter )
        then ResolveImport( ... ) & Iter
    else
        when def( skip )  (* condition is always true *)
        skip (* succeeds always without any effects *)
    end
end;
```

For further details concerning these control structures see /5. Zün 92, 5. Zün 96a/.

The main advantage of our control structures in comparison to other programmed graph rewriting approaches, as for instance /5. Dör 95, 5. Göt 88/, is that whole transactions have the same characteristics as single productions:

(a) They are *atomic* with respect to their effects onto a given host graph. Any execution attempt either succeeds as a whole or aborts without any graph modifications.

(b) They are *consistency preserving*, i.e. manipulate schema consistent graphs only.

(c) They make their own *nondeterministic choices* and initiate *backtracking* when a particular decision leads into a dead-end later on.

As a consequence, transactions over here fulfill (more or less) the well-known *ACID properties of database transactions*: <u>a</u>tomicity, <u>c</u>onsistency, <u>i</u>solation, and <u>d</u>uration. In the single user PROGRES environment (cf. section 3.6), the principle of *isolation*, which requires that the parallel execution of a set of transactions has the same effects as their serialized execution, makes no sense. Generated stand-alone prototypes of specified tools fulfill this requirement in a rudimentary way by locking the whole host graph for the duration of a top-level transaction. The last property, *duration* of the effects of a completed transaction, is guaranteed for top-level transactions, which are called from an "external" client. This is irrelevant in the single user PROGRES environment, but it is in turn important for generated tool prototypes. In this case, backtracking before "commit" points of top-level transactions is no longer useful and the still available ability of the basic execution machinery for undoing effects of any kind of transactions is only offered in the form of explicitly activated undo (and redo) commands (see section 4.2 about the underlying database system GRAS).

The execution of the presented transaction CreateConfig (with an empty set of requirements) applied to the graph of 3.2 (without the Config node 5 which will be created now) may, therefore, proceed as follows:

(a) The call to the production InitConfig selects the only viable variant of the root module "Main". Afterwards, the local variable ReqProps is still the empty set.

(b) The first call to the production ResolveImport in the loop decides to deal first with the imported module "Files" in the selected variant of "Main" and chooses by accident its "MSDOS" variant. Afterwards, the variable ReqProps is the singleton set { "OS:MSDOS" }.

(c) The next call to the production ResolveImport fails, since no variant of the still needed module "UserInterface" exists for "MSDOS". This terminates the loop successfully.

(d) The next line tests whether the constructed configuration is complete. This is apparently not the case such that the called test succeeds and its negation fails. This initiates backtracking.

(e) The execution returns then to the last choice point of the ongoing execution process and cancels all immediately executed graph transformations and variable or parameter assignments.

(f) As a result the second call to the production ResolveImport is reactivated and another remaining match is selected instead of the previous one. This leads to the selection of the "UNIX" variant of the module "UserInterface".

(g) Afterwards, the third call to ResolveImport succeeds and selects the only existing variant V1 of the third needed module "Files".

(h) Finally, the loop terminates again and the previously failed completeness test is now successful, thereby allowing a "commit" of the whole transaction execution process.

3.1.6 Advanced Features

Within previous sections we did not talk about *efficiency problems* and we developed a new specification from scratch, instead of *reusing* already existing *parametrized specification fragments*. Both topics are not relevant as long as PROGRES is used as a pure specification language for toy examples. But these aspects cannot be neglected once the language is used to describe and prototype real software engineering tools (as promised at the beginning of chapter 3). Then additional language constructs are needed. They are

(a) *pragmas* within graph schemata which have significant influence onto the runtime behavior of pattern matching strategies,

(b) formal *node parameters* by means of which information about already found subgraph matches may be passed from one rewrite rule to the next one,

(c) *meta attributes* which are attributes of node types instead of node instances and which allow for the definition of parametrized graph schemata, and

(d) advanced forms of *parametric polymorphism*, where one formal node parameter may have another formal node type parameter as its type.

These language constructs are the topic of this subsection and will be needed later on, especially in section 3.3 for the specification of syntax-directed editors. We will start with the discussion of efficiency matters and continue then with the definition of parametrized graph schemata and graph transformations.

The transaction Test of fig. 3.14 is inefficient with respect to its runtime behavior due to the following reasons:

(a) That part of production CreateModule which guarantees that a software system does not already contain a module with name MName computes first the set of all MODULE nodes of the selected System node and then checks the restriction name(MName) of fig. 3.9 for any node in this set.

(b) The following production CreateMUse loops even twice through the set of all MODULE nodes for finding those nodes which have the name ClientMName and ServerMName.

(c) Even worse, the knowledge of the first two CreateModule production calls of transaction Test about the nodes with name "UI" and "Files" is not used in the third production call.

(d) Finally, the transitive closure of the path dependsOn with the match of node pattern '2 as input is recomputed within any call to the production CreateMUse.

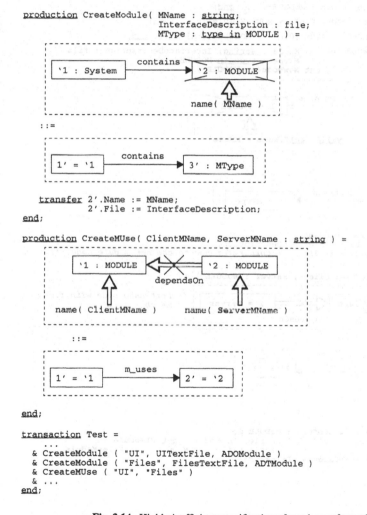

```
production CreateModule( MName : string;
                         InterfaceDescription : file;
                         MType : type in MODULE ) =
```

```
transfer 2'.Name := MName;
         2'.File := InterfaceDescription;
end;
```

```
production CreateMUse( ClientMName, ServerMName : string ) =
```

```
end;
```

```
transaction Test =
  ...
  & CreateModule ( "UI", UITextFile, ADOModule )
  & CreateModule ( "Files", FilesTextFile, ADTModule )
  & CreateMUse ( "UI", "Files" )
  & ...
end;
```

Fig. 3.14. Highly inefficient specification of graph transformation

It is a matter of debate whether the last point (d) above is really a source of inefficiencies. Any successful call to the production `CreateMUse` modifies indeed the derived relation `dependsOn`. Therefore, it might be more efficient to compute any application of `dependsOn` to a specific node from scratch instead of maintaining and reusing previously computed results. In the latter case, we have the additional overhead for invalidating and recomputing inconsistent results. But it is beyond any doubts that the "materialization" of the results of the restriction `isMain` and the path `needs` of fig. 3.9 would accelerate the execution of the transaction `CreateConfig` of fig. 3.13 considerably. In this case, their results are needed again and again within called productions, but are not affected at all.

```
node class UNIT
   ...
   intrinsic index Name : string;
end;
   ...

static restriction isMain : MODULE = ... end;
static path needs : ATOM [0:n] -> MODULE [0:n] = ... end;
static path dependsOn : ATOM [0:n] -> MODULE [0:n] = ... end;
production CreateModule(     MName : string; InterfaceDescription : file;
                             MType : type in MODULE;
                        out NewModule: MODULE ) =
```

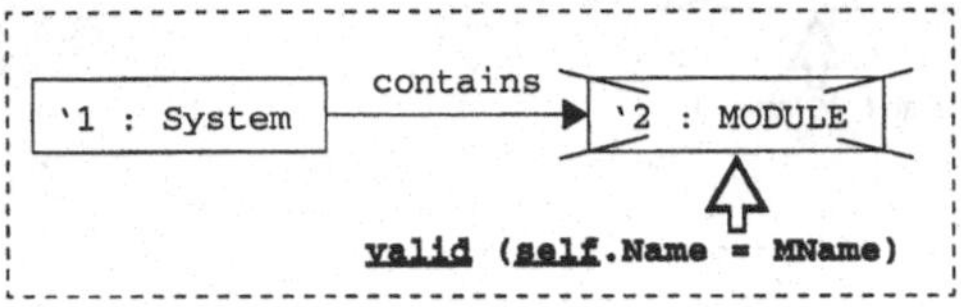

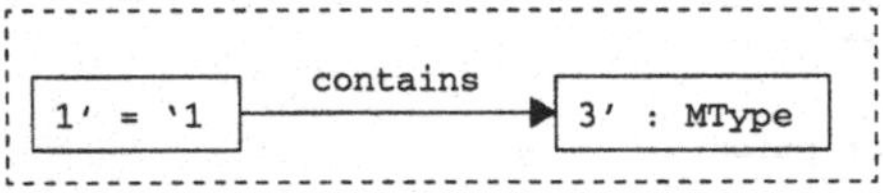

```
transfer 2'.Name := MName;
         2'.File := InterfaceDescription;
   return   NewModule := 3'; (* return reference to the new module node. *)
end;
production CreateMUse( Client, Server : MODULE ) =
```

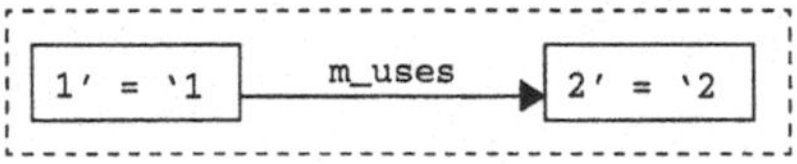

```
end;
transaction Test =
   ...
   & use UIModule, FilesModule : MODULE do
      & CreateModule( "UI", UITextFile, ADOModule, out UIModule )
      & CreateModule( "Files", FilesTextFile, ADTModule, out FilesModule )
      & CreateMUse( UIModule, FilesModule )
      & ...
      end
   & ...
end;
```

Fig. 3.15. Runtime improving modifications of a specification fragment

Fig. 3.15 contains a specification fragment, where all above mentioned problems are eliminated. All modified pieces of "code" are highlighted in boldface:

(a) The *pragma* <u>index</u> within the declaration of attribute Name causes the creation of an *attribute index* which allows for the efficient computation of the set of all UNIT nodes with a distinct name. Using the index, the loop over all MODULE nodes within production CreateModule is no longer necessary (another pragma <u>key</u> should be used if different UNIT nodes with the same Name value may not exist).

(b) The *pragma* <u>static</u> before the restriction isMain and the paths needs and dependsOn causes their *materialization*. An extended version of the incremental attribute evaluation algorithm is used to maintain materialized results in a consistent state (cf. section 4.2). Materialized (parameterless) restrictions are explicitly stored node sets with certain properties, whereas materialized (parameterless) paths correspond to explicitly stored derived binary relations.

(c) Finally, the pattern matching process of the production CreateMUse is considerably improved by *providing the production with matches* for the node patterns in its left-hand side. For this purpose, the production CreateModule returns *handles* to created MODULE nodes in its out-parameter NewModule. These handles are stored within the local variables UIModule and FilesModule and then used as in-parameter values for production CreateMUse.

These *improvements* have the effect that the pattern matching process for the production CreateModule accesses first an always existing index for all System nodes (which is always a singleton set in the running example), accesses then the index for the attribute Name (which returns in our case at most one MODULE node), and checks finally the existence of a contains edge between retrieved nodes. The pattern matching process for the production CreateMUse is even simpler. It has just to check whether the provided nodes Client and Server module are connected via a materialized dependsOn-edge.

In such a way, it is possible to write quite *efficiently executable* graph transformations *aside the considerable overhead* for storing graphs in a database, maintaining logs for backtracking (and recovery) purposes, and keeping indexes as well as derived data in a consistent state (on demand). It is the subject of ongoing research activities to develop new means for getting rid of unnecessary backtracking logs, pruning useless execution paths of our depth-first search and backtracking strategy, and keeping graphs in main memory, if required.

Moving from the discussion of efficiency matters onto the subject of *parametrized specification fragments* we will alter the decision that different types of modules do not have different types of variants. Therefore, we will replace the node type Variant of fig. 3.3 by three new node types FunctionVariant, ADTVariant, and ADOVariant. The type system of the current PROGRES version is not able to guarantee that has-edges connect only MODULE nodes and VARIANT nodes of corresponding types, i.e. that FunctionModules have only FunctionVariants, etc. It is again the subject of ongoing research activities to find out whether it is possible to extend the type system appropriately.

Currently, there are *two ways to circumvent the problem*. The first one is *type safe* and replaces the single edge type declaration has by three edge type declarations of the form

<u>edge type</u> xHas: xModule -> xVariant <u>end</u>;

with x being either Function or ADT or ADO. This solution has the undesirable consequence that we need a separate production for creating each type of VARIANT nodes (formal edge type parameter are not supported due to unsolved type checking problems of such a urgently needed language extension). Furthermore, any occurrence of the subexpression -has-> within path expressions must be replaced by the new subexpression -FunctionHas-> <u>or</u> -ADOHas-> <u>or</u> -ADTHas-> (subexpressions of the form <-has- must be treated analogously).

Therefore, another solution is preferred which is *not type safe*, but which is much more elegant and compact. It uses so-called meta attributes to define a kind of *parametrized node classes* and parametric polymorphism with node and node type parameters to define *parametrized graph transformations* (a primitive form of parametric polymorphism was already used in previous versions of the production `CreateModule`).

```
node class MODULE is a SPECIFICATION, ATOM
   ...
   meta
      VType: type in VARIANT;
   derived
      index Ok = for all Variant := self.-has-> :: Variant.type = self.VType end;
end;

node type ADOModule : MODULE
   redef meta
      VType = ADOVariant;
end;

   ...

node class VARIANT is a REALIZATION, ATOM end;

node type ADOVariant : VARIANT end;

   ...

production CreateModule(     MName : string;
                             InterfaceDescription : file;
                             MType : type in MODULE;
                         out NewModule : MType ) =
   ...
end;

production CreateVariant( Module : MODULE;
                          VName  : string ;
                          PSet : string [0:n] ) =
```

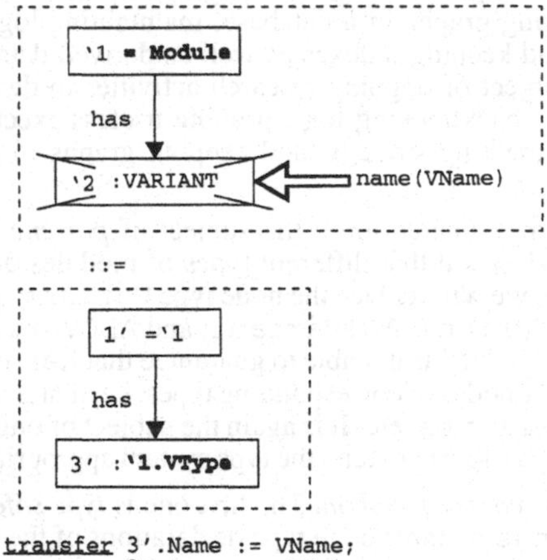

```
   '1 = Module

        | has
        ↓

   '2 :VARIANT  ⇐  name(VName)
```

```
   ::=
```

```
   1' ='1

        | has
        ↓

   3' :'1.VType
```

```
   transfer 3'.Name := VName;
            3'.Props := PSet;
end;

transaction Test =
   ...
   & use UIModule : ADOModule do
      & CreateModule( "UI", UITextFile, ADOModule, out UIModule )
      & CreateVariant( UIModule, "V1", PSet )
      & ...
   end
   & ...
end;
```

Fig. 3.16. Meta node type attributes and parametric polymorphism

The specification fragment in fig. 3.16 contains a single production CreateVariant, which creates for any existing type of MODULE a VARIANT node of the corresponding type. The correct VARIANT type for a given MODULE node is stored in its *meta attribute* VType. The value of such a meta attribute is defined within the graph schema (similar to derived attributes) and may not be modified at runtime (in contrast to intrinsic attributes). It has the same value for all nodes of a distinct type or, more precisely, it is not an attribute of a node instance but an *attribute of its node type*. Assuming that '1 matches a node of type ADOModule, the following equivalences hold:

'1.VType = '1.type.VType = ADModule.VType = ADOVariant

As a consequence, the new node pattern 3' : '1.VType always creates a node of the correct VARIANT type.

Nevertheless, an additional derived attribute Ok is defined for demonstration purposes, which offers direct access to all modules which have at least one variant of the wrong type (or which have only proper variants). It is again subject of ongoing research activities to extend the language PROGRES in such a way that it supports the definition of *complex integrity constraints in graph schemata* (not only via the workaround of using derived boolean attributes) and checks these integrity constraints automatically at runtime.

The declarations of fig. 3.16 also resolve another deficiency of the declarations of fig. 3.15. The formal parameter list of production CreateModule reveals now the fact that the returned MODULE node in the formal parameter NewModule has always the actual input value of the type parameter MType as its type (the old type definition MODULE is replaced by a new type definition MType). As a consequence, it is also possible to replace the unspecific type MODULE of the local variable UIModule in transaction Test by the new type ADOModule. The type check of the CreateModule call in transaction Test proceeds now as follows:

(a) A *first pass* over the parameter list assigns each node type in-parameter the static type of its actual parameter. In our case, MType is bound to the node type ADO-Module.

(b) A *second pass* then checks the compatibility of formal parameter types and actual parameter types by using the assembled information of the first pass. It replaces in our case the occurrence of MType within the declaration of NewModule by its actual type ADOModule and checks then that the type of the local variable UIModule is compatible with the type of the out-parameter NewModule.

This was just one example of "true" *parametric polymorphism* in PROGRES. The general rule is that visible node type parameter identifiers may be used at any place, where node class or node type identifiers are allowed. A polymorphic path or function which returns for a given System node the set of all MODULE nodes of a specified type may for instance be defined as shown within fig. 3.17. In this way it is possible to write highly parametrized specification fragments without loosing the *safety of an almost statically typed language*. The word "almost" refers to the fact that potentially failing *type restrictions* are supported in various forms (instance of clauses within expressions, node patterns within subgraph tests and productions, ...). These constructs are a strict necessity for a pattern matching based language and should not be mixed up with unsafe *type casts* of programming languages like Modula-2 or C. Type casts never fail and enforce the interpretation of an element of an arbitrary type as an element of the given type, instead of checking whether a given element has the required type or not at runtime.

```
path module(MType : type in MODULE): System [1:1] -> MType [0:n] =
    -contains-> & instance of MType
end;

function myModules(MType: type in MODULE; SystemNode : System) -> MType [0:n] =
    self.-contains->.instance of MType
end;
```

Fig. 3.17. Another two examples for parametric polymorphism

3.1.7 Summary and Open Problems

Within this section we presented the IPSEN graph grammar specification language PROGRES and its model-oriented approach to the specification of software engineering tools or, more precisely, the specification of their document manipulating activities. Our approach, called *graph grammar engineering*, is *model-oriented* due to the fact that we use directed, attributed, node and edge labeled graphs to model complex document structures and programmed graph rewriting systems to specify operations on these documents in terms of their effects on their internal graph representation (cf. /5. ELN 92, 5. ES 85, 5. Zün 96a/ for further details). PROGRES may be classified as a *very high level programming language* /5. Schü 91b/ which is a kind of

(a) *object-oriented database definition language* with graphical as well as textual constructs for the declaration of graph database schemata,

(b) *relational (logic-oriented) language* with various means for the definition of derived graph properties,

(c) *hybrid visual/textual database query language* which allows for the definition of rather complex subgraph patterns,

(d) *rule-oriented visual specification language* with support for the construction of parametrized graph rewrite rules (productions) with complex preconditions, and an

(e) *imperative/procedural programming language* with deterministic and nondeterministic control structures for programming complex graph transformation processes.

The language's implementation uses complex incrementally working algorithms to *materialize and update (read only) graph views* in the form of derived attributes and relationships. Furthermore, it uses *backtracking* to escape out of dead-ends caused by wrong nondeterministic selections. The most important difference between PROGRES and other rule-oriented languages (like OPS-5 or Prolog) is its very *elaborate type checking system*. Experience shows that especially novice users need some time to remove all reported analysis errors from their specifications. But afterwards, the chance is very high that the specification does what it is expected to do.

Having finished the implementation of the presented language version within the last months, we are now starting to evaluate first experiences with the language within various projects (e.g. in /5. AE 94, 5. Wes 95a/) and to develop the language's *programming-in-the-large part*. Some existing specifications are already about 150 pages long and require new means for their decomposition into separate, reusable, and encapsulated subspecifications. It is subject of ongoing work to develop a suitable *module concept* for this purpose.

In summary, we provided the reader with a brief *introduction* to the language PROGRES and demonstrated the very basic principles of *graph grammar engineering* by specifying a software design and configuration editor, which are the following (cf. /5. Zün 96a/):

(a) *Model document instances* as graphs and study "*use cases*" of typical document querying or modifying operations.

(b) *Refine the graph model* step by step and add any information needed or produced by graph processing tools in the form of additional nodes, edges, and attributes.

(c) Identify sets of node objects which have the same properties (own attributes as well as possible relationships to other nodes): This leads to the *definition of node and edge types* as well as node attributes.

(d) *Distinguish* between *intrinsic and derived data* and find needed computation rules for all kinds of derived data as well as useful initialization rules for intrinsic attributes.

(e) *Identify* node types which share subsets of their properties and arrange them in the form of a *multiple inheritance hierarchy* (lattice) of node classes with node types as leafs.

(f) *Introduce* for any needed document transformation (query) a corresponding *graph manipulating transaction* (query).

(g) Keep control structures within transactions and queries as simple as possible and *specify reusable basic actions* in the form of parametrized subgraph tests and rewrite rules.

(h) Repeat the steps (a) through (g) if it is not important whether a specification is efficiently executable or not, otherwise continue with steps (i) through (l).

(i) *Refine* the initial *graph model* (the result of steps (a) through (e)) by adding cardinality constraints, index or key attribute pragmas, and by "tuning" evaluation strategies for derived data.

(j) *Reorganize* not efficiently executable *subgraph patterns* by breaking them down into smaller subpatterns and by passing information about already found subpatterns from one test/rewrite rule to the next one via node parameters.

(k) *Eliminate nondeterminism* on the level of control structures and especially within loops, whenever possible.

(l) Iterate the steps (a) through (k) as long as necessary.

We are aware of the fact that the sketched procedure is still rather naive. But we will present later on in section 3.3 a more *useful and systematic approach for the specification of syntax-directed software engineering tools*. This approach is based on many years of experience with the design of abstract syntax graphs and with specifying typical tool activities like syntax-directed editing, identifier binding, type checking, etc. There, we shall see in more detail how highly reusable specification fragments may be written in PROGRES by using parametric polymorphism and meta attributes.

3.2 The Formal Background of PROGRES

A. Schürr

The previous section introduced the latest version of the language PROGRES in a completely *informal manner*, without giving any precise definitions of its context-free syntax, type-checking rules, and its dynamic semantics. Being a language which supports quite different programming paradigms within a single framework it has many constructs with a clear intuitive meaning in the usual case, but with perhaps unexpected behavior under pathological circumstances. Therefore, it was necessary to develop a *complete formal definition* of the language's static and dynamic semantics which guarantees that any possible combination of language constructs has a well-defined meaning.

Suspecting in advance that PROGRES is continuously changing and growing due to experience reports from actual users, it was natural to *divide the formal specification into three parts*:
  (a) the definition of the language's *context-free syntax* as a context-free string grammar plus an informal definition of needed graphical representations,
  (b) the definition of a more or less PROGRES language independent *programmed graph rewriting system kernel*, and
  (c) and the construction of a *semantic function* which maps any context-free correct PROGRES specification onto a graph rewriting system with well-defined meaning.

The *description of the initial language version* consists of 70 pages for the definition of the underlying graph rewriting system kernel and more than 200 pages for the definition of the language itself on top of the kernel /5. Schü 91a/. Repeating the description for the currently used PROGRES version here is neither useful nor possible. Therefore, we will just present a subset of the underlying graph rewriting system formalism (see /5. Schü 94a, 5. Schü 96/ for further details), and we will use a small number of examples (from section 3.1) to give the reader an impression of how the semantic function looks.

The *presentation is organized* as follows: Subsection 3.2.1 is a short summary of the history of programmed graph rewriting systems and explains our motivations for the development of just another new graph rewriting system approach. Subsection 3.2.2 discusses afterwards available means for the description of specific graph data models, graph schemes, and schema consistent graphs. Subsection 3.2.3 contains the formal definition of the match of a rewrite rule's left-hand side. Subsection 3.2.4 presents graph rewriting itself as a special case of rewriting (relational) structures. The formal treatment of control structures is divided into two parts. Subsection 3.2.5 introduces our basic means for defining the semantics of recursively defined control structures. The following subsection sketches the construction of a fixpoint semantics definition. The last subsection 3.2.7 is a summary, including a discussion of future work.

3.2.1 Basic Ideas and Related Work

The history of graph rewriting systems starts 25 years ago with *two seminal papers* about so-called "web grammars" /8. PR 69/ and "Chomsky systems for partial orders" /8. Schn 70/. Within the following ten years two main families of graph rewriting systems were developed which have both their roots at the University of Erlangen. The first one is the so-called *algorithmic graph grammar approach* which uses set theory to define the semantics of graph rewrite rules. The second one is the so-called *algebraic graph grammar approach* which uses category theory to define graph rewrite rules and their semantics.

From the very beginning graph rewriting systems were used and developed to solve "real world" problems in the fields of computer science itself, biology, etc. /5. CER 79/. One of the first surveys about graph rewriting systems /5. Nag 79/ distinguishes three different *types of applications*:

(a) Describing or *generating known languages of graphs* which have for instance certain graph-theoretical properties or model growing plants.

(b) *Recognizing languages of graphs* which model for instance the underlying logical structure of natural language sentences or scanned images and office documents.

(c) *Specifying new classes of graphs* and graph transformations which represent for instance databases and database manipulations or software documents and document manipulating tools.

For solving problems in the first category pure graph rewriting systems are often sufficient and accompanying tools are not urgently needed. The second category of problems requires classes of graph rewriting systems which are powerful enough to describe interesting languages of graphs, but which are restricted enough so that efficiently working parsing or execution tools can be realized. The design of adequate classes of graph rewriting systems is still subject of ongoing research activities and outside the scope of this paper (cf. /5. FB 93/ and /5. RS 96/ for getting a survey about this area).

The third category of problems needs graph rewriting systems as a kind of executable specification or even *very high level programming language*. In order to be able to fulfill the resulting requirements, many new concepts had to be added to "pure" first generation graph rewriting systems (see /5. EHK 91/ and especially /5. BFG 96/ for a discussion of needed extensions). One of the most important extensions was the introduction of new means for controlling the application of graph rewrite rules. This lead to the definition of *implemented programmed graph rewriting systems* like PAGG /5. Göt 88/ and PROGRES.

For historical reasons mainly, almost all earlier proposals for programmed graph rewriting systems /5. Bun 79, 5. Bun 82, 5. Eng 86, 5. Göt 88, 4. Lew 88, 5. Nag 79, 8. Schn 76/ belong to the algorithmic branch of graph rewriting systems and not to the algebraic branch. At the beginning, programmed graph rewriting systems were just a *set of simple rewrite rules* plus more or less *imperative control structures* (control flow graphs). But soon it became evident that *additional means* for defining complex rule application conditions, manipulating node attributes etc. are needed. Appropriate extensions were for instance suggested in /5. Eng 86/ and later on in /4. Lew 88/. But even then there was no support for

(a) separating the definition of *static graph integrity constraints* from dynamic graph manipulating operations — as database languages separate the definition of database schemata from the definition of database queries or manipulations,

(b) specifying *derived attributes and relations* in a purely declarative manner instead of writing lots of graph rewrite rules which keep them in a consistent state — in a similar style as attribute tree grammars or relational languages deal with derived data,

(c) and solving typical *generate and test* or *inference* problems by using implicitly available means for depth-first search and backtracking in the same manner as Prolog deals with these problems.

To overcome these remaining deficiencies, various *additional extensions* were needed and studied which finally resulted in the development of PROGRES. Adding more and more concepts to programmed graph rewriting systems had the consequence that their *formal definition* by means of set theory became more and more *difficult* or even infeasible. Formal definitions for control structures, (derived) attributes, and graph schemata did not exist in many cases. And switching from set theory to the competing formalism of category theory did not solve the problem at all. Both the category based Double Push Out (DPO) and the Single Push Out approach [5. EKL 90] had about the same difficulties with the definition of integrity constraints, derived information, and the like. Furthermore, they were even less suited for the formal treatment of complex embedding rules, typical for PROGRES and its predecessors.

Therefore, serious research efforts were necessary to establish a *new framework* for the formal definition of these application-oriented graph rewriting systems. The following observations had a major influence on the development of such a framework:

(a) *Relational structures* are an obvious generalization of various forms of graphs or hypergraphs /5. MW 91/.

(b) *Logic formulas* are adequate means for defining required properties of generated graph languages /5. Cou 91/.

(c) *Nonmonotonic reasoning* is successfully used for computing derived information and verifying integrity constraints in deductive databases /5. Min 88, 5. NT 89/.

(d) *Fixpoint theory* is well-suited for specifying the semantics of partially defined, non-deterministic, and recursive graph rewriting programs /8. Man 74, 5. Nel 89/.

Combining these sources of inspiration, first logic based graph rewriting systems were developed and used to produce a complete definition of the language PROGRES /5. Schü 91a/. Later on they were generalized to Logic Based Structure Replacement (LBSR) systems /5. Schü 94a/ and Programmed Logic based Structure Replacement (PLSR) systems /5. Schü 96/, which are the topic of this section. These generalizations have not only a value of their own, but will be needed to produce formal definitions of new considerably modified versions of PROGRES (cf. section 5.2 about future development plans). Please note (again) that the following subsections present just a short version of the formal definitions and theorems for PLSR systems. For further details the reader is referred to the above mentioned papers /5. Schü 94a, 5. Schü 96/.

3.2.2 Structure Schemata and Schema Consistent Structures

This subsection introduces basic terminology of predicate logic. Furthermore, it explains modelling of node and edge labeled graphs as special cases of *schema consistent structures*, i.e. as sets of formulas with certain properties. Afterwards, our running example (of section 3.1) of a MIL graph will be translated into a structure. In this way, we are able to demonstrate that directed (attributed) graphs are a special case of structures and that graph rewriting is a special case of structure rewriting. Nevertheless, all definitions and propositions of the following sections are independent of the selected graph model and its encoding.

Definition 1   Signature.

A 5-tuple $\Sigma := (\mathcal{A}_F, \mathcal{A}_P, \mathcal{V}, \mathcal{W}, \mathcal{X})$ is a *signature* if:

(1) $\mathcal{A}_F$ is an alphabet of function symbols (including constants as a special case).

(2) $\mathcal{A}_P$ is an alphabet of predicate symbols.

(3) $\mathcal{V}$ is a special alphabet of object identifier constants.

(4) $\mathcal{W}$ is a special alphabet of identifier constants for sets of objects.

(5) $\mathcal{X}$ is an alphabet of logical variables used for quantification purposes only.   ❑

The signature of the following example may be used for the definition of software architectures, or more precisely, their MIL graph representations as sets of formulas (cf. sample graph in fig. 3.2 on page 251 and graph schema in fig. 3.3 on page 253).

Example 2   Signature for MIL Graphs.

The graph signature for the graph of fig. 3.2 is $\Sigma := (\mathcal{A}_F, \mathcal{A}_P, \mathcal{V}, \mathcal{W}, \mathcal{X})$ with:

(1) $\mathcal{A}_F := \{$ System, FunctionModule, ... , contains, has, ... ,
            UNIT, MODULE, ... , Name, Size, ... , integer, +, -, ... $\}$.

(2) $\mathcal{A}_P := \{$ node, edge, attr, type, ... $\}$.

(3) $\mathcal{V} := \{$ 1, 2, 3, ... $\}$.

(4) $\mathcal{W} := \{$ ... $\}$.

(5) $\mathcal{X} := \{$ x1, x2, ... $\}$.   ❑

Note that the alphabet $\mathcal{A}_F$ above contains a constant symbol for any schema declaration of our MIL specification (of section 3.1). This includes types of nodes and edges as well as node classes and (derived) attributes. It even contains entries for all needed built-in types, constants, and functions of PROGRES. The following alphabet $\mathcal{A}_P$ contains four standard predicate symbols which are very important for the more or less arbitrarily selected encoding of any directed, attributed, node and edge labeled graph. They have the following interpretation:

(a) `node(x,l)`: graph contains a node x with label l,
(b) `edge(x,e,y)`: graph has edge with label e from source node x to target node y,
(c) `attr(x,a,v)`: attribute a at node x has value v,
(d) `type(v,t)`: attribute value v has type t.

The remaining three alphabets $\mathcal{V}$, $\mathcal{W}$, $\mathcal{X}$ are needed for the following purposes:

(a) $\mathcal{V}$ contains all constants which may be used to identify nodes within graphs and graph rewrite rules. They denote always a fixed node in a graph or a node pattern in a graph rewrite rule which matches exactly one node of a given host graph.
(b) $\mathcal{W}$ contains all constants which may be used to identify node set patterns within graph rewrite rules (cf. subsection 3.1.5). They match a set of nodes in a given host graph, i.e. a constant of $\mathcal{W}$ will be related to a set of constants of $\mathcal{V}$ in the sequel.
(c) $\mathcal{X}$ is an alphabet of usual logical variables which may be used for quantification purposes. Note that we do not need quantification over sets, i.e. the distinction between $\mathcal{V}$ and $\mathcal{W}$ constants is transparent for the underlying predicate logic formalism.

From now on, we will always assume that Σ is a signature over the above mentioned alphabets.

Definition 3 Σ-*Term and* Σ-*Atom.*

$\mathcal{T}_X(\Sigma)$ is the set of all *terms* (in the usual sense) which contain function symbols and constants of $\mathcal{A}_F$, free variables of $\mathcal{X}$, and additional identifier symbols of $\mathcal{V}$ and $\mathcal{W}$. $\mathcal{A}(\Sigma)$ is the set of all *atomic formulas* over $\mathcal{T}_X(\Sigma)$ which contain predicate symbols of $\mathcal{A}_P$ and "=" for expressing the equality of two Σ-terms. Finally $\mathcal{T}(\Sigma) \subset \mathcal{T}_X(\Sigma)$ is the set of all those terms which do not contain any symbols of $\mathcal{X}$, $\mathcal{V}$, and $\mathcal{W}$, i.e. do not have variables or object (set) identifiers as their leaves. ❑

Definition 4 *Closed* Σ-*Formula and Derivation of* Σ-*Formulas.*

$\mathcal{F}(\Sigma)$ is the set of all sets of *closed first order predicate logic formulas* which have $\mathcal{A}(\Sigma)$ as atomic formulas, $\wedge$, $\vee$, ... as logical connectives, and $\exists$, $\forall$ as quantifiers. Furthermore with Φ and Φ' being sets of Σ-formulas,

$$\Phi \vdash \Phi'$$

means that all formulas of Φ' are *derivable* from the set of formulas Φ using any (consistent and complete) inference system of first order predicate logic with equality. ❑

In the following, elements of $\mathcal{F}(\Sigma)$ will be used to represent structures, structure schemes, schema consistent structures, and even left- and right-hand sides as well as pre- and postconditions of structure rewrite rules.

Definition 5 Σ-*Structure.*

A set of closed formulas $F \in \mathcal{F}(\Sigma)$ is a Σ-*structure* (write: $F \in \mathcal{L}(\Sigma)$) :$\Leftrightarrow$
$F \subseteq \mathcal{A}(\Sigma)$ and F does not contain formulas of the form "$\tau_1 = \tau_2$". ❑

Example 6 *A MIL Graph Structure.*

The following structure F is a set of formulas which has the graph of fig. 3.2 on page 251 as a model:

```
F := { node(1,System), node(2,FunctionModule), ... ,
       attr(1,Name,"Example"), attr(1,Size,11600), ... ,
       edge(1,contains,2), ...                              }.◻
```

The set of formulas F has many different graphs as models. One of those models is the graph of fig. 3.2 on page 251, but there are many others in which we are not interested in. Some of them may contain additional nodes and edges, and some of them bind for instance different identifiers like 1 and 2 to the same node. In definition 7, we will introduce a so-called *completing operator*, which allows us to get rid of unwanted models of Σ-structures and to reason about properties of *minimal models* on a pure syntactical level. Therefore, models of structures are not introduced formally and will not be used in the sequel.

The following example 8 demonstrates our needs for a completing operator in more detail. It presents the definition of a MIL graph which represents an empty software architecture, i.e. consists of a single System node only. It explains our difficulties to prove that the given graph contains indeed a single node. A related problem has been extensively studied within the field of deductive database systems and has been attacked by a number of quite different approaches, either based on the so-called *closed world assumption* or by using *nonmonotonic reasoning* capabilities (cf. /2. MBJ 90, 5. Naq 86a/). The main idea of (almost) all of these approaches is to distinguish between basic facts and derived facts and to add only negations of basic facts to a rule base, which are not derivable from the original set of facts.

It is beyond the scope of this section to explain nonmonotonic reasoning in more detail. Therefore, we will simply assume the existence of a *completing operator* C which adds a certain set of additional formulas to a structure. The resulting set of formulas has to be consistent and "sufficiently complete" such that we can prove the above mentioned properties by using the axioms of first-order predicate logic only.

Definition 7   Σ-*Structure Completing Operator.*

A function $C: \mathcal{L}(\Sigma) \rightarrow \mathcal{F}(\Sigma)$ is a Σ-*structure completing operator* :⇔
For all structures $F \in \mathcal{L}(\Sigma)$: $F \subseteq C(F)$ and $C(F)$ is a consistent set of formulas
$$\text{and}\quad C(\rho(F)) = \rho(C(F))$$
with ρ: $\mathcal{F}(\Sigma) \rightarrow \mathcal{F}(\Sigma)$ being a substitution which renames object identifiers of $\mathcal{V}$ and object set identifiers of $\mathcal{W}$ in F without introducing name clashes; i.e. consistent renaming of identifiers and completion of formula sets are compatible operations.   ◻

Example 8   Nonmonotonic Reasoning.

The singleton set $F := \{$ node(1,System) $\}$ is a structure which has all graphs containing at least one System node as models. Being interested in properties of minimal F graph models only, we should be able to prove that F contains a single node. For this purpose, the operator C has to be defined as follows (omitted sets of formulas deal with edges etc.):
$$C(F) := F \cup ... \cup \quad \{ \ \forall\, x, l: node(x, l) \rightarrow (x = v_1 \vee ... \vee x = v_k)$$
$$\mid v_1, ... , v_k \in \mathcal{V} \text{ are all object ids in F} \} \, .$$
Now, we are able to prove that F contains just the System node 1:
$$C(F) \vdash (\forall\, x, l: node(x, l) \rightarrow x = 1 \ ) \ \wedge \ node(1, System) \, .   ◻$$

Completing operators may have definitions, which are specific for a regarded class of structures. Therefore, they are part of the following definition of *structure schemes*:

Definition 9   Σ-Structure Schema.

A tuple $S := (\Phi, C)$ is a Σ-*structure schema* (write: $S \in \mathcal{S}(\Sigma)$) :⇔
(1) $\Phi \in \mathcal{F}(\Sigma)$ is a consistent set of formulas without references to specific object (set) identifiers of $\mathcal{V}$ or $\mathcal{W}$ (it contains integrity constraints and derived data definitions).
(2) C is a Σ-structure completing operator.   ◻

Definition 10   Schema Consistent Structure.

Let $S := (\Phi, C) \in \mathcal{S}(\Sigma)$ be a schema. A Σ-structure $F \in \mathcal{L}(\Sigma)$ is *schema consistent with respect to* S (write: $F \in \mathcal{L}(S)$) :$\Leftrightarrow$
$C(F) \cup \Phi$ is a consistent set of formulas. ❑

This definition of schema consistency is very similar to a related definition of the knowledge representation language Telos /2. MBJ 90/. It states that a structure is inconsistent with respect to a schema, if and only if we are able to derive contradicting formulas from the completed structure and its schema.

The following example is the definition of a MIL graph schema. Its set of formulas Φ consists of three subsets:

(a) A first subset defines *integrity constraints for* the specific *data model* of directed graphs and excludes "dangling" edges and attributes of nonexisting nodes.
(b) The second subset contains all *MIL graph specific integrity constraints*, like "any SPECIFICATION node is also a UNIT node" and "any REALIZATION is the target of exactly one has-edge with a SPECIFICATION node as source".
(c) The last subset deals with *derived graph properties* like the derived Size-attribute of any MIL graph node, which is e.g. for a SPECIFICATION node the maximum of the Size-attribute values of its REALIZATION nodes.

Example 11 A Structure Schema for MIL Graphs.

A structure schema $S := (\Phi, C)$ for the graph F in fig. 3.2 on page 251 has about the following form (the definition of the structure completing operator C, a considerably extended version of the definition in example 8, is omitted due to lack of space):

$\Phi := \{$ $\forall$ x, e, y: edge(x, e, y) $\rightarrow$ $\exists$ xl, yl: node(x, xl) $\wedge$ node(y, yl),
   $\forall$ x, a, v: attr(x, a, v) $\rightarrow$ $\exists$ l: node(x, l), ... $\}$

$\cup \{$ $\forall$ x: node(x, SPECIFICATION) $\rightarrow$ node(x, UNIT),
   $\forall$ x: node(x, SYSTEM) $\rightarrow$ node(x, SPECIFICATION),
   ... ,
   $\forall$ x, y: edge(x, has, y)
      $\rightarrow$ node(x, SPECIFICATION) $\wedge$ node(y, REALIZATION),
   $\forall$ x, y, z: edge(x, has, z) $\wedge$ edge(y, has, z) $\rightarrow$ x = y,
   $\forall$ x $\exists$ z: edge(x, has, z),
   $\forall$ x, v: attr(x, Size, v) $\rightarrow$ type(v, integer),
   $\forall$ x: node(x, UNIT) $\rightarrow$ $\exists$ v: attr(x, Size, v),
   ... $\}$

$\cup \{$ $\forall$ x: node(x, SPECIFICATION)
      $\rightarrow$ $\exists$ v: att(x, Size, v)
         $\wedge$ (($\exists$ y, v': edge(x, has, y) $\wedge$ att(y, Size, v)) $\vee$ v = 0)
         $\wedge$ ($\forall$ y, v': edge(x, has, y) $\wedge$ att(y, Size, v') $\rightarrow$ v' $\geq$ v),
   ... $\}$.

$C(F) := F \cup ... .$ ❑

Please note that a *syntactically correct* specification of MIL graphs may never violate constraints which are mentioned within the first subset of example 11. Furthermore, the language's *static semantics rules* guarantee that a consistent specification respects all constraints of the second subset, except the cardinality constraints, which have to be checked at runtime (at least in the general case). Finally, all constraints of the third subset determine a specification's *runtime behavior*. The already mentioned incrementally working attribute evaluator (in section 3.1) has for instance the task to maintain Size-attribute values in a state which is consistent with the presented formula.

3.2.3 Substructures with Additional Constraints

This subsection formalizes the term "match with additional constraints" by means of morphisms. This term is central to the definition of "structure rewriting with pre- and postconditions", which follows afterwards. It determines which substructures of a structure are legal targets for a structure rewriting step, i.e. match a given rule's left-hand side. The main difficulty with the definition of the new structure rewriting approach was the requirement that it should include the expression-oriented algorithmic graph grammar approach /5. Nag 79, 5. Nag 87/ with its *powerful embedding rules* (which are able to delete, copy, and redirect arbitrary large bundles of edges).

We will handle embedding rules of algorithmic graph grammar approaches by introducing special *object set identifiers* on a structure rewrite rule's left- and right-hand side. These set identifiers match an arbitrarily large (maximal) set of object identifiers in a given structure (see example 20 and definition 21). As a consequence, morphisms between structures, which select the affected substructure for a rewrite rule in a structure, are neither total nor partial functions. In the general case, these *morphisms are relations* between object (set) identifiers. These relations are required to preserve the properties of the source structure (e.g a rule's left-hand side) while embedding it into the target structure (e.g the structure we have to rewrite) as usual and to take additional constraints for the chosen embedding into account.

Another problem comes from the fact that we have to deal with attributes, i.e. rewrite rules must be able to write, read, and modify attribute values in the same way as they are able to manipulate structural information. Therefore, it is not sufficient to map object (set) identifiers onto (sets of) object identifiers, but we need also the possibility to map them onto (sets of) attribute value representing Σ-terms.

Definition 12 Σ-Term Relation.

Let F, F' $\in$ $\mathcal{F}(\Sigma)$ be two sets of formulas which have $\mathcal{V}_F$, $\mathcal{W}_F$ and $\mathcal{V}_{F'}$, $\mathcal{W}_{F'}$ as their object (set) identifiers. Furthermore, $\mathcal{T}(\Sigma)$ is the set of all variable and object identifier free Σ-terms (cf. def. 3). A relation

$$u \subseteq (\mathcal{V}_F \times (\mathcal{V}_{F'} \cup \mathcal{T}(\Sigma))) \cup (\mathcal{W}_F \times (\mathcal{W}_{F'} \cup \mathcal{V}_{F'} \cup \mathcal{T}(\Sigma)))$$

is a Σ-*term relation* from F to F' :$\Leftrightarrow$

(1) For all $v \in \mathcal{V}_F$: $|u(v)| = 1$ with $u(x) := \{ y \mid (x, y) \in u \}$,
   i.e. every object identifier will be mapped onto a single object identifier or onto a single attribute value representing Σ–term.

(2) For all $w \in \mathcal{W}_F$: $|u(w)| = 1$ or $u(w) \subseteq \mathcal{V}_{F'} \vee u(w) \subseteq \mathcal{T}(\Sigma)$,
   i.e. every object set identifier will be mapped either onto another object set identifier or onto a set of object identifiers or attribute value representing Σ-terms. $\square$

The definition above defines relations between object identifiers and Σ-terms only. Their extensions to relations between arbitrary formulas are defined as follows:

Definition 13 Σ-Relation.

Let u be a Σ-term relation according to definition 12. The extension of u to a Σ-relation u*, i.e. to a binary relation between Σ-formulas, is defined as follows.

$u*(\phi, \phi')$:$\Leftrightarrow$ $\exists$ ψ with free variables $x_1, \dots, x_n$ but without any $\mathcal{V}$or $\mathcal{W}$identifiers
   $\wedge$ $\exists$ $v_1, \dots, v_n \in \mathcal{V} \cup \mathcal{W}$ with $v_i \neq v_j$ for i, j $\in \{1, \dots, n\}$
   $\wedge$ $\exists$ $\tau_1, \dots, \tau_n \in \mathcal{V} \cup \mathcal{W} \cup \mathcal{T}(\Sigma)$ with $u(v_1, \tau_1), \dots, u(v_n, \tau_n)$:
      $\phi = \psi [v_1 / x_1, \dots, v_n / x_n] \wedge \phi' = \psi [\tau_1 / x_1, \dots, \tau_n / x_n]$,
   where $[\rho_1 / x_1, \dots, \rho_n / x_n]$ denotes the consistent substitution of any x_i by its corresponding ρ_i.
Furthermore, with $\Phi \subseteq \mathcal{F}(\Sigma)$, the following short-hand will be used in the sequel:
   $u*(\Phi) := \{ \phi' \in \mathcal{F}(\Sigma) \mid \phi \in \Phi$ and $(\phi, \phi') \in u* \}$. $\square$

The definition of u* above simply states that two formulas ϕ and ϕ'are related to each other if they differ with respect to u-related terms only. Any object identifier v in ϕ must be replaced by the uniquely defined u(v) in ϕ'. Any object set identifier w in ϕ must be replaced by some element u(w) in ϕ' such that all occurrences of w in ϕ get the same substitute.

Definition 14   Σ-(Structure-)Morphism.

Let F, F' $\in$ $\mathcal{H}(\Sigma)$. A Σ-relation u from F to F' is a Σ-*morphism* from F to F' (write: u: F $\Rightarrow$ F') :$\Leftrightarrow$

F' $\vdash$ u*(F) .

With F, F' $\in$ $\mathcal{L}(\Sigma) \subseteq \mathcal{H}(\Sigma)$ u will be called Σ-*structure morphism.* ❏

The definition of a morphism u: F $\Rightarrow$ F' requires in the simplest case that u*(F) is a subset of F', as in the following example:

Example 15 A Simple Structure Morphism.

Let F' be the structure of example 6 which represents the graph of fig. 3.2 on page 251 and

```
F := {  node('1,ADTModule),
        attr('1,Name,ValName),attr('1,File,ValFile),
        edge('1,m_uses,Servers),edge('1,has,Variants),
        edge(ModClients,m_uses,'1),edge(System,contains,'1),
        edge(VariantClients,v_uses,'1) }
```

with

```
'1,ValName,ValFile,System ∈ 𝒱, and with
Servers,Variants,... ∈ 𝒲.
```

There is one Σ-relation from F to F' which is a structure morphism:

```
u := { ('1,4),(ValName,"Files"),(ValFile,FileHandle),
       (Variants,8),(Variants,9),(ModClients,3),
       (System, 1),(VariantClients, 6) }.
```
❏

The structure F above corresponds to the left-hand side of a simplified production ChangeModuleType (cf. fig. 3.10 on page 265), which matches a module node with its direct context. It contains an additional attr formula for any needed attribute value and an additional edge formula for any of its five embedding directives. It is simplified due to the fact that it matches any ADTModule node in F' instead of matching any MODULE node with a given Name. Later on, we will modify F such that it matches any MODULE node with a given name MName. But we will assume that MName is a constant, thereby avoiding the formal definition of in- and out-parameters of productions. The definition and manipulation of formal parameters and local variables (within transactions) is rather straightforward, but lengthy. Therefore, it is omitted here and may be found in /5. Schü 91a/.

The selected example shows that a object set identifier may be mapped onto an arbitrarily large set of identifiers (terms), with the empty set being a permitted special case. In the sequel, we will show that any morphism between two structures defines a kind of subset (substructure) relationship which is transitive, reflexive, and associative. The relation u is even maximal with respect to the number of object identifiers in F' which are bound to set identifiers in F. This is an important property of Σ-relations which are involved in the process of structure rewriting (within the following subsection).

Proposition 16   The Category of Σ-Structures.

Assume "∘" to be the usual composition of binary relations. Then, $\mathcal{H}(\Sigma)$ together with the family of Σ-morphisms defined above and "∘" is a *category*; the same holds true for the set of Σ-structures $\mathcal{L}(\Sigma)$ and the family of Σ-structure morphisms.

Proof:

Σ–Morphisms are closed w.r.t. "$\circ$", i.e. u: $F \Rightarrow F'$, u': $F' \Rightarrow F'' \Rightarrow (u \circ u'): F \Rightarrow F''$:

u and u' are Σ-relations $\Rightarrow_{def. 12}$ $(u \circ u')$ is a Σ-relation and

           def. 13 $(u \circ u')^* = u^* \circ u'^*$.

u, u' are morphisms $\Rightarrow_{def. 14}$ $F' \vdash u^*(F)$ and $F'' \vdash u'^*(F')$

$F' \vdash u^*(F)$ $\Rightarrow_{\text{substitution preserves proofs}} u'^*(F') \vdash u'^*(u^*(F)) = (u \circ u')^*(F)$

                            $\Rightarrow_{\text{modus ponens}}$ $F'' \vdash (u \circ u')^*(F)$,

                            i.e. $(u \circ u')$ is a morphism from F to F''.

Existence of neutral Σ–morphism id_F for any $F \in \mathcal{F}(\Sigma)$:

Obviously, the relation id_F, which maps any object (set) identifier in F onto itself, is a neutral element for the family of Σ-relations. Then,

    $id_F^*(F) = F \Rightarrow F \vdash id_F^*(F) \Rightarrow id_F: F \Rightarrow F$,

i.e. id_F is the required neutral morphism.

Associativity of "$\circ$" for Σ-morphisms:

Follows directly from the fact that "$\circ$" is associative for binary relations.

In order to obtain the proof that the family of Σ-structure morphisms together with $\mathcal{L}(\Sigma)$ and "$\circ$" is a category we simply have to replace any $\mathcal{F}(\Sigma)$ above by $\mathcal{L}(\Sigma)$. $\square$

Definition 17   Substructure.

F, F' $\in \mathcal{L}(\Sigma)$ are structures. F is a *substructure* of F' with respect to a Σ-relation u (write: $F \subseteq_u F'$) :$\Leftrightarrow$ u: $F \Rightarrow F'$. $\square$

This definition coincides with the usual meaning of a homomorphic substructure (or subgraph), if F does not contain any object set identifiers.

Proposition 18   Soundness of Substructure Property.

For F, F' $\in \mathcal{L}(\Sigma)$ being structures, the following properties are equivalent:

    F is a substructure of F' with respect to a Σ-relation u

$\Leftrightarrow$ u*(F) is a subset of F'.

Proof:

                 $F \subseteq_u F'$

$\Leftrightarrow_{\text{see def. 17}}$ u: $F \Rightarrow F'$

$\Leftrightarrow_{\text{see def.14}}$ $F' \vdash u^*(F)$

$\Leftrightarrow_{u^*(F), F' \in \mathcal{L}(\Sigma)}$ $u^*(F) \subseteq F'$.

The last step of the proof follows from the fact that F and F' are sets of atomic formulas without "=", such that "$\subseteq$" (normal set inclusion) and "$\vdash$" are equivalent relations. $\square$

Definition 19   Substructure with Additional Constraints.

$S := (\Phi, C)$ is a Σ-structure schema, F, F' $\in \mathcal{L}(S)$, and $\Psi \in \mathcal{F}(\Sigma)$ is a set of constraints with references to object (set) identifiers of F only. F is a *constrained substructure* of F' with respect to a Σ-relation u and a set of constraints Ψ (write: $F \subseteq_{u,\Psi} F'$) :$\Leftrightarrow$

(1) $F \subseteq_u F'$, i.e. $F' \vdash u^*(F)$.

(2) u: $\Psi \cup F \Rightarrow \Phi \cup C(F')$, i.e. $\Phi \cup C(F') \vdash u^*(\Psi \cup F) = \Phi \cup u^*(F)$. $\square$

Informally speaking, a structure F is a substructure of F' with respect to additional constraints, if and only if we are able to prove that all constraints for the embedding of F in F' are fulfilled. We may use the basic facts of F' including all formulas generated by the completing operator C and the set of formulas Φ of the structure schema S for this purpose.

Example 20 Substructure Selection.

Let S := (Φ, C) be the schema of example 11 and F' the MIL graph of example 6. The structure F $\in$ $\mathcal{L}$(S) and its accompanying set of constraints Ψ $\in$ $\mathcal{F}(\Sigma)$, defined below, represent the (now almost correct) left-hand side of production `ChangeModuleType` (cf. fig. 3.10 on page 265):

```
F := { node('1,MType),
       attr('1,Name,ValName),attr('1,File,ValFile),
       edge('1,m_uses,Servers),edge('1,has,Variants),
       edge(ModClients,m_uses,'1),edge(System,contains,'1),
       edge(VariantClients,v_uses,'1) }
```
Ψ := { node('1,MODULE),ValName = MName }.   ❑

The chosen encoding of the new left-hand side and its additional preconditions is rather straight-forward except the treatment of the node ‘1itself. The set F allows us to bind ‘1to any node in F', thereby binding `MType` to the selected node's type. The additional precondition that ‘1 belongs to class `MODULE` is part of the additional set Ψ. This is necessary due to the fact that `node('1,MODULE)` is a *derived* fact which is not directly stored in F'. The set of formulas Φ of the graph schema S is needed to prove that

node(4,ADTModule) $\Rightarrow$ node(4,MODULE),

but these formulas are only available for proving constraints in Ψ and not in F.

3.2.4 Schema Preserving Structure Rewriting

Having presented the definitions of structure schemata, schema consistent structures, and structure morphisms, we are now prepared to introduce *structure rewrite rules* as quadruples of *sets of closed formulas*.

Definition 21 Structure Rewrite Rule.

A quadruple p := (AL, L, R, AR) with AL, AR $\in$ $\mathcal{F}(\Sigma)$) and with L, R $\in$ $\mathcal{L}(\Sigma)$ is a *structure rewrite rule (production)* for the signature Σ (write: p $\in$ $\mathcal{P}(\Sigma)$)) $\Leftrightarrow$

(1) The set of left-hand side application/embedding conditions AL contains only object (set) identifiers of the left-hand side L.

(2) The set of right-hand side application/embedding conditions AR contains only object (set) identifiers of the right-hand side R.

(3) Every set identifier of L is a set identifier in R and vice-versa; they are used for deleting dangling references and for establishing connections between new substructures created by a rule's right-hand side and the rest of the modified structure. ❑

The following example defines a structure rewrite rule which is based on the structure selecting example 20 and its extension in example 22. It is the now complete translation of the production `ChangeModuleType` of 3.10 on page 265 into a structure rewrite rule.

Example 22 A MIL-Structure Rewrite Rule.

With F and Ψ defined as in example 20, `ChangeModuleType` := (AL, L, R, AR) consists of the following components:

(1) AL := Ψ.

(2) L := F.

(3) R := { node(1',NewMType),
```
       attr(1',Name,ValName),attr(1',File,ValFile),
       edge(1',m_uses,Servers),edge(1',has,Variants),
       edge(ModClients,m_uses,1'),edge(System,contains,1')
       edge(VariantClients,v_uses,1') }.
```

(4) AR := { }.   ❑

Definition 23 Schema Preserving Structure Rewriting.

$S := (\Phi, C) \in S(\Sigma)$ and F, F' $\in \mathcal{L}(S)$. Furthermore, $p := (AL, L, R, AR) \in \mathcal{P}(\Sigma)$. The structure F' is *direct derivable* from F by applying p (write: F ~p~> F') $\Leftrightarrow$

(1) There is a morphism u: L $\twoheadrightarrow$ F with:
   L $\subseteq_{u,AL}$ F ,
   i.e. the via u selected match in F respects the preconditions AL.

(2) There is no morphism û : L $\twoheadrightarrow$ F with:
   L $\subseteq_{\hat{u},AL}$ F   and   u $\subset$ û ,
   i.e. u selects a maximal substructure in F (with $\subset$ being the inclusion for relations).

(3) There is a morphism w: R $\twoheadrightarrow$ F' with:
   R $\subseteq_{w,AR}$ F' ,
   i.e. the via w selected subgraph in F' respects the postconditions AR.

(4) The morphism w maps any new object identifier of R, which is not defined in L, onto a separate new object identifier in F', which is not defined in F.

(5) With K := L $\cap$ R the following property holds:
   v := { (x, y) $\in$ u | x is identifier in K } = { (x, y) $\in$ w | x is identifier in K } ,
   i.e. u and w are identical with respect to identifiers in the "gluing" structure K.

(6) There exists a graph H $\in$ $\mathcal{L}(\Sigma)$:
   F \ (u*(L) \ v*(K)) = H = F' \ (w*(R) \ v*(K)) ,
   i.e. H represents the intermediate state after the deletion of the old substructure and before the insertion of the new substructure. $\square$

It is a straightforward task to transform the definition of schema preserving structure rewriting above into an *effective procedure* for the application of a rule p to a schema consistent structure F. Unfortunately, we cannot guarantee that the process of computing derived data or checking pre- and postconditions as well as integrity constraints terminates in the general case. Therefore, we will introduce a special symbol "∞" for nonterminating computations in subsection 3.2.6, when we define the semantics of structure rewriting programs (and thereby of transactions). Finally note that the last step of the execution of a structure rewrite rule has to check that the produced result F' is indeed a schema consistent structure. In the case of PROGRES rewrite rules it is at least necessary to check cardinality constraints of edges and to update values of derived attributes (or better to mark them as being invalid).

Note that the definition of structure rewriting does not prohibit the selection of *homomorphic redices* with two identifiers o1 and o2 in L being mapped onto the same object in F. A complete translation of the PROGRES production ChangeModuleType would therefore extend the set of productions AL in example 22 with the following inequalities:
   '1 ≠ Servers, '1 ≠ Variants, '1 ≠ ModClients, ... ,
although any possible match of a generated (correct) MIL graph will never violate these inequality constraints (remember that isomorphic matching is the PROGRES default behavior which can be overwritten by so-called folding directives; cf. subsection 3.1.5). "Sharing" of matches is even permitted if o1 belongs to R and o2 not (the static semantics rules of PROGRES disallow this kind of sharing with sometimes rather unexpected results). These *deleting/preserving conflicts* are resolved in favor of preserving objects.

Finally note that we have to take care about "dangling" references in the case of rewrite rules, where L is not a subset of R. We have to guarantee that any node(x, 1) is removed together with all related edge(x, e, y), edge(y, e, x), and attr(x, a, y) formulas. This may be accomplished by adding appropriate formulas with set identifiers (instead of y) to the rule's left-hand side. In this way, we are able to overcome the problem of the algebraic double pushout approach with the prohibited deletion of nodes with unknown context /5. Ehr 79/.

3.2.5 Basic Control Flow Operators and Transformations

The definition of a fixed set of control structures for programmed graph transformations is complicated by contradicting requirements. From a *theoretical point of view* the set of offered control structures should be as small as possible, and we should be allowed to combine them without any restrictions. But from a *practical point of view* control structures are needed which are easy to use and to understand, which cover all frequently occurring control flow patterns, and the application of which may be directed by a number of context-sensitive rules.

Therefore, it was quite natural to distinguish between basic control flow operators, called *BCF operators*, of an underlying theory of recursively defined structure transformations and more or less complex higher level programming mechanisms in PROGRES. Starting with a formal definition of basic control flow operators, we will then be able to define the meaning of any control structure by translating it into a equivalent BCF expression.

<Transformation> ::=   <TransformationId> "=" <BCFExpr> ;
<BCFExpr> ::=   <BasicAction> | <ActionCall> | <BCFTerm> ;
<BasicAction> ::=   "skip" | "loop" ;
<ActionCall> ::=   <RuleId> | <TransformationId> ;
<BCFTerm> ::=   "def" "(" <BCFExpr> ")"
       | "undef" "(" <BCFExpr> ")" |
       "(" <BCFExpr> ";" <BCFExpr> ")" |
       "(" <BCFExpr> "[]" <BCFExpr> ")" ;

Fig. 3.18. Syntax of structure rewriting transformations and BCF expressions

Fig. 3.18 contains the definition of BCF expressions themselves and of structure trans-formations (in contrast to PROGRES transactions) as functional abstractions of BCF ex-pressions. It distinguishes between *basic actions* like
- (a) skip, which represents the always successful identity operator and relates a given graph G to itself, and
- (b) loop, which neither succeeds nor terminates for any given structure and represents therefore "crashing" or forever looping computations,

calls of basic rewrite rules or other transformations, and finally between two unary and two binary *BCF operators* with
- (c) def(a) as an action which succeeds applied to a given structure F, whenever a applied to F produces a defined result, and returns F itself,
- (d) undef(a) as an action which succeeds applied to a structure F, whenever a applied to F terminates with failure, and returns F itself,
- (e) (a;b) as an action which is the sequential composition of a and b, i.e. applies first a to a given structure F and then b to any "suitable" result of the application of a,
- (f) and (a[] b) as an action which represents the nondeterministic choice between the application of a or b.

Note that the operators suggested above are intentionally similar to those proposed by Dijkstra /8. Dij 75/ and especially to those presented by Nelson /5. Nel 89/ with one essential difference: Due to the Boolean nature of basic structure rewrite rules and complex transformations, we are not forced to distinguish between side effect free Boolean expres-sions and state modifying actions. This has the consequence that complex guarded com-mands of the form

($Cond_1$ → $Body_1$ [] ... [] $Cond_n$ → $Body_n$)

are no longer necessary but may replaced by expressions like

(def($Cond_1$) ; $Body_1$) [] ... [] (def($Cond_n$) ; $Body_n$)

where "<u>def</u> (Cond$_i$)" tests either the applicability of a single rewrite rule or of a whole transformation without modifying the given input structure.

Having presented the syntax of BCF expressions, we are now prepared to discuss the intricacies of their intended semantics. A first problem comes with the definition of the meaning of (a;b) as "apply b to *any suitable* result of a". Let us assume that the application of a transformation a to a structure F has three possible results named F1, F2, and F3, respectively. Furthermore, let us assume that the graph transformation b applied to F1 fails, but applied to F2 and F3 succeeds. In this case we may either select F2 or F3 but not F1 as a suitable result of the application of a. This means that we need knowledge about future states of an ongoing transformation process in order to be able to discard those possible results of a single transformation step, which cause failure of the overall transformation process. It should be quite obvious that a more realization-oriented definition of this kind of clairvoyant nondeterminism requires a kind of *depth-first search* semantics with *backtracking* out of "dead-ends".

Another problem comes with the definition of expressions like (a [] b), where a loops forever applied to a certain structure F, but b has a well-defined set of possible results. Having a depth-first search semantics in mind, we are forced to define the outcome of the expression (a [] b) as being either a nonterminating computation or any defined result produced by b.

This means that the kind of *nondeterminism* we are going to define is not "angelic" but more or less "*erratic*": Using backtracking we are able to discard nondeterministic selections which lead to defined failures of basic actions or structure rewrite rules, but not selections which cause nonterminating computations.

The following example uses nondeterministic depth-first search and backtracking. It defines a graph transformation, which applies first a rewrite rule InitConfig and applies then another graph rewrite rule ResolveConfig as long as possible. It succeeds if a final test UnresolvedImportExists fails and fails otherwise (a PROGRES test is a structure rewrite rule with identical left- and right-hand side). It is a simplified version of the transaction CreateConfig of fig. 3.13 on page 270, where all parameters and local variables are omitted.

Example 24 A Complex MIL Graph Rewriting Transformation.

```
CreateConfig =
    (InitConfig ; (MyLoop;undef(UnresolvedImportExists)))
MyLoop =
    ((ResolveImport;MyLoop) [] undef(ResolveImport)))        ❑
```

3.2.6 Fixpoint Semantics of Transformations

After an informal introduction of structure rewriting transformations as named BCF expressions we will now define their intended semantics: This is a *semantic function* from the domain of BCF expressions onto the range of (extended) binary relations over abstract structures. In order to be able to deal with recursion and nondeterminism in the presence of an atomic sequence operator ";" we had to follow the lines of /5. Nel 89/. There, a new form of the fixpoint theorem is used to give an axiomatic definition of so-called nondeterministic commands. For being able to apply the fixpoint theorem to BCF expressions an appropriate partially ordered semantic domain is needed:

Definition 25 Extended Semantic Domain.

With $\mathcal{L}(S)$ being a class of schema consistent structures for a schema $S \in \mathcal{S}(\Sigma)$, the *semantic domain* of transformations is defined to be the following power set of binary relations:

$$\mathcal{D} := 2^{\mathcal{L}(S) \times (\mathcal{L}(S) \cup \{\infty\})}.$$

The semantics of a transformation is a binary relation between abstract structures, where the symbol "∞" in a second component represents *potentially nonterminating computations*. The word "potential" includes computations with partially unknown effects, i.e. computations which may abort or loop forever. A relation $R_\infty := \mathcal{L}(S) \times \{\infty\}$ for instance, which maps any structure F onto "∞", represents a computation with completely unknown outcomes.

In order to be able to apply fixpoint theory to recursively defined transformations we have to construct a *suitable partial order* for our semantic domain $\mathcal{D}$. "Suitable" means from a practical point of view that the relation R_∞ defined above should be less than any other element in $\mathcal{D}$ and that "R_1 less than R_2" means that R_2 is a better approximation of a given transformation than R_1. And "suitable" means from a theoretical point of view that we have to proof that any chain in $\mathcal{D}$ has a join, i.e. that any sequence of ordered elements in $\mathcal{D}$ has a least upper element.

Definition 26 Partial Order on Semantic Domain.

With R, R' ∈ $\mathcal{D}$ and S being the underlying structure schema, a suitable *partial order* "≤" is defined as follows:
$$R \leq R' :\Leftrightarrow \forall F, F' \in \mathcal{L}(S):$$
$$(F, F') \in R \Rightarrow (F' = \infty \vee (F, F') \in R')$$
$$\wedge (F, \infty) \notin R \Rightarrow ((F, F') \in R \Leftrightarrow (F, F') \in R').$$

The relation R of the definition above *approximates* R' such that any input F is either related to the same set of outputs by R and R' or is related to the symbol "∞" in R and to a potentially greater set of outputs in R' (by eventually dropping "∞"). The proof that the new partial order has indeed all required properties for constructing least fixpoints may be found in /5. Schü 96/. Now, we are prepared to define a semantic function $\mathcal{R}$ from the syntactic domain of BCF expressions or transformations onto the semantic domain $\mathcal{D}$ inductively:

Definition 27 BCF Expressions, Transformations, and their Semantics.

S and $\mathcal{D}$ are defined as in def. 26, and $P \subseteq \mathcal{P}(\Sigma)$ is a set of structure rewrite rules. Then, $\mathcal{E}(P)$ denotes the set of all *BCF expressions* and $\mathcal{T}(P)$ the set of all *transformations* over P. Their context-free syntax was already displayed in fig. 3.18, and a *semantic function* $\mathcal{R}_P: \mathcal{E}(P) \rightarrow \mathcal{D}$ is defined as follows with F, F', F'' ∈ $\mathcal{L}(S)$ and with a, b ∈ $\mathcal{E}(P)$:

(1) $(F, F') \in \mathcal{R}_P[\![\texttt{skip}]\!] :\Leftrightarrow \quad F = F'$.

(2) $(F, F') \in \mathcal{R}_P[\![\texttt{loop}]\!] :\Leftrightarrow \quad F' = \infty$.

(3) $(F, F') \in \mathcal{R}_P[\![\texttt{p}]\!] :\Leftrightarrow \quad F \sim\!p\!\rightarrow F'$,   for any production p ∈ $\mathcal{T}(\Sigma)$
$$\vee F' = \infty, \qquad \text{if execution of p may not terminate.}$$

(4) $(F, F') \in \mathcal{R}_P[\![\underline{\texttt{def}}(\texttt{a})]\!] :\Leftrightarrow \quad \exists F'' \neq \infty: (F, F'') \in \mathcal{R}_P[\![\texttt{a}]\!] \wedge F = F'$
$$\vee (F, \infty) \in \mathcal{R}_P[\![\texttt{a}]\!] \wedge F' = \infty.$$

(5) $(F, F') \in \mathcal{R}_P[\![\underline{\texttt{undef}}(\texttt{a})]\!] :\Leftrightarrow \quad (\neg \exists F'': (F, F'') \in \mathcal{R}_P[\![\texttt{a}]\!]) \wedge F = F'$
$$\vee (F, \infty) \in \mathcal{R}_P[\![\texttt{a}]\!] \wedge F' = \infty.$$

(6) $(F, F') \in \mathcal{R}_P[\![(\texttt{a;b})]\!] :\Leftrightarrow \quad \exists F'' \neq \infty: (F, F'') \in \mathcal{R}_P[\![\texttt{a}]\!] \wedge (F'', F') \in \mathcal{R}_P[\![\texttt{b}]\!]$
$$\vee (F, \infty) \in \mathcal{R}_P[\![\texttt{a}]\!] \wedge F' = \infty.$$

(7) $(F, F') \in \mathcal{R}_P[\![(\texttt{a} \; [\!] \; \texttt{b})]\!] :\Leftrightarrow \quad (F, F') \in \mathcal{R}_P[\![\texttt{a}]\!] \vee (F, F') \in \mathcal{R}_P[\![\texttt{b}]\!]$.

The definitions above are rather straightforward except for the treatment of the operators $\underline{\texttt{def}}$ and $\underline{\texttt{undef}}$. The expressions $\underline{\texttt{def}}(\texttt{a})$ and $\underline{\texttt{undef}}(\texttt{a})$ loop forever if a returns not a single defined result but loops forever. Furthermore, $\underline{\texttt{def}}(\texttt{a})$ may return its input if a returns at least one defined result, even if a may loop forever. It terminates with failure if a terminates with failure. On the other hand, <u>undef</u>(a) returns its input if and only if a fails, and it fails if and only if a has at least one defined result and may not loop forever.

Therefore, <u>undef</u> is *stricter* than <u>def</u> with respect to the treatment of looping computations; the expression <u>def</u>(a) may return a defined result even if a may loop forever. From a practical point of view, this distinction may be justified as follows:

(a) Often, we would like to know whether a computes at least one defined result without evaluating all possible execution paths of a after a successful path has been found.

(b) On the other hand, answering the question whether a fails is not possible without taking all execution paths of a into account, thereby running into any nonterminating execution branch of a.

In order to be able to use the fixpoint theorem of /5. Nel 89/ we have still to prove that BCF expressions correspond to *monotonic functionals*. A BCF expression which contains for instance applied transformation identifiers t_1 to t_n, must be interpreted as a functional with the following signature:

$$\mathcal{R}_P[\![\, E \,]\!] : \mathcal{D}^n \rightarrow \mathcal{D}.$$

Provided with the semantics $\mathcal{R}_P[\![\, t_1 \,]\!], \ldots, \mathcal{R}_P[\![\, t_n \,]\!]$ of t_1 to t_n the semantics of E is given by definition 27 and is denoted as follows:

$$\mathcal{R}_P[\![\, E \,]\!] \, [\, \mathcal{R}[\![\, T_1 \,]\!], \ldots, \mathcal{R}_P[\![\, T_n \,]\!] \,].$$

In such a way we are able to define the semantics of all BCF expressions and transformations bottom-up in the absence of recursion. But having a *recursively defined transformation* like

```
MyLoop =
    ((ResolveImport;MyLoop) [] undef(ResolveImport)))
```

we are looking for a least element $R \in \mathcal{D}$ such that the following fixpoint equation

```
R = 𝓡ₚ[ ((ResolveImport;MyLoop) [] undef(ResolveImport)))][R]
```

holds.

The proof that all presented BCF expressions are monotonic with respect to the introduced order is straightforward but lengthy and, therefore, omitted over here (it may be found in /5. Schü 96/). We are now able to define a fixpoint semantics for a given set of transformations, which may *call each other in an arbitrary manner*:

Proposition 28   Fixpoint Semantics for Transformations.

Let $T := \{\, t_1, \ldots, t_n \,\} \in \mathcal{T}(P)$ be transformations which contain in their bodies E_1 to $E_n \in \mathcal{E}(P)$ at most calls to transformations t_1 through t_n and calls to rewrite rules of $P \subseteq \mathcal{P}(\Sigma)$, i.e.

$$t_1 = E_1[\, t_1, \ldots, t_n \,], \ldots, t_n = E_n[\, t_1, \ldots, \tau_n \,].$$

With $\mathcal{L}(S)$ being the corresponding class of schema consistent structures, the following propositions hold and define a new *semantic function* $\mathcal{R}_{P,T}: T \rightarrow \mathcal{D}$:

(1) $t_1, \ldots, t_n$ have unique least fixpoints $\mathcal{R}_{P,T}[\![\, t_1 \,]\!], \ldots, \mathcal{R}_{P,T}[\![\, t_n \,]\!] \in \mathcal{D}$.

(2) Approximations of these fixpoints may be constructed in the following way:

$R_1^0 := \mathcal{L}(S) \times \{\, \infty \,\}; \ldots; R_n^0 := \mathcal{L}(S) \times \{\, \infty \,\},$

$R_1^{k+1} := \mathcal{R}_{P,T}[\![\, E_1 \,]\!] \, [\, R_1^k, \ldots, R_n^k \,]; \ldots; R_n^{k+1} := \mathcal{R}_{P,T}[\![\, E_n \,]\!] \, [\, R_1^k, \ldots, R_n^k \,],$

where $\mathcal{R}_{P,T}[\![\, E_i \,]\!] : \mathcal{D}^n \rightarrow \mathcal{D}$ takes approximations for transformations $t_1, \ldots, t_n$ and yields a new approximation for t_i by applying definition 27 to expression E_i.

Proof:

See /5. Schü 96/.   ❑

Note that the proposition above is not only interesting from a theoretical point of view by guaranteeing the existence of least fixpoints for any recursively defined set of transformations. Additionally, it provides us with an *algorithm* which *computes the results of terminating structure transformations* and approximates the results of (potentially) non-terminating transformations. Equipped with such a fixpoint computing function $\mathcal{R}$ we are now able to define programmed structure rewriting systems and their generated languages.

Definition 29   Programmed Logic Based Structure Rewriting Systems.

Assuming the vocabulary of definition 27, a quadruple PLSR := (A, P, T, t) is a *programmed structure rewriting (PLSR) system* with respect to a given structure schema $S \in \mathcal{S}(\Sigma)$ if:

(1) $A \in \mathcal{L}(S)$ is the schema consistent initial structure.

(2) $P \subseteq \mathcal{P}(\Sigma)$ is a set of structure rewrite rules.

(3) $T \subseteq \mathcal{T}(P)$ is a set of (recursively) defined transformations over P.

(4) $t \in T$ is the "main transformation" of PLSR.   ❑

Definition 30   Language of a Programmed Structure Rewriting System.

With PLSR := (A, P, T, t) as in def. 29, the *language* $\mathcal{L}$(PLSR) is defined as follows:
$$F \in (\text{PLSR}) :\Leftrightarrow (A, F) \in \mathcal{R}[\![\, t \,]\!]\,).$$ ❑

The definition above states that the language of a programmed structure rewriting system consists of all those structures which may be generated by applying a main transformation t to the initial structure A. The transformation t calls structure rewrite rules from P and other transformations from T, which in turn contain calls of rewrite rules and transformations.

If PLSR systems are used to define *abstract data types* instead of structure (graph) languages only, it might be useful to replace the single main transformation "t" above by a set of *exported transformations* $t_1, \ldots, t_n$. This would be a first step towards a module concept for structure rewriting systems. But even in that case the language of all possibly generated structures is definable as the result of the new main transformation

$$t' = ((t_1 \,\square\, \ldots \,\square\, t_n) \; ; \; t') \,\square\, \underline{\text{skip}}),$$

which either returns its input or applies the transformations $t_1, \ldots, t_n$ an arbitrary number of times.

3.2.7 Summary and Open Problems

The definitions and propositions of the preceding subsections constitute a *logic based framework* for the formal treatment of programmed graph rewriting systems as special cases of programmed structure rewriting systems. It allows for the formal treatment of graph rewriting systems, where

(a) the consistency of graph rewrite rules may be checked against a separately defined graph scheme,

(b) derived graph properties can be defined in a declarative style of programming,

(c) nodes, edges, and attributes are manipulated in a uniform manner,

(d) graph rewrite rules may possess complex pre- and postconditions,

(e) and graph rewrite rules may create, redirect, and delete edge bundles of arbitrary size (i.e. use complex set-oriented embedding rules).

The most important property mentioned above is *uniformity*. All static components of graph rewriting systems, like attributed graphs, their graph schemes, left- and right-hand sides of rewrite rules as well as additional application conditions, are modelled as sets of predicate logic formulas. And all aspects concerning the dynamic behavior of graph rewriting systems are defined by means of nonmonotonic reasoning and simple formula set manipulations.

Our formalism tries thereby to *close the gap* between the *operation-oriented manipulation* of data structures by means of rewrite rules and the *declaration-oriented description* of data structures by means of logic based knowledge representation languages. In this way, both disciplines - graph grammar theory and mathematical logic theory - might be able to profit from each other:

(a) Structure (graph) rewrite rules might be a very comfortable and well-defined mechanism for manipulating knowledge bases or deductive data bases (cf. /5. Cou 91/), whereas

(b) many logic based techniques have been proposed for efficiently maintaining derived properties of data structures, solving constraint systems, and for proving the correctness of certain kinds of data manipulations (cf. /5. BMM 91, 5. NT 89, 5. Tha 89/).

Last but not least the presented approach provides us with a *denotational semantics* based formal definition of partial, nondeterministic, and even recursive *structure rewriting programs*, termed transformations. We added a symbol "∞" to the domain of structures, which represents unknown results or nonterminating computations. Thereby, we were able to overcome the difficulties with operators, which test success or failure of subprograms, in the presence of recursion (cf. /5. Schü 91a/ for a more detailed discussion about these problems). These operators are a prerequisite for writing programs like "try first to execute subprogram A and, if and only if A fails, try to execute B".

Note that /5. Nel 89/, which presents an *axiomatic semantics definition* for nondeterministic partial commands, gave us the initial impulse for the introduction of the symbol "∞" as well as for the selection of the adequate fixpoint theorem version. Nevertheless, we had to prefer the "denotational" instead of the "axiomatic" approach, since structure rewrite rules play here about the same role as simple assignments in /5. Nel 89/. The definition of their intended semantics as binary relations is given in definition 23, but it is a yet unsolved problem how to "push" postconditions through rewrite rules in order to obtain their corresponding weakest preconditions (see question (b) below).

Beside the problem of extending the presented new approach such that *parallel structure rewriting* is supported, the following question should be studied in the future:

(a) Can we characterize a "useful" subset of rewrite rules and consistency constraints such that an effective proof procedure exists for the "are all derivable structures schema consistent" problem (which has already been considered in /5. Cou 91/ for restricted forms of graph grammars and monadic second order logic formulas)?

(b) Can we develop a general procedure which transforms any set of rewrite rule postconditions into weakest preconditions?

The problems (a) and (b) above are related to each other by transforming global consistency constraints into equivalent postconditions of individual rewrite rules using techniques proposed in /5. BMM 91/. Having such a procedure which translates postconditions into corresponding preconditions, problem (a) is reducible to the question whether these new preconditions are already derivable from the original sets of preconditions of rewrite rules.

But note that the main motivation for the development of the new formalism of PLSR systems was not to investigate these problems, but to provide us with a solid foundation for a *precise description of the PROGRES language's static and dynamic semantics*, which is more than 200 pages long. Therefore, it was impossible (and useless) to present a complete formal definition here. We hope, nevertheless, that section 3.1 and section 3.2 together contain a sufficiently complete informal description of the language PROGRES itself and a sufficiently complete definition of its formal background. Furthermore, we hope that the presented examples give the reader at least an impression of how the translation of a PROGRES specification into a programmed structure rewriting system looks like.

3.3 Specification of Logical Documents and Tools

A. Schürr / A. Zündorf

Section 3.1 presented the specification of a syntax-directed editor for software architectures and an accompanying configuration management tool. It did not cover any aspects concerning the user interface of these tools, but was a precise description of all needed internal data structures and operations on them. These data structures together with their access operations are called internal *logical documents* (cf. subsection 1.5). They are the topic of this section. For further details concerning the translation of logical documents into so-called *representation documents* and pixel-oriented *presentations* within windows, the reader is referred to section 4.1 and 4.3.

Used only for demonstration purposes, the specification of section 3.1 was written from scratch in a rather *ad hoc fashion*. In reality, software engineering tools and their internal documents are orders of magnitude more complex. Developing a complete specification as well as implementation for these tools is much work and requires a lot of expertise. Based on our experiences with the realization of all tools presented in chapter 2 and the PROGRES environment of section 3.6, we developed a *domain specific graph grammar engineering methodology*, which replaces the rather naive modelling approach of subsection 3.1.7. Its latest form, first presented in /5. Zün 96a/, is the topic of this section; intermediate stages are documented in /5. ES 85, 4. Lew 88, 5. ELN 92/.

The graph grammar engineering methodology starts with any available information about the syntax or semantics of a certain *software engineering language* and the external representation of manipulated documents. This information is used to derive an adequate logical document specification. "Adequate" means in this case that specified logical documents and their interface operations are well-suited for efficiently implementing tools like syntax-directed editors, analyzers, interpreters, etc. on top of them.

Subsection 3.3.1 contains a short comparison with *related work*, mainly in the area of compiler construction. The following subsection 3.3.2 discusses then the development of our graph grammar engineering methodology over the time and introduces the *basic ideas* of designing logical documents. The next subsection 3.3.3 has its main focus on modelling the *syntax of textual languages*. It starts with extended Backus-Naur forms and shows a systematic way to derive equivalent abstract syntax graph specifications. Subsection 3.3.4 deals with the *syntax of diagrammatic languages* and uses an Entity/Relationship like approach to specify their internal graph structures. These syntax specifications determine the functionality of (context-free) syntax-directed textual and graphical editors completely.

Subsection 3.3.5 sketches how *static and dynamic semantics* aspects of languages (their context-sensitive syntax) may be handled, independent of the fact whether they have a textual or a diagrammatic representation. It has a main focus on identifier binding rules and discusses only briefly how type checking and execution tools may be specified in a similar manner. For further details concerning these topics the reader is referred to /5. Zün 96a/. There, he will find adaptable specifications of type checking rules as well as an in-depth explanation of an abstract graph rewriting machinery. Such a machinery is the core of any interpreter and compiler in IPSEN. Finally, subsection 3.3.6 summarizes the state of the art of logical document modelling and sketches still unsolved problems, which will be explained in more detail in chapter 5.

3.3.1 Related Work

We have already mentioned that PROGRES specifications are not directly descriptions of IPSEN tools, but of their underlying main data structures, called logical documents. These logical document specifications are mainly *definitions of the syntax and semantics* of a certain software engineering language. All aspects concerning specific functions of considered tools, like cut&paste of a syntax-directed editor, are either provided by standard specification components or outside the scope of graph grammar engineering (like the design of a user interface). These additional aspects are taken into account during the transition process from a complete logical document specification to the implementation of corresponding IPSEN tools (cf. section 4.1 and 4.3 for further details).

Such a proceeding is common practice among (almost) all formal approaches for generating programming environments or compilers. It raises the following question: How can we *structure large specifications* of languages and how can we *reuse expert knowledge* of how these specifications should look like? There are two answers for this question. The first one is based on the combination of *multiple formalisms* within a common framework. Compiler generator tool kits like Optran /5. LMW 89/ or Eli /5. GHL 92/ and programming environment generators like Centaur /2. BCD 88/ or PSG /2. BS 86/ offer separate formalisms for purposes like defining lexical syntax, context-free syntax, static and dynamic semantics of a given language. There exist even specific languages for defining identifier binding rules /5. VL 88/ or code generating compiler backends /5. AGT 89/. These different formalisms determine the structure of a language specification and represent available expert knowledge about a specific subdomain at the same time.

The second answer is based on the idea to offer a general purpose formalism together with a suitable *module and abstraction concept.* All formalisms (we are aware of) belonging to the second category, are based on attribute grammars and were developed within the last few years. Composable attribute grammars /5. FMY 92/ offer the possibility to define separate *abstract subgrammars* for tasks like identifier binding etc. But using these subgrammars for the definition of a concrete language is a tedious task. A so-called glue grammar must be written which constructs subtrees of all needed subgrammars as syntactical attributes and combines or propagates these subtrees as needed. Modular attribute grammars /5. DC 90/, on the other hand, do not need a separate composition step. They use *production patterns* with attached attribute evaluation rules to specify common subproblems in a rather abstract manner. Any concrete production inherits then the attribute evaluation rules of all matching production patterns. The main problem with this approach is that definable production patterns are rather unspecific and match often too many productions. To avoid unwanted matches, artificial attributes or productions must be added which destroy the elegance of the approach to a great extent.

Another category of attribute grammars uses *inheritance* as the main paradigm for defining and reusing abstract subgrammars. TOOLS /5. KP 90/ is one example of a system which supports the construction of nonterminal class hierarchies. In this way, subnonterminals inherit attributes from supernonterminals, but inheritance of structural properties is not possible as in Mjolner/Orm /5. Hed 89/. This system offers the construction of class hierarchies for both nonterminal symbols and productions. It is for instance possible to define first a production for all binary arithmetic operators and to specialize the production afterwards for operators like "+", "-", etc. by redefining inherited attribute evaluation rules. Nevertheless, even Mjolner/Orm has the following restrictions compared with PROGRES: multiple inheritance is excluded, subclasses may not possess inherited attributes (use information from parent nodes), and an equivalent feature to path expressions is not existent.

All above mentioned approaches and many others (cf. /5. KW 94, 5. Paa 95/ for more detailed surveys about attribute grammars), suffer from the fact that basic components have serious *difficulties to abstract* from the syntactical structure of a regarded language. Possibilities for generalizing, inheriting, and redefining syntactical properties are either not present or very limited.

Finally, we have to emphasize that all presented approaches above are only well-suited for languages, which have a textual representation and a dominant syntax tree skeleton. PROGRES, on the contrary, with its graph-based data model is well-prepared for the *definition of visual languages*, as shown in /5. AE 94/ (see also subsection 3.3.4). Compared with other visual language description formalisms, like those presented in /5. GM 93, 5. MV 95, 5. CM 95/, it gives better support for the description of a language's static or dynamic semantics and for defining complex transformation processes. This a consequence of the fact that the language offers elaborate schema definition, parametrization, pattern matching, and imperative programming concepts at the same time (cf. section 3.1).

To conclude, PROGRES belongs to those approaches which offer a *single formalism* for all aspects concerning the syntax and semantics of logical documents. Any available knowledge about how specifications of specific subaspects (like identifier binding or type checking rules) should look like is not encoded in specific language constructs, but made available in the form of *highly parametrized abstract subspecifications*.

3.3.2 Logical Document Modelling with Parameterized Subspecifications

We will now present the basic ideas of our *logical document modelling approach* and its development over the time. We will focus our interest onto its most important properties, the avoidance of many similar document type specific rewrite rules by introducing generic rewrite rules, and the replacement of a pure operational style of specification by a more and more declarative schema based modelling approach.

A logical document specification is divided into various *subcomponents* which represent different aspects like abstract syntax trees, identifier binding rules, etc. Currently, these subcomponents are different sections of one specification document and not modules with well-defined interfaces and import/export relationships between them (cf. section 5.2).

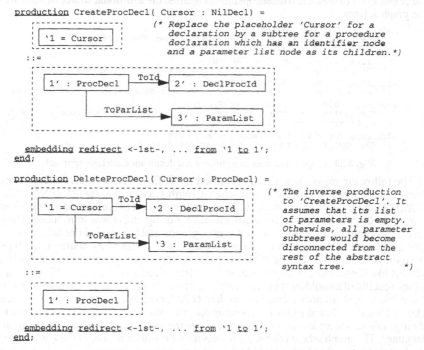

Fig. 3.19. The straight-forward document modelling approach

For some years, these subcomponents were just sets of rather *similar rewrite rules* (cf. /5. ES 85, 4. Lew 88/ for further details). Fig. 3.19 contains two typical examples of rewrite rules which create and delete the abstract syntax tree skeletons of procedure declarations. The `CreateProcDecl` production receives the currently selected placeholder for an arbitrary declaration as input and replaces it by a `ProcDecl` node which has an unexpanded identifier as its first child and the head of a still empty parameter list as its second child. The `DeleteProcDecl` production is the inverse operation.

The definition of a language's context-free syntax in this way had the following disadvantages:
(a) Many very similar productions had to be written down, as many inserted or deleted increments share the same structure if we forget about concrete node and edge labels.
(b) The declarative definition of a language's syntax by means of context-free string grammars is replaced by an operational definition of editing commands.
(c) Both create and delete operations have the same knowledge about the syntax of a specific construct.
(d) The introduction of many different edge labels makes the definition of standard tree traversals like "up to a node with a certain type" very tedious.

As a result, it was very *difficult* and time-consuming to *extend or modify the syntax* of a logical document's language.

The first improvement of this methodology, presented in /5. ELN 92/, was the introduction of a *separate graph schema* in addition to the set of graph rewrite rules. The part of such a graph schema for `ProcDecl` is displayed in fig. 3.20. As a consequence, specifications contained the knowledge about a language's context-free syntax three times, namely within the right-hand side of the corresponding create production, the left-hand side of its delete production, and within the graph schema. However, it was now feasible to check the consistency of create and delete operations against the additional source of information, the graph schema.

```
node class DECLARATION end;
   (* The node class for the nonterminal of the EBNF rule *)
   (* 'DECLARATION ::= ProcDecl | ... '.                   *)
node type NilDecl : DECLARATION end;
   (* The node type for 'DECLARATION' placeholders in a syntax tree. *)
node type ProcDecl : DECLARATION end;
   (* The node type for the roots of procedure declaration syntax subtrees. *)
edge type ToId : ProcDecl -> DeclProcId;
   (* The syntax tree edge from a procedure declaration root node to its *)
   (* first syntax child, its identifier node.                          *)
edge type ToParList : ProcDecl -> ParamList;
   (* The syntax tree edge to the parameter list.
```

Fig. 3.20. Graph schema for straight-forward document modelling approach

The following major step, already sketched in /5. ELN 92/, uses the concept of *parametric polymorphism*. A basic graph schema (with classes like INCREMENT, PLACE-HOLDER, and BINARY_OP of fig. 3.21) together with a set of parametrized graph rewrite rules (like `CreateBinary` or `DeleteBinary` of fig. 3.21) was introduced. They describe the general structure of abstract syntax graphs and the needed operations on them. The adaptation to the syntax of a given language was achieved by adding node types to the basic schema and by instantiating basic rewrite rules appropriately (in additional transactions like `CreateProcDecl` and `DeleteProcDecl` of fig. 3.21). All types of language specific placeholders (like `NilDecl`) are now descendants of a common superclass PLACEHOLDER, all nodes with two children (like `ProcDecl`) have a common ancestor class BINARY_OP, and so forth. Resulting specifications were much more compact, but their *graph schemata lost* any *information* about the syntactical structure of the modelled language. The graph schema of fig. 3.21 contains for instance no longer the knowledge that the first child (target of 1st-edge) of a `ProcDecl` node is a `DeclProcId` and its second child (target of 2nd-edge) a `ParamList`.

```
node class INCREMENT end;
   (* The superclass of all abstract syntax tree nodes. *)
node class PLACEHOLDER is a INCREMENT end;
   (* The common superclass of all placeholders for unexpanded subtrees. *)
node class BINARY_OP is a INCREMENT end;
   (* All nodes with (at least) two children in the syntax tree. *)
edge type 1st : BINARY_OP -> INCREMENT;
   (* The edge to the first child. *)
edge type 2nd : BINARY_OP -> INCREMENT;
   (* The edge to the second child. *)
 node type NilDecl : PLACEHOLDER end;
   (* The type for declaration placeholders which may be replaced by *)
   (* subtrees for procedure and type declarations.                  *)
node type ProcDecl : BINARY_OP end;
   (* The root node type for procedure declaration subtrees. Allows any    *)
   (* type of nodes as 'ProcDecl' children. The proper node types for its  *)
   (* children are defined as actual parameters of its 'CreateBinary' call.*)
production CreateBinary( Cursor    : PLACEHOLDER ;
                         NilType   : type in PLACEHOLDER ;
                         RootType  : type in BINARY_OP ;
                         1stType, 2ndType : type in INCREMENT)
=
```

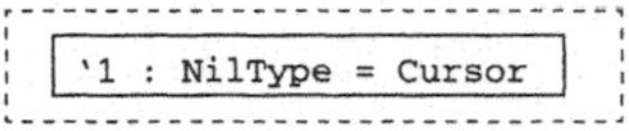

```
  ,-------------------------------,     (* Replaces given node 'Cursor' of type
  |                               |         'NilType' by a subtree with 2 child
  |   '1 : NilType = Cursor       |         nodes. The types of all 3 new nodes
  |                               |         are defined as input parameters.  *)
  '-------------------------------'
```

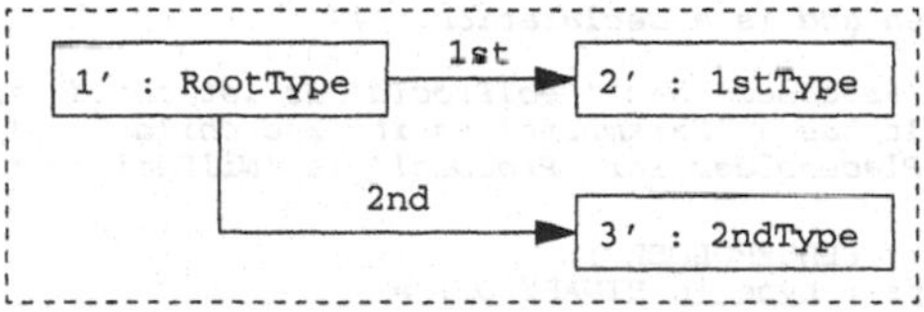

```
::=
```

```
  ,---------------------------------------------------,
  |                            1st                    |
  |   1' : RootType      ------------->  2' : 1stType |
  |                                                   |
  |              2nd                                  |
  |          ------------------>  3' : 2ndType        |
  |                                                   |
  '---------------------------------------------------'
```

```
   embedding redirect <-1st-, ... from '1 to 1';
end;
production DeleteBinary( Cursor    : BINARY_OP ;
                         NilType   : type in PLACEHOLDER ;
                         RootType  : type in BINARY_OP ;
                         1stType, 2ndType : type in INCREMENT)
=
```

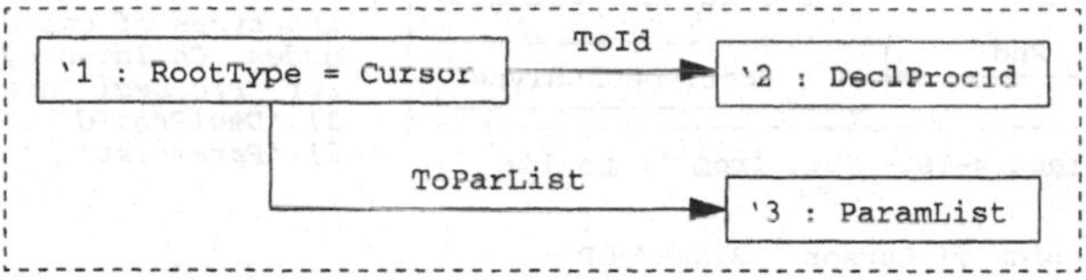

```
  ,---------------------------------------------------------,
  |                             ToId                        |
  |   '1 : RootType = Cursor    -------->  '2 : DeclProcId   |
  |                                                         |
  |              ToParList                                  |
  |          --------------------->  '3 : ParamList         |
  |                                                         |
  '---------------------------------------------------------'
```

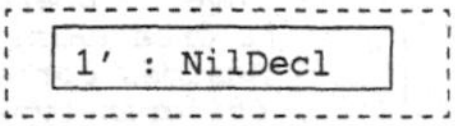

```
::=
  ,-----------------------,     (* Inverse operation to 'CreateBinary. *)
  |                       |
  |   1' : NilDecl        |
  |                       |
  '-----------------------'
```

```
   embedding redirect <-1st-, ... from '1 to 1';
end;
transaction CreateProcDecl( Cursor : NilDecl) =
   (* Transforms placeholder 'Cursor:NilDecl' into procedure declaration. *)
   CreateBinary ( Cursor, NilDecl, ProcDecl, DeclProcId, ParamList )
end;
transaction DeleteProcDecl( Cursor : ProcDecl) =
   (* Inverse operation to 'CreateProcDecl'. *)
   DeleteBinary ( Cursor, NilDecl, ProcDecl, DeclProcId, ParamList )
end;
```

Fig. 3.21. Document modelling with parametrized graph rewrite rules

Therefore, a third approach was developed (cf. fig. 3.22). It defines the context-free syntax of a language by means of *meta attributes* only. Any `BINARY_OP` type has for instance three meta attributes, which define the type of its first child (`1stType`) and its second child (`2ndType`) as well as the type of a placeholder for the regarded subtree (`NilType`). Generic graph rewrite rules need these meta attributes instead of additional rule parameters, in order to be able to generate correct abstract syntax trees only. The presented graph rewrite rule `CreateBinary` has for instance no input parameters for the children types of its parameter `RootType`. They are computed within its right-hand side by accessing the meta attributes `RootType.1stType` and `RootType.2ndType`, respectively. These meta attributes return the values `DeclProcId` and `ParamList`, if `RootType` is instantiated with `ProcDecl`. The remaining production `DeleteBinary` uses the meta attribute `NilType` in a similar manner to determine the correct type of the placeholder node which replaces the deleted subtree.

```
node class BINARY_OP is a INCREMENT
  meta
    1stType : type in INCREMENT; (* determines type of first child node *)
    2ndType : type in INCREMENT; (* determines type of second child node *)
    NilType : type in PLACEHOLDER; (* placeholder for binary subtree *)
end;
edge type 1st : BINARY_OP -> INCREMENT;
edge type 2nd : BINARY_OP -> INCREMENT;
node class DECLARATION is a INCREMENT end;
node type NilDecl : PLACEHOLDER, DECLARATION end;
node type ProcDecl : BINARY_OP, DECLARATION
  (* 'ProcDecl' has two children and is a declaration. *)
  redef meta
    1stType := DeclProcId ; (* 'ProcDecl' has 'DeclProcId' as 1st child. *)
    2ndType := ParamList ;  (* It has a 'ParamList' as its 2nd child.     *)
    NilType := NilDecl ;    (* Placeholder for 'ProcDecl' is 'NilDecl'    *)
end;
production CreateBinary( Cursor : PLACEHOLDER ;
                         RootType : type in BINARY_OP) =
```

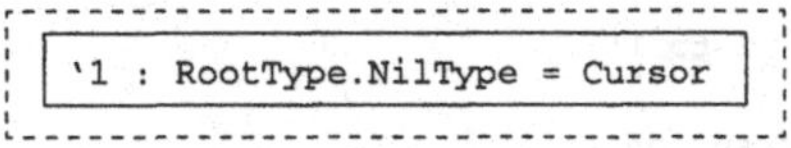


```
(* 'Cursor' points to unexpandend
   subtree. The type of the placholder
   must be the placeholder type for the
   'RootType' of the new subtree.     *)
::=
```

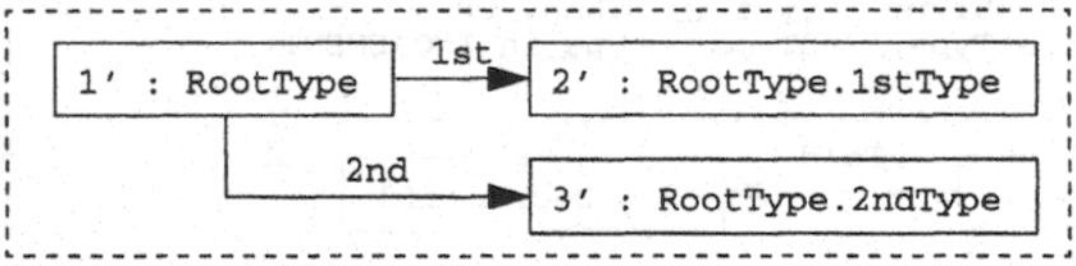


```
(* Meta attributes
   '1stType' and '2ndType'
   of 'RootType' determine
   the types of children
   nodes. Children types
   for 'ProcDecl' are:
   1) 'DeclProcId'
   2) 'ParamList'. *)
  embedding redirect <-1st-, ... from '1 to 1';
end;
production DeleteBinary( Cursor : BINARY_OP ;
                         RootType : type in BINARY_OP) =
```

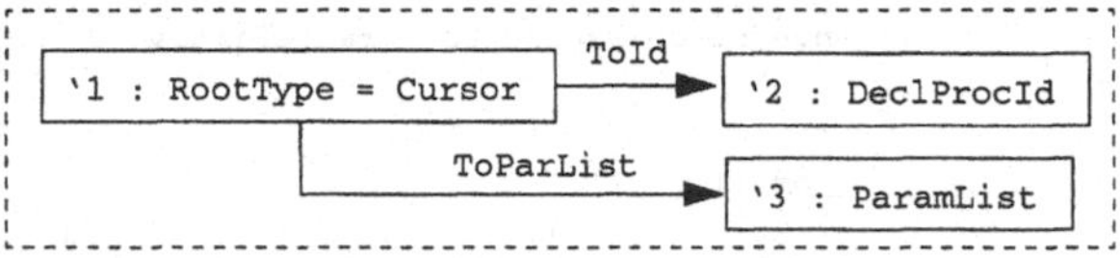


```
(* Inverse operation
   to CreateBinary'.
   Assumes correct
   children types. *)
::=
```

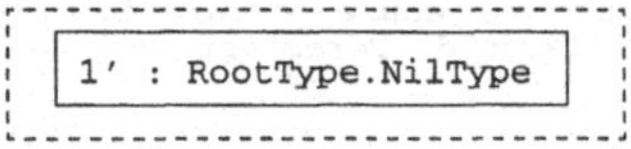


```
  embedding redirect <-1st-, ... from '1 to 1';
end;
```

Fig. 3.22. Document modelling with meta attributes

We will show in the next subsections in more detail, how meta attributes allow us to define the syntax and semantics of a textual or visual language in a uniform manner. In all cases, a basic layer of *abstract node classes* and *generic rewrite rules* represents our common knowledge about a specific language specification subtask. The missing details about a given concrete language are then added by combining needed abstract class hierarchies for several subproblems via multiple inheritance and extending the resulting class hierarchy with new node types. These node types redefine mainly inherited meta attributes.

3.3.3 Modelling the Syntax of Text Documents

The module interconnection language (MIL) of section 3.1 has a rather coarse-grained diagrammatic representation. Boxes represent modules and arrows between boxes import/export relationships between them. The contents of a single module is a set of variants (with certain properties not considered here). It does not contain any information about exported resources. Here, we will use a more *fine-grained textual representation* of software system architectures. The import of a module interface or an implementation variant is still a simple list of other modules, but its interface consists of certain type and procedure declarations. Procedure declarations in turn have a name and a formal parameter list with three different categories of parameters (in, out, and inout).

```
system Example;
   function_module Main;
      interface
         export procedure main();
      end
      variant V1;
         import UserInterface, Files, StandardTypes;
      end
   end;
   ado_module UserInterface;
      interface
         import StandardTypes, Files;
         export procedure Start( in ConfigurationFile: Files.File;
                                 out Ok: StandardTypes.Boolean);
                 procedure Edit( inout TextFile: Files.File;
                                 out Ok: StandardTypes.Boolean );
      end
      variant V1;
         import Files;
      end
   end;
   adt_module Files;
      interface
         import StandardTypes;
         export type File;
                procedure New(in FileName: StandardTypes.String;
                              out NewFile: File;
                              out Ok: StandardTypes.Boolean);
      end
      variant V1;
         import UNIX-Files;
      end
      variant V2;
         import MSDOS-Files;
      end
   end;
   collect_module StandardTypes;
      export type Boolean; type String;
   end;
end.
```

Fig. 3.23. Textual description of sample architecture

(1)	System ::=	**"system"** DeclSystemId ";" ModuleList **"end"** "."
(2)	ModuleList ::=	{ Module } Module
(3)	Module ::=	ADTModule I ADOModule I FunctionModule I CollectModule
(4)	ADTModule ::=	**"adt_module"** DeclModuleId ";" Definition **"end"** ";"
(5)	ADOModule ::=	**"ado_module"** DeclModuleId ";" Definition **"end"** ";"
(6)	FunctionModule ::=	**"function_module"** DeclModuleId ";" Definition **"end"** ";"
(7)	CollectModule ::=	**"collect_module"** DeclModuleId ";" ExportList **"end"**
(8)	Definition ::=	Interface VariantList
(9)	Interface ::=	**"interface"** ImportList ExportList **"end"** ";"
(10)	VariantList ::=	{ Variant } Variant
(11)	Variant ::=	**"variant"** DeclVariantId ";" ImportList **"end"** ";"
(12)	ImportList ::=	**"import"** { ADModuleId "," } ADModuleId ";"
(13)	ExportList ::=	**"export"** { Decl } Decl
(14)	Decl ::=	TypeDecl I ProcDecl
(15)	TypeDecl ::=	**"type"** DeclTypeId ";"
(16)	ProcDecl ::=	**"procedure"** DeclProcId [ParameterList] ";"
(17)	ParameterList ::=	"(" { Parameter ";" } Parameter ")"
(18)	Param ::=	InParameter I OutParameter I InOutParameter
(19)	InParameter ::=	**"in"** DeclParameterId ":" ParameterType
(20)	OutParameter ::=	**"out"** DeclParameterId ":" ParameterType
(21)	InOutParameter ::=	**"inout"** DeclParameterId ":" ParameterType
(22)	ParameterType ::=	ImportType I ApplOwnTypeId
(23)	ImportType ::=	ApplModuleId "." ApplTypeId

Fig. 3.24. EBNF of MIL language

Fig. 3.23 shows an extended textual representation of the architecture of fig. 3.1 of section 3.1. It contains four modules belonging to four different types. The module Main is a *function module* that exports a single parameterless procedure main. The next module UserInterface is an *abstract data object*. It exports resources for starting the user interface with a given configuration file, editing text files, etc. These resources have parameters of imported types. The needed type File and its access operations are defined within the following *abstract data type module* Files. This module has two variants. The first one (V1) uses the UNIX file system for its implementation, the second one (V2) is based on resources from an MSDOS file system. The *collection module* Standard-Types offers just a set (collection) of primitive data types, which are usually built-in types of a selected programming language.

The following fig. 3.24 contains the *concrete syntax definition* of the textual module interconnection language. It uses a kind of extended Backus Naur form (EBNF) with three different types of rules:

(a) *Structure rules*, like rule (1) for the structure nonterminal System, define language elements with a fixed number of logical components. These components are either mandatory, like DeclSystemId in rule (1), or optional, like ParameterList in rule (16). They are separated from each other by an arbitrary number of keywords.

(b) *List rules*, like rule (2) for the list nonterminal ModuleList, define the structure of language constructs which have a varying number of homogeneous subcomponents. Optional keywords are permitted at the beginning and the end of subcomponent lists as well as in between as subcomponent separating symbols.

(c) *Variant rules*, like the rule (3) for the variant nonterminal Module, introduce a common name for a set of logically related language elements. The right-hand side is a set of arbitrary nonterminals. This set may even contain another variant nonterminal, which is then a subclass of the defined variant nonterminal class.

The concrete syntax definition of fig. 3.24 is not complete. It does not contain any rules which define the *lexical syntax of identifiers*. These rules have no influence onto the design of abstract syntax trees/graphs and are, therefore, omitted.

The design of a language's *abstract syntax* is a task which is closely related to the task of designing a language's concrete syntax. Nevertheless, many programming environment generators treat concrete and abstract syntax separately from each other. The Cornell Program Synthesizer Generator /4. RT 88a/ requires for instance *separate definitions* of a language's concrete syntax, its abstract syntax, the transition from concrete to abstract syntax (for parsing purposes), and the transition from abstract to concrete syntax (in the form unparsing schemes).

The IPSEN meta environment (cf. section 4.4) offers less flexibility. It assumes an (almost) *one-to-one correspondence* between concrete and abstract syntax. As a consequence, abstract syntax definitions, parsing rules, and unparsing schemes are derivable from a single source of information, a language's EBNF. This simplifies the development of logical documents and accompanying tools (editors, parsers, etc.) in many cases.

Fig. 3.25 displays a cutout of an abstract syntax definition, which is automatically derivable from the EBNF definition of fig. 3.24. It uses a slightly modified version of the *operator/phylum notation* in /4. RT 88a/. Operators define concrete labels of syntax tree nodes, whereas phyla are a kind of nonterminal classes. Interpreted as an heterogeneous algebra definition phyla define sorts of elements with common properties. Operators are functions which take a number of subtrees of certain sorts as input and produce a new composite subtree of a specified sort as output.

(1)	phylum SYSTEM	
(2)	operator NilSystem:	() → SYSTEM
(3)	operator System:	(DECL_SYSTEM_ID, MODULES) → SYSTEM
(4)	phylum MODULES	
(5)	operator NilModules:	() → MODULES
(6)	operator ModuleList:	(MODULE⁺) → MODULES
(7)	phylum MODULE	
(8)	operator NilModule:	() → MODULE
(9)	operator ADTModule:	(DECL_MODULE_ID, DEFINITION) → MODULE
(10)	operator ADOModule:	(DECL_MODULE_ID, DEFINITION) → MODULE
(11)	operator FunctionModule:	(DECL_MODULE_ID, DEFINITION) → MODULE
(12)	operator CollectModule:	(DECL_MODULE_ID, EXPORT) → MODULE
(13)	...	

Fig. 3.25. Abstract Syntax of MIL language in operator/phylum notation

Structure and list rules are translated into operator definitions which take certain subtrees as input and produce a new composite subtree as output. Any constructed subtree belongs to a well-defined sort, its *phylum class*. The operator System takes for instance a subtree (node) of sort DECL_SYSTEM_ID and a subtree of sort MODULES as input and produces a new subtree of sort SYSTEM. The new abstract syntax tree contains the two given subtrees as its first and second child. The definition (6) of ModuleList is an example of an operator which takes a (nonempty) list of subtrees as input and returns a new subtree, the root of the given list of children nodes. The separate treatment of operators with a fixed number of arguments and operators with a variable number of arguments reflects the fact that abstract syntax graphs will not model lists of items as nested binary trees (as it is done in the Cornell Program Synthesizer Generator and other attribute grammar based systems).

Any phylum declaration D is directly followed by a distinguished operator declaration NilD with an empty parameter list. These declarations (NilSystem, NilModules, etc.) act as *defaults* for any parameter of sort D of any defined complex operator. They are used as

306

placeholders for still missing increments from a user's point of view, who edits a MIL document (cf. chapter 2 about IPSEN tools). An abstract syntax tree with a single NilSystem node represents for instance an empty MIL document. The subtree with root 4 of fig. 3.26 is the result of the application of the operator FunctionModule to the following two leaf nodes 5 := DeclModuleId() and 6 := NilDefinition(), i.e. 4 := FunctionModule(5, 6).

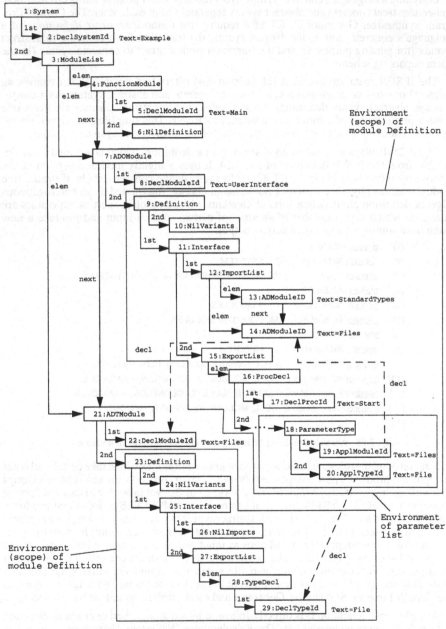

Fig. 3.26. Internal MIL graph representation of a sample architecture (cutout)

Fig. 3.26 displays a cutout of the *abstract syntax graph/tree* of the system architecture in fig. 3.23. Any node in the graph has an operator name as its type. The arguments of an *operator* node n *with fixed arity* are connected to n via edges of types 1stChild, 2ndChild, etc. The arguments of a *list operator* node n are connected to n via edges of type elem. Additional next edges model the order of list elements. The abstract syntax graph contains also three different categories of leaf nodes, beside the just mentioned two categories of complex nodes. Nodes of type "Nil..." are *placeholders* for still missing (optional) subtrees. Nodes of type "Decl...Id" and type "Appl...Id" represent *declarations* and *applied occurrences* of identifiers, respectively. They possess a string-valued Text attribute, their concrete name. The distinction between declarations and applied occurrences of identifiers as well as the distinction between identifiers and other literals (not present within our running example) is not a proper part of a language's abstract syntax definition. It will be discussed later on in subsection 3.3.5 together with the formal definition of identifier binding and scope nesting rules for the MIL language. For the purpose of this subsection it is sufficient to know that all kinds of identifiers belong to a common superclass LITERAL and that already visible dashed binding edges and visibility regions (environments) of fig. 3.26 are explained within subsection 3.3.5.

The graph schema of fig. 3.27 introduces all needed abstract syntax graph classes and their properties. The class INCREMENT is the root of our inheritance hierarchy. It may be decorated with an arbitrary number of *error messages*, which will be introduced later on. The purpose of its two subclasses LEAF and COMPLEX as well as the purpose of the two subclasses LITERAL and PLACEHOLDER of LEAF was already explained above. Please note that we use a Boolean attribute to distinguish optional from mandatory placeholders (instead of introducing two different placeholder classes which are treated in the same manner by all abstract graph inspection or modification operations). The only purpose of this attribute is to determine all incomplete abstract syntax (sub-)trees and to mark them as erroneous (cf. fig. 3.28).

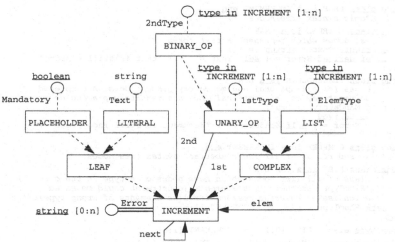

Fig. 3.27. Abstract syntax graph schema (overview)

The remaining three node classes of fig. 3.27 represent all nodes which are roots of abstract syntax subtrees, i.e. they have to be subclasses of COMPLEX. The subclass LIST represents all list operators of our abstract syntax definition. It has a set-valued meta attribute ElemType that contains for any node type of class LIST the types of all permitted children nodes. The meta attribute ElemType of ModuleList has, for instance, the set of all four module types plus the placeholder NilModule as value. This set is just the extension of the node class MODULES, which will be introduced later on (cf. fig. 3.29).

The subclass UNARY_OP, on the other hand, represents all nodes which have a fixed number of children greater equal one. Its meta attribute 1stType stores the information about all legal node types of its first child. Its value for System nodes is for instance the set { DeclSystemId, NilDeclSystemId }, i.e. the type of a proper system identifier plus the type of its placeholder. This set is the extension of another node class named DECL_SYSTEM_ID (it is possible to use identifiers with empty Text-attributes as their own placeholders, but this destroys the uniformity of abstract syntax graph schemata).

The subclass BINARY_OP of UNARY_OP represents in turn all complex nodes with (at least) two subtrees. The new meta attribute 2ndType determines all legal expansions for the second child of a node of this class. The inherited attribute 1stType still determines the permitted expansions for its first child. Please note that the MIL language does not have language elements with more than two subcomponents (with the exception of lists). Therefore, we do not introduce additional node classes for complex nodes with three or more subtrees. The only alternative to the presented approach would be to model subtrees with a fixed number of child nodes as lists, too. These lists could no longer be created by applying a single graph rewrite rule. As a consequence, complex transactions would be necessary for this purpose and modelling as well as checking the syntactical correctness of abstract syntax trees would be very difficult.

The *diagrammatic representation* of fig. 3.27 was mainly useful as a compact survey of the graph structure we are going to define. As soon as details concerning attribute evaluation functions, concrete meta attribute values, path implementations etc. have to be added to a graph schema, one has to switch from the diagrammatic representation to the corresponding *text representation* of fig. 3.28, which is maintained in parallel.

```
node class INCREMENT
    (* Superclass of any abstract syntax tree node. *)
    derived Error : string [0:n]; (* attribute for set of error messages *)
end;
node class LEAF is a INCREMENT end;
    (* Atomic syntax tree nodes. *)
node class LITERAL is a LEAF
    (* Leaf nodes which represent a text token. *)
    intrinsic Text : string := "";
    redef derived Error = [ self.Text = "" :: "text is still missing"];
end;
node class PLACEHOLDER is a LEAF
    (* Class for all optional and mandatory placeholders. A completed   *)
    (* document may contain optional, but not mandatory placeholders.   *)
    meta Mandatory := true;
    redef derived
        Error = [ self.Mandatory :: "document is still incomplete" ];
end;
node class COMPLEX is a INCREMENT end;
    (* The superclass of all inner abstract syntax tree nodes. *)
node class LIST is a COMPLEX
    (* Class of all list nodes which have nodes of a type in the set   *)
    (* 'ElemType' as their list elements (constraint could be added    *)
    (* which issues an error message for list elements of wrong type). *)
    meta ElemType : type in INCREMENT [1:n];
end;
edge type elem : LIST [0:1] -> INCREMENT [1:n];
edge type next : INCREMENT [0:1] -> INCREMENT [0:1];
node class UNARY_OP is a COMPLEX
    (* Class of all nodes with a fixed number of children. The type of *)
    (* the first child should be an element of the set '1stType'.      *)
    meta 1stType : type in INCREMENT [1:n];
end;
node class BINARY_OP is a UNARY_OP
    (* Class of all nodes with at least two children. *)
    meta 2ndType : type in INCREMENT [1:n];
end;
```

Fig. 3.28. Abstract syntax graph schema (text representation)

The specification fragment of fig. 3.28 contains the already mentioned Error attribute definitions for incomplete document parts, i.e. for unexpanded literals and still existing mandatory placeholders. Please note that more sophisticated specifications of logical documents (and implementations of IPSEN tools) distinguish between error messages for document inconsistencies and warnings for incomplete document parts.

The next fig. 3.29 presents a part of the *instantiation* of the abstract syntax graph schema *for the language MIL*. Its definition is rather straightforward. Any phylum of fig. 3.25 is translated into a node class (like SYSTEM, MODULES, and MODULE), any operator into a node type declaration (like NilSystem, System, etc.). These node type declarations have two superclasses. The first one is language specific and represents the corresponding operator's phylum class (as superclass SYSTEM of node type System). The second one is one of the general classes of fig. 3.27 and determines the structural properties of the regarded node type (as superclass BINARY_OP of node type System).

Please note that we use node type declarations with more than one superclass (as in fig. 3.22). They are not supported by the currently existing PROGRES language implementation and have to be read as an abbreviation for an additional node class declaration with more than one superclass and a simple node type declaration which belongs then to a single node class. This kind of standard transformation was used to define the common properties of all four types of modules in a separate class Module.

```
node class SYSTEM is a INCREMENT end;
    (* Class of MIL graph root nodes. *)
node type NilSystem : SYSTEM, PLACEHOLDER end;
    (* Placeholder type for an unexpanded MIL syntax tree*).
node type System : SYSTEM, BINARY_OP
    (* Root node type of a (partially) expanded MIL syntax tree. *)
    redef meta
        1stType := DECL_SYSTEM_ID;
        (* First child must belong to type of class 'DECL_SYSTEM_ID. *)
        2ndType := MODULES;
        (* Second child must belong to class 'MODULE'. *)
end;
node class MODULES is a INCREMENT end;
    (* The superclass for module lists. *)
node type NilModules : MODULES, PLACEHOLDER end;
    (* The placeholder for an unexpanded module list. *)
node type ModuleList : MODULES, LIST
    (* Module list with at least one element (cf. 'elem' edge decl.) *)
    redef meta
        ElemType := MODULE;
        (* Any element must belong to class 'MODULE'. *)
end;
node class MODULE : INCREMENT end;
    (* Class for all types of modules, including omitted placeholder *)
    (* type 'NilModule' which is needed for editing module lists.    *)
node class Module is a MODULE, BINARY_OP
    (* Class of all proper module types (without placeholder. *)
    redef meta
        1stType := DECL_MODULE_ID;
        2ndType := Definition;
end;
node type ADTModule : Module end;
    (* Abstract data type module with identifier and Definition. *)
node type ADOModule : Module end;
    (* Abstract data object module with identifier and Definition. *)
node type FunctionModule : Module end;
    (* Function module with identifier and Definition. *)
node type CollectModule : Module
    (* Module with
    redef meta
        2ndType := EXPORTS;
end;
```

Fig. 3.29. Instantiation of the abstract syntax graph schema for MIL language

Using the data stored within meta attributes it is simple to determine all possible types of expansions for the children of a given node (type). But *additional functions* are necessary to construct default completions (placeholder) for the children of a new complex node or and for determining the class (set of all node types) of all legal replacements for a given subtree root. These functions are listed in fig. 3.30 together with a number of frequently needed syntax *tree traversing path expressions*. The function class determines the types of all legal replacements of an already existing subtree by inspecting the corresponding meta attribute of its parent node. The function default returns the default replacement for a given subtree (root). It uses for this purpose the function class and selects the (hopefully) uniquely defined node type of class PLACEHOLDER in the result set of class. The function elT, finally, determines the default completion for the single child of a nonempty list (additional functions are omitted which compute the default completion of the first child of UNARY_OP node, the second child of a BINARY_OP node, etc.).

```
function class : ( I : INCREMENT ) -> type in INCREMENT [1:n] =
    (* Returns the set of permitted types which may replace a given node. *)
    (* This is the value of the 'ElemType' meta attribute of the source   *)
    (* of the 'elem' edge if 'I' is the target of an 'elem' edge, etc.     *)
    (* 'I.<-x-.ElemType' is a short-hand for 'I.<-x-.type.ElemType' since  *)
    (* 'I.<-x-' returns a node and not a node type which is the owner of   *)
    (* a meta attribute.                                                   *)
    [ I.<-elem-.ElemType | I.<-1st-.1stType | I.<-2nd.2ndType ]
end;

function default : ( I : INCREMENT ) -> type in PLACEHOLDER =
    (* Determines the placeholder which may replace an expanded abstract   *)
    (* syntax subtree. This is the only and always existing placeholder type *)
    (* in the set of all expansion alternatives for node/subtree 'I'.      *)
    class( I ) : type in PLACEHOLDER [1:1]
end;

function elT : ( T : type in LIST ) -> type in PLACEHOLDER =
    (* Computes the placeholder type for the elements of a list of type 'T'. *)
    elem( T.ElemType ) : type in PLACEHOLDER [1:1]
end;

path downTo ( Types : type in INCREMENT [1:n] ) : COMPLEX [0:1] -> Types [0:n] =
    (* Returns for a 'COMPLEX' node (subtree root) the set of all nodes in the *)
    (* subtree (without the start node) which have a type of the set 'Types'.  *)
    down & { not instance of Types :: down }
end;

path down : INCREMENT [0:1] -> INCREMENT [0:n] =
    (* Returns for any syntax tree node the set of all its children. This is *)
    (* either set of all 'elem' edge targets for list nodes or the union of  *)
    (* the '1st' and '2nd' edge for nodes with two children or just the target *)
    (* of the '1st' edge in the case of a 'COMPLEX' node with one child.       *)
    [ (instance of LIST & -elem->)
    | (instance of UNARY_OP & -1st->) or (instance of BINARY_OP & -2nd->) ]
end;

path upTo(Types : type in COMPLEX [1:n] ) :  INCREMENT [0:n] -> Types [0:1] =
    (* Ascends in the syntax tree from a given node until a node of a type of *)
    (* the set 'Types' is reached. It returns nothing if such a node does not *)
    (* exist. It returns the start node if it already has the required type.  *)
    { not instance of Types :: up }
end;

path up : INCREMENT [0:n] -> COMPLEX [0:1] =
    (* Returns the parent node of a node. *)
    [ <-elem- | <-1st- | <-2nd- ]
end;
```

Fig. 3.30. Auxiliary functions and complex syntax tree navigations

The two path declarations downTo and upTo (together with auxiliary path declarations up and down) are rather similar to built-in features of attribute grammar formalisms, which support *remote attribute access*. The path downTo returns the roots of all maximal subtrees of a given subtree which have a type in the given parameter set ChildTypes. The other path upTo returns either a single node, which is the closest parent with a type in ParentTypes, or fails.

311

These path declarations (and others like the combination of upTo and downTo into upDown) are quite handy for the specification of complex static semantic rules and allow to a certain degree the abstraction from the syntax of a given language. This has two benefits. The first one is that even some static semantics rules can be specified for a whole class of similar languages (like identifier binding rules for block structured languages in subsection 3.3.5). The second one is that minor changes of the syntax of a given language have less impact on those specification parts which use the offered path declarations instead of constructing less readable path expressions like "<-1stChild- & <-2ndChild- & -1stChild->" (cf. subsection 3.3.5).

Based on these functions and path declarations it is now easy to declare *generic graph rewrite rules* which construct and delete consistent abstract syntax subgraphs (consistent with respect to a given language's context-free syntax definition). All these graph rewrite rules are very similar to each other and the graph rewrite rules for manipulating binary abstract syntax trees in subsection 3.3.1. Therefore, we will only present a single expansions rule in fig. 3.31. It creates an arbitrary list with a placeholder as its first child. The condition T in class(PL) of CreateList guarantees that a list of the given parameter type T is a legal replacement for the selected placeholder node PL. Furthermore, the function elT computes the needed placeholder type for the additionally created list element. The other rewrite rule DeleteSubtree is even more general. It deletes any abstract syntax graph/tree node with all its children, the result of the transitive closure of the path down. It uses the function default to determine the type of a placeholder node which replaces the removed subtree.

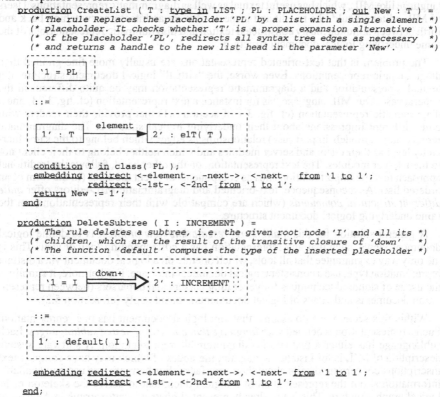

Fig. 3.31. General syntax graph/tree manipulating operations

In a similar way, it is even possible to define *generic graph transformations* for more complex tasks like copy&paste or three-way merging of logical documents, as it was done in /4. Wes 91/. All constructed basic rewrite rules and more complex transactions get any needed knowledge about a specific logical document's syntax through the inspection of introduced meta attributes.

The only drawback of this approach is that graph transformations of the abstract syntax layer are not designed to take *context-sensitive relationships* into account. Luckily, this is not necessary as long as these relationships are *automatically derived* from explicitly manipulated abstract syntax tree skeletons of logical documents (cf. subsection 3.3.5, where static semantics rules are defined by means of derived attributes and relationships only). As a consequence, only abstract syntax tree skeletons are explicitly manipulated. All additional graph data, necessary for type checking or execution purposes, are automatically kept in a consistent state by the PROGRES runtime system.

3.3.4 Modelling the Syntax of Diagrammatic Documents

The previous subsection presented a systematic way of designing the underlying graph data models of logical documents with text-oriented representations. It is the purpose of this subsection to discuss a similar methodology for logical documents with *diagrammatic (graphical) representations*. From a theoretical point of view, the internal logical document graph structure should be independent from the fact whether a document or its corresponding language has a textual or diagrammatic representation. This is especially true for a language like MIL, which has useful textual as well as diagrammatic representations. Users of MIL-editors would like to edit and inspect software architectures switching back and forth between simultaneously constructed textual and diagrammatic representations of the same underlying logical document structure.

The problem is that text-oriented representations are usually more fine-grained than diagrammatic representations. Even worse, the "virtual" logical document structure of a textual representation and a diagrammatic representation may be quite different in the general case. Our MIL language has for instance a text representation (cf. fig. 3.23) and a diagrammatic representation (cf. fig. 3.1 of section 3.1) that provide their readers with quite different impressions about their underlying logical structure. The diagrammatic representation models import (use) relationships as edges which belong to the same hierarchy level as their client and server modules and which neither belong to their client nor to their server modules. The text representation, on the other hand, follows the traditional approach to view import relationships as components of client modules (in the form of an ordered list). As a consequence, text-oriented and diagrammatic MIL-editors offer *quite different structural commands* (which are compatible with their representations) on the same underlying logical document structure.

A general solution for this *multiple representation/view problem* is to define logical document views, such that any representation has a corresponding *logical view*. This is the only way to guarantee that all tools, which operate on a logical document via a distinct representation type, use a consistent logical document interface. Furthermore, it simplifies the usage of standard techniques for generating parsers and unparsers (between representation documents and views of logical documents) considerably (cf. section 5.2).

Within this section, we do assume that any logical document has one representation. Such a representation is defined via a *language that consists of nested sublanguages*. Each sublanguage has either a textual or a diagrammatic representation. A software system description of MIL is for instance a diagram, the nodes of which may have complex text inscriptions concerning details about their interfaces. Furthermore, we use any available information about the representation of a logical document to derive the skeleton of its logical graph structure. This is the already presented *abstract syntax graph* in the case of text (sub-)representations, it is a *diagram graph* in the case of diagrammatic (sub-)representations.

EBNF is the widely accepted formalism for defining the concrete syntax of textual languages. Therefore, it was used in subsection 3.3.3 as the starting point of our logical document modelling process. A similar popular formalism for defining the syntax of diagrammatic languages is still missing as well as a formalism which offers the possibilities for defining the concrete syntax of textual and diagrammatic languages. As a consequence, we will use a rather ad hoc *notation to define the syntax of our diagrammatic MIL language*. It is a variant of the PROGRES schema notation with boxes for entity classes of modelled diagrams, attached circles for names and labels of entities, dashed edges for inheritance relationships between entity classes, and solid edges for binary relationships between entities.

Fig. 3.32 contains the *syntax definition* of our mixed diagrammatic/textual MIL language. Its axiom is the nonterminal class System. Any System instance is the root of a diagram which contains modules as entities with import/export relationships between them. Please note that the names and labels of entity boxes are nonterminals of an *accompanying EBNF definition*. Any Module entity has a name belonging to the nonterminal class DeclModuleId. CollectModules are then a specific type of modules with ExportList definitions as labels. All other types of modules, like ADTModules, have a more complex Definition as a second child, which is an ExportList plus a list of implementation variants (see EBNF on right-hand side of fig. 3.32).

The diagram syntax definition contains only one relationship declaration. This is the Uses relationship which connects any type of modules. It replaces the import lists of Interface declarations in fig. 3.24. Variant imports are still modelled as textual import lists within a module's body, its text label of type Definition. This is a consequence of the fact that Variants do not have a graphical representation over here. This shows that there are often many different possibilities in designing the concrete syntax of a mixed textual/diagrammatic language, even if the underlying concepts are precisely defined in advance. Finally note that the presented cutout of an EBNF does not, but might in turn contain nonterminals which are the names of other diagram language definitions.

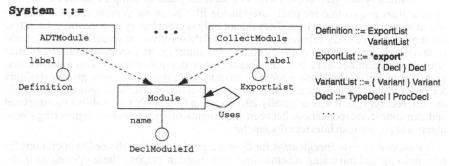

Fig. 3.32. Syntax definition of diagrammatic MIL language

Fig. 3.33 shows the *generic graph schema for diagram graphs* as an extension of the abstract syntax graph schema of subsection 3.3.3 in fig. 3.27. Any UNIT of a diagram graph is either an ENTITY or a binary REL(ATION)SHIP. Meta attributes are again used to instantiate the abstract schema for a specific diagram (sub-)language. Node types of class UNIT have a meta attribute that determines the set of all permitted label types, node types of class RELSHIP have two meta attributes FromType and ToType to determine their legal source and target node types, types of class ENTITY have a meta attribute that defines the syntax of their names, and types of class COMPLEX_ENTITY have a meta attribute that contains the types of all legal child units.

The *transition* between *text-oriented* abstract syntax graph modelled logical document parts and *diagrammatic* document parts and vice versa is realized as follows:

314

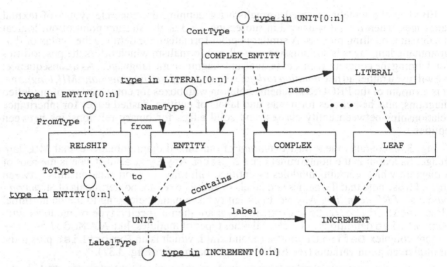

Fig. 3.33. Graph schema for diagrammatic logical MIL document

(a) Any UNIT may have a label which belongs to the abstract syntax graph root class
INCREMENT, i.e. its contents may be a sentence of any definable textual language.

(b) Any ENTITY has a name which belongs to the class LITERAL (declarations and
applied occurrences of identifiers will be introduced later on as important special
cases of literals; cf. subsection 3.3.5).

(c) Any subdiagram node of class COMPLEX_ENTITY is also a COMPLEX node in the
sense of the abstract syntax graph schema. It is, therefore, possible to construct
abstract syntax graphs/trees which contain diagrams as complex subtrees.

The *diagram graphs* that are really used inside IPSEN are *much more complex* than the
primitive version presented here. They do not only support binary relationships, but allow
for the creation of n-ary relationships. These relationships have so-called labeled *grabs*
(roles) which connect them to their entities. Relationships may even be complex entities
with an own identifier and a complex diagrammatic internal structure. This extended diagram data model is called *meta model* and was successfully used to realize graphical editors
for Entity Relationship diagrams, Structured Analysis diagrams, the language PROGRES,
etc. (cf. section 1.5). It was originally introduced in /7. Jan 92/ for establishing structural
and semantic correspondences between increments of requirements engineering documents and program architecture documents.

A *complete generic specification* for diagram graphs contains all needed operations for
manipulating and traversing schema consistent diagram graphs. These operations in the
form of complex path declarations, productions, etc. are constructed in a rather similar
manner as the operations for abstract syntax graphs and, therefore, omitted over here. They
preserve the correctness of diagrams by evaluating meta attributes of created instantiations.

Such an *instantiation* for our MIL language is displayed in fig. 3.34. A System contains
MODULE entities and Uses relationships. MODULE entities have a DECL_MODULE_ID
as their identifier and are the only permitted sources and targets of Uses relationships.
These facts are defined within the first three declarations of fig. 3.34. The following declarations in fig. 3.34 introduce then the different types of modules and their complex text
labels. An ADTModule has for instance an increment of class DEFINITION as its label.
DEFINITION in turn is either a placeholder (not defined here) or a proper Definition
increment. A Definition increment is finally a complex subtree with two children,
where the first one belongs to the class EXPORT_LIST and the second one to the class
VARIANT_LIST.

```
node type System: COMPLEX_ENTITY
   (* 'System' is a diagram with 'MODULE' entities and 'Uses' relationships. *)
   redef meta ContType := MODULE or Uses;
end;

node class MODULE is a ENTITY
   (* A module has a textual name of nonterminal class 'DECL_MODULE_ID'. *)
   redef meta NameType := DECL_MODULE_ID;
end;

node type Uses: RELSHIP
   (* The import/uses relationships connect modules with modules. *)
   redef meta FromType := MODULE;
               ToType := MODULE;
end;

node type ADTModule: MODULE
   (* The definition (of the interface and the body) of an abstract data     *)
   (* type module is modelled as a text label/increment of class 'DEFINITION' *)
   redef meta LabelType := DEFINITION;
end;

   . . . (* declarations of ADOModule and FunctionModule are omitted. *)

node type CollectModule: MODULE
   redef meta LabelType := EXPORTS;
end;

node class DEFINITION is a INCREMENT end;

node type Definition: DEFINITION, BINARY_OP
   (* The definition of a module consists of the description of its export *)
   (* interface and a list of implementation variants.                     *)
   redef meta 1stType := EXPORTS;
               2ndType := VARIANTS;
end;
```

Fig. 3.34. Instantiation of MIL language diagram graph schema (cutout)

3.3.5 Modelling the Semantics of Documents

Using the above presented document modelling methodology, we are able to develop specifications which capture the *behavior of syntax-directed editors* for partly textual, partly diagrammatic languages. These editors or their corresponding specifications check and guarantee the syntactical correctness of manipulated logical documents. Still missing is any advice on how to deal with static and dynamic semantics aspects, i.e. how to specify an analyzer, interpreter, compiler, or debugger in IPSEN.

An *analysis tool,* which checks the correctness of logical documents with respect to their *static semantics* rules, adds derived edges and attributes to abstract syntax or diagram graphs. These additional edges and attributes materialize any available and needed information about visibility scopes, bindings of identifiers, types of expressions, and so forth. *Execution tools,* on the other hand, deal with a language's *dynamic semantics.* They are usually realized as a hybrid solution in between a pure interpreter and a pure compiler. They translate basic blocks of a given document into intermediate code and interpret the produced code. All basic blocks are linked to each other via derived control flow edges, whereas the intermediate code itself is stored within derived attributes.

All these semantics processing tools deal with data which is completely determined by the underlying abstract syntax or diagram graph of a logical document. As a consequence, we will use the following (debatable) *distinction between syntax and semantics* within this section: Everything which is extensionally modelled in the form of abstract syntax (tree) or diagram graphs belongs to a language's (context-sensitive) syntax, everything else derived from abstract syntax or diagram graphs belongs to a language's static or dynamic semantics. As a consequence, derived attributes and materialized path expressions are the appropriate means of specifying the functionality of incrementally working analyzers and compilers in the sequel (the implementations of these tools are still hand-coded in IPSEN, mainly for reasons of efficiency; cf. section 4.4).

Our MIL language has a rather "poor" static semantics and no dynamic semantics at all. It models just the structural aspects of software system architectures and not their runtime behavior. Nevertheless, we can use our running example to demonstrate the principles of specifying

(a) *identifier binding* and scope nesting rules of block structured languages with import clauses,

(b) additional *consistency checks*, which could have been part of the MIL language's syntax, but are part of its static semantics,

(c) and the translation of MIL documents into Modula-2 module interfaces as a simple, but nevertheless typical *compilation* task.

For further details concerning the definition of more complex type checking rules and especially the construction of interpreters, the reader is referred to /5. Zün 96a/.

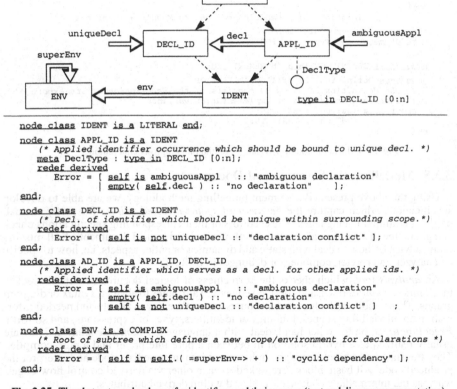

```
node class IDENT is a LITERAL end;

node class APPL_ID is a IDENT
    (* Applied identifier occurrence which should be bound to unique decl. *)
    meta DeclType : type in DECL_ID [0:n];
    redef derived
        Error = [ self is ambiguousAppl   :: "ambiguous declaration"
                | empty( self.decl ) :: "no declaration"     ];
end;

node class DECL_ID is a IDENT
    (* Decl. of identifier which should be unique within surrounding scope.*)
    redef derived
        Error = [ self is not uniqueDecl :: "declaration conflict" ];
end;

node class AD_ID is a APPL_ID, DECL_ID
    (* Applied identifier which serves as a decl. for other applied ids. *)
    redef derived
        Error = [ self is ambiguousAppl   :: "ambiguous declaration"
                | empty( self.decl ) :: "no declaration"
                | self is not uniqueDecl :: "declaration conflict" ]   ;
end;

node class ENV is a COMPLEX
    (* Root of subtree which defines a new scope/environment for declarations *)
    redef derived
        Error = [ self in self.( =superEnv=> + ) :: "cyclic dependency" ];
end;
```

Fig. 3.35. The abstract graph schema for identifiers and their scopes (text and diagram representation)

Fig 3.35 displays the needed abstract classes, their attributes, and the main relationships between them for specifying *identifier binding and scope nesting rules*. The class IDENT is a subclass of LITERAL (cf. fig. 3.27) and has in turn two subclasses APPL_ID and DECL_ID for applied identifier occurrences and their declarations, respectively. Any node of class APPL_ID is (hopefully) bound to a uniquely defined compatible declaration, a node of class DECL_ID. "Compatible" means for instance that a parameter type identifier must be bound to a type declaration identifier and not to a procedure declaration identifier. The meta attribute DeclType determines the set of all *compatible declaration types* for a certain type of applied identifier occurrences.

```
static path env : IDENT -> ENV [1:1] =
    (* Relates any identifier to its closest surrounding environment. The key *)
    (* 'static' indicates that the path 'env' is materialized and may be       *)
    (* traversed in both directions efficiently (like 'superEnv' and 'decl'). *)
    upTo( ENV ) : ENV [1:1] (* Environment is unique and has to exist! *)
end;
static path superEnv : ENV -> ENV [0:1] =
    (* Relates any environment to its closest surrounding environment. *)
    upTo( ENV ) (* Surrounding environment is unique, but need not exist. *)
end;
static path decl : APPL_ID -> DECL_ID =
    (* Binds applied identifier to visible declaration of required 'DeclType'. *)
    boundTo( self.DeclType )
end;
path boundTo( ToType : type in DECL_ID ) : APPL_ID -> ToType =
    '1 => '3 in
```

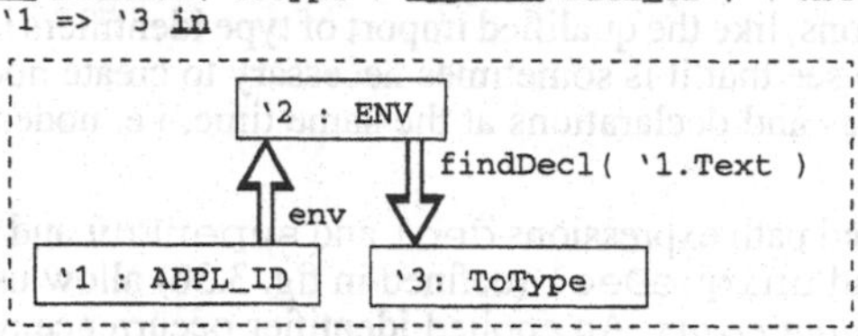

(* An applied identifier is
bound to a declaration with
the same name visible in the
surrounding environment
(block, scope).   *)

```
end;
restriction ambiguousAppl : APPL_ID =
    '1 in
```

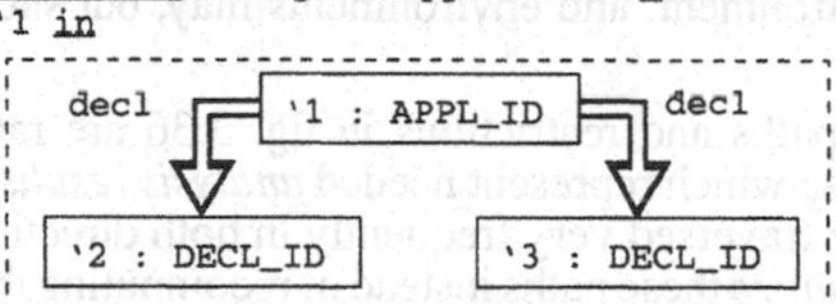

(* An applied identifier occurrence
does not have a uniquely defined
declaration if bound to at least
two visible declarations of its
name (overloading is not taken
into account).   *)

```
end;
restriction uniqueDecl : DECL_ID =
    '1 in
```

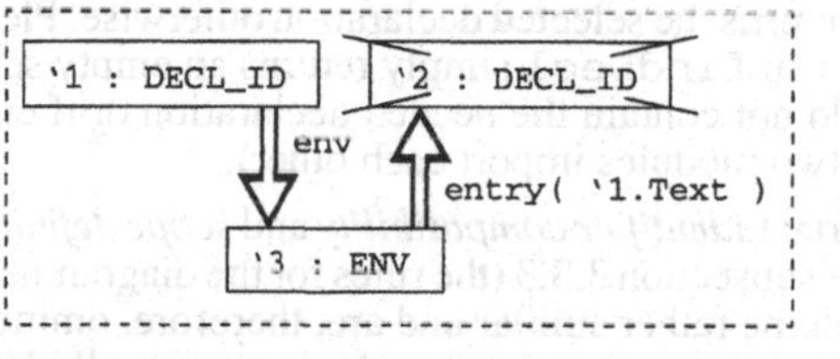

(* A declaration is unique in its
surrounding environment (scope)
if it is the only one with its
name. Again overloading is
disregarded. Furthermore, we do
assume that "inherited" id
declarations are concealed by
local declarations of the same
name such that they are not in
conflict with each other.   *)

```
end;
path findDecl ( Name : string ) : ENV -> DECL_ID =
    (* Returns all visible declarations of a given name in an environment. *)
    (* The '{ ... }' loop visits one surrounding environment after the other *)
    (* one, until an environment contains a declaration of the given name or *)
    (* there is no more surrounding env. '=entry( Name )=>' returns in the    *)
    (* first case this declaration, it returns nothing in the second case.   *)
    { not with entry( Name ) :: =superEnv=> } & =entry( Name )=>
end;
path entry( Name : string ) : ENV -> DECL_ID =
    '1 => '2 in
```

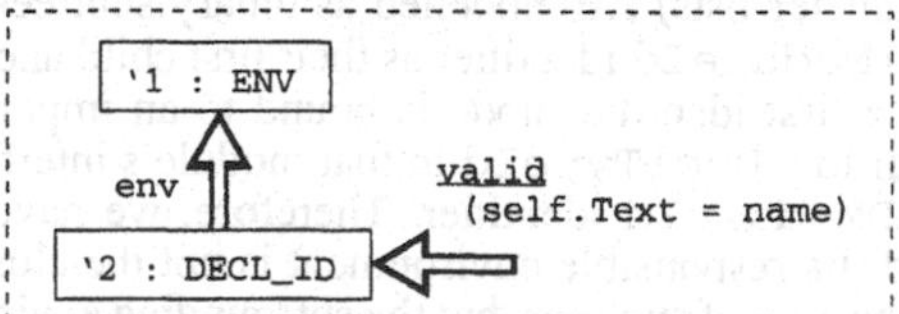

(* Returns for an environment
all its declarations with
name 'Name'. Its execution
relies on the fact that path
'env' is materialized and may
be efficiently traversed in
reverse direction.   *)

```
end;
```

Fig. 3.36. Needed path declarations and restrictions for identifier binding purposes

Bindings of identifiers are represented as derived decl-edges or, more precisely, as materialized path expressions. These path expressions determine first the closest surrounding scope of an applied identifier and then try to find the closest surrounding scope, where a declaration with the same identifier name is present (cf. fig. 3.36). *Visibility scopes* of languages are represented by nodes which belong to the class ENV. Any environment node is a kind of local symbol table which manages all identifier declarations and applications of a certain document region (a subtree in the usual case). These identifiers are bound to their ENV node via the path env. Furthermore, ENV nodes are connected via the path superEnv to all those ENV nodes which propagate their declarations to them. The default realizations of both the path env and the path superEnv are defined in fig. 3.36 as upTo(ENV) (cf. fig. 3.30). This is the correct definition for pure block structured languages. We shall see later on in fig. 3.37 how it is possible to override the default definition of these paths for more complex situations, like the qualified import of type identifiers into a module interface. There we will also see that it is sometimes necessary to create nodes which are applied identifier occurrences and declarations at the same time, i.e. nodes of class AD_ID.

Finally note that the already explained path expressions decl and superEnv and the two restrictions ambiguousAppl and uniqueDecl (defined in fig. 3.36) allow us to characterize all kinds of *identifier binding errors*: An applied identifier occurrence may have more than one possible declaration or no compatible declaration at all, a declaration may not be uniquely defined within its environment, and environments may, but should not reference each other.

The declarations of all aforementioned paths and restrictions in fig. 3.36 are rather straightforward. The first three paths are those which represent needed *analysis results* for consistency checking tools. They have to be traversed very frequently in both directions. As a consequence, it is worth-while to *materialize* these paths instead of recomputing them again and again (indicated by keyword <u>static</u>). The path findDecl is the most important one. It starts at a certain Env node and checks whether this environment contains a declaration of the given identifier name. It proceeds to the next enclosing environment as long as the declaration check fails and returns the selected declaration otherwise. Please note that the conditional repetition { . . . } in findDecl simply returns an empty set of results if all environments up to the top do not contain the needed declaration or if environments form a cyclic chain (e.g. when two modules import each other).

The next fig. 3.37 shows the most important *identifier compatibility* and *scope definition* rules for the text-oriented *MIL language* of subsection 3.3.3 (the rules for the diagrammatic language version in subsection 3.3.4 would be rather similar and are, therefore, omitted). Nodes of type Definition and Variant are environments, which manage all identifiers in their subtrees. A Definition is responsible for all interface declarations and propagates these declarations to its own nested Variant environments and to all its client modules.

Client modules have import clauses which are lists of ADModuleId nodes. Any AD-ModuleId node is an applied identifier occurrence and a declaration at the same time. It is the declaration for all occurrences of an imported module name within a module and it is bound to a corresponding DeclModuleId defined within the overall System. Occurrences of imported types (within parameter lists) are modelled as binary subtrees of type ImportType, which have an ApplModuleId identifier as their first child and an ApplTypeId as their second child. The first identifier node is bound to an imported ADModuleId node, the second identifier to a DeclTypeId in that module's interface which is determined by the imported ADModuleId identifier. Therefore, we have to redefine the path env for ApplTypeId. Its responsible environment is not the closest surrounding environment with respect to nesting of subtrees, but the surrounding environment of the binding of the binding of its ADModuleId qualifier.

```
node type System : SYSTEM, BINARY_OP, ENV
    (* A system has a name as its first child and contains a list of  *)
    (* modules as its second child. It is the topmost environment.    *)
    redef meta
        1stType := DECL_SYSTEM_ID;
        2ndType := MODULES;
end;

... (* Node classes for module lists etc. are omitted. *)

node class Module is a MODULE, BINARY_OP
    (* Class of all proper module types (without placeholder. *)
    redef meta
        1stType := DECL_MODULE_ID;
        2ndType := Definition;
end;

node type Definition : DEFINITION, BINARY_OP, ENV
    (* Interface and body = list of variants of a module. *)
    (* It is the scope (env.)for all local declarations.  *)
    redef meta
        1stType := INTERFACE ;
        2ndType := VARIANTS ;
end;

node type ImportType : PARAMETER_TYPE, BINARY_OP
    (* A import type name consists of a module qualifier *)
    (* followed by a simple type name.                   *)
    redef meta
        1stType := ApplModuleId ;
        2ndType := ApplTypeId ;
end;

node type Variant : VARIANT, BINARY_OP, ENV
    (* A variant is an environment with a name and a list of imports. *)
    redef meta
        1stType := DeclVariantId ;
        2ndType := IMPORTS ;
end;

node type DeclModuleId : DECL_ID end;

node type ADModuleId : AD_ID
    (* Item of omitted import list. It must be bound to a module name, *)
    (* a node of type DeclModuleId, and serves as a local declaration. *)
    redef meta
        DeclType := DeclModuleId ;
end;

node type ApplModuleId : APPL_ID
    (* Local true applied occurrence of module name (as type qualifier) *)
    (* which must be bound to an identifier of the module import list.  *)
    redef meta
        DeclType := ADModuleId ;
end;

node type ApplTypeId : APPL_ID
    (* Applied import type identifier. It is bound to a declaration in *)
    (* another imported module determined by its module name qualifier. *)
    redef meta
        DeclType := DeclTypeId ;
    redef derived
        env = self.( =upTo( ImportType )=>
                   & =downTo( ApplModuleId )=>
                   & =boundTo( ADModuleId )=>
                   & =boundTo( DeclModuleId )=>
                   & =upTo( Module )=>
                   & =downTo( Definition )=> );
end;

node type ApplOwnTypeId : PARAMETER_TYPE, APPL_ID
    (* Simple type identifier which must be bound to a type declaration *)
    (* in its own export list, i.e. 'Definition' is surrounding scope.  *)
    redef meta
        DeclType := DeclTypeId ;
    redef derived
        env = self.=upTo( Definition )=>;
end;
```

Fig. 3.37. Identifier binding rules of MIL language (cutout)

The MIL graph of fig. 3.26 on page 306 contains an example of an import type instance and its binding relationships. The procedure parameter type `Files.File` of procedure `Start` in module `UserInterface` (represented by nodes 18 through 20) is bound to the exported type `File` (node 29) of module `Files` (subtree with root node 21). Its qualifier `Files` establishes the needed connection to the export interface of module `Files` via its import node 14.

The following fig. 3.38 contains two examples for *static semantics rules* of our MIL language. The first one requires that abstract data type modules export one and only one type declaration, which must be used within the parameter list of any exported operation. The next one prohibits the existence of type declarations in the interface of function modules (a similar condition exists for `ADO_Modules`). Please note that the most complex condition that *import relationships do not form cycles* is already part of the basic identifier binding model. Any module interface is an environment which references other module interface environments via import clauses. The last condition of fig. 3.36 checks whether these interface environments do import each other directly or indirectly.

```
node type ADT_Module : Module
    (* An abstract data type module exports only one type declaration, *)
    (* the principal type of all its exported operations.              *)
    redef derived
        Error = [ card( self.downTo( TypeDecl )) # 1 ::
                    "single (principal) type declaration required"
                | exist Proc := self.downTo(ProcDecl) ::
                    empty(Proc.downTo(ApplOwnTypeId))
                  end ::
                    (* Condition is true if any procedure declaration in *)
                    (* the export interface of the module has a parameter *)
                    (* list without an occurrence of a private type decl. *)
                    (* ('ApplOwnTypeId' is applied identifier occurrence *)
                    (* of a 'TypeDecl' declaration).                      *)
                    "module operations must operate on principal type" ];
end;

node type Function_Module : Module
    (* A function module should not export own type declarations. *)
    redef derived
        Error = [ card( self.downTo( TypeDecl )) > 0 ::
                    "type declaration not allowed"         ];
end;
```

Fig. 3.38. Additional consistency rules of MIL language

The last specification fragment of this subsection in fig. 3.39 sketches the definition of a rather primitive *translation tool*, which takes the internal graph structure of a logical document as input and produces an unstructured piece of text as output. The specification translates any module subtree into an equivalent Modula-2 module interface definition. It is rather straight-forward, but exemplifies nevertheless very well one methodology to specify compiler backends, i.e. to deal with *dynamic semantics* aspects. It resembles the well-known approach of attribute grammar based compiler generators to specify abstract or target machine code generation by means of *synthesized attributes*.

This approach is no longer favored in modern compiler generator tool kits. Nowadays, dedicated rule-oriented specification languages, like *twig* /5. AGT 89/, are used for this purpose. The basic elements of twig (and similar languages) are *tree rewriting rules*. Each rule consists of a certain (source) tree pattern, a corresponding (target) machine code sequence and its estimated costs. The goal is now to cover the input, an intermediate tree representation of a program, by appropriate tree patterns, such that the costs of the corresponding target machine code sequence are minimized. Such a specification of a tree-to-string translation problem may be seen as a very special case of two coupled grammars. We will see later on in section 3.4 how *coupled graph grammars* may be used to construct document-to-document translators in the general case. For further details concerning the specification of abstract machine code compilers and interpreters the reader is referred to /5. Zün 96a/.

```
from LongStrings import

types
    LongString; (* Externally defined data type (in C). *)

functions         (* Some access operations for externally defined type. *)
    && : ( LongString, LongString ) -> LongString, (* concatenation *)
    word : ( string ) -> LongString,               (* conversion *)
    nl: () -> LongString,                           (* make newline *)
    indent: () -> LongString,                       (* begin indentation *)
    noIndent: () -> LongString;                     (* end of indentation *)

end;

node class CODE
    (* Superclass for any node in the abstract syntax graph which contributes *)
    (* to the text representation of a Modula-2 definition module.            *)
    derived
        DefCode : LongString;
end;

node class Module is a MODULE, BINARY_OP, CODE
    redef meta
        1stType := DECL_MODULE_ID;
        2ndType := DEFINITION;
    redef derived
        (* Text:  "definition module <Name>;
                      <Interface>
                   end. "                         *)
        DefCode =    word( "definition" )
                  && word( "module" )
                  && word( self.downTo( DeclModuleId ).Name )
                  && word( ";" ) && nl && indent
                  && self.downTo( Interface ).DefCode && noIndent
                  && word( "end" )
                  && word( "." ) ;
end;

node type Interface is a INTERFACE, BINARY_OP, CODE
    redef meta
        1stType := IMPORTS;
        2ndType := EXPORTS;
    redef derived
        (* Text:  "<ImportList>;
                   <ExportList>"   *)
        DefCode =    self.downTo( ImportList ).DefCode
                  && word( ";" )
                  && self.downTo( ExportList ).DefCode;
end;

node type ImportList is a IMPORTS, LIST
    redef meta
        ElemType := AD_MODULE_ID;
    redef derived
        (* Text:  "import <ModuleName_1), ... <ModuleName_n" *)
        DefCode = use Names := word( self.downTo( ADModuleId ).Name ) ::
                    [ empty(Names) :: word("")
                    | use 1stName := elem(Names) ::
                        concat( word( "import" ) && 1stName,
                            all (Names but not 1stName) )
                    end ]
                  end;
end;

function concat : ( prefix, next : LongString ) -> LongString =
    (* Is used above to construct a comma separated list of names from *)
    (* an unordered set of names. The input values of 'concat' are:    *)
    (*   1) prefix = "import Name_1" and next = "Name_2"                *)
    (*   2) prefix = "import Name_1, Name_2" and next = "Name_3"        *)
    (* and so forth.                                                    *)
    (* Result is "import Name" in the case of a single module import,   *)
    (* it is "import Name_1, ... , Name_n" in the case of n imports.    *)
    prefix && word( "," ) && next
end;
```

Fig. 3.39. Translating MIL modules into Modula-2 modules (cutout)

The specification of 3.39 computes for any MIL language module the corresponding Modula-2 module interface (definition module) by means of derived attributes. These derived attributes may become considerably longer than the maximum size of built-in string attributes. Therefore, it was necessary to program first a new type Long-Strings either in Modula-2 or in C and to import this type afterwards into our specification. Two functions support the conversion of simple string instances into Long-String instances and the concatenation of two given LongString instances. Using these functions, we can model our translation problem as a bottom-up attribute evaluation process. Any relevant node type inherits the attribute DefCode from the superclass CODE and defines its own evaluation rule. These evaluation rules are rather straightforward, except the case of abstract syntax tree lists. Fig. 3.39 shows one example of this kind, the evaluation rule of node type ImportList. It computes first the set of all imported module identifiers via the expression downTo(ADModuleID).Name, converts then the returned set of names into a set of LongString instances, and concatenates these instances (in random order) by calling the function concat for all elements of the determined set. The first element of the list has to be treated separately. It has the prefix "import" and not the prefix "," as all remaining list items. Furthermore, the case of an empty list had to be taken into account. Its text representation is the empty string.

3.3.6 Summary and Open Problems

Modelling logical documents and their operations by means of graphs and graph rewriting systems has a long history in IPSEN. This section discussed first the development of logical document modelling in IPSEN and related work in the research area of attribute grammars. It then presented the current *"state of the art" of graph grammar engineering* for this application area. Various subtasks, like the definition of abstract syntax graphs or identifier binding rules, were identified. For each of these subtasks a generic graph (meta) data model together with parameterized graph transformations is available. Specifying *logical documents for a certain language* works as follows:

(a) All needed generic subspecifications have to be identified and to be brought together into a single specification. There exist more or less elaborate subspecifications for purposes like type checking, interpreter construction, etc., beside the subspecifications presented here.

(b) Any language construct is translated into a node type declaration (plus an additional placeholder node type declaration) which belongs to a number of abstract node classes. The MIL language construct module Definition is for instance a subtree with two children (BINARY_OP), a significant object for scope nesting rules (ENV), and a relevant item for the translation into Modula-2 (CODE) at the same time.

(c) Specific properties of a language construct are specified by instantiating inherited meta attributes and by redefining inherited derived attributes and path declarations. A syntax tree node type thereby specifies the permitted types of its children, an applied identifier type its compatible types of declaration and its closed surrounding scope, and so forth.

(d) All inherited path declarations and graph transformations from generic subspecifications need not be modified. They instantiate themselves by reading appropriate meta attributes or have appropriate type parameters.

(e) Additional language specific graph transformations may be defined if needed. Typical examples of this kind are in our running example the transformation of one type of module into another type of module or the MIL specific creation of configurations with certain properties.

This procedure builds the conceptual background for the IPSEN tool generation machinery, which is described in more detail in section 4.4. There we will see in more detail how different subtasks like the definition of a language's concrete syntax, its corresponding abstract syntax, its identifier binding rules, and so forth interact with each other and how they are supported by a kind of *meta software engineering environment*.

The still existing *main drawbacks* of the presented methodology in practice are the absence of a suitable module concept for PROGRES and the inefficiency of the generated code for a complete logical document specification. This means that reuse of generic specification fragments is currently a matter of cut&paste and that a logical document specification is a single, more or less unstructured specification document.

The quality of the generated code is good enough for prototyping purposes (cf. section 3.6), but it has to be replaced by manually written code for creating software engineering tools, which may be used in practice (cf. section 4.4). It is the subject of ongoing work to develop first a suitable module concept (cf. section 5.2) and then a library of generic specification modules, where each PROGRES specification module has an accompanying (carefully tuned) generic implementation module written in C or C^{++}. It is our hope that the mixed usage of manually implemented basic modules together with completely generated instantiation modules allows us to *generate complete efficiently working* software engineering tools in the future.

3.4 Specification of Integration Tools

M. Lefering, A. Schürr

Until now, we have learned how to specify *tools*, which operate on *a single logical document*, like syntax-directed editors or type checkers. We have even seen an example of a transformation tool in subsection 3.3.5 that translates a given logical document into a sequence of string tokens. Derived attribute were used to define the desired output of this tool. Using simple derived attributes for the specification of transformation tools is no longer possible, when the output is another logical document instead of an unstructured text stream. Hence, another graph-based approach had to be developed for the construction of integration tools, which check and preserve the external consistency of *different logical documents*, i.e. operate on a set of graphs simultaneously (cf. section 1.6).

This section describes our approach to *specify the integration* of different documents, whereas section 2.2 and 2.3 dealt with the user interface of document integrating tools, and section 1.6 presented a classification scheme for them. The specification of a document integrator starts with the definition of a *graph grammar* for any involved class of logical documents. These graph grammars have a different purpose than any graph rewriting system specification presented until now. They do not define a complete set of document manipulating operations (of a syntax directed editor), but generate merely all documents (graphs) which are relevant as sources or targets for a document integration tool. Please note that a class of documents may contain many instances which represent intermediate editing states, but which are not relevant for the purpose of a document integration tool.

Correspondences between related documents are then defined by *coupling related productions* of different graph grammars. The resulting specification describes a whole family of integration tools on a very high, abstract level. It may be translated automatically into usual graph rewriting system specifications. These specifications determine the operational behavior of different types of document integration tools (like a transformation tool or a consistency checker; cf. section 1.6). The executable code of any integration tool is afterwards derived from such a graph rewriting system specification. This is done manually until now, but will be automated in the future. In the following, we describe how a mapping between two logical document languages can be specified in more detail and how various integration tools can be generated out of it. The derivation of code from this specification is discussed in section 4.6, when the implementation of rules is described.

The basic ideas and advantages of this approach, compared with related work, are discussed in subsection 3.4.1. Subsection 3.4.2 then introduces the running example of this section, the transformation of requirements engineering (RE) documents into module interconnection language (MIL) or programming-in-the-large (PiL) documents. It is a simplified version of the RE to PiL transformation of section 2.3. Subsection 3.4.3 defines needed shorthand notations. Subsection 3.4.4 shows afterwards in more detail, how coupling of graph grammars may be used to specify functional dependencies between logical documents and how a coupled graph grammar may be interpreted as the specification of a whole suite of integration tools. The last subsection 3.4.5 is a summary of our achievements concerning the specification of integration tools and discusses some open problems.

For any details concerning the *realization of integration tools* in IPSEN, the reader is referred to section 4.6. An in-depth discussion of the selected example may be found in /7. Jan 92/ and /4. Lef 93a/. A more detailed description of the requirements engineering (RE) language is presented in /7. Jan 92/, the simple software design language MIL was already introduced in section 3.1.

3.4.1 Basic Ideas and Related Work

The specification and the realization of *integration tool*s in software engineering environments is a "hot topic" for more than ten years. Nevertheless, the state of the art, especially concerning high-level specifications of integration tools and generation of integration tools from these specifications, is still unsatisfactory. The most popular integration approach used in practice is based on so-called *message servers*. Typical examples of this kind are the academic ancestor Field /6. Rei 90b/ and commercial products like HP-Soft-Bench /6. Fro 90/ or ToolTalk /6. Fra 91/. These systems offer *control-oriented mechanisms* for the integration of already existing tools, but give no support for specifying functional dependencies between complex structured documents.

Other projects follow a more *data-oriented integration* approach. They integrate tools by constructing so-called compatibility maps /5. Gar 88/ for a common database or views /6. Schi 93b/ onto a common database. This approach is useful as long as considered tools operate on a *common database*. It gives only rather limited support for defining functional dependencies between separate documents with very different syntax and semantics.

Furthermore, there are some (meta) software engineering environments which model whole project databases as *attributed syntax trees*. In the simplest case, a project database is a set of documents, where each document has its own attribute grammar. Mercury is a system, which follows this line of research /5. KKM 87/. It offers some support for *propagating changed attributes* of one document's syntax tree to another related document's syntax tree. In this way, it is possible to specify and generate *analysis tools* which check interdocument consistency rules. Other systems offer a refined version of this concept, which allows arbitrary nesting of documents. *Gate nodes or door attributes* model transitions from one context-free document language to another one. Systems of this kind are Gandalf /2. HN 86/ and Centaur /2. BCDI 88/. All of them have problems with the specification of active transformation tools, which do not only check interdocument integrity constraints, but modify related documents in order to reestablish required constraints.

The logical consequence of this deficiency is that evaluation rules are needed which determine the values of door attributes in abstract syntax trees. These values are abstract syntax trees in turn, which belong to another attribute grammar. This leads to the definition of *attribute coupled grammars* in /5. GG84/. A variant of this approach is nowadays used in the Cornell Program Synthesizer Generator, mainly for specifying the transition from concrete to abstract syntax /4. RT 88a/. Another approach for specifying translations of syntax trees into sentences of other languages is presented in /5. AGT 89/. It is based on *tree pattern matching* and *dynamic programming*. It is targeted at generating compiler backends, where abstract syntax trees are translated into target machine code programs.

A *severe drawback* of all syntax-tree oriented approaches presented above is that specified translation processes are *unidirectional and batch-oriented*. Assuming the case, where we need one integration tool for transforming requirements engineering documents into design documents and another tool for transforming design documents back to RE documents (reverse engineering), we have to write two hopefully consistent specifications for these two tools. Even worse, generated tools would not be able to propagate changes of one document into the related document incrementally.

The system TransformGen /4. SKG 87/ is a first attempt to treat source and target documents of transformation processes symmetrically, by defining appropriate *relationships between EBNFs* of source and target documents. The system has its main focus on mechanizing the translation of old document versions into new ones, when the corresponding language syntax has been modified slightly. With TransformGen transformation tools between different versions of documents are built (semi-)automatically, while the user is editing changes in the EBNF. Again, generated transformation tools are uni-directional and batch-oriented.

All approaches mentioned above suffer from the fact that context-sensitive relationships must be encoded as complex structured attributes. Therefore, it was quite natural to generalize the idea of relating grammars for different tree languages to graph languages. This was already done 25 years ago by T.W. Pratt /5. Pra 71/. He introduced the concept of *pair graph grammars* to describe transformations between different representations of programs. Context-free graph grammars (left-hand sides are single nonterminal nodes) describe isolated program representations as graph languages. Correspondences between nonterminal node labels are used to couple productions of graph grammars as needed. The transformation of one program representation into another works then as follows: The input representation is *parsed* with respect to its own graph grammar, yielding a sequence of productions. Afterwards, a related sequence of productions of the second graph grammar is determined and used to *generate* another program representation. This *process works in both directions*, if necessary, by exchanging the roles of input and output graph grammar.

Note that the *output* of a pair graph grammar based transformation process is *not uniquely determined* in the general case. The output graph grammar may possess rules which have the same nonterminal label on their left-hand sides. As a consequence, we have several possibilities how to translate a sequence of rules of the input graph grammar into a related sequence of rules of the output graph grammar. Being able to specify nondeterministic transformation processes is very important for the running example of the following subsection. There are many different possibilities how to translate an RE document into a MIL document. Some of them are incompatible and lead into dead-ends of the overall transformation process, but some of them are indistinguishable from a transformation tools point of view. It is up to the user of such a tool to the select those possibilities which produce finally a "good" software design.

When we tried to use *pair graph grammars* for the specification of transformation tools in IPSEN, we were faced with the following *severe problems*:
(a) Context-free productions without any additional preconditions are not able to deal with situations, where the transformation of a single document portion may depend on certain properties of its embedding context.
(b) Even worse, all existing parsing approaches for rather restricted classes of context-free graph grammars are batch-oriented, i.e. not very useful for the realization of incrementally working transformation tools.
(c) Defining (one-to-one) correspondences between (nonterminal) node labels is a good idea, but additional many-to-many correspondence definitions are needed, which relate possibly corresponding left- and right-hand side nodes of coupled productions.

To overcome these problems, a new variant of pair graph grammars was developed (cf. /5. Schü 94b, 4. Lef 94, 5. Lef 94/). Logical document graph classes are defined as attributed graph grammars with *context-sensitive productions*. Many features of PROGRES may be used (like path expressions) for defining these productions, except the modification of attribute values, the deletion of nodes and edges, and certain types of negative application conditions. These restrictions make the generation of an *incrementally working transformation algorithm* feasible. Such an algorithm maintains a set of left-hand side matches, which covers the given input graph and fulfills all required attribute and context conditions (cf. section 4.6). Please remember that these graph grammar productions must just be able to generate all legal input graphs for a given transformation process, but they do not have to specify document modifying tool operations. Thus, the restriction to non-deleting productions is tolerable in many cases. Nevertheless, a parsing algorithm, which is able to deal with more general classes of graph grammars, is under development /5. RS 96/.

Our variant of pair graph grammars uses a *separate correspondence relation* for each pair of productions which has to be glued together. Any triple of a source document production, a target document production, and their correspondence relation is a production of a higher level grammar, a so-called *triple graph grammar*. It generates pairs of consistent documents only, together with a set of interdocument links. These links realize many-to-many relationships between corresponding increments of involved documents.

3.4.2 The Running Example

The transformation of a data flow diagram (DFD) hierarchy into a corresponding software architecture as part of the integrator between requirements engineering (RE) and programming-in-the-large (PiL) or its simplified version MIL of this chapter was already described in section 2.3. There we had a main focus on the direction RE → MIL, whereas we will also consider the reverse direction MIL → RE and the simultaneous modification of RE and MIL documents here. It is a good example for demonstrating our needs for complex (nondeterministic) transformation rules, which establish many-to-many relationships between corresponding document portions of an RE document and a MIL document.

The main idea of the transformation rules is as follows: There are *three possibilities* to transform a DFD. Thus, the rule set is not unique and the specified RE → MIL integrator is a semi-automatic tool. The user has to select one of the following cases, which were already discussed in section 2.3.1 (cf. fig. 3.40):

(a)   a DFD A in RE corresponds to a functional module A in MIL that exports a (single) procedure A,

(b)   a process D together with its own DFD D used within another DFD B is translated into an exported procedure D of the functional module B,

(c)   or a process C with its DFD C becomes a local procedure of a module which is not part of the MIL document, but of a related module implementation document.

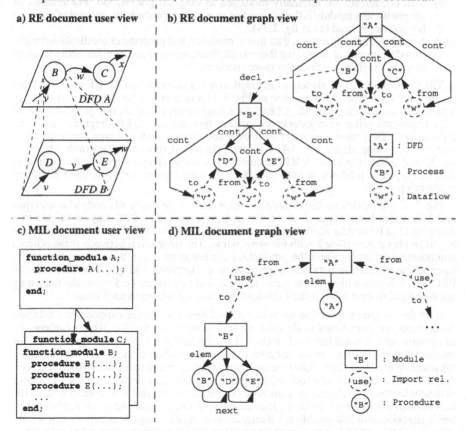

Fig. 3.40. External representation and internal graph structure of related documents

The last choice (c) establishes a consistency relationship between an RE document, a MIL document, and an a priori unknown number of module implementation documents. It shows that we need integration tools which inspect and manipulate sets of documents instead of tracing consistency relationships between pairs of documents only. An appropriate extension of triple graph grammars is still subject of ongoing work. Therefore, we will not consider case (c) above any longer and present only rules for cases (a) and (b) in the following subsection 3.4.3.

Fig 3.40.a and 3.40.c display (cutouts of) a small DFD hierarchy and one possible translation into a corresponding software system architecture (cf. fig. 2.18). The two visible DFDs A and B are translated into two function modules. The process B in A, an applied occurrence of the DFD B, is translated into an import (Uses) relationship from module A to module B. The process C in A has no counterpart in the MIL document. The remaining processes D and E in DFD B become exported procedures of the module B.

The internal *graph representations* of both documents are depicted in fig. 3.40.b and 3.40.d using the following assumptions:

(a) RE documents are internally modelled as diagram graphs (cf. section 3.3). They contain DFDs as complex entities, processes as atomic entities (bound to their corresponding DFD declarations via decl edges), and data flows as binary relationships (sources/targets of diagram crossing data flows are omitted in fig. 3.40.b).

(b) MIL documents are internally modelled as diagram graphs, too. For reasons of simplicity, any module is the list head of its exported procedures, instead of containing such a list head (as in fig. 3.34).

(c) Names of DFDs, processes, data flows, modules, and procedures are displayed within nodes, instead of displaying them as attributes of separate identifier nodes in order to make graph representations more succinct.

The following fig. 3.41 sketches the *graph schema declarations* for RE and MIL document graphs and their *correspondences*. Fig. 3.41.a requires that an RE_Document has a name and contains a set of RE_COMPLEX components. DFDs are one possible type of RE components (other components are control flow diagrams, ER diagrams, and data dictionaries). They have a name of their own and contain nodes of type Process and Dataflow among others. Fig. 3.41.b is just a simplified version of the graph schema in fig. 3.34 of subsection 3.3.4. A MIL document is a single complex entity which contains different types of modules as entities and Uses relationships between them as binary relationships.

Fig. 3.41.c then defines the desired *correspondences* between RE node classes/types and MIL node classes/types. It shows that a Process plus a DFD may be related to a ProcDecl, a Process alone to a Uses relationship, and a DFD alone to a Function-Module plus a ProcDecl with the same name. The interaction between these schema component relationships and the production correspondences in the next section is the same as the interaction between graph schema declarations and graph rewrite rules in PROGRES. Nodes within left- or right-hand sides of two corresponding productions may not be related to each other if their classes/types are not related to each other.

Both the *correspondences* on the schema level here and the correspondences between productions are *interpreted in different ways* depending on the fact which category of integration tool is considered (cf. section 1.6). An editor coupling tool guarantees for instance that any insertion of a Process instance in an RE document is accompanied by the insertion of a ProcDecl instance or a Uses relationship in the related MIL document. An RE to MIL transformation tool, on the other hand, translates already existing Process instances later on into ProcDecl instances or Uses relationships, whereas a MIL to RE transformation tool translates Uses relationships into Process instances. And a consistency checking tool just establishes interdocument relationships between Process instances and ProcDecl instances or Uses relationships which correspond to each other.

a) RE document graph schema:

```
node type RE_Document : COMPLEX_ENTITY
   redef meta
      NameType := Decl_RE_Id;
      ContType := RE_COMPLEX;
end;

node class RE_COMPLEX is a COMPLEX_ENTITY

node type DFD : RE_COMPLEX
   redef meta
      NameType := Decl_DFD_Id;
      ContType := DFD_ITEM or Dataflow;
end;

node type Dataflow: RELSHIP
   redef meta
      FromType := DFD_ITEM;
      ToType := DFD_ITEM;
end;

node type Process: DFD_ITEM
   redef meta
      NameType := Appl_DFD_Id;
end;

node class DFD_ITEM is a ENTITY end;
```

b) MIL document graph schema:

```
node type MIL_Document : COMPLEX_ENTITY
   redef meta
      NameType := Decl_MIL_Id;
      ContType := MODULE or Uses;
end;

node class MODULE is a ENTITY, LIST end;

node type FunctionModule : MODULE
   redef meta
      NameType := DeclModuleId;
      ElemType := ProcDecl;
end;

node type ProcDecl : BINARY_OP
   redef meta
      1stType := DeclProcId;
      2ndType := Parameters;
end;

node type Uses: RELSHIP
   redef meta
      FromType := MODULE;
      ToType := MODULE;
end;
```

c) RE↔MIL graph schema correspondences:

```
RE_Document      ↔ MIL_Document       RE_COMPLEX  ↔ MODULE
Decl_RE_Id       ↔ Decl_MIL_Id

Process, DFD     ↔ ProcDecl           DFD           ↔ FunctionModule, ProcDecl
Decl_DFD_Id      ↔ DeclProcId         Decl_DFD_Id ↔ DeclModuleId, DeclProcId

Process          ↔ Uses                ...
Appl_DFD_Id      ↔ DeclModuleId
```

Fig. 3.41. Corresponding logical document graph schemata (cutouts)

3.4.3 Shorthand notations for Triple Graph Grammars

Based on the graph schemata for RE and MIL graphs, presented within the previous subsection, we will now define functional dependencies between RE and MIL in more detail using triple graph grammars. Such a *triple graph grammar* is a set of triples with the following components:

(a) All first components are graph extending productions. They generate the language of all RE graphs which can be translated into corresponding MIL graphs (or the other way round).

(b) All third components are graph extending productions, too. They generate the language of all MIL graphs which can be translated into corresponding RE graphs (or the other way round).

(c) All second components establish needed relationships between left- and right-hand side nodes of first and third component productions.

The *formal definition of triple graph grammars* in /5. Schü 94b/ uses an additional correspondence production together with two morphisms to model many-to-many relationships between left- and right-hand side nodes of first and third component productions. In such a way, it is possible to represent all needed concepts as graphs (productions are just pairs of graphs) and total morphisms between graphs. This simplifies formal definitions and correctness proofs considerably, but leads to a notation which contains many redundancies and which is hard to read. We will therefore use a more succinct and readable textual notation within this book: Production correspondences are denoted as lists of related left- and right-hand sided nodes of involved productions.

In order to make definitions of triple graph grammars even more compact and readable, we will *merge left- and right-hand sides* of their production components. All those nodes and edges which are part of left- and right-hand sides have thin grey border lines. All those nodes and edges which are part of right-hand sides only have bold black border lines. This is possible due to the necessary restriction to graph extending productions. Nodes and edges which are part of a left-hand side, but not of a right-hand side would be deleted and are forbidden. The transition from the original PROGRES notation to the more compact one is excmplified in fig. 3.42.a and 3.42.b.

The fig. 3.42.c introduces *another shorthand notation* which is specific for our running example and not used elsewhere. Some nodes and edges within left- and right-hand sides of productions are needed for technical reasons, but of no importance for understanding specified transformation rules. These are the root nodes and identifier nodes of our logical document graphs. Any top level increment of a document (like DFD or FunctionModule) is the child of the corresponding document's root node, and any document increment with a name stores this name in an attribute of a separate identifier node. We will omit these technical nodes and their incident edges from now on. This last simplification step is shown in the transition from fig. 3.42.b to fig. 3.42.c.

a) Usual PROGRES production notation:

production InsertDFD(N : string) =

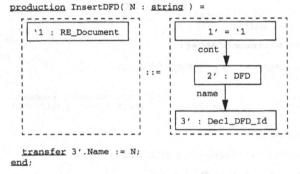

transfer 3'.Name := N;
end;

b) Shorthand notation for graph extending productions (of triple graph grammars):

production InsertDFD(N : string) =

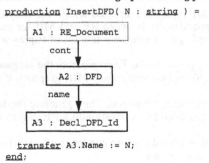

transfer A3.Name := N;
end;

c) Simplified shorthand notation omitting "technical" document root and identifier nodes:

production InsertDFD(N : string) =

    ┌─────────────┐
    │ A2 : DFD   │
    └─────────────┘

transfer A2.Name := N;
end;

Fig. 3.42. Compact notation for logical document creating productions

3.4.4 Specification of the Running Example

Fig. 3.43 contains the definition of the first RE ↔ MIL transformation rule as a triple graph grammar production plus a number of *derived interpretations* of the production. All these interpretations are regular graph rewrite rules which access and modify an RE graph (document), a MIL graph (document), and an intermediate correspondence graph (document) simultaneously. All three graphs are treated as subgraphs of a common project graph structure (due to the absence of a hierarchical graph data model in PROGRES). The new *intermediate correspondence graph* keeps track of all many-to-many relationships between RE and MIL nodes in the form of hyperedges. These hyperedges are realized as LinkNode instances with source edges to all related RE nodes and target edges to all related MIL nodes. It provides the necessary support for implementing hypertext-like browsing tools as well as for implementing incrementally working transformation tools.

The five subdiagrams of fig. 3.43 display a triple graph grammar production plus four different ways to interpret it as part of the specification of a specific transformation tool. They have to be read as follows:

(a) The *triple graph grammar production* itself in fig. 3.43.a tells us that a DFD node in an RE document may be related to a FunctionModule node and a ProcDecl node in a MIL document, which have the same name as the DFD node.

(b) The following production InsertDFDAndFM in fig. 3.43.b represents the most straightforward interpretation of the given triple graph grammar production, a scenario where all *documents are constructed simultaneously*. This is useful only if coupled productions correspond directly to document modifying commands offered at the user interface (which is usually not the case). It is part of the specification of a so-called *coupling tool* (cf. section 1.6) which enforces simultaneous editing of related documents.

(c) The next production TransformDFDToFM in fig. 3.43.c represents the standard scenario of a *forward transformation*, where a somehow modified RE document contains a new DFD node, which is not yet propagated into the MIL document. The production inserts the corresponding FunctionModule and ProcDecl nodes into the MIL document and updates the intermediate correspondence document. It is part of the specification of a *forward transformation tool* which propagates any update of an RE document into the related MIL document on demand.

(d) Production TransformFMToDFD in fig. 3.43.d realizes the *inverse transformation process*, where MIL document changes are propagated back into the related RE document. It translates any function module with an exported procedure of the same name back into a DFD with the same name. It is part of the specification of a *reverse transformation tool* which propagates any update of a MIL document into the related RE document on demand.

(e) The last production of fig. 3.43.e is needed for realizing a pure *consistency checker* or, more precisely, a *binding tool* which does not merely check the consistency of existing interdocument relationships, but establishes new ones on demand (cf. section 1.6). Here, both documents have been created already and the integrator searches for corresponding parts and installs the interdocument links between them.

The translation of a data flow diagram into a function module was just one of the possibilities mentioned at the beginning of subsection 3.4.2. Furthermore, it is still incomplete as long as import relationships between generated modules are not regarded, too. Therefore, two additional triple graph grammar productions are needed to complete our running example. They are listed in fig. 3.44. The first one in fig. 3.44.a shows that the creation of a Process within a DFD corresponds possibly to the creation of a Use relationship between two FunctionModules. The server module (target of to edge) is the result of translating the DFD which "implements" the regarded Process node. The client module (source of from edge) is the result of translating the DFD which contains the regarded Process node. Hence, the specified transformation is only useful (and possible) if both involved DFD nodes are translated into FunctionModule nodes.

a) Triple graph grammar production for relating RE and MIL documents:

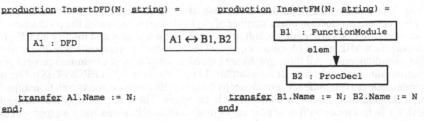

```
production InsertDFD(N: string) =        production InsertFM(N: string) =
```

A1 : DFD   A1 ↔ B1, B2   B1 : FunctionModule
elem
B2 : ProcDecl

```
    transfer A1.Name := N;                    transfer B1.Name := N; B2.Name := N
end;                                      end;
```

b) Derived synchronous editing rule for RE and MIL:

```
production TransformDFDToFM =
```

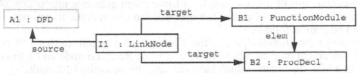

```
    transfer B1.Name := A1.Name; B2.Name := A1.Name;;
end;
```

c) Derived forward transformation rule from RE to MIL:

```
production TransformDFDToFM =
```

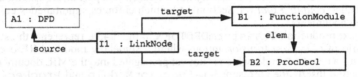

```
    transfer B1.Name := A1.Name; B2.Name := A1.Name;;
end;
```

d)Derived inverse transformation rule from MIL to RE:

```
production TransformFMToDFD =
```

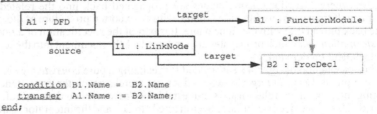

```
    condition B1.Name = B2.Name
    transfer  A1.Name := B2.Name;
end;
```

e) Derived consistency checking/binding rule between RE and MIL:

```
production TransformFMToDFD =
```

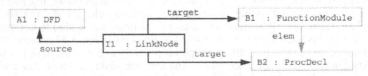

```
    condition A1.Name = B1.Name; A1.Name = B2.Name;
end;
```

Fig. 3.43. Derivation of transformation rules from triple graph grammar specification

a) Translation of DFD with possibly more than one applied process occurrence:

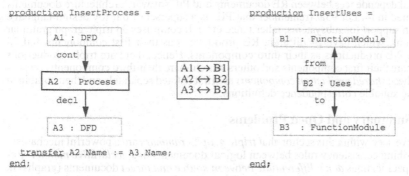

b) Translation of DFD with single applied process occurrence:

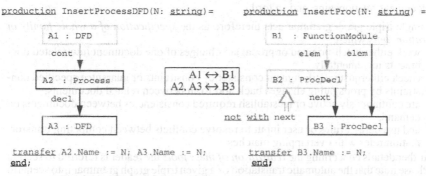

Fig. 3.44. Missing triple graph grammar rules for DFDs and function modules

The following triple graph grammar production in fig. 3.44.b defines an alternative transformation for a DFD node A3, which has one and only one Process occurrence A2 within another DFD A1 (A1 matches for instance the DFD node B and A2 the Process node E in fig. 3.40.b). Both nodes are translated into a single ProcDecl node B2 (exported procedure) of the corresponding module B which is appended as the new last one in the list of exported procedures (B1 matches for instance the FunctionModule B and B3 its procedure E in fig. 3.40.d). The transformation of a Process node together with its DFD into an exported procedure is not possible if its surrounding DFD was already translated into an exported procedure of another module M. An additional rule is then needed which translates these processes into local procedures of the same module M. But note that it would be possible to use the corresponding RE → MIL transformation rule for translating a DFD with more than one Process occurrence into a exported procedure. Such a local decision leads later on the overall transformation process into a dead-end.

It is sometimes, but not always possible to prohibit *incorrect local transformation decisions* by adding appropriate (negative) context-conditions to coupled productions. Especially in the case of *incremental document transformations*, it may always happen that once correct decisions become invalid later on, when the related documents are directly modified. Implementations of incrementally working transformation tools must, therefore, be able to keep track of all made (user) decisions including their preconditions and their consequences, and to correct inconsistencies when required. Fortunately, triple graph grammar users do not have to worry about these aspects of document integrations. They are taken into account within a common architectural framework for integration tools, which will be presented later on in subsection 4.6.

Finally, we should mention that the *complete triple graph grammar specification* of functional dependences between RE documents and PiL software architecture documents is presented in /4. Lef 93a/ (remember that PiL is a superset of our toy design language MIL with support for subsystems, inheritance etc.). It comprises 33 triple graph grammar productions, which have 24 different RE productions as their first components and 28 different PiL productions as their third components. Hence, there are triple productions which share their first components and others which share their third components, respectively. These *shared production components* are first defined separately and then combined by adding suitable correspondence definitions.

3.4.5 Summary and Open Problems

We have seen within this section that *triple graph grammars* are a powerful mechanism for describing consistency rules between logical documents in a *declarative manner*. Resulting specifications *don't differentiate between source and target* documents (graphs) in regarded transformation processes. They are even free from implementation specific considerations, like the selection of applicable transformation rules, the maintenance of needed interdocument relationships, and so forth.

A single triple graph grammar acts therefore as the *specification of a whole family of integration tools* which
(a)   work either batch-oriented or propagate changes of one document into related documents incrementally,
(b)   check either just interdocument consistency constraints or guarantee specified constraints by propagating changes back and forth between related documents,
(c)   are continuously active or reestablish required consistencies between documents on demand,
(d)   and use default rules or user input to resolve conflicts between competing transformation rules with overlapping matches.

For further details concerning the *realization of these tools* the reader is referred to section 4.6. Please note that the automatic translation of a given triple graph grammar into scenario specific parts of integration tools is possible, but not yet offered by the IPSEN meta software development environment.

Beside the lack of (meta) tool support for specifying and generating integration tools, there are also some *conceptual problems* that still have to be solved. Realized integration tools as well as their specifications need not and should not have complete knowledge about the internal graph structures of related documents. The "classical" solution for this requirement would treat each document specification as an *abstract data type* that hides its internal graph structure completely and offers access to the internal graph structure only via a set of interface operations. This approach fails in our case, where integration tools are specified by coupling graph rewrite rules (graph grammar productions). These rewrite rules have in almost all cases transformation specific graph patterns on their left- and right-hand sides and are, therefore, not part of (the interface of) involved logical document specifications. Nevertheless, they need access to the internal graph structures of logical documents. This is a consequence of our approach to specify integration tools by drawing and coupling graph patterns instead of writing down sequences of procedure calls.

The only viable solution for combining integration scenario specific graph rewrite rules with the requirement of data abstraction for related graph structures is based on the definition of *graph views*. These views have the same purpose as views in the world of databases, i.e. they allow us to hide certain data modelling details, which are irrelevant for the regarded integration problem. The difficult question remains how the idea of graph views can be incorporated into a future graph rewriting language and, especially, how the well-known view-update problem can be solved. First ideas concerning these problems are presented in section 5.2, where triple graph grammars are again used to define views on graphs for other triple graph grammars.

3.5 Specification of the Management of Products, Processes, and Resources

B. Westfechtel

This section presents a *case study* for the use of programmed graph rewriting. PROGRES is used to specify the *management tools* which were described in section 2.5. We assume the reader to be familiar not only with these tools, but also with the PROGRES language which was introduced in section 3.1.

Management of products, processes, and resources is an ideal application for programmed graph rewriting because complicated graph structures are involved and complex transformations are performed on these graphs. In contrast to section 3.3, we do not use abstract syntax graphs to model the internal data structures of management tools. Rather, *graphs* are employed somewhat *more directly*. While abstract syntax graphs play an important role for builders of IPSEN tools, they are not well suited to modelling the information to be maintained by management tools in a direct and intuitive way (see below).

In the first subsection 3.5.1, we summarize how PROGRES has been applied to management problems. The next subsections 3.5.2 to 3.5.4 describe cutouts of a PROGRES specification for managing products, processes, and resources, respectively. Afterwards, the parameterization of the management environment is discussed (3.5.5). Finally, a summary and a comparison to related work are given (3.5.6).

3.5.1 Specifying Management Tools with PROGRES

As all IPSEN tools, the management tools of section 2.5 are internally based on *abstract syntax graphs* (section 3.3). Not only textual, but also graphical (and hybrid) documents are represented by abstract syntax graphs. However, when trying to specify management tools on a high level of abstraction, we observed that abstract syntax graphs do not provide a satisfactory foundation. Basically, naturally occurring graph structures have to be encoded by trees augmented with context-sensitive edges. Furthermore, attributes (e.g. version number or creation date) cannot be represented directly. Rather, each attribute attached to an entity is typically represented by an own node carrying a single attribute. This results in a very fine-grained representation and graph rewrite rules with large left-hand and right-hand sides. Finally, basic syntax graph operations such as expanding placeholders, changing lexical units, or deleting subtrees do not match closely the commands to be offered by management tools.

For these reasons, we decided to specify management tools much more directly with the help of *genuine graph structures*. This approach is in line with the PROGRES environment (see next section) which deals with general graphs rather than with abstract syntax graphs. In this way, the structures, constraints, and operations of management graphs can be modeled more naturally.

Following this general remark, we briefly discuss in a slightly more detailed manner important *features* of *PROGRES* and examples of their *application* to management of products, processes, and resources (fig. 3.45):

(a) In the specification of the management model, the *schema* is used to define the static structure of version, configuration, and document group graphs. The schema also includes graphical constraints from which consistency-preserving graph rewrite rules may be derived in a systematic way.

(b) Furthermore, we use the *stratified type system* to distinguish between generic model (level of classes) and specific model (level of types). Thus, the management model is adapted to a specific application domain with the help of the stratified type system.

(c) *Derived attributes* and *relations* are used for specifying efficient generation of derived objects (object code derivation for Modula-2 programs in our running example to be introduced below).

(d) We use *graph rewrite rules* for graph transformations which need not be decomposed any further (e.g. creation of a history relation between two versions).

(e) *Control structures* and *transactions* are used to specify composite graph transformations. For example, a transaction which deletes a version and reorganizes the evolution history (by connecting all predecessors to all successors) is included in the specification of the product management model.

(f) Last but not least, PROGRES deals with *non-determinism* which is inherent in the notion of graph rewrite rules. Although we have not yet used this feature in the specification of the management model, it may be applied e.g. to construct a configuration based on (non-deterministic) selection rules (as has already been demonstrated in section 3.1 for variant selections in software architectures).

features of PROGRES	application to product, process, and resource management
graph schema	structure of version, configuration, and document group graphs
stratified type system	separation between generic and specific model
derived attributes and relations	object code generation
graph rewrite rules	atomic graph transformations (e.g. create history relation)
transactions, control structures	complex graph transformations (e.g. delete version and reorganize history)
non-determinism, backtracking	construction of a configuration based on selection rules

Fig. 3.45. Application of PROGRES to product, process, and resource management

3.5.2 Product Management

To illustrate the graph rewriting system for product management, we use a similar scenario as in section 2.5. Again, we refer to the development and maintenance of a *multi-pass compiler*. However, we constrain the scenario to the working area programming-in-the-small, i.e. coding modules of the compiler. We assume that the multi-pass compiler is written in *Modula-2*. Below, the term "module" is used according to the Modula-2 language definition. It denotes a compilation unit and therefore differs from the notion of module as used in programming-in-the-large (e.g. data type or function modules).

Fig. 3.46 shows an *ER-like diagram* which describes the structure of Modula-2 programs: Document groups of type Program contain modules of various types. Each program contains exactly one ProgramModule acting as main program, but it may contain many DefinitionModule and ImplementationModule instances. A module interface is specified in a DefinitionModule and realized in the corresponding ImplementationModule (there exists a one-to-one correspondence between both types of modules). A DefinitionModule exports resources (e.g. types or procedures) which may be imported by an arbitrary number of modules of any type.

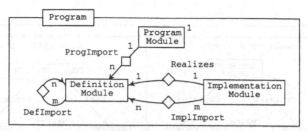

Fig. 3.46. ER-like diagram for Modula-2 programs

An example of a *configuration graph* for the multi-pass compiler is given in fig. 3.47 (using the informal notation of section 2.5). Control plays the role of the main program which sequentially invokes the passes LexAna, SynAna, SemAna, Optimize, and CodeGen (lexical, syntactical, static semantic analysis, optimization, and code generation, respectively). The TextFile submitted to the compiler is transformed step by step (-> TokenSeq -> ParseTree -> GraphCode ->) into a BinFile. Both TextFile and BinFile are realized using a general-purpose module File.

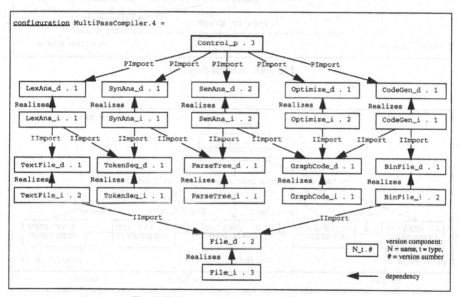

Fig. 3.47. Example of a configuration graph

Fig. 3.48 displays a *schema diagram* for the product management model. Boxes, dashed and solid arrows denote node classes, inheritance relations, and edge types, respectively. Relations which were represented as arrows in the screen dumps of section 2.5 are modeled as nodes and adjacent edges. A history relation is modeled as a HISTORY node with Predecessor and Successor edges. Similarly, a dependency relation is modeled as a VERSION_DEPENDENCY (or OBJECT_DEPENDENCY) node and Master and Dependent edges. This solution allows for attaching attributes to relations, and establishing relations between relations. In general, relations can be modeled either directly as edges, or they have to be simulated by nodes and connecting edges.

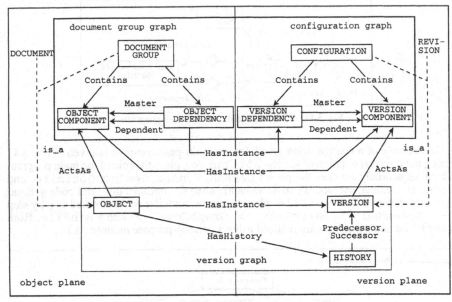

Fig. 3.48. Schema diagram

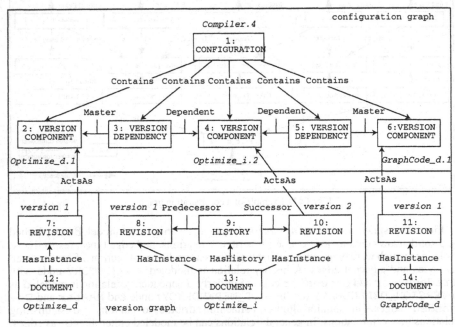

Fig. 3.49. Cutout of a schema-compatible graph

Each subgraph of the *product management graph* (which contains all information about products on the administrative level) is represented by a root node which is connected to all nodes belonging to this subgraph (a configuration graph is for instance represented by a CONFIGURATION node which is connected to VERSION_COMPONENT and VERSION_DEPENDENCY nodes by Contains edges). The graph model is constructed such that subgraphs are mutually disjoint. This leads to a clear separation of concerns. All applied occurrences of objects and versions (in document groups and configurations, respectively) are modeled as nodes to which context-specific information may be attached (represented either by node attributes or by incoming/outgoing relations). For example, object code generated by a compiler does not only depend on the source code of the corresponding module version, but it also depends on the context of this version in a configuration. In particular, compilation of a module version may succeed in one configuration and may fail in another one (see subsection 3.5.5).

Fig. 3.49 displays a cutout of a *schema-compatible graph*. The example refers to the multi-pass compiler which was introduced above. The upper half of the figure shows a cutout of a configuration graph for configuration 4 of the Compiler. Among others, the configuration contains version components Optimize_d.1, Optimize_i.2 (the definition and implementation module for the optimization pass, respectively), and GraphCode_d.1 (definition module for the intermediate code representation). These three components are connected by two dependencies: Optimize_i.2 realizes Optimize_d.1, and it imports GraphCode_d.1. The lower half of the figure illustrates cutouts of three version graphs. In the version graph for Optimize_i, versions 1 and 2 are connected by a history relation. Elements of version graphs and the configuration graph are linked by ActsAs edges. Since configurations are connected to component versions via a level of indirection, context-dependent information such as e.g. compiled code may be attached to VERSION_COMPONENT nodes.

```
section VersionGraphs

    node class OBJECT
        intrinsic
            key Name : string;
            NextVersionNo : integer := 1;
    end;

    edge type HasInstance : OBJECT [1:1] -> VERSION [0:n];

    node class VERSION
        intrinsic
            VersionNo : integer;
            Stable : boolean := false;
            CreationDate : string := CurrentDate;
            LastModificationDate : string := CurrentDate;
    end;

    edge type HasHistory : OBJECT [1:1] -> HISTORY [0:n];

    node class HISTORY end;

    edge type Predecessor : HISTORY [0:n] -> VERSION [1:1];

    edge type Successor : HISTORY [0:n] -> VERSION [1:1];

    path HasSuccessor : VERSION [0:n] -> VERSION [0:n] =
        <-Predecessor- & -Successor->
    end;

end;
```

Fig. 3.50. Textual schema for version graphs

Fig. 3.50 shows a part of the *textual schema* (in PROGRES) which refines the overview diagram displayed in fig. 3.48 by definitions of attributes and cardinalities. Each OBJECT node carries an intrinsic Name attribute which serves as a unique key. NextVersionNo denotes the number of the next version to be created. Edge type HasInstance connects OBJECT to VERSION nodes. Each object may have any number of versions; conversely, each version is attached to exactly one object (lower and upper bounds of cardinalities are enclosed in square brackets). A VERSION node carries a number which identifies it uniquely among all versions of one object, a Stable attribute indicating whether the version is frozen or may be modified, and two date attributes (CreationDate and LastModificationDate). History relations are represented by HISTORY nodes and Predecessor/Successor edges, and they are connected to OBJECT nodes by incoming HasHistory edges. Finally, the path HasSuccessor connects a version to its successor by traversing incoming Predecessor and then outgoing Successor edges. Thus, path declarations allow for abstraction from the representation of relations as nodes and adjacent edges (paths for dependencies and composition relations are defined similarly).

So far, the graph schema is not powerful enough to express all kinds of consistency constraints. In fig. 3.50, node classes and attributes are defined; furthermore, for each edge type source and target class as well as cardinalities are specified. Further *structural constraints* are listed in fig. 3.51. These constraints are more complicated, e.g. cyclic dependency relations are prohibited. They cannot be checked locally. Rather, a non-trivial subgraph of the product management graph has to be considered, e.g. all components which are transitively reachable by dependency relations.

1 Objects must be named in a unique way.

2 Versions of one object have to be uniquely numbered.

3 An object must not act more than once as a component in the same document group.

4 History and dependency relations must be local, i.e. source and target must belong to the same subgraph.

5 A version which has a successor must be stable.

6 All components of a stable configuration must be stable, as well.

7 Cycles in history, dependency, and composition relations are not allowed.

8 Each version component (dependency) has to be mapped 'monomorphically' to the corresponding object component (dependency).

9 For each pair of versions (components), there must exist at most one connecting history (dependency) relation.

Fig. 3.51. Consistency constraints

Structural constraints are *formalized* in the following way (fig. 3.52.a): In the declaration of class NODE (the root of the class hierarchy, which has been omitted in previous figures for the sake of simplicity), a derived attribute Constraint is introduced. Defining expressions for this attribute are given in subclasses of NODE. In this way, each node class defines the constraints in which it is involved. These constraints extend the graph schema introduced so far. All nodes with Constraint=false are considered erroneous.

As an example, fig. 3.52 specifies the *constraints* which have to hold for *history relations*. The defining expression for the attribute Constraint in the class HISTORY refers to a restriction, i.e. a derived node set which may be specified either textually or graphically:
(a) The *graphical restriction* HistoryRestriction in fig. 3.52.b states that a node of class HISTORY (node '3) has to belong to a certain graph pattern. In particular, the restriction checks constraints 4, 5, 7, and 9 of fig. 3.51. Node '4 is used to express a negative application condition, i.e. the restriction is only met if no match for this node can be found.

(b) An equivalent *textual restriction* is given below the graphical restriction (fig. 3.52.c). This notation may be preferred by users who are familiar with predicate logic. Note that the textual restriction closely corresponds to the meaning which is attached to the graphical restriction by the semantics definition of section 3.2.

```
node class NODE;
    derived Constraint : boolean;                                          a)
end;

node class HISTORY is a NODE;
    redef derived Constraint = self is HistoryRestriction;
end;
```

```
restriction HistoryRestriction : HISTORY = '3 in                            b)
```

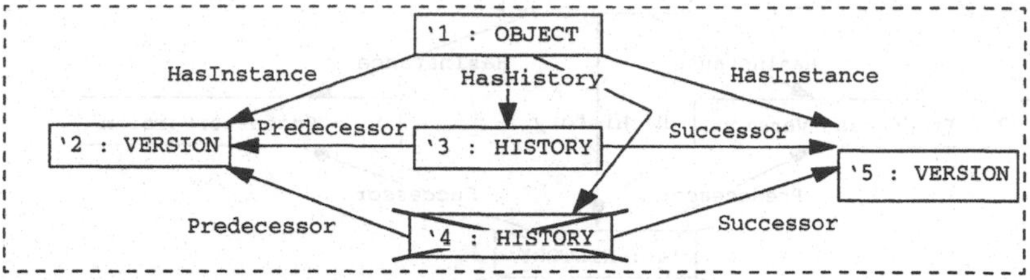

```
    condition '2.Stable; '2.VersionNo < '5.VersionNo;
end;
```

```
restriction HistoryRestriction : HISTORY =
    exist v1 : VERSION := self.-Predecessor->,
          v2 : VERSION := self.-Successor->,
           o : OBJECT := self.<-HasHistory- :                                c)
    (v1 in o.-HasInstance->) and (v2 in o.-HasInstance->) and
    (v1.Stable) and (v1.VersionNo < v2.VersionNo) and
    (not (exist h : HISTORY := o.-HasHistory-> :
            (h.-Predecessor-> = v1) and (h.-Successor-> = v2) and (h # self)
            end))
    end
end;
```

Fig. 3.52. Specification of consistency constraints: example HistoryRestriction, alternatively in graphical form and textual form

Let us briefly explain how the graphical restriction *checks* some (namely the relevant) of the *consistency constraints* listed in fig. 3.51:
(a) Each history relation is local because source '2 and target '5 belong to the same version graph of object '1 (constraint 4).
(b) Version '2, which has a successor ('5), must be stable as to be seen from the condition part (constraint 5).
(c) Cycles in history relations are excluded because version '5 must have a greater version number than version '2, see again condition part (constraint 7).
(d) Duplicate history relations are excluded by the negative application condition (there is no node with the properties of node '4; constraint 9).

During development of the specification, constraint definitions may be used in two ways:
(a) *Construction.* As we are going to demonstrate below, graphical restrictions provide valuable assistance in constructing constraint-preserving graph rewrite rules.
(b) *Testing.* In order to debug a specification, the Constraint attributes are evaluated to detect erroneous nodes.

In the sequel, we discuss the specification of *graph transformations* and *queries*. All operations are checked for consistency with the schema at specification time. However, some constraints cannot be checked statically. In particular, this applies to all structural constraints listed in fig. 3.51.

342

In the following, we give two examples of graph rewrite rules. The first one describes an insertion, the second one a deletion. In addition to showing the expressiveness of PRO-GRES, we also intend to demonstrate the *systematic construction* of *consistency-preserving rules*. In many cases, it is a straightforward task to derive a graph rewrite rule from the relevant constraints stated in the schema.

```
production CreateHistory
    ( PredecessorVersion, SuccessorVersion : VERSION ;
      Type : type in HISTORY ;
      out NewHistory : Type ) =
```

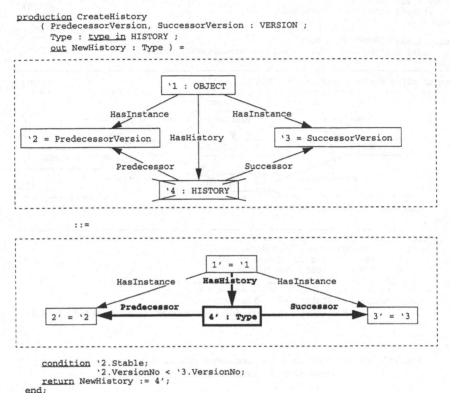

```
    condition '2.Stable;
             '2.VersionNo < '3.VersionNo;
    return NewHistory := 4';
end;
```

Fig. 3.53. Graph rewrite rule for creating a history relation

Let us first consider an *insertion rule*. Most (but not all) primitive insert operations create a single node and some adjacent edges. For each node class, a graphical restriction (see fig. 3.52 for an example) defines the constraints which have to hold for its instances. The following heuristic usually yields a consistency-preserving insertion rule:
(a) The header is constructed as follows: Supply the type of the node to be created as input parameter and its identifier as output parameter (each node has a unique identifier). Furthermore, supply (the identifier of) each context node occurring in the restriction as input parameter, provided that it cannot be determined uniquely from other nodes of the left-hand side. Finally, add an input parameter for each uninitialized intrinsic attribute.
(b) To obtain the left-hand side, remove the node to be created from the restriction graph, i.e. the graphical form of the restriction.
(c) To obtain the right-hand side, remove all positive and negative application conditions from the restriction graph and take the input type as type of the new node.
(d) The condition part is copied from the condition part of the restriction.
(e) Assign the values of intrinsic attributes in the transfer part.
(f) Assign the identifier of the new node to the output parameter in the return part.

The reader may easily verify that application of this *heuristic* to the graphical restriction of fig. 3.52 yields the rewrite rule for creating a history relation which is shown in fig. 3.53.

Fig. 3.54 displays another example of a graph rewrite rule which demonstrates the use of *set nodes* (dashed double rectangles). Provided there is no applied occurrence, DeleteVersion deletes a version, all incoming and outgoing history relations, and the contents of the corresponding configuration graph (if any) in a single rewrite step. To achieve this, set nodes are used which are mapped onto maximal sets of nodes in the host graph.

Let us describe this rule in greater detail:
(a) The <u>not</u> restriction is met if no outgoing ActsAs edge exists. This ensures that there is no configuration which contains the version to be deleted. In general, we do not allow deletion of declarations for objects which are still in use (this constraint has to hold in addition to the constraints listed in fig. 3.51).
(b) When a version is deleted from the version graph, all incoming and outgoing history relations have to be deleted, as well (set nodes '1 and '3, respectively). This could also be handled more restrictively, e.g. by prohibiting deletion of versions with successors.
(c) If the version to be deleted represents a configuration, this configuration may contain components and dependencies. These are deleted, as well. Note that nodes '4 and '5 cannot be connected directly to node '2 via Contains edges because this would cause a type error (Contains edges emanate from CONFIGURATION nodes and not from VERSION nodes in general). Therefore, a path is needed whose first element checks whether the source node actually belongs to class CONFIGU-RATION (the <u>instance of</u> clauses in the path expressions beside the double arrows act as filters).

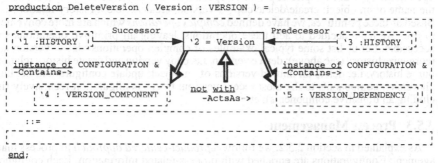

Fig. 3.54. Graph rewrite rule for deleting a version

The rule presented above serves as an example for a *deletion rule*. In general, a graph rewrite rule for deleting a node has to take its context into account. The following heuristic guides the construction of a graph rewrite rule for deleting a node n of class C (and in particular results in the graph rewrite rule presented above):
(a) Insert the node into the left-hand side.
(b) Determine all context nodes which may be affected by a deletion. In contrast to the rule shown above, it is in general not sufficient to take the 1-context into account. Rather, transitively affected nodes may have to be considered, as well.
(c) For each type of context node, decide whether its existence prohibits deletion of node n. If the answer is 'yes', add a negative application condition to the left-hand side. If the answer is 'no', then insert a single or set node (depending on the cardinality of the set of context nodes) into the left-hand side.
(d) Leave the right-hand side empty.

For specifying *complex graph transformations*, PROGRES provides control structures for the composition of graph rewrite rules. As an example for a complex graph transformation, fig. 3.55 shows a transaction which makes use of the graph rewrite rules presented in fig. 3.53 and fig. 3.54. The sample transaction deletes a version and reorganizes the evolution history by connecting all predecessors to all successors. The first statement asserts that there is no applied occurrence of the version to be deleted. If this assertion is violated, the sequence fails and leaves the host graph unaffected. The next statement consists of a loop iterating over all predecessors and successors of the current version. Each pair is connected by a history relation. Finally, the current version is deleted.

```
transaction DeleteVersionAndReorganizeHistory
   ( Version : VERSION ; Type : type in HISTORY )
=
   not ( Version is with -ActsAs-> )
   &
   for all PredecessorVersion : VERSION := elem ( Version.HasPredecessor );
           SuccessorVersion : VERSION := elem ( Version.HasSuccessor )
   do
        use NewHistory : HISTORY
      do
         CreateHistory
            ( PredecessorVersion, SuccessorVersion, Type, out NewHistory )
      end
   end
   & DeleteVersion ( Version )
end;
```

Fig. 3.55. Transaction for a complex operation

It is beyond the scope of this paper to give a complete description of product management operations. Typical examples of *primitive operations* are: create/delete an object; change the name of an object; create/delete/copy a version; create/delete a history relation; etc. Based on these primitives, we have defined *complex operations* which are more convenient to use. We have decided to add these operations, leaving all primitive operations still accessible. Let us list some typical examples of complex operations: delete version and reorganize history (see above); derive version, i.e. copy version and create history relation; purge history, i.e. delete all unused versions of an object; update configuration, i.e. bind all version components to the most recent version; freeze configuration recursively (including all transitive components); etc.

3.5.3 Process Management

As explained in section 2.5.2, we follow a *product-centered approach* to process management: Configurations are enriched with process-related information. Each configuration is interpreted as a process net, where components and dependencies correspond to processes and data flows, respectively. As a consequence, the specification for process management is based on the product management specification. The product management schema is extended with new node classes and edge types. The node classes for process management are subclasses of the node classes for product management. Product management operations can either be reused directly, or they must be redefined slightly to take process information into account. Furthermore, new process management operations are added, in particular operations corresponding to state transitions of processes. To sum up, process management *inherits* from product management. However, note that PROGRES does not yet support inheritance on graph level (only on node level). Therefore, inheritance has been simulated by extending the original specification for product management with new sections for process management. Below, we sketch how this simulation is performed.

A cutout of the *textual schema* for process management is given in fig. 3.56 In particular, the following elements are declared in the schema:

```
node class PROCESS is a VERSION_COMPONENT
    intrinsic
        ProcessState : State := Created;
        ReleaseSet : type in PROCESS [0:n];
end;

node class ACTOR end;

edge type ResponsibleFor : ACTOR [0:1] -> PROCESS [0:n];

node class DATA_FLOW is a VERSION_DEPENDENCY
    intrinsic
        Propagate : boolean := true;
        NeededForActivation : boolean := true;
end;

edge type RefersTo : DATA_FLOW [0:n] -> VERSION [0:1];

path ProducedBy : VERSION [0:1] -> PROCESS [0:n] =
    -ActsAs-> & (self : PROCESS)
end;

path Source : DATA_FLOW [0:n] -> PROCESS [0:1] =
    -Master-> & instance of PROCESS
end;

path Target : DATA_FLOW [0:n] -> PROCESS [0:1] =
    -Dependent-> & instance of PROCESS
end;
```

Fig. 3.56. Textual schema for process management

(a) PROCESS is a subclass of VERSION_COMPONENT. Attribute ProcessState represents the state of a process according to the state transition diagram given in section 2.5.2. ReleaseSet contains all the types of processes to which the result of the current process has been released so far (note the use of node types as ordinary attribute values; more about this topic in subsection 3.5.5). Recall that the release set is used to support simultaneous engineering.

(b) Node class ACTOR and edge type ResponsibleFor are introduced in order to take resource management into account. Although the process management model does not rely on specific assumptions with respect to the resource management model, it does assume that each process must be executed by some sort of actor. The node class ACTOR is used to represent general actors, and the edge type ResponsibleFor is used to relate actors and processes. In this way, the availability of resources can already be checked by certain process management operations (e.g. starting a process) without making a commitment to a specific resource management model.

(c) Node class DATA_FLOW inherits from VERSION_DEPENDENCY. Attribute Propagate controls whether propagation of data is enabled along the data flow. Similarly, attribute NeededForActivation states whether the source of the data flow must be available in order to start the process denoted by its target. Both attributes are needed for simultaneous engineering. Finally, edge type RefersTo relates the data flow to the last version which has been consumed via this flow.

(d) Finally, there are some path declarations which are used frequently in the following. All of these path declarations traverse a single edge and then check the class of the node reached by the traversal. ProducedBy relates a version to the process which produced it. Similarly, Source and Target relate a data flow to its source (corresponding to the master process) and its target (corresponding to the dependent process), respectively. Note that direct use of edge types results in type errors in the specification of the graph rewrite rules to be described below.

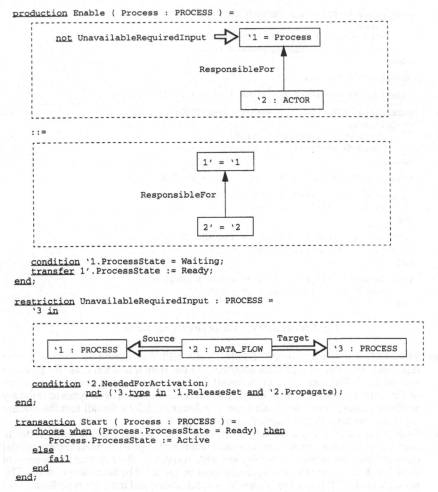

```
production Enable ( Process : PROCESS ) =
```

```
    not UnavailableRequiredInput  ⇒   '1 = Process

                                 ResponsibleFor

                                      '2 : ACTOR
```

```
::=
```

```
                            1' = '1

                         ResponsibleFor

                            2' = '2
```

```
    condition '1.ProcessState = Waiting;
    transfer 1'.ProcessState := Ready;
end;
```

```
restriction UnavailableRequiredInput : PROCESS =
    '3 in
```

```
    '1 : PROCESS  ⟵─Source─  '2 : DATA_FLOW  ─Target─⟶  '3 : PROCESS
```

```
    condition '2.NeededForActivation;
              not ('3.type in '1.ReleaseSet and '2.Propagate);
end;
```

```
transaction Start ( Process : PROCESS ) =
    choose when (Process.ProcessState = Ready) then
        Process.ProcessState := Active
    else
        fail
    end
end;
```

Fig. 3.57. Some operations for state transitions

As in the product management specification, we distinguish between basic operations and complex operations. The layer of *basic operations* comprises all operations which perform state transitions. Some of these operations for process management are specified in fig. 3.57. Note that each operation only changes the state of a single process without considering potential side effects on neighbor processes. This is left to the layer of complex operations which will be explained at the end of this subsection.

Let us now describe the operations specified in fig. 3.57:

(a) Enable performs a transition from Waiting to Ready. To this end, an actor must have been assigned to the process, i.e. node '2 serves as an application condition. Furthermore, all required inputs must actually be available. The restriction UnavailableRequiredInput is fulfilled if there is an input with the following properties (see condition part of the restriction): Firstly, the input is needed for activation. Secondly, propagation is either disabled along the corresponding data flow, or the master process has not yet released its result to the dependent process.

(b) After these preparations, `Start` only has to change the process state (all conditions have already been checked in the `Enable` transition). This simple modification is performed in a transaction which first checks the current state (<u>when</u> condition) and then changes the value of the state attribute (or <u>fails</u> if the condition is violated).

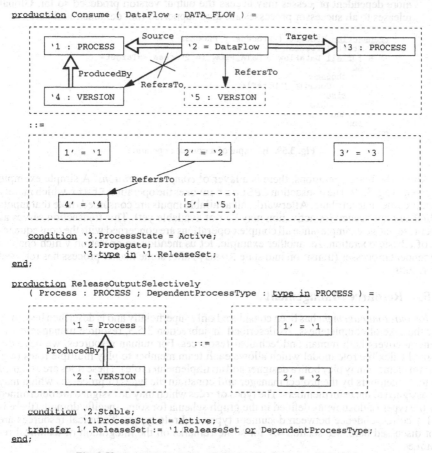

```
production Consume ( DataFlow : DATA_FLOW ) =
```

```
                      Source                    Target
    '1 : PROCESS ◄─────────── '2 = DataFlow ═══════════► '3 : PROCESS

         ▲                          │
  ProducedBy                        │ RefersTo
         │         ╳                ▼
    '4 : VERSION     RefersTo,┄┄┄┄┄┄┄┄┄┄┄┄┄┄
                              │ '5 : VERSION │
```

```
::=
```

```
    1' = '1              2' = '2              3' = '3

                  RefersTo
                 ◄─────────

    4' = '4              5' = '5
```

```
condition '3.ProcessState = Active;
          '2.Propagate;
          '3.type in '1.ReleaseSet;
end;
```

```
production ReleaseOutputSelectively
      ( Process : PROCESS ; DependentProcessType : type in PROCESS ) =
```

```
      '1 = Process                      1' = '1

    ProducedBy              ::=
         │
      '2 : VERSION                      2' = '2
```

```
condition '2.Stable;
          '1.ProcessState = Active;
transfer 1'.ReleaseSet := '1.ReleaseSet or DependentProcessType;
end;
```

Fig. 3.58. Some graph rewrite rules for simultaneous engineering

Fig. 3.58 lists two more graph rewrite rules which are used to formalize *simultaneous engineering*. Recall that consumption of inputs and production of outputs are decoupled from process start and termination to allow for simultaneous execution of master and dependent processes (i.e. processes which are connected by data flows):
(a) `Consume` is used to consume an input along some incoming data flow. By consuming a version of an input document, this version is added to the work context of the current process and can therefore be used by the actor of this process. Consumption may take place only when the process is active. Furthermore, the corresponding master process must have produced some version, and it must have released this version to the dependent process. Additionally, propagation must be enabled along the data flow, and the produced version must not have been consumed yet. If an old version has been consumed previously, the reference to the old version is deleted as the new version is consumed.

(b) As `Consume, ReleaseOutputSelectively` may only be applied to an active process. This graph rewrite rule changes the value of the `ReleaseSet` attribute by inserting an element into the set. As a consequence, dependent processes of the newly inserted type may consume the output of the current process. This means that more dependent processes may access the output version produced so far. Global releases to all successor processes are also supported (not demonstrated here).

```
transaction CPStart ( Process : PROCESS ) =
    Start ( Process )
    & for all DataFlow : DATA_FLOW := Process.<=Target=
    do
        choose
            Consume ( DataFlow )
        else
            skip
        end
    end
end;
```

Fig. 3.59. Example of a complex operation

Above the basic operations, there is a layer of *complex operations*. A simple example is given in fig. 3.59. The transaction `CPStart` invokes the operation `Start` which merely modifies the state attribute. Afterwards, all available inputs are consumed (note that inputs which are not needed for activation may be not available yet). This transaction serves as a representative example since all complex operations are concerned with the consequences of a basic operation. As another example, let us mention an operation which enables dependent processes (transition into state `Ready`) after some master process has released its results.

3.5.4 Resource Management

Resource management has been considered only superficially and is described here only for the sake of completeness. As described in subsection 2.5.3, resource management in general covers both human and technical resources. For human resources, we have designed a flexible role model which allows each team member to play multiple roles (e.g. a team member may play both a designer and an implementer role). These roles are assigned to team members by the project manager and constrain the types of processes which may be assigned to the team members. The types of roles which may be assigned are determined by the types of documents defined in the graph schema for some specific domain (there is a 1:1 correspondence between document types and role types). Technical resources are not discussed here; see section 4.7 for some remarks on the integration of technical resources.

The resource management specification is built on top of the process management specification. While process management strongly depends on product management, there is only a *loose coupling* between resource management and process management (note that in the future process and product management will be separated cleanly, resulting in a loose coupling, as well). The resource management specification makes use of the `ACTOR` class (and the `ResponsibleFor` edge type) introduced in the process management specification (alternatively, these declarations could have been factored out into a common base layer). So far, resource management does not rely on specific assumptions with respect to process management. Essentially, it only assumes that processes are typed, and uses these types to check the legality of work assignments. In this way, the process model may be replaced rather easily.

A cutout of the resource management *specification* is given in fig. 3.60. Node class `USER` is a subclass of `ACTOR` and defines attributes for the user name and the roles which may be played by the user. The first graph rewrite rule creates a user with a given set of roles. The second rule assigns a user to a process, provided that the role set allows for this assignment and the process resides in state Created or Suspended (work assignments are not allowed in other states). In case another user was responsible for the process, this responsibility is removed. So far, only assignment of one user is supported. Group work would require an extension of the model in order to organize cooperative work on the same process.

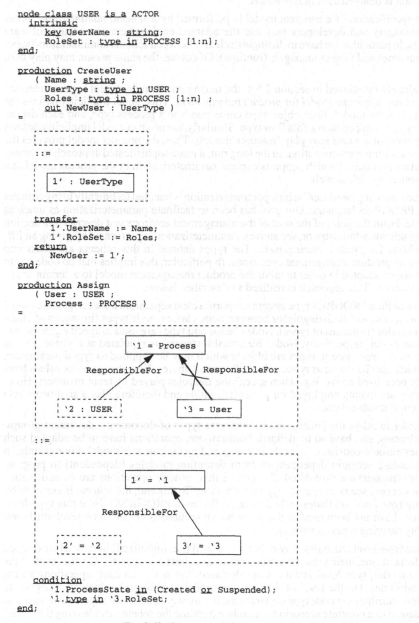

```
node class USER is a ACTOR
  intrinsic
    key UserName : string;
    RoleSet : type in PROCESS [1:n];
end;

production CreateUser
  ( Name : string ;
    UserType : type in USER ;
    Roles : type in PROCESS [1:n] ;
    out NewUser : UserType )
=

┌─────────────────────────────────┐
│                                 │
│                                 │
│ ::=                             │
│                                 │
│   ┌───────────────────┐         │
│   │ 1' : UserType     │         │
│   └───────────────────┘         │
└─────────────────────────────────┘

  transfer
    1'.UserName := Name;
    1'.RoleSet := Roles;
  return
    NewUser := 1';
end;

production Assign
  ( User : USER ;
    Process : PROCESS )
=

┌─────────────────────────────────────────────────┐
│                   ┌──────────────┐               │
│                   │ '1 = Process │               │
│                   └──────────────┘               │
│          ResponsibleFor      ResponsibleFor      │
│   ┌──────────────┐      ┌──────────────┐         │
│   │ '2 : USER    │      │ '3 = User    │         │
│   └──────────────┘      └──────────────┘         │
└─────────────────────────────────────────────────┘

┌─────────────────────────────────────────────────┐
│ ::=                                              │
│                   ┌──────────────┐               │
│                   │   1' = '1    │               │
│                   └──────────────┘               │
│                  ResponsibleFor                  │
│   ┌──────────────┐      ┌──────────────┐         │
│   │  2' = '2     │      │  3' = '3     │         │
│   └──────────────┘      └──────────────┘         │
└─────────────────────────────────────────────────┘

  condition
    '1.ProcessState in (Created or Suspended);
    '1.type in '3.RoleSet;
end;
```

Fig. 3.60. Resource management specification

3.5.5 Parameterization

So far, the specification has been independent of a specific application domain. The domain-independent part of the specification is called *generic model*. In the following, we discuss how the generic model is adapted to a specific domain. The result of such an adaptation is denoted as *concrete model*.

The specification of a concrete model is performed by a *schema administrator*. After that, managers and developers may use the adapted environment to execute software projects. In particular, we have to distinguish clearly between schema administrators (specification time) and project managers (runtime). Of course, the same person may play both roles.

As already mentioned in section 2.5.4, the management environment is parameterized by providing a *specific model* for *product management*. This model implicitly defines the specific process model: Each object type corresponds to a process type, and each dependency type is mapped onto a data flow type. Similarly, the product model implicitly defines the types of roles a user may play (resource model). Thus, the product model provides the only means for parameterization. In the long run, a more sophisticated approach to parameterization is required which supports explicit parameterization of the process model and the resource model, as well.

In the following, we describe how parameterization is handled technically using features of the PROGRES language. Our goal has been to facilitate parameterization as much as possible. From the point of the user of the management environment described in section 2.5 (the schema administrator, see above), parameterization is performed by giving an *ER-like schema* for *product management*. The types defined in this schema are taken into account by product management operations. In particular, this implies that no code has to be written or adapted in order to tailor the product management model to a certain application domain. This approach is realized as described below.

The stratified PROGRES type system supports a clear separation between generic model and concrete model.It distinguishes between node classes, node types (instances of classes), and nodes (instances of types). Node classes and types are used to specify generic and concrete model, respectively. Nodes are actual instances manipulated at runtime. Due to the stratified type system, types are objects which may be supplied as typed parameters, and which may be stored as typed values of node attributes. Note that types as values have already been used above, e.g. when specifying the roles played by team members. However, they are mainly employed for parameterization and therefore play a significant role in the current subsection.

In order to adapt the generic model, concrete types of documents, document groups, dependencies, etc. have to be defined. Furthermore, operations have to be adapted such that they enforce consistency constraints imposed by the concrete model. For example, in the Modula-2 scenario dependencies from definition modules (dependent) to program modules (master) are prohibited. To achieve this, generic operations are extended such that they access scenario-specific type information. To this end, the *schema* is *enriched* by defining *type-level attributes* (called meta attributes in PROGRES). Note that type-level attributes have not been used in the previous subsections (only instance-level attributes, possibly carrying types as values).

Since type-level attributes may only be assigned (i.e. initialized) in node class or node type declarations, their values are type- rather than instance-specific. On the level of the generic model, type-level attributes are declared, but not initialized; operations access these attributes. On the level of the concrete model, meaningful values are assigned to type-level attributes in node type declarations. In this way, product management *operations* are *adapted* to a concrete scenario by merely extending the schema and leaving the '*code*' of operations *unchanged* (see also section 3.3).

This approach is illustrated by the graph rewrite rule for *creating* a *version dependency* which is given in fig. 3.62 (to be explained later on). This rule checks the values of type-level attributes which are defined in fig. 3.61. These values are assigned according to the ER diagram of fig. 3.46.

In fig. 3.61, type-level attributes MasterType and DependentType are *type-valued attributes* which denote the type of master and dependent component, respectively. Boolean attributes MasterAtMostOnce and DependentAtMostOnce represent upper bounds of cardinalities; they are assigned <u>true</u> if a given component may play the master or dependent role at most once, respectively.

Fig. 3.61 also shows how these *type-level attributes* are *redefined* in case of import dependencies between program and definition modules. DependentType and MasterType are defined such that components representing program and definition modules may act as dependents and masters, respectively (the definition module acts as master because the contents of the program module depends on the contents of the imported definition module). DependentAtMostOnce is assigned <u>false</u> because a program module may import from multiple definition modules; conversely, each definition module may act as master at most once because each configuration contains at most one program module component.

```
node class VERSION_DEPENDENCY
   meta
      MasterType, DependentType : type in VERSION_COMPONENT;
      MasterAtMostOnce, DependentAtMostOnce : boolean;
end;
...
node type ProgModRevisionComponent : VERSION_COMPONENT
   ...
end;
node type DefModRevisionComponent : VERSION_COMPONENT
   ...
end;
...
node type ProgDefImportDependency : VERSION_DEPENDENCY
   redef meta
      MasterType := DefModRevisionComponent;
      DependentType := ProgModRevisionComponent;
      MasterAtMostOnce := true;
      DependentAtMostOnce := false;
end;
```

Fig. 3.61. Type-level attributes for specifying scenario-specific constraints

Fig. 3.62 presents the graph rewrite rule CreateVersionDependency which receives master and dependent component, and the dependency type as parameters. The rule has to *check* a lot of *constraints* enforced by the *generic model* (see fig. 3.51): master and dependent must belong to the same configuration, the configuration must be stable, a corresponding object dependency must exist, and there must not yet exist any dependency between master and dependent (the latter is ensured by the negative path condition between nodes ` 5 and ` 6). As in fig. 3.53, changes performed by the rule are emphasized in bold face.

Furthermore, all elements of the rule concerning *checks* of *scenario-specific constraints* are printed in italics. The dependency must be legal with respect to both master and dependent type (see condition part which accesses values of type-level attributes associated to dependency type Type), and no cardinality overflow must occur (see restrictions applying to nodes ` 5 and ` 6 of the left-hand side). MaxOutDegree (MaxInDegree) is a restriction which is fulfilled if a component already participates in a dependency of a given type with upper bound 1 (the cardinality is checked within the condition part of the restriction).

```
production CreateVersionDependency
    ( MasterComponent,
      DependentComponent : VERSION_COMPONENT ;
      VType : type in VERSION_DEPENDENCY ;
      out NewDependency : VType)
=
```

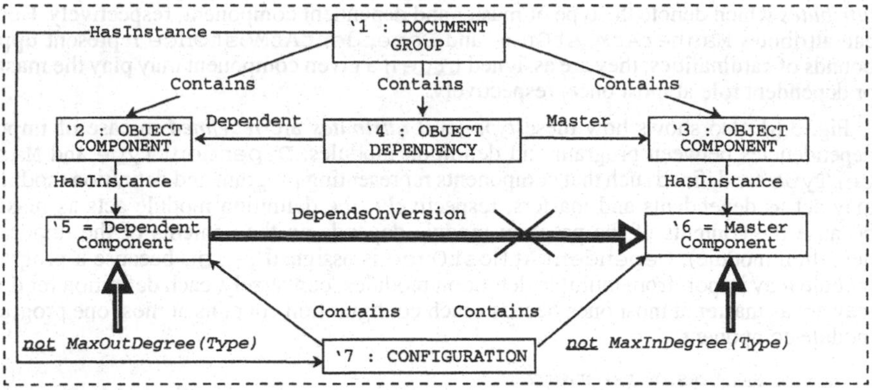

```
::=
```

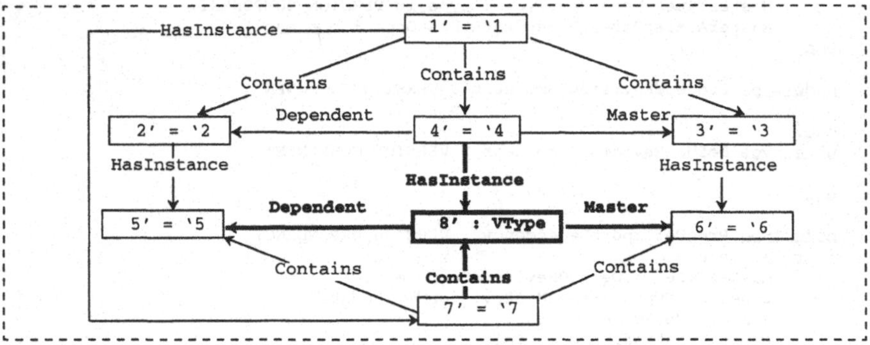

```
condition
    '5.type = Type.DependentType;
    '6.type = Type.MasterType;
    not '7.Stable;
transfer
    7'.LastModificationDate := CurrentDate;
return
    NewDependency := 8';
end;
```

```
restriction MaxOutDegree ( Type : type in VERSION_DEPENDENCY ) : VERSION_COMPONENT
= '1 in
```

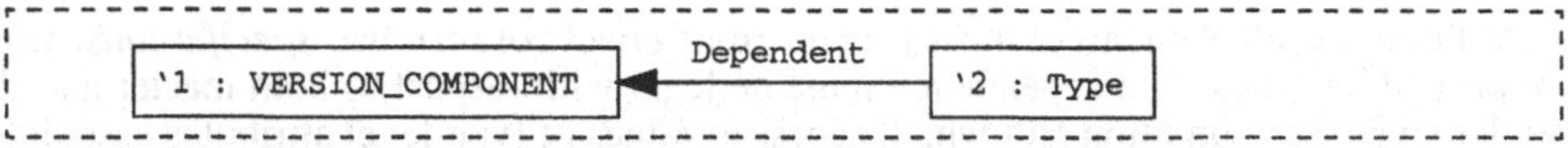

```
    condition Type.DependentAtMostOnce;
end;
```

Fig. 3.62. Graph rewrite rule for creating a version dependency.

To conclude this section, let us go into another feature of PROGRES which has a nice application in product management, namely *maintenance* of *derived information*. A significant portion of software version and configuration management research is devoted to system building. In large software systems, it is a rather complex task to build (the executable of) a system correctly, i.e. to trigger compile and link steps in the right order, with correct options, and with minimal effort.

In the sequel, we sketch how these tasks are supported by means of *derived attributes* (which have already been used to formalize structural constraints, see fig. 3.52). To maintain compiled code, derived attributes are used in the following way: The outputs of compilers and linkers are stored in derived attributes. Compilation and link steps are triggered by read accesses to these attributes. System building is controlled by the attribute evaluator which operates in an incremental and lazy fashion. As in Make /4. Fel 79/, only those modules whose object codes are out of date are recompiled in the correct order. The attribute evaluation rules are set up according to the compilation dependencies. During attribute evaluation, compilers and linkers are activated by calling external functions (i.e. functions which are not written in PROGRES, but may be used in a PROGRES specification through an import interface).

```
node class REVISION is a VERSION
    intrinsic
        SourceCode : File;
end;
...

node class PROGRAM_COMPONENT is a VERSION_COMPONENT
    intrinsic
        ObjectCode : File [0:1];
end;
...

node type ImplModComponent : PROGRAM_COMPONENT
    redef derived
        ...
        ObjectCode =
            [self.MastersCompiled and
            self.InterfaceCompiled and
            def (self.BoundTo.SourceCode)
            ::
            CompileImplMod
            (self.BoundTo.SourceCode,
             self.Realizes.ObjectCode,
             self.Import.ObjectCode)
            | nil ];
end;
...

transaction Make
    ( Component : PROGRAM_COMPONENT ; out CompiledComponent : File )
=
    CompiledComponent := Component.ObjectCode
end;
```

Fig. 3.63. Using derived attributes to specify compilations.

In the *Modula-2 scenario*, derived attributes are defined in the following way (fig. 3.63): To each module revision, its SourceCode is attached as an intrinsic attribute of type File. Object code attributes are attached to all component nodes contained in program configurations (class PROGRAM_COMPONENT). ObjectCode is declared as an optional attribute (cardinality enclosed in square brackets) because its evaluation will not always succeed. ObjectCode is a context-dependent attribute which in general varies across multiple configurations. Therefore, it cannot be attached to revisions. Rather, it has to be attached to component nodes which represent applied occurrences of revisions in configurations.

For implementation modules (node type `ImplModComponent`), a conditional expression denoted by [`expression1` | `expression2`] is given as *evaluation rule*. Since its second alternative `expression2` evaluates to <u>nil</u>, it will yield a defined value only if the first alternative `expression1` is selected. This alternative is a guarded expression of form `condition::expression` which is selected when the guard `condition` evaluates to <u>true</u> and then returns the value of its guarded body `expression`. The guard states that the source of the current component must exist, and that the corresponding definition module and all imported components must have been compiled successfully. In this case, the function `CompileImplMod` is called with three parameters, namely the source code, the object code of the corresponding definition module, and the set of object codes of all imported components. Within the body of this external function (not shown in the figure), the Modula-2 compiler is called. The function returns <u>nil</u> if compilation fails, and the compiled code otherwise.

After all, it is an easy task to simulate the functionality of the well-known *Make tool*. A call to the function `Make` (bottom of fig. 3.63) triggers all necessary compilations in the correct order with minimal effort - due to lazy evaluation of derived attributes - and delivers the requested object code, if possible. Linking may be handled in an analogous way (attach attribute `Executable` to program module components, define attribute evaluation rules, and provide a function `MakeExecutable`).

Fig. 3.64 presents an *example* which illustrates maintenance of compiled code by means of derived attributes. Dashed lines represent attribute dependencies. The `ObjectCode` attached to component `Optimize_i.2` (node 4) depends on the `SourceCode` of the revision (node 10) to which the component is bound (the path `BoundTo` traverses an `ActsAs` edge in negative direction). Furthermore, it depends on the `ObjectCode` attribute of the corresponding definition module component `Optimize_d.1` (node 2) and (among others) on the `ObjectCode` attribute of the imported component `GraphCode_d.1` (node 6). If the transaction `Make` is applied to `Optimize_i.2`, read access to its `ObjectCode` attribute will trigger all necessary recompilations in the correct order.

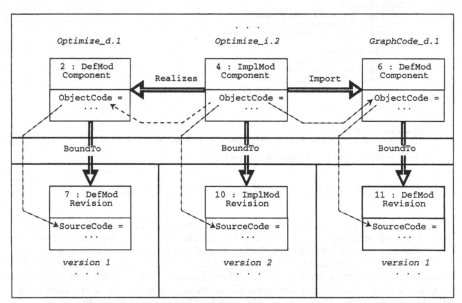

Fig. 3.64. Example for the use of derived attributes

3.5.6 Summary and Comparison

We have presented a programmed graph rewriting system for management of products, processes, and resources. The full specification covers about 50 pages PROGRES and has guided the implementation of the management environment described in section 2.5. We have shown how the rich language facilities for describing graph schemas (including consistency constraints and derived attributes) as well as graph transformations have helped us to *specify management* of products, processes, and resources on a *high level of abstraction*. To this end, we have decided not to rely on abstract syntax graphs. Rather, we use genuine graph structures which represent the concepts of product, process, and resource management more directly and naturally.

An analysis of *other management tools* and *environments* reveals that many of them *lack* a sound *formal foundation*. In the field of software configuration management, most approaches are based on file systems (e.g. Make /4. Fel 79/, RCS /4. Tic 85/, or DSEE /4. LCS 88/). Some are based on ER-like data models (e.g. PCTE /6. BMT 88/, which has a built-in version model for complex objects). Then, the formal description is limited to schema definition, but operations are not specified formally. In the field of software process management, some approaches do rely on a sound formal foundation, e.g. Petri nets /4. DG 90/. However, the formalism of Petri nets is only concerned with execution of static nets. In particular, Petri nets cannot be used to specify interleaving of editing and execution. On the other hand, both editing and execution can be described in a uniform way by graph rewrite rules.

3.6 Developing Tools with the PROGRES Environment

A. Schürr, A. Winter, A. Zündorf

The preceding sections of this chapter presented the language PROGRES, its underlying formalism, and its application for the specification of various types of IPSEN tools. It is now time to provide the reader with an overview on available tool support. For this purpose, we will use again the running example of section 3.1 to demonstrate the *functionality of various tools* for modifying, analyzing, and executing specifications.

Subsection 3.6.1 gives first a survey of the most important tools and their underlying main data structures. It shows that all these tools are connected with each other such that they form an *integrated specification environment*. Based on this survey the functionality of the PROGRES environment is compared with the functionality of other graph grammar environments we are aware of in subsection 3.6.2. The following three subsection present then available tools from a user's perspective. Subsection 3.6.3 deals with editing activities, subsection 3.6.4 with incremental analysis (type checking), and subsection 3.6.5 finally with all kinds of execution activities. Subsection 3.6.6 concludes the section and discusses presented highlights as well as major deficiencies which have to be tackled in the nearby future.

Finally, we have to emphasize that PROGRES tools form another instance of an integrated (meta) programming environment and are again implemented using *IPSEN graph technology*. They use the same basic components and have the same design as all other tools presented in chapter 2. For all details concerning the architecture and the realization process of the PROGRES environment the reader is, therefore, referred to chapter 4. For further details concerning *bootstrapping activities* the reader is referred to /5. Zün 96a/, which describes first attempts to specify a subset of the PROGRES environment with PROGRES itself and to generate a subset of the environment from the constructed specification.

3.6.1 Basic Components and their Interdependencies

Equipped with some knowledge about the language PROGRES, the reader probably can imagine the difficulties we had to face during the development of its integrated environment. It consists of the following *integrated set of tools* (with some of them being generic tools which are part of all IPSEN environments; cf. chapter 2):

(a) a mixed textual/graphical syntax-directed editor together with an incrementally working unparser and a layout editor for graph schemes, productions, etc.,

(b) an integrated (micro-)emacs like text editor together with an incrementally working LALR-parser,

(c) an incrementally working analyzer which detects all inconsistencies with respect to the PROGRES language's static semantics and explains highlighted errors,

(d) an import/export interface to plain text editors and text-processing systems (currently for FrameMaker from Adobe only),

(e) a browsing tool for finding declarations or applied occurrences of given identifiers, highlighting yet incomplete specification parts or unused declarations, and for displaying inferred type information,

(f) a browser which is an instantiation of the generic graph browser EDGE /4. New 91/ and displays graph schemes in an ER-like fashion,

(g) another instantiation of the generic graph browser EDGE which displays manipulated host graphs,

(h) a tcl/tk-based graph browser with simple view definition facilities for monitoring host graphs during an interpreter session,
(i) a hybrid interpreter/compiler which translates first a specification into intermediate code of an abstract graph rewriting machine and interprets the code afterwards,
(j) two compiler backends which translate the intermediate graph machine code into plain Modula-2 or C code,
(k) another backend which produces code fragments for the user interface toolkit tcl/tk /6. Ous 94/, and finally
(l) tools for version management and three-way merging of different versions of one specification document (cf. section 2.4).

The most important basic component of the PROGRES environment is the database system GRAS (cf. section 4.2). It supports efficient manipulation of persistent graph structures, incremental evaluation of derived graph properties, nested transactions, undo&redo of arbitrarily long sequences of already committed transactions, recovery from system crashes, and has various options of how to control access of multiple clients to their data structures. In this way, persistency of tool activities including undo&redo and recovery comes for free. Furthermore, integration of tools is facilitated by storing all data within a GRAS database as a set of related graphs.

The *editor* and *analyzer* are those tools of our environment that assist its users when creating and modifying specifications. Both tools are tightly coupled and they are even integrated with the interpreter tool. In this way, the tedious edit/compile/link/debug cycle is avoided and the environment's user is allowed to switch back and forth between editing, analyzing, and debugging activities. The editor itself is not a monolithic tool, but consists of a number of integrated subtools. These subtools support syntax-directed editing as well as text-oriented editing of specifications, pretty-printing, manual rearrangement of text and graphic elements as well as browsing and searching activities. PROGRES tools offer thereby about the same kind of support as the integrated set of tools for programming in Modula-2 of section 2.1 and the set of requirements engineering tools of section 2.2

Fig. 3.65 displays the major data structures of the environment and the transformation processes between them. Its right-hand side deals with compiling and executing specifications and is, therefore, specific for the PROGRES environment. Its left-hand side, on the otherhand, deals with editing and analyzing activities which are part of any integrated set of IPSEN tools, presented in section 2. It shows that specifications are stored in the form of two closely related documents which are internally realized as graphs (as already explained in section 1.5; cf. fig. 1.20). The *logical document* contains a specification's abstract syntax tree and all inferred type checking results. The accompanying *representation document* captures all concrete syntax information, including the chosen layout of (nested) text and graphic fragments.

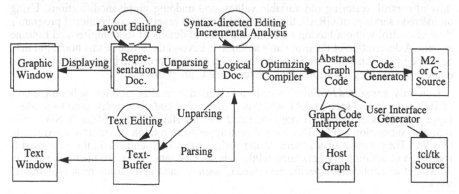

Fig. 3.65. Data Structures and Transformation Processes in the PROGRES Environment

An incrementally working *unparser* propagates updates of the logical document into its representation document. The unparser's counterpart is a *parser* which propagates changes in the reverse direction. It takes a line/column oriented text buffer and not a hierarchically structured representation document as input. Currently, "free" editing of graphical specification fragments with a micro-emacs like text editor is only supported via such a line/column oriented textual representation. For further details concerning these components the reader is referred to section 4.1 and 4.3. There she will find a more in-depth explanation of the left-hand side of fig. 3.65 and the realization of its components.

The right-hand side of fig. 3.65 reveals that there are two alternatives how to execute a given specification. The first one is based on *direct interpretation*. It is mainly used for debugging purposes, when intertwining of editing, analysis, and execution activities is advantageous. The second one is to *translate* a specification into equivalent Modula-2 or C code and to use the generated source code together with the graph DBMS GRAS as an abstract data type implementation in a larger program. In both cases, the execution process is divided into two phases:

(a) The initialization phase creates an empty host graph, processes all graph schema declarations and translates them into an internal format with a static attribute dependency graph as its main component.

(b) Afterwards, arbitrary productions or transactions may be executed step by step, and they may even be modified and recompiled if the PROGRES interpreter is used.

The diagram in fig. 3.65 shows that the editor and analyzer play the role of a conventional compiler's front-end and provide all information about a specification's underlying abstract syntax tree and its static semantics. An *incrementally working compiler* takes this information as input and translates executable increments (on demand) into intermediate code for an abstract graph rewriting machine. The compiler is the most important component of the whole execution machine and determines its efficiency to a great extent. This is especially true in the case of productions, where we have to choose between a large number of different intermediate code sequences. Any of these code sequences perform the required subgraph matching, but they may differ with respect to runtime efficiency considerably (for further details cf. /5. Zün 96a/).

The produced abstract graph code may be executed directly or serves as input for two compiler backends, which produce equivalent Modula-2 or C code. The underlying *abstract graph rewriting machine* combines the functionality of a conventional stack machine à la P-code with backtracking capabilities à la Warren Abstract Machine. Furthermore, its main component offers facilities for manipulating persistent graph structures stored in the database system GRAS.

The translation of abstract graph code into *readable Modula-2 or C source code* is rather straightforward with the exception of backtracking, which requires reversing a program's flow of control, restoring old variable values, and undoing graph modifications. Using undo&redo services of GRAS, the main problem is to reverse a conventional program's flow of control without having access to the internal details of its compiler and runtime system. A description of the problem's solution is beyond the scope of this book, but may be found in /5. Zün 96a/. It follows the lines of a proposal presented in /6. Liu 91/ how to embed backtracking constructs into conventional C programs.

Currently, *generated Modula-2 code* is mainly used for realizing certain subcomponents of IPSEN tools (cf. section 4.4), whereas *generated C code* is usually used to produce rapid prototypes of tools with graph-oriented user interfaces /5. SWZ 95a, 5. SWZ 95b/ (see also subsection 3.6.5). These rapid prototypes have a tcl/tk based user interface /6. Ous 94/. They consist of a generic framework, written in C and tcl/tk, the generated C sources, and additionally generated tcl/tk sources. The latter ones are mainly needed to glue together application specific generated C sources and the invariant prototype framework.

3.6.2 Related Work

All other graph grammar environments, we are aware of, offer only a subset of the above presented functionality of the PROGRES environment. The system *PAGG* (Programmed Attributed Graph Grammars) was as far as we know the first complete implementation of a programmed graph rewriting system. It supported graphical editing of graph rewrite rules and offered imperative control structures for programming activities. Graph rewrite rules and control structures were translated into Lisp code, but code for finding matches of left-hand sides of rules had to be added manually /5. Göt 87, 5. Göt 88, 5. GGN 90/. Nowadays, the compiler backend of the system is no longer available, but there are plans to realize a new backend which produces then C instead of Lisp code.

To the best of our knowledge, there is only one further graph grammar based system (except PROGRES and graph rewriting machines of functional programming languages) which is available as free software. This is the graph editing environment *GraphEd* developed at the University of Passau /4. Him 88/. It has its main focus on graph editing, graph layout, and classical graph-theoretic algorithms. But it offers also graph generation, parsing, and layout by means of context-free graph grammars. The specification of complex graph transformation algorithms or graph based tools is outside the scope of GraphEd. Therefore, PROGRES and GraphEd are more or less incomparable to each other.

Another system, developed at about same time at the University of Paderborn is called *PLEXUS* /4. Wan 91/. It is a kind of graph manipulation library plus a parser for a certain form of context-free graph grammars. The system is not an interactive programming environment in the sense of PROGRES or PAGG and, therefore, designed for rather different purposes.

A graph grammar compiler with a functionality similar to the C code generating backend of PROGRES was developed rather recently at the Free University of Berlin /5. Dör 95/. It uses the PROGRES editor and analyser as a front-end and the system GraphEd as a graph layout and browsing backend. The compiler translates a deterministic subset of PROGRES (left-hand sides of rules have to be trees with additional edges) into rather efficiently working C code. The system implementation is now finished, but was never released to external users.

Another system from the University of Erlangen, called *DiaGen*, follows also the compiler compiler approach /5. MV 95/. It takes a textual definition of a context-free hypergraph grammar plus additional layout constraints and graph transformation rules as input and produces a syntax-directed graphical editor for a specified visual language as output. Additional graph transformation rules are restricted to the manipulation of hypergraph derivation trees or may add further edges to a given hypergraph. Generated environments offer an incrementally working layout constraint solver. An incrementally working parser is under development.

The system *AGG* at the Technical University of Berlin presents another ongoing attempt to realize a graph grammar environment /5. LB 93/. It offers a rather sophisticated hierarchical graph data model, but its functionality is limited to hierarchical graph editing and basic category theory constructs (like pushout). It gives therefore currently no support for the specification of complex graph transformations or the (automatic) execution of graph rewrite rules.

Beside all these tools, which were developed more or less independently from certain application areas, there are some systems which were designed for rather specific purposes. There are systems like *GOOD* /6. GPT 93/ and *Spider* /4. RK 95/, which represent visual database query and manipulation tools, or *SESAM* /4. DM 95/, which supports the simulation of software engineering projects, or the graph rewriting machine described in /5. FB 93/, which was used to develop imagine recognition/pattern matching algorithms for mathematical expressions and music scores. All these systems were never used outside their original application areas and are not available for external users.

To summarize, not a single of the above mentioned tools or software packages supports the whole spectrum of "programming" activities ranging from syntax-directed editing, over analysis, to debugging and rapid prototyping of specified applications as PROGRES does. Furthermore, almost all of them employ a much more restrictive type of graph grammars, have no type concept and accompanying type checking rules, and do not support incremental evaluation of derived attributes and relationships or programming of back-tracking algorithms. But the presented comparison reveals also some deficiencies of our environment, which have to be resolved in the future. This is the lack of any *parsing algorithms* (for necessarily restricted subsets of graph grammars) as well as graph browsing and editing tools combined with *incrementally working graph layout algorithms*.

3.6.3 Building up and Maintaining Specifications

The *development process* of a new *specification* as presented at the end of section 3.1 starts with the design of a graph scheme. Afterwards, graph modifying operations are entered in the form of productions, transactions, etc. This order of processing has the advantage that any edited operation may immediately be checked for its correctness with respect to the language's static semantics rules. On the other hand, it might sometimes be advantageous to enter first (draft versions of) all kinds of operations and to develop then an appropriate graph scheme with more knowledge about needed node classes, attributes, and so forth. In this case, incremental static analysis is useless and should be deactivated until a first version of the graph scheme is completed. In many cases, the development process of a specification lies somewhere in between these two extremes. It starts with the creation of a basic graph scheme and proceeds then with the development of a core set of graph modifying operations. Later on, new scheme components and operations are added, analysed, and tested step by step.

Therefore, we will present a *guided tour* through the PROGRES environment that begins, when an initial version of the running example of section 3.1 is existent. We do assume that the graph schema of fig. 3.3 on page 253 for module interconnection language (MIL) graphs is created and that the basic operations for editing MIL graphs like the one in fig. 3.2 on page 251 were just entered. The following user actions are then:
- (a) Entering a simplified (erroneous) version of the production ResolveImport which was introduced in fig. 3.13 on page 270.
- (b) Adding a new node class for SUBSYSTEMS (for being able to model hierarchically structured software architectures) to the graph schema together with needed attribute evaluation rules, which resolve detected inheritance conflicts.
- (c) Defining another node class for SUBCONFIGURATIONS which are complex elements of CONFIGRATIONS as SUBSYSTEMS are complex elements of SYSTEMS.
- (d) This leads to an erroneous class hierarchy structure which is then changed appropriately by a suitable error repair command.
- (e) Afterwards, the modified specification is tested using the interpreter which results in the detection of the error in production ResolveImport.
- (f) Having removed the error by switching back and forth between editor and interpreter we will then generate code for the specification.
- (g) Finally, the generated code is compiled and linked together with the invariant part of an interactive diagram manipulating environment (for prototyping purposes).

Please note that the presentation of *syntax-directed editing* activities will be very brief and have a main focus on PROGRES specific commands. For further details concerning syntax-directed editing in general the reader is referred to chapter 2.

Our first announced editing step is to specify a variant of the production Resolve-Import of fig. 3.13. Its left-hand side matches any VARIANT node of a partially constructed configuration C which needs (imports) another module. This module should have a VARIANT with the required set of properties ReqProps which is not yet part of the constructed configuration. The first two screen dumps of fig. 3.66 display an intermediate state and the final result of entering the left-hand side of `ResolveImport`. The production's left-hand side in fig. 3.66.a has been created by activating first three times the command `OblNodeDecl` (the last one in the displayed list of executable commands). The command prompts the user for the position, the identifier (number), and the label of each node. It is not necessary to activate a node creating command like `OblNodeDecl` explicitly as long as the category of created nodes does not change (optional nodes or set nodes or negative nodes are the other categories). It is sufficient to select the desired node position with the right mouse button.

Node identifiers and their labels are usually entered using the built-in micro-emacs like text editor. Node identifiers are just single tokens such that the entered text must only be checked for its lexical correctness. The case is different for node labels. They are names of node types or classes preceded by a " : " or names of input parameters preceded by "=" or even more complex expressions. These expressions may either be entered by using a number of syntax-directed editing commands or by just typing in the whole text and forwarding it to the system's parser. Any user has his own *table of editing defaults* which determines for any nonterminal class wether it is usually entered using the syntax directed editing mode or whether the text editor is automatically activated for this purpose.

As soon as these three nodes are present, the `needs`-path or the `contains`-edge is created by (1) selecting its source node, (2) activating the appropriate command (`PathCond` or `EdgeDecl`), (3) selecting its target node, and (4) entering its label. *Shortcuts* are supported such that it is possible to create edges and paths without any needs to choose a command in the menu (by selecting the source node with the right mouse button, keeping the button pressed and draging the mouse pointer to the target node). The last previously selected edge or path creating command acts then as a kind of default.

The transition from fig. 3.66.a to fig. 3.66.b is the result of three further editing steps. They are initiated by activating for instance the commands `OblNodeDecl` (for node ` 2), `EdgeDecl` (for the `has`-edge from node ` 3 to node ` 2), and `NotEdgeDecl` (for the negative `contains`-edge from node ` 1 to node ` 2) in this order.

As soon as the left-hand side is complete, the command `CopyLeftToRight` adds a right-hand side to `ResolveImport` such that the production preserves the matched subgraph. All nodes and edges which are now added to or removed from the generated right-hand side will create or delete corresponding nodes and edges in the host graph at runtime. In our case, we have to add a further `contains`-edge from node ` 1 to node ` 2. Afterwards, the condition ` 2 . Props `are_in' ReqProps was entered as well as the left-hand side of the assignment for the out parameter `NewProps` in order to create the situation depicted in fig. 3.66.d. It shows a selected expression (with a bold text representation) and three possible syntax-directed extension command in the menu.

The two lower screen dumps of fig. 3.66 show the *graphical* as well as the *textual representation* of `ResolveImport` with a complete right-hand side. The displayed text representation gives the reader an impression of the format that is used for *free text editing* purposes with the built-in text editor. External text editors, like emacs, can be used to modify *exported ASCII files* of textual representations, where embedded comments contain essential graphical layout information about graph schemes as well as about left- and right-hand sides of productions or bodies of subgraph tests.

Modified text files may be re-imported by using a *multiple entry parser* (cf. section 4.4 for further details about the functionality of generated parsers in IPSEN). The parser compares first the modified text and the old specification document. It executes afterwards a more or less minimal sequence of syntax-directed editing commands to remove any differences between the new ASCII text file and the logical specification document. Additional layout editing commands are used to process (modified) layout comments of the text file if necessary. New ASCII text portions without embedded layout comments receive a default layout using appropriate text and graph layout algorithms (cf. section 2.4).

362

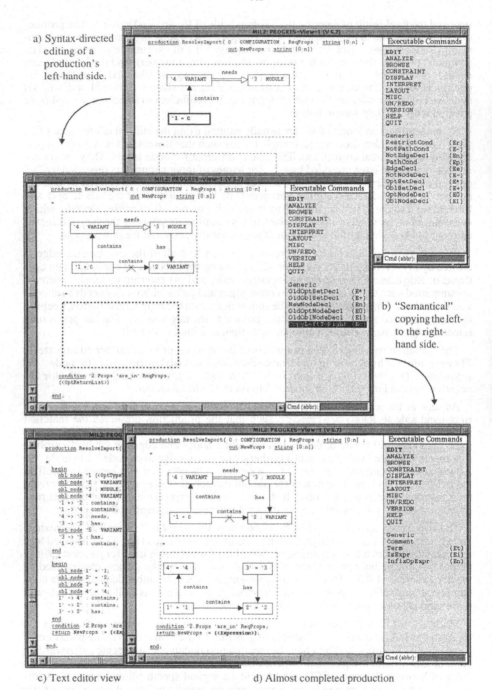

Fig. 3.66. Syntax-directed editing: entering a new production

3.6.4 Incremental Analysis and Error Repair

The PROGRES environment's analyser checks more than 400 *static semantics rule*s if activated (language constructs have about two consistency rules in the average case). Some of these rules are straightforward, some of them are rather complex. Simple rules for the production ResolveImport of fig. 3.66 are, for instance:
  (a) both in-parameters (C and ReqProps) are actually used,
  (b) the single out-parameter NewProps receives a value (a set of strings),
  (c) the identifier C of the node inscription '1 = C is a formal in-parameter with a node class or a node type as its type,
  (d) the labels contains and has are identifiers of edge type declarations,
  (e) CONFIGURATION nodes are legal sources and VARIANT nodes are legal targets of contains edges,

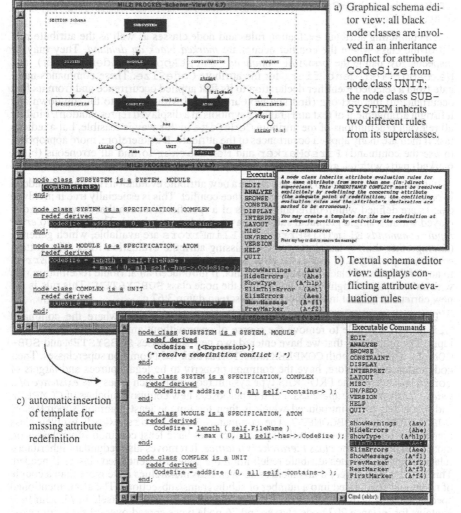

a) Graphical schema editor view: all black node classes are involved in an inheritance conflict for attribute CodeSize from node class UNIT; the node class SUB-SYSTEM inherits two different rules from its superclasses.

b) Textual schema editor view: displays conflicting attribute evaluation rules

c) automatic insertion of template for missing attribute redefinition

Fig. 3.67. Eliminating attribute redefinition conflicts

(f) MODULE nodes are legal sources and VARIANT nodes are legal targets of has edges,

(g) the label needs is the identifier of a path between VARIANT and MODULE nodes,

(h) MODULE nodes do have Props attributes and the infix operator 'are_in' takes two sets of strings as input and produces a Boolean value as output, and

(i) cardinality constraints allow for two contains edges which have the same source node.

The fig. 3.67 shows a first example of a more complex static semantics rule that deals with *attribute redefinition conflicts*. It involves one attribute declaration, a number of attribute redefinitions, and a class without any attribute redefinitions at all. The rule was violated by the introduction of the new node class SUBSYSTEM in the graphical schema view of fig. 3.67.a. This class inherits the attribute CodeSize from node class UNIT and two conflicting evaluation rules from its two direct superclasses SYSTEM and MODULE (which are the targets of dashed edges emanating from the new class node). These two superclasses replace both their inherited evaluation rules (from classes COMPLEX and ATOM) for the attribute CodeSize. The new rules are displayed in the text representation of fig. 3.67.b.

All conflicting attribute evaluation rules and node classes as well as the attribute rule list of the class where the conflict occurs are *marked black on demand*. They may be inspected by using the *browsing commands* FirstAppl(iedIdentifier) and NextAppl(iedIdentifier) for the attribute CodeSize. These commands navigate from a selected identifier declaration to its first applied occurrrence and from its first occurrence to the next one (first and next are defined with respect to the top/down and left/right arrangement of text and graphics symbols in a displayed representation). Finding all relevant redefinitions of the attribute CodeSize in this way is feasible, but a tedious task if their are many applied occurrences of the attribute. It is, therefore, more appropriate to use the commands FirstMarker and NextMarker to find all erroneous (black marked) parts within a given specification.

It is sometimes difficult to find out, where a new attribute evaluation rule has to be added in order to solve a reported multiple inheritance conflict. This is especially true if involved classes are defined within different sections of a specification such that they are not displayed within a single graphical subschema (as it is the case here). Therefore, two *error repair commands* ElimThisError and ElimErrors are available, which generate (among other things) templates for still missing attribute evaluation rules. The bottom screen dump of fig. 3.67 shows the effects of applying the command ElimThisError to any of the related black marked increments. It introduced an attribute redefinition rule with an unexpanded right-hand side within the node class SUBSYSTEM. This rule is the new current increment in the upper half of screen dump 3.67.c.

The following fig. 3.68 displays another specification error, where the command ElimErrors is able to remove the source of error without any needs for further user input. The problem is that we have entered two new subclasses SUBSYSTEM and SUB-CONFIG which have both COMPLEX and ATOM as their least common superclasses. Their node instances, therefore, have the common property to be legal sources and targets of contains edges. The PROGRES type system requires in such cases *the existence of a unique least common superclass*. For this purpose, a new common subclass of COMPLEX and ATOM has to be introduced which is then the unique least common superclass of SUBSYSTEM and SUBCONFIG. The command ElimErrors extends a given class hierarchy with new classes, until all pairs of classes have least common superclasses or, more formally, until the *class hierarchy is a lattice*. It removes also redundant inheritance relationships and creates attribute redefinition templates for generated classes if needed. This functionality is very convenient as soon as class hierarchies have more than a couple of nodes and are divided into a number of subdiagrams/subsections. The afore-mentioned specification of a subset of PROGRES by means of PROGRES itself in /5. Zün 96a/ contains for instance 207 node classes and 76 node types spread over 49 subsections. 63 of its node classes are generated.

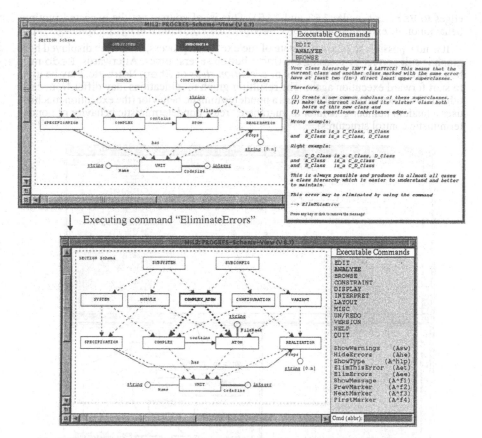

↓ Executing command "EliminateErrors"

Fig. 3.68. Automatic completion of class hierarchies with unique least common superclasses

3.6.5 Testing and Rapid Prototyping

Any entered specification is executable as soon as it is free of static semantics errors and reasonably complete. Experiences with small specifications of some pages as well as with large specifications of more than one hundred printed pages showed that (novice) PROGRES users need considerably more time to convince its analyser that a given specification is correct than to *debug a specification* afterwards with its interpreter. Furthermore, it is very helpful that

(a) an execution session may be interrupted, saved, and resumed later on, in the same manner as an editing session,

(b) the interpreter's Step, Next, ... commands are subject to undo and redo as any editing command, and that

(c) switching back and forth between editing and execution activities is supported (within certain limits; graph scheme modifications are not supported).

Fig. 3.69 displays an intermediate execution state of our running example. A small software system with three modules and four module variants is already constructed. We are now in the midst of building a configuration for the window system (WS) X (cf. value of variable ReqProps for "required properties" in the bottom/left window). The browser window in the right/bottom corner displays a host graph, where the new configuration contains two variants of the module Files (the Config node 173 has contains-edges to Variant-nodes 163 and 165). This is, of course, not the expected runtime behavior of the executed transaction CreateConfig (defined in fig. 3.13 on page 270).

It is now possible to return to a state of the execution process, where the displayed host graph is still correct by pressing the Undo button several times. Afterwards, Redo may be used to *replay* the same sequence of *execution steps* or Step, Next etc. may be used to start forward execution again. The resulting graph modifications may differ from each other if the executed piece of code has a nondeterministic behavior (the execution machine uses a random number generator to guarantee "real" nondeterministic behavior of nondeterministic control structures).

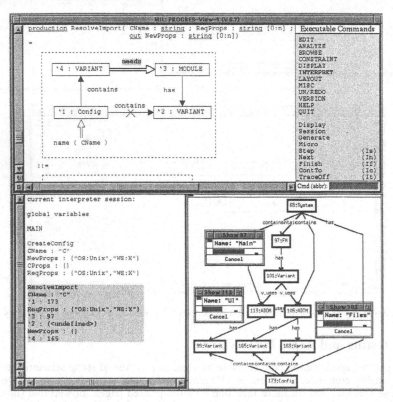

Fig. 3.69. Testing specifications with interpreter and graph browser

Using these facilities of the PROGRES environment plus already mentioned browsing commands, like GotoDecl, it is often possible to find the erroneous specification fragment in a short period of time without any needs for restarting the execution process from scratch. In our case, an incomplete left-hand side of the production ResolveImport is the source of malfunction (cf. fig. 3.66). It does not check whether a variant of the selected module is already part of the constructed configuration. Eliminating the error and testing the modified specification works now as follows:
(a) Undo commands are issued to reset the execution process to a state before the first erroneous call of production ResolveImport.
(b) Syntax-directed editing commands are then used to extend the production's left-hand side appropriately (cf. fig. 3.70).
(c) Afterwards, testing may continue with the already created host graph and a hopefully now correct version of ResolveImport.

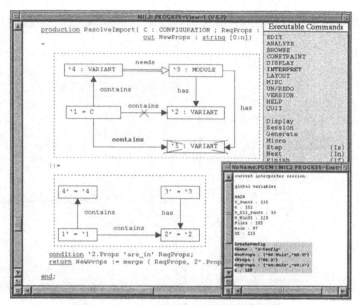

Fig. 3.70. Intertwining editing and debugging activities

As soon as we are (more or less) sure that a given specification has the expected runtime behavior it may be translated into Modula-2 or C code. The produced code has the same functionality as the interpreted code, but is about 10 times faster. The resulting compilation speed-up is considerably lower than usual, due to the fact that we do not interpret the specification itself, but lower level incrementally compiled abstract graph machine code. Furthermore, both the interpreted and the compiled code manipulate host graphs which are stored in the database system GRAS, i.e. we have to pay the price for persistency of and multiple user access to manipulated graphs.

The generated Modula-2 or C code together with the underlying database system GRAS can be used as an abstract data type implementation within any kind of software system. In this way, it will be possible to use translated specifications directly as *logical document implementations of IPSEN tools* (cf. section 4.4)

Another possibility is to combine the generated C code with additionally generated code fragments and an invariant framework which is built on top of the user interface toolkit tcl/tk /6. Ous 94/. This results in a *stand-alone prototype* of a tool which has a graphical user interface and offers selected transactions (productions) as available commands. The main differences between the execution of a specification in the PROGRES environment and the interaction with a generated prototype are (beside a speedup of factor 10):

(a) A user of the generated prototype is not aware of the existence of programmed graph rewriting systems as the underlying specification language.

(b) The execution of a transaction (production) is triggered by selecting a corresponding menu entry with a meaningful name for the end user (it may be different from the specification name of the activated transaction).

(c) The prototype offers various means to enter needed transaction parameters (different kinds of mouse selections, default values, text editor, binding to global variables).

(d) View definition mechanisms may be used to tailor the visible portion of the underlying graph structure such that it fulfills the needs of the end user.

(e) Multiple users may manipulate the same graph database concurrently via prototype instances with maybe different views and different sets of offered commands.

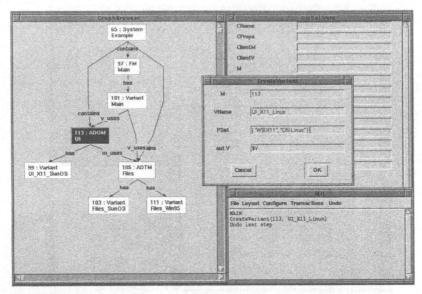

Fig. 3.71. A generated prototype's user interface

Explaining all these features of generated prototypes in detail is outside the scope of this book. Therefore, we will just have a closer look onto a single screen dump of a prototype (generated from the MIL specification) in fig. 3.71. It displays three main windows:

(a) The left window shows a view of the manipulated host graph, where certain types of nodes and edges or nodes with certain attribute values are visible and where node inscriptions (node icons) are determined from user defined attributes.

(b) The top/right window contains a list of variables. These variables store intermediate computation results and may be used as actual parameters of called operations.

(c) The small window in the center of the screen dump is one example for a generated input mask. It provides the activated command CreateVariant with its input values and binds its out-parameter V, a pointer to the created variant node, to the global variable V.

(d) The bottom/right window, finally, displays a protocol of all successfully executed commands, including undo/redo commands which have the same effects as undo/redo commands of the PROGRES environment.

3.6.6 Summary and Future Work

The *PROGRES environment* is the result of ten years of work with contributions from too many programmers, master thesis students, and Ph.D. students to list them all here. It offers assistance for creating, analyzing, compiling, and debugging graph rewriting system specifications. Being an *integrated set of tools* (as any set of IPSEN tools) with support for intertwining these activities, PROGRES combines the flexibility of interpreted languages with the safeness of compiled and statically typed languages.

A novice user finds the *syntax-directed editor* very useful for creating specifications which are correct with respect to the languages context-free syntax. Later on he may deactivate syntax-directed editing for selected (textually represented) language constructs and use a plain text editor for entering these constructs as a whole. The built-in incrementally working *analyzer* offers valuable assistance for eliminating many inadvertantly made errors which pass the checks for context-free correctness. Almost all "typos" and many types of usual specification errors, which have more subtle reasons, are caught in this way.

The *interpreter* offers further means to validate an entered specification interactively and to repair incorrect implementations of productions or transactions "on the fly". Especially the possibility for undo and replay of execution steps is helpful for tracing back erroneous graph states to the erroneous piece of specification. Two additionally available *compiler backends*, which produce C-code and Modula-2-code allow elimination of the interpretation overhead as soon as a specification is reasonably complete and correct. The generated code is more or less human readable and may either be used for throw away prototyping purposes or even for incremental/evolutionary prototyping.

The latest PROGRES version is always available as free software for Sun workstations via ftp from ftp-i3.informatik.rwth-aachen.de in the directory /pub/PROGRES or from ftp.qucis.queensu.ca in the directory /pub/PROGRES or via its www-homepage http://www-i3.informatik.rwth-aachen.de/research/progres/index.html.

The PROGRES environment is nowadays *used at various sites* for specification and rapid prototyping activities:
(a) Collegues at the University of Technology Aachen need PROGRES for rapid prototyping configuration management and process modelling tools (cf. section 3.5).
(b) Software engineers from the University of Leiden have been using PROGRES for the specification of visual (database query) languages and for prototyping a process modelling tool /4. And 96, 4. Zamp 96/.
(c) Software engineers from the University of Paderborn are going to prototype database reverse engineering applications with PROGRES /4. JSZ 96/.
(d) And people from Kingston University, Ontario, are redesigning already implemented graph rewriting pattern matching algorithms for mathematical expressions (music scores) with PROGRES /5. BFG 96/.

It is subject of future research activities to develop a new compiler backend for *generating C++ programs*, which store their graphs either in main memory or in an object-oriented database systems (based on the ODMG-93 standard /7. Cat 93/ of C++ bindings for OODBs). Current research activities are mainly focused on extending the functionality of *generated prototypes* with respect to constraint-based semi-automatic graph layout algorithms, display of nested diagram structures, new modes of interaction, and so forth.

3.7 Summary and Specification Lessons Learned

M. Nagl / A. Schürr

The aim of this section is (1) to *summarize* the main ideas of this chapter and to discuss (2) what we have *learned* in graph grammar engineering over the time. In relation to (2) we mainly restrict ourselves to reporting on experiences in specifying internal documents or subconfigurations.

Lessons learned corresponding (2.a) to the development of the PROGRES *language* or (2.b) to the PROGRES *environment* are *not explicitly* given. The reason for (2.a) is that this is not a book on PROGRES (see /5. Schü 91a, b,/, /Schü 94d, e/) but on SDEs. The reason for (2.b) is that the PROGRES environment is, internally, built up rather similarly to the IPSEN environment which will be discussed in the next chapter.

So, three of the following subsections summarize the main features of the PROGRES *language*, the *specification* state of the art, and the *environment*, respectively. A further subsection characterizes how graph grammar *specifications* have *changed* over the years and thus, implicitly, the progress we have made with/in PROGRES.

Before going into the discussion of these different topics let us look on fig. 3.72 which describes the *relationships* between the language, its underlying formalism, its tools for specification or programming activities, and the environments which were generated from these specifications. Thus, this figure is a cutout, a coarsening, and a refinement of fig. 1.49.

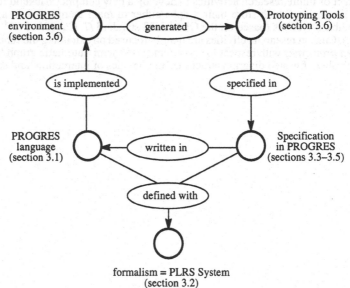

Fig. 3.72. PROGRES language, tools, formalisms and their "products"

3.7.1 The Main Features of the Formally Defined PROGRES Language

PROGRES is a *domain specific, high–level specification language* (cf. section 3.1 and following sections). Its main use in our group is to specify the internal data structures, called documents, appearing in an integrated SDE. However, the language is not restricted to SDE tool specification. It can be used as a knowledge–oriented language whenever changes on a highly–structured, semantical structure have to be specified. So, for example, in /5. Schü 94d/ a well–known example from AI was specified making extensive use of the backtracking facilities, in /5. Zün 96a/ the language was used to specify the internals of a small knowledge–based medical system. Other examples for uses outside the group have been mentioned at the end of section 3.6

The static and structural part of a graph–class specification is described by the *schema part* of a PROGRES specification. In particular, this part *defines*:
  (a) node structure internals and their similarity by node class inheritance hierarchies,
  (b) local graph structures by node types, types of incident edges,
  (c) derived relationships (by paths) and derived sets (by restrictions),
  (d) derived attributes of node classes/types and their possible redefinition in a subsequent class/type.

The dynamic part, i.e. the possible queries and updates, are determined by the *transaction part* within a PROGRES specification. Especially, there are *features* for
  (e) queries by complex pattern matching, namely subgraph tests, containing derived relationships and sets, negative and positive conditions, thereby using single nodes and node sets, optional and obligatory substructures, which can be combined by control structures,
  (f) updates by complex structure changes, namely rewrite rules which may use the same features as subgraph tests and which may either do simple or complex embedding changes,
  (g) control structures either being formulated nondeterministically (inducing backtracking) or deterministically, consisting of sequences/alternatives, conditions, and loops.

Advanced features in the schema as well as transaction parts (see section 3.1) *serve for*
  (h) pattern matching efficiency, namely pragmas for node lookup and path materialization,
  (i) generic query and update formulation by using parametric polymorphism and meta attributes for node type determination.

Although having all these high–level and complex features, the language is *strongly* and nearly *statically typed* using a stratified type system. It distinguishes between classes, types (belonging to a certain class), and instances (belonging to a certain type) of nodes as well as types and instances of binary relations (edges).

Thus, in the terminology of chapter 1, PROGRES is a *multiparadigm*, high–level visual language for knowledge–oriented *modelling* of *data structures*, their *static properties*, and data manipulating *operations* with
  (1) object–oriented features: used for the graph schema definition (node class hierarchies),
  (2) relational or logic–based features: for derived graph properties (attributes, sets, relations),
  (3) pattern– and rule–oriented features: for the definition of complex pattern matching and pattern changing operations (tests, rules),
  (4) imperative and procedural features: in the form of usual control structures, also occurring in nondeterministic form, to build up complex queries and transactions.

The PROGRES language is *formally defined* as it was outlined in section 3.2. This formal definition was *necessary* to (i) have a clear meaning of language construct combinations when having so many and different constructs serving for different paradigms. Furthermore, the implementation of the language was (ii) guided by its formal definition. Finally, the language (iii) has changed and grown considerably over the last six years, its formal foundation having been used as a guide for development.

The *procedure* of formal *definition* was to define the context–free syntax of the language, to determine a language independent programmed graph rewriting system kernel, and to construct a semantic function which maps any syntactically correct PROGRES program onto a graph rewriting system with a well–defined meaning. This is done by using programmed, logic–based structure replacement systems (PLRS) as formalism for the rewriting system kernel. Basically, a PROGRES program is expressed as a set of predicate logic formulas. So, the formal definition, by the way, closes the gap between graph rewriting and logic based techniques.

At the time of writing this book the use of PROGRES is practically *restricted* to specifying a *single document* of an internal overall configuration (see chapter 1). There is an expedient of this restriction by regarding the whole internal configuration to be one big graph. Then, different sections may be used to keep subspecifications for different internal documents, their coupling (unparsing/parsing between logical and representation documents), and their integration (logical documents via integration documents for integration tools) separate from each other. This is, however, not a practical solution due to the fact that sections are only a kind of structured comments without offering any means for information hiding.

The right alternative is to extend the language such that documents, coupling, integration, etc. can be defined by different *specification modules* with clear *relationships* between them. Our ideas in this direction are presented in section 5.2. The integration tool specification presented in section 3.4 was already a first step into this direction. It is given in a language extension which supports the definition of coupled graph grammars.

3.7.2 The Current State of Graph Grammar Engineering

This subsection tries to grasp the main ideas used for graph grammar based specifications of logical documents (section 3.3), integration tool specification (section 3.4) and administration environment functionality specification (section 3.5). The state of *graph grammar engineering*, as it is current practice now, was sketched at the end of section 3.1 as a procedure of 12 steps (see /5. Zün 96a/ for details) starting from instance graph "use cases" and ending with making specification executions more efficient by eliminating nondeterminism through introduction of more structural knowledge about the underlying class of graphs.

Logical Documents

In section 3.3 the modelling of logical documents which have a textual representation was discussed first. There, we start with an EBNF of the external representation of the underlying language in a normal form (structure, list, and variant rules). Internally, graphs are built up by abstract syntax trees together with context–sensitive edges, named *AST–graphs*. However, generic graph rewrite rules are used which factorize out the commonalities of all rewrite rules which differ only with respect to node labels and attribute values used used within their left– and right–hand sides. This is mainly achieved by making use of meta attributes at root nodes of subtrees. One generic rewrite rule, which accesses meta attribute values of provided (root) node types, acts as an abbreviation of a large set of specific rewrite rules which are instantiated with graph class specific node types and attribute values. Context–sensitive relationships can be automatically derived from explicitly manipulated tree skeletons and, therefore, are automatically kept in a consistent state by the PROGRES runtime system.

This AST–graph modelling was extended in order to cope with logical documents having a diagrammatic representation, the approach having been termed *metamodelling*. It was only sketched in section 3.3 for a portion of the MIL example. The essential idea is to describe commonalities of graphical representations by a graph schema extending the abstract syntax schema. Again, meta attributes are used to instantiate this generic schema in order to describe a specific diagram language. So, two different schema and transaction parts are put together and interrelated in order to specify a logical document such that it is suitable to have both a textual and diagram representation.

All above specification tasks deal with editor tool functionality specification. To have examples for *analyzers* and *"execution"* tools the static semantics and the translation of MIL to module frames in Modula–2 were presented in 3.3. The way is as above to start with generic graph schemata and to have it adapted by meta attributes. So, the philosophy of logical document modelling is essentially to unify generic subspecifications and to instantiate them by meta attributes. This approach can be used for all tools, from editors to executors.

Integration Tool Specification

Section 3.4 was devoted to specification of *integration tools*. We remember that such tools have to take care of fine–grained, increment–to–increment dependencies between different documents and, furthermore, that they have different appearances as checkers, binders, transformators, browsers, etc. Tools range from automatic to manual and, in any case, they must be incremental.

The specification was a *coupling* of graph grammars for source and target documents in a declarative manner by defining *correspondences* (triple rules) of language constructs on both sides. The advantage of this approach is that it is independent of the tool implementation, and independent from the tool characteristics (see chapter 1). Thus, it can be used for batch or incremental, continuously active or on demand active tools etc.

Rules for changing the source, integration, and target documents which reflect the specific properties of an integration tool (e.g. incremental, interactive transformer) can easily be *derived* by determining what is given and what is to be changed in a triple rule. Triple rules are denoted in an extension of PROGRES which is not supported up to now by the environment. Derived rules are only PROGRES if the integration is regarded to work on a single flat graph which contains all to be integrated graphs as subgraphs. Triple and derived rules are the basis for generating integration tools.

Administration Tool Specification

Administration configurations, in section 3.5 regarded as administration graphs, are a class which is not determined by the underlying AST–structure, but contains many application–specific edges. So, the graph grammar specification approach given in this section is different from that of section 3.3. It starts with *graph restrictions* as schema extensions describing the structural and static (sub–)graph structure. *Heuristics* are given to construct *consistency preserving* rewrite *rules* from these graphical restrictions.

In addition to the consistency preserving rules, complex transactions are defined for the different aspects of project organisation (product, process, resources). This yields a specification which is still independent of the development application (software engineering, CIM, etc.). So, what has been achieved are the two *layers* of the *application independent part* of fig. 1.24.c).

Then, as shown above for logical document modelling, there is an *adaptation* by the meta attribute mechanism to get tool behavior for application–specific project organization (here SE). However, different from above and due to the more complex and inherent graph structure the application–specific productions cannot be just parameterized at runtime. Rather, the generic productions can be reused only as a template for manual modifications by the specifier.

3.7.3 Lessons Learned by Writing Specs

This subsection describes what we have *learned* by writing specifications (and, implicitely, by improving the language in which a specification is described). Current work and open problems are discussed in section 5.2. The knowledge results from specifying logical documents (see 3.1 to 3.3), integration between logical documents (see 3.4), and specifying the administration configuration (see 3.5). We restrict ourselves to the aspect of *simplifying specification writing*. The security aspect is only touched, the efficiency aspect is omitted here (see end of 3.1).

If we look at the specifications of this chapter we see that we have tried to factor out as much *structural knowledge* for a graph class as possible of the operational part of a specification by describing this structural knowledge in a *declarative way*. This is especially true for the schema part where the node class hierarchy reflects similarities in the internal structure of nodes (their attributes), similarities in the local graph structure (incoming/outgoing edges of a certain type), and attribute evaluation (rules for all nodes of a type corresponding to a class). The node type and edge type declarations determine those graph elements which are allowed to occur within the graph class to be specified.

But we find also *declarative* elements in the *transaction part* of a specification in the form of path expressions which are derived relations between nodes each belonging to a certain class/type. The same holds true for restrictions being derived node sets. Even the elementary operations on graphs are described declaratively, namely by graph rules. Application conditions are directly specified as patterns. Specification of trial and error situations is supported by nondeterministic control structures.

A third branch of factorization is to *avoid redundancy in specifications*. This appeared in section 3.3 by describing how to handle structural changes of the tree part of a logical document by making use of generic specifications and giving instantiations for specific logical documents by the meta attribute mechanism. Even more, this mechanism can be used for all tool specifications on one document, i.e. editor, analyzer, etc. This idea has also been used for integration tool specification. Here, using graph grammars for the source and target documents means concentrating on the integration issue. Furthermore, correspondences describe integration tool unspecific specifications, i.e. they are the common core of any integration tool behavior.

Table 3.73 *summarizes* what we *have learned* over the years in making specifications more readable but also to reduce effort in specifying. The table is by no means complete. We restrict ourselves here to specification of changes. Testing complex structural situations has also been improved but is not discussed. The part (a) of table 3.73 summarizes what we have learned by specifying single logical documents, part (b) how specifications of integration issues between two logical documents or of a subconfiguration was improved. Topics which are still in evolution are marked and will be taken up again in chapter 5.

What are the *benefits* of the *declarative* and *common description* of *structural knowledge*? These benefits are threefold: Firstly, extracting declarative knowledge offers (1) the possibility to define a rich context–sensitive syntax (for a specification language). This, in turn, can be used to check a specification (by tools) at specification time thereby guaranteeing some kind of correctness (see below). Secondly, (2) the operational part of a specification decreases. It is cut down to its very core making a specification more readable. Therefore, it is no longer necessary to specify in an operational manner what can be specified declaratively at the very beginning. Examples for reduction of operational specifications are given in table 3.73. Thirdly, (3) writing generic specifications at one hand (3.a) again serves for readability, as common properties are separated from specific ones. On the other hand (3.b) it allows to reuse the generic specifications, thus reducing the effort for writing specifications.

In order to emphasize the *security aspect*, table 3.74 sketches how declarative descriptions can be used for checking specifications. The table is only a summary of about 400 con-

	purpose	formerly done by	now expressed as	advantage
(a)	changing remote attribute values of other nodes	sequences of rewrite rule applications propagating the intermediate changes of attributes	attribute equation sets, depending on each other	declarative description, no transactions needed, attribute evaluation machinery does update automatically
	building up connections between nonneighbouring nodes	rule application sequences testing for the structure in between these nodes	path expression within one single rule	intermediate rules not needed, path is a declarative description of the connection structure
	handling of trial and error situations	trial and backtracking was explicitly programmed as well as the necessary bookkeeping	nondeterministic control structures	no explicit bookkeeping of trials and errors necessary, automatically done by the PROGRES system (abort and undo transactions)
	handling sets of modification/ reevaluation patterns	explicitly programmed for all members of the set	set valued nodes, set valued attributes	avoids loop programming for all members of the set, one production defines declaratively and in a rule-based way the handling of a set of members
	application conditions to check internal connections (see above), nonexistence of connections, availability or nonavailability of context structures	tests and programming of control flow	restrictions, path declarations, negative nodes, edges, and paths	makes positive/negative structure within and outside the rule directly visible
	handling similar structural changes of (tree part) pattern rewriting	redundancy (multiple appearance) of rules and transactions	one rule with node type parameters, node class parameters, using meta attribute mechanism	generic rules which are instantiated by corresponding actual types for nodes, meta attributes of nodes define substructures
*1	uniform handling of editor, analysis, monitoring, execution part of tool specification (one logical document)	writing different specifications which have to fit together, having been written again and again for any logical document	generic specification portions for editor, analyser, ... part, specialization of node class hierarchy for a given language, instantiation by meta attributes	generic parts have to be written only once, adaptation to a specific document is much less effort (extension of generic spec), instantiation is easily done by meta attribute mechanism

(b)			
*1, *2	integration issue specification between different logical documents	regarding the whole situation namely source, target, and integration to be one graph, "programming" each integration tool (transformer, checker etc.) separately without seeing their common part	source and target document specification can be taken, common part of all integrator tools determined by correspondences, tool specific specs need not be written but can be mechanically derived
*1	integrating a subconfiguration	regarding the whole subconfiguration to be one big graph	still one graph, with clearly distinguished subgraph portions, different spec portions for subgraphs and their integration	clear separation of concern, logical graphs and integration issues

Table 3.73. (a) Specifying Document Classes and (b) Integration Issues: What we have learned
*1: still ongoing work, *2: Uses an extension of PROGRES

(1) general checks:
  • unused declarations of any kind
  • applied identifier occurrence without declaration
  • double declaration
  • applied and declared occurrences belong to consistent syntax classes (e.g. parameter type name cannot be a transaction name)

(2) class hierarchy:
  • is–a relationships are acyclic
  • any two classes have at most one common smallest superclass (greatest subclass)
  • attribute redefinitions are resolved by the specifier

(3) path expressions:
  • concatenation: result class of first subexpression is subclass of input class for second subexpression
  • intersection and union: result classes of subexpressions have a common subclass or superclass, respectively

  • iteration: cardinality constraints of a graph schema check whether iteration conditions are always true (e.g. test for existence of an edge in a specification is forbidden, if the edge declaration says that the edge must always exist)

(4) productions:
  • structure of left– or right–hand side have to conform to graph schema
  • assignments to derive attributes are prohibited
  • two nodes of left–hand side may only match the same node of the host graph if their classes have a common subclass

(5) Parameters and control structures:
  • types/classes of actual and formal parameters conform
  • one variable is not bound to more than one out–parameter (alias ban)
  • out–parameter receives unique return value
  • assignments to input–parameters are disallowed
  • out–parameters must not be read (used)
  • loop and branch conditions of transactions are side effect free (no production/transaction calls, assignments to local variables only)

Table 3.74. Checking PROGRES specifications: collection of context–sensitive checks (out of 400 corresponding rules)

text–sensitive rules. Some advanced examples, how these checks appear to the PROGRES specifier have been given in section 3.6. Topics (2)–(5) correspond to the different paradigms used within specifications. So, (2) corresponds to OO constructs, (3) to logical/relational constructs of the classification given in 3.7.1. Strong and mostly static typing turns out to be of great value, if large and complex specifications are written. This, of course, is the case for the specification of any practically usable tool. In our view a statically typed language is therefore an absolute must to get specifications which can be checked at specification time and therefore are likely to behave "correctly" at runtime.

3.7.4 The PROGRES Environment Supporting the Specification Process

In the same way as outlined in chapter 2 for PiS, RE, and other development processes, the *process* of *elaborating* a *PROGRES specification* is again rather complex. It is not a straightforward and linear process, but contains many backtracking steps. Furthermore, it is full of trial and error. Therefore, we need tools such that commands for building up, maintaining, analyzing, and evaluating specifications can be invoked in any interleaved order (in the same way as for any integrated set of IPSEN tools).

So, the external functionality and characteristics of the different PROGRES environment tools is similar to that of the IPSEN tools. Thus, the usual tools for structure–oriented editing or changing a PROGRES specification by syntax–directed, graphical/textual editor tools with immediate report of context–sensitive errors were not presented in detail. They behave exactly as those of section 2.2, 2.4, and 2.5. More complex *editor/analysis* operations were shown, namely "semantic" copying of left–hand sides into right–hand sides and correcting a node class schema in order to reestablish its lattice property.

Analogously, there are many similarities to the behavior of *execution* tools of 2.1 and 2.2. So, again, the execution tool description in 3.6 was rather short. Interpretative execution can proceed step–wise back and forth. This allows for tracing an execution back to the first application of a rule/transaction, changing the rule/transaction, and then rerunning the PROGRES program again.

Aside from building up and *testing specifications* which are later translated and put into the IPSEN framework as abstract data types (cf. chapter 4), the PROGRES environment can also be used as a stand–alone *modelling environment* for different purposes. For that – which is outside the IPSEN SDE building application – a PROGRES specification can be presented to a user as a parameterized modelling environment. Thereby, parameterization is twofold: (a) a specific specification reflects a certain application domain. Furthermore, (b) its outside representation is such that instead of internal graphs suitable application–dependent objects and relations are presented together with invocation possibilities for transactions.

So, for both purposes, either testing/prototyping an abstract data type which appears later as kernel data structure of an IPSEN–like SDE or developing a modelling environment for knowledge–based applications, the used PROGRES specification can be *directly executed* or *translated* into equivalent Modula–2 or C–code. The first is useful, if a specification is still in flux, the second to evaluate the dynamic behavior of a complex specification.

4 Realization:
Derivation of Efficient Tools

The *aim* of this *chapter* is to discuss the practical work of realizing different IPSEN prototypes and to report on the experiences we have obtained in these realization processes. Following the argumentation of chapter 1, it is clear that architecture modelling is one main topic. So, a lot of architecture diagrams will be shown and a large part of the discussion is on design decisions.

As in the last two chapters, we proceed from simple to complicated: We start from different tools on one document forming a technical *single environment*, switch over to *integration* tools serving for fine–grained integration on technical configurations, and end up with *administration* tools for managing collaborative work.

The discussion is based on an overview of the IPSEN *overall* architecture given in section 4.1. This architecture consists of a *framework* being built up by components which can be taken as they are, if an IPSEN–like SDE or DE in another application domain is built. It also identifies all *specific* components to be realized for a certain IPSEN instance and to be hooked into the framework in order to end up with an overall environment. Even more, there is a mechanical way to get these specific components, in the best case by using a generator tool.

This explains the title of this chapter: Efficient IPSEN tools for various purposes are derived rather than realized by handcrafting. So, the main concern of this chapter is *reuse*, i.e. what the reader can learn from the IPSEN project if he wants to apply the knowledge described to build an SDE or another intelligent and interactive system. To summarize the reuse results is one purpose of the concluding section of this chapter.

To give an overview of the chapter, its *contents* are as follows:
Section 4.1 discusses the structure of a technical environment by refining its static structure, and discussing its runtime dynamics, and by giving details on specific aspects, as e.g. visualization or its modification by the user. Then, it is indicated how single environments are extended by integration tools and by "front ends" to serve both for fine–grained (technical) and coarse grained (management) integration.
Section 4.2 explains in detail the graph–oriented and nonstandard DBS underlying all IPSEN instances. It consists of a kernel, for handling graph–like data structures, and further layers on top, for event handling, change control, schemata and attributes, and distribution. Performance results demonstrate the suitability for SDE applications.
Section 4.3 goes into the central part of a technical environment: It discusses how logical documents are structured to be suitable both for textual and graphical representations, how representation documents are built up, and how parsers/unparsers look like.
Section 4.4 deals with the meta SDE for producing single environments. Starting with an EBNF–environment, context free editors are generated. The EBNF grammar is translated to a PROGRES skeleton, to be extended by specs for context sensitive syntax rules. The corresponding code is again generated.
The next section discusses execution tools, taking the most complex one (execution of a requirements spec) as example. The main purpose is to show how adaptability of the execution machinery was achieved.
The topic of section 4.6 is the realization of incremental integration tools. Here again, all reusable components build up an integrator framework, the specific components are manually derived from an integrator spec of triple rules.
The last section deals with the administration environment to be used for coordinating different developers. It shares a lot of similarities with technical environments, but also shows some specifics. Furthermore, the realization of the "front end", necessary to bind technical developers to the administration database is discussed.

4.1 The Framework Revisited:
A More Detailed View on the IPSEN Architecture

P. Klein

In this section, we are going to take a more detailed look at some selected parts of the IPSEN architecture as presented in subsection 1.6.2, cf. fig. 1.28. The figure is repeated here (fig. 4.1) for convenience. The *purpose of* and *interactions between* the architecture's subsystems will be explained in the following.

In *contrast* to *section 1.6*, where an explanation of a single environment and a description of design decisions by level was the center of interest, this section provides more information on the architectural structure and the dynamic interaction of components at runtime. Furthermore, we focus on some specific parts of the IPSEN architecture. Finally, we discuss the structure of an integrated technical environment and of an IPSEN overall environment.

These elucidations serve two purposes: On the level of subsystem design, the *functionality* of the subsystems will become clearer if their cooperation in certain standard situations is understood. Furthermore, on the next deeper level of detail, the reader will get a more concrete insight into the *structure* of the subsystems. Together with sketches of discussions concerning adaptability and maintainability, the explanations comprise a *rationale* for parts of the architecture in section 1.6 and substantiate its design decisions.

The *content* of this section is as follows: After commencing with an explanation of the architectural components on subsystem level in 4.3.1, we continue by discussing the runtime behavior of a single environment in the next subsection. The following two subsections (4.1.3 and 4.1.4) describe specific parts of single technical environments. The former shows how representations (visualization structures of logical documents) and presentations (document contents visible on the screen) are maintained and which possibilities the user has to influence both. The latter demonstrates how commands and complex commands are handled internally. Subsection 4.1.5 gives a view on the architecture of an overall IPSEN environment for distributed work. The section concludes on a short summary of the main topics presented here.

4.1.1 The Static Structure of a Technical Environment Revisited

This subsection will give an *explanation* of the *subsystems* shown in the coarse architecture of fig. 4.1. It represents a simple (technical) environment like a Programming–in–the–Large environment for the designer. As in the overview given in subsection 1.6.2 (cf. table 1.29), we will proceed bottom–up, this time discussing some details of the architectural structure.

The bottom layer of the IPSEN framework contains data abstraction components which hide the details of the underlying *infrastructure*, e.g. operating system, window system, and the like. Ideally, porting IPSEN to another target environment influences only this layer. It contains the following *components*:

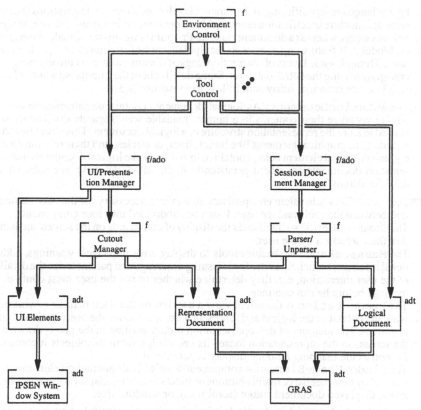

Fig. 4.1. Coarse architecture of a technical environment

GRAS: The GRAph Storage subsystem is the basic database component in IPSEN. GRAS allows the persistent maintenance of directed, attributed, node– and edge–labelled graphs and supports incremental computation of derived attributes, arbitrary undo/redo, error recovery, and version control mechanisms. In its current state, GRAS has full multi–client/multi–server abilities, i.e. one IPSEN application may use several GRAS servers for different documents, and several IPSEN applications can operate on one (remote) document. Since GRAS is a complex and comparatively large subsystem, a dedicated section (4.2) is devoted to the discussion of its design and implementation.

IPSENWindowSystem: This subsystem handles the mapping of an abstract, system–independent window system onto a concrete realization, possibly with the help of an existing window system. Historically, the first workstation version of IPSENWindowSystem in the IPSEN'88 prototype was implemented on top of the SunView library. In the IPSEN'91 version, SunView was replaced by the X Window System. The current prototypes additionally employ parts of the InterViews library.

The next level of the framework provides application–specific *logical document classes* and additional structures serving the *interaction* between user and application. The *components* are:

LogicalDocument: Logical documents contain the actual information the user is working with. Every logical document is an instance of a document class (an abstract data type) which is based on a certain language, i.e. it can store documents written in the underlying language. Accordingly, the interface of a logical document data type is language–specific, e.g. a document class for architecture descriptions (based on an architecture specification language) has operations to insert and delete modules or subsystems, whereas a document class for Programming–in–the–Small (based e.g. on Modula–2) features operations to manipulate control structures or type declarations. Through some layers of abstraction, logical documents are eventually mapped onto graphs using the GRAS database. Some details about the internal structure of the LogicalDocument subsystem follow in subsection 4.3.1.

RepresentationDocument: As logical documents contain no information about how to visualize their contents in a human–readable way, separate documents are needed to store the representation structure of a logical document. This structure may contain text, graphical elements like boxes, lines, or circles, and their relationships, e.g. one graphical element being contained in another. Like logical documents, representation documents are stored persistently in the GRAS database, see subsection 4.3.3 for details.

UIElements: This subsystem encapsulates all services necessary for the communication between the tools and the user. It can be subdivided into four components.
The CommandHandler facilitates the display of commands on the screen and handles their selection by the user.
The MessageHandler enables tools to display error messages, warnings, additional information, or help texts. Tools issuing a message can parameterize the details of the user interaction, e.g. they determine whether or not the user must confirm a message before he can continue.
The Presentation is the actual view a user has on the document he is working with. In contrast to the logical and representation documents, the presentation is not persistent. The memory of the representation is only existent in the pixels drawn on the screen, so the representation looses its knowledge about the objects it contains as soon as the mapping onto the display is performed.
The WindowFrameElements component deals with all interaction elements not covered by the other parts, mainly buttons or sliders to modify display parameters like zoom, displayed document cutout (scrollbars), or window size.

Although already discussed in chapter 1, it is appropriate to recapitulate on the reasons why we consider it to be of crucial concern to model *logical*, *representation*, and *presentation* data structures *separately*: (1) Decisions about how a *representation* for a given logical document should look like are *independent* of the structure of the logical document itself. While the internal structure of the logical document mainly depends on the underlying grammar, the representation document deals with issues such as indentation and spacing in text, how to represent certain logical structures graphically, and the arrangement of textual and graphical elements. The presentation on the other hand encapsulates details about how a portion of a representation document is mapped onto the screen with regard to scaling and the like. With our separate modeling of these data structures, representation decisions can be changed readily without affecting other parts of the environment. (2) There can be *more than one representation* for a logical document, and several presentations for any representation document. Although this is not apparent from the architecture, we do not support representation documents for more than one logical document or presentations for more than one representation document; this will be discussed later. (3) In most cases, a tool works on only one of these documents. A structure–based editor or an analyzer for example only operate on the abstract syntax tree structure of the logical document. All their operations are completely independent of how this structure is displayed to the user. Thus, separating the data structures creates a framework for if and how certain tools may access certain data and thereby prevents them from utilizing information outside their provided scope.

As useful as the separation of logical documents, representation documents, and document presentations might be from the data encapsulation point of view, it leaves the system with the problem of *synchronizing* them continuously in accordance to modifications made by a tool or the user. This coupling is performed by the next architecture layer.

`Parser/Unparser`: In order to create a representation for a given logical document, the table–driven `Unparser` uses document–class–specific layout information to insert appropriate textual and graphical objects into the representation graph. Vice versa, the `Parser` can infer the logical structure from a given textual representation. A more detailed description of this subsystem follows in subsection 4.1.3.

`CutoutManager`: The `CutoutManager` is the corresponding functional subsystem for the coupling between representations and presentations. The `CutoutManager` determines which part of the document is visible to the user and creates screen objects corresponding to the objects in the representation graph with respect to zooming and other display parameters.

A noticeable point about this architecture layer is that both functional subsystems have to respect performance issues to operate in satisfactory time bounds, e.g. performing a complete unparsing of a logical document after some insertion of an increment would be unbearable. Therefore, the `Unparser` and `CutoutManager` employ one of the fundamental ideas of the whole IPSEN system, namely an *incremental approach* (also see subsection 1.2.4). In our context we understand incremental as implying that the transformators only update the portion of the target structure which directly relates to *the changed part* in the source structure. The `Unparser` and the `CutoutManager` must therefore be able to act on arbitrary increments and not necessarily on all of the source document. Although the transformators are allowed to inspect source document parts which were not directly affected by the change, they modify the target document only to a minimal extent. Subsection 4.1.3 will give some more information on this topic.

The fourth level of the framework comprises components which know about all *documents* and *presentations* and their *relationships*, i.e. which representation document depends on which logical document etc.

`SessionDocumentManager`: The `SessionDocumentManager` is responsible for the coupling of logical and representation documents. In a wider sense, it contains the transient administrative knowledge about all documents in one user session. Besides controlling the mapping of logical to representation documents and vice versa, it is in charge of access control to documents, keeping track of versioning information, and controlling incremental updates between documents. Since documents are all stored persistently in the GRAS database, the information held by the `SessionDocumentManager` must also be preserved over session boundaries. On the other hand, this information is merely a cutout (specific to the current technical environment) of the global administrative knowledge maintained (persistently) by the corresponding environment, see fig. 1.34 in subsection 1.6.4 and subsection 4.1.5. In this sense, the `SessionDocumentManager` can be viewed as a transient mirror of the relevant cutout of the global administrative data: whenever a new task in a technical environment is started, the `SessionDocumentManager` of this environment receives the relevant information from the administrative database and maintains it for the duration of the session. Whenever an operation in the document manager induces a change in the working context of the technical environment, e.g. the creation of a new revision of a technical document, the corresponding updates in the administrative database are arranged via the `SessionDocumentManager`.

`UI/PresentationManager`: The `SessionDocumentManager`'s counterpart for the coupling of representation documents and document presentations is the `UI/PresentationManager`. The `UI/PresentationManager` keeps track of a representation document's open presentations, its display parameters such as zoom and the absolute position of the upper–left corner of the screen in the representation document, and a pointer to the currently active presentation. The latter is used to determine the position of user interface elements which should be placed "close" to the focus of the user, like menus or certain message windows.

Because the different aspects of a document are modeled with different data structures, it is possible to establish *m:n relationships* between logical documents, representation documents, and document presentations. This means that the architecture allows for one logical document to have several different representation documents, one representation document to have several presentations etc. Although this is not apparent from the architecture, we currently do not exploit all the possibilities of this model; the relationships are all 1:n. Apart from the fact that such 1:n relationships are easier to implement, a more fundamental reason for this restriction exists: If aspects and facts from more than one logical document were merged into one representation, the unparser would not only visualize a given logical structure. In fact, it would integrate disjoint logical structures into a new, virtual logical structure which is then visualized. In such cases, we therefore favour the cleaner approach and model the integrated logical structure explicitly. The same argument holds for the relationship between representation and presentation documents.

The next two layers consist of *components* for controlling one tool and all tools of an environment, respectively.

ToolControl: For every tool attached to an IPSEN environment, there is exactly one ToolControl subsystem. Depending on the type(s) of the underlying logical document(s), there are control modules e.g. for editor, analyzer, execution, monitoring, and integration tools. This subsystem is in charge of executing the commands selected by the user; this will be explained in detail later (cf. subsection 4.1.4). Note that currently, mainly for technical reasons, it is not possible to dynamically attach or detach tools to or from an environment at runtime: the corresponding subsystems are linked into the system at development time.

EnvironmentControl: This top–level module manages the interaction between the user and the tools and is responsible for the consistency of logical, representation, and presentation documents. Again, see subsection 4.1.4 for details.

4.1.2 Dynamic Aspects of a Single Environment

As a complementary view on the framework from fig. 4.1, we now illustrate the dynamic behavior of the system on a course–grained level, i.e. the *selection* and *execution* of *tool commands*. As an example, we assume that the user is working with a structure–based editor. This editor modifies a logical document in accordance to user input.

In a first step, the system has to provide an outside view on the logical document. This is achieved in two transformations: First, at least one *representation document* for the logical document has to be created (or updated). Therefore, the corresponding unparser will analyze the logical document and insert graphical and textual elements into the representation document accordingly. As was already mentioned in the previous subsection, both logical and representation documents are actually stored in the GRAS database. Second, for one or more representation documents, a *presentation* has to be maintained. This is achieved by the cutout manager which determines the visible part (cutout) of the representation document and draws screen objects into the current presentation. The technical details of accessing the screen are encapsulated by the basic services in the UIElements subsystem.

Now, after the user has some document presentation he wants to interact with, a decision has to be made about *which* subset of all *commands* is currently *executable*. This decision can only be made by the tool in charge of executing a certain command. The superset of all commands available in the integrated system is specified in a command table. The command table defines all possible commands of all tools through unique logical names. This table will be explained in greater detail in subsection 4.1.4.

After displaying one of possibly many presentations of a logical document to the user, the EnvironmentControl module asks all attached tools via a standardized operation provided by all ToolControl modules about their *current set of commands*. In order to select a sensible set of executable commands, the tools may of course investigate the current state of the representation and the logical document.

Of special concern is the so–called *current increment* of the representation document. At all times, exactly one increment in every representation document is marked as current. This increment is appropriately highlighted in the document presentation and denotes the focus of the user. Most editor operations like cut, copy, expand, append etc. act on the current increment, therefore an editor tool will most likely decide about the applicability of one of its commands depending on the type of the current increment. Considering a Programming–in–the–Small editor as an example, the command to expand a placeholder to a frame for an if–statement will be appropriate only if the current increment denotes a placeholder and the type of the placeholder corresponds to a nonterminal which allows derivation to an if–statement.

A noticeable point here is that the notion of a current increment is *known* only in *representation documents* and not in logical documents. The reasons for this become obvious when we consider one or more users working with different representations of the same logical document: If the current increment would be anchored in the logical document, operations in all representations would act on the same increment, i.e. selecting an increment (and thereby a current set of commands) would select the same increment in all representations. It would not be possible to act on the document from independent views, rendering the possibility of multiple representations useless.

The *information* about the commands offered is *returned* by every tool as a *set* of the above mentioned logical *command names*, together with an additional flag defining whether the tool wants the command to be selectable by the user or not and a callback pointer denoting the tool procedure to be activated if that command is selected (cf. subsection 4.1.4).

The next step the environment control takes is to *activate* the *command selection process* controlled by the UI/presentation manager. The UIElements interface offers operations to display a set of commands to the user and to acquire the selection of a command. (Internally, this step involves creating a menu window which is attached to the currently active presentation window.) The EnvironmentControl module then waits for the user interface to signal a command selection. When it receives such a selection, the control module delegates the *execution* of the corresponding command to the *tool* which offered the command using the callback pointer. Alternatively, the tool could offer a single standardized operation to be called on every command activation concerning this tool. This operation would then decide about the further steps to take using some sort of case–statement. To avoid the well–known maintainability problems resulting from such a structure, we decided to provide the tool operation directly with the respective command. In the course of the command execution, the tool will generally modify one or more increments in the underlying documents.

Finally, the system has to *synchronize* the *dependent structures* (representation document and presentation) in accordance to modifications made by a tool. The incremental updating of documents is achieved by the following scheme (cf. subsection 4.1.3 for more details): (1) The editor has changed the logical document and informs the document manager about this. (2) For each representation document, the document manager lets the corresponding unparser generate new representation increments for the changed logical increments. Note that the unparser might have nothing to do for a certain representation because it is not affected by the change in the logical document. (3) The editor demands an incremental update of the open presentations from the UI/presentation manager. (4) For each presentation, the UI/presentation manager activates a redrawing of affected parts of the window using the cutout manager. After all dependent data structures are updated, a new command cycle starts with the retrieval of executable commands for the current increment by the environment control.

Note that, apart from selecting modification commands with respect to the current increment, it is also possible for the user to *change* his respective *focus of work*. For example, he can (1) always select a new current increment in the same logical document. In this case, the generic selection tool updates the pointer to the current increment in the active represen-

386

tation, and the cutout manager takes care of the appropriate highlighting in the corresponding presentations. Furthermore, the selection tool may be (2) accompanied by a language–dependent browsing tool allowing navigation from an applied to a declaring occurrence of an identifier etc. (cf. subsection 2.4.4). A related example is to execute a step in an interpreter tool which makes the representation increment corresponding to the executed logical increment current. In both cases, intradocument links are used to automatically select a new current increment. But the user can also (3) choose to change his focus to another document by opening or creating it using operations in the document manager. Analogous to intradocument links, interdocument links can also be followed automatically e.g. by (4) executing an integration tool command selecting a dependent target document increment for some changed source document increment (see subsection 4.6.1).

We can observe that, although these navigation operations have a different quality for the user than e.g. editor commands for expanding a placeholder or deleting an increment, they fit into the same general scheme of command selection and execution. This is generally true also for all user activity resulting in the execution of tool commands. In other words, the tools attached to some environment *behave equally* from the framework point of view.

The following list *summarizes* the description of the *activities* occurring during one *command execution* cycle (cf. fig. 4.2 which, for reasons of simplicity, is drawn slightly different compared to fig. 4.1):

(1) The `EnvironmentControl` module asks all tools in turn which set of commands they offer with respect to the current document and increment. Note that a focus switch as described above (possibly changing the current document and/or increment and thereby the current set of commands) is also caused by some command.
(2) The `EnvironmentControl` module then triggers the display of all executable commands and the selection of a command by the user.
(3) The selected command is deferred to the tool offering the command.
(4) Eventually, changes made by the tool in some document are propagated to related documents.

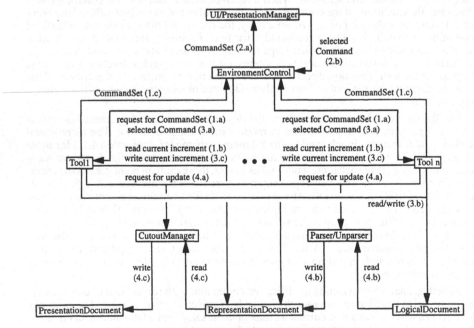

Fig. 4.2. The command cycle (simplified)

4.1.3 Document Visualization and Modification

As is apparent from the description of the command cycle in the previous subsection, a major part of the user interface handling in the IPSEN system is performed by a general mechanism. In fact, the developer of a technical environment deals with the user interface *strictly on logical level*, i.e. he is not concerned with the specification of representation aspects. These aspects can be divided – according to the basic services of the UIElements subsystem – into (1) maintaining a user visible view on the logical document (Presentation), (2) handling screen elements (WindowFrameElements), (3) displaying messages (MessageHandler), and (4) the coordination of command selection and tool execution (CommandHandler). This subsection is devoted to the former two subjects ((1) and (2)), the latter two ((3) and (4)) will be examined in the next subsection.

We already mentioned in the previous subsections that the Unparser component is responsible for computing a representation for some logical document, and that it has to update this representation incrementally. As long as only *textual representations* are involved, the unparser can be *generated completely* from the underlying grammar specification: When the representation for some logical increment is computed for the first time, the layout of textual parts is determined according to the layout of the context–free grammar which served as the input for generating the editor. More precisely, the layout of the right–hand sides of the corresponding productions serve as a template for the placing of keywords, identifiers, line–breaks, and tabulators in the representation.

In the case of *graphical representations* or, in general, mixed graphical/textual representations, the unparsing process is more complicated. Additional information is needed to determine how logical information should be mapped onto representation elements. In IPSEN, this information is split into two parts: (1) The *grammar specification* for the underlying language contains *descriptions* of which grammar elements are mapped onto graphical elements. This specification is restricted to the structural level, i.e. it only describes which elements are to be represented as nodes or edges. (2) The information whether a node shall be represented as a box, circle, ellipse etc. or an edge as solid, dashed, an arrow etc. is supplied in an *additional table*. Currently, this table is read and evaluated at startup time to avoid recompilation after modifications. This also allows different users to tailor the representation to their needs (with respect to the graphical elements offered by UI elements) by writing their own unparser tables. Furthermore, we have recently included graph layout algorithms to compute a sensible default placing of graphical (node) objects. The unparser receives further treatment in subsection 4.3.4 when we have said more about internal document structures.

Of course, the user may manipulate any component of the layout afterwards. The system therefore incorporates a language independent *layout editing tool* which allows arbitrary modifications to a representation document. This LayoutTool component – in contrast to the generic ToolControl shown in fig. 4.1 – does not operate on logical, but on representation documents only. In other words, the general usability edge between ToolControl and LogicalDocument is replaced by a general usability edge between LayoutToolControl and RepresentationDocument. If a representation document is in layout mode, the layout tool offers commands to move/resize boxes and lines, insert or delete tabulators and line–breaks, hide or show specific increments etc. These representation modifications are only on instance level, i.e. changing the representation for one increment does not affect the representation of other increments of the same representation type. Note that being in layout mode is a property of a representation document: So–called handles have to be attached to graphical and textual objects to enable the user to move or resize them. How and where such handles are shown is solely representation information, they are not part of the logical information and therefore not present in edit mode. Note also that, due to the separation of the representation information from the logical structure of the document, one or more users may create quite different representations of the same logical document.

When logical and representation documents are consistent, the cutout manager can *display* (a cutout of) the *representation*. For each representation element in the visible cutout, pixels are drawn accordingly onto the screen using UIElements's basic services. The parameters for this mapping like which document part should be visible in the window, zooming factor etc. can be changed by the user through special window frame elements, e.g. buttons or scrollbars. One possible solution for the realization of this behavior is to employ a separate high–level UI library. Such libraries generally provide a virtual window of arbitrary size ("canvas"), and the library itself takes care of the coordination of scrolling, zooming, redrawing, and the like. The virtual screen can be accessible through high–level library operations for drawing circles, boxes, lines etc. and/or on pixel level. Both access possibilities are not suitable for our approach, though. Setting up a virtual screen on pixel level for the complete representation document would be far too memory–intensive, so only the use of high–level operations remains. This, on the other hand, would require a fourth data structure in the visualization process, namely the representation structure of the UI library: The representation document (which cannot be dispensed with due to its persistency) would have to be transformed into the internal data structure of the library which itself then draws the screen objects. Therefore, IPSEN has an own component for these tasks, namely the CutoutManager.

Subsection 4.1.1 already stated the importance of an incremental approach for the integration of logical documents, representation documents, and document presentations. This *incrementality* is achieved by *maintaining additional information* about which parts of a document were affected by a modification. In detail, the logical document features a resource computing the subtrees of the document's abstract syntax tree which have changed due to modification operations in the LogicalDocument subsystem interface. This information is already optimized regarding containment, overlapping, multiple operations concerning the same subtree etc. When the unparser is activated by the document manager, it operates only on those subtrees needing an update. As a result of the corresponding operations the unparser performs on the representation document, it receives a list of changed rectangles, again optimized to avoid redundant updates. This list is passed via the document manager to the UI/presentation manager. When the UI/presentation manager receives a request for presentation update, it checks whether some presentation window intersects with a changed area and calls the cutout manager accordingly. Note that this mechanism only works if the containment structure in the logical document's abstract syntax tree matches the containment structure of the representation. Although the metamodel described in subsection 4.3.2 allows complete independence of logical and representation structure, the incremental update scheme as presented here needs some modification in this case.

It should be noted that the unparser is actually a special variant of an *integration tool* as discussed in section 4.6. The main differences are: (1) The unparser never uses editor commands to manipulate the target (i.e. representation) document or to read the source (logical) document. Instead, it directly operates on the document interface. (2) The unparser does not require an integration document. This would be too inefficient to maintain and is not necessary because of the restriction to 1:n relationships between logical and representation documents. Instead, we use a short–circuit realization of increment–to–increment links across document boundaries: Every representation increment contains a reference to the logical increment it depends on. (3) Whereas an integrator as described in section 4.6 generally operates on demand (even automatic integration can be turned off by the user), unparsing is an integral part of IPSEN's dynamic behavior.

Until now, we have only discussed the transformation from logical to representation to presentation structures. In a perfectly symmetric system, these *transformations* would be possible in the *other direction* analogously. Currently, this is not realized in the IPSEN system. For the step from presentation to representation document, a backward transformation fails because the presentation is not a document and has no knowledge about the objects it contains. The only operation the cutout manager offers concerning the direction from a presentation to a representation document is therefore the mapping of some screen coordinates to the representation increment displayed at that position. The transformation from representation to logical documents is equally impossible due to the absence of a general parser for structured data. Just as above, the transformator is only able to compute the logical increment for a given representation increment.

Nevertheless, IPSEN offers the possibility to enter arbitrary text into a document. This provides a loophole for users who find manipulating the document in a strictly command–driven fashion inconvenient at times. The same mechanism facilitates loading given textual representations into the editor. This process of *free input* can be regarded as a manipulation of the *representation* document which is *transformed* into corresponding *changes* in the *logical document* performed by an incremental parser. But the representation document is actually a complex structured graph, not plain text as provided by the user. This plain text has to be parsed yielding a corresponding substructure of the logical document as will be explained in subsection 4.3.4. This new part of the logical document can then be redisplayed according to the "forward" transformation steps mentioned above. In this sense, the user never manipulates the representation document directly.

As mentioned above, free editing is *only possible for textual parts* of a document. It would be more symmetric if graphical parts could be handled similarly, but this is overly costly to realize. The most general case (and the one directly corresponding to free text input) would be to parse free–hand drawings. Here, the benefit for the user would be out of all proportion to the implementation efforts. Even the parsing of input delivered by a graphic editor which respects the type of the objects in the drawing would be enormous. Furthermore, the benefits for the user gained by using an arbitrary graphic editor instead of a corresponding IPSEN editor would be marginal.

4.1.4 Command Handling and Complex Commands

The description of the command cycle already showed that the IPSEN system is *command–driven*, i.e. all tool activity is performed on behalf of a command selection. With the exception of implicit command activation which will be explained later, this selection is made by the user through menus. The process of *menu creation, command selection, and command execution* is the subject of this subsection.

First of all, we should note that there are three different logical levels (represented by corresponding architectural levels) on which we could use the term "menu": On the highest level of abstraction, a menu simply denotes an (unstructured) set of commands the user can select from. This is the notion the tools and the environment control have of a menu, and we prefer to talk about command sets instead of menus when we look at the UI/Presentation Manager's interface and its clients (cf. subsection 4.1.2). On the next deeper level, a menu additionally contains structural representation information, i.e. a menu is an ordered list of choices grouped into a hierarchy of submenus. When we talk about menus in the following, we refer to this level offered by the CommandHandler's interface. Finally, a menu can be thought of as a number of buttons with a respective size, color, label, font, positioning etc. as well as a certain behavior (pull–down, pop–up, folding etc.). This is what we call a menu presentation, and the above mentioned details are encapsulated by the UIElements subsystem. Menu presentations are realized using the IPSEN window system (which actually delegates many of its tasks to a UI library) and are of no further concern in this subsection. In short, the term menu as defined here does include a hierarchical structure, but it does not imply a certain presentation style – in fact, it is even independent of whether the system's user interface is graphical or textual.

Before a menu can be created, the already mentioned command set has to be computed, i.e. every tool has to decide *which commands* it can offer with respect to the current state of the related documents, notably the current increment in the active representation document. *Several models* can be thought of here: (1) All possible commands are selectable at any time by the user. The tool rejects a command if it detects that the command is inapplicable. (2) All possible commands are visible to the user, but the user interface denies selecting any command which cannot be executed currently. (3) Only the set of executable commands is visible (and selectable) for the user. Note that any of these models is possible within the frame architecture from above. In the IPSEN implementation, both the second and the third model are supported. Especially model (3) is necessary for syntax–oriented command–driven editors, since every rule in the underlying grammar results in at least one possibly executable command. For a realistic grammar, the number of all commands therefore runs to several hundreds, only a small fraction of which are actually executable in any given situation. To confine the corresponding editor menu to reasonable and manageable sizes, it is obliged to display only the currently executable commands. Since the actual content of every menu may change during runtime, we call them *dynamic menus*.

On the other hand, for tools with a rather small set of possibly executable commands, it is preferable to display all of these commands but to disable their selection if appropriate. The advantage of this approach is that the corresponding menus retain a certain stability and the user is able to browse through the set of commands even if some of them are currently not executable. Our implementation features dynamic as well as *static menus* with disabled entries.

To reduce the task of creating and modifying the user interface for a specific tool, we encapsulate as much of the menu handling as possible in a *general mechanism*. This is fairly easy and well–supported by existing UI libraries as far as static menus are concerned. In contrast, providing an easy–to–use interface to a UI system covering dynamic menus as well requires some thought.

The key element of our menu handling/command selection mechanism is the *command table*. This table describes all possible commands with their (unique) logical command name, their menu entry label, and their keyboard shortcut. Furthermore, it specifies the structure of menus and submenus and the relative placement of entries in a (sub–)menu. Whereas a default version of the command table featuring all logical command names has to be provided at development time, every user may *override all aspects* of the menu at system startup time by providing his own command table, i.e. he can rename menu entries, hide commands from menus, completely rearrange the hierarchical structure of the menu, and insert alias menu entries for the same logical command. In other words, the command table contains all the information to map command sets onto menus and offers a single point where tool developers and users alike can configure the user interface.

At system development time, the command table is parsed and an *enumeration type* is generated containing an element for every logical command name. As was already mentioned in subsection 4.1.2, every tool interface provides an operation to compute the current set of commands the tool wants to offer. This operation returns a set of elements of the generated enumeration type. For each element, the tool also specifies whether the command should be selectable and the tool operation to call on selection.

To start the command selection process, the environment control uses this operation to *query all attached modules* about their current command set and stores the results using the CommandSet subsystem which is part of the UI/PresentationManager subsystem. Fig. 4.3 shows the internal data structures involved in this functionality: the LogicalCommands module contains the definition of the enumeration type generated from the command table. The CmdTblEntry data type represents entries in the table, such entries are either descriptions of command groups (which set up the hierarchical structure) or of command entries (directly related to logical commands). To allow easy access to the hierarchical structure of the table at runtime, it is internally organized as a graph (in the current implementation actually a tree) with CmdGrpEntrys as inner nodes and CmdEntrys as leaf nodes. They are connected with CmdTblEdges. The *graph structure* is constructed at startup time from the contents of the command table. Each node in this graph contains attributes describing whether the corresponding command (group) should be displayed and, if so, whether it should be selectable by the user. Finally, the CmdSet module provides operations to store the current set of commands offered by the tools. Internally, the CmdSet module toggles the above mentioned attributes in the CmdGraph nodes accordingly.

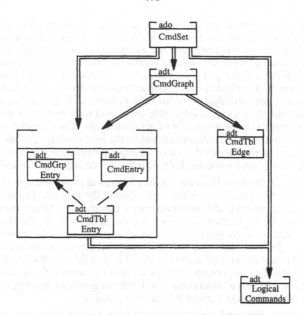

Fig. 4.3. Architecture of the CommandSet subsystem

When the environment control has completed the construction of the command set, it instructs the UI/presentation manager to *create an appropriate menu*. Since the UI/presentation manager has access to the hierarchical structure of the command set (via the CmdGraph interface), it can traverse the underlying tree in top–down order and create submenus as well as menu entries for each command offered by some tool. The actual drawing of screen objects with a certain menu style (pop–up, pull–down, folding etc.) is performed by the CommandHandler subsystem in UIElements.

Next, the UI/presentation manager asks the command handler for a *command selection*. In the current implementation, this selection can be made by clicking at an entry from a menu with the mouse or by entering a keyboard shortcut. The command handler has access to the menu entry labels and shortcut codes for associated commands via an appropriate view on the command table. The UI/presentation manager is neither aware of what interaction elements the command handler offers to the user, nor how a command is selected. It just receives a notification when some selection has been performed in the form of an element of the generated enumeration type. This selection is passed to the environment control which in turn calls the appropriate tool operation.

The second part of this subsection is devoted to explaining how *complex commands* are handled. By complex commands we understand commands which do not give back control to the user after an increment modification, instead they may involve subdialogs or a sequence of simple commands to perform complex document modifications.

The first point to discuss here is the so–called *automatic* or *implicit command activation*. Implicit command activation is motivated by the following scenario: A user is working with a syntax–directed editor. When he inserts a new structure, like expanding the placeholder for a statement to an if–statement, he will probably want to continue with expanding placeholders for a newly introduced substructure, in our case entering e.g. the condition for the if–statement. Furthermore, it is most likely that he prefers typing the expression in free input mode rather than creating it using structure–based commands. The general idea behind this example is that, after a command has been executed, the system can sometimes guess with sufficient reliability what the user wants to do next.

Several mechanisms can be thought of to realize the sort of intelligent tool behavior sketched above. In our current environment, the idea is as follows: When the collection of command sets from the tools is complete, the environment control does not directly start the menu construction and command selection process. Instead, it tries to determine a sensible command itself and, if this is possible, executes it directly, bypassing menu construction and user interaction. In order to determine such a command, the command table is extended with an additional priority number entry for each command. Before a menu is generated, the environment control looks for a selectable command with maximum priority. If some unique command has the highest priority of all commands, it is executed directly. Otherwise, the usual user interaction is required to select the next command. Note that this functionality is not necessarily restricted to one subsequent operation; in fact, some user–selected operation may trigger a whole chain of implicit command activations.

An important point about implicit command activation as presented here is that it is rather useless if the current increment stays the same during the process. In the example from above, the current increment is at first the statement placeholder. After the expansion to an if–statement, it will be the if–statement since its root node replaces the placeholder node in the abstract syntax tree. Now it is necessary to *advance the current increment* to the Boolean expression inside the if–statement before the implicit activation of the command "open free input on the current increment" makes sense. Whereas the actual activation of the command is parameterized by the command table as sketched above, the increment selection is currently hard–wired into an operation which tries to guess, depending on the previous user interaction, what the next current increment should be.

Note that implicit command activation, apart from keeping dynamic menus small, is another reason for maintaining exactly *one current increment*. On the other hand, this has proved to be no severe restriction: Experience shows that a vast majority of tool operations acts on one increment only. Some of the remaining commands operate on two increments, like drawing an edge in a PROGRES production or inserting a link in an integration tool. In such cases, IPSEN works by offering the command if the current increment is suitable as one element of the required increment pair, and the tool requests the selection of the other element if the command is activated. Especially in the case of integration tools, we can also think of manipulating an increment–to–increment link as an operation on the corresponding increment in the integration document.

Another extension to the basic command selection model is useful when a user wants to execute an explicitly given command sequence several times. In this case, it is necessary to provide some sort of *macro mechanism*, i.e. the possibility to define command sequences and to execute them with little effort. Such a macro feature is currently integrated in IPSEN's user interface. It will allow the user to define, store, and edit sequences of logical command names which can be executed at a single keystroke or mouse selection.

A far more general idea than what was discussed so far is to introduce *method–oriented tools* or *semantical tools*. Such a tool provides operations on a higher level than the tools described earlier; it groups simple tool or document operations to semantical operations. Again using a syntax–directed editor for Modula–2 as an example, the editor offers a command to insert a case–statement where all nonterminals inside the statement still have to be expanded manually. A semantical tool on the other hand could feature a command to insert a case–statement with respect to a certain enumeration type where an alternative for each element of the type is already present. Another example would be to create an abstract data type module: An appropriate tool could insert an opaque type declaration and create and destroy operations for the type's instances. For the implementation part, the tool could create templates for the operations declared in the interface. In this sense, the tool is indeed method–oriented because it augments the basic editor operations with operations to use the underlying language in a certain way. In contrast to changing the language itself, i.e. wiring the language extensions into the grammar, we can observe as a major difference that in this case, all users have to use exactly this extension. This can be an advantage (the methodical use of the basic language has to be obeyed), but it can also be a disadvantage (the tool cannot support extensions on which there is no general agreement, and changing the grammar possibly requires modifications in all corresponding documents).

Furthermore, it is easy to see that implicit command activation and macro mechanisms are subsumed under the notion of method–oriented tools. Whereas implicit command activation currently requires a special consideration in the command handling mechanism and quite some experience to parameterize correctly, an appropriate method–oriented tool could provide the same functionality without affecting the basic mechanism at all. Even more, a table–driven version of such a tool would offer the user a convenient way to influence its behavior. Note also that an integration tool as described in section 4.6 fits exactly into the notion of a semantical tool.

At the end of this subsection, we want to remark that a *command–driven approach* as presented here allows the encapsulation of the complete command handling mechanism in general and generated components. On the other hand, this paradigm is sometimes unwieldy, especially when a tool wants to *interact with the user directly*. In the current implementation, a restricted form of communication is possible using notification windows. Such windows can be created by the tool via the UI/presentation manager. The tool can specify the presentation the notification window should be attached to, whether or not the user has to confirm the window before the system will continue execution, and a message text to be shown in the window. These notification windows are useful for (error) messages or warnings the tool wants to display, but they provide *tool–to–user communication only*, which is not sufficient in special situations.

As an *example*, consider a tool which wants the user to select from a list of alternatives or to enter some additional information. In some cases, this functionality can be integrated into the general mechanism, e.g. one command is offered for each of the alternatives the user can choose from. Sometimes though the need for additional information arises during the execution of a tool operation. The tool might not be able to stop this execution, letting the user provide the information via a command selection. First, the tool itself cannot guarantee that the user will continue the execution of the "dangling" operation once the command cycle has returned to the environment control. Second, the tool, being a functional component, cannot preserve state between operation activations, i.e. even if the user selects the command to continue execution, the tool has lost all information already acquired before the user interaction.

For these reasons, we are currently working on a *generalized scheme* of interaction between tool and user. The UI/presentation manager offers a variety of *dialog elements* to tools which they may use to perform arbitrary communication with the user. These elements are realized with appropriate basic services from the UIElements subsystem. In contrast to the specification of commands in the command table, the tool developer and user may specify such dialog elements down to the representation level, i.e. they can freely determine the composition of dialogs from basic elements as sliders, buttons, scrollbars etc. The general look–and–feel though is still encapsulated in the UIElements subsystem.

Another alternative to strictly command–driven interaction concerns mainly structure–based editor tools. For example, IPSEN currently provides commands to expand a placeholder to an appropriate structure and alternatively the free input of (textual) document parts. In the first case, the editor actually manipulates the logical structure of the document which is then unparsed to yield a representation. Using the second method, the textual representation of some increment is handed over to a conventional editor, and the text is parsed back into the logical structure after the user finished his modifications. Other systems try to integrate these approaches into a *uniform model*: The user may type text like in IPSEN's free input mode, but the text is automatically parsed in the background, i.e. the logical structure is created and modified continuously as the user edits the text. This mechanism, sometimes called syntax–driven approach, combines well with some sort of *completion functionality*: When the parser recognizes the beginning of a structure, it can complete the rest of the structure automatically ("aggressive completion") or on user demand ("polite completion"). This model is currently not supported within the IPSEN framework. Although completion could be readily integrated into the editor used for free input, the simulation of background parsing with one command for each character the user might type would be rather awkward.

4.1.5 A Complete View on the IPSEN Architecture

In this subsection, we turn our attention from single technical environments to *integrated overall environments* (cf. subsection 1.6.4). As was already described, such an environment consists mainly of single technical environments (as presented earlier in this section) or of integrated environments (containing integration tools) together with an administration environment. The architectural structure of the administration environment is identical to that of a technical environment. At the top layer of the overall environment, a new `Over-allEnvironmentControl` component provides a frame for the contained environments, i.e. the role of this component for the overall environment is comparable to that of an `EnvironmentControl` component for single environments. Its major task is to allow the user to select a specific technical environment he wants to work with. Each of the technical environments is connected to the framework by an `ExtendedEnvironment-Control` component which coordinates the interaction between the technical environment and the administration environment.

Subsection 1.6.4 gave a conceptual overview considering all components used for the handling of an overall configuration. Here, we narrow our focus to a specific instance of an integrated environment for some subconfiguration. This means that we understand the term "integrated" here on the level of bound environments consisting of single technical environments with integration tools for the consistency and transformation between corresponding technical documents.

Fig. 4.4 shows an *example architecture* featuring three technical environments, namely one for Requirements Engineering, one for Programming–in–the–Large, and one for Programming–in–the–Small. This yields a (bound) system for a user who can take on either of the corresponding roles in the project. Note that the extended environment control of the administrative environment is missing: The user of the resulting system is not supposed to take on the role of the administrator. On the other hand, he might change administrative data implicitly, e.g. by creating a new Programming–In–The–Small document. In this sense, he has to have access to the administrative configuration via a corresponding view on the administrative documents.

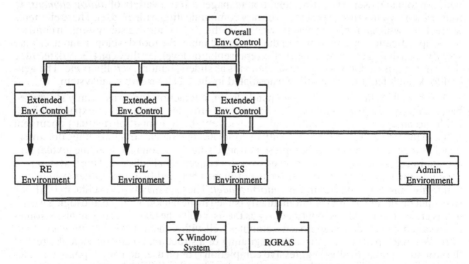

Fig. 4.4. Coarse example architecture of an overall environment

The actual access to data shared with other users working with similar environments is realized employing the *distributed* multi–user version of the *database*, RGRAS. This can be regarded as an *alternative* to the architecture of fig. 1.34 where each technical environment contained an own instance of the (undistributed) GRAS database and remote access was implemented on file system level. This does not necessarily mean that the environments have no local copy of the database: It is not unlikely that some environment uses a local GRAS for representation documents, whereas it accesses logical documents through the RGRAS interface. Whatever solution is chosen is of course apparent in the architecture specifications of the respective environment subsystems.

As an example of how an *integration tool fits* into this coarse *architecture*, we take a look at the RE/PiL integrator (cf. subsection 1.6.3 and section 4.6). Since this integrator is used to create and maintain an architecture document consistent with the requirements specification, it is part of the PiL environment. Fig. 4.5 shows the relevant subarchitecture in more detail. For reasons of simplicity, we have omitted all components concerned with document visualization and user interaction from this figure, so it focuses on logical documents and tools.

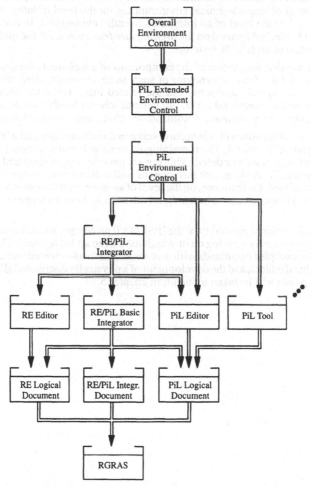

Fig. 4.5. Integration between technical environments

As was already mentioned earlier, we support only *statically bound* IPSEN prototypes currently. The only exception so far is distribution below the GRAS interface, i.e. access to remote documents via the distributed database (cf. subsection 4.2). Apart from the possibilities offered by RGRAS, we are currently investigating other aspects of physically distributing an IPSEN system, like dynamically attaching and detaching tools to or from a technical environment or technical environments to or from an overall environment. Some considerations about this topic follow in chapter 5.

Note that the RELogicalDocument component appears in the RE as well as in the PiL environment. Both interfaces may operate on the *same actual document* though using the distributed RGRAS database which inherently coordinates concurrent access to the document from either environment. In our case, this coordination is rather simple since the PiL environment accesses the RE document read–only; the RE/PiL integration tool is a transformator in the sense of subsection 1.6.3, cf. fig. 1.32.

4.1.6 Summary

In this section, we described the architecture of the IPSEN system on three levels of granularity: on the level of single technical environments, on the level of integrated technical environments, and on the level of an integrated overall environment. In contrast to other sections of this chapter, we focused on the *architecture framework*, i.e. the global static and dynamic properties of an IPSEN system.

After a more detailed *description* of the components of a *technical environment*'s architecture, we sketched the *dynamic behavior* of such an environment. Here, we emphasized the visualization of logical documents and the related incremental techniques. Another focus was the so–called command cycle, our general scheme for the coordination of command set evaluation, menu creation, command selection, and command execution.

In this sense, the discussions of this section serve as an introduction and a framework for the following parts of chapter 4. The remaining sections will explain some of the components mentioned here in greater detail. This covers generic components and mechanisms not dedicated to specific environment instances as well as how an environment for a certain purpose can be realized. Furthermore, on the level of an integrated overall environment, the administrative environment and its interaction with technical environments receive further treatment.

Besides sketching the functionality of the IPSEN 4.0 prototype, we also mentioned some *extensions* we are currently working on or which have been added recently. This comprises better support for complex commands with macros and method–oriented tools, layout algorithms for graphical editors, and the development of a physically distributed IPSEN system. Some of these points will be taken up again in chapter 5.

4.2 GRAS: A Graph–Oriented Software Engineering Database System

N. Kiesel, A. Schürr, B. Westfechtel

Building integrated, interactive, and incrementally working tools and environments for application areas like software engineering, CAD, or office automation has been a great challenge. Complex documents such as requirements definitions, software architectures, or module implementations have to be represented, and efficient storage, retrieval, read and update operations have to be supported. To this end, we have developed the graph–based database system *GRAS* /6. BL85, KSW 93, KSW 95a, KSW 95b, LS 88/. As emphasized throughout the whole book, attributed graphs are a well–suited data model for nonstandard application areas such as those mentioned above. GRAS provides tool builders with an *abstract interface* so that they need not care about basic implementation issues, e.g. mapping of graphs onto files, concurrency control, distribution, or maintenance of derived data.

GRAS is a *reusable subsystem* which is heavily employed in all environments described in this book: IPSEN (sections 2.1 – 2.4), PROGRES (section 3.6), and also SUKITS (sections 2.5 and 4.7). GRAS has also been applied in other software engineering projects, including Rigi /4. MK 88b/, CADDY /4. EHH 89/, Merlin /4. PS 92/, and Melmac /4. DG 90/. The application spectrum covers software engineering, CIM, office automation, information systems, visual languages, etc. In contrast to traditional business applications with large amounts of flat, regularly structured data, all of these *nonstandard applications* are characterized by complex data of many different types for which fairly sophisticated consistency constraints have to be maintained.

GRAS has a long *history* (cf. section 1.8). The first prototype of the GRAS system was completed in 1985 /6. BL 85/. Based on the kernel facilities provided by this implementation, several extensions (event handling, transactions, undo/redo, deltas, graph schemes, derived attributes) were gradually added which are part of the current official GRAS release. All of these parts were implemented in Modula–2 (and are currently ported to Modula–3). Furthermore, a layer for client/server distribution and concurrency control was implemented in C. This layer has been released internally and has been in use since 1993.

4.2.1 Introduction: GRAS as Nonstandard Database System

Database systems for *business applications*, e.g. airline reservation, library management, or accounting, are not well suited for *nonstandard applications*, e.g. software engineering, CAD, or office automation. Business and nonstandard applications differ as follows (/6. Ber87/, see also subsections 1.3.4, 1.5.1 and 1.5.5):

(a) In business applications, large amounts of *regularly structured data* have to be managed. Nonstandard applications are characterized by *many different types* of objects and relations.

(b) Database systems for business applications offer a data manipulation language which allows for performing *simple operations* on *large amounts* of *data* (e.g. raise the salary of all employees by 3 %). In nonstandard applications, *complex operations* have to be performed on small sets of objects (e.g. commands of a syntax–aided editor which checks context–sensitive correctness).

(c) Business applications access data in *short transactions* with classical ACID properties (atomicity, consistency, isolation, and duration). In nonstandard applications, design activities are carried out in *long transactions* which require cooperation and data exchange before commit. Due to these differing requirements, long transactions typically possess only a subset of the ACID properties.

(d) While database systems for business support primitive *data types* of *limited size* (e.g. integer, real, or boolean), nonstandard database systems also have to manage *long fields*, e.g. for storing bitmaps.

(e) Nonstandard applications must manage multiple *versions* of data, e.g. multiple versions of a software architecture. In addition to sequential revisions (ordered by creation time), parallel variants have to be supported, as well. Most business application only provide access to the current data; historical databases assume a *linear time axis* which is too restrictive for nonstandard applications.

GRAS has been designed to meet the requirements of nonstandard applications, especially of software engineering. GRAS provides *operations* on *attributed graphs* which are well suited for representing complex structured data. In addition to short transactions, GRAS supports cooperation support for long work sessions through its concurrency control layer. Data of arbitrary size can be stored in node attributes. Furthermore, GRAS provides basic operations for efficiently storing multiple versions through deltas which are simultaneously used to implement undo/redo operations, e.g. for syntax–aided editors.

On the one hand, GRAS is an independent component which has been used in multiple environments (see above). On the other hand, there are some close relations between GRAS and the PROGRES development environment:

(a) GRAS and PROGRES share the *same data model*, namely attributed graphs.

(b) GRAS provides merely an *operational interface*, while PROGRES comes with a *specification language*.

(c) A specification written in PROGRES in particular defines a *graph scheme*. It is the task of the PROGRES compiler/interpreter to translate the specification of a graph scheme into a sequence of operations exported by GRAS. These operations build up the internal representation of a graph scheme.

(d) Furthermore, a PROGRES specification contains high–level graph transformations, i.e. *graph rewrite rules*. These rules are mapped onto primitive operations provided by GRAS (creation/deletion of single nodes and edges, assignment of attribute values).

4.2.2 The Kernel of GRAS: Architectural Description

In the next two subsections, we discuss the internal architecture of the GRAS system. In order to provide for reusability and flexibility, we have designed a layered software *architecture* which is divided into two parts:

(a) Its lower part (the *kernel*), which is depicted in fig. 4.6 and will be explained in this subsection, consists of layers for data abstraction.

(b) By way of contrast, all layers of the *upper part*, which will be explained in the following subsection, rely on a common, graph–oriented data model. Each layer incrementally adds a set of logically related services to the functionality of the layer beneath it.

When proceeding through the layers of the architecture, we describe their *functionality* (i.e. the interface provided to upper layers) as well as their *realization*. We motivate our central design decisions not only with respect to individual layers, but also with respect to their arrangement (i.e. their position within the architecture).

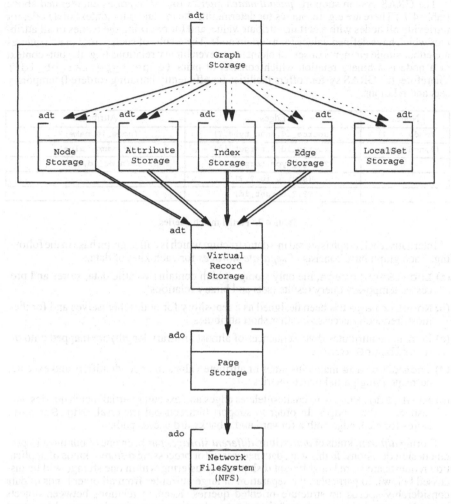

Fig. 4.6. Lower layers of the GRAS architecture

Graph Storage

The GraphStorage is the topmost data abstraction layer. It provides a *graph–oriented interface* consisting of GRAS resources (procedures) for creating, deleting, and accessing all kinds of graph components. In particular, the interface offers write operations for creating and deleting typed nodes, for creating and deleting typed directed edges, for initializing and modifying arbitrarily long node attributes, and finally for maintaining attribute indexes.

To characterize all read operations, graphs are considered *sets* of *tuples* of the following three forms:

(a) node := (node_id, node_type).

(b) edge := (source_id, edge_type, target_id).

(c) attribute := (node_id, name, value).

The GRAS system supports *partial match queries* for the relations enumerated above (table 4.7). There are e.g. resources for determining the in– and out–context of a node, for retrieving all nodes with a certain attribute value, and for returning the names of all attributes which have defined values for a certain node. The results of such partial match queries are either single elements or sets of elements or even binary relations (e.g. the out–context of a node is a binary relation which consists of pairs (edge_type, target_id)). Therefore, the GRAS system offers facilities for efficiently handling (ordered) temporary sets and relations.

Nodes	Edges	Attributes
(node_id, ?)	(source_id, edge_type, ?)	(node_id, name, ?)
(?, node_type)	(source_id, ?, target_id)	(?, name, value)
	(?, edge_type, target_id)	(node_id, ?, ?)
	(source_id, ?, ?)	
	(?, ?, target_id)	

Table 4.7. Partial match queries

Internally, each graph is stored in a data structure which is called graph base in the following. Each graph base consists of *separate storages* for each kind of data:

(a) LocalSetStorage, the only storage which contains volatile data, stores and processes temporary query results (sets and binary relations).

(b) NodeStorage has been designed as a repository for nodes themselves and for their most frequently accessed, rather short attributes.

(c) Long node attributes (byte sequences of almost arbitrary length) are mapped onto the AttributeStorage.

(d) IndexStorage maintains maps of attribute values to node identifiers and executes corresponding partial match queries.

(e) Finally, EdgeStorage creates/deletes edges and executes partial match queries with respect to these edges. In order to support bidirectional traversal, EdgeStorage stores for each edge both a forward and a backward access path.

Storing *different* kinds of *data* within *different storages* has been one of our most important design decisions. In this way, data necessary for processing different kinds of application requests are stored on different disk pages (clustering within one storage will be discussed below). In particular, the separation of large attributes from all other kinds of data considerably speeds up structure–oriented queries. Keeping relations between objects (nodes) separately is a proven technique for accelerating navigational queries. In contrast to "path indexes" in /6. KD 92/ and "access support relations" in /6. KM 92/, GRAS even avoids duplication of intrinsic relations within an additional index structure.

On the other hand, *operations* which affect a node including all its attributes and edges (as creation and deletion) need access to a greater *number* of *pages*. This disadvantage seems to be negligible if the database system's cache has a reasonable size. In this case, it makes no difference whether all needed nodes are stored on n1 pages, their attributes on separate n2 pages, and their edges on separate n3 pages or whether nodes are stored together with their attributes and edges on n1+n2+n3 pages (see also benchmark results in subsection 4.2.4).

Virtual Record Storage

All permanent storages described above *share* the following *characteristics*:

(a) They contain persistent data of dynamically varying size, ranging from a few hundred bytes up to some megabytes.

(b) Each data portion stored in one of these storages has to be identified by a unique identifier. These identifiers are internally used for establishing cross–references between different portions of data. They are also used for representing nodes in application–specific data structures. Unique identifiers must not vary during the whole lifespan of the data portions they belong to.

(c) Furthermore, some of these storages have to support efficient retrieval of data portions, selected by (only a part of) their identifiers (partial match queries).

Having these common characteristics in mind, we have implemented one *parametric* `VirtualRecordStorage` (cf. fig. 4.6) with a *record–oriented interface*. This storage realizes all specialized permanent storages mentioned above. The parameters mainly define the structure of records. Any record has an identifier of fixed size and additionally may consist of a data area of fixed size (e.g. for storing node types), a number of data areas of dynamically varying size (e.g. for storing long attributes), and a number of areas for ordered sets of identifiers (e.g. for storing references to other records).

In order to clarify the process of *implementing substorages* as special instances of the `VirtualRecordStorage` let us consider the most complicated case, the realization of the `EdgeStorage`. As already explained before, the components of this storage are tuples of the form

    `(source_node_id, edge_type, target_node_id),`

and we have to answer partial match queries with two specified components

    `(source_node_id, edge_type, ?)` and
    `(?, edge_type, target_node_id),`

as well as partial match queries with one specified component

    `(source_node_id, ?, ?)` and `(?, ?, target_node_id).`

For efficiently processing queries with a specified source (target) node identifier, this node identifier must be a prefix of the corresponding record identifier (see below). Therefore, we have to store two *permutations* of edge triplets as records with the following layout:

(a) The record's identifier consists of a source (target) node identifier i followed by a permutation flag (distinguishing between source and target identifiers) and an edge type t.

(b) The fixed size data area has length 0.

(c) And the last record component is an ordered set for all those target (source) node identifiers which belong to any edge with source (target) i and type t.

Records of the virtual storage are mapped onto locations on external storage pages in the following way: The unique database identifiers which identify records are hashed onto physical addresses. A special variant of binary index trees, so-called *tries* (cf. e.g. /6. ED 88/), is used for selecting a record's page, and *static hashing* is used for determining an appropriate position on a selected page.

Fig. 4.8 contains a trivial *example* of a substorage with five records distributed over three pages. In this case, the first identifier bit of the record 10000 and the first two bits of all other records are used to determine their pages (the first page contains all records with 1 as identifier prefix, the second page all records with 01 as identifier prefix , and the third page all records with 00 as identifier prefix). All remaining identifier bits are input to the static hashing function which computes positions of records on selected pages.

Each *substorage* has its *own index tree* so that structural data (e.g. edges) and nonstructural data (e.g. attribute values) are kept on separate pages. The data representing index trees are stored on separate pages, too. Beside this overall strategy for storing different kinds of data on different pages, the GRAS system additionally tries to cluster records within one substorage in the following way: The algorithms which generate database identifiers for new records and thus determine the page positions of new records are sensitive to requests of the application layer, i.e. the application may specify neighborhoods for records

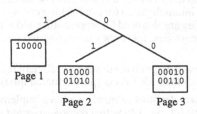

Fig. 4.8. Indexing and clustering records

which are often accessed together (e.g. nodes connected by certain edges). This information is used for *clustering logically related records* onto adjacent storage locations. More precisely, the computation of a database identifier for a new record may be influenced by the database identifier of an already existing record, so that

(a) the hashing function maps the new record onto the same page as the already existing record whenever possible,

(b) subsequent splitting of pages does not destroy these record clusters,

(c) and the index trees do not degenerate in the case of splitting an old page into two new pages by mapping almost all records of the old page onto one of the new pages.

Note that it is difficult and sometimes even impossible to find an *optimal solution* for both the conditions (b) and (c). Consider again the situation of fig. 4.8 which contains a somewhat artificially constructed but illustrative example for this problem: When creating a new record "nearby" record 0101, we have the following alternatives for the new record identifier:

(a) An identifier with prefix 010: this choice has the disadvantage that a splitting of page 2 produces one empty page and one page containing all records of the old page.

(b) An identifier with prefix 011: this choice has the disadvantage that a splitting of page 2 maps the old record 0101 and the new record onto different pages.

Therefore, we have tested different *identifier creation heuristics* which try to find the right balance between the risk of producing unbalanced index trees and the risk of scattering logically related portions of data over many pages. Furthermore, the creation of database identifiers and thus the selection of physical record addresses may even be controlled completely by a GRAS application which may exploit *application specific knowledge* to improve clustering (see benchmark results in subsection 4.2.4).

To summarize, the presented indexing scheme and its accompanying identifier creation algorithm have the following *characteristics*:

(a) The hashing function, which maps record identifiers onto page locations, is order preserving and thus allows for efficiently retrieving all records with a given identifier prefix.

(b) Order preserving hashing functions in general are not able to guarantee a uniform distribution of records over pages. This is the task of our identifier creation algorithm.

(c) The algorithms for inserting, deleting, and searching records are rather simple and straightforward to implement.

(d) Nevertheless, they can deal with data of rather dynamically varying size without any needs for maintaining overflow pages or for global reorganizations of data or index structures.

(e) And the index trees themselves (tries) are very small in comparison to the data they are used to address and, therefore, may and should normally be kept in main memory.

Page Storage and Network File System

The `PageStorage` (cf. fig. 4.6) provides a *page–oriented interface*; each page is a sequence of bytes which has a fixed length. Graphs are not required to fit into main memory; therefore, the page storage maintains a page cache in main memory and controls transfer of pages between disk and main memory. Paging is driven by an LRU strategy which takes additional factors such as frequency of access and priority into account (log pages are assigned the highest priority, followed by index pages and data pages). The size of the page cache may be fixed as needed. If the underlying operating system provides a sufficiently large virtual memory, the size may be chosen so that all graph operations are eventually performed in virtual memory. In this way, paging is delegated to the operating system.

Finally, the `NetworkFileSystem` layer provides the interface to the underlying operating system's *distributed file management*. It maps page sequences onto files. Since its interface is independent of a particular operating system, it is an easy task to port the GRAS system to another operating system. To this end, only few pages of source code implementing the file system layer have to be adapted or written anew.

4.2.3 Enhancing Layers: Architectural Description

All layers on top of the GRAS system's kernel `GraphStorage` (see fig. 4.9) rely on a common, graph–oriented data model. Each layer incrementally adds a set of *logically related services* to the functionality of the layer beneath it. They are to be explained below.

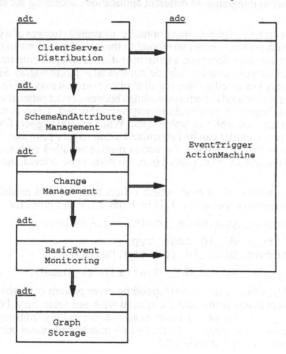

Fig. 4.9. Upper layers of the GRAS architecture

The *layers* of the *upper part* introduce event handling (`BasicEventMonitoring`), transactions, undo/redo, and deltas (`ChangeManagement`), graph schemes and management of derived attributes and relations (`SchemeAndAttributeManagement`), and concurrency control and distribution (ClientServerDistribution). Orthogonal to these layers, an EventTriggerActionMachine provides common functions for event handling which are used in all layers. Note that event handling cannot be introduced once and for all in BasicEventMonitoring. Rather, it has to be extended as new functionality is added in higher layers.

Arrangement of upper *layers* will be motivated at the end of each layer description part, respectively. Since at first glance the extensions provided by these layers seem to be independent of each other, it is attempting to follow a 'toolkit' approach: Firstly, for each extension a corresponding subclass of GraphStorage is provided; secondly, all desired combinations are realized by multiple inheritance. However, a severe drawback of this approach consists in the fact that one extension cannot be implemented with the help of another (e.g. management of derived attributes cannot exploit event handling). Furthermore, combination of different extensions is not for free and may involve a great deal of re–implementation.

Basic Event Monitoring

Event/Trigger mechanisms are a fundamental concept of most so–called *active database systems* /6. BM 91, 6. Day 88, 6. DKM 86/. They are also used in modern applications for separating the user interface component from the functional part of the application. Event/ Trigger mechanisms may be used for incremental supervision of certain consistency constraints, incremental computation of derived data like derived attribute values or relations, and a–posteriori integration of different applications accessing the same data structure.

In GRAS, *events* refer to database transitions, i.e. to atomic changes of a graph database. Roughly, these database transitions correspond to the write operations introduced in subsection 4.2.2. In some cases, however, a write operation is mapped onto multiple database transitions (e.g. deletion of a node includes deletion of all adjacent edges). Since an application is interested only in a specific subset of all evoked events, it may define event patterns. Furthermore, *triggers* are used to perform bindings between event patterns and corresponding *action routines*. In general, m:n bindings may be established. Triggers may be activated and deactivated at any time while a graph is open. When several triggers fire for a database transition, the execution order can be determined using trigger priorities. When an event matches an event pattern of a trigger, the action routine is called with actual parameters which depend on the type of event pattern (e.g. the node to be deleted, the source node of a new edge, etc.).

GRAS supports various *event types* which reflect both the data model and the set of change and administration operations. This includes e.g. event types for

(a) nodes: (node_type, node_id, {Create, Delete}),

(b) edges: (src_node_id, edge_type,
              target_node_id, {Create, Delete}),

(c) attributes: (node_type, node_id, attribute_name).

For each event type there exists a corresponding *event pattern type* which allows to replace arbitrary event components with the special wildcard value Any. For example, the event pattern (NT$_1$, Any, Create) matches all events resulting from creation of a node of type NT$_1$, whereas (Any, Any, 100, Delete) matches all events occurring from the deletion of an incoming edge of node 100.

Event management is realized using a generic *event–trigger–action machine* (see e.g. /6. TN 92/ for a general discussion about such machines), which is instantiated by GRAS–specific event patterns and corresponding compare operations (cf. fig. 4.9). Relevant state transitions in GRAS are transformed into events and sent (via procedure calls) to this instantiated machine, whereas the definition of event patterns, triggers and actions are performed by the application. The machine also allows for the definition of event patterns, triggers, and actions, which are automatically activated when accessing the graph. In this way, dynamic constraints may be enforced in addition to static constraints of the graph scheme.

As event management is based on the concept of monitoring state transitions to the database kernel, the *layer* evoking events due to database transitions has to be as *close* as possible to the *kernel*. Otherwise, database operations performed by layers between the kernel and the event management layer would be undetectable. For other event classes concerning e.g. change management or concurrency control which do not necessarily result in database transitions, corresponding events must be evoked directly from within these layers. This results in an architecture with a basic event management layer placed above the kernel, and an event–trigger–action machine standing vertically aside all enhancing layers.

Change Management

The ChangeManagement /6. Wes 89/ layer is placed above BasicEventMonitoring and adds to this layer all functions for logging, storing, and executing sequences of change operations (cf. fig. 4.9). Change management provides for *user recovery* (undo/ redo of user commands), *system recovery* (recovery from system failures), and *deltas* (efficient storage of versions). These tasks are handled by GRAS in an integrated way by maintaining logs of change operations.

Following /4. ACS 84/, we define *user recovery* as recovery actions which are controlled by the user rather than by the system which he uses. For example, the user may undo a command which was activated inadvertently or switch back and forth between breakpoints when debugging a program. GRAS supports implementation of user recovery in the following way: While a graph is open, an application may define checkpoints. Typically, this is done when the execution of a user command terminates. By means of *undo* and *redo* operations, the application may switch back and forth between arbitrary checkpoints (within the limits of the current session initiated by OpenGraph). Checkpoints are ordered sequentially. Undo and redo are constrained such that they always yield a semantically consistent state. This could not be guaranteed if e.g. selective undo were supported (undo command i, but not commands $i+1, \ldots, n$).

Checkpoints are also used for *system recovery*: On system failure, GRAS tries to restore the most recent checkpoint. Furthermore, system recovery is supported by *nested transactions* which are useful for implementing user commands in a layered architecture: Each application layer defines a corresponding level of consistency and uses transactions to guarantee atomicity of the operations which it provides. In particular, each layer is able to abort operation sequences of the next lower level which lead to an inconsistent state from its point of view. Note that checkpoints are treated as boundaries of top–level transactions.

In addition to supporting undo/redo "in the small", a software engineering environment has to provide for undo/redo "in the large". This is the task of version control /4. Tic 85/. While GRAS does not incorporate a specific model of version control (which is nearly always subject to debate), it does provide flexible mechanisms for efficient storage of versions by *graph deltas* /6. Wes 89/. Here, the term "delta" denotes a sequence of operations that, being applied to a version v1, yields another version v2. Instead of storing all versions of one document completely, it suffices to store a few of them completely and reconstruct the others by means of deltas.

GRAS provides for flexible delta control: Deltas save storage space at the cost of access time. Before a version may be operated on, it may have to be reconstructed. Thus, (optional) use of deltas is controlled by the application in order to achieve an appropriate balance of storage and runtime efficiency. Thereby, the application may choose between *forward* and *backward deltas*. This is illustrated in fig. 4.10 which shows a version tree (part a) and different examples for the storage of its four graph versions (parts b–d):

(b) Only forward deltas are used.

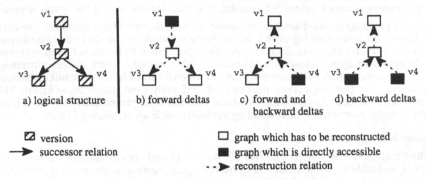

a) logical structure b) forward deltas c) forward and d) backward deltas
                                            backward deltas

⬛ version   ☐ graph which has to be reconstructed
⟶ successor relation   ■ graph which is directly accessible
                            - -▶ reconstruction relation

Fig. 4.10. Flexibility of delta control

(c) The most recent version on the main trunk is stored completely; all other versions are reconstructed by means of backward and forward deltas. This solution was pioneered by RCS /4. Tic 85/.

(d) Only backward deltas are used. In this case, there may be multiple ways to reconstruct a version. Then, GRAS selects the most efficient one automatically.

Virtually all functions of change management are implemented in a uniform way by *logs* of change operations on graphs. Two kinds of logs are needed: The forward log is used to implement redo, forward deltas, and recovery from system crashes, while the backward log is used analogously for undo, backward deltas, and transaction abort. Thus, logs are reused in an elegant manner for multiple purposes. Particularly, logging of change operations yields a delta on the side so that its costly a–posteriori reconstruction may be avoided. However, direct use of logs may be inefficient because the effect of one operation may be overridden by subsequent operations. Therefore, logs are compressed a–posteriori by removing redundant operations.

In order to execute coarse–grained operations (e.g. Open, Close, Delete, Copy operations on graphs), GRAS maintains an internal data structure which is invisible for applications. This data structure is modeled and realized as a graph which is called *delta graph*. Delta graphs are maintained within the ChangeManagement layer. Fig. 4.11 shows an example of an (internal) delta graph and its relations to a corresponding (external) version graph. In general, a delta graph consists of the following components:

(a) Graph state nodes represent states which may be classified as follows: Firstly, a state is either directly accessible, or it is reconstructed by application of deltas. Secondly, a state is either visible to the application, or it is used internally as an intermediate state that is produced when reconstructing a visible state.

(b) Delta nodes represent sequences of graph operations which have been executed within one session (from Open to Close).

(c) By means of reconstruction edges, a delta is related to the source state to which it is applied, and to the target state which it produces.

For example, when the application invokes an Open operation on version v1, GRAS retrieves the corresponding state node which represents an indirectly accessible state. Then, it searches for directly accessible states from which this state may be reconstructed (in this case, the nodes for v3 and v4 of fig. 4.11). The state with the shortest distance (measured in accumulated byte size of deltas) is selected for *reconstruction* (this may well be the state for v4 even though the numbers of deltas is larger than for v3).

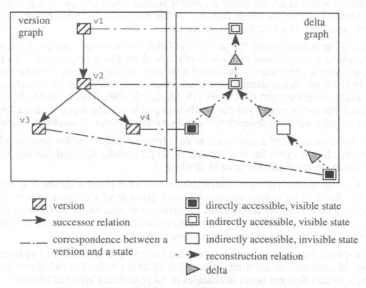

version graph — v1 — delta graph

v2

v3 — v4

▨ version	■ directly accessible, visible state
→ successor relation	▢ indirectly accessible, visible state
—·— correspondence between a version and a state	▢ indirectly accessible, invisible state
	⤍ reconstruction relation
	▶ delta

Fig. 4.11. Example of a delta graph (right–hand side) and its relations to the corresponding version graph (left–hand side)

To conclude this subsection, let us comment on the *position* of the ChangeManagement layer *within the GRAS architecture* (cf. fig. 4.9): In order to keep deltas short, ChangeManagement has been placed in the upper part of the GRAS architecture which relies on a common graph–oriented data model. Logging of graph–oriented operations is much more space–efficient than logging on any layer below GraphStorage.

Originally, ChangeManagement was *placed below* BasicEventMonitoring for the following reason: If events are raised during execution of the undo log, it cannot be guaranteed in general that the corresponding action routines do not modify the graph. Such modifications would lead to a state which, in general, is different from the state to be reconstructed. However, this approach has the following disadvantage: applications which do not support undo/redo themselves are not able to react on changes caused by undo/redo.

Therefore, BasicEventMonitoring and ChangeManagement have been *switched* recently. In order to cope with undo/redo, event handling has been extended in the following way:

(a) Undo/redo events are introduced (in the ChangeManagement layer). Such events are used by applications featuring an undo/redo facility.

(b) Each event handler has to declare whether its action routine is to be invoked during undo/redo. If activation is required, the action routine must not modify the host graph (rather, it is used for updating dependent information outside the host graph).

Scheme and Attribute Management

While presenting the GRAS system's basic graph operations, we have neglected one important requirement. The system has to preserve a graph's consistency with respect to its graph scheme by rejecting forbidden graph modifications and by recomputing derived attribute values. In order to be able to fulfill these tasks, information about a graph's class hierarchy, its attribute dependencies, evaluation functions, etc. must be available at run-time. Therefore, GRAS supports the construction of internal *graph schemes* which provide all these informations in an efficiently accessible format. Such a graph scheme may be extended arbitrarily during its whole lifetime so that the upward–compatibility of graph–based tools and their data structures is guaranteed.

Discussing the realization of this part of the GRAS architecture, we focus on its most important task: the incremental evaluation of derived attributes (cf. section 3.1). For this purpose, we have implemented a variant of a *two–phase, lazy attribute evaluation algorithm* /5. Hud 87/ which has already been used successfully within another graph–oriented database management system (Cactis /6. HK 88, 6. HK 89/). This demand–driven algorithm uses a static and potentially cyclic attribute dependency graph containing all information about possible attribute dependencies and evaluation rules. It works as follows:

Phase 1: The assignment of a new value to an intrinsic attribute or the insertion/deletion of certain edges triggers the *invalidation* of all potentially affected derived attributes (propagation stops at already invalid attributes).

Phase 2: The reevaluation of an invalid attribute will be delayed until the first attempt to read its value. During its then necessary *reevaluation*, read accesses to other attributes' values may raise evaluation processes for these attributes, too (a bookkeeping mechanism guarantees the abortion of the attribute evaluation process at runtime in the presence of forbidden cyclic attribute dependencies).

The two–phase attribute evaluation algorithm has an optimal behavior (with respect to the number of attribute reevaluations after graph updates) in the following two cases: (1) all graph (attribute) changes result in changes of all potentially affected attributes or (2) a graph contains many rarely accessed attributes with often changing values.

For example, consider *technical documentation* which is structured into sections (a similar example will be used in subsection 4.2.4 for performance evaluation). Each section is composed of a list of components, where each component is either a paragraph (leaf node of the hierarchy) or a nested section. Sections are numbered hierarchically, as is done in this book (for example, "4.2.3" is the number of the current subsection). The (sub–)section number is specified by means of derived attributes attached to nodes of class SECTION. The attribute Position describes the position of the current section in the surrounding list. The attribute Number constructs the string for the section number by concatenating the number of the father, a dot, and the string representation of Position.

```
node class SECTION;
   derived Position : integer =
      [self.Predecessor.Position + 1 | 1 ];
   derived Number : string =
      [self.Father.Number + "." + string(self.Position) |
      string(self.Position)];
end;
```

A *structure–oriented editor* for technical documentations provides commands for manipulating the text and displays a cut–out of this text on the screen. Each insertion or deletion of a section changes Number and Position attributes of all following sections and their subsections, but only Number and Position attributes of currently displayed sections (and their predecessors) must be up–to–date. Therefore, lazy attribute evaluation performs well in this example. For a more detailed discussion of the advantages and disadvantages of different graph–based incremental attribute evaluation algorithms, the reader is referred to /6. ACR 87, 5. Schü 91b/.

During the adaptation of the algorithm to the special needs of GRAS we encountered one major problem which has not yet been addressed by the graph attribute evaluation algorithms of /6. ACR 87, 6. HK 88, 6. HK 89/. The language PROGRES allows for the definition of complex *n–context attribute dependencies* : An attribute A1 of a node N1 may depend on an attribute A2 of a node N2, where N1 and N2 are connected via a path of arbitrary length n (n edges have to be traversed to reach N2 from N1). Therefore, graph modifications at remote locations may influence an attribute's value. The example given above demonstrates the usefulness of n–context attribute dependencies: the Position of a section will be computed by incrementing the Position of its preceding section (or by assigning the value 1 in the case of the first section). In order to find this preceding Section, we have to follow a potentially unrestricted number of Precedes edges from targets to sources, skipping all components without a Position attribute (for example, a section may have some introductory paragraphs before the first subsection starts). To this end, the path Predecessor is defined as follows:

```
path Predecessor: SECTION [0:1] -> SECTION [0:1] =
    <-Precedes- & {not instance of SECTION :: <-Precedes-}
end;
```

In order to be able to handle these remote attribute dependencies, we have introduced the concept of *virtual attributes* (cf. /5. Schü 91b/) in GRAS. These attributes are invisible to application programs, and they do not even possess values on their own (with exception of an invalid flag). Their only purpose is to reduce the difficult problem of propagating invalid flags in the case of n–context dependencies to the already solved 1–context problem. In the case of our documentation example we have to introduce one virtual attribute VAtt which propagates changes of Position attributes across an arbitrary number of components without Position attributes. Consider e.g. the deletion of the first section 3.1 in fig. 4.12. This operation initiates the following propagation process:

(a) the VAtt attribute of the first paragraph is invalidated because its incoming Precedes edge is deleted,

(b) this invalidation propagates to the VAtt attribute of the next paragraph,

(c) the Position attribute of the next section is invalidated in response to the invalidation of the VAtt attribute of the previous component,

(d) and Number and VAtt attributes at the same node are invalidated according to their dependency on the position attribute.

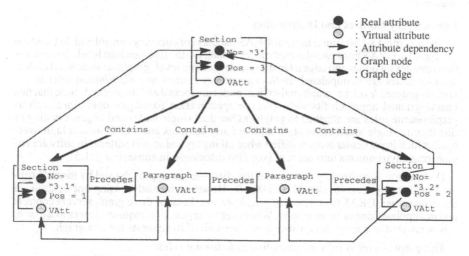

Fig. 4.12. Cut–out of a documentation's actual attribute dependency graph

All these attributes remain invalid as long as their values are not required by the application, i.e. they will be *recomputed on demand* (and propagation processes of subsequent insertions or deletions immediately stops at already invalid attributes). Reading e.g. the Number attribute of a section has the side effect of recomputing Number and Position attributes of all preceding sections and of "validating" the VAtt attribute of all preceding paragraphs. Similarly, accessing the index of a derived attribute A (not present in our example) triggers the reevaluation of all invalid A attributes of a graph. Otherwise, the GRAS system would not be able to answer queries like "find all nodes with a derived attribute A which has the value V".

Last but not least it was a straightforward idea to use the same concepts and techniques for the *incremental computation* of *derived relations*, which are (recursively) defined by means of complex path expressions. By viewing them as a special form of derived node reference attributes, our attribute evaluation algorithm is able to materialize their values on demand.

In this way, GRAS is able to efficiently maintain derived information about graphs in a similar way as e.g. in the object–oriented database system GOM /6. GKK 92, 6. KM 92/. But note that the actual attribute (and relation) dependencies of our sample graph in fig. 4.12 do not really exist in the form of additional relations, as in the system GOM, but will be deduced during the propagation process by means of a *static attribute dependency graph* (for further details, see /6. KSW 92b/).

We conclude the discussion of the SchemeAndAttributeManagement layer with a final remark about its *location* in the *GRAS architecture* on top of the ChangeManagement layer(cf. figure 4.9). This position has the advantage that undo/redo handles derived and intrinsic data in a uniform way, i.e. all computed derived data are still available after undo/redo operations. By exchanging the positions of both layers, we could follow the approach of Cactis /5. Hud 87, 6. HK 88/. Cactis does not log the values of derived data, but invalidates them during undo/redo and recomputes them on demand. Whereas the position of the SchemeAndAttributeManagement layer on top of ChangeManagement is debatable, there are no doubts about its cooperation with GRAS' EventTriggerActionMachine. New resources for manipulating graph schemes and derived data result in new types of events and event patterns that must be monitored and handled within this machine.

Concurrency Control and Distribution

The top–most architectural layer of GRAS handles concurrency control and distribution (cf. fig. 4.9). GRAS has a two–layered object model: On the fine–grained level, the application operates on nodes and edges. On the coarse–grained level, graphs as structured collections of nodes are manipulated. Both *concurrency control* and *distribution* refer to the *coarse–grained level*, i.e. graphs rather than nodes are locked and distributed. Note that this coarse–grained approach fits well with our specification paradigm: operations such as graph rewrite rules are attached to graphs rather than single nodes and edges. Locking or distributing single graph elements would be fairly complex and would incur a high overhead, which in particular is not justified when taking typical access patterns in software engineering environments into account (see also discussion in subsection 1.1.5).

Distribution is realized by a variant of the client–server approach used by most distributed database systems /6. Deu 91, 6. DM 90/. However, instead of using one centralized database server, GRAS uses a *pool of graph servers*. Each of these graph servers controls and manipulates one or more graphs. Whenever an application requests access to a graph, it is connected to a graph server which performs all of its requests for this graph.

This graph server is *selected* according to *following rules*:

(a) If the graph is already open due to a request from another application, the corresponding graph server is used.

(b) If a graph server exists which is willing to accept another graph, this server is selected. Acceptance is calculated within the servers based on current host load and number of served graphs.

(c) Otherwise, a new graph server is started. The location of this server is determined by the current load of a set of trusted hosts. It is even possible to start more than one server on a host.

A *special control* server – not depicted in fig. 4.13 – keeps track of the mapping of open graphs to graph servers. This control server also serializes open and close requests for graphs to avoid race conflicts and interconnection between different graph servers. Fig. 4.13 shows a typical scenario with three client and two graph server processes (without the control server). Notice that both Client2 and Client3 access the same graph G3, and that Client2 communicates with more than one server.

The interoperability of clients and servers is realized by inserting a communication layer consisting of two parts – the client side communication interface (CSCI) and the server side communication interface (SSCI). The procedural database interface is offered to clients through the CSCI, which uses a *remote procedure call* library to forward calls down to the SSCI of the appropriate server. These interfaces are also responsible for concurrency control and error handling. Furthermore, they handle communication failures and client or server shutdown using follow–up–RPCs and heartbeat protocols.

To organize concurrent accesses of applications to the same graph, GRAS supports an *access group model*: Each application accessing a graph belongs to a group which has an own copy of the accessed graph. Groups are temporary collections of applications which access the same graph. Groups are created explicitly by one application (which becomes the initial member of this group), potentially joined by other applications (which want to share their view of the graph with other members of that group), and terminate implicitly when the last group member leaves it (by closing the graph). This is analogous to the UNIX file access model where a file is physically closed when the last accessor (using the same handle) closes the graph.

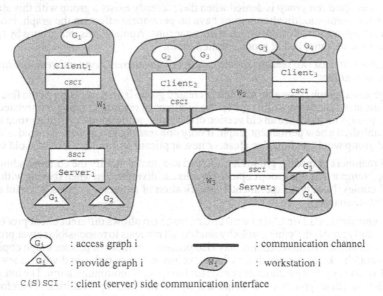

G : access graph i
G : provide graph i
C(S)SCI : client (server) side communication interface

: communication channel
W : workstation i

Fig. 4.13. A typical distributed GRAS scenario

Concurrency of members within a group is controlled by the *interaction granularity* attribute determining exclusive access units within the time space. Access conflicts due to concurrency conflicts are solved by either delaying or aborting the execution of the conflicting operation (the actual reaction is eligible at operation invocation). GRAS supports three different levels of interaction granularity:

(a) *Operational access* provides for a graph lock during the execution of one basic GRAS operation. This is the lowest level of locking over time and, therefore, yields the highest possible rate of concurrency. Allowing even concurrent execution of these operations is possible (although not yet implemented), but should be transparent for the application.

(b) The next level, *transactional access*, allows application access only within mutually exclusive top–level transactions which perform consistency–preserving transformations. As the whole graph is locked for the time span of the top–level transaction, lock conflicts cannot occur during its execution. This allows the application to perform operations without interfering with other applications. This decoupling of applications can be seen as a great advantage, as they can operate on shared graphs without knowing or even noticing (besides delay of transaction processing) the presence of other applications. These top–level transactions are also the units of undo and redo, because the SSCI automatically checkpoints the graph after each successful top–level transaction.

(c) The *sessional access* mode reserves the graph for one group member. This mode virtually provides for a single–user database system. Accessing the graph is allowed for exactly one member of the group, and all other members are delayed (or rejected) upon the OpenGraph operation. When the active member leaves the group (by closing the graph), the next pending member of this group becomes the active one.

As groups operate on own copies of the graph, interaction between different groups only take place when groups terminate. To avoid update conflicts between access groups of the same graph, at most one group is allowed to replace the original version of the graph by its copy on termination (i.e. to make its modifications permanent). The creation of such a *persistent–modification group* is denied when there already exists a group with this attribute. As nonpersistent–modification groups have no permanent effect on the graph, more than one of these groups is allowed to exist at the same time. Applications join groups by specifying their names (supplied at group creation time).

There are at least two reasons for the concept of *concurrent nonpersistent–modification groups* of a graph:

(a) The initial graph belonging to a newly created group is an exact copy of the final graph of the last terminated writing group. As lifetimes of reading groups are unrelated, reading groups may still see an old version of the graph while another writing group already established a new permanent graph. If only one reading group were allowed, either the old group would be forced to close, or new applications would still see the old version.

(b) As members of reading groups are allowed to actually modify the corresponding graph copy temporarily, the group copies of graphs can diverge even when starting with identical copies. Note that experimental modification of temporary copies is useful e.g. for what–if analyses.

To *summarize*, ClientServerDistribution allows different client processes to concurrently access the same graphs by sending all requests to responsible server processes via rpc–calls. Furthermore, clients may also possess a number of private graph copies (via check–out/check–in) for which they have exclusive access rights and which they are allowed to modify locally without any needs for interprocess communication. The integration of different client processes is supported by event handling facilities. Therefore, the ClientServerDistribution layer needs the services of the EventTrigger-ActionMachine, and it distributes events raised by one client to all other clients that are interested in them. Finally, ClientServerDistribution is realized on top of SchemeAndAttributeManagement in order to maximize the complexity of services provided at the GRAS system's interface. This minimizes the number of necessary rpc–calls between client and server processes that are necessary to perform a given task.

4.2.4 Performance Evaluation

The presentation of a database system's functionality and implementation is at least incomplete if it is not accompanied by some tables and charts which provide the reader with an overall impression of the *system's performance*, and which demonstrate the effects of important design and implementation decisions.

Therefore, we were looking for a *benchmark definition* which is tailored to the special needs of software engineering or hypertext system applications. This benchmark should comprise a set of operations for creating, querying, and modifying complex object structures containing many (cross-)references and attributes of rather different size. Furthermore, it should be well-suited for testing a database system's capability of efficiently executing different kinds of partial match queries (i.e. graph traversals), range queries, and especially for testing the effectiveness of its incorporated caching and clustering algorithms.

Unfortunately, many benchmarks proposed in the *literature* do not fulfill all of these requirements. For example, all benchmarks — except OO1 — described in /6. Gra 91/ have been designed for business-oriented and/or relational database system applications, and even the OO1 benchmark for object-oriented database systems /6. CS 92/ uses a database which contains only one type of relationship (connecting randomly selected objects), and is therefore not well-suited for testing the effects of different clustering algorithms with respect to different types of queries.

The Hypermodel Benchmark

Finally, we have selected the so-called *hypermodel benchmark* /6. ABM 90/ which does not propose any delete or structure-oriented update operations but is otherwise well-suited for our purposes. A hypermodel database's dominant structure is a totally balanced tree with fan-out 5. Every NODE within this tree possesses a couple of integer attributes with one of them playing the role of a unique node key. INNER nodes of this tree are sources of an ordered hierarchical one-to-many-relationship (1n-rel) connecting any node of level n with its five children nodes at level n+1. An additional hierarchical many-to-many-relationship (mn-rel) connects each INNER node with five randomly chosen nodes of the next lower level. Finally, there is a third type of attributed many-to-one relationships (m1a-rel). Every NODE of the database is the source of exactly one attributed reference to another randomly chosen node (cf. fig. 4.14).

The LEAF nodes of our tree are instances of two node classes. The majority of them are TEXT nodes attributed with a sequence of words (between 10 and 100 words). But every 125th node is a so-called FORM node which possesses a bitmap of a randomly selected size (between 100*100 and 400*400). Thus, a test database of depth 7 (with levels 0–6) contains 19531 objects belonging to three different classes, 58591 relationships of three different types, and many attributes with a total size of more than 6.5 MB.

The benchmark itself comprises *operations* for

(a) *creating* the initial test database with clustering along the one-to-many-relationship,

(b) *incremental modifications* of large text- or bitmap-attributes at a number of randomly selected LEAF nodes

(c) *range queries* of the form "find all nodes the integer attribute Hundred/Million of which has a value in a randomly chosen interval",

(d) so-called *group lookups (reference lookups)*, following a specified type of relationship from 50 randomly chosen sources to their targets (targets to their sources),

(e) and, finally, *closure operations* recursively following a specified type of relationship from 50 randomly chosen nodes on level 3 up to 25 steps in the case of potentially cyclic m1a-relations with some of them performing attribute read and write operations.

```
node class NODE;
    intrinsic key UniqueId: integer;
    intrinsic index Hundred: integer;
    intrinsic Ten: integer;
    intrinsic Thousand: integer;
    intrinsic Million: integer;
    derived index MillionIndex: integer = self.Million div 10000;
end;

node class INNER is a NODE end;

node class LEAF is a NODE end;

edge type 1stChild: INNER [0:1] -> NODE [1:1] ;
    (* ordered one-to-many-relationship with fan-out 5 *)
    . . .
edge type 5thChild: INNER [0:1] -> NODE [1:1] ;
    (* represented by 5 different one-to-one-relationships *)

edge type Part: INNER [0:n] -> NODE [0:n] ; (* many-to-many-relationship *)

node class LINK; (* representation of attributed many-to-one-relationship *)
    intrinsic OffsetFrom, OffsetTo: integer;
end;
edge type From: NODE [1:1] -> LINK [1:1] ;
edge type To: LINK [0:n] -> NODE [1:1] ;

node class TEXT is a LEAF;
    intrinsic TextAtt: string;
end;

node class FORM is a LEAF;
    intrinsic FormAtt: Bitmap;
end;
```

Fig. 4.14. Cutout of the hypermodel benchmark's graph scheme in PROGRES notation

In order to be able to measure the effects of caching and clustering, every test out of groups (b) through (e) is performed twice. The first run (*cold*) has to start with empty operating system's file buffers and database caches, and the second run (*warm*) with file buffers and caches the state of which is determined by the cold run. In total, the hypermodel test suite consists of about 35 different tests with many of them measuring similar performance characteristics of the underlying database system (at least in the case of our GRAS). Therefore, the following charts only display the performance results for significant subsets of all benchmark operations. These operations and their abbreviations are explained in more detail in table 4.15. For a more precise description of the whole benchmark the reader is referred to /6. ABM 90/.

When we started to implement the hypermodel benchmark on top of the GRAS system, we discovered three *major problems* with two of them concerning our data model (cf. section 3.1) and one of them concerning the GRAS system's functionality:

(a) Our simple data model of attributed graphs does not allow for the definition of *ordered relationships*. Thus, we were forced to introduce 5 different edge types in order to be able to distinguish between the 1st, 2nd, 3rd, . . . child node of an INNER node.

(b) Our data model does not support *attributed edges*. Therefore, attributed relationships are represented by attributed LINK nodes which are related to their sources and targets by From and To edges, respectively.

(c) The GRAS system supports partial match queries for indexed attributes but no *range queries* for integer attributes. In the case of the Hundred attribute it was acceptable to replace a range query of the form "find all nodes whose Hundred attribute has a value in the range [x..x+n]" by at most one hundred partial match queries of the form "find all nodes whose Hundred attribute has the value x, x+1, ...". But in the case of the Million attribute we had to introduce an auxiliary indexed attribute whose value is 1/10000 of the value of the Million attribute. Thus, we were able to replace every Million range query by at most one hundred MillionIndex partial match queries.

Abbreviation	Short description of benchmark operation
C.INNER	Creation of all INNER nodes of the database.
C.LEAF	Creation of all LEAF nodes of the database, i.e. TEXT and FORM nodes.
C.1n-rel	Creation of all 1n-relationships (Child edges) of the database.
C.mn-rel	Creation of all mn-relationships (Part edges) of the database.
C.m1a-rel	Creation of all m1a-relationships (LINK nodes, To and From edges).
Chg.Text c.	Cold search and replace of words in 50 randomly chosen Text attributes.
Chg.Text w.	Repetition of Chg.Text c. with warm cache and same Text attributes.
Gr.1n c./w.	Group lookup for 1n-rel (traversal of Child edges) starting at 50 nodes.
Gr.m1a c./w.	Group lookup for m1a-rel (traversal of From and To edges) at 50 nodes.
1n* c./w.	Closure of Group lookup for 1n-rel starting at 50 nodes.
mn* c./w.	Closure of Group lookup for mn-rel starting at 50 nodes.
1n*-S. c./w.	Same as 1n* c./w. + summing up all visited Hundred attributes.
m1a*-S. c./w.	Closure of Gr.m1a c./w. + summing up all visited Offset attributes.

Table 4.15. Descriptions and abbreviations of benchmark operations

Benchmark Results for Different Database Sizes

After this brief description of the hypermodel benchmark, we will now present and analyze the performance results of its implementation on top of the Modula-2 GRAS interface on the following *hardware platform*: a Sun 4/390 in multi-user mode with 32 MB main memory and a 1000 MB CDC IPI 9720 disk under Sun OS 4.1.1.

The benchmark implementation does *not exploit* the GRAS system's *facilities* for undo/ redo of graph modifications, event-handling, incremental attribute evaluation, and communication of multiple clients with multiple server processes. Application code and GRAS system code are both belonging to the same address space, and their communication is not based on time-consuming rpc-calls. Furthermore, the EventManagement and SchemeManagement layers of GRAS are almost inactive during the whole benchmark. Thus, their contribution to the overall processing time is negligible. The ChangeManagement layer, on the contrary, spends a considerable amount of time for creating logs, although all tasks based on these logs, like abortion of transactions, recovery from system crashes etc., are not part of the hypermodel benchmark suite, too. As a consequence, the hypermodel benchmark implementation is more a test suite for the *GRAS system's kernel* than for the system as a whole. Suitable extensions have to be designed and implemented in the future.

In the following, we will present and discuss our experiences with the GRAS hypermodel benchmark and especially with *varying the parameters* database size, cache size, and object clustering strategy. In detail, the following results will be presented as charts and tables:

(a) Space consumption and database creation, cold and warm query times for databases of varying size with fixed cache size and fixed clustering strategy (fig. 4.16 and 4.17).

(b) Characteristic database creation/query times for fixed database size and clustering strategy, but with varying cache size (fig. 4.17)

(c) Characteristic database creation/query times for fixed database and cache size, but with varying clustering strategies (cf. fig. 4.19 and table 4.20).

The charts of fig. 4.16 and 4.17 present the performance results for four *databases* of *different sizes* with each database being five times larger than the next smaller one. All reported times in these charts and the chart of the following subsection are given in milliseconds and have been divided by the overall number of affected objects or binary relationships (e.g. the elapsed time for creating all 3906 INNER nodes of the level 0-6 database is 39067 milliseconds; cf. fig 4.16). Furthermore, the GRAS system's cache has been set to the required upper limit, i.e. to 4 MB.

Fig. 4.16 presents also the *disk storage consumption* of each database (varying from 164 kB to 21000 kB) and the *database creation times* for all types of nodes and relationships as well as the times for updating randomly selected text attributes. Note that the disk storage consumption of each database is directly proportional to its net size. Furthermore:

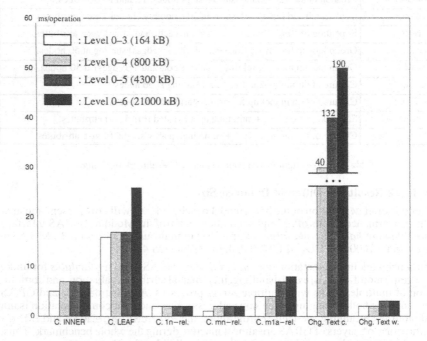

Fig. 4.16. Create ops. with varying graph size and fixed cache size (4 MB)

(a) Times reported for creating INNER nodes are identical for all databases but the first one. This is due to the fact that the benchmark starts with the creation of all INNER nodes and that all INNER nodes fit into a 4 MB cache.

(b) Times reported for creating LEAF nodes are always higher than those for INNER nodes (especially in the case of the largest test database). This has the following two reasons: (1) LEAF nodes possess additional large attributes the creation of which is rather time- and space-consuming, and (2) each LEAF node will be placed onto the same page as its already existing INNER parent node (cf. clustering strategy position). Therefore, this operation permanently creates new attribute containing pages and additionally accesses old node pages. This causes many page faults in the case of the largest database.

(c) Creation times for 1n- and mn-relations are very low and remain nearly constant for all databases. This is a result of the design decision to store large attributes as well as all relationships (edges) on separate pages. Thus, this operation affects only a small number of edge containing pages. Furthermore, additional "node existence" consistency checks, which prevent the creation of edges between non-existent nodes, demand only read accesses to a limited number of node containing pages.

(d) Creation times of m1a-relations are always higher than those for 1n- and mn-rel, and they are noticeably influenced by the size of a database. To understand this fact, the reader has to remember that the creation of one m1a-relation requires the creation of one attributed node and two edges, in contrast to the creation of one edge in the case of simple relationships. Therefore, this operation demands additional write accesses to node containing pages. This leads to a significantly greater number of "dirty" page transfers from cache to disk (at least in the case of larger databases).

(e) The operation "Change Text attribute cold" has the most significant increase in time from small databases to large databases. This is a consequence of the fact that all touched attributes are selected randomly. Therefore, the probability for two Text attributes belonging to the same page is inverse proportional to the size of a database, i.e. growing databases require a growing number of page transfers.

(f) Finally, the excellent performance results for the operation "Change Text attribute warm" are easy to explain: In this case all necessary pages are already stored in the database system's cache and transferring these pages back to the disk is part of a separate "Close database" operation (transaction commit only forces log pages but not data containing pages back to the disk).

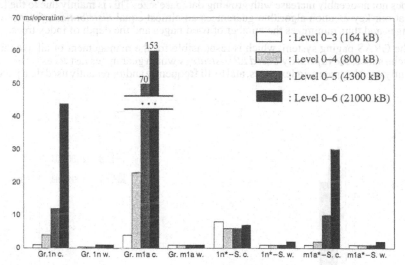

Fig. 4.17. Query ops. with varying graph size and fixed cache size (4 MB)

Similar reasons may be given for the *query performance results* displayed in fig. 4.17:

(a) The reasons for cold performance results of group lookup operations 1n c. and m1a c., which determine all outgoing 1n or m1a edges at a small number of randomly selected nodes, are the same as those for "Change Text attribute cold" of fig. 4.16.

(b) And the reasons for all displayed warm execution results of group lookup operations 1n w., m1a w., 1n*-S.w., 1m1a*w.) are trivial, too: Almost all accessed data are already present in the GRAS system's cache. Note that in the case of the closure operation 1n*-S.w. and m1a*-S.w. and the level 0-6 database only the separation of different kinds of data ensures that almost all accessed data fit into a 4 MB cache (both operations reach about 40% of the nodes of a 21 MB large database).

(c) Finally, we have to discuss the quite different cold performance results for the closure operations 1n*-S.c. and m1a*-S.c.. Traversals along 1n-relations with read accesses to Hundred attributes initially are more expensive than traversals along m1a-relations with read accesses to Offset attributes (read accesses to the larger number of NODE attributes require more page transfers than read accesses to LINK attributes). This initial effect is soon compensated by the fact that traversals along 1n-relations are compatible with our clustering strategy (strategy position). Therefore, the probability for crossing page boundaries is almost independent of the database's size. Traversals along m1a-rel, on the contrary, lead from randomly selected sources to randomly selected targets and touch a considerably greater number of pages. In this case, the probability for crossing page boundaries is proportional to the overall database size.

To *summarize*, our hypermodel performance results for growing databases and constant cache size are mainly determined by the following design decisions:

(a) The order in which objects and 1n-relationships are created is compatible with the system's *clustering strategy* along 1n-relationships.

(b) Especially 1n- and mn-relationships are *concentrated* on a *small number* of *pages*: This is caused by the system's strategy to store different types of information on different pages.

(c) The hashing overhead for mapping logical database keys onto physical page addresses does not noticeably increase with growing database size: This is mainly due to the fact that our key creation algorithm guarantees an almost equal *distribution of data* over pages and thus minimizes the number of used pages and the depth of index trees.

(d) The GRAS paging system, which is responsible for the management of all available cache space, uses a *priority-based LRU-strategy* which guarantees fast access to all currently used log pages, index pages, and to all frequently and/or recently used data pages.

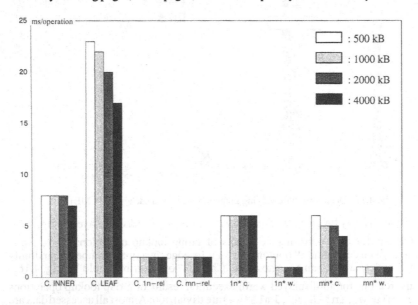

Fig. 4.18. Varying cache size and fixed graph size (4.3 MB)

Varying the cache size within a wide range while keeping the database size constant causes only minor changes of almost all warm performance results and influences the cold performance results in the same way as varying database sizes do in the presence of a constant cache (cf. fig. 4.18). The reasons are as above.

Benchmark Results for Different Clustering Strategies

The last important parameter to be changed is the GRAS system's *clustering strategy*. In order to be able to study its influence on the system's storage consumption and on its overall performance, we have executed the hypermodel benchmark with four different node clustering algorithms:

(a) *Random distribution* (random): Nodes are randomly distributed over pages, so that every page contains about the same number of nodes. The performance results of this method for graph traversals along 1n-relationships can be considered as upper boundaries for all possible clustering algorithms.

(b) *Heuristic page clustering* (page): New nodes receive an internal node key such that they are stored on a randomly selected position on the same pages as their already existing parent nodes (with respect to 1n-relationships). Therefore, subsequent page splits distribute a parent node's children randomly over different successor pages.

(c) *Heuristic position clustering* (position): New nodes receive an internal node key such that they are stored on a carefully selected position on the same page as their already existing parent node. In this case, subsequent page splits normally preserve the physical neighborhood of a parent node's children (as long as this is possible without producing unbalanced index trees or almost empty successor pages).

(d) *Optimal distribution* (optimal): Guided by the application's knowledge about the final size and form of the test database it is possible to compute optimal page positions for all nodes (with respect to breadth first graph traversals along 1n-relationships). Although the GRAS system's interface offers resources for directly determining a node's position, this possibility won't be used by "normal" applications. The main reason for presenting this method here is to find lower boundaries for graph traversals along 1n-relationships.

The chart of fig. 4.19 presents the anticipated *results* for all node positioning algorithms. Note that we were forced to use a *very small cache* (100 kB) in order produce remarkable *execution time differences* between the different clustering algorithms. This is a consequence of the fact that mainly interesting 1n–relation traversals of the hypermodel benchmark access only edge data which are stored on a relatively small number of pages in GRAS.

Considering the increasing execution times for traversing mn-relations and the decreasing execution times for creating/traversing 1n-relations from algorithm random to algorithm optimal, the position *algorithm* is considerably *better* than the page algorithm. For the most important operation, the warm traversal along 1n-relations, the position algorithm even performs as well as the optimal solution.

Concerning the *overall database size*, the algorithm random outperforms all other algorithms. This might be due to the fact that a random distribution of data over pages is the best way to guarantee balanced index trees and to avoid almost empty pages. Therefore, in a number of cases the strategy random needs the smallest number of page transfers and its performance results for creating the initial database and for following randomly chosen paths through the database along mn-relations are better than those for other algorithms. For similar reasons, the database size and the cold performance results for closure MN*c. of strategy page are better than those for strategies position and optimal.

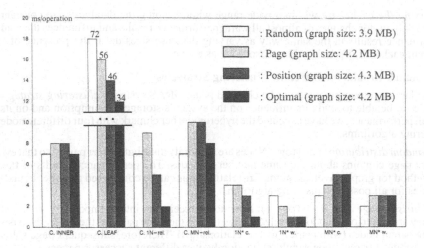

Fig. 4.19. Different clustering strategies with fixed cache size (100 kB)

Beside these not very significant runtime performance differences of clustering strategies, we were also curious to compare their *page access patterns* directly. Therefore, we were looking for some *metrics*

(a) which are easy to compute (based on a number of page access counters),

(b) which do not depend on the database system's cache or the benchmark's database size,

(c) and which are proportional to the expansion of a query and its locality.

The *expansion factor* EF of a query simply measures the overall number of accessed pages. It is low if all accessed data is concentrated on a very small number of pages. The *locality factor* LF of a query takes its concrete page access pattern into account. It is high, if all accesses to a distinct page are not interleaved with accesses to other pages (counted by the metric "interleaving accesses" IA). Thus, the overall number of page faults becomes minimal even in the case of a cache space which is considerably smaller than the expansion of a query.

With Q being one of the benchmark's queries (e.g. closure 1n-rel), TS being a certain *traversal strategy* for this query (e.g. depth first traversal), CS being an arbitrary *clustering strategy* (e.g. random), and (OTS, OCS) being the best traversal strategy and the best clustering strategy for a given query, our metrics are defined as follows:

EF(Q,CS) =
no. of touched pages (Q,CS) / no. of touched pages (Q,OCS)

LF(Q,TS,CS) =
IA(Q,OTS,OCS) / IA(Q,TS,CS), where

IA(Q,TS,CS) =
avg. no. of data accesses between two accesses to same page for (Q,TS,CS)
(= ∞, if every portion of data resides on a different page!)

The paper /6. TN 92/ already suggests comparing *different clustering strategies* with respect to the expansion as well as the locality of a query. However, this paper does not contain a proposal for the definition of the "locality factor", and proposes an "expansion factor" which is difficult to compute. This is due to the fact that the suggested formula depends on a database system's minimal number of bytes/pages necessary for storing a given number of objects, relationships etc. This number is not computable without very intimate knowledge about a database system's internal storage layout (in GRAS, the layout of pages changes during runtime in order to adapt it to the special needs of a certain application).

Strategy:	random	page	position	optimal
EF(1n*)	4.6	1.8	2.9	1.0
LF(1n*,DF)	0	0.17	0.21	0.32
LF(1n*,BF)	0	0.20	0.25	1.0

Table 4.20. Expansion and locality factors of different clustering strategies

Table 4.20 contains the expansion and the locality factors of the above introduced clustering strategies for a *depth first traversal* DF and a *breadth first traversal* BF along 1n-relations of a hypermodel database with levels 0–5. Note that

(a) the expansion, i.e. the total amount of accessed data, is always independent of the selected traversal order (therefore, EF is independent of the traversal strategy),

(b) the expansion of the strategy random is much greater than the expansion of all other strategies, although the strategy random creates the smallest database,

(c) the strategy page places the traversed part of the database on a smaller number of pages than the strategy position but is considerably less successful in minimizing the locality of both a depth first and a breadth first traversal (the dominant factor for the number of page faults if the database cache is much smaller than the whole database),

(d) for the page, position, and optimal strategy LF(DF) < LF(BF) always holds true, because all these strategies attempt to position children nodes near their parents and not nearby neighboring siblings,

(e) in the case of the strategy random every portion of accessed data resides on a new page (→ LF(1n*,DF,random) = LF(1n*,BF,random) = 0), and

(f) the clustering strategy *optimal* is most sensible to changes in access patterns (→ LF(1n*,DF,optimal) ≈ LF(1n*,BF,optimal) / 3).

Our *conclusions* from these analysis results are the following: Time consuming and sophisticated clustering strategies which depend on very specific assumptions about database access patterns are superior to more heuristically working algorithms with respect to our metrics, but they might degrade considerably in the case of rapidly changing databases with rather different applications on top of them. Furthermore, runtime performance results — especially in the case of warm and not artificially small caches — even show less differences between "dumb" and "intelligent" clustering strategies (at least in our system GRAS, where object references and node attributes are treated differently and stored on different pages). Therefore, the GRAS system only provides a rather primitive *incrementally and heuristically working clustering algorithm* (the aforementioned algorithm *position*), and it does not spend any efforts on analyzing access patterns of queries or on batch-oriented reorganizations of data clusters. Nevertheless, its interface allows for the implementation of such algorithms on top of it, as e.g. those proposed or analyzed in /6. HK 89, 6. BDK 92, 6. GKK 92, 6. TN 92/.

Comparing our GRAS benchmark results directly with published *results for other systems* is very difficult, even in the case where the same hypermodel benchmark was used. They refer to old versions of database systems, use different hardware platforms, etc. Even subtle differences in the interpretation of a standard benchmark description may have significant impact on presented results. Therefore, we will not try to compare available material about benchmarks for nonstandard database systems (like /6. ABM 90, 6. CDN 93, 6. DHK 90, 6. EK 92/ with our benchmark results nor to discuss our own three years old benchmark experiments with OBST /6. UTS 93/ and PCTE /6. ECM 90/ in /6. Fro 93/.

Our general impressions from studying published benchmark results and performing our own experiments are as follows:

(a) In other systems, the differences between *cold and warm performance* execution times for random database accesses tend to be more significant. This is a consequence of the fact that GRAS uses the same representation for data on disk and in main memory and makes no usage of recently developed pointer swizzling techniques.

(b) Page server based database systems have a better performance than GRAS if multiple client processes need *concurrent access* to the same graph, but where *event–based propagation* of graph changes to clients is not an issue; in this case, it is more efficient to send pages to client processes instead of sending operations to server processes.

(c) Finally, the *main strengths* of GRAS, compared with space and time efficiency of other nonstandard database systems, are the manipulation of fine–grained object structures with small attributes and many bidirectional mn–relationships.

Further differences between GRAS and other systems, which are not observable by inspecting hypermodel benchmark results, are the topic of the following subsection.

4.2.5 Related Work

The GRAS system's *kernel* consists of layers of data abstraction each of which has an own, carefully designed data model: the graph–oriented layer has been implemented on top of a record–oriented layer which in turn relies on a page–oriented layer and a network file system layer. Furthermore, the central subsystem of the GRAS kernel, the `Virtual-RecordStorage`, is highly parameterized and allows for the instantiation of rather different persistent data storages, as e.g. the attribute and edge storages of our graph–oriented layer. In this way, the GRAS system's implementation follows the so–called "tool kit" approach of systems like Exodus /6. CDR 89/. Therefore, it may be reused to realize persistent data stores for a wide spectrum of different applications.

The implemented *indexing scheme* of `VirtualRecordStorage` uses tries for addressing all relevant data pages within one storage, and static hashing with an order preserving function for locating relevant (ranges of) records within selected pages. Furthermore, a special record identifier creation algorithm (cf. /6. KSW 92b/) guarantees clustering of logically related data and uniform distribution of records over pages. Thus, our indexing scheme is well–suited for dynamically growing and shrinking medium sized databases (with each database having the size of a typical engineering document). In this case, attempts for addressing pages but not the addressed data itself fit into main memory. On the contrary,

(a) main memory indexing schemes – like those described in /6. AP 92/ and /6. LC 86/ – are tuned for the case that a whole database fits into main memory,

(b) whereas B–trees /6. BM 72/ and their variants assume that index structures themselves do no longer fit into main memory and that traversing these structures requires disk accesses, too,

(c) and dynamic hashing techniques /6. ED 88/ which either use directories – like 'extendible hashing' /6. FNP 79/, 'virtual hashing' /6. Lit 78/ etc. – or which address their data without any index at all – like 'linear hashing' /6. Lar 80/, 'modified dynamic hashing' /6. Kaw 85/ etc. – suffer from the following drawback: They require global reorganizations of index structures or data from time to time in order to avoid expensive maintenance of overflow chains

On the other hand, *analysis* and *simulation results* of /6. Fla 83/ and /6. Lar 88/ indicate that the above mentioned dynamic hashing techniques might be superior to our approach in the case of large databases, which consist of many thousands of pages and which would require deep tries.

The *event management layer*, the first one on top of the GRAS kernel, monitors all basic graph state transitions and forwards them to a generic `EventTriggerAction-Machine`. As already indicated by its name, the event mechanism provided by GRAS does not follow the lines of the wide–spread event–condition–action paradigm (cf. e.g. /6. MD 89/), where an action is triggered whenever a certain event happens and a specified condition is fulfilled. In our opinion, it is sufficient to have more or less complex event patterns and event triggered actions which may be composed of GRAS interface operations in an arbitrary manner. Events and actions may be used – as in other active database systems /6. BM 91, 6. Day 88, 6. DKM 86/ – to control dynamic integrity constraints and to extend the functionality of already defined transactions, and they may even be used to integrate different applications on top of GRAS (in a similar way as in so–called broadcast/message server architectures /6. Rei 90/).

The *change management layer* extends the functionality of the kernel by providing undo/redo, nested transactions, and deltas. During a session (between `Open` and `Close`), the application can set an arbitrary number of checkpoints which define boundaries of top–level transactions and act as targets of undo/redo operations. Use of graph deltas is controlled by the application; furthermore, deltas are supported without introducing a logical model for version control. All services mentioned above are implemented in a uniform way by logs of graph operations. In order to keep deltas short, logs are maintained on a high level of abstraction (operations such as creation/deletion of nodes/edges rather than byte–oriented operations).

Comparing our approach to other work, we observe that *traditional version control systems* such as SCCS /4. Roc 75/ or RCS /4. Tic 85/ are different in the following respects: Applications cannot control the use of deltas, modeling of version control is mixed up with its realization, and deltas are constructed a–posteriori such that undo/redo has to be supported by a different mechanism. In contrast, more recent systems such as Gypsy /4. CHW 88/ and EXODUS /6. CDR 89/ are closer to GRAS inasmuch as they provide for flexible delta control and separate modeling from realization of version control.

While Gypsy (unlike GRAS) relies on a–posteriori construction of deltas, EXODUS constructs deltas on the side when performing change operations. In contrast to GRAS, EXODUS relies on *data sharing*: Data which are common to multiple versions are physically shared among them. This is achieved by applicative operations on tree–like structures (EXODUS uses B+ trees for storing file objects). Similar techniques have been applied e.g. in /4. FM 87/ and /6. Ald 88/. Although this approach seems attractive because versions are always immediately accessible, it has been ruled out for the following reason: Data sharing techniques as they have been applied in other systems operate on a low level of abstraction. Within the GRAS system, such a technique would have to be applied on the page level. Each graph is realized by an index tree whose leaves point to storage pages. Small changes on the graph level (e.g. creation of a single node) may imply comprehensive physical reorganizations on the page level. Therefore, deltas on this level would become too large to be useful for an application. Note that this is not an argument against data sharing in general. Rather, we argue against the use of data sharing on a low level of abstraction. To the best of our knowledge, adequate techniques for high–level data sharing in attributed graphs have not yet been developed.

The *scheme* and *attribute management layer* is mainly responsible for computing intensionally defined facts in the form of derived attributes and relations. Table 4.21 summarizes the properties of our incremental evaluation algorithm in comparison to approaches used in a number of quite different systems:

(a) GOM /6. KM 92, 6. MD 89/, an object–oriented database system, which supports the materialization of arbitrary functions and path expressions,

(b) Relational Attribute Grammars /4. HT 86/, RAG, which are an attempt to combine the tree–oriented data model of attribute grammars, found in CPSG /4. RT 88/, with the relational data model,

(c) and finally the already mentioned graph–based system Cactis /6. HK 88, 6. HK 89/.

	GOM	RAG	Cactis	GRAS
Lazy evaluation	+	–	+	+
Eager evaluation	+	+	–	–
Space efficiency	–	–	+	+
Incrementality	+	–	+	+
N–context dep.	+	–	–	+

Table 4.21. Comparison of different incremental, derived data evaluation algorithms

All presented systems, with the exception of RAG, use a two–phase *lazy evaluation algorithm* for recomputing derived data. Furthermore, the system GOM offers a second eager evaluation algorithm which recomputes invalid data immediately after any changes to the underlying object base. In this way GOM avoids the invalidation of data that depends on potentially affected, but in fact still valid data. In rare cases, this algorithm may require exponential time because data are recomputed too early. Relational attribute grammars in contrast exploit very sophisticated attribute evaluation techniques to circumvent the above mentioned "exponential time complexity" trap. On the other hand, they have problems with mutual attribute/relation dependencies. Furthermore, the propagation of changed information from relations to attributes is very coarse–grained. It suffers from the fact that even small modifications of relations lead to reevaluation of all attributes which depend on these relations.

Concerning space overhead, Cactis and GRAS, which both rely on *static dependency graphs*, are superior to GOM and RAG: the system GOM creates large dependency tables on the instance level, and the incremental relation maintenance algorithm of RAG relies on the construction of many intermediate relations. Comparing the ability of the four systems to maintain n–context dependent relations, the systems GOM and GRAS are equal to each other. The system Cactis is restricted to the 1–context case, and RAG seems to have problems to deal with transitive closure for arbitrary relations.

The *concurrency* and *distribution layer* extends the kernel by allowing different applications to share graphs in a secure and efficient way. In contrast to other distributed (object–oriented) database systems which exchange data (normally in page or object units) between clients and servers (e.g. /6. BOS 91/ or /6. LLO 91/), GRAS exchanges operation calls and results. This concept has been successfully used e.g. in the X Window system /6. SG 86/. Although data exchange on the physical or logical level as realized by page servers or object servers shows a better performance in general (because much of the actual work can be shifted from the server to the clients), this approach has been chosen because, in most cases, a graph is used either by only one application exclusively or by many applications for frequent but short times:

(a) When many applications access a graph for short updates or queries, e.g. when operating on a project configuration graph, the lock protocols between clients and servers for ensuring consistency in the case of data exchanges are even more expensive than simple remote procedure calls.

(b) For achieving high performance of exclusively working applications as e.g. an analyzer checking a large graph, all kind of interprocess communication should be avoided at all, that is the database engine should better be linked directly to the application.

The layered architecture of GRAS allowed a straightforward realization of the *direct linking* of one application to a graph server. An implementation is currently under way that even performs an automatic and transparent shift from direct linking to network coupling when a graph is accessed by more than one application.

4.2.6 Summary

We have presented the functionality and the architecture of GRAS, a nonstandard database system which is based on attributed graphs. The GRAS system has a layered software architecture which may be divided into two parts. The lower part, which is called the *kernel*, provides basic operations for storing and manipulating graph structures. In order to execute such operations efficiently, the following techniques have been applied:

(a) *Different* kinds of *data* (e.g. nodes, long attributes, and edges) are mapped onto *separate substorages*. In this way, data necessary for processing different kinds of application requests are stored on different disk pages.

(b) Furthermore, an indexing scheme based on so-called *tries* and *static hashing* is used to map data of varying size and structure onto storage locations. By means of an *incrementally* and *heuristically working clustering algorithm* logically related data are mapped onto adjacent storage locations (i.e. on the same storage page wherever this is possible). This algorithm only incurs a negligible overhead in contrast to profiling–based and batch-oriented clustering algorithms which reorganize whole databases.

The upper part of the GRAS architecture consists of *enhancing layers* which incrementally extend the functionality provided by the kernel:

(a) The *change management* layer comprises all functions which are concerned with logging, storing and executing sequences of change operations. Change management is performed to provide for user recovery (undo/redo), system recovery (from system failures), and deltas (efficient storage of versions). These tasks are handled by GRAS uniformly by maintaining logs of change operations.

(b) The *event management* layer supports the definition of triggers and associated actions which are called when specified events occur within GRAS.

(c) The *scheme* and *attribute management* layer checks and ensures that all graph operations are consistent with a scheme defining types of graph components and their interrelations. In addition to optional runtime type checking, this layer supports attributes, i.e. node attributes which are calculated from attributes of neighbor nodes, where neighborhood is not confined to the 1-context, but includes arbitrarily far reaching attribute dependencies.

(d) The *concurrency control* and *distribution* layer manages concurrent access of different applications to shared graphs. It allows for the description of the intended interaction mode with other applications by means of a flexible group-oriented access model. In contrast to most other approaches, an operation exchange protocol instead of a data exchange protocol was chosen for interprocess communication.

GRAS has been *in use* for more than *10 years* now. It has been applied successfully in different projects. On top of GRAS, interactive tools have been built which operate on complex internal data structures. GRAS is available as free software, under similar conditions as software distributed by Gnu. The current release is both stable and efficient. Ongoing work addresses schema evolution, modularization of schemata, hierarchical graphs, and more general support for undo/redo and transactions.

4.3 Reuse in the Central Part: The Structure of Logical and Representation Documents, Parser, and Unparser

P. Klein

After discussing architectural aspects of the global IPSEN framework structure in section 4.1 and the GRAS database in section 4.2, we now describe the *design* of the *central layers* of the IPSEN architecture (cf. fig. 4.1) in detail. Since the step from representation to presentation (cf. section 4.1) is rather technical and presents no conceptual problems, we focus on the logical portion of this layer (right part of fig. 4.1). Fig. 4.22 shows the subarchitecture of a single technical environment we are dealing with.

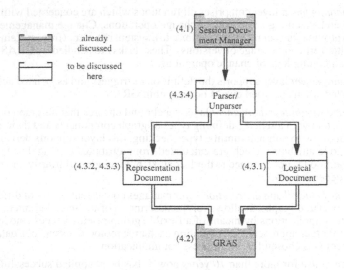

Fig. 4.22. Subarchitecture to be discussed in section 4.3

In subsection 4.3.1, we show how logical documents are internally structured (for the specification of logical documents see section 3.3). This closes the gap between the interface of logical documents from the framework point of view (cf. section 4.1) and the GRAS interface (cf. section 4.2). Before subsection 4.3.3 gives an analogous description for representation documents, we turn our attention in 4.3.2 to the metamodel, a concept to provide views on logical documents used for graphical representations. From the conceptual point of view, this was discussed in section 3.3, now we add the corresponding architectural details. The discussion of the parser/unparser technology employed in IPSEN (cf. subsection 4.1.3) will be taken up in subsection 4.3.4. To conclude this section, we give a short summary in subsection 4.3.5.

4.3.1 The Layered Structure of Logical Documents

In general, we can distinguish *several kinds* of *logical documents* in IPSEN's technical environments. Most important, there are internal counterparts of external documents as described in subsection 1.5.1. They represent documents in the sense of the working area model, i.e. they result from activities in one working area. These documents are written in a certain language, like SA/RT/IM for Requirements Engineering or Modula–2 for Programming–in–the–Small. Any of these languages comprises at least a context–free and a context–sensitive syntax. Apart from language–based documents, we have for example logical documents related to the execution (cf. section 3.3) or the consistency (cf. section 4.6) of one or more documents.

In this section, we will only consider *language–based internal documents* and neglect the latter types of logical documents for the following reasons:

(1) Historically, we have gathered quite some experience with language–based documents. The technology we present here can therefore be regarded as mature in contrast to other classes of logical documents.

(2) Integration documents and other types of non–language–based documents are generally not visualized, or at least not with the mechanisms described here. In this sense, they are not as much relevant to the rest of this section.

(3) The internal structure of language–based documents is, partially due to the extensive work we have done on this subject, much more complicated than that of other documents.

First of all, we have to *recapitulate* what was said in section 3.3 about the *specification* of *logical documents*. This section showed how a document specification can be constructed in a number of consecutive steps, each one adding some properties to the underlying structure. The first step is to map the syntax description of the language, given in an EBNF derivative, onto a graph schema with node types for the language's nonterminals and edge types to set up an abstract syntax tree structure. This allows us to represent a document in the respective language as a graph reflecting its abstract syntax tree. In the following steps, context–sensitive properties are defined in the AST framework. It was also shown how the specification consists of language–specific and language–unspecific parts which are defined separately and then related to each other by subtyping. In this sense, the developer's task is to extend the language–independent graph schema with language–specific classes, types, and operations. We will see that the architectural structure exactly reflects this approach.

Let us now take a look at the *internal structure* of *language–based logical documents*, cf. fig. 4.23. The subarchitecture is symmetric with respect to language–specific and language–unspecific parts. The right half contains several layers of data abstraction components. Each component extends the schema of the underlying graph with appropriate node classes and edge types and defines an interface with corresponding resources. The left half provides, if necessary, the language–specific implementations of these resources and assigns the increment types of the language to the node classes.

The *individual layers* and *components* of the subsystem are described next.

(X) Graph: The Graph component is realized directly on top of the GRAS database for the persistent management of directed, attributed, node– and edge–labeled graphs (cf. section 4.2). Its purpose is to provide basic services used for the realization of the other layers. All operations are language–unspecific; the sole purpose of the XGraph component is to define a unique graph type for the respective document class.

(X) ASTGraph: On this level, the (X) Graph interface is extended with operations to treat the underlying graph as an abstract syntax tree. This includes resources for the construction, manipulation, and traversal of the tree structure. The language–independent ASTGraph part defines a frame graph schema containing node classes e.g. for placeholders, identifiers, and operators. It is the responsibility of the corresponding XASTGraph component to define node types for the language's nonterminals and to establish subtype relationships between these node types and the corresponding node classes in the graph schema. Again, the major part of AST graph operations can be implemented in a language–independent manner, including the management of change logs needed for incremental updates of dependent structures (cf. subsection 4.3.4).

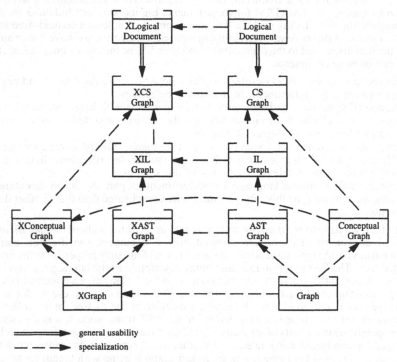

general usability
specialization

Fig. 4.23. The internal structure of logical documents

(X) ILGraph: Identifier linkage graphs introduce the notion of declaring and applied occurrences of identifiers in the syntax tree. As a fundamental prerequisite of many context–sensitive operations, edges are drawn between these occurrences. ILGraph therefore augments the AST schema with node classes for scopes (name spaces), declaring identifiers, applied identifiers, and an edge type to connect them. Analogous to the level below, XILGraph has to insert subtype relationships between the specific AST node types of XASTGraph and the IL node classes. Thereby it determines for example which abstract syntax subtree spawns a scope in the respective language. In the MIL example from section 3.3, a module definition introduces a name space, so the node type for the Definition nonterminal will be defined as a subtype of the Env class (representing a scope) defined in ILGraph. Furthermore, the language–specific realization of operations, e.g. for navigating between scopes or declaring and applied occurrences of identifiers, has to be implemented.

(X) ConceptualGraph: Just like the infrastructure for handling declaring and applied identifiers is provided by (X) ILGraph, this independent specialization of (X) Graph extends the basic graph structure with a notion of types and relationships between types. ConceptualGraph offers for example a node class TypeDef for type definitions and an edge type ToSuperTypes for connecting a TypeDef node with the TypeDef node(s) of its/their supertype(s). Again, the language–specific part has to identify which increments denote a type in the underlying language by extending the graph schema accordingly, e.g. the node type for the TypeDecl nonterminal in the MIL EBNF would become a subtype of TypeDef. Corresponding operations, e.g. to test two types for assignment compatibility or to navigate from a type to its super– or subtypes, have to be realized as well. Analogous to ILGraph, Conceptual–Graph materializes the respective increment relationships with edges of appropriate types (like ToSuperTypes). Note that this specialization does not depend on the under–lying structure being an abstract syntax tree, it operates directly on graph level.

(X) CSGraph: This top level of the specialization hierarchy implements a framework for handling context–sensitive relationships in internal logical graphs. All operations necessary for the incremental analysis of type compatibility and other structural prop–erties in the graph are realized here. The language–dependent part is responsible for the actual analysis using the basic services from XConceptualGraph and XIL–Graph. The abstract architecture component CSGraph takes care of removing analysis information from AST parts affected by manipulation operations and orga–nizes their reevaluation in the correct order.

(X) LogicalDocument: At the top of the subsystem we find the abstract and the lan–guage–specific interfaces of LogicalDocument and XLogicalDocument, respectively, comprising the interface of the subsystem. They realize a view on the respective graphs passing through operations preserving the document structure but hiding direct access to the graph internals from the subsystem's clients. This makes it impossible for the rest of the IPSEN framework to manipulate the document in a way violating its context–free and context–sensitive properties with respect to the underlying language.

Obviously, the *right part* of the logical document subsystem consists of *general compo–nents* only. They can be reused for every language an IPSEN system supports. Conversely, new developments in this subarchitecture can be used for all languages. The basic services implemented here have reached an extent which allows a wide variety of conventional as well as quite intricate languages to be managed as IPSEN documents. The ILGraph layer for example supports arbitrary nested scopes, imports, renaming, overloading, and many other concepts found in programming and specification languages. The Conceptual–Graph component can handle strong or weak typing, inheritance, polymorphism, or sev–eral compatibility models like name equivalence or structural equivalence.

A task which remains to be completed in order to yield logical documents for a certain language is to supply the language–specific *left subarchitecture* from fig. 4.23. The above description of the corresponding components shows that their realization mainly consists of the implementation of query and manipulation operations as well as schema extensions on the underlying graph structure. In this sense, it is a natural approach to *specify* these operations in terms of *graph grammars* as described in section 3.3. How the implementa–tion of the language–specific components can be generated from appropriate specifications will be discussed in section 4.4.

4.3.2 The Metamodel and Graphical Documents

As was described in the previous subsection, the view on an abstract internal logical doc–ument at its interface is that of a *graph* with a *dominant (spanning) tree* and *additional edges* reflecting context–sensitive relations between nodes. In general, the tree corresponds to the abstract syntax tree of the document with respect to the language it is written in. Concerning the visualization of a logical document, the non–tree edges can be neglected because they have no corresponding representation. This becomes obvious when we consider that con–text–sensitive information can always be inferred from the context–free structure. In other words, it is exactly the abstract syntax tree of the document which is visualized by the unparser.

430

As long as the document representation is *textual*, its *generation* from the logical structure is rather *straightforward*. A major advantage here is that the containment structure of the representation, i.e. the nesting of constructs in other constructs, always reflects the subtree relationship in the abstract syntax tree: Some increment's representation is covered by another increment representation if and only if the latter increment is a parent of the former in the tree. Furthermore, there are no structural relationships between increments in the representation document other than containment.

If we look at *graphical* representations though, this is not necessarily the case. First of all, we can distinguish several *types* of representation *objects*, noticeably first–order (vertex) and second–order (link) objects. Second, there are several *types* of *relationships* between these objects, e.g. a link is attached to exactly the two vertices it connects. Finally, the *containment structure* in the representation may be *different* from the hierarchy in the syntax tree.

As a consequence, a logical document as presented in the previous subsection contains not all the information necessary to create a corresponding graphical representation. In addition to the abstract syntax tree, the unparser needs information about the *representation properties* of the *logical increments*, like which increment should be represented as a vertex, how to determine which vertices are attached to a given link etc. In order to isolate the mapping of an abstract syntax tree onto a graphical representation from the logical and representation document structure, a special *view* on the LogicalDocument component is needed to *encapsulate* this *mapping*. The conceptual framework for providing such views is called *metamodel*, and the view is accordingly called the *metaview* of the document. We find its realization in the (X)MetaViewDocument component in fig. 4.24 (also cf. fig. 4.28).

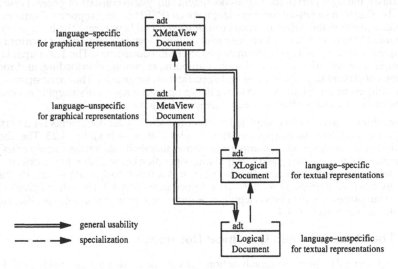

Fig. 4.24. The MetaView document

Just like logical documents, metaview documents have an abstract superclass (MetaViewDocument) defining the operations in the document's interface and language–specific subclasses (XMetaViewDocument) implementing them. Note that the abstract MetaViewDocument uses only the abstract LogicalDocument interface, whereas the realization of an XMetaViewDocument instance uses only the corresponding XLogicalDocument interface.

To get a better idea of the view a metamodel gives on the document, we now sketch the *class hierarchy* of MetaViewDocument increments, cf. fig. 4.25. The purpose of an XMetaViewDocument implementation is to map abstract syntax tree increments onto one of the classes in this hierarchy. In the following, we will continue to use the MIL introduced in section 3.3 as an example.

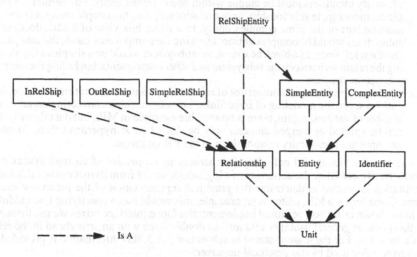

Fig. 4.25. Class diagram of MetaView documents

In detail, the *classes* are:

Unit: An arbitrary increment of a logical document. In particular, this can be a direct view on the underlying abstract syntax tree, possibly with a complex internal structure.

Entity: Every unit which might be source or target of a relationship. Entities are distinguishable by an identifier. An example for a graphical MIL document representation would be a module (eventually to be depicted as a box).

Relationship: A unit connecting entities. Relationships are existence–dependent on the entities they connect, i.e. they may not exist without them. Usability relations between a client and a provider module would be Relationships in the MIL example.

Identifier: If an entity is to be the source or the target of a relationship, and the relationship is not in the abstract syntax subtree under the entity, then there has to be a unit in this subtree serving as the (unique) identifier of the entity. If we look at the MIL example again, we find that Relationships for usability relations between modules are induced by the client entity, i.e. the relationship actually corresponds to the import clause in the client. In this case, the logical document increment related to the relationship (the import clause) is part of the client module subtree, so there is no need for the client to provide an Identifier in order to be the source of the relationship. For the provider module though, it is necessary to assign some identifier in its subtree as the module's Identifier to be able to determine the target entity of the relationship. Obviously, this would be the identifier denoting the module name in the MIL example.

SimpleRelShip: A (directed) relationship connecting exactly one source and one target entity, like the usability relation from above.

InRelShip: A (directed) relationship with exactly one target and no source entity, used for depicting half–edges. There are no good examples of half–edges in our MIL, but if we look at the SA language, we find data flows entering a data flow diagram from "outside", i.e. they have no source entity (in this diagram).

OutRelShip: A (directed) relationship with no target and exactly one source entity.

SimpleEntity: Some part of a complex entity. Only simple entities may be source or target of a simple relationship, in relationship, or out relationship. Modules are again an example in MIL.

ComplexEntity: A collection of simple entity, simple relationship, in relationship, and out relationship instances. Complex entities spawn a scope for entity identifiers, i.e. simple entity identifiers must be unique within one complex entity. Furthermore, a simple relationship, in relationship, or out relationship and the simple entity it connects must be part of the same complex entity. In a white box view of a MIL document, subsystems would be complex entities showing the components inside the subsystem and their relations. In a black box view, the subsystem would be a simple entity showing the relations between the subsystem and other components, but hiding the internal subsystem structure.

RelShipEntity: Combining the properties of relationships and simple entities, relationship entities serve the modeling of hyperlinks, i.e. relationships connecting an arbitrary number of entities. Again, there is no sensible example in MIL, but data flows in SA can be splitted or merged and can only be described as hyperlinks then. Another example are non–binary relationships in the ER language.

Note that the metamodel only describes *structural properties* of abstract syntax tree increments. To complete the unparsing of a logical document from its metaview, *additional information* is needed to determine the graphical representation of the metaview increments. Considering a MIL editor as an example, this would mean specifying that modules are to be shown as the sort of closed implementation/open interface boxes we use throughout this book or general usability relations as double lines with an arrowhead in the relation's direction. For the reasons stated in subsection 4.1.3, this information is provided in a *separate table* used by the graphical unparser.

For a more in–depth discussion of metaview documents from the graph grammar specification point of view, see subsection 3.3.4. Our diagram 4.25 differs from fig. 3.33 in that it does not show the connections between the metaview and the logical document's node class hierarchies. On the other hand, it is more detailed concerning the metaview schema. Furthermore, subsection 4.4.2 will show how the XMetaViewDocument instances are generated from an extended grammar specification and what role the metaview node classes play in the generation process. We only emphasize here that, using the technique of an extended grammar specification, we are always able to yield a textual representation of any document as well. Both the textual and the graphical unparser are generated from the same source.

4.3.3 Structuring Representation Documents

In contrast to the logical documents discussed in subsection 4.3.1, representation documents are not realized in a sequence of data abstraction layers, since no complex functionality is needed below their interface. A representation document is simply a container for objects with some relationships between them. In fact, as far as the representation is concerned, neither the objects nor their relationships carry any semantics beyond their type and their attributes. Accordingly, a representation document is not more than a graph with a certain schema, so their *mapping* onto the GRAS interface is rather *straightforward*. The only tasks of the RepresentationDocument component of fig. 4.1 are therefore (1) to provide a document interface (which differs in its administrative operations slightly from the graph interface) towards the document manager (which records the relationship between the representation document and its logical document), and (2) to set up the representation graph schema in GRAS. Since the major structural properties of representations can be found in this schema (which all representation graphs have in common), we now show its important elements and their relationships, cf. fig. 4.26.

433

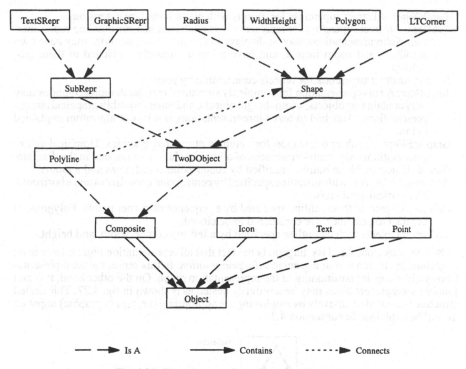

Fig. 4.26. Class diagram of representation graph nodes

A representation graph mainly consists of a spanning tree with complex inner nodes and atomic leaf nodes connected by "contains" edges. The diagram in fig. 4.26 allows the following node *classes* to *appear* in the *graph* of a representation document:

Object: Abstract superclass for all elements of a representation graph. All other classes inherit x and y coordinate attributes from this class describing the object's position.

Composite: Abstract superclass for composite objects, i.e. objects consisting of other objects. In terms of document visualization, a composite object covers the contained objects and contained objects are positioned relative to their composite. In terms of graph structure, inner nodes of the spanning tree have to be composites. Note that, keeping the idea of a PROGRES graph schema in mind, the property to possibly contain other objects (being the source of a "contains" edge in the representation graph) is inherited by all subclasses of composite.

Icon: Atomic class of scalable bitmap images.

Text: Atomic class of basic (i.e. unstructured) text blocks.

Point: Atomic class of objects with no extension. Although points are given some extension in the actual document visualization, their size can be changed neither explicitly (by the user through layout modification operations) nor implicitly (by zooming, scaling etc.).

Polyline: Polylines are used to connect shape objects. In contrast to what the term "line" suggests, they are composites because they may have a complex internal structure, e.g. for various graphical elements (lines, bullets, arrowheads etc.) or (possibly complex) text labels. Polylines are connected to the corresponding shapes through "toSource" and "toTarget" edges (summarized as "connects" edges in the class diagram). These are exactly the non–tree edges in a representation graph, i.e. they may connect objects regardless of the tree structure given by "contains" edges. Note that the positioning of a polyline is computed with respect to the shapes it connects.

TwoDObject: Abstract superclass for objects with given boundary extensions.

SubRepr: Abstract superclass for representations contained in a surrounding representation. Subrepresentations may be displayed in an individual window, may have own scrollbars and zoom factors, and have a layout algorithm attached to them (see below).

Shape: Abstract superclass for objects connectable by polylines.

TextSRepr: A subrepresentation for complexly structured text. Such representations may only contain text objects, width–height objects, and other (possibly graphical) subrepresentations. Attached to text subrepresentations is a layout algorithm explained below.

GraphicSRepr: A subrepresentation for complex structured graphics. Graphical subrepresentations may contain instances of all object classes mentioned in the diagram.

Radius: Objects with an outline specified by center point coordinates and a radius.

WidthHeight: Objects with an outline specified by center point coordinates and a horizontal and vertical semi–axis.

Polygon: Objects with an outline specified by a sequence of corner points. Polygons, in contrast to polylines, are considered to be closed.

LTCorner: Objects with an outline specified by a left top corner, width, and height.

Not obvious from the class diagram is the fact that all representation *objects* have to be *contained* in either a text or a graphic *subrepresentation*. In this sense, the subrepresentations yield a disjoint partitioning of the representation graph. On the other hand, text and graphic subrepresentations may be arbitrarily nested as is shown in fig. 4.27. This nested structure is created recursively by employing the appropriate (i.e. text or graphic) unparser as will be explained in subsection 4.3.4.

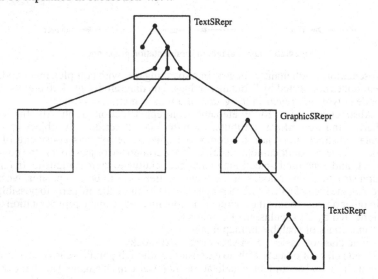

Fig. 4.27. Example of an overall representation graph structure

To conclude this subsection, we want to add a note concerning the *automatic layout* of subrepresentations. Subsection 4.1.3 already stated that the default layout for *textual* document parts is derived from the grammar specification of the underlying language, i.e. the layout of the right–hand sides of the grammar productions serve as templates for the placement of keywords, identifiers, line–breaks, and tabulators in the representation. To be more precise, in the course of the generation of an unparser from the grammar, certain layout attributes are derived from the respective rules. These attributes describe every rule's right hand side *layout* in terms of *constraints* like "line end after this keyword", "indent this substructure to the left", or "if this sequence of substructures fits into one line, arrange them horizontally, if not, put all elements in a separate line and align the lines vertically". These layout attributes are passed from the unparser to the corresponding text subrepresentation which resolves them in accordance to the bounding size of the subrepresentation area.

Currently, this layout facility is available for text only, but we are working on an analogous *constraint–based layout* for *graphic* subrepresentations. Here, the corresponding parts of the grammar are augmented with constraint descriptions like "if two vertex objects are connected by an edge object of a given type, align them vertically" and the like. As in the text case, a constraint–solving algorithm built into graphic subrepresentations is in charge of computing actual object positions from the constraints. Already implemented though are *standard layout algorithms* for graphic subrepresentations. These algorithms will generate constraints instead of object positions when the constraint–solving component is available. Then, a basic set of constraints resulting from some layout algorithm may be freely manipulated and augmented with user–defined constraints on class or instance level.

4.3.4 Parser and Unparser in Detail

After we have shown the internals of logical and representation documents in the previous subsections, we now turn our attention to the components serving the *consistency* of and *transformation* between them. For the direction of logical to representation structures, this is the *unparser* component which will be described first. Then we explain the *parser* component for the opposite direction in greater detail. To start with, we discuss the architecture of a general unparser in the IPSEN framework.

Section 4.1 already gave a sketch of the unparser's functionality. Essentially, an *unparser* is called by the session document manager when a logical document has been changed by a tool. It is now up to the unparser to update the representation document accordingly. This update is performed *incrementally* as discussed in subsection 4.1.3. With the more detailed information about internal document structures given in this section, we can now take a closer look at the unparser architecture.

Fig. 4.28 shows the *components participating* in the *unparsing* process:

LogicalDocument: This is an abstract supertype for logical documents. It contains no implementation, instead this component only describes the operations all logical documents have to offer. These operations comprise administrative resources for the creation and deletion of documents as well as resources to manipulate its contents. The interface view of a logical document is that of an abstract syntax tree with context–sensitive relations between increments, see subsection 4.3.1 for details.

XLogicalDocument: For every document type the environment might support, a language–specific subtype of LogicalDocument is provided. These subtypes inherit the logical document interface and implement the operations exported there.

RepresentationDocument: Each logical document may be assigned one or more representation documents describing how the contents of the document should be represented to the user. The internal structure of a representation document was shown in subsection 4.3.3.

MetaViewDocument: Metaview documents describe a view on a logical document containing the structural information needed to generate graphical representations. Analogous to logical documents, this is an abstract supertype determining a metaview document's interface, but without any implementation.

XMetaViewDocument: The language–specific subtype of MetaViewDocument implementing its interface.

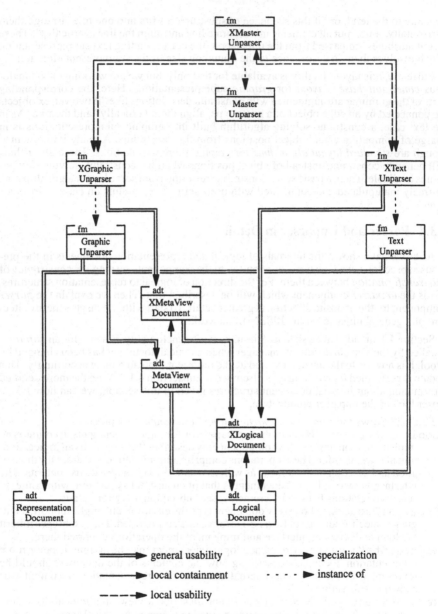

Fig. 4.28. Unparser architecture

GraphicUnparser: This is the generic unparser for creating graphical representations. Its purpose is to check the logical document for changed increments and to insert or delete appropriate graphical representation increments in the representation document.

XGraphicUnparser: A language–specific instance of the GraphicUnparser component. As generic parameter serves a table which determines the mapping between increment types in the metaview document and representation increments.

`TextUnparser`: Analogous to `GraphicUnparser` for textual representation increments.

`XTextUnparser`: Analogous to `XGraphicUnparser` for textual representation increments.

`MasterUnparser`: The generic control module for the unparser. Essentially, it looks up whether some increment should be represented textually or graphically and calls the corresponding text or graphic unparser, respectively.

`XMasterUnparser`: The instance of `MasterUnparser` determining if `XTextUnparser` or `XGraphicUnparser` should be used for some document part.

To *summarize* the *dynamic behavior* of the unparser, we assume that some increment in the logical document has been changed by a tool. The session document manager will now activate the unparser through the language–specific `XMasterUnparser` component. The master unparser decides whether the corresponding increment should be represented as text or as graphic and calls the corresponding unparser. If the logical increment is complex (i.e. a complex entity in the metaview for graphical document parts or an inner node in the spanning AST of the logical document for textual document parts), the text or graphic unparser first creates root representation nodes for all children of the complex increment. Then, it recursively calls the master unparser to process the corresponding substructures. After all substructures are created, the text or graphic unparser assembles them by creating a composite object (if no change in the representation kind has occurred between the increment and its substructures) or a new subrepresentation to reflect a change in the representation kind. Finally, the substructures are attached to the composite or inserted into the subrepresentation respectively. In the course of assembling the substructures, the unparser calls the subrepresentation's layout algorithms to compute the relative positioning of simpler objects within their complex object.

The unparser's counterpart for the reverse direction is the *parser component* as described in subsection 4.1.3. We already discussed that the parser is restricted to textual input due to the serious efforts necessary to parse input delivered by an arbitrary drawing tool or even free–hand drawings. Furthermore, since there is always a textual representation for all documents as noted in subsection 4.3.2, it is still possible to modify any document circumventing syntax–directed command–based editing. Fig. 4.29 shows the details of the parsing/unparsing subarchitecture.

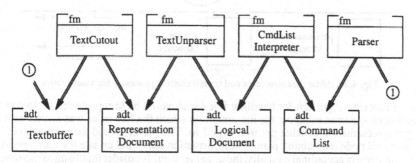

Fig. 4.29. Parser/Unparser subarchitecture for textual representations

When the user activates free input on an arbitrary increment of the document, the `Text-Cutout` module transforms the appropriate part of the representation document into a plain text representation which is stored in a `Textbuffer`. The user may then edit this text with any conventional editor. When the user quits the editor, a multiple–entry LALR *parser* (i.e. one that can parse arbitrary fragments of a document) *creates* a minimal sequence of logical *editor commands* which reflects the changes made by the user. So, what our parser does is not really parsing in the sense of constructing (parts of) the logical document. Instead, it determines only how this construction has to be done. To enhance the performance of this process, the parser does not consider the whole textbuffer but only the changed text fragments. The list of editor commands is then executed by the CmdListInterpreter. In this sense, free editing is reduced to parsing and editor command execution. As a consequence, if context–sensitive analysis is switched on, the user gets corresponding error/warning messages immediately during the update of the logical document.

Note that the *parser* and the associated *scanner* components are not hand–coded, instead they are *generated* using the well–known yacc and lex tools, respectively (see subsection 4.4.2 for details). Since these tools are not part of IPSEN, we treat their output as black box here and do not consider the parser's internal structure.

Fig. 4.30 *summarizes* the *transformations* participating in the *editing* process. (See fig. 3.65 in section 3.6 on how these transformations can be embedded into a more general environment including interpretation and code generation.)

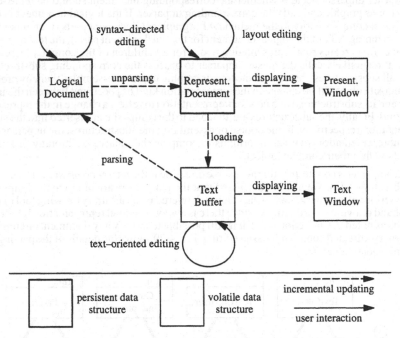

Fig. 4.30. Editor data structures and transformation processes for visualization

An *alternative approach* for handling free input would be to replace the subtree in the representation document under the increment on which the free input was issued with the textual representation of what the user typed in. The parser would then investigate this unstructured node (containing plain text information only) and update the corresponding logical document accordingly. Finally, the unparser would consider the changed increments in the logical document and replace the plain text node in the representation document with the correct representation structure. This solution would unify the textbuffer and representation document components in fig. 4.29, making parser and unparser symmetrical between logical and representation document as in fig. 4.22. The command list interpreter's purpose is only to avoid the reimplementation of commands in the parser which are already realized in the editor.

Again, we want to conclude this description with a short sketch of the *dynamic behavior* of the process of *free input* (also see subsection 4.1.3). When free input is issued on some increment, the increment is unparsed into textual form and passed to a text editor. The user may then edit the text. After he quits editing, the text is scanned and parsed. During parsing, a sequence of editor commands is created which, after successful completion, is passed to a command interpreter. The command interpreter eventually modifies the logical document in accordance to the command sequence and under close consideration of the existing AST structure, i.e. the interpreter ignores commands which only reproduce the already existing subtree.

4.3.5 Summary

The subject of this section was to describe the *structures* and *mechanisms* in the *central part* of the IPSEN architecture, especially the logical and representation documents and their coupling by the parser/unparser component. We have shown that, due to extensive experience and the use of graph–grammar technology, hand–coding has been almost completely banished from this subarchitecture. This part of IPSEN is dominated by general (i.e. independent of the concrete environment) and generated components. More details about the generators and their in– and outputs can be found in the next section, 4.4.

In the first subsection, we turned our attention to the *internal structure* of *logical documents*. There, we found two orthogonal inheritance hierarchies: the vertical hierarchy presenting several layers of data abstractions, adding new properties on each layer. The horizontal hierarchy on the other hand separates language–specific from language–unspecific parts of the corresponding layers. The resulting architecture exactly reflects the specification structure of logical documents as presented in section 3.3.

The next subsection discussed the question which additional information is necessary to represent a logical document graphically. We discovered that, in order to be able to obtain such a graphical representation, the logical increments have to be attributed to describe their spatial properties and relationships. To keep the corresponding representation decisions separate from the pure logical information, we introduced a special view on logical documents encapsulating these properties. We called this the *metaview* of the document.

To complete the description of the document layer of the IPSEN architecture, we took a closer look at *representation documents*. We saw that these documents consist of subrepresentations hierarchically structured according to a spatial containment relationship, a technique known as recursive composition. Subrepresentations are either graphical or textual and may, in accordance to their type, contain a variety of graphical or textual objects and other subrepresentations, possibly of another type.

Finally, we devoted a subsection to an in–depth view on the *parser* and *unparser mechanisms* necessary for providing consistency between logical and representation information. We discussed details of both transformation directions and how we realized an incremental behavior of the corresponding components.

Unfortunately, *comparing* the IPSEN concepts presented in this section to *related work* is *not possible*. As far as the behavior towards a tool developer is concerned, i.e. how a technical environment is built with IPSEN, such a comparison can be found in sections 3.3 and 4.4. The internal architectural structures and concepts as presented here are rather unique, and not much is known about comparable systems on the same level of detail.

We can, however, *compare* at least one aspect on an *abstract level*, namely the coupling of logical and representation documents with the MVC approach /6. KP 88/. Apart from the fact that we employ a three–level separation (logic, representation, and presentation; cf. subsection 4.1.1) compared to the two–level separation (model and view) in MVC, we can observe that our parser/unparser is a very specific form of MVC's generic controller. In this sense, we take the idea of separating the data structures and their coupling further to offer a complete mechanism handling bidirectional updates between logic and representation. Since we know very much about the internal structure of the documents we are dealing with, we can pin down the task of managing logic/representation dependencies to a formalized transformation. This enables us to offer a generator machinery (cf. section 4.4) which relieves the programmer from handcoding a controller.

4.4   Generating Single Document Processing Tools

P. Klein, A. Schürr, A. Zündorf

The preceding section 4.3 presented the architecture of single document processing tools with a main focus on syntax–directed editors for mixed textual/graphical languages. It showed that the implementations of these tools consist of some language–specific subcomponents embedded into the invariant IPSEN architecture framework. These *specific components encapsulate* any *information* needed about

(a) the (abstract) syntax of a given language,

(b) textual or graphical representations,

(c) static semantics (type checking) rules,

(d) complex context–sensitive editing operations,

(e) and execution or compilation rules.

Here, we will discuss how these *language–specific components* are *generated* by using some *meta programming tools*. These meta tools form in turn an integrated environment, called meta SDE, which has the same architecture as any other IPSEN environment and which was (partly) generated by means of itself (bootstrapping, cf. section 1.7).

The following subsection 4.4.1 provides the reader with an overview of the IPSEN meta environment, i.e. it shows its most important meta tools and their interdependencies. Subsection 4.4.2 then presents the subenvironment for editing EBNFs and for generating context–free editors. Subsections 4.4.3 and 4.4.4 explain the role of the PROGRES environment (already presented in section 3.6) for specifying and generating non–context–free operations of IPSEN tools. Subsection 4.4.3 has a main focus on the relationships between EBNF and PROGRES tools and subsection 4.4.4 explains the translation of (context–sensitive tool) specifications into ordinary (Modula–2) source code fragments. Finally, subsection 4.4.5 summarizes the main properties of the IPSEN meta environment and its state of development.

4.4.1   Overview

This subsection resumes the discussion of section 3.3 concerning the *specification* of *logical documents* and *logical document processing tools*. The specification of a module interconnection language (MIL) editor, our running example, started with the definition of its concrete and abstract syntax in the form of EBNF rules (cf. fig. 3.24 and fig. 3.25 in section 3.3). These EBNF rules are used to generate the core functionality of a syntax–directed MIL editor with text–only document representations. The given EBNF with a specific layout of its rules is also used to generate the appropriate text parser and unparsing tables (cf. section 4.3). Additional EBNF rule annotations may be used to specify graphical MIL language representations and to generate graphical editors.

The diagram of fig. 4.31 and especially its subdiagram A show how a *context–free editing environment* is generated from these sources of input. An EBNF editor (box 1) is used to define a language's context–free syntax (including all above mentioned annotations). The EBNF generator (box 4) then takes a complete EBNF document (box 2) plus a number of text file skeletons (box 3) as input and generates all language–specific Modula–2 sources (box 5) which are needed to realize syntax–directed and free editing of MIL documents via mixed graphical/text–oriented user interfaces.

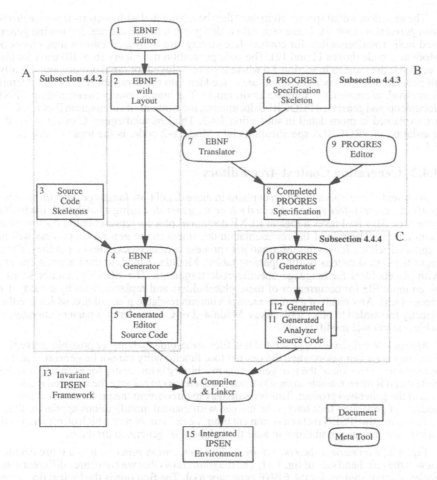

Fig. 4.31. The IPSEN meta environment: overview

The generated sources together with the invariant IPSEN framework (box 13) are compiled and linked (box 14) to *construct* a *basic version* of the *environment* (box 15). This environment does not yet offer any analysis or complex document transformation commands, e.g. for preventing cyclic import relationships or producing configurations with certain properties (cf. subsection 3.1). Its overall structure and most important basic components were discussed in sections 4.1 through 4.3. Further details about the generation process sketched in subdiagram A of fig. 4.31 are presented in subsection 4.4.2.

The *specification* of *complex document processing operations* for any kind of analysis or execution tools by means of programmed graph rewriting systems was the main topic of chapter 3. Its section 3.3 showed a systematic way for deriving an initial PROGRES document specification from a given EBNF. This kind of modelling knowledge is currently hardwired into an incrementally working EBNF translation tool (box 7) which takes an EBNF (box 2) and a language–independent specification skeleton (box 6) as input and produces a corresponding context–free logical document specification as output (box 8). It thereby forms the connection between the EBNF and PROGRES tools.

The generated initial specification must then be augmented with *context–sensitive graph transformations* (box 9). These manually added graph transformations, but not the generated basic transformations for context–free editing, are translated into various pieces of Modula–2 code (boxes 11 and 12). The code generation machinery (box 10) used for this purpose is the same as in section 3.6 where it was employed for rapid prototyping. Finally, all generated source code fragments are embedded into the invariant IPSEN architecture framework to construct a complete environment. The interactions between editing EBNF documents and generated PROGRES documents, the contents of subdiagram B of fig. 4.31, are explained in more detail in subsection 4.4.3. The last subdiagram C of fig. 4.31, the translation of PROGRES specifications into Modula–2 code, is the topic of subsection 4.4.4.

4.4.2 Generating Context–free Editors

As stated above, this subsection explains in more detail how *language–specific components* of a *context–free* syntax–directed *editor* are *generated* using a batch tool, the EBNF generator. This tool takes a logical EBNF document plus its representation document as main inputs. (The role of the representation document in the generation process will be explained below). It uses this information to process various types of text input files. These input files are skeletons of (un–)parsing tables, Modula–2 module implementations etc. with placeholders for language–specific code fragments. The EBNF generator scans a given input file for occurrences of these placeholders and replaces them by a computed piece of text. Any result of a replacement is a human readable piece of text which is either directly forwarded to other tools, like a Modula–2 or C compiler or a parser generator, or subject to manual modifications.

Manual modifications of generated text files are *avoided* whenever possible. Nevertheless, they are a last resort when the desired tool functionality cannot be generated and an appropriate extension of the tool generation machinery is too costly (or even impossible). Note that it is often feasible to *modify input file skeletons* to achieve the required modification of the generated product. This is a safe way to circumvent the problem that automatic updates of generated files have to be merged with manual modifications applied to them. In this sense, the IPSEN meta environment is an *"open" machinery* which offers an experienced user various possibilities to alter the behavior of generated products.

Fig. 4.32 *summarizes* the *context–free editor generation process*. It is a more detailed view at the left–hand side of fig. 4.31. The diagram shows that we have three different categories of input sources for the EBNF generator tool. The first one is the logical document containing the respective language's EBNF. The second source is the accompanying text representation document which contains text layout data involved in the generation process for text unparsing tables. The last category comprises all source text skeletons (ranging from the logical document to the master unparser table skeleton) which eventually result in the architecture components described in sections 4.1 and 4.3.

Note that the diagram of fig. 4.32 *hides* many *details* of the actual editor *generation process*, e.g. concerning certain preprocessing steps of EBNF documents for reasons of efficiency and tools for generating make files (for coordinating tool activations when building a new environment executable).

Some *skeletons* and corresponding *source code files* even *represent* whole *subsystems* on architecture level. This is noticeably the case for the LogicalDocument component. Its internal architecture is presented in fig. 4.23 of subsection 4.3.1. The most important subcomponent for a certain language X is the abstract data type XASTGraph. It is completely generated by the EBNF generator. All other language–specific components mentioned in fig. 4.23 (like XILGraph for identifier binding purposes) are included in the form of rather primitive default implementations. The default behavior of these context–sensitive subcomponents may be altered and refined by using PROGRES related tools (cf. subsections 4.4.3 and 4.4.4).

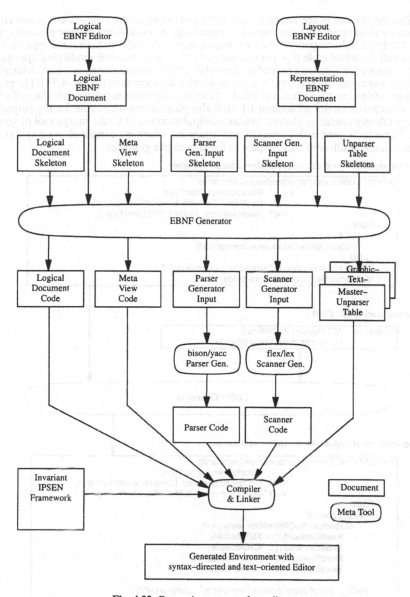

Fig. 4.32. Generating context–free editors

For *further details* concerning the internal structure and purpose of generated components, the reader is also *referred* to *section 4.3*: the MetaView component is explained in subsection 4.3.2 and the Unparser in subsection 4.3.4. Generated files for parsing and scanning purposes play a special role. They are in turn input files for scanner and parser generators which eventually produce the architecture components discussed in section 4.3.4. This will be explained in more detail at the end of this subsection.

444

The *structure* of generated *code fragments* and the generation *algorithms* involved are rather *straightforward* in most cases. Generated logical documents (or more precisely, their XASTGraph subcomponent) for two languages mainly differ in their node type declarations and the actual node type parameters permitted in syntax–tree modifying operations. They contain for instance a procedure ExecutablePlaceholderCommands which determines all legal expansion alternatives for a given placeholder increment (cf. fig. 4.33). The procedure is used to construct a menu of valid expansion commands at the user interface of a syntax–directed editor (cf. subsection 4.1.4). It also plays an important role for any language–independently operating abstract syntax manipulation tool, like the merge tool of section 2.4. These tools need such a procedure to determine whether a certain abstract syntax tree manipulation is allowed with respect to the language's grammar.

Text fragment of logical document implementation skeleton:

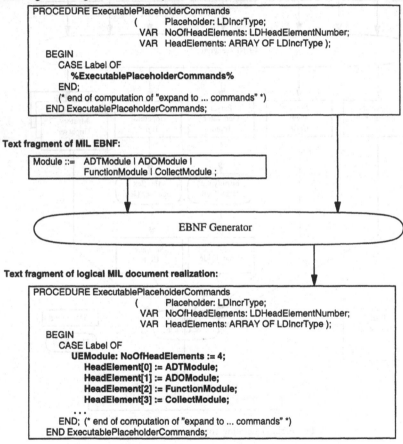

```
PROCEDURE ExecutablePlaceholderCommands
                    (       Placeholder: LDIncrType;
                    VAR  NoOfHeadElements: LDHeadElementNumber;
                    VAR  HeadElements: ARRAY OF LDIncrType );
    BEGIN
       CASE Label OF
          %ExecutablePlaceholderCommands%
       END;
       (* end of computation of "expand to ... commands" *)
    END ExecutablePlaceholderCommands;
```

Text fragment of MIL EBNF:

```
Module ::=   ADTModule | ADOModule |
             FunctionModule | CollectModule ;
```

EBNF Generator

Text fragment of logical MIL document realization:

```
PROCEDURE ExecutablePlaceholderCommands
                    (       Placeholder: LDIncrType;
                    VAR  NoOfHeadElements: LDHeadElementNumber;
                    VAR  HeadElements: ARRAY OF LDIncrType );
    BEGIN
       CASE Label OF
          UEModule: NoOfHeadElements := 4;
             HeadElement[0] := ADTModule;
             HeadElement[1] := ADOModule;
             HeadElement[2] := FunctionModule;
             HeadElement[3] := CollectModule;
          . . .
       END; (* end of computation of "expand to ... commands" *)
    END ExecutablePlaceholderCommands;
```

Fig. 4.33. Generating the logical document implementation

Generated *text unparser tables* are one–to–one *translations* of the structure and the layout of *EBNF rules* into the required internal format. The rule

```
ADTModule ::=    "adt_module" DeclModuleId ";"
                     Body
                 "end" ";"
```

will be translated into an unparsing table entry which requires that the textual ADTModule representation starts with the keyword **adt_module**, followed by a blank, its identifier, and a semicolon. The textual representation of its Body starts indented on a new line and is followed by the keyword **end** on a new line and another semicolon.

The generated logical document and the text unparsing table are the main components of a syntax–directed editor with a pure text–oriented representation. If we are going to build an *editor* with a *graphical document representation*, additional input has to be provided (cf. subsection 4.3.2). These are certain annotations (pseudo–comments) in the EBNF which define correspondences between nonterminals of the concrete text representation syntax and graphical nonterminal classes of a desired diagrammatic representation. In the MIL grammar example, we find something like

```
ADTModule (* @CC_EBNFMeta Entity @*) ::= . . . ;
DeclModuleId (* @CC_EBNFMeta Identifier @*) ::= . . . ;
```

These *annotations* determine the *structure* of a *graphical representation* of the underlying logical document, i.e. they assign the language's nonterminals to the metaview node classes of fig. 4.25. Here, they denote that an ADTModule is a graphical object with a Decl-ModuleId as its identifier. This information is encapsulated within another abstract data type implementation, the *metaview document* (cf. subsection 4.3.2). Further information about the appearance of graphical objects (shapes of objects, line styles, default sizes, default positions of identifiers and text labels etc.) is provided in the form of a *graphical unparsing table*. Finally, a generated *master unparsing table* is responsible for coordinating textual and graphical unparsing (cf. subsection 4.3.4).

The remaining document skeletons and generated documents deal with *scanning and parsing* of *text representations* (cf. subsection 4.3.4). They are generated in a two–stage process. In the first step, scanner and parser generator input files are generated from the grammar describing the underlying language. The second step employs the well–known lex (flex) and yacc (bison) tools for generating a scanner/parser implementation from the input files provided by step one. The latter step as well as the construction of the lex scanner generator input are fairly straightforward and will not be discussed here. The first step – the construction of the yacc input file – may also seem quite trivial insofar as it is customarily exactly the purpose of yacc to produce a parser from a grammar.

In our case though there is the *special difficulty* that the parser's *input* is generally *not complete*. In "upward" direction (from the syntax tree point of view) this means that the input is possibly an arbitrary small increment of the source language and not necessarily some complete document. In "downward" direction, the text to be parsed may still contain placeholders, i.e. there may be unexpanded subtrees in the syntax tree corresponding to the input.

To approach the first problem, the yacc input grammar has to allow the start nonterminal to be derived to any other nonterminal in the language. This way, every document increment may be parsed to a tree with a corresponding nonterminal at its root which in turn can be resolved to the start nonterminal, thereby completing the parsing process. As a consequence, generated parsers have the so–called *multiple entry* property.

The second problem is solved by introducing a new set of keywords in the yacc input grammar. For every nonterminal in the source grammar, a new keyword is inserted which denotes a placeholder. Accordingly, each nonterminal in the yacc grammar may be derived to either the corresponding placeholder keyword or the actual right hand side of the rule as given in the source grammar, i.e. generated parsers are able to process *incomplete input files*.

The following *example* should *illustrate* the *general ideas*. We start again with the MIL grammar specification in the restricted EBNF language described in subsection 3.3.3. The rules given here are an excerpt of the grammar describing that a module interface consists of the keyword **interface** followed by an optional import list (the import list has been made optional here to be able to explain the treatment of optional language elements), an mandatory export list, the keyword **end**, and another semicolon. Exports are given by a non–empty list of single declarations, each of them being either a type or a procedure declaration, whereas import items are simply applied occurrences of module identifiers.

```
Interface ::= "interface"
               [ ImportList ] ExportList
               "end" ";"
ImportList ::= "import" { ApplModuleId ","} ApplModuleId ";"
ExportList ::= "export" { Decl } Decl
Decl ::= TypeDecl I ProcDecl
TypeDecl ::= . . .
ProcDecl ::= . . .
```

Generating a *yacc input* yields the *following result*. First, a ROOT nonterminal is defined which serves as the start symbol. At first sight, there is one derivation option for each nonterminal in the EBNF above. We also note that each option consists of an E_xxx R_xxx sequence. The reason is that, in spite of the introduction of an appropriate root rule, the parser is still unable to operate on arbitrary increments if it has no information about the type of increment it should parse. Therefore, this information is passed to the parser as a special encrypted identifier denoted as E_xxx (with E standing for entry) in the rule. When free input is issued on an increment, the editor generates the identifier corresponding to this increment's type and prepends it to the text passed to the parser. The R_xxx (R for rule) nonterminal allows the actual derivation of ROOT according to the source EBNF; examples follow below.

```
ROOT :  E_Interface R_Interface
     I  E_ImportList R_ImportList
     I  E_ApplModuleId R_ApplModuleId
     I  E_Y_ImportList R_Y_ImportList
     I  E_ExportList R_ExportList
     I  E_Y_ExportList R_Y_ExportList
     I  E_Decl R_Decl
```

As was pointed out above, we generally enable the parser to derive all other nonterminals from ROOT. The example though shows that this is not always desirable: Consider the case that the user selects free input on some declaration. Now it is useful to allow him to *replace* a former *type declaration* by a *procedure declaration* or vice versa. To achieve this behavior, the yacc grammar is designed to resolve the given increment (TypeDecl or ProcDecl in our case) to the most general nonterminal possible (which is Decl here) before in turn resolving this nonterminal to ROOT. In the yacc grammar, we see that ROOT cannot be derived to type or procedure declarations directly: These alternatives have to be resolved to the more general declaration nonterminal first. Correspondingly, the editor does not always generate the entry identifier directly related to the increment type free input was issued on (as stated above). Instead, the entry for the most general nonterminal at the top of the increment's subtree in the abstract syntax tree is used.

The last detail we can see so far is the introduction of R_Y_xxx rules (and corresponding E_Y_xxx identifiers). The reason behind these rules, again, is to make free input easier. These rules *allow* the *extension* of a *list* with new elements during free input originally started on one list element only. For the example, the user does not need to activate free input on the whole list of imports to insert a new import clause, this is possible with free input on one import clause as well. We explain this below when we see an example definition of an R_Y_xxx nonterminal.

The following part shows the yacc *grammar generated* for *structure rules* like the one defining the nonterminal Interface. As the first alternative we see that the yacc rule allows the nonterminal to be replaced by a special placeholder identifier P_Interface (P for placeholder). This is necessary to achieve parsing of incomplete increments as sketched above: As long as an increment is not expanded, its position in the AST is taken over by a corresponding placeholder. The second alternative allows the derivation of an interface to the structure given by the input grammar. (The K_xxx nonterminals will be derived to the respective keywords.)

```
R_Interface : P_Interface
            | K_interface
              R_ImportList
              R_ExportList
              K_end Semicolon
  { cpsc(2, ToInterface); }
```

The rule itself is straightforward; more interesting here is the *yacc action* which is *triggered* by the *parsing* of an according increment (or, to be precise, by resolving the right-hand side to the R_Interface nonterminal). Subsection 4.1.3 already mentioned that the abstract syntax tree of the document is not directly changed during the parsing process. Instead, a sequence of editor commands is created reflecting the changes the user made in the document. This way, the implementation of editor commands with the accompanying tree modification and traversal operations is reused for the handling of free input. The construction of the command stream is performed by corresponding yacc triggered functions with the help of a stack of command subsequences. The cpsc (for concatenate, push, swap, concatenate) action in the example first concatenates the top two subsequences on the stack (containing the commands to create the import and export list subtrees) into one stack entry, then pushes the one–command–sequence "expand placeholder to an interface", swaps the two top stack entries, and concatenates them. The result is one stack entry containing the sequence to set up the complete right–hand side subtree.

The *translation* of *variant rules* into parser generator input is very simple. It is more or less a one–to–one translation of the original EBNF rule into the required yacc syntax. Consider for instance the yacc rule for declarations below. Its first alternative deals again with placeholders, the remaining two alternatives model the expansion of a declaration placeholder to either a type or a procedure declaration. In this case, we do not have any needs for yacc actions: The syntax tree remains unchanged.

```
R_Decl : P_Decl
       | R_TypeDecl
       | R_ProcDecl
```

The last yacc grammar excerpt shows the *handling* of *list rules* considering the R_ImportList nonterminal as example. Since the import list may be empty according to the rule for interfaces in the original grammar, R_ImportList may be derived to the empty symbol. Alternatively, either the corresponding placeholder or the keyword **interface** followed by a (non–empty) list of actual imports may appear. The action functions here extend the list of imports one clause at a time. Furthermore, we see here that the actual list structure is set up using R_Y_ImportList nonterminals, the Y depicting that a list and an item together form a new, extended list. When free input was issued on one element of the list (an R_ApplModuleId), the parser will be instructed to analyze an R_Y_ImportList afterwards, because this is the most general appropriate nonterminal (see above). Since this nonterminal allows derivation to a list of R_ApplModuleIds, we exactly achieve the behavior described in the discussion of the root rule.

```
R_ImportList : { empty (); }
             | P_ImportList
             | K_import R_Y_ImportList { pspc(); }

R_Y_ImportList : R_Y_ImportList R_ApplModuleId { psc(); }
               | R_ApplModuleId
```

4.4.3 Developing Context–sensitive Tool Specifications

Until now, we have seen how (textual and graphical) context–free editors are generated using the IPSEN meta environment, or better, its EBNF subenvironment. The PROGRES language and its tools are needed as soon as *context–sensitive operations* of *analysis* or *execution tools* are considered. The EBNF Translator supports the transition from the con- crete context–free syntax of languages to context–sensitive aspects. It takes an EBNF docu- ment as input and produces a PROGRES frame specification which defines the behavior of context–free editors. The output is again divided into a language–independent part with syntax tree (graph) modifying operations and a language–specific graph schema declara- tion.

Fig. 4.34 shows on its left–hand side a cutout of the MIL language *EBNF input* (cf. fig. 3.24 of section 3.3) and on its right–hand side the corresponding *translator output* of graph schema declarations (cf. fig. 3.29, section 3.3). Any EBNF rule which defines the structure of a certain syntax subtree is translated into a node type declaration. Concrete meta attribute values of such a node type declaration correspond to required nonterminal classes of its children (cf. translation of rule System on the left–hand side of fig. 4.34 into node type System on the right–hand side). Additional node types with prefix "Nil", like NilMo- dules for empty module lists, are necessary as placeholders for unexpanded subtrees. Fi- nally, node classes are introduced to define groups of node types which belong to the same nonterminal class and which share certain properties. The class Modules for example is the superclass of all four types of modules, i.e. ADTModule, ADOModule, Function- Module, and CollectModule.

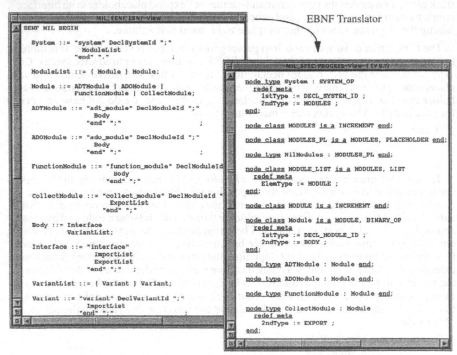

Fig. 4.34. Translating an EBNF into a PROGRES graph schema

For further details of the EBNF to PROGRES translation process, the reader is referred to section 3.3. Note that the generated class hierarchy displayed in fig. 4.34 differs slightly from the class hierarchy presented in section 3.3. The current version of PROGRES does not support the declaration of node types which belong to more than one class. Therefore, it is necessary to *replace* a *declaration* like

```
node type NilModules : MODULES, PLACEHOLDER end;
```

by *two declarations* of the form

```
node class MODULES_PL is a MODULES, PLACEHOLDER end;
node type NilModules : MODULES_PL end;
```

The generated PROGRES specification (or, more precisely, its expanded specification skeleton; cf. box 6 of fig. 4.31) includes the basic functionality for specifying identifier binding and type–checking rules. It is now the task of the meta environment's user to *modify* the generated *graph schema* and to *add* further *declarations* of language–specific *document properties*. He may also add special purpose context–sensitive graph transformations, like changing an abstract data object module into an abstract data type module or vice versa (cf. section 3.3). As a consequence, any generated part of such a PROGRES specification may and must be modified afterwards.

The screen dump on the right–hand side of fig. 4.34 already contains some *manual modifications*. The original generated version suggested the following node class and type declarations for modules:

```
node class MODULE_BINARY_OP is a MODULE, BINARY_OP end;
node type ADTModule : MODULE_BINARY_OP
  redef meta 1stType := DECL_MODULE_ID ;
  redef meta 2ndType := BODY ;
end;
. . .
node type CollectModule : MODULE_BINARY_OP
  redef meta 1stType := DECL_MODULE_ID ;
  redef meta 2ndType := EXPORT ;
end;
```

The meta environment user (tool specifier) then decided to *rename* the first generated *declaration* from MODULE_BINARY_OP to Module and to *move* common *redefinitions* of *meta attributes* from node types to their common node class Module:

```
node class Module is a MODULE, BINARY_OP
  redef meta 1stType := DECL_MODULE_ID ;
  redef meta 2ndType := BODY ;
end;
node type ADTModule : Module end;
. . .
node type CollectModule : Module
  redef meta 2ndType := EXPORT ;
end;
```

This new version of the class hierarchy emphasizes the fact that all types of modules have an increment of class DECL_MODULE_ID as their first child and, with the exception of collection modules, an increment of class BODY as their second child.

As a consequence of manually editing generated documents, special support is necessary to *propagate changes* of a language's EBNF into the related graph grammar specification *incrementally*, i.e. without destroying user updates to the generated PROGRES document. Fig. 4.35 shows how the EBNF translator manages to keep related EBNF and PROGRES documents in a consistent state, although both types of documents may be modified arbitrarily. It relies heavily on a context–sensitive *3–way merge tool* (cf. section 2.4) which takes care of a document's context–free syntax and its identifier binding rules.

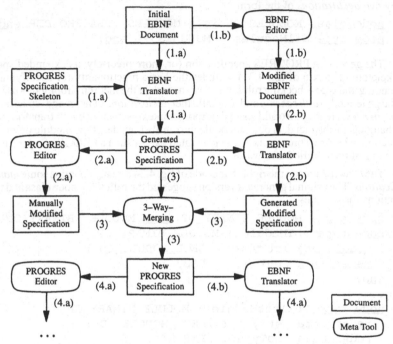

Fig. 4.35. Generating, modifying, and incremental updating of tool specifications

An *initial EBNF document* is the input for the *first activation* of the EBNF translator and an editing session. It may be the empty document or an already existing definition of the respective language, as for instance the definition of the MIL language in fig. 3.24/fig. 4.34. The EBNF translator needs an additional document with a PROGRES specification skeleton as input and produces an extended version of this document with language–specific information as output (arrows with label 1.a in fig. 4.35). A slightly modified cutout of such a generated MIL specification document was displayed in fig. 3.29/fig. 4.34.

At any time, a *new version* of the *EBNF document* may be created using the EBNF editor (1.b in fig. 4.35) in order to change or extend the context–free syntax of the language. An example for a sensible extension of the MIL language was already suggested in section 3.6. It concerned the introduction of hierarchically structured (sub–)systems and (sub–)configurations.

Now, the *initial* graph grammar *specification* may be *modified* with the PROGRES editor (2.a) in order to "beautify" the generated class hierarchy or to specify context–sensitive aspects of the language. One example for a rearrangement of node classes was already given earlier in this subsection, various examples for specifying context–sensitive aspects of the MIL language were discussed in section 3.3.

The *new version* of the *EBNF document* may be used to *generate* a *new specification* (2.b). The next step is then to *merge* the manually modified specification and the new generated specification with the old generated specification as the base document (3). This part of the overall transformation process is semi–automatic due to the fact that the user has to resolve various types of context–free as well as context–sensitive *merge conflicts*. For example, it could happen that the user defined a node class declaration manually with the same name as a new generated node class declaration. This conflict has to be resolved by selecting a new name for one of the two declarations. The result of the preceding EBNF editor session and the specification merge process may now be subject to *further editing activities* (4).

Combining a batch–oriented document transformation tool and the interactive merge tool in the presented way results in a *"low cost" document integration tool*. This tool translates changes in one document into incremental updates of the related document and requires user assistance in cases of doubt. Please note that the design and implementation of less batch–oriented and even more "intelligent" document transformation tools is the topic of section 4.6.

4.4.4 Generating Context–sensitive Tool Implementations

All *context–sensitive* IPSEN tools presented in chapter 2 and the PROGRES tools of section 3.6 were realized by *translating* their specifications *manually* into hopefully equivalent Modula–2 implementations. With the availability of the PROGRES code generation machinery, already used in section 3.6 for rapid prototyping purposes, it is now possible to *avoid manual coding activities* for language–specific components of analysis or execution tools.

Consider for instance *production* `DeleteSubtree` of fig. 4.36.a (already introduced in fig. 3.31 of section 3.3) and its *translation* into a number of intermediate graph code sequences. These code sequences are attached to the specification's underlying abstract syntax graph and call each other via `Gosub` or `CallProc` operators.

Fig. 4.36 displays two (out of more than ten) *intermediate code sequences* which are needed to execute the production `DeleteSubtree`. All variable names in the intermediate as well as in the Modula–2 code carry an integer suffix to ensure uniqueness. We will omit this suffix in the text to improve readability.

The first code sequence in fig. 4.36.b starts at address [0] with the definition of the *header* of the *translated production* with its in and out parameters (the first parameter is an out parameter, the following three parameters are in parameters) and their types. The first parameter `OutBtI` and the third parameter `InBtI` are both of type `BacktrackInfo`. They are needed for backtracking purposes and will be explained below. The second parameter, `HostGraph`, has the type `GraphNumber`. It is the handle to the manipulated MIL document graph instance. The last parameter, `I`, is the only parameter which is explicitly defined within the displayed specification. It has the type `NodeNumber` and represents a pointer to a specific node in the given `HostGraph`. It is used to enforce the application of the production to a certain subgraph.

The next graph code instruction at address [62] is a subroutine (differing from a procedure in that no activation record on the runtime stack is created) call to the code which *implements* the specified *graph rewriting step* and modifies the parameter `InBtI` to signal success or failure of the step. The following instruction at address [68] is a simple assignment of the modified `InBtI` parameter value to the production's out parameter `OutBtI`. The last instruction `EndProcDef` terminates the code sequence and acts as a "return from procedure call".

452

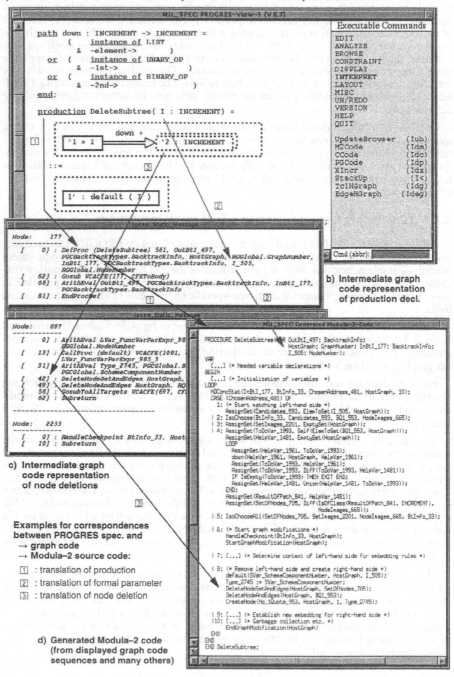

a) Production which deletes an abstract syntax subtree and creates a placeholder node

b) Intermediate graph code representation of production decl.

c) Intermediate graph code representation of node deletions

Examples for correspondences between PROGRES spec. and
→ graph code
→ Modula–2 source code:

1 : translation of production
2 : translation of formal parameter
3 : translation of node deletion

d) Generated Modula–2 code
(from displayed graph code
sequences and many others)

Fig. 4.36. Translating specifications into Modula–2 code

The window of fig. 4.36.c shows one graph code sequence which is part of the *production body implementation*. It is called after a match for the production's left–hand side is computed. Its precise contents is partially hidden and will not be explained in detail here.

Instead, we take a look at the more readable sequence of *Modula–2 instructions* generated from this intermediate code, cf. fig. 4.36.d. This is the result of an *abstract interpretation* of the presented graph machine code (cf. fig. 3.65, section 3.6).

In normal *forward execution mode*, the control flow is equivalent to the execution of the procedure without the outer loop statement and where the branches of the case statement are executed one after the other. This kind of behavior is realized by the procedure NDConcStat which implements a standard control flow automaton. The first two parameters of the procedure call, InBtI (for incoming backtracking information) and BtInfo (for computed backtracking information), keep track about success or failure of pattern matching steps. If these parameters signal that the execution of the next case statement branch has succeeded, then the parameter ChosenAddress is incremented by one.

If the execution of a case statement branch fails, ChosenAddress is decremented by one. Then, the *backtracking mode* is entered where old variable values are restored (not necessary in the running example) and already performed graph modifications are cancelled (within HandleCheckpoint of case statement branch 6). The control flow automaton switches back to forward execution mode as soon as one of its case statement branches signals that it has another possibility to execute its body.

The ten branches of the generated Modula–2 case statement have the following purposes:

1: Guarantees that the contents of the in parameter I is used as the only possible candidate for a match of node pattern `1 in DeleteSubtree.

2: Selects the only possible match for node pattern `1 (B(ack)Q(uote)1) and records the selected match in the node set NodeImages in order to avoid multiple matches of the same host graph node later on (cf. step 4).

3: Creates an empty set of nodes SetImages which is needed in steps 4 and 5.

4: Determines the set of nodes which is matched by the set node pattern `2. The first two instructions initialize two node sets. The following loop builds the transitive closure of the path down starting at the match of node `1. The instruction after the loop assigns the computed result (all nodes in the subtree rooted at the match of `1) to the variable ResultOfPath. All INCREMENT nodes of this result set minus the set of already matched nodes from step 2 are the match for the set node pattern with name `2.

5: Records the set of matched nodes in step 4 in SetImages in order to avoid multiple node matches. This implements a behavior which is called isomorphic subgraph selection and replacement (cf. section 3.1).

6: Marks the current state of the host graph with a checkpoint (so that it may be reconstructed later for backtracking purposes) and signals "begin of graph modification" to all possibly active graph browsers.

7: (Omitted) Computes the context of the left–hand side match for redirecting embedding edges.

8: Performs the actual graph modification. The first two statements determine the type for the node to be created by applying the function default to the given node I. The function returns an appropriate placeholder node type (cf. fig. 3.30, section 3.3). The next two statements delete the matched set of nodes `2 and the matched node `1 with all incident edges. The last statement creates a new node 1' (No_1Quote) with the correct type.

9: (Omitted) Implements the embedding rules which redirect any incoming edge of the deleted node `1 to the new node 1'.

10: (Omitted) Deletes temporary node sets and signals "end of graph modification".

The generated Modula–2 code for a PROGRES specification is still considerably *less efficient* than *handcoded subroutines* because

(a) handcoded update procedures for identifier binding relationships may use more *knowledge* about possible *effects* of *editing operations* in the presence of usual scoping rules than the standard attribute evaluation algorithm,

(b) manually implemented pattern matching algorithms (for left–hand sides of productions) can often use additional implicit *knowledge* about unlikely or impossible *graph structures*,

(c) and handwritten implementations can completely *avoid* unnecessary *overhead* for nondeterministic graph rewriting and *backtracking*.

If we look at fig. 4.36 again, we find some *examples* where the generated code is *less efficient* than a *handwritten solution*. The first three case statement branches of DeleteSubtree simply set up auxiliary data structures. They could be improved considering the facts that the root of the subtree to be deleted is uniquely defined (by parameter I) and that the result of the transitive closure of the path down returns all nodes of the selected subtree, but never the subtree root itself. Therefore, it would not be necessary to emit isomorphy testing code which guarantees that the match of the node pattern ‘1 and the match of the node set pattern ‘2 do not overlap. Furthermore, the code of the fourth branch could be simplified exploiting the knowledge that the transitive closure of the path down is an irreflexive relation. As a consequence, some lines of code could be deleted which guarantee the termination of the inner loop in branch 4 under any circumstances.

Last but not least, all lines dealing with *nondeterminism* and *backtracking* could be removed because the execution of the production DeleteSubtree never fails and does not involve any nondeterministic decisions. The match of its node pattern ‘1 is already determined by its in parameter I and the match for its dashed node set pattern ‘2 is a maximal (but possibly empty) set.

It is clear that a human implementor of the production DeleteSubtree would avoid the above mentioned sources of inefficiencies, maybe even unaware of the implicit assumptions which guarantee the correctness of the handwritten piece of code. Please note that the reasons for a deterministic or always successful execution are often not as straightforward as in the selected example. Therefore, we have to follow *two strategies* to *improve the efficiency* of generated tools.

The first one is simply to *combine* already existing *handwritten* pieces of code for *invariant parts* of specifications with *generated* code fragments for *language–specific aspects*. The handwritten pieces are the modules ASTGraph, ILGraph, etc. of fig. 4.23 in section 4.3, whereas the generated fragments correspond to modules XASTGraph, XILGraph etc. First experiences with this approach are reported in /5. Sob 96/.

The second strategy is to *add* some *additional pragmas* to PROGRES which mark possible sources of nondeterminism and failure within a given specification more clearly. Given the fact that software engineering tools show almost always a deterministic behavior and may often be realized without any needs for backtracking algorithms, we do hope that a forthcoming compiler version will be able to translate many tool specifications into Modula–2 (or C) source code without any overhead for backtracking purposes.

It is completely beyond the scope of this book to explain the translation of PROGRES specifications into intermediate graph code and the translation of graph code into equivalent Modula–2/C code in more detail. For *further information* about the incremental generation of abstract graph machine code sequences, the realization of the abstract graph machine itself, and the treatment of nondeterminism and backtracking within Modula–2 or C, the reader is referred to /5. Zün 96a, b/. Furthermore, we will meet the PROGRES execution machinery again in section 4.5 where it is used to animate requirements engineering specifications.

4.4.5 Summary

At the time being, the IPSEN meta SDE supports the *development* of *single document processing syntax–directed tools*. Its meta tools for generating context–free editors, unparsers, and parsers were used for the development of all tools presented from section 2.2 to section 2.5 of this book. Extensions already discussed for generating complex context–sensitive editing operations, incrementally working type checkers, and execution tools are still under development. They rely heavily on the existence of the PROGRES environment which was the main topic of section 3.6. An EBNF translator takes a context–free grammar as input and produces an equivalent graph grammar specification as output. PROGRES tools may then be used to specify context–sensitive operations and to translate them into plain Modula–2 or C code. This offers tool developers the opportunity to start with the development of a language's context–free concrete syntax and appropriate tools, a topic he should be familiar with. Afterwards, programmed graph rewriting systems may be used as a kind of visual logical document manipulation language.

All generated (Modula–2 or C) *source code documents* have their *specific places* in the overall *IPSEN architecture* framework. This framework (discussed in sections 4.1 and 4.3) offers all the functionality needed for building standard user interfaces and a handcoded graph library with basic routines for implementing incrementally working analysis, interpreter, and compiler tools.

Apart from the main characteristic of our approach, the usage of graphs and graph grammars instead of trees and attribute grammars, the following *characteristics* of the *meta SDE* should be mentioned:

(a) A language's abstract syntax is automatically derived from its concrete syntax. This reduces on one hand the flexibility of the generator machinery. It has on the other hand the often underestimated advantage that the specifier is relieved from the burden of keeping a concrete syntax description, an abstract syntax description, and the definition of mappings between them in a consistent state.

(b) Text unparsing information is not provided using a separate text layout description language but entered in a "what you see is what you get"–like style by modifying the layout of the involved EBNF document directly.

(c) Even any input necessary for generating graphical editor interfaces is stored within annotations of the corresponding EBNF document. This is a consequence of the fact that each logical document may be manipulated via a text–oriented user interface, but only some of them have simultaneously available graphical representations.

(d) The context–free editor generator operates as a UNIX filter. It may be called from makefiles or shell scripts and processes source file skeletons with certain placeholders as input. These skeletons are often subject to small modifications to adapt them to new versions of the IPSEN framework or to realize additional functionality.

(e) Any produced generator output has the form of human readable source text files. These source text files may be modified as a last resort to realize a required nonstandard behavior of otherwise generated tools.

To summarize, the generation machinery is a more or less *open combination* of *UNIX filter like tools* with *closed integrated environments* as subcomponents for editing, analyzing, and directly executing specifications. A makefile generation machinery builds the interface between IPSEN–specific components and standard UNIX tools for preprocessing text file skeletons or postprocessing generated output files. For example, the PROGRES environment's multiple entry parser is generated by executing the following steps:

(1) The original input file skeleton is extended with some lines which tell the yacc/bison parser generator how to resolve possible reduce/reduce conflicts.

(2) The corresponding output file is the input for an sed script which adjusts some generated yacc/bison rules for still supported syntax variants.

(3) The resulting file is then fed to the parser generator which produces an ordinary C file as output.

(4) This file in turn has to be compiled and included into certain libraries.

In this way, the IPSEN meta SDE is *less closed* (for a sophisticated user) than other meta SDEs, like the Cornell Program Synthesizer Generator /4. RT 88a/, Pan /5. BGV 92/, or PSG /2. BS86/, where any desired functionality of generated tools must be captured within their input specification languages. Another important difference of our approach, the usage of a *graph data model* instead of a tree data model and the usage of *graph rewriting systems* instead of context–free grammars or tree rewriting systems (combined with attribute evaluation rules or a relational/logical calculus), was already discussed in section 3.3.

Finally, we should mention two major points of criticism concerning the current state of the presented meta SDE. We still have some problems to find an appropriate representation for the implemented standard graph library on the level of graph grammar specifications. This a consequence of the *lack* of any *module concept* on specification level (cf. summary of section 3.1 and section 5.2). Furthermore, no support is offered for generating application–specific parts of *integration tools*. Until now, some basic components have been realized which are very helpful for implementing tools of this category (cf. section 4.6). But the automatic translation of a triple graph grammar specification (cf. section 3.4) of a new integration tool into the implementation of scenario–specific components is still outside the scope of the IPSEN meta SDE. An appropriate extension will be the main subject for future work (cf. section 5.2).

4.5 Execution Tools Within Environments

Ch. Kohring

This section reports about our *experience* in *building execution* and *monitoring tools*. Such tools have been developed within the PiS, the PROGRES, and the RE environment. In this section we give arguments why the RE environment tools are the most complex ones. Therefore they have been chosen and their internal structure is discussed here. The characteristics of all three environments is that execution and monitoring is tightly integrated with editing and analysis (see section 2.1, 2.2, and 3.6 for the corresponding outside behavior of tools and their level of integration).

Reuse in this section means reuse of *architectural patterns*, but also of *components* as code. There is no mechanical derivation of RE execution tools, as it was demonstrated for editor and analysis tools in section 4.3 and 4.4. The reason is that specifying the runtime behavior of an RE spec is very complicated and beyond the ability of the specification language PROGRES up to now (concurrency, explicit control of execution etc., see 2.2 and below). However, such runtime specifications have been delivered for the simpler execution model of PROGRES (see /5. Zün 96a/) for which code generation is possible. Nevertheless, to know how to build a complex execution/monitoring tool as for RE is also of great value. So, an execution/monitoring framework architecture is presented in this section on architecture pattern level.

The section's focus is not only to show how to build such tools but also to demonstrate that the solution described here is *flexible* and *adaptable*. Subsection 4.5.2 describes what flexibility/adaptability means in detail and subsection 4.5.5 summarizes that these goals were achieved.

This section discusses the design and implementation results of /4. Koh 96/. Especially, the *contents* of the core part, subsection 4.5.3 and 4.5.4, are as follows: After giving the coarse architecture of the RE execution and monitoring tool in subsection 4.5.3 the corresponding interpreter details are discussed. The next subsection discusses the internal structure of the monitoring and statistics tool. In this subsection, furthermore, the functionality of an editor tool is given to determine the various forms of a simulation run (target hardware spec, scheduling, processor assignment, but also interactive input).

4.5.1 Execution and Simulation in the RE Environment

This subsection describes *commonalities* but also *differences* between the RE, the PiS and the PROGRES environment. Common to the three environments is the tight integration of editor, static analysis, instrumentation, execution, and monitoring tools. Depending on the particular language (or languages) underlying each environment, the tools are more or less comprehensive and "intelligent". For example, analysing an RE spec demands much more knowledge about the context sensitive syntax and the semantics of the underlying languages than that needed for analysing a PiS document. Especially, this is true for execution tools. Therefore, we took the RE execution and simulation tools to be discussed in this section as they are the most complex execution tools of IPSEN environments.

One common aspect of the RE, the PROGRES, and the PiS environment is the *incremental compilation tool*. In particular, all executors make use of a two–step compilation process. In the first step an incremental compiler translates the source code into an intermediate code. In the second step the intermediate code will be interpreted. Interpretation can be done directly which is done in the RE environment and in the rapid prototypes for PROGRES applications (see section 3.6). Alternatively, intermediate code can be translated to a more efficient form as it was done for the PiS environment or for more efficient versions of PRO-GRES applications.

The RE execution simulation tools are different from PiS and PROGRES execution tools not only in the more complex execution model but also because they allow different *execution modi* to be used by the specifier, mainly due to different forms an RE spec can have during the RE development process (see section 2.2). The model is elaborated step by step during this process (refinement of DFDs, adding PSPECs, adding CSPECs for explicit control etc.). The various forms of such a process were sketched in section 2.2. The execution tools have to handle all *different* forms of *elaboration stages* of the RE model coming out from different processes. So the execution tools have to be designed carefully to allow these different stages/execution modi of/for execution documents.

Furthermore, execution can be done with or without *monitoring*. There are various forms of execution information to be collected and to be shown during simulation runs. Another difference is that the RE model can be executed in order to simulate a certain *target system behavior*. This was done to check wether a certain RE model can be implemented on a certain target hardware. There are various forms of specifications which have been sketched in section 2.2 and which are discussed in the following section.

Summing up, different execution forms are due to:
(i) symbolic execution or execution of specified processes down to atomic processes and PSPECS,
(ii) implicit control by activation or deactivation due to data flows or explicit control by a control model,
(iii) switching on monitoring and statistic features or switching them off,
(iv) including a target system specification or regarding execution on the logical model only.

4.5.2 Requirements for Adaptability and Flexibility of Tools

In this context *adaptability* deals with exchangeability and extensibility of the (RE) language, whereas *flexibility* deals with the functionality and the power of the tools integrated in the RE environment. In the following we discuss three *aspects* of adaptability and flexibility.

(1) An RE document may consist of various model parts, i.e. functional model, information model, control model objects. Here, the requirements engineer is free to *choose* only the *language* objects currently needed. Fig. 4.37 shows a small example of an RE spec. This document comprises a context diagram and one DFD including the atomic data processes A, B and C and a control process CP. The data processes are refined by PSPECs, the control process is refined by a state transition diagram (STD). This example contains some language elements which have to be used obligatory (e.g. context diagram, DFD, data processes and data flows). On the other side, the use of control processes, control flows and STDs is optional.

During the *design* and *implementation* of the RE environment we took care that the tools are as *independent* from the concrete *language* definition as possible. In /4. Koh 96/ some alternative language dialects for the concrete definition of the three RE model parts (see subsection 4.5.5 for some examples) are presented. All these alternatives can be realized within the basic layers of the tool implementations. Thus, the modularity of the architecture of tools guarantees easy adaptability to extended or changed RE languages.

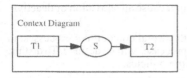

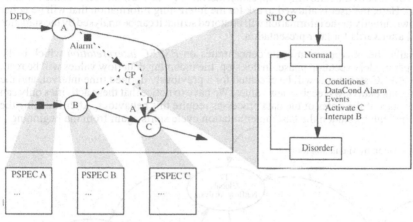

Fig. 4.37. Example of an executable RE document

(2) Because of the different language parts mentioned above to be used and because of the incrementality of all tools, a *flexible* and step by step development *process* for an RE spec is supported by the tools (see arguments given above). Thus, it is possible to evaluate firstly a simple RE model without control model objects and without PSPECs. Later on, the specification will be extended by using other language parts. Finally, the user is allowed to specify a simple hardware model. In this case the execution tool simulates the behaviour of the software model based on the specified properties of the target hardware. Consequently, the RE environment, especially the execution tool, has to be very flexible to influence and analyse different simulation runs which are different due to elaboration stage and execution modus.

(3) Finally, the RE environment has to allow an *intertwined construction, validation* and *modification* process (see again section 2.2). There, we mentioned that the RE process which creates, validates, and modifies an RE document can be structured in various ways. Therefore, we need flexible, highly integrated, and incremental tools. Especially, editor, analysis, and execution tools have to be tightly integrated to achieve the desired flexibility.

4.5.3 Architecture of the RE Simulation Tool

To understand the full behaviour of the simulation tool we should firstly describe the so–called basic *interpretation cycle*. Fig. 4.38 presents the working cycle of the execution tool consisting of five steps.

(1) In the first step, the interpreter has to analyse the whole net of data flow processes to find out the actual states of all processes. We call this phase *global netflow analysis*. Depending on the states of all data flow processes and the internal states of control flow processes the interpreter determines the actual states of all data flow and control processes.

(2) For that purpose the tool has to check and, if necessary, has to change the actual states of CSPECs (i.e. of state transition diagrams), too. This task is called *CSPEC interpreta-*

tion. For example, a state transition in a CSPEC might cause an activation or deactivation of a data flow process.

(3) If the tool has to simulate a concurrent system with several competitive processes, in the next step a certain execution order for dataflow processes will be defined. To do this, the user may choose one of nine different *scheduling* policies.

(4) It is the task of the following step, called *monitoring*, to show and store some run time data. Here, the user is allowed to ask for the interesting information that will be either shown directly or the information will be stored so that it can be analysed by the statistics tool afterwards for later presentation.

(5) Finally, the interpretation cycle concentrates on *PSPEC interpretation* which is the proper model execution phase. In this step, the incoming data flow values will be read, the PSPEC statements will be executed for a previously defined time interval, and the outgoing data flows receive new values. We have to notice that these activities only can take place if the states of the data processes require this behaviour. After finishing the PSPEC interpretation the basic interpretation cycle starts again from the beginning.

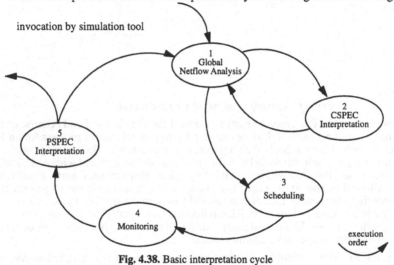

Fig. 4.38. Basic interpretation cycle

Corresponding to the basic interpretation cycle the *overall architecture* of the RE simulation tool was designed. Fig. 4.39 presents on one hand the embedding of the different RE tools within the RE environment. On the other hand, it shows the coarse architecture of the RE execution tool (here called RESI interpreter).

The *design* of the editor and analyser of the RE environment corresponds to the standard architecture of editor and analysis tools within the IPSEN environment (see sections 4.3 and 4.4). Hence, in this section we concentrate our discussion on the realization of the *simulation* tool. The RESI Interpreter consists of the Global Netflow Interpreter (GNI), the CSPEC Interpreter and the PSPEC Interpreter. Furthermore, fig. 4.39 shows the EnvP Editor, the Scheduler, the Monitoring, and the Statistics tool. The EnvP Editor enables the specification of target hardware properties. The role of the Scheduler and the Monitoring tool, have been mentioned above in the presentation of the basic interpretation cycle. The Statistics tool enables the subsequent statistical analysis of interesting runtime data (e.g. deadline violations, number of process activations etc.). These tools, from EnvP Editor to Statistics tool, will be discussed in more detail in subsection 4.5.4. The other parts of fig. 4.39 are now explained.

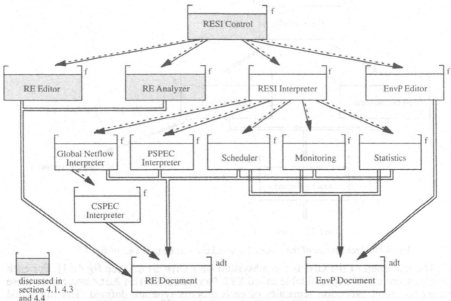

Fig. 4.39. The RE simulation tool within the RE environment

In the *basic layer* of the environment's architecture we see the RE Document and the EnvP Document. Both modules are abstract data types designed for the storage of an RE spec. These documents are constructed as abstract syntax trees like most IPSEN documents (see section 4.3).

The most tricky phase of the RE interpretation cycle is the global netflow analysis. We will now discuss the example of fig. 4.37 once again to explain roughly *how* the *GNI* is *working* and how the corresponding *subarchitecture* looks (see fig. 4.40).

The GNI starts with an *initialization process* to establish the start states of all processes (see GNI Initialization in fig. 4.40). The start state of a process depends on the different execution semantics of implicitly or explicitly controlled processes. Explicitly controlled processes have incoming control signals of type 'activate' and 'deactivate'. Implicitly controlled processes will only be activated by incoming data flows that actually carry a value. The abstract data type module Process Hierarchy (see fig. 4.40) stores all run time data that will be used by the GNI and the scheduler. This module is one level above the RE Document and the EnvP Document. All information needed for the initialization of the process hierarchy will be read from the RE Document and EnvP Document, respectively.

After initialization, the GNI analyses the top level of the DFD hierarchy (i.e. the context diagram) and determines the state of the system process. Afterwards, the GNI *analyses each level* of the DFD hierarchy from top to bottom (see GNI One Step in fig. 4.40). Referring to the example of fig. 4.37 we find out that the system process S is active and hence the control process CP is active, too. The inner state of CP changes from 'normal' to 'disorder' because the data condition 'alarm' reaches CP. Moreover, this event causes the activation of process C and an interrupt of process B. Thus, process B changes its state to 'interrupted', process C is now in state 'activated' and process A changes to state 'data awaiting' because it has reached the end of the PSPEC statement sequence.

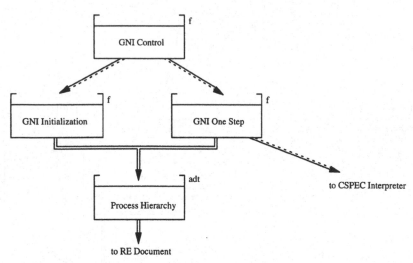

Fig. 4.40. Architecture of the Global Netflow Interpreter of fig. 4.39

The main part of the GNI is the subsystem GNI One Step (see fig 4.41). For each process there exists a special table called XYZ Process State Automaton. In these tables the exact execution semantics of each process type are defined. The functional module Next State of Process *determines* the *new state* of each process. Therefore, the old state of a process can be read in the process hierarchy while the conditions for a state change can be found in XYZ Process State Automaton.

The module Interrupt Handling (cf. fig. 4.41 again) realizes the *state changes* in case of an *interrupt event*. Here, we need a separate mechanism because the GNI has to check all processes in the DFD hierarchy above of the currently analysed atomic data process up to the abstract data process that was initially interrupted. Finally, the outside module CSPEC Interpreter executes the state changes inside of the CSPECs, i.e. within the state transition diagrams.

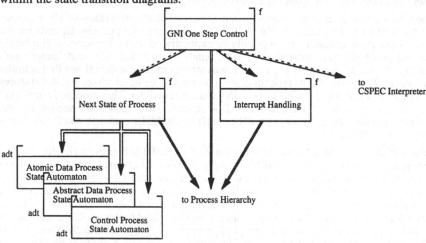

Fig. 4.41. Architecture of the subsystem GNI One Step of fig.4.40

The next component PSPEC Interpreter of fig. 4.39 to be explained has been realized by reusing the concept and the implementation of the existing PROGRES interpreter (/5. Zün 96a/, see section 3.6). Both interpreters compile in the first step the source code incrementally into intermediate code. Afterwards, the permanently stored intermediate code will be directly interpreted. This two–step compilation process is in most cases faster and less expensive than traditional compilation.

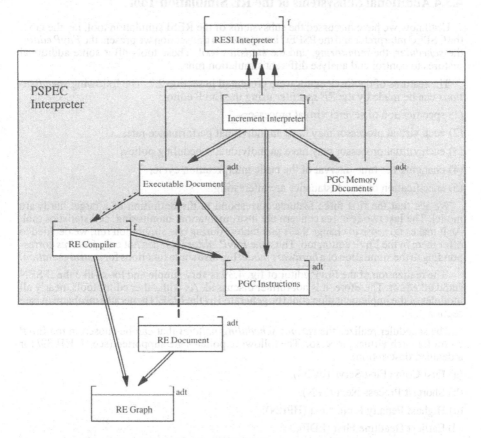

Fig. 4.42. Architecture of the PSPEC Interpreter of fig. 4.39

The architecture of the PSPEC Interpreter is shown in fig. 4.42. It is shown inline in its context to explain its mutual relations with neighboring components of the RE environment. The RESI Interpreter needs services from three modules, namely Increment Interpreter, Executable Document, and PGC Memory Documents. The functional module Increment Interpreter executes the instructions of the intermediate code. So, execution of code, corresponding to the fifth step of the interpretation cycle (cf. fig. 4.38), represents the top level of the PSPEC Interpreter. This module also represents the control module of the PSPEC Interpreter. All needed information about the executable code can be asked from the interface of Executable Document. This is implemented in the body of Executable Document which is a specialization of RE Document. The compilation of the source code to intermediate code will be done by the module RE Compiler. This module generates code and stores the code with the aid of PGC Instructions (PGC is an abbreviation of PROGRES Graph Code). Finally, the module PGC Memory Documents serves as storage for all run time data. This is an abstract data type module and realizes the so called machine graph. The machine graph represents the individual run time data corresponding to each instance of a PSPEC. This is necessary because the RE language supports concurrent execution of several PSPECs of the same type. Hence, we need for each process instance an own run time graph (the machine graph).

4.5.4 Additional Subsystems of the RE Simulation Tool

Until now we have discussed the subsystems of the RESI simulation tool, i.e. the GNI, the CSPEC interpreter and the PSPEC interpreter. In this section we present the *EnvP editor*, the *scheduler*, the *monitoring,* and the *statistics* tool. These tools offer some additional features to control and analyse different simulation runs.

The features of the EnvP editor were presented in section 2.2. The following *specifications* can be made by the *RE specifier* using the EnvP editor:

(1) specification of several virtual processors,

(2) each virtual processor may have an individual performance rate,

(3) each virtual processor may have an individual scheduling policy,

(4) changing the time interval of the basic interpretation cycle,

(5) specification of which statistics are interesting.

We see that the first three features correspond to the definition of a target hardware model. The last two features concern the instrumentation, monitoring, and statistics tool. As it makes no sense to change these parameters during one simulation run, we decided to offer them in the EnvP editor, too. Thus, the *EnvP editor* includes not only *features* corresponding to the simulation of a *hardware model* but also some functions for *instrumentation*.

The realization of the EnvP editor of fig. 4.39 is very simple and looks like the IPSEN standard editor. Therefore, it is not further discussed. As with other editor tools, nearly all modules of the implementation could be generated by the IPSEN generator mechanism (see section 4.4).

The scheduler realizes the *various scheduling policies* that can be chosen in the EnvP editor for each virtual processor. The following policies are supported (see /7. HH 89/ for a detailed description).

(a) First Come First Serve (FCFS),

(b) Shortest Process Next (SPN),

(c) Highest Penalty Ratio Next (HPRN),

(d) Earliest Deadline First (EDF),

(e) Least Late Tasks (LLT),

(f) Least Laxity First (LLF),

(g) Round Robin (RR),

(h) Selfish Round Robin (SRR),

(i) Multiple–level Feedback (FB).

These scheduling policies can be *divided* into three *groups*. Some of them (i.e. FCFS, SPN and HPRN) do not follow user defined priorities nor process deadlines. Others (i.e. EDF, LLF and LLT) use deadlines to make the right schedule. The policies of the last group (i.e. RR, MF and SRR) pay attention to user defined process priorities.

Fig. 4.43 shows the *architecture* of the *scheduler tool*. We see a global control module Scheduler Control that uses the different XYZ Scheduler modules. These modules represent the scheduling algorithms and were implemented as a specialization of Generic `Scheduler`. The `Generic Scheduler` uses a `Scheduling Queue` to store the actual execution sequence of processes (see `Atomic Process` in fig. 4.43). Moreover, the `Generic Scheduler` uses a component `XYZ Processor` on which this scheduling policy actually runs. Finally, the module `Time` serves as a global clock to control the process execution sequence corresponding to the individual process deadlines.

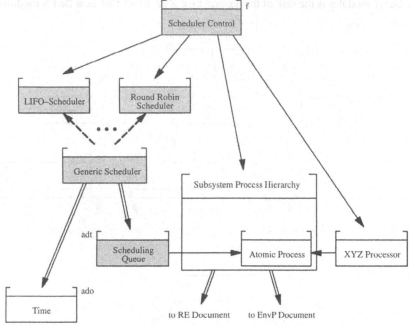

Fig. 4.43. Architecture of the `Scheduler` of fig. 4.39 (grey part)

Above, we have mentioned just two features concerning the monitoring and the statistics tool. *Additional instrumentation* and *monitoring features* are offered by the RE environment:

(6) assignment of virtual processors to data processes,

(7) definition of priorities for data processes,

(8) specification and change of data flow and control flow values.

The monitoring tool works in the background of the RE environment while the simulation tool is active. So, it shows some run time information continuously and others on demand. E.g. active processes will be highlighted, while the waiting queue of a special virtual processor will only be presented on user demand. The *implementation* of these *instrumentation* and *monitoring functions* was quite simple because all needed information can be read from the RE document and the process hierarchy. The presentation at the user interface is realized by use of an object oriented class library (InterViews /6. May 92, 6. LCI 92/).

Now, we discuss the *architecture* of the *statistics tool*, see fig. 4.44.a and b. The task of the statistics tool is to read the relevant run time information during model execution, to store this information in an appropriate manner, and finally, to analyse and present the statistics data to the RE specifier.

In fig. 4.44 we see three abstract data object *modules* `DP Stat Data`, `Deadline Stat Data`, and `Processor Stat Data`. In these modules all relevant *statistics information* is *gathered*. DP Stat Data embodies data concerning process states, Deadline Stat Data concentrates on deadline information and Processor Stat Data comprises information about processor states, waiting queues etc. All information that is stored in XYZ Stat Data will be extracted from Process Hierarchy, EnvP Document, and Scheduling Queues. Searching for this runtime data and reorganizing them in the XYZ Stat Data modules is the task of the Transfer XYZ Statistics Data modules.

a) data gathering

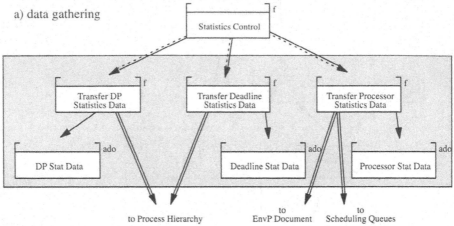

b) data evaluation

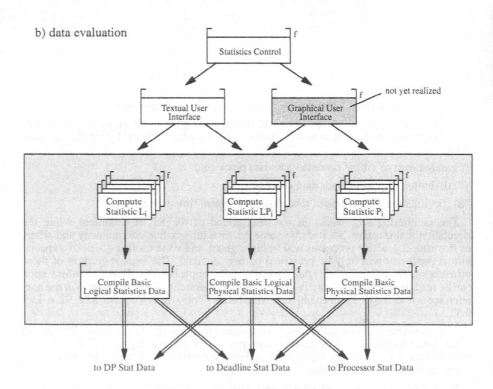

Fig. 4.44. Architecture of the statistics tool

Fig. 4.44.b shows the statistics tool architecture from the *data evaluation* point of view. In the basic level, we see again the abstract data objects DP Stat Data, Deadline Stat Data, and Processor Stat Data.

In the next level in upwards direction of the statistics tool architecture there are three Compile Basic XYZ Statistics Data and another level up are ten Compute Statistic XYZ. All these functional modules serve to analyse the stored information and to produce the various statistics asked by the user.

In the following we list the offered statistics. Corresponding to these statistics the above mentioned functional modules compute the required information. The existing tool implementation includes only a textual user interface but a graphical interface is planned as an extension.

1. Logical statistics:

● deadline violation of one data process

● number of activations of one data process

● number of interrupts of one data process

● state changes of one data process over time

2. Physical statistics:

● average occupation of virtual processors

● deadline violations at one processor

3. Logical–physical statistics:

● processor occupation over time

● average waiting and execution time at one processor

● average length of one (or more) scheduling queue(s) at one processor

● deadline violations of one data process at one processor

4.5.5 Summary of Adaptability and Corresponding Design Decisions

We stated at the beginning of this section that the RE environment is very flexible and adaptable corresponding to different parameters. In this section we want to explain *how* this *flexibility* and *adaptability* has been *realized*. We discuss three examples to prove these properties of the RE environment.

The most important facts for adaptability are (a) the *modular design* of all tools integrated in the RE environment and (b) the strict *separation* of the different *features* between individual tools. Especially, we have distinguished between proper execution, instrumentation, monitoring, and statistics evaluation. Furthermore, the specification of a modular RE software model (divided into FM, CM and IM parts) and a separated hardware model has been realized.

A first example to show the available flexibility is the PSPEC language. If we *change* the *syntax* of the *PSPEC language* we have to adapt the RE editor, the analyser and the PSPEC interpreter. Adapting the editor and analysis tool is quite simple because these tools are mostly generated. The PSPEC interpreter has to be adapted manually but we have to concentrate only on the first compilation phase where the intermediate code will be generated. If the syntax of the source code language changes, surely the compilation process must be adapted to the new language. But the second step, namely interpretation of the intermediate code, may remain unchanged.

The second example for flexibility deals with *changing* the *activation semantics* of the different process types. Actually, we distinguish between implicitly and explicitly controlled processes. Additionally, we can imagine defining a more complex activation semantics for the data processes, e.g. that individual incoming data flow must carry a value before the process becomes active. All those changes in the activation semantics may be simply realized by adapting the corresponding XYZ Process State Automaton module. This module belongs to the GNI subsystem and comprises all knowledge that will be needed for process activation.

Finally, we will discuss the example of *changing* the *functionality* of the *instrumentation/monitoring tool*. E.g., it is desirable to use so called watchpoints. Those watchpoints make it feasible to supervise special runtime information (e.g. actual dataflow values, process states etc.) continuously. The realization of watchpoints could be made by use of the InterViews library. We only need to design the desired windows for the user interface. All information concerning the actual runtime data could be read from the RE document and the process hierarchy.

In this section we described architectural details of the RESI environment which consists of editor, analysis, as well as flexible and adaptable simulation tools. Of course, it would be interesting to compare the RESI architecture with that of other RE environments (e.g. STATEMATE, Foresight, Teamwork/ES, ShortCut, Proto, for literature see section 2.4). However, we do not know very much about the internal organization of these environments as most of them are commercial tools. Neither the software architecture nor the corresponding design decisions have been published.

4.6 Realization of Incremental Integration Tools

M. Lefering

This section describes the architecture and realization of the *integrator framework* for fine–grained increment–to–increment coupling. All integrators the behavior of which was introduced in sections 2.2 and 2.3 were built using this framework. The main idea of the framework is to have the application–independent and hence reusable parts of an integrator extracted on architectural level and to identify those modules that have to be rebuilt for every new integration application.

The only *application–dependent* parts are the transformation rules which have to be formulated for every integration task. Therefore, the implementations of these rules are put into separate modules. They build up the non–reusable part of an integrator. The main part of an integrator tool's implementation consists of *reusable* building blocks. Therefore, the architecture is the same for all integration tools and we can speak of a *standard architecture* for integration tools.

Throughout this section we speak of *transformation tools* instead of integration tools. We do this even if the tool is only a consistency checker. The reason is that (a) transformation tools are the most complex integration tools, the discussion of which needs the longest explanation. Furthermore, as already mentioned, (b) integration tools of IPSEN in the classification of subsection 1.6.3 have a mixed character including transformations. Finally, any integrator can be described by triple rules (cf. section 3.4) and (c) at least one part of the triplet performs a transformation.

This *section* is as *follows*: After a short discussion of the coarse architecture in the first subsection, the control component of a transformation tool is explained in subsection 4.6.2. The next subsection describes how transformation rules are realized and how their implementation is derived from the specification introduced in section 3.4. Finally, subsection 4.6.4 deals with the memory of transformation tools, the integration document, and its realization as a graph. As usual, a short summary concludes this section.

4.6.1 A Framework for Integrators

The coarse architecture of integrators already introduced in subsection 1.6.3 is recalled in fig. 4.45. Three main *features* and corresponding *components* of an integrator can be identified:

(1) Our integrators work incrementally. That means that only the inconsistent parts are regarded in each step. To identify consistent and inconsistent parts, the tool has to *remember* and to *analyze* the recorded *integration relations*. For that, it requires its own memory. In our framework this memory is realized in an extra document, called `IntegrationDocument` (see below). The realization of the integration document is independent of the documents that have to be integrated, therefore it is one of the application–independent parts and can be reused without modifications.

(2) There is a standard functionality for *creating* and *controlling simple links* between the related documents which is required by every integration tool. It is also independent of the current application and, therefore, reusable. This functionality is realized by the component `BasicIntegrator`. It can be seen as an editor for the integration document that is used by the control component of an integration tool with a restricted functionality, namely to manipulate links. If only simple links are required, as in the case

of the manual or hypertext integrator described in subsection 2.3.4, the integration tool just presents these elementary commands to the user. As the BasicIntegrator can be implemented rather straightforwardly on top of IntegrationDocument, we do not discuss it in detail here (cf. /4. Lef 95/).

(3) The control component of an integration tool is realized in the subsystem XYIntegrationTool. Besides the realization of the tool execution control, this subsystem embodies the current set of transformation rules, i.e. the transformation algorithm of the specific integration task. Since this set of transformation rules is different for every integration tool, this subsystem contains application–dependent parts and is therefore called XYIntegrationTool in fig. 4.45. The code for the transformation rules can be derived from the specification introduced in section 3.4. We will discuss this derivation later.

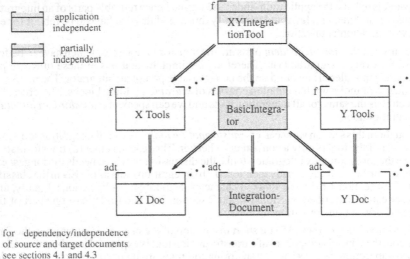

for dependency/independence
of source and target documents   • • •
see sections 4.1 and 4.3

Fig. 4.45. Coarse architecture of an integration tool

In the following we *concentrate* on *specific topics* of the transformation tool architecture of fig. 4.45. After explaining the internal structure of the control component XYIntegrationTool and its runtime behavior in the next subsection, we go into the application–dependent part of this component which realizes the transformation rules. There, we discuss how our approach is dealing with the most complex case of interactive transformation tools, like the RE–PiL transformation of section 2.3, and how the corresponding transformation rules inside of XYIntegrationTool can be derived. In the last subsection, we especially discuss how the integration document is structured internally in order to maintain and update the knowledge of a fine–grained transformation process.

4.6.2 The Subsystem IntegrationTool

The subsystem XYIntegrationTool realizes the *execution control* and the rule base of the integrator. Its *tasks* are to offer commands to the environment control (and, hence, to the user) and to execute the selected commands. We have commands to set and store tool parameters, to select rules, to install or remove integrations, and to assign priorities to rules.

The architecture of this *subsystem* is presented in fig. 4.46. (Relationships to modules outside the subsystem are omitted for the sake of clarity.) The *interface* of the subsystem consists of three modules: IntegratorCommands, ParamCommands, and RulePrioEditor which are discussed now in this order.

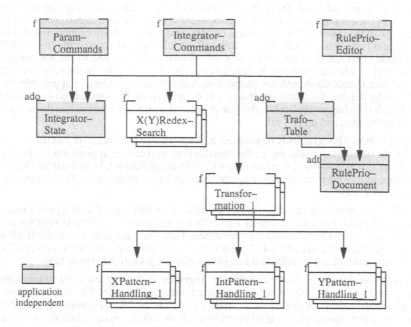

Fig. 4.46. Architecture of the subsystem `XYIntegrationTool`

`ParamCommands` *sets* and *changes* the *parameters* for the *execution control*. It stores the current values of these parameters in the abstract data object `IntegratorState`. The current values of these parameters are considered by the component that realizes the execution control, i.e. the module `IntegratorCommands`.

The following *parameters* were implemented in `ParamCommands` to allow the integrator framework to *support* several *integration* scenarios:

(1) *Protection of generated increments*: An integrator can protect the increments it has inserted in the target document against modification by the user. Then, the editor of the target document has no write access on these increments. When setting this parameter, inconsistencies can only occur after changes in the source documents, the integration is an adaptation of the target document to changes in the source document. This scenario is used in the PiL–PiS integration of subsection 2.3.3.

(2) *Deleting generated increments*: When an inconsistency occurs, the integrator can automatically delete the generated target increments to erase an integration relation. Otherwise, it will inform the user who then has to decide whether the increments should be deleted. For instance, in the RE–PiL integrator, increments are not deleted automatically. When the protection of the generated increments is enabled (e.g. in the PiL–PiS integration), these increments are usually also deleted since the integrator is the only tool with write access to these increments.

(3) *Usage of priorities*: Priorities can be assigned to transformation rules. If priority usage is switched on, the user has to assign a valid priority document to the integration (see below). Otherwise, all rules have the same priority, i.e. priority values are effectively ignored.

(4) *Checking of applied rules*: There are two levels of consistency checking: On the first level, only the completeness of the links is examined, i.e. inconsistencies can occur only when one of the connected increments is deleted and the link becomes incomplete. On the second level it is checked, additionally, if the rule that has created the link is still applicable. This needs no longer be the case when a context in one of the documents is changed or when a mastering integration relation has changed. In the case that the context in a source document has changed so that the rule is no longer applicable the link will be deleted. Furthermore, if a rule is dependent on the application of another rule which is no longer applicable, the link is deleted, too. With a parameter, the second level can be switched on and off.

(5) *Execution mode*: It was already mentioned in chapter 2 that the integrator can run in two modes. In (semi–)automatic mode, the transformation rules are applied automatically whenever this is possible (i.e. when only one rule is applicable). In manual mode, the tool stops before every integration step and the user has to select one of the options (cf. subsection 2.3.1).

Fig. 4.46 also contains the module `RulePrioEditor` that is used to *assign priorities* to the rules. The editor and the according `RulePrioDocument` realize a simple textual syntax–directed environment to edit rule priorities. They were generated with the IPSEN generator mechanism (cf. section 4.4). `RulePrioDocument` is used by `TrafoTable` to determine the set of active rules and assign the current priorities to these rules.

`ParamComands` and `RulePrioEditor` together with their memory documents `IntegratorState` and `RulePrioDocument` are used to adapt the control component of a transformation tool to achieve a certain tool behavior. This *adaptation* is possible only *before* a transformation tool is used for an integration task, i.e. no adaptation at *runtime* is possible. For that adaptation, `TrafoTable` at the beginning reads the relevant rules and their priorities. Then, the values stored in `IntegratorState` and `TrafoTable` are used to adjust the control component.

The module `TrafoTable` is used at runtime to determine the set of active rules and the priorities which, eventually, have been assigned by the user. Furthermore, this module determines for a rule the type of the dominant source increment. A dominant source increment serves as an anchor and starting point for the match of an arbitrarily complex pattern of the source document which has to be transformed (see below). Conversely, the applicable rules for a dominant source increment can also be determined by this component. So, `Trafo-Table` serves as the *memory* of *suitable rules* to be applied or gives *information* to *control* rule applications.

For any transformation *rule* there is a corresponding *module* in the architecture of a transformation tool (`Transformation_i` in fig. 4.46). This module has *three operations* at its interface: (a) to check the applicability of this rule, (b) to apply this rule and make a transformation, and (c) to check whether an applied transformation yields a valid state of integration. These operations are needed for carrying out incremental integration steps.

The component `IntegratorCommands` *controls* the *steps* of an *integration* tool's run. Therefore, we now give a closer look on these steps and we explain how `IntegratorCommands` realizes this control by using resources of the other modules which provide for certain subtasks (cf. fig. 4.46):

(1) If the use of rule priorities is switched off by the above–mentioned parameter, all *transformation rules* have to be *loaded* into a table inside the module `TrafoTable`. If priorities are switched on, the user has to select a `RulePrioDocument`. `TrafoTable` uses this document to determine the rules that are switched on. Only these rules, together with their priority, are then included in the transformation table. As this `Rule-PrioDocument` also contains (see fig. 2.21) the dominant source increments, the relation between rules and dominant source increments and vice versa, this information can also be made accessible through `TrafoTable`.

(2) Each transformation rule has a particular increment (more precisely an increment type) marked as its dominant source increment. In this second step the *dominant source increments* of all active rules of the transformation table are *collected* by `Integrator-Commands`. Increments the type of which is in this collection are candidates for the current integration run.

(3) In the following steps, the *redexes* for the integration, i.e. the source increments with inconsistent links, have to be *determined*.

   (3a) In the first step, all *links* of the `IntegrationDocument` are *checked* to see if they have become *inconsistent*. In any case, a link is marked inconsistent if increments of its source or target pattern have been deleted since the last integration run. This first step can be carried out using the resources of `BasicIntegrator`. If the above mentioned applied rules parameter is switched on, also those links are marked as inconsistent where the rule that has established the link is no longer applicable (because a context in the source document that is checked by the rule or a mastering transformation has changed). This is done by using the applicability check operation offered by the module corresponding to that rule and the functionality of `BasicIntegrator`. How a link is marked inconsistent is explained below.

   (3b) Additionally, all *source increments* that have *not* been *transformed* yet, i.e. the increments that have been inserted since the last integration run, have to be *collected*. To do this, `IntegratorCommands` uses the module `XRedexSearch` that exists for each source document. This module scans the source document. For each source increment that is a dominant source increment, i.e. its type is in the collection of step (2), a new inconsistent link is inserted into the integration document. So, `XRedexSearch` is nothing else than a complete scan through `XDoc` which determines all increments of a certain type (necessary here for a dominant source increment). This operation could also have been offered by `XTools`. Insertion of a new link is again done using `BasicIntegrator`. At this step, all locations that have to be integrated are determined by inconsistent links in the integration document. The transformation tool from now on does not distinguish whether an inconsistent link comes from a destroyed integration relation or from a newly inserted source increment.

(4) Now, for each inconsistent link it is examined which rules are applicable to transform this link, assuming that other rules might have been used before to integrate certain other source increments and their links. In this case, a rule application depends on the former execution of another rule. This shows that the order of rule execution is not arbitrary. Therefore, a *dependency graph* according to these rule dependencies is *built up* in the integration document and is used to determine the possible orders of incremental transformation. To do this, `IntegratorCommands` uses `TrafoTable` to determine the applicable rules and makes them examine their search pattern by delivering information which is necessary to build up the dependency graph. The latter is done using the resources of `BasicIntegrator`.

(5) In this main step the integration tool *executes integration steps* according to the possible orders of execution determined by the dependency graph. If automatic mode is selected, the control component `IntegratorCommands` proceeds automatically according to the dependency graph as long as a unique rule is applicable to make a certain inconsistent link consistent. If several rules are applicable, the user has to select one of them to solve this conflict (cf. sections 2.2 and 2.3). If manual mode is selected, the integrator presents all locations to the user that can be integrated independently of other inconsistent links. The user can then select an arbitrary increment and transform it.

All these steps are either *initiated* or *controlled* by `IntegratorCommands` which uses the `BasicIntegrator` to manipulate the integration document directly. The transformation itself or the necessary information about transformations is realized with the help of the transformation table module `TrafoTable` and by the operations of the corresponding rules.

Each *rule* is implemented in several *modules*. Provided that two documents X and Y have to be integrated as in fig. 4.46 and assuming a transformation from X to Y, they consist of four modules: The module `Transformation_i` controls this single integration step. It has the knowledge which patterns have to be searched and which have to be inserted as target patterns. Every rule can search a pattern in source documents (e.g. `XPatternHandling_i` in fig. 4.46). `IntPatternHandling_i` searches for a pattern in the integration document, i.e. for a former execution of a rule at another link. `YPatternHandling_i` searches a pattern in the target document and might additionally insert a certain pattern there. To indicate that these modules exist for every rule, they are numbered and carry shadows in fig. 4.46.

In fig. 4.46, the invariant or *reusable components* of an integration tool are marked in grey. They are `ParamCommands`, `IntegratorState`, `IntegratorCommands`, `RulePrioEditor`, `RulePrioDocument`, and `TrafoTable`.

The remaining modules are *application–specific* in three *different ways*: Whereas (1) `Transformation_i` is only specific for a certain kind of transformation tool (e.g. transformator plus binder) and is not dependent on certain documents to be integrated, (2) `XPatternHandling_i`, `IntPatternHandling_i`, and `YPatternHandling_i` have to be realized for every corresponding document type. Finally, (3) `XRedexSearch` (or possibly `YRedexSearch`) are dependent on the type of the source or target document. However, this dependency is rather weak as both components only use a standard pass through an AST–modelled document.

4.6.3 Realization of Transformation Rules

In this subsection, we shall discuss the techniques to *model* and to *implement* the *transformation rules* of transformation tools and we shall sketch how rule *implementations* are *derived* from triple graph grammar specifications. There are three main characteristic features of our rule realization: The concept of dominant source increments, dependencies between rules, and operational implementation of rules. They are explained now in this order.

Dominant source increments

Rules can search for arbitrarily complex patterns in source or target documents of the specific integration. The matching of an arbitrary subgraph in a graph is a complicated problem and can in general not be realized efficiently (cf. /5. Zün 95b/). Therefore, we introduced the concept of a *dominant source increment*. A dominant source increment is a part of the left hand side of a triple rule (source rule). Every transformation rule is related to one single dominant source increment. For example, in fig. 4.47.b the process application B is the dominant source increment of the source pattern. However, the process declarations A and B and the `ApplToDecl` relation between process application B and process declaration B are regarded as context as well. Two rules are in conflict if both transform the same dominant source increment.

Additionally, this increment is used as the *starting point* for *pattern matching* in the specific source document. The pattern itself can be arbitrarily complex (dominant increment embedded in a context). The dominant source increment dramatically facilitates pattern matching in the source document and, as a dominant source increment is always related to one transformation rule, it also facilitates the determination of the transformation rule to be applied.

Since (1) every rule has exactly one dominant source increment, (2) only one rule can be applied to transform an increment, and (3) every rule application inserts exactly one link in the integration document, there is a *1:1:1 relation* between dominant source increments, rule applications, and links in the integration document.

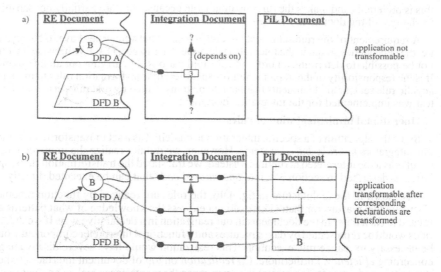

Fig. 4.47. Dependencies between rule applications

Dependencies between rule applications

As already mentioned in section 2.3 and above, the *application* of a transformation *rule* can *depend* on the former *application* of *another rule* on another increment. Fig. 4.47.a shows an example from the context of integrating RE and PiL. A process application (e.g. process application B and link 3) cannot be transformed unless the according declarations are transformed. Only if the process declarations have already been transformed, it is possible to transform the application in the sequel.

A *rule* that *realizes* the *transformation* of a process application as in the example of fig. 4.47.b would search for the process application B (dominant source increment) and the respective declarations in the source document (declarations of processes A and B), then search for the transformations of the declarations in the integration document, and, finally, search for the targets of both transformations in the target document. Hence, a rule tries to match source, integration, and target patterns.

In the architecture in fig. 4.46 it was shown that a rule implementation is realized by several modules. The match/manipulation of each pattern is realized in a single module. Hence, each of these modules realizes an operation of a rule on specific documents. The *implementation* of the *rule* in fig. 4.47 consists of the module Transformation_i and three modules REPatternHandling_i, IntPatternHandling_i, PiLPattern-Handling_i. To indicate that there are multiple patterns for multiple rules we simply added a number suffix to the module names in fig. 4.46. The realization parts of these pattern handling modules can be derived from the specifications presented in section 3.4 (see below).

The target pattern of a rule fulfills a second task besides insertion: A *rule* needs to *know* the correct *location* in the *target document* where its target pattern has to be inserted (if it is a real transformation rule and not just a consistency checking rule). Now it can determine that location relative to the target pattern instead of defining an absolute address in the document. In this way, the rules do not need to know the complete internal structure of the document but just a certain area around the target pattern. From the data abstraction point of view this is preferable and makes the rules maintainable because they are partially not sensitive to changes of the document structure.

A requirement of the rule set is that the *dependencies* between rules have to be *acyclic*, i.e. the dependency graph in the integration document has to be a DAG. Otherwise it would not be possible to determine an order of rule applications for carrying out an integration. It is the responsibility of the implementor (or specifier) of transformation rules to model an acyclic rule set (for all documents that have to be transformed by that rule set), as no cycle test was implemented for the integration document.

Operational implementation of rules

Since the algorithm of a specific integration is modelled as a set of transformation rules, our integrators are *rule–based* systems. However, we did not realize the implementation of rules as to be interpreted at runtime. Instead, we translated the transformation rules, specified as described in section 3.4, into *operational code* that can be executed directly.

As shown in the architecture in fig. 4.46, the rules are realized by function modules. There are two reasons for that: (1) We did not express the knowledge of what patterns are related to each other in the documents in our realization in a declarative way. If we did, the rules would be represented by data structures and a functional interpreter component would be necessary to realize rule execution. This realization would have severe disadvantages concerning *efficiency*. Furthermore, (2) *realization* on top of document interfaces (where integrators and other tools operate) is *easier*, since these interfaces realize an operational view on documents. For example, one can easily navigate through a document, read and modify single increments, and, thus, build up complex patterns to be searched for or inserted. However, it is not possible to pass complex patterns to the document interface for searched or insertion. These are the reasons that the declarative description of rules in the *specification* is *translated* into a functional description of how to execute rules.

Thus, the declarative knowledge is not contained in the architecture, but only in the specification. The *disadvantage* of this solution is that rules cannot be changed without recompiling and relinking the system. So, rule modification is not possible at runtime. This, however, is not a big disadvantage, as the rules are fixed by the integration tool builder and not by the tool user. The user's possibilities for adjustment are constrained to switching rules on and off, setting priorities etc. (see 2.3).

There are *two* possible *ways* to *derive code* from the specification of the rules. Firstly, the triple graph grammar specifications could be inserted into a framework specification. This complete specification could be translated (e.g. manually derived or automatically compiled) into source code (cf. fig. 4.48.a). Secondly, the rule specifications are translated into code and this code is integrated into a framework implementation (which itself is translated, either manually or automatically, cf. fig. 4.48.b). The advantage of the second approach is that it is more efficient and easier to implement. Therefore, we decided to follow this approach. Instead of specifying the framework and translating it, we implemented it manually. So, the upper right box in Fig. 4.48.b and its translation is missing. However, rules are specified and translated.

The *code* that has to be *translated* (at the moment manually) from a rule specification i comprises the procedure bodies of the resources of the XPatternHandling_i, YPatternHandling_i, and IntPatternHandling_i modules in fig. 4.46. That code is derived directly from the left–hand sides or right–hand sides of the triple rules specified in section 3.4. Which side has to be inserted into a search or replacement operation depends on the type of integration that is to be realized (left–to–right, right–to–left, or consistency check, cf. section 3.4) and has to be decided at generation time (not at specification time). So, code generation starts with the triple rule specifications of section 3.4 by determining the direction of a translation, what is to be inserted or already available, and not with the transformation rules (which themselves are derived from these determinations). For more details on the code derivation see /4. Lef 95/.

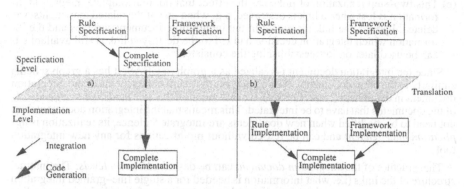

Fig. 4.48. Two ways of deriving an integrator implementation

In section 1.6.3, we presented a classification for integration tools and their coarse architecture. It was stressed that the *architecture* is *independent* of the concrete *type* of *integration tool* that has to be realized (except for the question of how many documents have to be used). This is to be sketched now w.r.t. the internal structure of XYIntegration-Tools (the reuse discussion on the coarse architecture of fig. 4.45 was already given above). Hence, the architecture is indeed stable for all studied types of integration tools and can be viewed as a standard architecture for fine–grained technical integration tools.

In the short discussion of this section we have seen that indeed the only variation of realization between different integrator types takes place within the *procedure bodies* corresponding to the *rules*. This is a matter of the implementation of modules and not of architecture modelling. The rule implementations also determine whether the tool is just a consistency checker or a transformation tool. The browsing facility is implemented in the *framework* (namely in module IntegratorCommands) and, therefore, included in all integrators without modification. Additionally, the *order* in which documents are used is realized in the body of modules Transformation_i of the rules, respectively. Whether they only read or also modify documents is again a question of the implementation of rules.

4.6.4 The Integration Document

The *integration document* was identified as one of the major and reusable parts of the integration tool framework of fig. 4.45. This subsection explains its *internal structure* and motivates why this structure looks as it is.

The relations that an integrator installs between increments of source and target documents are stored as links in an extra document that is internal to the integrator, i.e. cannot be viewed by the user. This *explicit realization* of *links* has a lot of *advantages* compared to other approaches, like realizing pointers in each of the related documents or combining the documents by a global hyperdocument:

(a) There is one central location where all integration information is stored instead of being distributed over several information units.

(b) The documents that have to be integrated are independent of the integrations they are involved in. That means especially that they need not be modified when a new integration is realized.

(c) The documents are still single work units that can be concurrently accessed by different users at the same time.

(d) The realization of m:n relations is simplified considerably since they can be reduced to an m:1 and a 1:n relation.

(e) This two–step realization of links has the effect that not the complete integration information is lost when a link is destroyed, e.g. when one of the related increments was deleted. Instead, the link increment in the integration document survives and the information which integration decision had led to the destroyed link is still available. It can be used later on for reestablishing the consistency.

Since the integration document is realized as a graph in GRAS, it has a graph schema similarly to the other documents. We do not want to describe the schema of the integration document in detail here (cf. /4. Lef 95/), we just mention that it is *modelled independently* of the documents that have to be integrated. This means that the integration document does not need to be modified when new documents are integrated. Hence, its realization is *application–independent* and can be reused without modifications for any new integration tool.

The structure of the *integration document* can be described on *two levels*: The internal structure of the links (i.e. what information is needed for a single fine–grained integration relation) and the structure of the integration document on top of these links, i.e. regarding the integration document structure with links as atomic units. Both levels are to be explained in this subsection. We start with the internal structure of links.

A *link* is not only an edge in a graph but a complex subgraph in the integration document. It contains all the information that is needed for an integration step. This *information* is concerned about which rules are applicable, which one has been applied, dependency of rules, corresponding source and target increments, and how a rule was created.

A link is either consistent or *inconsistent*. We distinguish *two different states* of inconsistent links (cf. fig. 4.49):

(a) *Unchecked inconsistent*: Such links are created in the steps (3a) and (3b) of the integration process described in subsection 4.6.2. Hence, these links simply mark the redexes for integration, i.e. the dominant source increments to be transformed. A link in this state can be seen in fig. 4.49.a. It consists of a link node that carries a state attribute value (here Unchecked) and a node that represents the dominant source increment.

(b) *Checked inconsistent*: A link of this state is the result of the integration step (4) of 4.6.2. It is still inconsistent, but the integrator has checked which rules are applicable to make it consistent. If a rule is applicable, i.e. its source pattern can be matched, the rule and the match pattern are stored as a subgraph at the link, as to be seen from fig. 4.49.b. These rules are called potentially applicable rules. Whether they are actually applicable might depend on the former integration of other links which is examined by the integration pattern later. If such a dependency to the integration of other links exists, dependency edges are drawn to these links (see below).

When the *links* are made *consistent* in integration step (5) of 4.6.2, they are changed to one of the following *three consistent* states:

(c) *Rule based*: Such a link has been made consistent by the application of a transformation rule. The rule is stored as the applied rule at the link, together with the matches of the source, integration, and target patterns (cf. fig. 4.49.c). Other rules which were potentially applicable are deleted. The pattern matches are stored at the link as they are needed if the parameter 'checking of applied rules' is switched on in the next integration step run, i.e. it has to be checked whether all patterns still have the same match (cf. subsection 4.6.2).

(d) *Manual*: A link in this state was drawn manually by the user. That means that it was drawn using a manual integrator like the one described in section 2.3 or the user selected the manual option in a semi–automatic integration tool, like the one also described in section 2.3. A link in state manual is shown in fig. 4.49.d. Such a link is always a 1:1–link since the user can select only one target increment.

479

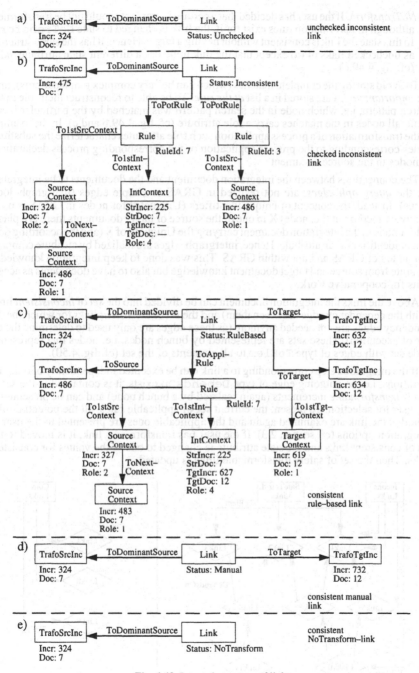

Fig. 4.49. Internal structure of links

(e) *NoTransform*: If the user has decided that a certain increment should not be transformed, although transformation rules exist for it, the link is changed to state `NoTransform`. In this state the link is consistent without having a target. Hence, it has the same structure as unchecked links of (a) except that the link node has a different state attribute value (cf. fig. 4.49.e).

To avoid storing the complete matches (which can be very complex graph patterns), only the *important nodes* are stored in a list *at the rule*. To be able to reconstruct their role in the search pattern, i.e. which node in the search pattern was matched by the particular increment, all nodes in the matches carry a role attribute (cf. fig. 4.49.b and c). In the example of the transformation of a process application such role attributes characterize the substitute nodes corresponding to the process application or the corresponding process declarations of nodes in the source document.

The connections between the integration document and the documents to be integrated, i.e. the *intergraph edges*, are not realized in GRAS as simple edges (like graph–local edges). Instead, the concept of unique identifiers (UniqueId) for nodes in GRAS is used. For every increment (i.e. node) X in one of the source or target documents there is a place-holder node in the integration document carrying the UniqueId of X (and the according document identifier) as an attribute. Hence, intergraph edges are realized by attribute comparison on top of GRAS and not within GRAS. This was done to keep integration knowledge separate from source and target document knowledge but also to have documents as access units for cooperative work.

Above the links the integration document can be divided into the *set* of *inconsistent* links (with the dependency edges between them) and the set of *consistent links* for which the dependency edges are not needed anymore (as these edges are only used to determine the order of execution). These sets are represented by bunch nodes, i.e. nodes that represent a node set with edges of type `ToElem` to all elements of the set (cf. fig. 4.50).

If the integration step corresponding to a link can be executed independently of other integrations, i.e. no outgoing edge of type `DependsOn` exists, it is contained in the set of *safely transformable* increments (again realized by a bunch node) and can be presented to the user for selection. To present the current set of applicable rules, all the potential rules stored at the link are examined again and the applicable ones are presented to the user as integration options (cf. section 2.3). If the user has transformed a link, it is moved to the set of consistent links and the state attribute is changed to one of the values for consistent links. Then the set of safely transformable links is updated.

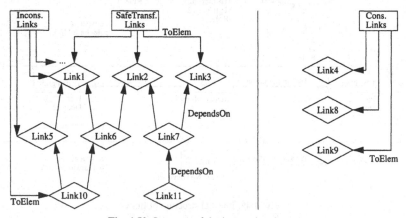

Fig. 4.50. Structure of the integration document

Fig. 4.50 gives an *example*: If link 1 was transformed, link 5 would become a safely transformable link, since it now only depends on the transformation of consistent links. Link 6 would not become safely transformable as it also depends on the transformation of link 2. After link 2 were transformed, link 6 would be safely transformable as well.

The realization of the integration document is very flexible, since links of arbitrary complexity can be realized. At the moment the *complexity* of *links* is, however, *restricted* by the specification approach presented in section 3.4. With that approach, only rules that relate arbitrary patterns in two documents can be specified. Hence, every single link only connects two documents in our integrators, although the integration document is able to realize links that connect an arbitrary number of documents. Such integrations have to be implemented completely manually at the moment.

4.6.5 Summary and Comparison

In this section we have discussed the *framework* and the *machinery* for realizing fine-grained integrators in IPSEN. There are two *components independent* of the type and application area of an integrator, namely IntegrationDocument and BasicIntegrator, see fig. 4.45. The component IntegrationDocument was discussed in detail here.

The subsystem XYIntegrator has to be modified when building an integrator of a specific type (transformer, consistency checker etc.). Even there, most of its internal components are *application–independent*, as ParamCommands or RulePrioEditor. The *application–specific* part within this *control subsystem*, therefore, is clearly identified as well (see fig. 4.46).

To *get* the *code* for these specific parts, a *special procedure* is applied: From triple rule and correspondence specification (see section 3.4), the bodies of the corresponding match and update operations are mechanically derived by the integration tool builder. This is a good starting point for automatically generating parts of those specific components or, in the long run, for completely generating these application–specific and integrator type specific parts.

The approach for integrators introduced within this book was *separation* into different documents to be constructed/modified by different persons but also *integration* in order to support change processes. So, there is a clear distinction to other approaches regarding the product of a process to be one complex whole. Furthermore, change processes can only in some cases be carried out automatically (as between PiL and PiS in 2.3). So, what we need is intelligent and fine–grained support for *interactive change processes* between depending documents or documents representing different perspectives.

The author is not aware of any paper discussing the *architecture* of such integration tools. Furthermore, links or hyperlinks between different documents either only serve for manual processes (e.g. for browsing) or methods are attached to these links which are only suitable for automatic change processes. Also, no paper is known to the author introducing an *integration document* of rich internal structure, keeping track of source and target patterns, checking contexts, fixing applicable or applied rules, or defining dependencies between rules, altogether necessary for interactive integration processes.

4.7 Realizing Management Environments and Embedding Technical Environments

P. Heimann, B. Westfechtel

In section 2.5, we described the functionality and user interface of tools for managing administration configurations. These tools constitute an environment which manages products, processes, and resources on the coarse–grained level. So far, administration is performed within one project only, and integration between different projects is not supported yet. The project administration environment does not only comprise *management tools* for running projects, it also includes *parameterization tools* which are used to adapt management tools to a certain application domain (e.g. CIM or software engineering). These tools are part of an overall administration system which in addition contains components for *embedding technical environments*.

As we already pointed out in section 2.5, the administration system was developed and applied in the SUKITS project which is devoted to the mechanical engineering domain. Concerning administration of engineering design applications in general, we believe that there are strong similarities between software engineering and mechanical engineering (see also subsection 1.1.4). Therefore, the application domain does not have a strong impact on design and realization of the administration system.

However, IPSEN and SUKITS differ with respect to the embedding of technical environments: In IPSEN, we follow an *a priori approach* to integration, i.e. an integration concept is developed before tools are realized according to that concept. In contrast, SUKITS addresses *a posteriori integration*: Technical environments are realized in isolation without taking integration into account. Therefore, we have to cope with heterogeneity concerning operating systems, networks, data management systems, and user interfaces. Under these prerequisites, it is often difficult (or even impossible) to achieve the same level of tight integration as realized in IPSEN environments.

The current section describes the *realization* of the *administration system* developed in the SUKITS project. After an architectural overview (subsection 4.7.1), we describe the realization of the project administration environment (subsection 4.7.2) and the embedding of technical environments (subsections 4.7.3 and 4.7.4). A conclusion is given in subsection 4.7.5.

4.7.1 Architectural Overview

Fig. 4.51 shows a simplified picture of the *structure* of the *overall integrated environment*. The *project administration environment*, which consists of management and parameterization tools, is based on the IPSEN machinery. The *administration configuration database* contains both schema data (for parameterization) and instance data (for running a project). The project administration environment may access the administration configuration database directly, i.e. through services which are available in a homogeneous network.

Technical environments (e.g. CAD systems or NC programming systems in mechanical engineering, CASE tools or programming environments in software engineering) have to be connected to the administration system. To this end, each technical environment is extended with a component which is responsible for its interaction with the administration system (and other technical environments). The result of this extension is called *extended technical environment* in the following.

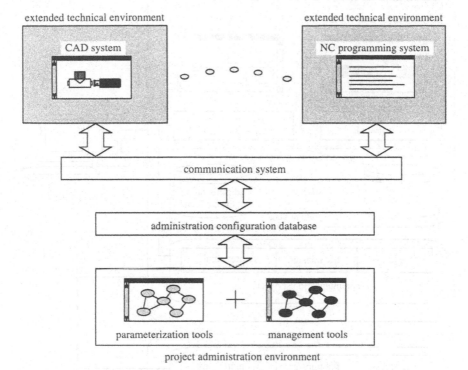

extended technical environment   extended technical environment

CAD system   NC programming system

communication system

administration configuration database

parameterization tools   management tools

project administration environment

Fig. 4.51. Overview of the system structure

The overall integrated environment operates in a heterogeneous network of workstations running under different operating systems and using varying communication protocols. Therefore, a *communication system* enables interoperation in such a heterogeneous network (the communication system is provided by one of our partners in the SUKITS project /6. HS 96, HE 94/). The components for extending technical environments use the communication system e.g. for file transfer and access to the administration configuration database.

Fig. 4.52 refines the overview given in fig. 4.51. The figure shows a *client machine* hosting an extended technical environment, and a *server machine*, on which the project administration environment runs and on which the administration configuration database is stored.

On the server machine, a database server provides access to the *administration configuration database*. In the current realization, each project has its own administration configuration database, and integration between multiple databases is not yet supported. The database maintains only coarse–grained data, i.e. the contents of document revisions are stored outside the administration configuration database which merely contains references to fine–grained data. The database comprises both schema data (definition of document types, dependency types, etc.) and instance data conforming to the schema. These data refer to products, processes, and resources as described in section 2.5. Schema– and instance level operations are accessed directly by the project administration environment. Extended tech-

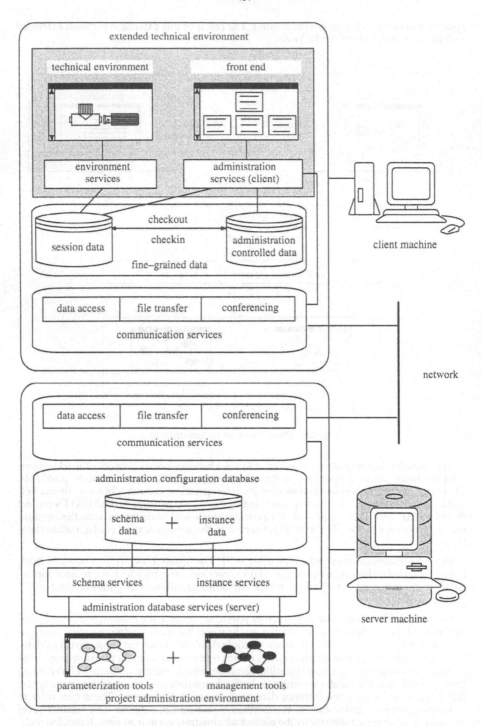

Fig. 4.52. Detailed view of the system structure

nical environments use the database access services provided by the communication system.

The communication system is partly based on ISODE /6. ROR 92/, a development environment for OSI–conforming applications, and offers services for *database access*, *file transfer*, and *conferencing*. The database is accessed via a service (ROSE) which is similar to remote procedure calls. In contrast to RPCs, where each procedure call is sent individually, a connection is established in ROSE before a sequence of operations is sent to a remote server. File transfer is used to supply technical environments with local data to be accessed in a working session. Finally, the communication system provides novel services for synchronous, multi–party communication (conferencing).

On the client machine, a *front end* is used to supply an engineer with an agenda of assigned tasks. For each task, a working context is established which includes input and output documents, guidelines, auxiliary documents, and annotations (see section 2.5). All technical environments are activated through the same front end. In this way, all administrative commands are presented to the engineer in a uniform way (environment–specific extensions would destroy this uniformity and would put high demands on the extensibility of technical environments).

For each technical environment, there is a *wrapper* which prepares the working session, calls the environment, and finally saves the results. These wrappers are part of the administration services called by the front end. Each wrapper is realized as a Perl script (see section 4.7.4). To prepare the working session, the (temporary) session workspace is populated with documents. To this end, documents may have to be copied from a remote machine (file transfer), and they may also have to be converted into a representation which can be processed by the technical environment. Subsequently, the technical environment operates on the session workspace using its native services (i.e. the technical environment itself need not be modified). After the session is finished, changed documents are put under control of the administration system.

Fig. 4.52 shows just one example of how logical components are *physically distributed*. In general,

(a) the project administration environment need not run on the machine hosting the administration configuration database,

(b) fine–grained, administration controlled data may be stored on a different machine (e.g. a file server) than session data contained in a local workspace,

(c) fine–grained, administration controlled data for one project may be distributed across different machines, and

(d) administration configuration databases for different projects may be located on different machines,

(e) a technical environment may even be started on a remote machine (using a remote execution service), provided that the display can be directed to the front end machine (this is supported e.g. by the X window system).

4.7.2 Realization of the Project Administration Environment

The project administration environment relies on the IPSEN machinery. For the sake of simplicity, the administration configuration database of one project is stored in a *single logical document* which comprises both schema and instance data referring to products, processes, and resources. In this respect, we have followed the same approach as in the realization of the requirements engineering environment, where different perspectives of a requirements definition (functional model, information model, etc.) are stored in different portions of the same logical document (section 2.2). Although a general framework for realizing integration tools has been developed (section 4.6), division of the administration configuration database into multiple logical documents would have required substantial additional implementation effort and seemed not to be necessary as there are no different roles and persons on management level for process, product, and resource administration, respectively.

Specification and Implementation

In section 3.5, we presented a *formal specification* for project administration. Recall that administration configuration graphs, as defined in the formal specification, are not abstract syntax graphs. Actually, abstract syntax graphs are much too "concrete" and fine–grained to be used for a high–level specification of the project administration model. For the purpose of realization, however, administration configuration graphs had to be mapped onto abstract syntax graphs, and all operations on these graphs had to be realized by syntax graph operations.

On the one hand, realization is straightforward after a formal specification has been written. On the other hand, manual transformation of the specification into an implementation is still time–consuming and error–prone. The following approaches may be pursued to solve (or at least reduce) this problem:

A high–level initial specification is transformed into a more low–level specification which is based on abstract syntax graphs. Subsequently, an efficient implementation is generated from this specification (with the help of special–purpose tools for abstract syntax graph specifications). Note that the transformation on the specification level would still have to be carried out manually.

An implementation is generated directly from the formal specification. Initial work on generating environments from a PROGRES specification was reported in section 3.6. Note that such a generated environment would not be based on the IPSEN machinery. This alternative seems to be promising, but only limited experience has been gained so far.

In the formal specification, *parameterization* is performed by extending the PROGRES schema. Node types are defined for domain–specific object and relation types, and meta attributes are assigned values such that operations preserve domain–specific consistency constraints. If a prototype were created directly from the specification, this approach would require compilation of the adapted specification before a project may be executed. Furthermore, *evolution* of the domain–specific schema could only be supported to a limited extent since the PROGRES environment only allows for schema extensions after population of the database.

In the current realization, we wanted to avoid compilation, and we also wanted to support schema evolution in a more general way. Therefore, the domain–specific schema is represented on the *instance level*, i.e. object and relation types are modeled as instances which are created and deleted in the same way as their applied occurrences. This allows for providing operations which modify the schema and check their implications on already created instances. Any schema modification may be performed (not only extensions), provided that no inconsistencies would be introduced into the administration configuration database. For example, types can only be deleted if there are no applied occurrences, and cardinalities can only be constrained if the new constraints are not violated on the instance level.

Architectural Description

Fig. 4.53 displays a cutout of the *architecture* of the project administration environment. Below, we explain this architecture bottom–up.

As mentioned above, the administration configuration database is realized as a *logical document* (module LogicalDocuments at the bottom). When an editor is developed for a language XYZ, a datatype module XYZDocuments is introduced as a specialization of LogicalDocuments (implementations for syntax tree operations are provided according to the context–free and context–sensitive syntax of XYZ). Here, this module is denoted as ProjectAdminDocuments.

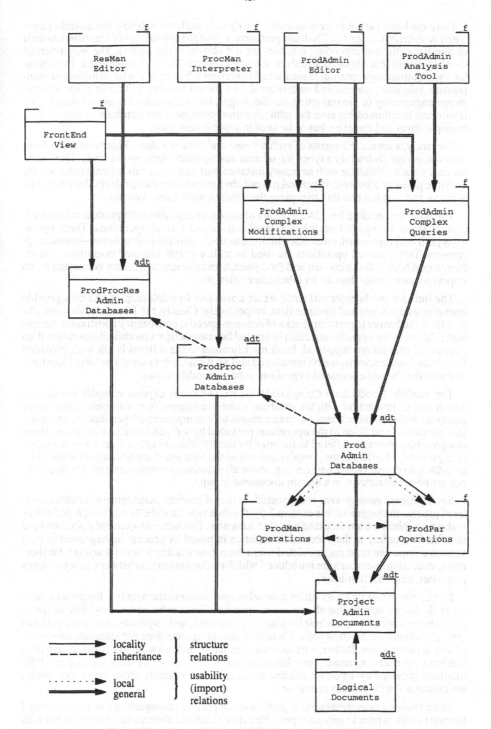

Fig. 4.53. Architecture of the project administration environment

Only the basic part of *context–sensitive analysis* is performed below the module `ProjectAdminDocuments`. The basic part merely comprises bindings of identifiers to their declarations (the corresponding modules are not shown in the figure). The major part of context–sensitive analysis is carried out above `ProjectAdminDocuments`. In particular, most consistency constraints mentioned in section 3.5 (e.g. no cycles in history or composition relations) are checked on this level. In contrast to other editors (e.g. for requirements engineering or programming–in–the–large), inconsistencies are not tolerated. This restriction is enforced because the administration configuration database is accessed by multiple users and therefore has to be kept in a consistent state.

Currently, a database consists of both *schema* and *instance data*. This means that there are no separate abstract data types for schema and instance data, respectively. Of course, we may create a database with an empty instance part and reuse this schema database for multiple projects. However, in general it is not obvious whether two projects share the same schema, and it is not possible to replace the schema with a new version.

The data type module `ProdAdminDatabases` encapsulates the product administration database. It exports both schema–level and instance–level operations. These operations perform graph transformations which are more complex than simple tree–oriented operations. Tree–oriented operations are used to realize graph–oriented operations. Therefore, `ProdAdminDatabases` and `ProjectAdminDocuments` are connected by an import relation rather than by an inheritance relation.

The function modules `ProdParOperations` and `ProdManOperations` provide operations on schema and instance data, respectively. Clearly, the latter module must import from the former to perform checks of domain–specific consistency constraints. An import relation in the opposite direction is needed because schema modifications rather than schema extensions are supported. Each modification to the schema is allowed, provided that no inconsistencies would be introduced and no instance data would be lost. Therefore, instance data must be accessed to perform schema modifications.

The module `ProdAdminComplexModifications` exports *complex operations* which makes interaction with the database more convenient (e.g. complete a document group according to the schema, i.e. create mandatory components/dependencies which are still missing). In addition to the operations provided by `ProdAdminDatabases`, these complex operations are offered to the user by the `ProdAdminEditor`. `ProdAminAnalysisTool` offers some *complex queries* at the user interface which are provided by `ProdAdminComplexQueries` (e.g. show all mandatory component types which have not yet been instantiated in a certain document group).

Since *process management* is supported on top of product management (product–centered process management, see section 2.5), the data type module `ProdProcAdminDatabases` inherits from `ProdAdminDatabases`. Product management operations are redefined according to the execution semantics imposed by process management (e.g., a version component must not be deleted when the corresponding process is active). Furthermore, execution operations are introduced which realize transitions between process states (e.g. start, suspend, terminate).

`ProcManInterpreter` offers *execution operations* to the user (i.e. the project manager). So far, we assume that all execution operations have to be initiated by humans (project managers, who use the administration environment, and engineers, who may perform state transitions via the front end). Therefore, the interpreter does not automate execution of whole process nets. Rather, it executes a command, updates state information, and then waits for the next command. Note that `ProcManInterpreter` only uses a part of the interface provided by `ProdProcAdminDatabases` (namely those operations which are concerned with process execution).

Since *resource management* is defined on top of process management (the roles attached to team members refer to process types), `ProdProcAdminDatabases` is extended with resource management operations by defining a subtype `ProdProcResDatabases`.

`ResManEditor` offers commands for resource management to project managers (and again only accesses the relevant part of the interface provided by `ProdProcResData-bases`).

In analogy to the *inheritance hierarchy* rooted at `ProdAdminDatabases`, we would expect a similar inheritance hierarchy above `LogicalDocuments`. However, this is not supported by the current machinery, i.e. there is only one level of inheritance (no subtypes of `ProjectAdminDocuments`). In general, inheritance on the level of logical documents may involve extensions of the underlying grammar. The IPSEN machinery does not support grammar extensions. Therefore, the module `ProjectAdminDocuments` is based on the complete grammar for all administrative data.

Finally, the module `FrontEndView` realizes an external interface to the administration configuration database. This view is used by front ends to access administrative data (see below). Although only limited administrative functionality is offered through the front end (e.g. a developer may not modify a task net), the realization of this functionality requires access to the modules `ProdProcResAdminDatabases`, `ProdAdminComplex-Queries`, and `ProdAdminComplexModifications`. However, `FrontEndView` only imports a restricted subset of the large set of operations provided by these modules.

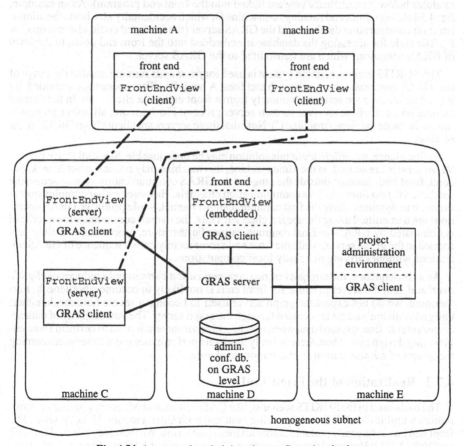

Fig. 4.54. Access to the administration configuration database

The database system *GRAS* is used to store and operate on administration configuration databases. (The logical part of) an administration configuration database is stored in a single graph which is accessed by multiple applications (front ends and project administration environments). As described in section 4.2, a graph server synchronizes accesses from multiple clients. To this end, GRAS provides a *communication system* which starts graph servers on appropriate machines in the network and transmits procedure calls from graph clients to servers. Since GRAS – like IPSEN in general – can only be used in a homogeneous subnet, its communication system has a limited range.

Fig. 4.54 illustrates how the communication systems of GRAS and SUKITS are combined to *access* the *administration configuration database*. Machines C, D, and E belong to the homogeneous subnet which is covered by the GRAS communication system. The SUKITS communication system is not responsible for database access within this subnet. The project administration environment (on machine E) contains the components which were shown in fig. 4.53 and accesses the administration configuration database via a client stub.

A *front end* which runs *within* the *homogeneous subnet* accesses the administration configuration database through the front end view, which is linked into the application (i.e. all modules below FrontEndView are linked into the front end program). As an example, fig. 4.54 shows a front end running on machine D, which accidentally also hosts the administration configuration database and the GRAS server (the front end could also run on C or E). The code for accessing the database is embedded into the front end down to the level of GRAS operations which are transmitted to the GRAS server.

The SUKITS communication system is used for *front ends* running *outside* the range of the *GRAS communication system* (machines A and B). The operations provided by FrontEndView are activated remotely from a front end via a client stub. In the current realization, each client receives its own server process. Furthermore, all server processes run on the same machine (machine C). Note that these servers are clients from GRAS' point of view.

At first glance, the *efficiency* of this solution may be questionable. Since all FrontEnd-View servers are started on the same machine, this machine may become a bottleneck. Second, front ends running outside the range of the GRAS communication system access the database via two inter–process communication channels. However, rather complex operations are transmitted along the first communication channel, while primitive GRAS operations are transmitted along the second channel. Thus, the overall communication overhead is dominated by GRAS–internal communication. Furthermore, processing is mainly performed in the graph server, while the front end server merely calls a sequence of GRAS operations without carrying out costly local computations.

As a consequence, the *interplay* of *two communication systems* only induces *negligible overhead*, and the server machine for front ends is not likely to become a bottleneck. Furthermore, we do not expect the graph server itself to become a severe bottleneck, either: Only administrative data is accessed through the graph server. The vast majority of data accesses refer to fine–grained data when a technical environment is used to perform some engineering design task. Thus, there are only moderate performance requirements concerning the access of administration configuration databases.

4.7.3 Realization of the Front End

The tools used in the SUKITS scenario, like CAD editors and NC programming systems, require a multitude of different operating systems, both Unix and non–Unix systems. The front end has to be easily portable across all these platforms. We therefore selected the *XVT toolkit* /6. XVT 93/ to build the user interface. The main part of XVT is a library of window–related procedures. They abstract from window systems specifics and allow creation and manipulation of windows and window contents in a portable way. An editor allows to interactively define window types and window components. A generator turns these definitions into C code, which has to be compiled and linked against the platform–specific XVT base library.

Portability does not come for free, however. XVT offers only a *limited subset* of the *functions* of the native window system. While it makes defining and using menus, buttons, scroll lists and text edit fields easy, support for graphic displays is only rudimentary. High level graphics packages with automated constraint–based layout algorithms, on the other hand, are bound to specific window systems and cannot be used on top of the XVT library. An integrated solution with the best of both worlds would have been useful for the front end.

The use of XVT or a similar toolkit mandates an architecture for the user interface subsystem that differs from the usual IPSEN approach. In a standard IPSEN environment, both the data storage and the user interface subsystem are at the bottom of the architecture, and tools are on the next layer up. They get connected by a small control module at the top which passes a list of allowed commands from the tools to the command module in the user interface subsystem and calls the corresponding tool when the user has selected a command. In the front end, the user interface is *event driven*. The user may keep an unlimited number of windows open at a time and may arbitrarily press keys or generate mouse events. Therefore, the user interface is at the top of the subsystem hierarchy, and the predefined main program loop is contained in the XVT library. When the user presses a key or clicks with the mouse onto a window element, when a window gets created or destroyed, or when a timer expires, this main loop calls a corresponding event handler. The event handler uses database calls to query or change the administration configuration and uses XVT procedures to change the display. The user interface handling thus gets scattered across a myriad of small code pieces. In addition to the generated code, the current front end consists of about 140 event handlers in as many files.

Below these event handlers, the module FrontEndView offers a limited view onto the administrative database. The operations exported here are targeted at the information needs of a technical developer and present the database in terms of agendas, tasks, tools, and working contexts with documents and annotations. Besides queries, possible operations include task state transitions, release management of documents, and creation of auxiliary documents. Operations to extend the schema or to define new configurations are not offered, as such commands are reserved for the project administration environment.

An important development goal for the front end has been to *make* the *implementation independent* both from the *database realization* and from the *product* and *process model* used. The module FrontEndView plays an important role for this independence. It shields the front end developer from the graph structure. Information about tasks, documents, versions, annotations and tools is presented in the form of object attributes. The front end does not see whether an attribute gets realized in the database as an attribute to a node or as a node of its own. Existence of a few attributes, e.g. name and type of documents, is required. The front end picks up all other attribute names and values from the database at runtime. Similarly, the front end gets informed whether the user may change the value of an attribute, and, in case of enumerated attribute types, which values are allowed. Neither are transitions between task states hardcoded. The front end queries the database before building a menu of allowed transitions which gets presented to the user. The front end just contains the user interface, the complex database operations which incorporate the product and process model are realized on the server side, below FrontEndView. Each scenario may therefore define additional task and document attributes, or use other task states and transitions, without the need to recompile the front end.

Besides decreasing programmer's effort in the front end and gaining flexibility, the definition of FrontEndView plays an important role for communication efficiency. By putting the cut between client and server exactly here in the architecture, *network traffic* is *minimized*. A typical operation at the FrontEndView interface translates into dozens of GRAS operations, so a cut on a lower level would mean a greater number of remote procedure calls per user command. Moving higher up into the user interface and transferring display elements across the network would increase the traffic as well.

4.7.4 Embedding Technical Environments

The front end itself only works on coarse grained administrative data. To modify document or annotation contents, external technical environments get called. To *start a technical environment*, the user just has to select a document version and click on the WORK_ON button. The front end then offers a list of those tools that are appropriate for the type of the selected document. The user gets shielded from the specifics of transferring the document into a session workspace and calling the environment with the necessary parameters. The front end presents to the user only a limited set of options for starting the tool. A selection between read–only and write access is usually all that is needed.

An environment specific *wrapper* realizes this abstraction. The wrapper first sets up a temporary session workspace to prevent unwanted interactions with other users. The document gets transferred from the global document storage into this private workspace. Then the environment gets started on the document copy. When the user quits the environment, and if the document has been modified, the changed version gets transferred back into the global storage. Finally, the temporary workspace is deleted. Fig. 4.55 shows the databases concerned and the calling and data transfer relations.

Some environments use a *set of related files* to store a document. In this case, the wrapper ensures (by packing the file set into a single archive before the file transfer, and by unpacking after a transfer) that the global database never contains inconsistent document components. Similarly, the wrapper calls a converter if an input document does not have the format which is required by the used technical environment.

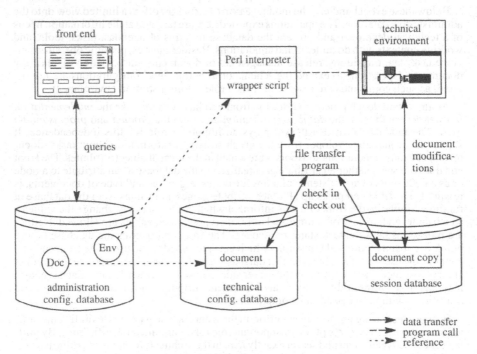

Fig. 4.55. Data transfer and program call relations

When calling a wrapper, the front end supplies an *access path* that refers to the document version. It gets this path from the administration database and passes it uninterpreted to the wrapper. This path contains the file transfer method used as well. The wrapper uses this information to call the right file transfer program. In this way, flexibility in the use of file transfer programs gets achieved. In the current implementation, local file copy and FTP are used.

The framework can be used as well for environments that store their documents not in files, but in a *database* of their own. The access path in this case contains a database specific path to the document. The environment has to meet several requirements in order to make this possible. As a session workspace cannot be set up by file copying, the database has to offer a programmatic interface that the wrapper can use to implement the check out and check in operations on the database, and to set the required locks to prevent modifications by other users. Furthermore, it must be possible to confine the running technical environment onto the part of the database that contains the checked out document version.

The wrappers have been implemented in *Perl* /6. WS 91/ for portability reasons. Interpreters for this language are available for a wide range of different platforms. Especially, file access and manipulation and start of external programs can be easily programmed in a way that runs unmodified on all platforms in our scenario, easier than writing them in C. For debugging purposes, the script can be run manually without a front end attached. By using wrappers, new environments can be added by writing a Perl script and extending the database. The front end itself remains unchanged.

4.7.5 Summary

We have described the *realization* of an *administration system* which is composed of a project administration environment and an extension for embedding technical environments. The project administration environment provides tools for managing products, processes, and resources in an integrated way, and it also includes parameterization tools for adapting management tools to a certain application domain. Technical environments are embedded via a front end which displays agendas, provides working contexts for task execution, offers commands for activating technical environments, and supplies these environments with technical documents.

In order to compare our approach to related work, let us refer to sections 2.5 and 3.5, where the main ideas underlying the project administration environment are described and compared. Furthermore, when realizing the project administration environment, we have used IPSEN components as described in the previous sections of this chapter. Embedding of technical environments has been realized in a rather straightforward manner with the help of scripts. According to the restrictions imposed by technical environments, integration has been performed on the coarse-grained level only (e.g. no fine-grained links between different documents).

There are still a lot of open problems to be solved by future work. Some of these concern the models for product, process, and resource management, as well as their parameterization. These problems have been discussed briefly at the end of section 2.5. Current work and future steps addressing these problems will be presented in section 5.1. Furthermore, integration on the fine-grained level (in contrast to coarse-grained integration of technical environments as supported by the current SUKITS prototype) has already been discussed partly in section 4.6. A major future challenge consists in achieving tight integration under the prerequisites of a posteriori integration.

4.8 Summary and Reuse

M.Nagl

The aim of this section is on one hand to *summarize* the main results of this chapter and on the other to make clear that developing an IPSEN instance is a *reuse* process.

Summarization is done by taking the *different outputs* of sections 4.1 – 4.7 as a scheme for structuring subsection 4.8.1: We summarize what we have learned for technical environments, the administration environment, and their major components. We also summarize how to integrate single environments by fine–grained tools on technical level. Furthermore, the environments have to be bound to form an overall environment for different developers working collaboratively. This is achieved by the so–called front ends. Integration tools on one side and front ends on the other form extensions on fine– and coarse–grained level, respectively, which are necessary to build up an integrated overall environment from specific environments, which support the activities of one developer in a specific role.

The reuse section one one side makes clear which different *forms of reuse* can be extracted from IPSEN's practical results. There is (1) pattern reuse if we regard the various forms of architectures for environments, their internal structure, the structure of basic components, integration tools, and front ends. Furthermore, there is (2) component reuse if IP-SEN–components of single environments or of the extensions are taken to build up another environment. Even more, the whole framework can be reused if the environment is IPSEN–like. Finally, there is (3) process reuse showing how to derive an environment or its specific components. A development process for an SDE is dramatically facilitated if we regard those parts for which the IPSEN meta environment gives substantial support.

4.8.1 Summary

Let us now go through the different products of the IPSEN project and summarize their main *realization* ideas and *design* decisions.

Single Environments

Technical Environments for elaborating a perspective of the requirements, the design for a subsystem, the program according to a module etc. have been discussed in section 4.1. There, the *overall architecture* was given in figure 4.1, and the corresponding design decisions were discussed in detail. The main characteristics are to distinguish internally between logical and representation documents to be stored in the graph storage, and the presentation realized with the help of a generalized input/output component. Parsers/Unparsers and the Cutoutmanager serve for coupling. The SessionDocumentManager administrates the session dependent part of the administrative knowledge and serves for actualization of all representations. Analogously, the CutoutManager controls the actualization of all presentations. ToolControl executes the commands selected by the user, Environmentcontrol manages the interaction between user and tools and serves for consistency of internal documents and their presentation. The dynamics of a single environment were discussed in detail (cf. fig. 4.2.).

Details of this architecture for a single environment were given: (1) Subsection 4.1.3 described how document visualization by a two–step mapping on one hand and modification of the representation by the user on the other hand are handled within an environment. In the case of a textual environment the mapping also exists in the other direction from representation to logical documents. (2) In subsection 4.1.4 it was described how commands are handled inside the SDE (see fig. 4.3). There, it was especially discussed how complex commands are handled by a generalized scheme of interaction between tool and user. The most important detail for the internal structure of technical environments, however, were given in section 4.3 dealing with (3) editor and analyzer functionality and in 4.5 discussing (4) the internal structure of execution tools. The corresponding refined architectural structures are discussed below.

The *administration* environment which serves for coordination functionality necessary to organize collaborative labour in a group (cf. section 2.5) is built along the same line of ideas as technical environments. Indeed it offers editor, analysis, and execution functionality at its user interface to structure, restructure, evaluate, and carry out the work of different developers. However, there are three *differences* in the architecture as compared to that of technical environments: Firstly, (1) complex operations and queries are built on top of the corresponding logical document (cf. fig. 4.53) and not inside this document. The reason is that these operations/queries are more complex than those needed for other software documents in textual or graphical form. Furthermore, (2) the administration configuration as underlying logical document is not only accessed by the administration environment but also by technical environments via restricted ops/queries through the front end. Finally, (3) there are possibilities to change the structure of the underlying administration configuration (e.g. for parameterization purposes) at project runtime which is not possible for technical environments.

Major Components of Single Environments and Their Architectural Details

The biggest component for single environments which is also used for integrated environments is the *nonstandard database system* GRAS developed to store, update, and retrieve all logical and representation documents as graphs. It was divided in section 4.2 into a *kernel* offering a general graph–orientated interface and enhancement layers. The kernel deals with updating/querying nodes, edges, attributes, indexes, and local sets. It is internally realized using a virtual record storage as common subsystem and advanced hashing techniques for mapping the record storage on pages/locations (cf. fig. 4.6). *Enhancements* (cf. fig. 4.9) deal with (1) event/trigger handling for binding action routines and their execution. Furthermore, (2) change management for user (undo/redo) and system recovery (transactions), deltas for versioning forward and backward are provided. Both are realized uniformly by logs of change ops on graphs. The third layer of enhancements (3) serves for a schema and attribute management. Internal graph schemes are used to check consistency of ops according to a schema. Attribute evaluation/reevaluation is necessary if and when attribute values are changed. Finally, (4) client/server distribution is provided. For IPSEN this means a coarse–grained distribution scheme where graphs are locked and distributed. GRAS may provide a pool of graph servers, each for handling a graph pool.

Another major component for a single environment is its core part dealing with how to structure a logical document, a representation document, and how to build the corresponding parsers and unparsers (cf. section 4.3). A *logical document* is internally represented as an inheritance hierarchy being composed of a general and a specific part (cf. fig. 4.23). The general part is built up from ASTGraph, handling the tree structure, ILGraph for identifier linkage, and ConceptualGraph for typing facilities. They are composed to CSGraph dealing with the context sensitive rules of a language. The latter is used to implement update and retrieval ops observing both the context free and the context sensitive rules of a certain language. The second branch of the inheritance hierarchy introduces the specifics of a certain language (for all above topics). The corresponding functionalities are "implemented" using the general and language–unspecific features. This, usually, means to assign specific to general language constructs. Some effort was necessary to adapt logical documents such that they can serve also for graphical tools. This was done by introducing a metamodel view (cf. figs. 4.24, 25). This is again achieved using general and specific functionality and by mapping the specific onto the general one.

The *representation document* is directly implemented on top of GRAS, i.e. there are no software layers in between. One representation document is introduced for all representations (cf. figs. 4.26, 27). Its schema part contains all appropriate structural properties of representations. However, a representation may be an arbitrary nesting of textual and graphical subrepresentations.

Unparsers are each built using a general corresponding unparser scheme (cf. fig. 4.28). Specific unparsers are instances, a corresponding table determining the mapping between logical increments and their textual and graphical increments, respectively. A master unparser is used for mixed textual/graphical representations, invoking the corresponding unparser for the corresponding subrepresentation. *Parsers* exist for good reasons only for text representations. They are multiple–entry parsers not building up the logical document but generating editor command sequences. The corresponding tables are generated from a suitable modification of the textual input grammar.

A further main component corresponds to *execution functionality* of a environment (cf. section 4.5). We chose to describe in this chapter the internal structure of the most complex execution and monitoring tool which was built in the IPSEN project, i.e. the RESI tools. Complexity is due to the execution model (e.g. concurrent execution), various forms of elaboration (e.g. symbolic vs. detailed execution), adding target hardware features, and including or excluding monitoring and statistics features. Execution tools of such complexity cannot be generated, as it was demonstrated for editor/analysis tools in section 4.3. So, reuse in this section means to introduce architectural patterns of how to do it right. The overall structure of the execution and simulation tool was presented (cf. fig. 4.39), as well as the architectures for components as global network interpreter (fig. 4.40), PSPEC interpreter (fig. 4.42), scheduler (fig. 4.43), and monitoring/statistics tool (fig. 4.44).

Further components of single environments have been mentioned above, when describing the overall architecture of a single environment in section 4.1. They could have been discussed here as well. They provide general and abstract UI functionality, command selection/tool execution functionality, and the corresponding coupling devices on two logical levels. They have been discussed above because they are a part of the framework, as they are also reusable even in the case that internal documents are not structured IPSEN–like, i.e. as graphs.

Fine– and Coarse–grained Integration

Integration is on *two levels*: For fine–grained integration on technical level integration tools have been developed. They form one part of the extensions of technical documents. Technical environments together with integration tools build up integrated environments. Thereby, "integrated" means to have close connection to other environments or to have integration within one environment serving for developers with different roles (cf. subsection 1.2.4). Integration tools can also be used to bridge the gap between the technical level (technical configuration) and management level (administration configuration, see section 5.1). Besides integration tools, front ends serve for coupling single or integrated environments to the administration configuration by using a restricted form of interface, the management functionality of which was delegated to a developer.

Integration tools (cf. section 4.6) have been classified according to their different forms and to their behavior (see subsection 1.6.3). Integration tools in IPSEN summarize different forms (e.g. transformers, consistency checkers, binders) and have different appearances (automatic, interactive, manual). All integration tools, however, work incrementally. There is an underlying reusable framework architecture (cf. fig. 4.45) for integration tools consisting of an integration document and the basic integrator component and the component XY-IntegrationTool which is partially reusable. Inside this latter component, further components for parameterization, priority handling and the trafo table are application independent, the contents of rules are application specific (cf. fig. 4.46). The integration document component is able to control detailed integration information as state information for rule applications, source and target patterns, rule application dependencies, and integration tool behavior (cf. figs. 4.49 and 50).

The second extension to a technical environment, namely the *front end*, serves for integration on management level. Not very much is to be discussed. Front ends have limited access to the administration functionality. This access is independent of the internal structure of the administration configuration and, therefore, especially from the underlying administrative database. This functionality corresponds to management functions delegated to developers. Front end views are realized as client interfaces at developer clients and as server interfaces (cf. fig. 4.54), both connected via machine–independent communication services abstracting from heterogeneous hardware. Front ends in clients also serve for checkout/checkin of technical documents which are not stored in the administration configuration but are under its control. Technical documents either are stored on the client machine or are transported to the client machine possibly using a converter program. This latter functionality is for a posteriori integration. In the case of a priori, i.e. in IPSEN, all documents are stored and accessed via one distributed database system (here GRAS). So, no converter functionality is necessary as all data components of the IPSEN system see graphs, either in unspecific forms, as `ASTGraph`, or in specific forms, as `ContextSensitiveGraph`.

Integrated Overall Environments

Technical environments, either single environments or integrated ones, are combined in order to build up an *integrated overall environment*. The administration environment is also a specific environment, namely for coordination. This overall environment was presented in figs. 1.31 and 4.4, respectively. Whereas in fig. 1.31 each specific environment has its own instance of a GRAS system, in fig.4.4 there is one distributed system (RGRAS) which is brought together on the level of a network file system. This short discussion makes clear that different overall architectures are possible depending on where different functionalities are located in a distributed system.

There is a more general discussion on where to have possible cuts within an overall environment, how to replicate components, how to concentrate components and, finally, how to reorganize an overall architecture such that it reflects its *distribution* on a net of distributed machines. We call the starting point of this procedure (containing no distribution details) a virtual architecture, the final result a concrete and physically distributed architecture. Steps towards a *methodology* for the process of deriving physical architecture have been elaborated and shall be presented in section 5.3.

How distribution was handled within RGRAS (see 4.2), in the current IPSEN prototype (see 4.1), and for SUKITS (see 4.7) was also discussed in this chapter.

4.8.2 Reuse Forms

As mentioned in the preface of this section, reuse is summarized under pattern reuse , product reuse, and process reuse. The discussion of the first two topics will be rather short as it only gives another perspective on the corresponding details having been explained in the first summary subsection. The topic process reuse is discussed in more detail, as it is also a summary of section 4.4, the contents of which have not been summarized yet.

Architecture Pattern Reuse

Pattern Reuse means to make advantage of conceptual patterns on architecture level. This is in the sense of "how to do" if the same or a similar situation has to be realized. So, these architectures are taken as patterns as they are or taken as patterns to be adapted before realizing an SDE, DE in another application domain, or any intelligent, integrated, and interactive application. Thus, pattern reuse means to apply *experience* previously proven in the field which, therefore, need not be gathered in a project.

These architectural patterns have been presented for *different purposes* and on different *levels* (cf. table 4.56 where the corresponding references to figures are given). There are patterns on *coarse* level, how to structure a technical environment, administration environment, fine–grained integration tools, altogether being large basic blocks of an overall environment. Furthermore, there are *detailed* patterns of these building blocks describing their internal structure. They give details on how to structure a technical environment, internal logical and representation documents, the unparser(s)/parser(s), execution and monitoring tools etc. In the same way details of the administration environment, of integrators, and of frontends are presented. Last but not least, the internal structure of the GRAS systems was explained.

All these patterns were given on the level of *architecture diagrams* and design decision explanations. A more detailed architectural specification(export and import details) would be valuable for someone willing to reuse the patterns. This, however, needs much more space than available here, therefore, it was not presented.

coarse architectural pattern of a technical environment: fig. 4.1   and its dynamics: figure 4.2 coarse architecture of fine–grained integration tools: figs. 4.5, 4.45 coarse architecture of an overall environment: fig. 4.4
structure of logical documents for textual representations: fig. 4.23 adaptation to graphical representation: figs. 4.24, 25 parser/unparser details: fig. 4.28 execution, monitoring tools and their internal structure, i.e. global net flow interpreter,   PSPEC interpreter, scheduler, monitoring tool: figs. 4.40, 4.42, 4.43, 4.44 integration tools' internal structure: fig. 4.46 administration environment's internal structure: fig. 4.53 frontend internal structure: fig. 4.54 GRAS system internal details: fig. 4.6 Layers on top of GRAS kernel:fig. 4.9

Table. 4.56. Summary of architecture patterns given in this chapter: coarse and detailed patterns

Product reuse

Product reuse is meant here as taking the *code* of a component, a group of components, or even a framework. So, reuse is not only on the level of "learning how to do" but "is not to be developed as it can be taken". So, product is not only a hint or the corresponding knowledge but a *realization* delivery from outside.

It need not be discussed that the development *process* is facilitated, looks different, or is even dramatically *reorganized* if not only a single product component but in the extreme case the whole IPSEN framework is reused in the product reuse sense (see discussion in section 1.1).

Large product reuse is only possible if an SDE, DE, or integrated, interactive system is *IPSEN–like*. Product reuse of single components, or groups of components is also possible if the architecture of the system does not follow the ideas presented in this chapter.

Table 4.57 summarizes the components, groups of components, and frameworks presented in this chapter which are *candidates* for *product reuse*. It also characterizes to which extent the product reuse of these building blocks is bound to have similarity with IPSEN architectural patterns. Trivially, product reuse is also restricted by the implementation language, dialect of the language, standard modules, etc. So, actual product reuse may be restrained by many trivial details which are not discussed here.

Tool execution components of fig. 4.1: requires distinction between logical, representation documents, presentation, and corresponding coupling

I/O part components of fig. 4.1: requires abstract I/O handling

GRAS systems and extensions of figs. 4.6, 4.9: requires graph–like internal documents

Fine–grained integration tools of fig. 4.45: requires separation and integration of graph–like documents, integration documents and the integrator framework

Administration environment, frontends of figs. 4.53, 4.54: nearly no requirements; however, there may be other ideas of an administration environment functionality

Logical documents, parsers, unparsers of figs. 4.23, 4.24, 4.28: requires the internal structure of a document to be IPSEN–like

Representation document of fig. 4.26: requires a representation to be built up by standard text and graphical subrepresentations

Framework of a technical environment of fig. 4.1: requires the environment to be IPSEN–like

Framework of an overall environment of fig. 4.4: requires the environment to be IPSEN–like

Administration system consisting of administration component, administration database, and frontends of figs. 4.53, 4.54: requires that models for processes, products, and resources are accepted

Table 4.57. Product reuse when building an SDE, DE: summary of possibilities, the explanation characterizes if and which similarity to IPSEN is necessary for reuse

Process Reuse

Process reuse can take place on different *levels* of *maturity*. Trivially, (1) using the knowledge of patterns of above avoids problems and corresponding development backtracking steps. Furthermore, (2) reusing products of IPSEN changes the process as those components need not be developed. Maybe they have to be changed, or the context in which they are reused has to be changed. The most advanced product reuse is to take all components of the framework for technical and overall environments. This was done in IPSEN's later prototypes. Then the development process is restricted to develop the specific components to be hooked into the framework. Finally, (3) there is process reuse in the sense of supporting or automating the development process, or steps of it.

We restrict our summary to the most advanced form of (2) namely reusing the framework, thus restricting the development process to the remaining specific components and discussing, according to (3), how to mechanize the remaining development process. In the terminology of chapter 1, therefore, the development of an IPSEN instance is a *reuse process*. Figure 4.58 summarizes this procedure. It can be applied to the development of a single technical environment, to an integrated technical environment, to the administration system, as well as to the development of an overall environment.

Mechanization is on *different levels* at the time of writing this book. Whereas building editor and analysis tools for technical environments is rather automated (see section 4.4 and the following discussion), building execution and monitoring tools (see section 4.5) is in the stage of providing knowledge on how to do it manually. Between both is the process for developing integration tools (see section 4.6) where this manual implementation process is guided by a gra gra spec which is written before. This is outlined by giving different refinements for the process of fig. 4.58.a in the other parts of the following figure.

So, in the rest of this subsection we concentrate on these *advanced* forms of reuse *processes* available up to now, namely building editor and analysis tools for technical environments (cf. fig. 4.58.b), and the integration tool subprocess (cf. fig. 4.58.c) and give a summary of these processes. Our current investigations on reuse improvement are given in chapter 5.

Let us start with the simpler development process of *developing* an *integration tool*, which is a subprocess of the development of an integrated technical environment. So, the framework of fig. 4.58.a is now restricted to the framework for integration tools containing the integration document, basic integrator etc. (see section 4.6). Iterations of the process are omitted. The spec process is two–level, in abstract form specifying triple rules and and in the next step specifying the concrete integrator (e.g. transformer, consistency checker, and binder). The corresponding code is derived manually from the specs by taking the spec as pattern.

The most advanced form of a reuse process is the *development* of an *editor* and *analysis tool* of technical environments, i.e. for a programming in the large environment. The process given in fig. 4.58.b is simplified (cf. section 4.4), as diverse skeletons are used, generation of the context–free part is made in two substeps (e.g. generating parser generator input from which, by the parser generator, the code of the parser is generated, see fig. 4.32), and the process is usually iterative (cf. fig. 4.35). Essentially, from an EBNF plus layout spec the code of the editor tool and a PROGRES spec is generated. This spec is then elaborated by the specifier to describe analysis tool behavior. Another generator then automatically derives the analyzer source code. The reader should notice that the process described only derives those source code building blocks which are not invariant. Invariant parts, also being on a rather detailed level, as e.g. the component of the right part of the inheritance hierarchy of fig. 4.23 are contained in the framework for a single environment and, thus, are not touched. So, only portions of the LogicalDocument of fig. 4.23, the XMetaViewDocument of fig. 4.24, the TextUnparser or GraphicUnparser of fig. 4.28, namely the corresponding unparser tables, are handled. The rest is contained in the framework source code. The reader should also note that the process of getting an environment is described likely different here in comparison to section 4.4, as compiling and linking source code is omitted in this summary section.

All the reused components either on specification or on source code level and all the tools to to be used, either specification tools or generators have been called the *IPSEN meta environment*. So, a meta environment can be rather poor for processes which are programming processes and where the specs are elaborated in paper and pencil mode and only experience is reused. It is rich if a process is well understood such that specific tools for the process have been developed.

a) framework reuse process

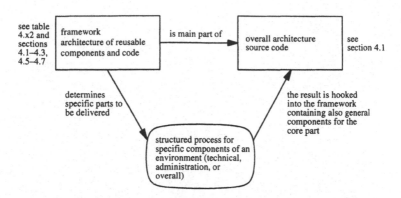

b) derivation of editor/analysis tools (simplified, for details see figs. 4.31, 32, processes are iterative, see fig. 4.35)

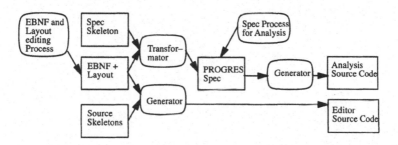

c) derivation of integrator tools (see section 4.6, the process given here is a subprocess of developing an integrated technical environment, iteration is omitted)

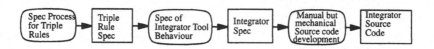

Fig. 4.58. Reuse processes and different forms of deriving specific components

5 Current and Future Work, Open Problems

This chapter describes the *current* work of the group in relation to IPSEN. Current work has produced some *intermediate results*. They are sketched rather than described in detail. The main purpose of this chapter, therefore, is to lay ground for the discussion of *open problems*, and *future steps* towards solving these open problems. In some cases there are rather elaborate plans, intermediate steps, and prototypes, in others only some vague ideas.

The *contents* of this chapter are four sections and a summary.

The first main section describes our current work/future plans w.r.t. improving *administration* for development processes such that such processes can be *parameterized* and *adapted* at development project runtime and from project to project. The aim is to improve administration tools such that they support the management of such processes, which is not achieved either by existing tools on the market or by research prototypes.

The next section 5.2 sketches our ideas to *structure* and restructure *large gra gra specs* by an extension of the PROGRES language and the corresponding tools. This is necessary for (a) laying the basis for future mechanical derivation of more complex tools than we are able to generate now and (b) for describing interaction of different environments.

The third section 5.3 describes our plans in direction of *distributed* overall development environments. Languages for expressing distributed architectures, corresponding tools, and resulting distributed architectures are our goals. Reengineering of existing systems and placement on a hardware platform by using available services are included in this task. As IPSEN also deals with a posteriori integration and a posteriori integration also appears in other projects, this section deals not only with distribution but also with *integration* of the environments.

A further section sketches two projects just started in the group, namely on a class *reuse environment* and a *writer* and *learner* environment. Both profit from the IPSEN knowledge on how to build environments. Furthermore, as both projects are distributed environments, existing and future results on distribution have to be applied. The use of multimedia is a new topic coming up in these two projects.

The concluding section *summarizes* the main ideas of this chapter but also makes clear that between different topics discussed here there exist some similarities and commonalities. Therefore, the summary also explains how the internal structure and coupling of environments is improved, how results are application–specific or can be adapted, and how distribution of IPSEN systems in the future is achieved.

Corresponding to the ideas and structure of this book, this chapter describes future *plans* on different *levels*: Firstly, (1) the behavior or *user* functionality of future tools is given (however only sketched, as no screendumps are available). For the *developer* of such future tools, our goals in direction of (2.a) specification of the core part of an integrated environment are presented (as in chapter 3) as well as (2.b) our future plans for extending the software engineering results (architecture, mechanization, generators, as in chapter 4), thereby concentrating on the distribution and integration aspects.

5.1   An Adaptable and Reactive Project Management Environment

P. Heimann, C.-A. Krapp, M. Nagl, B. Westfechtel

In subsections 1.1.4 to 1.1.6, we have introduced an *administration model* distinguishing between organization of processes, products, abstract and actual resources. It was also stressed in 1.1.6 and 1.4.1 that administration configurations are either dynamic at project runtime or static and definable before a project starts due to technologies available. In section 2.5, the functionality of an administration *environment* was described, supporting all these administration submodels and their mutual dependencies. It also integrates the activities of structuring/restructuring, analyzing, and executing a project. There, a product–centered approach was presented which interprets configuration descriptions as task nets. A formal *gra gra spec* for this environment was discussed in detail in section 3.5. The realization of this administration component as a distributed system was explained in section 4.7. This gives a starting point for this section.

We present here a *generalized workflow system* for the coordination of overall software development processes, again called administration system. It is generalized inasmuch as existing systems (1) do only regard certain aspects of coordination, as e.g. processes, but not the integration of all above submodels. Furthermore, as to be explained below, (2) existing systems do not handle the dynamic problems usually occurring in a development project, either not at all or not as needed. Even more, they (3) do not regard the integration between technical and administration processes and products or not in the desired degree. Finally, (4) they cannot be parameterized and configured to be useful in a certain context (lab or a company).

To all topics (1)–(4), the administration system discussed so far in the above mentioned sections has already demonstrated its use. Nevertheless, these results have to be improved as to be discussed in this section. What we need, in general, is an *adaptable* administration system where adaptability means to be able to change administration data, improve or exchange administration models due to knowledge coming up in a project or in a family of projects. The administration system has to be *reactive* such that project management can make use of that knowledge. There, we find immediate reactivity or long–term–reactivity (from project to project, or from a member of a family to the next). We also have adaptability in the sense of parameterization and configuration on one hand and adapting chosen models on the other.

The *contents* of this *section* are as follows: In subsection 5.1.1, we discuss the problems for which administration systems have to give an answer, make clear what adaptability and reactiveness means, and which dimensions of both are needed. The next subsection is devoted to discussing the current form of administration models and their integration, respectively. The following subsection introduces the different components of the future administration system and their interrelations. Up to this point, we describe ongoing work. The next subsection sketches future plans. We first generalize the administration and overall models by introducing layers, then we make a new step towards configuration and parameterization. Both latter topics are necessary for interproject coordination and collaboration between different companies, respectively. A summary and a list of open problems conclude this section.

5.1.1 Problems, Goals, and Comparison

In this *subsection*, we first give a list of problems occurring during development projects in practice. Then, we sketch the goal of an adaptable and reactive administration system to overcome these problems. Thereby, we make clear which different dimensions for adaptability exist. Finally, we briefly discuss existing approaches from literature to demonstrate that problems are not handled at all or not as required.

Dynamics of Development Processes

We start with a list of *problems* from *project organization* which come from the nature of development processes. Some of them have already been discussed in chapter 1 or 2, respectively. In this explanation, we concentrate on the administration configuration and, especially, on the part of coordinating development processes. We shall see later in this section that these problems occur also in other parts of an overall configuration.

The following problems from practice of development processes yield the *requirements* for a *future administration system* and the structure of complex development processes:

(1) *Structuring due to technical results*: The type and number of processes necessary to solve is, in general, due to technical results elaborated in the process itself. So, for example, after having finished the design of a subsystem, the number of implementation, test etc. processes can be determined as well as their mutual relations.

(2) *Using a schema for determination of structure*: In many cases it is possible to develop a schema, i.e. type information, saying how a complex process is structured in detail on administration level. For the subsystem development, the schema may determine types of processes and mutual relations. This is much more than knowing only which process types or which relation types are allowed to occur. For the problem (1), structuring may now be reduced to the determination of multiplicity of process objects, the types and relations of which are fixed in the schema. In other cases, more complex operations are necessary than determining only multiplicity.

(3) *Using given inline replacement patterns*: For some processes we may, only or in addition to (2), have schematic information on object pattern level. For example, for the implementation of a module body, there may be a fixed process pattern to be used (programming task, followed by a parallel white box test and a review task, concluded by a documentation task). Case (2) means to follow a type pattern, case (3) to insert an object pattern.

(4) *Selection and mutual insertion of schemata*: For processes, different alternatives for their internal structure may exist. For example, there may exist different schemata for a subsystem development, one of which is chosen at a certain time in the development process (e.g. using white or black box module test, incremental or big bang integration test etc.). As in the development of a subsystem the necessity for an inner subsystem may occur after its design, schemata are built up from subschemata at project runtime. It is no good solution to compose such subschemata in a flattened schema beforehand, as the composed structure is not readable because of combinatorial explosion.

(5) *Selection and mutual insertion of replacement patterns*: Accordingly, we may have different replacement patterns, one of which to choose in a certain situation. Again, a process in a pattern may be structured by another pattern. As above, to offer all inline combination of patterns is not reasonable due to combinatorial explosion.

(6) *Mutual use of manual and knowledge–based operations*: The use of type schemata to structure/restructure a process net yields processes for which object patterns may be used for their refinement, and vice versa. Furthermore, as not for all manipulations schematic information in the form of type schemata or object replacement patterns may be available or useful to apply, a manager should be able to reorganize a net freely

in problem situations. Thereby, we only obey structural information of low level, i.e. using processes of available types and relations of the available relations.

(7) *Changes due to administration information*: In the above discussion, it was technical information which gave the input how to proceed on administration level (the architecture of a subsystem) or schematic information on administration level (schemata, patterns chosen or inserted according to technical information) how to coordinate subsequent technical processes. On the other hand, administration information may also give rise to changes of the administration information (a new tool arrives, being capable of replacing a manual, possibly complex process; a tool is no longer available for supporting a process, another one gives different support; a new developer has to be assigned as an old one left the company). For these changes, also a schema or patterns may be available (e.g. a group organization model, or alternatives thereof).

The following three topics deal with upcoming *problems*, either on technical or administration level, rather than with information of both levels evolving at project runtime.

(8) *Backtracking by undo*: A problem was recognized, localized, and analyzed. It is due to the results of a process already finished (backtracking, feedback). The simplest situation is to trace a project history back to the point where the error was made, start again, and proceed differently.

(9) *Backtracking with reuse of subsequent results*: Undo (8) is not a practical solution, as one tries to reuse the results of subsequent processes after the point where the error was made. Some of the results may still be valid, some have to be changed as modification is cheaper than making a new development, others are thrown away as a new decision was followed.

(10) *Prereleasing and changing ongoing processes*: If a new or alternative design decision is made during a project, it is useful to ask all subsequent processes whether this decision is implementable or may give rise to problems (prereleasing). For that, not the elaborate result of a process is necessary, but only a sketch or an intermediate result. Conversely, if a problem report arrives when a former process is still active, this process should be able to consume this report, change existing results, and proceed differently. This yields another type of activation semantics on process nets.

The following two topics deal with *reuse* and their influence on process coordination.

(11) *Reuse of procedures/results and changing processes*: (a) Within a process, one may detect that a complicated process can be carried out as in an already finished process. Then, for organizing this process, it is not reasonable to build up the process net for coordination again and in the same way. Instead, it can make sense to reuse a big subnet of the old administration configuration to be inserted into the administration configuration of the new process. (b) Within a development process, there may be the decision to reuse a component or platform from outside. If the process has not started, its development is structured differently as if the corresponding components were developed in the project. If the development process has already started, we have a backtracking situation. Then, in addition, modification processes may be necessary to change already developed products such that the reused components may be incorporated. In any case, the process using components looks differently than the process in which such components are developed.

(12) *Structuring or restructuring reuse processes*: If, for a certain application, a framework or a standard platform exists, the specific components are identified, and methodologies or generators for them are available, we speak about a mechanical process or a reuse process. In chapter 1 (and below) the compiler example is discussed, chapter 4 gives details for a reuse process of IPSEN – like SDEs. Such a process is the result of similar projects, thereby developing application, structure, and project technologies. In any case, from project to project or within an ongoing project the process is reorganized to incorporate another reuse idea.

(13) *Transformation patterns for following alternatives*: A system may have been partly or fully realized and an alternative solution may have been chosen in the same project (backtracking) or from the old project to the new one. Then, there may be a clear idea of how to come from one solution to the next (for example replacement of a hardwired solution by a table–driven one, replacement of a self–developed component or platform by a standard one, replacing a mechanical but manually developed solution by the result of a generator etc.). In these cases, it is possible to develop complex transformation patterns supporting the reorganization of the corresponding administration configuration. This gives greater support than changing the administration configuration by the manager, even if solutions according to the above problems are used.

The last topics deal with the topic that *schematic information*, used to support structuring/restructuring of the administration configuration according to developing processes, backtracking situation, or reuse, may evolve within a project or from project to project.

(14) *Evolution of schematic process knowledge*: Type schemata according to (2), (4), (7), object patterns according to (3), (5), (7), example nets as in (11), transformation patterns of (13) all may be available before a project starts, possibly from the last project. Alternatively, they may evolve in the same project. For example, a new subsystem development schema including quality assurance processes is defined and may be used immediately in a project, a transformation pattern on administration level for product reuse was detected, is formalized, and immediately used.

(15) *Subproject and multi–project management*: If a project is structured into subprojects or different projects are combined to one big project, these projects are decoupled as much as possible and have to be integrated, as only their coordination delivers the complex result. Thereby, for example, backtracking situations occur across subproject borders (coupling). On the other hand, projects need not necessarily follow the same procedures (decoupling). So, for example, a specialized software house which might deliver a certain component is not able or willing to follow the same model for coordination. Also, schematic information according to (14) may have developed differently. Summing up, as having been occurred several times in this book, separation is needed (different subprojects or projects, different models) but also their integration (integration of administration and technical models). In the extreme case, selecting appropriate administration models and parameterizing them may take place at project runtime in a multi–project.

Nearly all of the examples for the above topics (1)–(15) have been chosen from the process part of an administration configuration. They could also have been chosen from the *product, abstract* resources, or *actual resources* part. So, for example, the configuration description also evolves at project runtime, it can also only partially be described by schematic information. Thus, and also as the above parts have mutual relations, the whole *administration configuration* is *evolving*. As was argued above, changes are often due to changes of the extended technical configuration. Therefore, the complete *overall* configuration is changing within a project and, if it is reused, from project to project.

As a dual aspect, we can state that all processes can only be partially structured and fixed before a project starts. This is immediately to be seen if we recall that technical processes are vague and chaotic and are in tight relation to administration processes, which also evolve at runtime producing changing results. So, a development process is an *interplay* of *loosely coupled processes*, where we do not know how their interaction exactly looks but where, nevertheless, mechanisms for their mutual influence have to be offered. The above examples only dealt with the coordination of such processes. So, in accordance to the philosophy of this book, we are looking for tool support without trying to restrict these processes.

Another remark may be in order: The above problems only dealt with *products*. Neither the process of how a manager is restructuring the administration configuration to be consistent with the technical development or how he makes a plan for it, nor the process of a person defining a schematic information was directly regarded. Again, our aim is to give help by *supporting* these *processes* by adequate tools such that they produce good results without restricting them. So, we call our approach *indirect* process support. In other projects at Aachen outside our group /7. PDJ 94/, direct support by inferring how a project was carried out, by defining methodological rules for handling processes etc. is regarded.

The Goal: Adaptability and Reactiveness of the Administration System

Before defining our goal, it is reasonable to look on our problems (1)–(15) and to give some *classification* for the underlying *mechanisms* or *models*:

(a) An administration model has to handle *object* information about processes, results, and resources as the organization of such items is our concern. We have to be able to say in which state a process is and how to reorganize it. On the other hand, as pointed out, *type information* in the form of subschemata gives valuable help for a manager or allows to build intelligent tools.

(b) After an administration model has (a) been *configured* and *parameterized* for a certain development project, it is (b) *changed* according to the knowledge coming up in the process or in a family of processes. Then it is (c) *used* in order to coordinate a certain project. In our case, this coordination determines how labor or developers are organized. On the other side, technical results enforce changes of the administration configuration.

(c) So, the necessity for changes, i.e. adaptation, arises not only for the administration configuration, but also for the schematic information used to manipulate the administration information. It is also necessary for configuring and parameterization if we have multi-project organizations in mind. So, *adaptation* in the above title has *four* different *semantics* to be explained below (see fig. 5.1).

(d) Adaptation may (a) be *short*-term, if the administration configuration is changed to describe the next planning step of organization. It may be (b) *middle*-term if a new type schema is created in a project to be used there or in the next project. Finally, it may be *long*-term if we (c) configure and parameterize an administration model to be used in a sequence of projects or a project family.

(e) *Support* by tools for involved people, i.e. the manager of a subproject, can be on *different levels*: There may be (a) simple operations following the parameterization information (which processes, relations are allowed) where the manager is manipulating the administration configuration by inserting processes, relations etc. Tools may (b) use the schematic information, e.g. a development type schema or a big object net, the rest is done by the manager himself. Finally, there may be (c) intelligent tools which infer management information from technical information and make a complex change to an administration configuration.

(f) *Schematic information* can be of *different kinds*: It can be (a) subschema information and (b) object insertion pattern information. It can be (c) predefined nested information (as a subschema where for all subprocesses corresponding object insertion patterns are defined), or a big net of the last project is used as 'how to do'. So, nesting or predefinition can be either on type, or on object level, or a mixture of both. It can also be (d) on transformation level (see the above example for organizing a reuse step) where a bigger portion of the administration configuration is altered.

(g) Due to the different kinds of information (cf. fig. 5.1 again) we shall see later that *different environments* will be necessary. These environments, however, are in *close relation* to each other.

Due to existing knowledge, due to evolving knowledge, and due to information coming up at project runtime, the administration system supporting all different aspects of coordination (configuring and parameterization, development of schematic information, project administration itself) has to be adapted. After being *adapted* the system is suitable for use (configuring, parameterization), offers improved functionality (use of schematic informa-

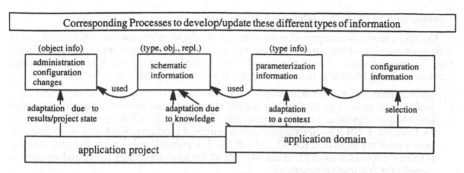

Fig. 5.1. Different levels of adaptation (sketch, to be detailed) in an administration system consisting of different environments

tion), or is able to coordinate a specific project (changing the administration configuration such that it is consistent with the state of a project). So, the administration system is *reactive* in the sense of being suitable, having better functionality, being able to react on project information (cf. fig. 5.2).

Adaptability for *improvement* and, therefore, improved *reactivity* is done *iteratively*: (a) the administration configuration is held in accordance to the current state of the project during its whole runtime, (b) schematic information can be developed and immediately used, (c) subprojects may demand a new parameterization. The subscription of fig. 5.2 indicates that this adaptation/reactivity improvement is a matter of the whole development process and, therefore, integrated overall environment. However, we shall concentrate on how to structure and improve coordination and the administration system in this section.

Definition and Use of Schematic Information

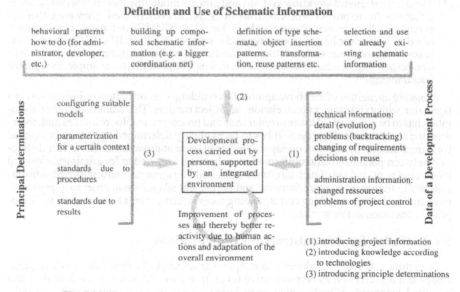

Fig. 5.2. Influences on a development process and reactivity of the integrated overall development environment

Comparison to Process Modelling Approaches

Existing approaches on project organization/coordination have some *deficiencies*. In the following we give a brief survey thereby trying to classify various approaches from literature. Neither the classes found nor the references cited are complete. It is also a personal view on existing literature, from the perspective of above problems (1)–(15).

(1) Most approaches neglect that processes, products, abstract, and actual resources *altogether* have to be *regarded* as they are different and separate *views* on administration knowledge. Version and configuration tools /3. Win 88, 3. WT 89/ or CAD frameworks /6. HNS 90, 1. SB 93/ only support organization of products. Workflow tools and process modelling tools /7. CKO 92, 3. FKN 94, 3. FuWo 96/ only regard the process side, resource allocation tools /3. BuJa 94/ aim at optimal schedules for actual resources, namely for fabrication processes.

(2) The *mutual relations* between these different submodels/perspectives as indicated in chapter 1 are not seen. So, the mutual influences, e.g. process model changes induce product model changes and vice versa, are not supported and, therefore, have to be obeyed by a project manager himself.

(3) Even if we concentrate on the process aspects, we find severe drawbacks. Approaches from process improvement, process certification etc. /7. Hum 89, 7. Bas 95/ mostly regard processes on a level of granularity such that workloads of single developers cannot be seen (*coarsest grain* as lifecycle models). Such approaches have their benefits, but they are not applicable to the coordination of developers.

(4) Most workflow systems /3. Bul 94, 3. Jab 95/ and process modelling tools /3. Huf 96, 3. GJ 96/ demand that process nets can be built up before a project starts. This is only useful if processes are well–understood, *invariant* over the time, and can be *statically composed*. It was often argued above that this is not the case for development processes. It may be the case for business administration processes or fabrication processes.

(5) The other extreme of workflow systems and process modelling tools is that *composition* structures due to project evolvement are *not explicitly* determined. They are either put in mutual calls of process object chunks /4. Fer 93, 4. HKB 92/ or dynamic manipulation of a data base according to process type schemata /4. DG 90, 4. BFG 93/. In both cases, composition of process administration structures is within the runtime data structure of a corresponding enactment machine. This makes it impossible, for example, to organize backtracking.

Summing up, neither of the above approaches builds up the complete administration configuration with its inherent mutual relations at project runtime. This administration configuration has to be an object structure in order to see all processes, results, resources and, therefore, the current state of a project. It has to be explicitly determined and has to be opened for reorganization by a project manager. Neither of these approaches makes a clear distinction between parameterization information, schematic knowledge for administration and its development, and use of such information for building up or restructuring an administration configuration. Even more, iterative and permanent adaptation in order to improve administration processes making corresponding tools reactive seems to be specific to the approach discussed in this section.

5.1.2 Models for Administration Configurations

In section 1.1.5, we introduced a conceptual framework for managing products, processes and resources on an administrative level. In section 2.5 and 3.5, we described and specified management tools which were based on preliminary administrative models. These models succeeded in several aspects and failed in others. In the following, we describe ongoing work on modeling administration configurations. We have *developed three submodels*:

(a) The *CoMa model* /6. SW 93, 6. GHM 93, 6. Wes 95a, 6. WEs 96/ supports version and configuration control for software documents. This submodel was already described in section 3.5.2.

(b) *DYNAMITE* /6. Joe 95, 6. HJK 95, 6. HJK 96/ replaces the process model as described in section 3.5.3. By combining CoMa and DYNAMITE, we obtain a clean separation between product and process model. Furthermore, DYNAMITE provides improved support for managing feedbacks, separation between control and data flow, and information hiding (a task has an interface which hides its realization).

(c) *RESMOD* /6. Krü 96, 6. Kra 97/ is used to model both resources required in a project and actual resources which exist independently from certain projects. The RESMOD model supports mapping of required onto actual resources, control of consistency and completeness of resource configurations, and uniform modeling of human and technical resources.

Process Model

The process model plays a central role for managing development activities. During planning, a model of all processes and their interactions forms the basis for identifying required resources and for estimating development times and costs. During enactment, it controls when tasks appear on the agenda of a developer and when tools are automatically started. Section 2.5.3 showed how such an agenda is presented to the developer, and section 4.7 described the technical framework for displaying agendas and starting external tools. This framework will be reused for the new model.

The product–centered process model presented in section 2.5 has severe limitations, however. To overcome these deficiencies, we have proposed the DYNAMITE model /6. HJK 96/, which is based on dynamic nets where each node represents a task instance. The *separation between products and processes* is an important difference between these two models.

In the product–centered model, there is a one–to–one correspondence between tasks and created documents. This is suitable for goal–oriented modeling, i.e. the model describes what to build, but not how this gets achieved. For activity–oriented modeling, where several subtasks that produce a single document shall be described, a richer model is needed. Tasks can e.g. review a document produced by a predecessor, without creating a document of their own. Furthermore, the separation allows for a task to produce several output documents. An implementation task, for example, may deliver both the source and the object code of a module. The following black box test task just gets the object code, not the source as input, therefore modeling both documents as a unit would be awkward.

Another drawback of the old model is the missing *abstraction*. In a complex task net, the user of a document does not care about the way it has been produced. A task should not be affected if the internals of a preceding task change. Therefore, we distinguish between the interface and the realization of a task, analogous to module interfaces and bodies in programming–in–the–large. The interface describes what to produce, it therefore includes definitions for input and output data. The realization describes how to achieve this goal (the process for solving the task). Realizations can be atomic, if we do not want to detail them further, or they can be refined by a subnet of tasks. Many different realizations can match an interface. They have to use the inputs defined at the interface, and produce the required outputs. The stepwise refinement results in a hierarchy of tasks. Enactment has to take this hierarchy into account and has to respect the abstraction.

Within a subnet, tasks are connected by several kinds of relations. *Control flow* relations determine the order of task execution. They create an acyclic graph. *Data flows* between tasks are used to pass documents along. A data flow can connect the output of a task interface to the input of another task interface within the same subnet, or it can connect the task interface to its realization. During enactment, a task may consume and produce sequential

512

versions of inputs and outputs. Tokens on the data flows track which versions have been passed.

As already explained in section 2.5.2, the process model has to cope with highly intertwined editing and enactment of task nets. Nets cannot be completely planned in advance, but evolve according to the contents of documents produced during execution. We use *feedback flows* to model error situations. These flows connect the task identifying a mistake to the task that has to correct the error. Feedbacks are therefore oriented oppositely to control flows. Usually, a data flow to send the error report to the receiving task accompanies a feedback.

As in the product–centered model of section 2.5, several connected tasks in a net can be active at the same time to support simultaneous engineering. The default state transition diagram and the transition conditions are similar and will therefore not be explained again. An important difference is the handling of error situations. If the target task of a feedback has been terminated, we model the reactivation by creating a *new task version*. Previous results can be reused in this situation. This way, the execution can be better monitored than if we would simply restart the task. Furthermore, we may decide to proceed differently from the first execution in order to correct the error and select another realization for the task without losing information about the realization that failed.

The evolution of task nets is controlled by a schema which defines domain–specific types of tasks and relations. A *generic model* defines a schema, operations on task nets and default conditions, which are then *adapted* to the specific application. Besides the adaptation beforehand, the specific model can be extended and adapted during execution.

We use the example "develop a simple software subsystem" to describe the process model. This task has a requirement specification as input, and produces a tested subsystem as output. To realize this task, we build a refining task net. At this point, we can select between *different realization types*: we can choose to test each module individually and finish with a big bang test, we may decide for a top down or a bottom up integration test strategy. Each variant would fulfill the conditions of the task interface, and users of the subsystem do not depend on the way it was built.

In our example, we select the bottom up strategy. Initially, the refining net contains only a design task and a subsystem regression test task (fig. 5.3). We know that there will be module implementation and test tasks, but their number is unknown at this moment, as it depends on the output of the design task. Once the coarse design has been *completed*, i.e. all modules and their export/import relations have been fixed (as seen in fig. 5.4), the task net gets *extended* according to the selected test strategy. For each module, an implementation and a test task are introduced, and they are connected by control flows so that a bottom up integration test results (fig. 5.5).

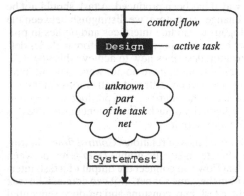

Fig. 5.3. Initial net

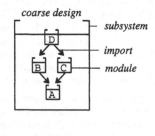

Fig. 5.4. Subsystem design

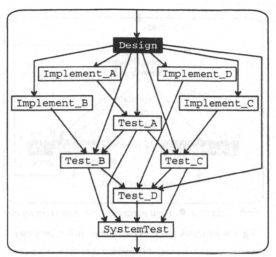

Fig. 5.5. Extended net according to design results

Control flows are refined by *data* flows: they describe which documents are passed between tasks. Implementation of a module may start after its export interface and the interfaces of all imported modules have been defined. The design task does not have to deliver all interface definitions at the same time. Some implementation tasks may therefore start before the design task has been completely finished. This is an example that tasks connected by control flows can be concurrently active. Before a task can be successfully finished, all preceding tasks must be terminated, and the specified output documents have to be produced. Furthermore, a task may consume different inputs as long as it is not completed.

Development does not always proceed smoothly as planned. During implementation of an importing module, an error can be identified in a module interface. The interface might miss a required procedure. In this case, we add a *feedback flow* from the implementation task to the (still active) design task (fig. 5.6). Along this feedback flow, a data flow propagates the error report. The design task uses this information to produce a corrected version of the interface definition. A *selective release* can be used: in a first step, the new definition gets released only to the implementation task for the changed module. After it has been checked and found to be implementable, other tasks may consume the new version as well. While forward control flows are added when building the net, feedback flows are only added when needed. Otherwise, a task net cluttered with all possible error situations would result, and hopefully only few of them are actually needed during enactment. The task net schema, however, contains all allowed feedback situations.

If the target task of a feedback flow is no longer active, the error situation is more severe. Fig. 5.7 shows the detection of an implementation error during the subsystem test. In this case, we want to give the project manager the chance to later trace what has happened. Sometimes, the person who executed the design task for the first time is no longer available, and someone else has to be assigned. We therefore create a *new version of the task* instead of reactivating the old one. The new task version gets copies of the inputs of the original task version, plus the new error information. All subsequent tasks are potentially affected by the new task version. If they have been finished before a new input version arrives, a new version of these tasks gets created as well. (In order to enhance legibility, inputs and outputs of old task versions have been omitted in fig. 5.7.)

An error detected during development may even affect the coarse design. If new modules are introduced, implementation and test tasks for them have to be added. The control flow

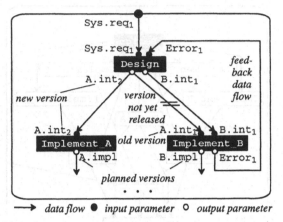

Fig. 5.6. Feedback and selective release (dataflow view)

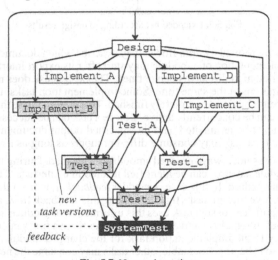

Fig. 5.7. New task versions

relations between existing tasks usually change, and some tasks may be abandoned because the modules they produce will be no longer needed. If even the realization type is changed, e.g. switching from a bottom up to a top down test strategy, a new version of the whole development task results. So, in general, a *feedback* may result in the fact that some existing results can be reused, others have to be modified, thrown away, or newly inserted.

The evolution of task nets is governed by an application specific *schema*. Fig. 5.8 shows a schema for the system development task nets described above. According to this schema, a correct net must contain exactly one Design and one SystemTest task instance and at least one Implement and one Test task each. The schema also defines names and document types for required and optional inputs and output ports of tasks, and it regulates the structure of control, feedback and dataflow relations. While a task of type Implement, for example, has to deliver a module Body to a Test task, all feedbacks and their accompanying data flows are optional.

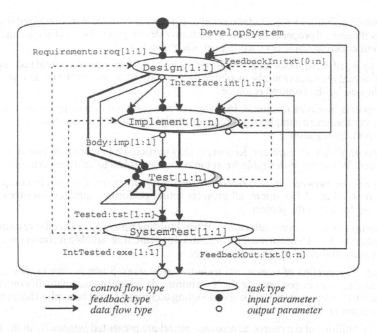

Fig. 5.8. Schema cutout for the DevelopSystem type

The DYNAMITE model has been formally specified by a graph rewriting system /6. Joe 95/. This PROGRES specification consists of a generic part and a *project specific extension*. In the simplest case, only the schema gets extended by new task and realization types, and the default operations and conditions are used. This is the case for the DevelopSubsystem example of above. If required, the enactment behavior can be adapted, as well. For example, new conditions for task state transitions can be defined. The degree of concurrency can thus be adapted to the application domain.

As we have seen, the DYNAMITE model offers support for many problems of dynamics. Task nets can be extended during enactment depending on the contents of documents produced. The schema can fix the tasks to insert beforehand, but their multiplicity must be determined at runtime. The interface–realization abstraction allows selection between several predefined alternatives. Error situations are modeled by feedbacks, and previous results can be reused and modified in this situation. The schema that controls the evolution can be extended at runtime as well: evolving process knowledge can result in new realization types.

Resource Model

Resource management is an important task within a company. Resources like computers, software licenses, and technical staff have to be distributed among all actual performed projects. Cost and time estimation, as well as the investment plan of a company are based on the resource management information. A resource management system deals with this kind of information and may give considerable support for this management task. The underlying data model has to fulfill the following requirements in order to be suitable in a development scenario:

(a) *Characterizing resources.* In order to deal with resources, they must be characterized and classified by some attributes as well as dependent resources which are needed when using the resource. This is highly company– and project–specific and must be defined by a user of the system.

516

(b) *Distinction between required resources and actual resources*. While required resources specify desired properties in order to perform a development task, actual resources represent concrete resources carrying certain properties.

(c) *Mapping of actual resources to required resources*. When a development task is carried out, actual resources must be available for a certain time, having the desired properties indicated by the required resource.

(d) *Support of complex resources*. In many cases, a resource is built up by several subresources forming a complex resource. The model for actual and required resources must support aggregation.

(e) *Support of shared resources*. Resources may participate in more than one complex resource. While this is desirable for some resources, it has to be avoided in other cases.

(f) *Distinction between project resources and company resources*. While company resources are available among all projects actual performed, project resources are reserved for a specific project.

(g) *Framework for resource allocation*. When building up a project specific resource configuration, a mechanism must be available for searching suitable resources within the company and checking their availability.

(h) *Uniform modeling of human and technical resources*. Since in many cases development tasks may be performed either by a human developer or automatically by a sophisticated development tool, the same modeling techniques must be applied for both kinds of resources.

The capabilities of the proposed *resource model* are presented *informally* in the following by means of a simple development project. A graph grammar specification for the resource model can be found in /6. Krü 96/.

```
resource type WS
      name : string;
      Mem  : integer;
      HD   : integer;
      OS   : OS2,ULTRIX,SunOS4,SunOS5;
end;
resource type SPARC isa WS          resource type    GCC
      OS   : SunOS4,SunOS5;               ver    : string;
      Kern : Sun4,Sun4c,Sun4m,Sun4u;      runs_on : SPARC, PC, ULTRIX;
end;                                end;


act resource SPARC#1 : SPARC-STATION     act resource GCC-SUNOS4 : GCC
      name := "Mahler";                   ver        := "gcc2.7.0";
      Mem  := 128;                        runs_on := SPARC;
      HD   := 1024;                       needs SPARC-STATION with
      OS   := SunOS4;                         OS = SunOS4;
      Kern := Sun4m;                      end;
end;
```

Fig. 5.9. Declarations of resource types and actual resources

In order to distribute all available resources within a company among several development projects, resources have to be *listed*, *characterized*, and *classified*. In the proposed resource model this can be done by a resource declaration. A resource declaration consists of a resource name and a set of user defined attributes, characterizing the resources (cf. fig 5.9). For instance, a workstation is characterized by a name, its main memory, the hard disk size, and the operating system running on the workstation. The gcc compiler runs under several platforms and has a version number. Kind and number of attributes are user defined and highly domain–, company– or even project–specific. Resource types can be classified by means of an object–oriented type hierarchy. A SPARCstation, for instance, is a special kind of workstation, characterized by a restricted range of operating systems and a further attribute containing the kernel architecture of the SPARCstation. Hence, a resource type is a named set of resources' attribute values. Besides the definition of resource properties, a resource manager has to define the number of available resources with different attribute values. In our example, the resource manager lists one SPARCstation and one gcc compiler. Of course, several incarnations of the compiler may exist.

Only rarely, a single resource is to be used. Often, *other resources* are necessary to make the single resource useful. For instance, the gcc compiler can only be used in connection with a SPARCstation running under Sun OS 4.x. For this reason, the resource declaration contains a field where such needed resources with required properties can be specified. As in most cases it does not matter which concrete resource will be used, only *conditions* are specified, which an actual resource must *satisfy* when using the resource. Internally within the management system, if a suitable resource is available, this resource is assigned to the resource which needs it. For instance, the SPARCstation Mahler may be assigned to the gcc compiler GCC-SUNOS4. Suitable resources may be sought and assigned automatically by the resource management system or manually by the manager.

The presented resource declarations show only the properties of resources. In many cases resources are *built* up *from subresources*. Fig. 5.10 shows the declaration of a work place for a designer. This complex resource consists of a programming–in–the–large (PiL) editor and the SPARCstation with name Mahler. The definition of a complex resource ensures that needed resources are only searched among all subresources. In this case, it is ensured that the PiL editor gets the SPARCstation with name Mahler as needed resource.

```
act resource DESIGN#1 : DESIGN          act resource PiL-Editor : PIL
      name := "Design-Mahler";               name := "pilv3.2"
contains                                 needs SPARC with
      SPARC#1;                                 OS = SunOS4;
      PiL-Editor;                        end;
end;
```

Fig. 5.10. Complex and needed resources

The declaration of all available actual resources is a prerequisite for planning and enacting a development project. When defining the activities of the software process, the project manager does not want to be bothered with technical details of resources, availability of technical staff, etc. Rather he wants to *specify* for each task the *resource properties* in a declarative way by defining the resource type and declaration of attribute conditions. In the case of an implementation task, for instance, a SPARCstation is required which runs under Sun OS 4.x and has a hard disk drive of size greater than 500 MB. The values of non–listed attributes are not important from the manager's point of view.

```
req resource                            req resource
REQ_SPARC1 : SPARC with                 REQ_IMPL : IMPL-PLACE with
      HD    > 500;                             supports = C++;
      OS    = SunOS4;                          containing REQ_SPARC1;
end;                                           containing REQ_EDITOR
                                                  using REQ_SPARC1;
                                               containing REQ_GCC
                                                  using REQ_SPARC1;
                                        end;
```

Fig. 5.11. Declarations of required resources

Not only the properties of resources can be specified, but also parts of the *desired resource structure*. For instance, for an implementation task the project manager requires a complex resource consisting of a SPARCstation, an editor, and a compiler running on the SPARCstation. The declaration of the required resource is shown in fig. 5.11. Since the editor and the compiler need a SPARCstation, as well, the using expression ensures that both tools run on the station REQ_SPARC1 which is part of the complex resource REQ_IMPL.

After finishing the declaration of all available resources within a company and the specification of required resources within a project, the management system must build up a project specific *resource configuration* which is consistent with respect to the desired properties and structure. To this end, for each required resource an actual resource may be either chosen randomly by the management system or manually by the project manager. The chosen actual resource is called allocated resource. In case the allocated resource needs some other resources (needs statement in the actual resource declaration), suitable resources are allocated, as well. If a complex resource is required in a project, such a complex actual resource satisfying the properties and structure is searched first among the actual resources. In case no such resource could be found, a project specific complex resource is built up by allocating its subresources. A resource configuration is consistent and complete, if for each required resource an actual resource with its needed resource could be allocated and if for all required subresources consistent and complete resources configurations could be allocated.

When we were speaking about resources, we do not only mean technical resources like machines or software. *Human* developers may be modeled, as well. Fig. 5.12 gives an example of the declaration of a *development team* which is built up in the same way as a complex resource. A development team has several properties and consists of different developers which in turn are defined as atomic actual resources.

```
resource type DEVELOPER                    resource type DEV-TEAM
        prog_lang : {C++,Mod2,Fortran};        expert_in : {DB, UI, COM};
        experience : integer;              end;
end;
                                           act resouce DB-Team : DEV-TEAM
act resource Peter : DEVELOPER                     expert_in : DB;
        prog_lang := Mod2;                         containing Peter;
        experience := 12;                          containing Klaus;
end;                                               containing Maria;
                                           end;
```

Fig. 5.12. Human resources

We presented a resource *model* which is suitable for *planning* and *enacting* a development project. By means of required resources, a manager can define the properties of resources needed in a project. Out of all specified resources, suitable ones can be found and their availability can be checked by the resource management system. The construction of project specific resource configurations from company resources is supported. Thus, a project manager can define arbitrary requirements without being bothered about technical and managerial details. The resource management system offers warnings in case of incomplete or inconsistent configurations.

Integration between Submodels

All submodels described above have been specified in PROGRES. However, *integration* of these models is currently being studied and has not been specified formally yet. Insofar, the material presented below represents ongoing work in a preliminary status.

Integration between *product* and *process model* is performed in the following way: Tasks communicate via data flows along which tokens are transmitted. Each token refers to an object. In order to keep the process model as general as possible, any object may be referenced by a token. When the DYNAMITE process model is integrated with the CoMa product model, tokens typically refer to versions of objects (in general, any entity declared in the product model can be passed along a data flow, including e.g. a version graph for a software document).

In order to *integrate* the *process* and *resource model*, we have to establish connections between resources and tasks. So far, the DYNAMITE model only takes inputs and outputs of tasks into account, but neglects the resources which are required to execute tasks.

Required resources are *assigned* to *tasks* rather than actual resources. In this way, we may abstract from the actual resources to be used and rather concentrate on their required properties. The mapping of a required resource onto an actual resource may be deferred until a task is executed. Furthermore, a different actual resource may be selected later without affecting the relationship between task and required resource.

We distinguish between *acting* and *assisting resources*. An acting resource is in charge of executing a task. It employs assisting resources in order to transform inputs into outputs. For example, an implementor is an acting resource which uses assisting resources such as an editor, a compiler or a debugger (or an integrated programming environment such as described in section 2.1) in order to implement a module interface. Note that if such an implementation task were refined by a task net, an assisting resource like this editor would "mutate" to an acting resource on the next lower level.

The DYNAMITE model distinguishes between an interface and a realization of a task. Accordingly, we distinguish between *resource assignments* to *task interfaces* and *realizations*. This results in the extended model shown in fig. 5.13.

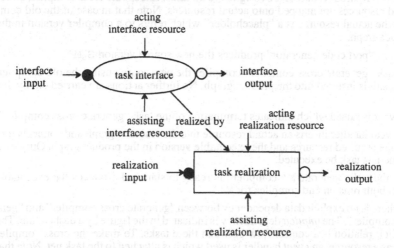

Fig. 5.13. Inputs, outputs, and resources of task interface and task realization

Inputs and *outputs* of an interface describe the functionality of a task from an outside perspective. Inputs and outputs of a realization describe what is actually needed and produced by the selected realization. A realization input may be obtained from the interface, but we also allow for additional inputs not specified in the interface. Conversely, a realization output is passed upwards to the interface. It is forbidden to pass realization outputs to other tasks because this would break abstraction (the receiving task would depend on the realization of the sending task).

Resources assigned to a realization are used to perform a task. Thus, an acting realization resource is in charge of performing state transitions such as Start, Suspend, Resume, Abort, and Commit. The realization must have been selected previously by an acting interface resource which has in turn been assigned in the task definition phase.

This *model* is *powerful* because it allows to express realization–dependent inputs, outputs, and resources. In particular, we can model both goal–oriented task assignment (the realization can be selected by the assigned acting resource) and procedure–oriented assignment (no acting interface resource, the assigned acting realization resource can merely execute a previously selected realization). The model introduces many degrees of freedom which can be resolved through default rules. For example, an acting interface resource might be assigned to the realization by default.

The integration between all submodels is illustrated by an example which describes *porting* of a *compiler* through *bootstrapping* (fig. 5.14, see also /6. NW 94/ and fig. 1.7). $S_S M$ denotes a compiler which translates from S to M and is itself written in S. First, the code generator is modified, resulting in a compiler $S_S M'$ (the source of a compiler which translates from S to a different machine M'). Then, a cross compiler $S_M M'$ is generated by compiling the source $S_S M'$ with the old compiler $S_M M$ (the executable on M which translates from S to M). Eventually, the cross compiler is used to generate the final compiler $S_{M'} M'$.

The *product graph* shows both source and executable versions of the compiler. The *resource* graph comprises both required and actual resources and mappings between them. In the *task* graph, we have not distinguished between interfaces and realizations since the distinction is not essential for this example.

In this example, a task generates an output which is used as a resource later on. The cross compiler *changes* its *role*. This is handled as follows:

(a) Initially, required resources are assigned to all tasks. Except the cross compiler, all required resources are mapped onto actual resources. Note that in case of the old compiler, the actual resource is a "placeholder" which refers to a compiler version in the product graph.

(b) The task "port code generator" produces the new source version $S_S M'$.

(c) The task "generate cross compiler" compiles the new source using the old compiler. The result is inserted into the product graph. No further actions are carried out by this task.

(d) An event is raised which indicates termination of the task "generate cross compiler".

(e) The event handler inserts an actual resource into the resource graph and connects it to both the required resource and the executable version in the product graph. Only then can the last task be executed.

(f) Now, the task "generate M' compiler" is ready to start and produces the executable which both runs on and compiles for M'.

Thus, there is no explicit data dependency between "generate cross compiler" and "generate M' compiler". The *implicit* dependency is indicated in the figure by a dashed line. The only explicit relation is a control flow between these tasks. To make the cross compiler available as a resource, an *event* handler is used which is attached to the task net. Note that a similar construction is required in the previous example (development of a subsystem) if we want to automate completion of the task net. Then, we need an event handler which is executed as soon as the coarse architecture is available.

5.1.3 The Administration System Consisting of Integrated Components

Based on the models presented in the last subsection, an *administration system* is currently under development which supports integrated and reactive management of products, processes, and resources. This system differs from the IPSEN environments described in chapter 2 inasmuch as it is based directly on programmed graph rewriting. We employ the PROGRES environment described in section 3.6 for developing specifications and generating prototypes. This approach has the advantage that there is a direct route from specification to implementation. On the other hand, abstraction is needed to shield end users from the complexities of large and complicated graphs and sophisticated graph rewrite rules. Therefore, user–friendly *views* and *tools* have to be offered by the administration system.

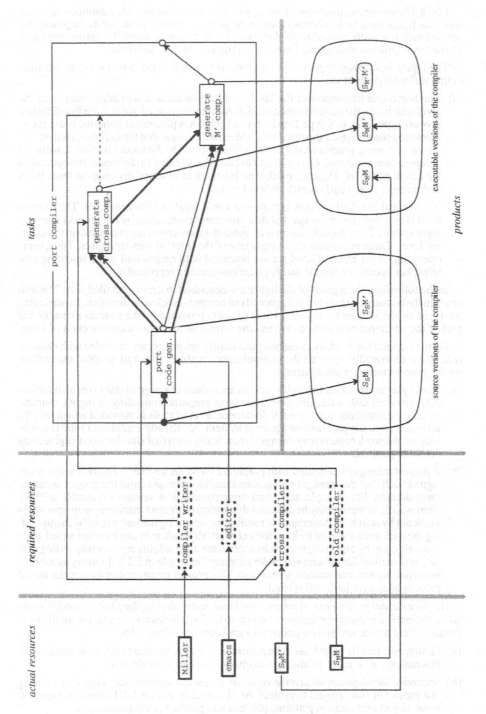

Fig. 5.14. Example for the integration between submodels

Fig. 5.15 provides an overview of our *approach* to *constructing* the *administration system*. The figure (and the text below) focuses on process management, but the approach described here is equally applied to product and resource management. Therefore, we speak of the term "process management system" in the rest of this subsection.

The figure describing the *process management system* is divided into four regions indicating different *parts* of the system:

(a) The horizontal line separates the level of administration model adaptation from the level which uses the administration model. Adaptation is used in the sense that different process types (e.g. task type `Implement`), object replacement patterns, reuse transformation patterns, etc., are introduced. (We shall later see that the definition is in accordance with some generic model to be defined first.) On the model use level, software processes are structured, changed, and executed according to the model introduced on the adaptation level. Thus, the model use level refers to actual instances of these types and patterns (e.g. `Implement Module A`).

(b) The vertical line distinguishes between *external level* and *internal level*. The internal level is concerned with the internal data structures maintained by the process management system. User–friendly views onto these data structures are presented on the external level. These views hide the complexity of the internal data structures. Thus, users operating on the external level are not bothered with graphs and graph rewriting systems, but operate on simple and application–specific representations.

In the following, the regions of the figure are described in a more detailed way. The tour starts in the bottom–right region and proceeds in counter–clockwise direction. In particular, we focus on the *support* for *different kinds of users* provided by the process management part of the administration system. We use the term *role* to denote a certain class of users.

On the *external use level*, users carrying out a software project are provided with customized and user–friendly views on the internal data structures (e.g. task graphs) maintained by the process management system:

(a) A user playing the *developer* role receives an *agenda* of assigned tasks (see also section 2.5). For each task, a detailed *work context* is prepared consisting of inputs, outputs, auxiliary documents, etc. For each document, a set of tools is provided which may be activated from the process management system. As already explained in the last subsection, the work context may change dynamically such that simultaneous engineering can be supported.

(b) A *project manager* is supplied with graphical *views on task nets*. The task nets are designed such that the manager recognizes familiar concepts from the project management domain. For example, tasks and their control flow relations resemble a PERT chart which, however, may be adjusted dynamically. Project managers may operate on a task net by activating commands for analyzing or editing the task net, or by manipulating the execution states of tasks in the net. Partially, task nets can be constructed automatically, e.g. by analyzing the product structure and building up a corresponding task net, as described for the subsystem development example in 5.1.2. In many situations, however, human intervention is required. The project manager can then make use of patterns that were built beforehand.

On the *external process model adaptation level*, users playing the *process modeler* role adapt the generic process management system to be discussed later to a specific application domain. Here again, we see two main tasks and corresponding roles:

(a) Firstly, one generic model has to be *parameterized* to a certain application context. To this end, types of tasks, relations, and attributes need to be defined.

(b) Secondly, *development* of diverse types of *schematic information* takes place during one project or from project to project. As sketched in section 5.1.1, there are type patterns, object replacement patterns, process and product reuse patterns etc.

523

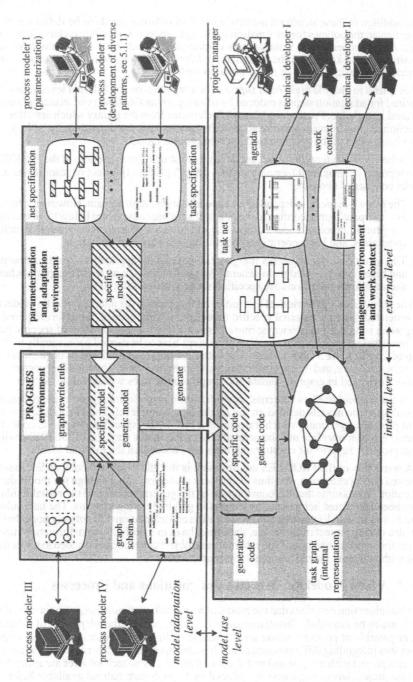

Fig. 5.15. An administration system based on programmed graph rewriting

In addition to these structural aspects, *execution behavior* needs to be defined as well. In particular, the policies for information exchange between work contexts have to be fixed (e.g., ACID properties vs. simultaneous engineering). Furthermore, conditions for state transitions (of tasks) have to be specified, and the reactions to events (e.g. suspension of a predecessor task) have to be determined, as well.

We intend to provide *high–level support* for adaptation on the external level. The effort required for adaptation steps is reduced by offering a *reusable library* of structural and behavioral knowledge. Process modelers pick elements from the library which are offered in selection menus. In this way, adaptation steps may be performed quite easily without intimate knowledge of the sophisticated internal process model.

On the *internal adaptation level*, models are constructed with the help of the PROGRES development environment (see also section 3.6). A process (product or resource as well) model consists of two parts:

(a) The *generic model* is independent of a specific application domain. However, it follows a certain paradigm according to the needs of a certain context (see below). For example, the generic process model defines the constituents of task nets, general structural constraints, and basic operations for editing, analysis, and execution.

(b) The *specific model* augments the generic model with application–specific structural and behavioral knowledge. In general, type definitions are added to the graph schema, and additional operations are specified using graph rewrite rules.

The arrow crossing the vertical line indicates that parts of the internal specific model can be generated from the external specific model. As a consequence, the effort required for adaptation is reduced in two ways: *reuse* of generic parts and *generation* of specific parts. We nevertheless expect that some adaptation steps have to be carried out manually with the help of the PROGRES environment. The better the library of model parts is, the less work has to be done here, and we expect this library to grow over time. The need for process modelers experienced in graph schemata and graph rewrite rules will therefore decrease.

On the *internal use level*, internal *administration configuration graphs* are maintained according to the models defined on the model adaptation level. The PROGRES environment provides a generator which transforms a PROGRES specification into C code. Furthermore, a user interface may be generated, as well. In this way, the PROGRES environment provides support for constructing the views needed on the external level.

A restriction of the PROGRES environment is that the generated code code cannot be changed during execution, and thus the process modelers cannot change the model during execution. We assume that the construction of the generic model and the reusable library have been completed beforehand by experts in graph rewriting systems. The next subsection, however, will discuss that parameterization and adaptation will not only occur before, but also during project runtime. We, therefore, have to modify the transformation mechanisms for C code generation. Type schemata and object patterns can be added to a specification without losing the old administration information.

5.1.4 A New Model for Overall Configurations and Processes

This subsection describes that the model of an *overall configuration*, introduced in chapter 1, has to be *extended*. This extension is necessary to describe adaptation of models to occur possibly at project runtime and to handle multi–project situations or development processes integrating different companies. It is also necessary to describe the difference between a project with a vague and undetermined process as no technologies are at hand, and a reuse project where vagueness is replaced by fixed determinations available before the project starts. The results presented are on the level of prestudies.

Layered Structure of the Overall Configuration

In section 5.1.2, we have described models for different parts of an administration config-uration and their integration. In the current section, a *layered administration model* and sub-sequently, overall configuration model, is introduced which is based on the previously de-scribed "flat" model (see fig. 1.4). As to be shown, all layers are structured in a uniform way. First, we introduce the structure of one layer. Then, we describe the full model, including the relations between different layers.

Fig. 5.16 displays the *generic structure* of one *layer*. Each layer is divided into four parts. The horizontal line separates products and processes, the vertical line distinguishes be-tween application of models and model definition/adaptation. We explain the structure of one layer by taking administration of projects as an example.

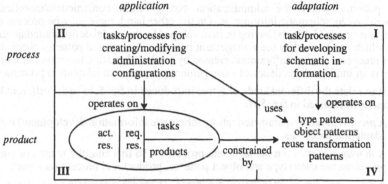

Fig. 5.16. Uniform layer structure

What we have discussed so far in subsection 5.1.2 corresponds to the *product* level of a layer. An administration configuration such as displayed in fig. 5.14 (bootstrapping of a compiler) is located in quadrant III. The corresponding schematic information belongs to quadrant IV. For example, a type pattern for task nets was given in fig. 5.8. Object patterns specify fixed replacement patterns which can be formalized by graph rewrite rules (see also subsection 5.1.1). The distinction between application and definition/adaptation on the product level has also been made in subsection 5.1.3 (horizontal line in fig. 5.15).

The notion of product is applied here on administration level and not on technical devel-opment level. All objects contained in administration configurations are seen as products, but also the diverse schematic information used (process patterns, product patterns of di-verse kinds, see 5.1.1). So, we have made a *generalization* of the term *product* as used up to now, as we also take schematic information of a layer into account, regarding them as products. They are used to produce products (here the administration configuration) in the sense the term was used above.

Furthermore, it is the *process* level which has not been considered explicitly so far. Pro-cesses create, analyze, modify, and execute configurations. The conceptual distinction be-tween process and product is essential. To understand this, let us consider the relation be-tween the *management process* (quadrant II) and task nets (in quadrant III). On a task net, operations of different types are executed (e.g., editing, analysis, or execution). It is the *trace* of these operations which constitutes the process.

This *trace* resembles more a transaction log of a database (i.e. traces as known from the database domain) than an execution trace of a program (i.e. traces as known from program-ming languages). The reason is that the structure of the task net changes dynamically, while a program structure is usually considered static. Thus, the trace does not only contain what would be called execution operations in the programming language domain. Rather, they contain other kinds of operations, as well (in particular, those operations which modify the structure of the task net). The reader should remember that structuring, modifying, and executing an administration configuration by a project manager is a *human task/process* which is only supported by corresponding tools. So, rather seldom a task net is available to precisely describe how this is done.

The distinction between the *adaptation process* and its product is more easy to understand. Here, the product consists of type and object patterns for different purposes; no execution is involved here. The process is composed of those operations which are used to create, analyze, and modify schematic information.

The arrows in fig. 5.16 denote *dependencies* between the different parts of a layer. Management and model adaptation processes *operate on* their respective products. Furthermore, schematic information is *used by* management processes, e.g. either by applying object patterns, where the administration configuration construction/modification is *constrained by* schematic information. On the other hand, there may be process patterns (elements or complete nets) having been developed by the model definition/adaptation process which can be used by the management process as behavioral patterns. Since management processes can use information created by model adaptation processes of both kinds, there is an implicit dependency of management processes on adaptation processes.

Let us relate the different kinds of actors introduced in fig. 5.15 to the different kinds of processes introduced in fig. 5.16:

(a) A *process modeler* (parameterization, schematic information development) carries out adaptation processes.

(b) A *manager* carries out management processes. To this end, the results of adaptation processes are used (type and object patterns, product and process patterns).

(c) A *developer* carries out technical processes. These are represented in a coarse–grained manner by tasks in the administration configuration located in quadrant III. In this way, the appropriate level of abstraction is provided to managers in order to coordinate/control technical processes. Technical developers change the execution state information of the administration configuration (take up a task, suspend a task, etc.).

There are a couple of further points to notice here:

(d) Usually, adaptation processes are carried out *before* a *project* starts. However, it may be necessary to modify schematic information *while* a project is being carried out. Thus, there need not be a hard borderline between management and its adaptation. To what degree dynamic schema modifications can be supported depends largely on 'technical issues' (e.g. support for schema modifications by the underlying database management system).

(e) On the management level, a process trace also comprises operations related to the execution of technical tasks (e.g., start or termination of the implementation of a module body). These operations are carried out by developers and not by managers. We may view this as *management functionality delegated* to developers.

(f) *Management processes* (and also corresponding model adaptation processes) are usually *implicit*. Planning, analysis, control, and modification are often highly intertwined. When designing dynamic task nets, it has been a major concern to support seamless integration of these different kinds of operation. Therefore, we can draw an analogy between management and technical processes, in particular those which are supported by an environment such as the IPSEN programming environment (section 2.1). However, if sufficient knowledge is available, we may also make these processes *explicit*. For example, process chunks are proposed in /4. Poh 95/ for those parts of (fine–grained) processes which are well–known and can therefore be coded into some sort of process model.

The *full model*, consisting of multiple layers, is displayed in fig. 5.17. So far, we have described *layer 1* of the full model. On the product level of layer 1, we have administration configurations which, as already argued earlier, represent an abstraction of *technical configurations*. These are located on *layer 0*, where technical developers operate on fine-grained technical configurations. For example, a programmer implements a module body. The corresponding technical processes are fine-grained, as well. Again, these processes are

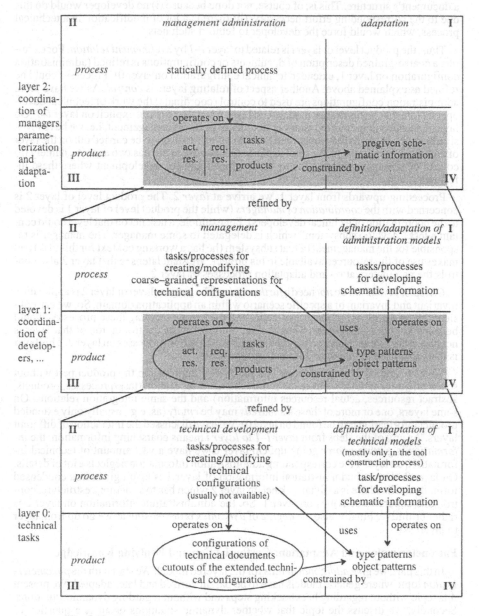

Fig. 5.17. The full process/product model for an overall development process

usually only implicit, i.e. the process of implementing a module's body is not given by a predefined net. Note that the product level of layer 0 contains "real" products, i.e. software documents such as requirements definitions, software architectures, or module bodies.

There is *no need* for further *refining layer 0*. In principle, we could determine and explicitly structure all technical processes down to the level of tool activation processes. In this case, a next layer would describe how corresponding tools would e.g. build up or maintain a document's structure. This is, of course, not done because (i) no developer would do this due to the corresponding effort necessary, (ii) there is a lot of modification in a technical process, which would force the developer to rebuild such nets.

Thus, the product level of layer i is related to layer $i-1$ by a *refinement relation*. For example, a coarse-grained description of documents or configurations is refined (administration configuration on layer 1, extended technical configuration on layer 0). Processes could be refined as explained above. Another aspect of relating layers is *control*. As we have seen, administration configurations are used to control (coordinate) the work of technical developers. Note that resources are modeled on layer i, but they are not explicit on layer $i-1$. On layer i, we have to introduce resources in order to perform management, i.e. we have to assign resources such as developers and tools on layer 1 to tasks to be carried out on the layer of technical development. We shall later see that control again has two aspects, namely (a) control of schematic information to be developed and (b) development where these information is used.

Proceeding upwards from layer 1, we arrive at *layer 2*. The product level of layer 2 is concerned with the *coordination* of *managers* (while the product level of layer 1 is devoted to the coordination of technical developers). For example, a task net on that level could contain a task "develop subsystem" which is delegated to some manager. The manager is responsible for the management of that subsystem (he has a working context for this task) and makes use of the resources available in his project. We shall later see that layer 2 also controls the parameterization and adaptation processes of layer 2.

On top of *layer 2* we do *not* need a *further layer*. The process level of layer 2 is application invariant and invariant of a specific scenario within an application domain. So, we can consider the process level of layer 2 as static, and the actor executing these processes would be some kind of "super user". Thus, further administration control on top of that layer is not necessary. We also have no parameterization/adaptation processes on layer 2. This layer is later also used to integrate different (sub)projects.

We have argued that on any layer i of our 3-layer approach in the product part without schematic information, we have the same scheme of separation (task/processes, products, abstract resources, actual resources information) and the same integration relations. On some layers, one or more of these 4 *subareas* may be *empty* (as, e.g., usually only extended product information is to be found on level 0). We have discussed the interaction of different layers. As any of the steps from *layer i-1 to layer i* means coarsening information, the *information* is *getting poorer* going up: On layer 0 we have a vast amount of technical information, on layer 1 the corresponding administration information neglects a lot of details. On layer 2, the total administration information of layer 1 is again given in a condensed form. Basically, there is a trivial task net on layer 2 which has to structure, restructure, control, and supervise activities on layer 1. So, the administration information on layer 2 is rather primitive. Finally, also the *degree* of *dynamics* is *decreasing* as we go up from layer to layer.

Parameterization and Adaptation: Customization and Evolving Knowledge

In this part, we give *additional details* for the layered model. We start with the *parameterization* topic where generic models have to be parameterized and later adapted. We present this topic without regarding backtracking steps and without regarding dynamic situations. Secondly, we discuss the topic that whether dynamic situations occur is a question of technology available. This gives rise to a short discussion on *reuse*. Finally, we regard the interaction of *subprojects* within a project and how this can be handled in the layered model.

When performing a project, the *generic models* of the administration model have to be *parameterized* and *adapted*. To this end, the administration subconfiguration in quadrant III of layer 2 is built up to coordinate the parameterization/adaptation process. Tasks for type schema development, task pattern definition, object pattern definition, as well as tasks for manipulating the administration subconfiguration in the product part of layer 1 are introduced. So layer 2 controls the parameterization/adaptation as well as the management process. Furthermore, supporting tools and human actors are assigned being responsible for the development of schematic information on layer 1 and, later on, for the manipulation of the administration subconfiguration.

During the execution of the parameterization/adaptation process on *administration level*, *schematic information* is *elaborated* in detail on layer 1. When this schematic information is available, it can be *used* to *manipulate* the subconfiguration in quadrant III of layer 1, i.e. development activities on the next level down are introduced, resources are assigned, product structures are determined, etc. Again, the task net in quadrant III of layer 1 may contain tasks to develop schematic information for layer 0. After defining the schematic information for layer 0 and having assigned resources, the development on fine–grained level can start.

The *technical developers* assigned on layer 1 or corresponding *method developers* can again develop *schematic information* for layer 0. These information may define which concepts, languages, methodologies, design patterns should be used by a technical developer. If the technology is available, there may be detailed process nets to be developed or even be predetermined (see below). Executing the tasks, which are managed on layer 1, then yields to the fine–grained extended technical configuration. We have argued in the last subsection that the overall process ends at that level.

We have seen that *schematic information* is developed on layer 1 and possibly on layer 0. Such information is also necessary on *layer 2* and, therefore, on any layer. There, however, it may be regarded as *predetermined* in the same way as the nets to be found there. At least we need information of the kind, which task types, configuration component types, roles, etc. can be used to structure the product information of layer 2.

The parameterization discussion we have given so far is a top–down approach. The process is carried out sequentially within and between layers. This, however, is not realistic. Often, the coarse–grained models are derived from the fine–grained ones. Technical knowledge is taken and used for their administration. So the *parameterization process* is at least partially *bottom–up* and *not* necessarily *sequential*. To give one example for a dynamic situation: Only when the first task of a certain kind is started (e.g. a design task) may we know which languages, methods, restrictions, etc. are to be used. So, parameterization can overlap with development.

On the other hand, *not every dynamic situation* can be *handled*. For example, it would be hard to change type schemas, if already corresponding objects and relations have been introduced. Such situations are not necessarily needed. Schematic information, however, can be extended. As we see from the discussion on reuse below, is is our aim to determine more details statically.

We are now discussing the *second topic* of this section. *Reuse* has been classified in chapter 1 as model reuse, process reuse, and product reuse. The discussion shows that reuse in any form depends on application and structure technology available for a system to be developed.

Model reuse corresponds to our parameterization/adaptation process. Model reuse means that we start a new system development taking the same models that have been introduced for a previous system development. This is very often the case: Any lab, any company division, any company, etc. has fixed proceedings for any domain class. If we have model reuse, we may have the same technical and administration concepts, languages, methods, tools, etc. as in other projects. Results of the parameterization/adaptation processes are taken as given. Therefore, we can omit the definitions for the parameterization model definition/adaptation processes. Thus, model reuse is that all task nets of the layered model start in states after model definition. Task nets shrink and the overall configuration gets smaller.

Reuse of *processes* takes place if we take an available process description e.g. for building up the administration information. In case the architecture of a software system is elaborated, for example, we can reuse the process description, which takes a software architecture and extends the task net. The process may describe that for each module an implementation and test task is inserted, control and data flows are derived from corresponding import relations. The responsible manager has just to follow the predefined steps in order to get a suitable task net, resource configuration, and product structure. The corresponding management task to build an administration configuration or to change it need not be coordinated on level 2. Again, the overall configuration gets smaller.

Dual to process reuse is *product reuse*. We may have product reuse, i.e. of a software component, being no longer interested in the process which has delivered this component. Another case is that we consider the organization of a technical process as a product of the administration process (e.g. bootstrapping a compiler, see fig. 5.14). Corresponding processes need not be carried out again. Therefore, task nets shrink again as the corresponding products are available. In the very extreme case, problem solving is just looking for and taking a given configuration.

The whole *reuse discussion* gets a *new interpretation* in the layered model. Reuse either on model, process, or product level means that we avoid performing processes by just taking the results of previous successful completions of processes (patterns of how to do are also process results). We take existing models, existing task nets, or existing products. We have argued that the information for structuring an overall configuration evolves at project runtime. Other structure information is clear before the project starts and, therefore, can be determined at the time of configuring the overall environment. The runtime dependency of an overall configuration is related to vagueness of processes. The more application and structure technology is at hand, the more runtime independent and statical the overall configuration is. In the bootstrapping example, we have an elaborated task and its organization for porting the compiler. In preceding projects, dynamic situations (evolvement, backtracking) have been eliminated. So, only two layers with rather static and rich information are responsible for what is happening at project runtime. If there are runtime dependencies left, they are reduced to that part which really can only be determined at runtime. With application and structure information at hand, we are able to structure technical processes, we are able to carry out processes by high level tools, etc.

As the *last topic* of this section, let us regard the question of *subprojects* and their interrelation (or, correspondingly, multi–projects). The aim of dividing a development project into subprojects is to reduce complexity by creating a clear problem to solve, and by assigning precise responsibilities and duties. So, an essential point is to have a logically separable task which has characterizations similar to what is known from subsystems or module characterizations. A subproject may be carried out using the same context (concepts, languages, methods, tools, etc.) or a different one.

On the other hand, the results of a subproject have to fit into the configuration of the enclosing subproject or using subprojects. Dynamic situations have to be handled across subproject borders. So, *integration* of *different subprojects* is an essential point. Separation and complexity reduction on one side facilitate integration as a logically independent task. On the other side, separation, loose coupling, and the freedom to proceed differently in subprojects may also cause severe problems for defining suitable languages and methods, for getting the right result.

If a project is divided into several subprojects, the relation between the project defining subprojects and the subproject itself has to be fixed by a *contract*. The contract is related to all layers of the model. There is usually technical information for the subproject (the input, determination of the results to be produced, determination of technical methods, languages, etc.). There is also management information (time/money restrictions, tools to use, etc.). There may also be parameterization information, the details being on layer 1, their administration on layer 2. As *all layers* are *involved* in a subproject, subproject handling is *orthogonal* to the layered model. There may be an arbitrary hierarchy of subprojects in one project. Subprojects may also be shared by different projects.

The determination of information may not be complete, therefore leaving some freedom for the subproject to proceed differently. In this case, the information on different layers within the subproject has to be *completed* in a way that the *contract* is *not violated*. The logical coupling is very much dependent on whether the same models are shared. Depending on this logical coupling, the result of a subproject can be more or less easily integrated into the overall configuration of the defining project.

Compared to the overall configuration model as introduced in chapter 1, we have made some *extensions* resulting in an even broader understanding of "product" of a development process. (1) Schematic information is regarded to be a part of the product. (2) Layers are explicitly introduced. The reader should note that any of these layers can deal with arbitrary hierarchical structures. So, on layer 0 there may be an architecture document containing arbitrarily many subsystems of subsystems. (3) A further layer and its product (coordination of management, parameterization, adaptation) has been taken into account. (4) In general, we must regard the model of fig. 5.17 not only for one project, but also for a project of different projects. So, the "product" structure has to take different products in the sense introduced up to now and has to combine them (see below). Finally, also (5) the processes are regarded as resulting not only in a product, but also in a *process/product* model. Conversely, if we neglect all the extensions listed here, we end up with overall configurations as used in the main part of this book if layers are forgotten.

Model Customization, Configuring, and Subsequent Adaptation

In this part, we further detail the discussion given above. We try to make clear which *parameters* for making models suitable are *found* and when these parameters are *fixed* (cf. fig. 5.18). At the left side of the vertical bar we have steps to build up our model, which is the base of the reactive administration system or, more generally, a reactive overall environment. At the right side, we have steps to parameterize and adapt the model to a certain project due to structural/procedural knowledge, general reuse, methodology, specific policies etc. We concentrate in the discussion again on the administration level. In general, all layers of our 3–layer approach have to be regarded.

(1) We start with the development of (a) *basic assumptions* about submodels of an administration domain model (in our case process, product, abstract and actual resources), (b) basic assumptions corresponding to their *integration*, (c) basic assumptions about the *relations* between different *layers* (dots on top of fig. 5.18), and (d) basic assumptions about relations between different *subprojects*. Thus, during step (1) modeling paradigms for the different subareas must be selected. For instance, for the process management area, a rule based modeling approach may be chosen.

(2) In the next step, we *determine* (e) the *detailed submodels* for administration (e.g. a detailed process model) and (f) their interrelation. Correspondingly, (g) integration corresponding to layers and (h) integration corresponding to subprojects now becomes more detailed and substantial. The result is what we call a *generic* model. The structure of the models have been determined, and operations are introduced which describe how the administration information can be modified. The generic model is not application specific, nor it is specific to a certain scenario of an application domain. Generic parameters serve as placeholders which are bound in subsequent steps. The generic model was the starting point for the discussion in the previous part.

Configuring suitable Models   **Parameterization and Adaptation**

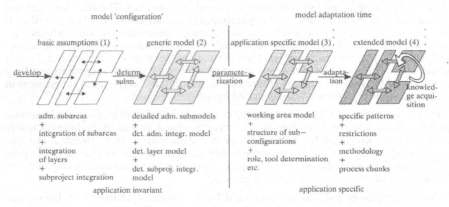

Fig. 5.18. Parameters of the layered model

(3) The following step is devoted to the process of getting a *specific model* for a concrete scenario in an application domain. This process was called parameterization above. We develop general models for an application domain, as e.g. software for business administration. These models may also reflect or may be derived from practices in a certain context (e.g. company). We end up with an application domain and context specific layered model. This was described as a project runtime process above, but in practice often takes place before the project starts. Application specific determinations fix the models we have left open on the technical and administration side. So what we do during this step is the definition of diverse *object* and *relation types*. These type definitions determine which combinations of task types, product types, and resource types are allowed.

(4) In the last step, we introduce *specific information* depending on *structure knowledge* of the application class of a system/its processes, reflecting local procedures/restrictions of a certain project into our layered model, or introducing transformation and reuse knowledge. This corresponds to the development of schematic information for different purposes in this section. In this case, we add fixed replacement *patterns* or *subconfigurations* on different layers of our model. For example, we can determine a fixed task/ process net for the bootstrapping example on layer 1. These patterns reflect certain specific procedures, assumptions, and/or restrictions. So, in this case we determine any knowledge we can get before a project starts. This knowledge is developed in preceding projects where the technology is invented. Therefore, step (4) corresponds to a bunch of projects being carried out in a specific application domain and handling systems of a certain structure class, and it is interleaved with carrying out projects. Introducing this specific object pattern information is again done according to our layered model. So, fixed nets are introduced by the administration, the corresponding processes being layer 0, fixed components to be used and their technical details are on layer 0, the corresponding administration information being inserted as resources on layer 1.

The steps on the left side of the vertical bar take place before runtime. Therefore, the corresponding processes are not explicitly modeled by a process model. The steps on the right side of the bar may take place at any time. Structural and methodical knowledge evolve permanently and should be added at any time. Schematic information can be extended dynamically and can be used immediately. Not only specific patterns are introduced permanently, but in case of introducing a new subproject, new types of object and relation are introduced, as well. Therefore the application specific model can be modified, in principle, also at project runtime.

5.1.5 Summary and Open Problems

Starting with administration problems of technical development processes, we have detected some nontrivial technical problems to be handled. It is the *dynamic* aspect which is our main research interest in the process modeling, control, and supervision business.

This lead to two main results described in this section: On one hand, we aim at developing an *administration system* which can handle diverse problems for different application domains in engineering disciplines. For adaptation in different semantics, we need two environments which are tightly coupled; one for coordinating/management itself, and one for parameterization and schematic information development. Tight coupling is also needed for the technical environments of developers.

The other result of this section is not restricted to the administration of development processes. In order to understand parameterization/adaptation, project runtime dependency or static definition of models, and multi–projects and integrated development processes, an *overall process* and *product* model has to be defined. It describes all the aspects mentioned above. The model is still in a preliminary form with respect to understanding, formalization, etc.

We are now going to describe the *state* of the *project*. We have studied coarse–grained integration on the administration level. Models, languages, and tools have been developed for configuration control, process and resource management. Dynamic situations arising from technical problems can be handled (evolution, feedback, backtracking). The models are adaptable to a specific development project by specifying a type schema and introducing type and object patterns. The models are formalized by various PROGRES specifications for which source code can be generated. We are currently on the way to develop a comprehensive framework for an integrated management environment. Graphical user interfaces for managers are provided and a communication infrastructure for different tools is being developed. So far, various parameters such as type schemata and object patterns are defined by extending a corresponding PROGRES specification.

There is a long list of *open problems* still to be studied. We concentrate on some of them in the following.

(a) The *integration between* the three *administrative submodels* has to be *formally* defined before it can be molded into tools. This integration has to take into account that we want to keep the *flexibility* to exchange one of the submodels at model configuration time (cf. fig. 5.18).

(b) Our system cannot strive for completeness. For example, there is a great number of concepts and tools in the literature for capacity control of actual resources, automatic scheduling of actual resources, etc., which we cannot include. The submodels and the system will therefore be *continuously extended* according to the needs of the current project, and the model must take this extension at runtime into account.

(c) The model currently concentrates itself on the formal communication between actors by exchange of product versions. Besides this, developers and managers often engage in *informal communication* like personal discussions, conferences, telephone calls, etc. in order to identify and solve problems, to evolve strategies, and to find decisions. As in these situations products are often discussed (e.g. a conference resolution is a formal document also subject to the product model), informal communication has to be tightly integrated both into the model and the tools.

(d) As described in 5.1.4, activities of managers for planning, analysis, control and modification are often intertwined, and *management processes* are implicit. Parts of these processes can be well–known in advance, however, so that a manager can be supported by predefined process chunks. We can regard tool actions as such chunks. The handling of certain error situations can e.g. be predefined: certain documents get locked, tasks suspended, new tasks for error identification and eradication created, error documentation documents produced, etc. The task model has to allow that a model for *fine–grained* processes or chunks can be plugged in here.

(e) Most of the *environments* sketched in fig. 5.15 still have to be built. While initial versions of the *administration tools* for technical developers already exist (as described in 4.7), tools that present task nets in a user–friendly way are as yet missing. Forcing a manager to work in the internal representation is not a long–term solution. For the typical situations a manager encounters, these new tools should include integrated commands that modify product, process and resource part consistently, e.g. creation of a new task with definition of inputs and outputs and assignment of a suitable resource.

(f) Similarly, an *environment for process modelers* has to be created that shields them from PROGRES details and allows for the adoption of the generic model to the application domain by selecting from common modeling variants. We are currently in the process of developing specialized easy to use formalisms and languages for these activities. As a prerequisite for building useful parameterization tools, the parameterization process itself has to be *formalized*.

(g) *Parameterization* takes place not only before, but also *during project runtime*. Extension of schemata and definition of new object patterns can e.g. occur as a consequence of an intermediate product contents or in order to react upon an error situation.

5.2 Specification in the Large for Graph Grammars

M. Nagl, A. Schürr, A. Winter

In chapter 3 we discussed conceptual *modelling* of *logical graphs* by writing graph grammar (PROGRES) specifications. The central idea of the approach sketched there was first to develop generic graph schemata and accompanying operations and then to instantiate schemata for a specific class of graphs without any need to instantiate generic graph rewrite rules (but additional language specific graph rewrite rules may be added). This was achieved by allowing generic graph rewrite rules to access meta level information at runtime, which is stored in the form of meta attributes in schema graphs. Any instantiation of a generic graph schema defines graph class specific values for these meta attributes.

At different stages of a specification development process the schema had to be extended with new information. This process started with pure syntax and extended the AST graph structure with identifier binding information, type information, and so on (cf. section 3.3). The main problem with this procedure for specifying logical graphs was that there was no support for *splitting specifications* into parts with clear mutual relations. For example, it would be desirable to keep (sub–)specifications of a document's abstract syntax, its identifier binding rules, etc. separate from each other and to state explicitly how these subspecifications interact via well–defined interfaces.

Moving from single logical graph processing tool specifications to integration tool specifications in section 3.4, we observe similar problems. Triple graph grammars (TGGs) were our means for specifying *integration tools* or better, for defining corresponding subgraph patterns of related logical graphs. Such a TGG specification regards coupled graphs as to be completely open, i.e. it has access to all details of involved graph structures. This is neither necessary for specifying integration tools nor desirable from the information hiding point of view. Again, concepts are missing which allow for the *definition* of graph grammar *specification interfaces*.

The two examples mentioned above may suffice to motivate our needs for a new graph grammar engineering approach, which supports the decomposition of complex specification into small pieces with well–defined interfaces between them. It is called *specification in the large* due to our expectation that it has the same benefits for writing graph grammar specifications as programming in the large has for developing software systems:

(1) Large specifications get a clear structure (understanding, correctness).
(2) They are open now for development by different specifiers (coordination).
(3) Maintenance of large specifications is improved (adaptability of specifications, planned process).
(4) Reuse of (parameterized) specification portions is possible (product reuse).

The following subsection 5.2.1 lists IPSEN tool specification problems in more detail, which have to solved by specification in the large concepts. Subsection 5.2.2, afterwards, explains how TGGs may be used for information hiding purposes by constructing updateable views. Subsection 5.2.3 reviews our experiences with using TGGs for (data) integration in comparison to other approaches, like broadcast message servers or event/trigger/action based mechanisms. Subsection 5.2.4 then explains our needs for developing a hierarchical graph data model together with hierarchical (meta) graph schemata and schema modifying graph rewrite rules. These ideas and their consequences for the PROGRES language and its implementation are summarized in subsection 5.2.5.

5.2.1 A List of Specification Problems

In the following subsection we sketch *specification problems* which should be solved by applying new concepts for specification in the large. All these problems were detected when building intelligent and integrated tools which are either presented in chapter 2, section 3.6, or in sections of this chapter. The problems are given here to outline their spectrum and to introduce what is discussed in this section. Investigated problems range from local (structuring a graph class) to global (integration) problems within an internal overall configuration, from specific (a certain configuration) to generic procedures (expressing commonalities) and their parameterization.

(1) Even one *logical* internal *document* is a rather *complex graph class*. It can be built up from a tree spec part (abstract syntax tree), consistency relations spec part (e.g. for context sensitive syntax relations) and in the case of an executable document, also from a part describing runtime behavior. Such spec parts may be using each other or inheriting from each other resulting in complex spec interrelation patterns. Whereas in AST graph handling (cf. section 3.3) such a pattern has to be composed from simple to more extended functionality, in other cases we saw the necessity to compose a complex structure from different hierarchies.

(2) In any case, general and reusable specification portions can and should be factored out (e.g. for general abstract syntax tree handling) and used for writing a specific specification. The advantage is that the spec writing process is simpler. *General* components are, usually, not suitable for all situations. So, they have to be *generic* to be parameterizable. The ideal case is that the whole spec for a logical document, being an arbitrary specification in the large structure, is generic and may be instantiated in order to derive a specific structure for a logical document.

(3) The problems (1) and (2) dealt with composing the internals of logical documents. For any kind of integration specifications, the integration tool need not and must not see all the internals of involved documents. So, we need a *view concept* hiding unimportant details and offering the information needed for the specific integration problem. The view has to be coupled with the underlying graph class it is derived from.

(4) For any logical document there may exist different representations (e.g. in graphical, tabular, or text form). Conversely, also for different logical documents there may exist one combined representation. So, a *corresponding view* of a logical document or of different logical documents for a certain *representation* has to be defined (e.g. the meta view for graphical representations) to prepare a logical document for interaction with a specific tool.

(5) Representations are also internally handled as graphs. Therefore, *logical* and *representation* documents have to be *coupled*, in order to describe the behavior of incremental unparsers and parsers. Applying the view concept, a specific unparser or parser needs only read or write access to views of the involved logical representation documents. So, parsing/unparsing is a specific integration situation.

(6) Within an overall configuration and, correspondingly, an internal overall configuration many integration problems occur. The first was called *horizontal integration*. This means, that different documents of one working area (e.g. requirements engineering, project organization) are seen as parts of one subconfiguration. Two forms of horizontal integration can be identified: Integrating different *perspectives* (as e.g. application process and data modelling within requirements engineering; process, product, and resources administration in project organization) or the integration between a *master* document (e.g. a design defining a subsystem) and its *dependent* document (e.g. the detailed design of that subsystem).

(7) *Vertical integration* is integration of documents belonging to different working areas and, therefore, to different subconfigurations (e.g. integration between requirements engineering and design). Although being quantitatively more complex the situation

is often *conceptually easier* to handle: In vertical integration usually master and dependent documents may be distinguished, such that document updates must be propagated in one direction only (from master to dependent documents).

(8) IPSEN environments mainly give product support by offering intelligent tools for the construction/change of a (sub)configuration, thereby guaranteeing structural integrity. The process itself is mostly left open and the developer or the group of developers may carry out quite different processes to deliver the same product (see chapter 1). In so–called process–centered environments the process itself is explicitly stored for analysis, evaluation, retracing, etc. purposes. Following such an approach means that within a product– and process–supporting environment *process* and *product* descriptions have to be *integrated* (cf. section 5.1). This is true for all parts of the overall process (a design process and its design spec) as well as for the whole development process (the overall process and the overall configuration).

(9) The administration configuration of an overall configuration contains coarse–grained descriptions of information contained in the extended technical configuration, but also of the processes, resources etc. in order to control and to support the cooperation of technical developers. This is only possible, if both *layers* (technical and administration layer) are *integrated*. The relation between both layers (cf. section 5.1) is on one side refinement (placeholder information on administration layer and detailed information on technical layer) but also control (administration configurations are used to coordinate technical developers). The suitable coupling of these layers guarantees that project administration is able to react on technical information thus reflecting or planning the current state of a project.

(10) Adaptation in 5.1 is also used for *incorporating administration knowledge* already available, developing from project to project, or evolving at project runtime (type schemata, object replacement patterns etc.). Furthermore, it was argued that the administration configuration has to be parameterized for a certain context. In gra gra terms this means that the *schema* of the administration configuration as well as *productions* and *transactions* change at project runtime. A 3–layer model was introduced in order to structure an overall configuration and to make clear, where configuring, parameterization, and adaptation of schematic information takes place.

(11) Moreover, for subproject interaction or multi–project coordination the interaction of layered overall configurations has to be regarded. It is not clear at this moment what this means in gra gra terms. Roughly, different *dynamic gra gras* have to interact such that *decoupling* is possible (different projects being carried out differently) but are *coupled* at the same time (e.g. for handling a backtracking step across subproject borders).

This is a vast *variety* of *specification problems* which are *non–trivial*. There is no hope of solving them in the next months or even years. However, without specification in the large, the solution is even more difficult to arrive at and the results cannot be reused, either as spec portions or as patterns of how spec portions interact.

In any case, how complicated a solution to problems (1)–(11) may be, abstracting from the details of such spec portions is necessary to understand the complete specification. We call such an abstraction from a specification portion a *specification module*. Clear relationships for coupling spec modules are necessary as well as clear build–plans of large specs, called *spec architectures* or spec *MiL patterns*.

From the above list of problems we mainly address (1) and (2) in subsection 5.2.2, (3), (4), and (5) in subsection 5.2.3, as well as (6) and (7) in subsection 5.2.4 . We shall see that quite different solutions are possible, having their specific advantages and disadvantages. From these examples we can derive different *coupling mechanisms* between specification modules. The discussion also gives rise to study *formalisms* for spec modules or graph class structuring mechanisms in the future.

5.2.2 Different Implementation Patterns for Logical Views

Chapter 3 discussed the specification of logical graph structures with PROGRES. It used a module interconnection language MIL as the running example. The resulting graph data type, which represents the logical structure of the given MIL language, was called *logical MIL document* or *MIL graph*. It offers graph access operations for all logical document processing tools like syntax–directed editors, analyzers, etc.. There were good reasons to require a 1:1 *correspondence* between the internal graph *structure* of logical (MIL) documents and their textual and/or graphical *representations*. Otherwise, it would have been very difficult to generate incrementally working parsers and unparsers (cf. section 4.3 and 4.4) and to guarantee end users a "what you see is what you manipulate" behavior of software engineering tools (presented in chapter 2).

This was our main motivation in section 3.3 for developing different underlying logical graph structures for textually and graphically represented MIL documents. Recall that we proposed different logical graph schemata and graph rewrite rules for textually and graphically represented MIL documents (cf. subsections 3.3.3 and 3.3.4). Unfortunately, the described situation in chapter 3 was simplified; it only took care of *one representation type of a logical document at a time*. This gave us the opportunity to model the logical graph corresponding to the representation that we had in mind.

For a language like MIL, it makes sense to switch back and forth between a *textual and a graphical representation* of the same document. As a consequence and in contradiction to the "a logical structure is similar to its representation structure" requirement, the pure logical state of a MIL document should be the same, regardless of the representation we are working with. One solution for dealing with these contradicting requirements is to define a *separate logical view* for *each* type of *representation*, thereby fulfilling the requirement of a 1:1 correspondence between logic and representation. It is then the task of additional mechanisms to keep these different logical views in a consistent state. This approach has the advantage that any representation dependent tool (like a syntax–directed editor or a browser) operates on logical graph structures which fulfil its specific needs.

In the following we will examine the variety of choices we have to model such a situation. We may either establish a *common logical base graph* and treat needed logical views as derived data or we may maintain each *logical view as a graph* in its own right, which is directly coupled to all related logical views. In the first case, we have still one graph which contains all data about a logical document. In the second case, the information which builds a logical document unit from a user's point of view is maintained as a set of graphs with partially "overlapping" contents.

In both cases, it is absolutely mandatory that all involved logical *graphs* (views) of a logical document and their *representations* remain *consistent* and up–to–date throughout time, regardless of which representation is used to select and manipulate the underlying (virtual) logical document. A manipulation through the textual view may affect the graphical view and vice versa. This means that we have to find a way to couple different logical graphs (view graphs and/or common base graphs) and to propagate changes between them. This problem is closely related to the well–known *view update problem* of the database community.

Starting with the state of the art of IPSEN tool implementations we have to recall that, mainly due to historical reasons, *abstract syntax graphs* (AST graphs) are our *common base* for all kinds of tools. This solution was well–suited for realizing syntax–directed text editors, but caused lots of problems during the development of graphical editors. This is due to the fact that the textual representation of a document and its abstract syntax tree structure are closely related to each other. The textual containment relationship corresponds to the AST subtree relationship and context–sensitive information is seldom expressed explicitly in the structure of textual representations, but inferred by binding applied identifier occurrences to declarations of the same name.

For *diagrammatic* representations (views) the AST model is *not appropriate* (and was discarded in favour of meta modelled graphs in section section 3.3). In most cases graphical representations do not offer fine–grained information, but are used to abstract from details of a textual representation. Furthermore, containment relationships (of nodes in subdiagrams) are less important and context–free as well as especially context–sensitive relationships are represented as edges between nodes. For example, the textual MIL language representation of section 3.3 models imports as lists of type and procedure names within the client module (the corresponding server is determined by name), whereas the diagrammatic representation introduces a single use–edge between the client and its server module.

Our solution for eliminating the mismatch between the AST graph model and the needs of diagrammatic representations was already explained in section 4.3. It is based on the construction of a *meta modelled view* on top of the AST modelled logical document (graph), which is closely related to the class of meta modelled logical graphs in section 3.3. This situation is summarized in fig. 5.19. Note that it omits the distinction between generic logical document implementations and their language specific instantiations, which is of no importance for the rest of this subsection. The language specific logical document is realized by instantiating an AST graph implementation. The meta view hides the AST graph structure behind a new class hierarchy for the meta model, thus making unparsing from a meta model consistent graph to its presentation possible in a rather straightforward way.

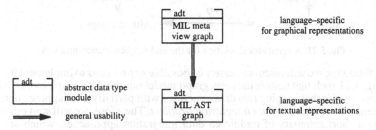

Fig. 5.19. Language specific MIL document architecture (revisited)

How do we have to *interpret* the *usability relationship* between the meta modelled graph view and the underlying AST graph in fig. 5.19? For clarification purposes, we have a closer look at a typical scenario of how MIL editors operate on MIL graphs. Assume that a graphical MIL editor modifies the underlying logical MIL instance graph (cf. fig. 5.20).

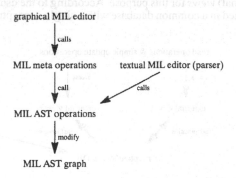

Fig. 5.20. Call/modify graph for MIL editors and their underlying data structures

In order to be able to reason about the *processing of command calls* in the graphical MIL editor, the architecture of fig. 5.19 has been replaced by the more fine–grained diagram of fig. 5.20, which distinguishes between operations offered at the interface of an abstract data type module and their underlying encapsulated data structures. This point of view will be more appropriate throughout the rest of this section, when we discuss various solutions for data (view) integration which violate more or less the principals of data abstraction.

Graphical editor commands of fig. 5.20 invoke corresponding operations of the MIL meta view realization. These operations are in turn mapped onto sequences of AST graph operations which, finally, perform the desired modification of the logical graph structure. Note that the transition from meta view operations to suitable AST operations is merely procedural. This means that a meta modelled MIL graph instance does not really exist, but is just a kind of *virtual view* onto the really existing MIL AST graph. The selected solution has as main disadvantage that we are forced to create AST graph instantiations even for those document classes which possess diagrammatic representations only.

In general, it would be much more appropriate if both MIL meta operations and MIL AST graph operations would manipulate their *own graph instances*, such that meta modelled graphs and AST modelled graphs can be used independently from each other. But in that case, an additional *coupling mechanism* must be provided which keeps related meta modelled and AST modelled graphs consistent to each other (as depicted in fig. 5.21).

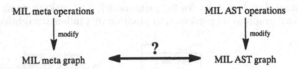

Fig. 5.21. A symmetrical solution for the multi representation problem

In the following we will discuss a *variety* of possible *approaches* to implement the situation of fig. 5.21 such that neither the meta graph model nor the AST graph model is dominant. Please notice that keeping two data structures with partially overlapping contents in a consistent state is a kind of *data integration problem*. Therefore, we will start our discussion with a short summary of traditional data integration approaches, which are well-known in the software engineering or the database design communities.

Traditional Data Integration Approaches

Customizing data stored within a database towards the specific needs of different clients is one of the main database design and implementation problems. It is state–of–the–art to use (external) *views* for this purpose. According to the usual database architecture, all data are collected in a common database with a single conceptual database schema defining its structure.

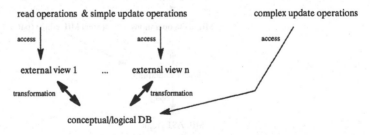

Fig. 5.22. Excerpt from a database architecture

Fig. 5.22 depicts how external views on the conceptual database are used. *External views emulate* the existence of user *specific databases*. In the simplest case, these views merely hide certain details (substructures, relations) of the underlying common database. More complex restructuring operations are supported by views which are defined as the result of (complex) database queries. In the later case, it is a major problem to keep defined views in a consistent state with their underlying database (without continuously recomputing them) and, especially, to translate view updates into corresponding changes of the underlying database.

Usually, *complex* database *updates* have to be performed on the *conceptual database* itself. This clearly does not satisfy our needs. Tools working on our graph views must be able to perform complex graph modifications without accessing other views or a common underlying graph base. In general, database technology is at the moment not able to provide us with sufficiently powerful view update mechanisms. It is subject of ongoing database research to develop incrementally working algorithms which propagate view updates to an underlying database and vice versa /5. AB 91, 5. Ber 92/.

Another standard solution for our data integration problem, advertised by the software engineering community and the closely related OO community, is sketched in fig. 5.23. Again, a single common data structure has to be designed which fulfils the needs of all its clients. The main difference between the solution of fig. 5.22 above and fig. 5.23 here is that the common data structure may not be accessed directly, but is encapsulated as an *abstract data type* with appropriate interface *operations*. The main drawback of this solution is again that we have to anticipate the *needs* of *all* eventually forthcoming client tools and to implement a single abstract data type which offers required resources simultaneously. Another drawback of this solution is a very broad and unstructured module interface of the common abstract data type. This problem may be eliminated by using a state of the art programming language like Modula-3 /7. Nel 91/. It allows for the definition of a separate (sub–)interface for each client on top of a shared data type implementation.

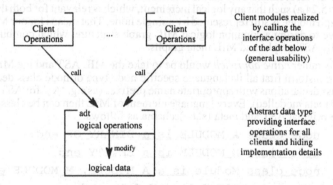

Fig. 5.23. A software engineering solution based on abstract data types

Merging AST Modelled Graphs and Meta Modelled Graphs

All revisited standard solutions for our data integration or multi representation problem are based on the idea of creating a common database, which contains all needed views as substructures. Therefore, we return to our starting point in section 3.3, where different graph structures were proposed for different (representation) purposes. Applying the proposed standard solution to such a scenario, we have to develop a *common graph model* which contains the AST model and the meta model as special cases.

Due to the existence of generic AST/meta graphs as well as language specific instantiations we have *two possibilities* of how to develop the common AST/meta graph model for a specific language like MIL. We may either (a) first instantiate the generic models to MIL specific graph models and then merge the resulting MIL graph models or (b) first merge the involved generic graph models and then instantiate the resulting generic model.

Following the second alternative and *merging generic graph models* (cf. fig. 5.24.b) seems to be infeasible. This is due to the combinatorial explosion of possibilities for how node classes of the meta graph schema may be related to node classes of the AST graph schema. In some cases it might, for instance, be advantageous to treat a logical increment as an ENTITY of the meta model and as a BINARY_OP of the AST model, in other cases it might be more appropriate to treat an ENTITY of the meta model as a LIST_OP of the AST model.

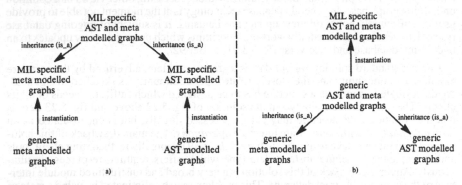

Fig. 5.24. Merging language specific graph models

So, there remains only the other alternative to *merge language specific graph models* (cf. fig. 5.24.a) such that any logical increment, which is relevant for both the AST and the meta graph model, is still represented by a single node. That means for our MIL example that we have to design a common logical MIL graph structure, which combines all properties of MIL AST graphs and MIL meta graphs.

A rather *naive approach* would be to take the MIL AST and the MIL meta schema and to transform first all its language specific node type or node class declarations into node class declarations with appropriate name prefixes (as e.g. 'A_' for AST modelled and 'M_' for meta modelled). Every language element of MIL then can be classified with respect to the original AST and meta (sub–)schema as follows:

```
node class A_MODULE is a BINARY_OP end;

node class M_MODULE is a ENTITY end;

node class Module is a A_MODULE, M_MODULE end;

node type ADOModule : Module end;

    ...

node class A_APPL_MOD_ID is a APPL_ID end;

node class M_USE_REL is a RELSHIP end;

node class IMPORT_ID is a A_APPL_MOD_ID, M_USE_REL end;

node type GeneralUseId : IMPORT_ID end;
```

Fig. 5.25 shows a possible *instance graph* corresponding to the new *"mixed"* logical MIL *graph schema*, where nodes with AST and meta model superclasses have bold borders. This figure shows once again the differences between AST and meta modelled graphs. The meta graph model for coarser–grained diagram representations uses a single node (with number 14) together with a pair of from and to edges for representing import relationships between modules (nodes 7 and 21). The AST graph model for more fine–grained text representations treats the same import of a server module into a client module as an applied identifier occurrence, which is part of the client module's import list via a context–free

elemedge and which is connected to the server module's identifier via a context–sensitive
ApplToDecl edge.

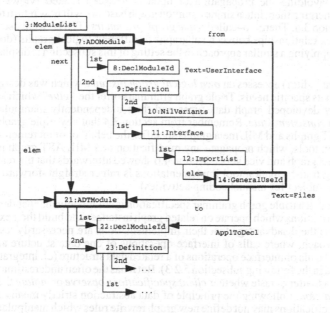

Fig. 5.25. A combined AST and meta modelled MIL instance graph

Having defined a common graph schema which allows MIL graph instances to be seen
as AST and meta modelled graphs at the same time solves only the first (easy) part of our
problem. We have to develop a complete MIL graph specification which fulfils both the
needs of text–oriented and diagram–oriented MIL tools. The still missing second step is to
re–implement all MIL specific graph transformations which are associated with its AST
and meta model such that they are able to process instances of the combined graph data
model.

Such a re–implementation of MIL specific operations may not rely exclusively on already existing generic AST and meta model operations. They offer for instance no means
to manipulate nodes which have incident AST and meta model edges (like the node 14 in
fig. 5.25). As a consequence, *new generic* graph rewrite *rules* are *needed* which are somehow combinations of generic AST and meta graph rewrite rules. But constructing these missing *combined* graph rewrite rules leads again to the task of developing a combined generic
AST and meta graph model, which was already rejected as infeasible beforehand.

Furthermore, suppose we could present a general super logical document. How could we
solve the problem that *client views* operate on *different* levels of *granularity*? Recall the
import relationship which specifies the imported resource for text–oriented representations
and only adds a use–edge between modules for the diagrammatic representation. Even
with a general underlying logical document, the diagram–oriented tool has to provide some
information about fine–grained imports, even if it does not "know" about it, because potentially, some different client might need and try to access this information. To summarize,
although different views may abstract from different details, they all have to provide the
information which is needed by others.

Having seen the almost unsurpassable problems with the design of a common graph data
model which contains the original AST and meta models as subsets, we will now follow
a completely *different approach* to tackle the fundamental problem of fig. 5.21.

Coupling of AST and Meta Model Graph Instances

Instead of avoiding the propagation of updates between related (views of) graph instances by merging them into a single common graph base, we will now return to the techniques of section 3.4. There, so–called *triple graph grammars* (TGGs) were used to define rather complex relationships between subgraphs of different logical graphs (documents). The result of applying a similar approach in the setting of this subsection is displayed in fig. 5.26.

Every client (editor) accesses an *own logical graph instance* which was designed in accordance with its specific needs. Triple graph grammars offer the *"glue"* which keeps these independently developed graph data types and their independently manipulated graph instances in a *consistent state*. Remember from section 3.4 that any triple graph grammar over MIL AST graphs and MIL meta graphs specifies the behavior of incrementally acting transformation tools, which propagate any modification of a MIL AST graph into the related MIL meta graph and vice versa. Section 4.6 showed afterwards that the realization of corresponding transformation tool implementations is rather straight–forward (although still being the subject for manual coding activities).

Please note that a triple graph grammar specification is completely independent from the graph transformations which operate on related graph instances and build their export interfaces. This has the disadvantage that their implementations are necessarily less efficient than any approach, where calls of interface operations of one data structure are directly translated into calls of interface operations of a related data structure (cf. integration strategies discussed in the following subsection 5.2.3). But it has the often underestimated *advantage* that it is a matter of taste whether *client specifications observe* or *violate* the *principle of data abstraction*. Following the principle of data abstraction strictly means in our case that client specifications may not define new graph rewrite rules which manipulate their underlying graph structure directly. They have to build more complex graph transformations exclusively by constructing graph rewriting "programs" on top of exported operations of the underlying graph data type. As a consequence, we loose the main advantage of programmed graph rewriting systems, the possibility of visual programming with graph rewrite rules in favour of being able to encapsulate all design decisions of basic graph data models.

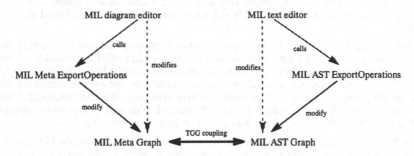

Fig. 5.26. Maintaining and coupling separate graph instances

Fig. 5.27 shows a *cutout* of a *triple graph grammar* specification which defines the logical correspondences between the client–specific MIL graph views. It associates the corresponding (sub–)graph patterns for AST– and meta–modelled function modules and import relationships. It reveals for instance that a single function module node of the meta modelled MIL graph (B1) corresponds to three nodes (A1, A1.1, and A1.2) and two edges (1st and 2nd) of the AST–modelled MIL graph. For further details concerning the notation of related subgraph patterns as related graph extending productions, the reader is referred to section 3.4. There, we suggested to introduce correspondences between graph schema components, too, and to use these additional relationships for consistency checking purposes. We have omitted explicit schema correspondences here. They would be defined in accordance with the pairs of AST and meta model node classes which were built in the previous subsection. Each pair of node classes was used there to determine the common superclasses of a single node class of the "merged" MIL graph schema.

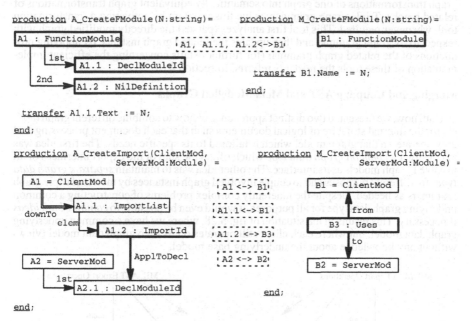

Fig. 5.27. Triple graph grammar schema correspondences and productions

How do we use the presented triple graph grammar to *keep related meta and AST graphs in a consistent state*? Let (and afterwards integrating)us regard the situation that a new import has been created with the text–oriented editor. In the underlying AST graph structure a new node `ModuleId` was added to the `Import-List` and connected via a `ApplTo-Decl` edge to the declaration of the corresponding module. We abstract from the details that the list of imports is realized by a linked list of possibly already existing imports. The coupling mechanism in fig. 5.27 may be interpreted as a translation of the AST graph transformation into a corresponding transformation on the diagram–oriented logical graph (cf. fig. 3.43 in section 3.4.4 for the discussion of different interpretations of TGG productions). The given production establishes the import relation by creating a new node of type `Uses` connected by two edges `from` and `to` to the importing and exporting module, respectively. Note that in the textual logical graph the import is modelled as a directed/asymmetric binding relationship from an applied identifier to its declaration, whereas in the graphical logical graph we have a bidirectional and symmetrical use relationship between two modules.

The situation gets more complex when, in the above sketched import situation, the textual client not only imports a module B, but also imports resources (type/procedure) of that module B. These fine–grained dependencies are not modelled in the diagram–oriented logical document. Therefore, provided that the diagram–oriented editor was first used to insert a import relation between two modules, the textual editor has to be used afterwards to add the *missing information about imported resources*. As long as this information is not available, a placeholder has to signal the incompleteness of the text–oriented AST graph.

In contrast to the above introduced idea of a common logical document graph, we have now the *other extreme* point of view. On one hand the idea of a private logical graph for each client supports its specific needs by offering a suitable logical document structure. Each client's logical graph structure can be developed independently from others. But this advantage is at expense of the *integration problem* of propagating graph updates, i.e. to translate graph transformations of one graph into semantically equivalent graph transformations of related graphs. Triple graph grammars solve this problem by activating a transformation tool, whenever required. This tool first analyzes (parses) the directly modified graph with respect to its graph grammar and then updates the related graph instance by applying productions of the related graph grammar (for further details concerning the efficient implementation of these tools the reader is referred to section 4.6).

Merging and Coupling AST and Meta Modelled Graphs

Until now, we presented two distinct approaches of how to combine different graph models for the internal structure of logical documents such that each document processing tool may operate on that graph model which is tailored to its specific needs. The first idea was to construct a *common graph data type* which offers the sum of the export interfaces of all involved graph models as its interface. The other idea was to maintain *separate graph data types* for different purposes and to couple involved graph instances by means of triple graph grammars as needed. Despite the inherently complex problems of constructing a common underlying graph data type for all purposes, it would even be possible to *combine both ideas* if necessary. This results in the situation of fig. 5.28, where we have a common underlying graph data model, but where each client still operates on its own graph data model (view) without any knowledge about the underlying base model.

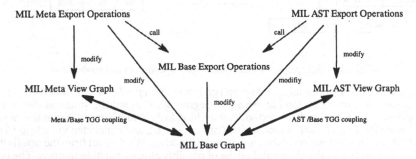

Fig. 5.28. Defining updateable views by means of triple graph grammars

The resulting framework of fig. 5.28 now contains various previously mentioned *data integration strategies as special cases*:

1) *Abstract data type layers*: all meta and AST graph operations are exclusively implemented by calling exported operations of a common abstract graph data type (the MIL base graph and its operations). Any abstract graph operation is, therefore, implemented by calling already existing concrete graph operations. These concrete graph operations modify in turn the actually existing MIL base graph instance. Separate meta and AST graph instances are not (yet) needed.

2) *Read only database views*: meta and AST graph modifying operations access directly a common underlying MIL base graph instance. Any update of the common base graph is then propagated to its related meta and AST graph instances (views) as defined by corresponding TGGs. These additionally maintained view graph instances may be used to realize meta or AST specific queries directly without any need to access the common base graph.

3) *Updateable database views*: All needed meta and AST graph operations are implemented exclusively on top of their own graph data models (views). Any update of one view via its interface operations is first propagated via the corresponding TGG to the common base graph and then via another TGG to the other view.

Let us *discuss* the *pros* and *cons* of the solution in fig. 5.28. Logical document *views* allow the client–specific modelling of behavior customized to tools and representations. Every client operates on an isolated graph and has the impression of total independence of other clients. It has direct access to all needed graph elements without danger of destroying overall consistency of a common graph database. The connection between all these client specific graphs is established by the common MIL base graph. It constitutes the representation and client independent logical data model of the regarded document class. Every logical client view is attached to the MIL base graph as an *updateable view*, i.e. we do not only have passive views which abstract from graph details, but we have a coupling that works in both directions. This allows for propagation of changes from a logical view to the logical base graph and back from the base graph to all its other associated logical graph views.

Direct access to the logical base graph is allowed by its interface operations and the explicitly revealed graph structure. *Consistency* of the logical base graph can be *guaranteed* as long as it is only changed by calling its interface operations or by propagating view updates through its associated triple graph grammars. Furthermore, the views are not coupled among each other which avoids distribution of client–specific information over several graphs. Consider also the situation that a *new client* with a very special logical view should be added. In that case it is only necessary to provide a bidirectional coupling via suitable triple graph grammar rules from logical base document to logical view. This coupling allows to propagate all changes from any view to the logical document and back to all coupled views.

It is still an unsolved problem and subject of current research, though, *how* such a *central* logical *graph* structure actually *looks like in the general case*. On one hand, its purpose is to hold the logical contents of a document without any needs to offer suitable services for representation–oriented clients, but, on the other hand, we need to specify a coupling from and to the views which gets more and more complicated if the coupled document views structure and represent the same data in very different ways.

5.2.3 Integration of different logical document specifications

During the discussion of IPSEN tools in chapter 2, their specification in chapter 3, and their implementation in chapter 4, we have seen the importance of *coupling or integrating logical documents* which belong to the same or different working areas. From a technical point of view it makes no difference whether we have to keep the internal logical graph structures of two different logical documents or two different logical graph structures of a single document in a consistent state. Therefore, it is possible to *apply* the discussed data *coupling* and *integration concepts* of the previous subsection to the problem of maintaining related logical documents in a consistent state. And indeed, the main coupling concept of the previous subsection, triple graph grammars, was first used (in section 3.4) to specify logical document integrating tools.

Therefore, it seems to be superfluous to have another subsection discussing the topic of integrating logical documents here. But the main purpose of this subsection is very different from the one of section 3.4, which had a main focus on explaining the new concept of triple graph grammars. As a consequence, we disregarded to a certain extent the discussion of *related data coupling concepts* and still open problems. We will see that a solution of these problems is again based on the definition of *logical graph views*, i.e. could not be presented beforehand.

As mentioned above, the graph coupling concepts presented in the previous subsection are also applicable to the integration of graphs representing different logical documents.

The main question is not which kinds of graphs have to be integrated, but rather *how tight the relationship* between those graphs is. The *tightness* of *coupling* and *integration* covers a wide *spectrum*. It ranges from a very tight coupling with an immediate bidirectional propagation of graph changes to loosely coupled graphs with a batch–like integration in only one direction. In the last subsection, we assumed a scenario, where logical graph views are very tightly coupled. It gave us the motivation to develop step by step the general and powerful view integration pattern of fig. 5.28. This pattern does not provide the only feasible solution for all kinds of data coupling and integration, especially when we integrate graphs from different logical documents. We will discuss in this subsection the suitability of our integration patterns and some alternative approaches for the solution of some concrete integration tool (data) integration problems, which were already sketched in section 2.1 through 2.3.

Recall the integration of documents within Requirements Engineering. SA document graphs and ER document graphs offer almost orthogonal perspectives on the same working area (horizontal integration, cf. section 2.2). But due to this fact, it is very difficult to specify correspondences between involved logical graphs. The only dependence between SA and ER graphs consists of edges which set applied occurrences of datastore or dataflow type identifiers in SA in relation to data (entity) type definitions in ER. In this situation it is not appropriate to establish a coupling with triple graph grammars between the graphs. Instead, both documents are merged together in a common RE graph (cf. fig. 5.29). The integration of SA with ER is an example, where it is not worthwhile to couple graph specifications and their graphs via TGGs. Rather we are aiming for a RE graph built as the aggregation of the SA and ER graph which remain more or less independent from each other. This specialized data integration approach will be discussed in more detail in the following subsection 5.2.4.

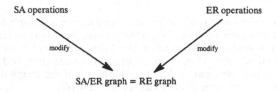

Fig. 5.29. Data integration in RE

Fig. 5.30 repeats the vertical integration of the RE and MIL document, a running example in sections 2.3 and 3.4. We have already presented a solution for this problem in detail. Triple graph grammars were defined in section 3.4 to specify the correspondences between RE and MIL graph schemata and graph instances. Note, that we have only one document for each working area, RE and MIL, comprising all necessary information. The functionality and the implementation of specified RE/MIL integration tools was discussed in section 2.3 and section 4.6, respectively. Note again that coupling with TGGs is based on parsing one of the coupled graphs, thereby extracting a sequence of productions the application of which would yield the actual graph. A sequence of productions, which is associated with the extracted sequence of productions, is then applied to the related graph instance. The main *advantage of coupling with triple graph grammars* is the bidirectional nature of the specified integration. That means that updates can be propagated in both directions for two given graphs. It is also possible to use TGGs for consistency checking purposes only.

The *main disadvantage* of TGGs is that the underlying graphs have to be parsed w.r.t. to TGG productions. In order to be able to realize an incremental and efficiently working parsing algorithm, TGG productions were restricted to be monotonous, i.e. their left–hand sides have to be subgraphs of their right–hand sides. Another drawback is that the schemata (structure) of the to be coupled graphs have to be revealed completely in order to be able to define appropriate graph grammar productions.

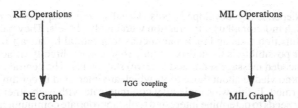

Fig. 5.30. Data integration with triple graph grammars

Immediate or tight coupling of graphs can be achieved by other, less expensive solutions. Fig. 5.31 depicts the situation of a rather popular data integration strategy known from the area of databases. *Active databases* provide *event mechanisms* for this purpose /6. WC 96/. Graph elements are not coupled via schema and production correspondences explicitly. Transformations working on one graph database raise events which inform other tools about graph changes, they might be interested in. Each of these tools may react with appropriate operations on its own graph database, thereby keeping it consistent with others. Of course, these reactions may in turn raise events. Technically speaking, the MIL document graph provides a separate event handler (operation) for each possible event that could be raised by relevant changes in the RE graph (and the other way round if propagation of MIL graph changes to RE graphs is an issue, too). These handlers are called automatically, when their associated graph changing events actually happen (cf. section 4.2 for a detailed discussion of how events and event handlers are managed in GRAS).

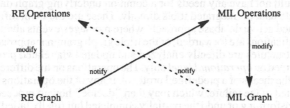

Fig. 5.31. Event–driven integration

Such a realization is suitable if relevant graph changes are *simple and mainly propagated in one direction*. Because transformations of both graphs at a time lead to conflicting calls of event handlers very soon. That means, changes in one graph invoke event handlers which, in turn, adapt the other graph notifying again event handlers, etc. This leads to a looping control flow from operations in one graph to operations in the other and back, which may – in the worst case – not terminate. Alternatively, the *invocation of event handlers can be delayed* and the corresponding events can be collected. Conflicting or contradicting events (like the delete event for a still delayed create event) should be eliminated and the remaining events may be sorted by priorities. Eventually, delayed events are released and call their handlers in the appropriate order. Depending on the desired behavior of the integration, immediate or delayed, a suitable strategy can be chosen.

To conclude, the main problem is to find suitable operations that have to be invoked if one of the underlying graphs is transformed. These operations have to be hard–wired as event handlers for possible transformation events. This approach has been used within the IPSEN project to integrate a "third party" graph browser with the PROGRES interpreter. There we have an unidirectional propagation of graph changes from the interpreter's host graph to the representation data structures of the browser (cf. section 3.6).

Completing the discussion about alternative integration strategies, we now turn our interest from the data–driven realizations of integration to *control integration* approaches (cf. fig. 5.32). Control integration is the most popular concept to achieve the *a posteriori in-*

tegration of independently developed tools. Usually, tool wrappers or envelopes are constructed which monitor all user interaction with involved tools. They pass information about relevant function calls and their parameters to a central broadcast message server (BMS). Another possibility is to modify a tool's source code directly (if accessible) such that it contains needed message send (and receive) statements. The central broadcast message server has knowledge about those tools which are interested in certain messages and keeps them informed. In this way, tools may communicate with each other and exchange data without any needs to determine interested tools, appropriate communication channels, protocols, and the like on their own.

Fig. 5.32. Control integration with Broadcast Message Servers

In our world, where graph transformations are specified by means of graph rewrite rules, a broadcast message server would receive and distribute *messages about called graph rewrite rules*. It would not have any needs for a common underlying graph database system or to access private data of integrated tools directly. These are the main differences to the previously sketched active database approach, where messages/events about actually performed data modifications are forwarded, or the triple graph grammar approach, where modified subgraph structures are directly analyzed and updated via related productions. The coupling is performed on *operational level* only. The operations on the different graphs may communicate by the means of a predefined protocol. If any of the operations fails, the partners may be notified of the failure, which may then "decide" how to proceed. They might either keep on transforming or undo the partially completed but finally failed operation and try an alternative operation. On one hand, with coupling on operational level only, there is no fine–grained dependency information available. We are only able to distinguish success or failure of operations, but there is no way to keep track of the reasons for failures. But, on the other hand, it is not necessary to reveal internal graph structures and, therefore, it is possible to *use data abstraction* on the corresponding documents. This realization is especially well–suited for *distributed tools* working on different graphs, if we can identify matches between the operations on these graphs.

Describing possible integration approaches based on active databases or broadcast message servers, we have pretended that involved logical graphs for different kinds of documents are suitable for integration. But, both, the RE and the MIL document are actually *realized by AST graph structures*. In contrast, the integration shown in section 3.4 was based on a *more natural* description by meta modelled graphs. But it is neither our aim to adapt the AST document structures for integration, nor to establish new logical document structures which are more appropriate for integration. Instead, we have seen that for different application purposes (e.g. integration) it is possible to let the underlying logical document graph untouched and to provide adapted *problem–specific logical views*. This solution allows us to specify logical documents *independently* from each other and to define appropriate consistency relationships a posteriori.

In fig. 5.33 we benefit from the realization pattern for coupling views of one logical document graph in fig. 5.28 and extend it to the integration of views for different logical document graphs. Note that for each of the underlying logical graphs (e.g. RE or MIL) there may exist further views for other purposes, but we are currently only interested in *those integra-*

tion views, which facilitate our document integration task at hand. The integration views can be realized using any of the mechanisms discussed in section 5.2.2.

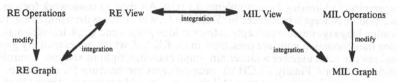

Fig. 5.33. Final document integration solution

Assuming that we have constructed suitable integration views for the documents which shall be integrated, we may now choose the *realization of the integration* itself from the above mentioned alternatives. Either we define correspondences on schema and operation level (TGG), consequently revealing graph internals. Or we rather aim for an immediate control–driven integration (BMS). In that case we have to equip the integration views with interface operations which can be invoked from and exchange results with the partner of the integration. In the first case we might again consider the specifications of the RE and the MIL documents of section 3.4 as specifications for the integration view needed here.

5.2.4 Structuring Graphs and Specifications

The previous two subsections explained how to use *triple graph grammars* to solve the following problems:
(1) keeping pure logical graphs and additionally needed representation–oriented views in a consistent state,
(2) defining updateable views on graphs which are not merely subgraphs of the underlying graph, but restructure the underlying graph significantly, and
(3) propagating changes from one logical graph to related logical graphs which represent logical documents of one or different working areas (horizontal/vertical integration).

This solves the problems (3) through (9) listed in subsection 5.2.1. Still missing are any concepts for *decomposing huge graphs* into subgraphs and for *decomposing huge specifications* into subspecifications with well–defined interfaces between them (cf. problems (1) and (2) in subsection 5.2.1). Furthermore, more complex means must be developed for constructing generic specifications, which are later instantiated with domain specific knowledge. Such an instantiation process may be divided into several partial instantiation steps. There are even needs for extending or *modifying instantiations* of tool specifications and implementations "on the fly", i.e. *during the runtime* of specified tools and/or the life time of their graphs (cf. problems (10) and (11) of subsection 5.2.1).

All *currently used* graph data models and graph grammar specification languages are not able to offer solutions for these problems. More precisely, they have serious deficiencies with respect to the following requests:
(1) It is unacceptable that all data of a specified complex system has to be modelled as a single flat graph. In contrast, a *hierarchical graph data model* would be useful, where certain details of encapsulated subgraphs may be hidden, but subgraph crossing edges are not excluded.
(2) There are real needs for a *graph grammar module concept* with support for import/export relationships as well as for inheritance such that big specifications may be constructed as refinements and/or assemblies of smaller (generic) subspecifications with well–defined interfaces between them.
(3) And even the already established idea of combining graph rewrite rules for specifying dynamic data manipulations and graph schemata for declaring static data properties has to be improved. Additional means would be welcome for defining *meta schemata*

of graph schemata and for specifying schema and graph rewrite rule modifying *meta graph rewrite rules*.

First proposals addressing these problems do exist. An abstract framework for a graph grammar module concept is introduced in /5. EE 95a,b/, which adapts the world of algebraic specification language module concepts to the world of graphs and graph transformations. So–called transformation units are presented in /5. KK 96/, which are essentially groups of related rewrite rules together with certain graph class descriptions and rule controlling application conditions. Finally, /5. CH 95/ proposes new mechanisms for refinement and combination of typed graph grammars. All three papers address thereby topic (2) of our problem list above.

Two–level graph grammars /8. Göt 77, 5. GH 96/ offer means to adapt a given graph grammar specification towards more specific scenarios and are thereby related to topic (3) above. Furthermore, various papers /5. Him 96, 5. HLW 92, 5. Pra 79, 5. PL 94, 5. PP 95, 5. Tae 96/ are already published dealing with topic (1) above, the definition of a hierarchical graph data model. Unfortunately, these papers do not address the problem of *information hiding* or disallow even *subgraph crossing edges*.

Therefore, we felt the necessity to first study concepts centered around hierarchical graphs and graph types before being able to design a more concrete graph grammar module concept. The result of these studies, or more precisely, our attempts to transfer already known software engineering, knowledge engineering, and database design concepts to the world of graphs and graph grammars is a formal definition of a *hierarchical graph data model* which supports

(1) *Encapsulation* (information hiding) as a means of hiding nodes and edges within graphs from the outside world.

(2) *Classification* as a means of defining static graph properties in the form of graph schemata, schemata of graph schemata, and so forth.

(3) *Aggregation* as a means of defining hierarchical graphs, where subgraphs (clusters) build complex nodes and where edges between visible nodes of different clusters are permitted.

(4) *Modularization* as just another name for the aggregation concept on the level of hierarchical graph schemata or meta schemata.

(5) *Import/export* relationships between modules as a means to declare for instance edge types of cluster crossing edges which are defined within one module, but reference node type definitions of another module.

(6) *Refinement* (inheritance) as a means of using already existing schema definitions and extending them as needed for the description of more specific graph classes.

These concepts and their relationships are studied extensively in /5. ES 95/. It is the main focus of current research activities to explore the relationships between encapsulated hierarchical graphs defined there and PROGRES graph rewrite rules. This will lead to a *graph grammar module concept*, where each module is a kind of complex node class definition. Schema declarations define the class of graphs which are legal internal states of a regarded node class. Associated graph rewrite rules manipulate the internal graph state of a regarded complex node and its external relationships (edges) to nodes within other complex nodes.

It is beyond the scope of this section to repeat all formal definitions presented in /5. ES 95/. Therefore, we will conclude this subsection with a short *informal discussion* of how these concepts may be applied to the example of fig. 5.34. It shows the external representations of a module interconnection language (MIL) graph and its dependent logical graphs. These are a Modula–2 definition module and a Modula–2 implementation module for each module of the MIL graph. Each module in the MIL graph is a complex subgraph with a list of all exported resources and a module import list.

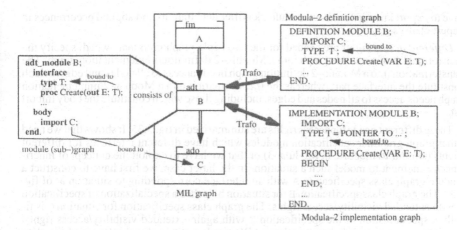

Fig. 5.34. A hierarchical graph and (sub–)graph dependencies

Using the current version of the language PROGRES, we have to model the MIL graph with all its module subgraphs as a *single flat graph*. Its schema and its access operations build a *single specification*, with no distinction between the schema and the operations of the coarse grained MIL graph on one hand and the schema and the operations of its module subgraphs on the other hand. As a consequence, changing design decisions concerning the internal structure of module subgraphs is a difficult task.

Furthermore, we have a number of *problems* concerning the usage of *triple graph grammars* for the specification of integration tools which keep a MIL graph and its Modula–2 module graphs in a consistent state. Triple graph grammars establish relationships between the contents of two fixed graphs and not between a subgraph of one graph and another graph or between a single graph on one side and a dynamically growing and shrinking number of graphs on the other side. Last but not least, a triple graph grammar has unrestricted access to all internal details of coupled graphs. They offer no concept for the a priori definition of needed access rights to related graph structures, except the suggested definition of views in subsection 5.2.3. But these views are in turn defined by means of triple graph grammars, i.e. the access right problem is shifted from one triple graph grammar to another one. Furthermore, using a triple graph grammar just for hiding certain nodes and edges within a (sub–)graph is an overkill.

The most obvious solution for all these problems is to define MIL graphs as *hierarchical graphs*, which contain complex module nodes which contain, in turn, module graphs as their internal states. Triple graph grammars are then defined between pairs of graphs as required, i.e. between module graphs (embedded in MIL graphs) and Modula–2 definition or implementation graphs. The definition of the internal graph structure of a complex module node and the accompanying graph rewrite rules builds a separate *specification module*, which is used/imported in the specification of MIL graphs.

Please note that we have to deal with *module graph boundary crossing edges*. Fig. 5.34 contains one example of such an edge. Its source is the applied occurrence of the module identifier C in the import clause of module B. Its target is the declaration of the identifier C in the module C. Let us assume that the graph rewrite rule that creates import clauses is also responsible for creating these edges. This has the consequence that a module (sub–)graph may not hide its internal structure completely, but has to allow for external accesses to its module identifier declaration nodes. Another possibility, which is less asymmetrical, would be to manipulate these module graph boundary crossing edges by graph rewrite rules of the "surrounding" MIL graph specification. In this case, module graphs have to export knowledge about module identifier declarations and applied occurrences in import clauses.

Different access rights are needed for the two triple graph grammars which specify the transformation of a module graph into a Modula–2 definition/implementation graph. The transformation into a Modula–2 definition graph needs access to all nodes and edges which constitute the interface part, whereas the transformation into a Modula–2 implementation graph needs access to all nodes and edges, including those which constitute the body import list.

These different needs for access rights are summarized in fig. 5.35. It shows that we need either graph grammar specification modules which have different interfaces for different clients (similar to modules in Modula–3) or that we have to exploit the concept of inheritance/refinement to model such a situation. In the latter case, we first have to construct a module graph class specification A with an interface corresponding to situation a) of fig. 5.35. The graph class specification B for situation b) is then a specialization of specification A with extended visibility/access rights. The graph class specification for situation C is finally a specialization of the specification B with again extended visibility/access rights. Any instance of a module graph within a MIL graph is then a direct instance of the class C and an indirect instance of classes A and B. Any module graph accessing tool specification may then use the interface of the most abstract graph class which offers all needed resources.

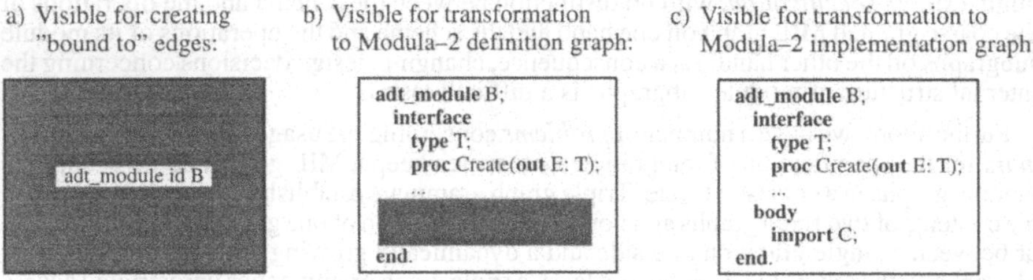

a) Visible for creating   b) Visible for transformation   c) Visible for transformation to
   "bound to" edges: to Modula–2 definition graph: Modula–2 implementation graph:

adt_module id B	adt_module B; interface type T; proc Create(out E: T); ... end.	adt_module B; interface type T; proc Create(out E: T); ... body import C; end.

Fig. 5.35. Needed access rights to the internal details of module graphs for different purposes

5.2.5 Summary

The language PROGRES and its tools, as presented in chapter 3, are the result of many years of *application–oriented graph grammar research* activities. Nowadays, they are used at various sites for specifying and prototyping software, database, and knowledge engineering tools. Despite our success in demonstrating the usefulness of graph grammar engineering concepts and tools for software development, we still have to solve many problems, until they are really usable in medium to large–scale projects. Compared with the history of programming languages, PROGRES has now reached the state of languages like Algol–68 or Pascal. It has a sophisticated type system and enforces a well–structured programming style. But it offers almost no support for *programming/specification in the large activities*, the description of *distributed systems* with concurrently active and communicating graph data types, or the development of generic specifications which are *instantiated at runtime*.

It was the purpose of this section to explain these deficiencies and to sketch how we are planning to overcome them. We have seen that *triple graph grammars* are a very promising concept for coupling independently developed subspecifications and for building updateable graph views, thereby resolving the conflict between our needs to access certain internal details of graph types and our wish to comply to the principle of data abstraction as far as possible. Furthermore, we have argued that other specification problems require the development of *hierarchical graph data models* together with *meta graph schemata* and meta graph rewrite rules.

The incorporation of these new concepts into future graph grammar based languages is a *long term research goal*. It requires a complete redesign of the formal foundations, the language definition, and the environment implementation of PROGRES. In the mean time we have to find *short–term solutions* for those PROGRES system users, who are already struggling with 100 to 200 pages long specifications. They urgently need (primitive) means to split their specification documents into smaller packages, which may be modified and analyzed independently of each other.

These *PROGRES packages* will offer them the same assistance as packages in Ada or modules in Modula–2, i.e. they will provide their users with closed name spaces for arbitrary sets of (related) declarations. They may for instance be used to realize abstract graph data types, which hide all details of their internal graph structure, or they may just contain and export a number of somehow related node class declarations. It is still an open problem how the concept of specification packages is related to the concept of aggregation, where complex nodes of one graph are graphs in turn which are exclusively manipulated via their own interface operations. There are some reasons to restrict the usage of packages such that each package constitutes the definition of a complex node type. But there are also some reasons to treat packages and aggregation as two concepts which are orthogonal to each other.

Another line of short–term research is centered around the previously discussed concept of *broadcast message servers*. We are planning to extend our prototype generation machine such that generated prototypes are able to communicate with a standard broadcast message server like ToolTalk. This gives future PROGRES users the opportunity to integrate realizations of independently developed specifications afterwards or to integrate generated prototypes with already existing standard tools. Finally, we will also offer a variant of the data integration technique based on *active databases* and their event/trigger mechanisms.

5.3 Distribution Aspects of Integrated Systems

R. Baumann, K. Cremer, P. Klein, A. Radermacher

Over the recent years, the term *distributed system* has become one of the major keywords in software development. More and more computers are not isolated processors, they are linked into a network of communicating agents forming a sort of "super processor". Correspondingly, it is possible to build software systems which do not run on a single computer but are distributed over the network. Some systems even have to be realized in a distributed fashion, especially whenever different users need to work with the software from different physical locations. If their activities are totally unrelated, it might be sufficient for them to operate with a stand–alone instance of the application. In general, though, this is impossible.

The *reasons* for *distribution* are:
(1) *Availability*: Some system functionality or data might be available only on certain machines in a network. This can be related to hardware or platform software requirements, security issues etc.
(2) *Sharing*: If several clients need to access the same functionality or data, the participating software components have to interact in some way to exchange the corresponding information.
(3) *Efficiency*: Although communication between software components generally introduces some overhead, there can still be an overall gain in software performance if the system is distributed. For example, functionality can be deferred to computers with dedicated hard– or software or low load. Data can dynamically migrate to machines with optimal access paths with respect to the current clients etc.
A distributed system is therefore desirable if not a necessity in many software application areas of today and the future.

The reasons listed here indicate what was already mentioned at several occasions in chapter 1: Obviously, there is a close connection between distributed work in a distributed project and the (physical) distribution of a development environment supporting this project. As this statement holds for SDEs in particular, the problem area of *distributed systems* is *relevant* to *IPSEN* in two ways. First, IPSEN and its tools have to support the construction of distributed software systems, offering dedicated solutions to the special problems arising here. Second, a future version of the IPSEN prototype has to be distributed itself. Section 4.1 already mentioned the limitations of our current implementation with respect to distribution, and section 4.2 discussed an approach we have investigated so far (a distributed version of IPSEN's database GRAS). All of these points will be taken up in this section.

Distribution has two facets which are closely related, yet contrary to some extent: the aspects of *separation* and of *integration*. With separation, we mean that the system is decomposed into a number of components with a certain autonomy. In general, these components may run concurrently, in different address spaces, on different platforms, and/or on different computers. On the other hand, these components need to interact in some way to achieve the system's overall behavior. If they run concurrently, they will have to synchronize themselves with other processes in certain situations. If they run on different platforms, the system has to deal with an inhomogeneous environment. If they run on different computers, communication lines have to exist between the different hosts. Furthermore, apart from these technical aspects, it might also be necessary to integrate the components on conceptual level first. In this sense, building distributed software means to break down systems into separated components and to assemble them into an integrated whole again.

As we will see, the tension between separation and integration confronts the developer of a distributed system with a *new dimension* of *problems*. The subject of this section is to sketch the approaches and ideas we are currently investigating in this area. Like in the other sections of chapter 5, we mainly describe ongoing work here. The emphasis therefore does not lie on the presentation of mature results; we also present open problems and try to outline future directions of our research.

The *structure* of this *section* is as follows: In subsection 5.3.1, we introduce some basic terminology about distributed and concurrent systems. Furthermore, we sketch our future plans in the direction of expressing distribution and concurrency on architectural level and the construction of appropriate tools. The next subsection outlines a methodology for distributing applications. Because, in most cases, systems have to be reengineered in order to prepare them for distribution, subsection 5.3.3 describes our corresponding approach. The following subsection gives some details about our current work concerning the distribution of the underlying object storage for IPSEN–like systems. Finally, the last subsection discusses current developments of middleware and platform services and how to use them in distributed applications. A summary concludes this section.

5.3.1 Structuring Distributed and Concurrent Applications

In this subsection, we turn our attention to the description of distributed systems on architectural level. First of all, this raises the question: To what extent does *distribution influence* some system's *architecture*? If we look at the IPSEN architecture of a technical environment as presented in section 4.1, we can observe that the diagrams make no statements concerning what components could run in different address spaces, how usability relations are implemented etc. Furthermore, we notice that realizing IPSEN as a distributed system would have to have some impact on the architecture. Components for process communication would have to appear, interfaces would have to change to access a certain location for a service and more. But this does not necessarily mean that the architecture in 4.1 describes a monolithic system only. In fact, design decisions related to distribution (how the system is decomposed into processes, what middleware is used for communication etc.) are largely independent of the system's core functionality.

Virtual and Concrete Architectures

This leads us to the conclusion that a software system actually has *two architectures*. The *virtual* architecture reflects the logical internal structure of the system. It is only concerned with aspects directly related to the abstractions of the application domain, and it is strictly adherent to the concepts of modularity and encapsulation. The *concrete* architecture reflects the additional realization aspects not covered by the virtual architecture, and it may even violate design rules in case there is a good reason.

To give some *examples* of things the designer might want to denote on concrete level, we can consider among others:
(1) Annotation of *concurrency properties* of components, like which components comprise a process, synchronization semantics of interface operations etc.
(2) Introduction of components to handle *distribution*, e.g. for parameter marshaling, finding a service provider etc.
(3) Extension or adaptation of the architecture in order to *integrate* components with a *different architectural structure*, e.g. if external libraries or components generated by external tools are used.
(4) Specification of the implementation of *usability relationships*, e.g. via (remote) procedure calls, exceptions, interrupts, event–triggering, or other forms of callback mechanisms.
(5) "Opening up" an abstract data type to *increase efficiency*.

As we can see, there are numerous possible reasons for deviations between a virtual and a concrete architecture. In some cases, we find *dependencies* between the corresponding *realization decisions*: As an example, suppose we want to separate a data object (e.g. a database) from the rest of an application to make it remotely accessible by different users. We could implement the incoming usability relationships as RPCs (cf. (4)). This also requires corresponding components as those mentioned in (2) to be introduced. These components might use existing data conversion libraries and generated stubs, so we may have to make some changes to the virtual architecture as in (3). Consequently, we might want to denote the synchronization semantics necessary due to the concurrent access to the data object as in (1) etc.

Although virtual and concrete architectures of a system are naturally *related*, they should be treated as *individual results* of the design process. The virtual architecture is necessary to understand the system's structure and it remains the central document for the implementation and maintenance activities. The aspects described by the concrete architecture are an important step towards the realization of the system, but they should not undermine its logical structure. In other words, each of the architectures represents a set of orthogonal design decisions which should be made, described, and maintained separately.

On the other hand, the relationship between virtual and concrete architecture is close enough to view them as a pair of *integrated documents* in the sense of this book (cf. sections 2.2 and 4.6). Ideally, the architectures are even related by a formalized set of transformation rules. In the presence of such rules, the concrete architecture could be semi–automatically derived from the virtual architecture through rule application, transformations would be reversible if they are not appropriate in a different context, and the rules would be an encapsulation of know–how which is reusable to a high degree in other projects. In general, though, it will not be possible to formalize a specific transformation as a rule, i.e. the increment dependencies between the architecture documents will have to be maintained manually (but possibly supported by a consistency checking integration tool as described in subsection 2.3.4).

As was mentioned above, the specific transformations from virtual to concrete architecture are driven by specific needs, and they may or may not be applicable independently. As a consequence, the concrete architecture will *evolve* in a *sequence* of *incremental transformation steps* from the virtual architecture as shown in fig. 5.36. (We will see an example of such a transformation and the resulting concrete architecture in the next subsection, 4.1.5). All of these steps select a realization variant for some abstract situation given by the virtual architecture, like a specific implementation of a usability relationship, use of a certain distribution middleware etc. In this sense, a virtual architecture contains the logical essence of a host of concrete architectures describing special realization choices.

Concrete Architectures and Corresponding Notions

So far, introducing virtual and concrete architectures allows us to model a software system on a pure logical level without having to implement it exactly that way. On the other hand, adaptations or extensions of the architecture necessary to fulfil certain realization constraints are still planned and prepared during the design process (and not, as frequently found in practice, as an "on–the–fly" activity during the implementation phase). Consequently, a corresponding *architecture description language* is needed which allows the notation of design decisions beyond the logical structure of the system.

The architecture description language used throughout this book (cf. /7. Nag 90/) is aimed at describing virtual architectures and has to be *extended* and/or *complemented* by (an)other language(s) to cover concrete architectures as well. Since the kind of design decisions we want to express in the concrete architecture largely depends on the nature of the transformation step, we narrow our focus to the description of concrete architectures of distributed systems.

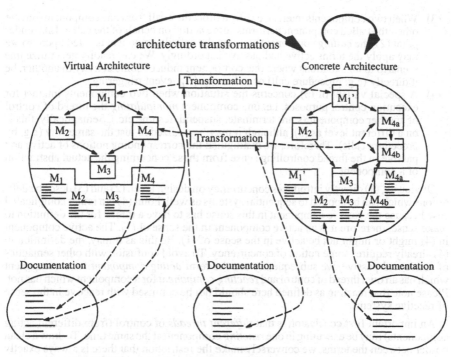

Fig. 5.36. Incrementally transforming virtual into concrete architectures

Firstly, we can observe that *concurrency* is a crucial *prerequisite* for *distribution*. It hardly makes sense to distribute an application over different computers if there is not a certain degree of independence of what is executed by their processors. Even more, it is natural for processes in different address spaces (and noticeably on different computers) to run concurrently until explicit synchronization occurs. Conversely, distributing concurrent components with the help of the rapidly evolving middleware/platform technology (cf. subsection 5.3.5) is becoming more and more a technical rather than a conceptual issue.

If we now want to describe concurrency on (concrete) architecture level, we first have to decide what a concurrent component actually is. The notion of *active objects* is frequently used in current literature to introduce concurrency on design level. Since the term active generally appears in different semantics, we sketch some definitions here.

(1) /7. Boo 94/ defines active objects as objects which encompass an own *thread* of *control*. This definition and others closely relate threads or processes with single components, noticeably data type or data object modules (classes/objects). A similar approach, although not restricted to data abstraction components, can be found in the task concept of the Ada programming language /7. DoD 83/.

(2) Although not explicitly discussed, the architecture descriptions in this book showed that we distinguish between data type, data object, and functional modules (and, to some extent, subsystems) in our architecture specification language. Functional modules are abstractions of operations; they have no state and serve transformation or controlling purposes. Data object modules encapsulate state, they hide the internal representation of this state and allow access to it only via a set of corresponding operations preserving the abstraction's semantics. Data type modules are templates for states, these states can be instantiated at run–time and are encapsulated like the state of a data object module. In this sense, *functional* components act and data abstraction components are acted upon, and it seems natural to apply the term active to functional and passive to data abstraction components.

(3) When two components interact, e.g. by a procedure call from one component into the other, the called component performs some action on behalf of the caller. Like under point (2), the *calling* component acts and the called component is acted upon, so we may apply the terms active and passive accordingly. We can readily generalize this scenario to all situations where one component induces some activity in another, be it directly (e.g. procedure call) or indirectly (e.g. event triggering).

(4) A special variant of (3) concerns the situation when two components interact for execution control purposes, i.e. one component *manipulating* the thread of control of another component (start, terminate, suspend, resume etc.). Semantically, this is on a different level as (3), although it may be realized in just the same way (e.g. by procedure calls). Therefore, we distinguish the corresponding notions of active and passive in the thread controlling sense from those concerning the actual abstraction of a component.

Obviously, (1) directly introduces concurrency on design level. (2) and (3) describe definitions which can be applied to sequential systems as well. Point (4) is a rather complicated case because the passive component in this sense has to have a thread for the definition to make sense, therefore it is an active component in the sense of (1). The active component in (4) might or might not be active in the sense of (1). Be this as it may, the definition in (4) already requires some notion of concurrency. To avoid confusion with other semantics of active and passive, we subsequently use the term *acting component* for a component which has an own thread of control and *reacting component* for a component which has not. Please note that reacting as defined here should not be confused with reactive in the sense of reactive systems.

An important first conclusion is that *different threads* of control (from different acting components) may be executing in one *reacting* component at the same time. To draw a clean border between the terms, we conversely make the restriction that there is always exactly *one thread* executing in an *acting* component (the thread owned by the component).

Choosing the semantics described in (1) as the foundation for our terminology does not mean that the other semantics for active and passive play no role in the design of an architecture description language for concurrent systems. In fact, *relating* the notions of *acting* and *reacting* components to *active* and *passive* components in the sense of (2) to (4) yields some valuable ideas presented in the following.

Comparing the definitions of acting and reacting to those of functional and data abstraction components shows that there is an intuitive relationship between the property of owning a thread of execution and the abstraction decision represented by a module's type. If a data abstraction component's purpose is to hide the details of some state's internal representation, to define what operations are semantically sensible on the state, and to map these operations onto some manipulation of the internal representation, we observe that there is no need for such a component to own a thread of control. The execution of access operations of the component is always triggered by some functional component and can therefore be performed in the corresponding thread of control. On the other hand, the execution of transformation or controlling activities may or may not happen concurrently. Therefore, we *restrict acting components* to *functional abstractions*, i.e. functional components may or may not be acting, while data abstraction components are always reacting.

Relating our definitions to the active/passive semantics described by (3) leads to the question whether an *acting component* can be *acted upon* in the sense of (directly or indirectly) calling one of its interface operations. A negative answer would result in the restriction that an acting component may have no interface. In the reverse direction, we see that a component with an empty interface surely has to be acting: If it has no own thread of control and no other control flow can enter through the interface, the component is obviously useless. But may an acting component have an interface and be passive in the sense of (3)? The intuitive notion that a component either does something of its own or it acts on behalf of other components leads us to the preliminary conclusion that this is not the case.

Considering some typical *examples* of *functional abstractions*, we observe:

(a) A collection of comparably *simple transformation* operations, e.g. trigonometric functions, is surely not a candidate for an acting component. As for data abstraction components, it is natural that the corresponding computations take place in the thread of the calling component. Even more, making such a component acting would result in the situation that only one computation may take place at the same time (because they all have to be executed by the component's own thread).

(b) The example of a functional component with a single *complex function* at its interface shows that the conclusion from above might be too restrictive: If we look at the Unparser component in the IPSEN architecture from fig. 4.1, it apparently makes sense to let different unparsers for different documents (within a technical environment) run concurrently. In such a concurrent solution, we can see though that the interface operation combines two aspects: Firstly, in the sense of point (3) from above, it abstracts from the realization of the unparsing functionality. Secondly, it is a thread controlling operation as in (4), because it implicitly starts the unparser's thread in which the actual code is executed.

(c) Many *controller* components, e.g. the main event loop in a graphical user interface, have no interface by nature. It is started when the application is initialized and terminated when the application is quitted.

(d) Other controllers or components for *continuous data processing* may have interface resources to suspend and resume their operation. These are pure thread controlling operations in the sense of (4).

This short survey suggests that, in a number of situations, there are indeed some sensible interface operations for acting components. But we also see that these are operations which directly or indirectly manipulate the component's thread of control. We therefore allow exactly such *thread controlling operations* in the interface of acting components. The kind of functional component described in (b) shows that the control semantics of an interface operation might be implicit; it is an open question whether this is desirable or whether the two aspects of functional abstraction and of thread control should be separated. A closely related question is whether there should be a predefined interface for acting components with a fixed set of operations.

An important point not mentioned so far is concerned with the question of *function type components*. It may seem trivial at first sight that an operation in an acting component's interface creates a new thread of control instead of manipulating a given one. Up to now, we have considered acting components only on instance level, i.e. equipped with exactly one thread of control. But just like we do for data abstraction components, we can shift the concepts for functional components to type level. This allows us to distinguish between function object and function type components: The former represent a single (set of) computation(s), and the latter are templates for instantiating such computations at run–time. In sequential systems, we do not need to bother with function types, because a single instance of every function is sufficient. However, in a concurrent system, function types are necessary since their instantiation is the logical counterpart of the creation of a new thread of control. We will not discuss this subject in detail here as most of the results for function objects can be transferred to function types in a way similar to their data abstraction analogues.

To summarize, we define acting components in a software system as functional components the interface of which consists at most of thread controlling operations. All other components are defined as being reacting. Although this terminology unites rather different notions of active and passive as described above, it is more or less remote from other concurrency approaches. To substantiate that the introduction of acting and reacting components is neither too restricted nor too redundant for the description of concurrent systems, we consider some classical *examples* of *concurrency situations* in the following.

Examples for Concurrency

If we look at a *single–threaded program* as a denaturated case, we can readily attach the thread of control to the "main program", e.g. the `EnvironmentControl` module of the IPSEN architecture from fig. 4.1. This component is functional and has no interface, hence it is obviously acting. All other components, functional or not, are reacting. The same holds for the main event loop module in a purely event–driven system.

The next example is known as the *producer/consumer situation*: A component is producing some data which is consumed by another component. The producer and the consumer execute concurrently. Both components are clearly functional because they perform some sort of transformation activity. Producer and consumer should not call each other directly, e.g. in that the consumer explicitly demands something to be produced. If this would be the case, we actually do not need concurrent execution of the components. Instead, it is sensible to place a buffer between producer and consumer to decouple their activities. The producer fills the buffer with data, and the consumer reads the data from there. Consequently, we have producer and consumer as acting components and the buffer as a reacting component.

Before we discuss more examples, we should note here that *reacting components* in a concurrent architecture might have to *synchronize* different *threads of control*. In the producer/consumer situation, the buffer will have some critical sections in its read and write operations, i.e. pieces of code which may only be executed atomically. As long as the buffer is in such a critical section, no other buffer operation may be executed at the same time. From the architecture modeling point of view, we can see that the synchronization semantics are a property of a reacting component's interface: Statements like whether two operations may be called concurrently or not are important information for the client of the component. As far as the implementation of these semantics is concerned, there is a variety of possibilities mostly depending on the support given by the programming language or the platform. For example, a possible Ada '83 /7. DoD 83/ solution for the buffer would be to implement it as a task. Note that, although we thereby assign a thread of control to the buffer, it remains a reacting component on architecture level. We simply use the Ada rendezvous concept to implement the synchronization semantics of the buffer's operations.

A bit more complicated than the consumer/producer situation is one of the classical active object examples: a data object module representing a *sensor* in some *reactive system*. The sensor, e.g. a thermometer, should notify the occurrence of certain situations by calling some operation of another component, e.g. a heater controller. At first sight, it seems that the sensor should have a thread to continuously watch the temperature, check whether an "interesting" situation occurs, and call some other operation if necessary. But modeling the sensor that way would be wrong: We would mix up two abstractions. First, we have a data abstraction decision concerning the sensor itself. This abstraction translates some voltage or bits at some physical port of a hardware unit into data which is meaningful for the application, namely the temperature. Second, we have a process watching the thermometer, checking the situation, and act accordingly. This is a functional abstraction encapsulating how often the thermometer is checked, what the interesting situations are, and what to do when they occur. The fact that these are different abstractions becomes even clearer when we consider the case that interesting situations are defined through the states of different sensors, e.g. a certain combination of temperature and pressure values, or that the notification can be implemented via a procedure call, event triggering etc. So, we have to separate the data object abstraction of the sensor and the functional abstraction of the sensor controller, and the controller is obviously acting while the sensor is reacting.

Finally, we consider the example of *asynchronous procedure calls*, e.g. in a data type module for files. Internally, the access operations for the file should be executed in an own thread which is forked at the time of invocation. For example, if the client calls the operation to write a record to a file, the operation forks a thread actually writing the record and immediately returns to the client which does not have to wait for completion of the operation. This case differs from the previous example in that there is no functional abstraction mixed into the data type, the file is a perfectly valid data abstraction component. Indeed, we have no functional component here to which the thread for writing the record could be attached. But even this does not make the file an acting component. The reason for this is the fact that the concurrency involved in this example is not visible on architecture level at all. Executing the write operation in a thread is merely an implementation decision concerning the file component and therefore not a subject of architecture specification.

The situation changes, of course, when an *asynchronous activation* might *affect* the *client* at a later point of execution. In the file example, this means that if the concurrent write operation may fail, the interface semantics of the file's write operation changes if it is implemented in a thread: The client cannot expect that the success or failure of the operation is known at the time the flow of control returns. In this case, the concurrent approach is not just a matter of implementation, but of architecture as well. On the other hand, a clean solution has to separate the realization of the write operation from the mechanism used to notify the client about success or failure. The latter is again a functional abstraction. In fact, the resulting situation is akin to the sensor example from above.

Distribution

Now that we have separated our architecture into acting and reacting components, we can think of *decomposing* the system into *distributable parts*. Between these parts, some sort of communication has to be realized. In a statically bound system, concurrent or not, this communication generally takes the form of procedure calls and their realization is straightforwardly delivered by the corresponding constructs of the programming language. In a distributed system, this is not necessarily the case, and the (concrete) architecture might need to cope with components for parameter marshaling, finding a service provider, establishing communication lines, handling communication errors etc.

As the concurrency discussion above mainly dealt with questions of the semantics of components, distribution requires the clarification of the *semantics* of *usability relationships* between components. This is, in general, a two–stage process: First, we have to decide about a mechanism for the interaction, and second, we have to choose an implementation of this mechanism.

As far as the *mechanism* is concerned, we can think of options like direct procedure call, exception, interrupt, or different variants of callbacks (event triggering, event broadcasting etc.). Distribution and concurrency considerations might have some impact on the corresponding decisions, but the problem itself is the same as for sequential systems. Therefore, we will not discuss this point here in more detail, although an evaluation of the different mechanisms, their advantages and disadvantages, their interoperation, and architecture transformations between them is a highly interesting subject in the area of concrete architectures.

The next question is how some usability relationship is *implemented*. This comprises aspects of when and how it will be determined which code is responsible for the execution of a certain resource, or how control is transferred to this code. In the following, we focus our attention to direct or indirect procedure calls because these are the most important interaction mechanisms. Furthermore, if and how other mechanisms like exceptions should be implemented in a distributed context is rather unclear up to now. Concerning the questions from above, i.e. when and how the connection between using and used component is established and how the communication is realized, we distinguish two main possibilities:

(1) Usability relations are bound at *development time* by a linker. Usage will take place as a procedure call as provided by the programming language. Using and used component run in the same address space and sequentially unless threading and concurrency support is also linked into the system. We can divide this case into two subcases: (1a) the linker collects all components into one single executable (static linking) or (1b) it may configure the core executable to load some or all remaining components at startup time (dynamic linking). In both cases, a completely linked system will be available once the actual execution starts.

(2) Usability relations are managed, i.e. established and possibly dismissed, at *run–time*. Usage will be realized using interprocess communication, e.g. remote procedure calls. Using and used component run in different address spaces and concurrently. Again, we can distinguish two subcases: (2a) the interface of the used component is linked into the using component, but the implementation is remote, or (2b) the using component does not know the interface and has to query its properties at run–time.

Accordingly, a truly *distributed system* can be *characterized* as a set of acting and reacting components with run–time management of (some) usability relations. As was already mentioned above, dynamic usability relations in the sense of (2) usually require new components to appear in the concrete architecture. We will come back to this point in the example of subsection 4.1.5.

Resuming the discussion of virtual and concrete architectures from the beginning of this subsection, we have to consider the question under what circumstances (if any) is *concurrency/distribution* a *property* of the application's *logical structure*. Obviously, an answer to this question depends largely on the specific application domain we are dealing with. As was stated in the introductory paragraph of this subsection, an integrated software development environment like IPSEN is not inherently distributed. Realizing it as a distributed system may or may not be an essential requirement for the realization, but the logical structure of the system (as discussed in chapter 4) is not directly affected by these considerations. In fact, it is quite common that software components are not concurrent/distributed by themselves, instead they are "forced" to deal with multiple threads of control in the application. Examples for the latter are systems which have to accommodate multi–user operation (which is not different from single–user operation at least from the logical point of view), like a flight reservation system realized by a transaction monitor, or components which have to be integrated into a concurrent system. In these cases, we can state that concurrency and/or distribution is a property of the concrete architecture only. A different situation arises if we look at an embedded real–time system, e.g. for controlling a welding robot in a car factory. Here, synchronization, coordination, and communication between different components of the system play a crucial role even in the logical structure of the system and consequently need appropriate coverage in the virtual architecture.

Open Problems and Future Work

To conclude this subsection, we state some open problems which are currently investigated:

(1) What is needed to *describe architectures* of *distributed systems*? As a result from the elucidations above, we can state that we need means to express concurrency on component level and different forms of communication on usability relationships level. For acting components, there are questions of who controls (creates, aborts, suspends, resumes) the thread, how it is scheduled, how it is realized etc. For reacting components, there are questions about whether the component is completely thread–safe (can cope with different threads simultaneously) or which operations can be called concurrently. For usability relations, we might want to know when they are bound, how the binding takes place, what components are necessary to realize the binding, how different mechanisms combine with different implementations etc. It has to be evaluated if and how the answers to these questions should be denoted in the architectural specification and in which cases they belong to the virtual or to the concrete architecture of the system.

(2) What *modeling* or *consistency rules* can we find in the context of distributed concurrent systems? For example, a (reacting) data object module operating as a buffer between acting producer and consumer processes should be thread–safe in the sense that simultaneous access to its read and write operations is either in some external way inhibited or handled internally by the buffer. Or, if two parts of the system are separated by a run–time usability relationship (i.e. possibly running on different machines), there has to be at least one acting component in each part. If an architec-

ture specification language would allow us to express concurrency and distribution, we could formulate context–sensitive rules on the level of concrete architectures as we can for virtual architectures.

(3) Are there formalizable *rules* for the *transformation* of virtual into concrete architectures and, if so, what do they look like? It is a very interesting topic to elaborate more knowledge in the area of concurrency and distribution and to formalize it using transformation rules in the sense of sections 2.2 and 4.6. Unfortunately, such knowledge is rare and mostly not up to the recent developments concerning distribution and concurrency middleware (cf. subsection 5.3.5). Furthermore, the corresponding changes often reach deeply into the implementation of components which cannot be described on architectural level at all. Formulating the mapping of a virtual architecture onto a concurrent, distributed concrete architecture as a set of (applications of) transformation rules is more a vision for the time being.

(4) Accompanying the development of a language facilitating the formulation of concrete architectures for concurrent and distributed software, an *IPSEN environment* is implemented which allows the creation and analysis of corresponding architecture specification documents. The environment shall support the language's context–free syntax, the context–sensitive rules, and possibly some transformation rules between virtual and concrete architectures.

(5) The IPSEN prototype itself is subject to a transformation into a distributed system. Compared to the current implementation, a *distributed IPSEN* could dynamically attach or detach code (e.g. single tools, a GRAS instance, or complete technical environments) to/from an overall environment. This run–time (re–)configuration could happen on user demand or implicitly (for performance reasons, code sharing etc.). Of course, shared data or functionality could be accessed from local or remote address spaces. Apart from a description of such a distributed IPSEN's concrete architecture, this also raises questions concerning the programming system, middleware platforms, and tools needed to realize the concurrency/distribution on implementation level.

To summarize, the *long–term vision* is that the designer models the system architecture on virtual level first. This architecture is mapped in several steps onto the concrete level in consideration of concurrency aspects, binding mechanisms, replication/concentration of code and/or data, and distribution support from platforms etc. As many of these steps as possible should be performed as applications of (semi–)formal architecture transformations. The complete process, from virtual architecture modeling to the final concrete architecture (possibly with some components already given by reuse or code generation), should be supported by a corresponding development environment which itself is distributed and dynamically configurable.

5.3.2 A Methodology for Distributing Complex Applications

As was already mentioned in the previous subsection, we have been working for some time on a *methodological approach* for *distributing* software systems /6. KKN 94, 6. KLM 95, 6. Möc 95, 6. CKN 96/. Though originally focused on the context of business administration systems, the resulting procedure is general enough to be applicable to arbitrary software systems. In this subsection, we show how this procedure guides the distribution of a software system in that it structures the planning and realization tasks in a number of well–defined consecutive steps. As running example, we choose an integrated SDE like IPSEN as a software system subject to be realized or restructured as a distributed system.

The first step to be taken is the *design* of the system's architecture on *logical level*, i.e. the development of its virtual architecture in the sense of subsection 5.3.1. If we are not realizing a new system but want to distribute an already existing system, this might require some re–engineering steps to understand and clean up the existing system's structure. Since this is the topic of subsection 5.3.3, we skip these preliminary measures here and assume that we have the freedom to devise a clean virtual architecture for the system. For our SDE example, we have already presented such an architecture in chapter 4.

The second step is to investigate the *possible decompositions* of the system into parts which could be assigned to different address spaces (and, thereby, computers, network nodes etc.). Between these parts, we introduce what we call potential cutting lines.

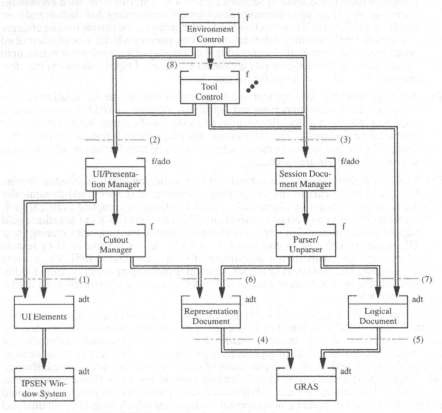

Fig. 5.37. Potential cutting lines in a technical environment

Fig. 5.37 shows some potential cutting lines on the level of a single *technical environment*:

(1) Separating the *user interface*: In this scenario, we only have a user interface on the local machine. The complete logic of the system is handled elsewhere (in itself distributed or not). This is a high–level version of distribution in window systems where each console is managed by a server and clients (whether they run on the computer the console is connected to or somewhere else) can request painting operations or query the mouse or keyboard.

(2) Separating *user interface management*: In this case, not only a presentation, but also the functionality to generate it from a representation is handled locally. Tools and environment control are still remote.

(3) Separating *persistent documents*: Here, the main program control (Environment-Control) is local, and all persistent (i.e. logical and representation documents) are remote.

(4) Separating the *database* for *representation* documents: Describes the situation that the representation documents are local, but the database in which they are stored (GRAS) is remote.

(5) Separating the *database* for *logical* documents: Like (4) for logical documents.

(6) Separating *representation* documents: Presentations are local here and their representation documents remote.

(7) Separating *logical* documents: Representation documents are local, logical documents remote.

(8) The environment control is local, and one or more *tools* are remote.

Note that, in general, not only one line but a *combination* of several *lines* makes up a *distribution scenario*, and some lines are even sensible only in combination with others. For example, lines (4) and (5) describe the situation that we are using a distributed database. It is still sensible though to use line (5) on its own, then we have a remote database for logical documents (e.g. for multi–user access to the documents) and a local database instance for representations. Using line (4) on its own does not make much sense: Why should we have local logical and remote representation documents? The same holds, on the next higher level of abstraction, for lines (6) and (7). Another good combination is that of lines (2) and (6): We have a local user interface (with document presentations and command handling), but the program control as well as all documents are remote.

Leaving the level of single technical environments, we find some more *potential cutting lines* in the integrated *overall environment*. Annotating them in fig. 1.34 (cf. subsection 1.6.4) yields fig. 5.38. Here, we find the separation of one technical environment in (9) or a group of technical environments in (10). Furthermore, we might have a remote administration environment as depicted by (11). Finally, we could employ a distributed file system (below the database level) as marked by line (12).

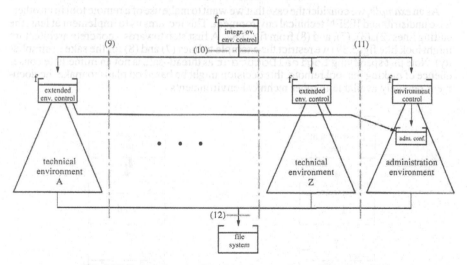

Fig. 5.38. Potential cutting lines in an integrated overall environment

After we have found the sensible potential decompositions of the system, the third step involves an *analysis* of *replication* and *concentration* in the desired distribution scenario. This means that we have to decide which parts appear exactly once and which parts appear several times in the distributed system. For example, we may choose to have one global database in our system which is accessed by all environments and one administrative environment (concentration). But we want to have several instances of each technical environment, e.g. for Programming in the Small or Requirements Engineering (replication).

The fourth step comprises the *selection* of *actual cutting lines* from the set of potential lines. The decisions about replication and concentration are a major guideline for this decision: At each boundary of concentrated and replicated parts, an actual cut has to be realized because the concentrated part has to be accessible from each instance of the replicated part. But, as we already stated in the introduction to this section, there may be reasons for implementing other cutting lines as well. An example would be to run a particular tool remotely even if it is replicated together with the environment it is used from, e.g. because some machine in the network is especially suited to execute this tool (hardware/software requirements, low load, license conditions etc.).

Next, we must think about the *implementation* of the *actual cutting lines* we have selected. As will be explained in more detail in subsection 5.3.5, there is a variety of distribution middleware/platform software which aids us in the realization of the cuts. Specific requirements may lead to different realization strategies for different cuts: To access some tool remotely, using a CORBA implementation might be sensible because we want to make use of high–level services for establishing communication lines etc. When accessing the database, it could be necessary to directly operate on RPC or even TCP/IP level for efficiency reasons (cf. subsection 5.3.4). At still other points, it could be useful to choose very lightweight network objects in order to support fast object migration.

Eventually, formulating our realization decisions on architecture level yields the *step* from a *virtual* to a *concrete architecture* (with respect to distribution) as explained in subsection 5.3.1: At the place of usability relationships in the virtual architecture, new components will be introduced for marshaling/unmarshaling parameters, handling communication errors, waiting for an incoming service request etc. Depending on the employed middleware, the new components can be rather small modules or complete subsystems (e.g. CORBA).

As an *example*, we consider the case that we want to make use of a remote tool in an otherwise undistributed IPSEN technical environment. This requires us to implement at least the cutting lines (2), (3), (7), and (8) from fig. 5.37. A first step towards a concrete architecture might look like fig. 5.39 (we restrict the example to lines (7) and (8) for the sake of simplicity). Note that specifying LogicalDocument as thread–safe is not an immediate consequence of making the tool remote, this decision might be based on plans to make the document remotely available to other technical environments.

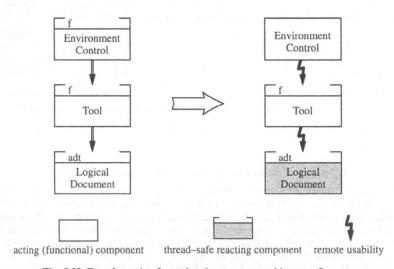

acting (functional) component   thread–safe reacting component   remote usability

Fig. 5.39. Transformation from virtual to concrete architecture, first step

569

In the second step, we might want to specify *detailed architectures* of the client and server parts of the resulting system. Using RPCs (cf. subsection 5.3.5) as the base technology for implementing the remote usability between `EnvironmentControl` and `Tool` in fig. 5.39, we obtain the diagrams from fig. 5.40. In this scenario, the environment control uses the `ToolClientStub` component instead of using `Tool` directly. The client stub converts the parameters for the tool into a flat byte stream using the `XDRMarshaling` component and sends a corresponding message together with the parameters into the network. On the server side, an event loop inside the `RPCBasicServices` subsystem continuously watches the net for such messages. If the message arrives, it notifies the `ToolServerStub` via callback. The server stub now decodes the parameters using XDRUnmarshaling's services and calls the actual tool resource. After execution of the tool command, the client stub is notified over the net that the RPC is finished and client execution may continue. (In the case that the tool sends back return values to the client, the corresponding marshaling/unmarshaling components have to be included in the server and client part, respectively.) Note that this step is rather mechanical compared to the first one. Once a decision has been made about the middleware to implement the remote usability, the corresponding architecture changes follow more or less schematically. It remains to be discussed in the work described in subsection 5.3.5 how these schemes look like for specific middleware platforms.

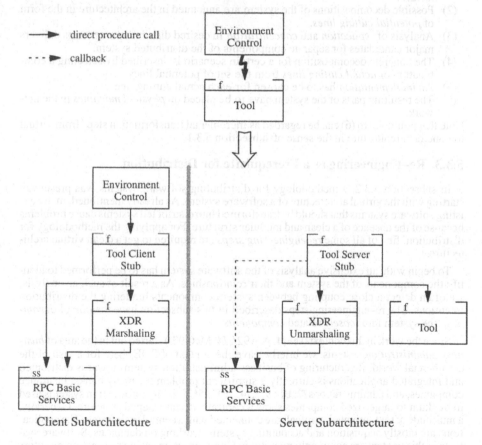

Fig. 5.40. Transformation from virtual to concrete architecture, second step

The last step of our distribution procedure concerns the *placement* of the isolated components on *physical machines* in the network. In some cases, this question is easy to answer, because the corresponding component requires some specific environment to run in (e.g. a large IMS database will run on an appropriate mainframe only). Most of the time, though, we are rather free to select an executing machine for the component. Note that separated components might end up running on the same machine, e.g. technical environments initially realized to run on different computers may of course be found on one computer in practice. The actual cutting lines only give us the opportunity to run components distributedly, this need not be the case in an actual assignment of components to computers. Also note that, especially in the SDE example, this assignment might not be a static decision. In fact, it may change permanently as users start or terminate a session with a specific environment. The last step of the procedure then only has to consider the placement of concentrated components, e.g. the database, and even this may be omitted if the network is very homogeneous and the corresponding support for dynamical service location is provided by the system.

To *summarize* the methodological approach to the distribution of a software system as described in this subsection, we can state that the following steps have to performed:
(1) Designing the system on logical level results in the specification of its *virtual architecture*.
(2) Possible decompositions of the system are annotated in the architecture in the form of *potential cutting lines*.
(3) Analysis of *replication* and *concentration* in desired distribution scenarios delivers major candidates for separate components of the distributed system.
(4) The concrete decomposition for a certain scenario is described by selecting a combination of *actual cutting lines* from the set of potential lines.
(5) An *implementation* has to be chosen for each actual cutting line.
(6) The resulting parts of the system have to be placed on *physical machines* in the network.
Note that points (2) to (6) can be regarded as incremental transformation steps from virtual to concrete architecture in the sense of subsection 5.3.1.

5.3.3 Re–Engineering as a Prerequisite for Distribution

In subsection 5.3.2, a methodology for distributing software systems was presented, starting with the virtual architecture of a software system. As already mentioned, many existing software systems that should be transformed into distributed systems cause problems because of the absence of a clean and modular structure. For applying the methodology for distribution, first of all some *re–engineering steps* are required to get a clean virtual architecture.

To begin with, an extensive analysis of the software system has to be performed to identify the components of the system and their relationships. As a result of such an analysis, we often detect a close coupling between system components hindering the distribution intentions. The re–engineering steps described in this subsection have the *aim* of *decompose* the system into *loosely* related *components*.

Since the work in this context (see /4. Arn 92/, /4. McC 92/) started out in the area of *business administration* systems, we briefly leave the context of SDEs here for a visit of the commercial world. Restructuring of business administration systems towards distributed and integrated applications is currently a significant problem for many banks, insurance companies, and administrations /7. BSt 95/, /4. IEE 95/. Existing information systems used in medium to large sized companies show a central and star–shaped structure. Generally, a multitude of text–oriented terminals are connected with a central mainframe. The applications are mostly acquisition and accounting systems working on databases. Software systems in this context are commonly monolithic Cobol programs using transaction monitors on mainframes.

Two driving forces stand behind the desire of companies to distribute their software. On one hand, the *need* for *restructuring* existing monolithic software systems is promoted by the availability of new hardware components (workstations, PCs, networks). On the other hand, existing systems lack the support for cooperative work to solve more complex problems.

Indeed, many deliberations for distributing business administration systems can be transferred to the context of SDEs. As shown in subsection 5.3.1 considerations regarding distribution are ongoing in this application domain as well to achieve distributed SDEs. Furthermore, the context of SDEs in the area of business administration system is important insofar as we have distinctly identified the necessity for *tools* assisting the *re–engineering process*. The restructuring process has to be supported by tools because of the size and the complexity of the respective application systems.

For several reasons, it is sensible *not* to completely *substitute* existing systems by newly developed applications, but to prepare the distribution of existing systems by re–engineering:
(1) Reliability and security of existing systems are well known, the development of new distributed applications comprises many non–predictable *risks*.
(2) Often, high *investment* is linked in existing applications.
(3) The development and introduction of completely new systems raises great *expenses*. Therefore, it is required to reuse (parts of) existing applications and to adapt them to the requirements of distributed environments.

As already mentioned in the introduction of this section, distribution has two facets which are closely related: separation and integration. The examination of existing systems basically shows two different system types. On one hand, there are *monolithic* systems operating in the mainframe environment, and on the other hand, we find a multitude of *stand–alone* systems co–existing in a non–integrated fashion. As a result, we have (1) separation steps for monolithic applications with the aim to break down large systems into loosely coupled components and (2) strategies for the integration of stand–alone systems. In the following we will deal with these two re–engineerings facets.

Re–engineering for monolithic software systems

In the context of business administration systems, we cannot assume the existence of a clean virtual architecture. Fig 5.41 shows the virtual *architecture* for *business administration* applications we intend to achieve with the help of the re–engineering steps described below. It is not necessary to obtain *exactly* the shown architecture, e.g. the details of the data accesses can be separated without the introduction of an application specific view and its access mechanism due to performance aspects.

We assume that the architecture is tailored to support one event of a business process. The application contains four *layers* (cf. fig. 5.41). Layer 1 is responsible for the control of a single application. The control for the single steps of an application is realized in layer 2. Layer 3 is separated into two parts. The view for the data accesses of the application resides on the right hand side. The left hand side contains the handling of in/output hiding the details of the realization. Layer 4 abstracts from the concrete realization of the DBMS and the I/O elements. To obtain such a virtual architecture, we have to encapsulate certain details in separated modules before discussing the distribution of the system. Having this view of a virtual architecture in mind, there are four main re–engineering steps /6. CKN 96/.

Step 1: Hiding the User Interface Details

The first step is the *elimination* of dependencies between the realization of the *user interface* and the program code. Currently, in most systems, various aspects of the user interface are scattered throughout the code. These aspects are (1) the layout of the screen masks, (2) the syntactical check of the input, (3) the control of transitions from one field of a mask to another, and (4) the interface operations of special I/O devices (frequently text–oriented terminals).

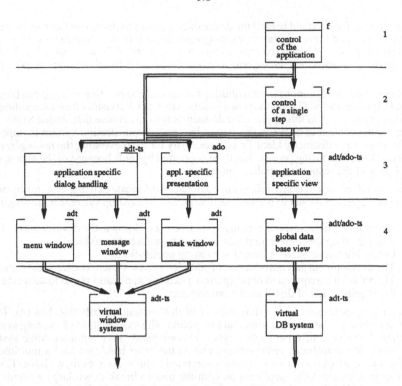

Fig. 5.41. Virtual architecture of a business administration application

Changes of elements of the user interface are hardly feasible or cause a big maintenance effort, as the locations of the appropriate code fragments are difficult to find. The absence of abstractions leads to the situation that the program appears as one large "block". The aim of this step is the extraction of the individual aspects of the user interface and their *encapsulation* in separated components. The result is a slimmer program code. The interaction between the application components is handled only with the help of abstract commands, messages, and data objects as shown in section 4.1.

Step 2: Elimination of Data Access Details

The data management is influenced by many *dependencies* concerning the underlying DBMS. Firstly, they *result* from the data model used (relational, hierarchical). Secondly, DBMSs offer only simple data manipulation mechanisms. Complex data manipulation has to be emulated by extensive code in the application. Thirdly, this code mostly depends on a concrete DBMS from an appointed vendor.

The details of data handling are again distributed throughout the program code. Changes of the data model, the underlying application schema as well as the DBMS are only possible at great expense. These deficits will be eliminated by the introduction of data abstractions. By this re–engineering step, the remaining program code is freed from all details of data handling. Data manipulations are performed only through *abstract* and *application–specific* operations. After the realization of the first two re–engineering steps, only the control of the application is left in the program code.

Step 3: Re–Organization of the Core Functionality

After eliminating user interface and data handling details, we recognize many parts of the program code offering the *same or very similar functionality*. For example, there may exist many command controllers operating in the same way. They are replaced by a common module. Generally, one should search the program code for parts with the same functionality and substitute them by common or generic components.

The technical functionality can remain in *hard–coded* style (the control of the application is contained in the program code). Alternatively, the control is represented in a finite automaton or net and the technical functionality is appended. The advantage of the first solution is efficiency, because in the second case, the finite automaton has to be interpreted at runtime. The advantage of the second strategy is its flexibility concerning the reorganization of business processes. The second approach offers the possibility to easily link stand–alone functionality together.

Step 4: Adaptation for Superior Control

As already mentioned, business processes can be modelled explicitly with the help of finite automata, nets, etc. The aim of the next re–engineering step is to *adapt* existing applications to the concepts of *business process modelling*. In the best case, applications that passed through the first three re–engineering steps are already suitable for a business process or event.

In the awkward and most likely case, we find applications not fitting into a business process model and not supporting a clean application subprocess. Then, some parts of the applications have to be *separated*, other parts have to be *added* until we get appropriate units for the support of business processes.

By applying these re–engineering steps, we get applications with the clean virtual architecture of fig. 5.41. These application systems may be integrated by a superior control component to build compounds used for the processing of complex business processes as we have seen for integrated technical environments in development applications.

Integration of stand–alone software systems

While re–engineering of monolithic systems pursues the aim of separating components, the focus for stand–alone systems is the *integration* aspect. Furthermore, separated systems resulting from the above mentioned re–engineering steps have to be integrated. The aim of the integration process is to merge stand–alone systems according to the *supported business process*. We find examples for such systems in the domains of service and subsidiary companies. Often, the field service assistant communicates with the company only by telephone/fax or mail. He prints his information, originally in electronic form, on paper and sends it to the company. Here the information is transformed back into electronic form by typists. So, the necessity for data integration is obvious.

Computers which are not permanently connected to a central server (nomadic computing) cause several problems which have to be solved for the integration of stand–alone systems:

(1) Databases should remain on a central server. For field service assistants, data from the central server has to be replicated. Now the question arises how field service assistants handle data changes on central servers.

(2) Another problem is the distribution of software releases. Often, changes of software have to be activated at certain deadlines.

(3) For data accesses from the field service assistants, competence and security functions have to be realized. Field service assistants should only have access to data relevant to them.

(4) Data which is transmitted via public networks has to be encrypted so that it cannot be intercepted or altered.

Furthermore, together with the integration effort, we have to examine the granularity of the stand–alone systems with respect to their support for business processes. Commonly, we find that one stand–alone system implements several steps of a business process. In this case, it has to be decided whether separation steps should be applied or the existing system should be kept as is, i.e. performing a complex process which is left unstructured in the business process model.

Comparison, Approach and Further Work

Re–engineering of large software systems is only possible with *tool support* because of the extent and the complexity of the respective systems. This fact is well known and a multitude of tools for reverse and re–engineering exists. However, these tools are not tailored to a specific application domain (like CIM, business application systems, technical process control etc.), instead they offer general functionality like the disentangling of GOTOs or the visualization of the occurrence of variables.

This kind of tools commonly operates on *program code level.* They allow for changing the code structure or representing it in an alternative style. We think that manipulating a program's structure through its implementation is inappropriate, because manipulating structure is a design issue, not an implementation issue. In particular, the program text contains information that is irrelevant for the manipulation of the structure, and it represents the program at a level ill–suited to support modification of its structure. Moreover, the implementation contains details that are *unrelated to the structure* of the system such as syntax added for readability or the sequence of operations performed by a procedure. To get a structural overview of a system, we have to regard the *design level.*

For these reasons, we need tools that *present* the regarded systems at an appropriate level of detail (the design level) and offer functionality to *manipulate* the presented design. Although the system is presented at the design level, the performed transformations have to *be passed through* to the implementation. The required tools not only have to offer presentation and manipulation functionality on the design level but they also have to *interlock* the design with the program code level.

Besides regarding the difficulty of re–engineering on the correct level of abstraction, additionally we have to consider the *application domain* and the *structural properties* of software systems as was already mentioned in chapter 1. For this purpose, we have to develop re–engineering tools which are tailored to specific application domains (e.g. business administration systems, scientific/technical applications, control of technical processes). Furthermore, although software systems have their origin in different application domains, there are manifold common structural properties. The common characteristics of several applications are summed up in *structure classes* (e.g. transformation systems, parallel systems, interactive systems, reactive systems, distributed systems). For the future development, we have to specialize re–engineering tools towards special application and structure classes. A possible solution is the development of a *general framework* for re–engineering tools which can be *parameterized* for special purposes.

As already mentioned in the previous sections, distribution and integration are problems occurring in many application domains. A *commonality* that we find throughout different application areas is the appearance of a central database server. A desired cutting line processes above the database (cf. fig. 5.37, cutting lines (4) and (5)), the database itself should remain *non–distributed.* Furthermore, the application domain influences the re–engineering process insofar as that either more distribution or more integration strategies overbalance. For example, in the area of monolithic business administration applications, distribution is the primary accent, while in the CIM domain integration aspects dominate.

The focus of the ongoing work lies on the development of tool support for the first two re–engineering steps (elimination of I/O and data handling details). Technical hurdles have to be removed first to allow distribution. Accordingly, the tool support for the business process re–engineering (re–engineering steps three and four) will be realized. The developed tools will work on the right level of abstraction and will be suitable for different application and structural classes.

5.3.4 An Active Database System for Distributed Design Applications

In subsection 5.3.2, we have seen that one possible line for distribution in an application architecture is the interface between the application program and the database system (lines (4) and (5) in fig. 5.37). In this section we will investigate what *support for* the *distribution* of an application a *database system* is able to *offer*.

Distribution in this context means that a number of *processes* concurrently *work* on the *same data*. These processes might be parts of one big application that was distributed as described in 5.3.2, or independent programs that use the database to communicate and synchronize with each other. We do not consider here what could be called a–posteriori integration of different database systems, i.e. applications using different databases with a unified schema (federated databases /6. SL 90/) for application areas like data mining and data warehousing.

Context

Distributing applications above a database system is common practice and probably the best understood distribution paradigm. One reason for this is that – regardless of where in a software architecture the control–flows are separated – the different processes of a distributed application share some data they work on. To avoid unnecessary data replication, it makes sense to use a *centralized component* that manages this shared data. Figure 5.42 depicts this situation.

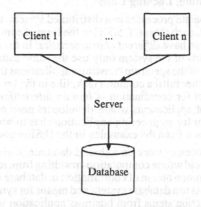

Fig. 5.42. Distributed system with a central database system

In IPSEN, we have the following *examples* for *distribution scenarios* like the one above:
(1) The PROGRES environment uses a graphical browser to display schema and host graph information (cf subsection 3.6.1). This browser is a separate process that is controlled by the PROGRES environment as well as by the user.
(2) Several instances of a prototype generated with PROGRES (cf. subsection 3.6.5) may run concurrently. These instances are controlled by different users and only interact with each other via shared data manipulation.
(3) The SUKITS environment (cf. section 2.5) provides the possibility to edit a project configuration document by more than one administrator.

From these examples we see that distributed applications have very *different* characteristics according to the *degree* of *interaction* between their different parts. While in one case the processes know each other and actively synchronize, they may not know anything about other clients working on the same database in the other case.

In this section, we will discuss distribution in the context of the database system GRAS that contributes persistence services to IPSEN. Currently, two different versions of GRAS are in use. For the sake of clarity we will give a short *version history* of the system and point out to which version we will refer in the text. The very first version of GRAS was written in Pascal on IBM PCs. This version contained all basic layers of the GRAS architecture, i.e. everything up to GraphStorage (cf. fig 4.9). We could call this version GRAS 1, but we will not refer to it later in the text. The next step was porting GRAS to UNIX systems and Modula–2. This version of GRAS was enhanced by the layers BasicEventMonitoring, ChangeManagement, and SchemeAndAttributeManagement as well as the EventTriggerActionMachine. We call this version GRAS 2. It offers all the functionality of the currently used GRAS version except for client/server distribution. GRAS 2 together with this distribution layer is called RGRAS (Remote GRAS) and this is the version used by the current implementations of IPSEN and PROGRES. This version has reached a considerable degree of maturity.

As already mentioned, RGRAS has a distribution layer that realizes a multi–client/multi–server scenario. This distribution layer resides on top of the GRAS 2 architecture (cf. sub-section 4.2) which implies several *consequences* for *concurrency control* and *locking* that we will point out later. These consequences lead us to reconsider the distribution architecture of GRAS, as we will see below. The second version of GRAS that is currently in use is a complete new implementation in the programming language Modula–3 and is still under construction. It is used to test new concepts and improve the functionality of the system. In the long run, this version – that we will refer to as GRAS 3 – will replace RGRAS.

Transactions, Versioning, Locking Units

When we speak of separate processes in a distributed system, this implies that the parts of the system interact with each other (cf. 5.3.1) in the form of communication and synchronization. This *coupling* can have *different characteristics*. In the simplest case, as in most business applications, parts of the system only use the same database and are unaware of each other. The other end of the spectrum constitute applications that communicate directly with each other and together fulfil a common task, like in the browser–example of above. Another important aspect for coordination is *human interaction*, especially in complex cooperative development applications where developers need access to the same documents. A database system for engineering applications has to support the whole range of this spectrum as we can see from the examples in the IPSEN context given above.

When two or more processes work on a shared database, their access to data has to be coordinated in order to avoid wrong computations resulting from reading intermediate database states. The most common notion of coordination in database access is the *transaction*. They are the units of access to a database system and means for synchronization. The classical definition of a transaction stems from business application where short sequences of read and write operations on a database are seen as a unit. These sequences are executed atomically, i.e. either all of the operations of a transaction are executed or none of them. Atomicity is the first of the *ACID properties* that classical transactions possess. The other three are consistency – the database state is transformed by a transaction from a consistent state into another consistent state –, isolation – no intermediate database states are visible to other transactions (clients) –, and durability – the database state after executing a transaction is persistent even if the system crashes.

Many authors have realized that the *ACID properties* are *not feasable* for applications that support design tasks (/6. Elm 92, 6. CR 90, 6. NZ 92, 6. KP 91/). The main reason for this is that transactions in a design application are not short sequences of simple read and write commands, but long running interactively performed activities in a design process. An example for a long lasting transaction is the implementation of a module as part of the development of a big software project.

When we treat such transactions as ACID–transactions, we encounter two main *drawbacks*. First of all, atomicity enforces that either all effects of a transaction on the database or none apply. But it is of course unacceptable to *reset* a long lasting *transaction* and to waste the work of days or even weeks just because of a conflict with another transaction or a detected inconsistency. What makes this situation worse is that conflicts with other transactions are much more likely to occur in long running activities than in short. The second problem of the ACID properties in this context is isolation. In modern design processes, the phases of development are not strictly sequential but intertwined and overlapping. This enforces that *intermediate results* of one phase have to be *visible* for other phases. In the example of a software project, part of the module implementation may be needed for an early integration test (see section 5.1). So it is clear that only part of the ACID properties are reasonable for long lasting transactions in a design database system.

On the other hand, the single steps that one developer performs when he implements a module have the characteristics of classical transactions. Inserting a variable declaration or a statement in a program text requires only few accesses to the database. On this abstraction level of the design process, it is very important that the database only reflects consistent states (this is, of course, a different notion of consistency than above). We conclude that it is necessary for a design *database system* to *support* both kinds of transactions: *short* transactions with ACID properties as well as *long* running design transactions with only a subset of the ACID properties.

One possibility to allow information exchange between the members of a design team and to support long lasting transactions are group transactions /6. KSU 85/. Unlike other transaction models, *group transactions* allow more than one client to participate in one transaction. Every group gets a local copy of the database it is working on (check out). After completion, the edited database is copied back into the repository (check in). All members of a group can work on the group's private database. This model is hierarchical, so that within a group subgroups can start transactions and work on copies of the database of their direct ancestor. The leaves of this hierarchy form transactions in that only one user participates which we, therefore, call *user* transactions. This transaction model was adapted for GRAS 3 by /6. Kl 96/.

Closely related to long lasting transactions is *version management*. The problems of long lasting transactions that we stated above become less critical when different transactions work on different versions of the same object. In the example of a module implementation this means that one version of the object will be released for the integration test while the implementation can proceed on a different version. This works well as long as only one transaction alters a version of an object. If two designers work on the same version of an object and both change it, the two different versions have to be merged into a new version or form different branches of the version graph. This problem also arises when group transactions allow more than one group to change its local copy of a database. In general, merging two versions of a design document cannot be done automatically but needs human interaction (see subsection 2.4.6).

Version management and long running transactions heavily interfere with *project management* (cf. section 2.5). When an actor has to perform a task, this can be regarded as a long lasting transaction on the database. Complex tasks contain subtasks that run concurrently. If output data of one subtask is input data for another subtask, then the second subtask normally has to wait until the first finishes its work and releases its output. This situation is depicted in fig. 5.43.a with a very simple task net. To improve concurrency, it is possible to propagate intermediate results from one task to a sibling. This propagation can be done in two ways:

(1) Every *document* may exist in *different versions* (cf. fig. 5.43.b). If a task modifies a version X of a document, this version is private to the modifying task and cannot be read or written by other tasks. To propagate an intermediate result of a document to a sibling, a task creates a new version X+1 of the document which contains all the changes made to version X so far. Version X and X+1 of the document are identical at this point. Now version X is released and can be used by other tasks, while the first task can continue to modify version X+1. The advantage of this possibility for document propagation is that it can be implemented with any database system that supports some form of versioning. The disadvantage is that the versioning concept is in

some way misused for internal communication. The version history of a document should reflect its main development phases and not arbitrary intermediate states. Though, of course, if a task shows an intermediate result to a sibling, this will not be in a truly arbitrary state but in some usable form. Nevertheless, it is an intermediate result which might not be of any interest for others than the two communicating tasks.

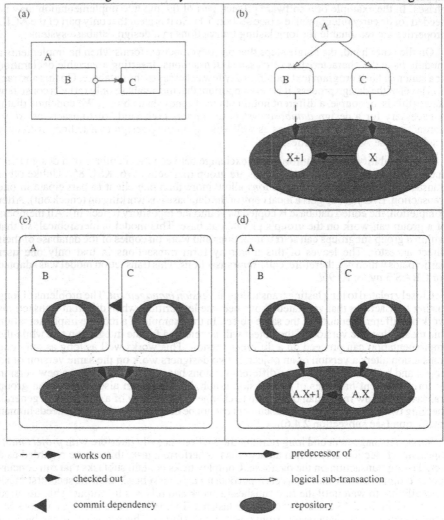

Fig. 5.43. Mapping a task net to database transactions

(2) Every *task* of a task–net is mapped on a *group transaction* of the database system (cf. fig 5.43.c). Every transaction has its own private workspace and if intermediate results of one task should be visible to others, the document in question is checked in to the workspace of the father transaction. Now a sibling of the modifying task may check out this document from the workspace of their common father task and both tasks can work on private and actual copies of the document. The advantage here is that we use a concept that was developed for this kind of communication and do not

misuse versioning. But a disadvantage is that the second task depends on the first one. If the first task decides to abort the transaction and roll back its changes made to the document, the second task also has to abort, since its input data is no longer valid.

To overcome the disadvantages of the two possibilities, we can combine them in the following way (cf. fig 5.43.d): We map each task of a task-net on a group transaction of the database system as in (2). But now every group transaction not only has its private workspace but also its private versioning system, i.e. not all versions of a document that exist in the workspace of a subtask are visible to its ancestors. When a task wants to propagate an intermediate result, it explicitly exports this result as a new version to its ancestor. This new version can be used by siblings without developing a commit dependency, since the modifying task works on a different version of the document and an abort would only affect this version. The version history of the document is local for every transaction. In this way, every task has to cope only with those versions of a document that are relevant to it.

The presented solutions show only a few ways to realize inter-task communication with database means in a process model. It is still an open problem how this is done best and what kind of support from a database system such an implementation needs.

GRAS 3 also supports the other end of the spectrum of transaction models. Closed nested transactions provide a solid basis for concurrent access to data. In contrast to the old RGRAS system and to group transactions, the *unit* of *locking* for these transactions is a *memory page* rather than a complete graph. This infringement of the old design was done for the following reasons.

(1) Concurrency control of the old system was done on top of all other architectural layers (cf. section 4.2). In this way, the only locking granularity that can be implemented with reasonable time and space complexity are complete graphs. But the larger the unit of locking in a system is, the more potential concurrency conflicts it causes. So, a *smaller* locking *granularity* like memory pages is likely to *improve* the overall *performance* of the system.

(2) The concurrency control layer of a database system is closely connected to the part of the system that realizes client/server communication. The *costs* for a call between client and server are divided into a constant amount for connection built-up and the costs for data transfer. For small messages, the costs for establishing a *connection* are unproportionally high compared to the amount of *data transferred* as can be seen in table 5.44 taken from /6. DFM 90/. The first column of this table lists different message sizes for which measures were taken. The second column shows the execution time of an RPC for these message sizes, i.e. data of the size in column 1 are sent in reply to a call from a client. The ratio between these two figures is the throughput that can be achieved with this message size. It is listed in column 3 of table 5.44. When the communication between client and server is done on top of a procedural interface like that of GRAS, the messages naturally become rather small (a few bytes for the parameters). Hence, much of the time spent in communication is overhead for the connection. This can be circumvented when the communication interface – and in this way concurrency control – lies deeper in the architecture, so that bigger data portions can be transferred with each client-server call.

(3) Situations exist in which it is unacceptable that one application exclusively locks a complete document for a longer period of time. The documents of administration and configuration management for example have different access patterns than the documents that a single developer edits. While the latter can normally be locked exclusively for one developer as long as he edits them, administration and configuration information has to be available for more than one user all the time: When a process manager reconfigures a task net, he will work on the configuration document for a considerable long time. But during this time it has to be possible for developers to access this document and change information about the state of the documents they work on. Hence, one must either lock complete documents for short periods of time

only or introduce smaller locking granularities so that concurrent write access at least to different parts of a document is possible.

Size of message in bytes	Execution Time in ms	Throughput in kByte/s
1	7.8	0.13
10	7.9	1.27
100	8.2	12.20
1000	9.7	103.09
4000	17.9	223.46
8000	28.4	281.69

Table 5.44. Influence of message size on communication costs from /6. DFM 90/.

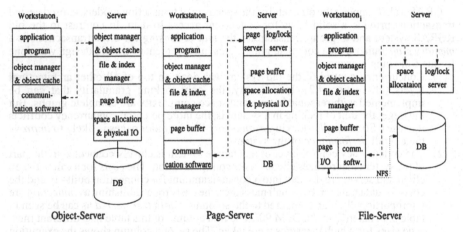

Fig. 5.45. Three alternatives for communication in client–server ODBMS from /6. DFM 90/.

When communication is not done on top of the system but internally, a question similar to the discussion of 5.3.3 arises: which parts of the architecture are suited for this purpose, i.e. which are well understood and encapsulated so that only a small interface for communication has to be realized. In /6. DFM 90/ three *alternatives* for *data–shipping client/server architectures* of object–oriented database systems are discussed and compared quantitatively with respect to communication overhead: object–server, page–server, and file–server architectures. As depicted in fig. 5.45, the interface for communication in the architecture lies highest in the object–server and lowest in the file–server. The measures performed in /6. DFM 90/ suggest that the page–server architecture gives the best trade–off between a stable behavior under heavy load (avoiding thrashing) and good performance during normal work load.

The data–shipping approach has the drawback that data from the server is temporarily cached by the client. This implies the need to keep different copies of data coherent. In /6. Nix 96/ we developed and implemented an *integrated cache–coherency and concurrency–control* protocol for the page–server realization of GRAS 3. The communication between client and server was realized with the network objects of Modula–3 /6. BNO 94/. This was done mainly for ease of implementation. In the long run, the RPC–based communication services for RGRAS should be used, since these were developed especially for efficient communication in client/server environments with a high rate of callbacks /6. Rei 96/. Nevertheless, it would also be possible to use the mechanisms discussed in 5.3.5, e.g. of CORBA. In this case, every GRAS graph could be a CORBA object and access to this graph would be realized by the standard CORBA mechanisms. Though this would be a very pleasant solution, the currently available CORBA implementations do not offer the flexible callback and exception mechanisms offered by /6. Rei 96/.

Active Database Systems

The discussion so far dealt with databases for distributed systems in general. As the title of this subsection already suggests, we are also interested in *active database systems* (/6. WC 96/) that we will discuss in the following. Active database systems, in contrast to conventional or passive ones, offer additional functionality in that they are able to automatically detect certain situations in a database and execute specific actions when these situations occur.

In general, we speak of *rules* for active database systems where a rule constitutes from *three parts*: An *event* that triggers the execution of the rule, a *condition* that is checked when the event occurs, and an *action* that is taken when the condition holds. Such actions are called ECA–rules, referring to these three components /6. WC 96/. Events of an active database system are either *primitive* or *composite*. Primitive events may be defined by the system (e.g. creation/deletion of objects) or synthetic, i.e. user–defined. Composite events are composed of other events (primitive or composite) with certain event–operators (e.g. sequence, disjunction, conjunction).

Coupling modes between event occurrence and condition evaluation as well as between condition evaluation and action execution determine when condition and action of a rule are processed. Three *coupling modes* are distinguished in general: immediate, deferred, and decoupled. An immediate coupling between event and condition of a rule means that the condition is evaluated directly after detection of the event. Deferred means that the condition is evaluated at commit–time of the transaction in which the event occurred. Finally, decoupled states that the condition is evaluated in a separate transaction, independent from the triggering one. The same holds, analogously, for coupling between condition and action.

In RGRAS, active behavior is realized by an *event–trigger–machine* as described in section 4.2. Events are write operations on a graph such as insertion/deletion of nodes and edges. *No explicit conditions* can be attached to rules, though it is possible to specify that the action of a rule is only executed when the nodes affected still exist at that time. Actions are application–defined procedures that are executed via callbacks to the application. RGRAS also has *no explicit coupling modes*. Normally the coupling is immediate, though action execution can be arbitrarily deferred. A special case arises for events that are triggered by a different database client than the one which declared an action for this event. In this case, RGRAS defers action execution up to the commit of the top–level transaction of the triggering transaction.

Active capabilities of a database system can be used for *two* main *purposes*. Firstly, rules can be used to maintain *consistency* or check *constraints* on the data. An example from the IPSEN–context is maintenance of context sensitive information in a document editor. Here, node– and edge–deletion events are used to keep track of application–to–declaration relationships. The second purpose is *synchronization* between clients. When a client specifies interest in certain events, it is normally not interested whether the event was triggered by itself or a different client. In this way, clients are able to keep track of the data, even if changes are made by other clients. When two clients agree upon a certain protocol, synthetic events can even be used to synchronize upon abstract conditions. This is done in PROGRES to synchronize the graph browser and the PROGRES environment. Another example for synchronization again stems from project management. For coordination between two or more tasks, it is necessary to know the state of the work a task performs. Especially, it is interesting whether a task has produced an intermediate result that can be used by some of his siblings, or, vice versa, a task can be notified that siblings are interested in intermediate results.

The *architecture* of GRAS 3 is very similar to the one of RGRAS that is discussed in section 4.2. It is shown in fig. 5.46. Two *differences* to the old architecture can be identified: (1) The `ClientServerDistribution` layer on top of the architecture of RGRAS is replaced by the `PageServer` layer just above the network file system. This realizes the already discussed distribution of GRAS as a data–shipping system. The second difference in the architectures affects the active components of the system. First of all, we can see that (2.a) now also the deeper layers of the architecture use the `EventTriggerActionMachine`. One of the reasons for this is that a transaction commit/abort event from a different client has to be propagated by the `PageServer`. Therefore, the `PageServer` needs access to the event trigger action machine. We also note that (2.b) the layer `BasicEventMonitoring` that was directly above the `GraphStorage` does not appear in the new architecture. The functionality of this layer moved into the subsystem `GraphStorage`. In this way, every layer of the system monitors its corresponding event occurrences. With the `BasicEventMonitoring` layer, the events of the subsystem `GraphStorage` had to be detected outside of it.

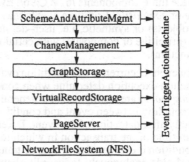

Fig. 5.46. Architecture of GRAS 3

There are two problems related to active behavior in a distributed database management system for engineering applications like GRAS. The first is technical in nature: How are *events propagated* in a client/server system? Especially, is there a *central* component for event detection/propagation or can a *distributed solution* be found? This is even more interesting for composite events. A composite event can comprise events that were triggered by different clients, so composite event detection needs information about all occurring events of a system.

The two alternatives are depicted in figure 5.47. The left side of the figure shows four GRAS clients and the connections between them that are necessary if every client (actually the event trigger action machine of every client) has to be informed about every event the other clients monitor. This means that not only the database server needs information about all its clients, but also every client. This is rather unacceptable. The right part shows a solution with a central event propagation component (EP) that mediates event occurrences between the four clients. Here, the information about the clients and the events they are interested in is stored only in this central component. Nevertheless, client information is still replicated since it also resides in the database server. A possible solution would be to combine the server and the event propagation component so that this information needs to be maintained in one place only. The drawback of every centralized solution is, of course, that the central component is a communication and hence a performance bottle–neck and a single point of failure.

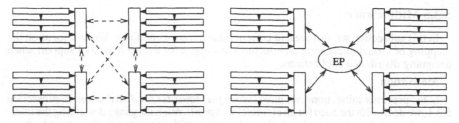

Fig. 5.47. Event–propagation in a distributed system

The second problem is a conceptual one. An advanced database system offers means for synchronization, concurrency control, and recovery. It is not clear how all these features can be used for engineering environments like IPSEN. Especially, the interaction between the different features is not well studied. For example: How do transaction management and the sophisticated undo/redo mechanism of GRAS interact. If transactions are subject to this mechanism, this means that the last of the ACID–properties – durability – is not longer guaranteed. Another example is the interplay of active behavior with transactions, multi–user facilities, and undo/redo. These *conceptual problems* are rarely discussed in the literature on (active) databases.

Future work

We will investigate the problems stated above in more detail. The main focus of the work will be on *active functionality* of GRAS. This seems to be a very promising facility for all kinds of problems of distributed systems, since it offers a communication mechanism between different clients.

Concrete *research topics* are:

(1) Development of a *distributed architecture* for *event detection* and event *propagation* that realizes a compromise between a centralized component and a purely distributed solution.

(2) Investigation of *other kinds* of use for *active* behavior. For example, it could be possible to maintain derived structural information with the event mechanism.

(3) When clients communicate via event occurrences, it is necessary that these occurrences are also propagated to clients that are not active at the time the event occurs. As an example, consider the integration tools of sections 2.2 and 2.3. It is a very natural approach to notify the integrator about changes in a document via the event mechanism of GRAS. But to be sure to be notified, the integrator would need to run every time an application (potentially) modifies the document. This can be circumvented if we introduce *event logs*. An event log collects all occurring events that a certain application is interested in. In this way, the integrator needs to be started only from time to time. It then reads the event log associated with the integration relationship to perform the relevant changes.

(4) Another main problem is the already mentioned *relationship* between the different *mechanisms* that GRAS offers (undo/redo, transactions (ACID and log–lasting), versioning, and active behavior). We will investigate their interrelationships and try to identify typical scenarios and the way the different mechanisms should be used in these scenarios.

(5) Identifying the *basic mechanisms* that this class of nonstandard–DBS for development applications needs to be able to realize the required services. An example for such a basic mechanism are the command logs of RGRAS. They are used to implement nested transactions, undo/redo, deltas for versioning, and crash recovery. When we have identified a set of basic mechanisms with *orthogonal functionality*, we also have to investigate how they can be used to *realize* the *services* (possibly in different variations) of a database.

5.3.5 Middleware

In this subsection we will present current middleware technology. We will focus on the mapping of virtual to concrete architectures and argue for the need for tool support when designing distributed applications.

Motivation

In the previous subsections, we have shown *prerequisites for distribution*. In subsection 5.3.1, we dealt with the need for an architecture specification language describing the interactions between components by particularly coping with concurrency. Systems which are subject to distribution, must at least have an *object–based* architecture. As we have determined in subsection 5.3.3, many existing systems do not comply to this architecture or even lack a clean structure. Thus, re–engineering tools are needed to transform the system towards the desired architecture.

Assuming we now have an object–based structure in which communication is only done via the interfaces, a technology to perform the actual distribution on a network of computers is still required. The application program should not have to deal with all the nitty gritty details of network programming which, in addition, are likely to be non–portable between different operating systems and hardware architectures. The network protocols and runtime support should comply to a standardized technology allowing the use of products from different vendors and guaranteeing interoperability in a *heterogeneous environment*. This technology is known as *middleware*, because it is located between the application and the underlying operating system.

The concrete architecture of a distributed system is affected by the employed middleware, e.g. by generated modules. We aim to support the transformation from the virtual to concrete architecture as a semi–automatic process in interaction with the developer (see subsection 5.3.1).

Available technology

Let us first examine available *middleware technology* and its potential. Common technologies today are OMG's CORBA, RPC from the OSF/DCE, and the telecommunication standard TINA–C. We will now have a closer look at RPC and CORBA.

RPC

A very common and mature technology is the *remote procedure call* (RPC). The remote procedure call behaves like a "normal" procedure call: There is only one flow of control. The calling process blocks until the result is returned from the remote server. The key abstraction of the RPC is *transparency*. Local and remote procedure calls should be semantically as similar as possible (except pointer valued parameters which are usually not allowed as they would involve the deep copy of memory structures to the remote system).

Fig. 5.48 shows the communication between client and server with the layered RPC structure (left hand side) and the corresponding architectural view (right hand side). The former is similar to the typical OSI/ISO representation, the latter to our architecture diagrams. The stubs, generated from a description of the procedural interfaces, bind to a server and *marshal* arguments and return values. Marshaling comprises the transformation of variables to a flat data stream and vice versa. Thus, the stubs hide the details of network programming from the developer.

Besides its advantages, RPC is not a standardized technology, although there are de facto standards like ONC RPC from SUN or the DCE RPC from the Open Software Foundation (OSF). An overview of RPC concepts is found in /6. Sch 92/. In the next paragraph, we will have a closer look at the *CORBA standard* from the OMG which has advanced to the most important middleware technology.

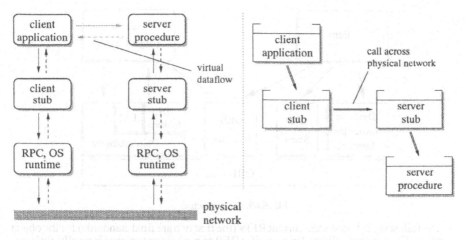

Fig. 5.48. RPC technology

CORBA

The Common Object Request Broker Architecture is developed by the *Object Management Group* (OMG) since 1991. The Object Management Group is a consortium of now about 600 information technology companies, among them –to name but a few– Sunsoft, IONA, Hewlett–Packard, IBM, Novell, and Microsoft.

The goal of CORBA is to ease the creation of distributed, object–oriented/object–based applications. This is achieved by a uniform *object model* in which each object (class) has an interface consisting of operations. The invocation of operations is the only way to manipulate the object's internal state. The object model thus reflects the state of the art in most object–based and object–oriented languages without adhering to a specific language.

The interfaces of objects are described in a standardized *interface definition language* (IDL). The structure of CORBA is shown in fig. 5.49. Besides of a stub object generated from the IDL source, CORBA has also a dynamic invocation interface (DII) which allows a client to bind to a server object with an interface unknown at compile time. We will examine the generated files in the following paragraph about concrete CORBA architectures. With the 2.0 revision of the CORBA standard /6. OMG 95b/, interoperability between the brokers of different vendors is addressed. Besides environment–specific interoperability protocols, each object request broker must support the internet interoperability protocol (IIOP).

Apart from the synchronous control flow in a "normal" object invocation, CORBA has the notion of a *oneway call* which is restricted to methods returning no value. This call is useful for notification purposes in event driven systems or interactions between active objects (see subsection 5.3.1).

CORBA has a notion of *object services*. These services implement basic tasks which support the use and management of objects. The CORBA services, with their operations defined in IDL, are standardized in the *Common Object Services Specification* (COSS, /6. OMG 94/). The OMG organizes the standardization process by issuing a request for proposal (RFP) and evaluates the contributed submissions.

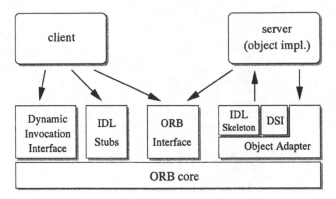

Fig. 5.49. ORB structure

The following list shows the current RFPs (the first two are final standards) for the object services. The services collected in a specific RFP do not belong together logically, the compilation being mainly driven by the idea to complete the most important services first.

(1) *RFP1*   Event Management, Life Cycle, Naming, Persistency
(2) *RFP2*   Concurrency, Externalization, Relationship, Transaction
(3) *RFP3*   Security, Time
(4) *RFP4*   Licensing, Property, Query
(5) *RFP5*   Change Management, Collections, Trader, Startup

The object services fulfil basic requirements in a distributed system, higher–level services in CORBA are called *Common Facilities*. They are divided further into those facilities targeted at a horizontal and those for a vertical market. The former focus on *general purpose* tasks (e.g. user interface), the latter are *specific* for an *application domain* (say medical imaging). The OpenDoc framework –supported by IBM, Apple, Novell, and CIL (Component Integration Labs, founded by the former companies)– is already adopted by the OMG as part of the Common Facilities. OpenDoc is mainly a framework of classes which supports user interface programming and a uniform storage model. The advantage of a framework in CORBA compared to a "traditional" one is that the usage is not restricted to the programming language it was developed in. There is also no need to incorporate the –possibly huge– source code of the framework in the application.

Fig. 5.50 shows the metaphor of CORBA as a *software bus* connecting Object Services, Common Facilities, and the Application Objects.

Compared with RPC, the CORBA technology offers a higher abstraction layer (an implementation of CORBA might choose RPCs as its underlying messaging layer). Object Services and Common Facilities of CORBA offer rich functionality in a homogeneous way, e.g. more flexibility due to means of a name service or trader finding an appropriate server dynamically at runtime.

Application of CORBA

Consequently, CORBA is suitable for integrating components. *Application specific frameworks* can be defined within the scope of the Common Facilities. However, this process has just started to gain momentum and there is no suitable framework for business applications yet /6. OMG 95a/.

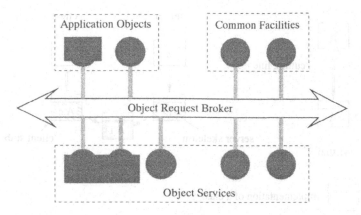

Fig. 5.50. Metaphor software bus

Database systems are an essential part of distributed client/server environments. As discussed in subsection 5.3.4 and /6. DFM 90/, three different cutting lines between client and server are useful. Common systems often use a proprietary protocol, because the available CORBA implementations are not very efficient in the sense that they are not optimized to handle the specific needs say of a page server or the large number of callbacks that might occur in GRAS. But there is a more important benefit using CORBA: If the application programming interface (API) of the database (to be specific: the client part of the database) is defined in IDL, the *database* can act as a *CORBA server* and thus being called from any programming language supporting CORBA. In the case of GRAS, we were able to separate application code and the object manager of the database (cf. 5.3.4).

Concrete Architectures in CORBA Systems

We will now look at the concrete, distributed architecture of CORBA systems by examining some very small example architectures. The concrete architecture is enriched by stubs and skeletons generated from the IDL of an interface. Fig. 5.51 shows the situation that module B uses module A. The notation distinguishes generated, interface, and implementation modules (the latter provide the desired functionality).

The IDL compiler generates a pure interface class, a client stub, and a server skeleton from the interface description of module A. The resulting concrete architecture (class hierarchy) on the client side is similar to the virtual architecture: module B uses module A. On the server side, the original implementation (A) must inherit from the skeleton (A.s) which in turn inherits from the abstract interface (A.i). However, this hierarchy is not the only possible solution. The new C++ binding employs the *tie approach* as an alternative to inheritance on the server side: the generated stub *delegates* requests to the object implementation. The tie approach has the advantage that it builds a *separate hierarchy* of CORBA classes and does not affect the existing one. On the other hand the creation of objects is non-trivial. Some CORBA implementations do not generate pure interface classes but rather incorporate the interface directly in the stubs and skeletons. This simplifies the resulting hierarchies but does not affect the following considerations (in contrast to the tie approach which is not treated here).

Let us look at a simple, object–oriented example. The following reflections are interesting as they state that badly designed OO–systems must be regarded as legacy code with respect to distribution.

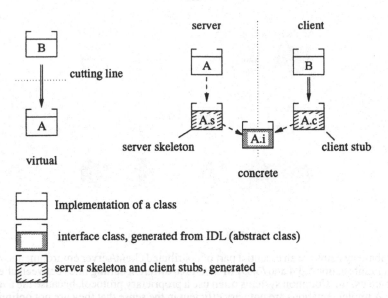

Fig. 5.51. Virtual and concrete architecture

Fig. 5.52 shows the situation that class X inherits from class Y, both X and Y are used by class B. The resulting distributed class hierarchy is already non–trivial and specifically uses multiple inheritance on the server side: class X inherits from the implementation of Y and its generated stub. Assuming that the classes X and Y are not closely related, we might want to implement X and Y on different servers, employing cutting line (2). The implementation inheritance between the two classes –originated from a bad design– could make this task difficult:

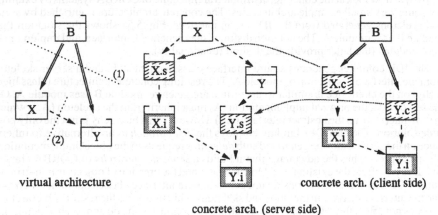

Fig. 5.52. Inheritance relationship in CORBA architectures

(1) The implementation of a method belonging to class X calls a method of the superclass Y. The call can be *delegated* to the remote server Y using CORBA. This means that the call of a method might include nested CORBA calls degrading performance.

(2) If the called method of the superclass Y is state dependent, a 1:1 relationship between instances of the sub– and superclass must be enforced in addition to the delegation.

In general, the above situation is not desirable and prior re–engineering steps are recommended. The considerations above are important because they emphasize the need for strong encapsulation which is often violated by unreflected (OO) design. The strong encapsulation of CORBA components is not always easy to achieve, but it eases *distribution* and *reuse* of a software system and is therefore also worthwhile in non–distributed systems.

Problems and Approach for Future Work

Many applications require a highly available system which also must enforce *data integrity/security*. This problem is beyond the focus of our work, nevertheless we want to use existing and upcoming solutions. Reliable systems are currently achieved by applying group communication to CORBA /6. Maf 95/. Data security is supported by encryption methods (PGP), encapsulated in standards like secure socket layer (SSL).

As was shown in subsection 5.3.1 an architecture specification language suitable for distributed systems with their inherent concurrency must be specified. We must also be able to map the virtual to the concrete architecture of the application, defined in an extended architecture specification language, and thus to a technological basis like CORBA. Here, we are currently mainly concerned about the *mapping* between the *virtual* and the *concrete architecture* that reflects the *underlying middleware*. This mapping is restricted by properties of the middleware: considering CORBA, the existing system must adhere to strong encapsulation and should not employ implementation inheritance between unrelated classes. Other influences on the mapping include e.g. CORBA's asynchronous calls which allow different interaction models and thus a different concrete architecture compared to a RPC system.

The mapping is ideally supported by an integrated environment inheriting parts of the IPSEN machinery. We also want to incorporate the re–engineering facilities of section 5.3.3 which are –as we have stated– unique to the application domain or even to a specific class of systems. Thus it is important that the environment allows the integration of different components in an easy way (preferably at runtime).

One possibility to achieve this goal is to model the development environment itself as a distributed system. It could be specified in a bootstrapping process in its own MIL. Another advantage of a distributed environment, using the technologies described above, is the ability to *exchange, add or delete* components of the environment depending on the developers needs. Take, for example, the possibility to configure either a volatile or a persistent graph storage (e.g. GRAS, see section 5.3.4) or the support for different underlying middleware technologies.

Future work will concentrate first on possible concrete architectures for CORBA and study the mapping for some examples. The next step is to formalize the mapping using e.g. graph transformations. The formalization is a prerequisite to an automatic tool support for this task. Finally, embedding and integration in an integrated environment is desirable, as the mapping process is cross connected with the definition of the virtual architecture and re–engineering steps.

5.3.6 Summary

In this section, we presented our current *research efforts* related to the area of *distributed systems*. We started the discussion with our concept of stepwise incremental adaptations, extensions, and annotations of an architecture specification to reflect design decisions beyond the level of pure object–based/object–oriented modeling. The distinction between a clean virtual architecture and corresponding concrete architectures allows us to specify scenario–specific details of the system's realization structure on architecture level without blurring the original design concepts.

As the specification of concrete architectures requires us to annotate additional properties of a system's components and their relationships, the descriptive capabilities of an architecture specification language for virtual architectures are exceeded. Focusing on the context of concrete architectures for concurrent distributed systems, subsection 5.3.1 showed our first results concerning an *extended architecture specification language* with means to express concurrency, different mechanisms for usability relations, distribution aspects, and the like. Subsection 5.3.2 showed by example how the transformation from a virtual architecture to a concrete architecture implementing a certain distribution scenario can be made in a number of well–planned steps and how the result, denoted in a prototypical version of a corresponding language, might look. As a long–term vision, we are working on a language allowing the complete specification of concurrent and distributed systems together with appropriate context–sensitive consistency rules. The language shall be supported by IPSEN–like editing and analyzing tools. Furthermore, not only the specification of virtual and concrete architectures, but also dependencies and transformations between them (as in 5.3.2) will be handled by the environment.

Since the starting point of distribution considerations is often an existing implementation, the need arises to analyze and understand the given system before the transformation activities sketched in 5.3.1 can be tackled. Therefore, we are working on a *re–engineering methodology* supporting the analysis of a software system and corresponding restructuring steps. In a sense, these activities are preliminary measures for applying the concepts of subsections 5.3.1/5.3.2. On the other hand, they can be seen as a reverse transformation of a concrete architecture (that of the given system) towards its virtual architecture. Beginning with the recognition of dependencies between virtual and concrete architecture (where is a certain part of the logical structure implemented and vice versa), we can think of architecture transformations reverting the effects of ill–considered design like code redundancy, violation of encapsulation etc. These transformations, the resulting virtual and concrete architectures, and their relationships should be the basis for corresponding implementation changes, i.e. adapting the code to the restructured design. But even if this is not feasible, they are still a foundation for future maintenance and restructuring activities. For the application area of business administration systems, we have shown such transformation steps in subsection 5.3.3. In the future, we will further investigate these steps and try to find similar approaches for other application domains. As before, IPSEN–like tools are under development which support the activities of analyzing, understanding, and restructuring a software system on architecture level.

Distribution of complex applications is seldom implemented directly on top of physical networks. Mostly, the technical details of the realization of component interaction in a distributed system are encapsulated in general and/or generated components. In this section, we have seen two basic examples for such distribution support. Subsection 5.3.4 discussed *distribution within* a complex part of the overall system, in this case the non–standard *database system* GRAS. As was pointed out several times throughout this section, databases are generally attractive candidates for (internal) distribution because remote access to shared data is one of the main reasons why a system should be distributed at all. Furthermore, databases offer a high degree of reusability which makes it worthwhile to incorporate polished distribution and synchronization mechanisms. Finally, databases have been realized in a multi–user fashion for some time now resulting in many experiences concerning synchronization of concurrent access and optimized communication techniques. Unfortunately, not all of these experiences can be transferred directly to databases for engineering environments. Subsection 5.3.4 sketched some of the major differences which force us to abandon classical database technology and presented our approaches how concurrency and distribution can be realized inside a database like GRAS. The next generation of GRAS will be a distributed, multi–user/multi–client active database with specific support for the scenario of distributed and integrated engineering environments.

Of course, not all distribution scenarios can be handled inside large reusable subsystems like the database or the window system. In general, arbitrary components which use each other directly on logical level are subject to being separated by physical boundaries in a distributed system. Quite some technology has emerged to realize the corresponding network communication, ranging from remote procedure calls (with semantics as close as possible to direct procedure calls) to CORBA (with a host of additional services and mechanisms necessary or useful for the realization of distributed systems). In the future, we will have broad, standardized middleware platforms supporting the construction of distributed and concurrent applications by defining protocols, tools, general services etc. This, however, does not solve the problem of *how to use a certain platform* for a specific system. The work described in subsection 5.3.5 will bridge this gap. In cooperation with the other projects mentioned here, we investigate how transformation steps realizing a desired distribution scenario with a given middleware technology look like. Corresponding tools will support the designer by offering guidance through the process of preparing a system, introducing new or modifying existing components etc. in order to use certain middleware.

In sum, the work described in this section will provide concepts, languages, and an IPSEN–like integrated development environment for concurrent distributed systems. The environment will support preliminary re–engineering steps, the (re–)design of the system on architecture level, architecture transformations to denote concurrency and distribution under consideration of certain middleware platforms, and the mapping of the resulting architectures onto implementations. In a *bootstrapping step*, this environment is subject to distribution considerations, i.e. the resulting application itself will also be a distributed system. Based on a distributed GRAS and standard middleware platforms, this system will offer collaboration across physical locations and between different users as well as dynamically configurable (technical) environments etc.

5.4 Specific Application Environments

A. Behle, A. Deparade, P. Klein, M. Nagl

This section describes *two application specific projects* and corresponding *environments* which are currently studied and developed. One is a writer and reader environment for future books in electronic form and the other one an environment for product reuse of software documents and components.

A characteristic feature of both projects is that we can *apply* SDE *technology* developed in the IPSEN context. So, both projects can be regarded as IPSEN *transfer projects*. In both cases, however, new platforms and implementation languages (WWW and Java, respectively) play an important role.

A closer look at both projects, described in the following two subsections, shows that they deal not only with one, but with a *set* of closely related *environments*. This is similar to the situation sketched in section 5.1 where we found a management environment, an environment for defining administrative knowledge, a management administration environment etc.

The *contents* of this section are as follows: The first two subsections describe the two projects, discuss the corresponding literature, and sketch the open problems which have to be solved by future work. The last subsection, on one hand, summarizes the main ideas and, on the other, describes the commonalities between the projects and their environments. From the structural point of view, we will see that they are rather similar although the application domains are completely different.

5.4.1 Supporting Writing, Distribution, and Reading of Electronic Books

In the following, we sketch how *writing* and *reading books* can be improved using ideas of this book and upcoming new technology. We first justify that a new kind of support is necessary, sketch the structure of corresponding environments, and close with a list of open problems.

Structured Electronic Books: Reader and Writer Support

In the course of the increasing presence of powerful computers and network connections in average households, many publishers, authors, and teachers will want to exploit the capacities of this infrastructure to present and distribute information /9. FAF 95, 9. DS 95/. Currently, the vast majority of information like books, course material, manuals, newspapers, magazines etc. is published in paper form, possibly accompanied (and sometimes even replaced) by audio or video tapes and CDs. Making this material available in some electronic form does not only enhance its accessibility by transmission over a network or on high capacity storage media, it also opens completely new ways for the reader to explore and use it. So, the future of *electronic books* (as an example for the above mentioned publications) is not simply converting printed information into bitmap or character sequences.

All kinds of publications *consist* of logically related *units*, i.e. the text is structured by fragments with different semantical properties (paragraphs, section headings, footnotes, figures etc.) and *relationships* between these fragments. On the lowest level, these relationships (1) describe the hierarchical structure of the book consisting of sequences of words, sections, chapters etc. Furthermore, there are (2) rather obvious references to figures or sections in the text or in the table of contents etc. Finally and most important, there are also

(3) complex dependencies and implicit references, e.g. from a term to the section in which the term is defined, from a summary section to the chapter in which the topic is discussed in detail, between different explanation variants for a topic, or connecting a train of thoughts needed for the understanding of an idea. Fig. 5.53 depicts a sketch of such a structure. Note also the coarse–grained structural dependencies in this book which has been shown in fig. 1.54.

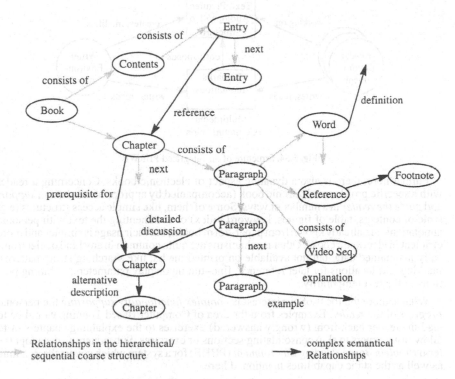

Fig. 5.53. Semantical Structure of a Book

Although the writer has this *complex semantical structure* in mind when preparing the material, the limitations of the paper distribution obstruct the structure from the view of the reader. Partially, it can be visualized by using different fonts, page references, and the like, other structural aspects are completely lost in the transition. In principle, the structure is only implicitly present in the publication, and the reader has to infer it from the plain text.

The prospect for the future is therefore to utilize the advanced technology and infrastructure to incorporate *intelligent tools* into the *reading*, *distribution*, as well as the *writing process*. These tools allow the explicit creation, maintenance, and usage of the structure of an electronic book (cf. fig. 5.54). The features and components of these tools are explained next.

Looking at an electronic book from a static point of view, it is now possible to *tailor* or *parameterize* a given book to specific *reader profiles*. The writer may want to take into consideration that a more or less widespread variety of different people will read the book: depth of topic–specific knowledge, general education, or experience and expertise in related areas are typical features which split up the target group into a host of subgroups, each having different prerequisites, aims, and needs when working with the book. An electronic book in our sense is therefore not one book, but a template allowing to extract several variants according to a given set of parameters reflecting a reader profile. Note that this idea of using the semantical structure to obtain customized profile–specific variants can be applied to the domain of conventional books as well.

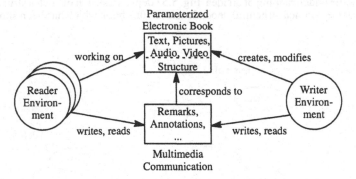

Fig. 5.54. Structure of an Integrated PBRWE

Furthermore, there is also a dynamic aspect of electronic books. Concerning a reader with a specific profile, an electronic book (accompanied by appropriate tools) can *support* and *guide the reader* in a number of ways. Some of them, like simple access structures (e.g. table of contents, table of figures, keyword index) or commenting the text with personal annotations, are already known from paper–form books, but their usage is simpler and more efficient in electronic books. Other mechanisms are quite common in any kind of electronically maintained data, but not available on printed media, like searching string patterns, marking text locations for later reference, fine–tuning display parameters, or hiding portions of the text temporarily.

What is more the focus of our interest is *complex functionality supporting* the personal *progress* of the *reader*. Examples from the area of Computer Based Training would be to lead the reader back from (wrongly answered) exercises to the explaining chapters or to allow fast learners to skip consolidating sections or exercises. Subsequently, we adopt the term *Problem Based Reading Environment* (PBRE) for a system which covers the dynamic as well as the static capabilities mentioned here.

Another important improvement gained by the employment of electronic books, especially in the educational area, is the ability to *monitor* the reader's *activities*. Keeping track of user interactions with the book provides means not only to rate an individual reader's progress, but it facilitates *feedback* to the *writer* of the book as well. Watching one or more readers working with the book may reveal that certain sections are too easy or too hard, or parts which should be omitted from or included in a variant for a specific user profile. In general, such a continuous evaluation of the material makes it necessary for the writer to restructure the book according to reader experience. In turn, the modified book can be directly republished circumventing the usual efforts of a complete new edition.

A problem which may be underestimated currently is that, just as tools have to be developed for the reader to exploit the information as effectively as possible, there arises also the need to *support the writer* in a similar fashion /9. SG 96/. In accordance to a PBRE as described above, it is equally important to develop a *Problem Based Writing Environment* (PBWE). The essential purpose of this environment is to allow the writer to explicitly model the structure of the book, i.e. to identify the basic information fragments and to specify the properties of and relationships between these fragments. Even more, a PBWE is not only a necessity if the book is to be published electronically, but it is also a major help for the writing of conventional books. As was already mentioned, the derivation of customized variants is one of the features which are useful for a printed book as well. More important though is that a PBWE supports the writer in that it allows him to think about the semantical structure above text level.

The monitoring and evaluation problem shows that the communication between reading and writing environments is bidirectional, so the desired overall result of the efforts to support electronic books is an *integrated Problem Based Reading and Writing Environment* (PBRWE). Besides the implicit form of interaction between reader and writer found in the monitoring and evaluation context, it is also necessary to facilitate *explicit communication* between reader and writer on one hand and between different readers on the other. Often, some learner will want to discuss problems with his peers (this kind of interaction being especially important for course material), or he wants to ask questions or make suggestions to the writer. To stress the notion that this kind of interaction is not bound to certain rules or schemes, we call it *informal communication*. Although quite a few (electronic and non-electronic) media like letters, phone calls, or electronic mail make informal communication over arbitrary distances feasible, a sophisticated PBRWE should support it to a degree which resembles the classroom/conference room situation as close as possible. This includes features like shared displays to enable participants to "show" each other parts of the text as well as own textual and graphical remarks (synchronous communication), and means to create and distribute annotations to an interested group of readers (asynchronous communication).

A Practical and Bottom–Up Approach

After outlining this general scenario of Problem Based Learning and Writing Environments, we now sketch our *approach* to the *realization* of such environments. As was described above, the basic notion is to think of a book as a fine–grained configuration of information fragments. This internal structure provides the basic information the reader environment needs to implement the above mentioned functionality, but, of course, it is not accessible if the book is represented as a plain sequence of bitmaps or characters. Our aim is therefore to *make the semantics* in the book *explicit*.

Ideally, we can think of an integrated writer environment which allows to *define*, *establish*, *maintain*, and *monitor* this *semantical structure*. The extraction of structural information from the plain material has to be accompanied by the specification of how the structure should be presented to and used by the reader. Ranging from purely passive links which the reader may investigate at any time to active links which lead the reader through the book according to his specific profile and progress, the writer will want to attribute semantic information to the links. Partly, the structure will provide standard semantics for certain link types, and for other links, the writer should be able to explicitly lay down how the reader can or must deal with the link.

Apparently, the tasks and data models necessary for a PBRWE as described above are *closely related* to *development environments* as discussed in this book. We will further investigate the analogies by comparing it to IPSEN. Just as the writing of an electronic book, the software development and maintenance process requires a host of documents to be created and updated, like requirements specifications, architecture specifications, or module implementations. Inside these documents, we find a complex structure relating some fragments in the document to others (cf. section 1.4). These links may have different semantics (e.g. by being optional or obligatory in the SDE case, or tagged as explanatory, consolidating, defining etc. in PBRWEs) which influence their handling by the environment. One important type of links in PBRWEs as well as in SDEs are links between applied and declaring uses of terms (i.e. identifiers in IPSEN).

There is also a *global structure* concerning *links* between fragments in possibly *different documents*. In the PBRWE we have for example links from the table of contents to the book's sections, links between a manual and a teaching book, or links from literature references to the corresponding sources. An example for such a fine–grained relationship in IPSEN is a link from a procedure import in some module to the procedure declaration in another module. Finally, in both cases we find not only fine–grained relationships between fragments of documents, but also coarse–grained relationships between whole documents. These links might reflect successor/predecessor information with respect to the development history of a document, relate different variants of a document (group) or the like. In either application area, the environment is responsible for *maintaining* this *structural information* and offering the user adequate *means to exploit* it. For the writer/maintainer of the structure, this means that some types of links can be created by the environment automatically, for others, it lets the user select (fragments in) documents to be linked from a given set of choices. Still others may be inserted by the user completely manually.

The conceptual kinship observed above suggests that the *technological experience* gathered throughout the past years with IPSEN should be *applied* to the *design* of a *PBRWE*. With the technology and the implementation framework described in this book, we could indeed develop a PBRWE with all the required features as described above. On the other hand, we do not consider this to be a realistic approach. First of all, despite the available technology, the implementation efforts for a completely new integrated reader/writer environment would still be respectable. But even more, we deem it out of the question to follow an approach which demands that all books have to be (re–)written to suit the purposes of the PBRWE.

A practicable solution to this situation has to *make use* of the *available infrastructure*, especially the already existing books. Although electronic books in the above sense will become a widespread and important tool in the educational area, even with a long–term perspective there will remain a wide gap between books dedicated to a usage in PBREs and other publications. Furthermore, the topic of preparing interactive course material is already investigated for quite some time in the context of Computer Based Training (CBT) and related research efforts /9. JM 90, 9. JW 92, 9. LGS 94, 9. MP 94, 9. RMS 93/. Our aim is not to compete with the results from these areas or to reinvent their ideas, instead we follow a *bottom–up approach*: we concentrate on the issue of enriching arbitrary plain material with semantical information.

The main aspect of a bottom–up approach is to *model* the *structural information* needed in the PBRWE *separate* from the plain textual and/or graphical information already present in the book (cf. fig. 5.54). The writer environment starts with the *plain version* of the material prepared for example by a scanner or, if possible, by the text processing system the material was originally written with. In the next step, the writer can *establish* the *structural level on top* of the plain information (possibly in view of already available data). This is done by identifying relevant text fragments and introducing links of corresponding types between them. Thereby, the writer constitutes a graph structure reflecting the basic components of the text, their properties, and the logical dependencies and relationships between these components. Of course, the environment should support the writer with the usual features of a text processing system for browsing and examining the underlying material (but not necessarily for creating or modifying it). More important though is that the PBWE can feature functionality to recognize some structural properties heuristically or on the basis of general schemes /9. Bot 92, 9. RRS 95/. This context–sensitive knowledge enables the PBWE to partially support the establishment of the graph structure automatically or semi–automatically.

The reader on his part may later load the two components either in semantical portions or on a one–off basis. In general, he should be able to examine the plain material just as the writer does and/or he can use the structural information accessible through the graph in the way the writer intended. The reader environment may or may not utilize the graph to collect statistical information about the reader's interactions for monitoring and evaluation purposes.

Analogously to focusing on a bottom–up approach for the writing of electronic books, we also have to consider existing infrastructure which can be used for *distributing* and *reading* them. In contrast to the creation and maintenance of semantical structure on top of existing text material, the technology needed for the expected PBRE functionality is much more advanced. In fact, many of the problems encountered here are closely related to issues known from the application area of *hypertext/hypermedia systems*. Questions like how to present and manage links between information fragments or how to guide the reader through complex document structures are already dealt with and partially solved in this field /9. Con 87, 9. Nie 90, 9. Rad 95, 9. RBS 94/.

Remaining true to the principle of engaging available technology and tools if possible, we consider the use of the *World Wide Web* (WWW) /9. BCL 94, 9. Man 95/ as an appropriate basis for the PBRE. On one hand, this is a very widespread technology offering a broad acceptance and a multitude of increasingly sophisticated tools, on the other, this solution covers the distribution as well as the reading aspect of electronic books (in the future probably including copyrighting and other legal issues /9. Cuf 96, 9. Sam 95/). Furthermore, it allows us to concentrate on the more important issue of bottom–up structure modeling first without having to solve all problems in one step. For the PBWE, this means that the semantical graph structure of the document(s) has to be mapped onto a link structure in the corresponding *Hyper Text Markup Language* (HTML) /7. W3C/ document(s). The distribution and reading of these HTML documents can then be left to conventional WWW technology. Of course, this choice is not perfect with respect to the desired features of a PBRWE: HTML offers neither active links nor different link types with different semantics, and no real integration of PBRE and PBWE is possible (besides being able to perform bookkeeping and statistical evaluation on the single accesses to the documents). The future will show whether WWW/HTML will evolve in the desired direction providing solutions to these problems or if at some time the development of more suitable tools is reasonable.

Open Problems and Future Work

To conclude, we sketch the *concrete topics* which are covered by our future work. The essential aim is to develop tools and techniques which support the *creation*, *maintenance*, and *utilization* of the *graph structure* representing the logical components and relationships of the basic material. As a prerequisite, the available conceptual and technological infrastructure has to be examined and evaluated with respect to its suitability in the given context.

For the *writer environment* (PBWE), a prototype will be developed which allows the writer to define, establish, and maintain the semantical structure of text material given in plain (ASCII) text format, possibly accompanied by figures, pictures, drawings, and audio/video information in respective formats. Using this tool, the writer can decompose the text into fragments with certain attributes, and he can establish links of different types between the fragments. The environment will be able to support the user with the functionality known from text processing systems (with respect to browsing) as well as with context–sensitive operations guiding his activities in an automatic or semi–automatic way. A revisioning/versioning component will be integrated for controlling document history and assembling sets of document variants into releasable configurations. Eventually, the environment will be able to prepare the material for distribution by mapping it onto an HTML file hierarchy. To start with, it has to be investigated how the tools and machinery developed in the IPSEN context can be used or adopted to design an application with the desired functionality. The next stage will deal with the issue of active links, i.e. links triggering some kind of action (in the reader or the writer environment) when followed. So far, a general concept of active links is available neither in our integration technology nor in WWW and related tools. Whether upcoming approaches in the WWW/HTML context (like Java /7. HSS 96, 7. Dec 95/ etc.) will solve these problems remains to be seen.

The *distribution component* as well as the *reader environment* (PBRE) is covered by conventional technology; the World Wide Web and the accompanying *Hyper Text Transfer Protocol* (HTTP) /7. W3C/ approach, although not perfectly suited, are considered to provide a sound and widespread basis for this. Accordingly, the reader environment can start off with one of the rapidly improving applications for WWW browsing. In the next project stage, new PBREs might be necessary to support active links and a tighter integration with the PBWE.

Furthermore, the topic of *informal communication* between users of the PBRWE has to be explored. Again, there should be an incremental development starting with conventional media (like dedicated front–end applications using electronic mail as a transport medium) and working towards a support for the desired functionality including shared windows and synchronous group communication. As was already the case for WWW, it cannot be estimated yet in what way current developments like metamail for the transmission of multimedia information accommodate our needs in the future.

5.4.2 Environments for Retrieving Components For Reuse

In this subsection, we introduce *tools* necessary to support *reuse* of *software components*. As in the last subsection, we first motivate the necessity of such tools, then present our approach of reuse support thereby describing the project into which these tools are incorporated, and finally give a list of problems to be solved.

Motivation

Today, nobody doubts that *software reuse* is necessary in the long term to improve the process of software development. The expected and proven benefits are increasing productivity, quality, and shorter development cycles /7. LHK 91/, /4. Kar 95/, /4. Iso 95/, /7. Tra 90/.

In subsection 1.1.2, we explained *different kinds* of software reuse. Here, we will examine the reuse of documents and components especially at *product* level. Reuse of patterns, frameworks, and processes at the level of architecture (see section 1.6) could also be supported by the tools and environments presented in the following. This topic, however, is not discussed.

Software reuse refers to all documents built in the process of software development /7. FF 95/. So, we need a *library* appropriate for requirement definitions, design specifications, source code, test documents, and documentation. But the existence of such a library is not enough. Software reuse needs *active support*.

Therefore, we need languages and tools assisting (a) creation and maintenance of a library containing reusable components, (b) search and retrieval of components, and (c) the integration of components into a new system. Present reuse activities attend to the stage of implementation and mainly consider source code or binary libraries which we want to refer to as *reusable components*. However, in /7. Bör 94/, reuse is related to design documents specified in a special programming–in–the–large language called EMIL.

There are two kinds of software reuse. *Internal reuse* is the use of components which were created in earlier projects in the same enterprise and stored in a repository containing all software documents. *External reuse* is performed when components are received from the public domain or bought from another company.

For easy integration of components into a new system, their possible reuse has to be considered at the time of creation. Multiple reuse projects have shown that the so–called *development for reuse* is expensive and that the costs for building software repositories containing reusable components are high /4. Iso 95/. Furthermore, Biggerstaff's *rule of three* /7. Tra 95/ was confirmed by different reuse projects. According to this rule, software must be developed three times until it is really reusable and must be reused three times until it is sound and generalized so that reuse is of economic advantage. Therefore, most software producers can not afford internal reuse.

Today, in almost every branch of industry, enterprises buy components if they do not have the know–how to build them by themselves or if it would take too much time to learn how to build them in the desired quality. In the software industry, the situation is still exceptional. Only a few software companies use commercially or freely available software components. However, the broader reuse of commercial components could contribute to change the software producing enterprises into an *industry*.

Until now, there are only a few tools supporting external reuse. Later, we will describe the features such tools should provide. In the RSB project described below, our aim is to create a *component information system* in a community of software producing enterprises. Here, the main idea is to separate the component description from the component. The sources of supply are part of the component description.

In section 5.1, we discussed three different kinds of environments. In our reuse systems, we also have three environments. The *reuse administrator* creates and maintains the classification scheme which is used for efficient storage and retrieval of component information. The *reuse manager* decides which components or component descriptions are fed into the database. He has to create and maintain reuse descriptions and he has to control the access to components. The *user* is the software designer or developer searching in the information system for a component suitable for his problem. In contrast to section 5.1, there are less strong dependencies between these environments. The classification scheme maintained by the administrator will not be changed frequently. But if changes are made, these changes will affect both the manager, which has to maintain the data, and the user, which has different possibilities to search or different paths to navigate in the information system. Changes made by the manager result in new component entries or in the update of component entries, so the user will get more or other retrieval information for his next component search.

Derived from the different environments, *tools* are needed to *assist* the *different users* for the following tasks:
1. Administrator
   - Input and maintenance of the classification scheme.
   - Check of the consistency of the classification scheme.
2. Manager
   - Check and re-installation of the integrity of component descriptions when the classification scheme changes.
   - Input and maintenance of the component description.
3. User
   - Query specification and navigation through the reuse information system.
   - Check and evaluation of the reusability of a retrieved component.
   - Integration of a found component into a new system including necessary adaptations.

There are several ways to integrate an existing component into a new system. If the component needs no changes (*black box reuse*), only the context in the new system must be adapted. In the majority of cases, however, a component found in a repository has to be adapted for integration (*white box reuse*). Especially reusing object–oriented class hierarchies is not trivial and specific tool support is difficult.

All these tools can be integrated into a software development environment like IPSEN, but their isolated use is also important if no integrated software development environment is available.

Literature and Comparison of Selected Approaches

We will now present a brief *survey* of *existing approaches* to and properties of software reuse libraries. Software reuse systems can be classified by the following criteria:

(1)   The method used to represent components
Methods for representing reusable software come from three areas: indexing languages from library and information science, knowledge–based methods from AI, and hypertext, which roots in information science and AI /5. FG 90/.
Indexing methods from library and information science are based on controlled or uncontrolled vocabulary. *Controlled vocabulary* is used in classification systems and keyword systems. We distinguish faceted, enumerated, and feature–oriented classification. The *faceted* classification /7. PF 87, 7. Pri 91/ uses a fixed number of facets and a pre–defined vocabulary for each facet to describe a component. Similarities between the terms of this vocabulary are defined in conceptual distance graphs. If the classification scheme consists of classes created by pre–combination of all facet terms, this is called *enumerated* classification. The *feature–oriented* classification /4. Bör 93, 7. Bör 94/ is a further development of faceted classification also supporting multiple terms which describe one facet (feature). Furthermore, the refinement of features helps structuring the classification scheme and generates a hierarchical classification structure. Moreover, arbitrary relations between terms can be defined, e.g. to define similarities. Instead of classes, some systems use controlled keywords. The RSL system /4. BAB 87/ uses classification by a combination of category code and five keywords. *Uncontrolled vocabulary* is used at *free–text indexing* methods. /4. HM 91/ presents a software reuse system using the source code and the documentation for indexing. The CATALOG system /4. FN 87/ uses a prologue in the source code. However, /4. Hen 96/ points to the difficulties of applying free–text methods to source code.
Knowledge based methods use semantic nets /4. SWT 89/ or frames. The *frame representation* is used in PEEL/CodeFinder /4. Hen 95, 4. Hen 96/, LaSSIE /4. DBS 91/, AIRS /4. OHP 92/, and the reuse system presented in /4. WS 88/.
A *hypertext* approach representing used–by and import relationships determined from the source code is used in /4. Fre 94/.

(2)   Creating the indexes: degree of automation
The possible degree of automation depends on the method used to create the index. While free–text indexing and the hypertext approach can be executed automatically or at least semi–automatically, the classification of components is performed rather manually as the semantic aspects are difficult to specify.

(3)   The mechanisms to support retrieval
Generally, we distinguish between two methods to find reusable components: *searching* and *browsing*.
When searching a component, the user specifies a keyword (keyword search), a term to search in the whole database (full text search), or a question in natural language. Systems using algebraic specification use the definition of the signature or specification /4. MW 95a, 4. MW 95b/. In addition, the search can be gradually refined, e.g. in the relevance–feedback method /7. SB 90/.
Browsing the database is necessary if the user has no concrete idea about terms describing the required component. He can navigate through the database following links or navigation paths. Comfortable systems combine searching and browsing facilities so that the search space can be reduced while browsing.

There are many other criteria to classify reuse systems. We want to present briefly the characteristics of *three interesting* software *reuse libraries.*
(a)   The SEL (Software Engineering Library, /4. Fre 94/) is a hypertext system developed for internal reuse of software at BMW. One main idea is the separation of component and component description. Relations between components, e.g. uses–used and imports–imported, are represented by directed links and established semi–automatically.
(b)   PEEL/CodeFinder /4. Hen 95, 4. Hen 96/ is frame–based and, like SEL, developed for internal reuse. Similarities are represented by an associative network. One interesting aspect of this system is that the classification system is extensible. Developers

601

becoming familiar with an application domain can modify the classification system. There is no logical separation between administrator, manager, and user. Furthermore, this system is developed for storing functions only. Neither modules containing several functions nor class hierarchies, classes, or objects are supported.

(c) The Feature–Oriented Classification System (FOCS) /4. Bör 93, 7. Bör 94/ was created using the IPSEN machinery. The syntax of FOCS is specified in the SENF language. The SENF specification serves as basis for the generation of tools and analyzers for input and maintenance of the classification scheme as well as the component descriptors. Furthermore, a tool has been generated to check and re–establish database consistency when simple changes are made to the classification scheme. The syntax–oriented editor used for input is also applied for defining a descriptor of the requested component. Thus, in this tool, there is no logical separation of the different environments, too.

Project Description

The RSB project takes place in cooperation between the Aachen University of Technology and the REGINA (Regionaler Industrieclub Informatik Aachen e.V.), an association of many software producing companies in the Aachen area.

The aim of the *REGINA Software Library* project (RSB for the German term REGINA Software Bibliothek) /4. Beh 97/ in which nine companies are participating is to create a software component information system suitable to support external reuse. If a new software system is developed and several components are needed, this system gives information about all suitable components which are commercially or freely available. It should contain descriptions of different kinds of components: source code, static or dynamic libraries, and the new generation of binary components, the so–called VBXs (VB Custom Controls) and OCXs (OLE Custom Controls).

All project participants should have access to the information system. Hence, we decided to place the system in the World Wide Web (WWW) /7. For 95, 7. W3C/ in the Internet. The World Wide Web is a special service in the Internet provided by the hypertext transfer protocol (HTTP). By HTTP and the underlying TCP/IP, nearly all kinds of platforms can be connected. The browsers necessary to access the Web provide a uniform user interface on all platforms.

We index the components through *classification* and use an extension of the feature–oriented classification approach. Our classification approach allows the nested combination of view and is relations. Moreover, we have taken a more general approach concerning links. Instead of links specifying similarities we can formulate arbitrary links to other component descriptions (i.e. see–also) or to other nodes in the classification scheme. The creation of the component description is performed manually. This is due to the fact that we have different sources of information and that, in general, the source code of commercial components will not be available.

The supported *search facilities* are keyword search, browsing and advanced search where keywords can be combined by the operators AND and OR. Furthermore, the advanced search enables the combination of search and navigation. We will not implement search by algebraic specification because (a) it is difficult to decide if two algebraic specifications are equivalent, (b) the user has to learn how to write algebraic specifications, and (c) it is difficult to write sound algebraic specifications. The underlying database is not GRAS as in FOCS; instead we use the relational database ORACLE7.

The decision to use the World Wide Web as distribution platform implies several properties of the user interfaces and the design. First of all, the standard format to present and transfer data is the *Hypertext Markup Language* (HTML) /7. Gra 95, 7. W3C/. The client needs a special browser to access the WWW and to view HTML pages. The interaction between client and server takes place through HTML forms and is, in general, limited to a question–

answer process initiated by the client. Because the communication in the WWW is stateless, the server never starts to communicate to a client. The only exception is the mechanism provided by the Java language described below. A main characteristic of HTML is the use of *hyperlinks* pointing to arbitrary HTML pages in the WWW specified by a unique identifier called URL (Uniform Resource Locator).

The following fig. 5.55 depicts the *scenario* described above. The user, manager, and administrator environments are represented in HTML format by WWW browsers. They are connected via the Internet to the WWW server. The WWW server consists of a Web Request Broker responsible for the access to the Internet, two different database interfaces, and the static HTML pages. The standard database interface sends queries to the database, receives the results, and creates HTML pages containing the results. These pages are returned to the WWW clients. The Java database interface and the reason for additional user data will be explained in the following. The database is not part of the WWW server and can be accessed through other user interfaces, too.

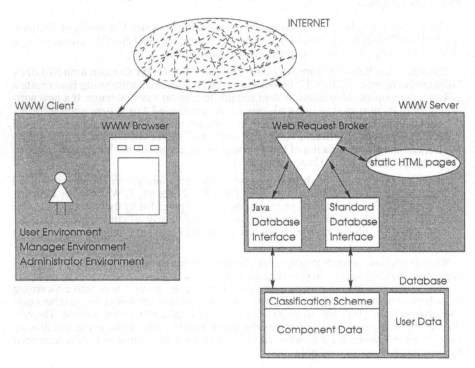

Fig. 5.55. The component information system and the Internet

At the time of writing, we implemented a simple prototype realizing searching and browsing via the World Wide Web on an ORCALE7 database using SQL and PL/SQL scripts as well as HTML forms. However, no tool support is implemented yet. In the near future, we will implement the tools described above.

Especially, we have to consider the the following *aspects*:

(1) Java interface
We will develop a user–friendly interface using the object–oriented programming language Java /7. Rit 95, 7. Nau 96, 7. Anu 96, 7. JM 96/. The user interface provided by Java applets is copied on demand to any client WWW browser supporting Java. The Java applet will recognize the user profile and notify the server if the user profile

changes. Java also allows distributed computation through client/server communication. The Java applet can load additional information from the server without changing the URL or HTML page on the client's WWW browser /9. KBA 95/. The two possibilities to realize communication between client applet and server are (a) socket communication supported by standard Java classes and (b) the Java/CORBA connection realizing the communication between distributed objects. We have to examine whether the Java user interface has in fact advantages compared to the standard HTML interface.

(2) Evaluation of reusability

If multiple components are found as a query result, the user should have a tool to judge and compare the reusability of different components and to see which one can be integrated most easily. /7. DKM 96, 7. CB 91/ describe some reusability metrics. A tool is needed to determine the reusability if the source code is available.

(3) User profile

In the first step, the parts building the user profile must be examined. In the second step, rules must be developed and implemented to determine the profile from the user's behavior. The profile is the main part of the user data mentioned above.

(4) Classification scheme

A major problem designing this system is the fact that the classification scheme has to be extensible. The operation of the information system will be started on an incomplete classification system because a complete domain analysis for all known domains is too expensive. Furthermore, new domains will emerge during run time. The classification system and the component descriptions should be extensible when new experiences are made or when there is concrete demand. Our classification approach meets this extensibility, but we have to map this onto a relational database and so we need an appropriate database scheme. We developed a meta scheme which manages the tables in the database and which guarantees that the classification system can be modified as necessary. This meta scheme, tools to maintain it, and tools to propagate structural changes to the database will be implemented soon.

Implementing the system described above, we can reuse the following parts of the IPSEN philosophy and technology. Firstly, we can reuse existing tools, structural considerations, and architecture specifications. Secondly, we reuse the division of the environment into the three parts for administrator, manager, and user as described above. Thirdly, we can use the mechanisms to generate tools. To some extent, these tools can be IPSEN instances. However, the external representation of data must be in HTML format or through a Java interface due to the connection to the World Wide Web. So, we have to create tools generating user interfaces based on HTML or on Java. Fig. 5.56 shows a survey of the different parts planned for our component reuse system.

Future Work

Until now, we simply considered separated components. Only the manager can specify special relations. In the next step, components at *different levels of granularity* must also be admitted to the information system. So, we have to support components containing object classes, complex class hierarchies, and their interrelations. If we look at the software development process, we neglected all other documents so far, e.g. design specifications which could also be reused. In IPSEN, all these documents are established with one system. Obviously, the interconnections between documents from different working areas can be very important for users. For example, if (a part of) the design document is reused, probably also the (corresponding parts of the) source code and test documents can be reused.

Following the retrieval of components, the next step is their *integration* into the new system. A tool is necessary to assist the user in integrating the different kinds of components. Noticeably object–oriented components are difficult to reuse /7. BT 95a, 7. BT 95b/. It is even worse to reuse multiple class hierarchies /7. Ber 90/. An integration tool transforming two or more conflicting or redundant class libraries into one sound class library can be created using PROGRES and graph rewrite rules.

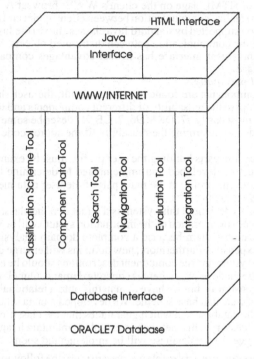

Fig. 5.56. The reuse environment

Another aspect which will be increasingly important in the future is the preparation of knowledge available in the Internet for usage in local databases. So far, we have the hard contrast between the open World Wide Web with its large amount of unstructured information and the dedicated information system with its structured information about software components. We have to examine if and how we can use *search engines* to enrich our information system with valuable data without influencing its performance and search facilities.

At the beginning of this subsection, we explained the differences between internal and external reuse. We want to examine the differences, restrictions, and potentials of these two kinds of reuse. Our component information system can also be used to manage *internal reuse*. The corresponding modifications of the information system and the classification system to adapt the component information system to be suitable for internal reuse have to be investigated.

Since the classification scheme represents a graph and changes to the classification system are nothing else but graph transformations, we will also consider the use of the PRO-GRES environment (section 3.6) and the underlying database GRAS (sections 4.2 and 5.3).

5.4.3 Summary

In this section, we have presented two *ongoing projects* which are not directly related to the application domain of software development environments. At closer consideration, though, we have found that the corresponding systems and tools to be developed are very similar to the IPSEN environment presented in this book.

In the first subsection, we described our vision of the *electronic book* as an interactive multimedia information source. To exploit the advantages of electronic books over conventional ones, dedicated environments for the reader and writer have to be devised. These environments support the creation and usage of structural information about the semantics of a book. On the basis of this logical structure, the reader can be supported by providing him a special book variant tailored to his specific needs and profile. Furthermore, a parameterized, dynamically adaptable reading process can be realized by intelligent tools within the reader's environment.

On the other hand, we need corresponding support for the writer of electronic books. We plan to realize a writer environment which allows the author to identify and adapt the structural properties of the book. Finally, an *integrated reader/writer environment* allows the bidirectional communication between both applications for monitoring, evaluation, and informal feedback purposes.

In the second subsection, we presented an *environment* supporting the *reuse* of documents and components on product level. The project's objective is to facilitate internal and external reuse using an extension of the feature–oriented classification approach. The main tools consider the extensible classification scheme, input and search of components, and the integration of components into a new system.

In both projects, the resulting overall environment consists of a *set* of closely *related subenvironments* (reader and writer environment in 5.4.1, administrator, manager, and user environment in 5.4.2) as was already found in the project described in section 5.1. The overall environment, therefore, is a distributed system in the sense of section 5.3 with corresponding needs for integration and separation.

The focus in the two projects discussed here though is different from those in section 5.3: The aspect of separation, i.e. how to decompose a logically monolithic system into distributable parts, is pushed into the background since the subenvironments already are "stand–alone" applications on top of shared data. Correspondingly, the *integration* of these subenvironments by means of exchanging information gains importance.

The *realization approach* concerning the communication between the subenvironments is, in both cases, based on *World Wide Web technology*. Internally, shared data is stored in a database (structure–oriented in the reader/writer environment, relational in the reuse environment). For external access, the information is represented in HTML format. This allows WWW middleware and tools to be used for network communication and document visualization.

A final note should be made about the employment of "remote code" in the form of Java applets or the like. Both projects make use of the possibility to *load* not only data, but also *code* from a server which is then executed in the client application. This is a very interesting variant of distribution with a wide range of applications: it can be used (1) internally to replicate functionality to a client who needs it, (2) to parameterize or configure the client application dynamically, or (3) even to load or replace a complete client application at run–time. The projects will evaluate the usefulness of this approach in the face of concrete distribution scenarios.

5.5 Summary and Synergy

M. Nagl

This chapter reported on *ongoing* work. So, the topics presented here were more than visions or ideas. On the other hand, results are intermediate, have to be detailed and substantiated and, therefore, are still open to modification.

As can be seen from the contents of this chapter, the group is moving towards certain *applications outside* of *software engineering*, or of SDEs. This is to be seen from 5.1 where we discussed means of how to organize development processes for arbitrary engineering disciplines. Furthermore, in section 5.3 we saw that reengineering in business administration applications is studied as well as means for structuring reactive and concurrent systems. The application studies in section 5.4 are furthest away from software engineering, namely the writer/learner environment for electronic books and the retrieval system where its specific instantiation for reusing OO classes is only one of its possible forms.

Conversely, the problems found there give rise to an extension or *improvement* of *IPSEN tools* and of the *machinery* to produce such tools. For example, developing different environments which are tightly coupled in a different sense than technical environments (by fine–grained integration tools) are a new challenge. Also, the new tools of 5.3 build up a machinery for reengineering, distributing, or integrating application systems and offer new IPSEN functionality. According to the philosophy of this book, these new functionalities or this different type of coupling has first to be solved on graph grammar spec level where new ways of structuring specifications have to be found (section 5.2).

The first characterization of the results of this chapter can be given if we relate its contents to the list of *future directions* in the field SDEs given in subsection 1.8.3: (1) 'Future platform approaches' are discussed in the distribution section 5.3. Furthermore, in the SU-KITS project, the definition of future generalized platform services and the mapping of tool structures (data, control, UI, direct communication of developers) on this generalized platform is studied, which was not discussed in this chapter. (2) 'Integrated administration services' are directly addressed in section 5.1. There, exchangeability, configurability, and adaptability of administration models due to information available before or at project runtime is the main topic. Also, a closer and more intelligent integration between the technical and the administration level is discussed. (3) 'Completeness, Combination, and Configurability', (4) 'Intelligence, Integration, and Flexibility', as well as (5) 'Structuring, Mechanization' all need a better understanding of the development process to build integrated environments. There are two contributions: The main contribution is 5.2, where our plans for structuring large specs are described, this is a prerequisite for all topics (3)–(5). This is because exchangeability of technical or administration models but also the integration of specific models has to be handled first on spec level. Furthermore, distributed architectures of 5.3 and the way to get them is a contribution to these topics. (6) 'Specific environments' are handled in 5.4 where some application–specific environments are sketched.

The *contents* of this short summary section are as follows: Firstly, we summarize the main ideas of the above sections 5.1 to 5.4, respectively. This is done in the first subsection. Then, we characterize the variety of future IPSEN products sketched in this chapter from their external behavior, their new internal structure or new type of interaction, from their new philosophy (bottom–up approaches), and from the fact how they are realized on a distributed platform.

5.5.1 Summary of this Chapter

We now go through the sections of this chapter and *summarize* their *main ideas*. Thereby, we try to introduce different perspectives than taken in the sections themselves to avoid redundancy and to give new viewpoints.

Organization and Coordination of Development Processes

In section 5.1 we discussed *project organization* thereby concentrating on the *dynamics* aspect of processes, products, but also resources. Concentrating on the administration and middle–grain level, we detected that permanent changes are also found on technical level (results of developers) or, even more, changes of this level mostly induce dynamics on administration level. The starting point for this project was to organize and manage arbitrary development processes in engineering disciplines like CIM, chemical process control etc. The approach introduced in 5.1, after introducing the problems to be handled and sketching the goal, lead to three main results.

A *new model* for an *administration configuration* was introduced consisting of a submodel for processes, products, and abstract/actual resources, respectively. Furthermore, the *integration* relations between these submodels have been made clear. The administration model has been formalized in order to "derive" the next version of an administration system.

Starting from this generalized model for an administration configuration, a *new* model for an *overall configuration* compared to that of the introductory chapter was given. The differences are: (1) A layered structure of three layers where the extended technical configuration is found at the bottom and management of management/parameterization/adaptation at the top. Furthermore, (2) not only the products but also the corresponding processes are taken into account resulting in an overall process/product model. In addition, (3) the interaction of different overall configurations in the case of cooperating projects is regarded. Finally, (4) the question of generic model construction and exchangeability of its submodels was sketched.

The third result is a coherent set of *different environments* (for the manager, the parameterizer, process modeler, technical developer) working tightly together. The integration of such environments is new when compared to the integration of technical environments by integration tools discussed in the main chapters of this book. This is discussed below in more detail. *Adaptation* due to changes of different kinds and *reactivity* of human processes is handled by the interaction of corresponding supporting environments.

Future Gra Gra Specs and Their Support

In section 5.2 it was argued that in order to handle *large gra gra specs* (understandability, handling the process of their development, adaptability, reuse etc.) it is necessary that such specs are modularized with a formal interrelation of such spec modules. This results in a *specification in the large* approach and corresponding MIL patterns. Especially, the various integration problems studied in the IPSEN project enforce this approach.

After introducing various spec structuring problems to be solved, section 5.2 contained the following main results:
(1) It was detected that *layer* adt *structures* invented in the SE or OO DBMS context do *not serve* our *needs* for handling integration problems occurring in a tightly integrated SDE. There, it is not possible to completely abstract from a document's structure on a certain layer. Instead, we need on one side abstraction forgetting realization details but on the other hand we need access to certain underlying structural details to achieve tight integration.
(2) Different *interaction mechanisms* were studied as well as their *advantages* and *disadvantages*. It was shown that different coupling situations can be mapped onto the same

interrelation patterns (different representations for a logical document, integration views and their coupling etc.).

(3) Especially, there is the need for formalizing partial abstraction needed in the above coupling patterns. For this the notion of *"hierarchical" graphs* was introduced.

Distribution by and within Environments

In subsection 5.3.2 a *methodology* for *distribution* was introduced which was developed in the business administration context but which is also applicable to engineering development systems, like SDEs. It consisted of different *steps*: (a) reengineering of existing application systems to make them suitable for distribution, (b) determination of potential cutting lines, (c) determination of replicated and concentrated systems and components, (d) selection of actual cutting lines, (e) implementation of the distributed system using platform services like CORBA and, finally, (f) placement of the system on a physical hardware platform. These steps can also be applied for *integrating* systems to support cooperative processes which are not integrated yet. Then, some of the above steps may become trivial.

Distribution and integration may be supported by methods, corresponding tools, components or platforms helping to restructure a system, being parts of the final system, or customizing corresponding components/platforms. Section 5.3 suggested (a) *tool support* for the above steps, or used (b) the IPSEN system (or parts of it, like R–GRAS) as *example* for this restructuring process.

In detail, 5.3.3 introduced corresponding *reengineering tools* for existing application systems to prepare them for distribution or integration resulting in a corresponding clear and modular object–based building plan, the virtual architecture. These steps extract UI details and place them in a separate subsystem, hide data structuring details by introducing a layer of abstractions for accessing persistent data, reorganize the application functions' core part, and adapt the system to the structure of development/business processes.

The virtual architecture is then prepared for distribution as was shown in 5.3.1 resulting in a corresponding *concrete architecture*. It was also described there that the mechanisms or implementation details of concrete architecture are necessary for describing concurrent reactive systems or event–based systems, for specifying efficiency improvements, and for determining binding mechanisms. The suggestion was to have the concrete architecture as a separate software document (subconfiguration) and to build *incremental transformation tools* to transform a virtual to a concrete architecture. These tools can be used to support the above steps (b)–(d).

Finally, for the above steps (e) and (f) tool support has to be developed to choose a suitable platform, according to the desired coordination and communication mechanisms and requirements, to select corresponding available features, to parameterize the platform, and to use it in order to configure a corresponding distributed system on a certain hardware platform. Introducing available *platform technology* and suggesting corresponding *tools* was the aim of 5.3.5.

So, subsections 5.3.3, 5.3.1, and 5.3.5 propose a *coherent tool support* by corresponding environments for the whole process for distributing as well as integrating (of separately placed) existing systems. Essentially, there are two integration lines: (i) The underlying data of a business and development system offered to the application systems in an appropriate abstract data form, and (ii) the coordination of corresponding development or business processes. All tools suggested emphasize the architecture level, are specific to a certain application domain, or to a certain class of software systems.

Although being classical from the outside perspective (environments plus integration tools as introduced in the core chapters of this book), we shall later see that a different realization strategy is used compared to the tools discussed above. The results of subsection 5.3.4 are described later.

New Application–Specific Environments

Two *examples* of *application–specific* systems have been introduced in section 5.4. One is for writing, parameterizing, reading of future electronic books and the other one for structuring a retrieval context, for inputting and maintaining corresponding information, and for using the retrieved information. From that short characterization it is seen that any of both systems is not a single environment but, again as in 5.1, an *ensemble* of *tightly cooperating environments*. The different form of coupling of these environments is introduced in the next subsection.

In the writer/reader system we have the following different *functionalities*:

A *writer environment* helps to explicitly structure the semantic net of a book. This improves book writing as it is at the moment. (i) No writer builds up such a structure, he usually has only a rough and vague form of it in mind. In addition, (ii) he can structure a book not only for one but for different reader profiles (see below). Furthermore, (iii) electronic books can take advantage of audio or video information. Such an electronic book can (iv) be parameterized according to different reader profiles (experience, educational background, interest in specific topics, degree of detail etc.).

A *reader environment* gives (v) an improved access to the book contents either for personalized statically determined traces, for lookup, for studying specific subtopics etc. It gives (vi) support for a personalized reading process by offering dynamic traces due to gained understanding (checking and evaluating the results of exercises, forward and backward jumps). Even more, (vii) a personalized reading context can be built up by personal annotations, remarks etc. which can be utilized for browsing, lookup, or rereading.

Both types of environments can be coupled for *interaction* of different readers and for interaction of readers and a writer. MM techniques of other projects outside the group can be used.

The *reuse system* supports reuse of OO classes but also of subarchitectures and the integration of reused results, either for external (e.g. public domain) or internal reuse (within the company). An extension of feature–oriented classification is used. After a short comparison of existing literature on product reuse the outside functionality was described. Again, *different functionality* is needed:
(a) To structure/restructure a reuse domain by an reuse *administrator*. Specific tools are needed for this purpose.
(b) A reuse *manager* needs tools for filling, updating, and restructuring the reuse library.
(c) A *user* (developer) needs intelligent access to a reuse library and tools for integrating found classes and subsystems, for their modification, and for the modification of the system under development to incorporate the reused results.

Both projects described in 5.4 follow a *bottom–up approach* (see below for more details): Existing products are (i) reused (existing books, classes). Tool support is (ii) needed to prepare existing products for advanced functionality. Existing modern technology is (iii) taken, namely WWW, internet, Java etc. Existing further tools are (iv) integrated as book writing and preparation systems, or search engines over existing data stores. So, transfer of IPSEN results is mostly on the conceptual level of how to build the tools. For the writer environment or the reuse administrator/manager tools IPSEN–like realizations are possible. This is, because of overhead reasons, not suitable for the book reader or the reuse user tools.

Now that we have summarized the contents of the different sections of this chapter, the rest of this section is devoted to make clear that these *projects* are not isolated but *interact* in various ways. So, from an integration viewpoint we now characterize commonalities and interrelations of these projects.

5.5.2 Future IPSEN Products and Their Different Realization Structure

This subsection summarizes chapter 5 under different perspectives: (1) Which new functionality is offered by the tools under investigation/construction, (2) How does the internal structure of environments and their interaction deviate from that described in the main chapter of this book, (3) In which different respects bottom–up approaches are used, and (4) How IPSEN is becoming a distributed system.

New Outside Functionality

Going through sections 5.1–5.4 we *summarize* the new *outside functionality* by table 5.57. We see that tools under development belong to quite different aspects within or outside software engineering. Some are in the state of prestudies, in other cases preliminary prototypes are available. So, table 5.57 gives some program for ongoing work rather than making an announcement of compulsory delivering dates.

From the vast variety of tools for software engineering or other applications outside of SE we *concentrate* on certain *topics*. These topics are *interesting* because of the following *reasons*: (1) There are new scientific and realization problems behind which lead to new environment structures or new coupling patterns between environments. (2) We can generalize results gained in the SDE field to cope with other application areas. (3) We can transfer structural knowledge compiled in IPSEN and apply it to other fields outside SDEs. (4) The functionality is necessary to improve existing tool construction or to allow the realization of tools under investigation.

All tools under development emphasize the *architectural* view. This is clear from the distribution/integration machinery built up as described in section 5.3. It is also true for the generalized administration system of 5.1 as it is ''*architectural*'' information on technical development level which is important for management (schematic information for administration is mostly derived from architectures or from documents with a similar character), and subproject, multiproject, and overall processes between companies are only possible, if some determination on architectural level (built plan level) has been made. It is even true for the new gra gra spec tools of 5.2 as they are based on the assumption that architectures for large specs have to be introduced.

A further common aspect is that all new tools developed are *adaptable* to a certain context (application domain, structure of systems or products to be built, type of project etc.). So, future tools contain as little fixed determinations as possible and leave freedom for introducing the specifics of a certain context without triggering a complete restart of the tool development machinery. In some cases adaptation can even yield a different external functionality. This is to be seen from the OO–classes reuse system: The underlying mechanisms allow that the system can be parameterized to build up an intelligent retrieval system in a completely different domain, e.g. literature enquiry.

organizing engineering development processes and embedding technical development processes (1)
reactive management environment for handling administration configurations (reactive w.r.t. evolving technical details, management problems, parameterization to an application domain, evolving schematic information)   front end for technical developers (introducing a working context for a task, giving a passive view on the enclosing process, containing an incremental transformer for management information derived from technical information)   parameterization tools and schematic information specification tools of the parameterization and administration methods environment (introducing parameterization information for a generic model, developing or extending schematic information of different types, see 5.1)   environment for supporting subprojects, multi–projects, and processes between companies (managing management cooperation, determining parameterization, contract definition etc.)
restructuring systems for distribution, integrating isolated systems, structuring embedded systems
reengineering environment (for developing an object–based architecture from existing code, extracting application functionality, splitting integrated systems, preparing isolated systems for integration)

concrete architecture development environment (for transforming usability relations into concrete MI mechanisms, handling concurrency, handling distribution preparation, inserting concrete binding mechanisms) environment for utilizing advanced platform services (for selecting a platform, parameterizing it, developing/generating needed stubs, inserting traders/brokers, placement of a distributed system on a hardware platform)

application–specific systems

knowledge–based writer/reader system
    environment for defining and extending the underlying logical structure of a book (book structure knowledge development)
    environment for structuring/restructuring a certain book (writer environment)
    personalized reader environment
    reader and writer communication tools
intelligent and interactive software reuse systems (2, 3)
    environment for defining and extending reuse structure knowledge (reuse administrator environment)
    environment for inputting/maintaining/restructuring the reuse data store (reuse manager)
    environment for using reusable classes, hierarchies, restructuring them/the system under development (reuse user)

specifying large gra gra specs, deriving prototypes and code for frameworks

future PROGRES environment
    support for storing spec modules in different logical spec documents of a project database, with multiple user access and incremental analysis across module boundaries
    editing/analyzing/executing tools for triple graph grammars
    tools for hierarchical graph models
prototyping of environments
    enhancing user interfaces of generated prototypes: interaction of multiple views onto a common graph database, textual views, graphical editing support, manual/semiautomatic layout of graphs
code generation (2)
    generating efficient integration tools from triple gra gra specs
    translating specs onto C++ code where graphs are either stored in ODMG–standard compliant OODB (replacement of GRAS by a commercial DBS) or kept in main memory (performance improvement)

Table 5.57. New tools under development: (1) means current versions having been described in chapter 2, (2) first version of a new prototype is available or nearly available, (3) experience available not described in this book

Structure and Coupling of Environments

The main chapters of this book described various tools for working areas, mainly in the field of software engineering or their integration. Working areas/integration are on technical development (RE, PiL, transformation between both etc.) or administration (process and corresponding product administration etc.) level. Even for the integration of both means have been developed in the form of front ends (working context, delegation of management functionality etc.). All tools developed so far are *application–specific* (for software development), *language–specific* (as an EER editor), or *method–oriented* (as the integration tool between RE and PiL). So all tools incorporate some application, structure, or method knowledge.

Tools are *adapted* to (1) a specific application domain, (2) corresponding languages, or (3) to method knowledge of how to apply a language or corresponding languages in the case of integration tools. Knowledge according to (1)–(3) is (a) how products are structured, (b) which sensible relations between product parts (increments) in the form of fine–grained relations exist and have to be regarded, and (c) which sensible steps of the processes of constructing/maintaining a certain portion of a configuration can be supported by incremental and interactive tools. This adaptation to dimensions (1)–(3) and how it is achieved through (a)–(c) lies in the *process* of *developing tools*, ranging from specification of the core part of IPSEN systems to their translation into efficient and executable code. In the case of the presentation part of an IPSEN–like system it is found in the code development for presentation purposes (cf. sections 4.1, 4.3). So, once the tools have been developed, adaptation is found in hardwired form in the tool code.

Extension or *modification* of *tools* due to changes in one of the dimensions (1)–(3) means (i) to restart the tool development process which is not itself easy, (ii) that users have to be reeducated to get along with new tool behavior, and (iii) products produced with the old tools cannot be reused. The positive message in this problem statement is that the manpower for tool production is reduced by the mechanized process. The situation is even better for the rapid prototyping tools introduced in 3.6 where only a specification has to be changed. However, problems (ii) and (iii) remain.

If underlying *knowledge* is *available* and is *not changing*, then there is no problem with this procedure. This is mostly the case for language–specific tools for a standardized language, as a programming language (only method knowledge may change). In this sense all IPSEN tools developed so far and described in the main part of this book are language–specific. If they are method–oriented, then these methods are put into an extended language syntax incorporating methodological rules. However, we have seen in the administration system discussion of 5.1, in the reengineering/distribution/integration discussion of 5.3, as well as in the electronic book or OO classes retrieval/reuse discussion of 5.4 that such knowledge is *not available*, or is available but still *in development*, or is even *changing during a project* itself as it also contains project–specific knowledge or knowledge which is only detected when carrying out such a project.

So, how to overcome problems (i)–(iii) of above in these cases? Before we go into the discussion of this question, let us make clear which different situations arise for the IPSEN tools described in the main chapters of this book or in ongoing work of this chapter. The necessary characterization is given by *answering* two *questions* (cf. fig. 5.58): (a) Is the knowledge to be incorporated in the tools "closed" and definite at some time? (b) How is knowledge development time related to tool construction and use time?

There is the extreme situation which seldom occurred in the IPSEN project (cf. 5.58.a) that *knowledge* was *available before* tool development. This is the case for programming language tools. Knowledge is here syntactic and semantic language knowledge. The typical situation is given in fig. 5.58.b. Underlying knowledge and tool construction *overlap*, as this knowledge was not clear enough before building tools (RE tools, RE–PiL integration tools). Knowledge is here again syntactic and semantic knowledge or method knowledge how to relate both languages, thereby defining some "integration" language. The situations of fig. 5.58.c and .d are those occurring for ongoing projects. In 5.58.c underlying knowledge is developed in *parallel*, there may be different versions of tools such that "use" is overlapping with tool construction. So we need flexibility of tool construction as underlying knowledge is changing. Modifying and extending knowledge induces a corresponding tool development process. In the last case 5.58.d there is *no end point* for knowledge development and, therefore, tools have to be *adapted incrementally*.

So, the above discussion of interesting cases for this summary, namely .c and .d of fig. 5.58, reduce to the question whether a *knowledge modifier* is a *user* of the overall development process or whether a knowledge modifier is only a *specialist* which occurs during the *tool construction* process. In the first case, knowledge, tool behavior, as well as their use changes as knowledge is evolving. Here, we need a different implementation strategy that knowledge is not once and for ever translated to code. In the second case, we need a flexible tool construction process for easy rapid prototype construction and a mechanization of the efficient tool construction process. As we have already discussed results for the second case (see section 3.6 for rapid prototyping, section 4.4 for the flexible and iterative tool specification process, the rest of chapter 4 for the tool development machinery), we concentrate in the following discussion on the first case. Trivially, also for the second case some progress has to be made in the future.

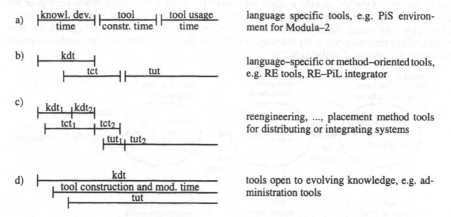

a) | knowl. dev. | tool | tool usage | — language specific tools, e.g. PiS environ-
     time | constr. time | time   ment for Modula–2

b) | kdt | — language–specific or method–oriented tools,
     | tct | tut   e.g. RE tools, RE–PiL integrator

c) | kdt_1 | kdt_2 | — reengineering, ..., placement method tools
     | tct_1 | tct_2 | for distributing or integrating systems
     | tut_1 | tut_2 |

d) | kdt | — tools open to evolving knowledge, e.g. ad-
     | tool construction and mod. time | ministration tools
     | tut |

Fig. 5.58. Relating knowledge development to tool construction and use time

Let us now *summarize* the situations we have discussed in this chapter for the first case (cf. 5.59).

For the *administration system* let us concentrate on administration of a project and coupling between the administration layer and that of technical developers (cf. fig. 5.59.a). So, multi–project, company–integrating projects, configuring suitable models and its coordination is omitted, see section 5.1. A parameterization and method development adaptation environment is used to develop underlying structure rules and patterns of various kinds to support management. This knowledge is used to make the management environment reactive in the sense of incorporating these patterns for application–specific development, reuse etc. processes. Administration knowledge is used to structure and coordinate technical developer processes and to control the status of a project (planning, management, control, supervision).

A similar situation is found in the knowledge–based *writer* and *learner* system (cf. fig. 5.59.b) and the OO–classes and hierarchy reuse system (cf. fig. 5.59.c), both of section 5.4. The "method developer" is now structuring a book in general, for certain classes, certain styles etc. by defining structural product and process method knowledge which is used by an intelligent writing environment, see section 5.4. Analogously, in the *reuse* case general and specific reuse domain knowledge is built up which is to be used by a FOCS–based reuse library system.

Common to all three cases is that a "knowledge developer" is incorporated in the process of developing a certain application environment's functionality (reactive management system, writer system, reuse library system). The knowledge developed is not only once developed and used but is due to permanent changes. This is true in the first case as argued carefully in 5.1 and in both latter cases at least during the whole process of application system development. The *difference* between the cases (a)–(c) is found on the left side as environments found here have quite different characteristics and coupling between them and the systems of the middle column is quite different. Whereas in (a) it is coordination and control of technical developers (only coarse–grained information is relevant for the management environment), in case (b) it is transformation to a parameterized version and MM interaction, in (c) it is retrieval query and result communication.

So, the *coupling* between method development environments and corresponding environments incorporating this method knowledge (cf. right column and middle column of fig. 5.59) is completely *different* from horizontal and vertical integration tools coupling (fine–grained coupling on technical development level), or from coupling technical environments to the administration system by front–ends (course–grained abstraction coupling) we have discussed in the main part of this book. It is also different from the coupling between the environments of the left and the middle column of fig. 5.59. Coupling is made here in order to influence the behavior of an environment to make it more intelligent, specific, or change-able. This has some *implications* for *implementing* this type of coupling, which was sketched in subsection 5.1.3. By the way, coupling is also on a different platform in the cases (b) and (c), compared to the case (a).

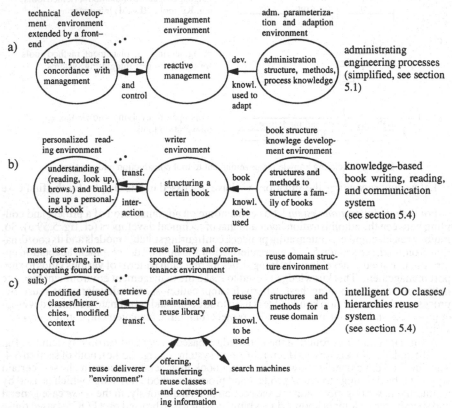

Fig. 5.59. Different method or structure development environments occurring in ongoing projects

The *advantage* of the approach to have method development in the development process is that *knowledge* of *different kinds* can be *handled uniformly*. There may be knowledge of how underlying products are structured, integration knowledge for their interrelation, meth-od knowledge of how to structure products (type or object patterns of 5.1) which altogether give rise to structure or integration knowledge of a higher level. Also, as we have seen, this knowledge may be product (how results look like) or process knowledge (how the process looks to produce these results). We have also argued above that this knowledge may be re-lated to forward development, to backtracking, to different types of reuse, to reengineering situations up to knowledge of an advanced (application, structure class, and project type) technology–driven process. Whereas classical IPSEN tools are mostly language–specific (where language is to be used in a general sense as the language reflects the application do-main, structure knowledge expressed by the language, methodological use can be incorpo-rated in the language, the language may be an "integrated" language etc.) this new way of-

615

fers the possibility for method–oriented tools in the sense of various patterns to be defined, extended, and exchanged.

The *flexibility* which is offered by having the knowledge developer included in a software development process also has some *disadvantages*: (a) Tool construction is more complicated, as tool "construction" is now the tight coupling between method development and method use by another environment. (b) Tool behavior is now changing which hinders portability of developers. Thus, we may get different understandings for underlying products, their processes etc. in every development context. (c) Efficiency of tools is harder to achieve as some interpretation mechanism is necessary for flexibility in adaptation process. (d) In any case it is not possible to change underlying knowledge, it is only possible to extend it due to the product reuse problem (iii) of above.

Thus, this flexibility should be applied only in those situations where it is necessary. So, once *knowledge* has gained some *fixed*, commonly agreed, and standardized *status*, it is preferable to *encode* knowledge into tool behavior. This means to put knowledge into the code of tools. In the light of the discussion given here, therefore, the proceeding taken in the main part of this book is sensible if underlying knowledge of tools has gained some fixed status. We then have clear role–specific support shared by all persons of a role in the development process. This was the approach taken for technical environments in this book.

Of course, it is also possible to *handle different parts* of *knowledge differently*: (a) Knowledge corresponding to the structure of underlying products is encoded into tools. (b) Method knowledge which is evolving is treated interpretatively. (c) Once method knowledge is fixed it is encoded. This offers the possibility of higher–level knowledge being developed, which the first time is interpreted and then encoded. This procedure can be iterated.

Used Bottom–up Approaches

In chapter 1 the *difference* between a priori or *top–down* SDE development or *bottom–up* or a posteriori tool construction was explained. It is clear that most of this book falls into the top–down approaches' category. Only the SUKITS results, also applicable to coordinate software developers (see section 2.5, 3.5, and 4.7), have been developed in the context of a general bottom–up approach. Inside the administration system, again a top–down approach was followed, so no existing workflow system, configuration management system etc. was taken for integration but a new and general administration system was developed.

This has changed if we regard ongoing projects. We are now *summarizing* where *bottom–up ideas* came up in the *ongoing projects* described in this chapter.

Administration systems: The general philosophy remains to be bottom–up. The aim still is to integrate existing engineering development systems. Inside of the administration system we study now how and if existing systems for subtopics can be used and integrated. This is not easy, as it seems to be in contradiction to the tight integration needed within administration systems. Also, reactivity will be hindered. However, certain aspects such as scheduling of actual resources are to be integrated. Furthermore, patterns of the administration system can be reused and need not be developed in the process where the administration system is applied. It was argued that this is the solution needed in order to have an adaptable administration system accepted in engineering disciplines.

Specification systems: Specification in the large allows the reuse of spec modules or spec subarchitectures. Although they have to be formalized in the PROGRES language and by a new PROGRES system and cannot be taken from outside (internal spec product reuse), this allows building up specs from reusable spec portions. So, in future, bottom–up spec development processes are possible. A further project, not described in this book, is to build fine–grained integration tools by taking existing environments to be integrated. As argued in section 5.2, this induces that on spec level views for the corresponding internal structures of environments have to be defined.

Distribution and integration systems: Reengineering with the aim of distribution is a bottom–up idea as it takes existing systems. A similar reengineering process is necessary for integrating existing isolated systems. As above in the administration system, reengineering rules can be applied (although they are not developed in the reuse process). Furthermore, it is a bottom–up idea to take existing and future platform technology, as the platform is not developed inside the project. This was not the case for the IPSEN platform described in the main part of this book. It was also argued, that with platform technology utilities come along as e.g. stub generators.

Application–specific systems: In the writer/reader system we take existing books by putting a semantical net on top of a plain text structure. Book preparation systems are incorporated. Existing new technology is taken, as internet, WWW, HTML format, or Java as implementation language. Existing multimedia techniques are used for communication between readers and a writer. In the same way, in the reuse system we take existing usable classes or OO hierarchies from public domain or market. So, again, only a classification structure is built on top of existing products. As in the case of the writer/reader system existing new technology is taken (WWW, internet etc.), in this case also an OO DBS from the market. Search engines are included to retrieve results from external data stores.

The term *bottom–up* has been used in *different senses* above: (a) using a general philosophy (developing a suitable administration system for arbitrary engineering development processes), (b) the use of existing tools (as a scheduler for concrete resources), (c) use of existing products to be taken for modification (specs, books, classes), (d) use of existing and available technology (WWW, MM), (e) use of existing and available platform technology for environments (CORBA, OO DBS), and (f) supporting a bottom–up philosophy (as by the adaptation environment to support administration or reuse processes).

Distributed IPSEN Systems

Distribution started in IPSEN with distributing the underlying object storage GRAS. *R–GRAS* with R standing for "remote" was described in section 4.2. The current ongoing work was discussed in subsection 5.3.4. Before summarizing what is done or planned in direction of IPSEN itself, we make up a summary of this project 'future active distributed GRAS' which was left out in subsection 5.5.1.

One stream of research activities comes from the *bottom*. Transactions with their ACID property are not suitable for engineering processes with long running 'transactions'. So, these properties have to be weakened. Engineering data bases have to support short as well as long transactions (group transactions). Transactions are one mechanism of change control (undo/redo, recovery, versioning and delta logs, locking etc.). They all have to be seen together to offer a suitable basic functionality of an engineering data base system. Especially, locking units for concurrency control which at the moment are complete graphs (either a developer possesses a version; or a process to guarantee mutual exclusion of access has to be implemented) must be finer–grained, and there has to be a universal mechanism for different levels of granularity. Furthermore, data communication should be flexibly implemented such that existing page servers can be used.

The other stream is *top–down*. What is the functionality of an engineering DBS or different DBSs as part of an advanced platform for distributed applications such that (i) they are suitable for extended technical configurations with arbitrary internal, interrelated, and hierarchical structure, for (ii) corresponding human and automatic technical processes of developers or tools where certain process chunks or complete processes are realized by tools, for (iii) coordination of diverse developers, for (iv) the adaptation of the process due to different adaptation dimensions, up to handling (v) integrated processes across borders of companies? What are the basic functionalities to be offered and commonly used? How is the mapping between both levels done?

The *aim* is to restructure R–GRAS as an *active, distributed data base system* with different data base actors. Is there a universal mechanism like the ECA–rules with a corresponding event–trigger machine such that all mutual influences of portions of an overall configuration and their corresponding mutually influencing subprocesses (see section 5.1) can be mapped on this mechanism? How does the architecture look like, especially on top of the kernel (see fig. 4.9 for a first discussion)? How is distribution according to certain requirements and needs achieved and how can the architecture be adapted to a certain distribution platform? Handling underlying data is, of course, only one feature of a future services platform for distributed applications, the mutual relations between these different services being not clear at the moment, nor is the implementation of such a platform and, therefore, the placement of a distributed DBS. So, there are a lot of questions to be answered.

R–GRAS is one example of a system to be distributed or where distribution is improved. The other one is the IPSEN system itself. So, we can (a) use the method sketched in section 5.3 to be applied to the restructuring and distribution process of IPSEN. Especially, they can be used to "derive" the next R–GRAS version. This is a kind of a *conceptual bootstrapping* step. If corresponding tools of the tightly integrated environment for reengineering, ..., distribution support of section 5.3 were available, we can (b) apply these tools for a real bootstrapping step. It is probable that distributed IPSEN is available at that time such that the tools can on one side (i) demonstrate the procedure to get the distributed results for a nontrivial system, and (ii) give possible hints for improvement of the distributed IPSEN system's structure.

Future IPSEN systems are not only distributed. They should also be based on a platform such as CORBA or, even better, on a general services platform for distributed development systems which is either an improvement of existing systems like CORBA or a general layer on top of it. IPSEN systems should also be *dynamically loadable* such that the functionality of a specific environment or of an integrated environment is built according to the functionality corresponding users need.

6 Conclusion: Summary, Evaluation, and Vision

M. Nagl

The purpose of the last chapter is on one side to *summarize* the essential ideas, concepts, mechanisms, and their corresponding solutions of this book after the reader has gone through chapters 1 to 5. This summary, therefore, has another character than the introductory overview of chapter 1 as (1) all technical details have been explained (chapters 2–4) from which the main ideas are extracted now, (2) future plans and still open problems have been discussed (chapter 5) and can be included. So, it is a detailed and broader perspective from which this chapter is given and it is a summary, not a introduction or overview.

The second topic of this chapter and an output of the summary is (1) to *characterize* the project's approach, thereby implicitly discussing the differences to other projects. Furthermore, (2) the contributions of IPSEN to overcome problems of software engineering, to give solutions in software engineering, and to follow future trends in SDEs are given. Finally, (3) some related projects are sketched, and (4) the different facets of the IPSEN project are summarized.

The third goal of this chapter is to demonstrate the practical *relevance* of the project. Trivially, the contributions (2) of the last paragraph could be mentioned again for this purpose. Although being a research project, IPSEN has contributed to the solution of problems of practical relevance. Moreover, most of the structural knowledge on how to build an SDE can be transferred for developing environments in other application domains, within and outside engineering. Especially, the view of underlying and nested graph complexes to be handled inside an SDE is applicable to other domains and also to other approaches (as a posteriori).

The second and third topic deliver the *evaluation* part of this summary. So, we are not going to enumerate achieved results but give a self–critical view on our work. Finally, there is also a *vision* part summarizing the future goals and the long–term aims. As to be seen, there are more ideas on how to proceed than there will be available resources for their investigation.

The *contents* of this chapter are the following: In section 6.1 we summarize the underlying philosophy of IPSEN tools. It is clear separation of concern accompanied by integration and, therefore, not putting everything together into an unstructured bag. From this discussion we derive how future support for development processes must look. The second section is to indicate the role of graphs and graph grammars in this book and how future tool support is to be handled on graph grammar specification level. Section 6.3 emphasizes IPSEN's practical contributions either to current problems of software engineering or for tool builders. Then, we take up a discussion of the introduction and demonstrate that IPSEN has contributed to technologies due to a corresponding specialization and concentration on specific topics. In section 6.4 we summarize graph–based environments of this book or from other groups. Finally, section 6.5 gives a condensed chapter summary but also a characterization, evaluation, and vision of IPSEN.

6.1 Integration and Development Processes

The *aim* of this *section* is to summarize the *philosophy* underlying current and future IP-SEN tools. The main topic is *integration*. However, integration is based on separation due to concern, roles, rules etc. Integration overcomes separation in a regulated way. This section summarizes how we see a development process, the corresponding product, suitable future support, and which implications this has for the realization structure of an overall environment.

6.1.1 Separation, Integration, and Distribution

After pleading for a clear separation of concern in this *section* to avoid unprecise terms and insufficient support (there are different products and processes in a development process), we discuss how integration of separated topics has to be achieved and is supported by a distributed overall environment containing specific support for separate processes and for the integration of their results.

Separation of Concern

It was argued in the introduction that *separation* of concern, i.e. the distinction of different matters, is necessary to *handle* the *complexity* of development processes in engineering applications, like SE. Separation is found on the product side, the process side itself, and the resources side. A working area model roughly structuring the process or its product (cf. fig. 1.2) made this clear.

Regarding the *product* of a development process we argued in section 1.1 that we need a wide understanding of product resulting in the term 'overall configuration'. This discussion was taken up in 5.1 again, where we saw that this product contains even more *complexity* and *structure*. We now regard this extended version of an overall configuration and find what is to be separated.

Separation has *to do* (a) with a *logical perspective* which can clearly be differed from others resulting in a separately handled unit (separation unit) as, e.g. a requirements spec. Such a unit can (b) in general be represented with a different *degree* of *detail* (overview, detailed description), and (c) be *elaborated* to a certain *level*, as the different stages of a requirements model in 2.2. A separation unit can (d) be *atomic*, so not further divided into parts or (e) *composed*. Separation is found at the border of a separation unit to others.

Separation is due to the following *dimensions*: We separate (1) different technical *activities* and their corresponding results (requirements spec, architecture) and, thereby, (2) different *parts* as a structural part, consistency relations, execution preparation etc. In technical results but also in others to be discussed we find (3) separate *compositions* in form of subconfigurations (e.g. a subsystem's architecture with corresponding code, a complex architectural design with corresponding subsystem designs). *Technical* results are (4) separated from *administration* results (as a process net to coordinate developers) and, even more, from results for management of administration. One can separate (5) what is *available* for a certain development (a subsystem to be included in a system) or what has to be *developed* in the project. We differ also (6) between results to be *elaborated* for the development of a certain software system, either on technical or other level, or schematic information developed to *facilitate* the process of developing another product. (The discussion of this topic concentrated on administration aspects in 5.1. This distinction, however, is also applicable on technical level, see discussion in 5.5.) Furthermore, we (7) distinguish between different states of time of separation units, called *revisions*, or (8) different *variants* of it. Finally, (9) we separate what is produced in one (sub)project or different *projects* if an integrated project or a family of projects is regarded.

So, one can regard the overall configuration of section 5.1 (cf. fig. 5.17) for a certain project, and use cutting lines to determine what is a suitable unit of *separation*. For the software development context table 6.1 gives *examples* discussed in this book where most of them are, correspondingly, supported by IPSEN tools.

To any of the above separation units either 'atomic', as the functional model of a requirements spec, or 'composed', as a complete requirements spec, we find a corresponding *subprocess* within the overall development process. This subprocess may belong to a certain fixed degree of product detail and it may be in a certain elaboration state. As *integration* is also handled as a subprocess (e.g. RE–PiL integration, which can be handled quite differently by a designer), we may regard any integration item to be also a "derived" separation unit. Indeed, internally, we have introduced documents for integration. Subprocesses *interact* with each other (see below).

Separation of a part of the overall configuration corresponds to the *independence* of the corresponding subprocess. This independence makes it possible that a person with a specific role (or a group) with corresponding capabilities is able to carry out the subprocess. Alternatively, in the rare case that the subprocess can be automatically performed, a complex tool execution delivers the subprocess result. So, *resources*, either human or automatic (tool), can be assigned to subprocesses. The result of a subprocess may be either an active or a passive resource for another subprocess (see subsection 1.1.5). Usually, a resource supports a human subprocess (a tool or environment). For this, it has to have the corresponding functionality (a Modula–2 editor for implementing or maintaining module bodies). Usually, more or less big process steps are carried out by a corresponding tool (insertion of a while-statement). Different tools of an environment correspond to different process steps within a subprocess.

---

results of technical development subprocess
    requirements spec:
        a perspective as function, data, or control model; a refinement hierarchy of a
        perspective; a coarse (graphical) or detailed (textual) requirements spec; an
        elaboration stage for a requirements model
    architectural design:
        overall coarse architecture; subsystem design containing subsystems and
        modules; modules with detailed interfaces; sketch of an architecture (rough plan
        down to a certain layer)
    programming:
        a body to a module interface; a module body revision as result of a 3–way
        merging process
    documentation:
        user documentation; technical documentation; parts of it as design rationale,
        explanation of analysis determinations
results of administration processes:
    a configuration description; a process net; abstract resources together with their
    current actual resources; an administration configuration for a subproject; a
    composition of administration configurations of subprojects for a project
results of technical or administration processes to be reused:
    an architectural design to be taken; a subsystem together with its code to be used in
    a system; a net for development coordination adopted for another subproject
administration knowledge developed for use in the corresponding process:
    type patterns for a subsystem development; object patterns for module
    implementation; reuse transformation pattern etc.
result of an configuration or adaptation process:
    basic administration models; parameterized administration model

---

Table 6.1. Separation units within the results of a development process
(only some examples from SE and the IPSEN context)

Any of the separation units of above are built up, or their corresponding processes are supported by *different* kinds of *tools*, *environments*, or parts of them. So we can go through the separation discussion for the products of above and assign corresponding specific support.

Atomic separation units are internally handled as documents, *composed* to subconfigurations. Different levels of *representation* degrees are mapped on different representation documents for a logical document/subconfiguration and parsers/unparsers, respectively. Different degrees of *elaboration* are related to a sketchy or detailed structure of the corresponding document/subconfiguration.

Specific environments contain *different tools* (editor, analyzer etc.). Integration tools of different kinds (transformer, checker etc.) support to handle specific separation units to be composed. Administration functionality is available for technical environments (by front ends). Development environments differ from reuse support environments/tools. Method development environments produce results which are used by specific environments. Specific tools are needed for handling revisions and variants, either on administration level (e.g. configuration description) or on technical level (melting two document revisions). As pointed out in the last chapter, future specific support for handling multi–projects is needed.

Integration of Development Processes, their Results, and Corresponding Support

The *aim* of *integration* is to overcome separation units. So, it is the border of separation units integration has to deal with, as a separation unit can already be composed. Separation units in any case are given: In a priori approaches they are or may be the result of a considered separation process, in a posteriori approaches they are given and there, usually, no clear separation is underlying.

Integration means *composition* and not putting everything together to an unstructured and amorphic whole. Integration, using this latter kind of understanding, does not mean to more easily handle complexity but makes it impossible, as different topics are wildly merged together. Integration does not come for free but needs a *clear understanding* and corresponding formalization. So, the formerly separated parts are still existing, their integration is made clear, and corresponding support is given. Former separation may be "hidden", either partially or totally. Integration must not narrow but allow *freedom*. This was often emphasized in this book by pointing out that usually various different forms of processes exist. We now go through the same discussion of products, processes, resources, and their corresponding support of above. The discussion is shorter as we only take another viewpoint.

On the *product side* we take up the separation discussion of above where we detect the borderlines which have to be *integrated*.

Different representations (graphical, detailed textual), substructures (consists of, consistency relations etc.), elaboration stages (rough, detailed by elaboration), different activities on the same unit (editing, analyzing) are handled inside a specific environment based on the unit of a *document*, more precisely an internal form of it. The document contains not only its parts (increments) but also all necessary logical relations between increments.

So, a document is a basic separation unit to be further composed. Documents deal with logical separation (e.g. architectural design) of a certain size (a subsystem's architecture) to be elaborated. Documents are built up to *subconfigurations* for different purposes, as handling consistency of different views (in RE) or introducing different separate units dependent on each other (a PiL architecture and its subsystems). Both were termed horizontal integration when taking place in the same working area. Vertical integration builds up subconfigurations having documents or subconfigurations of different working areas (as RE–PiL).

So, a *subconfiguration* may contain different documents with clear *integration relations* between its parts. On technical level we find *two–sided fine–grained* relations between increments of corresponding documents. These relations are built up and retrieved from (internal) integration documents. A subconfiguration can be built up from documents or sub-configurations developed in the same project, or it is taken from outside. In the latter case, usually only some interface description is necessary.

Subconfigurations are classified in technical, administration, and administration management subconfigurations. So, it is necessary to integrate subconfigurations of these levels which is done by one-sided *fine*-grained and *coarse-grained relations*.

To deal with schematic information in the form of diverse patterns *another type* of *relations* is needed expressing that action or product patterns are to be used as inline patterns to be placed, patterns to be obeyed etc. Here, it may or may not be necessary to keep the relations after the pattern was used. It is necessary if we keep track of which patterns have to be used and where. Then, a subconfiguration between pattern documents/subconfigurations and where patterns are used is necessary, together with relations of another type. It is not necessary if knowledge of patterns is only used for construction. (The reader might remember that we also do not keep track of which structure operation, e.g. of an editor, was applied. This is possibly kept in logs.) In the latter case we end up with a loose integration of documents/subconfigurations.

Different *versions* and variants of documents/subconfigurations are seen together only on administration level. On technical level, it is kept in logs, it is up to analysis tools to determine what has changed, or it is up to a developer to see what is structured differently.

Finally, to put different overall configurations together to build up the overall configuration of an integrated project (or a family of projects), *other* integration *mechanisms* are needed. We need variants of the above forms as relations abstract from certain specifics, but keep track of other details (correspondence relations of patterns which are not equal but similar etc.).

So, we see that an *overall configuration* consists of different documents/subconfigurations. We have also seen that *different integration mechanisms* are used within an overall configuration as fine-grained intradocument relations, fine-grained interdocument relations to be stored in integration documents, use of patterns, logs, determining difference by analysis tools, keeping track of a similarity of structure. It depends on the integration task which mechanism is taken. It, furthermore, depends on the underlying products to be integrated. So, for example, for a posteriori integration some of these mechanisms may not applicable as corresponding structures are not available, it is too complicated to realize them etc.

Integration from the *process side* means having *clear interaction* of subprocesses. Integrated processes are usually carried out collaboratively. If one person (or a tool) makes up an integration process, then integration is done by the person with the help of different tools (or by the tool itself). Collaborative processes have to be supported not only for their specific processes but also for integration of technical or other results, as well as for their management. On the other side, such processes must not be restricted. *Loose* interaction allowing different processes is a must. We shall later see that interaction of processes has quite different semantics. Integrated subprocesses are ordered corresponding to logical order of their parts and corresponding to time when they are elaborated. This ordering is administrated (in an extended task/process net). The process produces a complex result, which is administrated, too. There are restrictions corresponding to time, money etc. which also are under consideration of administration. Integrated subprocesses need resources (roles, support) to which actual resources (persons, environments/tools) have to be assigned.

Integration or *coupling* for the underlying *tools/environments* supporting interacting processes producing complex (integrated) products is summarized in table 6.2. This topic is discussed in the following subsection.

integration topics in the environments	their realization in IPSEN
specific environments	
different representations	one logical document, different representations/ presentations, parser/unparser
different parts of structures	composing a logical document from different structures
different elaboration stages	extending/modifying a logical document
different tasks	integrating different tools on one document
different versions	analysis tools, logs, merging
integrated environments for technical or administration tasks	
different views	integration tool, integration document between view documents
different subtasks of one problem area	integration tools, integration document
vertical integration	integration tools, integration document(s)
reuse	integration tool, integration document(s) containing interface descriptions of reused results
coupling of environments	
administration for a complex process	administration configuration, front–ends, technical environments
schematic knowledge and its use in the process	coupling of method development environment with a corresponding environment where this methodology is used
overall projects consisting of different projects	coupling of overall environments (still to be studied)

Table 6.2. Different topics of integration (or coupling) handled by IPSEN tools

Distribution and Binding

Distribution and binding has firstly *administration* aspects. As processes are mostly human collaborative processes, they must have a corresponding structure before distribution. Distribution has first to do with determining the right person or group profile (roles and group structures), assigning corresponding abstract actors (responsibility for performing tasks or producing results). Actors have to be supported by suitable tools with a certain support profile which has to be assigned, correspondingly. All necessary information for a task has to be available (working context). Actual resources (certain persons, environments etc.) have to be assigned (bound) corresponding to availability, workload of resources etc. This all is managed on administration level, a corresponding state information being contained in the administration configuration. Certain aspects like quality assurance, reuse, adaptation due to parameterization or evolving knowledge, or multi–projects severely influence administration processes and, therefore, also distribution and binding.

Another topic of distribution/binding is on *technical* level, technical level here w.r.t. structure location, structure of tools/environments, underlying integration platform, down to a hardware net. First of all, (1) there has to be state information of another kind not contained in the administration configuration of above but in close relation to it. On which workstation a developer is currently working, where are the corresponding data located and where can they be accessed from, what are the connection structures of a net? From this concrete information one can abstract, yielding some virtual location, connection etc.

The most important type of technical distribution/binding information, from the tool builder's view, (2) corresponds to the *internal structure* of *environments*. The corresponding topics were discussed in section 5.3 and are later taken up again.

6.1.2 Mutually Interacting Subprocesses and Their Support

The aim of this subsection is to *summarize* the available IPSEN *support* or that of ongoing work for collaborative software development processes. Even more important is the following discussion on the *nature* of development processes and the conclusion on how *future* support must look.

Specific Support for Subprocesses

Interacting and *collaborative* processes have to be *supported* by tools and environments. This means substantially supporting their specific technical subprocesses, their integration, as well as their coordination. We now characterize the *approach for support* taken in IPSEN:

(1) For *specific subprocesses* on one document corresponding intelligent support is available which allows building up, maintaining, analyzing, executing, and monitoring their corresponding results. Intelligence of tools corresponds to how they incorporate the structure of underlying documents, or methods to handle such structures. Especially, change support is given by analysis tools and by the tight integration with other tools.

(2) *Changes* made in results of subprocesses are not handled by another developer (of another dependent document or a parallel document) by human interpretation and determination of the corresponding changes. Also, it is not only determined which corresponding document is possibly or actually affected. Instead, tools support interdocument relations and their construction/maintenance/use (integration tools of integrated environments). Here, intelligence corresponds to language–language correspondence knowledge.

(3) Processes are often not planned, structured, or formalized. This is true for most technical development subprocesses. So, support of *subprocesses* by tools, either personal or collaborative subprocesses, must give *freedom* to allow *different forms* (order of process steps). Also, changes in complex configurations can be handled differently. Therefore, the intelligence of above is to be combined with freedom of corresponding tool activations. This demands incrementality of tools.

(4) Collaborative processes are not handled such that any developer changes anyone's result. Instead, corresponding management has to take place. This *management* usually cannot be made before a project starts but has to react on the project's status. This demands for solutions handling certain forms of *dynamics*. Especially, management has to be in tight *interaction* with technical development (offering complete working contexts and derivation of management information from technical information).

(5) In general, processes have to be seen in relation to their product they produce. It is sometimes not easy to answer whether we have product– or process–centered support, it is sometimes only a question of implementation mechanisms. IPSEN now offers *product–centered* support (support for process steps which are carried out by tool activations and ensure consistency of underlying documents). *Process–centered* support on top of that is due to further work.

(6) Especially, in long lasting processes, it must be possible to *incorporate knowledge* (product/process patterns of different kinds, for different purposes) gained in the process itself as well as from project to project.

(7) Processes are not only new construction processes. It was often stressed that even construction means *maintenance*. So, *"permanent changes"* of the overall configuration have to be supported (topics (1)–(6) of above) occurring anywhere and at any time.

(8) Equally important is that we learn how to carry out processes to produce complex results. Here in IPSEN, the topic is not coarse–grained process improvement on a lifecycle level but introduction of *application*, *structure* class, and *project* type knowledge into a project or a project family to end up with an understood, structured, and efficient reuse process and corresponding support.

We have given some answers in this book on how to achieve this development support in order to deal with productivity improvement of processes and quality improvement of products and their processes. Therefore, the *approach* of available IPSEN tools or tools under investigation is far *away* from what is found in *everyday practice* (human interpretation of results and corresponding human derived processes).

Subprocesses and Their Mutual Influence

Subprocesses are usually composed, the *composition* structure may not have been made explicit. The latter is usually the case for technical development processes (of a single developer, or a composed process of how to carry out a requirements change for a software system in detail). We shall later argue that composition cannot be statically defined for most development processes in advance. On administration level composed processes are *organized* to coordinate different developers. Even there, we have argued that this organization is only due to a certain project state (see section 5.1).

A subprocess of a certain type (e.g. design) produces an atomic or composed *result* of a certain type (e.g. architecture). Both types are related 1:1. This result can be *used* by another subprocess. This is dependant on the *type* of the result, the *type* of the using subprocess, and the *kind* (e.g. input) how the result is used. For example, an architecture can either be used as input for an implementation or for a technical documentation subprocess. A result is either *new* (internally, in its construction process, it has often been modified) or *changed*, a process is either a new construction or a modification process.

By only regarding *kinds of use*, remembering some *situations* in software engineering of this book, we can get the following distinction for *interaction* of subprocesses:

(a) A technical result is used as (part of an) *input* for another *dependent* and following technical task (e.g. a requirements subconfiguration as input of a design task). Chains of tasks occur rather often on technical level.
(b) A technical result is used as (part of an) *input* for a *parallel* task where parallel tasks are mutually dependent (e.g. a changed function model for the data model modification process).
(c) A result of an administration task is used to *coordinate* other technical tasks (task/process net for coordinating technical developers) or, conversely, the result of a technical task gives rise to an *adjustment* of administration (subsystem's architecture yields an actualization of an administration task net).
(d) The software product as result of an outside process is to be *reused* in another development process (product reuse). The technical as well as the administration process looks differently than when a corresponding component were developed inside the development process. The difference depends on the quantity of the used product (module, subsystem, platform, framework).
(e) The product of a process is used to *support* another construction process, e.g. products are process or product schematic information, see 5.1 (e.g. a type schema for subnets to support the construction of task/process nets on administration level). Here, the result is not input of the task but some part of the 'program' for a corresponding construction process.
(f) The result of a task is a *program* of a *tool* to *support* another human task (e.g. tool construction in a development process). In some cases, where a task is carried out automatically by a tool, the result can be the program *of* the tool. The result may also be a part of this program or the program of some runtime support for this program etc.
(g) If a task is solved, the corresponding process is usually structured as a sequence of an analysis task, a structuring (planning) task, an execution task, and a supervision task. Errors are made, so usually these tasks and their corresponding processes are tightly intertwined. Furthermore, all tasks, but especially a construction task, produces a plan (e.g. a task/process net) of arbitrary depth. For any of these tasks the above situations (a)–(f) can hold true. So, the result of a task may be a *part* of any of these *subtasks*.

The *interaction* of subprocesses *also depends* on the *contents* of *results* produced by another subprocess (how done, to which detail, what has been changed etc.). This can be discussed by only taking the first case (a) of the above classification (a technical result R_A

of a task A is (a part of the) input to another technical task B) and regarding the maintenance situation (see discussion on incrementality, different orders of subprocesses in chapter 1, fig. 1.17): (i) There may be different ways how to make the change within the document R_A to get consistency in that document. Depending on how the repair has been achieved there are different possibilities of maintaining R_B and achieving interdocument consistency between R_A and R_B. (ii) Secondly, even for a fixed way of doing changes according to (i), there are different orders to organize this maintenance process (batch–like, trace–like etc.). So, how something is made determines what is to do next, and this again can be performed differently in subsequent processes. This can be organized in a huge number of different processes.

Thus, due to the type of processes and results, the kind of interaction, and due to the contents of corresponding results we can state that there is a huge amount of possible interactions of subprocesses. Most of these interactions can only be fixed at project execution time. Even on the coarse–grained administration level we have a lot of project runtime dependencies. An overall development process is, therefore, a *dynamic interaction* of *loosely coupled subprocesses*. Nevertheless, it has to be organized according to its current state to avoid getting into chaos. The situation is only different if deep application, structure class, and project technologies are available which, however, is seldom the case.

Understanding Development Processes

So, a *future product/process model*, as sketched in 5.1, *cannot be* structured and *fixed*, neither for an application domain, nor for a certain system development process, nor for a certain type of project, nor for certain restrictions of a development context. The above dynamic interaction of loosely coupled subprocesses is unavoidable and is necessary for any creative development process in any engineering discipline. What we can *achieve* is to get clearly understood subprocesses or chunks of subprocesses and clearly described, formalized, and correspondingly supported interaction mechanisms between different subprocesses. These subprocesses and their *interaction mechanisms* must be adaptable to application domains, structures of systems, types of projects, procedures and techniques applied in a certain context etc. This all is not clearly understood yet. This understanding, however, is the key for quality and productivity improvement.

So, despite the results contained in this book, the following *questions* have to be answered in the *future*:
(a) to get a clear understanding of the *product* structure of an overall development process, assuming a broad understanding of the term 'product', especially in the case of multi–projects or integrated projects,
(b) the corresponding structure of the overall development *process*,
(c) product/process *interrelation*, in general, for any subprocess, either atomic or composed,
(d) the variety of *interactions* of different subprocesses occurring in a development process and the *integration* of their corresponding results,
(e) the *configuration/parameterization/adaptation* steps to be made for a general process/ product approach,
(f) the interdependencies of processes of project families and their results, especially if technologies are developed in such families such that a vague development *process* is *changed* to a clear *reuse* process (trivially, the product itself is also changed).

For providing 'complete' and intelligent support for development processes which regards their nature of loosely coupled and tightly interacting subprocesses, it is not only sufficient to give answers to the above questions. Indeed, we have to answer *specific questions* on how *to build* corresponding tools of *environments*:
(1) Which different *representations* for results of subprocesses or subprocesses themselves are to be given and which kind of tool support is necessary for the interaction of subprocesses, integration of their products, corresponding adaptation, reuse etc. (called *external* level in this book).

(2) Furthermore, the *internal structure* for products/processes in an overall environment to support such development processes has to be defined (which was called *conceptual* level in this book).

(3) Finally, different *services* of a future service platform for distributed overall development environments have to be defined to be used in environments. Even more, it has to be clearly determined how they are realized taking new platform technologies.

So, we have to describe which different forms of *representations* we need on different *levels* for the construction of overall environments or in such environments. These levels, their representations, the corresponding interaction mechanisms, and the *mapping* between levels is to be described in the future architecture of an overall environment supporting such development processes.

Our investigations do *not cover* the *full spectrum* of problems of development processes. The following topics are, for example, not the center of our interest:

(a) For coordination of technical developers we concentrate on management. To achieve this, in the forefield, group agreement, negotiations etc. have to take place which also have to be structured, organized, and supported.

(b) There are human processes which are not formalizable at all, as no underlying structures of products or no process knowledge are available. We concentrate on processes where resulting products have some sort of clear structure (any degree of richness) and at least partial process support can be given.

(c) In collaborative processes besides cooperation some interaction between developers (to check whether there is a problem, to eliminate a misunderstanding etc.) have to take place. For that, documents can be annotated by remarks, questions, 'to do'–topics etc.

(d) Individual aspects of developers to organize their results, to structure their working context, to adapt the UI interface of tools etc. are not specific topics of our work.

All these topics (and others) are investigated in a large project for which a proposal has been written. They are covered by other groups if this project is to start. The corresponding results have to be integrated with that of our future work.

6.2 The Role of Graphs and Specifications

The goal of this section is to summarizes the role of *graphs* and the *use* of their *formal treatment* in this book. For this, we (1) firstly remember for which different purposes graphs appear in this book. More precisely, it (2) is not graphs but complexes of graphs we mainly dealt with. Then, (3) we highlight the use of graph grammar specifications and, furthermore, (4) sketch how coupling of future environments has to be specified.

6.2.1 Graphs and Complex Graph Structures

It is useful to go through the book and to have a look for those different *purposes* for which *graphs* or graph complexes were *used*. This is the aim of this subsection.

Graphs in Different Roles

Graphs appeared in *different roles* in this book. Table 6.3 gives a *summary*. Graphs are only meant here in the sense of a graphical representation of graphs as mathematical structures, so not as pictures in general. Nevertheless, the list of table 6.3 is far away from being complete. In this table we also say which type of user (role) is dealing with different graphs.

The graphs belong to different *categories* w.r.t. their *use*: On the language or method definition level (1) we determine structure, find methods, either on coarse and vague (only pictures) or formalized level (clear syntax/semantics of graphic/text representations). This is necessary before we are able to think about support by tools. This was called 'method work' in chapter 1. Some of these determinations are later supported by tools, others are obeyed/carried out by humans. On external level (2) we have made determinations for corresponding support by environments (what is seen, how it is represented, which tool functionality is offered). The next two categories (3) and (4) of table 6.3 are clearly related to chapter 3 or 4, respectively. Finally, there may be (5) graphs for explanation purposes in this book, the corresponding list only giving some of them.

To any of the above categories (1)–(4) where graphs occurred, we may have used graphs not being listed in table 6.3, for *elucidation* as to prepare the reader, to explain a definition, to motivate some tool behavior etc. For example, 'attribute dependency graphs' of fig. 4.12 or use of 'derived attributes' of fig. 3.64 are both graphs introduced to explain attribute dependency and evaluation, as incorporated in the PROGRES language and system, and to be used in a certain specification. Other pictures are introduced to prepare the reader for architectural considerations (fig. 1.10), or introducing the term 'incrementality' (figs. 1.12, 1.16) or 'different orders of processes' (fig. 1.17) to give an understanding of 'tight integration and loose coupling of tools'.

Especially, the graphs of category (3) '*internal modelling*' of table 6.3 serve for quite different purposes, i.e. *different roles* of users are involved. They serve for (a) either for language definition/explanation of PROGRES, (b) for defining/explaining a clear use of the language (c) for the use of the language in a method for specification, as e.g. AST graph modelling, or their explanation, (d) for using the PROGRES environment to interactively handle a spec and to produce code, or explaining that, and (e) for explaining the overall outside functionality of the PROGRES system.

The *main use* of graphs in this book is for *tool building*. As already explained, we use graphs for representing logical documents, their mutual fine–grained relations, and their representation. This all is on *internal* conceptual level. For logical graphs we specify their changes due to graph local tools ops and due to integration tool ops. Their external representation (what is to be seen and how) and the behavior of corresponding representation tools was realized by the IPSEN system after the definition of representation documents. So, category (2) of above, after tools are developed, is '*derived*'. Category (1) topics are a *prerequisite*, corresponding to method work, and have only been explained to impart an understanding of the development process for the environments incorporating these methods. So, we concentrate on the internal conceptual level in the following.

---

1 SE language/method definition level (language/method designer, and user)
    structuring a universe: working areas 1.2, 1.6, overall configuration of software
      systems 1.4, 1.5, product/process model 5.17
    specific models: object and their versions, configurations 2.34, merging 2.31
    specific processes: RE process 2.17, reuse processes 4.58, understood processes 5.14
    processes in general: structure 1.7, 5.7, 5.13, state diagram 2.41
    hierarchies: SA 2.18
    fine–grained relations: for horizontal integration 2.12, vertical integration 2.18
    schematic information for some product or its corresponding process: 5.8
2 external level, i.e. external behavior of environments (user, mostly software engineer)
    representation of hierarchical structures: 2.11
    fine–grained graph relations: 2.13, 2.18
    execution of a model: by graph sequences 2.15 ff.
    incremental behavior of tools: by graph sequences 2.10 ff., 3.67
    inspecting runtime state: 3.69
    determining automatic layout: 2.27
    administration of processes: version graph 2.37, configuration graph 2.38
    schema graph: 2.47
3 internal level (specifier of IPSEN tools, rapid prototyping tool builder, PROGRES user)
    logical document: 1.22, 3.26
    representation document: 4.27
    integration document: 4.49
    internal configurations: 1.21
    schema for a graph class: 3.3, 3.6
    graph test pattern: 3.7
    graph productions in various forms: 3.10 ff.
    abstract graph productions: 3.31 ff.
    triple rules: 3.34
    constraints: 3.52
    gra gra module interaction patterns: 5.21 ff.
    interaction of schema parts and corresponding host graphs: 5.5, 5.8
4 architecture of an SDE or a software system in diagram form (designer, especially of
    SDEs)
    sketch level: 1.25, 4.13
    coarse level: technical environment 1.28, 1.32, overall environment 1.34, 4.4,
      integration of technical environments 4.5
    detailed graphical level: technical environment 4.3, 4.23
    runtime behavior: 4.2
    overview of meta environment: 4.31
    "architectural" pictures: 1.26, 5.56
5 Explanation level (reader of this book)
    interrelations of languages, tools, formalisms and their products for PROGRES 3.72
    structuring a book by semantical relations: 5.53
    classification scheme for SDEs: 1.35–1.45
    structures in classification schemes: 1.46
    structure of this book: 1.54
    dependency of IPSEN prototypes: 1.49

Table 6.3. Graphs and different roles in this book (corresponding different user roles), references corresponding to figures

Table 6.3 impressively summarizes the wide variety of applications of graphs and, thereby, demonstrates *their universal character* for encoding *structural knowledge* of any application domain. Structural knowledge is meant here for discrete structures which may have continuous value information. This ranges from internal document handling of graphs for tool construction to classification of SDEs or the used classification structures.

Graph Complexes for Internal Overall Configurations

By looking on an internal configuration as the internal pendant of how an overall configuration is handled inside an SDE, we see that we have to deal with complex graphs for logical, integration, and representation purposes. These graphs, but especially the logical graphs, themselves are arbitrarily complex (intragraph structure) but, nevertheless, clearly structured (see chapter 3, or section 5.2 for their specification structure). However, the various relations between these graphs also have to be regarded (intergraph structure). So, an overall configuration is internally mapped on a *graph complex*.

Integration relations between logical graphs are of *different forms* in available IPSEN systems. We find (1) double–sided, fine–grained relations within the subconfiguration representing the external technical configuration. For coupling of administration and technical configurations (2) one–sided coarse–grained (a logical document of the technical configuration) and on the other side fine–grained relations (an increment in the administration configuration representing that document) are used. The first type (1) is internally mapped on integration documents containing various additional information (cf. fig. 4.49). The second type (2) is internally handled by attribute values (corresponding document name) in the administration configuration.

Looking at the *future* form of an internal overall configuration even more information and corresponding graphs as well as *integration mechanisms* are necessary (cf. section 5.1 and discussion in 5.5, 6.1). Mechanism (2) of above can also be used for coupling level 2 and 1 of fig. 5.17. Furthermore, fine–grained integration mechanisms are necessary to extract management information from technical information (upwards coupling of levels). Further integration mechanisms have to be developed to relate schematic information (patterns) to the products where they are used, if these patterns are not only used to facilitate construction and pattern–product–relations are forgotten afterwards. Finally, as outlined in 5.1 for multi–projects, new mechanisms are necessary to couple two sides, and to allow freedom between both. Also, for representing the processes corresponding to products and for relating both to each other, future steps are needed. So, the future form of an internal product/process model is even more complicated than internal overall configurations underlying realized tools.

We have, furthermore, sketched in chapter 5 that *a posteriori* integration has to be handled on internal configuration level. For that, in 5.2 the view problem was introduced. Looking from our current discussion to a posteriori integration means that either on specification level (or later on realization level) the available and application system dependent data structures are abstracted to view graphs representing that structure of a document to be integrated with others (cf. fig. 6.4). For integration of these view graphs any of the above discussed integration mechanisms may be applicable.

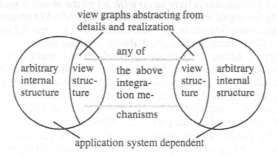

Fig. 6.4. A posteriori integration and view graphs

6.2.2 Specification and Graph Grammars

In the following *section* we firstly *explain* for which purposes graph grammars are used in this book as a means for specification of an overall development environment. Then, we sketch what has been *achieved* with graph grammars and what still has to be done.

The Role and Purpose of Graph Grammar Specifications

Specification is one of the most semantically *overloaded* terms in computer science. So we should firstly explain which different *types* of specifications exist, for which one we have applied graph grammars, and for which other types it could be used (but was not used) as well. For this, we take up the discussion we already begun in subsection 1.5.5. For explaining different types of specifications we only discuss the most popular forms (or what, in our view, the mostly used forms should be; often specification is used for mixed purposes). Furthermore, we restrict the use of graph grammar specifications in the discussion to the environment construction process. A specification always has underlying abstractions as it describes details and abstracts from others.

We find the following *forms* of *specifications* and underlying abstractions:
(1) A *requirements specification* describing the complete 'outside behavior' of a software system (function model, the underlying data (information model), the coordination of functions (control model), the user interface (UI model), and other topics for embedded/ reactive system, complex computation systems etc.). Furthermore, in the so–called non-functional RE spec other topics such as safety, efficiency etc. are handled which are of no interest here. Abstraction of an RE spec is neglectful of how the system is realized, it only describes its external perspective.
(2) A *design spec* or architecture describes the realization structure of the system, as the architecture is a complete build plan (all layers, hierarchies of subsystems etc.) without regarding implementation details. It can concentrate on the structural aspects (how a system is composed from components) but may also contain the semantics of components (as algebraic specifications) or runtime behavior of components, or their concrete interaction, binding etc. (cf. section 5.3). Abstraction is used here quite differently, namely forgetting the details of component bodies.
(3) In case a new or a very complex system is built, a third form of specification may be used. For *behavioral aspects* of the system, a prestudy in the form of a formal treatment is given to make sure that the complexity is manageable. This was the first use of gra gras in the group to convince ourselves (by gra gras in paper and pencil form) that complexity of internal data structures can be treated. Abstraction is used here in the sense of (a) forgetting the rest of the system and/or (b) not going down to details (in our case, e.g., how graphs are implemented).

Graph grammar specifications have *to do with all* of the above topics (1)–(3) but they are *not* used exactly for *one* of these purposes only (cf. fig. 6.5). We assume now that a complete graph grammar specification in the form sketched in section 5.2 handling the future form of overall configurations, as discussed above, is available.
(a) This gra gra spec contains *RE information* (tools, data model). Even, the behavior of tools is specified which is necessary for seeing the later outside behavior of an SDE (e.g. an incremental analysis tool) but which is usually not given. On the other side in RE specs on complex data, the UI details are not specified (see below).
(b) It also contains *architectural information* (spec modules and MiL patterns), which can be used 1:1 to structure the core part of an SDE. The code for components can be derived, from handcoding to generation, according to this architecture. (Even more, the complete code can be generated so as to obey this architectural structure.)
(c) By taking the complete specification, disregarding its MiL structure but examining its behavior only, we have a *behavioral description* which can be used for rapid prototyping of the core part of an SDE.

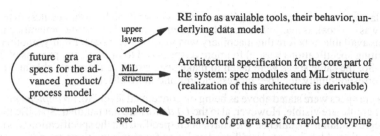

RE info as available tools, their behavior, underlying data model

Architectural specification for the core part of the system: spec modules and MiL structure (realization of this architecture is derivable)

Behavior of gra gra spec for rapid prototyping

Fig. 6.5. Future gra gra specs and their use for other types of specifications

The Purpose for which Graph Grammar Specifications Have Been Used

The task of *graph grammar specifications* in the tool construction process is to specify tool behavior. As stated above, this is done by (a) concentrating on the most interesting part, namely to determine the effect of tools by regarding their changes on underlying data structures. This specification is on conceptual internal level ignoring implementation details. Tools of any kind (editor, analyzer, execution, monitoring, simulation, transformer, consistency checker, binder etc.) have an impact on these data structures, in our case *graph complexes*, in the way that they inspect them and make changes on them (insertion of local structure, ..., insertion of relations). We have called this the specification of *graph processors* in chapter 1. Specification did not only describe structures but also tool effects. So, the *behavior* of *tools* on a conceptual level was described (what is going on inside, but no implementation details, no presentation details).

Specifications were given for a *graph class* by determining the behavior of all *tools operating* on a graph of that class (cf. sections 3.3, 3.5). The methodology for writing such specs underwent a long development ranging from 'done to see whether it is possible to master the underlying complex topic' to 'a method of how to do it for a certain type of graph classes' (those representing textual documents (AST graph), graphical documents ('graphical' graph), administration documents (application–specific relations and heuristics)). Most effort was spent to factor out commonalities of these graph classes and between these graph classes. The current state of this *graph grammar engineering* is to make use of genericity, their adaptation being achieved by the meta attribute mechanism (cf. section 3.7 for a summary). In section 5.2 we argued that it is necessary to impose a clear spec *module structure* on these specs, separating the different parts of a large spec and integrating these spec modules by a clear interconnection pattern. This improves the methodology of a spec process as reuse and parameterization of specs (modules but also subarchitectures) is facilitated.

According to the separation and integration discussion of above, integration tools' behavior was not specified by taking one 'large' underlying graph class. Coupling of graph grammars for describing fine–grained *integration tools*, therefore, was another topic of the specification business (cf. section 3.4). This was done by triple graph grammars firstly on a declarative level, namely relating language constructs on both sides. Then, the behavior of the corresponding tools was introduced. Corresponding integration knowledge of a tool's execution process and of the documents on both sides was put into the structure of integration documents. So, such specs operate not on one graph class but on a *graph class triple*. Although this specification approach assumed a clear separation of concern w.r.t. structure of underlying documents and tool behavior, it was argued again in section 5.2 that this has to be explicitly incorporated in the structure of a gra gra spec by separating different *spec modules* and their *interconnection*. Especially, the integration views were regarded to be expressed explicitly within such a modularized spec.

All specifications *written* for the construction of environments were *not complete, even on conceptual level*. We remember (a) that the role of gra gra specs was mostly the management of complex matters. So, if something was clear in its handling, as gra gra specs for a similar topic have been written before, no spec was written. (b) Completeness in this sense never was our goal, as many of the tools have been developed before the generation machinery was available or before this machinery was in a complete state. Finally, another reason for writing specifications was (c) to improve specs and to improve the process of creating specs. So, the same specs were taken to make spec structure more readable and reusable and, correspondingly, the spec process clearer and more efficient.

Gra gra specs were stated above as being on conceptual level. So, *no implementation* details of graphs are visible. However, also the *UI details* are not handled. Specification ends with representation documents. They have been specified but the specification was not used for generation. Also, layout algorithms developed for representations are not based on gra gras but on constraint algorithms. Even the translation/coupling between logical documents and their representation documents is not covered by gra gras. The reason was, as explained in 4.1 and 4.3, that we implemented a simpler coupling scheme underlying unparsers than fine–grained coupling, namely 'functional' coupling by events directly incorporated in the code of the unparser. Conversely, the parsing process for textual documents is only on syntactical input level as ops of the logical document are used to change the logical graph. Presentation is not a topic where graphs can sensibly be used (certain forms of boxes, arrows, and how to present them). The same is true for how menus, messages etc. are presented at the user interface.

So, all *presentation* details are not a topic of gra gra specs but can be found in the reusable code of the framework. The same is true for *representation* and *parsing/unparsing*, the corresponding code not being derived from a spec. Of course, gra gra specs could have been used to determine the complete internal state or the corresponding changes of an environment up to representation level, ignoring the presentation. However, it was not done for good reasons.

There are others *uses* of gra gra specs *outside* the *tool development* context. Semantics of programming languages have been operationally defined by gra gras (e.g. /5. Göt 77, 5. Jac 86/). Even a graph grammar specification was given to operationally define a graph grammar language (bootstrapping for language definition /5. Zün 96a/). Methods how to use a language or a correspondence of language increments have been developed (e.g. /7. Jan 92/). Many further applications inside or outside of computer science can be found (see section 6.4).

Future Gra Gra Specs and Their Development Processes

Future gra gra *specifications* are still on what we have called the *conceptual* level, therefore without UI details, concentrating on the logical part of an internal overall configuration. As above, we rather aim at treating interesting problems than achieving complete specs (also for the future problems, no generation machinery will be available in the first run). The first *list of problems* to be tackled is given from sections 5.1, 5.2, the summary section 5.5, and the discussion of complex processes and their products in this chapter.

As discussed, development processes consist of loosely coupled subprocesses producing corresponding results, where these results and the corresponding processes are mutually influencing. We have seen that we need process *interaction* mechanisms, suitable *integration* mechanisms for their results, and *coupling mechanisms* for the corresponding environments. To *formalize* these mechanisms is the task of graph grammar specifications. In the long run, the resulting specs, making use of these mechanisms, have a clear modular structure. The processes of getting these specifications must get the same degree of understanding than those introduced in chapter 3. Thus, a future graph grammar engineering methodology has to be developed.

The *internal conceptual* pendant of what we have called a future *process/product model* for development processes has to be *formalized* by *graph grammars*. This specification is, according to the philosophy of this book, a prerequisite of building environments supporting these mechanisms. The emphasis will lie on formalizing interaction/integration portions of processes/products to get an understanding of suitable mechanisms to be applied. Thereby, we use existing knowledge on how to model graph classes or subconfigurations for describing the results of these subprocesses.

Suggestions for *some* of these *mechanisms* have already *been made* in section 5.2. The emphasis of the discussion there was more on improving internal graph class structuring or structuring fine–grained integration tools behavior or, more precisely, their underlying description in the product/process model. These problems are rather well–understood compared to the interaction/integration problems introduced later. However, we believe that some of the coupling mechanisms suggested there will be applicable also for the other types of problems. Especially, the view problem discussed there for fine–grained integration, will also have an application for subproject coupling or upward coupling of layers. It should also be applicable for the a posteriori case of integration tools. Clearly, *further* mechanisms are *necessary* for the adaptation problem (development of patterns and their use in the same project), for the downward layer coupling problem (e.g. results of administration processes are used to coordinate developers or, conversely, management information is inferred from technical information and used for administration processes). Finally, as this problem has to do with both, namely adaptation and layer coupling, these mechanisms are necessary for the subproject interaction problem.

The first idea is to understand the *formalization* of a *process/product* model for loosely coupled and mutually influencing subprocesses on internal conceptual level as *coupling of graph grammars* (cf. fig. 6.6). These graph grammars serve for different purposes, see the above separation and integration discussion. Any of these separate graph grammars can have a composite internal structure (e.g. for expressing the composition of a product graph class as described in chapter 3). Such a graph grammar can also abstract from underlying details (as in the view problem discussed for integration tools) not to be seen outside. It seems that for all interaction/integration problems the coupling situation of fig. 6.6 is applicable where for realizations of relations (1), (2), (3) different mechanisms have to be applied.

To *give* some first and rather sketchy *indications*:
(a) *Process/product coupling* is the coupling of a graph grammar with its product. We remember that graph grammars up to now only describe tiny portions of the process, namely the corresponding tool operations. If there is knowledge on how to structure a process, either partially or totally, then a process chunk (e.g. a subnet) or a complete net is available controlling the graph grammar execution. This net is the result of another process (relation (2)). We have clearly stated that we are interested in processes which are formalizable, either partially or totally.
(b) If a process generates *schematic information to be used* by another process (structural product information, process information), then this product is used by another graph grammar to build up a corresponding product. So, it is again a product (relation (2)) which controls another graph grammar. Control may now have another meaning: The example that an object pattern is defined means that a new transaction of another graph grammar is defined. If a type schema is defined, this is a new 'transaction' interpretatively executed such that a right hand side is parameterized by corresponding information.
(c) We have also regarded the case that administration *information* is *derived* from technical information to be put into the administration configuration. This information is used either to parameterize productions (cf. figs. 5.5, 5.8), or it already has subnet/subconfiguration description form to be inserted into the administration configuration (relations (2) or (3), respectively).
(d) *Control between layers* is similar to (a). A task/process net, for example, is used to 'control' developers, in other words for enacting the corresponding graph grammars. Thus, again, relation (2) is involved. A different sense of control is used, namely enactment (start) not controlling the execution of a graph grammar.

(e) Relation (1) has occurred by coupling graph grammars for *integration tool* construction. Then, their products are integrated (relation (3)).

Of course, these are only vague ideas. Especially, the problem is to deal with *human processes* which are not structured and defined and, therefore, cannot be formalized. So, a formalization must express the arbitrariy of using underlying tiny and formalized portions of the process (e.g. offered by a tool).

Despite of difficult problems to be solved, graph grammars seem to be a *suitable formal model* for these problems. *How else* should such interaction/integration mechanisms be specified *than* in an *operational* way? Arguments, from above, are: different kinds of product uses by other processes, or the elaboration state of a product portion allows different ways to react, or various processes are possible. This all can hardly be described by other semantical approaches (as denotational, axiomatic, or purely declarative ones).

Furthermore, also the *mapping problem* indicated in 6.1 to get down to an underlying layer of common services for distributed applications could be studied by graph grammars. On this layer, again, interaction and integration is necessary, namely interaction of computational processes and integration of data bases. So, there is a chance of handling this mapping problem again by coupling of graph grammars, where the different graph grammars either belong to one of the layer, or deal with the mapping. Alternatively, if this mapping is not regarded to be dependent on the development process or its results, or the elaboration stages of these results, it may be defined such that a mapping process described by a graph grammar produces the lower level graph grammar.

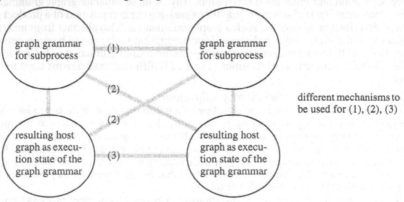

Fig. 6.6. Coupled graph grammars for describing subprocess interaction and product integration

6.3 The IPSEN Project's Value for Software Engineering

The *aim* of this *section* is to summarize the practical results of IPSEN for software engineering. These are (1) results for the development of arbitrary or specialized types of software systems. Here, we find (i) method knowledge how to understand or how to do software development better, and (ii) the demonstration of the value of IPSEN tools for supporting software development processes. The second goal (2) is to summarize the impact of the IPSEN project on tool building. After (iii) explaining the achieved results we, finally, (iv) evaluate the IPSEN project w.r.t. specialization in software engineering and development of specific technologies.

6.3.1 Results for Software Engineers

In this *subsection* we summarize the results of this book for *arbitrary* or *specific software engineering processes*. There are on one side 'method' results to get a better understanding of the software process for construction, maintenance, reuse, or reengineering, and of the underlying languages to describe the products or methods to achieve them. Furthermore, we have developed various tools with specific functionality to give advantageous support in these processes.

'Method' Results

In subsection 1.1.2 we have identified the *main problem fields* we see in software engineering. One dimension of the discussion was to explain that requirements engineering, architecture modelling, and project organization are the most risky working areas. Another dimension was to detect deficiencies of current software engineering practices, namely the lack of quality, the unpayable effort of maintenance, the rare use of reuse, and the missing support of cooperation. We now give a brief summary on our *method work* to overcome the problems in these fields which, as often stated, is a prerequisite of building suitable tools.

Languages used in *requirements engineering* are usually not precisely defined, not expressive enough, and there exist no methods how to use them. Our contribution in the RE area was to find out deficiencies of SA, and EER, to name them, and to provide some rules on how to apply these insufficient languages /7. Jan 92, 4. Lef 95, 4. Koh 96/. Furthermore, a formal control model was added /7. Bee 96/. The mutual dependencies of these sublanguages of requirements engineering were carefully studied, and an integrated requirements engineering language was defined. With this language, one should be able to specify the functional requirements of most software systems. It was even demonstrated in section 2.2 that, due to the control model part and due to sublanguages to be used according to the elaboration stage in the RE process, the integrated languages are suitable even for reactive systems. Various forms of requirements engineering development processes can be carried out (see end of section 2.2).

For describing the architecture of a software system, called *programming in the large* or architecture modelling, a corresponding language was defined by ourselves /7. Nag 90, 7. Bör 94/. It incorporates different design paradigms (locality, layers of software systems, OO), handles different granularities (interface parts of modules, modules, subsystems, subarchitectures, complete systems), offers means for reuse by OO and genericity, and has two representations for graphical overviews and detailed textual descriptions. A lot of rules (patterns) have been derived for different purposes (mechanism patterns, style patterns, translation patterns, framework patterns etc.). Further work, as described in 5.3, is on developing languages and methods for concrete architectures which are especially important in the context of reactive and/or distributed systems. The relation between the RE language and PiL constructs was made clear so that the designer has a well–defined set of choices for translation (see section 2.3).

In *project organization* we concentrated on how to handle the coordination of different developers in a software development process (see 5.1). So important subtopics, like cost estimation, human engineering etc. were not our focus. There, we made clear that planning (structuring and maintaining), evaluation (analyzing), control (executing), and supervising (monitoring an administration configuration) are tightly intertwined. Furthermore, it is not sufficient to regard subtopics as task/process control, revision/configuration control, and resources control separately as all have to be seen together. An administration configuration is permanently changed, analyzed, executed, and monitored in correspondence with the project's state, either the technical development state or the administration state. This was one aspect of adaptation discussed in this area. Another was that the administration configuration and corresponding tool support can be reused for any type of software projects (and other engineering development projects as well) if parameterization according to the specific context is achieved. Finally, adaptation is necessary for evolving knowledge on how to handle the administration process on product or process side, and specific software processes such as reuse processes or multi project processes.

All of the above was for arbitrary software development in any application domain. As stated in section 5.3 distributing 'integrated' systems or integrating isolated systems in BA applications is one of our current research topics. Sketches for a reengineering methodology and a distribution methodology were given there. The result of this work is planned to be a coherent methodology for the whole process from reengineering existing BA systems to distributing reengineered systems on different underlying modern platforms. So, these considerations are *specific* w.r.t. (a) the *application domain* and (b) certain *types* of *projects*. In section 5.3 our current work on architecture modelling was also described. The idea of developing concrete architectures, studying interaction, binding, and distribution mechanisms, and mapping virtual onto different concrete architectures is, in particular, necessary for the development of reactive (technical control) systems. Finally, in 5.4 a retrieval system for OO classes and hierarchies was sketched. As finding suitable components is only one task, others are to modify them and the corresponding context where they are to be used, a corresponding reuse methodology has to be developed.

These are also our contributions to the topics *maintenance* (long term) and *reuse* of above. Other contributions to short term (maintenance) or to process/product quality improvement are due to tools as sketched below. On the method side our contribution to quality improvement is, furthermore, to give clear underlying languages for the most important working areas, methods to use them, and methods how to interrelate them.

The above topics are also a contribution to *quality* improvement of products and quality and *efficiency improvement* of the corresponding processes. A further contribution are our general investigations towards understanding a (software) development process (see 5.1, 6.1). As long as we do not have a clear understanding of the 'product' of a software development, maintenance, reuse etc. process, the corresponding subprocesses, and their interaction, existing practice will be limited as well as the underlying tool support.

Tools for Software Construction, Maintenance, Reuse, and Reengineering

Lots of *prototypes* were developed to demonstrate improved tool functionality for software engineering processes. Prototypes are meant here as rather stable and efficient *demonstrators* (cf. table 1.14), so not in the sense of rapid prototyping. However, they are not industrial quality to be used in a large industrial or research project. Thus, they have also not been used in the development of IPSEN systems. However, industrial tools can be built along the IPSEN results having the features of these demonstrators (see section 6.4). Demonstration was to show the value of new tool behavior (see discussion in subsection 1.4, 1.5 on tightly–integrated, ..., project organization – oriented). The aim of the following discussion is to evaluate what has been achieved w.r.t. the above problems in the sense of demonstrating improvement.

Existing IPSEN tools have been summarized in table 1.50, 1.53, the external functionality for some of them has been explained in chapter 2. Current work on tools was summarized in table 5.57. This is not to be repeated here. The following table 6.7 gives a *summary* under another perspective, namely for what *purpose* these *tools* can be *used*. As long as IPSEN is not an industrial system, and a software system has already been developed with it, environments can demonstrate their use only for new development (entry 1) which, however, is a permanent change, see chapter 1. The currently investigated environments of entry 2 can demonstrate their value for restructuring systems (for which most of them are developed) or for new system development. The organization tools of the administration system are usable for both, new development as well as maintenance (entry 3).

1 new software development (including maintenance) for arbitrary software systems:
     RE environment (see 2.2, specific use for reactive systems)
     PiL environment including RE–PiL integration tools (see 2.3, PiL environment was not
       discussed)
     PiS environment including PiL–PiS transformation tools (see 2.1, only PiS version 2.5 discussed)
     DOC environment with integration tools to other documents (see 2.3)
     further general tools (see 2.5)

2 specific software development:
     reengineering environment (see 5.3.3, in connection with a PiL environment)
     concrete architecture development environment (see 5.3.1, in connection with a PiL
       environment)
     environment for utilizing advanced platform services (see 5.3.5, in connection with a PiL
       environment)
     reuse environment (see 5.4.2, in connection with a PiL environment)

3 coordination of arbitrary (software) projects, usable for 1 and 2:
     administration environment for products, processes, and resources (see 2.5, 5.1)
     parameterization (see 2.5), adaptation due to a projects state (see 2.5, 5.1)
     adaptation due to other dimensions (see 5.1)

Table 6.7. Existing and currently developed IPSEN tools under the perspective of their use for different software processes

The value of the corresponding environments of entry 1 for RE, PiL etc., and the value of the administration environment for coordination of arbitrary software projects should be clear now. So, let us concentrate on the maintenance, reuse, quality of products, and quality/ efficiency aspects of development processes. Short term *maintenance support* is given by tools regarding the structure and consistency of documents. So, it is not only human interpretation dealing with that to be done but there is constructive maintenance support. Of specific importance is maintenance support by integration tools to get the underlying overall configuration into a consistent state. Again, not human interpretation using a suitable environment for a dependent document is the concern but provision of active support by integration tools. *Quality* of products and quality of processes/*efficiency* of processes, therefore, is due to constructive support (for doing it right) and incremental analytic support (to immediately see what was wrong). Efficiency of processes is, furthermore, supported as different processes are possible (see corresponding discussion of chapter 1).

The *specific maintenance support* in the sense of reengineering and reuse, thereby also productivity/quality improvement of products, is given by the specific tools of entry 2, if and when the corresponding tools are available. This is to be demonstrated for the restructuring/maintenance process of BA systems and reuse processes for systems using OO components. The quality of developed systems is, especially, improved by getting a clear structure corresponding to tools for reengineering, distribution, and the use of advanced platforms.

There has already been made a remarkable *step* by the available IPSEN tools in *direction* of *mutually interacting* but *loosely coupled* subprocesses such that different forms of corresponding processes can be carried out and tight integration of their products is given (see discussion in 6.1). The RE, PiL, PiS, DOC environments of IPSEN already have these characteristics. They give intelligent support for subprocesses, but also for their interaction, allow various forms of processes, but give tight integration for the corresponding results. Especially, various forms of processes are supported by the administration system and its integration with corresponding technical development environments. Furthermore, application– and project–specific support of the same kind (see entry 2 of table 6.7) can also be demonstrated in the future.

Of course, there is still a *long way to go* to demonstrate suitable tool support for development processes in general (see section 6.1): Support for adaptation in the sense of using evolving knowledge has to be given, especially for the purpose of reuse. Interaction of technical developers and corresponding coordination has to be improved as well as the integration of their results. Support for large projects has to be given, especially for nonlocal development processes or multi–projects.

6.3.2 Results for Environments Builders

The second *subsection* concentrates on the tool developer's view. After summarizing the corresponding results achieved within the IPSEN project, we take up the principal discussion of subsections 1.1.2 and 1.1.6 to demonstrate the value of IPSEN in software engineering, which is due to its specialization and corresponding specific technologies.

How to Build Software Development Environments

An overview of the general approach of a mechanized tool production process was already given in sections 1.5 and 1.6 and was substantiated in chapters 3 and 4. So, we can give a brief *summary* concentrating on *including* the ongoing projects described in chapter 5 and, especially, their new *problems* due to the *visions* resulting from ongoing projects.

In order to see the *available state* of the *art* of the *construction process* for an overall environment, let us regard fig. 6.8. There was a construction process for developing the framework for a single environment, which was not described in chapter 4 but whose results were. The framework can be used either for constructing technical environments (e.g. a PiL environment) as well as administration environments. For getting the specific parts of single environments structured processes are available. These are more or less supported by generator tools. In the same way, a framework development process for integration tools delivered an integrator framework. Its specific core part is delivered again by a structured process. A rather manual development process produced the front ends. Specific environments and integration tools build up integrated environments which are combined together with the parameterized administration system and front ends to an integrated overall environment. The corresponding configuring and binding process is not shown. The reader should keep in mind that parameterization of the administration environment at project runtime is a topic of current work.

So, we see an advanced software construction process or *reuse process* which is well–understood. We have pattern reuse, product reuse, and process reuse, as summarized in subsection 4.8.2. The efficiency of the process can be seen from fig. 6.8 as the processes delivering products to be reused are no longer interesting. Only the processes painted in grey remain, they deliver the specific components.

These processes have a *different degree* of understanding, corresponding to their *structure* and, therefore, also *support*. The best understood and supported process is to derive editor/analysis tools (see figs. 4.31, 4.32, 4.35, for a summary 4.58.b). So, for the development of execution and monitoring tools some work is still due to handcoding. The process for delivering the specific parts of an integrator is well–understood (cf. fig. 4.58.c) but the translation of specific integration rules to code is a mechanical process which is still up to handcoding.

All the corresponding support for the development of environments was called the *IPSEN meta SDE*. Corresponding tools were summarized in table 1.52, the necessary PRO-GRES environment translation tools in table 1.51. The meta SDE is not an environment for arbitrary software construction processes. It is an environment for a *specialized software* construction *process* which follows an underlying idea of reuse. This specialized process has a clear *method* and an underlying *machinery*: (a) Graph grammar specifications of the core part of an environment/integration tool. There, it is clear how to do it (graph grammar engineering). (b) Mechanical derivation of the corresponding code with different degrees of automation. (c) The results of that subprocess are hooked into a framework. (d) Tool support is given either at specification level for prototyping a spec (see 3.6) as well as on translation level to efficient code (generators). This all needs an underlying clear understanding of specific environments, integration tools, their coupling to integrated environments, and coupling of technical environments by front ends to a parameterized administration environment.

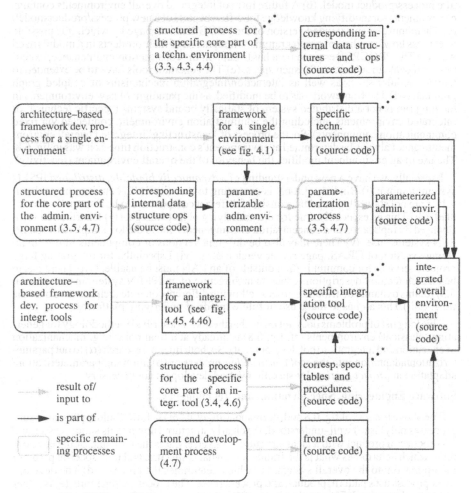

Fig. 6.8. The available process for developing an integrated overall environment (without ongoing work of chapter 5, simplified, references correspond to sections)

As argued in subsection 5.5.2, future environments cannot assume the underlying knowledge of their product structures or of the corresponding human processes being available before tool construction time. Instead, that knowledge must be extensible as it is incomplete or it must be adaptable even at project runtime. The discussion in section 6.1 about interacting subprocesses and integrating products demands, at least in some cases, a new methodology for environment construction. There, however, one has to make a clear distinction between (a) tools where the corresponding knowledge is available before construction time, including reconstruction as the knowledge is extended, and (b) tools where the underlying knowledge is due to permanent changes. The second case demands more complicated tool interaction and product integration mechanisms which should not be used if it is not necessary.

So to handle these *problems* of *ongoing* and *future* work the whole *machinery* for producing environments has to be *extended*: (a) There has to be a clear understanding of interacting processes and integrating products and how to map this on an internal logical level of a future process/product model. (b) A future form of integrated overall environments contains environments for modifying knowledge for different parts of a new process/product model. (c) There must be an extended version of the PROGRES language by which it is possible to express how coupling of graph grammars/integration of their products in a modularized way. (d) The PROGRES environment has to support the construction/maintenance, execution, and evaluation process for such specs. (e) The generator tools have to be extended to handle modular specs as well as interaction/integration mechanisms of coupled graph grammars. (f) The framework has to be modified, as the paradigm of new environments in the long run is not a distributed system of statically bound systems (specific technical or integrated environments, including the administration environment, connected via fixed communication components). So, the process of 'constructing' integrated overall environments cannot always be determined at environment's construction time as it was in fig. 6.8. The use of an environment modifies the behavior of the overall environment (reactivity).

Especially, we have a new understanding of a *dynamically bindable, distributed* IPSEN system in mind: (i) Binding of tools is according to use. (ii) IPSEN environments themselves are not statically bound but consist of different components to be eventually distributed. (iii) This is, especially, true for the underlying object storage. (iv) Distribution is influenced by replication and concentration of components due to the load implied by the IPSEN systems' use. (v) There may also be different versions of components in use (main storage version of GRAS, page server version etc.). (vi) Especially, for integrating large projects services for communication outside of an LAN must be usable. (vii) There has to be an architectural description (concrete architecture of an IPSEN system in the sense of 5.3) for this dynamic distribution process allowing different concrete architectures over the time. (viii) This all has to make use of future trends of underlying platforms.

This long list of problems does not mean that the above described methodology for generating 'classical' environments (cf. fig. 6.8) is already at a final point (e.g. mechanization of execution and integration tool development). So, both lines of research (α) to put parameterization/adaptation into the *tool construction process* or (β) allowing parameterization/adaptation at *project runtime* by specific method developers are necessary.

Software Engineering, Specialization, and Technologies

The above *process* of fig. 6.8 and, correspondingly, its *reuse* form (boldly presented subprocesses only) is (a) well–understood, (b) clearly structured down to its subprocesses and (c) produces a product with a clear structure. Conversely, it is the structure of the environment which determines what is the framework, what is specific, and how specific parts are incorporated into the overall system, i.e. which determines the process. (d) The development process uses pattern, product, and process reuse. The process, even more, (e) is rather statically determined. This is obviously *different* to common software development processes.

A prerequisite for developing such processes is *specialization*. As indicated in the introduction there are three dimensions (cf. table 6.9). The application domain is (i) 'support of software construction and maintenance'. The structure class is (ii) 'interactive, integrated development environments'. The project type is (iii) 'new development' (of an SDE) what we have called a priori approach.

The corresponding application, structure class and project *technology* in the terminology of chapter 1 does not come for free. There were series of projects (cf. fig. 1.49) in which these technologies have been developed, the vagueness, nondeterminism, the backtracking steps, the insufficient intermediate results, and the pure handcrafting having been eliminated in predecessor projects. So, SDE development processes are a good example of development processes with *deep knowledge*. This, by the way, is not only true for IPSEN.

Such a deep understanding of processes and their results evidently demonstrates 'product improvement' or 'process quality/efficiency improvement'. Figures about the time needed to develop an environment using the available machinery could be given. This all cannot be gained on the level of improving a process in order to carry it out in nearly the same way as the last time. Instead, there are *highly creative* steps involved *to arrive at* such a *reuse process* by (a) determining a good structure for a system, (b) finding those components which the system may share with others (from reusable components, to platforms, basic layers, to the whole framework). Even more, (c) trying to mechanize the processes for the remaining specific parts, either manually or automatically by generators, introduces a new quantum leap. So, (1) deep technology *needs time for probing* and creativity. Furthermore, (2) the best indication of deep technology in software projects is the availability of a rich application–specific environment (in our case the meta SDE).

Let us now go through the different entries of table 6.9 *to apply* the *specialization* discussion *to different IPSEN projects*.

IPSEN 4.0 tools support the development of new software systems and their subsequent maintenance. The tools are not specific to a certain type of software system. The structure class is an intelligent development system with special emphasis on incremental mechanisms allowing various processes. The project type is a priori development using a meta SDE and a self–developed platform.

The current work of the next three entries *transfers results* of IPSEN systems (neglecting new problems in the first run) and thereby *extends* and *modifies* technologies. Not new software development is the goal for the tools described in entry 2 but reengineering of existing systems. Analogously, reuse is the topic of entry 4. Furthermore, the application domain is specialized for entries 2 and 3, namely BA systems, or reactive technical control systems. The structure class is as above but specific topics (cf. section 5.5 for the time of introducing knowledge) are introduced. The project type is mixed a priori/a posteriori with different dimensions for this distinction (using outside tools, platforms from outside).

The *IPSEN meta SDE* of entry 5 is the most specific tool support we have developed up to now. It requires a clear imagination of the product, its reusable framework, and the process of getting specific parts. It *shares* its architectural structure with IPSEN systems and also the outside characteristics of interactive tools. However, specific emphasis is laid on specification and generation.

The *administration system* was not developed for software development but for coordinating CIM development processes (cf. section 2.5, 5.1). However, it can also be applied for software development coordination. As reuse and maintenance are investigated now from the coordination point of view, this administration system should in the future give specific coordination support for such development processes. The available/future corresponding environments (for management, parameterization, knowledge development) are IPSEN–like. A mostly a priori approach was/is used for its construction, although its necessity came up in the problem of a posteriori integration of existing development systems.

system	application domains for which the system is built	structure class of the system	project type of the construction process
1 IPSEN tools 4.0, see table 1.50 and chapter 2	support of new software development (including its permanent maintenance) for arbitrary software systems	interactive, intelligent development environments (emphasis: incrementality allowing various processes)	new development (a priori approach) using a meta SDE, our platform

2 Environments from section 5.3	Reengineering (distributing and integrating) BA applications and supporting their distribution on new platforms	as above in 1 (but pattern definition involved in the tool construction processes)	new development, using available tools from outside, prototyping included in the tools construction process, using new platforms
3 RE environment section 2.2 plus environment of 5.3.1	developing software for reactive systems (as control systems for technical processes)	as in 2	new development using new platforms
4 Reuse environment of subsection 4.5.2	support for reusing OO components and hierarchies, including their maintenance and that of their context	as above in 1 (but structure knowledge changes during use)	a posteriori approach (WWW, OODBS), using IPSEN knowledge to be applied
5 IPSEN meta SDE (see tables 1.51, 1.52, sections 3.6, 4.4)	support for developing IPSEN–like SDEs, very specific construction process needing a clear understanding of product, specification, and corresp. translation	interactive development environment (emphasis on specification and generation)	a priori approach using our platform
6 Administration system (see table 1.53, section 2.5)	support of coordinating arbitrary software development processes but also specific processes, as reengineering, reuse, developing deep knowledge	as above in 1 for the management and parameterization environment, different for front end and its connection	a priori approach using our platform for environments; front ends using existing communication services in UI systems

Table 6.9. Specialization in the development of software systems, here applied to IPSEN tool construction

Availability of *technologies* offers new *qualities* for *support*. To describe this for a software process we regard fig. 6.10: (1) Current industrial tools offer support for software processes but they are mostly on representation level (some graphics) or the pure decomposition level (a structure–oriented programming language editor without context–sensitive checking). They demand human interpretation to see what has changed, especially on the border of different subprocesses, to do the development right (see section 6.1). (2) Available IPSEN tools demonstrated how this can be improved by (i) making underlying notions precise, (ii) giving support for fine–grained tight integration, (iii) allowing various processes, and (iv) giving adequate means for coordination. This all is of particular value for maintenance processes. (3) Specializing the application domain (as BA systems) or specializing the task (reuse, reengineering) delivers more specific support for a certain development process. (4) The most advanced form is an application–specific environment for development, if corresponding knowledge is available. Our example for a technology–driven process supported by corresponding tools is development of IPSEN–like systems using the IPSEN meta SDE.

Application–specific development environments are not only possible for SDE construction (here meta SDEs) but *for arbitrary software systems*. It demands that program construction means to specify the specific parts of a system within an otherwise invariant system frame. Specification can mean different things as specifying by doing (e.g. for UI presentations) or building up a formal spec. Also, generation can mean either direct interpretation or translation by generators. The borderline between (3) and (4) of fig. 6.10 is determined by whether software development still means handling large portions of code (case (3)) or whether (i) code handling appears either only in some portions of system development or (ii) code development is obsolete as system development only deals with application–specific notions (see discussion in subsection 1.8.3, topics (5) and (6)).

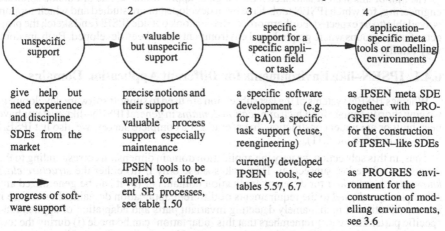

give help but need experience and discipline	precise notions and their support	a specific software development (e.g. for BA), a specific	as IPSEN meta SDE together with PRO-GRES environment
SDEs from the market	valuable process support especially maintenance	task support (reuse, reengineering)	for the construction of IPSEN–like SDEs
→ progress of software support	IPSEN tools to be applied for different SE processes, see table 1.50	currently developed IPSEN tools, see tables 5.57, 6.7	as PROGRES environment for the construction of modelling environments, see 3.6

Fig. 6.10. Different degrees of support by tools and examples for software development
(see also section 1.7)

The *future lines* of *research* for IPSEN tools are:
(a) Improvement of the mechanical tool construction process. There are still manual subprocesses which could be structured and mechanized (building executors, building integrators).
(b) For the application–specific tools or tools supporting specific processes of table 6.7, entry 2, we need more flexibility in the tool construction process as the corresponding knowledge the tools incorporate is changing at tool development time (see discussion in 5.5).
(c) Future administration tools need a new coupling of environments serving for knowledge development at project runtime (see sections 5.1 and 6.1).
(d) Developing tools outside the SE context following the direction of (c), see table 5.57.
(e) A posteriori integration of existing development tools but nevertheless trying to get tight integration (outside of SE).

In all these cases we face new *problems*. So, there will again be a vague research and development process, full of backtracking steps due to errors made or due to insufficient results achieved. Mechanized production of corresponding new tools is not provided (probing, handcrafting). Only after we know how to deal with these problems, mechanization considerations will be taken up again. So, it will take some time until tool construction processes handling problems (a)–(e) are in the mature state of IPSEN tool development as shown in fig. 6.8. Thus, *extending* SDE or DE *construction technology* will *require* some *time* and *creativity*, as argued above.

6.4 Graph–Based Environments in Different Domains

The *aim* of this *section* is to sketch the range of applications, inside or outside software engineering, for which IPSEN tools have been developed or are studied and which support is available/to be expected. Furthermore, we have a look outside IPSEN and sketch the projects of other groups where graph–based environments have been developed. Both are done very briefly.

6.4.1 IPSEN–like Environments for Different Application Domains

Whereas IPSEN systems of the last subsection are used to support software development we now shortly explain for which *application domains* in general IPSEN–like systems have been built or are under construction. In order to get a complete survey, we also list IPSEN SDEs again (cf. table 6.11).

Thus, in this subsection we vary the application domain dimension corresponding to the discussion of the last subsection. This makes sense only if (a) either the *structure class knowledge* is *invariant* for different application domains or (b) it can be generalized and subsequently *adapted* to the requirements of different application domains. In our case it is a combination of both, namely detecting invariant parts and adaptation of application–specific parts. The reader remembers that this 'adaptation' can be made (i) during the tool construction process or (ii) it is even to be supported by corresponding environments (see corresponding discussion in 5.1, 5.5). Either one of these possibilities (i) or (ii) is used, as required.

System	Application domain
1 IPSEN 4.0	demonstrating support for arbitrary software system construction and maintenance
2 Reengineering, Reuse etc. Environments (see 2., 3., 4. of table 6.9)	supporting specialized software construction processes in the field BA, reactive systems, specific subprocesses as reengineering, or reuse in the OO context
3 IPSEN meta SDE (including PROGRES system)	supporting the construction of IPSEN–like SDEs
4 PROGRES system	supporting specification processes and generation of rapid prototypes
5 Administration system new form	supporting the coordination of arbitrary development processes (approved for CIM development processes, to be applied for developing processes in chemical process control)
6 Retrieval systems	classifying retrieval domains, structuring the retrieval data stores, retrieving from complex data stores (the OO reuse case is only one application) where the underlying structure of the store can be modified
7 KBLW system	structuring electronic books, preparing parameterized books for personalization, supporting the reading process
8 A posteriori integration tools	supporting maintenance of technical development processes as in chemical process engineering

Table 6.11. IPSEN–like tools for various application domains, inside and outside software engineering

If we look on the ongoing projects of chapter 5, summarized in the last section, then we see that applying IPSEN technology for *specified* processes *in software engineering* or for applying the technology *outside* of software engineering is our main concern. There has already been an application in the CIM area (cf. sections 2.5, 3.5, 4.7, and 5.1). There are efforts towards a large project in the field of development support in the area chemical process control.

6.4.2 Some Graph–based Systems from other Groups

We shortly sketch some *systems* having been developed *outside* our group. The reason for this is (1) to see that similar ideas are used by other groups, (2) to demonstrate that it is a larger community which follows the idea that graphs are a means for structuring application systems or specification systems.

The discussion does not aim to be complete. We concentrate here on that work in which *graphs* are used to *build application systems*. So, (i) neither results where graphs are used only as formal models for applications (as programming language definition, data base definition etc.) are discussed here (many examples in /CEE 96, CER 79, CM 95, EKR 91, ENR 83, ENR 87, Nol 76, NP 83, SB 92, Tin 94, SE 94, VFR 95/, all bibl. chapter 5). Furthermore, also (ii) graph specification languages are not summarized, as they already have been discussed in subsections 3.1.1 or 3.2.1. The same holds (iii) for references demonstrating the use of specification languages (see section 3.3). We, furthermore, (iv) do not discuss specification systems being based on graphs or graph grammars here, as they already have been surveyed in subsection 3.6.2 as competitors of PROGRES.

From the graph–based application system approaches which are candidates for this short subsection, we only give examples for those systems where *non specialized forms* of graphs (attributed trees, attributed trees with links etc.) are taken, or where non specialized *implementations* of graphs are used such that graphs are not explicitly handled.

So, if the reader wants a *survey* of *all research topics where graphs* or graph grammars are *used* either explicitly or implicitly, either formal or informal, either only in paper and pencil mode or with corresponding support, either as an idea or a means to construct systems, either for theoretical or for rather practical work, he has to look into all these different sources. There is quite a large community dealing with graphs in this broad sense.

A rather closely related outside system is *OPUS* /4. FS 94/ of the Univ. of Dortmund. Indeed, this system can be regarded as a refined (e.g. allowing multi–user operation) version of the IPSEN 2.5 system (PiL, PiS, DOC working areas) which, however, was brought to an industrial standard. Other work of that group was on process modelling and its application in software development processes. The corresponding *MERLIN* system /2. JPS 94/ internally uses a Prolog–like definition of software processes. The abstract syntax structure of these programs is graph–like and stored in a graph DBS. Fine–grained configuration management is planned to be adapted.

The *SESAM* system /4. DM 95/ from the Univ. of Stuttgart is an educational tool for project managers of software projects. They learn how to build up a corresponding process. A simulation and animation component allows to execute the model and evaluate the achieved result.

The *CADDY* system /3. EL 92, 4. EHH 90/ developed at the Univ. of Braunschweig is a database design environment. Structural aspects of the schema can be put in/are maintained by a syntax–directed editor for ER diagrams. The ER schema is mapped on a relational schema, internally achieved by graph transformations. There exists also a graphic query language SQL/EER, a query being again internally handled as a graph and translated to a relational query.

Similar to the last approach is the *SPIDER* system /4. RK 95/ of the Univ. of London which offers a visual data base query language based on graph grammars and an experimental visual data base programming language. A similar functionality is offered by the *GOOD* system /6. GPT 93/ of the Univ. of Antwerp, i.e. a graphical and user–friendly interface to a data base system.

Graphs and a formal treatment of graphs (not by graph grammars but in the Z–like specification language GRAL) is underlying the *KOGGE* system of the Univ. of Koblenz /5. Ebe 87, 7. EWD 96/. The system is a meta SDE for graphical DEs using the CAD system Vario-

CAD. Emphasis is laid on a homogeneous representation of tool description and data structures resulting from interactive handling of tools.

The *DIAGEN* system from the Univ. of Erlangen /5. MV 95/ is a generic tool for the construction of graphical editors to build up structural and also executable models. In the tool construction process the corresponding parameterization to an application domain (structures, layout, execution models) is built in.

Rather *specific* to a certain *application area* is the approach of the Univ. of Mainz described in /5. GGN 91/ using graph grammar–based systems for CAD of kitchens. Even farer away from the above applications in computer science or engineering are systems of Queen's Univ., Canada, for either manipulating mathematical formulae or even music scores /5. FB 93, 5. BFG 96/. Finally, there is a system from the Univ. of Bremen, based on different concepts of formal rewriting /5. DHT 96, 5. FHK 95/, using a syntactical approach for picture processing. Regular structures are generated, put into pictures, regarded from different viewpoints, lighted etc. and put together to scenes.

6.5 Summary and Evaluation of IPSEN

In this *section* we lean back and *ask* (a) what has been achieved, (b) how this can be classified, (c) how the results are to be evaluated, and (d) what is the vision for future work.

6.5.1 Summary and Characterization

Here, we *summarize* this chapter and the results of this book under different *perspectives*: We give a summary of the contents of this chapter and we characterize IPSEN.

Contents of this Chapter

In sections 6.1–6.4 the results of this book have been summarized by *answering* specific *questions*.

In 6.1 we asked for an understanding of software development *processes* and the corresponding *suitable support*. A software process has to be divided into specific subprocesses with corresponding distinguished results. A process is not the same as another one, nor is the result of a process the same as another result. Separation of concern, integration of results, loose subprocesses and their interaction, separate environments and their coupling was the corresponding view. We have got corresponding results in IPSEN by tight integration of different tools on one document, by tight coupling of technical environments, and by coupling technical environments to the administration system to allow the corresponding coordination of development processes. Ongoing work continues this line with new forms of interaction, integration, and coupling.

In section 6.2 we put our emphasis on the most *specific* part of the IPSEN project, namely to use *graphs* and graph grammars for *specification* and subsequent *implementation*. We saw that graphs have different roles in this book and we explained how graph grammar specifications are related to other types of specifications. We have demonstrated a broad use of graph grammars for tool construction processes inside and outside software engineering. Mutually influencing subprocesses and their support by coupled environments yield, on the specification level, coupled and mutually influencing graph grammars to specify the behavior of an integrated overall and reactive environment supporting these mutually influencing subprocesses.

The next subsection asked for the *practical impact* of the IPSEN project. There, it was argued that current IPSEN tools demonstrate broad and new support for development processes. This was the value for software developers, or a demonstration of new functionality for tool builders. Then, we asked what practical results we got for the specialized tool building process by our machinery supporting mechanized tool construction. Finally, a discussion from chapter 1 that software engineering needs specialization and deep results, was taken up and it was discussed how we achieved to get corresponding technologies for the specialized tool construction process.

The last section gave on one side an overview for which *different application domains* IPSEN tools have been or are to be developed and, therefore, technology can be transferred. This is only possible if, on one side, the underlying structure class technology offers product parts being invariant of the application domain thus being applicable to the construction of various 'development' systems and other parts which can be suitably adapted on the other side. In this section we also sketched approaches of other groups to demonstrate that graph–based system construction is a broader initiative.

Characterization of IPSEN

It was discussed at the beginning of chapter 5 how the IPSEN project fits into the discussion of *future trends* in SDEs given in section 1.8. If the reader accepts the personal view of future trends given there, it should be clear now, how achieved results or ongoing work correspond to these future lines of SDE research.

One other aspect of characterization is the *type* of the IPSEN project. It is *not an industrial project* which aims at developing a new integrated overall SDE to be used for large software projects. Instead, we studied principle and ambitious questions where new concepts and solutions are necessary and did not only collect available knowledge to produce an SDE with the current state of the art. So, the systems built are *demonstrators* and no industrial products. We have never been under time pressure to show the next results on a forthcoming fair which is the usual situation in industry. We also have not been interested only in producing some SDE but, in a series of projects (cf. subsection 1.8.1), asked the question *what did we learn* by building SDEs, how could we better understand its product or process, or how could we mechanize the process to produce such a result. There, we had time to investigate and were not forced to produce only.

On the other side IPSEN is a *practical research project*. We have not been interested in getting scientific results as such. Instead, all these results are more or less directly related to the question of how to build (software) development environments. This, as an extreme case, is also true for the formal foundation of the PROGRES language. We also have built various prototypes demonstrating what can be achieved. As already stated above, prototypes are *large systems* (cf. subsection 1.8.2) which are quite efficient, some of them are very stable. Therefore, the software results produced in the group have been and are used by other groups (PROGRES system, GRAS system etc.).

The languages and *concepts* we took from the software engineering world to be supported were quite *conventional* (RE language, integrated architecture language, programming languages such as Modula–2, C etc.). This was to demonstrate the new tool behavior to available software engineers and not to their next generation. However, the results for the tool construction process could also be applied for any *avantguardistic* languages, or understanding of the development process.

Furthermore, the underlying philosophy of a software development process was *engineering–like* (different working areas, different roles, different results are involved, the coordination of different developers has to be achieved for clearly defining complex tasks and integrating their results). This, again, can be replaced by other philosophies for a software process. However, the editor believes that complex development processes have to be structured and organized in this way.

There are also some *transfer* results to industrial practice: The RE–PiL translation tool results have been incorporated by industrial tools of Cap debis SSP. Furthermore, the system OPUS, as sketched in 6.4.2, can be regarded as an industrial version of the IPSEN 2.5 prototype (with the corresponding improvements). There are also various transfer results in the research community.

Another aspect of characterization is *prototyping*. Here, we do not mean the various IPSEN systems having been built as demonstrators (although they are prototypes in the sense that they are not built for software development in large projects). We have discussed in chapter 3 that prototyping is possible for parts of an IPSEN system (see section 3.6). Furthermore, it was stressed that in the tool construction process for ongoing projects this prototyping subprocess has to be incorporated as the knowledge of tools encoded in tool behavior evolves at tool construction time. Finally, the IPSEN 4.0 prototype, due to its RE part, can be taken as a rapid prototyping tool (see section 2.2).

6.5.2 Evaluation and Vision

Many person years have been put into the IPSEN projects (cf. section 1.8). So, now the question is to *evaluate* the results on a perspective level and to sketch the *vision* in which directions further investigations are to go.

Evaluation of IPSEN Results

As stated above, the *highlights* of IPSEN are not on the language and method side for which they give support. Instead, it is the tool behavior, understanding of the tool construction process, and developing a machinery for this process. The main chapters 2–4 contain the corresponding results.

(1) *New tool behavior* is due to tight coupling of environments supporting mutual interaction of technical processes due to their current products (fine–grained integration) and to coordinate processes of developers due to the current state of a project (reactivity). This was carefully motivated in chapter 1 and demonstrated for the available tools in chapter 2. The list of IPSEN tool characteristics of subsection 1.4.5 summarizes tool behavior, section 2.6 verified that this was achieved by IPSEN tools.

(2) The second highlight, called *graph grammar engineering*, was to use graphs and graph grammars for specifying the behavior of tools as graph processors (their product structure, corresponding changes on products by tools). This spec is (a) formal as the underlying PROGRES is formal. (b) There are methodological rules on how to apply the language up to a (c) clear methodology for building up a spec by reusing other spec portions (e.g. editor/analysis tool, integration tool). Furthermore, (d) as these specs are operational, they can be evaluated by execution. (e) Corresponding tool support for the whole specification process is available.

(3) Software *construction* is to be improved to get rid of handcrafting where possible. This does not come for free but *needs* underlying *technologies*. In our case it was the derivation of a clean architecture of SDEs, to detect its invariant part (framework) and the corresponding specific parts. The specific parts in our case are components for handling the internal graph complexes and their changes. For these components, graph grammar specs are written and translated to efficient code. So it is a technical technology–driven process for the development of an IPSEN–like SDE.

The specific idea used in this book was to use graphs, corresponding formalisms, and techniques for the *whole process* of *tool construction*. In many cases corresponding outside languages/methods are not available or not precise. So, graph grammar specifications served (a) for this purpose to deliver language or method specifications, before tools can be built. Furthermore, as this specification was done on the conceptual internal level, we also got (b) the suitable preparation for tool construction. The architecture of the environment was designed (c) such that graph classes and their coupling play the central role in its core part. The corresponding specifications (after having been carefully constructed and evaluated, see graph grammar engineering) are (d) translated to efficient code. For the specification process, an environment (e) being again graph–based, is at hand. The translation process is (f) partially automated by generators. The underlying platform (g) supports handling of graphs (GRAS). This *uniform approach* was called *graph technology*. It ranges from language definition to implementation details of an underlying graph storage.

As demonstrated in this book, this approach is not only applicable for SDE but for general *DE construction*. This is why 'software' was put into parenthesis in the book's cover. Some examples for using IPSEN knowledge outside the software engineering field have been demonstrated. The adaptation to a new application domain was, for the available tools, done in the tool construction process.

Vision and Invitation

Although the *topic SDEs* still has a long list of *open questions* (improved outside functionality, configurability, framework development as a standard, mechanized tool construction process, development of a comprehensive meta SDE etc.) it is, surprisingly and regrettably, no longer a 'fashionable' topic. Many researchers in that field have moved to other topics, which can be verified when looking into current software engineering literature.

SDEs have their value as an *example* of the product of a *well–understood construction process* (as compiler construction for another class of systems). So, they should also be a topic of a computer science curriculum. Thereby, its aim is not to prepare students for later SDE construction processes in companies but to give an example of a good process. This was, by the way, one of the aims for writing this book. Such examples should stimulate the software engineering community to proceed on the way to inventing deep technology in different fields. This, in the opinion of the editor, is the only way to improve software engineering towards becoming a scientific discipline.

We have argued in section 6.1 that software *development processes* are *not really understood*. The same situation holds true for all development processes in any engineering discipline. So, one prerequisite for future development environments is to get this understanding. The open problems we are facing now, which have been summarized in sections 6.1–3, are derived from this question of understanding development processes. Thereby, as pointed out, processes are *not definable* by static and pregiven structures. Instead, they are due to permanent interaction of subprocesses and their intermediate results in a development process. This is, at least, true if a development process is not based on underlying technology. As pointed out in this book, such processes are rare cases. So, the major question is (a) to understand these processes, (b) to give suitable support even if they are in this premature state, and (c) to give support for their transition to technology–driven reuse processes.

One value of knowledge of SDE products and their processes is the *transferability* of results. Here we see two dimensions: (a) As it is the case with compiler construction, existing realization ideas, architectural patterns, underlying concepts etc. can be transferred even to systems outside engineering disciplines. The reader might remember that many advanced ideas for software construction come from compiler construction and are applied successfully outside this field. (b) As pointed out above and demonstrated for some studies, SDE construction knowledge can be transferred to building development environments for other engineering disciplines (but also the other way round). This offers the chance to extend the results of this book in the direction of a general methodology for building development environments in different engineering disciplines but also interactive systems outside of engineering.

One specific question, which is not easy to handle, is the *adaptation* topic with various semantics of adaptation as introduced in sections 5.1 and 6.1. Here, we detected some interesting problems the solutions of which are not easy to attain. However, we see no chance of circumventing these problems as this adaptation is due to mutually influencing subprocesses in an overall development process.

Another major question is what structure a development environment will have in the future in the light of 'arbitrary' *distributed systems*. At the moment we mostly think of bound systems for one or more roles being available on one computer. Upcoming distribution platforms suggests another metaphor. Distribution, on the other hand, is inherent as usually development environments are directly accessible by developers. So, the question is to generalize the ideas of this book of integrated environments consisting of different environments being placed on several machines to more general concepts as indicated in sections 5.3 and 6.3.

Of course, not all problems stated above in the book can be tackled and solved by one group. We shall concentrate on certain topics due to (a) availability of resources, (b) due to the probability that we get results, and (c) due to the topic whether we have the corresponding necessary know-how. So, let me conclude this book with an *invitation* to other researchers to take up one or the other load. The goal would be to *contribute* in a common effort to a special branch of software engineering and, thus, to *software engineering in general*.

7 Extended Bibliography

compiled by M. Nagl, R.P. Rössel, and C. Rövenich

Contents

The following is a comprehensive bibliography on Software Development Environments, Methods of Software Engineering, and Formalisms for Developing SDE's. Nevertheless, it is only a small selection of publications which appeared in the last 20 years. This is especially true for sections 7 and 8 of this bibliography which mainly contain only those papers which have a connection to the articles of this book. Furthermore, it should clearly be stated, that most of the following references come from academia or (industrial) research institutes. Rather little can be found on descriptions of existing industrial tools (some references collecting industrial papers are given in section 1).

Sections 1 to 3 give an overview on which SDE projects exists, which specifics these projects have, and which topics of software engineering they support, respectively. The main source for technical papers is section 4. Section 5 gives references to internal formalisms for tool building and section 6 summarizes the bibliography on basic components of SDEs, as object storages.

Citation in the text of the book and mutual citation in the bibliography is given by prefixing the number of the bibliographic section in which the corresponding reference is contained.

The following abbreviations are used throughout the bibliography:

ESEC :   European Software Engineering Conference
ICSE :   IEEE International Conference on Software Engineering,
             IEEE Computer Society Press
IFB :   Informatik–Fachberichte, Berlin: Springer–Verlag
LNCS :   Lecture Notes in Computer Science, Berlin: Springer–Verlag
POPL :   ACM Symposium on Principles of Programming Languages
TOPLAS :   ACM Transactions on Programming Languages and Systems
TOSE :   IEEE Transactions on Software Engineering
TOSEM: ACM Transactions on Software Engineering and Methodology

1 Software Development Environments in General: Books, Proceedings, Special Issues, and Overview Articles

/Ada 86/   Proc. IEEE 2nd Int. Conf. Ada Applications and Environments, Miami Beach, Fl., IEEE Comp. Soc. Press (1986).

/Bal 85/   H. Balzert (Ed.): Modern Software Development Systems and Tools (in German), Mannheim: Bibl. Institut (1985).

/BCM 94/   A.W. Brown/D.J. Carney/E.J. Morris/D.B. Smith/P.F. Zarrella: Principles of CASE Tools Integration, New York: Oxford University Press (1994).

/BF 85/   J. G. B. Barnes/G. A. Fisher, Jr. (Eds.): Ada in Use: Proc. Ada Int. Conf., London: Cambridge University Press (1985).

/Bre 88/   P. Brereton (Ed.): Software Engineering Environments, Chichester: Ellis Horwood (1988).

/BSS 84/   D. R. Barstow/H. E. Shrobe/S. Sandewall (Eds.): Interactive Programming Environments, New York: McGraw Hill (1984).

/CDW 86/   R. Conradi/T. M. Didriksen/D. H. Wanvik (Eds.): Proc. Int. Workshop on Advanced Programming Environments, LNCS 244 (1986).

/Cha 86/   R. N. Charette: Software Engineering Environments – Concepts and Technology, New York: McGraw–Hill (1986).

/Chi 88/   E. J. Chikofsky (Ed.): Computer–aided Software Engineering, IEEE Comp. Soc. Press (1988).

/CST 85/   Proc. 1985 IEEE Conf. on Softw. Tools, Washington, D. C.: IEEE Comp. Soc. Press (1985).

/DEF 87/   S. A. Dart/R. J. Ellison/P. H. Feiler/A. N. Habermann: Software Development Environments, in /1. HN 87/, 18–28.

/Deu 85/   L. P. Deutsch (Ed.): ACM SIGPLAN '85 Symposium on Language Issues in Programming Environments, ACM SIGPLAN Notices 20, 7 (1985).

/DS 83/   D. Degano/E. Sandewall (Eds.): Integrated Interactive Computing Systems, Amsterdam: North–Holland (1983).

/EW 91/   A. Endres/H. Weber (Eds.): Sofware Development Environments and CASE Technology, Proc. European Symp. Königswinter, LNCS 509 (1991).

/Fis 88/   A. S. Fisher: CASE – Using Software Development Tools, New York: Wiley (1988).

/Gli 90a/   E. P. Glinert: Visual Programming Environments: Paradigms and Systems, IEEE Comp. Soc. Press (1990).

/Gli 90b/   E. P. Glinert: Visual Programming Environments: Applications and Issues, IEEE Comp. Soc. Press (1990).

/Goo 81/   G. Goos (Ed.): Tools for Programming (in German), IFB 43 (1981).

/GTE 85/   Proc. GTE Workshop on Software Development Environments for Programming in the Large, Harwichport (Mass.) (1985).

/Hai 86a/   B. Hailpern (Ed.): Special Issue on Multiparadigm Languages and Environments, IEEE Software 3, 1, (1986).

/Hai 86b/   B. Hailpern: Guest Editor's Introduction: Multiparadigm Languages and Environments, in /1. Hai 86a/, 6–9.

/Hen 84/   P. Henderson (Ed.): Proc. 1st ACM SIGSOFT/SIGPLAN Software Engineering Symposium on Practical Software Development Environments, ACM SIGPLAN Notices 19, 5 (1984).

/Hen 87/   P. Henderson (Ed.): Proc. 2nd Symp., ACM SIGPLAN Notices 22, 1 (1987).

/Hen 88/   P. Henderson (Ed.): Proc. 3rd Symp., ACM Software Engineering Notes 13, 5 (1988).

/HMS 85/   H. L. Hausen/M. Müllerberg/H. M. Sneed: Software Production Environments (in German), Köln: Verlag Rudolf Müller (1985).

/HN 87a/   P. Henderson/D. Notkin (Eds.): Special Issue on Software Development Environments, IEEE Computer 20, 11 (1987).

/HN 87b/   P. Henderson/D. Notkin: Integrated Design and Programming Environments, in /1. HN 87a/, 12–16.

/Hün 81/   H. Hünke (Ed.): Software Engineering Environments, Amsterdam: North–Holland (1981).

/Lon 90/   F. Long (Ed.): Software Engineering Environments, Proc. Int. Workshop on Environments, Chinon, France, LNCS 467 (1990).

/Lon 91/   F. Long (Ed.): Software Engineering Environments – Volume 3, London: Ellis Horwood (1991).

/LT 87/   M. M. Lehman/W. M. Turski: Essential Properties of IPSEs, ACM Software Engineering Notes 12, 1, 52–55 (1987).

/McD 85/   J. McDermid (Ed.): Integrated Project Support Environments, London: Peregrinus (1985).

/MS 84/ H. Morgenbrod/W. Sammer (Eds): Programming Environments and Compilers (in German), German Chapter ACM Bericht, Stuttgart: Teubner–Verlag (1984).

/MSW 90/ N. H. Madhavji/W. Schäfer/H. Weber (Eds.): SD&F1 – Proc. 1st Int. Conf. on System Development Environments & Factories, Berlin 1989, London: Pitman (1990).

/Nag 93/ M. Nagl: Software Development Environments, Classification and Future Trends (in German), Informatik–Spektrum 16, 5, 273–280 (1993).

/NF 92/ R. J. Norman/G. Forte (Guest Ed.): CASE in the '90s, Special Issue, Comm. ACM 35, 4 (1992).

/RF 80/ W. E. Riddle/R. E. Fairley (Eds.) Software Development Tools, New York: Springer–Verlag (1980).

/Rid 86/ W. E. Riddle (Ed.): Proc. Software Environments Workshop, ACM Software Engineering Notes 11, 1 (1986).

/Rid 88/ W. E. Riddle (Ed.): Software Engineering Environment Architectures, Special Issue, TOSE 14, 6 (1988).

/SB 93/ D. Schefström/G. v.d.Broek (Eds.): Tool Integration, New York: Wiley (1993).

/Sch 89/ H.–J. Scheibl: Software Development Systems and Tools (in German), 3. Kolloq., Techn. Akademie Esslingen (1989).

/SEJ 94/ Special Issue on CASE, Software Engineering Journal 9, 4 (1994).

/SN 90/ F. Schönthaler/T. Nemeth: Software Development Tools: Methodological Foundations (in German), Stuttgart: Teubner–Verlag (1990).

/Sof 87/ Special Issue on Software Development Environments, IEEE Software 4, 6 (1987).

/Sof 88/ Special Issue on The Emergence of CASE, IEEE Software 5, 2 (1988).

/Sof 90/ Special Issue on Tools Fair, IEEE Software 7, 3 (1990).

/Sof 92/ Special Issue on 'Integrated CASE', IEEE Software 9, 2 (1992).

/Sof 93/ Special Issue on Tools Assessment, IEEE Software 10, 3 (1993).

/Som 86/ I. Sommerville (Ed.): Software Engineering Environments, IEEE Computing Series 7, London: Peregrinus (1986).

/SR 84/ W. Sammer/W. Remmele (Eds.): Programming Environments: Development Tools and Programming Languages (in German), IFB 79 (1984).

/Taf 87/ S. Tafvelin (Ed.): Ada Components: Libraries and Tools, Proc. Ada–Europe Intern. Conf. Stockholm, Cambridge: Cambridge University Press (1987).

/Tay 90/ R.N. Taylor (Ed.): Proc. 4th ACM SIGSOFT Symposium on Software Development Environments, ACM Software Engineering Notes 15, 6 (1990).

/TL 91/ V.–P. Tahvanainen/K. Lyytinen (Eds.): Proc. 2nd Workshop in The Next Generation of CASE Tools, Trondheim, Norway, Techn. Report 1, Dep. of Comp. Sci. & Inf. Syst., Univ. of Iyväskylä, Finland (1991).

/ToPL 86/ Special Issue on Programming Environments, TOPLAS 8, 4 (1986).

/TrSE 86/ Special Issue on Programming Environments, TOSE 12, 12 (1986).

/Was 81/ A.E. Wasserman (Ed.): Software Development Environments, Los Alamitos: IEEE Comp. Soc. Press (1981).

/Web 92/ Weber: Proc. 5th ACM SIGSOFT Symposium on Software Develpment Environments, ACM Software Engineering Notes 17, 5 (1992).

/WHB 87/ N.H. Weiderman/A.N. Habermann/M. W. Borger/M. H. Klein: A Methodology for Evaluating Environments, in /1. Hen 87/, 199–207.

2 Surveys on Special SDE-Projects

/Abb 86/   H. Abbenhardt: POINTE – Portable, integrated Development Tool (in German), Computer Magazin 10, 69–71 (1986).

/Bal 85/   R. Balzer: A 15 Year Perspective on Automatic Programming, TOSE 11, 11, 1257–1268 (1985).

/Bau 85,87/ F. L. Bauer et al.: The Munich CIP Project, Vol. I: The Wide Spectrum Language CIP–L, LNCS 183, Vol. 2: The Program Transformation System CIP–S, LNCS 292 (1985, 1987).

/BB 90/   T. J. Biggerstaff/L. Belady: A Vision of Leonardo, in /1. MSW 90/, 37–48.

/BBC 90/   K. Benali/N. Boudjlida/F. Charoy/J.–C. Derniame/C. Godart/P. Griffiths/V. Gruhn/P. Jamart/A. Legait/D. E. Oldfield/F. Oquendo: Presentation of the ALF Project, in /1. MSW 90/, 75–90.

/BCD 88/   P. Borras/D. Clement/Th. Despeyroux/J. Incerpi/G. Kahn/B. Lang/V. Pascual: Centaur: The System, in /1. Hen 88/, 14–24.

/BGH 86/   M. Broy/A. Geser/H. Hussmann: Towards Advanced Programming Environments Based on Algebraic Concepts, in /1. CDW 86/, 454–470.

/BL 95/   T. Batz/C. Lewerentz: Lessons from Building Complex SDEs (in German), Informatik – Forschung und Entwicklung 10, 2, 107–109 (1995).

/BOS 90/   J. Boarder/H. Obbink/M. Schmidt: ATMOSPHERE – Advanced Techniques and Methods of System Production in a Heterogeneous, Extensible, and Rigorous Environment, in /1. MSW 90/, 199–208.

/Bot 89/   F. Bott (Ed.): ECLIPSE – An Integrated Project Support Environment, London: Peregrinus (1989).

/Bro 91/   A. W. Brown (Ed.): Integrated Project Support Environments: The ASPECT Project, London: Academic Press (1991).

/BS 86/   R. Bahlke/G. Snelting: The PSG System – From Language Definitions to Interactive Programming Environments, in /1. ToPL 86/, 547–576.

/Bux 80/   J. Buxton: Requirements for the Ada Programming Support Environments: Stoneman, US Dept. of Defense, Washington, D.C.: OSD/R&D (1980).

/CCH 87/   A. Carle/K. D. Cooper/R. T. Hood/K. Kennedy/L. Torczon/S. K. Warren: A Practical Environment for Scientific Programming, in /1. HN 87/, 75–89.

/CL 93/   E. Casais/C. Lewerentz (Eds.): Issues in Tools' Integration, STONE Project Monograph, 167 pp., Karlsruhe (1993).

/CL 94/   E. Casais/C. Lewerentz (Eds.): Models and Tools for Object–oriented CASE Environments, STONE Project Monograph, 180pp, FZI Karlsruhe (1994).

/DHK 84/   V. Donzeau–Gouge/G. Huet/G. Kahn/B. Lang: Programming Environments Based on Structured Editors: The Mentor Experience, in /1. BSS 84/, 128–140.

/DKP 89/   P. De la Cruz/B. Krieg–Brückner/A. Perez Riereo: From Algebraic Specifications to Correct Ada Programs: The Esprit Project PROSPECTRA, in Alvarez (Ed.): Proc. Ada '89 Int. Conf., Madrid, 171–182, Cambridge: Cambridge University Press (1989).

/DoD 84/   Department of Defense (USA): Requirements and Design Criteria for the Common APSE Interface Set (CAIS), KIT Team Report (October 1984).

/Dow 87/   M. Dowson: Integrated Project Support with IStar, in /1. Sof 87/, 6–15.

/DT 80/   L. P. Deutsch/E. A. Taft (Eds.): Requirements for an Experimental Programming Environment, TR CSL 80–10, XEROX PARC (1980).

/ES 89/   G. Engels/W. Schäfer: Program Development Environments (in German), Stuttgart: Teubner–Verlag (1989).

/Eva 89/   M. W. Evans: The Software Factory – A Fourth Generation Software Engineering Environment, New York: Wiley (1989).

/FO 90/   C. Fernström/L. Ohlsson: The ESF Vision of a Software–Factory, in /1. MSW 90/, 91–100.

/Gol 84/   A. Goldberg: Smalltalk–80: An Interactive Programming Environment, Reading: Addison–Wesley (1984).

/GR 83/   A. Goldberg/D. Robson: Smalltalk–80 – The Language and its Implementation, Reading: Addison–Wesley (1983).

/Hab 82/   A. N. Habermann et al.: The Second Compendium of Gandalf Documentation, Techn. Report, Department of Computer Science, Carnegie–Mellon Univ. (1982).

/HK 85/   R. Hood/K. Kennedy: A Programming Environment for Fortran, Proc. 18th Hawaii Int. Conf. on Syst. Sci., 625–637 (1985).

/HN 86/   A. N. Habermann/D. Notkin: Gandalf: Software Development Environments, in /1. TrSE 86a/, 1117–1127.

/Hru 87/   P. Hruschka: ProMod at the Age of Five, in Nichols/Simpsom (Eds.): Proc. 1st ESEC, LNCS 289, 307–316 (1987).

/Hru 91/   P. Hruschka (Ed.): CASE in Application – Experiences with the Introduction of CASE (in German), München: Hanser–Verlag (1991).

/HSS 90/   H. Hormann/L. Schöpe/W. Stulken: Tool Integration such as shown in the RASOP–Project, in /1. MSW 90/, 209–218.

/Ivi 77/   E. L. Ivie: The Programmer's Workbench – A Machine for Software Development, Comm. ACM 20, 10, 746–753 (1977).

/Jac 90/   K. Jackson: ASPECT (Alvey) in Perspective, in /1. MSW 90/, 101–106.

/JPS 94/   G. Junkermann/B. Peuschel/W. Schaefer/S. Wolf: MERLIN: Supporting Cooperation in Software Development through a Knowledge–based Environment, in A. Finkelstein et al. (Eds.): Advances in Software Process Technology, 103–129, New York: Research Studies Press, Wiley (1994).

/Kad 92/   R. Kadia: Issues Encountered in Building a Flexible Software Development Environment – Lessons Learned from the Arcadia Project, in /1. Web 92/, 169–180.

/KM 84/   B. W. Kernighan/J. R. Marshey: The UNIX Programming Environment, Computer 14, 25–34 (1981), repr. in /1. BSS 84/, 175–197.

/KR 84/   B. W. Kernigham/R. P. Ritchie: The UNIX Programming Environment, Englewood Cliffs: Prentice–Hall (1984).

/MBJ 90/   J. Mylopoulos/A. Borgida/M. Jarke/M. Koubarkis: Telos: a Language for Representing Knowledge about Information Systems, ACM Transactions on Information Systems 8, 4, 325–362 (1990).

/Mic 85/   Microsoft Corporation: Windows – User Guide (1985).

/MR 84/   J. McDermid/K. Ripken: Life Cycle Support in the Ada Environment, Cambridge: Cambridge University Press (1984).

/Nag 90/   M. Nagl: A Characterization of the IPSEN–Project, in /1. MSW 90/, 141–150.

/Nag 93/   M. Nagl: Tightly Integrated Software Development Environment – An Experience Report about the IPSEN Project (in German), Informatik Forschung & Entwicklung 8, 105–119 (1993).

/NES 85/   D. Notkin/R. J. Ellison/B. J. Staudt/G. E. Kaiser/E. Kant/A. N. Habermann/V. Ambriola/C. Montangero: Special Issue on the GANDALF Project, Journal of Systems and Software 5, 2 (May 1985).

/Oss 86/   H. L. Ossher: A Mechanism for Specifying the Structure of Large, Layered, Object–oriented Programs, SIGPLAN Notices 21, 10, 143–152 (1986).

/Ost 81/   L. J. Osterweil: Software Environment Research: Directions for the Next Five Years, IEEE Computer 14, 4, 35–44 (1981).

/Ost 83/   L. J. Osterweil: Toolpack– An Experimental Software Development Environment Research Project, TOSE 9, 6, 673–685 (1983).

/PAC 86/   PACT: General Description by BULL, EUROSOFT, Syseca, ICL, GEC, Olivetti, Siemens, ESPRIT Project 1086 (1986).

/Pic 90/   P. Picard: SFINX: Tool Integration in a PCTE based Software Factory, in /1. MSW 90/, 219–228.

/Rei 95/   St.P. Reiss: The Field Programming Environment: A Friendly Integrated Environment For Learning and Development, Boston: Kluwer Academic Publishers (1995).

/RW 90/   C. Rich/R. C. Waters: The Programmer's Apprentice, New York: ACM Press (1990).

/San 78/   E. Sandewall: Programming in an Interactive Environment: The LISP Experience, ACM Comp. Surveys 10, 1, 35–71 (1978).

/SB 91/   H. Steusloff/T. Batz (Eds.): System Engineering for Realtime Systems (in German), Bericht über das Verbundproject PROSYT, Berlin: Springer–Verlag (1991).

/SKW 85/   D. R. Smith/G. B. Kotik/S. J. Westfold: Research on Knowledge–Based Software Environments at Kestrel Institute, TOSE 11, 11, 1278–1295 (1985).

/ST 83/   The DoD STARS Program, Software Technology for Adaptable, Reliable Systems, Special Issue, IEEE Computer, November 1983.

/Stu 87/   R. Studer: Concepts for a Distributed, Knowledge–based Software Development Environment (in German), IFB 132 (1987).

/Sun 86/   SunView Programmer's Guide, Mountain View: SunMicrosystems Inc. (1986).

/SW 89/   W. Schäfer/H. Weber: The ESF Profile, in R. Yeh/P. Ng (Eds.): Handbook of Computer Aided Software Engineering, 613–637, New York: van Nostrand (1989).

/TB 87/   R. N. Taylor/D. A. Baker et al.: Next Generation Software Environments: Principles, Problems, and Research Directions, Techn. Rep. 87–16, Univ. California: Irvine, CA (1987).

/Tei 84/   W. Teitelman: An Tour Through Cedar, IEEE Software 1, 2, 44–73 (1984).

/Tim 87/   M. Timm: The Software Development Environment UNIBASE (in German), in Moderne Software–Entwicklungssysteme und –Werkzeuge, Techn. Akademie Esslingen (1987).

/TM 84/   W. Teitelman/L. Masinter: The Interlisp Programming Environment, IEEE Computer 14, 4, 25–34 (1981), repr. in /1. BSS 84/, 83–96.

658

/TR 81/   T. Teitelbaum/T. Reps: The Cornell Program Synthesizer: A Syntax–directed Programming Environment, Comm. ACM 24, 9, 563–573 (1981), repr. in /1. BSS 84/, 97–116.

/TSY 88/   R. N. Taylor/R. W. Selby/M. Young/F. C. Belz/L. A. Clarke/J. C. Wileden/L. Osterweil/A. L. Wolff: Foundations for the Arcadia Environment Architecture, in /1. Hen 88/, 1–13.

/War 90/   B. Warboys: The IPSE 2.5 Project: Process Modelling as the Basis for a Support Environment, in /1. MSW 90/, 59–74.

659

3 Tool Support for Special Topics of Software Engineering: Books, Proceedings, and Surveys

/AM 81/   R. Abbot/D. Moorhead: Software Requirements and Specifications – A Survey of Needs and Languages, Journal of Systems and Software, 2, 4, 297–316 (1981).

/Bab 86/   W. A. Babich: Software Configuration Management, Reading: Addison Wesley (1986).

/Bei 83/   B. Beizer: Software Testing Techniques, New York: van Nostrand (1983).

/Bei 84/   B. Beizer: Software System Testing and Quality Assurance, New York: van Nostrand (1984).

/BES 95/   N.S. Barghouti/W. Emmerich/W. Schaefer/A. Skarra: Information Management in Process–Centered Software Engineering Environments – Trends in Software, in A. Fugetta/A. Wolf (Eds.): Special Issue on the Software Process, New York: John Wiley & Sons Ltd. (1995).

/BHS 80/   E. H. Bersoff/V. D. Henderson/ S. G. Siegel: Software Configuration Management – An Investment in Product Integrity, Englewood Cliffs: Prentice–Hall (1980).

/BJ 94/   C. Bußler/S. Jablonski: An Approach to Integrate Workflow Modeling and Organization Modeling in an Enterprise, in Proc. 3rd IEEE International Workshop on Enabling Technologies: Infrastructure for Collaborative Enterprises, 81–94 (1994).

/BKM 84/   R. Budde/K. Kuhlenkamp/L. Mathiassen/H. Züllighoven: Approches to Prototyping, Berlin: Springer–Verlag (1984).

/Boe 84/   B. W. Boehm: Verifying and Validating Software Requirements and Design Specifications, IEEE Software 1, 1, 75–88 (1984).

/BP 89/   T. J. Biggerstaff/A. J. Perlis: Software Reusability, Vol. I: Concepts and Models, New York: ACM Press (1989).

/BP 92/   W. Bischofberger/G. Pomberger: Prototyping–oriented Software Development – Concepts and Tools, Berlin: Springer–Verlag (1992).

/Bul 94/   H. J. Bullinger (Ed.): Workflow Management and Services (in German), FBO–Fachverlag für Büro– und Organisationstechnik (1994)

/BW 82/   Bartlett/Walter (Eds.): Proc. Int. Conf. on Systems Documentation, January (1982).

/Cho 85/   T. S. Chow: Software Quality Assurance, Silver Spring: IEEE Comp. Soc. Press (1985).

/CDS 86/   S. D. Conte/H. E. Dunsmore/V. Y. Shen: Software Engineering Metrics and Models, Menlo Park: Benjamin Cummings (1986).

/Con 86/   D. Conde: Bibliography on Version Control and Configuration Management, ACM Software Engineering Notes 11, 3, 81–84 (1986).

/CSM 89/   Conference on Software Maintenance 1989, Proceedings, IEEE Comp. Soc. Press (1989).

/Cur 86/   B. Curtis: Human Factors in Software Development, 2nd ed., Washington: IEEE Comp. Soc. Press (1986).

/Dow 86/   M. Dowson (Ed.): Proc. 3rd Int. Software Process Workshop, IEEE Comp. Soc. Press (1986)

/EL 92/   G. Engels/P. Löhr–Richter: CADDY: A Highly Integrated Environment to Support Conceptual Database Design, in G. Forte et al. (Eds.): Proc. 5th CASE (1992), Montreal (Canada), 19–22, Los Alamitos: IEEE Computer Society Press (1992).

/EM 87/   M. W. Evans/J. J. Marciniak: Software Quality Assurance and Management, New York: John Wiley (1987).

/FBB 82/   W. R. Franta/H. K. Berg/W. E. Boebert/T. G. Moher: Formal Methods of Program Verification and Specification, Englewood Cliffs: Prentice Hall (1982).

/Fei 91/   P. Feiler (Ed.): Proc. 3rd Int. Workshop on Software Configuration Management (SCM3), New York: ACM Press (1991).

/FKN 94/   A. Finkelstein/J. Kramer/B.A. Nuseibeh (Eds.): Software Process Modelling and Technology, Taunton: Research Studies Press (1994).

/Fre 87/   P. Freeman (Ed.): Software Reusability, Washington: IEEE Comp. Soc. Press (1987).

/FW 96/   A. Fuggetta, A. Wolf (Eds.): Software Process, Chicester: John Wiley & Sons (1996).

/GC 87/   R. B. Grady/D. R. Caswell: Software Metrics: Establishing a Company–wide Program, Englewood Cliffs: Prentice Hall (1987).

/Gil 88/   T. Gilb: Principles of Software Engineering Management, Reading: Addison Wesley (1988).

/GJ 96/   P. Garg, M. Jazayeri, Process–Centered Software Enigineering Environments: A Grand Tour, in /3. FW 96/, 25–52.

/Hal 77/   H. M. Halstead: Elements of Software Science, New York: Elsevier (1977).

/Hal 90/   M. Hallmann: ESF, Prototyping of Complex Software Systems (in German), Stuttgart: Teubner–Verlag (1990).

/How 87/   W. E. Howden: Functional Program Testing and Analysis, New York: McGraw–Hill (1987).

/Huf 96/   K. E. Huff: Software Process Modeling, in /3. FW 96/, 1–24.

/IEEE 87/   IEEE: Software Engineering Standards, New York: Wiley Interscience (1987).

/IEEE 94a/   IEEE Software Special Issue on Measurement–Based Process Improvement, IEEE Software 11, 4 (1994).

/IEEE 94b/   IEEE Software Special Issue on Systematic Reuse, IEEE Software 11,5 (1994).

/Jab 95/   S. Jablonski: Workflow Management Systems: Motivation, Modelling, Architecture (in German), Informatik Spektrum 18, 13–24 (1995).

/Kem 89/   R. A. Kemmerer (Ed.): Proc. 3rd Symp. on Software Testing, Analysis, and Verification (TAV 3), ACM Software Engineering Notes 14, 8 (1989).

/Man 81/   M. Mantei: The Effect of Programming Team Structures on Programming Tasks, Comm. of the ACM 24, 3, 106–113 (1981).

/MH 81/   E. Miller/W. E. Howden (Eds.): Software Testing and Validation Techniques, New York: IEEE Comp. Soc. Press (1981).

/MM 83/   J. Martin/C. McClure: Software Maintenance – The Problem and its Solution, Englewood Cliffs: Prentice Hall (1983).

/Mor 90/   M. Moriconi (Ed.): Int. Workshop on Formal Methods in Software Development, ACM Software Engineering Notes 15, 4 (1990).

/MS 91/   N. Madhavji/W. Schäfer (Eds.): Special Issue on Software Process and its Support, Software Engineering Journal 6, 5 (1991).

/Mye 79/   G. Myers: The Art of Software Testing, New York: John Wiley (1979).

/Ohn 87/   Y. Ohno (Ed.): Current Issues of Requirements Engineering Environments, Amsterdam: North–Holland (1982).

/Per 90/   D.E. Perry (Ed.): Proc. 5th Int. Software Process Workshop, Los Alamitos: IEEE Comp. Soc. Press (1990).

/Pep 83/   P. Pepper (Ed.): Program Transformation and Programming Environments, Berlin: Springer–Verlag (1983).

/Pfa 83/   P. E. Pfaff (Ed.): User Interface Management Systems, Proc. Seaheim Workshop UIMS, New York: Springer–Verlag (1983).

/Pot 89/   C. Potts (Ed.): Proc. 5th Int. Workshop on Software Specification and Design, Pittsburgh, ACM Software Engineering Notes 14, 3 (1989).

/PSS 81/   A. Perlis/F. Sayward/M. Shaw (Eds.): Software Metrics – An Analysis and Evaluation, Cambridge: MIT Press (1981).

/PTM 81/   Proc. ACM SIGPLAN/SIGSOFT Conf. Text Manipulation, Portland, Or., ACM Press (1981).

/PZ 83/   G. Parikh/N. Zvegintzov (Eds.): Software Maintenance, Silver Spring: IEEE Comp. Soc. Press (1983).

/Rei 86/   B. J. Reifer (Ed.): Software Management, 3rd ed., Washington: IEEE Comp. Soc. Press (1986).

/RO 85/   W. Rzepka/Y. Ohno (Eds.): Special Issue on Requirements Engineering Environments, IEEE Computer 18, 4 (1984).

/Rom 85/   G.C. Roman: A Taxonomy of Current Issues in Requirements Engineering, IEEE Computer 18, 4, 14–22 (1985).

/RW 86/   C. Rich/R. C. Waters: Artificial Intelligence and Software Engineering, Los Altos: Morgan Kaufman (1986).

/SBZ 82/   S. Squires/M. Branstad/M. Zelkowitz (Eds.): Proc. ACM SIGSOFT Engineering Workshop on Rapid Prototyping, ACM Software Engineering Notes 7, 5 (1982).

/Shn 86/   B. Shneiderman: Designing User Interfaces, Reading: Addison Wesley (1986).

/Suc 88/   L. Suchman (Ed.): CSCW 88 Proc. Conf. on Computer–Supported Cooperative Work, Portland, Or., New York: ACM Press (1988).

/TD 90/   R. H. Thayer/M. Dorfman: System and Software Requirements Engineering, IEEE Comp. Science Press (1990).

/Tha 88/   R. Thayer: Software Engineering Project Management, IEEE Comp. Soc. Press (1988).

/TP 84/   R. H. Thayer/A. B. Pyster: Special Issue on Software Engineering Project Managment, TOSE 10, 1 (1984).

/Tra 88/   W. Tracz (Ed.): Software Reuse – Emerging Technology, Washington: IEEE Comp. Soc. Press (1988).

/TrSe 86/   Special Issue on Software Design Methods, TOSE 12, 2 (1986).

/Tul 89/   C. Tully (Ed.): Proc. 4th Int. Software Process Workshop, ACM Software Engineering Notes 14, 4 (1989).

/WD 85/   J. C. Wileden/M. Dowson (Eds.): Proc. 2nd Int. Software Process Workshop, IEEE Comp. Soc. Press (1985).

/Win 88/   J. F. H. Winkler (Ed.): Proc. 1st Int. Workshop on Software Version and Configuration Control (SCM1), Bericht 30 German Chapter ACM, Stuttgart: Teubner–Verlag (1988).

/WT 89/   J. F. H. Winkler/W. Tichy (Eds.): Proc. 2nd Int. Workshop on Software Configuration Management (SCM2), ACM Software Engineering Notes 17, 7 (1989).

4 Publications on Special SDE Tools, Projects, Architectures

/ABL 81/ C. N. Alberga/A. L. Brown/G. B. Leeman/M. Mikelsons/M. N. Wegman: A Program Development Tool, Proc. 8th POPL, 92–104 (1981).

/ABL 84/ C. N. Alberga/A. L. Brown/G. B. Leeman/M. Mikelsons/M. N. Wegman: A Program Development Tool, IBM J. Res. Develop. 28, 60–73 (1984).

/ACM 90/ V. Ambriola/P. Ciancarini/C. Montangero: Software Process Enactment in Oikos, in /1. Tay 90/, 183–192.

/ACS 84/ J. E. Archer/R. Conway/F. B. Schneider: User Recovery and Reversal in Interactive Systems, TOPLAS 6, 1, 1–19 (1984).

/AD 86/ J.D. Ascher/M.T. Devlin: Rational's Experiences Using Ada for very Large Systems, Proc. 1st Int. Conf. Ada Progr. Lang. Appl., B.2.5.1–B.2.5.12 (1986).

/Ada 93/ D. Adamcyk: Scheduling for an SA/RT/IM Interpreter (in German), Master's Thesis, RWTH Aachen (1993).

/AEC 90/ A. Alderson/A. Elliott/J. Cartmell: The Eclipse Programme, in /1. MSW 90/, 187–198.

/AGM 86/ E. Adams/W. Gramlich/S. Muchnick/S. Tirfing: SunPro – Engineering a Practical Program Development Environment, in /1. CDW 86/, 86–96.

/AHM 89/ E. W. Adams/M. Honda/T. C. Miller: Object Management in a CASE Environment, Proc. 11th ICSE, 154–163 (1989).

/AHW 90/ F. Arefi/Ch. E. Hughs/D. A. Workman: Automatically Generating Visual Syntax–Directed Editors, in Comm. ACM 33, 3, 349–360, ACM Press (1990).

/AL 82/ J. Arnon/H. Lehrhaupt: Software Documentation: An Automated Approach, in Bartlett/Walter (Eds.): Proc. Int. Conf. on Systems Documentation, Carson, Cal., 1–8 (1982).

/Alf 85/ M. W. Alford: SREM at the Age of Eight: The Distributed Computing Design System, IEEE Computer 18, 4, 36–46 (1985).

/Ame 94/ G. v.Amerongen: Compilation of PROGRES Operations (in German), Master's Thesis, RWTH Aachen (1994).

/And 96/ M. Andries: Graph Rewrite Systems and Visual Database Languages, Doct. Diss., Rijksuniversiteit Leiden, Netherlands (1996).

/Ath 89/ Athena Systems, Inc.: Foresight: Modelling and Simulation Toolset for Real–Time System Development, Foresight Product Description (1989).

/BAB 87/ B.A. Burton/R.W. Aragon/S.A. Bailey/K.D. Koehler/L.A. Mayes: The Reusable Software Library, in /3. Tra 88/, 129–137.

/Bac 92/ V. Bacvanski: Software Engineering for Heterogeneous Knowlegde–Based Systems, in Awad (Ed.): Proc. 3rd Annual Symposium of the IAKE'92, 21–33, Kensington, MD: Software Engineering Press (1992).

/Bac 93a/ V. Bacvanski: Introducing Abstract Data Types into Production Systems, in Acharya (Ed.): Proc. IJCAI–93 Workshop on Production Systems and their Innovative Applications, 75–86, IJCAI Inc. (1993).

/Bac 93b/ V. Bacvanski: Applying Object–Oriented Software Engineering to Knowledge–Based Systems in Industrial Environments, in Dost (Ed.): Proc. 1993 Int. Simulation Technology Multiconference, 203–208, San Diego, CA: The Society for Computer Simulation (1993).

/Bac 93c/ V. Bacvanski: An Architecture for the Integration of Industrial Artificial Intelligence Systems, in Takamori/Tsuchiya (Eds.): Robotics, Mechatronics and Manufacturing Systems, 815–820, Amsterdam: Elsevier Science Publ. (1993).

/Bak 75/ F. T. Baker: Structured Programming in a Production Programming Environment, TOSE 1, 2, 241–152 (1975).

/Bar 92/ N.S. Barghouti: Supporting Cooperation in the MARVEL Process–Centered SDE, in /1. Web 92/, 21–31.

/BCG 83/ R. Balzer/T. Cheatham/C. Green: Software Technology in the 1990's: Using a New Paradigm, IEEE Computer 16, 11, 39–45 (1983).

/BD 80/ J. N. Buxton/L. E. Druffel: Rationale for Stoneman, in Proc. 4th Int. Comp. Software and Applications Conf. 1980, 66–72, repr. in /1. BBS 84/, 535–545.

/BE 87a/ N. Belkhatir/J. Estublier: Experiences with a data base of programs, in /1. Hen 87/, 84–91.

/BE 87b/ N. Belkhatir/J. Estublier: Software Management Constraints and Action Triggering in the Adele Program Database, in Nichols/Simpson (Eds.): Proc. 1st ESEC, LNCS 289, 47–58 (1987).

/Beh 97/ A. Behle: A Dynamic, Personalized Information System for Software Components in the World Wide Web (in German), EMISA Forum 1/1997, to appear.

/Ber 86/ V. Berzins: On Merging Software Extensions, Acta Informatica 23, 607–619 (1986).

/Ber 87/   E. Berens: Support of Technical Documentation within a Software Development Environment (in German), Univ. of Osnabrück (1987).

/BF 92/   A.W. Brown/P.H. Feiler: An Analysis Technique for Examing Integration in a Project Support Environment, in /1. Web 92/, 139–148.

/BFG 93/   S. Bandinelli, A. Fugetta, C. Ghezzi: Software Process Model Evolution in the SPADE Environment, IEEE Transactions on Software Engineering 19, 12, 1128–1144 (1993).

/BGH 86/   M. Broy/A. Geser/H. Hussmann: Towards Advanced Programming Environments Based on Algebraic Concepts, in /1. CDW 86/, 454–470.

/BGV 90/   R. Ballance/S. L. Graham/M. L. VanDeVanter: The Pan Language–Based Editing System for Integrated Development Environments, in /1. Tay 90/, 77–93.

/BH 88/   R. Blumofe/A. Hecht: Executing Real–Time Structured Analysis Specifications, ACM Software Eng. Notes 13, 3, 32–40 (1988).

/BJ 78/   J. C. Browne/D. B. Johnson: Fast: A Second Generation Program Analysis System, Proc. 3rd ICSE, 142–148 (1978).

/BJ 92/   J. Börstler/Th. Janning: Traceability Between Requirements Engineering and Design: A Transformational Approach, Proc. COMPSAC 92, 362–368 (1992).

/BKH 92/   I.Z. Ben–Shaul/G.E. Kaiser/G.T. Heineman: An Architecture for Multi–User Software Development Environments, in /1. Web 92/, 149–158.

/BKP 85/   V. R. Basili/E. E. Katz/N. M. Panlilio–Yap/C. Loggia Ramsey/S. Chang: Characterization of an Ada Support Development, IEEE Computer 18, 9, 53–65 (1985).

/BL 81/   Bell Labs: Source Code Control System User's Guide, UNIX System III Programmer's Manual, AT & T Inf. Systems (1981).

/BM 77/   L. A. Belady/P. M. Merlin: Evolving Parts and Relations: A Model for System Families, Res. Rep. RC–6627, T. J. Watson Research Center (1977).

/BM 92/   A.W. Brown/J.A. McDermid: Learning from IPSE's Mistakes, in /1. Sof 92/, 23–28.

/Bör 91/   J. Börstler: An Editor for Programming–in–the–Large as a Central CASE–Tool (in German), in Zorn/Bender (Eds.): Proc. Tool '91, 341–350, Berlin: VDE Verlag (1991).

/Bör 93/   J. Börstler: FOCS: A Classification System for Software Reuse, in Proc. 11th Pacific Northwest Software Quality Conf., 201–211, Portland: Pacific Agenda (1993).

/Bör 94/   J. Börstler: IPSEN: An Integrated Environment to Support Development for and with Reuse, in W. Schäfer et al. (Eds): Software Reusability, 134–140, Chichester: Ellis Horwood (1994).

/Bör 95/   J. Börstler: Feature–oriented Classification for Software Reuse, in Proc. 7th Int. Conf. Softw. Eng. and Knowl. Eng., 204–211, Skokie (USA): Knowledge Systems Institute (1995).

/Bor 86/   E. Borison: A Model of Software Manufacture, in /1. CDW 86/, 197–220.

/BR 81/   V. R. Basili/R. Reiter, Jr.: A Controlled Experiment Quantitatively Comparing Software Development Approaches, TOSE 7, 5, 299–320 (1981).

/BR 88/   V. R. Basili/H. D. Rombach: The TAME Project: Towards Improvement oriented Software Environments, in /1. Rid 88/, 758–773.

/BR 90/   J. C. Bicarregui/B. Ritchie: Providing Support for the Formal Development of Software, in /1. MSW 90/, 117–130.

/Bra 89/   H. Brandt: Syntax–oriented Editing allowing Inconsistencies (in German), Master's Thesis, RWTH Aachen (1989).

/Bru 91/   T. Bruckhaus: Incremental Analysis Tools for Integrating Requirements Specifications and Software Architecture Descriptions (in German), Master's Thesis, RWTH Aachen (1991).

/BS 84/   M. H. Brown/R. Sedgewick: A System for Algorithm Animation, Comput. Graphics 18, 177–186 (1984).

/BS 86/   R. Bahlke/G. Snelting: Context–sensitive editing with PSG environments, in /1. CDW 86/, 26–38.

/Bul 85/   G. M. Bull et al.: The PEACOCK paradigm of system development, in Proc. ESPRIT '85, Status report of ongoing work, 343–348, Amsterdam: North Holland (1985).

/CA 87/   R. P. Cook/R. J. Auletta: StarLite, A Visual Simulation Package for Software Prototyping, in /1. Hen 87/, 102–110.

/Cap 85/   M. Caplinger: Structured Editor Support for Modularity and Data Abstraction, in /1. Deu 85/ 140–147.

/CDG 90/   R. Conradi/T. M. Didriksen/B. Gulla/H. Eidnes/E.–A. Karlsson/A. Lie/P. H. Westby/S. O. Hallsteinsen/P. Holager/O. Sølberg: Design of the Kernel EPOS Software Engineering Environment, in /1. MSW 90/, 3–20.

/CDF 84/   M. Chesi/E. Dameri/M. P. Franceschi/M. G. Gatti/C. Simonelli: Systems Management, in /1. Hen 84/, 81–88.

/CDW 84/   R. Conway/D. DeJohn/S. Worona: A User's Guide to the COPE Programming Environment, Dep. Comput. Sci., Cornell Univ., Ithaca NY, Tech. Rep. 84–599 (April 1984).

/CGG 85/   R. Chandhok/D. Garlan/D. Goldenson/M. Tucker/P. Miller: Structure Editing–based Programming Environments: The GNOME Approach, in Proc. NCC 85, (July 1985).

/Che 84/   T. E. Cheatham, Jr.: A Computer–based Project Management Assistant, in Dig. Papers Fall COMP-CON, 156–160 (1984).

/CHO 85/   M. Clemm/M. Heimbigner/J. Osterweil/G. Williams: Keystone, A Federated Software Environment, in /1. GTE 85/, 80–88.

/CHW 88/   E. S. Cohen/D. A. Soni/R. Gluecker/W. M. Hasling/R. W. Schwanke/M. E. Wagner: Version Management in Gypsy, in /1. Hen 88/, 201–215.

/CK 84/   R. H. Campbell/P. A. Kirslis: The SAGA Project: A System for Software Development, in /1. Hen 84/, 73–80.

/CKT 87/   K. D. Cooper/K. Kennedy/L. Torczon: Editing and Compiling Whole Programs, in /1. Hen 87/, 92–101.

/CL 84/   R. P. Chase/D. Leblang: Computer–Aided Software Engineering in a Distributed Workstation Environment, in /1. Hen 84/, 104–112.

/Cle 88/   G. M. Clemm: The Workshop System – A Practical Knowledge–Based Software Environment, in /1. Hen 88/, 55–64.

/Clé 90/   D. Clément: A Distributed Architecture for Programming Environments, in /1. Tay 90/, 11–21.

/Coo 90/   St. Coors: Design of an Integrated Requirements Engineering Environment (in German), Master's Thesis, RWTH Aachen (1990).

/CR 90/   R. H. Campbell/H. S. Render: Formalizing Configuration Management with CLEMMA, in /1. MSW 90/, 159–170.

/CR 92/   J.L. Cybulsky/K. Read: A Hypertext–Based Software–Engineering Environment, in /1. Sof 92/, 62–68.

/CRZ 88/   L. A. Clarke/D. J. Richardson/S. J. Zeil: TEAM: A Support Environment for Testing, Evaluation, and Analysis, in /1. Hen 88/, 153–162.

/CSE 90/   Computer & Software Engineering: ShortCut User's Manual, CSE Salzburg (1990).

/CT 86/   R. H. Campbell/R. B. Terwilliger: The SAGA Approach to Automated Project Management, in /1. CDW 86/, 142–155.

/CV 87/   C. Childs/F. I. Vokolos: AWB–ADE: An Application Development Environment for Interactive, Integrated Systems, in /1. Hen 87/, 111–120.

/CWT 86/   L. Clarke/J. C. Wileden/R. N. Taylor/M. Young/L. J. Osterweil: ARCADIA: A Software Development Environment Research Project, in /1. Ada 86/.

/CWW 80/   E. Cristofar/T. A. Wendt/B. C. Wonsiewicz: Source Control + Tools = Stable Systems, in Proc. COMPSAC 80 (1980).

/CWW 86/   L. Clarke/J. C. Wileden/A. C. Wolfe: Graphite: A Meta Tool for Ada Environment Development, in /1. Ada 86/, 91–90.

/Däb 91/   D. Däberitz: An Integration Document for Incrementally Integrating Requirements Engineering and Programming–in–the–Large (in German), Master's Thesis, RWTH Aachen (1991).

/DBS 91/   P. Devanbu/R.J. Brachmann/P.G. Selfridge/B.W. Ballard: LaSSIE: A Knowledge–Based Software Information System, Comm. ACM 34, 5, 35–49 (1991).

/DeT 84/   J. DeTreville: Phoan: An Intelligent System for Distributed Control Synthesis, in /1. Hen 84/, 96–103.

/DG 90/   W. Deiters/V. Gruhn: Managing Software Processes in the Environment MELMAC, in /1. Tay 90/, 193–205.

/DG 91/   W. Deiters/V. Gruhn: Software Process Model Analysis based on FUNSOFT Nets, Journal of Mathematical Modeling and Simulation 8, 315–325 (1991).

/DGS 89/   W. Deiters/V. Gruhn/W. Schäfer: Process Programming: A Structured Multi–Paradigm Approach Could be Achieved, in /3. Per 90/, 54–57.

/DHK 75/   V. Donzeau–Gouge/G. Huet/G. Kahn/B. Lang/J. J. Levy: A Structure–oriented Program Editor: A First Step toward Computer Assisted Programming, Proc. Int. Comp. Symp., Amsterdam: North–Holland (1975).

/DHM 78/   T. A. Dolotta/R. C. Haight/J. R. Mashey: UNIX Time–sharing System: The Programmer's Workbench, Bell Syst. Tech. J., 57, 2, July–Aug. 1978, repr. in /1. BSS 84/, 353–369.

/Dic 92/   O. Dickoph: Identifier Binding in an Incremental Software Development Environment (in German), Master's Thesis, RWTH Aachen (1992).

/DKL 84/   V. Donzeau–Gouge/G. Kahn/B. Lang/B. Melese: Document Structure and Modularity in Mentor, in /1. Hen 84/, 141–148.

/DLM 84/   V. Donzeau–Gouge/B. Lang/B. Mélèse: Practical Applications of a Syntax–directed Program Manipulation Environment, Proc. 7th ICSE, 346–354 (1984).

/DLM 85/   V. Donzeau–Gouge/B. Lang/B. Mélèse: A Tool for Ada Program Manipulations: Mentor–Ada, in /1. BF 85/, 297–308.

/DM 95/   A. Drappa/R. Melchisedech: The Use of Graph Grammars in a Software Engineering Education Tool, in A. Corradini/U. Montanari (Eds.): Proc. Joint COMPUGRAPH/SEMAGRAPH Workshop on Graph Rewriting and Computation, Volterra (Pisa), Italy, August '95, Electronic Notes in Theoretical Computer Science (ENTCS), 85–94, Amsterdam: Elsevier Science Publ. (1995).

/DMS 84/   N. M. Deslisle/D. E. Menicosy/M. D. Schwartz: Viewing a Programming Environment as a Single Tool, in /1. Hen 84/, 49–56.

/Don 85/   J. Donahue: Integration Mechanisms in Cedar, ACM SIGPLAN Notices, 20, 7 in /1. Deu 85/, 245–251.

/Dow 87/   M. Dowson: ISTAR – An Integrated Project Support Environment, in /1. Hen 87/, 27–33.

/DS 86/   N. Delisle/M. Schwartz: Neptune: A Hypertext System for CAD Applications, Proc. Intern. Conf. on Management of Data, ACM SIGMOD 15, 2, 132–143 (1986).

/DS 87/   N. Delisle/M. Schwartz: A Programming Environment for CSP, in /1. Hen 87/, 34–41.

/EFR 86/   G. E. Estrin/R. S. Fenchel/R. R. Razouk/M. K. Vernon: SARA (System Architecture Apprentice): Modelling, Analysis, and Simulation for Design of Concurrent Systems, TOSE 12, 2, 293–311 (1986).

/EGK 84/   J. Estublier/S. Ghoul/S. Krakowiak: Preliminary Experience with a Configuration Control System, in /1. Hen 84/, 149–156.

/EHH 90/   G. Engels/U. Hohenstein/K. Hülsmann/P. Löhr–Richter/H.–D. Ehrich: CADDY – Computer Aided Design of Non–Standard Databases, in /1. MSW 90/, 151–158.

/EJS 88/   G. Engels/Th. Janning/W. Schäfer: A Highly Integrated Tool Set for Program Development Support, in Proc. ACM SIGSMALL Conference '88, Cannes, 1–10 (1988).

/Ell 86/   R. J. Ellison: Software Development Environments: Research to Practice, in /1. CDW 86/, 175–180.

/ELN 86/   G. Engels/C. Lewerentz/M. Nagl/W. Schäfer: On the Structure of an Incremental and Integrated Software Development Environment, Proc. 19th Hawaii Int. Conf. Syst. Sci., Vol. 2, 585–597 (1986).

/ENS 86/   G. Engels/M. Nagl/W. Schäfer: On the Structure of Structure–Oriented Editors for Different Applications, in /1. Hen 87/, 190–198.

/ES 85a/   R. J. Ellison/B. J. Staudt: The Evolution of the Gandalf System, J. Syst. Software 5, 107–119 (1985).

/ES 85b/   G. Engels/W. Schäfer: The Design of an Adaptive and Portable Programming Support Environment, in G. Valle/W. Bucchi (Eds.): Proc. 8th ICS, Florence, 297–308 (1985).

/ES 86/   G. Engels/A. Sandbrink: Experiences with a Hybrid–Interpreter Based on Incremental Compilation Techniques, in Proc. of the Workshop on Compiler Compilers and Incremental Compilation Techniques, Bautzen, Oct. 1986, iir – Informatik Informationen 12, 172–184, Berlin (Ost): Akedemie der Wissenschaften der DDR (1986).

/ES 87/   G. Engels/A. Schürr: A Hybrid Interpreter in a Software Development Environment, in Nichols/Simpson (Eds.): Proc. 1st ESEC, LNCS 289, 87–96 (1987).

/Est 85/   J. Estublier: A Configuration Manager: The Adele Data Base of Programs, in /1. GTE 85/, 140–146.

/Est 88/   J. Estublier: Configuration Management – The Notion and the Tools, in /3. Win 88/, 38–61.

/Fei 82/   P. H. Feiler: A Language–oriented Interactive Programming Environment Based on Compilation Technology, Doct. Diss., Dep. Comp. Sci., Carnegie–Mellon Univ., Pittsburgh, PA (1982).

/Fel 79/   S. I. Feldman: MAKE – A Program for Maintaining Computer Programs, Software Practice and Experience 9, 3, 255–265 (1979).

/Fer 93/   C. Fernström: PROCESS WEAVER: Adding Process Support to UNIX, in Proc. 2nd Int. Conf. Softw. Process, 12–26, Los Alamitos: IEEE Comp. Soc. Press (1993).

/Fey 92/   A. Feye: Compilation of PROGRES Path Expressions (in German), Master's Thesis, RWTH Aachen (1992).

/Fis 88/   G. Fisher: An Overview of a Graphical Multilanguage Application Environment, in /1. Rid 88/, 774–786.

/FJM 84/   C. N. Fisher/G. F. Johnson/J. Mauney/A. Pal/D. L. Stock: The POE Language–based Editor Project, in /1. Hen 84/, 21–29.

/FJS 86/   P. H. Feiler/F. Jalili/J. H. Schlichter: An Interactive Prototyping Environment for Language Design, in Proc. 19th Hawaii Int. Conf. Syst. Sci., Vol. 2, 106–116 (1986).

/FK 83/   P. H. Feiler/G. E. Kaiser: Display–oriented Structure Manipulation in a Multi–purpose System, in Proc. IEEE 7th Int. Comp. Software and Applicat. Conf., Nov. (1983).

/FM 81/   P. Feiler/R. Medina–Mora: An Incremental Programming Environment, in Proc. 5th ICSE, 44–53 (1981).

/FM 87/   D. Fraser/M. Myers: An Editor for Revision Control, TOPLAS 9, 2, 277–295 (1987).

/FN 87/   W.B. Frakes/B.A. Nejmeh: An Information System for Software Reuse, in /3. Tra 88/, 142–151.

/FPS 84/   C. N. Fischer/A. Pal/D. L. Stock/G. F. Johnson/Jon Mauney: The POE Language–Based Editors, in /1. Hen 84/, 21–29.

/Fre 94/   B. Freitag: A Hypertext–based Tool for Large Scale Software Reuse, in Proc. 6th Conf. on Advanced Information Systems Engineering, LNCS 811, 283–296, *xxx: xxx* (1994).

/Fri 84a/   P. Fritzson: Preliminary Experience from the DICE System, a Distributed Incremental Compiling Environment, in /1. Hen 84/, 113–123.

/Fri 84b/   P. Fritzson: Towards a Distributed Programming Environment based on Incremental Compilation, Linkoping Studies in Science and Technology Diss. No. 109, Dpt. of Comp. and Inf. Sci., Linkoping Univ., Linköping, Sweden (1984).

/Fri 86/   P. Fritzson: Incremental Symbol Processing, Techn. Rep. Lonköping Univ. (1986).

/FS 94/   R. Fehling/W. Schaefer: Cooperative Construction of Software Architectures with the Tool OPUS (in German), Informatik – Forschung und Entwicklung 9, 3, 141–152, Berlin: Springer–Verlag (1994).

/Gar 86/   D. Garlan: Views for Tools in Integrated Environments, in /1. CDW 86/, 314–343.

/GC 84/   N. Giddings/T. Colburn: An Automated Design Evaluator, Proc. ACM '84 Ann. Conf., 109–115 (1984).

/GCN 92/   D.A. Garlan/L. Cai/R.L. Nord: A Transformational Approach to Generating Application–Specific Environments, in /1. Web 92/, 58–67.

/GDR 90/   J.–L. Giavitto/A. Devarenne/G. Rosuel/Y. Holvoët: Adage: New Trends in CASE Environments, in /1. MSW 90/, 177–183.

/GF 84/   R. P. Gabriel/M. E. Frost: A Programming Environment for a Timeshared System, in /1. Hen 84/, 185–192.

/GHM 82/   E. Ganser/J. R. Horgan/D. J. Moore/P. T. Surko/D. E. Swartwout: SYNED–A Language–based Editor for an Interactive Programming Environment, in Dig. Papers Spring CompCon '83, IEEE Comp. Soc., Nov. (1982).

/GI 90/   D. Garlan/E. Ilias: Low–Cost, Adaptable Tool Integration Policies for Integrated Environments, in /1. Tay 90/, 1–10.

/GLB 83/   C. Green/D. Luckham/R. Balzer/T. Cheatham/C. Rich: Report on a Knowledge–based Software Assistant, Kestrel Institute, Palo Alto (1983).

/GM 84/   D. B. Garlan/P. L. Miller: GNOME – An Introductory Programming Environment Based on a Family of Structure Editors, in /1. Hen 84/, 65–72.

/Gol 90/   A. Goldberg: Reusing Software Developments, in /1. Tay 90/, 107–119.

/GRD 84/   A. Giacalone/M. C. Rinard/T. W. Doeppner, Jr.: IDEOSY: An Ideographic and Interactive Program Description System, in /1. Hen 84/, 15–20.

/Gru 91a/   V. Gruhn: Validation and Verification of Software Process Models, in /1. EW 91/, 271–286.

/Gru 91b/   V. Gruhn: The Software Process Management Environment MELMAC, in V. Ambriola et al. (Ed.): Proc. 1st European Workshop on Software Process Modeling, Milan, 191–202, Rom: AICA (1991).

/GS 88/   A. Giacalone/S. A. Smolka: Integrated Environments for Formally Well–Founded Design and Simulations of Concurrent Systems, in /1. Rid 88/, 787–802.

/Guh 93/   M. Guhl: Meta–modelling of Logical Documents Taking a Graphical SA/RT Editor as an Example (in German), Master's Thesis, RWTH Aachen (1993).

/Han 71/   W. J. Hansen: User Engineering Principles for Interactive Systems, AFIPS Fall Joint Conference 39, 523–532, Montval, N. J.: AFIPS PRESS (1971).

/Haß 92/   D. Haßl: An Editor for Developing Classification Schemata for Reusable Software (in German), Master's Thesis, RWTH Aachen (1992).

/Hav 85/   H. Haverkamp: Source Code Generation by an Unparser within a Software Development Environment (in German), Master's Thesis, Univ. of Dortmund (1985).

/Haw 90/   J. Hawgood: Project Management Support: PEGASUS out of PIMS, in /1. MSW 90/, 107–116.

/Hei 89/   P. Heimann: Document Administration in an Integrated Software Development Environment (in German), Master's Thesis, RWTH Aachen (1989).

/Hen 86/   P. B. Henderson: Data–Oriented Incremental Programming Environments, in /1. CDW 86/, 13–25.

/Hen 95/   S. Henninger: Information Access Tools for Software Reuse, The Journal of Systems and Software 30, 3, 231–247 (1995).

/Hen 96/   S. Henninger: Supporting the Construction and Evolution of Component Repositories, in Proc. 18th ICSE, 279–288 (1996).

/Her 89/   R. Herbrecht: A Graph Grammar Editor (in German), Master's Thesis, RWTH Aachen (1989).

/Him 88/   M. Himsolt: GraphED: An Interactive Graph Editor, in Proc. STACS 89, LNCS 349, 532–533 (1988).

/HJP 90/   H. Hünnekens/G. Junkermann/B. Peuschel/W. Schäfer/K.–J. Vagts: A First Step Towards Knowledge–Based Software Process Modelling, in /1. MSW 90/, 49–58.

/HK 85/   R. Hood/K. Kennedy: A Programming Environment for Fortran, in Proc. 18th Hawaii Int. Conf. Syst. Sci. Vol. 2, 625–637 (1985).

/HK 88/   D. Heimbigner/S. Krane: A Graph Transform Model for Configuration Management Environments, in /1. Hen 88/, 216–225.

/HKB 92/   G. T. Heineman, G. E. Kaiser, N. S. Barghouti, I. Z. Ben–Shaul: Rule Chaining in Marvel, IEEE Expert 7, 6, 26–33 (1992).

/HL 88/   K. E. Huff/V. R. Lesser: A Plan–Based Intelligent Assistant that Supports the Software Development Process, in /1. Hen 88/, 97–106.

/HM 84/   J. R. Horgan/D. J. Moore: Techniques for Improving Language–based Editors, in /1. Hen 84/, 7–14.

/HM 91/   R. Helm/Y.S. Marek: Integrating Information Retrieval and Domain Specific Approaches for Browsing and Retrieval in Object–Oriented Class Libraries, ACM SIGPLAN Notices 26, 47–61 (1991).

/Höf 92/   F. Höfer: Incremental Attribute Evaluation of Graph Expressions and their Realization (in German), Master's Thesis, RWTH Aachen (1992).

/Hor 85/   S. Horwitz: Generating Language–Based Editors: A Relationally–Attributed Approach, Doct. Diss., Department of Computer Science TR 85–696, Cornell Univ., Ithaka (1985).

/Hor 89/   P. Hormanns: Incremental, Table–driven Unparsers (in German), Master's Thesis, RWTH Aachen (1989).

/Hor 90/   S. Horwitz: Identifying the Semantic and Textual Differences between two Versions of a Program, in Proc. ACM SIGPLAN '90 Conf. on Programming Language Design and Implementation, SIGPLAN Notices Vol. 25, 6, 234–245 (1990).

/HP 81/   A. N. Habermann/D. E. Perry: System Composition and Version Control for Ada, in /1. Hün 81/, 331–343.

/HPR 89/   S. Horwitz/J. Prins/T. Reps: Integrating Non–Interfering Versions of Programs, TOPLAS 11, 3, 345–387 (1989).

/HS 90/   C. F. Hart/J. J. Shilling: An Environment for Documenting Software Features, in /1. Tay 90/, 120–132.

/HT 86/   S. B. Horwitz/T. Teitelbaum: Generating Editing Environments Based on Relations and Attributes, in /1. ToPL 86/, 577–608.

/HW 85a/   P. Henderson/M. Weiser: Continuous Execution: The Visiprog Environment, in Proc. 8th ICSE, 68–74 (1985).

/HW 85b/   E. Horowitz/R. C. Williamson: SODOS: A Software Documentation Support Environment – Its Use, in Proc. 8th ICSE, 8–14 (1985).

/HW 86/   E. Horowitz/R. C. Williamson: SODOS: A Software Documentation Support Environment – Its Definition, TOSE 12, 8, 849–859 (1986).

/Iso 95/   S. Isoda: Experiences of a Software Reuse Project, The Journal of Systems and Software 30, 3, 171–186 (1995).

/IWJ 90/   E. A. Isper, Jr./D. S. Wile/D. Jacobs: A Multi–Formalism Specification Environment, in /1. Tay 90/, 94–106.

/Jan 87/   Th. Janning: Access and Responsibility Control in a Software Development Environment (in German), Master's Thesis, Univ. of Osnabrück (1987).

/Jar 90/   S. Jarzabek: Specifying and Generating Multilanguage Software Development Environments, Software Engineering Journal, 125–137 (March 1990).

/Jar 92/   M. Jarke: Strategies for Integrating CASE Environments, in /1. Sof 92/, 54–61.

/JHW 86/   S. Jaehnichen/F. A. Hussain/M. Weber: Program Development by Transformation and Refinement, in /1. CDW 86/, 471–486.

/JL 88/   Th. Janning/C. Lewerentz: Integrated Project Team Management in a Software Development Environment, in Proc. IFBAC Workshop in Experiences with the Management of Software Projects, Sarajevo, 27.–29. Sept. (1988).

/Joe 92/   A. Joereßen: A Semantical Editor for Programming–in–the–Large (in German), Master's Thesis, RWTH Aachen (1992).

/Joh 82/   S. Johnson: A Computer System for Checking Proofs, Ann Arbor, Mich.: UMI Research Press (1982).

/Jor 90/   M. Jordan: An Extensible Programming Environment for Modula–3, in /1. Tay 90/, 66–76.

/JSZ 96/   J. Jahnke/W. Schäfer/A. Zündorf: A Design Environment for Migrating Relational to Object Oriented Database Systems, submitted for publication to ICSM '96.

/Kai 85/   G. E. Kaiser: Semantics for Structure Editing Environments, Doct. Diss., Carnegie–Mellon Univ., Pittsburgh (1985).

/Kam 82/   G. Kampen: SWIFBT: A Requirements Specification System for Software, in /3. Ohn 82/, 77–84.

/Kam 86/   R. F. Kamel: Software Development in a Distributed Environment, The XMS System, in /1. CDW 86/, 126–141.

/Kar 95/   E.–A. Karlsson: Software Reuse – A Holistic Approach, New York: John Wiley & Sons (1995).

/KCH 86/   S. M. Kaplan/R. H. Campbell/M. T. Harandi/R. E. Johnson/S. N. Kamin/J. W. S. Liu/J. M Purtilo: An Architecture for Tool Integration, in /1. CDW 86/, 112–125.

/KF 84/   G. E. Kaiser/P. H. Feiler: Generation of Language–oriented Editors, in /1. MS 84/, 31–45.

/KF 87a/   G. E. Kaiser/P. H. Feiler: Intelligent Assistance without Artificial Intelligence, in Proc. 32nd IEEE Comp. Soc. Int. Conf. (COMPCON), 236–241 (1987).

/KF 87b/   G. E. Kaiser/P. H. Feiler: An Architecture for Intelligent Systems in Software Development, in Proc. 9th ICSE, 80–88 (1987).

/KH 82a/   G. E. Kaiser/A. N. Habermann: An Environment for System Version Control, in Dig. Papers Spring Compcon '83, IEEE Comp. Soc., Nov. (1982).

/KH 82b/   G. E. Kaiser/ A. N. Habermann: A Description of the Correct Version Control Supported by the Gandalf Environment, in /2. Hab 82/.

/KK 88/   J. Karimi/B. R. Konsynski: An Automated Software Design Assistant, TOSE 14, 2, 194–210 (1988).

/Kle 93/   P. Klein: The PROGRES Graph–Code Machine (in German), Master's Thesis, RWTH Aachen (1993).

/KLM 86/   J. H. C. Kuo/K. J. Leslie/M. D. Maggio/B. G. Moore/H.–C. Tu: Information Structuring for Software Environments, in /1. CDW 86/, 97–111.

/KLN 96/   Ch. Kohring/M. Lefering/M. Nagl: A Requirements Engineering Environment within a Tighly–Integrated SDE, to appear in Requirements Engineering (1996).

/Kob 90/   H.–U. Kobialka: Configuration Edition, Generation and Test within Working Contexts, in /1. Tay 90/, 173–182.

/Koe 88/   S. Koenig: ISEF: An Integrated Industrial–Strength Software Engineering Framework, in /1. Hen 88/, 45–54.

/Koe 90/   R. Koether: An EBNF–Editor Generator (in German), Master's Thesis, RWTH Aachen (1990).

/Koh 93a/   Ch. Kohring: A Flexible Interpreter for Executable Requirements Specifications (in German), in Züllighoven/Altmann/Doberkat (Eds.): Requirements Engineering '93: Prototyping, German Chapter of the ACM 41, 193–208, Stuttgart: Teubner–Verlag (1993).

/Koh 93b/   Ch. Kohring: RESI – An Integrated Tool Set for Requirements Engineering and Simulation, in Short Paper Proceedings of ESS '93: European Simulation Symposium, 5–6, San Diego: Society for Computer Simulation (1993).

/Koh 96/   Ch. Kohring: Execution of Requirements Specifications for Rapid Prototyping: Requirements Engineering and Simulation (in German), Doct. Diss., RWTH Aachen, Aachen: Shaker Verlag (1996).

/Kos 92/   P. Kossing: Modeling of Abstract Syntax Graphs for EBNFs in Normal Form (in German), Master's Thesis, RWTH Aachen (1992).

/Kre 87/   M. A. Kret: An Information Workstation for Software Managers, in /1. Hen 87/, 59–69.

/KTC 85/   P. A. Kirslis/R. B. Terwilliger/R. H. Campbell: The SAGA Approach to Large Program Development in an Integrated Modular Environment, in /1. GTE 85/, 44–53.

/Lam 88/   A. van Lamsweerde et al.: Generic Lifecycle Support in the ALMA Environment, in /1. Rid 88/, 720–741.

/Lan 86/   B. Lang: On the Usefulness of Syntax Directed Editors, in /1. CDW 86/, 47–51.

/LBD 87/   A. van Lamsweerde/M. Buyse/B. Delcourt/E. Delor/M. Ervier/M. C. Schayes/J. P. Bouquelle/R. Champagne/P. Nisolle/J. Seldeslachs: The Kernel of a Generic Software Development Environment, in /1. Hen 87/, 208–217.

/LC 84/   D. B. Leblang/ R. P. Chase, Jr.: Computer–Aided Software Engineering in a Distributed Workstation Environment, in /1. Hen 84/, 104–112.

/LCS 88/   D.B. Leblang, R.P. Chase, H. Spilke: Increasing Productivity with a Parallel Configuration Manager, in /3. Win 88/, 21–38.

/LDD 88/   A. van Lamsweerde/B. Delcourt/E. Delor/M.–C. Schayes/R. Champagne: Generic Lifecycle Support in the ALMA Environment, in /1. Rid 88/, 720–741.

/Lef 90/   M. Lefering: Transition from Requirements Engineering to Programming in the Large (in German), Master's Thesis, RWTH Aachen (1990).

/Lef 93a/   M. Lefering: Tools to Support Life Cycle Integration, in Proc. 6th Software Engineering Environments Conference, 2–16, Washington: IEEE Comp. Soc. Press (1993).

/Lef 93b/   M. Lefering: An Incremental Integration Tool between Requirements Engineering and Programming in the Large, in Proc. 1st Int. Symposium on Requirements Engineering, 82–89, Washington: IEEE Comp. Soc. Press (1993).

/Lef 95/   M. Lefering: Integration Tools in a Software Development Environment (in German), Doct. Diss., RWTH Aachen, Aachen: Shaker–Verlag (1995).

/Lew 88a/   C. Lewerentz: Variant and Revision Control within an Incremental Programming Environment, in /3. Win 88/, 426–429.

/Lew 88b/   C. Lewerentz: Extended Programming in the Large within a Software Development Environment, in /1. Hen 88/, 173–182.

/Lew 88c/   C. Lewerentz: Interactive Design of Large Program Systems (in German), Doct. Diss., RWTH Aachen, IFB 194 (1988).

/LGH 85/   J. Ludewig/M. Glinz/H. Huser/G. Matheis/M. F. Schmidt: SPADES – A Specification and Design System and its Graphical Interface, in Proc. 8th ICSE, 83–91 (1985).

/Lie 91/   T. Liese: Support of Inheritance in a Design Environment (in German), Master's Thesis, RWTH Aachen (1991).

/Lin 84/   M. A. Linton: Implementing Relational Views of Programs, in /1. Hen 84/, 132–140.

/LM 85/   D. Leblang/G. McLean: Configuration Management for Large–Scale Software Development Efforts, in /1. GTE 85/, 122–127.

/LN 85/   C. Lewerentz/M. Nagl: Incremental Programming in the Large: Syntax–aided Specification Editing, Integration, and Maintenance, in Proc. 18th Hawaii Int. Conf. Syst. Sci., Vol. 2, 638–649, Honolulu (1985).

/LNW 88/   C. Lewerentz/M. Nagl/B. Westfechtel: On Integration Mechanisms within a Graph–Based Software Development Environment, in Göttler/Schneider (Eds.): Proc WG '87 Workshop on Graph–Theoretic Concepts in Computer Science, LNCS 314, 219–229 (1988).

/LPR 88/   P. Lee/F. Pfenning/G. Rollins/W. Scherlis: The Ergo Support System: An Integrated Set of Tools for Prototyping Integrated Environments, in /1. Hen 88/, 25–34.

/LS 79/   H. C. Lauer/E. H. Satterthwaite: The Impact of Mesa on System Design, in Proc. 4th ICSE, 174–182 (1979).

/LS 83/   B. W. Lampson/E. E. Schmidt: Organizing Software in a Distributed Environment, in Proc. SIGPLAN '83 Symp. Program. Lang. Issues in Software Syst., 1–13 (1983).

/LS 90/   A. Lockman/J. Salasin: A Procedure and Tools for Transition Engineering, in /1. Tay 90/, 157–172.

/MB 84/   N. Minsky/A. Borgida: The Darwin Software–Development Environment, in /1. Hen 84/, 89–95.

/McC 92/   C. McClure: The Three Rs of Software Automation Re–engineering, Ropository, Reusability, Englewood Cliffs: Prentice Hall (1992).

/Med 82/   R. Medina–Mora: Syntax–directed Editing: Towards Integrated Programming Environments, Doct. Diss., Carnegie–Mellon Univ., Pittsburgh PA. (1982).

/Meu 92/   M. Meuser: Graphical Representation of Executable SA/RT–Models (in German), Master's Thesis, RWTH Aachen (1992).

/MF 81/   R. Medina–Mora/P. Feiler: An Incremental Programming Environment, TOSE 7, 5, 472–482 (1981).

/MH 86/   M. Moriconi/D. F. Hare: The PegaSys System: Pictures as Formal Documentation of Large Programs, in /1. ToPL 86/, 524–546.

/MHK 87/   H. A. Müller/R. Hood/K. Kennedy: Efficient Recompilation of Module Interfaces in a Software Development Environment, in /1. Hen 87/, 180–189.

/Mit 87/   C. Z. Mitchell: Engineering VAX Ada for a Multi–Language Programming Environment, in /1. Hen 87/, 49–58.

/MK 88a/   J. Micallef/G. E. Kaiser: Version and Configuration Control in Distributed Language–Based Environments, in /3. Win 88/, 119–143.

/MK 88b/   H. A. Müller/K. Klashinsky: Rigi: A System for Programming–in–the–large, in Proc. 10th ICSE, 80–86 (1988).

/MKB 87/   R. M. Mital/M. M. Kim/R. A. Berg: A Case Study of Workstation Usage During the Early Phases of the Software Development Life Cycle, in /1. Hen 87/, 70–76.

/Mil 86/   T. Miller: The Unified Programming Environment: Unobtrusive Support, in /1. CDW 86/, 507–518.

/ML 88/   A. Mahler/A. Lampen: An Integrated Toolset for Engineering Software Configurations, in /1. Hen 88/, 191–200.

/ML 90/   A. Mahler/A. Lampen: Integrating Configuration Management into a Generic Environment, in /1. Tay 90/, 229–237.

/MLV 85/   N. Madhavji/N. Leoutsarakos/D. Vouliouris: Software Construction Using Typed Fragments, in Ehrig (Ed.): Formal Methods and Software Development, Proc. TAPSOFT Conf., LNCS 186, 163–178 (1985).

/MN 81a/   R. Medina–Mora/D. S. Notkin: ALOE Users' and Implementors' Guide, Tech. Rep. CMU–CS–81–145, Dpt. of Comp. Science, Carnegie–Mellon Univ., Pittsburgh, PA (November 1981).

/MNE 82/   R. Medina–Mora/D. S. Notkin/R. Ellison: ALOE Users' and Implementors' Guide, in /2. Hab 82/.

/Mor 86/   M. Moriconi: PegaSys and the Role of Logic in Programming Environments, in /1. CDW 86/, 52–58.

/Mor 88/   T. M. Morgan: Configuration Management and Version Control in the Rational Programming Environment, in Proc. Ada–Europe Int. Conf. 1988, 17–28, Cambridge: Cambridge University Press (1988).

/MR 90/   N. H. Minsky/D. Rozenshtein: Configuration Management by Consensus: An Application of Law–Governed Systems, in /1. Tay 90/, 44–55.

/MR 92/   S. Meyers/S.P. Reiss: An Empirical Study of Multiple–View Software Development, in /1. Web 92/, 47–57.

/MS 81/   J. M. Morris/M. D. Schwartz: The Design of a Language–directed Editor for Block–structured Languages, in Proc. ACM SIGPLAN–SIGOA Symp. on Text Manipulation, ACM SIGPLAN Notices 16, 6, 28–33 (1981).

/MS 91/   N. Madhavji/W. Schäfer: Prism – Methodology and Process–Oriented Environment, TOSE 17, 12, 1270–1283 (1991).

/MS 92/   P. Mi/W. Scacci: Process Integration in CASE Environments, in /1. Sof 92/, 45–53.

/Mug 85/   Mughal. K.: Control–Flow Aspects of Generating Runtime Facilities for Language–based Programming Environments, in /1. CST 85/, 85–91.

/MW 80/   M. Mikelsons/ M.N. Wegman: PDE1L: The PL1L Programs Development Environment (Principles of Operation), IBM T. J. Watson Research Center, Yorktown Heights, N.Y., Tech. Rep. RC 8513 (1980).

/MW 86/   K. Marzullo/D. Wiebe: Jasmine: A Software System Modelling Facility, in /1. Hen 87/ 121–130.

/MW 95a/   Z.A. Moormann/J.M. Wing: Specification Matching of Software Components, ACM Software Engineering Notes 20, 4, 6–17 (1995).

/MW 95b/   Z.A. Moormann/J.M. Wing: Signature Matching: A Tool for Using Software Libraries, TOSEM 4, 2, 146–170 (1995).

/Nad 91/   E. Nadarzinski: An Editor for Programming–in–the–Large for Supporting Subsystems (in German), Master's Thesis, RWTH Aachen (1991).

/Nag 85a/   M. Nagl: An Incremental and Integrated Software Development Environment, Computer Physics Communications 38, 245–276 (1985).

/Nag 85b/   M. Nagl: Graph Technology Applied to a Software Project, in /9. RS 86/, 303–322.

/Nag 89/   M. Nagl: An integrated Software Development Environment – An Alternative Conceptual Approach (in German), in Lippe (Ed.): Software–Entwicklung, Fachtagung Marburg, IFB 212, 21–42 (1989).

/Nag 93/   M. Nagl: Reuse and CASE – IPSEN as Example (in German), Online '93, Congress Software and Information Engineering, C630.01–C630.16, Velbert: Online Press (1993).

/New 86/   J. Newcomer: IDL: Past Experience and New Ideas, in /1. CDW 86/, 257–289.

/New 91/   F. Newbery Paulisch: The Design of an Extendible Graph Editor, LNCS 704 (1991).

/Not 84/   D. Notkin: Interactive Structure–oriented Computing, Doct. Diss., Carnegie–Mellon Univ., Pittsburgh PA (1984).

/Not 85/   D. Notkin: The Gandalf Project, J. Syst. Software 5, 91–106 (1985).

/Not 88/   D. Notkin: The Relationship Between Software Development Environments and the Software Process, in /1. Hen 88/, 107–109.

/NP 88/   R. L. Nord/F. Pfenning: The Ergo Attribute System, in /1. Hen 88/, 110–120.

/NS 85/   K. H. Narfelt/D. Schefstrom: Extending the Scope of the Program Library, in /1. BF 85/, 25–40 (1985).

/NS 87/   K. Narayasanaswamy/W. Scacchi: Maintaining Configurations of Evolving Software Systems, TOSE 13, 3, 324–334 (1987).

/NS 91/   M. Nagl/A. Schürr: A Graph Grammar Specification Environment, in /5. EKR 91/, 599–609.

/OH 90/   H. Ossher/W. Harrison: Support for Change in RPDE^3, in /1. Tay 90/, 218–228.

/OHP 92/   E. Ostertag/J. Hendler/R. Prieto–Dfaz/C. Braun: Computing Similarity in a Reuse Library System: An AI–based Approach, TOSEM 1, 3, 205–228 (1992).

/OO 84/   K. J. Ottenstein/L. M. Ottenstein: The Program Dependence Graph in a Software Develpment Environment, in /1. Hen 84/, 177–184.

/Opp 80/   D. C. Oppen: Prettyprinting, TOPLAS 2, 4, 465–483 (1980).

/Ost 86/   L. Osterweil: A Process–Object Centered View of Software Environment Architecture, in /1. CDW 86/, 156–174.

/Ost 87/   L. Osterweil: Software Processes are Software Too, in Proc. 9th ICSE, 2–13 (1987).

/Per 87/   D. Perry: Version Control in the Inscape Environment, in Proc. 9th ICSE, 142–149 (1987).

/Phi 92/   F. Philipp: Support of Genericity in a Design Environment (in German), Master's Thesis, RWTH Aachen (1992).

/Poh 87/   B. Pohlmann: A Tool for Diagrammatic Representation of Software Architectures (in German), Master's Thesis, Univ. of Osnabrück (1987).

/Poh 95/   K. Pohl: A Process Control Requirements Engineering Environment, Doct. Diss., RWTH Aachen (1995).

/Pol 86/   W. Polak: Framework for a Knowledge–Based Programming Environment, in /1. CDW 86/, 566–575.

/Pro 86/   R. Proudfoot: A Maintenance Environment for the C Programming Language, in Proc. 19th Hawaii Int. Conf. on Syst. Sci., 448–458 (1986).

/PS 92/   B. Peuschel/W. Schäfer: Concepts and Implementation of a Rule–based Process Engine, in Proc. 14th ICSE, 262–279 (1992).

/QJD 90/   X. Qian/R. Jullig/M. Daum: Consistency Management in a Project Management Assistant, in /1. Tay 90/, 34–43.

/RA 84/   T. Reps/B. Alpern: Interactive Proof Checking, in Proc. 11th POPL, 36–45 (1984).

/RDM 87/   L. A. Rowe/M. Davis/E. Messinger/C. Meyer/C. Spirakis/A. Tuan: A Browser for Directed Graphs, Software – Practice & Experience 17, 1, 61–76 (1987).

/Red 88/   U. S. Reddy: Transformational Derivation of Programs Using the Focus System, in /1. Hen 88/, 163–172.

/Rei 84a/   S. P. Reiss: PECAN: Program Development Systems that Support Multiple Views, in Proc. 7th ICSE, 324–333 (1984).

/Rei 84b/   S. P. Reiss: Graphical Program Development with PECAN Program Development Systems, in /1. Hen 84/, 30–41.

/Rei 86/   S. P. Reiss: GARDEN Tools: Support for Graphical Programming, in /1. CDW 86/, 59–72.

/Rei 87a/   S. P. Reiss: Working in the Garden Environment for Conceptual Programming, in /1. Sof 87/, 16–27.

/Rei 87b/   S. P. Reiss: A Conceptual Programming Environment, in Proc. 9th ICSE, 225–235 (1987).

/Rep 81/   T. Reps: The Synthesizer Editor Generator: Reference Manual, Cornell Univ., Ithaca, N.Y. (1981).

/Rep 83/   T. Reps: Generating Language–based Environments, Cambridge (Mass.): M.I.T. Press (1983).

/RG 87/   R. H. Reppy/E. R. Ganser: A Foundation for Programming Environments, in /1. Hen 87/, 218–227.

/RHP 88/   T. Reps/S. Horwitz/J. Prins: Support for Integrating Program Variants in an Environment for Programming in the Large, in /3. Win 88/, 197–216.

/Rid 81/   W. E. Riddle: An Assessment of DREAM, in /1. Hün 81/, 191–222.

/RJG 91/   T. Rose/M. Jarke/M. Gocek/C. Maltzahn/H. Nissen: A Decision–Based Configuration Process Environment, Software Engineering Journal, 332–346 (1991).

/RK 84/   J. Reppy/C. M. R. Kintala: Generating Execution Facilities for Integrated Programming Environments, Tech. Mem. 59545–84, A. T. & T. Bell Laboratories, Murray Hill, NJ (March 1984).

/RK 95/   P.J. Rodgers/P.J.H. King: A Visual Database Language Using Graph Rewriting, Techn. Report, Department of Computer Science, Birbeck College, http://web.dcs.bbk.ac.uk/~pjr/rodgers95a.ps (1995).

/RMT 86/   T. Reps/C. Marceau/T. Teitelbaum: Remote Attribute Updating for Language–based Editors, in Proc. 13th POPL, 1–13 (1986).

/Rob 85/   R. E. Robbins: BUILD: A Tool For Maintaining Consistency in Modular Systems, Techn. Report A.I.T.R. 874, MIT (1985).

/Rob 92/   S.A. Robert: Software Reengineering, Los Alamitos: IEEE Computer Society Press (1992).

/Roc 75/   M. Rochkind: The Source Code Control System, TOSE 1, 4, 364–370 (1975).

/Ros 87/   G. Ross: Integral–C – A Practical Environment for C Programming, in /1. Hen 87/, 42–48.

/ROT 92/   D.J. Richardson/T. Owen O'Malley/C. Tittle Moore/S. Leif Aha: Developing and Integrating ProDAG in the ARCADIA Environment, in /1. Web 92/, 109–119.

/RS 88/   J. Ramanathan/S. Sarkar: Providing Customized Assistance for Software Lifecycle Approaches, in /1. Rid 88/, 749–757.

/RSS 88/   T. Rodden/P Sawyer/I. Sommerville: Interacting with an Active, Integrated Environment, in /1. Hen 88/, 76–84.

/RT 84/   T. Reps/T. Teitelbaum: The Synthesizer Generator, in /1. Hen 84/, 42–48.

/RT 88/   T. Reps/T. Teitelbaum: The Synthesizer Generator Reference Manual, New York: Springer–Verlag (1988).

/Rze 92/   W.E. Rzepka: A Requirements Engineering Testbed: Concept and Status, in Proc. 2nd Int. Conf. System Integration, 118–126, IEEE (1992).

/San 86/   A. Sandbrink: Design and Implementation of an Interpreter Regarding Test and Runtime Support (in German), Master's Thesis, Univ. of Osnabrück (1986).

/SB 90/   G. Snelting/R. Bahlke: PSG: A Theory–Based Environment Generator, in /1. MSW 90/, 131–140.

/SBH 89/   W. Schäfer/P. Broekman/L. Hubert/J. Scott: ESF and Software Process Modelling, in /3. Per 90/, p. 178.

/SBK 86/   M. J. Stefik/P. G. Bobrow/K. M. Kahn: Integrating Access–oriented Programming into a Multiparadigm Environment, in /1. Hai 86a/, 10–18.

/Schä 86/   W. Schäfer: An Integrated SDE: Concepts, Design, and Implementation (in German), Doct. Diss., VDI Fortschrittsberichte 57, Düsseldorf: VDI–Verlag (1986).

/Sche 86/   W. L. Scherlis: Abstract DataTypes, Specialization, and Program Reuse, in /1. CDW 86/, 433–453.

/Schl 86/   U. Schleef: An Incremental Parser as Part of a Syntax–oriented Editor (in German), Master's Thesis, Univ. of Osnabrück (1986).

/Schü 87/   A. Schütte: Specification and Generation of Compilers for Graph Languages by Attributed Graph Grammars (in German), Doct. Diss., Berlin: EXpress–Edition (1987).

/SDB 84/   M. Schwartz/N. Delisle/V. Begwani: Incremental Compilation in Magpie, in Proc. SIGPLAN 84 Symposium on Compiler Construction, ACM SIGPLAN Notices 19, 6, 122–131 (1984).

/SHO 90/   S. M. Sutton, Jr./D. Heimbigner/L. J. Osterweil: Language Constructs for Managing Change in Process–Centered Environments, in /1. Tay 90/, 206–217.

/SK 88/   R. W. Schwanke/G. E. Kaiser: Living with Inconsistency in Large Systems, in /3. Win 88/, 98–118.

/SKG 87/   B. J. Staudt/C. W. Krueger/D. Garlan: A Structural Approach to the Maintenance of Structure–Oriented Environments, in /1. Hen 87/, 160–170.

/SN 90/   K. Sullivan/D. Notkin: Reconciling Environment Integration and Component Independence, in /1. Tay 90/, 22–33.

/SN 92/   K.J. Sullivan/D. Notkin: Reconciling Environment Integration and Software Evolution, TOSEM 1,3, 229–268 (1992).

/Sne 85/   G. Snelting: Experiences with PSG – Programming System Generator, in Ehrig (Ed.): Formal Methods and Software Development, Proc. TAPSOFT Conf., LNCS 186, 148–162 (1985).

/Sno 80/   R. Snowden: An Experience–based Assessment of Development Systems, in /1. RF 80/, 64–75.

/Sno 84/   R. Snodgrass: Monitoring in a Software Development Environment: A Relational Approach, in /1. Hen 84/, 124–131.

/Sol 84/   E. Soloway: A Cognitively–Based Methodology for Designing Languages/Envoronments/Methodologies, in /1. Hen 84/, 193–196.

/Som 88/   I. Sommerville: Interacting with an Active, Integrated Environment, in /1. Hen 88/, 76–84.

/Spi 89/   R. Spielmann: Development of a Basic Layer for Graph Grammar Interpretation (in German), Master's Thesis, RWTH Aachen (1989).

/SS 86/   R. Snodgrass/K. Shannon: Supporting Flexible and Efficient Tool Integration, in /1. CDW 86/, 290–313.

/ST 84/   T. A. Standish/R. N. Taylor: Arcturus: A Prototype Advanced Ada Programming Environment, in /1. Hen 84/, 57–64.

/Ste 87/   V. Stenning: On the Role of an Environment, in Proc. 9th ICSE, 30–34 (1987).

/Str 88/   T. Strelich: The Software Life Cycle Support Environment (SLCSE): A Computer Based Framework for Developing Software Systems, in /1. Hen 88/, 35–44.

/Swe 85/   R. E. Sweet: The Mesa Programming Environment, in /1. Deu 85/, 216–229.

/SWT 89/   J. Solderitsch/K. Wallnau/J. Thalhamer: Constructing Domain–Specific Ada Reuse Libraries, in Proc. 7th Annual National Conference on Ada Technology, 419–433 (1989).

/Sym 86/   A. J. Symonds: Creating a Software Engineering Knowledge Base, in /1. CDW 86/, 494–506.

/SZB 86/   D. C. Swinehart/P. T. Zellweger/R. J. Beach/R. B. Hagemann: A Structural View of the Cedar, in /1. ToPL 86/, 419–490.

/SZH 85/   D. C. Swinehart/P. T. Zellweger/R. B. Hagmann: The Structure of Cedar, in /1. Deu 85/, 230–244.

/Tei 72/   W. Teitelman: Automated Programming: The Programmer's Assistant, in Fall Joint Computer Conf. Proc., AFIPS Vol. 41, 917–921 (1972).

/Thi 89/   M. Thiele: Building Blocks for Diagram Editors (in German), Master's Thesis, RWTH Aachen (1989).

/Tho 89/   I. Thomas: Tool Integration in the Pact Environment, in Proc. 11th ICSE, 13–22 (1989).

/Tic 82/   W. Tichy: Design, Implementation, and Evaluation of a Revision Control System, in Proc. 6th ICSE, 58–67 (1982).

/Tic 85/   W. Tichy: RCS – A System for Version Control, Software – Practice & Experience 15, 7, 637–654 (1985).

/Tic 86/   W. Tichy: Smart Recompilation, TOPLAS 8, 3, 273–291 (1986).

/Tic 88/   W. Tichy: Tools for Software Configuration Management, in /3. Win 88/, 1–20.

/TL 85/   J. Thomas/T. Loerscher: MOSAIX – A Version Control and History Management System, in /1. GTE 85/, 128–139.

/Top 92/   B. Tophoven: Logic and Representation of Graph–like Software Documents (in German), Master's Thesis, RWTH Aachen (1992).

/TR 88/   J. Tsai/F. Ridge: Intelligent Support for Specifications Transformation, IEEE Software 5, 6, 28–35 (1988).

/TRH 81/   T. Teitelbaum/T. Reps/S. Horwitz: The Why and Wherefore of the Cornell Program Synthesizer, in Proc. ACM SIGPLAN/SIGOA Symp. Text Manipulation, 8–16 (1981).

/TSK 90/   L. Tan/Y. Shinoda/T. Katayama: Coping with Changes in an Object Management System Based on Attribute Grammars, in /1. Tay 90/, 56–65.

/Vai 94/   S. Vaillant: Integration of Logic and Representation by Constraints (in German), Master's Thesis, RWTH Aachen (1994).

/Ver 90/   M. Verrall: Tool Interaction and Integration in Software Engineering Environments, in /1. MSW90/, 229–240.

/Wan 91/   E. Wanke: PLEXUS: Tools for Analyzing Graph Grammars, in /5. EKR 91/, 68–79.

/War 87/   S. Wartik: Rapidly Evolving Software and the OVERSEE Environment, in /1. Hen 87/, 77–83.

/Wat 86/   R. C. Waters: Reuse of Cliches in the Knowledge–Based Editor, in /1. CDW 86/, 536–550.

/WBM 88/   J. Walpole/B. S. Blair/J. Malik/J. R. Nicol: A Unifying Model for Consistent Distributed Software Development Environments, in /1. Hen 88/, 183–190.

/WCW 85a/   A. L. Wolf/L. A. Clarke/J. E. Wileden: Ada–based Support for Programming in the Large, IEEE Software 2, 2, 58–71 (1985).

/WCW 85b/   A. L. Wolf/L. A. Clarke/J. G. Wileden: Interface Control and Incremental Development in the PIC Environment, in Proc. 8th ICSE, 75–82 (1985).

/WDT 76/   T. R. Wilcox/A. M. Davis/M. H. Tindall: The Design and Implementation of a Table Driven, Interactive Diagnostic Programming System, Comm. ACM 19, 11, 609–616 (1976).

/Weg 80/   M. Wegman: Parsing for Structural Editors, in Proc. 21st IEEE Symp. on Foundations of Computer Science, 320–327, Washington: IEEE Comp. Soc. Press (1980).

/Wes 89/   B. Westfechtel: Revision Control in an Integrated Software Development Environment, in /3. WT 89/, 96–105.

/Wes 91a/   B. Westfechtel: Revision and Consistency Control in an Integrated Software Development Environment (in German), Doct. Diss., RWTH Aachen, IFB 280 (1991).

/Wes 91b/   B. Westfechtel: Structure–Oriented Merging of Revisions of Software Documents, in /3. Fei 91/, 68–79.

/Wes 92/   B. Westfechtel: A Graph–Based Approach to the Construction of Tools for the Life Cycle Integration between Software Documents, in Forte/Madhavji/Müller (Eds.): Proc. CASE'92, 2–13, Los Alamitos: IEEE Comp. Soc. Press (1992).

/Wil 86/   D. S. Wile: Organizing Programming Knowledge into Syntax–Directed Experts, in /1. CDW 86/, 551–565.

/Win 85/   J. F. H. Winkler: Language Constructs and Library Support for Families of Large Ada Programs, in /1. GTE 85/, 17–28.

/Win 86/   J. F. H. Winkler: The Integration of Version Control into Programming Languages, in /1. CDW 86/, 230–250.

/Wit 94/   St. Witt: An RE–PiL.–Integrator with Application–independent Integration Document (in German), Master's Thesis, RWTH Aachen (1994).

/WP 87/   A. I. Wasserman/P. A. Pircher: A Graphical, Extensible Integrated Environment for Software Development, in /1. Hen 87/, 131–142.

/WPS 86/   A. I. Wasserman/P. A. Pircher/D. T. Shewmake/M. L. Kersten: Developing Interactive Information Systems with the User Software Engineering Methodology, TOSE 12, 2, 312–325 (1986).

/WS 88/   M. Wood/I. Sommerville: An information retrieval system for software components, Software Engineering Journal 3, 5, 198–207 (1988).

/Yeh 90/   R. T. Yeh: Specification Compiler – A Basis for Future CASE Systems, in /1. MSW 90/, 171–176.

/YHR 90/   W. Yang/S. Horwitz/T. Reps: A Program Integration Algorithm that Accomodates Semantics–Preserving Transformations, in /1. Tay 90/, 133–143.

/YI 86/   S. Yamamoto/S. Isoda: SOFTDA – A Reuse–Oriented Software Design System, in Proc. 10th COMPSAC '86, 284–290 (1986).

/YTT 88/   M. Young/R.N. Taylor/D.B. Troup: Software Environment Architectures and User Interface Facilities, in /1. Rid 88/, 697–708.

/Zam 96/   A. Zamperoni: GRIDS – Graph–based, Integrated Development of Software: Integrating Different Perspectives of Software Engineering, in Proc. ICSE 18, 48–59, IEEE Computer Society Press (1996).

/Zel 84/   M. V. Zelkowitz: A Small Contribution to Editing with a Syntax Directed Editor, in /1. Hen 84/, 1–6.

5 Formalisms for Specifying and Describing the Internals of SDEs

/AA 86/   G. Ausiello/P. Atzeni (Eds.): Proc. Int. Conf. on Database Theory, LNCS 243 (1986).

/AB 91/   S. Abiteboul/A. Bonner: Objects and Views, in J. Clifford/R. King (Eds.): Proc. Int. Conf. on Management of Data, Denver 91, ACM SIGMOD 20, 2, 238–247 (1991).

/ACR 88/   B. Alpern/A. Carle/B. Rosen/P. Sweeney/K. Zadeck: Graph Attribution as a Specification Paradigm, in /1. Hen 88/, 121–130.

/ACS 90/   M. Angelaccio/T. Catarci/G. Santucci: QBD*: A Graphical Query Language with Recursion, TOSE 16, 10, 1150–1163 (1990).

/AE 94/   M. Andries/G. Engels: Syntax and Semantics of Hybrid Database Languages, in /5. SE 94/, 19–36.

/AGT 89/   A.V. Aho/M. Ganapathi/S.W.K. Tjiang: Code Generation Using Tree Matching and Dynamic Programming, TOPLAS 11, 4, 491–516 (1989).

/Ait 84/   H. Ait–Kaci: A Lattice–Theoretic Approach to Computation Based on a Calculus of Partially–Ordered Type Structures, Ph.D. Thesis, Univ. of Pennsylvania, Philadelphia (1984).

/BEH 87/   P. Böhm/H. Ehrig/U. Hummert/M. Löwe: Towards Distributed Graph Grammars, in /5. ENR 87/, 86–98.

/Ber 92/   E. Bertino: A View Mechanism for Object–Oriented Databases, in A. Pivotte/C. Delabel/G. Gottlob (Eds.): Advances in Database Technology – Proc. 3rd Int. Conf. on Extending Database Technology (EDBT 92), LNCS 580, 136–151 (1992).

/BFG 95/   D. Blostein/H. Fahmy/A. Grbavec: Practical Use of Graph Rewriting, TR 95–373, Computing and Information Science, Queen's University, Canada (1995).

/BFG 96/   D. Blostein/H. Fahmy/A. Grbavec: Issues in the Practical use of Graph Rewriting, in /5. CEE 96/, 38–55.

/BGT 91/   H. Bunke/T. Glauser/T.–H. Tran: An Efficient Implementation of Graph Grammars Based on the RETE Matching Algorithms, in /5. EKR 91/, 174–189.

/BGV 92/   R. Ballance/S.L. Graham/M.L. Van der Vanter: The Pan Language–Based Editing System, TOSEM 1, 1, 95–127 (1992).

/BL 93/   B. Bell/C. Lewis: ChemTrains: A Language for Creating Pictures, in /5. VL 93/, 188–195.

/BMM 91/   F. Bry/R. Manthey/B. Martens: Integrity Verification in Knowledge Bases, in /5. Vor 91/, 114–139.

/BMS 81/   R. M. Burstall/ D. B. MacQueen/D. T. Sanella: HOPE – An Experimental Applicative Language, Techn. Report CSR–62–80, Edinburgh Univ. (1981).

/BMS 84/   M. L. Brodie/J. Mylopoulos/J. W. Schmidt (Eds.): On Conceptual Modelling, Berlin: Springer–Verlag (1984).

/Bra 88/   Th. Brandes: Formal Methods for Specifying Automatic Parallelization (in German), Doct. Diss., Univ. Marburg, Heidelberg: Hüthig Verlag (1988).

/Bun 79/   H. Bunke: Sequential and Parallel Programmed Graph Grammars (in German), Doct. Diss., Univ. of Erlangen, TR IMMD 12, 3 (1979).

/Bun 82/   H. Bunke: Attributed Programmed Graph Grammars and Their Application to Schematic Diagram Interpretation, IEEE Pattern Analysis and Machine Intelligence 4, 6, 574–582 (1982).

/CD 85/   R. J. Cunningham/ A. J. J. Dick: Rewrite Systems on a Lattice of Types, Acta Informatica 22, 149–169, Berlin: Springer–Verlag (1985).

/CEE 96/   J. Cuny/H. Ehrig/G. Engels/G. Rozenberg (Eds.): Graph Grammars and their Applications to Computer Science, Proc. 5th Int. Workshop, LNCS 1073 (1996).

/CER 79/   V. Claus/H. Ehrig/G. Rozenberg (Eds.): Proc. 1st Int. Workshop on Graph Grammars and Their Application to Computer Science and Biology, LNCS 73 (1979).

/CH 95/   A. Corradini/R. Heckel: A Compositional Approach to Structuring and Refinement of Typed Graph Grammars, in /5. CM 95b/, 167–176.

/CM 93/   M. Consens/A. Mendelzon: Hy+: A Hygraph–based Query and Visualization System, in Proc. ACM SIGMOD '93 Conf. on Management of Data, SIGMOD RECORD 22, 2, 511–516 (1993).

/CM 95/   S.S. Chok/K. Marriott: Automatic Construction of User Interfaces from Constraint Multiset Grammars, in Proc. of the 1995 IEEE Symp. on Visual Languages, 242–249, Los Alamitos: IEEE Computer Society Press (1995).

/CM 95b/   A. Corradini/U. Montanari (Eds.): Proc. Joint COMPUGRAPH/SEMAGRAPH Workshop on Graph Rewriting and Computation, Electronic Notes in Theoretical Computer Science (ENTCS), Amsterdam: Elsevier Science Publ. (1995).

/Cou 91/   B. Courcelle: Graphs as Relational Structures: An Algebraic and Logical Approach, in /5. EKR 91/, 238–252.

/CR 87/   M. Carroll/B. G. Ryder: An Incremental Algorithm for Software Analysis, in /1. Hen 87/, 171–179.

/CZ 84/   R. Constable/D. Zlatin: The Type Theory of PL/CV3, TOPLAS 6, 1, 94–117 (1984).

/DC 90/   G.D.P. Dueck/G.V. Cormack: Modular Attribute Grammars, Computing Journal 33, 164–172 (1990).

/DHK 95/   F. Drewes/A. Habel/H.J. Kreowski/S. Taubenberger: Generating self–affine fractals by collage grammars, Theor. Comp. Sci. 145, 159–187 (1995).

/DHT 96/   J. Dassow/A. Habel/S. Taubenberger: Chain–Code Pictures and Collages Generated by Hyperedge Replacement, in /5. CEE 96/, 412–427.

/Dör 95/   H. Dörr: Efficient Graph Rewriting and its Implementation, Doct. Diss., FU Berlin, LNCS 922 (1995).

/Dor 84/   H.J. Dorka: Specification of a Syntax–oriented Editor for the Programming Language Ada by Graph Grammars, Master's Thesis, Univ. of Dortmund (1984).

/DP 89/   J. Dassow/G. Paun: Regulated Rewriting in Formal Language Theory, EATCS 18, New York: Springer–Verlag (1989).

/DRT 81/   A. Demers/T. Reps/T. Teitelbaum: Incremental Evaluation for Attribute Grammars with Applications to Syntax–directed Editors, in Proc. 8th POPL, 26–28 (1981).

/DRZ 85/   A. Demers/A. Rogers/F. K. Zadeck: Attribute Propagation by Message Passing, in /1. Deu 85/, 43–59.

/Ebe 87/   J. Ebert: A Versatile Data Structure for Edge–oriented Graph Algorithms, Comm. ACM 30, 6, 513–519 (1987).

/EE 95a/   H. Ehrig/G. Engels: Pragmatic and Semantic Aspects of a Module Concept for Graph Transformation Systems, in /5. CEE 96/, 137–154.

/EE 95b/   G. Engels/H. Ehrig: Towards a Module Concept for Graph Transformation Systems: The Software Engineering Perspective, in /5. VFR 95/, 25–28.

/EE 96/   H. Ehrig/G. Engels: Pragmatic and Semantic Aspects of a Module Concept for Graph Transformation Systems, in /5. CEE 96/, 137–154.

/EER 96/   G. Engels/H. Ehrig/G. Rozenberg (Guest Eds.): Special Issue on Graph Transformation Systems, Fundamenta Informaticae 26, 3/4 (1996).

/EG 94/   G. Engels/L.P.J. Groenewegen: SOCCA: Specifications of Coordinated and Cooperative Activities, in A. Finkelstein/J. Kramer/B.A. Nuseibeh (Eds.): Software Process Modelling and Technology, 71–102, Taunton: Research Studies Press (1994).

/EGN 83/   G. Engels/R. Gall/M. Nagl/W. Schäfer: Software Specification using Graph Grammars, Computing 31, 317–346 (1983).

/EHK 91/   H. Ehrig/A. Habel/H.–J. Kreowski/F. Parisi–Presicce: From Graph Grammars to High–Level Replacement Systems, in /5. EKR 91/, 269–291.

/Ehr 74/   H. Ehrig: Introduction to the Algebraic Theory of Graph Grammars (a Survey), in /5. CER 74/, 1–69.

/Ehr 79/   H. Ehrig: Introduction to the Algebraic Theory of Graph Grammars (a Survey), in /5. CER 79/, 1–69.

/EKL 90/   H. Ehrig/M. Korff/M. Löwe: Tutorial Introduction to the Algebraic Approach of Graph Grammars Based on Double and Single Pushouts, TR 90/21, TU Berlin (1990).

/EKR 91/   H. Ehrig/H. J. Kreowski/G. Rozenberg (Eds.): Proc. 4th Int. Workshop on Graph Grammars and Their Application to Computer Science, LNCS 532 (1991).

/ELN 92/   G. Engels/C. Lewerentz/M. Nagl/W. Schäfer/A. Schürr: Experiences in Building Integrating Tools, Part I: Tool Specification, TOSEM 1, 2, 135–167 (1992).

/ELS 87/   G. Engels/C. Lewerentz/W. Schäfer: Graph Grammar Engineering – A Software Specification Method, in /5. ENR 87/, 186–201.

/Eng 86/   G. Engels: Graphs as a Central Data Structure in a Software Development Environment (in German), Doct. Diss., Univ. of Osnabrück, VDI Fortschrittsberichte 62, Düsseldorf: VDI–Verlag (1986).

/ENR 83/   H. Ehrig/M. Nagl/G. Rozenberg (Eds.): Proc. 2nd Int. Workshop on Graph Grammars and Their Application to Computer Science, LNCS 153 (1983).

/ENR 87/   H. Ehrig/M. Nagl/G. Rozenberg/A. Rosenfeld (Eds.): Proc. 3rd Int. Workshop on Graph Grammars and Their Application to Computer Science, LNCS 291 (1987).

/ES 85/   G. Engels/W. Schäfer: Graph Grammar Engineering: A Method User for the Development of an Integrated Programming Support Environment, in Ehrig et al. (Eds.): Proc. TAPSOFT Conf., Berlin, LNCS 186, 179–193 (1985).

/ES 95/   G. Engels/A. Schürr: Hierarchical Graphs, Graph Types, and Meta Types, in /5. CM 95b/, 75–84.

/EW 83/   R. Elmasri/G. Wiederhold: GORDAS: A Formal High–Level Query Language for the Entity–Relationship Model, in /7. Che 83/, 49–72.

/FB 93/   H. Fahmy/D. Blostein: A Graph Grammar Programmin Style for Recognition of Music Notation, Machine Vision and Application 6, 2, 83–99 (1993).

/FG 90/   W.B. Frakes/P.B. Gandel: Representing Reusable Software, Information and Software Technology 32, 10, 641–664 (1990).

/FMY 92/   R. Farrow/T.J. Marlowe/D.M. Yellin: Composable Attribute Grammars: Support for Modularity in Translator Design and Implementation, in Proc. ACM Symp. on Principles of Programming Languages, 223–234, New York: ACM Press (1992).

/Fur 91/   G. Furnas: New Graphical Reasoning Models for Understanding Graphical Interfaces, in Proc. CHI '91, 71–78 (1991).

/Gal 78/   H. Gallaire: Logic and Data Bases, New York: Plenum Press (1978).

/Gal 82/   R. Gall: Structured Development of Modular Software Systems – The Module Graph as Central Data Structure, in Proc. WG' 81, Workshop on Graphtheoretic Concepts in Computer Science, 327–338, München: Hanser–Verlag (1982).

/Gar 88/   D. Garlan: Views for Tools in Integrated Environments, Doct. Diss., Computer Science Department, Carnegie Mellon University, Pittsburgh (1988).

/Gen 69/   G. Gentzen: Investigations into Logical Deductions, in Szabo (Ed.): The collected Papers of Gerhard Gentzen, 68–131, Amsterdam: North–Holland (1969).

/Ger 75/   S. L. Gerhart: Correctness–preserving Program Transformations, in Proc. 2nd POPL, 54–56 (1975).

/GG 84/   H. Ganzinger/R. Giegerich: Attribute Coupled Grammars, in Proc. ACM SIGPLAN '84 Symp. on Compiler Construction, ACM SIGPLAN Notices 17, 6, 172–184 (1984).

/GGN 91/   H. Göttler/J. Günther/G. Nieskens: Use Graph Grammars to Design CAS–Systems, in /5. EKR 91/, 396–410.

/GH 96/   H. Göttler/B. Himmelreich: Modelling of Transactions in Object–Oriented Databases by Two–level Graph Grammars, in: Abstract Proc. 5th Int. Workshop on Graph Grammars and their Application to Computer Science, 151–156 (1996).

/GHL 92/   R.W. Gray/V.P. Heuring/St.P. Levi/A.M. Sloane/W.M. Waite: Eli: A Complete, Flexible Compiler Construction System, Comm. ACM 35, 2, 121–130 (1992).

/GM 79/   C. Ghezzi/D. Mandrioli: Incremental Parsing, TOPLAS 1, 1, 58–70 (1979).

/GM 80/   C. Ghezzi/D. Mandrioli: Augmenting Parsers to Support Incrementality, Journal ACM 27, 3, 564–579 (1980).

/GM 87/   J. Goguen/M. Moriconi: Formalization in Programming Environments, in /1. HN 87a/, 55–64.

/GM 93/   E. Golin/T. Magliery: A Compiler Generator for Visual Languages, in Proc. of the 1993 IEEE Symp. on Visual Languages, 314–321, Los Alamitos: IEEE Computer Society Press (1993).

/Göt 83/   H. Göttler: Attributed Graph Grammars for Graphics, in /5. ENR 83/, 130–142.

/Göt 87/   H. Göttler: Graph Grammars and Diagram Editing, in /5. ENR 87/, 216–231.

/Göt 88/   H. Göttler: Graph Grammars in Software Engineering (in German), IFB 178 (1988).

/Gre 86/   M. Green: A survey of three dialogue models, ACM Transactions on Graphics, 5, 3, 244–275 (1986).

/Gro 91/   J. Grosch: Puma – A Generator for the Transformation of Attributed Trees, Compiler Generation Report 26, GMD, Univ. of Karlsruhe (1991).

/GT 85/   J. Goguen/J. Tardo: An Introduction to OBJ: A Language for Writing and Testing Software Specifications, in Gehani/McGelwick (Eds.): Software Specification Techniques, 291–420, Reading: Addison Wesley (1985).

/Hed 89/   G. Hedin: An Object–Oriented Notation for Attribute Grammars, in S. Cook (Ed.): Proc. 3rd European Conf. on Object–Oriented Programming (ECOOP '89), 329–345, Nottingham: British Informatics Society Ltd. (1993).

/HH 89/   H.R. Hartson/D. Hix: Human–computer interface development: concepts and systems for its management, ACM Computing Surveys, 21, 1, 5–92 (1989).

/HHT 96/   A. Habel/R. Heckel/G. Taentzer: Graph Grammars with Negative Application Conditions, in /5. EER 96/, 287–314.

/Hil 86/   R.D. Hill: Supporting concurrency, communication, and synchronization in human–computer interaction – the Sassafras UIMS, ACM Transactions on Graphics, 5, 3, 179–210 (1986).

/Him 96/   M. Himsolt: Hierarchical Graphs for Graph Grammars, in: Abstract Proc. 5th Int. Workshop on Graph Grammars and their Application to Computer Science, 67–70 (1996).

/HK 87/   R. Hull/R. King: Semantic Database Modeling: Survey, Applications, and Research Issues, ACM Computing Surveys, Vol. 19, 3, 201–260 (1987).

/HLW 92/   F. Höfting/Th. Lengauer/E. Wanke: Processing of Hierarchically Defined Graphs and Graph Families, in: B. Monien, Th. Ottmann (Eds.): Data Structures and Efficient Algorithms, LNCS 594, 45–69 (1992).

/HMT 95/   R. Heckel/J. Müller/G. Taentzer/A. Wagner: Attributed Graph Transformations with Controlled Application of Rules, in /5. VFR 95/, 41–54.

/Hoa 69/   C. A. R. Hoare: An Axiomatic Basis for Computer Programming, Comm. ACM 12, 10, 576–583 (1969).

/Hud 87/   S.E. Hudson: Incremental Attribute Evaluation: an Algorithm for Lazy Evaluation in Graphs, TR 87–20, Univ. of Arizona (1987).

/Jac 86/   M. Jackel: Formal Specification of Concurrent Ada Constructs by Graph Grammars (in German), Doct. Diss., Univ. of Osnabrück (1986).

/JF 85/   G. F. Johnson/C. N. Fischer: A Meta–Language and System for Nonlogical Incremental Attribute
           Evaluation in Language–based Editors, in Proc. 12th POPL, 141–151 (1985).

/Kas 80/   U. Kastens: Ordered Attribute Grammars, Acta Informatica 13, 3, 229–256 (1980).

/Kau 85/   M. Kaul: Syntax Analysis of Graphs by Precedence Graph Grammars (in German), Doct. Diss., Univ.
           of Osnabrück (1985), appeared as Techn. Report, Univ. of Passau.

/KG 89/   S. M. Kaplan/S. K. Goering: Priority Controlled Incremental Attribute Evaluation in Attributed Graph
           Grammars, in Diaz/Orejas (Eds.): Proc. TAPSOFT '89, Vol. 1, LNCS 351, 306–320 (1989).

/KGC 87/   S. M. Kaplan/S. K. Goering/R. H. Campbell: Supporting the Software Development Process with At-
           tributed NLC Graph Grammars, in /5. ENR 87/, 309–325.

/KHZ 82/   U. Kastens/B. Hutt/E. Zimmermann: GAG – A Practical Compiler Generator, LNCS 141 (1982).

/KK 88/   H.–J. Kreowski/G. Rozenberg: On Structured Graph Grammars: Part I and II, TR 3/88, Univ. of Bre-
           men, FB Mathematik/Informatik (1988)

/KK 96/   H.J. Kreowski/S. Kuske: On the Interleaving Semantics of Transformation Units – A Step into
           GRACE, in /5. CEE 96/, 89–106.

/KKM 87/   G.E. Kaiser/S.M. Kaplan/J. Micallef: Multiuser, Distributed Language–Based Environments, IEEE
           Software 4, 6, 58–67 (1987).

/KLG 91/   S. Kaplan/J. Loyall/S. Goering: Specifying Concurrent Languages and Systems with Δ–Grammars, in
           /5. EKR 91/, 475–489.

/Kli 93/   P. Klint: A Meta–Environment for Generating Programming Environments, TOSEM 2, 2, 176–201
           (1993).

/KLM 83/   G. Kahn/B. Lang/B. Mélèse: Metal – A Formalism to Specify Formalisms, Science of Computer Pro-
           gramming 3, 151–188 (1983).

/KLM 90/   H. Kuchen/R. Loogen, J.J. Moreno–Navarro/M. Rodriguez–Artalejo: Graph–based Implementation
           of a Functional Logic Language, in Proc. ESOP '90, LNCS 432, 271–290 (1990).

/Kor 92/   M. Korff: Algebraic Transformation of Equationally Defined Graph Structures, TR 92/32, TU Berlin
           (1992).

/KP 90/   K. Koskimies/J. Paakki: Automating Language Implementation – A Pragmatic Approach, Chichester:
           Ellis Horwood (1990).

/KR 88/   H.–J. Kreowski/G. Rozenberg: On Structured Graph Grammars: Parts I and II, Techn. Report 3/88,
           University of Bremen (1988).

/KW 76/   K. Kennedy/S. K. Warren: Automatic Generation of Efficient Evaluators for Attribute Grammars, in
           Proc. 3rd POPL, 32–49 (1976).

/KW 94/   U. Kastens/M.W. Waite: Modularity and Reusability in Attribute Grammars, Acta Informatica 31,
           601–627 (1994).

/Lam 87/   D. A. Lamb: IDL – Sharing intermediate Representations, TOPLAS 9, 3, 297–318 (1987).

/LB 93/   M. Löwe/M. Beyer: AGG – An Implementation of Algebraic Graph Rewriting, in Proc. 5th Int. Conf.
           on Rewriting Techniques and Applications, LNCS 690, 451–456 (1993).

/Lef 94/   M. Lefering: Software Document Integration Using Graph Grammar Specifications, in Proc. 6th Int.
           Conference on Computing and Information, a special issue of Journal of Computing and Information
           1, 1, E6: 1222–1243 (1994).

/LKW 93/   M. Löwe/M. Korff/A. Wagner: An Algebraic Framework for the Transformation of Attributed Graphs,
           in /5. SPV 93/, 185–199.

/LMW 89/   P. Lipps/U. Möncke/R. Wilhelm: OPTRAN – A Language/System for the Specification of Program
           Transformations, System Overview and Experiences, LNCS 371, 52–65 (1989).

/LN 84/   C. Lewerentz/M. Nagl: A Formal Specification Language for Software–Systems defined by Graph
           Grammars, in Pape (Ed.): Proc. of WG '84 Workshop on Graphtheoretic Concepts in Computer Sci-
           ence, 224–241, Linz (Austria): Trauner–Verlag (1984).

/Löw 90/   M. Löwe: Algebraic Approach to Graph Transformation Based on Single Pushout Derivations, Doct.
           Diss. TR 90/5, TU Berlin (1990).

/MG 92/   D.W. McIntyre/E.P. Glinert: Visual Tools for Generating Iconic Programming Environments, in /5.
           VL 92/, 162–168.

/Mil 78/   R. Milner: A Theory of Type Polymorphism in Programming, Journal of Computer and System Sci-
           ences 17, 348–375 (1978).

/Min 88/   J. Minker: Perspectives in Deductive Databases, Jounal of Logic Programming, 33–60 (1988).

/MR 86/   A. M. Meyer/M. B. Reinhold: 'Type' is not a type, in Proc. 13th POPL, 287–295 (1986).

/MV 95/   M. Minas/G. Viehstaedt: DiaGen: A Generator for Diagram Editors Providing Direct Manipulation
           and Execution of Diagrams, in Proc. of the 1995 IEEE Symp. on Visual Languages, 203–210, Los Ala-
           mitos: IEEE Computer Society Press (1995).

/MW 91/   A. Maggioli–Schettini/J. Winkowski: Programmed Derivations of Relational Structures, in /5. EKR 91/, 582–598.

/Mye 92/   B.A. Myers (Ed.): Language for developing user interfaces, Jones and Bartlett Publishers (1992).

/Nag 79/   M. Nagl: Graph Grammars: Theory, Applications, and Implementation (in German), Braunschweig: Vieweg–Verlag (1979).

/Nag 87a/   M. Nagl: A Software Development Environment Based on Graph Technology, in /5. ENR 87/, 458–478.

/Nag 87b/   M. Nagl: Set Theoretic Approaches to Graph Grammars, in /5. ENR 87/, 41–54.

/Nag 90/   M. Nagl (Ed.): Proc. WG '89 15th Int. Workshop on Graphtheoretic Concepts in Computer Science, LNCS 411 (1990).

/Nag 94/   M. Nagl: Uniform Modelling in Graph Grammar Specifications, in /5. SE 94/, 296–311.

/Naq 86a/   Sh.A. Naqvi: Some Extensions to the Closed World Assumption in Databases, in /9. AA 86/, 341–348.

/Naq 86b/   Sh.A. Naqvi: Negation as Failure for First–Order Queries, in Proc. 5th ACM SIGACT–SIGMOD Symp. on Principles of Database Systems, 114–122 (1986).

/Nel 89/   G. Nelson: A Generalization of Dijkstra's Calculus, TOPLAS 11, 4, 517–561 (1989).

/NEG 83/   M. Nagl/G. Engels/R. Gall/W. Schäfer: Software Specification by Graph Grammars, in /5. ENR 83/, 267–287.

/NNG 90/   J. R. Nestor/J. M. Newcomer/P. Giannini/D. L. Stone: IDL: The Language and Its Implementation, Englewood Cliffs: Prentice Hall (1990).

/Nol 76/   H. Noltemeier (Ed.): Graphs, Algorithms, Data Structures, Proc. WG '76 2nd Workshop on Graph-theoretic Concepts in Computer Science, Applied Computer Science 4, Munich: Hanser Verlag (1976).

/Nor 87/   K. Normark: Transformations and Abstract Presentations in a Language Development Environment, Ph.D. Thesis, University of Aarhus, Denmark (1987).

/NP 83/   M. Nagl/J. Perl (Eds.): Proc WG '83 Int. Workshop on Graphtheoritic Concepts in Computer Science, Linz (Austria): Trauner–Verlag (1983).

/NS 96/   Nagl M., Schürr A.: Software Integration Problems and Coupling of Graph Grammar Specifications, in /5. CEE 96/, 155–169.

/NT 89/   Sh.A. Naqvi/Sh. Tsur: Data and Knowledge Bases, IEEE Computer Society Press (1989).

/Paa 95/   J. Paakki: Attribute Grammar Paradigms – A High Level Methodology in Language Implementation, ACM Computing Surveys 27, 2, 196–256 (1995).

/PL 94/   A. Poulovassilis/M. Levene: A Nested–Graph Model for the Representation and Ma nipulation of Complex Objects, ACM Transactions on Information Systems 12, 1, 35–68 (1994).

/PP 95/   F. Parisi–Presicce/G. Piersanti: Multilevel Graph Grammars, in: Proc. 20th Int. Workshop on Graph–Theoretic Concepts in Computer Science, WG '94, LNCS 903, 51–64 (1995).

/Pra 71/   T.W. Pratt: Pair Grammars, Graph Languages and String–to–Graph Translations, Journal of Computer and System Sciences 5, 560–595 (1971).

/Pra 79/   T.W. Pratt: Definition of Programming Language Semantics Using Grammars for Hierarchical Graphs, in /5. CER 79/, 390–400.

/Rep 82/   T. Reps: Optimal–time incremental semantic analysis for syntax–directed editors, in Proc. 9th POPL, 169–176 (1982).

/Rep 84/   T. Reps: Generating Language Based Environments, Doct. Diss., Cambridge (USA): MIT Press (1984).

/Roz 96/   G. Rozenberg (ed.): Handbook on Graph Grammars, vol. 1, to appear.

/RS 96/   J. Rekers/A. Schürr: Defining and Parsing Visual Languages with Layered Graph Grammars, Journal of Visual Languages and Computing 7, 3 (1996).

/RTD 83/   T. Reps/T. Teitelbaum/A. Demers: Incremental Context dependend Analysis for Language Based Editors, TOPLAS 5, 3, 449–477 (1983).

/Ryb 87/   H. Rybinski: On First–Order–Logic Databases, ACM Transactions on Database Systems 12, 3, 325–349 (1987).

/SB 92/   G. Schmidt/R. Berghammer: Proc. WG '91 Int. Workshop on Graph–Theoretic Concepts in Computer Science, LNCS 570 (1992).

/Schi 92/   G. Schied: About Graph Grammars: A Specification Method for Programming Languages and Distributed Systems (in German), Doct. Diss., Univ. of Erlangen, TR IMMD–25–2 (1992).

/Schn 93/   H.J. Schneider: On Categorical Graph Grammars Integrating Structural Transforma tions and Operations on Labels, Theoretical Computer Science (TCS) 109, 257–274 (1993).

/Schü 88/   A. Schürr: Modelling and Simulation of Complex Systems in PROGRES (in German), in Ameling (Ed.): Proc. 5. Symp. Simulationstechnik, IFB 179, 84–91 (1988).

679

/Schü 89/   A. Schürr: Introduction to PROGRES, an Attribute Graph Grammar Based Specification Language, in /5. Nag 90/, 151–165.

/Schü 91a/   A. Schürr: Operational Specification using Programmed Graph Rewriting Systems: Formal Definition, Application, and Tools (in German), Doct. Diss., RWTH Aachen, Wiesbaden: Deutscher Universitäts–Verlag (1991).

/Schü 91b/   A. Schürr: PROGRES – A VHL–Language Based on Graph Grammars, in /5. EKR 91/, 641–659.

/Schü 94a/   A. Schürr: Logic Based Structure Rewriting Systems, in /5. SE 94/, 341–357.

/Schü 94b/   A. Schürr: A Fixpoint Semantics for Programmed Graph Transformations, in /5. VFR 95/, 117–124.

/Schü 94c/   A. Schürr: Rapid Programming with Graph Rewrite Rule, Proc. USENIX Very High Level Language Conf., 83–100 (1994).

/Schü 94d/   A. Schürr: Specification of Graph Translators with Triple Graph Grammars, in /5. Tin 94/, 151–163.

/Schü 94e/   A. Schürr: PROGRES, A Visual Language and Environment for PROgramming with Graph REwrite Systems, Techn. Report AIB 94–11, RWTH Aachen (1994).

/Schü 94f/   A. Schürr: Programmed Graph Transformations and Graph Transformation Units in GRACE, in /5. CEE 96/, 122–136.

/Schü 96/   A. Schürr: Logic Based Programmed Structure Rewriting Systems, in /5. EER 96/, 363–385.

/SE 94/   H.J. Schneider/H. Ehrig (Eds.): Graph Transformations in Computer Science, LNCS 776, Berlin: Springer–Verlag (1994).

/SE 95/   A. Schürr/G. Engels: Hierarchical Graph Objects, Types, and Metatypes, Techn. Report 95–21, University of Leiden (1995).

/SMS 84/   J. F. Sowa/J. Mylopoulos/J. W. Schmidt: Conceptual Structures: Information Processing in Mind and Machine, Reading: Addison Wesley (1984).

/Sob 94/   G. Sobbe: Modelling and Generation of SDEs using Graph Grammars (in German), Master's Thesis, RWTH Aachen (1994).

/SPV 93/   M.R. Sleep/M.J. Plasmeijer/M.C. van Eekelen (Ed.): Term Graph Rewriting: Theory and Practice, New York: John Wiley & Sons Ltd (1993).

/SW 92/   A. Schürr/B. Westfechtel: Graphgrammatiken und Graphersetzungssysteme, Techn. Report AIB 92–15, RWTH Aachen (1992).

/SWZ 95a/   A. Schürr/A.J. Winter/A. Zündorf: Specification and Prototyping of Graph–based Systems (in German), in G. Snelting (Ed.): GI Conf. on Software Engineering, 86–97 (1995).

/SWZ 95b/   A. Schürr/A.J. Winter/A. Zündorf: Graph Grammar Engineering with PROGRES, in W. Schäfer/P. Botella (Eds.): Proc. 5th ESEC, LNCS 989, 219–234 (1995).

/SWZ 95c/   A. Schürr/A.J. Winter/A. Zündorf: Visual Programming with Graph Rewriting Systems, in V. Haarslev (Ed.): Proc. VL '95 11th Int. IEEE Symp. on Visual Languages, Darmstadt, Sept. 1995, 326–335, Los Alamitos: IEEE Computer Society Press (1995).

/Tae 96/   G. Taentzer: Hierarchically Distributed Graph Transformations, in /5. CEE 96/, 304–320.

/TB 94/   G. Taentzer/M. Beyer: Amalgamated Graph Transformations and Their Use for Specifying AGG – an Algebraic Graph Grammar System, in /5. SE 94/, 380–394.

/Ten 74/   A. Tenebaum: Automatic Type Analysis in a Very High Level Language, Doct. Diss., Computer Science Department, New York Univ. (1974).

/Tha 89/   A. Thaise (Ed.): From Standard Logic to Logic Programming, New York: John Wiley & Sons Ltd. (1989).

/Tin 94/   G. Tinhofer (Ed.): Proc. WG '94 Int. Workshop on Graph–Theoretic Concepts in Computer Science, LNCS 903 (1994).

/TS 95/   G. Taentzer/A. Schürr: DIEGO, another Step Towards a Module Concept for Graph Transformation Systems, in /5. CM 95b/, 85–94.

/VFR 95/   G. Valiente Feruglio/F. Rosello Llompart (Eds.): Proc. Coll. on Graph Transformation and its applications in Computer Science, Techn. Rep. B–19, Universitat de les Illes Balears (1995).

/VHe 89/   P. Van Hentenrynck: Constraint Satisfaction in Logic Programming, Cambridge: MIT Press (1989).

/VL 88/   S. Vorthmann/R.J. LeBlanc: A Naming Specification Language for Syntax–Directed Editors, in Proc. Int. Conf. on Computer Languages, 250–257, Los Alamitos: IEEE Computer Society Press (1988).

/VL 92/   Proc. 1992 IEEE Symp. on Visual Languages, Los Alamitos: IEEE Computer Society Press (1992).

/VL 93/   Proc. 1993 IEEE Symp. on Visual Languages, Los Alamitos: IEEE Computer Society Press (1993).

/VL 94/   Proc. 1994 IEEE Symp. on Visual Languages, Los Alamitos: IEEE Computer Society Press (1994).

/Vor 91/   A. Voronkov (Ed.): Logic Programming, LNCS 592 (1991).

/War 76/   S. K. Warren: The Coroutine Model of Attribute Grammar Evaluation, Doct. Diss., Dpt. of Mathematical Sciences, Rice Univ., Houston (1976).

/Wes 95a/   B. Westfechtel: Using Programmed Graph Rewriting for the Formal Specification of a Configuration Management System, in Mayer, Schmidt, Tinhofer (eds.): Proc. WG '94 Int. Workshop on Graph–Theoretic Concepts in Computer Science, LNCS 903, 164–179 (1995).

/Wes 95b/   B. Westfechtel: A Graph–Based Model for Dynamic Process Nets, in: Int. Conf. on Software Engineering and Knowledge Engineering SEKE 95, 126–130, Skokie: Knowledge Systems Institute (1995)

/Yeh 83/   D. Yeh: On Incremental Evaluation of Ordered Attributed Grammars, BIT 23, 308–320 (1983).

/ZS 92/   A. Zündorf/A. Schürr: Nondeterministic Control Structures for Graph Rewriting Systems, in /5. SB 92/, 48–62.

/Zün 89/   A. Zündorf: Control Structures of the Specification Language PROGRES (in German), Master's Thesis, RWTH Aachen (1989).

/Zün 92/   A. Zündorf: Implementation of the Imperative/Rule Based Language PROGRES, TR AIB 92–38, RWTH Aachen (1992).

/Zün 93/   A. Zündorf: A Heuristic for the Subgraph Isomorphism Problem in Executing PROGRES, Techn. Report AIB 93–5, RWTH Aachen (1993).

/Zün 96a/   A. Zündorf: An Environment for Programmed Graph Rewriting Systems: Specification, Realization, and Use (in German), Doct. Diss., RWTH Aachen, Wiesbaden: Deutscher Universitätsverlag (1996).

/Zün 96b/   A. Zündorf: Graph Pattern Matching in PROGRES, in /5. CEE 96/, 454–468.

6 Basic Components, Mechanisms, and Platforms for SDEs

/ABM 90/   T.L. Anderson/A.J. Berre/M. Mallison et al.: The Hypermodel Benchmark, in: Bancilhon/Thanos/ Tsichritzis (Eds.): Advances in Database Technology – EDBT '90, LNCS 416, 317–331 (1990).

/ACR 87/   B. Alpern/A. Carle/B. Rosen: Incremental Evaluation of Attributed Graphs, Techn. Report CS 87–29, Brown University (1987).

/ADG 87/   K. Abramowicz/K. R. Dittrich/W. Gotthard/R. Längle/P. C. Lockemann/T. Raupp/S. Rehm/T. Wenner: Database Support for Software Development Environments (in German), in Schenk/Schlageter: Datenbanksysteme in Büro, Technik und Wissenschaft, IFB 136, 116–131 (1987).

/Ald 88/   A. Alderson: A Space–Efficient Technique for Recording Versions of Data, Software Engineering Journal, 240–246, IEE & BCS Joint Publ. (1988).

/AP 92/   A. Analyti/S. Pramanik: Fast Search in Main Memory Databases, in: /6. Sto 92/, 215–224.

/ASN 87/   Specification of Abstract Syntax Notation One (ASN–1), ISO 8824 (1987).

/BCL 87/   B. Bershad/D. Ching/E. Lazowsky/J. Sanislo/M. Schwartz: A remote procedure call facility for interconnecting heterogeneous computer systems, TOSE SE–13, 880–894 (1987).

/BDK 92/   F. Bancilhon/C. Delobel/P. Kanellakis (Eds.): Building an Object–Oriented Database System, Los Altos: Morgan Kaufmann Publ. (1992).

/Bea 88/   M. Beaudouin–Lafon: User Interface Support for the Integration of Software Tools: an Iconic Model of Interaction, in /1. Hen 88/, 143–152.

/Ber 87/   P. A. Bernstein: Data Base System Support for Software Engineering, in Proc. 9th ICSE, 166–178 (1987).

/Bie 94/   R. Biermanns: Implementation of Project Administration Graphs for Exchangeable Scenarios (in German), Master's Thesis (1994).

/BJ 93/   J. Bertot/I. Jacobs: Sophtalk tutorials, Techn. Report 149, INRIA (1993).

/BKS 91/   T. Batz/D. Krömker/H.–P. Subel: Frameworks for open Toolsets: Interfaces and Standards (in German), Informationstechnik it 33, 150–159 (1991).

/BL 85/   Th. Brandes/C. Lewerentz: GRAS: A Non–Standard Database System within a Software Development Environment, in /1. GTE 85/, 113–121.

/BM 72/   R. Bayer/E.M. McCreight: Organization and Maintenance of Large Ordered Indices, Acta Informatica 1, 173–189, New York: Springer–Verlag (1972).

/BM 91/   C. Beeri/T. Milo: A Model for Active Object Oriented Database, in Proc. 17th Int. Conf. on Very Large Data Bases, 337–349, Los Alamitos: IEEE Computer Society Press (1991).

/BMT 88/   G. Boudier/R. Minot/I. M. Thomas: An Overview of PCTE and PCTE+, in /1. Hen 88/, 248–257.

/BNO 94/   A. Birrel/G. Nelson/S. Owicki/E. Wobber: Network Objects, Techn. Rep. 115, DEC Systems Research Center, Palo Alto (1994).

/Bos 88/   J. v.d.Bos: Abstract interaction tools: a language for user interface management systems, TOPLAS 14, 2, 215–247 (1988).

/BOS 91/   P. Butterworth/A. Otis/J. Stein: The GemStone Object Dabase Management System, Comm. ACM 34, 10, 64–77 (1991).

/Bra 84/   Th. Brandes: Design and Implementation of a Graph Storage (in German), Master's Thesis, Univ. of Dortmund (1984).

/Bre 92/   R. Breuer: Basic Mechanisms for Document Handling in Software Development Environments (in German), Master's Thesis, RWTH Aachen (1992).

/Bro 89/   A. W. Brown: Database Support for Software Engineering, London: Kogan Page (1989).

/Bro 90/   M. Broekmanns: Change Administration in a Non–standard Database System (in German), Master's Thesis, RWTH Aachen (1990).

/CA 89/   J. Cartmell/A. Alderson: The Eclipse Two–Tier Database, in /2. Bot 89/, 39–66.

/Cat 93/   R.G.G Catell (Ed.): The Object Database Standard: ODMG–93, San Mateo: Morgan Kaufmann Publ. (1993).

/CDN 93/   M.J. Carey/D.J. DeWitt/J.F. Naughton: The oo7 benchmark, 1993 SIGMOD conference (1993).

/CDR 89/   M. Carey/D. J. DeWitt/J. E. Richardson/E. J. Shekita: Storage Management for Objects in EXODUS, in Kim/Lochovsky (Eds.): Object–Oriented Concepts, Databases, and Applications, 341–369, New-York: ACM Press (1989).

/Chr 91/   G. Chroust: Software Development Environments: Synthesis and Integration (in German), IBM AS/E Product Support, Vienna (1991).

/CK 88/   H.–T. Chou/W. Kim: Versions and Change Notification in an Object–Oriented Database System, in Proc. 25th ACM/IEEE Design Automation Conference, 275–281 (1988).

682

/CKN 96/   K. Cremer/P. Klein/M. Nagl/A. Radermacher: Distribution of Environments and Their Integration (in German), in W. Wahlster (Ed.): Proc. Online '96 Congress VI, C.610.01–C.610.23, Velbert: Online Press (1996).

/CL 86/   G. M. Clemm: The Odin System – An Object Manager for Software Environments, Ph. D. Thesis, Dept. of Computer Science, Univ. of Boulder, Col. (1986).

/Clé 90/   C. Clément: A distributed architecture for programming environments, in /1. Tay 90/, 11–21.

/COR 93/   Digital Equipment Corporation, Hewlett–Packard Company, HyperDesk Corporation, NCR Corporation, Object Design Inc., SunSoft Inc.: The Common Object Request Broker: Architecture and Specification, Revision 1.2, Draft 29 December 1993, OMG Document Number 93.12.43

/Cou 85/   J. Coutaz: Abstractions for User Interface Design, IEEE Computer 18, 21–34 (1985).

/CR 90/   P.K. Chrysanthis/K. Ramamrithan: ACTA: A Framework for Specifying and Reasoning About Transaction Structure and Behavior, in Proc. of the ACM SIGMOD Int. Conf. on Managment of Data, 194–203 (1990).

/CS 92/   R.G.G. Cattell/J. Skeen: Object Operations Benchmark, ACM Transactions on Database Systems 17, 1, 1–31 (1992).

/Dal 93/   R. Daley (Ed.): Integration technology for CASE, Avebury Technical, Ashgate Publishing Company (1993).

/Day 88/   U. Dayal et al.: The HiPAC Project: Combining Active Databases and Timing Constraints, ACM SIGMOD 17, 1, 51–70 (1988).

/DD 86/   K. Dittrich/U. Dayal (Eds.): Int. Workshop Object–oriented Databases, Pacific Grove, Cal., Sept. 23–26 (1986).

/DEC 91/   Digital Equipment Corporation: CDD/Repository Architecture Manual, Techn. Report, Digital Equipment (1991).

/Deu 91/   O. Deux: The O_2 System, Comm. ACM 34, 10, 34–48 (1991).

/DFM 90/   D. DeWitt/P. Futtersack/D. Maier/F. Velez: A Study of Three Alternative Workstation Server Architectures for Object–Oriented Database Systems, Proc. 17th Int. Conf. on Very Large Data Bases, Brisbane, Australia, 107–121 (1990).

/DGL 86/   K. Dittrich/W. Gotthard/P. Lockemann: DAMOKLES: A Database System for Software Engineering Environments, in /1. CDW 86/, 353–371.

/DHK 90/   S. Dewal/H. Hormann/U. Kelter/D. Platz/ M. Roschewski/L. Schöpe: Evaluation of object management systems, Techn. Report 44, Lehrstuhl für Software–Technologie, University of Dortmund (1990).

/DHS 91/   S. Dewal/H. Hormann/L. Schöpe/U. Kelter/D. Platz/M. Roschewski: Evaluation of Object Development Systems for Software Development Environments (in German), in Appelrath (Ed.): Datenbank–Systeme in Büro, Technik und Wissenschaft, GI–Fachtagung, Kaiserslautern, IFB 270, 404–411 (1991).

/DKM 86/   K.R. Dittrich/A.M. Kotz/J.A. Mülle: An Event/Trigger Mechanism to Enforce Complex Consistency Constraints in Design Databases, ACM SIGMOD 15, 3, 22–36 (1986).

/DL 88/   K. R. Dittrich/R. A. Lorie: Version Support for Engineering Database Systems, TOSE 14, 4, 429–437 (1988).

/DM 90/   D.J. DeWitt/D. Maier: A Study of Three Alternative Workstation–Server Architectures for Object–Oriented Database Systems. in Proc. 16th Int. Conf. on Very Large Data Bases, 107–121, Los Alamitos: IEEE Computer Society Press (1990).

/DoD 88/   Department of Defense (USA): Proposed Military Standard DOD–STD–1838 A, Common Ada Programming Support Environment (APSE) Interface Set (CAIS) (1988).

/DS 86/   N. M. Delisle/M. D. Schwartz: Neptune – Hypertext System for CAD Applications, in Proc. ACM SIGMOD '86 Conference on Management of Data, 132–143 (1986).

/DS 87/   P. Dewan/M. Solomon: Dost: An Environment to Support Automatic Generation of User Interfaces, in /1. Hen 87/, 150–159.

/Ear 90/   A. Earl: A Reference Model for Computer Assisted Software Engineering Environment Frameworks, Techn. Report, Software Environments Group HP Labs, Bristol, England (1990).

/ECM 90/   European Computer Manufacturers Association (ECMA): ECMA–149: Portable Common Tool Environment (PCTE) Abstract Specification (1990).

/ED 88/   R. Enbody/H. Du: Dynamic Hashing Schemes, ACM Computing Surveys 20, 2, 85–113 (1988).

/Eic 89/   M. Eichstädt: Communication of Complex Software Documents in Computer Nets (in German), Master's Thesis, RWTH Aachen (1989).

/EK 92/   W. Emmerich/M. Kampmann: The merlin oms benchmark – definition, implementations and results, Techn. Report 65, Lehrstuhl für Software–Technologie, University of Dortmund (1992).

/Elm 92/   A.K. Elmagarmid (Ed.): Database Transaction Models for Advanced Applications, Los Altos: Morgan Kaufmann (1992).

/EM 88/ R. Engelmore/T. Morgan (Eds.): Blackboard Systems, Reading: Addison–Wesley (1988).

/EMN 92/ W. Eversheim/W. Michaeli/M. Nagl/O. Spaniol/M. Weck: The SUKITS–Project: An Approach to A posteriori Integration of CIM Components, in Proc. GI–Jahrestagung 92, Informatik Aktuell 494–504, Berlin: Springer–Verlag (1992).

/End 83/ G. Enderle: Report on the Interface of the UIMS to the Application, in /3. Pfa 83/, 21–29.

/Erd 86/ F. Erdtmann: Organization of an Internal Data Structure for Texts in Structure–oriented Editors (in German), Master's Thesis, Univ. of Osnabrück (1986).

/ESF 89/ ESF Technical Reference Guide, V.1.1 (July 1989).

/ESF 90/ ESF–Subproject Softwarebus: SWB User Guide, Vol. 2 Component Builder, V.1.2 (June 1990).

/ESW 93/ W. Emmerich/W. Schäfer/J. Welsh: Databases for Software Engineering Environments – The Goal Has not yet Been Attained, in I. Sommerville/M. Paul (Eds.): Proc. 4th ESEC, LNCS 717, 145–162 (1993).

/Fer 91/ C. Fernström: An ESF Pilot Factory for Real–Time Software, in /1. Lon 91/, 305–316.

/FHS 92/ J.C. Ferrans/D.W. Hurst/M.A. Sennet/B.M. Covnot/W. Ji/P. Kajka/W. Ouyang: HyperWeb: A Framework for Hypermedia–Based Environments, in /1. Web 92/, 1–10.

/Fla 83/ Ph. Flajolet: On the Performance Evaluation of the Extendible Hashing and Trie Searching, Acta Informatica 20, 345–367, New York: Springer–Verlag (1983).

/FNP 79/ R. Fagin/J. Nievergelt/N. Pippinger et al.: Extendible Hashing: A Fast Access Method for Dynamic Files, ACM Transactions on Database Systems 4, 3, 315–344 (1979).

/FO 90/ C. Fernström/L. Ohlsson: The ESF Vision of a Software Factory, in /1. MSW 90/, 91–100.

/Fra 91/ B. Frankel: The ToolTalk Service, Sun Microsystems Inc., Mountain View, California (1991).

/Fro 90/ B.D. Fromme: HP Encapsulator: Bridging the Generation Gap, Hewlett–Packard Journal, 59–68 (June 1990).

/Ger 88/ C. Geretty: HP softbench: a new generation of software development tools, Techn. Report SESD–89–25, Hewlett–Packard Software Engineering Systems Division, Fort Collins, Colorado (1988).

/GHM 93/ R. Große–Wienker/O. Herrmanns/D. Menzenbach/A. Pollack/S. Repetzki/J. Schwartz/K. Sonnenschein/B. Westfechtel: Das SUKITS–Projekt: A–posteriori–Integration heterogener CIM–Anwendungssysteme, Techn. Report AIB 93–11, RWTH Aachen (1993).

/GI 90/ D. Garlan/E. Ilias: Low–cost, adaptable tool integration policies for integrated environments, in /1. Tay 90/, 1–10.

/Gib 87/ P. Gibbons: A stub generator for multilanguage RPC in heterogeneous environments, TOSE SE–13, 77–87 (1987).

/GKK 87/ B. Gasch/U. Kelter/H. Kopfer/H. Weber: Reference Model for the Integration of Tools within the EUREKA Software Factory, in Proc. Fall Joint Comp. Conf., Dallas, 183–190 (1987).

/GKK 92/ C. Gerlhof/A. Kemper/Ch. Kilger et al.: Clustering in Object Bases, Techn. Report 6/92, Fakultät für Informatik, University of Karlsruhe (1992).

/GMT 87/ F. Gallo/R. Minot/I. Thomas: The Object Management System of PCTE as a Software Engineering Database Management System, in /1. Hen 87/, 12–15.

/GN 81/ R. Gall/M. Nagl: Software Implementation of Associative Storages (in German), Elektronische Rechenanlagen 23, 2, 61–71 (1981).

/Got 88/ W. Gotthard: Database Systems for Software Development Environments (in German), IFB 193 (1988).

/GPT 93/ M. Gemis/J. Paredaens/I. Thyssens/J.v.d. Bussche: GOOD: A Graph–Oriented Object Database System, in Proc. ACM SIGMOD '93 Conf. on Management of Data, SIGMOD RECORD 22, 2, 505–510 (1993).

/Gra 91/ J. Gray (Ed.): The Benchmark Handbook, Los Altos: Morgan Kaufmann Publ. (1991).

/Has 94/ H. Hassoun: Design and Realization of an Event Trigger Machine for GRAS (in German), Master's Thesis, RWTH Aachen (1994).

/HE 94/ O. Hermanns/A. Engbrocks: Design, Implementation and Evaluation of a Distributed File Service for Collaborative Engineering Environments, in Proc. 3rd IEEE Workshop on Enabling Technologies – Infrastructures for Collaborative Enterprises, 170–177, Los Alamitos: IEEE Computer Society Press (1994).

/Hei 92/ D. Heimbigner: The Process Wall: A Process State server Approach to Process Programming, in /1. Web 92/, 159–169.

/HJK 95/ P. Heimann/G. Joeris/C.–A. Krapp/B. Westfechtel: A Programmed Graph Rewriting System for Software Process Management, in /5. CM 95/, 123–132.

/HJK 96/ P. Heimann/G. Joeris/C.–A. Krapp/B. Westfechtel: DYNAMITE: Dynamic Task Nets for Software Process Management, Proc. 18th Int. Conf. on Software Engineering, Berlin, 331–341 (1996).

/HK 88/   S. E. Hudson/R. King: The Cactis Project: Database Support for Software Environments, in /1. Rid 88/, 709–719.

/HK 89/   S.E. Hudson/R. King: Cactis: A Self–Adaptive, Concurrent Implementation of an Object–Oriented Database Management System, ACM Transactions on Database Systems 14, 3, 291–321 (1989).

/HNS 90/   D. Harrison, A. Newton, R. Spickelmier, T. Barnes: Electronic CAD Frameworks, Proc. of the IEEE, vol. 78–2, 393–417 (1990).

/Høg 93/   F. Høgberg: Software Engineering Database Benchmark (in German), Master's Thesis, RWTH Aachen (1993).

/Hor 92/   C. Horbach: Integration and Cooperation Mechanisms in Software Development Environments (in German), Master's Thesis, RWTH Aachen (1992).

/HP 89/   Hewlett Packard: Exploring HP Softbench: A Beginner's Guide, Techn. Report (1989).

/HS 96/   O. Hermanns/M. Schuba: Performance Investigations of the IP Multicast Architecture, Computer Networks and ISDN Systems 28, 4, 429–439 (1996).

/HW 91/   B. Holtkamp/H. Weber: Object Management Machines: Concept and Implementation, Journal of Systems Integration 1, 3–4, 367–389 (1991).

/IBM 89/   IBM: AD/Cycle Concepts, Techn. Report GC26–4531–0, IBM (1989).

/IBM 93/   IBM Corporation: Open Blueprint Introduction, Techn. Report (December 1993).

/Imb 91a/ M. Imber: The CASE DataInterchange Format (CDIF) Standards, in /1. Lon 91/, 457–474.

/Imb 91b/ M. Imber: CASE DataInterchange Format Standards, Information and Software Technology 33, 9, 647–655 (1991).

/JH 94/   A.M. Julienne/B. Holtz: ToolTalk and Open Protocols: Inter–Application Communication, SunSoft Press/Prentice Hall (1994).

/Joe 95/   G. Joeris: Execution Semantics and Aspects of Dynamics in a Net–Based Process Model (in German), Master's Thesis, RWTH Aachen (1995).

/Jon 89/   O. Jones: Introduction to the X Window System, New Jersey: Prentice Hall (1989).

/KAC 85/   R. H. Katz/M. Anwarrudin/E. Chang: Organizing a Design Database Across Time, in Brodie/Mylopoulos (Eds.): On Knowledge Base Management Systems, 287–295, Berlin: Springer–Verlag (1985).

/Kaw 85/   K. Kawagoe: Modified Dynamic Hashing, in: Navathe (Ed.): Proc. of the ACM SIGMOD 1985 Int. Conf. on Management of Data, 201–213 (1985).

/KC 87/   R. H. Katz/E. Chang: Managing Change in a Computer–Aided Design Database, in Proc. 13th Conf. on Very Large Data Bases, 455–462 (1987).

/KD 92/   U. Keßler/P. Dadam: Evaluation of Complex Queries on Hierarchically Structured Objects by Path Indexes, in Appelrath (Ed.): Proc. Datenbanksysteme in Büro, Technik und Wissenschaft, IFB 270, 218–237 (1992).

/KH 87/   R. King/S. Hudson: Implementing A User Interface as a System of Attributes, in /1. Hen 87/, 143–149.

/KKN 94/   P. Klein/N. Kiesel/M. Nagl/J. Schmidt: Distribution in Business Applications: Some Remarks from Software Architecture Side (in German), in S. Jänichen (Ed.): Proc. Congress VI of Online '94, C 620.01–C 620.29, Velbert: Online (1994).

/KLN 95/   P. Klein/J. Lacour/M. Nagl/V. Schmidt: Restructuring Client Server Applications: An Example from Business Applications (in German), in F. Vogt (Ed.): Proc. Congress VI of Online '95, C.630.01–C.630.25, Velbert: Online Press (1995).

/Klo 83/   J. Kloth: Basic Software for Screen–Handling (in German), Master's Thesis, Univ. of Dortmund (1983).

/Klo 96/   U. Kloock: Transaction Management and Concepts for the Non–Standard Database Management System GRAS (in German), Master's Thesis, RWTH Aachen (1996).

/KM 92/   A. Kemper/G. Moerkotte: Access Support Relations: An Indexing Method for Object Bases, Information Systems 17, 2, 117–145, Pergamon Press Ltd (1992).

/KO 92/   M.I. Kellner/J. Over: Process Modelling, CACM 35, 9, 75–90 (1992).

/KP 88/   G.E. Krasner/S.T. Pope: A cookbook for using the model–view controller user interface paradigm in Smalltalk–80, Journal of Object–Oriented Programming 1, 3, 24–49 (1988).

/KP 91/   G.E. Kaiser/D.E. Perry: Making Progress in Cooperative Transaction Models, Data Engineering 14, 1, 19–23 (1991).

/Kra 96/   C.–A. Krapp: Parameterizing Dynamic Task Nets for Managing Software Processes (in German), Proc. Softwaretechnik '96, Koblenz, 33–40 (1996).

/Kra 97/   C.–A. Krapp: Formal Resource Management in the Software Process, submitted for publication.

/Krü 96/   S. Krüppel: A Resource Model to Support Software Development Processes (in German), Master's Thesis, RWTH Aachen (1996).

685

/KSU 85/   P. Kahold/G. Schlageter/R. Unland/W. Wolkes: A Transaction Model Supporting Complex Applications in Integrated Systems, in Proc. of the ACM SIGMOD Int. Conf. on Managment of Data, Austin, Texas, 388–401 (1985).

/KSW 92a/   N. Kiesel/J. Schwartz/B. Westfechtel: Objects and Process Management for the Integration of Heterogeneous CIM Components, in Proc. GI–Jahrestagung 92, Informatik Aktuell 484–493, Berlin: Springer–Verlag (1992).

/KSW 92b/   N. Kiesel/A. Schürr/B. Westfechtel: Design and Evaluation of GRAS, a Graph–Oriented Database System for Engineering Applications, Techn. Report AIB 92–44, RWTH Aachen (1992).

/KSW 93/   N. Kiesel/A. Schürr/B. Westfechtel: GRAS – A Graph–oriented Data Base System for (Software) Engineering Applications, in Lee et al. (Eds.): Computer–Aided Software Engineering (CASE '93), 272–286, Los Alamitos: IEEE Computer Society Press (1993).

/KSW 95a/   N. Kiesel/A. Schürr/B. Westfechtel: GRAS – A Graph–oriented (Software) Engineering Database System, Information Systems 20, 1, 21–51 (1995).

/KSW 95b/   N. Kiesel/A. Schürr/B. Westfechtel: Functionality and Applications of a Graph–Oriented Database System, in King (Ed.): Proc. ICSE Workshop on Databases and Software Engineering 94, 64–68 (1995).

/Lar 80/   P.A. Larson: Linear hashing with Parital Expansions, in Proc. 6th Int. Conf. on Very Large Databases, 224–232, IEEE Computer Society Press (1980).

/Lar 88/   P.A. Larson: Dynamic Hash Tables, Comm. ACM 31, 4, 446–457, ACM Press (1988).

/LC 86/   T.J. Lehmann/M. Carey: A Study of Index Structures for Main Memory Database Management Systems, in Proc. 12th Int. Conf. on Very Large Databases, 294–303, Los Alamitos: IEEE Computer Society Press (1986).

/LC 93a/   C. Lewerentz/E. Casais: Getting Started with OBST, STONE Project, System Documentation, 168 pp., Karlsruhe (1993).

/LC 93b/   C. Lewerentz/E. Casais: Models and Tools for Object–oriented Software Engineering Environments, STONE Project, Project Monograph, 210 pp., Karlsruhe (1994).

/LCI 92/   M.A. Linton/P.R. Calder/J.A. Interante/S. Tang/J.M. Vlissides: InterViews Reference Manual Version 3.1, Board of Trustees of the Leland Stanford Junior University (1992).

/Lee 86/   G. B. Leeman: A Formal Approach to Undo Operations in Programming Languages, TOPLAS 8, 1, 50–87 (1986).

/LH 88/   L.–C. Liu/E. Horowitz: Object Database Support for a Software Management Environment, in /1. Hen 88/, 85–96.

/Lit 78/   W. Litwin: Virtual Hashing: Dynamically Changing Hashing, in Proc. 4th Conf. on Very Large Databases, 517–523, Los Alamitos: IEEE Computer Society Press (1978).

/Liu 91/   Y. Liu: btc: A Backtracking Procedural Language, Techn. Report 203, University of Queensland, Key Center for Software Technology, Australia (1991).

/LLO 91/   O. Lamb/G. Landis/J. Orenstein et al.: The Objectstore Database System, Comm. ACM 34, 10, 50–63 (1991).

/LS 87/   C. Lewerentz/A. Schürr: A Database System for Software Documents (in German), GI Softwaretechnik–Trends 7–2, 148–163 (Oct. 1987).

/LS 88/   C. Lewerentz/A. Schürr: GRAS – A Management System for Graph–like Documents, in Beeri/ Schmidt/Dayal (Eds.): Proc. 3rd Int. Conf. on Data and Knowledge Bases, 19–31, San Matheo: Morgan–Kaufmann (1988).

/Lüc 94/   B. Lücken: A Configuration Tool for Engineering Applications (in German), Master's Thesis, RWTH Aachen (1994).

/Maf 95/   S. Maffeis: The Electra Object Request Broker, Doct. Diss., University of Zurich (1995).

/May 92/   S. Mayer: Introduction to InterViews (in German), Institut für Informatik, TU Munich (1992).

/MD 89/   D.R. McCarthy/U. Dayal: The Architecture of An Active Database Management System, in: Clifford/ Lindsay/Maier (Eds.): Proc. of the ACM SIGMOD 1989 Int. Conf. on Management of Data, 215–224 (1989).

/Mel 94/   R. Melchiesedech: Materialization of Linear and Graphical Paths in PROGRES (in German), Master's Thesis, RWTH Aachen (1994).

/Met 91/   C. Metzen: Revision Administration in an Integrated Software Development Environment (in German), Master's Thesis, RWTH Aachen (1991).

/Möc 95/   P. Möckel: Distribution Aspects in Integrated Software Development Environments (in German), Master's Thesis, RWTH Aachen (1995).

/MOP 88/   R. Munck/P. Obendorf/E. Ploederer/R. Thall: An Overview of DOD–STD–1838A Star War Standard (proposed), The Common APSE Interface Set, Revision A, in /1. Hen 88/, 235–247.

/MWW 84/   U. Möncke/B. Weisgerber/R. Wilhelm: How to Implement a System for Manipulation of Attributed Trees, in Proc. 8. Fachtagung Programmiersprachen und Programmentwicklung, IFB 77, 112–127 (1984).

/Nes 86/   J. R. Nestor: Toward a Persistent Object Base, in /1. CDW 86/, 372–394.

/Nix 96/   R. Nix: Distribution of a Database Management System: A Workstation/Server–Architecture Illustrated by the Non–Standard DBMS GRAS (in German), Master's Thesis, RWTH Aachen (1996).

/Nol 90/   C. Nolan: IPSE Integration using ATIS – An Object–Oriented View of Tools Integration, Techn. Report, Digital Equipment S.p.A., Varese, Italy (1990).

/NW 94/   M. Nagl/B. Westfechtel: A Universal Component for the Administration in Distributed and Integrated Development Environments, Techn. Report AIB 94–8, RWTH Aachen (1994).

/NZ 92/   M. Nodine/S. Zdonik: Cooperative Transaction Hierarchies, VLDB Journal, VLDB Endowment 1, 1, 41–80 (1992).

/Obe 88/   P. A. Oberndorf: The Common Ada Programming Support Environement (APSE) Interface Set CAIS, in /1. Rid 88/, 742–748.

/OMG 93/   Object Management Group: Object request broker architecture, Techn. Report OMG TC Document 93.7.2 (1993).

/OMG 94/   Object Management Group: Common Object Services Specification, Volume I, OMG Document 94–01–01 (January 1994).

/OMG 95a/   Object Management Group: OMG Business Application Architecture, White Paper, OMG Document 95–04–01 (April 1995).

/OMG 95b/   Object Management Group: The Common Object Request Broker: Architecture and Specification, Rev. 2.0, OMG Document 96–03–04 (July 1995).

/OSF 92a/   Open Software Foundation: Introduction to OSF DCE, Cambridge, USA 1992.

/OSF 92b/   Open Software Foundation: DCE Users Guide and Reference, Cambridge, USA 1992.

/OSF 92c/   Open Software Foundation: DCE Application DevelopmentGuide, Cambridge, USA 1992.

/OSF 92d/   Open Software Foundation: DCE Application Development Reference, Cambridge, USA 1992.

/OSF 92e/   Open Software Foundation: DCE Administration Guide, Cambridge, USA 1992.

/OSF 92f/   Open Software Foundation: DCE Administration Reference, Cambridge, USA 1992.

/OSF 92g/   Open Software Foundation: DCE 1.0 Porting and Testing Guide, Cambridge, USA 1992.

/OSF 92h/   Open Software Foundation: OSF Distributed Computing Environment Rationale, Cambridge, USA 1992.

/Ous 94/   J. Ousterhout: Tcl and the Tk Toolkit, Reading: Addison–Wesley (1994).

/Pfa 85/   G. E. Pfaff (Ed.): User Interface Management Systems, Eurographic Seminars, Berlin: Springer–Verlag (1985).

/PPT 88/   M. Penedo/E. Ploedereder/I. M. Thomas: Object Management Issues for Software Engineering Environments (Workshop Report), in /1. Hen 88/, 226–234.

/PS 85/   M. H. Penedo/E. D. Stuckle: PMDB – A Project Master Data Base for Software Engineering Environments, in Proc. 8th ICSE, 150–157 (1985).

/Pur 94/   J.M. Purtillo: The POLYLITHE software bus, TOPLAS 16, 1, 151–174 (1994).

/Que 92/   R. Quester: obTiOS: A CaX–Framework Service for Building Cuncurrent Engineering Environments, in /1. Web 92/, 32–40.

/Rei 88/   S. P. Reiss: Integration Mechanisms in the FIELD Environment, Techn. Report CS–88–18, Brown University, R. I., USA (October 1988).

/Rei 90a/   St. Reiss: Interacting with the FIELD Environment, Software: Practice and Experience 20, S1, 89–115, New York: John Wiley & Sons (1990).

/Rei 90b/   St.P. Reiss: Connecting Tools Using Message Passing in the Field Environment, IEEE Software 7, 4, 55–66 (1990).

/Rei 96/   W. Reimesch: A Communication System for GRAS (in German), Master's Thesis, RWTH Aachen (1996).

/ROR 92/   M.T. Rose/J. Onions/C.J. Robbins: The ISO Development Environment: User's Manual, Vol. 1–5, Vers. 7.0, Palo Alto (1992).

/Ros 91/   A. Rossow: A Graph Browser for GRAS–Graphs (in German), Master's Thesis, RWTH Aachen (1991).

/Röv 91/   M. Rövenich: An Exchange Format for Complex Objects with Generatable Communication Mechanisms (in German), Master's Thesis, RWTH Aachen (1991).

/Rud 86/   A. Rudmik: Choosing an Environment Data Model, in /1. CDW 86/, 395–404.

/Scha 90/   H. Scharrel: Mechanisms for Supporting Geographically Distributed Software Development Environments (in German), Master's Thesis, RWTH Aachen (1990).

/Schä 85/   W. Schäfer: The User Interface of an integrated Software Development Environment (in German), in Bullinger (Ed.): Software–Ergonomie 85, Bericht German Chapter ACM, Vol. 24, 420–430, Stuttgart: Teubner–Verlag (1985).

/Sche 91/   D. Schefström: ATMOSPHERE Tool Model, ATMOSPHERE–ID: D2.4.1.1.1–doc–1.2–Telesoft–DS, Version 1.2, Telesoft Sweden (1991).

/Schi 92/   A. Schill: Remote Procedure Call: Advanced Concepts and Systems – An Overview (in German), Informatik Spektrum 15, 2, 79–87 and 15, 3, 145–155 (1992).

/Schi 93a/   A. Schill: DCE – The OSF Distributed Computing Environment (in German), Berlin: Springer–Verlag (1993).

/Schi 93b/   B. Schiefer: Supporting Integration and Evolution with Object–Oriented Views, in /2. CL 93/, 129–149.

/SG 86/   R. W. Scheifler/J. Gettys: The X Window System, ACM Trans. Graphics 5, 79–109, (1986).

/SL 90/   A. Sheth/J. Larson: Federated Database Systems for Managing Distributed, Heterogenous and Autonoumous Databases, ACM Computing Surveys 22, 3, 183–236 (1990).

/SMB 88/   L. Schiavoni/M. Manchini/G. Bux/G. Le Saint: A Comprehensive Introduction to the Portable Common Tool Environment, SFINX Consortium, ESPRIT Project 1262 (1299) (March 1988).

/SS 90/   R. Snodgrass/K. Shannon: Fine Grained Data Management to Achieve Evolution Resilience in a Software Development Environment, in /1. Tay 90/, 144–156.

/SS 95/   S. Sachweh/W. Schaefer: Version Management for Tightly Integrated Software Engineering Environments, in M. Verall (Ed.): Proc. 7th Int. Conf. on Software Engineering Environments, 21–31, Los Alamitos: IEEE Computer Society Press (1995).

/ST 81/   J. W. Sullivan/S. W. Tyler (Eds.): Intelligent User Interfaces, New York: ACM Press (1981).

/Sto 92/   M. Stonebraker (Ed.): Proc. of the ACM SIGMOD Int. Conf. on Management of Data 21, 2 (1992).

/SUN 92/   Sunsoft: Designing and writing a ToolTalk procedural protocol, Techn. Report SunSoft (June 1992).

/SUN 93/   Sunsoft, Inc.: The ToolTalk Service: An Inter–Operability Solution, SunSoft Press/Prentice Hall (1993).

/SW 93/   J. Schwartz/B. Westfechtel: Integrated Data Management in a Heterogeneous CIM Environment, in Croisier et al. (Eds.): Proc. Conf. Computers in Design, Manufacturing, and Production, 248–257, Los Alamitos: IEEE Comp. Society Press (1993).

/SW 94/   J. Schwartz/B. Westfechtel: Configuration Control in a Heterogeneous CIM Environment (in German), in Buchmann (Ed.): Proc. STAK'94 (Softwaretechnik in Automatisierung und Kommunikation), 179–197, Berlin: vde–verlag (1994).

/SW 95/   W. Schaefer/S. Wolf: Cooperation Patterns for Process–centered Software Development Environments, in D. Hurley/R. Semmel (Eds.): Proc. 7th Int. Conf. on Software Engineering and Knowledge Engineering, 454–463, Rockville: Knowledge Systems Institute (1995).

/Thi 90/   H. Thimbleby: User Interface Design, New York: ACM Press (1990).

/Tho 88/   I. Thomas: The PCTE Initiative and the Pact project, ACM Software Engineering Notes 13, 4, 52–56 (1988).

/Til 86/   P. Tillmann: Physical Representation of Texts in Structured Editors (in German), Master's Thesis, Univ. of Osnabrück (1986).

/TN 87/   W. Tichy/F. J. Newberry: Knowledge–Based Editors for Directed Graphs, in Nichols/Simpson (Eds.): Proc. 1st ESEC, LNCS 289, 109–118 (1987).

/TN 92/   M.M. Tsangaris/J.F. Naughton: On the Performance of Object Clustering Techniques, in /6. Sto 92/, 144–153.

/TR 85/   A.S. Tanenbaum/R. v.Renesse: Distributed operating systems, ACM Computing Surveys 17, 4, 419–470 (1985).

/TTB 90/   M. Tedjini/I. Thomas/G. Benoliel/F. Gallo/R. Minot: A Query Service for a Software Engineering Database System, in /1. Tay 90/, 238–248.

/UTS 93/   J. Uhl/D. Theobald/B. Schiefer/R. Ranft/W. Zimmer/J. Alt: The object management system of stone – obst release 3.3, Techn. Report FZI.027.2, Forschungszentrum Informatik, available from gate.fzi.de:/pub/OBST, Karlsruhe (1993).

/VB 87/   V. Varadharajan/K. D. Baker: Directed Graph Based Representation of Software System Design, Software Engineering Journal, January, 21–28 (1987).

/Ver 91a/   J. Verrall: The Software Bus – Its Objective: The Mutual Integration of Distributed Software Engineering Tools, in /1. Lon 91/, 415–428.

/Ver 91b/   M. S. Verrall: Unity doesn't imply unification *or* Overcoming Heterogeneity Problems in Distributed Software Engineering Environments, Computer Journal, Special Issue on Distributed Systems 34, 522–533 (December 1991).

/VM 92/   M. S. Verrall/L. Morgan: Tool Integration in CASE Environments: The Software Bus, in 5th Int. Workshop in Computer Aided Software Engineering, Montreal, 46–49 (July 1992).

/WA 87/   D. S. Wile/D. G. Allard: Worlds: an Organizing Structure for Object–Bases, in /1. Hen 87/, 16–26.

/WC 96/   J. Widom/S. Ceri (Eds.): Active Database Systems: Triggers and Rules For Advanced Database Processing, Los Altos: Morgan Kaufmann (1996).

/Wel 88/   R. J. Welke: The CASE Repository: More than another database application, Techn. Report Meta Systems Ltd., Ann Arbor (1988).

/Wel 91/   T. Welsch: Digital's COHESION Environment, Reading: DEC (1991).

/Wes 89/   B. Westfechtel: Extensions of a Graph Storage for Software Documents with Primitives for Undo/ Redo and Revision Control, Techn. Report AIB 89–8, RWTH Aachen (1989).

/Wes 92/   B. Westfechtel: Basic Mechanisms for Data Administration in Structure–oriented Hypertext Systems (in German), Techn. Report AIB 92–2, RWTH Aachen (1992).

/Wes 95/   B. Westfechtel: Engineering Data and Process Integration in the SUKITS Environment, in: Windsor (ed.): Proc. International Conference on Computer Integrated Manufacturing ICCIM 95, 117–124, Singapore: World Scientific (1995).

/Wes 96/   B. Westfechtel: Integrated Product and Process Management for Engineering Design Applications, Integrated Computer–Aided Engineering, Special Issue on Integrated Product and Process Management 3, 1, 20–35 (1996).

/WKL 86/   D. Woelk/W. Kim/W. Luther: An Object–oriented Approach to Multimedia Databases, in Proc. ACM SIGMOD Conf., 311–325 (1986).

/WP 92/   E.L. White/J.M. Purtilo: Integrating the heterogeneous control properties of software modules, in /1. Web 92/, 99–108.

/WS 91/   L. Wall/R.L. Schwartz: Programming Perl, Sebastopol: O'Reilly & Associates (1991).

/WWF 88/   A. L. Wolff/J. C. Wileden/C. D. Fisher/P. L. Tarr: P Graphite: An Experiment in Persistent Typed Object Management, in /1. Hen 88/, 130–142.

/XVT 93/   XVT – Development Solution for C, Continental Graphics, Broomfield, Colorado (1993).

/YHM 88/   N. Yankelovich/B.J. Haan/N.K. Meyrowitz/S.M. Drucker: Intermedia: The Concept and the Construction of a Seamless Information Environment, IEEE Computer, 81–96 (1988).

/YTT 88/   M. Young/R. N. Taylor/D. B. Troup: Software Environment Architectures and User Interface Facilities, in /1. Rid 88/, 697–708.

/Zdo 86/   S. B. Zdonik: Version Management in an Object–Oriented Database, in /1. CDW 86/, 405–422.

/Zoh 92/   S. Zohren: The GRAS–Server: A Client–Server Realization of GRAS (in German), Master's Thesis, RWTH Aachen (1992).

689

7 Notions, Languages, and Methods of Software Engineering

/Agr 86/   W. Agresti (Ed.): New Paradigms for Software Development, Washington: IEEE Comp. Soc. Press (1986).

/Ala 88/   B. Alabiso: Transformation of Data Flow Analysis Models to Object–Oriented Design, in /7. OOPSLA '88/, 335–353.

/Alt 79/   W. Altmann: A New Module Concept for the Design of Reliable Software, in Raulefs (Ed.): Workshop on Reliable Software, 155–166, München: Hanser–Verlag (1979).

/Anu 96/   E. Anuff: Java sourcebook, New York: John Wiley & Sons (1996).

/Arc 81/   J. L. Archibald: The External Structure – Experiences with an Automated Module Interconnection Language, Journal of Systems and Software 2, 2, 147–157 (1981).

/ASM 89/   J.–R. Abrial/S. A. Schuman/B. Meyer: A Specification Language, in McNaughton/McKeag: On the Construction of Programs, Cambridge: Cambridge University Press (1989).

/Bai 89/   S. C. Bailin: An Object–Oriented Requirements Specification Method, Comm. ACM 32, 5, 608–623 (1989).

/Bas 95/   V.R. Basili: The Experience Factory and Its Relationship to Other Quality Approaches, Advances in Computers 41, 65–82 (1995).

/Bat 89/   C. Batini (Ed.): Entity–Relationship–Approach, Amsterdam: North Holland (1989).

/Bau 75/   F. L. Bauer (Ed.): Software Engineering, An Advanced Course, LNCS 30 (1975).

/BB 84/   D. S. Batory/A. P. Buchman: Molecular Objects, Abstract Datatypes, and Data Models: A Framework, in Proc. 10th Int. Conf. Very Large Data Bases, 172–184 (1984).

/BBL 76/   B. W. Boehm/J. R. Brown/M. Lipow: Quantitative Evaluation of Software Quality, in Proc. ICSE, 592–685 (1976).

/BBM 78/   B. W. Boehm/J. R. Brown/G. McLead/M. Lipow/M. Merrit: Characteristics of Software Quality, Amsterdam: North–Holland (1978).

/BDH 89/   M. v.d.Beeck/J. Derissen/P. Hruschka/Th. Janning/M. Nagl: Integrating Structured Analysis and Information Modelling, Techn. Report AIB 89–17, RWTH Aachen (1989).

/Bec 89/   J. Beckers: Discussion of Extensions of an Integrated Requirements Engineering Method (in German), Master's Thesis, RWTH Aachen (1989).

/Bee 93a/   M. v.d.Beeck: Improving Structured Analysis – Achieving Preciseness, Executability, and Real–Time Specification, in Züllighoven/Altmann/Doberkat (Eds.): Requirements Engineering '93: Prototyping, German Chapter of the ACM 41, 227–245, Stuttgart: Teubner–Verlag (1993).

/Bee 93b/   M. v.d.Beeck: Integration of Structured Analysis and Timed Statecharts for Real–Time and Concurrency Specification, in Sommerville/Paul (Eds.): Proc. 4th ESEC, LNCS 717, 313–328 (1993).

/Bee 93c/   M. v.d.Beeck: Enhancing Structured Analysis by Timed Statecharts for Real–Time and Concurrency Specification, in Cosnard/Puigjaner (Eds.): Proc. 5th Int. Conf. on Decentralized and Distributed Systems, IFIP Transactions A–39, 369–381, Amsterdam: North–Holland (1993).

/Bee 93d/   N. Beermann: Development of an Executable Version of Structured Analysis with Time–constraints (in German), Master's Thesis, RWTH Aachen (1993).

/Bee 94a/   M. v.d.Beeck: Method Integration and Abstraction from Detailed Semantics to Improve Software Quality, in Peters/Pohl/Starke (Eds.): Proc. 1st Int. Workshop on Requirements Engineering: Foundation of Software Quality, 102–111, Aachen: Verlag der Augustinus Buchhandlung (1994).

/Bee 94b/   M. v.d.Beeck: A Comparison of Statecharts Variants, in Langmaack/de Roever/Vytopil (Eds.): Proc. 3rd Int. Symposium on Formal Techniques in Real Time and Fault Tolerant Systems, LNCS 863, 128–148 (1994).

/Bee 96/   M. v.d.Beeck: A Control Model for Requirements Specifications (in German), Doct. Diss., RWTH Aachen (1996).

/BEP 87/   E. K. Blum/H. Ehrig/F. Parisi–Presicce: Algebraic Specification of Modules and their Basic Interconnections, Techn. Report, Univ. of Southern California, Los Angeles (1987).

/Ber 90/   L. Berlin: When Objects Collide: Experiences with Reusing Multiple Class Hierarchies, ACM SIGPLAN Notices 25, 10, 181–193 (1990).

/BG 81a/   G. D. Bergland/R. D. Gordon: Software Design Strategies, 2nd ed., New York: Springer–Verlag (1981).

/BG 81b/   R. M. Burstall/J. A. Goguen: An Informal Introduction to Specifications Using Clear, in Boyer/Moore: The Correctness Problem in Computer Science, 185–213, New York: Springer–Verlag (1981).

/BJ 88/   D. Bjørner/C. B. Jones: VDM '87 VDM – A Formal Method at Work, LNCS 252, Berlin: Springer–Verlag (1988).

/BJ 91/   J. Börstler/Th. Janning: Bridging the Gap between Requirements Analysis and Design, Techn. Report AIB 91–16, RWTH Aachen (1991).

/BJK 88/   W. Bruyn/R. Jensen/D. Keskar/P. Ward: ESML: An Extended Systems Modelling Language Based on the Data Flow Diagram, ACM Software Engineering Notes 13, 1, 58–67 (1988).

/Bjo 87/   D. Bjorner: On the Use of Formal Methods in Software Development, in Proc. 9th ICSE, 17–29 (1987).

/BMM 89/   A. Borgida/M. Mylopoulos/J.W. Schmidt/I. Wetzel: Support for Data–intensive Applications: Conceptual Design and Software Development, in Proc. 2nd Int. Workshop Database Programming Languages, Gleneden Beach (USA), Oct. 1989, 258–280, Palo Alto: Morgan Kaufmann (1989).

/Bob 86/   D. G. Bobrow et al: Common Loops: Merging Common Lisp and Object–oriented Programming, in /7. OOPSLA '86/, 17–29.

/Boe 76/   B.W. Boehm: Software Engineering, IEEE Transactions on Computers C–25, 12, 1226–1241 (1976).

/Boe 82/   B. W. Boehm: Software Engineering Economics, Englewood Cliffs: Prentice Hall (1982).

/Boe 86/   B. W. Boehm: A Spiral Model of Software Development and Enhancement, ACM Software Engineering Notes 11, 4, 22–42 (1986).

/Boe 89a/   B. W. Boehm: Software Risk Management, IEEE Comp. Soc. Press (1989).

/Boe 89b/   B. Boehm: Advanced Software Cost Estimating: Featuring the Most Sophisticated Tool Today COCOMO, Seminar Outline, The Higher Silver Video Learning Series No. 2 (1989).

/Boo 87/   G. Booch: Software Components with Ada, Menlo Park: Benjamin Cummings (1987).

/Boo 90/   G. Booch: Object–Oriented Design, Redwood City: Benjamin Cummings (1990).

/Boo 94/   G. Booch: Object–oriented Analysis and Design with Applications, 2nd ed., Menlo Park: Benjamin Cummings (1994).

/Bör 89/   J. Börstler: Reuse and Software Development: Problems, Approaches, and Bibliography (in German), Softwaretechnik–Trends 9, 2, 62–76 (1989).

/Bör 94/   J. Börstler: Programming–in–the–Large in Languages, Tools, and Reuse (in German), Doct. Diss., RWTH Aachen (1994).

/Bro 83/   M. L. Brodie: A Database Abstraction for Semantic Modelling, in /7. Che 83/, 577–602.

/BS 95/   M.L. Brodie/M. Stonebraker: Migrating Legacy Systems, Los Altos: Morgan Kaufmann (1995).

/BST 92/   G. Boloix/P. Sorenson/J. Trembley: Transformations using a meta–system approach to software development, IEE Software Engineering Journal 7, 6, 425–437 (1992).

/BT 95a/   R. Biddle/E. Tempero: Inheritance and Reusability, Techn. Report CS–TR–95/8, Victoria University of Wellington, New Zealand (1995).

/BT 95b/   R. Biddle/E. Tempero: Object–oriented Programming and Reusability, Techn. Report CS–TR–95/6, Victoria University of Wellington, New Zealand (1995).

/Buh 84/   R. J. A. Buhr: System Design with Ada, Englewood Cliffs: Prentice Hall (1984).

/BW 81/   H. Balzert/D. Weber: A Language for System Design (in German), Bericht German Chapter of the ACM 5, 175–200, Stuttgart: Teubner–Verlag (1981).

/BZ 91/   J. Börstler/A. Zündorf: Revisiting extensions to Modula–2 to support reusability, Techn. Report AIB 91–15, RWTH Aachen (1991).

/Cam 89/   J. R. Cameron: JSP & JSD: The Jackson Approach to Software Development, 2nd ed., Washington: IEEE Comp. Soc. Press (1989).

/CB 91/   G. Caldiera/V.R. Basili: Identifying and Qualifying Resable Software Components, Computer 24, 2, 61–70 (1991).

/CFG 91/   J. Cramer/W. Fey/M. Goedicke/M. Große–Rhode: Towards a Formally Based Component Description Languange – A Foundation for Reuse, Structured Programming 2, 12, 91–110, New York: Springer–Verlag (1991).

/Che 76/   P. P. Chen: The Entity–Relationship Model: Towards a Unified View of Data, ACM Transactions on Database Systems 1, 1, 9–36 (1976).

/Che 80/   P. P. Chen (Ed.): Entity Relationship Approach to System Analysis and Design, Amsterdam: North Holland (1980).

/Che 83/   P. P. Chen: Entity Relationship Approach to Information Modelling and Analysis, Amsterdam: North Holland (1983).

/CKM 93/   L. Chung/P. Katalagarianos/M Marakakis/M. Mertikas/J. Mylopoulos/Y. Vassiliou: Mapping Information System Requirements to Design, in /7. Jar 93/, 243–280.

/CKO 92/   B. Curtis/M. I. Kellner/J. Over: Process Modelling, Comm. of the ACM, 35, 9, 75–90 (1992).

/Coo 79/   L. W. Cooprider: The Representation of Families of Software Systems, Ph. D. Thesis, Carnegie–Mellon Univ., Techn. Report CMU–CS–79–116 (1979).

/Cox 86/   B. Cox: Object–oriented Programming – An Evolutionary Approach, Reading: Addison Wesley (1986).

/CP 89/   A. Carle/L. Pollock: Modular Specification of Incremental Program Transformation Systems, in Proc. 11th ICSE, 178–187 (1989).

/DC 83/   A. Dogac/P. P. Chen: Entity–Relationship Model in the ANSI/SPARC Framework, in /7. Che 83/, 357–374.

/DEC 82/   Digital Equipment Corporation: CMS/MMS: Code/Module/Management System Manual, Mainards, Mass. (1982).

/Dec 95/   J. December: Introducing Java, Indianapolis: Howard Sams (1995).

/Der 88/   J. Derissen: Integration of Structured Analysis and Information Modelling (in German), Master's Thesis, RWTH Aachen (1988).

/DeM 78/   T. DeMarco: Structured Analysis and System Specification, New York: Yourdon Press (1978).

/DGL 87/   K. R. Dittrich/W. Gotthard/P. C. Lockemann: Complex Entities for Engineering Applications, in /7. Spa 87/, 421–440.

/DHB 89/   J. Derissen/P. Hruschka/M. v.d.Beeck/Th. Janning/M. Nagl: Integrating Structured Analysis and Information Modelling, Techn. Report AIB 89–17, RWTH Aachen (1989).

/DJN 83/   C. G. Davis/S. Jajodia/P. A. Ng/R. T. Yeh (Eds.): Entity–Relationship–Approach to Software Engineering, Amsterdam: North Holland (1983).

/DK 76/   F. DeRemer/H. H. Kron: Programming–in–the–Large versus Programming–in–the–Small, TOSE 2, 2, 80–86 (1976).

/DKM 96/   P. Devanbu/S. Karstu/W. Melo/W. Thomas: Analytical and Empirical Evaluation of Software Reuse Metrics, in Proc. 18th ICSE, 189–199 (1996).

/Doc 91/   H. Docquier: ISADT – A Revised Structured Analysis Method (in German), Master's Thesis, RWTH Aachen (1991).

/DoD 83/   Department of Defense (USA): Reference Manual for the Ada Programming Language, ANSI–MIL–STD 1815 A (1983).

/Dow 93/   M. Dowson: Software Process Themes and Issues, in Proc. 2nd Int. Conf. Softw. Process, 54–63, Los Alamitos: IEEE Comp. Soc. Press (1993).

/DT 90/   M. Dorfman/R. H. Thayer: Standards, Guidelines, and Examples: System and Software Requirements Engineering, IEEE Comp. Soc. Press (1990).

/Edw 93/   J. Edwards: Real–Time Structured Methods – Systems Analysis, New York: J. Wiley & Sons (1993).

/EE 88/   J. Ebert/G. Engels: Concepts of a Language for Software Architectures (in German), IFB 212, 238–250 (1988).

/EE 94a/   J. Ebert/G. Engels: Design Representation, in J.J. Marciniak (Ed.): Encyclopedia of Software Engineering, 382–394 New York: John Wiley & Sons (1994).

/EE 94b/   J. Ebert/G. Engels: Stuctural and Behavioural Views on OMT–Classes, in E. Bertino/S. Urban (Eds.): Proc. Int. Symp. on Object–Oriented Methodologies and Systems (ISOOMS), Palermo, Italy, September 1994, LNCS 858, 142–157 (1994).

/EFP 86/   H. Ehrig/W. Frey/F. Parisi–Presicce: Distributive Laws of Composition and Union of Module Specifications for Software Systems, in Proc. IFIP WG 2.1, Workshop on Programm Specification and Transformations, 293–312, Amsterdam: North–Holland (1986).

/EG 92/   G. Engels/L.P.J. Groenewegen: Specification of Coordinated Behaviour in the Software Development Process, in J.C. Derniame (Ed.): Proc. 2nd European Workshop on Software Process Technology (EWSPT '92), Trondheim (Norway), LNCS 635, 58–60 (1992).

/EG 93/   G. Engels/L.P.J. Groenewegen: Modular, Visual Specifications of Software Processes, in W. Schäfer (Ed.): Proc. 8th Int. Software Process Workshop (ISPW '93), Wadern (Germany), March 1993, 66–68, Los Alamitos: IEEE Computer Society Press (1993).

/EG 94/   G. Engels/L.P.J. Groenewegen: Specification of Coordinated Behaviour by SOCCA, in B. Warboys (Ed.): Proc. 3rd European Workshop on Software Process Technology (EWSPT '94), Grenoble (France), Feb. 1994, LNCS 772, 128–151 (1994).

/EK 94/   G. Engels/G. Kappel: Object–Oriented System Development: Will the New Approach Solve Old Problems, in K. Duncan/K. Krueger (Eds.): Proc. IFIP Congress '94 – Vol. 3, Hamburg 1994, 434–441, Amsterdam: Elsevier Science B.V. (1994).

/EM 85, 89/ H. Ehrig/B. Mahr: Fundamentals of Algebraic Specification, Band 1, Berlin: Springer–Verlag (1985), Band 2, Berlin: Springer–Verlag (1989).

/EPE 83/   G. Engels/U. Pletat/H.–D. Ehrich: An Operational Semantics for Specifications of Abstract Data Types with Error Handling, Acta Informatica 19, 235–253 (1983).

/EW 86a/   H. Ehrig/H. Weber: Specification of Modular Systems, TOSE 12, 7, 784–789 (1986).

/EW 86b/   H. Ehrig/H. Weber: Programming in the Large with Algebraic Module Specifications, in Kugler (Ed.): Proc. of IFIP '86, 675–684, Amsterdam: Elsevier North–Holland (1986).

/EWD 96/   J. Ebert/A. Winter/P. Dahm/A. Franzke/R. Suttenbach: Graph Based Modelling and Implementation with EER/GRAL, in B. Thalheim (Ed.): 15th Int. Conf. on Conceptual Modelling, to appear.

/FBB 82/   W. R. Franta/H. K. Berg/W. E. Boebert/T. G. Moher: Formal Methods of Program Verification and Specification, Englewood Cliffs: Prentice Hall (1982).

/FFF 89/   J. P. Forrestier/C. Fornarino/P. Franchi–Zanettacci: Ada++ – A Class and Inheritance Extension for Ada, in Alvarez (Ed.): Proc. Ada Europe '89 Conf., Madrid, 16–25, Cambridge: Cambridge University Press (1989).

/FGH 88/   F. Flores/M. Graves/B. Hartfield/T. Winograd: Computer Systems and Design of Organizational Interaction, ACM Trans. Office Inform. Systems 6, 2, 153–172 (1988).

/FH 93/   P. Feiler/W. Humphrey: Software Process Development and Enactment: Concepts and Definitions, in Proc. 2nd Int. Conf. Softw. Process, 28–40, Los Alamitos: IEEE Comp. Soc. Press (1993).

/Fla 91/   M. Flavin: Fundamental Concepts of Information Modelling, New York: Yourdon Press (1981).

/Flo 84/   Ch. Floyd: A Systematic Look at Prototyping, in /3. BKM 84/, 1–18.

/Flo 92/   C. Floyd et al. (Eds.): Software Development and Reality Construction, Berlin: Springer–Verlag (1992).

/For 95/   A. Ford: Spinning the Web, London: Intern. Thomson Publ. (1995).

/FW 83/   P. Freeman/A. J. Wasserman (Eds.): Software Design Techniques, 4th ed., Silver Spring: IEEE Comp. Soc. Press (1983).

/GB 80/   I. Goldstein/D. Bobrow: A Layered Approach to Software Design, XEROX PARC, Techn. Report CSL–80–5 (1980).

/GC 91/   R. Guindon/B. Curtis: Control of cognitive process during software design: What tools are needed?, in Proc. of CHI '88 Conf: Human Factors in Computer Systems, 263–269, New York: ACM Press (1991).

/GE 95/   L. Groenewegen/G. Engels: Coordination by Behavioural Views and Communication Patterns, in W. Schäfer (Ed.): Proc. 4th European Workshop on Software Process Technology (EWSPT '95), Noordwijkerhout (The Netherlands), April 1995, LNCS 913, 180–192 (1995).

/GF 94/   O. Gotel/A. Finkelstein: An Analysis of the Requirements Traceability Problem, in Proc. 1st Int. Conf. on Requirements Engineering, Colorado Springs, 94–102, Los Alamitos: IEEE Computer Society press (1994).

/GG 89/   S.J. Garland/J.V. Guttag: An Overview of LP, The Larch Prover, in Proc. 3rd Int. Conf. Rewriting Techniques and Applications, LNCS 355, 137–151 (1989).

/GHM 90/   J.V. Guttag/J.J. Horning/A. Modet: Report on the Larch Shared Language, Version 2.3, Techn. Report SRC 58 (1990).

/GHW 85/   J. V. Guttag/J. J. Horning/J. M. Wing: The Larch Family of Specification Languages, IEEE Software 2, 5 (1985).

/GJ 82/   C. Ghezzi/M. Jazayeri: Programming Language Concepts, New York: Wiley (1982).

/GJH 93/   J.V. Guttag/J. Janies/J. Horming: LARCH – Languages and Tools for Formal Specification, New York: Springer–Verlag (1993).

/GM 86a/   N. Gehani/A. McGettrick (Eds.): Software Specification Techniques, Reading: Addison Wesley (1986).

/GM 86b/   J. A. Goguen/J. Messeguer: Extensions and Foundations of Object–oriented Programming, SIGPLAN Notices 21, 10, 153–162 (1986).

/Gra 95/   L.S. Graham: The HTML sourcebook: a complete guide to HTML, New York: Wiley (1995).

/GS 79/   C. Gane/T. Sarson: Structured Systems Analysis: Tools & Techniques, New York: Improved Systems Technologies (1979).

/GS 90/   P.G. Garg/W. Scacci: A Hypertext System to Manage Software Life–Cycle Documents, IEEE Software, 90–98 (1990).

/Gut 76/   J. Guttag: Abstract Data Types and the Development of Data Structures, in Conf. on Data, Salt Lake City, 1976, repr. Comm. ACM 20, 6, 396–404 (1977).

/Haa 94/   V. Haase et al.: Bootstrap – Fine–Tuning Process Assessment, IEEE Software 11, 7, 25–35 (1994).

/Hal 88a/   M. Hallmann: An Operational Requirements Description Model for Open Systems, in Proc. 10th ICSE, 286–295 (1988).

/Hal 88b/   M. Hallmann: Incorporating Transactions in a Requirements Engineering Method, in Proc. COMPSAC 88, 121–126 (1988).

/Har 87/   D. Harel: Statecharts: A Visual Formalism for Complex Systems, Sci. Comp. Prog. 8, 231–274 (1987).

/Har 90/   D. Harel et al.: STATEMATE: A Working Environment for the Development of Reactive Systems, TOSE 16, 4, 403–414 (1990).

/HB 95/   K. Holzblatt/H. R. Beyer (Eds.): Requirements Gathering: The Human Factor, Special Issue, Comm. of the ACM 38, 5 (1995).

/HCJ 92/   M. Hallmann/S. Coors/Th. Janning: SA/IM – HOOD Integration, in: Method Integration Handbook, 59–84, New York: John Wiley (1992).

/HGR 88/   C. Huizing/R. Gerth/W. P. de Roever: Modelling Statecharts Behavior in a Fully Abstract Way, in Dauchet/Nivat: Proc. CAAP '88, LNCS 299, 271–294 (1988).

/HH 89/   R. G. Herrtwich/G. Hommel: Cooperation and Competition: Concurrent, Distributed, and Realtime-dependent Program Systems (in German), Berlin: Springer–Verlag (1989).

/Hil 83/   P. Hilfinger: Abstraction Mechanisms and Language Design, Cambridge: MIT Press (1983).

/Hoa 90/   C. A. R. Hoare (Ed.): Proceedings of the International Conference on VDM and Z, LNCS 428, Berlin: Springer–Verlag (1990).

/HOO 89/   HOOD Working Group: HOOD Reference Manual, European Space Agency WME 89–173/JB (1989).

/HP 87/   D. J. Hatley/I. A. Pirbhai: Strategies for Real–Time Systems, New York: Dorset House (1987).

/HP 80/   A. N. Habermann/D. E. Perry: Well–formed System Compositions, Tech. Rep. CMU–CS–80–117, Carnegie–Mellon Univ. (1984).

/Hru 88/   P. Hruschka: New Approaches of Method Representation and Model Knowledge in Business Decision Support Systems (in German), Angewandte Informatik 4, 158–168 (1988).

/Hru 94/   P. Hruschka: A Process for System Development, in Conf. on Systems Engineering of Computer–Based Systems, 111–115, Stockholm (1994).

/HSD 90/   M. Heitz/I. Sneed/J. Derissen/J.–F. Muller: HOOD, a method to support RT&E system design, in Proc. Toulouse '90: Software Engineering & its Applications, Toulouse, France, 917–932, EC2, Nanterre (1990).

/HSS 96/   A.van Hoff, S/Shaio/O. Starbuck: Hooked on Jave, Reading, MA: Addison Wesley (1996).

/Hum 89/   W.S. Humphrey: Managing the Software Process, Reading: Addison Wesley (1989).

/IEE 88/   Tutorials on object–oriented Computing, Vol. 1, 2, IEEE Comp. Soc. Press (1988).

/IEE 95/   IEEE Software: Special Issue on Legacy Systems (January 1995).

/ISO 9000–3/   International Organization for Standardization: ISO 9000 – Quality Management and Quality Assurance Standards, Part 3: Guidelines for the Application of ISO 9001 to the Development, Supply, and Maintenance of Software (1991).

/Jac 83/   M. Jackson: System Development, Englewood Cliffs: Prentice Hall (1983).

/Jan 92/   Th. Janning: Requirements Engineering and Programming–in–the–Large: Integration of Languages and Tools (in German), Doct. Diss., RWTH Aachen, Wiesbaden: Deutscher Universitätsverlag (1992).

/Jar 93/   M. Jarke (Ed.): Database Application Engineering with DAIDA, Esprit Research Reports, Berlin: Springer–Verlag (1993).

/JL 90/   Th. Janning/M. Lefering: A Transformation from Requirements Engineering into Design – The Method and the Tool, in Proc. Toulouse '90: Software Eng. & its Appl., 223–238, EC2 (1990).

/JLM 88/   F. Jahanian/R. Lee/A. K. Mok: Semantics of Modcchart in Real Time Logic, in Proc. 21st Hawaii Int. Conf. Syst. Sci., 479–489 (1988).

/JM 96/   J.R. Jackson/A.L. McClellan: Java by example, Upper SaddleRiver, NY: Prentice Hall (1996).

/Joh 88/   W.L. Johnson: Deriving Specifications from Requirements, in Proc. 10th Int. Conf. on Software Engineering, 428–438, Singapore (1988).

/Jon 86a/   C. B. Jones: Systematic Software Development Using VDM, Englewood Cliffs: Prentice Hall (1986).

/Jon 86b/   T. C. Jones: Programming Productivity, New York: McGraw–Hill (1986).

/Jon 91/   K.J. Jones: LM3 – A Larch Interface Language for Modula–3, in /7. GJH 93/, 102–120.

/Jun 95/   G. Junkermann: A Dedicated Process Design Language based on EER–models, Statecharts and Tables, in D. Hurley/R. Semmel (Eds.): Proc. 7th Int. Conf. on Software Engineering and Knowledge Engineering, 487–496, Rockville: Knowledge Systems Institute (1995).

/Kar 87/   J. Karimi: An Automated Software Design Methodology Using CAPO, Journal of Management Information Systems 3, 3 (1987).

/KF 90/   M.I. Kellner/P.H. Feiler: Software Process Modeling Example Problem, in Proc. 6th Int. Software Process Workshop, 19–30, Los Alamitos: IEEE Comp. Soc. Press (1990).

/KG 87a/   G. E. Kaiser/D. Garlan: MELDing Data Flow and Object–Oriented Programming, in /7. OOPSLA '87/, 254–267.

/KG 87b/   G. E. Kaiser/D. Garlan: Melding Software Systems from Reusable Building Blocks, IEEE Software 4, 4, 17–24 (1987).

/Kla 83/   H. A. Klaeren: Algebraic Specification – An Introduction (in German), Berlin: Springer–Verlag (1986).

/KS 82/   R. Kling/W. Scacci: The Web of Computing: Computing Technology as Social Organization, in Yovits (Ed.): Advances in Computers, Vol. 21, 1–90, New York: Academic Press (1982).

/LB 85/   M. M. Lehmann/L. A. Belady: Program Evolution, London: Academic Press (1985).

/LC 88/   P. Loucopoulos/R. Champion: Knowledge–Based Approach to Requirements Engineering Using Method and Domain Knowledge, Knowledge–Based Systems 1, 3 (1988).

/LG 86/   B. Liskow/J. Guttag: Abstraction and Specification in Program Development, Cambridge: MIT Press (1986).

/LH 85/   D. Luckham/F.W.v. Henke: An Overview of Anna, a Specification Language of Ada, IEEE Software, 9–22 (1985).

/LH 89/   M. Lubars/M. Harandi: Addressing Software Reuse through Knowledge–based Design, in T. Biggerstaff/A. Perlis (Eds.): Software Reusability, Vol. II: Applications and Experience, 345–377, New York: ACM–Press/Addison–Wesley (1989).

/LHK 91/   J.A. Lewis/S.M. Henry/D.G. Kafura/R.S. Schulman: An Empirical Study of the Object–Oriented Paradigm and Software Reuse, in /7. OOPSLA/, 184–196 (1991).

/LL 95/   C. Lewerentz/T. Lindner: Case Study 'Production Cell' – A Comparative Study in Formal Specification and Verification, in M. Broy/S. Jähnichen (Eds.): KORSO: Methods, Languages, and Tools for the Construction of Correct Software – Final Report, LNCS 1009 (1995).

/LLR 95/   C. Lewerentz/T. Lindner/A. Rüping, E. Sekerinski: On Object–oriented Design and Verification, in M. Broy/S. Jähnichen (Eds.): KORSO: Methods, Languages, and Tools for the Construction of Correct Software – Final Report, LNCS 1009 (1995).

/LS 79/   H. C. Lauer/E. H. Satherswaite: The Impact of Mesa on System Design, in Proc. 4th ICSE, 174–182 (1979).

/LZ 74/   B. H. Liskov/S. Zilles: Programming with Abstract Data Types, SIGPLAN Notices 9, 4, 50–59 (1974).

/LZ 75a/   B. H. Liskov/S. Zilles: Specification Techniques for Data Abstraction, ACM SIGPLAN Notices, 10, 6, 72–87 (1975).

/LZ 75b/   B. Liskov/S. Zilles: Specification Techniques for Data Abstractions, in Int. Conf. on Reliable Software, Los Angeles, 72–87, New York: IEEE (1975).

/Mac 83/   B. MacLennon: Principles of Programming Languages, New York: Holt, Rinehart and Winston (1983).

/Mey 85/   B. Meyer: On Formalisms in Specifications, IEEE Software 2, 1, 6–26 (1985).

/Mey 88a/ B. Meyer: Object–oriented Software Construction, New York: Prentice Hall (1988).

/Mey 88b/ B. Meyer: Eiffel – A Language and Environment for Software Engineering, Journal of Systems and Software 8, 199 –246 (1988).

/Mit 88/   B. Mitschang: Towards a Unified View of Design Data and Knowledge Representation, in Kerschberg (Ed.): Proc. 2nd Int. Conf. Expert Database Systems, 133–160, Redwood City: The Benjamin/Cummings Publishing Company (1988).

/MM 88a/   J. Martin/C. McClure: Structured Techniques, 2nd ed., Englewood Cliffs: Prentice Hall (1988).

/MM 88b/   D. Marca/C. L. McGowan: SADT – Structured Analysis and Design Technique, New York: McGraw Hill (1988).

/MP 84/   S. M. McMenamin/J. F. Palmer: Essential Systems Analysis, New York: Yourdon Press (1984).

/MMS 79/   J. G. Mitchell/W. Mayburg/R. Sweet: Mesa Language Manual, Xerox PARC, Techn. Report CSL–79–3 (1979).

/Mül 86/   A. H. Müller: Rigi – A Model for Software System Construction, Integration, and Evolution based on Module Interface Specifications, Doct. Diss., Rice Univ., COMP TR 86–36, Houston TX (1986).

/Nag 82/   M. Nagl: Introduction to the Programming Language Ada (in German), Chapter 4, 1st ed., Braunschweig: Vieweg–Verlag (1982).

/Nag 90/   M. Nagl: Software Engineering: Methodological Programming–in–the–Large (in German), Berlin: Springer–Verlag (1990).

/Nag 91/   M. Nagl: The Importance of Software Architecture Modelling, in /1. EW 91/, 211–232.

/Nag 92/   M. Nagl: Ada – Introduction to the Software Engineering Programming Language (in German), 4th ed., Braunschweig: Vieweg–Verlag (1992).

/Nau 96/   P. Naughton: Java Handbook, Berkeley: McGraw–Hill (1996).

/Nel 91/   G. Nelson: Systems Programming with Modula–3, Englewood Cliffs : Prentice Hall (1991).

/Nor 87/   K. Normark: Transformations and Abstract Presentations in a Language Development Environment, Doct. Diss., Univ. of Aarhus (1987).

/NR 68/   T. Naur/B. Randell (Eds.): Software Engineering, Report on a Conference, Garmisch, 1968, Brussels: NATO Scientific Affairs Division (1968).

/OOPSLA/   Proceedings Conf. on Object–oriented Programming Systems, Languages and Applications, OOPSLA '86: SIGPLAN Notices 21, 11 (1986), OOPSLA '87: SIGPLAN Notices 22, 12 (1987), OOPSLA '88: SIGPLAN Notices 23, 11 (1988), OOPSLA '89: SIGPLAN Notices 24,10 (1989), OOPSLA '90: SIGPLAN Notices 25, 10 (1990), OOPSLA '91: SIGPLAN Notices 26, 11 (1991),

OOPSLA '92: SIGPLAN Notices 27,10 (1992), OOPSLA '93: ACM Press (1993), OOPSLA '94: SIGPLAN Notices 29, 10 (1994), OOPSLA '95, SIGPLAN Notices 30, 10 (1995).

/Pag 88/   M. Page–Jones: A Practical Guide To Structured Systems Design, 2nd ed., New York: Yourdon Press (1988).

/Par 72/   D. L. Parnas: On the Criteria To Be Used in Decomposing Systems into Modules, Comm. ACM 15, 12, 1053–1058 (1972).

/Par 78/   D. L. Parnas: Designing Software for Ease of Extension and Contraction, in Proc. 3rd ICSE, 264–277 (1978).

/Par 91/   H. Partsch: Requirements Engineering, Braunschweig: Oldenbourg (1991).

/Pau 93/   M.C. Paulk: Comparing ISO 9001 and the Capability Maturity Model for Software, Software Quality Journal 2, 4, 245–256 (1993).

/PCC 93/   M.C. Paulk/B. Curtis/M.B. Chrissis/C.V. Weber: Capability Maturity Model, Version 1.1, IEEE Software 10, 4, 18–27 (1993).

/PCW 85/   D. L. Parnas/P. C. Clements/D. M. Weiss: The Modular Structure of Complex Systems, TOSE 11, 3, 259–266 (1985).

/PDJ 94/   K. Pohl/R. Dömges/M. Jarke: Decission Oriented Process Modelling, in Proc. Int. Software Process Workshop, IEEE Computer Society Press, 124–128 (1994).

/Per 87/   D. E. Perry: Software Interconnection Models, in Proc. 9th ICSE, 61–69 (1987).

/PF 87/   R. Prieto–Dfaz/P. Freeman: Classifying Software for Reusability, IEEE Software 4, 1, 6–16 (1987).

/PHL 93/   I. Pyle/P. Hruschka/M. Lissandre/K. Jackson: Real–Time Systems – Investigating Industrial Practice, New York: Wiley (1993).

/PN 86/   R. Prieto–Diaz/J. M. Neighbor: Module Interconnection Languages, Journal of Systems and Software 6, 307–334 (1986).

/Pri 91/   R. Prieto–Dfaz: Implementing Faceted Classification for Software Reuse, Comm. ACM 34, 5, 88–97 (1991).

/PS 75/   D. L. Parnas/D. T. Siewiorek: Use of the Concept of Transparency in the Design of Hierarchically Structured Systems, Comm. ACM 18, 7, 401–408 (1975).

/PS 92/   B. Peuschel/W. Schäfer: Concepts and Implementation of a Rule–Based Process Engine, in Proc. 14th ICSE, 262–279 (1992).

/Raa 91/   J. Raasch: System Development with Structured Methods (in German), München: Hanser (1991).

/Ram 84/   C. V. Ramamourthy et al.: Software Engineering – Problems and Perspectives, IEEE Computer 17, 10, 191–209 (1984).

/RBP 91/   J. Rumbaugh/M. Blaha/W. Premerlani/ F. Eddy/W. Lorensen: Object–Oriented Modeling and Design, Englewoods Cliffs: Prentice Hall (1991).

/RE 93/   B. Ramesh/M. Edwards: Issues in the Development of a Requirements Traceability Model, in Proc. 1st Int. Symp. on Requirements Engineering, San Diego, 256–259, Los Alamitos: IEEE Computer Society Press (1993).

/Rit 95/   T. Ritchey: Programming with Java!, Beta 2.0, Indianapolis: New Riders (1995).

/Rob 92/   P.J. Robinson: Hierarchical Object–oriented Design, Englewood Cliffs: Prentice Hall (1992).

/Rom 85/   G. C. Roman: A Taxonomy of Current Issues in Requirements Engineering, IEEE Computer 18, 4, 14–22 (1985).

/Rom 90/   H.D. Rombach: Framework for Assessing Process Representations, in Proc. 6th Int. Software Process Workshop, 175–184, Los Alamitos: IEEE Comp. Soc. Press (1990).

/Ros 78/   D. T. Ross: Structured Analysis (SA): A Language for Communicating Ideas, in Gries (Ed.): Programming Methodology, 388–421, New York: Springer–Verlag (1978).

/Ros 85/   D. T. Ross: Applications and Extensions of SADT, IEEE Computer 18, 4, 25–34 (1985).

/RP 92/   C. Rolland/C. Proix: A Natural Language Approach for Requirements Engineering, in Proc. 4th Int. Conf. on Advanced System Engineering, LNCS 593 (1992).

/RS 77/   D.T. Ross/K.E. Schoman, JR.: Structured Analysis for Requirements Definition, TOSE 3, 1, 6–15 (1977).

/SB 90/   G. Salton/C. Buckley: Improving Retrieval Performance by Relevance Feedback, Journal of the American Society for Information Science 41, 4, 288–297 (1990).

/SB 92/   G. Starke/M. v.d.Beeck: SA/CM/IM for Process Modelling, in Derniame (Ed.): Proc. 2nd European Workshop on Software Process Technology, LNCS 635, 18–20 (1992).

/SC 88/   R. Simonian/M. Crone: InnovAda: True Object–oriented Programming in Ada, Journal of Object–oriented Programming 1, 4 (1988).

/Sca 84/   W. Scacchi: Managing Software Engineering Projects: A Social Analysis, IEEE Transactions on Software Engineering 10, 1, 49–59 (1984).

/Sha 84/   M. Shaw: Abstraction Techniques in Modern Programming Languages, IEEE Software 1, 4 (1984).

/Sha 86/   M. Shaw: Beyond Programming in the Large: The Next Challenges for Software Engineering, in /1. CDW 86/, 519–535.

/Shu 91/   K. Shumate: Structured Analysis and Object–Oriented Design are Compatible, ACM SIGADA Ada Letters XI, 4, 78–90 (1990).

/SI 90/   P.D. Sully/D.C. Ince: The Synthesis of Object–Oriented Designs from the Products of Structured Analysis, in P. Hall (Ed.): Proc. of Software Engineering '90, Brighton, 405–432, Cambridge University Press (1990).

/SJ 91/   S. C. Solsi/E. L. Jones: Simple Yet Complete Heuristics for Transforming Data Flow Diagrams into Booch Style Diagrams, ACM Ada Letters 11, 2, 115–127 (1991).

/SM 87/   I. Sommerville/R. Morrison: Software Development with Ada, Reading: Addison Wesley (1987).

/Som 93/   I. Sommerville et al.: Integrating Ethnography into the Requirements Engineering Process, Proc. 1st Int. Symp. on Requirements Eng., 165–173, IEEE Computer Society Press (1993).

/Spa 87/   S. Spaccapidra (Ed.): Entity Relationship Approach, Amsterdam: North Holland (1987).

/Spi 90/   J. M. Spivey: An introduction to Z and formal specifications, Software Engineering Journal 4, 1, 40–50 (1990).

/SS 77a/   J. M. Smith/D. C. P. Smith: Database Abstractions: Integration and Generalization, ACM Transactions on Database Systems 2, 2, 105–133 (1977).

/SS 77b/   J. M. Smith/D. C. P. Smith: Database Abstractions: Aggregation, Comm. ACM 20, 6, 405–413 (1977).

/SS 87/   E. Seidewitz/M. Stark: Towards a General Object–Oriented Software Development Methodology, ACM Ada Letters 7, 4, 54–67 (1987).

/SSW 80/   P. Scheuermann/G. Schiffner/H. Weber: Abstraction Capabilities and Invariant Properties Modelling within the Entity–Relationship Approach, in /7. Che 80/, 121–140.

/SSW 92/   T. Shepard/S. Sibbald/C. Wortley: A Visual Software Process Language, in /1. NF 92/, 37–44.

/ST 92/   C. Shekaran/J. Tremlett: Reasoning about Integration Issues during Requirements Definition: A Knowledge–Based Approach, in Proc. 2nd Int. Conf. on System Integration, Morristown (USA), 229–239, Los Alamitos: IEEE Computer Society Press (1992).

/Str 86/   B. Stroustrup: The C++ Programming Language, Reading: Addison–Wesley (1986).

/SUR 89/   ACM Computing Surveys (Guest Editor P. Wegner): Special Issue on Programming Language Paradigms 21, 3, 252–510 (1989).

/SUW 88/   G. Schlageter/R. Unland/W. Wilkes/R. Zieschang/G. Maul/M. Nagl/R. Meyer: OOPS – An object–oriented Programming System with Integrated File Management Component, in Carlis (Ed.): Proc. 4th Int. Conf. on Data Engineering, 118–125, IEEE Comp. Soc. Press (1988).

/SW 87/   B. Shriver/P. Wegner: Research directions in Object–oriented Programming, Computer Science Series, Cambridge: MIT Press (1987).

/TH 77/   D. Teichroew/E. A. Hershey: PSL/PSA: A Computer–aided Technique for Structured Documentation and Analysis of Information Processing Systems, TOSE 3, 1, 41–48 (1977).

/Tra 90/   W. Tracz: Where does reuse start?, ACM SIGSOFT Software Engineering Notes 15, 21, 42–46 (1990).

/Tra 95/   W. Tracz: Confessions of a Used Program Salesman: Institutionalizing Software Reuse, Reading, MA: Addison Wesley (1995).

/Tuc 85/   A. Tucker: Programming Languages, New York: McGraw–Hill (1985).

/VJT 92/   I. Vessey/S. L. Jarvenpaa/N. Tractinsky: Evaluation of Vendor Products: CASE Tools as Methodology Companions, in /1. NF 92/, 90–105.

/VMK 90/   Y. Vassiliou/M. Marakakis/P. Katalagarianos/L. Chung/M. Mertikas/J. Mylopoulos: IRIS – A Mapping Assistant for Generating Designs from Requirements, in Proc. of the CAiSE '90, LNCS 436, 307–338 (1990).

/W3C/   World Wide Web Consortium (W3C), URL: http://www.w3c.org/pub/WWW/.

/War 89/   P. T. Ward: How to Integrate Object Orientation with Structured Analysis and Design, IEEE Software 6, 2, 74–82 (1989).

/WB 89/   M. Wirsing/J. A. Bergstra (Eds.): Algebraic Methods: Theory, Tools, and Applications, LNCS 394 (1989).

/Web 83/   N. W. Webre: An Extended Entity–Relationship Model and Its Use on a Defense Project, in /7. Che 83/, 173–193.

/Web 91/   H. Weber: The Integration of Reusable Software Components, Journal of Systems Integration 1, 1, 55–79 (1991).

/Weg 87/   P. Wegner: The object–oriented Classification Paradigm, in /7. WS 87/, 479–550.

/Wel 89/   R. J. Welke: Meta systems on meta models, CASE Outlook 4, 35–45 (1989).

/Wir 88/   N. Wirth: Programming in Modula–2, 4th ed., Berlin: Springer–Verlag (1988).

/WHO 91/   G. M. Wijers/A. H. M. ter Hofstede/N. E. v.Oosterom: Representation of Information Modelling Knowledge, in Tahvanainen/Lyytinen: Proc. 2nd Workshop on The Next Generation CASE Tools, Techn. Report 1, Department of Comp. Sci. and Inf.Syst., Univ. of Jyväskylä, Finnland, 159–219 (1991).

/WM 85/   P. T. Ward/S. J. Mellor: Structured Development for Real–Time Systems, Vol. 1, 2, 3, New York: Yourdon Press (1985).

/Woo 88/   M. Woodman: Yourdon dataflow diagrams: A tool for disciplined requirements analysis, Inf. and Software Technology 30, 9, 515–533 (1988).

/WS 87/   P. Wegner/B. Shriver: Research Directions in Object–oriented Programming, Cambridge: MIT Press (1987).

/YC 78/   E. Yourdon/L. Constantine: Structured Design, New York: Yourdon Press (1978).

/YC 79/   E. Yourdon/L. Constantine: Structured Design, Englewood Cliffs: Prentice Hall (1979).

/You 89/   E. Yourdon: Modern Structured Analysis, New York: Yourdon Press (1989).

/Zav 82/   P. Zave: An operational approach to requirements specification for embedded systems, IEEE Transactions on Software Engineering 8, 3, 250–269 (1982).

/Zel 79/   M. Zelkowitz et al.: Principles of Software Engineering and Design, Englewood Cliffs: Prentice Hall (1979).

/Zil 75/   S. N. Zilles: Data Algebra: A Specification Technique for Data Structures, Doct. Diss., Project MAC, MIT (1975).

8 'Historical' Papers Important for this Book

/AHK 79/   B. Austermühl/W. Henhapl/H. H. Kron/R. Lutze: The Generation of Interactive Program Development Environments (in German), Notizen zum Interaktiven Programmieren 2 (1979).

/Alt 78/   W. Altmann: Description of Program Modules for the Design of Reliable Software, Doct. Diss., Univ. of Erlangen, Arbeitsberichte IMMD 11–16 (1978).

/BBN 77/   W. Brendel/H. Bunke/M. Nagl: Syntax–directed Programming and Incremental Compilation, IFB 10, 57–74 (1977).

/BG 73/   M. Berthaud/M. Griffiths: Incremental Compilation and Conversational Interpretation, Ann. Rev. Autom. Programming 7, 2, 95–114 (1973).

/BNW 78/   W. Brendel/M. Nagl/D. Weber: Implementation of Sequential and Parallel Graph Rewriting Systems, in Mühlbacher (Ed.): Proc. Workshop Graphtheoretic Concepts in Computer Science, Applied Computer Science 8, 79–106, München: Hanser–Verlag (1978).

/Bre 76/   W. Brendel: Implementation of Graph Grammars (in German), Techn. Report IMMD 9, 1, 126–127, Univ. of Erlangen (1976).

/Bre 77/   W. Brendel: Generation of Machine Code in Incremental Compilers (in German), Techn. Report IMMD 10, 8, 24–120, Univ. of Erlangen (1977).

/Bun 74/   H. Bunke: Description of a Syntax–directed Incremental Compiler by Graph Grammars, Master's Thesis, Univ. of Erlangen, TR IMMD 7,7 (1974).

/DFS 75/   E. Denert/R. Franck/W. Streng: PLAN2D – Towards a Two–dimensional Programming Language, LNCS 26, 202–213 (1975).

/Dij 75/   E.W. Dijkstra: Guarded Commands, Nondeterminacy, and Formal Derivation of Programs, Comm. ACM 18, 8, 453–457 (1975).

/EC 72/   J. Earley/P. Caizergues: A Method for Incrementally Compiling Languages with Nested Statement Structure, Comm. ACM 15, 12, 1040–1044 (1972).

/EW 74/   J. Encarnacao/D. Weck: An Implementation of DATAS (in German), Techn. Report A–74–1, Institut für Angewandte Mathematik und Informatik, Universität des Saarlandes (1974).

/Gal 83/   R. Gall: Formal Description of Incremental Programming–in–the–Large by Graph Grammars (in German), Doct. Diss., Univ. of Erlangen, Techn. Report IMMD 16, 1 (1983).

/Gal 78/   R. Gall: Restructuring the Associative Data Storage DATAS on a 32 Bit machine (in German), Master's Thesis, Univ. of Erlangen (1978).

/GJ 76/   E. Grötsch/B. Jahn: Graphersetzungssysteme: Zwei Beiträge zu Theorie und Implementierung, Techn. Rep. IMMD 9–6, University of Erlangen (1976).

/Göt 77/   H. Göttler: Two–Level Graph Manipulation Systems for the Semantics of Programming Languages (in German), Doct. Diss., Univ. of Erlangen, Techn. Report IMMD 10, 12 (1977).

/Hof 74/   H. J. Hoffmann: Programming by selection, in Proc. 1973 Int. Comp. Symp., 59–66, Amsterdam: North–Holland (1974).

/Kah 79/   M. Kahrs: Inplementation of an Interactive Programming System, in Proc. 1979 SIGPLAN Symp. on Compiler Construction, SIGPLAN Notices 14, 8, 76–82 (1979).

/Kar 80/   W. Karl: Implementation of an Associative Storage using Microprogramming (in German), Master's Thesis, Univ. of Erlangen (1980).

/Kat 69/   H. Katzan: Batch, conversational, and incremental compilers, in AFIPS Proc. 1969 SJCC, Vol. 34, 47–56 (1969).

/Man 74/   Z. Manna: Mathematical Theory of Computation, New York: McGraw–Hill (1974).

/Nag 76/   M. Nagl: Graph Rewriting Systems and Their Application to Biology, Lecture Notes in Biomathematics 11, 135–156, Berlin: Springer–Verlag (1976).

/Nag 80a/   M. Nagl: An Incremental Compiler as Component of a System for Software Development, IFB 25, 29–44 (1980).

/Nag 80b/   M. Nagl: GRAPL – A Programming Language for Handling Dynamic Problems on Graphs, in Pape (Ed.): Discrete Structures and Algorithms, 25–45, München: Hanser–Verlag (1980).

/Nag 81a/   M. Nagl: Application of Graph Rewriting to Optimization and Parallelization of Programs, Computing Suppl. 3, 105–124 (1981).

/Nag 81b/   M. Nagl: Graph Rewriting and Automatic, Machine–independent Program Optimization, in H. Noltemeier (Ed.): Proc. WG '80 Int. Workshop on Graphtheoretic Concepts in Computer Science, LNCS 100, 55–69 (1981).

/NZ 79/   M. Nagl/H. Zischler: A Dialog System for the Graphical Representation of Graphs, Proc. Int. Workshop on Graphtheoretic Concepts in Computer Science, Applied Computer Science 13, 325–339, München: Hanser–Verlag (1979).

/PR 69/   J. L. Pfaltz/A. Rosenfeld: Web Grammars, in Proc. Int. Joint Conf. Art. Intelligence, Washington, 609–619 (1969).

/Ris 70/   W. J. Rishel: Incremental Compilers, Datamation 16, 1, 129–136 (1970).

/Schm 72/   H. A. Schmid: A user oriented and efficient incremental compiler, in Proc. Int. Comp. Symp. Venice, 259–269 (1972).

/Schn 70/   H. J. Schneider: CHOMSKY – Systems for Partial Orders (in German), Techn. Report IMMD 3, 3, Univ. of Erlangen (1970).

/Schn 75/   H. J. Schneider: Syntax–directed description of incremental compilers, LNCS 26, 192–201 (1975).

/Schn 76/   H.J. Schneider: Conceptual Database Descriptions using Graph Grammars, in /5. Nol 76/, 77–98.

/Web 78/   D. Weber: Data Graphs and their Transformations: A Concept for the Specification of Data Types (in German), Doct. Diss., Univ. of Erlangen, Techn. Report IMMD 11, 8 (1978).

/Wei 80/   R. Weiß: Implementation of an Associative Storage using B–trees (in German), Master's Thesis, Univ. of Erlangen (1980).

9 Other Literature

/ACM 87/ The Full Computing Reviews Classification System, Computing Reviews (January 1987).

/ASU 86/ A. Aho/R. Sethi/J. Ullman: Data Structures and Algorithms, Reading: Addison Wesley (1987).

/BCL 94/ T. Berners–Lee/R. Cailliau/A. Luotonen/H. Nielsen/A. Secret: The World Wide Web, Comm. ACM 37, 8 (1994).

/BI 95/ M. Bieber/T. Isakowitz (Ed.): Designing Hypermedia Applications, Comm. ACM 38, 8, 26–112 (1995).

/BMS 84/ M. Brodie/J. Mylopoulos/J. W. Schmidt (Eds.): On Conceptual Modelling: Perspectives from Artificial Intelligence, Data Bases and Programming Languages, New York: Springer–Verlag (1984).

/Bot 92/ R. Botafogo: Structural Analysis of Hypertexts: Identifying Hierarchies and Useful Metrics, ACM Transactions Information Systems 10, 2 (1992).

/BR 69/ J. N. Buxton/B. Randell (Eds.): Software Engineering Techniques, Report on a Conference, Rome, 1969, Brussels: NATO Scientific Affairs Division (1969).

/CER 90/ B. Czejdo/R. Elmasri/M. Rusinkiewicz/D.W. Embley: A Graphical Data Manipulation Language for an Extended Entity–Relationship Model, IEEE Computer 23, 3, 26–37 (1990).

/CLR 90/ Th.H. Cormen/Ch.E. Leiserson/R.L. Rivest: Introduction to Algorithms, Cambridge: MIT Press (1990).

/Con 87/ J. Conklin: Hypertext: An Introduction and Survey, Los Alamitos: IEEE Computer Society Press (1987).

/Cuf 96/ L. Cuff: Commercial Hypertext Publishing: Electronic Books using Trails and the Author–Publisher–Reader Model, World Wide Web Journal: Special Issue: The Fourth International WWW Conference Proceedings, Sebastopol: O'Reilly & Associates (1996).

/DS 95/ P.J. Denning/B. Samuelson: The ACM Electronic Publishing Plan, Comm. ACM 38, 4, 97–109 (1995).

/FAF 95/ E. Fox/R. Akscyn/R. Futura (Eds.): Digital Libraries, Comm. ACM 38, 4, 22–96 (1995).

/GW 85/ G. Goos/J. Waite: Compiler Construction, New York: Springer–Verlag (1985).

/ISB 95/ T. Isakowitz/E.A. Stohr/P. Balasubramanian: RMM: A Methodology for Structured Hypermedia Design, Comm. ACM 38, 8, 34–43 (1995).

/JM 90/ D. Jonassen/H. Mandl (Eds.): Designing Hypermedia for Learning, New York: Springer (1990).

/JW 92/ M. Jones/P. Winne (Eds.): Adaptive Learning Environments, NATO ASI Series, New York: Springer (1992).

/KBA 95/ T. Kamba/K. Bharat/M. Albers: The Krakatoa Chronicle – An Interactive, Personalized Newspaper on the Web, 4th Int. World Wide Web Conference, Boston, Massachusetts, URL: http://www.w3.org/pub/Conferences/WWW4/Papers/93/ (1995).

/LGS 94/ G. Li/E. Gallant/J. Stasko: MMEDS: An Environment for Multimedia–Based Education Delivery, Techn. Report GVU 94–20, Geogia Institute of Technology (1994).

/LS 84/ J. Loeckx/K. Sieber: The Foundations of Program Verification, New York–Stuttgart: Wiley–Teubner (1984).

/Man 95/ J. Manger: The World Wide Web, Mosaic, and More, New York: McGraw–Hill (1995).

/Nie 90/ J. Nielson: Hypertext & Hypermedia, London: Academic Press (1990).

/NN 95/ J. Nanard/M. Nanard: Hypertext Design Environments and the Hypertext Design Process, Comm. ACM 38, 8, 49–56 (1995).

/MP 94/ J. Multisilta/S. Pohjolainen: Implementation of Authoring Tools for Hypermedia Based Learning Environments in Mathematics, Proc. of CALISCE '94 (1994).

/NR 68/ T. Naur/B. Randell (Eds.): Software Engineering, Report on a Conference, Garmisch, 1968, Brussels: NATO Scientific Affairs Division (1968).

/PD 82/ S. Pemberton/M. C. Daniels: Pascal Implementation – The P4 System, Chichester: Ellis Horwood (1984).

/Rad 95/ R. Rada: Interactive Media, New York: Springer (1995).

/RBS 94/ E. Rivlin/R. Botafogo/B. Shneiderman: Navigation in Hyperspace: Designing a Structure–Based Toolbox, Comm. ACM 37, 2 (1994).

/RMS 93/ J. Riedl/V. Mashayekhi/J. Schnepf/M. Claypool/D. Frankowski: SuiteSound: A System for Distributed Collaborative Multimedia, IEEE Transactions on Knowledge and Data Engineering 5, 4 (1993).

/RRS 95/ M. Recker/A. Ram/T. Shikano/G. Li/J. Stasko: Cognitive Media Types for Multimedia Information Access, Journal of Educational Multimedia and Hypermedia 4, 2/3 (1995).

/RS 86/ G. Rozenberg/A. Salomaa: The Book of L, New York: Springer–Verlag (1986).

/Sam 95/ P. Samuelson: Copyright and Digital Library, Comm. ACM 38, 4, 15–21 (1995).

/Schn 81/   H.J. Schneider: Problem–oriented Programming Languages (in German), Stuttgart: Teubner (1981).

/SG 96/   M. Sharples/T. van der Geest (Eds.): The New Writing Environment: writers at work in a world of technology, London: Springer (1996).

/SMS 84/   J. F. Sowa/J. Mylopoulos/J. W. Schmidt: Conceptual Structures: Information Processing in Mind and Machine, Reading: Addison Wesley (1984).

/Wir 86/   N. Wirth: Compiler Construction (in German), Stuttgart: Teubner (1986).

Index

A

abstract
  data type specification 87, 297
  syntax graph approach 90, 139, 307
access group model 411, 578
ACID properties 272, 576
acting component 560
active
  data base 575
  object 559
actor 24
adaptability
  of administration system 508, 528
  of execution tools 187
adaptation 611
administration
  component/system 160, 222, 485, 504, 522
  configuration 23, 65, 115, 222, 335, 485, 507
  document 53, 297
  of configurations, tasks, processes etc. 20, 22, 222, 510
  SDE 39, 115, 145, 152, 222, 485, 504, 522
  services, future 162
analyzer 33, 77, 174, 180, 209, 315, 426
a posteriori approach 36, 42, 144, 615
application
  area specizic SDEs 37, 151, 644
  conditions 262, 268
  system 8
  technology 28, 72, 642
a priori approach 36, 42, 144
architectural design 5
architecture 97
  client/server 569, 580
  diagrams 99
  graphs 86
  modelling 5, 9, 29, 49, 76, 97
  of a front end 492
  of a logical document 428
  of a reengineered system 572
  of a single/specific environment 100, 381
  of an administration environment 487, 523
  of an integration tool 111, 470
  of an overall environment 116, 394, 483, 567
  of a representation document 433
  of command handling 391
  of execution tools 461
  of GRAS 399, 403, 575
  of IPSEN meta environment 441
  of parser/unparser 436
  of the core part of the specific environment 426
  of the meta view document 430
  virtual and concrete 557
AST graph modelling 297, 539
atom 283
atomic increment 172
attribute
  condition 268
  dependencies 249
  evaluation mechanism 258, 408
  evaluation rule 257
  function 254

inherited, synthesized 249
intrinsic, derived 252
tree grammars 248
attributed graphs, trees 82, 248
attributes of a classification scheme 120, 123
automatic mode of integration tool 184, 203

B

backtracking
  in generated code 453
  of development processes 62, 70, 506, 513
  of subgraph test 260
basic
  component 104
  integrator 112
behavior of IPSEN tools 61, 243
benchmarking of GRAS 413
binder 112, 183, 324, 469
bootstrapping 30
bottom–up approaches 615
broadband language 34
browser 112, 184, 213, 324, 469
browsing through errors, warnings 214
business applications and SDEs 54, 85, 94

C

cardinality
  clause 254
  constraints 257
CASE 32
change management of GRAS 405
characterization of SDEs 33, 36, 119
characteristics of IPSEN tools 73, 243
CIM 15
class
  combinations 253
  of nodes 252
classes
  of a meta view document 431
  of a representation document 433
classifying software systems 28
classifying/classification scheme for SDEs,
  SDE projects, processes for SDEs 119
classification scheme nodes, edges 122
client/server architecture 569, 580
closed SDEs 36
clustering strategies 419
collaboration 26
combined (e.g. PiL/PiS) SDE 40
command
  –driven 74, 171, 393
  execution cycle 386
  selection 171, 385, 391
comments 209
compiler–oriented SDEs 37, 144
compilers 29, 72
completeness, combination and configurability of
  future SDEs 162, 503
completing operator 284
complex binder 112, 178, 324, 469
complexes of internal documents 79, 629

Springer
and the
environment

At Springer we firmly believe that an
international science publisher has a
special obligation to the environment,
and our corporate policies consistently
reflect this conviction.
We also expect our business partners –
paper mills, printers, packaging
manufacturers, etc. – to commit
themselves to using materials and
production processes that do not harm
the environment. The paper in this
book is made from low- or no-chlorine
pulp and is acid free, in conformance
with international standards for paper
permanency.

Springer

Lecture Notes in Computer Science

For information about Vols. 1–1099

please contact your bookseller or Springer-Verlag

Vol. 1135: B. Jonsson, J. Parrow (Eds.), Formal Techniques in Real-Time and Fault-Tolerant Systems. Proceedings, 1996. X, 479 pages. 1996.

Vol. 1136: J. Diaz, M. Serna (Eds.), Algorithms – ESA '96. Proceedings, 1996. XII, 566 pages. 1996.

Vol. 1137: G. Görz, S. Hölldobler (Eds.), KI-96: Advances in Artificial Intelligence. Proceedings, 1996. XI, 387 pages. 1996. (Subseries LNAI).

Vol. 1138: J. Calmet, J.A. Campbell, J. Pfalzgraf (Eds.), Artificial Intelligence and Symbolic Mathematical Computation. Proceedings, 1996. VIII, 381 pages. 1996.

Vol. 1139: M. Hanus, M. Rogriguez-Artalejo (Eds.), Algebraic and Logic Programming. Proceedings, 1996. VIII, 345 pages. 1996.

Vol. 1140: H. Kuchen, S. Doaitse Swierstra (Eds.), Programming Languages: Implementations, Logics, and Programs. Proceedings, 1996. XI, 479 pages. 1996.

Vol. 1141: H.-M. Voigt, W. Ebeling, I. Rechenberg, H.-P. Schwefel (Eds.), Parallel Problem Solving from Nature – PPSN IV. Proceedings, 1996. XVII, 1.050 pages. 1996.

Vol. 1142: R.W. Hartenstein, M. Glesner (Eds.), Field-Programmable Logic. Proceedings, 1996. X, 432 pages. 1996.

Vol. 1143: T.C. Fogarty (Ed.), Evolutionary Computing. Proceedings, 1996. VIII, 305 pages. 1996.

Vol. 1144: J. Ponce, A. Zisserman, M. Hebert (Eds.), Object Representation in Computer Vision. Proceedings, 1996. VIII, 403 pages. 1996.

Vol. 1145: R. Cousot, D.A. Schmidt (Eds.), Static Analysis. Proceedings, 1996. IX, 389 pages. 1996.

Vol. 1146: E. Bertino, H. Kurth, G. Martella, E. Montolivo (Eds.), Computer Security – ESORICS 96. Proceedings, 1996. X, 365 pages. 1996.

Vol. 1147: L. Miclet, C. de la Higuera (Eds.), Grammatical Inference: Learning Syntax from Sentences. Proceedings, 1996. VIII, 327 pages. 1996. (Subseries LNAI).

Vol. 1148: M.C. Lin, D. Manocha (Eds.), Applied Computational Geometry. Proceedings, 1996. VIII, 223 pages. 1996.

Vol. 1149: C. Montangero (Ed.), Software Process Technology. Proceedings, 1996. IX, 291 pages. 1996.

Vol. 1150: A. Hlawiczka, J.G. Silva, L. Simoncini (Eds.), Dependable Computing – EDCC-2. Proceedings, 1996. XVI, 440 pages. 1996.

Vol. 1151: Ö. Babaoğlu, K. Marzullo (Eds.), Distributed Algorithms. Proceedings, 1996. VIII, 381 pages. 1996.

Vol. 1152: T. Furuhashi, Y. Uchikawa (Eds.), Fuzzy Logic, Neural Networks, and Evolutionary Computation. Proceedings, 1995. VIII, 243 pages. 1996. (Subseries LNAI).

Vol. 1153: E. Burke, P. Ross (Eds.), Practice and Theory of Automated Timetabling. Proceedings, 1995. XIII, 381 pages. 1996.

Vol. 1154: D. Pedreschi, C. Zaniolo (Eds.), Logic in Databases. Proceedings, 1996. X, 497 pages. 1996.

Vol. 1155: J. Roberts, U. Mocci, J. Virtamo (Eds.), Broadbank Network Teletraffic. XXII, 584 pages. 1996.

Vol. 1156: A. Bode, J. Dongarra, T. Ludwig, V. Sunderam (Eds.), Parallel Virtual Machine – EuroPVM '96. Proceedings, 1996. XIV, 362 pages. 1996.

Vol. 1157: B. Thalheim (Ed.), Conceptual Modeling – ER '96. Proceedings, 1996. XII, 489 pages. 1996.

Vol. 1158: S. Berardi, M. Coppo (Eds.), Types for Proofs and Programs. Proceedings, 1995. X, 296 pages. 1996.

Vol. 1159: D.L. Borges, C.A.A. Kaestner (Eds.), Advances in Artificial Intelligence. Proceedings, 1996. XI, 243 pages. (Subseries LNAI).

Vol. 1160: S. Arikawa, A.K. Sharma (Eds.), Algorithmic Learning Theory. Proceedings, 1996. XVII, 337 pages. 1996. (Subseries LNAI).

Vol. 1161: O. Spaniol, C. Linnhoff-Popien, B. Meyer (Eds.), Trends in Distributed Systems. Proceedings, 1996. VIII, 289 pages. 1996.

Vol. 1162: D.G. Feitelson, L. Rudolph (Eds.), Job Scheduling Strategies for Parallel Processing. Proceedings, 1996. VIII, 291 pages. 1996.

Vol. 1163: K. Kim, T. Matsumoto (Eds.), Advances in Cryptology – ASIACRYPT '96. Proceedings, 1996. XII, 395 pages. 1996.

Vol. 1164: K. Berquist, A. Berquist (Eds.), Managing Information Highways. XIV, 417 pages. 1996.

Vol. 1165: J.-R. Abrial, E. Börger, H. Langmaack (Eds.), Formal Methods for Industrial Applications. VIII, 511 pages. 1996.

Vol. 1166: M. Srivas, A. Camilleri (Eds.), Formal Methods in Computer-Aided Design. Proceedings, 1996. IX, 470 pages. 1996.

Vol. 1167: I. Sommerville (Ed.), Software Configuration Management. VII, 291 pages. 1996.

Vol. 1168: I. Smith, B. Faltings (Eds.), Advances in Case-Based Reasoning. Proceedings, 1996. IX, 531 pages. 1996. (Subseries LNAI).

Vol. 1169: M. Broy, S. Merz, K. Spies (Eds.), Formal Systems Verification. XXIII, 541 pages. 1996.

Vol. 1170: M. Nagl (Ed.), Building Tightly Integrated Software Development Environments: The IPSEN Approach. IX, 709 pages. 1996.

Vol. 1171: A. Franz, Automatic Ambiguity Resolution in Natural Language Processing. XIX, 155 pages. 1996. (Subseries LNAI).

Vol. 1172: J. Pieprzyk, J. Seberry (Eds.), Information Security and Privacy. Proceedings, 1996. IX, 333 pages. 1996.

Vol. 1173: W. Rucklidge, Efficient Visual Recognition Using the Hausdorff Distance. XIII, 178 pages. 1996.

Vol. 1174: R. Anderson (Ed.), Information Hiding. Proceedings, 1996. VIII, 351 pages. 1996.

Vol. 1175: K.G. Jeffery, J. Král, M. Bartošek (Eds.), SOFSEM'96: Theory and Practice of Informatics. Proceedings, 1996. XII, 491 pages. 1996.

Vol. 1176: S. Miguet, A. Montanvert, S. Ubéda (Eds.), Discrete Geometry for Computer Imagery. Proceedings, 1996. XI, 349 pages. 1996.

Vol. 1177: J.P. Müller, The Design of Intelligent Agents. XV, 227 pages. 1996. (Subseries LNAI).